Exploring PSYCHOLOGY In Modules

Seventh Edition

D0022803

U18402 3167368

Exploring PSYCHOLOGY In Modules

Seventh Edition

DAVID G. MYERS

Hope College
Holland, Michigan USA

WORTH PUBLISHERS

Grateful acknowledgment is given for permission to reprint the following photos: p. 1: Corbis; pp. vii, 35: Mel Yates/Getty Images; p. 97: Paul Barton/Corbis; p. 141: Robb Kendrick/Getty Images; p. 191: Uli Wiesmeier/zefa/Corbis; pp. ix, 231: Walter Hodges/Corbis; p. 267: Thomas M. Barwick/Corbis; pp. x, 305: First Light/Getty Images; p. 355: Louisa Gouliamaki/epa/Corbis; p. 405: Tim de Waele/Corbis; p. 457: Foodpix/Picturequest; pp. xi, 497: Ansgar/zefa/Corbis; p. 539: Michael Newman/PhotoEdit, Inc.; pp. xii, 573: Patrik Giardino/Corbis.

Credits for timeline photos, inside front and back covers (by date): 1637, Corbis-Bettmann; 1859, Granger Collection; 1878, 1879, 1890, Brown Brothers; 1893, 1894, Wellesley College Archives; 1898, Yale University Library; 1905, Sovfoto; 1913, 1920, 1933, 1939, Archives of the History of American Psychology, University of Akron; 1924, Larsen/Watson Papers, Archives of the History of American Psychology, University of Akron; 1938, Bettmann/Corbis; 1945, Corbis; 1951, Courtesy of Carl Rogers Memorial Library; 1954, Ted Polumbaum/*Life* magazine, © 1968 TimeWarner, Inc.; 1959, Chris Felver/Archive Images; 1963, Courtesy of CUNY Graduate School and University Center; 1966, Courtesy of John Garcia; 1971, Courtesy of Albert Bandura, Stanford University; 1974, Russell Fernald, Courtesy of the Stanford University News Service; 1979, Courtesy of Elizabeth Loftus, University of California, Irvine; 1981, Courtesy of the Archives, California Institute of Technology; 1993, Chet Snedden/American Airlines Corporate Communications.

Publisher: Catherine Woods

Senior Acquisitions Editor: Kevin Feyen

Executive Marketing Manager: Katherine Nurre

Development Editors: Nancy Fleming, Christine Brune

Media Editor: Peter Twickler

Photo Editor: Bianca Moscatelli

Photo Researchers: Christina Micek, Julie Tesser

Art Director: Babs Reingold

Cover Designers: Lyndall Culbertson, Babs Reingold

Interior Designer: Lissi Sigillo

Layout Designer: Lee Ann Mahler

Associate Managing Editor: Tracey Kuehn

Project Editors: Dana Kasowitz
                Kat Strever, TSI Graphics

Illustration Coordinator: Bill Page

Illustrations: TSI Graphics, Alan Reingold, Matthew Holt, Christy Krames, Shawn Kenney, Bonnie Hofkin, and Demetrios Zangos

Production Manager: Sarah Segal

Composition: TSI Graphics

Printing and Binding: RR Donnelley

Cover Painting: Laura James, *Six O'Clock,* acrylic on canvas, 1997
               Collection of Warren Stein

paperback:
ISBN-13: 978-1-4292-0589-4
ISBN-10: 1-4292-0589-X

hardcover:
ISBN-13: 978-1-4292-0588-7
ISBN-10: 1-4292-0588-1

© 2008 by Worth Publishers
All rights reserved.

Printed in the United States of America

Second printing

All royalties from the sale of this book are assigned to the David and Carol Myers Foundation, which exists to receive and distribute funds to other charitable organizations.

Worth Publishers
41 Madison Avenue
New York, NY 10010
www.worthpublishers.com

About the Author

David Myers received his psychology Ph.D. from the University of Iowa. He has spent his career at Hope College, Michigan, where he is the John Dirk Werkman Professor of Psychology and has taught dozens of introductory psychology sections. Hope College students have invited him to be their commencement speaker and voted him "outstanding professor."

Myers' scientific articles have, with support from National Science Foundation grants, appeared in more than two dozen scientific periodicals, including *Science, American Scientist, Psychological Science,* and the *American Psychologist.* In addition to his scholarly writing and his textbooks for introductory and social psychology, he also digests psychological science for the general public. His writings have appeared in three dozen magazines, from *Today's Education* to *Scientific American.* He also has authored five general audience books, including *The Pursuit of Happiness and Intuition: Its Powers and Perils.*

David Myers has chaired his city's Human Relations Commission, helped found a thriving assistance center for families in poverty, and spoken to hundreds of college and community groups. Drawing on his experience, he also has written articles and a book *(A Quiet World)* about hearing loss, and he is advocating a transformation in American assistive listening technology (see http://www.hearingloop.org).

He bikes to work year-round and plays daily pick-up basketball. David and Carol Myers have raised two sons and a daughter.

Brief Contents

Contents

Preface

Two decades of time's ever-rolling stream have flowed swiftly by since publication of this book's first edition. And what an amazing two decades it has been. Hardly a day goes by without my feeling gratitude for the privilege of assisting with the teaching of psychology to so many students, in so many countries, through so many different languages. To be entrusted with discerning and communicating the wisdom of this humanly significant discipline is both an exciting honor and a great responsibility.

What sustains my motivation is, first, my ongoing appreciation for psychological science and its continually expanding understandings, and, second, my commitment to the students and teaching colleagues with whom this book enables me to have conversation. I love the mind-expanding learning that comes from my day-to-day reading of psychological science, and I love connecting with so many people (many hundreds of whom have written to share their experiences and gentle words of advice).

Although each new edition of this text appears every three years, it is a rare day in between those editions when I do not harvest new information about the field I love and its application to everyday life. Week by week, new information surprises us with discoveries about, for example, the neuroscience of our moods and memories, the reach of our adaptive unconscious, and the shaping power of our social and cultural context. No wonder this book has changed dramatically since I set to work on the first edition. Today's psychological science is more attuned to the relative effects of nature and nurture, to gender and cultural diversity, to our conscious and unconscious information processing, and to the biology that underlies our behavior (see **TABLES 1** and **2**). We today can also harness new ways to present information, both in books and via electronic media. These changes are exhilarating! Keeping up with new discoveries fills each day and connects me with many colleagues and friends.

The thousands of instructors and millions of students across the globe who have studied this book have contributed immensely to its development. Much of this has occurred spontaneously, through correspondence and conversations. Dozens of formal reviews from teaching psychologists and researchers around the world have also aided each revision. I look forward to continuing feedback as we strive, over future editions, to create an ever better book.

Why a Modular Book?

This 45-module text has been a longtime wish come true for me. It breaks out of the box by restructuring the material into a buffet of (a) *short, digestible chapters* (called modules) that (b) *can be selected from and assigned in any order.*

Have we not all heard the familiar student complaint: "The chapters are too long!" A text's typical 30- to 50-page chapter cannot be read in a single sitting before the eyes grow weary and the mind wanders. So why not parse the material into readable units? Ask your students whether they would prefer a 600-page book to be organized as thirteen 45-page chapters or as forty-five 13-page chapters. You may be surprised at their overwhelming support for shorter chapters. Indeed, students digest material better when they process in smaller chunks—as spaced rather than massed practice.

I have equally often heard from instructors bemoaning the fact that they "just can't get to everything" in the book. Sometimes instructors want to cover certain sections but not others in a traditional, long chapter. For example, in the typical States of Consciousness chapter, someone may want to cover Sleep and Hypnosis but not Drugs. In *Exploring Psychology, Seventh Edition in Modules,* instructors can easily choose to cover Module 15, Waking and Sleeping Rhythms, and Module 16, Hypnosis, but not Module 17, Drugs.

TABLE 1 Evolutionary Psychology and Behavior Genetics

*In addition to the coverage found in Module 5, the **evolutionary perspective** is covered on the following pages:*

Antisocial personality disorder, p. 518
Anxiety disorders, p. 514
Attraction, pp. 75–76
Biological predispositions in learning, p. 254
Brainstem, p. 48
Charles Darwin, p. 3
Electromagnetic spectrum, sensitivity to, p. 147
Emotion, pp. 314–315, 420–421
Emotion-detecting ability, p. 347
Evolutionary perspective, defined, p. 7
Fear, pp. 314–315
Hearing, p. 157
Hunger and taste preference, pp. 362, 363
Intelligence, pp. 345–347, 349

Language, pp. 319, 321–322
Love, p. 136
Need to belong, pp. 387, 597
Perceptual adaptation, pp. 182–183
Personality, p. 464
Puberty, onset of, pp. 120–122
Sensation, p. 143
Sensory adaptation, pp. 146–147
Sexual attraction, pp. 75–76
Sexual orientation, pp. 383–384
Sexuality, p. 375
Sleep, pp. 196–197, 203
Smell, pp. 166–167
Stress and the immune system, pp. 440–441
Taste, pp. 164–165
Weight, pp. 364, 366

*In addition to the coverage found in Module 5, **behavior genetics** is covered on the following pages:*

Abuse, intergenerational transmission of, p. 263
Aggression, pp. 599–600
Biomedical therapies, pp. 565–570
Depth perception, p. 173
Drives and incentives, p. 358
Drug use, pp. 226–228
Emotion and cognition, pp. 413–414
Happiness, pp. 429–432
Hunger, taste preference, pp. 362, 366
Intelligence, pp. 326, 340–350
Learning, p. 254
Motor development, p. 105
Perception, pp. 181–185

Personality traits, pp. 476, 478–479, 482–483
Psychological disorders:
    anxiety disorders, pp. 509–510, 514
    biopsychosocial approach, pp. 502, 524–525
    mood disorders, pp. 521–529
    personality disorders, pp. 515–518
    schizophrenia, pp. 531–537
Sexual orientation, p. 383
Sexuality, p. 375
Smell, pp. 166–167
Stress, personality, and illness, pp. 443, 438–439, 451
Traits, p. 346

TABLE 2 Neuroscience

In addition to coverage found in Modules 3 and 4, neuroscience can be found on the following pages:

Antisocial personality disorder, pp. 517–518
Autism, p. 111
Biofeedback, pp. 451–454
Brain activity and:
    aging, pp. 130–131, 134, 290
    dementia and Alzheimer's, p. 280
    dreams, pp. 207–208
    emotion, pp. 121, 167, 280–281, 410, 411, 413–414
    sleep, pp. 195–200
Brain development and:
    adolescence, pp. 121–122
    experience, pp. 79–81
    infancy and childhood, p. 105
    sexual differentiation in utero, p. 90
Drug dependence, p. 226
Emotion and cognition, pp. 413–414
Fear-learning, pp. 514–515

Fetal alcohol syndrome and brain abnormalities, p. 102
Hallucinations and:
    hallucinogens, pp. 223–224
    sleep, p. 207
Hormones and:
    abuse, p. 116
    development, pp. 90–91, 120–122
    emotion, p. 409
    memory, pp. 280–281
    sex, pp. 90, 120–121, 130, 349, 376–377, 409
    stress, pp. 410, 436–437, 438, 440, 448
    weight control, pp. 361–362
Hunger, pp. 361–362
Insight, pp. 308–309
Intelligence, p. 342
Memory, physical storage of, pp. 279–283
Mirror neurons, p. 261

Neuroscience perspective, explained, pp. 5, 6–7
Neurotransmitters and:
    biomedical therapy:
        anxiety, p. 566
        depression, pp. 481–482, 566–568
        ECT, pp. 568–570
        psychosurgery, pp. 570–571
        schizophrenia, pp. 533–534, 566
    child abuse, p. 117
    depression, pp. 502, 526
    drugs, pp. 217–223
    exercise, pp. 449–450
    obsessive-compulsive disorder, p. 551
    pain, pp. 162–164
    schizophrenia, pp. 533–534
Parallel vs. serial processing, p. 152
Perception and:
    brain damage, pp. 142, 152

color vision, pp. 154–155
feature detection, pp. 151–152
transduction, p. 80
visual information processing, pp. 151–153
Phantom limb pain, pp. 162–163
Prejudice, p. 595
Schizophrenia and brain abnormalities, pp. 533–534
Sensation and:
    body position and movement, pp. 167–168
    hearing, pp. 157–160
    sensory adaptation, pp. 146–147
    smell, pp. 166–167
    taste, pp. 164–165
Sexual orientation, pp. 382–384
Sleep:
    memory and, pp. 203, 207
    recuperation during, p. 203

How Is This Book Different from *Exploring Psychology,* Seventh Edition?

The primary differences between this book and my *Exploring Psychology,* Seventh Edition, text are the organization and the independence of the modules.

Organization

This book really IS *Exploring Psychology,* Seventh Edition—just in a different format. So this modular version contains all the updated research and innovative new coverage from *Exploring Psychology,* Seventh Edition. A very few sections have moved around to accommodate the modular structure. For example, "Rates of Psychological Disorders" is a separate section at the end of the Psychological Disorders chapter in *Exploring Psychology,* Seventh Edition, but it is covered in the first of the Psychological Disorders modules in this modular version. And Module 28, Motivation at Work, is an Appendix titled Psychology at Work in *Exploring Psychology,* Seventh Edition.

The Modules Are Independent

Each module in this book is stand-alone rather than dependent upon the others for understanding. Cross references to other parts of the book have been replaced with brief explanations. In some cases, illustrations or key terms are repeated to avoid possible confusion. No assumptions are made about what students have read prior to each module. This independence gives instructors ultimate flexibility in deciding which modules to use and in what order. Connections among psychology's subfields and findings are still made—they are just made in a way that does not assume knowledge of other parts of the book.

Trademark Features

Throughout its seven editions, my vision for *Exploring Psychology* has not wavered: *to merge rigorous science with a broad human perspective in a book that engages both mind and heart.* My aim has been to create a state-of-the-art introduction to psychology, written with sensitivity to students' needs and interests. I aspire to help students understand and appreciate the wonder of important phenomena of their lives. I also want to convey the inquisitive spirit in which psychologists *do* psychology. The study of psychology, I believe, enhances our abilities to restrain intuition with critical thinking, judgmentalism with compassion, and illusion with understanding.

Believing with Thoreau that "anything living is easily and naturally expressed in popular language," I seek to communicate psychology's scholarship with crisp narrative and vivid storytelling. Writing as a solo author, I hope to tell psychology's story in a way that is warmly personal as well as rigorously scientific. I love to reflect on connections between psychology and other realms, such as literature, philosophy, history, sports, religion, politics, and popular culture. And I love to provoke thought, to play with words, and to laugh.

Successful SQ3R Study Aids

1 Exploring Psychology, Seventh Edition in Modules' *complete system of learning aids includes numbered "preview questions," which appear in this format throughout the book.*

This text has retained its popular system of study aids, integrated into an SQ3R structure that augments the narrative without disrupting it. Each module opens with a module outline that enables students to quickly *survey* its major topics. Numbered

■ **key terms** Look for complete definitions of each important term in the margin near its introduction in the narrative.

In the margins of this book, students will find interesting and informative review notes, and quotes from researchers and others that will encourage them to be active learners and apply what they are learning.

preview *questions* at the start of each new major topic define the learning objectives that will guide students as they *read*. All **key terms** are defined in the margins for ready reference while students are being introduced to the new term in the narrative (see sample at left). Periodic Thinking Critically About and Close-Up boxes encourage development of critical thinking skills as well as application of the new concepts. *Rehearse It* quizzes at the end of each module will stimulate students to rehearse what they have learned. These test items offer a novel combination of crisp review of key ideas, and practice with the multiple-choice test format. The module-ending *Review* is structured as a set of answers to the numbered preview questions. Test Yourself questions at the end of each module offer students an opportunity to review and apply key concepts for even better retention. The Tips for Studying Psychology section at the end of Module 1 explains the SQ3R-based system of study aids, suggesting how students can *survey, question, read, rehearse,* and *review* the material for maximum retention.

Goals for the Seventh Edition

Although supplemented by added storytelling, this new edition retains its predecessors' voice and much of its content and organization. It also retains the goals—the guiding principles—that have animated the previous six editions:

1. *To exemplify the process of inquiry* I strive to show students not just the outcome of research, but how the research process works. Throughout, the book tries to excite the reader's curiosity. It invites readers to imagine themselves as participants in classic experiments. Several modules introduce research stories as mysteries that progressively unravel as one clue after another falls into place. (See, for example, the historical story of research on the brain's processing of language on pages 58–59.)

2. *To teach critical thinking* By presenting research as intellectual detective work, I exemplify an inquiring, analytical mind-set. Whether students are studying development, cognition, or statistics, they will become involved in, and see the rewards of, critical reasoning. Moreover, they will discover how an empirical approach can help them evaluate competing ideas and claims for highly publicized phenomena—ranging from subliminal persuasion, ESP, and hypnosis, to astrology, alternative therapies, and repressed and recovered memories.

3. *To put facts in the service of concepts* My intention is not to fill students' intellectual file drawers with facts, but to reveal psychology's major concepts—to teach students how to think, and to offer psychological ideas worth thinking about. In each module I place emphasis on those concepts I hope students will carry with them long after they complete the course. Always, I try to follow Albert Einstein's dictum that "everything should be made as simple as possible, but not simpler."

4. *To be as up-to-date as possible* Few things dampen students' interest as quickly as the sense that they are reading stale news. While retaining psychology's classic studies and concepts, I also present the discipline's most important recent developments. More than 400 references in this edition are dated 2004 or later.

5. *To integrate principles and applications* Throughout—by means of anecdotes, case histories, and the posing of hypothetical situations—I relate the findings of basic research to their applications and implications. Where psychology can illuminate pressing human issues—be they racism and sexism, health and happiness, or violence and war—I have not hesitated to shine its light.

6. *To enhance comprehension by providing continuity* Because this book has a single author, many significant issues—such as behavior genetics, cultural diversity, the bold thinking of intellectual pioneers, human rationality and irrationality, empathy for and understanding of troubled lives—weave throughout many modules, and students hear a consistent voice. "The uniformity of a work," observed Edward Gibbon, "denotes the hand of a single artist."

7. ***To reinforce learning at every step*** Everyday examples and rhetorical questions encourage students to process the material actively. Concepts are presented and then frequently applied to reinforce learning. The SQ3R system of pedagogical aids augments learning without interrupting the text narrative. A marginal glossary helps students master important terminology. Major sections begin with numbered preview questions, and modules end with Rehearse It! sections for self-testing on key concepts. End-of-module reviews repeat the preview questions and answer them. And the end-of-module Test Yourself questions invite students to review and apply key concepts in memorable ways.

8. ***To convey respect for human unity and diversity*** Especially in newly revised Module 5, Behavior Genetics and Evolutionary Psychology, and Module 6, Environmental Influences on Behavior, but also throughout the book, readers will see evidence of our human kinship—our shared biological heritage, our common mechanisms of seeing and learning, hungering and feeling, loving and hating. They will also better understand the dimensions of our diversity—our *individual* diversity in development and aptitudes, temperament and personality, and disorder and health; and our *cultural* diversity in attitudes and expressive styles, in child-rearing and care for the elderly, and in life priorities.

What's New?

Despite the overarching continuity, there is change on every page. There are updates everywhere and 650 new references—but overall this edition is slightly more streamlined than its predecessor. I have introduced the following major changes to *Exploring Psychology, Seventh Edition in Modules:*

Increased Coverage of Cultural and Gender Diversity

This edition presents an even more thoroughly cross-cultural perspective on psychology (**TABLE 3**)—reflected in research findings, and text and photo examples. Coverage of the psychology of women and men is thoroughly integrated (see **TABLE 4**). In addition, I am working to offer a world-based psychology for our worldwide student readership.

Thus, I continually search the world for research findings and text and photo examples, conscious that readers may be in Melbourne, Sheffield, Vancouver, or Nairobi. North American and European examples come easily, given that I reside in the United States, maintain contact with friends and colleagues in Canada, subscribe to several European periodicals, and live periodically in the U.K. This edition, for example, offers many dozens of Canadian, British, and Australian and New Zealand examples. We are all citizens of a shrinking world, thanks to increased migration and the growing global economy. Thus, American students, too, benefit from information and examples that internationalize their world-consciousness. And if psychology seeks to explain *human* behavior (not just American or Canadian or Australian behavior), the broader the scope of studies presented, the more accurate is our picture of this world's people. My aim is to expose all students to the world beyond their own culture. Thus, I continue to welcome input and suggestions from all readers. Our **revised Module 5, Behavior Genetics and Evolutionary Psychology, and Module 6, Environmental Influences on Behavior,** encourage students to appreciate cultural and gender differences and commonalities, and to consider the interplay of nature and nurture.

Many new photos showcase the diversity of cultures within North America, as well as across the globe. In addition to significant cross-cultural examples and research presented within the narrative, these new photos with informative captions freshen each module and broaden students' perspectives in applying psychological science to their own world and to the worlds across the globe.

Table 3 Culture and Multicultural Experience

*From the first to the last module, coverage of **culture and multicultural** experience can be found on the following pages:*

Table 4 The Psychology of Men and Women

*Coverage of the **psychology of men and women** can be found on the following pages:*

Greater Emphasis on the Biological, Psychological, Social-Cultural Levels-of-Analysis Approach in Psychology

This edition now systematically includes coverage of the biological, psychological, and social-cultural influences on our behavior. A significant new section in Module 1 introduces the levels-of-analysis approach, setting the stage for future modules, and new levels-of-analysis figures in many modules help students understand concepts in the biopsychosocial context.

Greater Sensitivity to the Clinical Perspective

With helpful guidance from clinical psychologist colleagues, I have been more mindful in this edition of the clinical angle on various concepts within psychology, which has sensitized and improved the Personality, Psychological Disorders, and Therapy modules, among others. For example, I now cover problem-focused and emotion-focused coping strategies in Module 31, Stress and Illness. And Module 25, Intelligence, includes several mentions of how intelligence tests are used in clinical settings.

New Teaching and Learning Resources

Our supplements and media have been celebrated for their quality, abundance, and accuracy. The package available for *Exploring Psychology, Seventh Edition in Modules,* raises the bar even higher. New media items include the *ActivePsych* classroom activity CD-ROMs, the new *Online Study Center 2.0* for students, and enhanced course management solutions. New print supplements include Martin Bolt's *Instructor's Media Guide,* Richard Straub's *Visual Concept Reviews,* and a thoroughly revised *Test Bank.* See pages xxvi-xxvii for details.

New Careers in Psychology Appendix, by Jennifer Zwolinski, University of San Diego

This highly applied and research-based appendix provides guidance to students considering a psychology major and/or career. Topics covered include the benefits of studying psychology and obtaining a psychology degree, psychology careers available and the job market landscape for students at all levels (bachelor's, master's, doctoral), career options within the subfields in psychology (such as clinical, counseling, community, school, forensic, and sports psychology), and early preparation tips for those considering graduate school.

Enhanced Critical Thinking Coverage

I aim to introduce students to critical thinking in a natural way throughout the book, with even more in the narrative that encourages active learning of psychology's key concepts. This new edition includes the following opportunities for students to learn or practice their critical thinking skills.

- *Module 2 takes a unique, critical thinking approach to introducing students to psychology's research methods,* emphasizing the fallacies of our everyday intuition and common sense and, thus the need for psychological science. Critical thinking is introduced as a key term in this module (p. 17).
- *"Thinking Critically About . . ." boxes* are found throughout the book, modeling for students a critical approach to some key issues in psychology. For example, see the new box "Thinking Critically About: ADHD—Normal High Energy or Genuine Disorder?" on p. 501.
- *Detective-style stories* throughout the narrative get students thinking critically about psychology's key research questions.

- *"Apply this"* and *"Think about it"* style discussions keep students active in their study of each module.
- *Critical examinations of pop psychology* spark interest and provide important lessons in thinking critically about everyday topics.
- *Appendix A: Statistical Reasoning in Everyday Life* encourages students to focus on thinking smarter by applying simple statistical principles to everyday reasoning (pp. A-1 to A-9).

See **TABLE 5** for a list of this text's coverage of Critical Thinking topics and Thinking Critically About boxes.

Innovative Multimedia Supplements Package

Exploring Psychology, Seventh Edition in Modules boasts a host of new electronic and print supplements titles.

Media Supplements

PsychPortal to accompany *Exploring Psychology, Seventh Edition in Modules* provides an Angel-based Course Management resource that includes an eBook, and an assessment system developed by top experts in online quizzing for introductory psychology, and a variety of engaging animations, videos, and tutorials.

Worth eBook for *Exploring Psychology, Seventh Edition in Modules,* offers the same first-rate content as the print book, with anytime access, fully integrated media,

---

TABLE 5 Critical Thinking and Research Emphasis

Critical thinking coverage, and in-depth stories of psychology's *scientific research* process, can be found on the following pages:

Thinking Critically About . . . boxes:

The Fear Factor—Do We Fear the Right Things?, pp. 314–315

Lie Detection, p. 412

Alternative Medicine: New Ways to Health or Old Snake Oil?, pp. 452–453

How to Be a "Successful" Astrologer or Palm Reader, pp. 480–481

ADHD—Normal High Energy or Genuine Disorder?, p. 501

Insanity and Responsibility, p. 505

Critical Examinations of Pop Psychology:

Perceiving order in random events, pp. 23–24

Do we use only 10 percent of our brains?, p. 57

Critiquing the evolutionary perspective, pp. 76–77

How great is the power of parenting?, pp. 80–81

Sensory restriction, pp. 181–182

Is there extrasensory perception?, pp. 186–187

Can hypnosis enhance recall?

Coerce action? Be therapeutic? Alleviate pain?, pp. 211–213

Has the concept of "addiction" been stretched too far?, p. 217

Is aerobic exercise therapeutic?, pp. 449–450

Spirituality and faith communities, pp. 454–456

How valid is the Rorschach test?, p. 465

Is repression a myth?, p. 466

Is Freud credible?, pp. 467–468

Post-traumatic stress disorder, pp. 512–513

Dissociation and Multiple Personalities, pp. 516–517

Evaluating alternative therapies, pp. 557–559

Do Video Games Teach, or Release, Violence?, p. 605

Thinking Critically with Psychological Science:

The limits of intuition and common sense, pp. 13–15

The scientific attitude, pp. 15–16

"Critical thinking" introduced as a key term, p. 16

The scientific method, pp. 17–18

Correlation and causation, pp. 21–22

Illusory correlation, p. 23

Exploring cause and effect, pp. 24–25

Evaluating therapies, p. 25

Is psychotherapy effective?, pp. 554–556

Statistical reasoning, p. A-1

Making inferences, pp. A-7–A-8

Scientific Detective Stories:

Is breast milk better than formula?, pp. 24–25

Language in the brain, pp. 58–59

Our divided brains, pp. 60–62

The twin and adoption studies, pp. 67–70

How a child's mind develops, pp. 107–112

Parallel processing, pp. 152–153

How do we see in color?, pp. 154–155

Why do we sleep?, pp. 200–203

Why we dream, pp. 206–208

Explaining the hypnotized state, pp. 213–214

How do we store memories in our brains?, pp. 279–283

Memory construction, pp. 295–302

Do animals exhibit language?, pp. 326–329

Why do we feel hunger?, pp. 360–362

What determines sexual orientation?, pp. 380–386

The pursuit of happiness: Who is happy, and why?, pp. 425–432

Why—and in whom—does stress contribute to heart disease?, pp. 438–439

How and why is social support linked with health?, pp. 447–449

Self-esteem versus self-serving bias, pp. 492–494

What causes mood disorders?, pp. 521–529

Do prenatal viral infections increase risk of schizophrenia?, pp. 534–535

Why do people fail to help in emergencies?, pp. 613–615

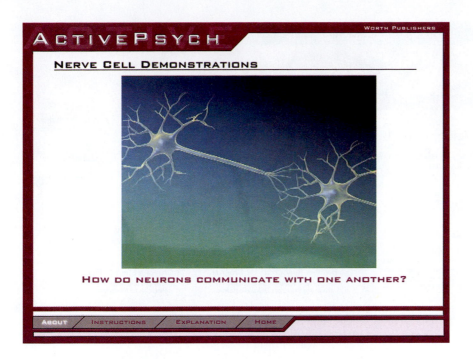

effective study tools, and easy customization for instructors at half the cost of the printed text. An access code for the eBook can also be packaged with the print book at no additional cost. Visit http://ebooks.bfwpub.com to learn more.

New! *ActivePsych: Classroom Activities, Projects, and Video Teaching Modules* Instructor's Classroom Exercise CD-ROMs include interactive activities designed for in-class presentation and group participation, with a robust library of new clips and animations. These activities require very little instructor preparation (just load the CD and launch the activity) and are designed to foster class discussion and critical thinking. The *ActivePsych* suite of instructor presentation CD-ROMs includes the following:

- Two powerful types of classroom activities: 32 Flash-based interactive demonstrations are designed to promote classroom discussion and critical thinking. 22 PowerPoint-based demonstrations, inventories, and surveys are designed to assess student understanding of various psychological topics. (These demonstrations work easily with the iClicker Classroom Response System.)
- **New! Digital Media Archive, Second Edition** Drawn from a variety of sources, the new edition of the Digital Media Archive includes more than 30 short video clips, plus numerous new animations. These clips are available in MPEG format for easy import into PowerPoint presentations.
- **New!** *Scientific American Frontiers* **Teaching Modules, Third Edition**, edited by Martin Bolt. The Third Edition offers you 15 edited clips from *Scientific American Frontiers* segments produced between 2003 and 2005.

New! Instructor's Media Guide (based on trusted Instructor's Resources author Martin Bolt's work) expands the Lecture Guides and offers instructors a simple way to incorporate instructor media, presentation, and video resources into their course.

New! Online Study Center 2.0 for *Exploring Psychology, Seventh Edition in Modules* The customized Online Study Center (OSC) offers students a variety of tools to help them master the course:

- *A Module-by-Module Self-Guided Study Plan With Diagnostic Tests.* Students may take a Self-Test to assess their current knowledge of a particular module, then view a Study Plan that identifies areas of weakness and offers a variety of resources for learning those concepts.

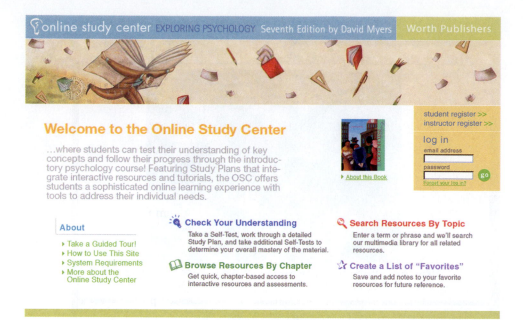

- *Self-Paced Tutorials* that allow students to revisit and master course concepts on their own.
- *Multiple Assessment and Review Tools,* organized by module. In addition to the Study Plan, students can Search by Topic or Browse by Module to access interactive demonstrations and review materials.
- *Dozens of Hands-On Activities.* Your students will be able to tackle classic experiments (condition a rat, probe the hypothalamus electronically), encounter perceptual illusions, test their memory, interpret facial expressions, and more.
- *Digitized Video Demonstrations* (for example, the effects of teratogens on development) and Animations (such as neural communication) bring text concepts to life.
- *A Sophisticated Search Engine* (similar to Google®) that allows students to search quickly by topic (not just by module).
- *Interactive Study Tools.* Students are able to add resources to their Favorites and even add Notes to specific resources.

New! Enhanced Course Management Solutions (WebCT, Blackboard, Desire2Learn, Angel) allow adopters to access all of this edition's teaching and learning resources in one central location (through their course management system) through one, seamless, guided experience.

New! eLibrary for *Exploring Psychology, Seventh Edition in Modules,* brings together the supplementary resources, such as the *Instructor's Resources, PsychSim* 5.0, and *PsychOnline,* in a single, easy-to-use Web site. Through sophisticated and seamless search and browse functions, the eLibrary allows instructors to quickly build free, premium student Web pages, construct lectures, and organize resources.

New! Expanded and Improved Book Companion Site The *Exploring Psychology, Seventh Edition in Modules* Book Companion site offers students a virtual study guide, 24 hours a day, seven days a week. Best of all, these resources are free and do not require any special access codes or passwords. In addition to self-tests, review materials, annotated Web links, simulations, and demonstrations, the site now includes an interactive, historical timeline and new Spanish-English Flashcards. The ***password-protected Instructor Site*** offers a full array of teaching resources, including a new suite of PowerPoint slides, electronic Lecture Guides, an online quiz grade book, and links to additional tools.

New! iClicker Radio Frequency Classroom Response System iClicker is Worth's hugely successful new polling system, created by educators for educators. This radio frequency system is the hassle-free way to make your class time more interactive. The system allows you to pause to ask questions and instantly record responses, as well as take attendance, direct students through lectures, gauge your students' understanding of the material, and much more.

Revised! *Instructor's Resources* **CD-ROM** Customized for *Exploring Psychology, Seventh Edition in Modules,* this CD-ROM contains pre-built PowerPoint presentation slide sets for each module, a digital photograph library, an electronic version of Martin Bolt's *Instructor's Resources and Lecture Guides,* and a complete illustration library. A new intuitive browser interface makes it easy to preview and use all elements in this CD-ROM.

- *Module Art PowerPoint® Slides* feature all of the text art and illustrations (including tables, charts, and graphs) within the PowerPoint format. This program also offers a number of layered PowerPoint slides for key biological and process diagrams.
- *Revised! Lecture PowerPoint® Presentation Slides* Developed by a longtime adopter of *Psychology* and informed by 20 reviewers, these slides focus on key concepts and themes from the text. The slides feature tables, graphs, and figures from the text and from outside sources.
- *New! Step Up to Psychology: A PowerPoint Review Game by John Schulte, Cape Fear Community College and University of North Carolina-Wilmington* This PowerPoint-based review adopts a game-show approach where students divide into teams to compete for points by answering questions related to text material. The questions are ranked for difficulty (four levels), and include both factual/definitional and conceptual/application questions.
- *New! Digital Photo Library* gives you access to all of the photographs from the Seventh Edition in Modules, organized by module.

PsychSim 5.0, Thomas Ludwig, Hope College, CD-ROM and Booklet These 42 interactive simulations involve students in the practice of psychological research by having them play the role of experimenter (conditioning a rat, probing the hypothalamus electronically, working in a sleep lab) or participant (responding to tests of memory or visual illusions, interpreting facial expressions). Other simulations provide dynamic tutorials or demonstrations. In addition, five-question, multiple-choice quizzes are available for each activity on the Companion Web site.

PsychInquiry for *Exploring Psychology, Seventh Edition in Modules***: Student Activities in Research and Critical Thinking CD-ROM, Thomas Ludwig, Hope College** Customized to work specifically with this new edition, this CD-ROM contains dozens of interactive activities designed to help students learn about psychological research and to improve their critical thinking skills.

PsychOnline (Course Management Version), Thomas Ludwig, Hope College Housed in both WebCT and Blackboard, *PsychOnline* is a comprehensive instructor and student online solution for introductory psychology. Designed for use as a supplement for either Web-enhanced lecture courses or complete online courses, *PsychOnline* offers a rich, Web-based collection of interactive tutorials and activities for introductory psychology.

PsychOnline 2.0 (Web-Based Version), Thomas Ludwig, Hope College *PsychOnline 2.0* is a comprehensive online resource for introductory psychology. *PsychOnline 2.0* looks like a Worth Web site, includes more than 100 interactive tutorials and over 250 activities, and also contains the following new features:

- A Web-based interface that is easy to use and incorporate within your course.

- A self-guided study plan that includes a multiple-choice Diagnostic Test for each topic. After the student completes the Diagnostic Test, the student is given a Diagnostic Test Report that offers test results and suggestions for re-examining and studying material.
- 20 modules from Thomas Ludwig's *PsychSim 5.0*

Diploma Computerized Test Bank (Available in Windows and Macintosh on one CD-ROM) This program allows you to add an unlimited number of questions, edit questions, format a test, scramble questions, and include pictures, equations, or multimedia links. With the accompanying grade book, you can record students' grades throughout a course, sort student records and view detailed analyses of test items, curve tests, generate reports, add weights to grades, and more. This CD-ROM is the access point for Diploma Online Testing. Blackboard and WebCT formatted versions of the Test Bank are also available within the Course Cartridge and ePack.

- *Diploma Online Testing at http://www.brownstone.net* With Diploma, you can easily create and administer exams over the Internet, with questions that incorporate multimedia and interactivity. Students receive instant feedback and can take the quizzes multiple times. Instructors can sort and view results, and can take advantage of various grade book and result-analysis features, as well as restrict tests to specific computers or time blocks.
- *Online Quizzing at http://www.worthpublishers.com/myers* Now you can easily and securely quiz students online using prewritten multiple-choice questions for each module. Students receive instant feedback and can take the quizzes multiple times. As the instructor, you can view results by quiz, student, or question, or you can get weekly results via e-mail.

Worth Image and Lecture Gallery at http://www.worthpublishers.com/ilg Using the Image and Lecture Gallery, you can browse or search and download text art, illustrations, outlines, and pre-built PowerPoint slides for *all* Worth titles. Users can also create personal folders for easy organization of the materials.

Video/DVD Resources

New! Worth Publishers Video Tool Kit for Introductory Psychology spans the full range of standard topics for the introductory psychology course, combining both research and news footage. With its superb collection of brief (one to 13 minutes) clips and emphasis on the biological basis of behavior, the **Video Tool Kit** gives students a fresh new way to experience both the classic experiments at the heart of psychological science and cutting-edge research conducted by the field's most influential investigators.

New! *Moving Images: Exploring Psychology Through Film* Available in VHS and DVD and edited by Martin Bolt (Calvin College), this completely new series (drawn from the Films for the Humanities and Sciences) contains 24 one-to-eight minute clips of real people, real experiments, and real patients. The series combines historical footage with cutting-edge research and news programming. Highlights include "Brain and Behavior: A Contemporary Phineas Gage," "Firewalking: Mind Over Matter," and "Social Rejection: The Need to Belong."

Worth Digital Media Archive **(available in dual platform CD-ROMs, VHS, and DVD)** This rich presentation tool contains 42 digitized video clips of classic experiments and research. Footage includes Bandura's Bobo doll experiment, Takooshian's bystander studies, Piaget's conservation experiment, Harlow's monkey experiments, and Milgram's obedience studies. The Digital Media Archive CD-ROM clips are available in MPEG for optimal visual presentation, and are compatible with PowerPoint.

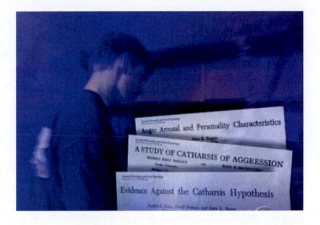

Moving Images: Exploring Psychology Through Film
(edited by Martin Bolt)

***Psychology: The Human Experience* Teaching Modules** This series includes more than 3 hours of footage from the Introductory Psychology telecourse, *Psychology: The Human Experience,* produced by Coast Learning Systems in collaboration with Worth Publishers. Footage contains noted scholars, the latest research, and striking animations.

***The Many Faces of Psychology* Video (available in VHS and DVD)** Created and written by Frank J. Vattano, Colorado State University, and Martin Bolt, Calvin College (produced by the Office of Instructional Services, Colorado State University), this video is a terrific way to begin your psychology course. *The Many Faces of Psychology* introduces psychology as a science and a profession, illustrating basic and applied methods. The 22-minute video presents some of the major areas in which psychologists work and teach.

***Scientific American Frontiers* Video Collection, Second Edition (available in VHS and DVD)** Hosted by Alan Alda, these 8-12 minute teaching modules from the highly praised Scientific American series feature the work of such notable researchers as Steve Sumi, Renée Baillargeon, Carl Rosengren, Laura Pettito, Steven Pinker, Barbara Rothbaum, Bob Stickgold, Irene Pepperberg, Marc Hauser, Linda Bartoshuk, and Michael Gazzaniga.

***The Mind* Video Teaching Modules, Second Edition (available in VHS and DVD)** Edited by Frank J. Vattano, Colorado State University, with the consultation of Charles Brewer, Furman University, and myself in association with WNET, these 35 brief, engaging video clips dramatically enhance and illustrate your lectures. Examples include segments on language processing, infant cognitive development, genetic

Scientific American Frontiers **Teaching Modules, Third Edition**
(edited by Martin Bolt)

factors in alcoholism, and living without memory (featuring a dramatic interview with Clive Wearing).

The Brain Video Teaching Modules, Second Edition (available in VHS and DVD) Edited by Frank J. Vattano and Thomas L. Bennet from Colorado State University, and Michelle Butler, from the United States Air Force Academy, this collection of 32 short clips provides vivid examples for myriad topics in introductory psychology.

Print Supplements for Instructors

New! Significantly Revised and Enhanced Printed Test Bank, Volumes 1 and 2, John Brink, Calvin College Broken down into two volumes of questions, the *Test Bank* provides over 5000 multiple-choice factual/definitional, conceptual/application, and conceptual questions, plus essay questions. In response to review input from over a dozen reviewers, Brink has changed the number of distracters from five to four to avoid confusion, and he has carefully edited each question for effectiveness and comprehension. As a result, this seventh-edition set includes over 20 percent new and significantly revised questions. Each question is keyed to a learning objective, page-referenced to the text, and rated for level of difficulty. The learning objectives are also listed in the *Instructor's Resources* and used to organize the Lecture Guides and the Module Review in the *Study Guide.* Also included are copies of the Student Book Companion site quizzes. The first *Test Bank* includes optional questions from the Study Guide (for instructors who incorporate or require the Study Guide in their courses). The second *Test Bank* includes optional questions on key Worth media tools, such as *PsychSim* 5.0, *The Brain* and *The Mind* video series, the *Scientific American* videos, the *Digital Media Archive,* and *Moving Images: Exploring Psychology Through Film.*

New! Instructor's Media Guide: This handy guide quickly and visually organizes the extensive instructor and student media resources available for *Exploring Psychology, Seventh Edition in Modules,* including every video, animation, student Web activity (including *PsychSim*), PowerPoint®, and more—all organized by module.

Instructor's Resources, Martin Bolt, Calvin College (also available electronically within the eLibrary) Well-known in the psychology community for its comprehensiveness and innovative teaching ideas, Martin Bolt's revised *Instructor's Resources* features more than 30 percent new, revised, and updated material and includes the following:

- *Outline of Resources,* organized by text topic, includes the relevant Instructor's Resources items by type (classroom exercise, lecture/discussion topic, etc.) with appropriate *Instructor's Resources* page number.
- *Module Objectives* highlight main concepts and terms and detail the key points of each text module. They can be used as essay questions in classroom examinations. The seventh edition *Test Bank,* and the seventh edition *Study Guide* fill-in questions are also keyed to these Objectives.
- *Module Outlines* follow the major text section headings (with page references), providing relevant instructional materials for each topic—including dozens of detailed lecture/discussion ideas, student projects, classroom exercises (many with ready-to-use handouts for in- or out-of-class use), and suggestions about how to use *PsychSim* modules and feature films (as they apply to psychological concepts discussed in the text). The videos provided by Worth Publishers (see pages xxiv-xxvi) are listed, by module, in the Preface and described in their Faculty Guides on the Worth Web site. All items from the *ActivePsych* CD-ROM are keyed to the module and section to which each pertains. Note that the films and videos from other sources are outlined in the Book Companion site. The Book Companion site also describes relevant Web sites and repeats the feature film descriptions that appear in the *Instructor's Resources.*

Martin Bolt's Lecture Guides, available in both print and easily modifiable Microsoft Word formats, offer you a terrific integrating resource for lecture preparation. For each text module, the Lecture Guides summarize the main ideas by major section and by Learning Objective. The Lecture Guides also list the lecture/discussion topics, exercises, projects, feature films, transparencies, *PsychSim* modules, and video segments (from the Worth library) that complement the topics within each major section.

Overhead Transparencies Our transparency set includes over 150 text images, charts, and tables from *Exploring Psychology, Seventh Edition in Modules* and other sources.

Print Supplements for Students

New! *Visual Concept Reviews,* **Richard Straub, University of Michigan-Dearborn** This full-color booklet—available for free when shrink-wrapped with the book or *Study Guide*—offers fill-in-the-blank style concept charts that allow students to apply their understanding of the concepts to real-life situations (with answers in an appendix).*

Study Guide, **Richard Straub, University of Michigan-Dearborn** Following the text's content, Richard Straub offers a Module Overview and Module Review, divided by major section. Each group of fill-in-the-blank and short-essay questions is preceded by the relevant learning objective. The learning objectives also appear in the *Instructor's Resources* and are keyed to questions in the *Test Banks*. Each module also has a self-test (including questions that encourage students to think critically about the module's concepts by applying them to real-life situations), answers (with explanations of why a choice is correct or incorrect), and a Focus on Language and Vocabulary section (by Cornelius Rea, Douglas College), which explains idioms and other phrases from the text that may not be clear to some readers.

Pursuing Human Strengths: A Positive Psychology Guide, **Martin Bolt, Calvin College** By using the scientific method in its efforts to assess, understand, and then build human strengths, positive psychology balances the investigation of weakness and damage with a study of strength and virtue. This brief *Positive Psychology Guide* gives instructors and students alike the means to learn more about this relevant approach to psychology.

Critical Thinking Companion, **Second Edition, Jane Halonen, University of West Florida, and Cynthia Gray, Alverno College** Tied to the main topics in *Exploring Psychology, Seventh Edition in Modules,* this engaging handbook includes six categories of critical thinking exercises: pattern recognition, practical problem solving, creative problem solving, scientific critical thinking, psychological reasoning, and perspective taking, which connect to the six categories used in the Critical Thinking Exercises available in the student *Study Guide.*

Scientific American Reader I hand picked these 14 classic and current articles to provide another tool for enhancing lectures, encouraging discussions, and emphasizing the relevance of psychology to everyday life.

Improving the Mind and Brain: A Scientific American Special Issue This single-topic issue from *Scientific American* magazine features findings from the most distinguished researchers in the field.

Scientific American Explores the Hidden Mind: A Collector's Edition This collector's edition includes feature articles that explore and reveal the mysterious inner workings of our minds and brains.

In Appreciation

If it is true that "whoever walks with the wise becomes wise" then I am wiser for all the wisdom and advice received from expert colleagues. Aided by nearly a thousand consultants and reviewers over the last two decades, this has become a better, more

*(The *Visual Concept Reviews* available for packaging uses chapter numbering from Myers' *Exploring Psychology, 7e,* so the package will have a conversion chart to allow it to be used with *Exploring Psychology, Seventh Edition in Modules.*)

accurate book than one author alone (this author, at least) could write. As my editors and I keep reminding ourselves, all of us together are smarter than any one of us.

My indebtedness continues to each of the teacher-scholars whose influence I acknowledged in the six previous editions, and also to the innumerable researchers who have been so willing to share their time and talent to help me accurately report their research. This new edition also benefited from the creative input and assistance of Jennifer Peluso, Florida Atlantic University, in revising Modules 21 to 24, which examine memory, thinking, and language.

My gratitude extends to the colleagues who contributed criticism, corrections, and creative ideas related to the content, pedagogy, and format of this new edition and its supplements package. For their expertise and encouragement, and the gifts of their time to the teaching of psychology, I thank these colleagues:

Richard Alexander,
Muskegon Community College

Viviette Allen,
Fayetteville State University

Alfred Atanda,
Ocean County College

Joyce Bishop,
Golden West College

Jeffrey Blum,
Los Angeles City College

Victor Broderick,
Lincoln Land Community College

Carrie Canales,
Los Angeles City College

Dominic Carbone,
East Stroudsburg University of Pennsylvania

Carol Chandler,
McHenry County College

Roxanna Conroy,
Jacksonville State University

Diane Cook,
Gainesville College

Mary Coplen,
Hutchinson County Community College

Damien Cronin,
Lake Superior College

William Davis,
Indiana University of Pennsylvania

Jonathan Durm,
Cy-Fair College

Andrea Ericksen,
San Juan College

Sussie Eshun,
East Stroudsburg University of Pennsylvania

Gaithri Fernando,
California State University—Los Angeles

Sandra E. Gibbs,
Muskegon Community College

Sheldon Helms,
Ohlone College

Nicole Korzetz,
Lee College

Frank LoSchiavo,
Ohio University—Zanesville

Judy McCalla,
University of Miami

Krista McClain-Rocha,
West Valley College

Amy Overman,
University of Pittsburgh

Susan Pinsker,
Berkshire Community College

Ron Salazar,
San Juan College

Moises Salinas,
Central Connecticut State University

Roger Sambrook,
University of Colorado

Tanya Scott,
College of Staten Island

Rochelle Sechooler
Los Angeles City College

Barbara Silver,
Cape Fear Community College

John Smith,
Indiana University of Pennsylvania

Melinda Spohn,
Spokane Falls Community College

Amy Sweetman,
Los Angeles City College

Victoria Van Wie,
Cy-Fair College

Marc Weinstein,
Gainesville College

Rob Weinstein,
College of Staten Island

Steve West,
Truckee Meadows Community College

Tanya Whipple,
Missouri State University

At Worth Publishers, a host of people played key roles in creating this edition. Although the information gathering is never ending, the formal planning began as the author-publisher team gathered for a two-day retreat. This happy and creative get-together included John Brink, Martin Bolt, Thomas Ludwig, Richard Straub, and me from the author team, along with my assistant Kathryn Brownson and manuscript developer Phil Vandervelde. We were joined by Worth Publishers' president Liz Widdicombe; publisher Catherine Woods; editors Christine Brune, Nancy Fleming, Tracey Kuehn, and Betty Probert; and sales and marketing executives Kate Nurre, Tom Kling, Guy Geraghty, Greg David, and Chuck Linsmeier. The input and brainstorming during this meeting of minds gave birth, among other things, to the thoroughly revised Module 5, Behavior Genetics and Evolutionary Psychology, and Module 6, Environmental Influences on Behavior.

Christine Brune, Chief Editor for the last six editions, is a wonder worker. She offers just the right mix of encouragement, gentle admonition, attention to detail, and passion for excellence. An author could not ask for more. Psychology Acquisitions Editor, Kevin Feyen, with whom we are pleased to now be working closely, has become a valued team leader, thanks to his dedication, creativity, and sensitivity. Development Editor Nancy Fleming is one of those rare editors who is gifted both at "thinking big" about a module—and with a kindred spirit to my own—while also applying her sensitive, graceful, line-by-line touches. Publisher Catherine Woods helped construct and execute the plan for this new edition and its supplements. Catherine was also a trusted sounding board as we faced the myriad discrete decisions along the way. Media and Supplements Editor Peter Twickler coordinated production of the huge supplements package for this edition. Betty Probert efficiently edited and produced the print supplements, and, in the process, also helped fine-tune the whole book. Editorial Assistants Sarah Berger and Leo Wilkinson provided invaluable support in commissioning and organizing the multitude of reviews, mailing information to professors, and numerous other daily tasks related to the book's development and production. Lee Mahler did a splendid job of laying out each page. Patricia Marx, Bianca Moscatelli, Christina Micek, and Julie Tesser worked together to locate the myriad new photographic illustrations.

Associate Managing Editor Tracey Kuehn displayed tireless tenacity, commitment, and impressive organization in leading Worth's gifted artistic production team and coordinating editorial input throughout the production process with the help of Project Editor Dana Kasowitz. Production Manager Sarah Segal masterfully kept the book to its tight schedule, and Babs Reingold skillfully directed creation of the distinctive design and art program. Production Manager Stacey Alexander, along with Production Editor Jenny Chiu, did their usual excellent work of producing the many supplements.

To achieve our goal of supporting the teaching of psychology, this teaching package not only must be authored, reviewed, edited, and produced, but also made available to teachers of psychology. For their exceptional success in doing that, our author team is grateful to Worth Publishers' professional sales and marketing team. We are especially grateful to Executive Marketing Manager Kate Nurre and Marketing Manager Amy Shefferd, both for their tireless efforts to inform our teaching colleagues of our efforts to assist their teaching, and for the joy of working with them.

At Hope College, the supporting team members for this edition included Project Manager Kathryn Brownson, who researched countless bits of information, proofed hundreds of pages, and, with the assistance of Sara Neevel, prepared the bibliography and name index. Kathryn has become a knowledgeable and sensitive adviser on many matters, and Sara has become our Quark-expert manuscript developer, par excellence. They were supported by Julia Roehling, who assisted with the bibliography preparation, and Merry Roberts, who assisted with research and photocopying. Laura Myers updated, with page citations, all the cross-reference tables.

Again, I gratefully acknowledge the influence and editing assistance of my writing coach, poet Jack Ridl, whose influence resides in the voice you will be hearing in the pages that follow. He, more than anyone, cultivated my delight in dancing with the language, and taught me to approach writing as a craft that shades into art.

After hearing countless dozens of people say that this book's supplements have taken their teaching to a new level, I reflect on how fortunate I am to be a part of a team on which everyone has produced on-time work marked by the highest professional standards. For their remarkable talents, their long-term dedication, and their friendship, I thank Martin Bolt, John Brink, Thomas Ludwig, and Richard Straub.

Finally, my gratitude extends to the many students and instructors who have written to offer suggestions, or just an encouraging word. It is for them, and those about to begin their study of psychology, that I have done my best to introduce the field I love.

The day this book went to press was the day I started gathering information and ideas for the eighth edition. Your input will again influence how this book continues to evolve. So, please, do share your thoughts.

David Myers

Hope College
Holland, Michigan 49422-9000 USA
davidmyers.org

Introduction to the History and Science of Psychology

Introduction to the History and Science of Psychology

Hoping to satisfy their curiosity about people and to remedy their own woes, millions turn to "psychology." They listen to talk-radio counseling, read articles on psychic powers, attend stop-smoking hypnosis seminars, and absorb self-help books on the meaning of dreams, the path to ecstatic love, and the roots of personal happiness.

Others, intrigued by claims of psychological truth, wonder: Do mothers and infants bond in the first hours after birth? Should we trust childhood sexual abuse memories "recovered" in adulthood—and prosecute the alleged predators? Does handwriting offer clues to personality? Does psychotherapy heal?

For these questioners, as for most people whose exposure to psychology comes from popular books, magazines, and TV, psychologists analyze personality, offer counseling, and dispense child-rearing advice.

Do they? Yes, and much more. Consider some of psychology's questions that from time to time you may wonder about:

- Have you ever found yourself reacting to something as one of your biological parents would—perhaps in a way you vowed you never would—and then wondered how much of your personality you inherited? *To what extent are person-to-person differences in personality predisposed by one's genes? To what extent by the home and neighborhood environments?*

- Have you ever played peekaboo with a 6-month-old and wondered why the baby finds the game so delightful? The infant reacts as if, when you move behind a door, you actually disappear—only to reappear later out of thin air. *What do babies actually perceive and think?*

- Have you ever awakened from a nightmare and, with a wave of relief, wondered why you had such a crazy dream? *How often, and why, do we dream?*

- Have you ever wondered what leads to success? Are some people just born smarter? *Does sheer intelligence explain why some people get richer, think more creatively, or relate more sensitively?*

- Have you ever become depressed or anxious and wondered whether you'll ever feel "normal"? *What triggers our bad moods—and our good ones?*

- Have you ever worried about how to act among people of a different culture, race, or gender? *In what ways are we alike as members of the human family? How do we differ?*

Such questions provide grist for psychology's mill because psychology is a science that seeks to answer all sorts of questions about us all: how we think, feel, and act. In Module 1, we trace psychology's roots and survey the scope of this field. In Module 2, we consider psychology's methods and some ways we can all benefit by thinking critically.

A smile is a smile the world around
Throughout this book are examples of our cultural and gender diversity and also of the similarities that define our human nature. People in different cultures vary in when and how often they smile, but a smile *means* the same thing anywhere in the world.

© Stock Image/Alamy

Sally Cassidy/The Picture Cube/Index Stock Imagery

Robert Caputo/Stock, Boston

The History and Scope of Psychology

Psychology's Roots

Once upon a time, on a planet in your neighborhood of the universe, there came to be people. Soon thereafter, these creatures became intensely interested in themselves and in one another. They wondered, *"Who are we? From where come our thoughts? Our feelings? Our actions? And how are we to understand—and to master or manage—those around us?"* Psychology's answers to these wonderings have developed from international roots in philosophy and biology into a science that aims to observe, describe, and explain how we think, feel, and act. Understanding the roots of today's psychology helps us appreciate psychologists' varied perspectives.

Psychological Science Is Born

1-1: How did the science of psychology develop?

To be human is to be curious about ourselves and the world around us. Before 300 B.C., the Greek naturalist and philosopher Aristotle theorized about learning and memory, motivation and emotion, perception and personality. Today we chuckle at some of his guesses, like his suggestion that a meal makes us sleepy by causing gas and heat to collect around the source of our personality, the heart. But credit Aristotle with asking the right questions.

Philosophers' thinking about thinking continued until the birth of psychology as we know it, on a December day in 1879, in a small room on the third floor of a modest building at Germany's University of Leipzig. There, two young men were helping an austere, middle-aged professor, Wilhelm Wundt, create an experimental apparatus. Their machine measured the time lag between people's hearing a ball hit a platform and their pressing a telegraph key (Hunt, 1993). Curiously, people responded in about one-tenth of a second when asked to press the key as soon as the sound occurred—and in about two-tenths of a second when asked to press the key as soon as they were consciously aware of perceiving the sound. (To be aware of one's awareness takes a little longer.) Wundt was seeking to measure "atoms of the mind"—the fastest and simplest mental processes. Thus began what many consider psychology's first experiment, launching the first psychological laboratory, staffed by Wundt and psychology's first graduate students.

This young science of psychology developed from the more established fields of philosophy and biology. Wundt was both a philosopher and a physiologist. Charles Darwin, who proposed evolutionary psychology, was an English naturalist. Ivan Pavlov, who pioneered the study of learning, was a Russian physiologist. Sigmund Freud, renowned personality theorist, was an Austrian physician. Jean Piaget, the twentieth century's most influential observer of children, was a Swiss biologist. William James, author of an important 1890 psychology textbook, was an American philosopher. This list of pioneering psychologists—"Magellans of the mind," as Morton Hunt (1993) has called them—illustrates psychology's origins in many disciplines and countries.

As these names illustrate, the early pioneers of most fields, including psychology, were predominantly men. When William James' student Mary Calkins completed all the requirements for a Harvard Ph.D., outscoring all the male students on their exams, Harvard denied her the degree she had earned, offering her instead a degree

Throughout the text you will find numbered Preview Questions to help focus your reading, and at the end of each module, the Rehearse It! and Test Yourself questions will help you review what you've read.

Information sources are cited in parentheses, with name and date. Every citation can be found in the end-of-book References, with complete documentation that follows American Psychological Association style.

Wilhelm Wundt
Wundt (far left) established the first psychology laboratory at the University of Leipzig, Germany.

Sigmund Freud
Famed personality theorist and therapist, whose controversial ideas influenced humanity's self-understanding.

from Radcliffe, its sister school for women. Calkins refused the degree, but she went on to become the American Psychological Association's (APA's) first female president. The first woman to receive a psychology Ph.D. was animal behavior researcher Margaret Floy Washburn, who became the second female APA president.

The rest of the story of psychology—the subject of this book—develops at many levels. With activities ranging from psychotherapy to the study of nerve cell activity, *psychology* is not easily defined. Psychology began as the science of mental life. Wundt's basic research tool became *introspection*—self-examination of one's own emotional states and mental processes. Wundt focused on *inner* sensations, images, and feelings. James, too, engaged in introspective examination of the stream of consciousness and of emotion. Freud emphasized the ways emotional responses to childhood experiences and our unconscious thought processes affect our behavior. Thus, until the 1920s, *psychology* was defined as "the science of mental life."

From the 1920s into the 1960s, American psychologists, initially led by flamboyant and provocative John B. Watson and later by the equally provocative B. F. Skinner, dismissed introspection and redefined *psychology* as "the scientific study of observable behavior." After all, said these **behaviorists,** science is rooted in observation. You cannot observe a sensation, a feeling, or a thought, but you *can* observe and record people's *behavior* as they respond to different situations.

Humanistic psychology was a softer, 1960s response to Freudian psychology and to behaviorism, which pioneers Carl Rogers and Abraham Maslow found too mechanistic. Rather than calling up childhood memories or focusing on learned behaviors, Rogers and Maslow both emphasized the importance of current environmental influences on our growth potential, and the importance of meeting our needs for love and acceptance.

Throughout the text, important concepts are *boldfaced*. As you study, you can find these terms with their definitions in a nearby margin and in the Glossary at the end of the book.

William James and Mary Whiton Calkins
William James was a legendary teacher-writer of psychology. He also mentored students, including Mary Whiton Calkins, who became a pioneering memory researcher and the first woman president of the American Psychological Association.

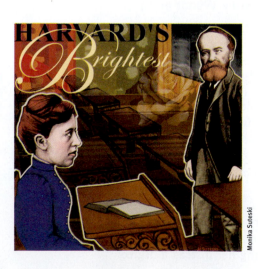

Margaret Floy Washburn
The first woman to receive a psychology Ph.D.; synthesized animal behavior research in *The Animal Mind.*

John B. Watson and Rosalie Rayner
Working with Rayner, Watson championed psychology as the science of behavior and demonstrated conditioned responses on a baby who became famous as "Little Albert."

Monika Suteski

B. F. Skinner
A leading behaviorist, who rejected introspection and studied how consequences shape behavior.

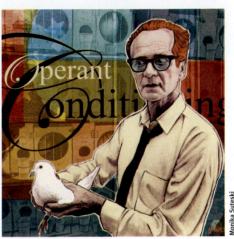

Monika Suteski

In the 1960s, psychology began to recapture its initial interest in mental processes through studies of how our mind processes and retains information. This *cognitive revolution* supported earlier psychologists' ideas about the importance of internal thought processes, but expanded those ideas to explore scientifically the ways we perceive, process, and remember information. Cognitive psychology, and more recently *cognitive neuroscience* (the study of brain activity underlying thought), has suggested new ways to understand and treat psychological disorders.

To encompass psychology's concern with observable behavior *and* with inner thoughts and feelings, today we define **psychology** as *the scientific study of behavior and mental processes.* Let's unpack this definition. *Behavior* is anything an organism *does*—any action we can observe and record. Yelling, smiling, blinking, sweating, talking, and questionnaire marking are all observable behaviors. *Mental processes* are the internal, subjective experiences we infer from behavior—sensations, perceptions, dreams, thoughts, beliefs, and feelings.

The key word in psychology's definition is *science.* Psychology, as I will emphasize throughout this book, is less a set of findings than a way of asking and answering questions. My aim, then, is not merely to report results but also to show you how psychologists play their game. You will see how researchers evaluate conflicting opinions and ideas. And you will learn how all of us, whether scientists or simply curious people, can think smarter when describing and explaining the events of our lives.

Contemporary Psychology

Like its pioneers, today's psychologists are citizens of many lands. The International Union of Psychological Science has 69 member nations, from Albania to Zimbabwe. Nearly everywhere, membership in psychological societies is mushrooming—from 4183 American Psychological Association members and affiliates in 1945 to more than 160,000 today, with similarly rapid growth in Britain (from 1100 to 34,000). In China, five universities had psychology departments in 1985; by the century's end, there were 50 (Jing, 1999). Worldwide, some 500,000 people have been trained as psychologists, and 130,000 of them belong to European psychological organizations (Tikkanen, 2001). Moreover, thanks to international publications, joint meetings, and the Internet, collaboration and communication cross borders more now than ever: "We are moving rapidly towards a single world of psychological science," reports Robert Bjork (2000). Psychology is *growing* and it is *globalizing.*

Today's psychologists debate some enduring issues and view behavior from differing perspectives. They also teach, work, and do research in many different subfields.

■ **behaviorism**   the view that psychology (1) should be an objective science that (2) studies behavior without reference to mental processes. Most research psychologists today agree with (1) but not with (2).

■ **humanistic psychology**   historically significant perspective that emphasized the growth potential of healthy people; used personalized methods to study personality in hopes of fostering personal growth.

■ **psychology**   the scientific study of behavior and mental processes.

A nature-made nature-nurture experiment
Because identical twins have the same genes, they are ideal participants in studies designed to shed light on hereditary and environmental influences on temperament, intelligence, and other traits. Studies of identical and fraternal twins provide a rich array of findings that underscore the importance of both nature and nurture.

■ **nature-nurture issue** the longstanding controversy over the relative contributions that genes and experience make to the development of psychological traits and behaviors. Today's science sees traits and behaviors arising from the interaction of nature and nurture.

■ **levels of analysis** the differing complementary views, from biological to psychological to social-cultural, for analyzing any given phenomenon.

■ **biopsychosocial approach** an integrated approach that incorporates biological, psychological, and social-cultural levels of analysis.

Psychology's Big Question

1-2 : What is psychology's historic big issue?

During its short history, psychology has wrestled with some issues that reappear throughout this book. The biggest and most persistent is the **nature-nurture issue**—*the controversy over the relative contributions of biology and experience.* The origins of this debate are ancient. Do our human traits develop through experience, or do we come equipped with them? Plato assumed that character and intelligence are largely inherited and that certain ideas are inborn. Aristotle countered that there is nothing in the mind that does not first come in from the external world through the senses. The nature-nurture debate weaves a thread from these ancient Greeks to our own time. Today's psychologists explore this issue by asking, for example:

- How are differences in intelligence, personality, and psychological disorders influenced by heredity and by environment?
- Is children's grammar mostly innate or formed by experience?
- Are sexual behaviors more "pushed" by inner biology or "pulled" by external incentives?
- Should we treat depression as a disorder of the brain or a disorder of thought—or both?
- How are we humans alike (because of our common biology and evolutionary history) and different (because of our differing environments)?
- Are gender differences biologically predisposed or socially constructed?

Such debates continue. Yet over and over again we will see that in contemporary science the nature-nurture tension dissolves: *Nurture works on what nature endows.* Our species is biologically endowed with an enormous capacity to learn and adapt. Moreover, every psychological event (every thought, every emotion) is simultaneously a biological event. Thus depression can be *both* a thought disorder and a brain disorder.

Psychology's Three Main Levels of Analysis

1-3 : What theoretical perspectives do psychologists take, and how does the biopsychosocial approach help integrate these perspectives?

Each of us is a complex system that is part of a larger social system, but each of us is also composed of smaller systems, such as our nervous system and body organs, which are composed of still smaller systems—cells, molecules, and atoms.

These tiered systems suggest different **levels of analysis,** which offer complementary outlooks. It's like explaining why grizzly bears hibernate. Is it because hibernation enhanced their ancestors' survival and reproduction? Because their inner physiology drives them to do so? Because cold environments hinder food gathering during winter? Such perspectives are complementary, because "everything is related to everything else" (Brewer, 1996). Together, different levels of analysis form an integrated **biopsychosocial approach,** which considers the influences of biological, psychological, and social-cultural factors (**FIGURE 1.1**). Each level provides a valuable vantage point for looking at behavior, yet each by itself is incomplete. Like different academic disciplines, psychology's varied perspectives ask different questions and have their own limits. One perspective may stress the biological, psychological, or social-cultural level more than another, but the different perspectives described in **TABLE 1.1** complement one another. Consider, for example, how they shed light on anger.

- Someone working from a *neuroscience perspective* might study brain circuits that produce the physical state of being "red in the face" and "hot under the collar."
- Someone working from the *evolutionary perspective* might analyze how anger facilitated the survival of our ancestors' genes.

Dennis Degnan/Corbis

Tim Wright/Corbis

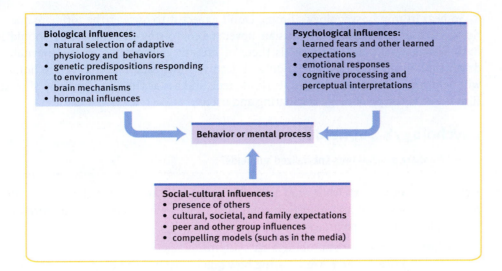

Biological influences:
• natural selection of adaptive physiology and behaviors
• genetic predispositions responding to environment
• brain mechanisms
• hormonal influences

Psychological influences:
• learned fears and other learned expectations
• emotional responses
• cognitive processing and perceptual interpretations

Behavior or mental process

Social-cultural influences:
• presence of others
• cultural, societal, and family expectations
• peer and other group influences
• compelling models (such as in the media)

FIGURE 1.1
Biopsychosocial approach
This integrated viewpoint incorporates various levels of analysis and offers a more complete picture of any given behavior or mental process.

- Someone working from the *behavior genetics perspective* might study how heredity and experience influence our individual differences in temperament.
- Someone working from the *psychodynamic perspective* might view an outburst as an outlet for unconscious hostility.
- Someone working from the *behavioral perspective* might study the facial expressions and body gestures that accompany anger, or might attempt to determine which external stimuli result in angry responses or aggressive acts.
- Someone working from the *cognitive perspective* might study how our interpretation of a situation affects our anger and how our anger affects our thinking.
- Someone working from the *social-cultural perspective* might explore which situations produce the most anger, and how expressions of anger vary across cultural contexts.

The point to remember: Like two-dimensional views of a three-dimensional object, each of psychology's perspectives is helpful but by itself fails to reveal the whole picture.

Gabe Palmer/Corbis

Views of anger
How would each of psychology's levels of analysis explain what's going on here?

TABLE 1.1

PSYCHOLOGY'S CURRENT PERSPECTIVES

Perspective	Focus	Sample Questions
Neuroscience	How the body and brain enable emotions, memories, and sensory experiences	How are messages transmitted within the body? How is blood chemistry linked with moods and motives?
Evolutionary	How the natural selection of traits promotes the perpetuation of one's genes	How does evolution influence behavior tendencies?
Behavior genetics	How much our genes and our environment influence our individual differences	To what extent are psychological traits such as intelligence, personality, sexual orientation, and vulnerability to depression attributable to our genes? To our environment?
Psychodynamic	How behavior springs from unconscious drives and conflicts	How can someone's personality traits and disorders be explained in terms of sexual and aggressive drives or as the disguised effects of unfulfilled wishes and childhood traumas?
Behavioral	How we learn observable responses	How do we learn to fear particular objects or situations? What is the most effective way to alter our behavior, say, to lose weight or stop smoking?
Cognitive	How we encode, process, store, and retrieve information	How do we use information in remembering? Reasoning? Solving problems?
Social-cultural	How behavior and thinking vary across situations and cultures	How are we—as Africans, Asians, Australians, or North Americans—alike as members of one human family? As products of different environmental contexts, how do we differ?

© The New Yorker Collection, 1986, J. B. Handelsman from cartoonbank.com. All Rights Reserved.

"I'm a social scientist, Michael. That means I can't explain electricity or anything like that, but if you ever want to know about people I'm your man."

Want to learn more? See Appendix B, Careers in Psychology, at the end of this book for more information about psychology's subfields and to learn about the many interesting options available to those with bachelor's, master's, and doctoral degrees in psychology.

Psychology: A science and a profession Psychologists experiment with, observe, test, and treat behavior. Here we see psychologists testing a child, recording children's behavior, and doing face-to-face therapy.

So bear in mind psychology's limits. Don't expect it to answer the ultimate questions, such as those posed by Russian novelist Leo Tolstoy (1904): "Why should I live? Why should I do anything? Is there in life any purpose which the inevitable death that awaits me does not undo and destroy?" Instead, expect that psychology will help you understand why people think, feel, and act as they do. Then you should find the study of psychology fascinating and useful.

Psychology's Subfields

1-4: What are psychology's specialized subfields?

Picturing a chemist at work, you probably envision a white-coated scientist surrounded by glassware and high-tech equipment. Picture a psychologist at work and you would be right to envision

- a white-coated scientist probing a rat's brain.
- an intelligence researcher measuring how quickly an infant becomes bored with (looks away from) a familiar picture.
- an executive evaluating a new "healthy life-styles" training program for employees.
- someone at a computer keyboard analyzing data on whether adopted teens' temperaments more closely resemble those of their adoptive parents or those of their biological parents.
- a therapist listening carefully to a client's depressed thoughts.
- a traveler en route to another culture to collect data on variations in human values and behaviors.
- a teacher or writer sharing the joy of psychology with others.

The cluster of subfields we call psychology has less unity than most other sciences. But there is a payoff: Psychology is a meeting ground for different disciplines and is thus a perfect home for those with wide-ranging interests. In their diverse activities, from biological experimentation to cultural comparisons, a common quest unites the tribe of psychology: to describe and explain behavior and the mind underlying it.

Some psychologists conduct **basic research** that builds psychology's knowledge base. In the pages that follow we will meet a wide variety of such researchers:

- *Biological psychologists* exploring the links between brain and mind
- *Developmental psychologists* studying our changing abilities from womb to tomb
- *Cognitive psychologists* experimenting with how we perceive, think, and solve problems
- *Personality psychologists* investigating our persistent traits
- *Social psychologists* exploring how we view and affect one another

These psychologists also may conduct **applied research** that tackles practical problems. So do other psychologists, such as *industrial/organizational psychologists,*

Michael Newman/Photo Edit Jeff Greenberg/PhotoEdit Michael Newman/Photo Edit

who use psychology's concepts and methods in the workplace to help organizations and companies select and train employees, boost morale and productivity, design products, and implement systems.

Although most psychology textbooks focus on psychological science, psychology is also a helping profession devoted to such practical issues as how to have a happy marriage, how to overcome anxiety or depression, and how to raise thriving children. **Counseling psychologists** help people cope with challenges (including academic, vocational, and marital issues) by recognizing their strengths and resources. **Clinical psychologists** assess and treat mental, emotional, and behavior disorders (APA, 2003). Both counseling and clinical psychologists administer and interpret tests, provide counseling and therapy, and sometimes conduct basic and applied research. By contrast, **psychiatrists,** who also often provide psychotherapy, are medical doctors licensed to prescribe drugs and otherwise treat physical causes of psychological disorders. (Some clinical psychologists are lobbying for a similar right to prescribe mental health–related drugs, and in 2002 the state of New Mexico was the first state to grant that right to specially trained and licensed psychologists.)

With perspectives ranging from the biological to the social, and with settings from the laboratory to the clinic, psychology relates to many fields, ranging from mathematics to biology to sociology to philosophy. And more and more, psychology's methods and findings aid other disciplines. Psychologists teach in medical schools, law schools, and theological seminaries, and they work in hospitals, factories, and corporate offices. They engage in interdisciplinary studies, such as psychohistory (the psychological analysis of historical characters), psycholinguistics (the study of language and thinking), and psychoceramics (the study of crackpots).[1]

Psychology also influences modern culture. Knowledge transforms us. Learning about the solar system and the germ theory of disease alters the way people think and act. Learning psychology's findings also changes people: They less often judge psychological disorders as a moral failing, treatable by punishment and ostracism. They less often regard and treat women as men's mental inferiors. They less often view and rear children as ignorant, willful beasts in need of taming. "In each case," notes Morton Hunt (1990, p. 206), "knowledge has modified attitudes, and, through them, behavior." Once aware of psychology's well-researched ideas—about how body and mind connect, how a child's mind grows, how we construct our perceptions, how we remember (and misremember) our experiences, how people across the world differ (and are alike)—your mind may never again be quite the same.

Tips for Studying Psychology

1-5: How can psychological principles help you as a student?

The investment you are making in studying psychology should enrich your life and enlarge your vision. Although many of life's significant questions are beyond psychology, some very important ones are illuminated by even a first psychology course. Through painstaking research, psychologists have gained insights into brain and mind, depression and joy, dreams and memories. Even the unanswered questions can enrich us, by renewing our sense of mystery about "things too wonderful" for us yet to understand. What is more, your study of psychology can help teach you *how to ask and answer important questions*—how to think critically as you evaluate competing ideas and claims.

Laura Dwight

I see you!
A biological psychologist might view this child's delighted response as evidence for brain maturation. A cognitive psychologist might see it as a demonstration of the baby's growing knowledge of his surroundings. For a cross-cultural psychologist, the role of grandparents in different societies might be the issue of interest. As you will see throughout this book, these and other perspectives offer complementary views of behavior.

"Once expanded to the dimensions of a larger idea, [the mind] never returns to its original size."

Oliver Wendell Holmes, 1809–1894

■ **basic research** pure science that aims to increase the scientific knowledge base.

■ **applied research** scientific study that aims to solve practical problems.

■ **counseling psychology** a branch of psychology that assists people with problems in living (often related to school, work, or marriage) and in achieving greater well-being.

■ **clinical psychology** a branch of psychology that studies, assesses, and treats people with psychological disorders.

■ **psychiatry** a branch of medicine dealing with psychological disorders; practiced by physicians who sometimes provide medical (for example, drug) treatments as well as psychological therapy.

---

[1]Confession time: I wrote the last part of this sentence on April Fools' Day.

■ **SQ3R** a study method incorporating five steps: *Survey, Question, Read, Rehearse, Review.*

Having your life enriched and your vision enlarged (and getting a decent grade) requires effective study. To master information you must *actively process* it. Your mind is not like your stomach, something to be filled passively; it is more like a muscle that grows stronger with exercise. Countless experiments reveal that people learn and remember material best when they put it in their own words, rehearse it, and then review and rehearse it again.

The **SQ3R** study method incorporates these principles (Robinson, 1970). SQ3R is an acronym for its five steps: Survey, Question, Read, Rehearse, Review.

To study a module, first *survey,* taking a bird's-eye view as you note its headings. Notice how the module is organized.

As you prepare to read each section, use its heading or the Preview Question to form a *question* that you should answer. For this section, you might have asked, "How can I most effectively and efficiently master the information in this book?"

Then *read,* actively searching for the answer. At each sitting, read only as much as you can absorb without tiring. Usually, a single module will do. Relating what you are reading to your own life will improve understanding and retention. Reading the occasional Close-Up and Thinking Critically boxes will also help.

Having read a section, *rehearse* in your own words what you read. Test yourself by trying to answer your question, rehearsing what you can recall, then glancing back over what you can't recall.

Finally, *review:* Read over any notes you have taken, again with an eye on the module's organization, and quickly review the whole module.

Survey, question, read, rehearse, review. I have organized this book to facilitate your use of the SQ3R study system. Each module begins with an outline that aids your *survey.* Headings and *Preview Questions* suggest issues and concepts you should consider as you *read.* The material is organized into sections of readable length. At the end of each module there are *Rehearse It* and *Test Yourself* questions that help you test your understanding before moving on. The answers to these questions help you *review* the module's essentials, and the list of key terms helps you check your mastery of important concepts. Survey, question, read. . . .

Five additional study tips may further boost your learning:

1. *Distribute your study time.* One of psychology's oldest findings is that "spaced practice" promotes better retention than "massed practice." You'll remember material better if you space your time over several study periods—perhaps one hour a day, six days a week—rather than cram it into one long study blitz. Spacing your study sessions requires a disciplined approach to managing your time. (Richard O. Straub explains time management in the helpful *Study Guide* that accompanies this text.)

2. *Learn to think critically.* Whether reading or in class, note people's *assumptions and values.* What perspective or bias underlies an argument? *Evaluate evidence.* Is it anecdotal? Correlational? Experimental? *Assess conclusions.* Are there alternative explanations?

3. *In class, listen actively.* As psychologist William James urged a century ago, "*No reception without reaction, no impression without . . . expression.*" Listen for the main ideas and sub-ideas of a lecture. *Write them down.* Ask questions during and after class. In class, as in your private study, process the information actively and you will understand and retain it better.

4. *Overlearn.* Psychology tells us that overlearning improves retention. We are prone to overestimating how much we know. You may understand a module as you read it, but by devoting extra study time to testing yourself and reviewing what you think you know, you will retain your new knowledge long into the future.

5. *Be a smart test-taker.* If a test contains both multiple-choice questions and an essay question, turn first to the essay. Read the question carefully, noting exactly what the instructor is asking. On the back of a page, pencil in a list of points you'd like to make and then organize them. Before writing, put aside the essay and work through the multiple-choice questions. (As you do so, your mind may continue to mull over the essay question. Sometimes the objective questions will bring pertinent thoughts to mind.) Then reread the essay question, rethink your answer, and start writing. When finished, proofread to eliminate spelling and grammatical errors that make you look less competent than you are. When reading multiple-choice questions, don't confuse yourself by trying to imagine how each choice might be the right one. Try instead to answer the question as if it were a fill-in-the-blank. First cover the answers, recall what you know, and complete the sentence in your mind. Then read the answers on the test and find the alternative that best matches your own answer.

While exploring psychology, you will learn much more than effective study techniques. Psychology deepens our appreciation for how we humans perceive, think, feel, and act. By so doing it can indeed enrich our lives and enlarge our vision. Through this book I hope to help guide you toward that end. As educator Charles Eliot said a century ago: "Books are the quietest and most constant of friends, and the most patient of teachers."

REVIEWING

>> MODULE REVIEW

1-1: **How did the science of psychology develop?**
Beginning with the first psychological laboratory, founded in 1879 by German philosopher and physiologist Wilhelm Wundt, psychology's modern roots can be found in many disciplines and countries.

Having begun as a "science of mental life," psychology evolved in the 1920s into a "science of observable behavior." After rediscovering the mind in the 1960s, *psychology* now views itself as a "science of behavior and mental processes."

1-2: **What is psychology's historic big issue?**
Psychology's long-standing issue concerns the relative contributions of *nature and nurture* (genes and experience). Today's science emphasizes the interactions of genes and experience, as genetic influences are expressed in specific environments.

1-3: **What theoretical perspectives do psychologists take, and how does the biopsychosocial approach help integrate these perspectives?**
Psychologists view behavior and mental processes from various perspectives, including neuroscience, evolutionary, behavior ge-

netics, psychodynamic, behavioral, cognitive, and social-cultural. The *biopsychosocial approach* integrates information from the biological, psychological, and social-cultural *levels of analysis.* By melding information gathered from many lines of research, this approach offers a more complete understanding than would usually be available from any single viewpoint.

1-4: **What are psychology's specialized subfields?**
Psychology's subfields encompass *basic research* (often done by biological, developmental, cognitive, personality, and social psychologists), *applied research* (sometimes conducted by organizational/industrial psychologists), and clinical applications (the work of *counseling* and *clinical psychologists*).

1-5: **How can psychological principles help you as a student?**
Experiments have shown that learning and memory are enhanced by active study. The *SQ3R* study method—survey, question, read, rehearse, and review—applies the principles derived from these experiments.

>> REHEARSE IT!

You can use these Rehearse It questions to gauge whether you are ready for the next module.

1. The science of psychology was born in December 1879, when a psychologist and his students measured the time lag between people's hearing a ball hit a platform and their pressing a key. The psychologist who ran this experiment and established the first psychology lab was

   a. Charles Darwin.
   b. William James.
   c. Edward Bradford Titchener.
   d. Wilhelm Wundt.

2. A prominent psychology text was published in 1890. Its author was

   a. Wilhelm Wundt.
   b. Mary Whiton Calkins.
   c. Charles Darwin.
   d. William James.

3. The definition of *psychology* has changed several times since the late 1800s. In the early twentieth century, _____ redefined *psychology* as "the science of observable behavior."

   a. John B. Watson
   b. Sigmund Freud
   c. William James
   d. Jean Piaget

4. *Psychology* is now defined as "the scientific study of behavior and mental processes." The perspective in psychology that focuses on how behavior and thought differ from situation to situation and from culture to culture is the

   a. cognitive perspective.
   b. behavioral perspective.
   c. social-cultural perspective.
   d. neuroscience perspective.

5. In the history of psychology, a major topic has been the relative influence of nature and nurture. Nature is to nurture as

   a. personality is to intelligence.
   b. biology is to experience.
   c. intelligence is to biology.
   d. psychological traits are to behaviors.

6. The behavioral perspective in psychology emphasizes observable responses and how they are acquired and modified. A behavioral psychologist would be most likely to study

   a. the effect of school uniforms on classroom behaviors.
   b. the hidden meaning in children's themes and drawings.
   c. the age at which children can learn algebra.

   d. whether certain mathematical abilities appear to be inherited.

7. A psychologist who treats emotionally troubled adolescents at the local mental health agency is most likely to be a/an

   a. research psychologist.
   b. psychiatrist.
   c. industrial/organizational psychologist.
   d. clinical psychologist.

8. A psychologist who conducts basic research to expand psychology's knowledge base would be most likely to

   a. design a computer screen with limited glare and assess the effect on computer operators' eyes after a day's work.
   b. treat older people who are overcome by depression.
   c. observe 3- and 6-year-old children solving puzzles and analyze differences in their abilities.
   d. interview children with behavioral problems and suggest treatments.

Answers: 1. d, 2. d, 3. a, 4. c, 5. b, 6. a, 7. d, 8. c.

>> TERMS AND CONCEPTS TO REMEMBER

humanistic psychology, p. 4
behaviorism, p. 5
psychology, p. 5
nature-nurture issue, p. 6

levels of analysis, p. 6
biopsychosocial approach, p. 6
basic research, p. 8
applied research, p. 8

counseling psychology, p. 9
clinical psychology, p. 9
psychiatry, p. 9
SQ3R, p. 10

>> TEST YOURSELF

The Test Yourself questions offer you a handy self-test on the material you have just read. Answers to these questions can be found in Appendix C at the back of the book.

1. What events defined the founding of scientific psychology?
2. What are psychology's major levels of analysis?

> Multiple-choice **self-tests** and more may be found at www.worthpublishers.com/myers.

Research Strategies: How Psychologists Ask and Answer Questions

2

M O D U L E

Although in some ways we outsmart the smartest computers, our intuition often goes awry. To err is human. Enter psychological science. With its procedures for gathering and sifting evidence, science restrains error. As we familiarize ourselves with its strategies and incorporate its underlying principles into our daily thinking, we can think smarter. *Psychologists use the science of behavior and mental processes to better understand why people think, feel, and act as they do.*

Thinking Critically With Psychological Science

What About Intuition and Common Sense?

2-1: Why are the answers that flow from the scientific approach more reliable than those based on intuition and common sense?

Some people think psychology merely documents what people already know and dresses it in jargon: "So what else is new—you get paid for using fancy methods to prove what my grandmother knew?" Others scorn a scientific approach because of their faith in human intuition. Advocates of "intuitive management" urge us to distrust statistical predictors and tune into our hunches when hiring, firing, and investing. Like *Star Wars'* Luke Skywalker, should we trust the force within?

Taxi/Getty Images

The limits of intuition
Personnel interviewers tend to be overconfident of their gut feelings about job applicants. Their confidence stems partly from their recalling cases where their favorable impression proved right, and partly from their ignorance about rejected applicants who succeeded elsewhere.

Actually, notes writer Madeleine L'Engle, "The naked intellect is an extraordinarily inaccurate instrument" (1972). Our intuition can lead us astray. We sometimes err in presuming that we could have foreseen what happened.

Did We Know It All Along? Hindsight Bias

How easy it is to seem astute when drawing the bull's eye after the arrow has struck. After each stock market downswing—after the bursting of the dot-com bubble, for example—investment gurus say "the market was obviously overdue for a correction." After the first World Trade Center tower in New York was hit on September 11, 2001, commentators said people in the second tower *should* have immediately evacuated (it became obvious only later that it was not an accident). But *before* the arrow strikes, the stock market drops, or the terrorists attack, these results are anything but obvious. Finding that something has happened makes it seem inevitable. Psychologists Paul Slovic and Baruch Fischhoff (1977) have called this 20/20 hindsight vision **hindsight bias,** also known as the *I-knew-it-all-along phenomenon.*

This phenomenon is easy to demonstrate: Give half the members of a group some purported psychological finding, and the other half an opposite result. Tell the first group, "Psychologists have found that separation weakens romantic attraction. As the saying goes, 'Out of sight, out of mind.'" Ask them to imagine why this might be true. Most people can, and nearly all will then regard this true finding as unsurprising.

> "Life is lived forwards, but understood backwards."
>
> Philosopher Søren Kierkegaard, 1813–1855

■ **hindsight bias** the tendency to believe, after learning an outcome, that one would have foreseen it. (Also known as the I-knew-it-all-along phenomenon.)

Tim Boyle/Getty Images

Hindsight bias

After the horror of 9/11, it seemed obvious that the U.S. intelligence analysts should have taken advance warnings more seriously, that airport security should have anticipated box-cutter–wielding terrorists, that occupants of the second World Trade Center tower should have known to play it safe and leave. With 20/20 hindsight, everything seems obvious. Thus we now spend billions to protect ourselves against what the terrorists did last time.

Tell the second group just the opposite—that "psychologists have found that separation strengthens romantic attraction. As the saying goes, 'Absence makes the heart grow fonder.'" People given this untrue result can also easily explain it, and they overwhelmingly see it as unsurprising common sense. Obviously, when both a supposed finding and its opposite seem like common sense, there is a problem.

Such errors in our recollections and explanations show why we need psychological research. Just asking people how and why they felt or acted as they did can sometimes be misleading—*not* because common sense is usually wrong, but because common sense more easily describes what *has* happened than what *will* happen. As physicist Neils Bohr reportedly said, "Prediction is very difficult, especially about the future."

Hindsight bias is widespread. Some 100 studies have observed it in various countries and among both children and adults (Bernstein & others, 2004; Guilbault & others, 2004). Nevertheless, Grandmother is often right. As Yogi Berra once said, "You can observe a lot by watching." (We have Berra to thank for other gems, such as "Nobody ever comes here—it's too crowded," and "If the people don't want to come out to the ballpark, nobody's gonna stop 'em.") Because we're all behavior watchers, it would be surprising if many of psychology's findings had *not* been foreseen. Many people believe that love breeds happiness, and they are right, according to researchers who have found that we have a deep "need to belong." Indeed, note Daniel Gilbert, Brett Pelham, and Douglas Krull (2003), "Good ideas in psychology usually have an oddly familiar quality, and the moment we encounter them we feel certain that we once came close to thinking the same thing ourselves and simply failed to write it down."

But sometimes Grandmother's intuition, informed by countless casual observations, has it wrong. Research has overturned many popular ideas—that familiarity breeds contempt, that dreams predict the future, and that emotional reactions coincide with menstrual phase. It has also surprised us with discoveries about how the brain's chemical messengers control our moods and memories, about animal abilities, and about the effects of stress on our capacity to fight disease.

> "Anything seems commonplace, once explained."
>
> Dr. Watson to Sherlock Holmes

Non Sequitur

THE IRRESISTIBLE FORCE MEETS THE IMMOVABLE OBJECT

THE FACTS AS THEY ARE

THE TRUTH AS I SEE IT

WiLEY 5-16

Reprinted by permission of Universal Press Syndicate. © 1997 Wiley.

Overconfidence

Our everyday thinking is also limited by our human tendency to be overly confident: We tend to think we know more than we do. Asked how sure we are of our answers to factual questions (Is Boston north or south of Paris?), we tend to be more confident than correct.[1] Or consider these three anagrams, which Richard Goranson (1978) asked people to unscramble:

WREAT → WATER
ETRYN → ENTRY
GRABE → BARGE

Reflect for a moment: About how many seconds do you think it would have taken you to unscramble each of these?

Once people know the target word, hindsight makes it seem obvious—so much so that they become overconfident. They think they would have seen the solution in only 10 seconds or so, when in reality the average problem solver spends 3 minutes, as you also might, given a similar anagram without the solution: OCHSA (see this module's final page to check your answer).

Are we any better at predicting our social behavior? To find out, Robert Vallone and his associates (1990) had students predict at the beginning of the school year whether they would drop a course, vote in an upcoming election, call their parents more than twice a month, and so forth. On average, the students felt 84 percent confident in making these self-predictions. Later quizzes about their actual behavior showed their predictions were correct only 71 percent of the time. Even when they were 100 percent sure of themselves, their self-predictions erred 15 percent of the time.

The point to remember: Hindsight bias and overconfidence often lead us to overestimate our intuition. But scientific inquiry, fed by curious skepticism and by humility, can help us sift reality from illusions.

The Scientific Attitude

2-2: What attitudes characterize scientific inquiry?

Underlying all science is, first, a hard-headed *curiosity,* a passion to explore and understand without misleading or being misled. Some questions (Is there life after death?) are beyond science. To answer them in any way requires a leap of faith. With many other ideas (Can some people demonstrate ESP?), the proof is in the pudding. No matter how sensible or crazy-sounding an idea, the hard-headed question is, Does it work? When put to the test, can its predictions be confirmed?

This scientific approach has a long history. As ancient a figure as Moses used such an approach. How do you evaluate a self-proclaimed prophet? His answer: Put the prophet to the test. If the predicted event "does not take place or prove true," then so much the worse for the prophet (*Deuteronomy* 18:22). Magician James Randi uses Moses' approach when testing those claiming to see auras around people's bodies:

Randi:	Do you see an aura around my head?
Aura-seer:	Yes, indeed.
Randi:	Can you still see the aura if I put this magazine in front of my face?
Aura-seer:	Of course.
Randi:	Then if I were to step behind a wall barely taller than I am, you could determine my location from the aura visible above my head, right?

Randi has told me that no aura-seer has agreed to take this simple test.

"They couldn't hit an elephant at this distance."
General John Sedgwick just before being killed during a U.S. Civil War battle, 1864

Fun anagram solutions from Wordsmith.org:
Elvis = lives
Dormitory = dirty room
Slot machines = cash lost in 'em

"We don't like their sound. Groups of guitars are on their way out."
Decca Records, in turning down a recording contract with the Beatles in 1962

"The telephone may be appropriate for our American cousins, but not here, because we have an adequate supply of messenger boys."
British expert group evaluating the invention of the telephone

"The scientist . . . must be free to ask any question, to doubt any assertion, to seek for any evidence, to correct any errors."
Physicist J. Robert Oppenheimer, Life, October 10, 1949

[1]Boston is south of Paris.

The amazing Randi
The magician James Randi exemplifies skepticism. He has tested and debunked a variety of psychic phenomena.

Courtesy of the James Randi Education Foundation

"A skeptic is one who is willing to question any truth claim, asking for clarity in definition, consistency in logic, and adequacy of evidence."

Philosopher Paul Kurtz, *The Skeptical Inquirer*, 1994

"My deeply held belief is that if a god anything like the traditional sort exists, our curiosity and intelligence are provided by such a god. We would be unappreciative of those gifts . . . if we suppressed our passion to explore the universe and ourselves."

Carl Sagan, *Broca's Brain*, 1979

Throughout this book, you will encounter Thinking Critically boxes. Each highlights careful thinking about some interesting or important issue.

"The real purpose of the scientific method is to make sure Nature hasn't misled you into thinking you know something you don't actually know."

Robert M. Pirsig, *Zen and the Art of Motorcycle Maintenance*, 1974

When subjected to such scrutiny, crazy-sounding ideas sometimes find support. More often, science relegates crazy-sounding ideas to the mountain of forgotten claims of perpetual motion machines, miracle cancer cures, and out-of-body travels into centuries past. To sift reality from fantasy, sense from nonsense, therefore requires a scientific attitude: being skeptical but not cynical, open but not gullible.

"To believe with certainty," says a Polish proverb, "we must begin by doubting." As scientists, psychologists approach the world of behavior with a *curious skepticism*, persistently asking two questions: What do you mean? How do you know?

In the arena of competing ideas, skeptical testing can reveal which ones best match the facts. Do parental behaviors determine their children's sexual orientation? Can astrologers analyze your character and predict your future based on the position of the planets at your birth? Tests of such claims have led most psychologists to doubt them.

Putting a scientific attitude into practice requires not only skepticism but also *humility*—an awareness of our own vulnerability to error and an openness to surprises and new perspectives. In the last analysis, what matters is not my opinion or yours, but the truths nature reveals in response to our questioning. If people or other animals don't behave as our ideas predict, then so much the worse for our ideas. This is the humble attitude expressed in one of psychology's early mottos: "The rat is always right."

Historians of science tell us that these attitudes of curiosity, skepticism, and humility helped make modern science possible. Many of its founders, including Copernicus and Newton, were people whose religious convictions made them humble before nature and skeptical of mere human authority (Hooykaas, 1972; Merton, 1938). Today's deeply religious people sometimes view science, including psychological science, as a threat. Yet, notes sociologist Rodney Stark (2003a, b), the scientific revolution was led mostly by deeply religious people acting on the religious idea that "in order to love and honor God, it is necessary to fully appreciate the wonders of his handiwork."

Of course, scientists, like anyone else, can have big egos and may cling to their preconceptions. We all view nature through the spectacles of our preconceived ideas. Nevertheless, the ideal that unifies psychologists with all scientists is the curious, skeptical, humble scrutiny of competing ideas. As a community, scientists check and recheck one another's findings and conclusions.

Critical Thinking

The scientific attitude prepares us to think smarter. Smart thinking, called **critical thinking**, examines assumptions, discerns hidden values, evaluates evidence, and assesses conclusions. Whether reading a news report or listening to a conversation, critical thinkers ask questions. Like scientists, they wonder, How do they know that? What is this person's agenda? Is the conclusion based on anecdote and gut feelings, or on evidence? Does the evidence justify a cause-effect conclusion? What alternative explanations are possible? Carried to an extreme, healthy skepticism can degenerate into a negative cynicism that scorns any unproven idea. Better to have a critical attitude that produces humility and its willingness to consider new perspectives.

Has psychology's critical inquiry been open to surprising findings? The answer is plainly yes. Believe it or not . . .

- massive losses of brain tissue early in life may have minimal long-term effects.
- within days, newborns can recognize their mother's odor and voice.
- brain damage can leave a person able to learn new skills, yet be unaware of such learning.

- diverse groups—men and women, old and young, rich and working class, those with disabilities and without—report roughly comparable levels of personal happiness.
- electroconvulsive therapy (delivering an electric shock to the brain) is often a very effective treatment for severe depression.

And has critical inquiry convincingly debunked popular presumptions? The answer is again yes. The evidence indicates that . . .

- sleepwalkers are *not* acting out their dreams and sleeptalkers are *not* verbalizing their dreams.
- our past experiences are *not* all recorded verbatim in our brains; with brain stimulation or hypnosis, one *cannot* simply "play the tape" and relive long-buried or repressed memories.
- most people do *not* suffer from unrealistically low self-esteem, and high self-esteem is not all good.
- opposites do *not* generally attract.

In each of these instances and more, what has been learned is not yet what is widely believed.

The Scientific Method

Psychologists arm their scientific attitude with the *scientific method*. Psychological science evaluates competing ideas with careful observation and rigorous analysis. In its attempt to describe and explain human nature, it welcomes hunches and plausible-sounding theories. And it puts them to the test. If a theory works—if the data support its predictions—so much the better for that theory. If the predictions fail, the theory will be revised or rejected.

Constructing Theories

2-3: How do psychologists use the scientific method to construct theories?

In everyday conversation, we tend to use *theory* to mean "mere hunch." In science, however, theory is linked with observation. A scientific **theory** *explains* through an integrated set of principles that *organizes* observations and *predicts* behaviors or events. By organizing isolated facts, a theory simplifies things. There are too many facts about behavior to remember them all. By linking facts and bridging them to deeper principles, a theory offers a useful summary. When we connect the observed dots, we may discover a coherent picture.

A good theory of depression, for example, helps us organize countless observations concerning depression into a short list of principles. Imagine we observe over and over that people with depression describe their past, present, and future in gloomy terms. We might therefore theorize that low self-esteem contributes to depression. So far so good: Our self-esteem principle neatly summarizes a long list of facts about people with depression.

Yet no matter how reasonable a theory may sound—and low self-esteem seems a reasonable explanation of depression—we must put it to the test. A good theory does not just sound appealing. It must produce testable predictions, called **hypotheses.** By enabling us to test and reject or revise the theory, such predictions give direction to research. They specify what results would support the theory and what results would disconfirm it. To test our self-esteem theory of depression, we might assess people's self-esteem by having them indicate their agreement to statements such as "I have good ideas" and "I am fun to be with." Then we could see whether, as we hypothesized, people who report poorer self-images also score higher on a depression scale (**FIGURE 2.1**).

■ **critical thinking** thinking that does not blindly accept arguments and conclusions. Rather, it examines assumptions, discerns hidden values, evaluates evidence, and assesses conclusions.

■ **theory** an explanation using an integrated set of principles that organizes observations and predicts behaviors or events.

■ **hypothesis** a testable prediction, often implied by a theory.

FIGURE **2.1**
The scientific method
A self-correcting process for asking questions and observing nature's answer.

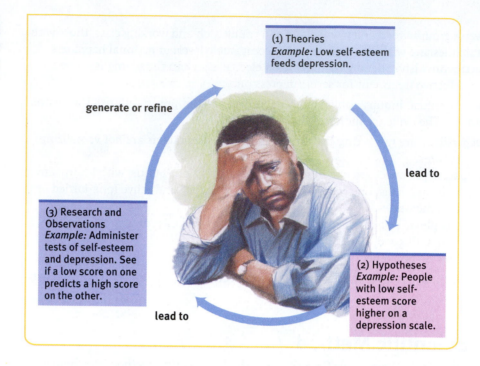

generate or refine

(1) Theories
Example: Low self-esteem feeds depression.

lead to

(2) Hypotheses
Example: People with low self-esteem score higher on a depression scale.

lead to

(3) Research and Observations
Example: Administer tests of self-esteem and depression. See if a low score on one predicts a high score on the other.

■ **operational definition** a statement of the procedures (operations) used to define research variables. For example, *human intelligence* may be operationally defined as what an intelligence test measures.

■ **replication** repeating the essence of a research study, usually with different participants in different situations, to see whether the basic finding extends to other participants and circumstances.

■ **case study** an observation technique in which one person is studied in depth in the hope of revealing universal principles.

■ **survey** a technique for ascertaining the self-reported attitudes or behaviors of people, usually by questioning a representative, random sample of them.

Good theories explain by
1. organizing and linking observed facts.
2. implying hypotheses that offer testable predictions and, sometimes, practical applications.

In testing our theory, we should be aware that it can bias subjective observations. Having theorized that depression springs from low self-esteem, we may see what we expect. We may perceive depressed people's neutral comments as self-disparaging. The urge to see what we expect is an ever-present temptation for all of us. For example, according to the bipartisan U.S. Senate Select Committee on Intelligence (2004), preconceived expectations that Iraq had weapons of mass destruction led intelligence analysts to wrongly interpret ambiguous observations as confirming that theory, and this theory-driven conclusion then led to the preemptive U.S. invasion of Iraq.

As a check on their biases, psychologists report their research—with precise **operational definitions** of concepts that allow anyone to **replicate** (repeat) their observations. If other researchers re-create a study with different participants and materials and get similar results, then our confidence in the finding's reliability grows. The first study of hindsight bias aroused psychologists' curiosity. Now, after many successful replications with differing people and questions, we feel sure of the phenomenon's power.

In the end, our theory will be useful if it (1) effectively *organizes* a range of self-reports and observations and (2) implies clear *predictions* that anyone can use to check the theory or to derive practical applications. (If we boost people's self-esteem, will their depression lift?) Eventually, our research will probably lead to a revised theory that better organizes and predicts what we know about depression.

As we will see next, we can test our hypotheses and refine our theories using descriptive, correlational, and experimental methods. To think critically about popular psychology claims, we need to recognize these methods and know what conclusions they allow.

Description

2-4: How do psychologists observe and describe behavior?

The starting point of any science is description. In everyday life, all of us observe and describe people, often drawing conclusions about why they behave as they do. Professional psychologists do much the same, though more objectively and systematically.

The Case Study

Among the oldest research methods is the **case study,** studying one individual in great depth in the hope of revealing things true of us all. Some examples: Much of our early knowledge about the brain came from case studies of individuals who suffered a particular impairment after damage to a certain brain region. Jean Piaget taught us about children's thinking after carefully observing and questioning but a few children. Studies of only a few chimpanzees have revealed their capacity for understanding and language. Intensive case studies are sometimes very revealing.

Case studies can suggest hypotheses for further study. They also show us what *can* happen. In everyday life, however, individual cases sometimes mislead us: An individual may be atypical. Unrepresentative information can lead to mistaken judgments and false conclusions. Indeed, anytime a researcher mentions a finding ("Smokers die younger: 95 percent of men over 85 are nonsmokers") someone is sure to offer a contradictory case ("Well, I have an uncle who smoked two packs a day and lived to be 89"). Numbers can be numbing (in one study of 1300 dream reports concerning a kidnapped child, only 5 percent correctly envisioned the child as dead [Murray & Wheeler, 1937]). Anecdotes—dramatic stories, personal experiences, even psychological case examples—often command attention. ("But I know a man who dreamed his sister was in a car accident, and two days later she was.") As psychologist Gordon Allport (1954, p. 9) said, "Given a thimbleful of [dramatic] facts we rush to make generalizations as large as a tub."

The point to remember: Individual cases can suggest fruitful ideas. What's true of all of us can be glimpsed in any one of us. But to discern the general truths that cover individual cases, we must answer questions with other methods.

The Survey

The **survey** method looks at many cases in less depth. A survey asks people to report their behavior or opinions. Questions about everything from sexual practices to political opinions get put to the public. Harris and Gallup polls have revealed that 72 percent of Americans think there is too much TV violence, 89 percent favor equal job opportunities for homosexual people, 89 percent say they face high stress, 95 percent believe in God, and 96 percent would like to change something about their appearance. In Britain, seven in ten 18- to 29-year-olds support gay marriage; among those over 50, about the same percentage oppose it (a generation gap found in many Western countries). But asking questions is tricky, and the answers may well depend on your wording and your choice of respondents.

Wording Effects Even subtle changes in the order or wording of questions can have major effects. Should cigarette ads or pornography be allowed on television? People are much more likely to approve "not allowing" such things than "forbidding" or "censoring" them. In one national survey, only 27 percent of Americans approved of "government censorship" of media sex and violence, though 66 percent approved of "more restrictions on what is shown on television" (Lacayo, 1995). People are similarly much more approving of "aid to the needy" than of "welfare," of "affirmative action" than of "preferential treatment," and of "revenue enhancers" than of "taxes." Because wording is such a delicate matter, critical thinkers will reflect on how the phrasing of a question might have affected the opinions respondents expressed.

Random Sampling You can describe human experience using your estimates of others, perhaps supplemented by dramatic anecdotes and personal experience. But for an accurate picture of the experiences and attitudes of a whole population, there's only one game in town—the representative sample.

The case of the conversational chimpanzee
In intensive case studies of chimpanzees, psychologists have explored the intriguing question of whether language is uniquely human. Here Nim Chimpsky signs *hug* as his trainer, psychologist Herbert Terrace, shows him the puppet Ernie. But is Nim really capable of using language? Cognitive theorists continue to debate that issue.

'Well my dear,' said Miss Marple, 'human nature is very much the same everywhere, and of course, one has opportunities of observing it at closer quarters in a village.'"

Agatha Christie, *The Tuesday Club Murders*, 1933

© The New Yorker Collection, 1969, D. Fradon from the cartoonbank.com. All Rights Reserved.

"How would you like me to answer that question? As a member of my ethnic group, educational class, income group, or religious category?"

With very large samples, estimates become quite reliable. *E* is estimated to represent 12.7 percent of the letters in written English. *E*, in fact, is 12.3 percent of the 925,141 letters in Melville's *Moby Dick*, 12.4 percent of the 586,747 letters in Dickens' *A Tale of Two Cities*, and 12.1 percent of the 3,901,021 letters in 12 of Mark Twain's works (*Chance News*, 1997).

■ **population** all the cases in a group, from which samples may be drawn for a study. (*Note:* Except for national studies, this does *not* refer to a country's whole population.)

■ **random sample** a sample that fairly represents a population because each member has an equal chance of inclusion.

■ **naturalistic observation** observing and recording behavior in naturally occurring situations without trying to manipulate and control the situation.

■ **correlation** a measure of the extent to which two factors vary together, and thus of how well either factor predicts the other. The *correlation coefficient* is the mathematical expression of the relationship, ranging from −1 to +1.

We can extend this point to everyday thinking, as we generalize from samples we observe, especially vivid cases. Given (a) a statistical summary of a professor's student evaluations and (b) the vivid comments of two irate students, an administrator's impression of the professor may be influenced as much by the two unhappy students as by the many favorable evaluations in the statistical summary. The temptation to generalize from a few vivid but unrepresentative cases is nearly irresistible.

The point to remember: The best basis for generalizing is from a representative sample of cases.

So how do you obtain a representative sample—say, of the students at your college or university? How could you choose a group that would represent the total student **population**, the whole group you want to study and describe? Typically, you would choose a **random sample**, in which every person in the entire group has an equal chance of participating. This means you would *not* send each student a questionnaire. (The conscientious people who return it would not be a random sample.) Rather, you would use, say, a table of random numbers to pick participants from a student listing, making sure you involve as many as possible. Large representative samples are better than small ones, but a small representative sample of 100 is better than an unrepresentative sample of 500.

Sampling voters in a national election survey is like sampling the student population: 1500 randomly sampled people, drawn from all areas of a country, provide a remarkably accurate snapshot of the opinions of a nation. Without random sampling, large samples—including call-in phone samples and TV Web site polls—often merely give misleading results.

The point to remember: Before believing survey findings, think critically: Consider the sample. You cannot compensate for an unrepresentative sample by simply adding more people.

Naturalistic Observation

A third descriptive research method involves watching and recording the behavior of organisms in their natural environment. These **naturalistic observations** range from watching chimpanzee societies in the jungle, to unobtrusively videotaping (and later systematically analyzing) parent-child interactions in different cultures, to recording students' self-seating patterns in the lunchrooms of multiracial schools.

Like the case study and survey methods, naturalistic observation does not *explain* behavior. It *describes* it. Nevertheless, descriptions can be revealing. We once thought, for example, that only humans use tools. Then naturalistic observation revealed that chimpanzees sometimes insert a stick in a termite mound and withdraw it, eating the stick's load of termites. Such unobtrusive naturalistic observations, recalls chimpanzee observer Jane Goodall (1998), paved the way for later studies of animal thinking, language, and emotion: "Observations, made in the natural habitat, helped to show that the societies and behavior of animals are far more complex than previously supposed," thus expanding our understanding of our fellow animals. We later learned that chimpanzees and baboons also use deception to achieve their aims. Psychologists Andrew Whiten and Richard Byrne (1988) repeatedly saw one young baboon pretending to have been attacked by another as a tactic to get its mother to drive the other baboon away from its food.

Naturalistic observations are also done with humans. Here are three findings you might enjoy.

- *A funny finding.* We humans laugh 30 times more often in social situations than in solitary situations. (Have you noticed how seldom you laugh when alone?) When we do laugh, 17 muscles contort our mouth and squeeze our eyes, and we emit a series of 75-millisecond vowel-like sounds that are spaced about one-fifth of a second apart (Provine, 2001).
- *Sounding out students.* What, really, are introductory psychology students saying and doing during their everyday lives? To find out, Matthias Mehl and James Pennebaker (2003) equipped 52 such University of Texas students with a belt-worn tape recorder that, for up to four days, captured 30 seconds of their waking hours every 12.5 minutes—thus enabling the researchers to eavesdrop on more than 10,000 half-minute life slices. On what percentage of the slices do you suppose they found the students talking with someone? What percentage captured the students at a computer keyboard? The answers: 28 and 9 percent, respectively. (What percentage of *your* waking hours are spent in these activities?)
- *Culture, climate, and the pace of life.* Naturalistic observation also enabled Robert Levine and Ara Norenzayan (1999) to compare the pace of life in 31 countries. By operationally defining *pace of life* as walking speed, the speed with which postal clerks completed a simple request, and the accuracy of public clocks, they concluded that life is fastest paced in Japan and Western Europe, and slower paced in economically less-developed countries. People in colder climates also tend to live at a faster pace (and are more prone to die from heart disease). As this study illustrates, naturalistic observation can also be used with correlational research, our next topic.

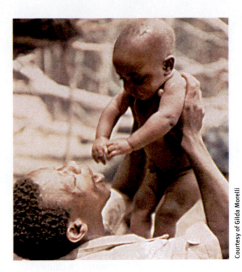

Naturalistic observation

For more than 20 years, psychologist Gilda Morelli has lived among and observed the Efe people of Central Africa, including the man and baby shown here, studying paternal and maternal care and observing children's development.

Correlation

2-5 : Why do correlations permit prediction but not explanation?

Describing behavior is a first step toward predicting it. When surveys and naturalistic observations reveal that one trait or behavior accompanies another, we say the two **correlate.** The *correlation coefficient* is a statistical measure of a relationship. It reveals how closely two things vary together and thus how well either one *predicts* the other. Knowing how much aptitude test scores *correlate* with school success tells us how well the scores *predict* school success.

A *positive correlation* (between 0 and +1.00) indicates a *direct* relationship, meaning that two things increase together or decrease together.

A *negative correlation* (between 0 and −1.00) indicates an *inverse* relationship: As one thing increases, the other decreases. Our earlier findings on self-esteem and depression illustrate a negative correlation: People who score *low* on self-esteem tend to score *high* on depression. Negative correlations could go as low as −1.00, which means that, like people on the opposite ends of a teeter-totter, one set of scores goes down precisely as the other goes up. A weak correlation, indicating little or no relationship, has a coefficient near zero.

Here are some recent news reports of correlational research. Can you spot which are reporting positive correlations, which negative?

- The more TV is on in the homes of young children, the less time they spend reading (Kaiser, 2003).
- The more sexual content teens see on TV, the more likely they are to have sex (Collins & others, 2004).
- The longer children are breast-fed, the greater their later academic achievement (Horwood & Fergusson, 1998).
- The more income rose among a sample of poor families, the fewer psychiatric symptoms their children experienced (Costello & others, 2003).

(These are negative, positive, positive, and negative correlations, respectively.)

Correlation need not mean causation
Length of marriage correlates with hair loss in men. Does this mean that marriage causes men to lose their hair (or that balding men make better husbands)? In this case, as in many others, a third factor obviously explains the correlation: Golden anniversaries and baldness both accompany aging.

A *New York Times* writer reported a massive survey showing that "adolescents whose parents smoked were 50 percent more likely than children of nonsmokers to report having had sex." He concluded (would you agree?) that the survey indicated a causal effect—that "to reduce the chances that their children will become sexually active at an early age" parents might "quit smoking" (O'Neil, 2002).

Though informative, psychology's correlations usually leave most of the variation among individuals unpredicted. For example, research shows a positive correlation between parents' abusiveness and their children's later abusiveness when they become parents. But this does not mean that most abused children become abusive. The correlation simply indicates a statistical relationship: Although most abused children do not grow into abusers, nonabused children are even less likely to become abusive. Correlations point us toward predictions, but usually imperfect ones.

The point to remember: A correlation coefficient helps us see the world more clearly by revealing the extent to which two things relate.

Correlation and Causation

Correlations help us predict. Low self-esteem correlates with (and therefore predicts) depression. But does that mean low self-esteem *causes* depression? If, based on the correlational evidence, you assume that it does, you have much company. A nearly irresistible thinking error is assuming that correlation proves causation. But no matter how strong the relationship, it does not!

How else might we explain the negative correlation between self-esteem and depression? As **FIGURE 2.2** suggests, we'd get the same correlation between low self-esteem and depression if depression caused people to be down on themselves, or if something else—a third factor such as heredity or brain chemistry—caused both low self-esteem and depression. Among men, for example, length of marriage correlates positively with hair loss—because both are associated with a third factor, age.

This point is so important—so basic to thinking smarter with psychology—that it merits one more example, from a survey of over 12,000 adolescents: The more teens feel loved by their parents, the less likely they are to behave in unhealthy ways—having early sex, smoking, abusing alcohol and drugs, exhibiting violence (Resnick & others, 1997). "Adults have a powerful effect on their children's behavior right through the high school years," gushed an Associated Press (AP) story on the study. But the correlation comes with no built-in cause-effect arrow. Said differently (turn the volume up here), *correlation does not prove causation.* Thus, the AP could as well have said, "Well-behaved teens feel their parents' love and approval; out-of-bounds teens more often think their parents are disapproving jerks."

The point to remember: Correlation indicates the *possibility* of a cause-effect relationship, *but it does not prove causation.* Knowing that two events are correlated need not tell us anything about causation. Remember this principle and you will be wiser as you read and hear news of scientific studies.

FIGURE 2.2
Three possible cause-effect relationships
People low in self-esteem are more likely to report depression than are those high in self-esteem. One possible explanation of this negative correlation is that a bad self-image causes depressed feelings. But, as the diagram indicates, other cause-effect relationships are possible.

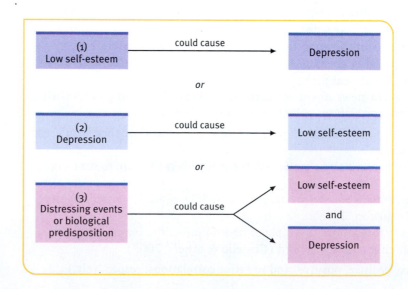

Illusory Correlations

2-6 : How accurately does the naked eye detect correlations?

■ **illusory correlation** the perception of a relationship where none exists.

Correlation coefficients make visible the relationships we might otherwise miss. They also restrain our "seeing" relationships that actually do not exist. A perceived but nonexistent correlation is an **illusory correlation.** When we *believe* there is a relationship between two things, we are likely to *notice* and *recall* instances that confirm our belief (Trolier & Hamilton, 1986).

Because we are sensitive to dramatic or unusual events, we are especially likely to notice and remember the occurrence of two such events in sequence—say, a premonition of an unlikely phone call followed by the call. When the call does not follow the premonition, we are less likely to note and remember the nonevent. Illusory correlations help explain many other superstitious beliefs, such as the presumption that more babies are born when the moon is full or that infertile couples who adopt become more likely to conceive (Gilovich, 1991).

Such illusory thinking helps explain why for so many years people believed (and many still do) that sugar made children hyperactive, that getting cold and wet caused one to catch a cold, and that weather changes trigger arthritis pain. We are, it seems, prone to perceiving patterns, whether they're there or not.

The point to remember: When we notice random coincidences, we may forget that they are random and instead see them as correlated. Thus, we can easily deceive ourselves by seeing what is not there.

Perceiving Order in Random Events

In our natural eagerness to make sense of our world—what poet Wallace Stevens called our "rage for order"—we look for order even in random data. And we usually find such, because *random sequences often don't look random.* Consider a random coin flip: If someone flipped a coin six times, which of the following sequences of heads (H) and tails (T) would be most likely: HHHTTT or HTTHTH or HHHHHH?

Daniel Kahneman and Amos Tversky (1972) discovered that most people believe HTTHTH would be the most likely random sequence. Actually, all three are equally likely (or, you might say, equally unlikely) to occur. A bridge or poker hand of 10 through Ace, all of hearts, would seem extraordinary; actually, it would be no more or less likely than any other specific hand of cards (**FIGURE 2.3**).

In actual random sequences, patterns and streaks (such as repeating digits) occur more often than people expect. To demonstrate this phenomenon for myself (as you can do), I flipped a coin 51 times, with these results:

1. H	11. T	21. T	31. T	41. H	51. T
2. T	12. H	22. T	32. T	42. H	
3. T	13. H	23. H	33. T	43. H	
4. T	14. T	24. T	34. T	44. H	
5. H	15. T	25. T	35. T	45. T	
6. H	16. H	26. T	36. H	46. H	
7. H	17. T	27. H	37. T	47. H	
8. T	18. T	28. T	38. T	48. T	
9. T	19. H	29. H	39. H	49. T	
10. T	20. H	30. T	40. T	50. T	

FIGURE 2.3

Two random sequences

Your chances of being dealt either of these hands are precisely the same: 1 in 2,598,960.

Looking over the sequence, patterns jump out: Tosses 10 to 22 provided an almost perfect pattern of pairs of tails followed by pairs of heads. On tosses 30 to 38 I had a "cold hand," with only one head in eight tosses. But my fortunes immediately reversed with a "hot hand"—seven heads out of the next nine tosses. Similar streaks happen, about as often as one would expect in random sequences, in basketball

Given enough random events, something weird will happen
Angelo and Maria Gallina were the beneficiaries of one of those extraordinary chance events when they won two California lottery games on the same day.

On March 11, 1998, Utah's Ernie and Lynn Carey gained three new grandchildren when three of their daughters gave birth—on the same day (*Los Angeles Times*, 1998).

Bizarre-looking, perhaps. But actually no more unlikely than any other number sequence.

shooting, baseball hitting, and mutual fund stock pickers' selections (Gilovich & others, 1985; Malkiel, 1989, 1995; Myers, 2002). These sequences often don't look random, and so get overinterpreted ("When you're hot, you're hot!").

What explains these streaky patterns? Was I exercising some sort of paranormal control over my coin? Did I snap out of my tails funk and get in a heads groove? No such explanations are needed, for these are the sorts of streaks found in any random data. Comparing each toss to the next, 24 of the 50 comparisons yielded a changed result—just the sort of near 50-50 result we expect from coin tossing. Despite seeming patterns, the outcome of one toss gives no clue to the outcome of the next.

However, some happenings seem so extraordinary that we struggle to conceive an ordinary, chance-related explanation (as applies to our coin-tosses). In such cases, statisticians often are less mystified. When Evelyn Marie Adams won the New Jersey lottery *twice*, newspapers reported the odds of her feat as 1 in 17 trillion. Bizarre? Actually, 1 in 17 trillion are the odds that a given person who buys a single ticket for two New Jersey lotteries will win both times. But statisticians Stephen Samuels and George McCabe (1989) report that, given the millions of people who buy U.S. state lottery tickets, it was "practically a sure thing" that someday, somewhere, someone would hit a state jackpot twice. Indeed, say fellow statisticians Persi Diaconis and Frederick Mosteller (1989), "with a large enough sample, any outrageous thing is likely to happen." "The really unusual day would be one where nothing unusual happens," adds Diaconis (2002). An event that happens to but one in 1 billion people every day occurs about six times a day, 2000 times a year.

Experimentation

2-7: How do experiments clarify or reveal cause-effect relationships?

Happy are they, remarked the Roman poet Virgil, "who have been able to perceive the causes of things." We endlessly wonder and debate *why* we act as we do. Why do people smoke? Have babies while they are still children? Do stupid things when drunk? Become troubled teens and open fire on their classmates? Though psychology cannot answer these questions directly, it has helped us to understand what influences drug use, sexual behaviors, thinking when drinking, and aggression.

Exploring Cause and Effect

Many factors influence our everyday behavior. To isolate cause and effect—say, in looking for causes of depression—psychologists statistically control for other factors. For example, many studies have found that breast-fed infants grow up with somewhat higher intelligence scores than those of infants bottle-fed with cow's milk (Angelsen & others, 2001; Mortensen & others, 2002; Quinn & others, 2001). Mother's milk correlates modestly but positively with later intelligence. But does this mean that smarter mothers (who more often breast-feed) have smarter children? Or, as some researchers believe, do the nutrients of mother's milk contribute to brain development? To help answer this question, researchers have "controlled for" (statistically removed differences in) certain other factors, such as maternal age, education, and intelligence. Still, breast-fed infants exhibit slightly higher intelligence as young children.

Although this suggests that breast-feeding gives a boost, correlational research cannot control for all other possible factors. Thus, the clearest and cleanest way to isolate cause and effect is to **experiment.** Experiments enable a researcher to focus on the possible effects of one or more factors by (1) *manipulating the factors of interest* and (2) *holding constant ("controlling") other factors*. With parental permission, a British research team led by Alan Lucas (1992) decided to experiment. They randomly assigned 424 hospital preterm infants to either the usual infant formula feedings or to donated breast milk feedings. When given intelligence tests at age 8, the children nourished with breast milk had significantly higher intelligence scores than their formula-fed counterparts. No single experiment is conclusive, of course. But by **randomly assigning** infants to one feeding group or the other, these researchers were able to hold constant all factors except nutrition. This eliminated alternative explanations and supported the conclusion that, so far as the developing intelligence of preterm infants is concerned, breast is best. (*Note:* The other infants were not harmed by the experiment, because they received the standard feeding.)

If a behavior (such as test performance) changes when we vary an experimental factor (such as infant nutrition), then we know the factor is having an effect. *The point to remember:* Unlike correlational studies, which uncover naturally occurring relationships, an experiment manipulates a factor to determine its effect.

Evaluating Therapies

Our tendency to seek new remedies when we are ill or emotionally down can produce misleading testimonies. If three days into a cold we start taking vitamin C tablets and find our cold symptoms lessening, we may credit the pills rather than the cold naturally subsiding. If, after nearly failing the first exam, we listen to a "peak learning" subliminal tape and then improve on the next exam, we may credit the tape rather than conclude that our performance has returned to our average. In the 1700s, blood-letting *seemed* effective. Sometimes people improved after the treatment; when they didn't, the practitioner inferred the disease was just too advanced to be reversed. (We, of course, now know that blood-letting is a *bad* treatment.) So, whether or not a remedy is truly effective, enthusiastic users will probably endorse it. To find out whether it actually is effective, we must experiment.

And that is precisely how investigators evaluate new drug treatments and new methods of psychological therapy. Often, the participants in these studies are *blind* (uninformed) about what treatment, if any, they are receiving. One group receives the treatment. Others receive a pseudotreatment—an inert *placebo* (perhaps a pill with no drug in it). Many studies use a **double-blind procedure**—neither the participant nor the research assistant collecting the data knows whether the participant's group is receiving the treatment. In such studies, researchers can check a treatment's actual effects apart from the participants' belief in its healing powers and the staff's enthusiasm for its potential. Just *thinking* you are getting a treatment can boost your spirits, relax your body, and relieve your symptoms. This **placebo effect** is well documented in reducing pain, depression, and anxiety (Kirsch & Sapirstein, 1998).

The double-blind procedure is one way to create an **experimental group,** in which people receive the treatment, and a contrasting **control group** without the treatment. By randomly assigning people to these conditions, researchers can be fairly certain the two groups are otherwise identical. Random assignment roughly equalizes the two groups in age, attitudes, and every other characteristic. With random assignment, as occurred with the infants in the breast milk experiment, we also can know that any later differences between people in the experimental and control conditions will usually be the result of the treatment.

■ **experiment** a research method in which an investigator manipulates one or more factors (independent variables) to observe the effect on some behavior or mental process (the dependent variable). By random assignment of participants, the experimenter aims to control other relevant factors.

■ **random assignment** assigning research participants to experimental and control conditions by chance, thus minimizing preexisting differences between those assigned to the different groups.

■ **double-blind procedure** an experimental procedure in which both the research participants and the research staff are ignorant (blind) about whether the research participants have received the treatment or a placebo. Commonly used in drug-evaluation studies.

■ **placebo** [pluh-SEE-bo; Latin for "I shall please"] **effect** experimental results caused by expectations alone; any effect on behavior caused by the administration of an inert substance or condition, which is assumed to be an active agent.

■ **experimental group** the group in an experiment that is exposed to the treatment, that is, to one version of the independent variable.

■ **control group** ■ the group in an experiment that contrasts with the experimental group and serves as a comparison for evaluating the effect of the treatment.

■ **independent variable** the experimental factor that is manipulated; the variable whose effect is being studied.

■ **dependent variable** the outcome factor; the variable that may change in response to manipulations of the independent variable.

Note the distinction between random *sampling* in surveys and random *assignment* in experiments. Random sampling helps us generalize to a larger population. Random assignment controls extraneous influences, which helps us infer cause and effect.

Independent and Dependent Variables

Here is an even more potent example: The drug Viagra was approved for use after 21 clinical trials, including an experiment in which researchers randomly assigned 329 men with impotence to either an experimental condition (Viagra) or a control condition (a placebo). It was a double-blind procedure—neither the men nor the person who gave them the pills knew which drug they were receiving. The result: At peak doses, 69 percent of Viagra-assisted attempts at intercourse were successful, compared with 22 percent for men receiving the placebo (Goldstein & others, 1998). Viagra had an effect.

This simple experiment manipulated just one drug factor. We call this experimental factor the **independent variable** because we can vary it independently of other factors, such as the men's age, weight, and personality (which random assignment should control). Experiments examine the effect of one or more independent variables on some measurable behavior, called the **dependent variable** because it can vary *depending* on what takes place during the experiment. Both variables are given precise *operational definitions*, which specify the procedures that manipulate the independent variable (the precise drug dosage and timing in this study) or measure the dependent variable (the questions that assessed the men's responses). These definitions answer the "What do you mean?" question with a level of precision that enables others to repeat the study. (See **FIGURE 2.4** for the breast milk experiment's design.)

Experiments can also help us evaluate social programs. Do early childhood education programs boost impoverished children's chances for success? What are the effects of different anti-smoking campaigns? Do school sex-education programs reduce teen pregnancies? To answer these questions, we can experiment: If an intervention is welcomed but resources are scarce, we could use a lottery to randomly assign some people (or regions) to experience the new program and others to a control condition. If later the two groups differ, the intervention's effect will be confirmed (Passell, 1993).

Let's recap. A *variable* is anything that can vary (infant nutrition, intelligence, TV exposure—anything within the bounds of what is feasible and ethical). Experiments aim to *manipulate* an *independent* variable, *measure* the *dependent* variable, and *control* all other variables. An experiment has at least two different groups: an *experimental group* and a *comparison or control group*. *Random assignment* works to equate the groups before any treatment effects. In this way, an experiment tests the effect of at least one independent variable (what we manipulate) on at least one dependent variable (the outcome we measure). **TABLE 2.1** compares the features of psychology's research methods.

FIGURE 2.4
Experimentation
To discern causation, psychologists may randomly assign some participants to an experimental group, others to a control group. Measuring the dependent variable (intelligence score) will determine the effect of the independent variable (type of milk).

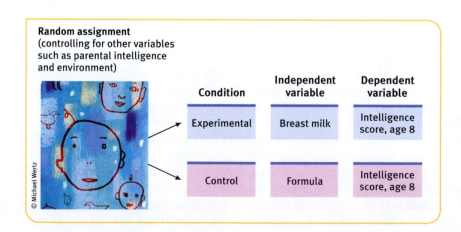

Random assignment
(controlling for other variables such as parental intelligence and environment)

	Condition	Independent variable	Dependent variable
	Experimental	Breast milk	Intelligence score, age 8
	Control	Formula	Intelligence score, age 8

© Michael Wertz

TABLE 2.1

COMPARING RESEARCH METHODS

Research Method	Basic Purpose	How Conducted	What Is Manipulated	Weaknesses
Descriptive	To observe and record behavior	Do case studies, surveys, or naturalistic observations	Nothing	No control of variables; single cases may be misleading.
Correlational	To detect naturally occurring relationships; to assess how well one variable predicts another	Compute statistical association, sometimes among survey responses	Nothing	Does not specify cause and effect.
Experimental	To explore cause and effect	Manipulate one or more factors; use random assignment	The independent variable(s)	Sometimes not feasible; results may not generalize to other contexts; not ethical to manipulate certain variables.

Frequently Asked Questions About Psychology

We have reflected on how a scientific approach can restrain biases. We have seen how case studies, surveys, and naturalistic observations help us describe behavior. We have also noted that correlational studies assess the relationship between two factors, which indicates how well one thing predicts another. We have examined the logic that underlies experiments, which use control conditions and random assignment of participants to isolate the effects of an independent variable on a dependent variable.

You are now prepared to understand what lies ahead and to think critically about psychological matters. Yet, even knowing this much, you may still be approaching psychology with a mixture of curiosity and apprehension. So before we plunge in, let's address some frequently asked questions.

2-8: Can laboratory experiments illuminate everyday life?

When you see or hear about psychological research, do you ever wonder whether people's behavior in the lab will predict their behavior in real life? For example, does detecting the blink of a faint red light in a dark room have anything useful to say about flying a plane at night? After viewing a violent, sexually explicit film, does an aroused man's increased willingness to push buttons that he thinks will electrically shock a woman really say anything about whether violent pornography makes a man more likely to abuse a woman?

Before you answer, consider: The experimenter *intends* the laboratory environment to be a simplified reality—one that simulates and controls important features of everyday life. Just as an aeronautical wind tunnel enables an engineer to re-create atmospheric forces under controlled conditions, a laboratory experiment enables a psychologist to re-create psychological forces under controlled conditions.

In aggression studies, deciding whether to push a button that delivers a shock may not be the same as slapping someone in the face, but the *principle* is the same. The experiment's purpose, notes Douglas Mook (1983), is not to re-create the exact behaviors of everyday life but to test theoretical principles. *It is the resulting principles—not the specific findings—that help explain everyday behaviors.*

When psychologists apply laboratory research on aggression to actual violence, they are applying theoretical *principles* of aggressive behavior, principles they have refined through many experiments. Similarly, it is the principles of the visual system, developed from experiments in artificial settings (such as looking at red lights in the

■ **culture** the enduring behaviors, ideas, attitudes, and traditions shared by a large group of people and transmitted from one generation to the next.

dark), that we apply to more complex behaviors such as night flying. And many investigations show that principles derived in the laboratory *do* typically generalize to the everyday world (Anderson & others, 1999).

The point to remember: As psychologists, our concerns lie less with particular behaviors than with the general principles that help explain many behaviors.

2-9: Does behavior depend on one's culture and gender?

If culture shapes behavior, what can psychological studies done in one culture, often with white Europeans or North Americans, really tell us about people in general? As we will see time and again, **culture**—shared ideas and behaviors that one generation passes on to the next—matters. Our culture influences our standards of promptness and frankness, our attitudes toward premarital sex and varying body shapes, our tendency to be casual or formal, our eye contact, our conversational distance, and much,

A cultured greeting
Because culture shapes people's understanding of social behavior, actions that seem ordinary to us may seem quite odd to visitors from far away. Yet underlying these differences are powerful similarities. Supporters of newly elected leaders everywhere typically greet them with pleased deference, though not necessarily with bows and folded hands, as in India. Here influential and popular politician Sonia Gandhi greets some of her constituents shortly after her election.

much more. Being aware of such differences, we can restrain our assumptions that others will think and act as we do. Given the growing mixing and clashing of cultures, our need for such awareness is urgent.

You will see throughout this book that gender matters, too. Researchers report gender differences in what we dream, in how we express and detect emotions, and in our risk for alcoholism, depression, and eating disorders. Not only is studying such differences interesting, it also is potentially beneficial. For example, many researchers believe that women carry on conversations more readily to build relationships, while men talk more to give information and advice (Tannen, 1990). Knowing this difference can help us prevent conflicts and misunderstandings in everyday relationships.

We also tend to exhibit and perceive the very behaviors our culture expects of males and females. But it's important to remember that psychologically as well as biologically, women and men are overwhelmingly similar. Whether female or male, we learn to walk at about the same age. We experience the same sensations of light and sound. We feel the same pangs of hunger, desire, and fear. We exhibit similar overall intelligence and well-being.

Our shared biological heritage unites us as a universal human family. The same underlying processes guide people everywhere:

- People diagnosed with dyslexia, a reading disorder, exhibit the same brain malfunction whether they are Italian, French, or British (Paulesu & others, 2001).
- Variation in languages—spoken and gestured—may impede communication across cultures. Yet all languages share deep principles of grammar, and people from opposite hemispheres can communicate with a smile or a frown.
- People in different cultures do vary in feelings of loneliness. But across cultures, loneliness is magnified by shyness, low self-esteem, and being unmarried (Jones & others, 1985; Rokach & others, 2002).
- Most Japanese prefer their fish raw and most North Americans prefer theirs cooked. But the same principles of hunger and taste influence us all when we sit down to a meal. We are each in certain respects like all others, like some others, and like no other. Studying people of all races and cultures helps us discern our similarities and our differences, our human kinship and our diversity.

The point to remember: Even when specific attitudes and behaviors vary across cultures, as they often do, the underlying processes are much the same. A children's song says it well: "We're all the same and different."

2-10 : Why do psychologists study animals, and is it ethical to experiment on animals?

Many psychologists study animals because they find them fascinating. They want to understand how different species learn, think, and behave. Psychologists also study animals to learn about people, by doing experiments permissible only with animals. Human physiology resembles that of many other animals. We humans are not *like* animals; we *are* animals. Animal experiments have therefore led to treatments for human diseases—insulin for diabetes, vaccines to prevent polio and rabies, transplants to replace defective organs.

Likewise, the same processes by which humans see, exhibit emotion, and become obese are present in rats and monkeys. To discover more about the basics of human learning, researchers even study sea slugs. To understand how a combustion engine works, you would do better to study a lawn mower's engine than a Mercedes'. Like Mercedes' engines, humans are complex. But the simplicity of the sea slug's nervous system is precisely what makes it so revealing of the neural mechanisms of learning.

If we share important similarities with other animals, then should we not respect them? "We cannot defend our scientific work with animals on the basis of the similarities between them and ourselves and then defend it morally on the basis of differences," noted Roger Ulrich (1991). The animal protection movement protests the use of animals in psychological, biological, and medical research. Researchers remind us that the world's 30 million mammals used each year in research are but a fraction of 1 percent of the billions of animals killed annually for food (which means the average person eats 20 animals a year). And for every dog or cat used in an experiment and cared for under humane regulations, 50 others are killed each year in humane animal shelters (Goodwin & Morrison, 1999).

Animal protection organizations, such as Psychologists for the Ethical Treatment of Animals (PETA), advocate naturalistic observation of animals rather than laboratory manipulation. Animal researchers have responded that the issue is not the morality of good versus evil but of compassion for animals versus compassion for people. How many of us would have attacked Louis Pasteur's experiments with rabies, which caused some dogs to suffer but led to a vaccine that spared millions of people (and dogs) from agonizing death? And would we really wish to have deprived ourselves of the animal research that led to effective methods of training children with mental disorders; of understanding aging; and of relieving fears and depression? The answers to such questions vary by culture. In Gallup surveys in Canada and the United States, about 6 in 10 adults deem medical testing on animals "morally acceptable." In Britain, only 37 percent do (Mason, 2003).

Out of this heated debate, two issues emerge. The basic one is whether it is right to place the well-being of humans above that of animals. In experiments on stress and cancer, is it right that mice get tumors in hopes that people might not? Should some monkeys be exposed to an HIV-like virus in the search for an AIDS vaccine? Is our use of other animals as natural as the behavior of carnivorous hawks, cats, and whales?

If we give human life first priority, the second issue is the priority we give to the well-being of animals in research. What safeguards should protect them? Most researchers today feel ethically obligated to enhance the well-being of captive animals and protect them from needless suffering. In one survey of animal researchers, 98 percent or more supported government regulations protecting primates, dogs, and

> "All people are the same; only their habits differ."
>
> Confucius, 551–479 B.C.

> Rats are very similar to humans except that they are not stupid enough to purchase lottery tickets."
>
> Dave Barry, July 2, 2002

> I believe that to prevent, cripple, or needlessly complicate the research that can relieve animal and human suffering is profoundly inhuman, cruel, and immoral."
>
> Psychologist Neal Miller, 1983

> Please do not forget those of us who suffer from incurable diseases or disabilities who hope for a cure through research that requires the use of animals."
>
> Psychologist Dennis Feeney (1987)

> The righteous know the needs of their animals."
>
> Proverbs 12:10

Animal research benefiting animals
Thanks partly to research on the benefits of novelty, control, and stimulation, these gorillas are enjoying an improved quality of life in New York's Bronx Zoo.

"The greatness of a nation can be judged by the way its animals are treated."
Mahatma Gandhi, 1869–1948

cats, and 74 percent supported regulations providing for the humane care of rats and mice (Plous & Herzog, 2000). Many professional associations and funding agencies already have such guidelines. For example, British Psychological Society guidelines call for housing animals under reasonably natural living conditions, with companions for social animals (Lea, 2000). American Psychological Association (2002) guidelines mandate ensuring the "comfort, health, and humane treatment" of animals, and of minimizing "infection, illness, and pain of animal subjects." Humane care also leads to more effective science, because pain and stress would distort the animals' behavior during experiments.

Animals have themselves benefited from animal research. One Ohio team of research psychologists measured stress hormone levels in samples of millions of dogs brought each year to animal shelters, and they devised handling and stroking methods that reduced stress and eased their transition to adoptive homes (Tuber & others, 1999). In New York, formerly listless and idle Bronx Zoo animals now stave off boredom by working for their supper, as they would in the wild (Stewart, 2002). Other studies have helped improve care and management in animals' natural habitats. By revealing our behavioral kinship with animals and the remarkable intelligence of chimpanzees, gorillas, and other animals, experiments have also led to increased empathy and protection for them. At its best, a psychology concerned for humans and sensitive to animals serves the welfare of both.

2-11: Is it ethical to experiment on people?

If the image of animals or people receiving supposed electric shocks troubles you, you may be relieved to know that most psychological research involves no such stress. With people, blinking lights, flashing words, and pleasant social interactions are more common.

Occasionally, though, researchers do temporarily stress or deceive people, but only when they believe it is essential to a justifiable end, such as understanding and controlling violent behavior or studying mood swings. Such experiments wouldn't work if the participants knew all there was to know about the experiment beforehand. Either the procedures would be ineffective or the participants, wanting to be helpful, might try to confirm the researchers' predictions.

Ethical principles developed by the American Psychological Association (1992) and the British Psychological Society (1993) urge investigators to (1) obtain the informed consent of potential participants, (2) protect them from harm and discomfort, (3) treat information about individual participants confidentially, and (4) fully explain the research afterward. Moreover, most universities today screen research proposals through an ethics committee that safeguards the well-being of every participant.

2-12: Is psychology free of value judgments?

Psychology is definitely not value-free. Values affect what we study, how we study it, and how we interpret results. Consider: Researchers' values influence their choice of research topics—whether to study worker productivity or worker morale, sex discrimination or gender differences, conformity or independence. Values can also color "the facts." As we noted earlier, our preconceptions can bias our observations and interpretations; sometimes we see what we want or expect to see (**FIGURE 2.5**).

Even the words we use to describe a phenomenon can reflect our values. Are the sex acts we do not practice "perversions" or "sexual variations"? Both in and out of psychology, labels describe and labels evaluate: The same holds true in everyday speech. One person's "rigidity" is another's "consistency," one person's "faith" is another's "fanaticism." Our labeling someone as "firm" or "stubborn," "careful" or "picky," "discreet" or "secretive" reveals our feelings.

Popular applications of psychology also contain hidden values. If you defer to "professional" guidance about how to live—how to raise children, how to achieve self-fulfillment, what to do with sexual feelings, how to get ahead at work—you are accepting value-laden advice. A science of behavior and mental processes can certainly help us reach our goals, but it cannot decide what those goals should be.

> "It is doubtless impossible to approach any human problem with a mind free from bias."
>
> Simone de Beauvoir, *The Second Sex*, 1953

© Roger Shepard

FIGURE 2.5
What do you see?
People interpret ambiguous information to fit their preconceptions. Did you see a duck or a rabbit? Before showing some friends this image, ask them if they can see the duck lying on its back (or the bunny in the grass). (From Shepard, 1990.)

2-13: Is psychology potentially dangerous?

If some people see psychology as merely common sense, others have a different concern—that it is becoming dangerously powerful. Is it an accident that astronomy is the oldest science and psychology the youngest? Exploring the external universe is one thing, but to some people, exploring our own inner universe seems more dangerous and threatening. Might psychology be used to manipulate people?

Knowledge, like all power, can be used for good or evil. Nuclear power has been used to light up cities—and to demolish them. Persuasive power has been used to educate people—and to deceive them. Although psychology does indeed have the power to deceive, its purpose is to enlighten. Every day, psychologists are exploring ways to enhance learning, creativity, and compassion. Psychology also speaks to many of our world's great problems—war, overpopulation, prejudice, family dysfunction, crime—all of which involve attitudes and behaviors. And psychology speaks to our deepest longings—for nourishment, for love, for happiness. True, psychology cannot address all of life's great questions, but it speaks to some mighty important ones.

>> MODULE REVIEW

2-1: **Why are the answers that flow from the scientific approach more reliable than those based on intuition and common sense?**

Intuition and common sense are not always trustworthy, and without scientific inquiry and critical thinking, we would readily succumb to *hindsight bias* (also called the I-knew-it-all-along phenomenon), the tendency to believe, after learning an outcome, that we would have foreseen it. We also are routinely overconfident of our judgments, thanks partly to our bias to seek information that confirms them. Although limited by the testable questions it can address, a scientific approach can help us sift reality from illusion, taking us beyond the limits of our intuition and common sense.

2-2: **What attitudes characterize scientific inquiry?**

Scientific inquiry begins with an attitude—a curious eagerness to skeptically scrutinize competing ideas and an open-minded humility before nature. This attitude carries into everyday life as *critical thinking*, which examines assumptions, searches for hidden values, evaluates evidence, and assesses outcomes. Putting ideas, even crazy-sounding ideas, to the test helps us winnow sense from nonsense.

2-3: **How do psychologists use the scientific method to construct theories?**

Research stimulates the construction of *theories*, which organize observations and imply predictive *hypotheses*. After constructing precise *operational definitions* of their procedures, researchers test their hypotheses (predictions), validate and refine the theory, and, sometimes, suggest practical applications. If other researchers can *replicate* (repeat) the study with similar results, we can then place greater confidence in the conclusion.

2-4: **How do psychologists observe and describe behavior?**

Psychologists observe and describe behavior using individual *case studies*, *surveys* among *random samples* of a *population,* and *naturalistic observations*. In generalizing from observations, remember: Representative samples are a better guide than vivid examples.

2-5: **Why do correlations permit prediction but not explanation?**

The strength of the relationship between one factor and another is expressed in their correlation coefficient. Knowing how closely two things are positively or negatively *correlated* tells us how much one predicts the other. But a correlation is only a measure of the strength of a relationship. It does not tell us whether either factor causes the other, or whether both are caused by some third factor.

2-6: **How accurately does the naked eye detect correlations?**

Correlations help us to see relationships that the naked eye might miss and to discount *illusory correlations* and random events that might otherwise look significant.

2-7: **How do experiments clarify or reveal cause-effect relationships?**

To discover cause-effect relationships, psychologists construct a controlled reality in an *experiment*. They can manipulate one or more factors (*independent variables*) and discover how these affect a particular behavior (the *dependent variable*). *Random assignment* minimizes preexisting differences between people chosen for the *experimental group* or the *control group*.

2-8: **Can laboratory experiments illuminate everyday life?**

Researchers test theoretical principles by creating a controlled, simplified environment in the lab. Their concern is not the particular behavior being studied, but rather the underlying principles that help explain many behaviors.

2-9: **Does behavior depend on one's culture and gender?**

Behaviors, ideas, attitudes, and traditions vary across *cultures*, but the principles that underlie them vary much less. Cross-cultural psychology explores both our cultural differences and the universal similarities that define our human kinship. Although gender differences tend to capture attention, males and females are biologically and psychologically much more alike than different.

2-10: **Why do psychologists study animals, and is it ethical to experiment on animals?**

Some psychologists study animals out of an interest in animal behavior. Others do so because knowledge of other animals' physiological and psychological processes helps them understand similar human processes. Under ethical and legal guidelines, animals used in psychological experiments rarely experience pain. Nevertheless, animal rights groups raise an important issue: Even if it leads to the relief of human suffering, is an animal's temporary suffering justified?

2-11: **Is it ethical to experiment on people?**

Occasionally researchers temporarily stress or deceive people to learn something important. Professional ethical standards, enforced by university ethics committees, safeguard research participants' well-being.

2-12: **Is psychology free of value judgments?**

Psychologists' own values influence their choice of research topics, their theories and observations, their labels for behavior, and their professional advice.

2-13: **Is psychology potentially dangerous?**

Psychology has the power to deceive, but so far, applications of psychology's principles have been overwhelmingly for the good. Psychology addresses some of humanity's greatest problems and deepest longings.

>> REHEARSE IT!

1. Psychology tells us what we already know from common sense, say some skeptics. *Hindsight bias* refers to our tendency to

a. perceive events as obvious or inevitable after the fact.
b. assume that two events happened because we wished them to happen.
c. overestimate our abilities to predict the future.
d. make judgments that fly in the face of common sense.

2. As scientists, psychologists view theories with skepticism, humility, and curiosity. This means that they

a. approach research with a negative cynicism.
b. assume that an article published in a reputable journal must be true.
c. realize that some issues should not be studied.
d. persistently ask questions, and are willing to reject ideas that cannot be verified by research.

3. A newspaper article describes how a "cure for cancer has been found." A critical thinker probably will

a. immediately dismiss the article as untrue because there is no evidence to back up the facts.
b. accept the information as a wonderful breakthrough.
c. question the article, evaluate the evidence, and assess the conclusions.
d. question the article but quickly accept it as true due to the author's excellent reputation.

4. In psychology, a good theory implies hypotheses, or predictions that can be tested. When hypotheses are tested, the result is typically

a. increased skepticism.
b. rejection of the merely theoretical.
c. confirmation or revision of the theory.
d. personal bias on the part of the investigator.

5. Psychologists use various research methods to observe and describe behaviors and mental processes. Which of the following would you use in an attempt to predict college grades from high school grades?

a. A case study
b. Naturalistic observation
c. Correlational research
d. A phone survey

6. You wish to take an accurate poll in a certain country by questioning people who truly represent the country's adult population. Therefore, you need to make sure the people are

a. at least 50 percent males and 50 percent females.
b. a small but intelligent sample of the population.
c. a very large sample of the population.
d. a random sample of the population.

7. Suppose a psychologist finds that the more natural childbirth training classes a woman attends, the less pain medication she requires during childbirth. The relationship between the number of training sessions and the amount of pain medication required is a/an

a. positive correlation (direct relationship).
b. negative correlation (inverse relationship).
c. cause-effect relationship.
d. illusory correlation.

8. Knowing that two events are correlated does not tell us what is the cause and what is the effect. However, it does provide

a. a basis for prediction.
b. an explanation of events.
c. proof that as one increases, the other also increases.
d. an indication that an underlying third factor is at work.

9. Some people wrongly perceive that their dreams predict future events. This is an example of a/an

a. negative correlation.
b. positive correlation.
c. illusory correlation.
d. naturalistic correlation.

10. A researcher wants to determine whether noise level affects the blood pressure of elderly people. For one group she varies the level of noise in the environment and records participants' blood pressure. In this experiment, the level of noise is the

a. control condition.
b. experimental condition.
c. dependent variable (the factor being measured).
d. independent variable (the factor being manipulated).

11. To test the effect of a new drug on depression, we randomly assign people to control and experimental groups. Those in the experimental group take a pink pill containing the new medication; those in the control group take a pink pill that contains no medication. Which statement is true?

a. The medication is the dependent variable.
b. Depression is the independent variable.
c. Participants in the control group take a placebo.
d. Neither the experimental nor the control group is told the purpose of the experiment.

12. To eliminate the biasing effect of a researcher's positive expectations on the outcome of a health clinic's research experiment,

a. patients are randomly assigned to the control and experimental groups (random assignment).
b. members of the experimental group are carefully matched for age, sex, income, and level of education with members of the control group.
c. neither the patients nor the researcher will know whether a given person has been assigned to the experimental or control condition.
d. people in the experimental group are chosen by selecting every tenth person in an alphabetical listing of all the clinic's patients.

13. Descriptive and correlational studies describe behavior, detect relationships, and predict behavior. But in order to begin to explain that behavior, psychologists use

a. naturalistic observation.
b. experimentation.
c. surveys.
d. case studies.

14. In a laboratory experiment, features of everyday life can be simulated, manipulated, and controlled. The laboratory environment is designed to
  a. exactly re-create the events of everyday life.
  b. re-create psychological forces under controlled conditions.
  c. create opportunities for naturalistic observation.
  d. minimize the use of animals and humans in psychological research.

15. Which of the following is true regarding gender differences and similarities?
  a. Differences between the genders outweigh any similarities.
  b. Despite some gender differences, the underlying processes of human behavior are the same.
  c. Both similarities and differences between the genders depend more on biology than on environment.
  d. Gender differences are so numerous, it is difficult to make meaningful comparisons.

16. The animal protection movement has protested the use of animals in all fields of scientific research. In defending their experimental research with animals, psychologists have noted that
  a. animals' physiology and behavior can tell us much about our own.
  b. they do not torture or needlessly exploit animals.
  c. advancing the well-being of humans justifies animal experimentation.
  d. All of the above are true.

Answers: 1. a, 2. d, 3. c, 4. c, 5. c, 6. d, 7. b, 8. a, 9. c, 10. d, 11. c, 12. c, 13. b, 14. b, 15. b, 16. d.

>> TERMS AND CONCEPTS TO REMEMBER

hindsight bias, p. 13
critical thinking, p. 16
theory, p. 17
hypothesis, p. 17
operational definition, p. 18
replication, p. 18
case study, p. 19
survey, p. 19

population, p. 20
random sample, p. 20
naturalistic observation, p. 20
correlation, p. 21
illusory correlation, p. 23
experiment, p. 25
random assignment, p. 25
double-blind procedure, p. 25

placebo effect, p. 25
experimental group, p. 25
control group, p. 25
independent variable, p. 26
dependent variable, p. 26
culture, p. 28

>> TEST YOURSELF

1. What is the scientific attitude, and why is it important for critical thinking?

2. What are the strengths and weaknesses of the three different methods psychologists use to describe behavior—case studies, surveys, and naturalistic observation?

3. Here are some recently reported correlations, with interpretations drawn by journalists. Further research, often including experiments, has clarified cause and effect in each case. Knowing just these correlations, can you come up with other possible explanations for each of these?
  a. Alcohol use is associated with violence. (One interpretation: Drinking triggers or unleashes aggressive behavior.)
  b. Educated people live longer, on average, than less-educated people. (One interpretation: Education lengthens life and enhances health.)
  c. Teens engaged in team sports are less likely to use drugs, smoke, have sex, carry weapons, and eat junk food than are teens who do not engage in team sports. (One interpretation: Team sports encourage healthy living.)
  d. Adolescents who frequently see smoking in movies are more likely to smoke. (One interpretation: Movie stars' behavior influences impressionable teens.)

4. Why, when testing a new drug for blood pressure, would we learn more about its effectiveness from giving it to half of the participants in a group of 1000 than to all 1000 participants?

5. How are human and animal research participants protected?

(Answers in Appendix C.)

Multiple-choice **self-tests** and more may be found at www.worthpublishers.com/myers.

>> ANSWER TO QUESTION WITHIN THE MODULE

Q. Can you unscramble this anagram? OCHSA

A. Did you figure it out? The answer is CHAOS.

Biology and Behavior

Biology and Behavior

No principle is more central to today's psychology, or to this book, than this: *Everything psychological—every idea, every mood, every urge—is simultaneously biological.* We find it convenient to talk separately of biological and psychological influences, but we need to remember: To think, feel, or act without a body would be like running without legs.

Today's science is riveted on the most amazing parts of our body—our brain, its component neural systems, and their genetic blueprints. The brain's ultimate challenge? To understand itself. How does our brain organize and communicate with itself? How does our heredity prewire the brain, and our experience modify it? How does the brain process the information we need to shoot a basketball? To delight in a guitarist's notes? To remember our first kiss?

We have come far since the early 1800s, when the German physician Franz Gall invented *phrenology,* a popular but ill-fated theory that claimed bumps on the skull could reveal our mental abilities and our character traits. Phrenology did, however, correctly focus attention on the idea that various brain regions have particular functions.

Within little more than the last century, we have also realized that the body is composed of cells; that among these are nerve cells that conduct electricity and "talk" to one another by sending chemical messages across a tiny gap; that specific brain systems serve specific functions (though not the functions Gall supposed); and that from the information processed in these different brain systems, we construct our experiences of sights and sounds, meanings and memories, pain and passion.

In these modules, we start small and build from the bottom up—from neurons and their interconnections (Module 3), to the brain (Module 4), to the genetic and evolutionary influences (Module 5) that interact with environmental and cultural influences (Module 6) to affect our behavior. We also work from the top down, as we consider how our thinking and emotions influence our brain and our health.

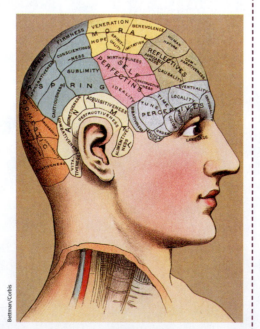

Bettman/Corbis

A wrongheaded theory
Despite initial acceptance of Franz Gall's speculations, bumps on the skull tell us nothing about the brain's underlying functions. Nevertheless, some of Gall's assumptions have held true. Different parts of the brain do control different aspects of behavior, as you will see throughout Modules 3 through 6.

Neural and Hormonal Systems

Neural Communication

The Nervous System

The Endocrine System

3-1: Why do psychologists study biology?

Throughout this book, you will find examples of how biology underlies our behavior and mental processes. By studying the links between biological activity and psychological events, **biological psychologists** are gaining a better understanding of such events.

Neural Communication

At all levels, psychologists examine how we process information—how we take it in; how we organize, interpret, and store it; and how we use it. For scientists, it is a happy fact of nature that the information systems of humans and other animals operate similarly—so similarly, in fact, that you could not distinguish between small samples of brain tissue from a human and a monkey. This similarity allows researchers to study relatively simple animals, such as squids and sea slugs, to discover how our neural systems operate, and it allows them to study other mammals' brains to understand the organization of our own. Cars differ, but all have engines, accelerators, steering wheels, and brakes. A Martian could study any one of them and grasp the operating principles. Likewise, animals differ, yet their nervous systems operate similarly. Though the human brain is more complex than a rat's, both follow the same principles. Here we look at the basics of the body's two communication systems: the nervous and hormone systems.

Neurons

3-2: What are neurons, and how do they transmit information?

Our body's neural information system is complexity built from simplicity. Its building blocks are **neurons,** or nerve cells. There are many different types of neurons, but all are variations on the same theme (**FIGURE 3.1**). Each consists of a *cell body* and its branching fibers. The bushy **dendrite** fibers receive information and conduct it toward the cell body. From there, the cell's **axon** passes the message along to other neurons or to muscles or glands. Axons speak. Dendrites listen.

■ **biological psychology** a branch of psychology concerned with the links between biology and behavior. (Some biological psychologists call themselves *behavioral neuroscientists, neuropsychologists, behavior geneticists, physiological psychologists,* or *biopsychologists.*)

■ **neuron** a nerve cell; the basic building block of the nervous system.

■ **dendrite** the bushy, branching extensions of a neuron that receive messages and conduct impulses toward the cell body.

■ **axon** the extension of a neuron, ending in branching terminal fibers, through which messages pass to other neurons or to muscles or glands.

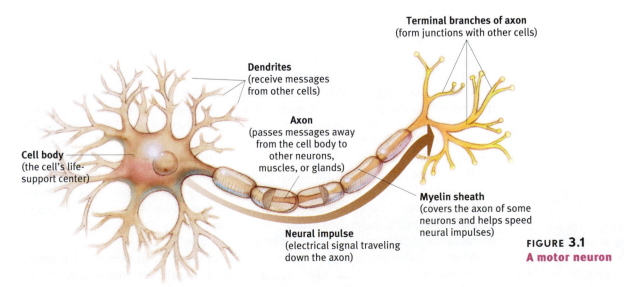

Terminal branches of axon
(form junctions with other cells)

Dendrites
(receive messages from other cells)

Axon
(passes messages away from the cell body to other neurons, muscles, or glands)

Cell body
(the cell's life-support center)

Myelin sheath
(covers the axon of some neurons and helps speed neural impulses)

Neural impulse
(electrical signal traveling down the axon)

FIGURE 3.1
A motor neuron

■ **action potential** a neural impulse; a brief electrical charge that travels down an axon.

■ **threshold** the level of stimulation required to trigger a neural impulse.

■ **synapse** [SIN-aps] the junction between the axon tip of the sending neuron and the dendrite or cell body of the receiving neuron. The tiny gap at this junction is called the *synaptic gap* or *cleft*.

■ **neurotransmitters** chemical messengers that traverse the synaptic gaps between neurons. When released by the sending neuron, neurotransmitters travel across the synapse and bind to receptor sites on the receiving neuron, thereby influencing whether that neuron will generate a neural impulse.

❝What one neuron tells another neuron is simply how much it is excited.❞

—Francis Crick, *The Astonishing Hypothesis*, 1994

Unlike the short dendrites, axons are sometimes very long, projecting several feet through the body. A neuron carrying orders to a leg muscle, for example, has a cell body and axon roughly on the scale of a basketball attached to a rope 4 miles long.

Neurons transmit messages when stimulated by signals from sensory receptors or when triggered by chemical signals from neighboring neurons. At such times, a neuron fires an impulse, called the **action potential**—a brief electrical charge that travels down its axon.

Depending on the type of fiber, the neural impulse travels at speeds ranging from a sluggish 2 miles per hour to a breakneck 200 or more miles per hour. But even this top speed (achieved with the help of a fatty sheath called *myelin*) is 3 million times slower than that of electricity through a wire. We measure brain activity in milliseconds (thousandths of a second) and computer activity in nanoseconds (billionths of a second). That helps to explain why, unlike the nearly instantaneous reactions of a high-speed computer, your reaction to a sudden event, such as a child darting in front of your car, may take a quarter-second or more. Your brain is vastly more complex than a computer, but not faster at executing simple responses.

Each neuron is itself a miniature decision-making device performing complex calculations as it receives signals from hundreds, even thousands, of other neurons. Most of these signals are *excitatory,* somewhat like pushing a neuron's accelerator. Others are *inhibitory,* more like pushing its brake. If excitatory signals minus inhibitory signals exceed a minimum intensity, or **threshold,** the combined signals trigger an action potential. (Think of it this way: If the excitatory party animals outvote the inhibitory party poopers, the party's on.) The action potential then travels down the axon, which branches into junctions with hundreds or thousands of other neurons and with the body's muscles and glands.

Increasing the level of stimulation above the threshold, however, will not increase the neural impulse's intensity. The neuron's reaction is an *all-or-none response:* Like guns, neurons either fire or they don't. How then do we detect the intensity of a stimulus? How do we distinguish a gentle touch from a big hug? A strong stimulus—a slap rather than a tap—can trigger *more* neurons to fire, and to fire more often. But it does not affect the action potential's strength or speed. Squeezing a trigger harder won't make a bullet go faster.

How Neurons Communicate

3-3: How do nerve cells communicate?

Neurons interweave so intricately that even with a microscope you would have trouble seeing where one neuron ends and another begins. Scientists once believed that the axon of one cell fused with the dendrites of another in an uninterrupted fabric. Then a Spanish anatomist, Santiago Ramón y Cajal (1852–1934), described gaps between individual nerve cells and concluded that individual neurons must function as independent agents within the nervous system. At the same time, British physiologist Sir Charles Sherrington (1857–1952) noticed that neural impulses were taking an unexpectedly long time to travel a neural pathway. Inferring that there must be a brief interruption in the transmission, Sherrington called the junction a **synapse.**

We now know that the axon terminal of one neuron is in fact separated from the receiving neuron by a *synaptic gap* (or *cleft*) less than a millionth of an inch wide. Cajal marveled at these near-unions of neurons, calling them "protoplasmic kisses." "Like elegant ladies air-kissing so as not to muss their makeup, dendrites and axons don't quite touch," notes poet Diane Ackerman (2004). How do the neurons execute this protoplasmic kiss, sending information across the tiny synaptic gap? The answer is one of the important scientific discoveries of our age.

When an action potential reaches the knoblike terminals at an axon's end, it triggers the release of chemical messengers, called **neurotransmitters** (FIGURE **3.2**). Within

❝All information processing in the brain involves neurons 'talking to' each other at synapses.❞

Neuroscientist Solomon H. Snyder (1984)

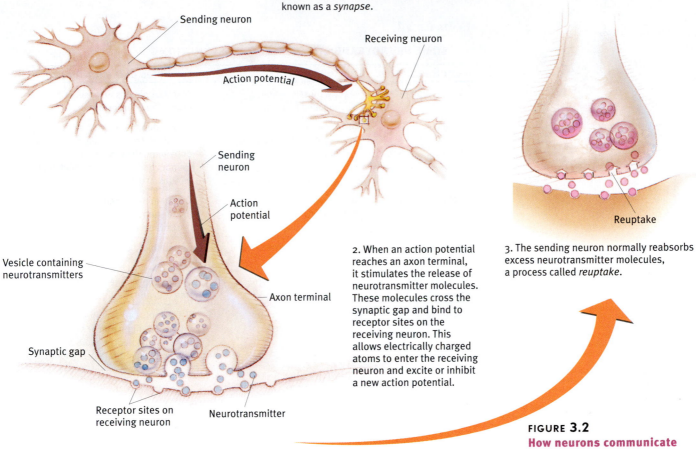

1. Electrical impulses (action potentials) travel down a neuron's axon until reaching a tiny junction known as a *synapse*.

Sending neuron

Receiving neuron

Action potential

Sending neuron

Action potential

Vesicle containing neurotransmitters

Axon terminal

Synaptic gap

Receptor sites on receiving neuron

Neurotransmitter

2. When an action potential reaches an axon terminal, it stimulates the release of neurotransmitter molecules. These molecules cross the synaptic gap and bind to receptor sites on the receiving neuron. This allows electrically charged atoms to enter the receiving neuron and excite or inhibit a new action potential.

Reuptake

3. The sending neuron normally reabsorbs excess neurotransmitter molecules, a process called *reuptake*.

FIGURE 3.2
How neurons communicate

1/10,000th of a second, the neurotransmitter molecules cross the synaptic gap and bind to receptor sites on the receiving neuron—as precisely as a key fits a lock. For an instant, the neurotransmitter unlocks tiny channels at the receiving site, and electrically charged atoms flow in, exciting or inhibiting the receiving neuron's readiness to fire. Then, in a process called *reuptake*, the sending neuron reabsorbs the excess neurotransmitters.

How Neurotransmitters Influence Us

3-4 : How do neurotransmitters influence human behavior?

In their quest to understand neural communication, researchers have discovered dozens of different neurotransmitters, and almost as many new questions: Are certain neurotransmitters found only in specific places? How do they affect our moods, memories, and mental abilities? Can we boost or diminish these effects through drugs or diet?

Among the many answers now flooding in are these: Neurotransmitters travel along their own designated neural pathways in the brain (**FIGURE 3.3**). And particular neurotransmitters may have specific effects on behavior and emotions (**TABLE 3.1**).

Acetylcholine (ACh) is one of the best-understood neurotransmitters. In addition to its role in learning and memory, ACh is the messenger at every junction between a motor neuron and skeletal muscle. When ACh is released to our muscle cells, the muscle contracts. If ACh transmission is blocked, as happens during some kinds of anesthesia, the muscles cannot contract and we are paralyzed.

"When it comes to the brain, if you want to see the action, follow the neurotransmitters."

—Neuroscientist Floyd Bloom (1993)

FIGURE 3.3
Neurotransmitter pathways
Each of the brain's differing chemical messengers has designated pathways where it operates, as shown here for serotonin and dopamine (Carter, 1998).

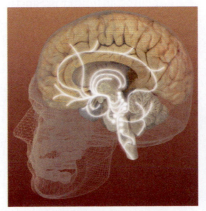

Serotonin pathways

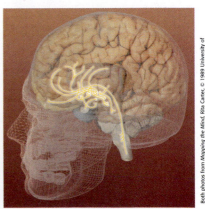

Dopamine pathways

Both photos from *Mapping the Mind*, Rita Carter, © 1989 University of California Press

TABLE 3.1

SOME NEUROTRANSMITTERS AND THEIR FUNCTIONS

Neurotransmitter	Function	Examples of Malfunctions
Acetylcholine (ACh)	Enables muscle action, learning, and memory.	With Alzheimer's disease, ACh-producing neurons deteriorate.
Dopamine	Influences movement, learning, attention, and emotion.	Excess dopamine receptor activity linked to schizophrenia. Starved of dopamine, the brain produces the tremors and decreased mobility of Parkinson's disease.
Serotonin	Affects mood, hunger, sleep, and arousal.	Undersupply linked to depression; Prozac and some other antidepressant drugs raise serotonin levels.
Norepinephrine	Helps control alertness and arousal.	Undersupply can depress mood.
GABA (gamma-aminobutyric acid)	A major inhibitory neurotransmitter.	Undersupply linked to seizures, tremors, and insomnia.
Glutamate	A major excitatory neurotransmitter; involved in memory.	Oversupply can overstimulate brain, producing migraines or seizures (which is why some people avoid MSG, monosodium glutamate, in food).

■ **endorphins** [en-DOR-fins] "morphine within"—natural, opiatelike neurotransmitters linked to pain control and to pleasure.

"Physician Lewis Thomas, on the endorphins: "There it is, a biologically universal act of mercy. I cannot explain it, except to say that I would have put it in had I been around at the very beginning, sitting as a member of a planning committee."

—*The Youngest Science*, 1983

Candace Pert and Solomon Snyder (1973) made an exciting discovery about neurotransmitters when they attached a radioactive tracer to morphine, showing where it was taken up in an animal's brain. The morphine, an opiate drug that elevates mood and eases pain, bound to receptors in areas linked with mood and pain sensations. But why would the brain contain these "opiate receptors" unless it had its own naturally occurring opiates? Why would it have a chemical lock, unless it also had a corresponding key? Researchers soon confirmed that the brain does indeed contain several types of neurotransmitter molecules similar to morphine. These **endorphins** (short for *endogenous* [produced within] *morphine*), are natural opiates released in response to pain and vigorous exercise. They may therefore help explain good feelings such as the "runner's high," the painkilling effects of acupuncture, and the indifference to pain in some severely injured people. But once again, new knowledge led to new questions.

How Drugs and Other Chemicals Alter Neurotransmission

If indeed the endorphins lessen pain and boost mood, why not flood the brain with artificial opiates, thereby intensifying the brain's own "feel-good" chemistry? One problem is that when flooded with opiate drugs such as heroin and morphine, the brain may stop producing its own natural opiates. When the drug is withdrawn, the brain may then be deprived of any form of opiate. For suppressing the body's own neurotransmitter production, nature charges a price.

Drugs and other chemicals affect brain chemistry at synapses, often by either exciting or inhibiting neurons' firing. *Agonists* excite. An agonist molecule may be similar enough to a neurotransmitter to mimic its effects (**FIGURE 3.4**) or it may block the neurotransmitter's reuptake. Some opiate drugs, for example, produce a temporary "high" by amplifying normal sensations of arousal or pleasure. Not so pleasant are the effects of black widow spider venom, which floods synapses with ACh. The result? Violent muscle contractions, convulsions, and possible death.

Antagonists inhibit. Some drug molecules inhibit a neurotransmitter's release from the sending neuron. Botulin, a poison that can form in improperly canned food, causes paralysis by blocking ACh release. (Injections of botulin—Botox—smooth wrinkles by paralyzing the underlying facial muscles.) Others are enough like the natural neurotransmitter to occupy its receptor site and block its effect, as in Figure 3.4, but are not similar enough to stimulate the receptor (rather like foreign coins that fit into,

FIGURE 3.4
Agonists and antagonists

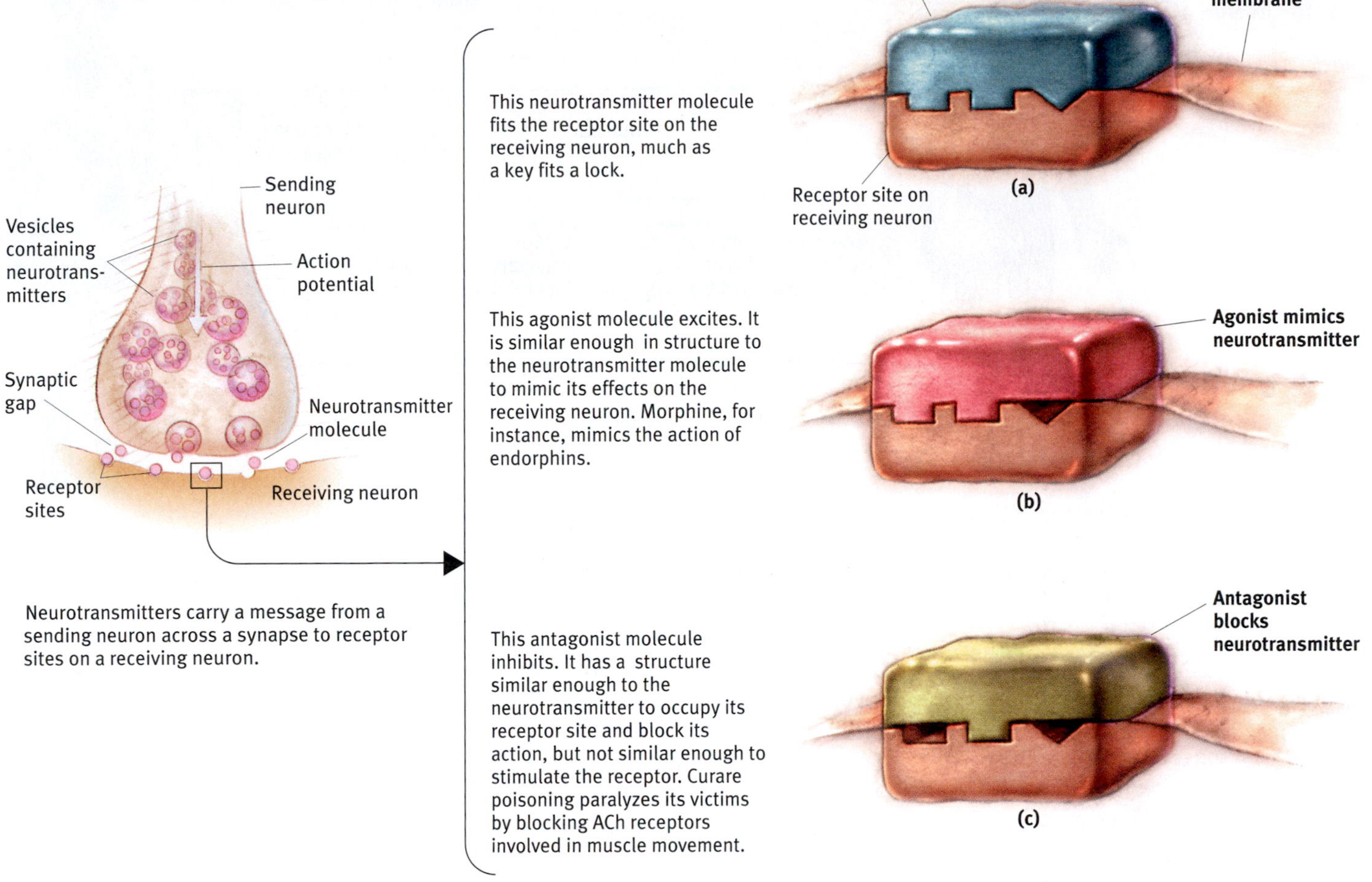

Neurotransmitter molecule

Receiving cell membrane

This neurotransmitter molecule fits the receptor site on the receiving neuron, much as a key fits a lock.

Receptor site on receiving neuron

(a)

Sending neuron

Vesicles containing neurotrans- mitters

Action potential

Synaptic gap

Neurotransmitter molecule

Receptor sites

Receiving neuron

This agonist molecule excites. It is similar enough in structure to the neurotransmitter molecule to mimic its effects on the receiving neuron. Morphine, for instance, mimics the action of endorphins.

Agonist mimics neurotransmitter

(b)

Neurotransmitters carry a message from a sending neuron across a synapse to receptor sites on a receiving neuron.

This antagonist molecule inhibits. It has a structure similar enough to the neurotransmitter to occupy its receptor site and block its action, but not similar enough to stimulate the receptor. Curare poisoning paralyzes its victims by blocking ACh receptors involved in muscle movement.

Antagonist blocks neurotransmitter

(c)

but won't operate, a soda or candy machine). Curare, a poison certain South American Indians have applied to hunting-dart tips, occupies and blocks ACh receptor sites, leaving the neurotransmitter unable to affect the muscles. Struck by one of these darts, an animal becomes paralyzed.

Neurotransmitter research is leading to new drugs for treatment of disorders. Designing such drugs is a challenge because a *blood-brain barrier* fences out unwanted chemicals circulating in the blood. Scientists know, for example, that the tremors of Parkinson's disease result from the death of dopamine-producing nerve cells. Giving the patient dopamine doesn't help, because dopamine cannot cross the blood-brain barrier. But some chemicals can slither through this barrier. One, L-dopa, a raw material the brain can convert to dopamine, enables many patients to regain better muscular control.

Throughout this text, you'll hear much more about neurotransmitter influences. For now, let's focus on the body's larger communication network.

The Nervous System

3-5 : What are the major divisions of the nervous system, and what are their basic functions?

To live is to take in information from the world and the body's tissues, to make decisions, and to send back information and orders to the body's tissues. All this happens thanks to our body's speedy electrochemical communications network, our **nervous system** (FIGURE 3.5). The brain and spinal cord form the **central nervous system**

■ **nervous system** the body's speedy, electrochemical communication network, consisting of all the nerve cells of the peripheral and central nervous systems.

■ **central nervous system (CNS)** the brain and spinal cord.

FIGURE 3.5
The functional divisions of the human nervous system

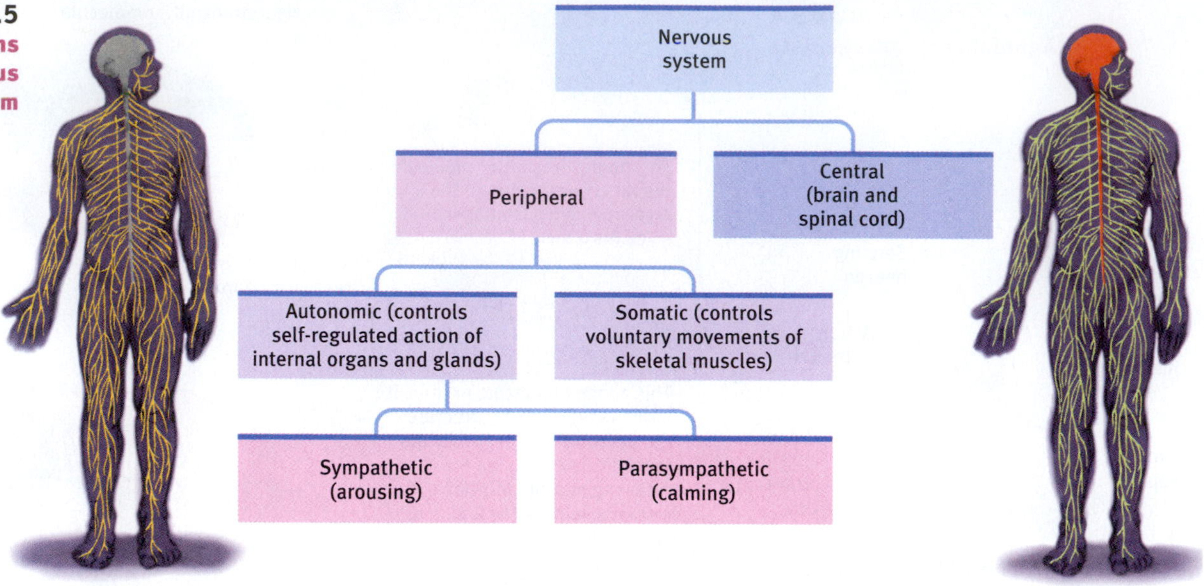

- **peripheral nervous system (PNS)** the sensory and motor neurons that connect the central nervous system (CNS) to the rest of the body.

- **nerves** neural "cables" containing many axons. These bundled axons, which are part of the peripheral nervous system, connect the central nervous system with muscles, glands, and sense organs.

- **sensory neurons** neurons that carry incoming information from the sense receptors to the central nervous system.

- **motor neurons** neurons that carry outgoing information from the central nervous system to the muscles and glands.

- **interneurons** central nervous system neurons that internally communicate and intervene between the sensory inputs and motor outputs.

- **somatic nervous system** the division of the peripheral nervous system that controls the body's skeletal muscles. Also called the *skeletal nervous system.*

- **autonomic** [aw-tuh-NAHM-ik] **nervous system** the part of the peripheral nervous system that controls the glands and the muscles of the internal organs (such as the heart). Its sympathetic division arouses; its parasympathetic division calms.

- **sympathetic nervous system** the division of the autonomic nervous system that arouses the body, mobilizing its energy in stressful situations.

- **parasympathetic nervous system** the division of the autonomic nervous system that calms the body, conserving its energy.

- **reflex** a simple, automatic response to a sensory stimulus, such as the knee-jerk response.

(CNS). The **peripheral nervous system (PNS)** links the central nervous system with the body's sensory receptors, muscles, and glands. Neurons are the elementary components of the nervous system.

Axons carrying PNS information are bundled into the electrical cables we know as **nerves.** The optic nerve, for example, bundles a million axon fibers into a single cable carrying the messages each eye sends to the brain (Mason & Kandel, 1991).

Information travels in the nervous system through three types of neurons. **Sensory neurons** carry messages from the body's tissues and sensory organs inward to the brain and spinal cord, for processing. The central nervous system then sends instructions out to the body's tissues via the **motor neurons.** In between the sensory input and motor output, information processing takes place in the CNS' internal communication system, via its **interneurons.** Our complexity resides mostly in our interneuron systems. Our nervous system has a few million sensory neurons, a few million motor neurons, and billions and billions of interneurons.

The Peripheral Nervous System

Our peripheral nervous system has two components—somatic and autonomic. The **somatic nervous system** enables voluntary control of our skeletal muscles. As you reach the bottom of this page, your somatic nervous system will report to your brain the current state of your skeletal muscles and carry instructions back, triggering your hand to turn the page.

Our **autonomic nervous system** controls our glands and the muscles of our internal organs, influencing such functions as glandular activity, heartbeat, and digestion. Like an automatic pilot, this system may be consciously overridden, but usually it operates on its own (autonomously).

The autonomic nervous system is a dual system (**FIGURE 3.6**). The **sympathetic nervous system** arouses and expends energy. If something alarms, enrages, or challenges you (such as a longed-for job interview), your sympathetic system will accelerate your heartbeat, raise your blood pressure, slow your digestion, raise your blood sugar, and cool you with perspiration, making you alert and ready for action. When the stress subsides, your **parasympathetic nervous system** produces opposite effects. It conserves energy as it calms you by decreasing your heartbeat, lowering your blood sugar, and so forth. In everyday situations, the sympathetic and parasympathetic nervous systems work together to keep us in a steady internal state.

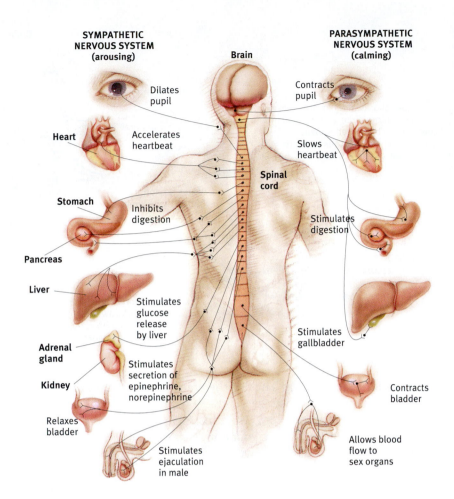

SYMPATHETIC NERVOUS SYSTEM (arousing)

PARASYMPATHETIC NERVOUS SYSTEM (calming)

Brain

Dilates pupil

Contracts pupil

Heart — Accelerates heartbeat

Slows heartbeat

Spinal cord

Stomach — Inhibits digestion

Stimulates digestion

Pancreas

Liver

Stimulates glucose release by liver

Stimulates gallbladder

Adrenal gland

Kidney

Stimulates secretion of epinephrine, norepinephrine

Contracts bladder

Relaxes bladder

Stimulates ejaculation in male

Allows blood flow to sex organs

FIGURE 3.6
The dual functions of the autonomic nervous system
The autonomic nervous system controls the more autonomous (or self-regulating) internal functions. Its sympathetic division arouses and expends energy. Its parasympathetic division calms and conserves energy, allowing routine maintenance activity. For example, sympathetic stimulation accelerates heartbeat, whereas parasympathetic stimulation slows it.

The Central Nervous System

From the simplicity of neurons "talking" to other neurons arises the complexity of the central nervous system that enables our humanity—our thinking, feeling, and acting. Tens of billions of neurons, each communicating with thousands of other neurons, yield an ever-changing wiring diagram that dwarfs a powerful computer. With some 40 billion neurons, each having roughly 10,000 contacts with other neurons, we end up with perhaps 400 trillion synapses—places where neurons meet and greet their neighbors (de Courten-Myers, 2005). A grain-of-sand–sized speck of your brain contains 100,000 neurons and one billion "talking" synapses (Ramachandran & Blakeslee, 1998).

Neurons cluster into work groups called *neural networks*. To understand why, Stephen Kosslyn and Olivier Koenig (1992, p. 12) invite us to "think about why cities exist; why don't people distribute themselves more evenly across the countryside?" Like people networking with people, neurons network with nearby neurons with which they can have short, fast connections. One of the great remaining scientific mysteries is how this neural machinery organizes itself into complex circuits capable of learning, feeling, and thinking.

The spinal cord is an information highway connecting the peripheral nervous system to the brain. Ascending neural fibers send up sensory information, and descending fibers send back motor-control information. The neural pathways governing our **reflexes,** our automatic responses to stimuli, illustrate the spinal cord's work. A simple spinal reflex pathway is composed of a single sensory neuron and a single motor neuron. These often communicate through an interneuron. The knee-jerk response, for example, involves one such simple pathway; a headless warm body could do it.

"You are your synapses."
—Joseph Le Doux, *The Synaptic Self*, 2002

"The body is made up of millions and millions of crumbs."

FIGURE **3.7**
A simple reflex

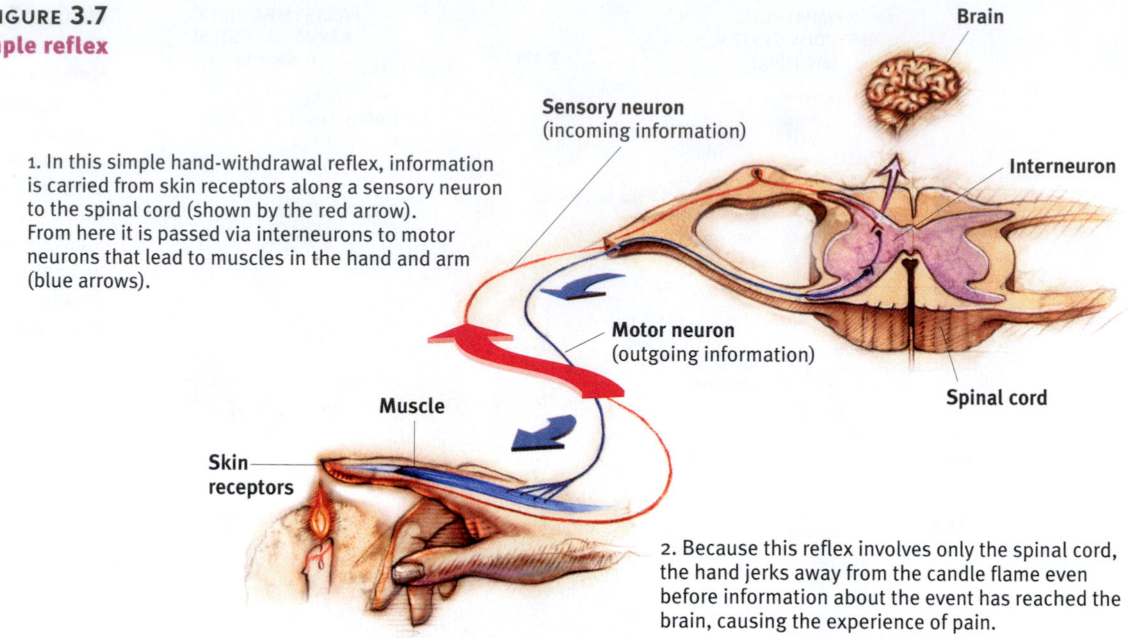

1. In this simple hand-withdrawal reflex, information is carried from skin receptors along a sensory neuron to the spinal cord (shown by the red arrow). From here it is passed via interneurons to motor neurons that lead to muscles in the hand and arm (blue arrows).

Brain

Sensory neuron (incoming information)

Interneuron

Motor neuron (outgoing information)

Spinal cord

Muscle

Skin receptors

2. Because this reflex involves only the spinal cord, the hand jerks away from the candle flame even before information about the event has reached the brain, causing the experience of pain.

Another such pathway enables the pain reflex (**FIGURE 3.7**). When your finger touches a flame, neural activity excited by the heat travels via sensory neurons to interneurons in your spinal cord. These interneurons respond by activating motor neurons leading to the muscles in your arm. That's why it feels as if your hand jerks away not by your choice, but on its own.

Because the simple pain reflex pathway runs through the spinal cord and out, your hand jerks from the candle's flame *before* your brain receives and responds to the information that causes you to feel pain. Information travels to and from the brain by way of the spinal cord. Were the top of your spinal cord severed, you would not feel such pain. Nor would you feel pleasure. With your brain literally out of touch with your body, you would lose all sensation and voluntary movement in body regions with sensory and motor connections to the spinal cord below its point of injury. You would exhibit the knee-jerk without feeling the tap. When the brain center keeping the brakes on erections is severed, men paralyzed below the waist may be capable of an erection (a simple reflex) if their genitals are stimulated (Goldstein, 2000). Females similarly paralyzed may respond with vaginal lubrication. But, depending on where and how completely the spinal cord is severed, they may be genitally unresponsive to erotic images and have no genital feeling (Kennedy & Over, 1990; Sipski & Alexander, 1999). To produce bodily pain or pleasure, the sensory information must reach the brain.

The Endocrine System

3-6 : How does the endocrine system—the body's slower information system—transmit its messages?

So far we have focused on the body's speedy electrochemical information system. Interconnected with your nervous system is a second communication system, the **endocrine system** (**FIGURE 3.8**). The endocrine system's glands secrete another form of chemical messengers, **hormones,** which travel through the bloodstream and affect other tissues, including the brain. When they act on the brain, they influence our interest in sex, food, and aggression.

FIGURE **3.8**
The endocrine system

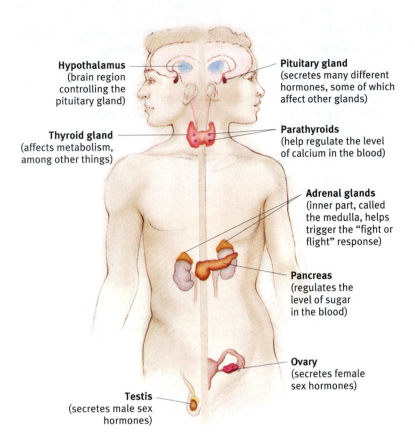

Hypothalamus
(brain region
controlling the
pituitary gland)

Pituitary gland
(secretes many different
hormones, some of which
affect other glands)

Thyroid gland
(affects metabolism,
among other things)

Parathyroids
(help regulate the level
of calcium in the blood)

Adrenal glands
(inner part, called
the medulla, helps
trigger the "fight or
flight" response)

Pancreas
(regulates the
level of sugar
in the blood)

Ovary
(secretes female
sex hormones)

Testis
(secretes male sex
hormones)

Some hormones are chemically identical to neurotransmitters (those chemical messengers that diffuse across a synapse and excite or inhibit an adjacent neuron). The endocrine system and nervous system are therefore kindred systems: Both secrete molecules that activate receptors elsewhere. But unlike the speedy nervous system, zipping messages from eyes to brain to hand in a fraction of a second, endocrine messages trudge along in the bloodstream, taking several seconds or more to travel from the endocrine gland to its target tissue. If the nervous system's communication delivers messages rather like e-mail, the endocrine system is the body's snail mail. These endocrine messages are often worth the wait, though, because their effects usually outlast the effects of a neural message. That helps explain why, after our conscious mind is distracted from some mildly stressful news, we sometimes have a lingering feeling that something isn't quite right. Under the influence of hormones and non-verbal brain areas, the feeling outlasts the thought—until we recapture the awareness and perhaps feel relief at recalling the reason for our discomfort.

The endocrine system's hormones influence many aspects of our lives—growth, reproduction, metabolism, mood—working to keep everything in balance while we respond to stress, exertion, and our own thoughts. In a moment of danger, for example, the autonomic nervous system orders the **adrenal glands** on top of the kidneys to release *epinephrine* and *norepinephrine* (also called *adrenaline* and *noradrenaline*). These hormones increase heart rate, blood pressure, and blood sugar, providing us with a surge of energy. When the emergency passes, the hormones—and the feelings of excitement—linger a while.

The most influential endocrine gland is the **pituitary gland,** a pea-sized structure located in the core of the brain, where it is controlled by an adjacent brain area, the hypothalamus. The pituitary releases hormones that influence growth, and its secretions also influence the release of hormones by other endocrine glands. The pituitary, then, is really a sort of master gland (whose own master is the hypothalamus). For example,

■ **endocrine** [EN-duh-krin] **system** the body's "slow" chemical communication system; a set of glands that secrete hormones into the bloodstream.

■ **hormones** chemical messengers, mostly those manufactured by the endocrine glands, that are produced in one tissue and affect another.

■ **adrenal** [ah-DREEN-el] **glands** a pair of endocrine glands just above the kidneys. The adrenals secrete the hormones epinephrine (adrenaline) and norepinephrine (noradrenaline), which help to arouse the body in times of stress.

■ **pituitary gland** the endocrine system's most influential gland. Under the influence of the hypothalamus, the pituitary regulates growth and controls other endocrine glands.

under the brain's influence, the pituitary triggers your sex glands to release sex hormones. These in turn influence your brain and behavior.

This feedback system (brain → pituitary → other glands → hormones → brain) reveals the intimate connection of the nervous and endocrine systems: the nervous system directing endocrine secretions, which then affect the nervous system. Conducting and coordinating this whole electrochemical orchestra is that maestro we call the brain.

>> MODULE REVIEW

3-1: Why do psychologists study biology?

Biological psychologists study the links between our biology and our thoughts, feelings, and behaviors, because everything psychological is simultaneously biological.

3-2: What are neurons, and how do they transmit information?

Neurons are the elementary components of the nervous system, the body's speedy electrochemical information system. The billions of neurons in this system send signals through their *axons,* and they receive signals from other cells through their branching *dendrites* and their cell body. If the combined signals are strong enough, the neuron fires, transmitting an electrical impulse (the *action potential*) down its axon by means of a chemistry-to-electricity process. The neuron's reaction is an all-or-none process.

3-3: How do nerve cells communicate?

When action potentials reach the end of an axon, they stimulate the release of *neurotransmitters.* These chemical messengers pass on their excitatory or inhibitory messages as they traverse the tiny gap (*synapse*) between neurons and bind to receptor sites on neighboring neurons.

3-4: How do neurotransmitters influence human behavior?

Neurotransmitters travel designated paths in the brain and have particular effects on behavior. Acetycholine affects muscle action,

learning, and memory. The *endorphins* are natural opiates released in response to pain and exercise. Some drugs (agonists) mimic particular neurotransmitters or block their reuptake; others (antagonists) block their release or effects.

3-5: What are the major divisions of the nervous system, and what are their basic functions?

One major division is the *central nervous system (CNS),* which consists of the brain and spinal cord. The other is the *peripheral nervous system (PNS).* The *interneurons* in the brain and spinal cord (the CNS) communicate with the *sensory neurons* and *motor neurons* that form *nerves* in the PNS. The PNS has two main divisions. The *somatic nervous system* enables voluntary control of the skeletal muscles. The *autonomic nervous system,* through its *sympathetic* and *parasympathetic divisions,* controls the involuntary muscles and the glands.

3-6: How does the endocrine system—the body's slower information system—transmit its messages?

Hormones released by the *endocrine system* glands travel through the bloodstream and affect other tissues, including the brain. During stressful or dangerous times, the autonomic nervous system activates the *adrenal glands.* The endocrine system's master gland, the *pituitary,* influences hormone release by other glands.

>> REHEARSE IT!

1. The neuron fiber that carries messages to other neurons is the
   a. dendrite.
   b. axon.
   c. cell body.
   d. myelin.

2. The neuron's response to stimulation is an all-or-none response, meaning that the intensity of the stimulus determines
   a. whether or not an impulse is generated.
   b. how fast an impulse is transmitted.
   c. how intense an impulse will be.
   d. whether the stimulus is excitatory or inhibitory.

3. There is a minuscule space between the axon of a sending neuron and the dendrite or cell body of a receiving neuron. This small space is called the
   a. axon terminal.
   b. sac or vesicle.
   c. synaptic gap.
   d. threshold.

4. When an action potential reaches the axon terminal of a neuron, it

triggers the release of chemical messengers called
   a. dendrites.
   b. synapses.
   c. neural impulses.
   d. neurotransmitters.

5. Endorphins are released in the brain in response to
   a. morphine or heroin.
   b. pain or vigorous exercise.
   c. antagonists.
   d. all of the above.

6. The autonomic nervous system controls internal functions, such as heart rate and glandular activity. The word *autonomic* means

   a. peripheral.
   b. voluntary.
   c. self-regulating.
   d. arousing.

7. Usually, the sympathetic nervous system arouses us for action and the parasympathetic nervous system calms us down. Together, the two systems make up the

   a. autonomic nervous system.
   b. somatic nervous system.

   c. central nervous system.
   d. peripheral nervous system.

8. The neurons of the spinal cord are part of the

   a. somatic nervous system.
   b. central nervous system.
   c. autonomic nervous system.
   d. peripheral nervous system.

9. The endocrine system, the body's second and slower communication system, produces chemical messengers that travel through the bloodstream and affect other tissues. These chemical substances are

   a. hormones.
   b. neurotransmitters.
   c. endorphins.
   d. glands.

10. The pituitary gland releases hormones that influence growth and the activity of other glands. The pituitary gland is part of the

   a. endocrine system.
   b. peripheral nervous system.
   c. sympathetic nervous system.
   d. central nervous system.

Answers:
1. b, 2. a, 3. c, 4. d, 5. b, 6. c, 7. a, 8. b, 9. a, 10. a.

>> Terms and Concepts to Remember

biological psychology, p. 37
neuron, p. 37
dendrite, p. 37
axon, p. 37
action potential, p. 38
threshold, p. 38
synapse [SIN-aps], p. 38
neurotransmitters, p. 38
endorphins [en-DOR-fins], p. 40

nervous system, p. 41
central nervous system (CNS), p. 41
peripheral nervous system (PNS), p. 42
nerves, p. 42
sensory neurons, p. 42
motor neurons, p. 42
interneurons, p. 42
somatic nervous system, p. 42

autonomic [aw-tuh-NAHM-ik] nervous system, p. 42
sympathetic nervous system, p. 42
parasympathetic nervous system, p. 42
reflex, p. 43
endocrine [EN-duh-krin] system, p. 44
hormones, p. 44
adrenal [ah-DREEN-el] glands, p. 45
pituitary gland, p. 45

>> Test Yourself

1. How do neurons communicate with one another?

2. How does information flow through your nervous system as you pick up a fork? Can you summarize this process?

3. Why is the pituitary gland called the "master gland"?

(Answers in Appendix C.)

*Multiple-choice **self-tests** and more may be found at www.worthpublishers.com/myers.*

48

MODULE

4 The Brain

Note: *Neurons* (the nervous system's basic building blocks) communicate electrochemically by transmitting *neurotransmitters* (chemical messengers) across the *synapses* (tiny gaps) that separate them.

Imagine that just moments before your death, someone removed your brain from your body and kept it alive by floating it in a tank of cerebral fluid while feeding it enriched blood. Would you still be in there? Further imagine that your still-living brain were transplanted into the body of a person whose own brain had been severely damaged. To whose home should the recovered patient return?

That we can imagine such questions illustrates how convinced we are that we live in our heads. And for good reason: The brain enables the mind—seeing, hearing, smelling, feeling, remembering, thinking, speaking, dreaming. The brain is what poet Diane Ackerman (2004, p. 3) calls "that shiny mound of being . . . that dream factory . . . that huddle of neurons calling all the plays . . . that fickle pleasure-drome."

Moreover, it is the brain that self-reflectively analyzes the brain. When we're thinking about our brain, we're thinking *with* our brain—by firing countless millions of synapses and releasing billions of neurotransmitter molecules. Indeed, say neuroscientists, the *mind is what the brain does*. But precisely where and how are the mind's functions tied to the brain? (To see how scientists explore such questions, turn the page to see Close-Up: The Tools of Discovery.)

Older Brain Structures

Brain structures determine an animal's capacities. In primitive vertebrate (back-boned) animals, such as sharks, a not-too-complex brain primarily regulates basic survival functions: breathing, resting, and feeding. In lower mammals, such as rodents, a more complex brain enables emotion and greater memory. In advanced mammals, such as humans, the brain processes more information, so we are able to act with foresight.

To enable this increasing complexity, species have elaborated new brain systems on top of the old, much as the Earth's landscape covers the old with the new. Digging down, one discovers the fossil remnants of the past—brainstem components still performing much as they did for our distant ancestors. Starting with the brainstem and working up to the newer systems, let's now explore the brain.

The Brainstem

4-1: What are the functions of the brainstem and its associated structures?

The brain's basement—its oldest and innermost region—is the **brainstem.** It begins where the spinal cord enters the skull and swells slightly, forming the **medulla.** Here lie the controls for your heartbeat and breathing. Just above the medulla sits the *pons,* which helps coordinate movements. If a cat's brainstem is severed from the rest of the brain above it, the animal will still breathe and live—and even run, climb, and groom (Klemm, 1990). But cut off from the brain's higher region, it won't purposefully run or climb to get food.

The brainstem is a crossover point, where most nerves to and from each side of the brain connect with the body's opposite side. This peculiar cross-wiring is but one of many surprises the brain has to offer.

© The New Yorker Collection, 1992, Gahan Wilson, from cartoonbank.com. All rights reserved.

"You're certainly a lot less fun since the operation."

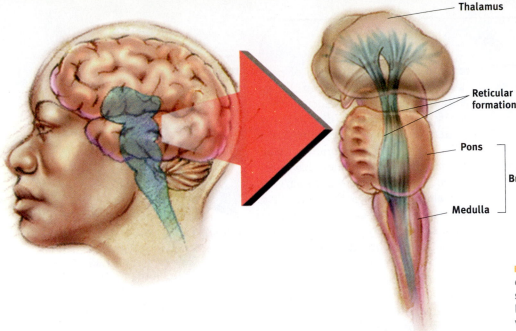

Thalamus

Reticular formation

Pons

Brainstem

Medulla

FIGURE 4.1

The brainstem and thalamus

The brainstem, including the pons and medulla, is an extension of the spinal cord. The thalamus is attached to its top. The reticular formation passes through both structures.

- **brainstem** the oldest part and central core of the brain, beginning where the spinal cord swells as it enters the skull; the brainstem is responsible for automatic survival functions.

- **medulla** [muh-DUL-uh] the base of the brainstem; controls heartbeat and breathing.

- **thalamus** [THAL-uh-muss] the brain's sensory switchboard, located on top of the brainstem; it directs messages to the sensory receiving areas in the cortex and transmits replies to the cerebellum and medulla.

- **reticular formation** a nerve network in the brainstem that plays an important role in controlling arousal.

- **cerebellum** [sehr-uh-BELL-um] the "little brain" attached to the rear of the brainstem; its functions include processing sensory input and coordinating movement output and balance.

The Thalamus

Atop the brainstem sits the brain's sensory switchboard, a joined pair of egg-shaped structures called the **thalamus** (FIGURE 4.1). It receives information from all the senses except smell and routes it to the brain regions that deal with seeing, hearing, tasting, and touching. Think of the thalamus as being to sensory input what London is to England's trains: a hub through which traffic passes en route to various destinations. The thalamus also receives some of the higher brain's replies, which it then directs to the medulla and to the cerebellum.

The Reticular Formation

Inside the brainstem, between your ears, lies the **reticular** ("netlike") **formation,** a finger-shaped network of neurons that extends from the spinal cord right up to the thalamus (Figure 4.1). As the spinal cord's sensory input travels up to the thalamus, some of it travels through the reticular formation, which filters incoming stimuli and relays important information to other areas of the brain.

In 1949, Giuseppe Moruzzi and Horace Magoun discovered that electrically stimulating the reticular formation of a sleeping cat almost instantly produced an awake, alert animal. When Magoun *severed* a cat's reticular formation from higher brain regions, without damaging the nearby sensory pathways, the effect was equally dramatic: The cat lapsed into a coma from which it never awakened. Magoun could clap his hands by the cat's ear, even pinch it; still, no response. The conclusion? The reticular formation is involved in arousal.

FIGURE 4.2

The brain's organ of agility

Hanging at the back of the brain, the cerebellum coordinates our movements, as when David Beckham directs the ball precisely.

The Cerebellum

Extending from the rear of the brainstem is the baseball-sized **cerebellum,** meaning "little brain," which is what its two wrinkled halves resemble (FIGURE 4.2). The cerebellum enables one type of nonverbal learning and memory. It helps us judge time, modulate our emotions, and discriminate sounds and textures (Bower & Parsons, 2003). And it coordinates voluntary movement. When soccer great David Beckham fires the ball into the net with a perfectly timed kick, give his cerebellum some credit. If you injured your cerebellum, you would have difficulty walking, keeping your balance, or shaking hands. Your movements would be jerky and exaggerated.

Cerebellum

Spinal cord

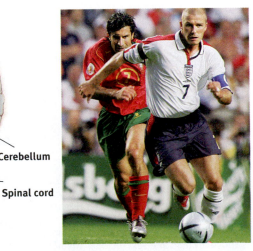

Lluis Gene/AFP/Getty Images

CLOSE-UP

THE TOOLS OF DISCOVERY

"You must look into people, as well as at them."

—Lord Chesterfield, *Letter to his son*, 1746

For centuries, we had no tools high-powered yet gentle enough to explore the living human brain. Clinical observations revealed some brain-mind connections. Physicians noted, for example, that damage to one side of the brain often caused numbness or paralysis on the body's opposite side, suggesting that the right side of the body is wired to the brain's left side, and vice versa. Others noticed that damage to the back of the brain disrupted vision, and that damage to the left-front part of the brain produced speech difficulties. Gradually, these early explorers were mapping the brain.

Now, within a lifetime, all that has changed. The known universe's most amazing organ is being probed and

Banking brains
Francine Benes, director of McLean Hospital's Brain Bank, sees the collection as a valuable database.

mapped by a new generation of neural cartographers. Whether in the interests of science or medicine, they can selectively **lesion** (destroy) tiny clusters of normal or defective brain cells, leaving the surrounding tissue unharmed. Such studies have revealed, for example, that damage to one area of the hypothalamus in a rat's brain reduces eating, causing the rat to starve unless force-fed. Damage in another area produces *overeating*.

Today's scientists can also electrically, chemically, or magnetically stimulate various parts of the brain and note the effects; snoop on the messages of individual neurons and eavesdrop on the chatter of billions of neurons; see color representations of the brain's energy-consuming activity. These techniques for peering into the thinking, feeling brain are doing for psychology what the microscope did for biology and the telescope did for astronomy. Let's look at a few of them in more detail.

Recording the Brain's Electrical Activity

Right now, your mental activity is giving off telltale electrical, metabolic, and magnetic signals that would enable neuroscientists to observe your brain at work. The tips of modern microelectrodes are so small they can detect the electrical pulse in a single neuron. For example, we can now detect exactly where the infor-

FIGURE 4.3

An electroencephalograph providing amplified tracings of waves of electrical activity in the brain
Here it is displaying the brain activity of this 4-year-old who has epilepsy.

mation goes in a cat's brain when someone strokes its whisker.

Electrical activity in the brain's billions of neurons sweeps in regular waves across its surface. An **electroencephalogram (EEG)** is an amplified read-out of such waves (**FIGURE 4.3**).

Neuroimaging Techniques

Newer windows into the brain give us a Supermanlike ability to see inside the living brain. One such tool, the **PET (positron emission tomography) scan** (**FIGURE 4.4**), depicts brain activity by showing each brain area's consumption of its chemical fuel, the sugar glucose (see Figure 4.18 in this module's discussion of language processing). Active neurons are glucose hogs. A person is

"Consciousness is a small part of what the brain does."

—Neuroscientist Joseph LeDoux, in "Master of Emotions," 2006

■ **limbic system** a doughnut-shaped system of neural structures below the cerebral hemispheres; associated with emotions such as fear and aggression and drives such as those for food and sex. Includes the *hippocampus, amygdala,* and *hypothalamus.*

Note: These older brain functions all occur without any conscious effort. This illustrates another of our recurring themes: *Our brain processes most information outside of our awareness.* We are aware of the *results* of our brain's labor (say, our current visual experience) but not of *how* we construct the visual image. Likewise, whether we are asleep or awake, our brainstem manages its life-sustaining functions, freeing our newer brain regions to dream, think, talk, or savor a memory.

The Limbic System

4-2: What are the functions of limbic system structures?

At the border ("limbus") of the brain's older parts and the *cerebral hemispheres*—the two halves of the brain—is the doughnut-shaped **limbic system** (**FIGURE 4.6**). One limbic system component, the *hippocampus,* processes memory. If animals or humans

FIGURE 4.4

The PET scan

To obtain a PET scan, researchers inject volunteers with a low and harmless dose of a short-lived radioactive sugar. Detectors around the person's head pick up the release of gamma rays from the sugar, which has concentrated in active brain areas. A computer then processes and translates these signals into a map of the brain at work. (See Figure 4.18 for an example of PET scans.)

given a temporarily radioactive form of glucose, and the PET scan locates and measures the radioactivity, thereby detecting where this "food for thought" goes. Rather like weather radar showing rain activity, PET scan "hot spots" show which brain areas are most active as the person performs mathematical calculations, listens to music, or daydreams.

In **MRI (magnetic resonance imaging)** scans, the head (or other body part) is put in a strong magnetic field, which aligns the spinning atoms of brain molecules. Then a brief pulse of radio waves disorients the atoms momentarily. When the atoms return to their normal spin, they release signals that provide a detailed picture of the brain's (and the body's) soft tissues. MRI scans have revealed a larger-than-average neural area in the left hemisphere of musicians who display perfect pitch (Schlaug & others, 1995). They have also revealed enlarged fluid-filled brain areas in some patients who have schizophrenia, a disabling psychological disorder (**FIGURE 4.5**).

A special application of MRI, **fMRI (functional MRI),** can reveal the brain's functioning as well as its structure. Where the brain is especially active, blood goes. By comparing MRI scans taken less than a second apart, researchers can watch

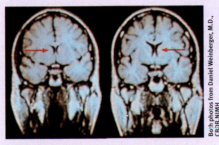

FIGURE 4.5

MRI scan of a healthy individual (left) and a person with schizophrenia (right)

Note the enlarged fluid-filled brain region in the image on the right.

the brain light up (with increased oxygen-laden bloodflow) as a person performs different mental functions. As the person looks at a face, for example, the fMRI machine detects blood rushing to the back of the brain, which processes visual information (see Figure 4.13). Such snapshots of the brain's changing activity provide new insights into how the brain divides its labor.

To be learning about the neurosciences now is like studying world geography while Magellan was exploring the seas. Clearly, this is the golden age of brain science.

■ **lesion** [LEE-zhuhn] tissue destruction. A brain lesion is a naturally or experimentally caused destruction of brain tissue.

■ **electroencephalogram (EEG)** an amplified recording of the waves of electrical activity that sweep across the brain's surface. These waves are measured by electrodes placed on the scalp.

■ **PET (positron emission tomography) scan** a visual display of brain activity that detects where a radioactive form of glucose goes while the brain performs a given task.

■ **MRI (magnetic resonance imaging)** a technique that uses magnetic fields and radio waves to produce computer-generated images that distinguish among different types of soft tissue; allows us to see structures within the brain.

■ **fMRI (functional magnetic resonance imaging)** a technique for revealing blood flow and, therefore, brain activity by comparing successive MRI scans. MRI scans show brain anatomy; fMRI scans show brain function.

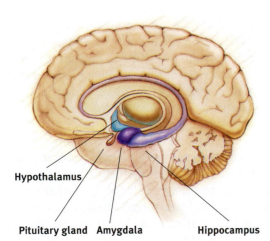

Hypothalamus

Pituitary gland   Amygdala   Hippocampus

FIGURE 4.6

The limbic system

Limbic structures form a doughnut-shaped neural system between the brain's older parts and its cerebral hemispheres. Although part of the hormonal (endocrine) system, not the brain, the pituitary gland is controlled by the limbic system's hypothalamus, just above it.

Moonrunner Design Ltd., UK

FIGURE 4.7
The amygdala

Frank Siteman/Stock, Boston

Aggression as a brain state
Back arched and fur fluffed, this fierce cat is ready to attack. Electrical stimulation of a cat's amygdala provokes reactions such as the one shown here, suggesting its role in emotions like rage. Which division of the autonomic nervous system is activated by such stimulation? (See this module's final page.)

lose their hippocampus to surgery or injury, they become unable to process new memories of facts and episodes. The limbic system also has important links to emotions such as fear and anger, and to basic motives such as those for food and sex.

The Amygdala

In the limbic system, two lima bean-sized neural clusters, the **amygdala,** influence aggression and fear (**FIGURE 4.7**). In 1939, psychologist Heinrich Klüver and neurosurgeon Paul Bucy surgically lesioned the part of a rhesus monkey's brain that included the amygdala. The result? The normally ill-tempered monkey turned into the most mellow of creatures. Poke it, pinch it, do virtually anything that normally would trigger a ferocious response, and still the animal remained placid. What then might happen if we electrically stimulated the amygdala in a normally placid domestic animal, such as a cat? Do so in one spot and the cat prepares to attack, hissing with its back arched, its pupils dilated, its hair on end. Move the electrode only slightly within the amygdala, cage the cat with a small mouse, and now it cowers in terror.

These experiments confirm the amygdala's role in rage and fear, not to mention the perception of such emotions and the processing of emotional memories (Anderson & Phelps, 2000; Poremba & Gabriel, 2001). Still, we must be careful. The brain is not neatly organized into structures that correspond to our categories of behavior. Both aggressive and fearful behavior involve neural activity in all brain levels, not solely in the amygdala. Even within the limbic system, stimulating structures other than the amygdala can evoke such behavior. If you charge your car's dead battery, you can activate the engine. Yet the battery is merely one link in an integrated system.

The Hypothalamus

Another of the limbic system's fascinating structures lies just below (*hypo*) the thalamus, and so is called the **hypothalamus** (**FIGURE 4.8**). By either lesioning or stimulating different areas, neuroscientists have identified hypothalamic neural networks that perform specific bodily maintenance duties. Some clusters influence hunger; others regulate thirst, body temperature, and sexual behavior.

The hypothalamus both monitors blood chemistry and takes orders from other parts of the brain. For example, thinking about sex (in your brain's cerebral cortex) can stimulate your hypothalamus to secrete hormones. These hormones in turn trigger the adjacent "master gland," the pituitary (see Figure 4.6), to influence hormone release by other glands. (Note the interplay between the nervous and endocrine systems: The brain influences the endocrine system, which in turn influences the brain.)

A remarkable discovery about the hypothalamus illustrates how progress in science often occurs—when curious, open-minded investigators make an unexpected observation. Two young McGill University neuropsychologists, James Olds and Peter Milner (1954), were trying to implant electrodes in the rats' reticular formations when they made a magnificent mistake. In one rat, they incorrectly placed an electrode in

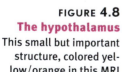

FIGURE 4.8
The hypothalamus
This small but important structure, colored yellow/orange in this MRI scan photograph, helps keep the body's internal environment in a steady state by regulating thirst, hunger, and body temperature. Its activity also influences experiences of pleasurable reward.

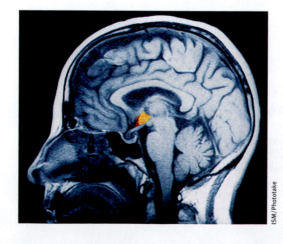

ISM/Phototake

what was later discovered to be a region of the hypothalamus (Olds, 1975). Curiously, the rat kept returning to the location where it had been stimulated by this misplaced electrode, as if seeking more stimulation. On discovering their mistake, Olds and Milner alertly realized they had stumbled upon a brain center that provides a pleasurable reward.

In a meticulous series of experiments, Olds (1958) went on to locate other "pleasure centers," as he called them. (What the rats actually experience only they know, and they aren't telling. Rather than attribute human feelings to rats, today's scientists refer to *reward centers,* not "pleasure centers.") When allowed to trigger their own stimulation in

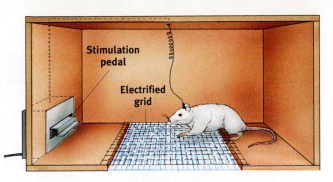

these areas by pressing a pedal, rats would sometimes do so at a feverish pace—up to 7000 times per hour—until they dropped from exhaustion. Moreover, to get this stimulation, they would even cross an electrified floor that a starving rat would not cross to reach food (**FIGURE 4.9**).

Similar reward centers in or near the hypothalamus were later discovered in many other species, including goldfish, dolphins, and monkeys. In fact, animal research has revealed both a general reward system that triggers the release of the neurotransmitter dopamine, and specific centers associated with the pleasures of eating, drinking, and sex. Animals, it seems, come equipped with built-in systems that reward activities essential to survival.

Reward center findings like these have led people to wonder whether humans, too, might have limbic centers for pleasure. Indeed we do. One neurosurgeon used electrodes to calm violent patients. Stimulated patients reported mild pleasure; however, unlike Olds' rats, they were not driven to a frenzy (Deutsch, 1972; Hooper & Teresi, 1986). Some researchers believe that addictive disorders, such as alcoholism, drug abuse, and binge eating, may stem from a *reward deficiency syndrome*—a genetically disposed deficiency in the natural brain systems for pleasure and well-being that leads people to crave whatever provides that missing pleasure or relieves negative feelings (Blum & others, 1996).

The Cerebral Cortex

Older brain networks sustain basic life functions and enable memory, emotions, and basic drives. Newer neural networks within the *cerebrum*—the two large hemispheres that contribute 85 percent of the brain's weight—form specialized work teams that enable our perceiving, thinking, and speaking. Covering those hemispheres, like bark on a tree, is the **cerebral cortex,** a thin surface layer of interconnected neural cells. It is your brain's thinking crown, your body's ultimate control and information-processing center. (**FIGURE 4.10** locates the cerebral cortex as well as other brain areas discussed in this module.)

FIGURE 4.9

Rat with an implanted electrode

With an electrode implanted in a reward center of its hypothalamus, the rat readily crosses an electrified grid, accepting the painful shocks, to press a lever that sends electrical impulses to its "pleasure centers."

■ **amygdala** [uh-MIG-duh-la] two lima bean-sized neural clusters that are components of the limbic system and are linked to emotion.

■ **hypothalamus** [hi-po-THAL-uh-muss] a neural structure lying below (*hypo*) the thalamus; it directs several maintenance activities (eating, drinking, body temperature), helps govern the endocrine system via the pituitary gland, and is linked to emotion.

■ **cerebral** [seh-REE-bruhl] **cortex** the intricate fabric of interconnected neural cells that covers the cerebral hemispheres; the body's ultimate control and information-processing center.

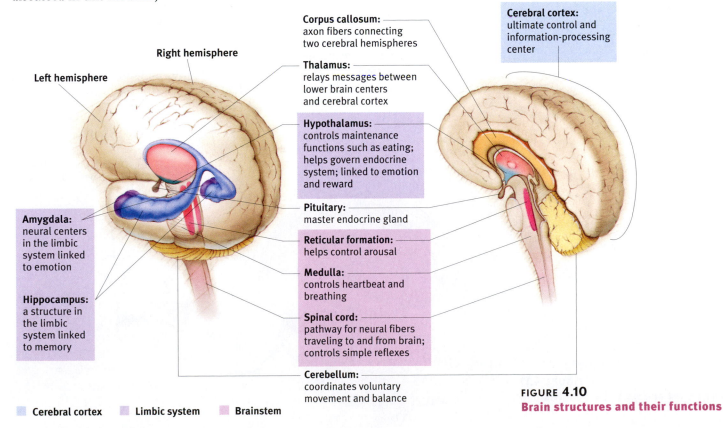

Left hemisphere
Right hemisphere

Corpus callosum:
axon fibers connecting two cerebral hemispheres

Thalamus:
relays messages between lower brain centers and cerebral cortex

Cerebral cortex:
ultimate control and information-processing center

Hypothalamus:
controls maintenance functions such as eating; helps govern endocrine system; linked to emotion and reward

Amygdala:
neural centers in the limbic system linked to emotion

Pituitary:
master endocrine gland

Reticular formation:
helps control arousal

Hippocampus:
a structure in the limbic system linked to memory

Medulla:
controls heartbeat and breathing

Spinal cord:
pathway for neural fibers traveling to and from brain; controls simple reflexes

Cerebellum:
coordinates voluntary movement and balance

■ Cerebral cortex   ■ Limbic system   ■ Brainstem

FIGURE 4.10

Brain structures and their functions

■ **frontal lobes** the portion of the cerebral cortex lying just behind the forehead; involved in speaking and muscle movements and in making plans and judgments.

■ **parietal** [puh-RYE-uh-tuhl] **lobes** the portion of the cerebral cortex lying at the top of the head and toward the rear; receives sensory input for touch and body position.

■ **occipital** [ahk-SIP-uh-tuhl] **lobes** the portion of the cerebral cortex lying at the back of the head; includes the visual areas, each receiving information from the opposite visual field.

■ **temporal lobes** the portion of the cerebral cortex lying roughly above the ears; includes the auditory areas, each receiving information primarily from the opposite ear.

■ **motor cortex** an area at the rear of the frontal lobes that controls voluntary movements.

The people who first dissected and labeled the brain used the language of scholars—Latin and Greek. Their words are actually attempts at graphic description: For example, *cortex* means "bark," *cerebellum* is "little brain," and *thalamus* is "inner chamber."

With the expansion of the cerebral cortex, tight genetic controls relax and the organism's adaptability increases. Frogs and other amphibians with a small cortex operate extensively on preprogrammed genetic instructions. The larger cortex of mammals offers increased capacities for learning and thinking, enabling them to be more adaptable. What makes us distinctively human mostly arises from the complex functions of our cerebral cortex.

Structure of the Cortex

4-3 : How is the cerebral cortex organized?

If you opened a human skull, exposing the brain, you would see a wrinkled organ, shaped somewhat like the meat of an oversized walnut. Without these wrinkles, a flattened cerebral cortex would require triple the area—roughly that of a very large pizza—to fit inside the skull. Eighty percent of the brain's weight lies in its ballooning left and right hemispheres, which are mostly filled with axon connections between the brain's surface and its other regions. The cerebral cortex—that thin surface layer—contains some 20- to 23-billion nerve cells and 300-trillion synaptic connections (de Courten-Myers, 2005). Being human takes a lot of nerve.

The cortex on each hemisphere is divided into four *lobes,* geographic subdivisions separated by prominent *fissures,* or folds (**FIGURE 4.11**). Starting at the front of your brain and going around over the top, there are the **frontal lobes** (behind your forehead), the **parietal lobes** (at the top and to the rear), the **occipital lobes** (at the back of your head), and the **temporal lobes** (on the sides of your head, just above your ears). Each lobe carries out many functions, and many functions require the interplay of several lobes.

Functions of the Cortex

4-4 : What are the functions of the cerebral cortex?

More than a century ago, autopsies of people partially paralyzed or speechless revealed damaged cortical areas. But this rather crude evidence did not convince researchers that specific parts of the cortex perform specific complex functions. After all, if control of speech and movement were diffused across the cortex, damage to almost any area might produce the same effect. A television would go dead with its power cord cut, but we would be deluding ourselves if we thought we had "localized" the picture in the cord.

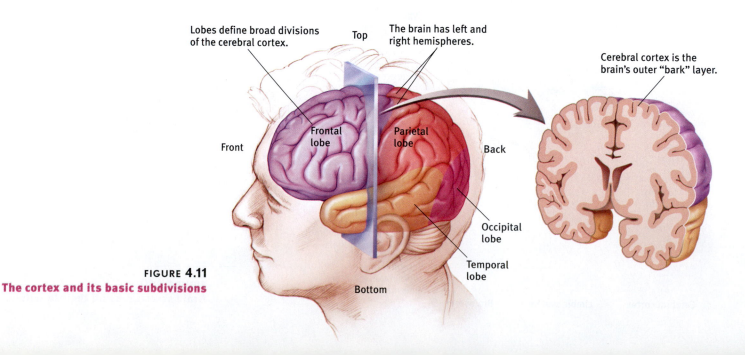

FIGURE 4.11
The cortex and its basic subdivisions

Lobes define broad divisions of the cerebral cortex.

Top

The brain has left and right hemispheres.

Cerebral cortex is the brain's outer "bark" layer.

Front

Frontal lobe

Parietal lobe

Back

Occipital lobe

Temporal lobe

Bottom

Motor Functions

Scientists had better luck in localizing simpler brain functions. For example, in 1870, when German physicians Gustav Fritsch and Eduard Hitzig applied mild electrical stimulation to dogs' cortexes, they made an important discovery: They could make different body parts move. The effects were selective: Stimulation caused movement only when applied to an arch-shaped region at the back of the frontal lobe, running roughly ear-to-ear across the top of the brain. Moreover, stimulating parts of this region in the left or right hemisphere caused movements of specific body parts on the *opposite* side of the body.

The arch Fritsch and Hitzig discovered is now called the **motor cortex** (**FIGURE 4.12**). More than a half-century ago, neurosurgeons Otfrid Foerster in Germany and Wilder Penfield in Montreal mapped the motor cortex in hundreds of wide-awake patients. Before putting the knife to the brain, the surgeons needed to know the possible side effects of removing different parts of the cortex. By painlessly (the brain has no sensory receptors) stimulating different cortical areas and noting the body's responses, they were able to map the motor cortex. Interestingly, they discovered that areas of the body requiring precise control, such as the fingers and mouth, occupied the greatest amount of cortical space.

Spanish neuroscientist José Delgado repeatedly demonstrated the mechanics of motor behavior. In one human patient, he stimulated a spot on the left motor cortex that triggered the right hand to make a fist. Asked to keep the fingers open during the next stimulation, the patient, whose fingers closed despite his best efforts, remarked, "I guess, Doctor, that your electricity is stronger than my will" (Delgado, 1969, p. 114). More recently, scientists have been able to predict a monkey's arm motion a tenth of a second before it moves—by repeatedly measuring motor cortex activity preceding specific arm movements (Gibbs, 1996). By similarly eavesdropping on the brain, researchers are seeking ways to help paralyzed people learn to move a robotic limb or command a cursor to write e-mail or surf the Web.

In 2004, the U.S. Food and Drug Administration approved the first clinical trial of neural prosthetics with paralyzed humans (Pollack, 2004.) The first patient, a paralyzed 25-year-old man, could mentally control a television, draw shapes on a computer screen, and play video games—all thanks to an aspirin-sized chip with 100 microelectrodes recording activity in his motor cortex (Patoine, 2005).

Demonstration: **Try moving your right hand in a circular motion, as if polishing a table. Now start your right foot doing the same motion synchronized with the hand. Now reverse the foot motion (but not the hand). Tough, huh? But easier if you try moving the left foot opposite to the right hand. The** *left* **and right limbs are controlled by opposite sides of the brain. So their opposed activities interfere less with one another.**

FIGURE 4.12

Left hemisphere tissue devoted to each body part in the motor cortex and the sensory cortex

As you can see from this classic though inexact representation, the amount of cortex devoted to a body part is not proportional to that part's size. Rather, the brain devotes more tissue to sensitive areas and to areas requiring precise control. Thus, the fingers have a greater representation in the cortex than does the upper arm.

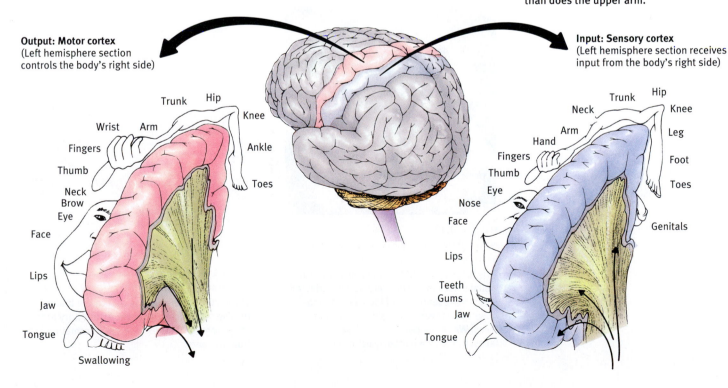

Output: Motor cortex
(Left hemisphere section controls the body's right side)

Input: Sensory cortex
(Left hemisphere section receives input from the body's right side)

■ **sensory cortex** the area at the front of the parietal lobes that registers and processes body touch and movement sensations.

■ **association areas** areas of the cerebral cortex that are not involved in primary motor or sensory functions; rather, they are involved in higher mental functions such as learning, remembering, thinking, and speaking.

Sensory Functions

If the motor cortex sends messages out to the body, where does the cortex receive the incoming messages? Penfield also identified the cortical area that specializes in receiving information from the skin senses and from the movement of body parts. This area, parallel to the motor cortex and just behind it at the front of the parietal lobes, we now call the **sensory cortex** (Figure 4.12). Stimulate a point on the top of this band of tissue, and a person may report being touched on the shoulder; stimulate some point on the side, and the person may feel something on the face.

The more sensitive a body region, the larger the sensory cortex area devoted to it; your supersensitive lips project to a larger brain area than do your toes (Figure 4.12). (That's one reason we kiss with our lips rather than touch toes.) Similarly, rats have a large area of the brain devoted to their whisker sensations, owls to their hearing sensations, and so forth.

Scientists have identified additional areas where the cortex receives input from senses other than touch. At this moment, you are receiving visual information in the occipital lobes at the very back of your brain (**FIGURES 4.13** and **4.14**). A bad enough bash there would make you blind. Stimulated there, you might see flashes of light or dashes of color. (In a sense, we *do* have eyes in the back of our head!) From your occipital lobes, visual information goes to other areas that specialize in tasks such as identifying words, detecting emotions, and recognizing faces.

Any sound you now hear is processed by the auditory areas in your temporal lobes (Figure 4.14). (If you think of your clenched fist as a brain, and hold it in front of you, your thumb would roughly correspond to the temporal lobe.) Most of this auditory information travels a circuitous route from one ear to the auditory receiving area above your opposite ear. If stimulated there, you might hear a sound. The sound needn't be real. MRI scans of people with schizophrenia reveal active auditory areas in the temporal lobes during auditory hallucinations (Lennox & others, 1999). Even the phantom ringing sound experienced by people with hearing loss is—if heard in one ear—associated with activity in the temporal lobe on the brain's opposite side (Muhlnickel, 1998).

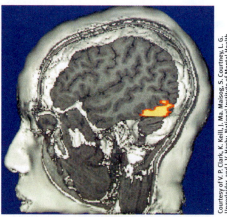

Courtesy of V. P. Clark, K. Keill, J. Ma. Maisog, S. Courtney, L. G. Ungerleider, and J. V. Haxby, National Institute of Mental Health

FIGURE 4.13
New technology shows the brain in action
This functional MRI (fMRI) scan shows the visual cortex in the occipital lobes activated (color representation of increased blood-flow) as a research participant looks at faces. When the person stops looking at faces, the region instantly calms down.

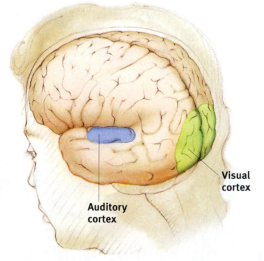

Visual cortex

Auditory cortex

FIGURE 4.14
The visual cortex and auditory cortex
The occipital lobes at the rear of the brain receive input from the eyes. An auditory area of the temporal lobes receives information from the ears.

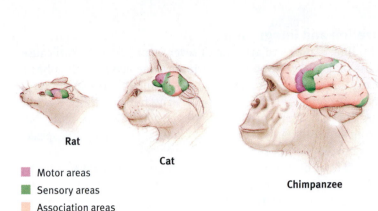
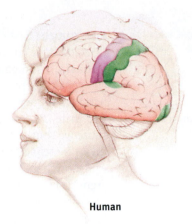

Rat

Cat

Chimpanzee

Human

■ Motor areas
■ Sensory areas
■ Association areas

FIGURE 4.15

Areas of the cortex in four mammals
More intelligent animals have increased "uncommitted" or association areas of the cortex. These vast areas of the brain are responsible for integrating and acting on information received and processed by sensory areas.

Association Areas

So far, we have pointed out small areas of the cortex that either receive sensory input or direct muscular output. In humans, that leaves a full three-fourths of the thin wrinkled layer, the cerebral cortex, uncommitted to sensory or muscular activity. What then goes on in this vast region of the brain? Neurons in these **association areas** (the peach-colored areas in **FIGURE 4.15**) integrate information, linking sensory inputs with stored memories—a very important part of thinking.

Electrically probing the association areas doesn't trigger any observable response. So, unlike the sensory and motor areas, association area functions can't be neatly mapped. Their silence has led to what Donald McBurney (1996, p. 44) calls "one of the hardiest weeds in the garden of psychology": that we ordinarily use only 10 percent of our brains. But the odds are *not* 90 percent that a bullet to your brain would land in an area you don't use. Surgically lesioned animals and brain-damaged humans bear witness that association areas are not dormant. Rather, these areas interpret, integrate, and act on information processed by the sensory areas.

Association areas are found in all four lobes. In the frontal lobes, they enable judgments, planning, and processing of new memories. People with damaged frontal lobes may have intact memories, score high on intelligence tests, and be able to bake a cake—yet be unable to plan ahead to *begin* baking the cake for a birthday party.

Frontal lobe damage also can alter personality, removing a person's inhibitions. Consider the classic case of railroad worker Phineas Gage. One afternoon in 1848, Gage, then 25 years old, was packing gunpowder into a rock with a tamping iron. A spark ignited the gunpowder, shooting the rod up through his left cheek and out the top of his skull, leaving his frontal lobes massively damaged (**FIGURE 4.16**). To everyone's amazement, he was immediately able to sit up and speak, and after the wound healed he returned to work. But the affable, soft-spoken Phineas Gage was now irritable, profane, and dishonest. Although his mental abilities and memories were intact, his personality was not. This person, said his friends, was "no longer Gage." He eventually lost his job and ended up earning his living as a fairground exhibit. With his frontal lobes ruptured, Gage's moral compass had disconnected from his behavior.

Association areas also perform other mental functions. In the parietal lobes, parts of which were large and unusually shaped in Albert Einstein's normal-weight brain, they enable mathematical and spatial reasoning (Witelson & others, 1999). An area on the underside of the right temporal lobe enables us to recognize faces. If a stroke or head injury destroyed this area of your brain, you would still be able to describe facial features and to recognize someone's gender and approximate age, yet be strangely unable to identify the person as, say, Katie Couric or even your grandmother.

FIGURE 4.16

Phineas Gage reconsidered
Using measurements of his skull (which was kept as a medical record) and modern neuroimaging techniques, researcher Hanna Damasio and her colleagues (1994) have reconstructed the probable path of the rod through Gage's brain.

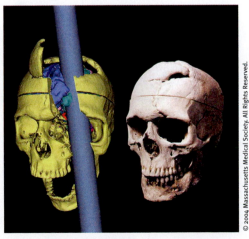

© 2004 Massachusetts Medical Society. All Rights Reserved.

■ **aphasia** impairment of language, usually caused by left hemisphere damage either to Broca's area (impairing speaking) or to Wernicke's area (impairing understanding).

■ **Broca's area** controls language expression—an area of the frontal lobe, usually in the left hemisphere, that directs the muscle movements involved in speech.

■ **Wernicke's area** controls language reception—a brain area involved in language comprehension and expression; usually in the left temporal lobe.

■ **plasticity** the brain's capacity for modification, as evident in brain reorganization following damage (especially in children) and in experiments on the effects of experience on brain development.

Language: Specialization and Integration

Consider this curious finding: Damage to any one of several cortical areas can cause **aphasia,** an impaired use of language. Even more curious, some people with aphasia can speak fluently but cannot read (despite good vision), while others can comprehend what they read but cannot speak. Still others can write but not read, read but not write, read numbers but not letters, or sing but not speak. This is puzzling, because we think of speaking and reading, or writing and reading, or singing and speaking as merely different examples of the same general ability.

Researchers began to sort out how the brain processes language after a discovery by French physician Paul Broca in 1865. Broca discovered that after damage to a specific area of the left frontal lobe, later called **Broca's area,** a person would struggle to form words, yet could often sing familiar songs with ease. A decade later, German investigator Karl Wernicke discovered that after damage to a specific area of the left temporal lobe (**Wernicke's area**), people could speak only meaningless words and were unable to comprehend others' words.

Almost a century later, Norman Geschwind assembled these and other clues into an explanation of how we use language (**FIGURES 4.17** and **4.18**). When you read aloud, the words (1) register in the visual area, (2) are relayed to a second brain area, the *angular gyrus,* which transforms the words into an auditory code that (3) is received and understood in the nearby Wernicke's area, and (4) is sent to Broca's area, which (5) controls the motor cortex as it creates the pronounced word. Depending on which link in this chain is damaged, a different form of aphasia occurs. Damage to the angular gyrus leaves the person able to speak and understand but unable to read. Damage to Wernicke's area disrupts understanding. Damage to Broca's area disrupts speaking.

When you read a word, your brain also computes the word's form, sound, and meaning using different neural networks (Posner & Carr, 1992). Thus, fMRI scans show that jokes playing on meaning ("Why don't sharks bite lawyers? . . . Professional courtesy") are processed in a different brain area than jokes playing on words ("What kind of lights did Noah use on the ark? . . . Flood lights") (Goel & Dolan, 2001). Think about it: *What you experience as a continuous, indivisible stream of perception is actually but the visible tip of the information-processing iceberg, most of which lies beneath the surface of your conscious awareness.*

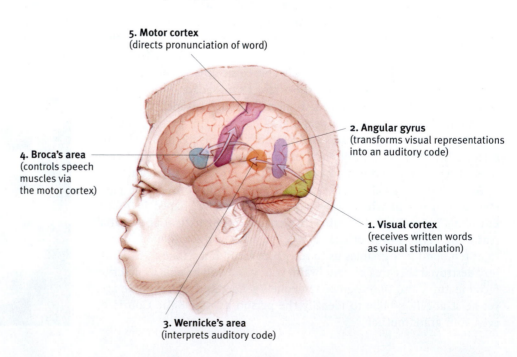

5. **Motor cortex**
(directs pronunciation of word)

2. **Angular gyrus**
(transforms visual representations into an auditory code)

4. **Broca's area**
(controls speech muscles via the motor cortex)

1. **Visual cortex**
(receives written words as visual stimulation)

3. **Wernicke's area**
(interprets auditory code)

FIGURE 4.17
Specialization and integration in language

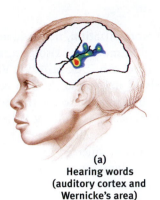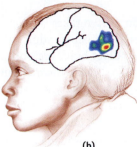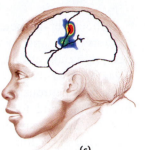

(a)
Hearing words
(auditory cortex and
Wernicke's area)

(b)
Seeing words
(visual cortex and
angular gyrus)

(c)
Speaking words
(Broca's area and
the motor cortex)

FIGURE 4.18

Brain activity when hearing, seeing, and speaking words

PET scans such as these detect the activity of different areas of the brain.

To sum up, the mind's subsystems are localized in particular brain regions, yet the brain acts as a unified whole. Moving your hand; recognizing faces; even perceiving color, motion, and depth—all depend on specific neural networks. Yet complex functions such as listening, learning, and loving involve the coordination of many brain areas. Together, these two principles—specialization and integration—describe the brain's functioning.

The Brain's Plasticity

4-5 : Is the brain capable of reorganizing itself if damaged?

Our brains are sculpted not only by our genes but also by our experiences. Evidence from studies of the brain's **plasticity** demonstrate its ability to modify itself after some types of damage.

Unlike cut skin, severed neurons usually do not regenerate (if your spinal cord were severed, you likely would be permanently paralyzed). And some brain functions seem preassigned to particular areas. One newborn who suffered damage to the facial recognition areas on both temporal lobes never regained a normal ability to recognize faces (Farah & others, 2000). But some neural tissue can *reorganize* in response to damage. It happens within all of us, as the brain repairs itself after little mishaps, but our brains are most plastic when we are young children (Kolb, 1989; see **FIGURE 4.19**).

The brain's plasticity is good news for those blind or deaf. If a blind person uses one finger to read Braille, the brain area dedicated to that finger expands as the sense of touch invades the visual cortex that normally helps people see (Barinaga, 1992a; Sadato & others, 1996). Temporarily "knock out" the visual cortex with magnetic stimulation, and a lifelong-blind person will make more errors on a *language* task (Amedi & others, 2004). In deaf people whose native language is sign, the temporal lobe area normally dedicated to hearing waits in vain for stimulation. Finally, it looks for other signals to process, such as those from the visual system. That helps explain why some studies find that deaf people have enhanced peripheral vision (Bosworth & Dobkins, 1999).

Plasticity is especially evident after serious damage. Lose a finger and the sensory cortex that received its input will begin to receive input from the adjacent fingers, which then become more sensitive (Fox, 1984). As Figure 4.12 shows, the hand is between the face and the arm regions on the sensory cortex. This explains a mysterious phenomenon: When stroking the arm of someone whose hand had been amputated, V. S. Ramachandran found the person felt the sensations not only on the area stroked but also on the nonexistent ("phantom") fingers. Sensory fibers that terminate on adjacent areas had invaded the brain area vacated by the hand. Note, too, that the toes region is adjacent to the genitals. So what do you suppose was the sexual intercourse experience of another Ramachandran patient whose lower leg had been amputated? "I actually experience my orgasm in my foot. And there it's much bigger than it used to be because it's no longer just confined to my genitals" (Ramachandran & Blakeslee, 1998, p. 36).

FIGURE 4.19

Brain plasticity

If surgery or an injury destroys one part of a child's brain or, as in the case of this 6-year-old, even an entire *hemisphere* (removed to eliminate seizures), the brain will compensate by putting other areas to work. One Johns Hopkins medical team, reflecting on the 58 child hemispherectomies they had performed, reports being "awed" by how well children retain their memory, personality, and humor after removal of either brain hemisphere (Vining & others, 1997).

Joe McNally/Joe McNally Photography

■ **corpus callosum** [KOR-pus kah-LOW-sum] the large band of neural fibers connecting the two brain hemispheres and carrying messages between them.

■ **split brain** a condition in which the brain's two hemispheres are isolated by cutting the fibers (mainly those of the corpus callosum) connecting them.

"You wouldn't want to have a date with the right hemisphere."
—Michael Gazzaniga (2000)

Although brain modification often takes the form of reorganization, new evidence suggests that, contrary to long-held belief, adult mice and humans can also generate new brain cells, at least in two older brain regions (Kempermann & Gage, 1999; Van Praag & others, 2002). Monkey brains form thousands of new neurons each day. These baby neurons originate deep in the brain and may then migrate to the thinking frontal lobe and form connections with neighboring neurons (Gould & others, 1999). Master stem cells that can develop into any type of brain cell have also been discovered in the human embryo. If mass-produced in a lab and injected into a damaged brain, might neural stem cells turn themselves into replacements for lost brain cells? Might we someday be able to rebuild damaged brains, much as we reseed damaged lawns? Might new drugs spur the production of new nerve cells? Stay tuned. Today's biotech companies are hard at work on such possibilities (Gage, 2003).

Our Divided Brain

For more than a century, clinical evidence has shown that the brain's two sides serve differing functions. This hemispheric specialization (or *lateralization*) is apparent after brain damage. Accidents, strokes, and tumors in the left hemisphere impair reading, writing, speaking, arithmetic reasoning, and understanding. Similar lesions in the right hemisphere seldom have such dramatic effects.

By 1960, many interpreted these differences as evidence that the left hemisphere is the "dominant" or "major" hemisphere, and its silent companion to the right is the "subordinate" or "minor" hemisphere. Then researchers found that the "minor" right hemisphere was not so limited after all. The story of this discovery is a fascinating chapter in psychology's history.

Splitting the Brain

4-6: What is a split brain, and what does it reveal about brain functioning?

In 1961, two Los Angeles neurosurgeons, Philip Vogel and Joseph Bogen, speculated that major epileptic seizures were caused by an amplification of abnormal brain activity reverberating between the two cerebral hemispheres. If so, they wondered, could they reduce seizures in patients with uncontrollable epilepsy by severing the **corpus callosum** (FIGURE 4.20), the wide band of axon fibers connecting the two hemispheres and carrying messages between them?

Vogel and Bogen had reason to believe such an operation would not be incapacitating. Psychologists Roger Sperry, Ronald Myers, and Michael Gazzaniga had divided the brains of cats and monkeys in this manner with no serious ill effects. So the surgeons operated. The result? The seizures were all but eliminated and the patients with

FIGURE 4.20
The corpus callosum
This large band of neural fibers connects the two brain hemispheres. To photograph the half brain (near right), a surgeon separated the hemispheres by cutting through the corpus callosum and lower brain regions. In the view on the far right, brain tissue has been cut back to expose the corpus callosum and bundles of fibers coming out from it.

Corpus callosum

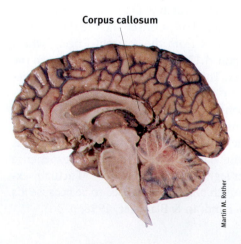

Martin M. Rother

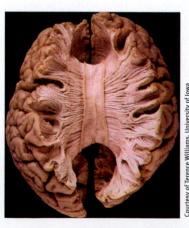

Courtesy of Terence Williams, University of Iowa

these **split brains** were surprisingly normal, their personality and intellect hardly affected. Waking from the surgery, one even managed to quip that he had a "splitting headache" (Gazzaniga, 1967). The subsequent studies of these people provided a key to understanding the two hemispheres' complementary functions.

As **FIGURE 4.21** explains, the peculiar nature of our visual wiring enabled Sperry and Gazzaniga to send information to a patient's left or right hemisphere—by having the person stare at a spot and then flashing a stimulus to its right or left. They could do this with you, too, but in your intact brain the hemisphere receiving the information would instantly pass the news to its partner across the valley. The split-brain surgery severed the phone cables—the corpus callosum—across the valley, enabling the researchers to quiz each hemisphere separately.

In an early experiment, Gazzaniga (1967) asked split-brain patients to stare at a dot as he flashed HE•ART on a screen (**FIGURE 4.22**). Thus, HE appeared in their left visual field (which transmits to the right hemisphere) and ART in the right field (which transmits to the left hemisphere). When he then asked what they had seen, the patients *said* they had seen ART. But when asked to *point* to the word, they were startled when their left hand (controlled by the right hemisphere) pointed to HE. Given an opportunity to express itself, each hemisphere reported only what it had seen. The right hemisphere (controlling the left hand) intuitively knew what it could not verbally report.

When a picture of a spoon was flashed to their right hemisphere, the patients could not *say* what they had viewed. But when asked to *identify* what they had viewed by feeling an assortment of hidden objects with their left hand, they readily selected the spoon. If the experimenter said, "Right!" the patient might reply, "What? Right?

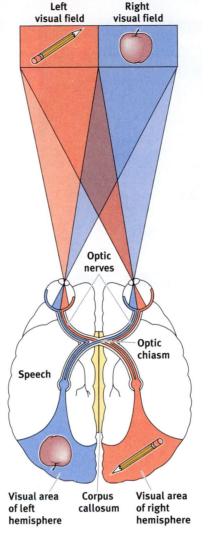

Left visual field | **Right visual field**

Optic nerves

Speech

Optic chiasm

Visual area of left hemisphere | Corpus callosum | Visual area of right hemisphere

FIGURE 4.21

The information highway from eye to brain

Information from the left half of your field of vision goes to your right hemisphere, and information from the right half of your visual field goes to your left hemisphere, which usually controls speech. (Note, however, that each eye receives sensory information from both the right and left visual fields.) Data received by either hemisphere are quickly transmitted to the other across the corpus callosum. In a person with a severed corpus callosum, this information sharing does not take place.

"Do not let your left hand know what your right hand is doing."

—Matthew 6:3

"Look at the dot."

Two words separated by a dot are momentarily projected.

"What word did you see?"

or

"Point with your left hand to the word you saw."

Art

FIGURE 4.22

Testing the divided brain

When an experimenter flashes the word HEART across the visual field, the split-brain person reports seeing the portion of the word transmitted to her left hemisphere. However, if asked to indicate with her left hand what she saw, she points to the portion of the word transmitted to her right hemisphere. (From Gazzaniga, 1983.)

FIGURE **4.23**
Try this!
Joe, a split-brain patient, can simultaneously draw two different shapes.

How could I possibly pick out the right object when I don't know what I saw?" It is, of course, the left hemisphere doing the talking here, bewildered by what the nonverbal right hemisphere knows.

A few people who have had split-brain surgery have been for a time bothered by the unruly independence of their left hand, which might unbutton a shirt while the right hand buttoned it, or put grocery store items back on the shelf after the right hand put them in the cart. It was as if each hemisphere was thinking "I've half a mind to wear my green (blue) shirt today." Indeed, said Sperry (1964), split-brain surgery leaves people "with two separate minds." With a split brain, both hemispheres can comprehend and follow an instruction to copy—*simultaneously*—different figures with the left and right hand (Franz & others, 2000; see **FIGURE 4.23**). (Reading these reports, I fantasize a split-brain person enjoying a solitary game of "rock, paper, scissors"—left versus right hand.)

When the "two minds" are at odds, the left hemisphere does mental gymnastics to rationalize reactions it does not understand. If a patient follows an order sent to the right hemisphere ("Walk"), the interpretive left hemisphere will offer a ready explanation ("I'm going into the house to get a Coke"). Thus, Michael Gazzaniga (1988), who considered split-brain patients "The most fascinating people on earth," concludes that the conscious left hemisphere is an "interpreter" that instantly constructs theories to explain our behavior.

Studying Hemispheric Differences in the Intact Brain

So, what about the 99.99+ percent of us with undivided brains? Have scientists found our hemispheres to be similarly specialized? Yes, they have, in several different types of studies.

When a person performs a *perceptual* task, for example, brain waves, bloodflow, and glucose consumption reveal increased activity in the *right* hemisphere; when the person speaks or calculates, activity increases in the *left* hemisphere. On occasion, hemispheric specialization (*lateralization*) has been dramatically shown by using magnetic stimulation to temporarily disrupt left- or right-brain activity (Knecht & others, 2002), or by briefly sedating an entire hemisphere. To check for the locus of language before surgery, a physician may inject a sedative into the neck artery that feeds blood to the hemisphere on its side of the body. Before the drug is injected, the patient is lying down, arms in the air, conversing easily. You can likely predict what happens when the drug flows into the artery going to the left hemisphere: Within seconds, the person's right arm falls limp. If the left hemisphere controls language, the patient also becomes speechless until the drug wears off. When the drug enters the artery to the right hemisphere, the *left* arm falls limp, but the person can still speak.

Which hemisphere would you suppose enables sign language among deaf people? The right, because of its visual-spatial superiority? Or the left, because of its processing language? Studies reveal that, just as hearing people usually use the left hemisphere to process speech, deaf people use the left hemisphere to read signs (Corina & others, 1992; Hickok & others, 2001). A stroke in the left hemisphere will disrupt a deaf person's signing, much as it would disrupt a hearing person's speaking. Broca's area is similarly involved in both spoken and signed speech production (Corina, 1998). To the brain, language is language, whether spoken or signed.

Although the left hemisphere is adept at making quick, literal interpretations of language, the right hemisphere excels in making inferences (Beeman & Chiarello,

---

Question: If we flashed a red light to the right hemisphere of a split-brain patient and flashed a green light to the left hemisphere, would each observe its own color? Would the person be aware that the colors differ? What would the person verbally report seeing? (Answers on this module's final page.)

Speech processing is somewhat correlated with handedness. Nearly 90 percent of us are primarily right-handed (Medland & others, 2004). Some 10 percent of us (somewhat more among males, somewhat less among females) are left-handed. (A few people write with their right hand and throw a ball with their left, or vice versa.) Almost all (95 percent) right-handers process speech primarily in the left hemisphere, which tends to be the slightly larger hemisphere (Springer & Deutsch, 1985). Left-handers are more diverse. More than half process speech in the left hemisphere, as right-handers do. About a quarter process language in the right hemisphere; the other quarter use both hemispheres.

1998; Bowden & Beeman, 1998; Mason & Just, 2004). Primed with the flashed word *foot,* the left hemisphere will be especially quick to recognize the closely associated word *heel.* But if primed with *foot, cry,* and *glass,* the right hemisphere will more quickly recognize another word distantly related to all three (*cut*). And if given an insightlike problem—what word

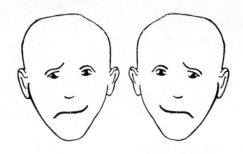

Which one is happier?
Look at the center of one face, then the other. Does one appear happier? Most people say the right face does. Some researchers think this is because the right hemisphere, which is skilled in emotion processing, receives information from the left half of each face (when looking at its center).

goes with *high, district,* and *house?*—the right hemisphere more quickly than the left recognizes that the solution is *school.* As one patient explained after suffering right-hemisphere stroke damage, "I understand words, but I'm missing the subtleties." The right hemisphere also helps us modulate our speech to make meaning clear—as when we ask "What's that in the road ahead?" instead of "What's that in the road, a head?" (Heller, 1990). The right side of the brain surpasses the left in some other areas as well, as the split-brain research has shown—at copying drawings, recognizing faces, perceiving differences, perceiving emotion, and expressing emotion through the more expressive left side of the face. Right-hemisphere damage therefore more greatly disrupts emotion processing and social conduct (Tranel & others, 2002).

Simply looking at the two hemispheres, so alike to the naked eye, who would suppose they contribute uniquely to the harmony of the whole? Yet a variety of observations—of people with split brains and people with normal brains—converge beautifully, leaving little doubt that we have unified brains with specialized parts.

Reflections on the Biological Revolution in Psychology

We have glimpsed the truth of an overriding principle: Everything psychological is simultaneously biological. We have focused on how our thoughts, feelings, and actions arise from our specialized yet integrated brain. Later in this text, we will further explore the significance of the biological revolution in psychology.

You and I are privileged to live in a time when discoveries about the interplay of our biology and our behavior and mental processes are occurring at an exhilarating pace. Yet what is unknown still dwarfs what is known. We can describe the brain. We can learn the functions of its parts. We can study how the parts communicate. But how do we get mind out of meat? How does the electrochemical whir in a hunk of tissue the size of a head of lettuce give rise to elation, a creative idea, or that memory of Grandmother?

The mind seeking to understand the brain—that is indeed among the ultimate scientific challenges. And so it will always be. To paraphrase cosmologist John Barrow, a brain simple enough to be understood is too simple to produce a mind able to understand it.

"If I were a college student today, I don't think I could resist going into neuroscience."

—Novelist Tom Wolfe, 2004

>> MODULE REVIEW

Clinical observations have long revealed the general effects of damage to various areas of the brain. But *MRI scans* now reveal brain structures, and *EEG, PET,* and *fMRI (functional MRI)* recordings reveal brain activity.

4-1: What are the functions of the brainstem and its associated structures?

Within the *brainstem,* the *medulla* controls heartbeat and breathing, and the *reticular formation* controls arousal and attention. On top of the brainstem is the *thalamus,* the brain's sensory switchboard. The *cerebellum,* attached to the rear of the brainstem, coordinates muscle movement.

4-2: What are the functions of limbic system structures?

The *limbic system* is linked to memory, emotions, and drives. One of its neural centers, the *amygdala,* is involved in aggressive and fearful responses. Another, the *hypothalamus,* is involved in various bodily maintenance functions, pleasurable rewards, and control of the endocrine system. A third, the hippocampus, processes memory.

4-3: How is the cerebral cortex organized?

The *cerebral cortex* is the thin layer of interconnected neurons covering the brain's hemispheres. Prominent folds divide each hemisphere into four lobes—the *frontal, parietal, occipital,* and *temporal.*

4-4: What are the functions of the cerebral cortex?

Some brain regions serve specific functions. One is the *motor cortex* (at the rear of the frontal lobes), which controls muscle movement. Another is the *sensory cortex* (at the front of the parietal lobes), which receives information from our senses. However, most of the cortex is devoted to uncommitted *association areas,* which integrate information involved in learning, remembering, thinking, and other higher-level functions. In general, these functions result from the intricate coordination of many brain areas. Language, for example, depends on a chain of events in several brain regions, particularly *Broca's area, Wernicke's area,* and the angular gyrus. Damage to any of these regions may cause one of several types of *aphasia.*

4-5: Is the brain capable of reorganizing itself if damaged?

If one hemisphere is damaged early in life, the other will pick up many of its functions. This *plasticity* diminishes later in life, although nearby neurons may partially compensate for damaged ones after a stroke or other brain injury.

4-6: What is a split brain, and what does it reveal about brain functioning?

A *split brain* is one whose *corpus callosum,* the large band of nerve fibers connecting the two brain hemispheres, has been severed. Split-brain research has demonstrated that in most people the left hemisphere is the more verbal, and the right hemisphere excels in visual perception and the recognition of emotion. Studies of healthy people with intact brains confirm that each hemisphere makes unique contributions to the integrated functioning of the brain.

>> REHEARSE IT!

1. The brainstem is the oldest and innermost region of the brain. The part of the brainstem that controls heartbeat and breathing is the
   a. cerebellum.
   b. medulla.
   c. cortex.
   d. thalamus.

2. The nerve network that governs arousal is the
   a. spinal cord.
   b. cerebellum.
   c. reticular formation.
   d. medulla.

3. The thalamus receives information from the sensory neurons and routes it to the higher brain regions that control the senses. The thalamus functions like a
   a. memory bank.
   b. pleasure center.
   c. breathing regulator.
   d. switchboard.

4. The part of the brain that coordinates voluntary movement is the
   a. cerebellum.
   b. medulla.
   c. thalamus.
   d. reticular formation.

5. The limbic system, a doughnut-shaped structure at the border of the brain's older parts and the cerebral hemispheres, is associated with basic motives, emotions, and memory functions. Two parts of the limbic system are the amygdala and the
   a. reticular formation.
   b. hippocampus.
   c. thalamus.
   d. medulla.

6. A cat's ferocious response to electrical brain stimulation would lead you to suppose that the electrode had been touching the
   a. medulla.
   b. pituitary.

   c. hypothalamus.
   d. amygdala.

7. The neural structure that most directly regulates eating, drinking, and body temperature is the
   a. cerebellum.
   b. hypothalamus.
   c. thalamus.
   d. amygdala.

8. The reward centers discovered by Olds and Milner were located in regions of the
   a. cerebral cortex.
   b. brainstem.
   c. hypothalamus.
   d. spinal cord.

9. The motor cortex is the brain region that controls voluntary muscle movement. If a neurosurgeon stimulated your right motor cortex, you would most likely
   a. see light.
   b. hear a sound.

c. feel a touch on the right arm.
d. move your left leg.

10. The sensory cortex registers and processes body sensations, with the more sensitive body regions having the greatest representation. Which of the following has the greatest representation?

a. Knee
b. Toes
c. Forehead
d. Thumb

11. About three-fourths of the cerebral cortex is not committed to any specific sensory or motor function. The "uncommitted" areas are called

a. occipital lobes.
b. fissures.
c. association areas.
d. Wernicke's area.

12. Judging and planning are enabled by the

a. occipital lobes.
b. parietal lobes.
c. frontal lobes.
d. temporal lobes.

13. The area in the brain that, if damaged, might impair your ability to form words is

a. Wernicke's area.
b. Broca's area.
c. the left occipital lobe.
d. the angular gyrus.

14. Plasticity refers to the brain's ability to reorganize itself after damage. Especially plastic are the brains of

a. split-brain patients.
b. young adults.
c. young children.
d. right-handed people.

15. The brain structure that enables the right and left hemispheres to communicate is

a. the medulla.
b. Broca's area.
c. Wernicke's area.
d. the corpus callosum.

16. An experimenter flashes the word HERON across the visual field of a split-brain patient. HER is transmitted to his right hemisphere and ON

to his left hemisphere. When asked to indicate what he saw, the patient

a. says he saw HER but points to ON.
b. says he saw ON but points to HER.
c. says he saw HERON but points to HER.
d. says he saw HERON but points to ON.

17. The study of split-brain patients has allowed us to observe the special functions of each hemisphere of the brain. The left hemisphere excels in

a. processing language.
b. visual perceptions.
c. recognition of emotion.
d. recognition of faces.

18. Damage to the brain's right hemisphere is most likely to reduce a person's ability to

a. recite the alphabet rapidly.
b. recognize the emotional content of facial expressions.
c. understand verbal instructions.
d. solve arithmetic problems.

Answers: 1. b, 2. c, 3. d, 4. a, 5. b, 6. d, 7. b, 8. c, 9. d, 10. d, 11. c, 12. c, 13. b, 14. c, 15. d, 16. d, 17. a, 18. b.

>> TERMS AND CONCEPTS TO REMEMBER

brainstem, p. 48
medulla [muh-DUL-uh], p. 48
thalamus [THAL-uh-muss], p. 49
reticular formation, p. 49
cerebellum [sehr-uh-BELL-um], p. 49
lesion [LEE-zhuhn], p. 50
electroencephalogram (EEG), p. 50
limbic system, p. 50
PET (positron emission tomography) scan, p. 50

MRI (magnetic resonance imaging), p. 51
fMRI (functional MRI), p. 51
amygdala [uh-MIG-duh-la], p. 52
hypothalamus [hi-po-THAL-uh-muss], p. 52
cerebral [seh-REE-bruhl] cortex, p. 53
frontal lobes, p. 54
parietal [puh-RYE-uh-tuhl] lobes, p. 54
occipital [ahk-SIP-uh-tuhl] lobes, p. 54
temporal lobes, p. 54

motor cortex, p. 55
sensory cortex, p. 56
association areas, p. 57
aphasia, p. 58
Broca's area, p. 58
Wernicke's area, p. 58
plasticity, p. 59
corpus callosum [KOR-pus kah-LOW-sum], p. 60
split brain, p. 61

>> TEST YOURSELF

1. Within what brain region would damage be most likely to disrupt your ability to skip rope? Your ability to sense tastes or sounds? In what brain region would damage perhaps leave you in a coma? Without the very breath and heartbeat of life?

(Answers in Appendix C.)

>> ANSWERS TO QUESTIONS WITHIN THE MODULE

Q. If you electrically stimulated a cat's amygdala, which division of the cat's nervous system would be aroused?

A. Its sympathetic nervous system.

Q. If we flashed a red light to the right hemisphere of a split-brain patient, and flashed a green light to the left hemisphere, would each observe its own color?

A. Yes.

Q. Would the person be aware that the colors differ?

A. No.

Q. What would the person verbally report seeing?

A. Green.

Multiple-choice **self-tests** and more may be found at www.worthpublishers.com/myers.

Behavior Genetics and Evolutionary Psychology

What makes you you? In important ways, we are each unique. We look different. We sound different. We have varying personalities, interests, and cultural and family backgrounds. But how different are we really?

We are also the leaves of one tree. Our human family shares not only a common biological heritage—cut us and we bleed—but also common behavioral tendencies. Our shared brain architecture predisposes us to sense the world, develop language, and feel hunger through identical mechanisms. Whether we live in the Arctic or the tropics, we prefer sweet tastes to sour. We divide the color spectrum into similar colors. And we feel drawn to behaviors that produce and protect offspring.

Our kinship appears in our social behaviors as well. Whether named Wong, Nkomo, Smith, or Gonzales, we start fearing strangers at about eight months, and as adults we prefer the company of those with attitudes and attributes similar to our own. Coming from different parts of the globe, we know how to read one another's smiles and frowns. As members of one species, we affiliate, conform, reciprocate favors, punish offenses, organize hierarchies of status, and grieve a child's death. A visitor from outer space could drop in anywhere and find humans dancing and feasting, singing and worshiping, playing sports and games, laughing and crying, living in families, and forming groups. Taken together, such universal behaviors reveal our human nature.

What causes our striking diversity and our shared human nature? How much are our human differences shaped by our differing genes? And how much by our **environment**—by every external influence, from maternal nutrition while in the womb to social support while nearing the tomb? More specifically, to what extent are we formed by our upbringing? By our culture? By our current circumstances? By people's reactions to our genetic dispositions? This module begins to tell the complex story of how our genes (*nature*) and environments (*nurture*) define us.

The nurture of nature
Parents everywhere wonder: Will my baby grow up to be peaceful or aggressive? Homely or attractive? Successful or struggling at every step? What comes built in, and what is nurtured—and how? Research reveals that nature and nurture together shape our development—every step of the way.

Jeffrey W. Myers/Stock, Boston

■ **environment** every nongenetic influence, from prenatal nutrition to the people and things around us.

■ **behavior genetics** the study of the relative power and limits of genetic and environmental influences on behavior.

Behavior Genetics: Predicting Individual Differences

5-1: How do behavior geneticists explain individual differences?

If Jaden Agassi, son of tennis stars Andre Agassi and Stephanie Graf, grows up to be a tennis star, should we attribute his superior talent to his Grand Slam genes? To his growing up in a tennis-rich environment? To high expectations? **Behavior geneticists** study our differences and weigh the effects and interplay of heredity and environment.

Genes: Our Codes for Life

5-2: Our genes predispose our biology; does this mean they determine our behaviors?

Behind the story of our body and of our brain—surely the most awesome thing on our little planet—is the heredity that interacts with our experience to create both our universal human nature and our individual and social diversity. Barely more than a century ago, few would have guessed that every cell nucleus in your body contains the genetic master code for your entire body. It's as if every room in the Empire State Building had a

© The New Yorker Collection, 1999, Danny Shanahan from cartoonbank.com. All Rights Reserved.

"Thanks for almost everything, Dad."

Nucleus
(the inner area of a cell that houses chromosomes and genes)

Chromosome
(threadlike structure made largely of DNA molecules)

Gene
(segment of DNA containing the code for a particular protein; determines our individual biological development)

Cell
(the basic structural unit of a living thing)

DNA
(a spiraling, complex molecule containing genes)

FIGURE 5.1

The genes: Their location and composition

Contained in the nucleus of each of the trillions of cells in your body are chromosomes. Each chromosome contains a coiled chain of the molecule DNA. Genes are DNA segments that, when expressed (turned on), form templates for the production of proteins. By directing the manufacture of proteins, the genes determine our individual biological development.

book containing the architect's plans for the entire structure. The plans for your own book of life run to 46 chapters—23 donated by your mother (from her egg) and 23 by your father (from his sperm). Each of these 46 chapters, called a **chromosome,** is composed of a coiled chain of the molecule **DNA** *(deoxyribonucleic acid)*. **Genes,** small segments of the giant DNA molecules, form the words of those chapters (**FIGURE 5.1**). All told, you have 30,000 or so gene words. These self-replicating units do not directly guide your behavior. They simply, when "turned on," provide the code for creating protein molecules, the building blocks of physical development.

Genetically speaking, every other human is close to being your identical twin. Human **genome** researchers have discovered the common sequence within human DNA. It is this shared genetic profile that makes us humans, rather than chimpanzees or tulips. Even the person you like least is your near-clone, sharing about 99.9 percent of your DNA (Plomin & Crabbe, 2000). But that 0.1 percent difference, in interaction with differing environments, can give us a Nelson Mandela or an Adolf Hitler.

Geneticists and psychologists are interested in the occasional variations found at particular gene sites in the DNA. Slight person-to-person variations from the common pattern give clues to our uniqueness—why one person has a disease that another does not, why one person is short and another tall, why one is happy and another depressed.

Human traits are influenced by many genes. How tall you are, for example, reflects the height of your face, the size of your vertebrae, the length of your leg bones, and so forth—each of which may be influenced by different genes interacting with your environment. Complex human traits such as intelligence, happiness, and aggressiveness are similarly influenced by groups of genes. Thus our genetic predispositions—our genetically influenced traits—help explain both our shared human nature and our human diversity.

Twin and Adoption Studies

To scientifically tease apart the influences of environment and heredity, behavior geneticists would need to design two types of experiments. The first would control the home environment while varying heredity. The second would control heredity while varying the home environment. Such experiments with human infants would be unethical, but happily for our purposes, nature has done this work for us.

Identical Versus Fraternal Twins

Identical twins, who develop from a single fertilized egg that splits in two, are *genetically* identical (**FIGURE 5.2**). They are nature's own human clones—indeed, clones who share not only the same genes but the same conception, uterus, birth date, and usually the same cultural history.

■ **chromosomes** threadlike structures made of DNA molecules that contain the genes.

■ **DNA (deoxyribonucleic acid)** a complex molecule containing the genetic information that makes up the chromosomes.

■ **genes** the biochemical units of heredity that make up the chromosomes; a segment of DNA capable of synthesizing a protein.

■ **genome** the complete instructions for making an organism, consisting of all the genetic material in that organism's chromosomes.

■ **identical twins** twins who develop from a single fertilized egg that splits in two, creating two genetically identical organisms.

" We share half our genes with the banana."
Evolutionary biologist Robert May, president of Britain's Royal Society, 2001

Identical?

Twins Morgan Hamm (left) and Paul Hamm (right), world-class gymnasts, are identical, yet their achievements are not. In the 2004 Olympics, Paul won more medals than the brother with whom he grew up. This small difference suggests the influence of slightly different environments (perhaps even prenatal environments) as well as the influence of their individual interactions with their environments after birth.

Adrian Dennis/AFP/Getty Lages

FIGURE 5.2

Same fertilized egg, same genes; different eggs, different genes

Identical twins develop from a single fertilized egg, fraternal twins from two.

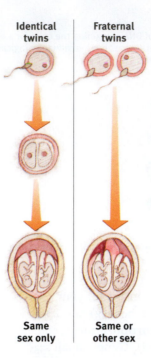

Identical twins

Fraternal twins

Same sex only

Same or other sex

Fraternal twins, who develop from separate fertilized eggs, share a fetal environment, but they are genetically no more similar than ordinary brothers and sisters. Shared genes can translate into shared experiences. A person whose identical twin has Alzheimer's disease, for example, has a 60 percent risk of getting the disease; if the affected twin is fraternal, the risk is only 30 percent (Plomin & others, 1997).

Are identical twins, being genetic clones of one another, also behaviorally more similar than fraternal twins (Bouchard, 2004)? Studies of nearly 13,000 pairs of Swedish twins, of 7000 Finnish twin pairs, and of 3810 Australian twin pairs provide a consistent answer: On both extraversion (outgoingness) and neuroticism (emotional instability), identical twins are much more similar than fraternal twins. And when John Loehlin and Robert Nichols (1976) gave a battery of questionnaires to 850 U.S. twin pairs, identical twins were much more similar than fraternals in many other dimensions—abilities, personal traits, and interests. However, the identical twins, more than fraternal twins, also reported being treated alike. So, did their experience rather than their genes account for their similarity? No, said Loehlin and Nichols; identical twins whose parents treated them alike were *not* psychologically more alike than identical twins who were treated less similarly. In explaining individual differences, genes matter.

Sweden has the world's largest national twin registry—140,000 living and dead twin pairs—which forms part of a massive registry of 600,000 twins currently being sampled in the world's largest twin study (Wheelwright, 2004). www.genomeutwin.org

Separated Twins

Imagine the following science fiction experiment: A mad scientist decides to separate identical twins at birth, then rear them in differing environments. Better yet, consider a true story:

On a chilly February morning in 1979, some time after divorcing his first wife, Linda, Jim Lewis awoke in his modest home next to his second wife, Betty. Determined that this marriage would work, Jim made a habit of leaving love notes to Betty around the house. As he lay in bed he thought about others he had loved, including his son, James Alan, and his faithful dog, Toy.

Jim looked forward to spending some of the day's free time in his basement woodworking shop, where he had derived many hours of satisfaction from building furniture, picture frames, and other items, including a white bench circling a tree in his front yard. Jim also liked to spend free time driving his Chevy, watching stock-car racing, and drinking Miller Lite beer.

Jim was basically healthy, except for occasional half-day migraine headaches and blood pressure that was a little high, perhaps related to his chain-smoking habit. He had become overweight a while back but had shed some of the pounds. Having undergone a vasectomy, he was done having children.

What was extraordinary about Jim Lewis, however, was that at that same moment (I am not making this up) there existed another man—also named Jim—for whom all these things (right down to the dog's name) were also true.[1] This other Jim—Jim Springer—just happened, 38 years earlier, to have been his womb-mate. Thirty-seven days after their birth, these genetically identical twins were separated, adopted by blue-collar families, and reared with no contact or knowledge of each other's whereabouts until the day Jim Lewis received a call from his genetic clone (who, having been told he had a twin, set out to find him).

Twins Lorraine and Levinia Christmas, driving to deliver Christmas presents to each other near Flitcham, England, collided (Shepherd, 1997).

■ **fraternal twins** twins who develop from separate fertilized eggs. They are genetically no closer than brothers and sisters, but they share a fetal environment.

[1] Actually, this description of the two Jims errs in one respect: Jim Lewis named his son James Alan. Jim Springer named his James Allan.

Identical twins are people two Identical twins Jim Lewis and Jim Springer were separated shortly after birth and raised in different homes without awareness of each other. Research has shown remarkable similarities in the life choices of separated identical twins, lending support to the idea that genes influence personality.

One month later, the brothers became the first twin pair tested by University of Minnesota psychologist Thomas Bouchard and his colleagues, beginning a study of separated twins that extends to the present (Holden, 1980a,b; Wright, 1998). Given tests measuring their personality, intelligence, heart rate, and brain waves, the Jim twins—despite 38 years of separation—were virtually as alike as the same person tested twice. Their voice intonations and inflections were so similar that, hearing a playback of an earlier interview, Jim Springer guessed "That's me." Wrong—it was his brother.

Identical twins Oskar Stohr and Jack Yufe presented equally striking similarities. One was raised by his grandmother in Germany as a Catholic and a Nazi, while the other was raised by his father in the Caribbean as a Jew. Nevertheless, they share traits and habits galore. They like spicy foods and sweet liqueurs, have a habit of falling asleep in front of the television, flush the toilet before using it, store rubber bands on their wrists, and dip buttered toast in their coffee. Stohr is domineering toward women and yells at his wife, as did Yufe before he and his wife separated. Both married women named Dorothy Jane Scheckelburger. Okay, the last item is a joke. But as Judith Rich Harris (2006) notes, it is hardly weirder than some other reported coincidences.

Aided by publicity in magazine and newspaper stories, Bouchard and his colleagues (1990; DiLalla & others, 1996; Segal, 1999) located and studied 80 pairs of identical twins reared apart. They continue to find similarities not only of tastes and physical attributes but also of personality, abilities, attitudes, interests, and even fears.

In Sweden, Nancy Pedersen and her co-workers (1988) identified 99 separated identical twin pairs and more than 200 separated fraternal twin pairs. Compared with equivalent samples of identical twins reared together, the separated identical twins had somewhat less identical *personalities*—characteristic patterns of thinking, feeling, and acting. Still, separated twins were more alike if genetically identical than if fraternal. Separation shortly after birth (rather than, say, at age 8) didn't amplify their personality differences.

Stories of startling twin similarities do not impress Bouchard's critics, who remind us that "the plural of anecdote is not data." They contend that if any two strangers were to spend hours comparing their behaviors and life histories, they would probably discover many coincidental similarities. If researchers created a control group of biologically unrelated pairs of the same age, sex, and ethnicity, who had not grown up together but who were as similar to one another in economic and cultural background as are many of the separated twin pairs, wouldn't these pairs also exhibit striking similarities (Joseph, 2001)? (Bouchard replies that separated fraternal twins do not exhibit similarities comparable to those of separated identical twins, and twin researcher Nancy Segal [2000] notes that "virtual twins"—same-age, biologically unrelated siblings—are also much more dissimilar.)

"In some domains it looks as though our identical twins reared apart are . . . just as similar as identical twins reared together. Now that's an amazing finding and I can assure you none of us would have expected that degree of similarity."
Thomas Bouchard (1981)

Coincidences are not unique to twins. Patricia Kern of Colorado was born March 13, 1941, and named Patricia Ann Campbell. Patricia DiBiasi of Oregon also was born March 13, 1941, and named Patricia Ann Campbell. Both had fathers named Robert, worked as bookkeepers, and at the time of this comparison had children ages 21 and 19. Both studied cosmetology, enjoyed oil painting as a hobby, and married military men, within 11 days of each other. They are not genetically related (from an AP report, May 2, 1983).

Even the more impressive data from personality assessments are clouded by the reunion of many of the separated twins some years before they were tested. Moreover, identical twins share an appearance, and the responses it evokes, and adoption agencies tend to place separated twins in similar homes. Despite these criticisms, the striking twin study results helped shift scientific thinking toward a greater appreciation of genetic influences.

If genetic influences help explain individual differences, do they also help explain group differences between men and women, or between people of different races? Not necessarily. Individual differences in height and weight, for example, are highly heritable; yet nutritional rather than genetic influences explain why, as a group, today's adults are taller and heavier than those of a century ago. The two groups differ, but not because human genes have changed in a mere century's eyeblink of time. Ditto aggressiveness, a genetically influenced trait. Thus, today's peaceful Scandinavians differ from their more aggressive Viking ancestors, despite carrying many of the same genes.

Biological Versus Adoptive Relatives

For behavior geneticists, nature's second type of real-life experiment—adoption—creates two groups of relatives: genetic (biological parents and siblings) and environmental (adoptive parents and siblings). For any given trait we can therefore ask whether adopted children are more like their biological parents, who contributed their genes, or their adoptive parents, who contribute a home environment. While sharing that home environment, do adopted siblings also come to share traits?

The stunning finding from studies of hundreds of adoptive families is that people who grow up together, whether biologically related or not, do not much resemble one another in personality (McGue & Bouchard, 1998; Plomin & others, 1998; Rowe, 1990). Adoptees' traits (such as outgoingness and agreeableness) bear more similarities to their biological parents than to their caregiving adoptive parents.

The finding is important enough to bear repeating: Environmental factors shared by a family's children have virtually no impact on their personalities. Two adopted children reared in the same home are no more likely to share personality traits with each other than with the child down the block. Heredity shapes other primates' personalities, too. Macaque monkeys raised by foster mothers exhibit social behaviors that resemble their biological, rather than foster, mothers (Maestripieri, 2003). Add all this to the similarity of identical twins, whether they grow up together or apart, and the effect of a shared rearing environment seems shockingly modest.

What we have here is perhaps "the most important puzzle in the history of psychology," contends Steven Pinker (2002): Why are children in the same family so different? Why do shared genes and shared family environment (the parents' personalities, marital status, and social class; day care versus home care; the neighborhood) have so little discernible effect on children's personalities? Is it because each sibling experiences differing peer influences and life events? Is it because sibling relationships ricochet off each other, amplifying their differences? Is it because siblings—despite sharing half their genes—have very different combinations of genes and may evoke very different kinds of parenting?

So is adoptive parenting a fruitless venture? No. The genetic leash may limit the family environment's influence on personality, but parents do influence their children's attitudes, values, manners, faith, and politics (Brodzinsky & Schechter, 1990). A pair of adopted children or identical twins *will* have more similar religious beliefs, especially during adolescence, if reared together (Kelley & De Graaf, 1997; Koenig & others, 2005; Rohan & Zanna, 1996). Parenting matters!

Moreover, in adoptive homes, child neglect and abuse and even parental divorce are rare. (Adoptive parents are carefully screened; natural parents are not.) So it is not surprising that, despite a somewhat greater risk of psychological disorder, most

"Mom may be holding a full house while Dad has a straight flush, yet when Junior gets a random half of each of their cards his poker hand may be a loser."

David Lykken (2001)

The greater uniformity of adoptive homes—mostly healthy, nurturing homes—helps explain the lack of striking differences when comparing child outcomes of different adoptive homes (Stoolmiller, 1999).

adopted children thrive, especially when adopted as infants (Benson & others, 1994; Wierzbicki, 1993). Seven in eight report feeling strongly attached to one or both adoptive parents. As children of self-giving parents, they grow up to be more self-giving and altruistic than average (Sharma & others, 1998). Many score higher than their biological parents on intelligence tests, and most grow into happier and more stable adults. In one Swedish study, infant adoptees grew up with fewer problems than were experienced by children whose biological mothers had initially registered them for adoption but then decided to raise the children themselves (Bohman & Sigvardsson, 1990). Regardless of personality differences between parents and their adoptees, children benefit from adoption.

Temperament and Heredity

As most parents will tell you after having their second child, babies differ even before gulping their first breath. Consider one quickly apparent aspect of personality. An infant's **temperament** is its emotional excitability—whether reactive, intense, and fidgety, or easygoing, quiet, and placid. From the first weeks of life, *difficult* babies are more irritable, intense, and unpredictable. *Easy* babies are cheerful, relaxed, and predictable in feeding and sleeping (Chess & Thomas, 1987).

Parents, being keenly sensitive to their children's differences, perceive their temperaments as even more different than they are (Saudino & others, 2004). Yet actual differences do exist and do persist. Consider these findings:

- The most emotionally reactive newborns tend also to be the most reactive 9-month-olds (Wilson & Matheny, 1986; Worobey & Blajda, 1989).
- Exceptionally inhibited and fearful 2-year-olds often are still relatively shy as 8-year-olds; about half will become introverted adolescents (Kagan & others, 1992, 1994).
- The most emotionally intense preschoolers tend to be relatively intense young adults (Larsen & Diener, 1987). In one study of more than 900 New Zealanders, emotionally reactive and impulsive 3-year-olds developed into somewhat more impulsive, aggressive, and conflict-prone 21-year-olds (Caspi, 2000).

Heredity may predispose temperament differences (Emde & others, 1992; Gabbay, 1992; Robinson & others, 1992). As we have seen, identical twins have more similar personalities, including temperament, than do fraternal twins. Physiological tests reveal that anxious, inhibited infants have high and variable heart rates and a reactive nervous system, and that they become more physiologically aroused when facing new or strange situations (Kagan & Snidman, 2004). Such evidence adds to the emerging conclusion that our biologically rooted temperament helps form our enduring personality (McCrae & others, 2000; Rothbart & others, 2000).

Nature *and* Nurture

Among our similarities, the most important—the behavioral hallmark of our species—is our enormous adaptive capacity. Some human traits, such as having two eyes, develop the same in virtually every environment. But others are expressed in particular environments. Go barefoot for a summer and you will develop toughened, callused feet—a biological adaptation to friction. Meanwhile, your shod neighbor will remain a tenderfoot. The difference between the two of you is, of course, an effect of environment. But it is also the product of a biological mechanism. Our shared biology enables our developed diversity (Buss, 1991).

An analogy may help: Genes and environment—nature and nurture—work together like two hands clapping. Genes not only code for particular proteins, they also respond to environments. An African butterfly that is green in summer turns brown in fall, thanks to a temperature-controlled genetic switch. Gary Marcus (2004) explains: "The genome is giving the butterfly two different choices, two different opportunities.

■ **temperament** a person's characteristic emotional reactivity and intensity.

"Oh, he's cute, all right, but he's got the temperament of a car alarm."

© The New Yorker Collection, 1999, Barbara Smaller from cartoonbank.com. All Rights Reserved.

❝Men's natures are alike; it is their habits that carry them far apart.❞
Confucius, *Analects*, 500 B.C.

It's not dictating, 'You must take this form.' It's saying, 'If you're in this situation you can take this form, if you're in this other situation you can take this other form.'" Thus, genes are *self-regulating*. Rather than acting as blueprints that lead to the same result no matter the context, genes react. People with identical genes but differing experiences therefore have similar though not identical minds. One twin may fall in love with someone quite different from the co-twin's love. And at least one known gene will, in response to major life stresses, code for a protein that controls neurotransmitter functions underlying depression. By itself, the gene doesn't cause depression, but it is part of the recipe.

Thus, asking whether your personality is more a product of your genes or your environment is like asking whether the area of a field is more the result of its length or its width. We could, however, ask whether the *differing* areas of various fields are more the result of differences in their length or width and whether person-to-person personality *differences* are influenced more by nature or nurture.

Gene-Environment Interaction

To say that genes and experience are *both* important is true. But more precisely, they interact. Imagine two babies, one genetically predisposed to be attractive, sociable, and easygoing, the other less so. Assume further that the first baby attracts more affectionate and stimulating care than the second and so develops into a warmer and more outgoing person. As the two children grow older, the more naturally outgoing child more often seeks activities and friends that encourage further social confidence.

What has caused their resulting personality differences? Neither heredity nor experience dances alone. Environments trigger gene activity. And our genetically influenced traits *evoke* significant responses in others. Thus, a child's impulsivity and aggression may evoke an angry response from a teacher who reacts warmly to the child's model classmates. Parents, too, may treat their children differently; one child elicits punishment, another does not. In such cases, the child's nature and the parents' nurture interact. Neither operates apart from the other. Gene and scene dance together.

Evocative interactions may help explain why identical twins reared in different families recall their parents' warmth as remarkably similar—almost as similar as if they had had the same parents (Plomin & others, 1988, 1991, 1994). Fraternal twins have more differing recollections of their early family life—even if reared in the same family! "Children experience us as different parents, depending on their own qualities," noted Sandra Scarr (1990). Moreover, as we grow older we also *select* environments well suited to our natures.

> "Heredity deals the cards; environment plays the hand."
>
> Psychologist Charles L. Brewer (1990)

Gene-environment interaction
People respond differently to Rowan Atkinson, left (shown here playing Mr. Bean), than to fellow actor Orlando Bloom, right.

Rex Features

Alessia Pierdomenico/Reuters/Corbis

So, from conception onward, we are the product of a cascade of **interactions** between our genetic predispositions and our surrounding environments. Our genes affect how people react to and influence us. Biological appearances have social consequences. So, forget nature *versus* nurture; think nurture *via* nature.

Evolutionary Psychology: Understanding Human Nature

5-3: How do evolutionary psychologists use natural selection to explain behavior tendencies?

Behavior geneticists explore the genetic and environmental roots of human differences. **Evolutionary psychologists** instead focus mostly on what makes us so much alike as humans. They use principles of **natural selection** in their attempt to understand behaviors and mental processes. To see these principles at work, let's consider a straightforward example in foxes.

Natural Selection

A fox is a wild and wary animal. If you capture a fox and try to befriend it, be careful. Stick your hand in the cage and, if the timid fox cannot flee, it probably will make a snack of your fingers. Familiar with foxes, Dmitry Belyaev, of the Russian Academy of Science's Institute of Cytology and Genetics, wondered how our human ancestors had domesticated dogs from their equally wild wolf forebears. Might he, within a comparatively short stretch of time, accomplish a similar feat by transforming the fearful fox into a friendly fox?

To find out, Belyaev set to work with 30 male and 100 female foxes. From their offspring he selected and mated the tamest 5 percent of males and 20 percent of females. (He measured tameness by the foxes' responses to attempts to feed, handle, and stroke them.) Over more than 30 generations of foxes, Belyaev and his successor, Lyudmila Trut, repeated that simple procedure. Today, more than 40 years and 45,000 foxes later, they have a new breed of foxes that, in Trut's (1999) words, are "docile, eager to please, and unmistakably domesticated. . . . Before our eyes, 'the Beast' has turned into 'beauty,' as the aggressive behavior of our herd's wild [ancestors] entirely disappeared." So friendly and eager for human contact are they, so inclined to whimper to attract attention and to lick people like affectionate cats, that the cash-strapped institute seized on a way to raise funds—marketing its foxes to people as house pets.

When certain traits are *selected*—by conferring a reproductive advantage to an individual or a species—those traits, over time, will prevail. Dog breeders, as Robert Plomin and his colleagues (1997) remind us, have given us sheepdogs that herd, retrievers that retrieve, trackers that track, and pointers that point. Psychologists, too, have bred dogs, mice, and rats whose genes predispose them to be serene or reactive, quick learners or slow.

Does natural selection also explain our human tendencies? Nature has indeed selected advantageous variations from among the **mutations** (random errors in gene replication) and the new gene combinations produced at each human conception. But the tight genetic leash that predisposes a dog's retrieving, a cat's pouncing, or an ant's nest building is looser on humans. The genes selected during our ancestral history provide more than a long leash; they endow us with a great capacity to learn and therefore to adapt to life in varied environments, from the tundra to the jungle. Genes and experience together wire the brain. Our adaptive flexibility in responding to different environments contributes to our fitness—our ability to survive and reproduce.

© The New Yorker Collection, 1999, Nick Downes from cartoonbank.com. All Rights Reserved.

"I thought that sperm-bank donors remained anonymous."

■ **interaction** in psychology, occurs when the effect of one factor (such as environment) depends on another factor (such as heredity).

■ **evolutionary psychology** the study of the evolution of behavior and the mind, using principles of natural selection.

■ **natural selection** the principle that, among the range of inherited trait variations, those that lead to increased reproduction and survival will most likely be passed on to succeeding generations.

■ **mutation** a random error in gene replication that leads to a change.

From beast to beauty

More than 40 years into the fox-breeding experiment, most of the offspring are devoted, affectionate, and capable of forming strong bonds with people.

L.N. Trut, *American Scientist* (1999) 87: 160–169

Yet in the big picture, our lives are remarkably alike. Visit the international arrivals area at Amsterdam's Schipol Airport, a world hub where arriving passengers meet their excited loved ones. There you will see the same delighted joy in the faces of Indonesian grandmothers, Chinese children, and homecoming Dutch. Although human differences grab our attention, our deep similarities also demand explanation. Evolutionary psychologist Steven Pinker (2002, p. 73) believes our shared human traits "were shaped by natural selection acting over the course of human evolution." No wonder, then, that our emotions, drives, and reasoning "have a common logic across cultures."

Our behavioral and biological similarities arise from our shared human genome. No more than 5 percent of the genetic differences among humans arise from population group differences. Some 95 percent of genetic variation exists within populations (Rosenberg & others, 2002). The typical genetic difference between two Icelandic villagers or between two Kenyans is much greater than the *average* difference between the two groups. Thus, noted geneticist Richard Lewontin (1982), if after a worldwide catastrophe only Icelanders or Kenyans survived, the human species would suffer only "a trivial reduction" in its genetic diversity.

Why are we all so much alike? At the dawn of human history, our ancestors faced certain questions: Who is my ally, who my foe? What food should I eat? With whom should I mate? Some individuals answered those questions more successfully than others. For example, some women's experience of nausea in the critical first three months of pregnancy predisposes their avoiding certain bitter, strongly flavored, and novel foods. Avoiding such foods has survival value, since they are the very foods most often toxic to embryonic development (Schmitt & Pilcher, 2004). Those disposed to eat nourishing rather than poisonous food survived to contribute their genes to later generations. Those who deemed leopards "nice to pet" often did not.

Similarly successful were those who mated with someone with whom they could produce and nurture offspring. Over generations, the genes of individuals not so disposed tended to be lost from the human gene pool. As genes providing an adaptive edge continued to be selected, behavioral tendencies and thinking and learning capacities emerged that prepared our Stone Age ancestors to survive, reproduce, and send their genes into the future.

As inheritors of this prehistoric genetic legacy, we are predisposed to behave in ways that promoted our ancestors' surviving and reproducing. We love the taste of sweets and fats, which once were hard to come by but which prepared our ancestors to survive famines. Ironically, with famine rare in Western cultures, and sweets and fats beckoning us from store shelves, fast-food outlets, and vending machines, obesity has become a growing problem. Our natural dispositions, rooted deep in history, are mismatched with today's junk-food environment (Colarelli & Dettman, 2003). We are, in some ways, biologically prepared for a world that no longer exists.

Charles Darwin's theory of evolution has been an organizing principle for biology for a long time. Jared Diamond (2001) notes that "virtually no contemporary scientists believe that Darwin was basically wrong." This theory lives on in "the second Darwinian revolution": the application of evolutionary principles to psychology. In concluding *On the Origin of Species,* Darwin anticipated this, foreseeing "open fields for far more important researches. Psychology will be based on a new foundation" (1859, p. 346).

Evolutionary psychologists have addressed questions such as these:

- Why do infants start to fear strangers about the time they become mobile?
- Why are biological fathers so much less likely than unrelated boyfriends to abuse and murder the children with whom they share a home?
- Why do so many more people have phobias about spiders, snakes, and heights than about more dangerous threats, such as guns and electricity?

Those who are troubled by an apparent conflict between scientific and religious accounts of human origins may find it helpful to recall that different perspectives of life can be complementary. For example, the scientific account attempts to tell us *when* and *how*; religious creation stories usually aim to tell about an ultimate *who* and *why.* As Galileo explained to the Grand Duchess Christina, "The Bible teaches how to go to heaven, not how the heavens go."

- How are men and women alike? How and why do men's and women's sexuality differ?

To see how evolutionary psychologists think and reason, let's pause to explore this last question.

An Evolutionary Explanation of Human Sexuality

Having faced many similar challenges throughout history, men and women have adapted in similar ways. Whether male or female, we eat the same foods, avoid the same predators, and perceive, learn, and remember similarly. It is only in those domains where we have faced differing adaptive challenges—most obviously in behaviors related to reproduction—that we differ, say evolutionary psychologists.

Gender Differences in Sexuality

Differ we do, report psychologists Roy Baumeister, Kathleen Catanese, and Kathleen Vohs (2001). They invite us to consider whether women or men have the stronger sex drive. Who desires more frequent sex, thinks more about sex, masturbates more often, initiates more sex, and sacrifices more to gain sex? The answers, they report, are men, men, men, men, and men. Indeed, "with few exceptions anywhere in the world," agree cross-cultural psychologist Marshall Segall and his colleagues (1990, p. 244), "males are more likely than females to initiate sexual activity." This difference is among the largest of **gender** differences in sexuality, but there are others:

- In a 2005 survey of 289,452 entering U.S. college students, 58 percent of men but only 34 percent of women agreed that "if two people really like each other, it's all right for them to have sex even if they've known each other for a very short time" (Pryor & others, 2005). "I can imagine myself being comfortable and enjoying 'casual' sex with different partners," agreed 48 percent of men and 12 percent of women a in survey of 4901 Australians (Bailey & others, 2000).
- In another survey of 3432 U.S. 18- to 59-year-olds, 48 percent of the women but only 25 percent of the men cited affection as a reason for first intercourse. And how often do they think about sex? "Every day" or "several times a day," acknowledged 19 percent of the women and 54 percent of the men (Laumann & others, 1994).
- In surveys, gay men (like straight men) report more interest in uncommitted sex, more responsiveness to visual sexual stimuli, and more concern with their partner's physical attractiveness than do lesbian women (Bailey & others, 1994; Doyle, 2005).

Natural Selection and Mating Preferences

As biologists use natural selection to explain the mating behaviors of many species, so evolutionary psychologists use natural selection to explain women's more relational and men's more recreational approaches to sex. Their explanation goes like this: While a woman normally incubates and nurses one infant, a male can spread his genes through other females. Our natural yearnings are our genes' way of reproducing themselves. In our ancestral history, women most often sent their genes into the future by pairing wisely, men by pairing widely. "Humans are living fossils—collections of mechanisms produced by prior selection pressures," says evolutionary psychologist David Buss (1995).

And what do heterosexual men and women find attractive in the other sex? Some aspects of attractiveness cross place and time. Men in 37 cultures, from Australia to Zambia (**FIGURE 5.3**), judge women as more attractive if they have a youthful appearance (Buss, 1994). Evolutionary psychologists say that men who were drawn to healthy, fertile-appearing women—women with smooth skin and a youthful shape suggesting many childbearing years to come—stood a better chance of sending their

■ **gender** in psychology, the biologically and socially influenced characteristics by which people define *male* and *female*.

> "It's not that gay men are oversexed; they are simply men whose male desires bounce off other male desires rather than off female desires."
>
> Steven Pinker, *How the Mind Works*, 1997

Canada's famed Starbuck Holstein bull sired more than 200,000 offspring.

FIGURE **5.3**
Worldwide mating preferences
If men more than women prefer attractive physical features suggesting youth and health—and reproductive potential—and if women more than men prefer mates with resources and social status, we can credit (or blame) natural selection. (The red dots indicate the 37 cultures studied [Buss, 1994].)

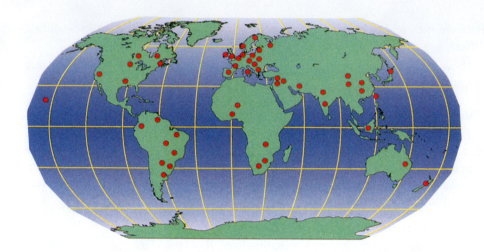

genes into the future. Regardless of cultural variations in ideal weight, men everywhere feel most attracted to women whose waists are roughly a third narrower than their hips—a sign of future fertility (Singh, 1993).

Women also feel attracted to healthy-looking men, but especially to those who seem mature, dominant, bold, and affluent (Singh, 1995). Such attributes, say the evolutionary psychologists, connote a capacity to support and protect (Buss, 1996, 2000; Geary, 1998). Women also prefer mates with the potential for long-term mating and investment in their joint offspring (Gangestad & Simpson, 2000). They prefer stick-around dads over likely cads. Long-term mates contribute protection and support, which give their offspring greater survival prospects. Thus, for men there are genetic tradeoffs between seeking to distribute one's genes widely and being willing to co-parent.

There is a principle at work here, say evolutionary psychologists: Nature selects behaviors that increase the likelihood of sending one's genes into the future. As mobile gene machines, we are designed to prefer whatever worked for our ancestors in their environments. They were predisposed to act in ways that would leave grandchildren—had they not been, we wouldn't be here. And as carriers of their genetic legacy, we are similarly predisposed.

Critiquing the Evolutionary Perspective

Without disputing nature's selection of traits that enhance gene survival, critics see problems with evolutionary psychology. It often, they say, starts with an effect (such as the gender sexuality difference) and works backward to propose an explanation. So let's imagine a different observation and reason backward. If men were uniformly loyal to their mates, might we not reason that the children of these committed, supportive fathers would more often survive to perpetuate their genes? Might not men also be better off bonded to one woman—both to increase the otherwise slim odds of impregnation and to keep her from the advances of competing men? Might not a ritualized bond—a marriage—also spare women from chronic male harassment? Such suggestions are, in fact, evolutionary explanations for why humans tend to pair off monogamously. One can hardly lose at hindsight explanation, which is, said paleontologist Stephen Jay Gould (1997), mere "speculation [and] guesswork in the cocktail party mode."

Some worry about the social consequences of evolutionary psychology. Does it suggest a genetic determinism that strikes at the heart of progressive efforts to remake society (Rose, 1999)? Does it undercut moral responsibility? Could it be used to rationalize "high-status men marrying a series of young, fertile women" (Looy, 2001)?

© The New Yorker Collection, 1999, Robert Mankoff from cartoonbank.com. All Rights Reserved.

"I had a nice time, Steve. Would you like to come in, settle down, and raise a family?"

Much of who we are is *not* hard-wired (which evolutionary psychologists do not dispute). What's considered attractive does vary somewhat with time and place. The voluptuous Marilyn Monroe ideal of the 1950s has been replaced by the twenty-first-century, leaner, athletic image. Moreover, cultural expectations can bend the genders. If socialized to value lifelong commitment, men may sexually bond with one partner; if socialized to accept casual sex, women may willingly have sex with many partners.

Gender differences in mate preferences are also influenced by social and family structures. Show Alice Eagly and Wendy Wood (1999; Wood & Eagly, 2002) a culture with gender inequality—where men are providers and women are homemakers—and they will show you a culture where men strongly desire youth and domestic skill in their potential mates, and where women seek status and earning potential in their mates. Show Eagly and Wood a culture with gender equality, and they will show you a culture with smaller gender differences in mate preferences. They draw their conclusions from an analysis of the same 37 cultures mentioned earlier.

Evolutionary psychologists reassure us that the sexes, having faced similar adaptive problems, are far more alike than different. They stress that humans have a great capacity for learning and social progress. (We come equipped to adapt and survive, whether living in igloos or tree houses.) They point to the coherence and explanatory power of evolutionary principles, especially those offering testable predictions (for example, that we will favor others to the extent that they share our genes or can later reciprocate our favors). And they remind us that the study of how we came to be need not dictate how we ought to act. Understanding our propensities sometimes helps us overcome them.

REVIEWING

>> MODULE REVIEW

5-1: **How do behavior geneticists explain individual differences?**

Behavior geneticists use methods such as twin and adoption studies to identify the extent to which genetics and *environment* influence our behavior creating individual differences. Studies of the inheritance of *temperament*, and of *identical* and *fraternal* twins and adopted children, provide scientific support for the idea that nature *and* nurture *interact* to influence our personality and our development.

5-2: **Our genes predispose our biology; does this mean they determine our behaviors?**

Genes (*DNA* segments that form the *chromosomes*) are the biochemical units of heredity. When "turned on," they trigger the production of protein molecules, the building blocks of our physical and behavioral development. Our genetic predispositions help explain our behaviors, but they do not determine them.

5-3: **How do evolutionary psychologists use natural selection to explain behavior tendencies?**

Evolutionary psychologists attempt to understand how *natural selection* has shaped behaviors found throughout the human species. They reason that if organisms vary, if only some mature to produce surviving offspring, and if certain inherited behavioral tendencies assist that survival, then nature must select those tendencies. They believe this helps explain *gender* differences in sexuality. Critics maintain that evolutionary psychologists start with an effect and work backward to an explanation; that they underestimate cultural and social factors; and that they absolve people from taking personal responsibility for their behaviors.

>> REHEARSE IT!

1. Every cell nucleus in your body contains the genetic master code for your entire body. ———— are threadlike structures made largely of DNA molecules.

   a. Gene complexes
   b. Nuclei
   c. Chromosomes
   d. Cells

2. Each person's genetic blueprint combines contributions from the mother's egg and the father's sperm. When the egg and sperm unite, each contributes

   a. one chromosome pair.
   b. 23 chromosomes.
   c. 23 chromosome pairs.
   d. 30,000 chromosomes.

3. Studies of identical and fraternal twins offer an opportunity to assess genetic and environmental influences on behavior. Fraternal twins result when

   a. a single egg is fertilized by a single sperm and then splits.
   b. a single egg is fertilized by two sperm and then splits.
   c. two eggs are fertilized by two sperm.
   d. two eggs are fertilized by a single sperm.

4. Adoption studies seek to reveal genetic influences on personality. They do this mainly by

   a. comparing adopted children with nonadopted children.
   b. evaluating whether adopted children more closely resemble their adoptive or biological parents.
   c. studying the effect of prior neglect on adopted children.
   d. studying the effect of one's age at adoption.

5. Although development is lifelong, there is stability of personality over time. For example,

   a. temperament is a product of learning and can therefore be unlearned.
   b. temperament seems to be biologically based and tends to remain stable throughout life.
   c. temperament changes significantly during adolescence.
   d. fraternal twins tend to have more similar temperaments than do identical twins.

6. Evolutionary psychologists study how we came to be who we are. They are most likely to focus on

   a. how we differ from one another.
   b. the links between biology and behavior.
   c. natural selection of the fittest adaptations.
   d. random assignment of genes over several generations.

Answers: 1. c, 2. b, 3. c, 4. b, 5. b, 6. c.

>> TERMS AND CONCEPTS TO REMEMBER

environment, p. 66
behavior genetics, p. 66
chromosomes, p. 67
DNA (deoxyribonucleic acid), p. 67
genes, p. 67

genome, p. 67
identical twins, p. 67
fraternal twins, p. 68
temperament, p. 71
interaction, p. 73

evolutionary psychology, p. 73
natural selection, p. 73
mutation, p. 73
gender, p. 75

>> TEST YOURSELF

1. What are the three main criticisms of the evolutionary explanation of human sexuality?

   (Answer in Appendix C.)

Multiple-choice **self-tests** and more may be found at www.worthpublishers.com/myers.

MODULE 6

Environmental Influences on Behavior

Parents and Peers

6-1: To what extent are our lives shaped by early stimulation, parental nurture, and peer influences?

Our genes, as expressed in specific environments, influence our developmental differences. But what about the part of us that is *not* hard wired? If we are formed by nature *via* nurture, what are the most influential components of our nurture? How do our early experiences, our family and peer relationships, and all our other experiences guide our development and contribute to our diversity?

Parents and Early Experiences

The formative nurture that conspires with nature begins at conception, with the prenatal environment in the womb, as embryos receive differing nutrition and varying levels of exposure to toxic agents. Nurture then continues outside the womb, where our early experiences foster brain development.

Experience and Brain Development

Our genes dictate our overall brain architecture, but experience directs the details, developing neural connections and preparing our brain for thought and language and other later experiences. But how do early experiences leave their "marks" in the brain? Mark Rosenzweig and David Krech reared some young rats in solitary confinement and others in a communal playground (**FIGURE 6.1**). When they later analyzed the rats' brains, those who died with the most toys had won. The rats living in the enriched environment, which simulated a natural environment, usually developed a heavier and thicker brain cortex.

Rosenzweig (1984; Renner & Rosenzweig, 1987) was so surprised by this discovery that he repeated the experiment several times before publishing his findings. So great are the effects that, shown brief video clips of rats, you could tell from their activity and curiosity whether their rearing was impoverished or enriched (Renner & Renner, 1993). "An extraordinary change," report Bryan Kolb and Ian Whishaw (1998), noting that after 60 days in an enriched environment, a rat's brain weight increases 7 to 10 percent and the number of synapses mushrooms by about 20 percent. Such results have motivated improvements in environments for laboratory, farm, and zoo

FIGURE 6.1

Experience affects brain development

Mark Rosenzweig and David Krech reared rats either alone in an environment without playthings, or with others in an environment enriched with playthings changed daily. In 14 of 16 repetitions of this basic experiment, rats in the enriched environment developed significantly more cerebral cortex (relative to the rest of the brain's tissue) than did those in the impoverished environment.

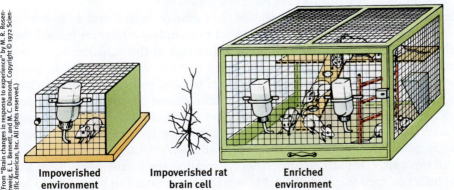

(From "Brain changes in response to experience" by M. R. Rosenzweig, E. L. Bennett, and M. C. Diamond. Copyright © 1972 Scientific American, Inc. All rights reserved.)

Impoverished environment   **Impoverished rat brain cell**   **Enriched environment**   **Enriched rat brain cell**

Courtesy of C. Brune

Stringing the circuits young
String musicians who started playing before age 12 have larger and more complex neural circuits controlling the note-making left-hand fingers than do string musicians whose training started later (Elbert & others, 1995).

"Genes and experiences are just two ways of doing the same thing—wiring synapses."

Joseph LeDoux, *The Synaptic Self*, 2002

animals—and for children in institutions. Stimulation by touch or massage also benefits infant rats and premature babies (Field, 2001; Field & others, 2004). "Handled" infants of both species develop faster neurologically and gain weight more rapidly. By giving preemies massage therapy, neonatal intensive care units now help them to develop faster and go home sooner.

Both nature and nurture sculpt our synapses. After brain maturation provides us with an abundance of neural connections, experience preserves our activated connections and allows those that are unused to degenerate. Sights and smells, touches and tugs activate and strengthen some neural pathways while others weaken from disuse. Similar to pathways through a forest, less-traveled paths gradually disappear and popular paths are broadened. The result by puberty is a massive *pruning* of unemployed connections.

Here, then, at the juncture of nurture and nature, is the biological reality of early childhood education. During early childhood—while excess connections are still on call—youngsters can most easily master such skills as the grammar and accent of another language. Lacking any exposure to written or signed language before adolescence, a person will never master any language.

Likewise, lacking visual experience during the early years, people whose vision is restored by cataract removal never achieve normal perceptions. The brain cells normally assigned to vision have died or been diverted to other uses. For us to have optimum brain development, normal stimulation during the early years is critical. The maturing brain seems governed by a rule: Use it or lose it.

The brain's development does not, however, end with childhood. Throughout life our neural tissue is changing. If a monkey is trained to push a lever with a finger several thousand times a day, the brain tissue controlling that finger will change to reflect the experience. Human brains work similarly (**FIGURE 6.2**). Whether learning to keyboard or skateboard, we perform with increasing skill as our brain incorporates the learning.

FIGURE 6.2
A trained brain
A well-learned finger-tapping task activates more motor cortex neurons (orange area, far right) than were active in the same brain before training (near right). (From Karni & others, 1998.)

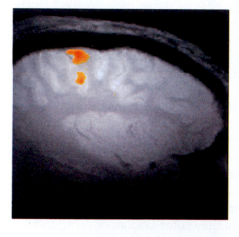 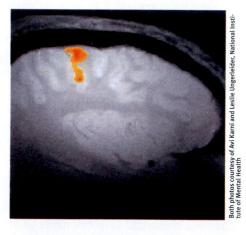

Both photos courtesy of Avi Karni and Leslie Ungerleider, National Institute of Mental Health

How Much Credit (or Blame) Do Parents Deserve?

In procreation, a woman and a man shuffle their gene decks and deal a life-forming hand to their child-to-be, who is then subjected to countless influences beyond their control. Parents, nonetheless, feel enormous satisfaction in their children's successes, and guilt or shame over their failures. They beam over the child who wins an award. They wonder where they went wrong with the child repeatedly called into the principal's office. Freudian psychiatry and psychology have been among the sources of such ideas, by blaming problems from asthma to schizophrenia on "bad mothering." Society reinforces such parent-blaming: Believing that parents shape their offspring as a potter molds clay, people readily praise parents for their children's virtues and blame them for their children's vices. Popular culture endlessly proclaims the psychological harm toxic parents inflict on their fragile children. No wonder then, that it can seem risky to have and raise children.

Even among chimpanzees, when one infant is hurt by another, the victim's mother will often attack the offender's mother (Goodall, 1968).

But do parents really produce future adults with an inner wounded child by being (take your pick from the toxic-parent lists) overbearing—or uninvolved? Pushy—or ineffectual? Overprotective—or distant? Are children really so easily wounded? If so, should we then blame our parents for our failings, and ourselves for our children's failings? Or does all the talk of wounding fragile children through normal parental mistakes trivialize the brutality of real abuse?

Parents do matter. The power of parenting to shape our differences is clearest at the extremes—the abused who become abusive, the neglected who become neglectful, the loved but firmly handled children who become self-confident and socially competent. The power of the family environment also frequently shows up in children's political attitudes, religious beliefs, and personal manners. And it appears in the remarkable academic and vocational successes of children of the refugee "boat people" fleeing Vietnam and Cambodia—successes attributed to close-knit, supportive, even demanding families (Caplan & others, 1992).

Yet in personality measures, shared environmental influences—including the home influences siblings share—typically account for less than 10 percent of children's differences. In the words of behavior geneticists Robert Plomin and Denise Daniels (1987), "Two children in the same family [are on average] as different from one another as are pairs of children selected randomly from the population." To developmental psychologist Sandra Scarr (1993), this implies that "parents should be given less credit for kids who turn out great and blamed less for kids who don't." Knowing children are not easily sculpted by parental nurture, then perhaps parents can relax a bit more and love their children for who they are.

Peer Influence

As children mature, what other experiences do the work of nurturing? At all ages, we are subject to group influences, as we seek to fit in with various groups.

Consider children's conformity (Harris, 1998):

- Preschoolers who disdain a certain food despite parents' urgings often will eat the food if put at a table with a group of children who like it.
- A child who hears English spoken with one accent at home and another in the neighborhood and at school will invariably adopt the accent of the peers, not the parents.
- Teens who start smoking typically have *friends* (rather than parents) who model smoking, suggest its pleasures, and offer cigarettes (Rose & others, 1999, 2003). Part of this peer similarity may result from a *selection effect,* as kids seek out peers with similar attitudes and interests. Those who smoke (or don't) may select as friends those who also smoke (or don't).

Howard Gardner (1998) concludes that parents and peers are complementary:

Parents are more important when it comes to education, discipline, responsibility, orderliness, charitableness, and ways of interacting with authority figures. Peers are more important for learning cooperation, for finding the road to popularity, for inventing styles of interaction among people of the same age. Youngsters may find their peers more interesting, but they will look to their parents when contemplating their own futures. Moreover, parents [often] choose the neighborhoods and schools that supply the peers.

As Gardner points out, parents can influence the culture that shapes the peer group, by helping to select their children's neighborhood and schools. And because neighborhood influences matter, parents may want to become involved in intervention programs for youth that aim at a whole school or neighborhood. If the vapors of a toxic climate are seeping into a child's life, that climate—not just the child—needs reforming.

© The New Yorker Collection, 2001, Barbara Smaller from cartoonbank.com. All Rights Reserved.

"So I blame you for everything—whose fault is that?"

❝If you want to blame your parents for your own adult problems, you are entitled to blame the genes they gave you, but you are not entitled—by any facts I know—to blame the way they treated you. . . . We are not prisoners of our past.❞

Martin Seligman, *What You Can Change and What You Can't,* 1994

❝Men resemble the times more than they resemble their fathers.❞

Ancient Arab proverb

❝It takes a village to raise a child.❞

African proverb

Peer power

As we develop, we play, mate, and partner with peers. No wonder children and youths are so sensitive and responsive to peer influences.

Ole Graf/zefa/Corbis

Cultural Influences

6-2 : How do cultural norms affect our behavior?

Compared with the narrow path taken by flies, fish, and foxes, the road along which environment drives us is wider. The mark of our species—nature's great gift to us—is our ability to learn and adapt. We come equipped with a huge cerebral hard drive ready to receive many gigabytes of cultural software.

Culture is the behaviors, ideas, attitudes, values, and traditions shared by a group of people and transmitted from one generation to the next (Brislin, 1988). Human nature, notes Roy Baumeister (2005), seems designed for culture. We are social animals, but more. Wolves are social animals; they live and hunt in packs. Ants are incessantly social, never alone. But "culture is a better way of being social," notes Baumeister. Culture supports survival and reproduction with social and economic systems that give us an edge. Wolves function pretty much as they did 10,000 years ago. You and I enjoy things unknown to most of our century-ago ancestors, including electricity, indoor plumbing, antibiotics, and the Internet. Culture works.

Primates exhibit the rudiments of culture, with local customs of tool use, grooming, and courtship. Younger chimpanzees and macaque monkeys sometimes invent customs—potato washing, in one famous example—and pass them on to their peers and offspring. But human culture does more. Thanks to our mastery of *language*, we humans not only know how to clean our food, we also enjoy one of culture's hallmarks: the *preservation of innovation*. Within the span of this day, I have, thanks to my culture, made good use of Post-It notes, Google, and a single-shot skinny latté. We also have culture's accumulated knowledge to thank for the last century's extension of our life expectancy from 47 to 76 years. Moreover, culture enables an efficient *division of labor*. Although one lucky person gets his name on this book's cover, the product actually results from the coordination and commitment of a team of women and men, no one of whom could produce it alone.

Across cultures, we differ in our language, our monetary system, our sports, which fork—if any—we eat with, even which side of the road we drive on. But beneath these differences is our great similarity—our capacity for culture. Culture provides the shared and transmitted customs and beliefs that enable us to communicate, to exchange money for things, to play, to eat, and to drive with agreed-upon rules and without crashing into one another. This shared capacity for culture enables our striking differences. Human nature manifests human diversity.

Uniform requirements
People in individualist Western cultures sometimes see traditional Japanese culture as confining. But from the Japanese perspective, the same tradition expresses a "serenity that comes to people who know exactly what to expect from each other" (Weisz & others, 1984).

Kevin R. Morris/Corbis

If we all lived in homogeneous ethnic groups in separate regions of the world, as some people still do, cultural diversity would be less relevant. In Japan, 99 percent of the country's 126 million people are of Japanese descent. Internal cultural differences are therefore minimal compared with those found in Los Angeles, where the public schools recently taught 82 different languages, or in Toronto or Vancouver, where minorities are one-third of the population and many are immigrants (as are 17 percent of all Canadians and 24 percent of Australians) (Iyer, 1993; Statistics Canada, 2002; Trewin, 2001). I am ever mindful that the readers of this book are culturally diverse. You and your ancestors reach from Australia to Africa and from Singapore to Sweden.

Variation Across Cultures

We see our adaptability in cultural variations among our beliefs and our values, in how we raise our children and bury our dead, and in what we wear (or whether we wear anything at all). Riding along with a unified culture is like biking with the wind: As it carries us along, we hardly notice it is there. When we try riding *against* the wind we feel its force. Face to face with a different culture, we become aware of the cultural winds. Visiting Europe, most North Americans notice the smaller cars, the left-handed use of the fork, the uninhibited attire on the beaches. Stationed in Iraq, Afghanistan, and Kuwait, European and American soldiers alike realized how liberal their home cultures were. Arriving in North America, visitors from Japan and India struggle to understand why many people wear their dirty *street* shoes in the house.

Each cultural group evolves its own **norms**—rules for accepted and expected behavior. Many South Asians, for example, use only the right hand's fingers for eating. The British have a norm for orderly waiting in line. Sometimes social expectations seem oppressive: "Why should it matter how I dress?" Yet, norms grease the social machinery and free us from self-preoccupation. Knowing when to clap or bow, which fork to pick up first at a dinner party, and what sorts of gestures and compliments are appropriate—whether to greet people by shaking hands or kissing each cheek, for example—we can relax and enjoy one another without fear of embarrassment or insult.

When cultures collide, their differing norms often befuddle. For example, if someone invades our **personal space**—the portable buffer zone we like to maintain around our bodies—we feel uncomfortable. Scandinavians, North Americans, and the British prefer more personal space than do Latin Americans, Arabs, and the French (Sommer, 1969). At a social gathering, a Mexican seeking a comfortable conversation distance may end up walking around a room with a backpedaling Canadian. (You can experience this at a party by playing Space Invader as you talk with someone.) To the Canadian, the Mexican may seem intrusive; to the Mexican, the Canadian may seem standoffish.

Cultures also vary in their expressiveness. Those with roots in northern European culture often perceive people from Mediterranean cultures as warm and charming but inefficient. The Mediterraneans, in turn, see northern Europeans as efficient but cold and preoccupied with punctuality (Triandis, 1981).

Cultures vary in their pace of life, too. People from time-conscious Japan—where bank clocks keep exact time, pedestrians walk briskly, and postal clerks fill requests speedily—may find themselves growing impatient when visiting Indonesia, where clocks keep less accurate time and the pace of life is more leisurely (Levine & Norenzayan, 1999). In adjusting to their host countries, the first wave of U.S. Peace Corps volunteers reported that two of their greatest culture shocks, after the language differences, were the differing pace of life and the people's differing sense of punctuality (Spradley & Phillips, 1972).

■ **culture** the enduring behaviors, ideas, attitudes, values, and traditions shared by a group of people and transmitted from one generation to the next.

■ **norm** an understood rule for accepted and expected behavior. Norms prescribe "proper" behavior.

■ **personal space** the buffer zone we like to maintain around our bodies.

Cultures differ
Behavior seen as appropriate in one culture may violate the norms of another group. In Arab societies, but not in Western cultures, men often greet one another with a kiss, or hold hands as a sign of friendship, as U.S. President George W. Bush did in 2005 while strolling with Saudi Crown Prince Abdullah.

■ **individualism** giving priority to one's own goals over group goals and defining one's identity in terms of personal attributes rather than group identifications.

■ **collectivism** giving priority to goals of one's group (often one's extended family or work group) and defining one's identity accordingly.

©The New Yorker Collection, 2000, Ziegler, from cartoonbank.com. All Rights Reserved.

Variation Over Time

Consider, too, how rapidly cultures may change over time. English poet Geoffrey Chaucer (1342–1400) is separated from a modern Briton by only 20 generations, but the two would converse with great difficulty. In the thin slice of history since 1960, most Western cultures have changed with remarkable speed. Middle-class people fly to places they once only read about, e-mail those they once snail-mailed, and work in air-conditioned comfort where they once sweltered. They enjoy the convenience of on-line holiday shopping, cellphone calling, and—enriched by doubled per-person real income—eating out more than twice as often as did their parents back in the culture of 1960. With greater economic independence, today's women are more likely to marry for love and less likely to endure abusive relationships out of economic need. Many minority groups enjoy expanded human rights.

But some changes seem not so wonderfully positive. Had you fallen asleep in the United States in 1960 and awakened today, you would have opened your eyes to a culture with more divorce, delinquency, and depression. You would also find North Americans—like their counterparts in Britain, Australia, and New Zealand—spending more hours at work, fewer hours sleeping, and fewer hours with friends and family (Frank, 1999; Putnam, 2000).

Whether we love or loathe these changes, we cannot fail to be impressed by their breathtaking speed. And we cannot explain them by changes in the human gene pool, which evolves far too slowly to account for high-speed cultural transformations. Cultures vary. Cultures change. And cultures shape our lives.

Culture and the Self

6-3 : How does the view of self differ in individualist and collectivist cultures?

Cultures vary in the extent to which they give priority to the nurturing and expression of one's personal identity or one's group identity. To grasp the difference, imagine that someone were to rip away your social connections, making you a solitary refugee in a foreign land. How much of your identity would remain intact? The answer would depend in large part on whether you give greater priority to the independent self that marks *individualism* or to the interdependent self that marks *collectivism*.

If as our solitary traveler you were the former, a great deal of your identity would remain intact—the very core of your being, the sense of "me," the awareness of your personal convictions and values. **Individualists** give relatively greater priority to personal goals and define their identity mostly in terms of personal attributes. They strive for personal control and individual achievement. In American culture, with its relatively big "I" and small "we," 85 percent of people say it is possible "to pretty much be who you want to be" (Sampson, 2000). Being more self-contained, individualists also move in and out of social groups more easily. They feel relatively free to switch places of worship, leave one job for another, or even leave their extended families and migrate to a new place. Marriage is often for as long as they both shall love.

If set adrift in a foreign land as a **collectivist**, you might experience a much greater loss of identity. Cut off from family, groups, and loyal friends, you would lose the connections that have defined who you are. In a collectivist culture, group identifications provide a sense of belonging, a set of values, a network of caring individuals, an assurance of security. In return, collectivists have deeper, more stable attachments to their groups, often their family, clan, or company, and define their identity in terms of group goals. In Korea, for example, people place less value on expressing a consistent, unique self-concept, and more on tradition and shared practices (Choi & Choi, 2002).

Valuing communal solidarity, people in collectivist cultures place a premium on preserving group spirit and making sure others never lose face. What people say reflects not only what they feel (their inner attitudes) but what they presume others feel (Kashima & others, 1992). Avoiding direct confrontation, blunt honesty, and uncomfortable topics, people defer to others' wishes and display a polite, self-effacing humility (Markus & Kitayama, 1991). In new groups, they may be shy and more easily embarrassed than their individualist counterparts (Singelis & others, 1995, 1999). Compared with Westerners, people in Japanese and Chinese cultures, for example, exhibit greater shyness toward strangers and greater concern for social harmony and loyalty (Bond, 1988; Cheek & Melchior, 1990; Triandis, 1994). Elders and superiors receive respect, and duty to one's family may trump personal career preference. When the priority is "we," not "me," that individualized latté—"decaf, single shot, skinny, extra hot"—that feels so good to a North American in an espresso shop might sound more like a selfish demand in Seoul, note Heejung Kim and Hazel Markus (1999).

Individualism offers benefits that come at a cost. People in competitive, individualist cultures have more personal freedom, take more pride in personal achievements, are less geographically bound to their families, and enjoy more privacy (**TABLE 6.1**). Their less-unified cultures offer a smorgasbord of life-styles and invite individuals to construct their own identities. These cultures also celebrate innovation and creativity, and they tend to respect individual human rights. Such may help explain Ed Diener, Marissa Diener, and Carol Diener's (1995) finding that people in individualist cultures report experiencing greater happiness than do those in collectivist cultures. When individualists pursue their own ends and all goes well, life can seem rewarding.

Kyodo News

Collectivism
By identifying with family and other groups, these women and children in Pakistan have gained a sense of "we," a set of values, a network of care. This collectivist support system may have helped these people struggle through the devastation of the October 2005 Kashmir earthquake, which leveled the house behind them.

"One needs to cultivate the spirit of sacrificing the *little me* to achieve the benefits of the *big me*."

Chinese saying

Individualist proverb: "The squeaky wheel gets the grease."

Collectivist proverb: "The quacking duck gets shot."

TABLE 6.1

VALUE CONTRASTS BETWEEN INDIVIDUALISM AND COLLECTIVISM

Concept	Individualism	Collectivism
Self	Independent (identity from individual traits)	Interdependent (identity from belonging)
Life task	Discover and express one's uniqueness	Maintain connections, fit in, perform role
What matters	Me—personal achievement and fulfillment; rights and liberties; self-esteem	Us—group goals and solidarity; social responsibilities and relationships; family duty
Coping method	Change reality	Accommodate to reality
Morality	Defined by individuals (self-based)	Defined by social networks (duty-based)
Relationships	Many, often temporary or casual; confrontation acceptable	Few, close and enduring; harmony valued
Attributing behavior	Behavior reflects one's personality and attitudes	Behavior reflects social norms and roles

Sources: Adapted from Thomas Schoeneman (1994) and Harry Triandis (1994).

Curiously, though, within individualist cultures, people with the strongest social ties express greatest satisfaction with their lives (Bettencourt & Dorr, 1997). Moreover, the seeming benefits of individualism can come at the cost of more loneliness, more divorce, more homicide, and more stress-related disease (Popenoe, 1993; Triandis & others, 1988). People in individualist cultures express more self-focused "narcissism," by agreeing, for example, that "I find it easy to manipulate people" (Foster & others, 2003). And they demand more romance and personal fulfillment in marriage, subjecting the relationship to more pressure (Dion & Dion, 1993). In one survey, "keeping romance alive" was rated as important to a good marriage by 78 percent of U.S. women but only 29 percent of Japanese women (*American Enterprise,* 1992). In China, love songs often express enduring commitment and friendship (Rothbaum & Tsang, 1998). As one song put it, "We will be together from now on . . . I will never change from now to forever."

Culture and Child-Rearing

Child-rearing practices reflect cultural values and vary from one time and place to another. Do you prefer children who are independent or children who comply with what others think? If you live in a Westernized culture, the odds are you prefer the former. "You are responsible for yourself," Western families and schools tell their children. "Follow your conscience. Be true to yourself. Discover your gifts. Think through your personal needs." But a half-century ago, Western cultural values placed greater priority on obedience, respect, and sensitivity to others (Alwin, 1990; Remley, 1988). "Be true to your traditions," parents then taught their children. "Be loyal to your heritage and country. Show respect toward your parents and other superiors." Cultures can change.

Many Asians and Africans live in cultures that value emotional closeness. Rather than being given their own bedrooms and entrusted to day care, infants and toddlers may sleep with their mothers and spend their days close to a family member (Morelli & others, 1992; Whiting & Edwards, 1988). These cultures encourage a strong sense of *family self*—a feeling that what shames the child shames the family, and what brings honor to the family brings honor to the self.

Children across place and time have thrived under various child-rearing systems. Upper-class British parents traditionally handed off routine caregiving to nannies, then sent their children off to boarding school at about age 10. These children generally grew

> "We recognize that we are the products of many cultures, traditions, and memories; that mutual respect allows us to study and learn from other cultures; and that we gain strength by combining the foreign with the familiar."
>
> U.N. Secretary-General Kofi Annan, Nobel Peace Prize lecture, 2001

Cultures vary
In Scotland's Orkney Islands' town of Stromness, social trust has enabled parents to park their toddlers outside of shops.

Copyright Steve Reehl

up to be pillars of British society, just like their parents and their boarding-school peers. In the African Gusii society, babies nurse freely but spend most of the day on their mother's back—with lots of body contact but little face-to-face and language interaction. When the mother becomes pregnant, the toddler is weaned and handed over to someone else, often an older sibling. Westerners may wonder about the negative effects of this lack of verbal interaction, but then the African Gusii would in turn wonder about Western mothers pushing their babies around in strollers and leaving them in playpens and car seats (Small, 1997). Such diversity in child-rearing cautions us against presuming that our culture's way is the only way to rear children successfully.

Parental involvement promotes development
Parents in every culture facilitate their children's discovery of their world, but cultures differ in what they deem important. Asian cultures place more emphasis on school and hard work than does North American culture. This may help explain why Japanese and Taiwanese children get higher scores on mathematics achievement tests.

Developmental Similarities Across Groups

Mindful of how others differ from us, we often fail to notice the similarities predisposed by our shared biology. Compared with the person-to-person differences within groups, the differences between groups are small. Regardless of our culture, we humans share the same life cycle. We speak to our infants in similar ways and respond similarly to their coos and cries (Bornstein & others, 1992a,b). All over the world, the children of warm and supportive parents feel better about themselves and are less hostile than are the children of punitive and rejecting parents (Rohner, 1986; Scott & others, 1991).

Even differences *within* a culture, such as those sometimes attributed to race, are often easily explained by an interaction between our biology and our culture. David Rowe and his colleagues (1994, 1995) illustrate this with an analogy: Black men tend to have higher blood pressure than white men. Suppose that (1) in both groups salt consumption correlates with blood pressure, and (2) salt consumption is higher among black men than among white men. The blood pressure "race difference" might then actually be, at least partly, a *diet* difference—a cultural preference for certain foods.

And that, say Rowe and his colleagues, parallels psychological findings. Although Hispanic, Asian, Black, and White Americans differ in school achievement and delinquency, the differences are "no more than skin deep." To the extent that family structure, peer influences, and parental education predict behavior in one of these ethnic groups, they do so for the others as well.

So in surface ways we may differ, but as members of one species we seem subject to the same psychological forces. As members of different ethnic and cultural groups, our languages vary, yet they reflect universal principles of grammar. Our tastes vary, yet they reflect common principles of hunger. Our social behaviors vary, but they reflect pervasive principles of human influence. Cross-cultural research can help us appreciate both our cultural diversity *and* our human kinship.

> "When someone has discovered why men in Bond Street wear black hats he will at the same moment have discovered why men in Timbuctoo wear red feathers."
>
> G. K. Chesterton, *Heretics*, 1908

Gender Development

6-4: How do nature and nurture interact to define us as male or female?

Cognitive psychologists have demonstrated that we humans have an irresistible urge to organize our worlds into simple categories. Among the ways we classify people—as tall or short, slim or fat, smart or dull—one stands out: At your birth, everyone wanted to know, "Boy or girl?" Our biological sex in turn helps define our *gender*, our assumed characteristics as male or female. In considering how nature and nurture together create social diversity, gender is the prime case example. Let's recap one of psychology's main themes—that nature and nurture together create our differences and commonalities—by considering some gender variations.

■ **aggression** physical or verbal behavior intended to hurt someone.

Gender Similarities and Differences

Having faced similar adaptive challenges, we are in most ways alike. Men and women are not from different planets—Mars and Venus—but from the same planet Earth. Tell me whether you are male or female and you give me virtually no clues to your vocabulary, intelligence, self-esteem, and happiness, or to the mechanisms by which you see, hear, learn, and remember. Your "opposite" sex is, in reality, your very similar sex. And should we be surprised? Among your 46 chromosomes, 45 are unisex.

But males and females also differ, and differences command attention. Some differences are obvious. Compared with the average man, the average woman enters puberty two years sooner and will outlive her male counterpart by five years. She also has 70 percent more fat, possesses 40 percent less muscle, and is 5 inches shorter. Throughout this book, we will also see some less obvious gender differences. Women are more likely to dream equally of men and women, to become sexually re-aroused immediately after orgasm, to smell faint odors, to express emotions freely, and in some situations to be offered help. Women are also doubly vulnerable to depression and anxiety and at 10 times greater risk for eating disorders. But then men are some four times more likely to commit suicide or suffer alcoholism and are far more often diagnosed with autism, color-blindness, hyperactivity (as children), and antisocial personality disorder (as adults). Choose your gender and pick your vulnerability.

How much does biology bend the genders, and what portion of our differences are socially constructed—by the gender roles culture assigns us, and by how we are socialized as children? To answer that question, let's look more closely at some gender differences in aggression, social power, and social connectedness.

Gender and Aggression

In surveys, men admit to more **aggression** than do women, and experiments confirm that men tend to behave more aggressively, such as by administering what they believe are more painful electric shocks (Bettencourt & Kernahan, 1997). The aggression gender gap pertains to *physical* aggression (such as hitting) rather than verbal, *relational* aggression (such as excluding someone). The gap appears in everyday life in various cultures and at various ages (Archer, 2004). Violent crime rates illustrate the difference. The male-to-female arrest ratio for murder, for example, is 9 to 1 in the United States and 7 to 1 in Canada (FBI, 2004; Statistics Canada, 2003).

Throughout the world, hunting, fighting, and warring are primarily men's activities (Wood & Eagly, 2002). Men also express more support for war. In one 2005 survey, 51 percent of American men but only 34 percent of American women expressed approval of George Bush's Iraq initiative (Gallup, 2005).

Gender and Social Power

Around the world, from Nigeria to New Zealand, people perceive men as more dominant, forceful, and independent, women as more deferential, nurturant, and affiliative (Williams & Best, 1990). Indeed, in most societies men *are* socially dominant. When groups form, whether as juries or companies, leadership tends to go to males (Colarelli & others, 2006). As leaders, men tend to be more directive, even autocratic; women tend to be more democratic, more welcoming of subordinates' participation in decision making (Eagly & Johnson, 1990; van Engen & Willemsen, 2004). When people interact, men are more likely to utter opinions, women to express support (Aries, 1987; Wood, 1987). In everyday behavior, men are more likely to act as powerful people often do—talking assertively, interrupting, initiating touches, staring, smiling less (Hall, 1987; Major & others, 1990).

Such behaviors help sustain social power inequities. When political leaders are elected, they usually are men, who held 84 percent of the seats in the world's governing parliaments in 2005 (IPU, 2005). When salaries are paid, those in traditionally male occupations receive more. Gender differences in power do appear to lessen with maturity, however, as middle-aged women become more assertive and men more empathic (Maccoby, 1998).

Question: Why does it take 200 million sperm to fertilize one egg?
Answer: Because they won't stop for directions.

❝In the long years liker must they grow;
The man be more of woman, she of man."
Alfred Lord Tennyson, *The Princess*, 1847

Every man for himself, or tend and befriend?
Gender differences in the way we interact with others begin to appear at a very young age.

Gender and Social Connectedness

To Carol Gilligan and her colleagues (1982, 1990), the "normal" struggle to create one's separate identity describes individualist males more than relationship-oriented females. Gilligan believes females differ from males both in being less concerned with viewing themselves as separate individuals and in being more concerned with "making connections."

These gender differences in connectedness surface early, in children's play. Boys typically play in large groups with an activity focus and little intimate discussion. Girls usually play in smaller groups, often with one friend. Their play is less competitive than boys' and more imitative of social relationships. Both in play and other settings, females are more open and responsive to feedback than are males (Maccoby, 1990; Roberts, 1991). And these differences continue with age. As teens, girls spend more time with friends and less time alone (Wong & Csikszentmihalyi, 1991). As adults, men enjoy doing activities *side-by-side*; women take more pleasure in talking *face-to-face* (Wright, 1989). And women, being more *interdependent,* use conversation more to explore relationships; men use it to communicate solutions (Tannen, 1990). This may help explain a recent finding about gender differences in phone communication in France, where women make 63 percent of telephone calls, and when talking to a woman stay connected longer (7.2 minutes) than men do when talking to other men (4.6 minutes) (Smoreda & Licoppe, 2000).

Women emphasize caring and provide most of the care to the very young and the very old. They also purchase 85 percent of greeting cards (*Time,* 1997). Although 69 percent of people say they have a close relationship with their father, 90 percent feel close to their mother (Hugick, 1989). Not surprising, perhaps. When wanting understanding and someone with whom to share worries and hurts, both men and women usually turn to women, and both report their friendships with women to be more intimate, enjoyable, and nurturing (Rubin, 1985; Sapadin, 1988). As friends, women talk more often and more openly (Berndt, 1992; Dindia & Allen, 1992). And when they themselves must cope with stress, women more often turn to others for support—they *tend and befriend* (Tamres & others, 2002; Taylor, 2002).

The Nature of Gender

What explains our gender diversity? Is biology destiny? Are we shaped by our cultures? A biopsychosocial view suggests it is both, thanks to the interplay among our biological dispositions, our developmental experiences, and our current situations (Wood & Eagly, 2002).

In domains where men and women have faced similar challenges—regulating heat with sweat, developing tastes that nourish, growing calluses where the skin meets friction—the sexes are similar. Even when describing the ideal mate, both men and

■ **X chromosome** the sex chromosome found in both men and women. Females have two X chromosomes; males have one. An X chromosome from each parent produces a female child.

■ **Y chromosome** the sex chromosome found only in males. When paired with an X chromosome from the mother, it produces a male child.

■ **testosterone** the most important of the male sex hormones. Both males and females have it, but the additional testosterone in males stimulates the growth of the male sex organs in the fetus and the development of the male sex characteristics during puberty.

■ **role** a set of expectations (norms) about a social position, defining how those in the position ought to behave.

■ **gender role** a set of expected behaviors for males or for females.

women put traits such as "kind," "honest," and "intelligent" at the top of their lists. But in domains pertinent to mating, evolutionary psychologists contend, guys act like guys whether they are elephants or elephant seals, rural peasants or corporate presidents. Such gender differences may be influenced genetically, by our differing *sex chromosomes* and, physiologically, from our differing concentrations of *sex hormones*.

Males and females are variations on a single form. Seven weeks after conception, you were anatomically indistinguishable from someone of the other sex. Then your genes activated your biological sex. Your sex was determined by your twenty-third pair of chromosomes, the two sex chromosomes. From your mother you received an **X chromosome.** From your father, you received the one chromosome out of 46 that is not unisex—either an X chromosome, making you a girl, or a **Y chromosome,** making you a boy. The Y chromosome includes a single gene that throws a master switch triggering the testes to develop and produce the principal male hormone, **testosterone,** which about the seventh week starts the development of external male sex organs. Females also have testosterone, but less of it.

Another key period for sexual differentiation falls during the fourth and fifth prenatal months, when sex hormones bathe the fetal brain and influence its wiring. Different patterns for males and females develop under the influence of the male's greater testosterone and the female's ovarian hormones (Hines, 2004; Udry, 2000). Recent research confirms male–female differences during development in brain areas with abundant sex hormone receptors (Cahill, 2005). In adulthood, parts of the frontal lobes, an area involved in verbal fluency, are reportedly thicker in women. Part of the parietal cortex, a key area for space perception, is thicker in men. Other studies report gender differences in the hippocampus, the amygdala, and the volume of brain gray matter (the neural bodies) versus white matter (the axons and dendrites).

Further evidence of biology's influence on gender development comes from studies of genetic males who, despite normal male hormones and testes, are born without penises or with very small ones. In one study of 14 who underwent early sex-reassignment surgery (which is now controversial) and were raised as girls, 6 later declared themselves as male, 5 were living as female, and 3 had unclear sexual identity (Reiner & Gearhart, 2004). In one famous case, the parents of a Canadian boy who lost his penis to a botched circumcision followed advice to raise him as a girl rather than as a damaged boy. Alas, "Brenda" was not like other girls. "She" didn't like dolls. She tore her dresses with rough-and-tumble play. At puberty she wanted no part of kissing boys. Finally, Brenda's parents explained what had happened, whereupon Brenda immediately rejected her female identity, cut her hair, took a male name and ended up marrying a woman, becoming a stepfather, and, sadly, later committing suicide (Colapinto, 2000).

Further research is needed, but this much seems clear, reports the National Academy of Sciences (2001): "Sex matters." In combination with the environment, sex-related genes and physiology "result in behavioral and cognitive differences between males and females."

The Nurture of Gender

Although biologically influenced, gender is also socially constructed. What biology initiates, culture accentuates.

Gender Roles

Sex matters. But from a biopsychosocial perspective, culture and the immediate situation matter, too. Culture, as we noted earlier, is everything shared by a group and transmitted across generations. We can see culture's shaping power in the social expectations that guide men's and women's behavior. In psychology, as in the theater, a **role** refers to a cluster of prescribed actions—the behaviors we expect of those who occupy a particular social position. One set of norms defines our culture's **gender roles**—our expectations about the way men and women behave. Thirty years ago, it

© New Yorker Collection, 2001, Barbara Smaller from cartoonbank.com All Rights Reserved.

"Sex brought us together, but gender drove us apart."

was standard for men to initiate dates, drive the car, and pick up the check, and for women to decorate the home, buy and care for the children's clothes, and select the wedding gifts. Gender roles exist outside the home, too. Compared with employed women, employed men in the United States spend about one hour more on the job and about one hour less on household activities and caregiving each day (Bureau of Labor Statistics, 2004). I do not have to tell you which parent, about 90 percent of the time in two-parent families, stays home with a sick child, arranges for the baby-sitter, or calls the doctor (Maccoby, 1995). In Australia, women devote 54 percent more time to unpaid household work and 71 percent more time to child care than do men (Trewin, 2001).

Gender roles can smooth social relations, saving awkward decisions about who does the laundry this week and who mows the lawn. But they often do so at a cost: If we deviate from such conventions, we may feel anxious.

Do gender roles reflect what is biologically natural for men and women? Or do cultures construct them? Gender-role diversity over time and space indicates that culture has a big influence. Nomadic societies of food-gathering people have only a minimal division of labor by sex. Boys and girls receive much the same upbringing. However, in agricultural societies, where women work in the fields close to home, and men roam more freely herding livestock, children typically socialize into more distinct gender roles (Segall & others, 1990; Van Leeuwen, 1978).

Among industrialized countries, gender roles and attitudes nevertheless vary widely. Would you say life is more satisfying when both spouses work for pay and share child care? If so, you would agree with most people in 41 of 44 countries, according to a Pew Global Attitudes survey (2003). Even so, the culture-to-culture differences were huge, ranging from Egypt, where people disagreed 2 to 1, to Vietnam, where people agreed by 11 to 1.

Attitudes about gender roles vary over time, of course. As we began the last century, only one country—New Zealand—granted women the right to vote (Briscoe, 1997). In that same century, with the flick of an apron, the number of U.S. college women hoping to be full-time homemakers plunged during the late 1960s and early 1970s (**FIGURE 6.3**). In 1960, one in 30 entering U.S. law students were women; by the early twenty-first century, half were (Glater, 2001).

The gendered tsunami
In Sri Lanka, Indonesia, and India, the gendered division of labor helps explain the excess of female deaths from the 2004 tsunami. In some villages, 80 percent of those killed were women, who were mostly at home while the men were more likely to be out at sea fishing or doing out-of-the-home chores (Oxfam, 2005).

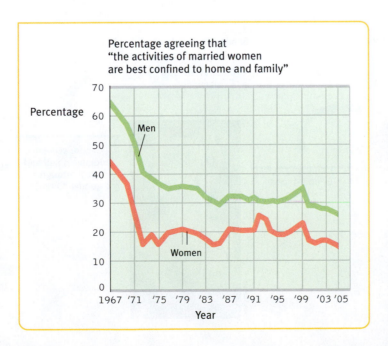

Percentage agreeing that "the activities of married women are best confined to home and family"

FIGURE 6.3
Changing attitudes about gender roles
U.S. college students' endorsement of the traditional view of women's role has declined dramatically. Men's and women's attitudes have also converged. (From Dey & others, 1991; Pryor & others, 2005.)

© The New Yorker Collection, 1999, John O'Brien from cartoonbank.com. All Rights Reserved.

"How is it gendered?"

Gender ideas also vary across generations. When families emigrate from Asia to Canada and the United States, the immigrant children often grow up with peers who assume gender roles different from those of the immigrant parents. Daughters, especially, may feel torn between competing sets of norms (Dion & Dion, 2001).

Gender and Child-Rearing

As society assigns each of us to a gender, the social category of male or female, the inevitable result is our strong **gender identity,** our sense of *being* male or female. To varying extents, we also become **gender-typed.** That is, some boys more than others exhibit traditionally masculine traits and interests, and some girls more than others become distinctly feminine.

Social learning theory assumes that children learn gender-linked behaviors by observing and imitating and by being rewarded or punished. "Nicole, you're such a good mommy to your dolls"; "Big boys don't cry, Alex." But modeling and rewarding is not done by parents alone, because the differences in the way parents rear boys and girls aren't enough to explain gender-typing (Lytton & Romney, 1991). In fact, even when their families discourage traditional gender-typing, children organize themselves into "boy worlds" and "girl worlds," each guided by rules for what boys and girls do.

Gender schema theory combines social learning theory with cognition: In your own childhood, as you struggled to comprehend the world, you—like other children— formed *schemas,* or concepts that helped you make sense of your world. One of these was a schema for your own gender (Bem, 1987, 1993). Gender then became a lens through which you viewed your experiences (**FIGURE 6.4**). Social learning shapes gender schemas. Before age 1, children begin to discriminate male and female voices and faces (Martin & others, 2002). After age 2, language forces children to begin organizing their worlds on the basis of gender. English, for example, uses the pronouns *he* and *she;* other languages classify objects as masculine ("*le* train") or feminine ("*la* table").

Young children are "gender detectives," explain Carol Lynn Martin and Diane Ruble (2004). Once they grasp that two sorts of people exist—and that they are of one sort— they search for clues about gender, and they find them in language, dress, toys, and songs. Girls, they may decide, are the ones with long hair. Having divided the human world in half, 3-year-olds will then like their own sex better and seek out their own kind for play. And having compared themselves with their concept of gender, they will adjust their behavior accordingly ("I am male—thus, masculine, strong, aggressive," or

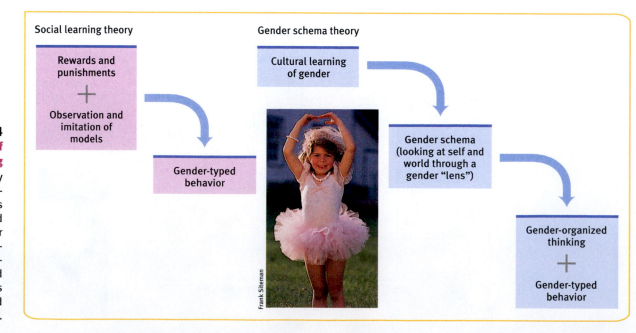

FIGURE 6.4
Two theories of gender-typing
Social learning theory proposes that gender-typing evolves through imitation and reinforcement. Gender schema theory proposes that one's concept of maleness and femaleness influences one's perceptions and behavior.

Social learning theory

Rewards and punishments
+
Observation and imitation of models
→ Gender-typed behavior

Gender schema theory

Cultural learning of gender
→ Gender schema (looking at self and world through a gender "lens")
→ Gender-organized thinking
+
Gender-typed behavior

Frank Siteman

"I am female—therefore, feminine, sweet, and helpful"). The rigidity of boy-girl stereo-types peaks at about age 5 or 6. If the new neighbor is a boy, a 6-year-old girl may just assume he cannot share her interests. For young children, gender schemas loom large.

Reflections on Nature and Nurture

"There are trivial truths and great truths," reflected the physicist Niels Bohr on some of the paradoxes of modern science. "The opposite of a trivial truth is plainly false. The opposite of a great truth is also true." It appears true that our ancestral history helped form us as a species. Where there is variation, natural selection, and heredity, there will be, on some scale, evolution. The unique gene combination created when our mother's egg engulfed our father's sperm also helped form us, as individuals. Genes predispose both our shared humanity and our individual differences. This is a great truth about human nature. Genes form us.

But it also is true that our experiences form us. In the womb, in our families, and in our peer social relationships, we learn ways of thinking and acting. Even differences initiated by our nature may be amplified by our nurture. If their genes and hormones predispose males to be more physically aggressive than females, culture may magnify this gender difference through norms that encourage males to be macho and females to be the kinder, gentler sex. If men are encouraged toward roles that demand physical power, and women toward more nurturing roles, each may then exhibit the actions expected of those who fill such roles and find themselves shaped accordingly. Roles remake their players. Presidents in time become more presidential, servants more servile. Gender roles similarly shape us.

But gender roles are converging. Brute strength has become increasingly irrelevant to power and status (think Bill Gates). Thus both women and men have become "fully capable of effectively carrying out organizational roles at all levels," note Wendy Wood and Alice Eagly (2002). And as women's employment in formerly male occupations has increased, gender differences in traditional masculinity/femininity and in what one seeks in a mate have diminished (Twenge, 1997). As the roles we play change over time, we change with them.

* * * * *

If nature and nurture jointly form us, are we "nothing but" the product of nature and nurture? Are we rigidly determined?

We *are* the product of nature and nurture (**FIGURE 6.5**), but we are also an open system. Genes are all-pervasive but not all-powerful; people may defy their genetic

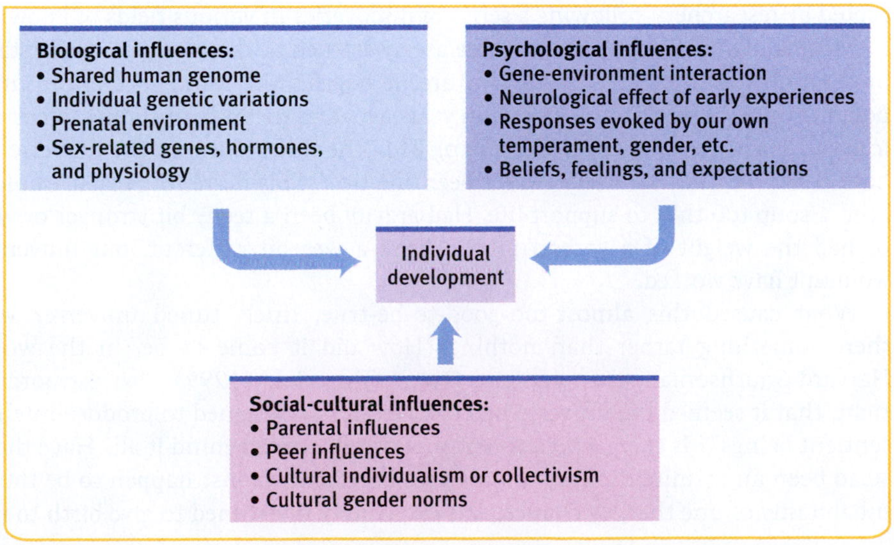

■ **gender identity** one's sense of being male or female.

■ **gender-typing** the acquisition of a traditional masculine or feminine role.

■ **social learning theory** the theory that we learn social behavior by observing and imitating and by being rewarded or punished.

■ **gender schema theory** the theory that children learn from their cultures a concept of what it means to be male and female and that they adjust their behavior accordingly.

"Genes, by themselves, are like seeds dropped onto pavement: powerless to produce anything."

Primatologist Frans B. M. de Waal (1999)

Biological influences:
- Shared human genome
- Individual genetic variations
- Prenatal environment
- Sex-related genes, hormones, and physiology

Psychological influences:
- Gene-environment interaction
- Neurological effect of early experiences
- Responses evoked by our own temperament, gender, etc.
- Beliefs, feelings, and expectations

Individual development

Social-cultural influences:
- Parental influences
- Peer influences
- Cultural individualism or collectivism
- Cultural gender norms

FIGURE 6.5
The biopsychosocial approach to development

bent to reproduce, by electing celibacy. Culture, too, is all-pervasive but not all-powerful; people may defy peer pressures and do the opposite of the expected. To excuse our failings by blaming our nature and nurture is what philosopher-novelist Jean-Paul Sartre called "bad faith"—attributing responsibility for one's fate to bad genes or bad influences.

In reality, we are both the creatures and the creators of our worlds. We are—it is a great truth—the products of our genes and environments. Nevertheless—another great truth—the stream of causation that shapes the future runs through our present choices. Our decisions today design our environments tomorrow. Mind matters. The human environment is not like the weather—something that just happens. We are its architects. Our hopes, goals, and expectations influence our future. And that is what enables cultures to vary and to change so quickly.

* * * * *

I know from my mail and from public opinion surveys that some readers feel troubled by the naturalism and evolutionism of contemporary science. They worry that a science of behavior (and evolutionary science in particular) will destroy our sense of the beauty, mystery, and spiritual significance of the human creature. For those concerned, I offer some reassuring thoughts.

When Isaac Newton explained the rainbow in terms of light of differing wavelengths, the poet Keats feared that Newton had destroyed the rainbow's mysterious beauty. Yet, notes Richard Dawkins (1998) in *Unweaving the Rainbow*, Newton's analysis led to an even deeper mystery—Einstein's theory of special relativity. Moreover, nothing about Newton's optics need diminish our appreciation for the dramatic elegance of a rainbow arching across a rain-darkened sky.

When Galileo assembled evidence that the Earth revolved around the Sun, not vice versa, he did not offer irrefutable proof for his theory. Rather he offered a coherent explanation for a variety of observations, such as the changing shadows cast by the Moon's mountains. His explanation eventually won the day because it described and explained things in a way that made sense, that hung together. Darwin's theory of evolution likewise is a coherent view of natural history. It offers an organizing principle that unifies various observations.

Although some people of faith may find the scientific idea of human origins troubling, many others find it congenial with their spirituality. In the fifth century, St. Augustine (quoted by Wilford, 1999) wrote, "The universe was brought into being in a less than fully formed state, but was gifted with the capacity to transform itself from unformed matter into a truly marvelous array of structures and life forms." Some 1600 years later, Pope John Paul II in 1996 welcomed a science-religion dialogue, finding it noteworthy that evolutionary theory "has been progressively accepted by researchers, following a series of discoveries in various fields of knowledge."

Meanwhile, many people of science are awestruck at the emerging understanding of the universe and the human creature. It boggles the mind—the entire universe popping out of a point some 14 billion years ago, and instantly inflating to cosmological size. Had the energy of this Big Bang been the tiniest bit less, the universe would have collapsed back on itself. Had it been the tiniest bit more, the result would have been a soup too thin to support life. Had gravity been a teeny bit stronger or weaker, or had the weight of a carbon proton been a wee bit different, our universe just wouldn't have worked.

What caused this almost-too-good-to-be-true, finely tuned universe? Why is there something rather than nothing? How did it come to be, in the words of Harvard-Smithsonian astrophysicist Owen Gingerich (1999), "so extraordinarily right, that it seemed the universe had been expressly designed to produce intelligent, sentient beings"? Is there a benevolent superintelligence behind it all? Have there instead been an infinite number of universes born and we just happen to be the lucky inhabitants of one that, by chance, was exquisitely fine-tuned to give birth to us? Or

"Let's hope that it's not true; but if it is true, let's hope that it doesn't become widely known."

Lady Ashley, commenting on Darwin's theory

"Is it not stirring to understand how the world actually works—that white light is made of colors, that color measures light waves, that transparent air reflects light . . . ? It does no harm to the romance of the sunset to know a little about it."

Carl Sagan, *Skies of Other Worlds*, 1988

does that idea violate *Occam's razor,* the principle that we should prefer the simplest of competing explanations? On such matters, a humble, awed, scientific silence is appropriate, suggested philosopher Ludwig Wittgenstein: "Whereof one cannot speak, thereof one must be silent."

Rather than fearing science, we can welcome its enlarging our understanding and awakening our sense of awe. In *The Fragile Species,* Lewis Thomas (1992) described his utter amazement that the Earth in time gave rise to bacteria and eventually to Bach's *Mass in B-Minor.* In a short 4 billion years, life on Earth has come from nothing to structures as complex as a 6-billion-unit strand of DNA and the incomprehensible intricacy of the human brain. Nature, says cosmologist Paul Davies (1992, 1999, 2004), seems cunningly and ingeniously devised to produce extraordinary, self-replicating, information-processing systems—us. Although we appear to have been created from dust, over eons of time, the end result is a priceless creature, one rich with potentials beyond our imagining.

> "The causes of life's history [cannot] resolve the riddle of life's meaning."
>
> Stephen Jay Gould, *Rocks of Ages: Science and Religion in the Fullness of Life,* 1999

REVIEWING

>> MODULE REVIEW

6-1: To what extent are our lives shaped by early stimulation, parental nurture, and peer influences?

Parents influence some areas of their children's lives, such as their political and religious beliefs, but they do not determine who we are or will become. Genetic influences, prenatal environments, early experiences (which help build neural connections in the brain), and social and cultural influences also help form our identities. Peers are especially influential in learning to cooperate with one another, achieve popularity, and interact with people of a similar age.

6-2: How do cultural norms affect our behavior?

Cultural *norms* are rules for accepted and expected behaviors, ideas, attitudes, and values. We become uneasy when we violate our culture's norms. *Cultures* differ in their norms for *personal space,* expressiveness, pace of life, and emphasis on the individual versus the group.

6-3: How does the view of self differ in individualist and collectivist cultures?

Individuals and cultures vary in giving priority to "me" or "we"— to personal control and individual achievement or to social connections and solidarity. Self-reliant *individualism* defines identity in terms of personal goals and attributes; socially connected *collectivism* gives priority to group goals and to one's social identity and commitments.

6-4: How do nature and nurture interact to define us as male or female?

Gender is a social definition of what it means to be male or female. Although similar in their overall genetic makeup, males and females have different sex chromosomes, leading to differing concentrations of sex hormones, which trigger differences in size, age of onset of puberty, and life expectancy. They also differ psychologically in some areas, such as *aggression* and connectedness. Gender differences vary widely, depending upon cultural socialization through *social learning* and *gender schemas.* Psychologists use a biopsychosocial approach to study the interaction of nature and nurture in these and other areas.

>> REHEARSE IT!

1. Normal levels of stimulation are important during infancy and early childhood because during these years,
    a. a rich environment can override a child's genetic limits.
    b. experience activates and preserves neural connections that might otherwise die off from disuse.
    c. experience stimulates the growth of billions of new brain cells.
    d. experience triggers the production of human growth hormones.

2. Children and youth are particularly responsive to influences of their
    a. peers.
    b. fathers.
    c. teachers and caretakers.
    d. mothers.

3. In psychology, *personal space* refers to the portable buffer zone we like to maintain around our bodies. This space varies according to cultural norms. Which of the following prefer less personal space than the others?

a. American
b. British
c. Arabs
d. Scandinavians

4. Cultural values vary over time and place. Western cultures are to _____ as Asian and African cultures are to _____.

   a. obedience; emotional closeness
   b. independence; social harmony
   c. loyalty; interdependence
   d. respect; morality

5. Human developmental processes tend to _____ from one group to another because we are members of _____.

   a. be the same; the same ethnic group

b. be the same; the same species
c. differ; different species
d. differ; different ethnic groups

6. The fertilized egg will develop into a boy if it receives

   a. an X chromosome from its mother.
   b. an X chromosome from its father.
   c. a Y chromosome from its mother.
   d. a Y chromosome from its father.

7. Gender roles vary across cultures and over time. "Gender role" refers to our

   a. sense of being male or female.
   b. expectations about the way males and females behave.
   c. biological sex.

d. beliefs about how men and women should earn a living.

8. Psychologists differentiate between our biological sex and our gender. As a consequence of the gender assigned to us by society, we develop a gender identity, which means that we

   a. exhibit traditional masculine or feminine roles.
   b. are socially categorized as male or female.
   c. have a sense of being male or female.
   d. have an ambiguous biological sex.

Answers: 1. b, 2. a, 3. c, 4. b, 5. b, 6. d, 7. b, 8. c

>> TERMS AND CONCEPTS TO REMEMBER

culture, p. 82
norm, p. 83
personal space, p. 83
individualism, p. 84
collectivism, p. 84

aggression, p. 88
X chromosome, p. 90
Y chromosome, p. 90
testosterone, p. 90
role, p. 90

gender role, p. 90
gender identity, p. 92
gender-typing, p. 92
social learning theory, p. 92
gender schema theory, p. 92

>> TEST YOURSELF

1. To predict whether a teenager smokes, ask how many of the teen's friends smoke. One explanation for this correlation is peer influence. What's another?

2. How do individualist and collectivist cultures differ?

3. What are gender roles, and what do their variations tell us about our human capacity for learning and adaptation?

   (Answers in Appendix C.)

Multiple-choice **self-tests** and more may be found at www.worthpublishers.com/myers.

Developing Through the Life Span

Developing Through the Life Span

As we journey through life—from womb to tomb—when, how, and why do we develop? Virtually all of us began walking around age 1 and talking by age 2. As children, we engaged in social play in preparation for life's work. As adults, we all smile and cry, love and loathe, and occasionally ponder the fact that someday we will die. *Developmental psychology* examines how people are continually developing, physically, cognitively, and socially, from infancy through old age. Much of its research centers on three major issues:

1. *Nature/nurture:* How do genetic inheritance (*our nature*) and experience (*the nurture we receive*) influence our development?

2. *Continuity/stages:* Is development a gradual, continuous process like riding an escalator, or does it proceed through a sequence of separate stages, like climbing rungs on a ladder?

3. *Stability/change:* Do our early personality traits persist through life, or do we become different persons as we age?

In other modules, we engaged the nature/nurture issue. In Modules 7 through 10, we reflect on the continuity and stability issues throughout the life span.

" Nature is all that a man brings with him into the world; nurture is every influence that affects him after his birth."

Francis Galton, *English Men of Science*, 1874

Developmental Issues, Prenatal Development, and the Newborn

From the union of sperm and egg to the birth of the newborn, development progresses in an orderly, though fragile, sequence. By birth, infants are equipped with perceptual and behavioral abilities that facilitate their survival. In this module, we look at what developmental biologists have learned about life before birth. We will also consider some of the findings of **developmental psychology**—the study of our lifelong physical, mental, and social development—about the newborn. But first let's focus on a couple of issues that preoccupy developmental psychologists.

Two Major Developmental Issues

7-1: What conclusions can we draw from research on the issues of continuity versus stages and of stability versus change in lifelong development?

Any survey of developmental psychology must consider three pervasive issues. The first—how development is steered by genes and by experience—recurs throughout this text. Here we consider the second issue, whether development is a gradual, continuous process or a series of discrete stages, and the third, whether development is characterized more by stability over time or by change.

■ **developmental psychology** a branch of psychology that studies physical, cognitive, and social change throughout the life span.

Continuity and Stages

Adults are vastly different from infants. But do they differ as a giant redwood differs from its seedling—a difference created by gradual, cumulative growth? Or do they differ as a butterfly differs from a caterpillar—a difference of distinct stages?

Generally speaking, researchers who emphasize experience and learning see development as a slow, continuous shaping process. Those who emphasize biological maturation tend to see development as a sequence of genetically predisposed stages or steps: Although progress through the various stages may be quick or slow, everyone passes through the stages in the same order.

Are there clear-cut stages of psychological development, as there are physical stages such as walking before running? Several *stage theories* of development have been proposed and tested over the years. For example, developmental psychologist Jean Piaget (pronounced Pee-ah-ZHAY) proposed that all children pass through four discrete, age-linked stages of cognitive development, each stage with its own specific conceptual (thinking) abilities. But subsequent research has suggested that cognitive development, though occurring basically in the sequence Piaget proposed, is more continuous, with some conceptual abilities occurring at earlier ages than Piaget supposed. Similarly, research has tested other stage theories and found that life does not occur through a fixed, predictable series of steps.

Although research casts doubt on the idea that life proceeds through neatly defined, age-linked stages, the concept of stage remains useful. The human brain does experience growth spurts during childhood and puberty that correspond roughly to Piaget's stages (Thatcher & others, 1987). And stage theories contribute a developmental perspective on the whole life span, by suggesting how people of one age think and act differently when they arrive at a later age.

Stages of the life cycle

TOO MUCH COFFEE MAN BY SHANNON WHEELER

LIFE:

PLAY, PLAY, PLAY, PLAY, PLAY, PLAY, PLAY, PLAY, PLAY, PLAY,
PLAY, PLAY, PLAY, PLAY, PLAY, PLAY, PLAY, PLAY, PLAY, PLAY,
PLAY, PLAY, PLAY, PLAY, PLAY, PLAY, PLAY, PLAY, PLAY, PLAY,
PLAY, SCHOOL, PLAY, SCHOOL, PLAY, SCHOOL, PLAY, SCHOOL,
SCHOOL, SCHOOL, SCHOOL, SCHOOL, SCHOOL, SCHOOL, SCHOOL,
SCHOOL, SCHOOL, SCHOOL, SCHOOL, SCHOOL, SCHOOL, SCHOOL,
SCHOOL, SCHOOL, SCHOOL, SCHOOL, SCHOOL, SCHOOL, SCHOOL,
FIRST LOVE, BRIEF HAPPINESS, BREAK UP, REGRET, SCHOOL,
SCHOOL, SCHOOL, SCHOOL, SCHOOL, SCHOOL, SCHOOL, SCHOOL,
SCHOOL, SCHOOL, SCHOOL, SCHOOL, SCHOOL, SCHOOL, SCHOOL,
PLAY, WORK, PLAY, WORK, PLAY, WORK, PLAY, WORK,
IDEALISM, EFFORT, REJECTION, FAILURE, WORK, EFFORT, FAILURE,
COMPROMISE, WORK, WORK, WORK, WORK, WORK, WORK, PLAY,
COMMITMENT, WORK, WORK, WORK, WORK, WORK, WORK, PLAY,
WORK, WORK, WORK, WORK, WORK, WORK, WORK, WORK, PLAY,
WORK, WORK, WORK, WORK, WORK, WORK, WORK, WORK, PLAY,
WORK, WORK, WORK, WORK, WORK, WORK, WORK, WORK, PLAY,
WORK, WORK, WORK, WORK, WORK, WORK, WORK, WORK, PLAY,
WORK, WORK, WORK, WORK, WORK, WORK, WORK, WORK, PLAY,
WORK, WORK, WORK, WORK, WORK, WORK, WORK, WORK, PLAY,
WORK, WORK, WORK, WORK, WORK, WORK, WORK, WORK, PLAY,
WORK, WORK, WORK, WORK, WORK, WORK, WORK, WORK, PLAY,
WORK, WORK, WORK, WORK, WORK, WORK, WORK, WORK, PLAY,
WORK, WORK, WORK, WORK, WORK, WORK, WORK, WORK, PLAY,
WORK, WORK, WORK, WORK, WORK, WORK, WORK, WORK, PLAY,
WORK, WORK, WORK, WORK, WORK, WORK, WORK, WORK, PLAY,
WORK, WORK, WORK, WORK, WORK, WORK, WORK, WORK, PLAY,
WORK, WORK, WORK, WORK, WORK, WORK, WORK, WORK, PLAY,
RETIRE, PLAY, DIE.

©Shannon Wheeler

© The New Yorker Collection, 1998, Peter Mueller from cartoonbank.com. All Rights Reserved.

As adults grow older, there is continuity of self.

> "At 70, I would say the advantage is that you take life more calmly. You know that 'this, too, shall pass'!"
>
> Eleanor Roosevelt, 1954

■ **zygote** the fertilized egg; it enters a 2-week period of rapid cell division and develops into an embryo.

■ **embryo** the developing human organism from about 2 weeks after fertilization through the second month.

Stability and Change

This leads us to the next question: Over time, are people's personalities consistent, or do they change? If reunited with a long-lost grade school friend, would you instantly recognize that "it's the same old Andy"? Or does a person befriended during one period of life seem like a different person at a later period?

Researchers who have followed lives through time have found evidence for both stability and change. There is continuity to personality and yet, happily for troubled children and adolescents, life is a process of becoming: The struggles of the present may be laying a foundation for a happier tomorrow. More specifically, researchers generally agree on the following points:

1. The first two years of life provide a poor basis for predicting a person's eventual traits (Kagan & others, 1978, 1998). Older children and adolescents also change. Although delinquent children later have elevated rates of work problems, substance abuse, and crime, many confused and troubled children have blossomed into mature, successful adults (Moffitt & others, 2002; Roberts & others, 2001; Thomas & Chess, 1986). As people grow older, personality gradually stabilizes (Johnson & others, 2005; Vaidya & others, 2002).

2. Some characteristics, such as temperament, are more stable than others, such as social attitudes (Moss & Susman, 1980). When a research team led by Avshalom Caspi (2003) studied 1000 New Zealanders from age 3 to 26, they were struck by the consistency of temperament and emotionality across time.

3. In some ways, we all change with age. Most shy, fearful toddlers begin opening up by age 4, and most people become calmer and more self-disciplined, agreeable, and self-confident in the years after adolescence (McCrae & Costa, 1994; Roberts & others, 2003, 2006). Conscientiousness increases especially during the twenties, and agreeableness during the thirties (Srivastava & others, 2003). Many a 20-year-old goof-off has matured into a 40-year-old business or cultural leader. Such changes can occur without changing a person's position *relative to others* of the same age. The hard-driving young adult may mellow by later life yet still be a relatively hard-driving senior citizen.

Finally, we should remember that life requires *both* stability and change. Stability enables us to depend on others, provides our identity, and motivates our concern for the healthy development of children. Change motivates our concerns about present influences, sustains our hope for a brighter future, and lets us adapt and grow with experience.

Conception and Prenatal Development

7-2 : How does life develop before birth?

Conception

Nothing is more natural than a species reproducing itself. Yet nothing is more wondrous. Consider human reproduction.

The process starts when a woman's ovary releases a mature egg—a cell roughly the size of the period at the end of this sentence—and the 200 million or more sperm deposited during intercourse begin their race upstream like space voyagers approaching a huge planet, 85,000 times their own size. The relatively few reaching the egg release digestive enzymes that eat away its protective coating (**FIGURE 7.1**). As soon as one sperm begins to penetrate and is welcomed in, the egg's surface blocks out the others. Before half a day elapses, the egg nucleus and the sperm nucleus fuse. The two have become one. Consider it your most fortunate of moments. Among 200 million sperm, the one needed to make you, in combination with that one particular egg, won the race.

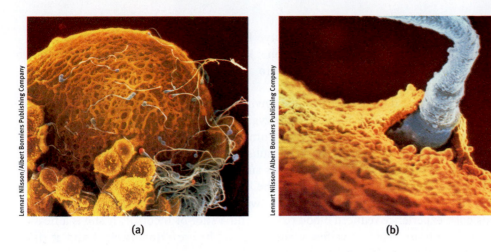

(a)   (b)

Lennart Nilsson/Albert Bonniers Publishing Company

FIGURE 7.1

Life is sexually transmitted

(a) Sperm cells surround an ovum.
(b) As one sperm penetrates the egg's jellylike outer coating, a series of chemical events begins that will cause sperm and egg to fuse into a single cell. If all goes well, that cell will subdivide again and again to emerge 9 months later as a 100-trillion-cell human being.

Prenatal Development

Fewer than half of all fertilized eggs, called **zygotes,** survive beyond the first 2 weeks (Grobstein, 1979; Hall, 2004). But for you and me, good fortune prevailed. One cell became 2, then 4—each just like the first—until this cell division had produced a zygote of some 100 cells within the first week. Then the cells began to differentiate—to specialize in structure and function. How identical cells do this—as if one decides "I'll become a brain, you become intestines!"—is a scientific puzzle that developmental biologists are just beginning to solve.

About 10 days after conception, the increasingly diverse cells attach to the mother's uterine wall, beginning approximately 37 weeks of the closest human relationship. The zygote's inner cells become the **embryo** (**FIGURE 7.2**). Over the next 6 weeks, organs begin to form and function. The heart begins to beat.

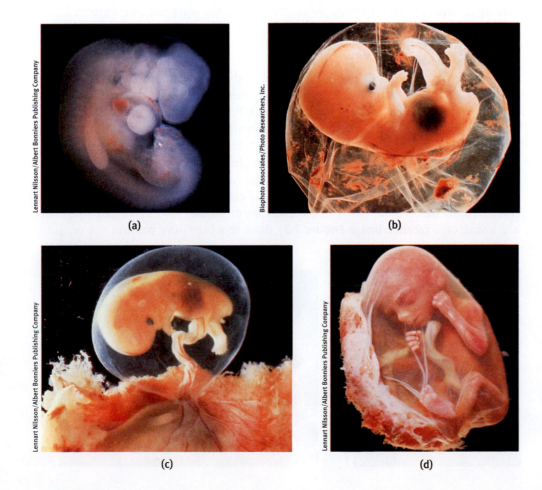

(a)   (b)

(c)   (d)

FIGURE 7.2

Prenatal development

(a) The embryo grows and develops rapidly. At 40 days, the spine is visible and the arms and legs are beginning to grow. (b) Five days later, the inch-long embryo's proportions have begun to change. The rest of the body is now bigger than the head, and the arms and legs have grown noticeably. (c) By the end of the second month, when the fetal period begins, facial features, hands, and feet have formed. (d) As the fetus enters the fourth month, its 3 ounces could fit in the palm of your hand.

By 9 weeks after conception, the embryo looks unmistakably human. It is now a **fetus** (Latin for "offspring" or "young one"). During the sixth month, organs such as the stomach are sufficiently developed to allow a prematurely born fetus a chance of survival.

At each prenatal stage, genetic *and* environmental factors affect our development. The *placenta,* which formed as the zygote's outer cells attached to the uterine wall, transfers nutrients and oxygen from mother to fetus. The placenta also screens out many potentially harmful substances. But some substances slip by, among them **teratogens,** harmful agents such as certain viruses and drugs. If the mother is a heroin addict, her baby will be born a heroin addict. If she carries the AIDS virus, her baby may also. A pregnant woman never smokes alone; she and her fetus both experience reduced blood oxygen and a shot of nicotine. If she is a heavy smoker, her fetus may receive fewer nutrients and be born underweight and at risk for various problems (Pringle & others, 2005).

There is no known safe amount of alcohol during pregnancy. Alcohol enters the woman's bloodstream—and her fetus'—and depresses activity in both their central nervous systems. Even light drinking can affect the fetal brain (Braun, 1996; Ikonomidou & others, 2000), and persistent heavy drinking will put the fetus at risk for birth defects and mental retardation. For 1 in 750 infants, the effects are visible as **fetal alcohol syndrome (FAS),** marked by a small, misproportioned head and life-long brain abnormalities.

The Competent Newborn

7-3 : What are some of the newborn's abilities?

Having survived prenatal hazards, we as newborns came equipped with automatic responses ideally suited for our survival. We withdrew our limbs to escape pain. If a cloth over our face interfered with our breathing, we turned our head from side to side and swiped at it.

New parents are often in awe of the coordinated sequence of *reflexes* by which their baby gets food. When something touches their cheek, babies turn toward that touch, open their mouth, and vigorously *root* for a nipple. Finding one, they automatically close on it and begin *sucking*—which itself requires a coordinated sequence of reflexive *tonguing, swallowing,* and *breathing.* Failing to find satisfaction, the hungry baby may *cry*—a behavior parents are predisposed to find highly unpleasant and very rewarding to relieve.

We are born preferring sights and sounds that facilitate social responsiveness, and our sensory and perceptual abilities will develop continuously over the next months. As newborns, we turn our heads in the direction of human voices. We gaze longer at a drawing of a facelike image (**FIGURE 7.3**) than at a bull's-eye pattern; yet we gaze

---

Prenatal development
zygote: conception to 2 weeks
embryo: 2 weeks through 8 weeks
fetus: 9 weeks to birth.

"You shall conceive and bear a son. So then drink no wine or strong drink."

Judges 13:7

■ **fetus** the developing human organism from 9 weeks after conception to birth.

■ **teratogens** agents, such as chemicals and viruses, that can reach the embryo or fetus during prenatal development and cause harm.

■ **fetal alcohol syndrome (FAS)** physical and cognitive abnormalities in children caused by a pregnant woman's heavy drinking. In severe cases, symptoms include noticeable facial misproportions.

Prepared to feed and eat
Animals are predisposed to respond to their offsprings' cries for nourishment.

more at a bull's-eye pattern—which has contrasts much like those of the human eye—than at a solid disk (Fantz, 1961). We prefer to look at objects 8 to 12 inches away, which, wonder of wonders, just happens to be the approximate distance between a nursing infant's eyes and its mother's (Maurer & Maurer, 1988).

Within days after birth, our brain's neural networks were stamped with the smell of our mother's body. Thus, a week-old nursing baby, placed between a gauze pad from its mother's bra and one from another nursing mother, will usually turn toward the smell of its own mother's pad (MacFarlane, 1978). At 3 weeks, if given a pacifier that sometimes turns on recordings of its mother's voice and sometimes that of a female stranger's, an infant will suck more vigorously when it hears its now-familiar mother's voice (Mills & Melhuish, 1974). So not only can we as young infants see what we need to see, and smell and hear well, but we are already using our sensory equipment to learn.

FIGURE 7.3

Newborns' preference for faces
When shown these two stimuli with the same elements, Italian newborns spent nearly twice as many seconds looking at the facelike image (Johnson & Morton, 1991). Canadian newborns—average age 53 minutes in one study—display the same apparently inborn preference to look toward faces (Mondloch & others, 1999).

REVIEWING

>> MODULE REVIEW

7-1: What conclusions can we draw from research on the issues of continuity versus stages and of stability versus change in lifelong development?

Later studies have modified some of the stage theories, but stage theories usefully alert us to differences among people of different ages. The discovery that people's traits continue to change in later life has intensified interest in lifelong development. Nevertheless, there is also an underlying consistency to most people's temperament and personality traits.

7-2: How does life develop before birth?

Developmental psychologists study physical, mental, and social changes throughout the life span. The life cycle begins at conception, when one sperm cell unites with an egg. The nuclei of the egg and sperm then fuse to form a *zygote*. Attached to the uterine wall, the developing *embryo's* body organs begin to form and function. By 9 weeks, the *fetus* is recognizably human. *Teratogens* are potentially harmful agents that can pass through the placental screen and harm the developing embryo or fetus.

7-3: What are some of the newborn's abilities?

Newborns are born with sensory equipment and reflexes that facilitate their survival and their social interactions with adults. For example, they quickly learn to discriminate their mother's smell and sound.

>> REHEARSE IT!

1. Developmental researchers who emphasize learning and experience tend to believe in _____; those who emphasize biological maturation tend to believe in _____.
   a. nature; nurture
   b. continuity; stages
   c. stability; change
   d. randomness; predictability

2. Although development is lifelong, there is stability of personality over time. For example,
   a. most personality traits emerge in infancy and persist throughout life.
   b. temperament tends to remain stable throughout life.
   c. few people change significantly after adolescence.
   d. people tend to undergo greater personality changes as they age.

3. Developmental psychologists tend to focus on three major issues. Which of the following is not one of those issues?
   a. Nature/nurture
   b. Reflexes/unlearned behaviors
   c. Stability/change
   d. Continuity/stages

4. The 9 months of prenatal development prepare the individual for survival outside the womb. The body organs first begin to form and function during the period of the _____; within 6 months, during the period of the _____, the organs are sufficiently functional to allow a chance of survival.

   a. zygote; embryo
   b. zygote; fetus
   c. embryo; fetus
   d. placenta; fetus

5. Teratogens are chemicals that pass through the placenta's screen and may harm an embryo or fetus. Which of the following is not a teratogen?

   a. Oxygen
   b. Heroin
   c. Alcohol
   d. Nicotine

6. Stroke a newborn's cheek and the infant will root for a nipple. This illustrates

   a. a reflex.
   b. sensorimotor learning.
   c. differentiation.
   d. a gender difference.

Answers: 1. b, 2. b, 3. b, 4. c, 5. a, 6. a.

>> TERMS AND CONCEPTS TO REMEMBER

developmental psychology, p. 99
zygote, p. 101

embryo, p. 101
fetus, p. 102

teratogens, p. 102
fetal alcohol syndrome (FAS), p. 102

>> TEST YOURSELF

1. Your friend—a heavy smoker—hopes to become pregnant soon and has stopped smoking. Why is this a good idea?

   (Answer in Appendix C.)

*Multiple-choice **self-tests** and more may be found at www.worthpublishers.com/myers.*

Infancy and Childhood

During infancy, a baby grows from newborn to toddler, and during childhood from toddler to teenager. We all traveled this path, developing physically, cognitively, and socially. From infancy on, brain and mind, neural hardware and cognitive software, develop together.

Physical Development

Cognitive Development

Social Development

Physical Development

8-1: How do the brain and motor skills develop during infancy and childhood?

Brain Development

In your mother's womb, your developing body formed nerve cells at the explosive rate of nearly one-quarter million per *minute.* On the day you were born, you had most of the brain cells you would ever have. However, your nervous system was immature: After birth, the neural networks that eventually enabled you to walk, talk, and re-member had a wild growth spurt. From ages 3 to 6, the most rapid growth is in the brain's frontal lobes, which enable rational planning (and which continue develop-ing into adolescence and beyond). The association areas—those linked with thinking, memory, and language—are the last cortical areas to develop. As they do, mental abil-ities surge ahead (Chugani & Phelps, 1986; Thatcher & others, 1987). Fiber pathways supporting language and agility proliferate into puberty, after which a *pruning process* shuts down excess connections and strengthens others (Paus & others, 1999; Thomp-son & others, 2000).

As a flower unfolds in accord with its genetic instructions, so do we, in the orderly sequence of biological growth processes called **maturation.** Maturation decrees many of our commonalities—from standing before walking, to using nouns before adjectives. Severe deprivation or abuse can retard development, and ample parental experiences of talking and reading will help sculpt neural connections. Yet the ge-netic growth tendencies are inborn. Maturation sets the basic course of development; experience adjusts it.

© The New Yorker Collection, 2001, Robert Weber from cartoon-bank.com. All Rights Reserved.

"This is the path to adulthood. You're here."

Motor Development

The developing brain enables physical coordination. As an infant's muscles and ner-vous system mature, more complicated skills emerge. With minor exceptions, the se-quence of physical (motor) development is universal. Babies roll over before they sit unsupported, and they usually creep on all fours before they walk (**FIGURE 8.1**). These behaviors reflect not imitation but a maturing nervous system; blind children, too, crawl before they walk.

There are, however, individual differences in timing. In the United States, for ex-ample, 25 percent of all babies walk by age 11 months, 50 percent within a week after their first birthday, and 90 percent by age 15 months (Frankenburg & others, 1992). The recommended infant "back-to-sleep" position (putting babies to sleep on their backs to reduce the risk of a smothering crib death) has been associated with some-what later crawling but not with later walking (Davis & others, 1998; Lipsitt, 2003).

Genes play a major role in motor development. Identical twins typically begin sit-ting up and walking on nearly the same day (Wilson, 1979). Maturation—including

■ **maturation** biological growth processes that enable orderly changes in behavior, rel-atively uninfluenced by experience.

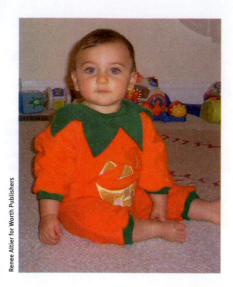

Renee Altier for Worth Publishers

Jim Craigmyle/Corbis

Phototake Inc./Alamy Images

Profimedia.CZ s.r.o./Alamy

FIGURE 8.1
Triumphant toddlers
Sit, crawl, walk, run—the sequence of these motor development milestones is the same the world around, though babies reach them at varying ages.

the rapid development of the cerebellum at the back of the brain—creates our readiness to learn walking at about age 1. Experience before that time has a limited effect. This is true for other physical skills, including bowel and bladder control. Before necessary muscular and neural maturation, no pleading, harassment, or punishment will produce successful toilet training.

Maturation and Infant Memory

Our earliest memories seldom predate our third birthdays. We see this *infantile amnesia* in the memories of some preschoolers who experienced an emergency fire evacuation caused by a burning popcorn maker. Seven years later they were able to recall the alarm and what caused it—*if* they were 4 to 5 years old at the time. Those experiencing the event as 3-year-olds could not remember the cause and usually misrecalled being already outside when the alarm sounded (Pillemer, 1995). Other studies confirm that the average age of earliest conscious memory is 3.5 years (Bauer, 2002). By 4 to 5 years, childhood amnesia is giving way to remembered experiences (Bruce & others, 2000).

Can you recall your first day of preschool (or your third birthday party)?

■ **cognition** all the mental activities associated with thinking, knowing, remembering, and communicating.

■ **schema** a concept or framework that organizes and interprets information.

■ **assimilation** interpreting one's new experience in terms of one's existing schemas.

■ **accommodation** adapting one's current understandings (schemas) to incorporate new information.

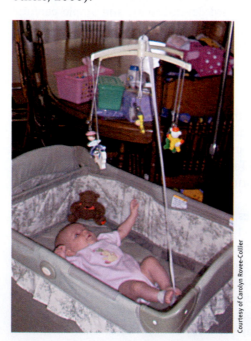

Courtesy of Carolyn Rovee-Collier

FIGURE 8.2
Infant at work
Babies only 3 months old can learn that kicking moves a mobile—and can retain that learning for a month. (From Rovee-Collier, 1989, 1997.)

Although we *consciously* recall little from before age 4, our memory is processing information during and beyond those early years. Given occasional reminders, 3-month-olds who learn to propel a mobile by moving their leg will retain that association for at least a month (**FIGURE 8.2**). And when 10-year-olds are shown photos of preschoolers and asked to spot their former classmates, they recognize only 1 in 5 of their onetime compatriots. Yet their physiological responses (measured as skin perspiration) are greater to their former classmates, whether or not they consciously recognize them (Newcombe & others, 2000). What the conscious mind does not know and cannot express in words, the nervous system somehow remembers.

Cognitive Development

8-2 : How did Piaget view the development of a child's mind, and what are current researchers' views?

"Who knows the thoughts of a child?" wondered poet Nora Perry. As much as anyone of his generation, developmental psychologist Jean Piaget (pronounced Pee-ah-ZHAY) knew. His interest began in 1920, when he was in Paris developing questions for children's intelligence tests. While administering tests, Piaget became intrigued by children's *wrong* answers to some questions. Where others saw childish mistakes, Piaget saw intelligence at work. The errors made by children of a given age, he noted, were often strikingly similar.

A half-century spent with children convinced Piaget that a child's mind is not a miniature model of an adult's. Thanks partly to his work, we now understand that children reason *differently* in "wildly illogical ways about problems whose solutions are self-evident to adults" (Brainerd, 1996).

Cognition refers to all the mental activities associated with thinking, knowing, remembering, and communicating. Piaget proposed that a child's mind develops through a series of stages, in an upward march from the newborn's simple reflexes to the adult's abstract reasoning power. Thus, an 8-year-old can comprehend things a 2- or 3-year-old cannot, such as the analogy that "getting an idea is like having a light turn on in your head," or that a miniature slide is too small for sliding, and a miniature car is much too small to get into (**FIGURE 8.3**). But our adult minds likewise engage in reasoning uncomprehended by 8-year-olds.

Jean Piaget (1896–1980)
"If we examine the intellectual development of the individual or of the whole of humanity, we shall find that the human spirit goes through a certain number of stages, each different from the other" (1930).

Bill Anderson/Photo Researchers, Inc.

Both photos: Courtesy Judy DeLoache

FIGURE 8.3
Scale errors
Psychologists Judy DeLoache, David Uttal, and Karl Rosengren (2004) report that 18- to 30-month-old children may fail to take the size of an object into account when trying to perform impossible actions with it. At left, a 21-month-old attempts to slide down a miniature slide. At right, a 24-month-old opens the door to a miniature car and tries to step inside.

Piaget believed the driving force behind this intellectual progression is our unceasing struggle to make sense of our experiences. His core idea is that "children are active thinkers, constantly trying to construct more advanced understandings of the world" (Siegler & Ellis, 1996). To this end, the maturing brain builds **schemas,** concepts or mental molds into which we pour our experiences (**FIGURE 8.4**). By adulthood we have built countless schemas, ranging from cats and dogs to our concept of love.

To explain how we use and adjust our schemas, Piaget proposed two concepts. First, we **assimilate** new experiences—we interpret them in terms of our current understandings (schemas). Having a simple schema for *dog,* for example, a toddler may call all four-legged animals *doggies*. But we also adjust, or **accommodate,** our schemas to fit the particulars of new experiences. The child soon

FIGURE 8.4
An impossible object
Look carefully at the "devil's tuning fork" at left. Now look away—no, better first study it some more—and then look away and draw it. . . . Not so easy, is it? Because this tuning fork is an impossible object, you have no schema for such an image.

learns that the original *doggie* schema is too broad and accommodates by refining the category. As children interact with the world, they construct and modify their schemas.

To appreciate how a child's mind grows, let's look at Piaget's stages in the light of our current thinking about cognitive development.

Piaget's Theory and Current Thinking

Piaget believed that children construct their understandings from interactions with the world and experience spurts of change followed by greater stability as they move from one cognitive developmental plateau to the next. These plateaus form four stages (**TABLE 8.1**), each with distinctive characteristics that permit specific kinds of thinking.

"Childhood has its own way of seeing, thinking, and feeling, and there is nothing more foolish than the attempt to put ours in its place."

Philosopher Jean-Jacques Rousseau, 1798

TABLE 8.1

PIAGET'S STAGES OF COGNITIVE DEVELOPMENT

Typical Age Range	Description of Stage	Developmental Phenomena
Birth to nearly 2 years	*Sensorimotor* Experiencing the world through senses and actions (looking, hearing, touching, mouthing, and grasping)	• Object permanence • Stranger anxiety
2 to about 6 or 7 years	*Preoperational* Representing things with words and images; using intuitive rather than logical reasoning	• Pretend play • Egocentrism
About 7 to 11 years	*Concrete operational* Thinking logically about concrete events; grasping concrete analogies and performing arithmetical operations	• Conservation • Mathematical transformations
About 12 through adulthood	*Formal operational* Abstract reasoning	• Abstract logic • Potential for mature moral reasoning

Milt and Patti Putnam/Corbis

Sensorimotor Stage

In the **sensorimotor stage,** from birth to nearly age 2, babies take in the world through their sensory and motor interactions with objects—through looking, hearing, touching, mouthing, and grasping.

Very young babies seem to live in the present: Out of sight is out of mind. In one test, Piaget showed an infant an appealing toy and then flopped his beret over it to see whether the infant would search for it. Before the age of 6 months, the infant did not. Young infants lack **object permanence**—the awareness that objects continue to exist when not perceived (**FIGURE 8.5**). By 8 months, infants begin exhibiting memory for things no longer seen. If you hide a toy, the infant will momentarily look for it. Within another month or two, the infant will look for it even after being restrained for several seconds.

FIGURE 8.5

Object permanence

Infants younger than 6 months seldom understand that things continue to exist when they are out of sight. But for this infant, out of sight is definitely not out of mind.

Doug Goodman

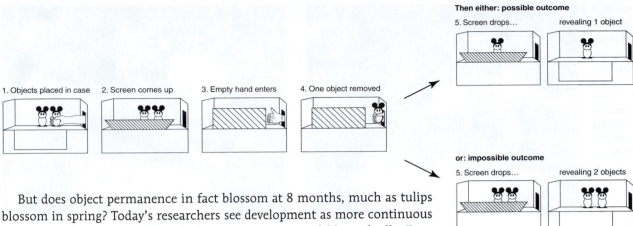

Then either: possible outcome

5. Screen drops...   revealing 1 object

1. Objects placed in case   2. Screen comes up   3. Empty hand enters   4. One object removed

or: impossible outcome

5. Screen drops...   revealing 2 objects

FIGURE 8.6
Baby math
Shown a numerically impossible outcome, 5-month-old infants stare longer. (From Wynn, 1992.)

But does object permanence in fact blossom at 8 months, much as tulips blossom in spring? Today's researchers see development as more continuous than Piaget did, and they believe object permanence unfolds gradually. Even young infants will at least momentarily look for a toy where they saw it hidden a second before.

Researchers believe Piaget and his followers underestimated young children's competence. Consider some simple experiments that demonstrate baby logic:

- Like adults staring in disbelief at a magic trick (the "Whoa!" look), infants look longer at an unexpected scene of a car seeming to pass through a solid object, a ball stopping in midair, or an object violating object permanence by magically disappearing (Baillargeon, 1995, 1998, 2004; Wellman & Gelman, 1992). Babies seem to have a more intuitive grasp of simple laws of physics than Piaget realized.

- Babies also have a head for numbers. Karen Wynn (1992, 2000) showed 5-month-olds one or two objects. Then she hid the objects behind a screen, and visibly removed or added one (**FIGURE 8.6**). When she lifted the screen, the infants sometimes did a double take, staring longer when shown a wrong number of objects. But were they just responding to a greater or smaller mass of objects, rather than a change in number (Feigenson & others, 2002)? Later experiments showed that babies' number sense extends to larger numbers and such things as drumbeats and motions (Lipton & Spelke, 2003; McCrink & Wynn, 2004; Spelke, 2000; Wynn & others, 2002). If accustomed to a Daffy Duck puppet jumping three times on stage, they show surprise if it jumps only twice. Clearly, infants are smarter than Piaget appreciated. Even as babies, we had a lot on our minds.

Preoperational Stage

Piaget believed that until about age 6 or 7, children are in a **preoperational stage**—too young to perform mental operations. For a 5-year-old, the milk that seems "too much" in a tall, narrow glass may become an acceptable amount if poured into a short, wide glass. Focusing only on the height dimension, this child cannot perform the operation of mentally pouring the milk back, because he lacks the concept of **conservation**—the principle that quantity remains the same despite changes in shape. Closed beakers with identical volumes seem suddenly to hold different amounts after one is merely inverted (see **FIGURE 8.7** on the next page).

Piaget did not view the stage transitions as abrupt. Even so, symbolic thinking appears at an earlier age than he supposed. Judy DeLoache (1987) discovered this when she showed children a model of a room and hid a model toy in it (a miniature stuffed dog behind a miniature couch). The 2½-year-olds easily remembered where to find the miniature toy, but they could not use the model to locate an actual stuffed dog behind a couch in a real room. Three-year-olds—only 6 months older—usually went right to the actual stuffed animal in the real room, showing they *could* think of the model as a symbol for the room. Piaget probably would have been surprised.

■ **sensorimotor stage** in Piaget's theory, the stage (from birth to about 2 years of age) during which infants know the world mostly in terms of their sensory impressions and motor activities.

■ **object permanence** the awareness that things continue to exist even when not perceived.

■ **preoperational stage** in Piaget's theory, the stage (from about 2 to 6 or 7 years of age) during which a child learns to use language but does not yet comprehend the mental operations of concrete logic.

■ **conservation** the principle (which Piaget believed to be a part of concrete operational reasoning) that properties such as mass, volume, and number remain the same despite changes in the forms of objects.

Question: If most 2½-year-olds do not understand how miniature dolls and toys can symbolize real objects, should anatomically correct dolls be used when questioning such children about alleged physical or sexual abuse? Judy DeLoache (1995) reports that "very young children do not find it natural or easy to use a doll as a representation of themselves."

Ontario Science Center

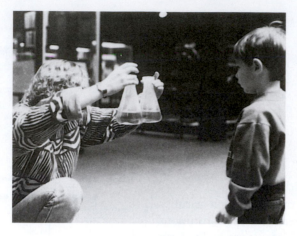

FIGURE 8.7
Piaget's test of conservation
This preoperational child does not yet understand the principle of conservation of substance. Closed beakers with identical volumes seem suddenly to hold different amounts after one is merely inverted.

> "It is a rare privilege to watch the birth, growth, and first feeble struggles of a living human mind."
>
> Annie Sullivan, in Helen Keller's *The Story of My Life*, 1903

Egocentrism Piaget contended that preschool children are **egocentric:** They have difficulty perceiving things from another's point of view. Asked to "show Mommy your picture," 2-year-old Gabriella holds the picture up facing her own eyes. Three-year-old Gray makes himself "invisible" by putting his hands over his eyes, assuming that if he can't see someone, they can't see him. Children's conversations also reveal their egocentrism, as one young boy demonstrated (Phillips, 1969, p. 61):

"Do you have a brother?"
"Yes."
"What's his name?"
"Jim."
"Does Jim have a brother?"
"No."

TV-watching preschoolers who block your view of the TV assume that you see what they see. They simply have not yet developed the ability to take another's viewpoint. Even as adults, we often overestimate the extent to which others share our opinions and perspective, as when we assume that something will be clear to others if it is clear to us, or that e-mail recipients will "hear" our "just kidding" intent (Epley & others, 2004; Kruger & others, 2005). Children, however, are even more susceptible to this "curse of knowledge."

Theory of Mind When Little Red Riding Hood realizes her "grandmother" is really a wolf, she swiftly revises her ideas about the creature's intentions and races away. Preschoolers, although still egocentric, develop this ability to infer others' mental states when they begin forming a **theory of mind** (a term first coined by psychologists David Premack and Guy Woodruff, to describe chimpanzees' seeming ability to read intentions).

As their ability to take another's perspective develops, children seek to understand what made a playmate angry, when a sibling will share, and what might make a parent buy a toy. And they begin to tease, empathize, and persuade. Between about 3½ and 4½, children worldwide come to realize that others may hold false beliefs (Callaghan & others, 2005; Wellman & others, 2001; Zimmer, 2003). Jennifer Jenkins and Janet Astington (1996) showed Toronto children a Band Aids box and asked them what was inside. Expecting Band Aids, the children were surprised to discover that the box actually contained pencils. Asked what a child who had never seen the box would think was inside, 3-year-olds typically answered "pencils." By age 4 to 5, the children's "theory of mind" had leapt forward, and they delighted in anticipating their friends' false belief that the box would hold Band Aids.

Children with autism (see Close-Up: Autism) have an impaired ability to infer others' states of mind. And so, sometimes, do abusive parents, who have no understanding of children's greater egocentrism (Larrance & Twentyman, 1983).

Family Circus ® Bil Keane

TELL ME, JEFFY, WHAT WAS THIS FUN DREAM ABOUT LAST NIGHT?

8-21

"Don't you remember, Grandma? You were in it with me."

©Bil Keane, Inc. Reprinted with special permission of King Features Syndicate.

CLOSE-UP

Autism and "Mind-Blindness"

For reasons still debated, **autism** diagnoses have been increasing in recent years. This disorder, characterized by mild to severe deficiencies in communication and social interaction, is related to malfunctions of brain areas that enable attending to others. Its symptoms also may include speech difficulty and clumsiness. Autism's underlying cause—altered brain circuitry involving the fibers connecting distant neurons and enabling communication among brain regions—appears to result from an unknown number of genes interacting with the environment (Blakeslee, 2005; Wickelgren, 2005).

People with autism have an impaired theory of mind (Klein & Kihlstrom, 1998; Yirmiya & others, 1998). They have difficulty inferring others' thoughts and feelings. They do not appreciate that playmates and parents might view things differently. Mindreading that you do intuitively—is that face conveying a happy smile, a self-satisfied smirk, or a contemptuous sneer?—is difficult. Most children learn that another child's pouting mouth signals sadness, and that twinkling eyes mean happiness

Daniel Hulshizer / Associated Press, AP

Autism

Both of Bobbie Gallagher's children were diagnosed with autism, which is marked by deficient social communication and difficulty in grasping others' states of mind.

or mischief, but a child with autism fails to understand these signals (Frith & Frith, 2001). *Asperger syndrome*, sometimes classified as a "high functioning" form of autism, is marked by normal intelligence, often accompanied by exceptional skill or talent in a specific area, but deficient social and communication skills (and thus an inability to form normal peer relationships).

In a provocative new theory, psychologist Simon Baron-Cohen (2004, 2005) proposes that autism represents

an "extreme male brain." Girls are naturally predisposed to be "empathizers," he contends. They are better at reading facial expressions and gestures—a challenging task for those with autism. And, although the sexes overlap, boys are, he believes, better "systemizers"—they understand things according to rules or laws, as in mathematical and mechanical systems. "If two 'systemizers' have a child, this will increase the risk of the child having autism," he theorizes. And because of *assortative mating*—people's tendency to seek spouses who share their interests—two systemizers will indeed often mate. "I do not discount environmental factors," he notes. "I'm just saying, don't forget about biology."

Elizabeth Spelke (2005), however, is skeptical. From other research, she sees "no male advantage for perceiving objects or learning about mechanical systems. In most studies, male and female infants are found to discover the same things at the same times." So, is there any merit to the idea that children with autism (most of whom are male) have extreme male brains? Stay tuned for more research to come.

Concrete Operational Stage

By about 6 or 7 years of age, said Piaget, children enter the **concrete operational stage.** Given concrete materials, they begin to grasp conservation. Understanding that change in form does not mean change in quantity, they can mentally pour milk back and forth between glasses of different shapes. They also enjoy jokes that allow them to use this new understanding:

> Mr. Jones went into a restaurant and ordered a whole pizza for his dinner. When the waiter asked if he wanted it cut into 6 or 8 pieces, Mr. Jones said, "Oh, you'd better make it 6, I could never eat 8 pieces!" (McGhee, 1976)

Piaget believed that during the concrete operational stage, children fully gain the mental ability to comprehend mathematical transformations and conservation. When my daughter Laura was 6, I was astonished at her inability to reverse arithmetic operations. Asked, "What is 8 plus 4?" she required 5 seconds to compute "12," and another 5 seconds to then compute 12 minus 4. By age 8, she could answer the second question instantly.

■ **egocentrism** in Piaget's theory, the preoperational child's difficulty taking another's point of view.

■ **theory of mind** people's ideas about their own and others' mental states—about their feelings, perceptions, and thoughts, and the behavior these might predict.

■ **autism** a disorder that appears in childhood and is marked by deficient communication, social interaction, and understanding of others' states of mind.

■ **concrete operational stage** in Piaget's theory, the stage of cognitive development (from about 6 or 7 to 11 years of age) during which children gain the mental operations that enable them to think logically about concrete events.

Piaget was hardly the only psychologist to describe children's cognitive development. By age 7, noted the Russian psychologist Lev Vygotsky (1896–1934), children become increasingly capable of thinking in words and of using words to work out solutions to problems. They do this, he said, by no longer thinking aloud. Instead they internalize their culture's language and rely on inner speech. Parents who say "No" when pulling a child's hand away from a cake are giving the child a self-control tool. When later needing to resist temptation the child may likewise say "No." Whether out loud or inaudible, talking to themselves helps children control their behavior and emotions and master new skills. And when parents give children words, they provide, in Vygotsky's words, a *scaffold* upon which children can step to higher levels of thinking.

Formal Operational Stage

By age 12, our reasoning expands from the purely concrete (involving actual experience) to encompass abstract thinking (involving imagined realities and symbols). As children approach adolescence, said Piaget, many become capable of solving hypothetical propositions and deducing consequences: *If* this, *then* that. Systematic reasoning, what Piaget called **formal operational** thinking, is now within their grasp.

Although full-blown logic and reasoning await adolescence, the rudiments of formal operational thinking begin earlier than Piaget realized. Consider this simple problem:

> If John is in school, then Mary is in school. John is in school. What can you say about Mary?

Formal operational thinkers have no trouble answering correctly. But neither do most 7-year-olds (Suppes, 1982).

Reflecting on Piaget's Theory

What remains of Piaget's ideas about the child's mind? Plenty—enough to merit his being singled out in 1999 by *Time* magazine as one of the century's 20 most influential scientists and thinkers and rated in a survey of British psychologists as the greatest twentieth-century psychologist (*Psychologist,* 2003). Piaget identified significant cognitive milestones and stimulated worldwide interest in how the mind develops. His emphasis was less on the ages at which children typically reach specific milestones than on their sequence.

Studies around the globe, from aboriginal Australia to Algeria to North America, have supported the idea that human cognition unfolds basically in that sequence (Lourenco & Machado, 1996; Segall & others, 1990).

However, today's researchers see development as more continuous than did Piaget. By detecting the beginnings of each type of thinking at earlier ages, they have revealed conceptual abilities Piaget missed. Moreover, they see formal logic as a smaller part of cognition than he did. Piaget would not be surprised that today, as part of our own cognitive development, we are adapting his ideas to accommodate new findings.

Implications for Parents and Teachers

Future parents and teachers remember: Young children are incapable of adult logic. Preschoolers who stand in the way or ignore negatively phrased instructions simply have not learned to take another's viewpoint. What is simple and obvious to you—getting off a teeter-totter will cause a friend on the other end to crash—may be incomprehensible to a 3-year-old. Also remember that children are not passive receptacles waiting to be filled with knowledge. Better to build on what they already know, engaging them in concrete demonstrations and stimulating them to think for themselves. And finally, accept children's cognitive immaturity as adaptive. It is nature's strategy for keeping children close to protective adults and providing time for learning and socialization (Bjorklund & Green, 1992).

"Assessing the impact of Piaget on developmental psychology is like assessing the impact of Shakespeare in English literature."

Developmental psychologist Harry Beilin (1992)

■ **formal operational stage** in Piaget's theory, the stage of cognitive development (normally beginning about age 12) during which people begin to think logically about abstract concepts.

■ **stranger anxiety** the fear of strangers that infants commonly display, beginning by about 8 months of age.

■ **attachment** an emotional tie with another person; shown in young children by their seeking closeness to the caregiver and showing distress on separation.

Social Development

8-3: How do the bonds of attachment form between caregivers and infants?

From birth, babies in all cultures are social creatures, developing an intense bond with their caregivers. Beginning with a newborn's attraction to humans in general, infants soon come to prefer familiar faces and voices, then to coo and gurgle when given their mother's or father's attention. Soon after object permanence emerges and children become mobile, a curious thing happens: In most cultures, at about 8 months, they develop **stranger anxiety.** They may greet strangers by crying and reaching for familiar caregivers. "No! Don't leave me!" their distress seems to say. At about this age, children have schemas for familiar faces; when they cannot assimilate the new face into these remembered schemas, they become distressed (Kagan, 1984). Once again, we see an important principle: *The brain, mind, and social-emotional behavior develop together.*

At 12 months, many infants cling tightly to a parent when they are frightened or expect separation. Reunited after being separated, they shower the parent with smiles and hugs. No social behavior is more striking than this intense and mutual infant-parent bond.

Stranger anxiety

A newly emerging ability to evaluate people as unfamiliar and possibly threatening helps protect babies 8 months and older.

Origins of Attachment

The **attachment** bond is a powerful survival impulse that keeps infants close to their caregivers. Infants become attached to those—typically their parents—who are comfortable and familiar. For many years, developmental psychologists reasoned that infants became attached to those who satisfied their need for nourishment. It made sense. But an accidental finding overturned this explanation.

Body Contact

During the 1950s, University of Wisconsin psychologists Harry Harlow and Margaret Harlow bred monkeys for their learning studies. To equalize the infant monkeys' experiences and to isolate any disease, they separated them from their mothers shortly after birth and raised them in sanitary individual cages, which included a cheesecloth baby blanket (Harlow & others, 1971). Then came a surprise: When their blankets were taken to be laundered, the monkeys became distressed.

The Harlows recognized that this intense attachment to the blanket contradicted the idea that attachment derives from an association with nourishment. But how could they show this more convincingly? To pit the drawing power of a food source against the contact comfort of the blanket, they created two artificial mothers. One was a bare wire cylinder with a wooden head and an attached feeding bottle, the other a cylinder wrapped with terry cloth.

When reared with both, the monkeys overwhelmingly preferred the comfy cloth mother (**FIGURE 8.8**). Like human infants clinging to their mothers, the monkeys would cling to their cloth mothers when anxious. When venturing into the environment, they used her as a *secure base,* as if attached to her by an invisible elastic band that stretched so far and then pulled them back. Researchers soon learned that other qualities—rocking, warmth, and feeding—made the cloth mother even more appealing.

FIGURE 8.8
The Harlows' mothers

Psychologists Harry Harlow and Margaret Harlow reared monkeys with two artificial mothers—one a bare wire cylinder with a wooden head and an attached feeding bottle, the other a cylinder with no bottle but covered with foam rubber and wrapped with terry cloth. The Harlows' discovery surprised many psychologists: The infants much preferred contact with the comfortable cloth mother, even while feeding from the nourishing mother.

Lee Kirkpatrick (1999) reports that for some people a perceived relationship with God functions as do other attachments, by providing a secure base for exploration and a safe haven when threatened.

Human infants, too, become attached to parents who are soft and warm and who rock, feed, and pat. Much parent-infant emotional communication occurs via touch (Hertenstein, 2002), which can be either soothing (snuggles) or arousing (tickles). Human attachment also consists of one person providing another with a safe haven when distressed and a secure base from which to explore. As we mature, our secure base and safe haven shift—from parents to peers and partners (Cassidy & Shaver, 1999). But at all ages we are social creatures. We gain strength when someone offers, by words and actions, a safe haven: "I will be here. I am interested in you. Come what may, I will actively support you" (Crowell & Waters, 1994).

Familiarity

Contact is one key to attachment. Another is familiarity. In many animals, attachments based on familiarity likewise form during a **critical period**—an optimal period when certain events must take place to facilitate proper development (Bornstein, 1989). For goslings, ducklings, or chicks, that period falls in the hours shortly after hatching, when the first moving object they see is normally their mother. From then on, the young fowl follow her, and her alone.

This rigid attachment process, called **imprinting,** was explored by Konrad Lorenz (1937). He wondered: What would ducklings do if he was the first moving creature they observed? What they did was follow him around: Everywhere that Konrad went, the ducks were sure to go. Further tests revealed that although baby birds imprint best to their own species, they also will imprint to a variety of moving objects—an animal of another species, a box on wheels, a bouncing ball (Colombo, 1982; Johnson, 1992). And, once formed, this attachment is difficult to reverse.

Attachment
When French pilot Christian Moullec takes off in his microlight plane, his imprinted geese, which he reared since their hatching, follow closely.

Alastair Miller

Children—unlike ducklings—do not imprint. However, they do become attached to what they've known. *Mere exposure* to people and things fosters fondness—children like to reread the same books, rewatch the same movies, reenact family traditions. They prefer to eat familiar foods, live in the same familiar neighborhood, attend school with the same old friends. Familiarity is a safety signal. Familiarity breeds content.

Attachment Differences

What accounts for children's attachment differences? Placed in a *strange situation* (usually a laboratory playroom), about 60 percent of infants display *secure attachment*. In their mother's presence they play comfortably, happily exploring their new environment. When she leaves, they are distressed; when she returns, they seek contact with her. Other infants show *insecure attachment*. They are less likely to explore

■ **critical period** an optimal period shortly after birth when an organism's exposure to certain stimuli or experiences produces proper development.

■ **imprinting** the process by which certain animals form attachments during a critical period very early in life.

their surroundings; they may even cling to their mother. When she leaves, they either cry loudly and remain upset or seem indifferent to her departure and return (Ainsworth, 1973, 1989; Kagan, 1995; van IJzendoorn & Kroonenberg, 1988).

Mary Ainsworth (1979), who designed the strange situation experiments, studied attachment differences by observing mother-infant pairs at home during their first six months. Later she observed the 1-year-old infants in a strange situation without their mothers. Sensitive, responsive mothers—those who noticed what their babies were doing and responded appropriately—had infants who exhibited secure attachment. Insensitive, unresponsive mothers—mothers who attended to their babies when they felt like doing so but ignored them at other times—had infants who often became insecurely attached. The Harlows' monkey studies, in which the artificial structures were certainly the ultimate unresponsive mothers, produced even more striking effects. When put in strange situations without their artificial mothers, the deprived infants were terrified (**FIGURE 8.9**).

But is attachment style the result of parenting, as children's early experiences form their thinking about relationships? Or is attachment style the result of genetically influenced *temperament*—one's characteristic emotional reactivity and intensity? Shortly after birth, some babies are noticeably *difficult*—irritable, intense, and unpredictable. Others are *easy*—cheerful, relaxed, and feeding and sleeping on predictable schedules (Chess & Thomas, 1987). By neglecting such inborn differences, chides Judith Harris (1998), the parenting studies are like "comparing foxhounds reared in kennels with poodles reared in apartments." So, to separate nature and nurture, Dutch researcher Dymphna van den Boom (1990) varied parenting while controlling temperament. (Pause and think: If you were the researcher, how might you have done this?)

Van den Boom's solution was to randomly assign one hundred 6- to 9-month-old temperamentally difficult infants to either an experimental condition, in which mothers received personal training in sensitive responding, or to a control condition, in which they did not. At 12 months of age, 68 percent of the experimental-condition infants were rated securely attached; only 28 percent of the control-condition infants received this rating. Other studies have also found that intervention programs can increase parental sensitivity and, to a lesser extent, infant attachment security (Bakermans-Kranenburg & others, 2003).

As these examples indicate, researchers have more often studied mother care than father care. Infants who lack a caring mother are said to suffer "maternal deprivation"; those lacking a father's care merely experience "father absence." This reflects a wider attitude in which "fathering a child" has meant impregnating, and "mothering" has meant nurturing. But fathers are more than just mobile sperm banks. Across nearly 100 studies worldwide, a father's love and acceptance have been comparable to a mother's love in predicting offsprings' health and well-being (Rohner & Veneziano, 2001). In one mammoth British study following 7259 children from birth to adulthood, those whose fathers were most involved in parenting (including outings, reading to them, and taking an interest in their education) tended to achieve more in school, even after controlling for many other factors such as parental education and family wealth (Flouri & Buchanan, 2004).

Whether children live with one parent or two, are cared for at home or in a day-care center, live in North America, Guatemala, or the Kalahari Desert, their anxiety over separation from parents peaks at around 13 months, then gradually declines (**FIGURE 8.10**). Does this mean our need for and love of others also fades away? Hardly. Our capacity for love grows, and our pleasure in touching and holding those we love never ceases. The power of early attachment does nonetheless gradually relax, allowing us to move out into a wider range of situations, communicate with strangers more freely, and stay attached emotionally to loved ones despite distance.

FIGURE **8.9**
Social deprivation and fear
Monkeys raised with artificial mothers were terror-stricken when placed in strange situations without their surrogate mothers. (Today's climate of greater respect for animal welfare prevents such primate studies.)

Fantastic father
Among the Aka people of Central Africa, fathers form an especially close bond with their infants, even suckling the babies with their own nipples when hunger makes the child impatient for Mother's return. According to anthropologist Barry Hewlett (1991), fathers in this culture are holding or within reach of their babies 47 percent of the time.

FIGURE **8.10**
**Infants' distress over separation
from parents**

In an experiment, groups of infants were left by their mothers in an unfamiliar room. In both groups, the percentage who cried when the mother left peaked at about 13 months. Whether the infant had experienced day care made little difference. (From Kagan, 1976.)

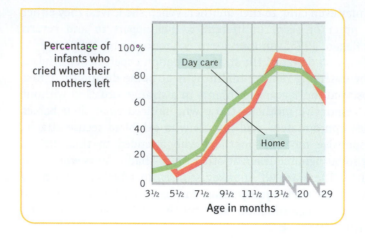

"Out of the conflict between trust and mistrust, the infant develops hope, which is the earliest form of what gradually becomes faith in adults."

Erik Erikson, 1983

"What is learned in the cradle, lasts to the grave."

French proverb

Developmental theorist Erik Erikson (1902–1994) would not have been surprised. Erikson, in collaboration with his wife, Joan Erikson, said that securely attached children approach life with a sense of **basic trust**—a sense that the world is predictable and reliable. He attributed basic trust not to environment or inborn temperament, but to early parenting. He theorized that infants blessed with sensitive, loving caregivers form a lifelong attitude of trust rather than fear. Nor would Erikson have been surprised that our adult styles of romantic love exhibit either secure, trusting attachment; insecure, anxious attachment; or the avoidance of attachment (Feeney & Noller, 1990; Mikulincer & Shaver, 2005; Rholes & Simpson, 2004). Although debate continues, many researchers now believe that our early attachments form the foundation for our adult relationships (Fraley, 2002).

Deprivation of Attachment

If secure attachment nurtures social competence, what happens when circumstances prevent a child from forming attachments? In all of psychology, there is no sadder research literature. Babies reared in institutions without the stimulation and attention of a regular caregiver, or locked away at home under conditions of abuse or extreme neglect, are often withdrawn, frightened, even speechless. Those abandoned in Romanian orphanages during the 1980s looked "frighteningly like Harlow's monkeys" (Carlson, 1995). If institutionalized more than 8 months, they often bore lasting emotional scars (Chisholm, 1998; Malinosky-Rummell & Hansen, 1993; Rutter & others, 1998).

Harlows' monkeys similarly bore scars if reared in total isolation, without even an artificial mother. As adults, when placed with other monkeys their age, they either cowered in fright or lashed out in aggression. When they reached sexual maturity, most were incapable of mating. If artificially impregnated, females often were neglectful, abusive, even murderous toward their first-born.

In humans, too, the unloved sometimes become the unloving. Most abusive parents—and many condemned murderers—report having been neglected or battered as children (Kempe & Kempe, 1978; Lewis & others, 1988). But does this mean that today's victim is predictably tomorrow's victimizer? The answer is no. Though most abusers were indeed abused, most abused children do *not* later become violent criminals or abusive parents. Most children growing up under adversity (as did the surviving children of the Holocaust) are resilient; they become normal adults (Helmreich, 1992; Masten, 2001).

But others, especially those who experience no sharp break from their abusive past, don't bounce back so readily. Some 30 percent of those abused do abuse their children—four times the U.S. national rate of child abuse (Kaufman & Zigler, 1987; Widom, 1989a, b).

■ **basic trust** according to Erik Erikson, a sense that the world is predictable and trustworthy; said to be formed during infancy by appropriate experiences with responsive caregivers.

Although children are resilient, extreme childhood trauma can leave footprints on the brain. Baby rats deprived of their care-giving adult for several hours a day form fewer new brain neurons later in life (Mirescu & others, 2004). Normally placid golden hamsters that are repeatedly threatened and attacked while young grow up to be cowards when caged with same-sized hamsters, or bullies when caged with weaker ones (Ferris, 1996). Such animals show changes in the brain chemical serotonin, which calms aggressive impulses. A similarly sluggish serotonin response has been found in abused children who become aggressive teens and adults. "Stress can set off a ripple of hormonal changes that permanently wire a child's brain to cope with a malevolent world," concludes abuse researcher Martin Teicher (2002).

Such findings may help explain why young children terrorized through physical abuse or wartime atrocities (being beaten, witnessing torture, and living in constant fear) suffer other lasting wounds—often nightmares, depression, and an adolescence troubled by substance abuse, binge eating, or aggression (Kendall-Tackett & others, 1993; Polusny & Follette, 1995; Trickett & McBride-Chang, 1995). Child sexual abuse, especially if severe and prolonged, places children at increased risk for health problems, psychological disorders, substance abuse, and criminality (Freyd & others, 2005; Tyler, 2002).

Child-Rearing Practices

Parenting styles vary. Some parents spank, some reason. Some are strict, some are lax. Some show little affection, some liberally hug and kiss. Do such differences affect children?

The most heavily researched aspect of parenting has been how, and to what extent, parents seek to control their children. Investigators have identified three parenting styles:

1. *Authoritarian* parents impose rules and expect obedience: "Don't interrupt." "Do keep your room clean." "Don't stay out late or you'll be grounded." "Why? Because I said so."
2. *Permissive* parents submit to their children's desires, make few demands, and use little punishment.
3. *Authoritative* parents are both demanding and responsive. They exert control not only by setting rules and enforcing them but also by explaining the reasons and, especially with older children, encouraging open discussion and allowing exceptions when making the rules.

Too hard, too soft, and just right, these styles have been called. Studies by Stanley Coopersmith (1967), Diana Baumrind (1996), and John Buri and others (1988) reveal that children with the highest self-esteem, self-reliance, and social competence usually have warm, concerned, *authoritative* parents. (Those with authoritarian parents tend to have less social skill and self-esteem, and those with permissive parents tend to be more aggressive and immature.) Although the participants in most studies have been middle-class white families, studies with families of other races and in more than 200 cultures worldwide confirm the social and academic correlates of loving and authoritative parenting (Rohner & Veneziano, 2001; Steinberg & Morris, 2001).

A word of caution: *Correlation is not causation.* The association between certain parenting styles (being firm but open) and certain childhood outcomes (social competence) is correlational. Perhaps you can imagine other possible explanations for this parenting-competence link.

Parents struggling with conflicting advice and with the stresses of child-rearing should remember that *all advice reflects the advice-giver's values.* For those who prize unquestioning obedience from a child, an authoritarian style may have the desired effect. For those who value children's sociability and self-reliance, authoritative firm-but-open parenting is advisable.

The investment in raising a child buys many years not only of joy and love but of worry and irritation. Yet for most people who become parents, a child is one's biological and social legacy—one's personal investment in the human future. Remind young adults of their mortality and they will express increased desire for children (Wisman & Goldenberg, 2005). To paraphrase psychiatrist Carl Jung, we reach backward into our parents and forward into our children, and through their children into a future we will never see, but about which we must therefore care.

"You are the bows from which your children as living arrows are sent forth."
Kahlil Gibran, *The Prophet*, 1923

REVIEWING

>> MODULE REVIEW

8-1: **How do the brain and motor skills develop during infancy and childhood?**

Within the brain, nerve cells form before birth. Sculpted by *maturation* and experience, their interconnections multiply rapidly after birth. We lose conscious memories of experiences from before age 3, in part because major areas of the brain have not yet matured. Our complex motor skills—sitting, standing, walking—develop in a predictable sequence whose timing is a function of individual maturation and culture.

8-2: **How did Piaget view the development of a child's mind, and what are current researchers' views?**

Piaget proposed that children's reasoning develops in stages, and that children actively construct and modify their understanding of the world as they interact with it. They form *schemas* that help them organize their experiences. In this way, children progress from the simplicity of the *sensorimotor stage* of the first two years to more complex stages of thinking, which include a developing *theory of mind*. Piaget viewed preschool children, in the *preoperational stage*, as *egocentric* and unable to perform simple logical operations. At about age 6 or 7 they enter the *concrete operational stage* and can perform concrete operations, such as those required to comprehend the principle of *conservation*. And by about age 12, children enter the *formal operational stage*, in which systematic reasoning is within their

grasp. Research supports the sequence Piaget proposed for the unfolding of human *cognition*, but it also shows that young children are more capable, and their development more continuous, than he believed. The cognitive abilities that emerge at each stage apparently begin developing in a rudimentary form in the previous stage.

8-3: **How do the bonds of attachment form between caregivers and infants?**

Infants form *attachments* not simply because caregivers gratify biological needs but, more important, because they are comfortable, familiar, and responsive. Ducks and other animals have a more rigid attachment process, called *imprinting*, that occurs during a *critical period*. Neglect or abuse can disrupt the attachment process and put children at risk for physical, psychological, and social problems. Once an attachment forms, infants separated from their caregivers will, for a time, display *stranger anxiety*. Infants' differing attachment styles reflect both their individual temperament and the responsiveness of their parents and child-care providers. Parenting styles—permissive, authoritative, and authoritarian—reflect varying degrees of control. Children with the highest self-esteem, self-reliance, and social competence tend to have authoritative parents.

>> REHEARSE IT!

1. The orderly sequence of biological growth is called maturation. Maturation explains why
   a. children with autism have difficulty inferring others' thoughts and feelings.
   b. most children have begun walking by about 12 months.
   c. enriching experiences may affect brain tissue.
   d. differences between the sexes are minimal.

2. Although we are born with most of the brain cells we will ever have, at birth our nervous system is still immature. Between ages 3 and 6, we experience the greatest growth in our _____ lobes, which we use for rational planning, and which continue developing at least into adolescence.
   a. parietal
   b. temporal
   c. frontal
   d. occipital

3. As the infant's muscles and nervous system mature, more complicated skills emerge. Which of the following is true of motor-skill development?
   a. It is determined solely by genetic factors.
   b. The sequence, but not the timing, is universal.
   c. The timing, but not the sequence, is universal.
   d. Environment creates a readiness to learn.

4. Piaget's preoperational stage extends from about age 2 to 6. During this period, the young child's thinking is

   a. abstract.
   b. negative.
   c. conservative.
   d. egocentric.

5. The principle of conservation explains why a pint of milk remains a pint, whether poured into a tall thin pitcher or a round one. Children acquire the mental operations necessary to understand conservation during the

   a. sensorimotor stage.
   b. preoperational stage.
   c. concrete operational stage.
   d. formal operational stage.

6. Piaget's stage theory continues to inform our understanding of cognitive development in childhood. However, many researchers believe that

   a. Piaget's "stages" begin earlier and development is more continuous than he realized.
   b. children do not progress as rapidly as Piaget predicted.
   c. few children really progress to the concrete operational stage.
   d. there is no way of testing much of Piaget's theoretical work.

7. After about 8 months of age, infants develop schemas for familiar objects. Faced with a new babysitter, they will show distress, a behavior referred to as

   a. conservation.
   b. stranger anxiety.
   c. imprinting.
   d. maturation.

8. Body contact facilitates attachment between infant and parent. In a series of experiments, Harry and Margaret Harlow found that monkeys raised with artificial mothers tended, when afraid, to cling to

   a. the wire mother.
   b. the cloth mother.
   c. whichever mother held the feeding bottle.
   d. other infant monkeys.

9. From the very first weeks of life, infants differ in their characteristic emotional reactions, with some infants being intense and anxious, while others are easygoing and relaxed. These differences are usually explained as differences in

   a. attachment.
   b. imprinting.
   c. temperament.
   d. parental responsiveness.

Answers: 1. b, 2. c, 3. b, 4. d, 5. c, 6. a, 7. b, 8. b, 9. c.

>> Terms and Concepts to Remember

maturation, p. 105
cognition, p. 107
schema, p. 107
assimilation, p. 107
accommodation, p. 107
sensorimotor stage, p. 108
object permanence, p. 108

preoperational stage, p. 109
conservation, p. 109
egocentrism, p. 110
theory of mind, p. 110
autism, p. 111
concrete operational stage, p. 111

formal operational stage, p. 112
stranger anxiety, p. 113
attachment, p. 113
critical period, p. 114
imprinting, p. 114
basic trust, p. 116

>> Test Yourself

1. Use Piaget's first three stages of cognitive development to explain why young children are *not* just miniature adults in the way they think.

   (Answer in Appendix C.)

Multiple-choice **self-tests** and more may be found at www.worthpublishers.com/myers.

9 Adolescence

Many psychologists once believed that childhood sets our traits. Today's developmental psychologists see development as lifelong. At a five-year high school reunion, former soul mates may be surprised at their divergence; a decade later, they may have trouble sustaining a conversation.

As this life-span perspective emerged, psychologists began to look at how maturation and experience shape us not only in infancy and childhood, but also in adolescence and beyond. **Adolescence**—the years spent morphing from child to adult—starts with the physical beginnings of sexual maturity and ends with the social achievement of independent adult status.

To G. Stanley Hall (1904), one of the first psychologists to describe adolescence, the tension between biological maturity and social dependence created a period of "storm and stress." Indeed, after age 30, many who grow up in independence-fostering Western cultures look back on their teenage years as a time they would not want to relive, a time when their peers' social approval was imperative, their sense of direction in life was in flux, and their feeling of alienation from their parents was deepest (Arnett, 1999; Macfarlane, 1964).

Adolescence can also be a time of vitality without the cares of adulthood, a time of rewarding friendships, of heightened idealism and a growing sense of life's exciting possibilities.

Physical Development

9-1 : What major physical changes occur during adolescence?

Adolescence begins with **puberty,** the time one is maturing sexually. Puberty follows a surge of hormones, which may intensify moods and which trigger a two-year period of rapid physical development, usually beginning at about age 11 in girls and at about age 13 in boys. About the time of puberty, boys' growth propels them to greater height than their female counterparts (**FIGURE 9.1**). During this growth spurt, the **primary**

FIGURE 9.1
Height differences
Throughout childhood, boys and girls are similar in height. At puberty, girls surge ahead briefly, but then boys overtake them at about age 14. (Data from Tanner, 1978.) Recent studies suggest that sexual development and growth spurts are beginning somewhat earlier than was the case a half-century ago (Herman-Giddens & others, 2001).

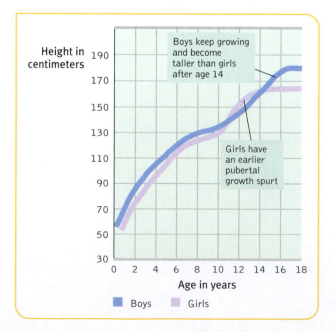

Height in centimeters

Boys keep growing and become taller than girls after age 14

Girls have an earlier pubertal growth spurt

Age in years

Boys   Girls

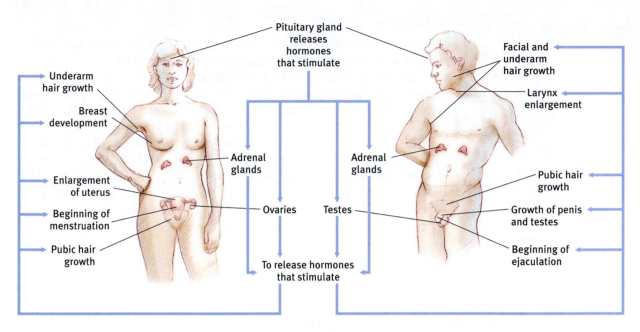

FIGURE 9.2
Body changes at puberty
At about age 11 in girls and age 13 in boys, a surge of hormones triggers a variety of physical changes.

Pituitary gland releases hormones that stimulate

Underarm hair growth

Breast development

Enlargement of uterus

Beginning of menstruation

Pubic hair growth

Adrenal glands

Ovaries

To release hormones that stimulate

Facial and underarm hair growth

Larynx enlargement

Adrenal glands

Testes

Pubic hair growth

Growth of penis and testes

Beginning of ejaculation

sex characteristics—the reproductive organs and external genitalia—develop dramatically. So do **secondary sex characteristics,** the nonreproductive traits such as breasts and hips in girls, facial hair and deepened voice in boys, pubic and underarm hair in both sexes (**FIGURE 9.2**). A year or two before puberty, however, boys and girls often feel the first stirrings of attraction toward those of the other (or their own) sex (McClintock & Herdt, 1996).

In girls, puberty starts with breast development, which now often begins by age 10 (Brody, 1999). But puberty's landmarks are the first ejaculation in boys, usually by about age 14, and the first menstrual period in girls, usually within a year of age 12. The first menstrual period, called **menarche** (meh-NAR-key), is a memorable event. Nearly all adult women recall it and remember experiencing a mixture of feelings—pride, excitement, embarrassment, and apprehension (Greif & Ulman, 1982; Woods & others, 1983). Girls who have been prepared for menarche usually experience it as a positive life transition. Most men similarly recall their first ejaculation (*spermarche*), which usually occurs as a nocturnal emission (Fuller & Downs, 1990).

Just as in the earlier life stages, the *sequence* of physical changes in puberty (for example, breast buds and visible pubic hair before menarche) is far more predictable than their *timing*. Some girls start their growth spurt at 9, some boys as late as age 16. Though such variations have little effect on height at maturity, they may have psychological consequences. For boys, early maturation pays dividends: Being stronger and more athletic during their early teen years, they tend to be more popular, self-assured, and independent, though also more at risk for alcohol use and premature sexual activity (Steinberg & Morris, 2001). But for girls, early maturation can be stressful. If a young girl's body is out of sync with her own emotional maturity and her friends' physical development and experiences, she may begin associating with older adolescents or may suffer teasing or sexual harassment. It is not only when we mature that counts, but how people react to our genetically influenced physical development. Remember: *Heredity and environment interact*.

Adolescents' brains are also a work in progress. Frontal lobe development during adolescence includes the continuing growth of *myelin,* the fatty tissue around axons that speeds neurotransmission. Frontal lobe maturation brings improved judgment, impulse control, and the ability to plan for the long term. But this maturation lags the emotional limbic system. The pubertal hormonal surge and limbic system development help explain teens' occasional impulsiveness, risky behaviors, emotional storms—slamming doors and turning up the music. No wonder younger teens (whose unfinished frontal lobes aren't yet fully equipped for making long-term plans

■ **adolescence** the transition period from childhood to adulthood, extending from puberty to independence.

■ **puberty** the period of sexual maturation, during which a person becomes capable of reproducing.

■ **primary sex characteristics** the body structures (ovaries, testes, and external genitalia) that make sexual reproduction possible.

■ **secondary sex characteristics** nonreproductive sexual characteristics, such as female breasts and hips, male voice quality, and body hair.

■ **menarche** [meh-NAR-key] the first menstrual period.

❝If a gun is put in the control of the prefrontal cortex of a hurt and vengeful 15-year-old, and it is pointed at a human target, it will very likely go off.❞
National Institutes of Health brain scientist Daniel R. Weinberger, "A Brain Too Young for Good Judgment," 2001

"**Young man, go to your room and stay there until your cerebral cortex matures.**"

and curbing impulses) so often succumb to the lure of smoking, which most adult smokers could tell them they will later regret.

So, when Junior drives recklessly and academically self-destructs, should his parents reassure themselves that "he can't help it; his frontal cortex isn't yet fully grown"? They can at least take hope: The brain with which Junior begins his teens differs from the brain with which he will end his teens; his frontal lobes will continue maturing until about age 25 (Beckman, 2004). In 2004, the American Psychological Association joined seven other medical and mental health associations in filing U.S. Supreme Court briefs, arguing against the death penalty for 16- and 17-years-olds. The briefs documented the teen brain's immaturity "in areas that bear upon adolescent decision-making." Teens are "less guilty by reason of adolescence," suggested psychologist Laurence Steinberg and law professor Elizabeth Scott (2003). In 2005, by a 5-to-4 margin, the Court concurred, declaring juvenile death penalties unconstitutional.

Cognitive Development

9-2: How did Piaget and Kohlberg describe cognitive and moral development during adolescence?

"When the pilot told us to brace and grab our ankles, the first thing that went through my mind was that we must all look pretty stupid."
Jeremiah Rawlings, age 12, after a 1989 DC-10 crash in Sioux City, Iowa

As young teenagers become capable of thinking about their thinking, and of thinking about other people's thinking, they begin imagining what other people are thinking about *them*. (Adolescents might worry less if they knew how similarly self-preoccupied their peers are.) As their cognitive abilities mature, many begin to think about what is ideally possible and compare that with the imperfect reality of their society, their parents, and even themselves.

Developing Reasoning Power

During the early teen years, reasoning is often self-focused. Adolescents may think their private experiences are unique, something parents just couldn't understand: "But, Mom, *you* don't really know how it feels to be in love" (Elkind, 1978).

Gradually, though, most achieve the intellectual summit Jean Piaget called *formal operations,* and they become more capable of abstract logic: *If* this, *then* that. We can see this abstract reasoning power as adolescents ponder and debate human nature, good and evil, truth and justice. Having left behind the concrete images of early childhood, they may now seek a deeper conception of God and existence (Elkind, 1970; Worthington, 1989). The ability to reason hypothetically and deduce consequences also enables them to detect inconsistencies in others' reasoning and to spot hypocrisy. This can lead to heated debates with parents and silent vows never to lose sight of their own ideals (Peterson & others, 1986).

"**Ben is in his first year of high school, and he's questioning all the right things.**"

Demonstrating their reasoning ability
Although on opposite sides of the Iraq War debate, these teens demonstrate their ability to think logically about abstract topics. According to Piaget, they are in the final cognitive stage, formal operations.

Developing Morality

A crucial task of childhood and adolescence is discerning right from wrong and developing character—the psychological muscles for controlling impulses. To be a moral person is to *think* morally and *act* accordingly.

Piaget (1932) believed that children's moral judgments build on their cognitive development. Agreeing with Piaget, Lawrence Kohlberg (1981, 1984) sought to describe the development of *moral reasoning,* the thinking that occurs as we consider right and wrong. Kohlberg posed moral dilemmas (for example, whether a person should steal medicine to save a loved one's life) and asked children, adolescents, and adults if the action was right or wrong. He then analyzed their answers for evidence of stages of moral thinking.

His findings led him to believe that as we develop intellectually, we pass through three basic levels of moral thinking:

- **Preconventional morality** Before age 9, most children's morality focuses on self-interest: They obey rules either to avoid punishment or to gain concrete rewards.
- **Conventional morality** By early adolescence, morality usually evolves to a more conventional level that cares for others and upholds laws and social rules simply because they are the laws and rules.
- **Postconventional morality** Those who develop the abstract reasoning of formal operational thought may reach a third level of morality, affirming people's agreed-upon rights or following self-defined, basic ethical principles.

Kohlberg claimed these levels form a moral ladder. As with all stage theories, the sequence is unvarying. We begin on the bottom rung and ascend to varying heights.

Research confirms that children in various cultures progress from Kohlberg's preconventional level into his conventional level (Edwards, 1981, 1982; Snarey, 1985, 1987). However, the postconventional level is more controversial. It appears mostly in the European and North American educated middle class, which prizes individualism—giving priority to one's own goals rather than to group goals (Eckensberger, 1994; Miller & Bersoff, 1995). Critics therefore contend that Kohlberg's theory is biased against the moral reasoning of those in collectivist societies such as China and India—and also against Western women, whose morality may be based slightly less on abstract, impersonal principles and more on caring relationships.

Nevertheless, as our *thinking* matures, our *behavior* also becomes less selfish and more caring (Krebs & Van Hesteren, 1994; Miller & others, 1996). Today's character education programs therefore tend to focus both on moral issues and on *doing* the right thing. They teach children *empathy* for others' feelings, and also the self-discipline needed to restrain one's own impulses—to delay small gratifications now to enable bigger rewards later. Those who do learn to *delay gratification* become more socially responsible, academically successful, and productive (Funder & Block, 1989;

> " It is a delightful harmony when doing and saying go together."
>
> Michel Eyquem de Montaigne (1533–1592)

"This might not be ethical. Is that a problem for anybody?"

> " I am a bit suspicious of any theory that says that the highest moral stage is one in which people talk like college professors."
>
> James Q. Wilson, *The Moral Sense,* 1993

Moral reasoning
New Orleans hurricane Katrina victims were faced with a moral dilemma: Should they steal household necessities? Their reasoning likely reflected different levels of moral thinking, even if they behaved similarly.

■ **identity** one's sense of self; according to Erikson, the adolescent's task is to solidify a sense of self by testing and integrating various roles.

■ **intimacy** in Erikson's theory, the ability to form close, loving relationships; a primary developmental task in late adolescence and early adulthood.

Mischel & others, 1988, 1989). In service-learning programs, teens tutor, clean up their neighborhoods, and assist the elderly, and their sense of competence and desire to serve increases and their school absenteeism and drop-out rates diminish (Andersen, 1998; Piliavin, 2003). Moral action feeds moral attitudes.

Social Development

9-3: What tasks and challenges do adolescents face en route to mature adulthood?

Theorist Erik Erikson (1963) contended that each stage of life has its own *psychosocial* task, a crisis that needs resolution. Young children wrestle with issues of *trust*, then *autonomy* (independence), then *initiative* (**TABLE 9.1**). School-age children strive for *competence*, feeling able and productive. The adolescent's task, said Erikson, is to synthesize past, present, and future possibilities into a clearer sense of self. Adolescents wonder "Who am I as an individual? What do I want to do with my life? What values should I live by? What do I believe in?" Erikson called this quest the adolescent's *search for identity*.

Forming an Identity

To refine their sense of identity, adolescents in Western cultures usually try out different "selves" in different situations—perhaps acting out one self at home, another with friends, and still another at school or on the Internet. If two situations overlap—as when a teenager brings home friends—the discomfort can be considerable. The teen asks, "Which self should I be? Which is the real me?" The resolution is a self-definition that unifies the various selves into a consistent and comfortable sense of who one is—an **identity.**

John Eastcott/Yves Momatiuk/The Image Works

Dex Image/Getty Images

TABLE 9.1

ERIKSON'S STAGES OF PSYCHOSOCIAL DEVELOPMENT

Stage (approximate age)	Issues	Description of Task
Infancy (to 1 year)	Trust vs. mistrust	If needs are dependably met, infants develop a sense of basic trust.
Toddlerhood (1 to 2 years)	Autonomy vs. shame and doubt	Toddlers learn to exercise will and do things for themselves, or they doubt their abilities.
Preschooler (3 to 5 years)	Initiative vs. guilt	Preschoolers learn to initiate tasks and carry out plans, or they feel guilty about efforts to be independent.
Elementary school (6 years to puberty)	Competence vs. inferiority	Children learn the pleasure of applying themselves to tasks, or they feel inferior.
Adolescence (teen years into 20s)	Identity vs. role confusion	Teenagers work at refining a sense of self by testing roles and then integrating them to form a single identity, or they become confused about who they are.
Young adulthood (20s to early 40s)	Intimacy vs. isolation	Young adults struggle to form close relationships and to gain the capacity for intimate love, or they feel socially isolated.
Middle adulthood (40s to 60s)	Generativity vs. stagnation	In middle age, people discover a sense of contributing to the world, usually through family and work, or they may feel a lack of purpose.
Late adulthood (late 60s and up)	Integrity vs. despair	When reflecting on his or her life, the older adult may feel a sense of satisfaction or failure.

But not always. Erikson noticed that some adolescents forge their identity early, simply by taking on their parents' values and expectations. (Traditional, less individualistic cultures inform adolescents about who they are, rather than encouraging their deciding on their own.) Other adolescents may adopt an identity defined in opposition to parents but in conformity with a particular peer group—jocks, preppies, geeks, goths.

The late teen years, when many people begin attending college or working full time, provide new opportunities for trying out possible roles. Many college seniors have achieved a clearer identity and a more positive self-concept than they had as first-year students (Waterman, 1988). In several nationwide studies, researchers have given young Americans tests of self-esteem. (Sample item: "I am able to do things as well as most other people.") During the early to mid-teen years, self-esteem falls and, for girls, depression scores often increase, but then self-image rebounds during the late teens and twenties (Robins & others, 2002; Twenge & Campbell, 2001; Twenge & Nolen-Hoeksema, 2002).

Erikson contended that the adolescent identity stage is followed in young adulthood by a developing capacity for **intimacy,** the ability to form emotionally close relationships. With a clear and comfortable sense of who you are, said Erikson, you are ready for close relationships. Such relationships are, for most of us, a source of great pleasure. When Mihaly Csikszentmihalyi (pronounced chick-SENT-me-hi) and Jeremy Hunter (2003) used a beeper to sample the daily experiences of American teens, they found them unhappiest when alone and happiest when with friends. As Aristotle long ago recognized, we humans are "the social animal."

Parent and Peer Influence

As adolescents in Western cultures seek to form their own identities, they begin to pull away from their parents (Paikoff & Brooks-Gunn, 1991). The preschooler who can't be close enough to her mother, who loves to touch and cling to her, becomes the 14-year-old who wouldn't be caught dead holding hands with Mom. The transition occurs gradually (**FIGURE 9.3**). By adolescence, arguments occur more often, usually over mundane things—household chores, bedtime, homework (Tesser & others, 1989).

For a minority of parents and their adolescents, differences lead to estrangement and to great stress (Steinberg & Morris, 2001). But for most, disagreement at the level of bickering is not destructive. One study of 6000 adolescents in 10 countries, from Australia to Bangladesh to Turkey, found that most liked their parents (Offer & others, 1988). "We usually get along but . . . ," adolescents often report (Galambos, 1992; Steinberg, 1987). Positive relations with parents support positive peer relations. High school girls who have the most affectionate relationships with their mothers tend also to enjoy the most intimate friendships with girlfriends (Gold & Yanof, 1985). And teens

Leland Bobbe/Getty Images   Matthias Clamer/Getty Images

Who shall I be today?
By varying the way they look, adolescents try out different "selves." Although we eventually form a consistent and stable sense of identity, the self we present may change with the situation.

© The New Yorker Collection, 2001, Barbara Smaller from cartoonbank.com. All Rights Reserved.

"How was my day? How was my day? Must you micromanage my life?"

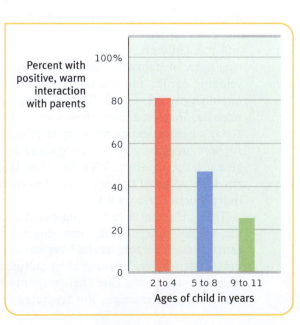

Percent with positive, warm interaction with parents

100%

80

60

40

20

0

2 to 4   5 to 8   9 to 11

Ages of child in years

Compared with teens in other Western countries, U.S. teens spend more time watching TV and hanging out with friends (both predictors of negative outcomes) and less time on schoolwork (Larson, 2001).

FIGURE 9.3
The changing parent-child relationship
Interviews from a large, national study of Canadian families reveal that the typically close, warm relationships between parents and preschoolers loosen among children of older ages. (Data from Statistics Canada, 1999.)

who feel close to their parents tend to be healthy and happy and to do well in school (Resnick & others, 1997). Of course, we can state this correlation the other way: Misbehaving teens are more likely to have tense relationships with parents and other adults.

Adolescence is typically a time of diminishing parental influence and growing peer influence. Asked in a survey if they had "ever had a serious talk" with their child about illegal drugs, 85 percent of American *parents* answered yes. But some teens apparently tuned out this earnest advice: only 45 percent could recall such a talk (Morin & Brossard, 1997).

Heredity does much of the heavy lifting in forming individual differences in character and personality, and parent and peer influences do much of the rest. Teens are herd animals. They talk, dress, and act more like their peers than their parents. What their friends are—what "everybody's doing"—they often become. In teen calls to hot-line counseling services, peer relationships are the most discussed topic (Boehm & others, 1999). For those who feel excluded, the pain is acute. "The social atmosphere in most high schools is poisonously clique-driven and exclusionary," observes social psychologist Elliot Aronson (2001). Most excluded "students suffer in silence. . . . A small number act out in violent ways against their classmates." Those who withdraw are vulnerable to loneliness, low self-esteem, and depression (Steinberg & Morris, 2001). Peer approval matters.

Teens see their parents as having more influence in other areas—for example, in shaping their religious faith and practices and in thinking about college and career choices (*Emerging Trends,* 1997). A Gallup Youth Survey reveals that most share their parent's political views, too (Lyons, 2005).

Nine times out of ten, it's all about peer pressure.

Emerging Adulthood

In young adulthood, emotional ties with parents loosen. During their early twenties, many people still lean heavily on their parents, but by the late twenties, most feel more comfortably independent and better able to empathize with parents as fellow adults (Frank, 1988; White, 1983). This graduation from adolescence to adulthood is now taking longer.

In the Western world, adolescence now roughly corresponds to the teen years, but at earlier times and in other parts of the world, this was not always the case (Baumeister & Tice, 1986). Shortly after sexual maturity, society bestowed adult responsibilities and status on the young person, often marking the event with an elaborate initiation—a public *rite of passage*. The new adult then worked, married, and had children. With compulsory schooling, adult independence began occurring later. In industrialized cultures from Europe to Australia, adolescents are developing earlier and are taking more time to finish college, leave the nest, and establish careers. In the United States, for example, the average age at first marriage has increased more than 4 years since 1960 (to 27 for men, 25 for women). Today's earlier sexual maturity is related both to increased body fat (which can support pregnancy and nursing) and to weakened parent-child bonds, including absent fathers (Ellis, 2004). Together, later independence and earlier sexual maturity have widened the once-brief interlude between biological maturity and social independence (**FIGURE 9.4**).

The time from 18 to the mid-twenties is an increasingly not-yet-settled phase of life, which some now call *emerging adulthood* (Arnett, 2000). No longer adolescents, these emerging adults have not yet taken on adult-level responsibilities and independence. Unlike some older cultures with an abrupt transition to adulthood, Westerners typically ease their way into their new status. Those who leave home for college, for example, are separated from parents and, more than ever before,

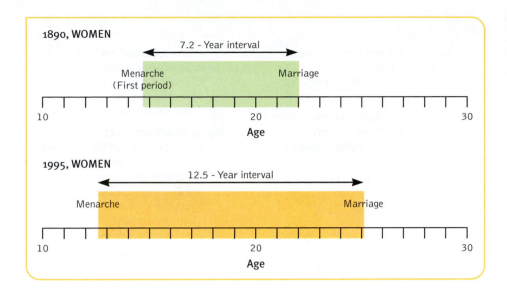

FIGURE 9.4
Adolescence is being stretched from both ends
In the 1890s the average interval between a woman's first menstrual period and marriage, which typically marked a transition to adulthood, was about 7 years; today in industrialized countries it is about 12 years (Guttmacher, 1994, 2000). Although many adults are unmarried, later marriage combines with prolonged education and earlier menarche to help stretch out adolescence.

managing their time and priorities. Yet they may remain dependent on their parents' financial and emotional support and may return home for holidays. For many others, their parents' home may be the only affordable place to live. Adulthood emerges, gradually.

REVIEWING

>> MODULE REVIEW

9-1: **What major physical changes occur during adolescence?**
Adolescence is the transition period between biological maturity and social independence. During these years, both *primary* and *secondary sex characteristics* develop dramatically. Boys seem to benefit from "early" maturation, girls from "late" maturation. The brain's frontal lobes mature during adolescence and the early twenties, enabling improved judgment, impulse control, and long-term planning.

9-2: **How did Piaget and Kohlberg describe cognitive and moral development during adolescence?**
Piaget theorized that adolescents develop the capacity for formal operations, which enables them to reason abstractly, but the rudiments of formal logic appear earlier than Piaget believed. Kohlberg proposed a stage theory of moral thinking, from a preconventional morality of self-interest, to a conventional morality concerned with gaining others' approval or doing one's duty, to

(in some people) a postconventional morality of agreed-upon rights or universal ethical principles. But morality also lies in actions. Kohlberg's critics also note that the postconventional level represents morality from the perspective of individualist, middle-class males.

9-3: **What tasks and challenges do adolescents face en route to mature adulthood?**
Erik Erikson theorized that a chief task of adolescence is solidifying one's sense of self—one's *identity*. This often means "trying on" a number of different roles. During adolescence, parental influence diminishes and peer influence increases. The transition from adolescence to adulthood is now taking longer. Emerging adulthood is the period from age 18 to the mid-twenties, when many young people in Western cultures are not yet fully independent.

>> Rehearse it!

1. Adolescence is marked by the onset of

    a. an identity crisis.
    b. puberty.
    c. concrete operational thought.
    d. parent-child conflict.

2. Dramatic developments in the sex characteristics take place during the adolescent growth spurt. Primary sex characteristics relate to _____; secondary sex characteristics refer to _____.

    a. ejaculation; menarche
    b. breasts and facial hair; ovaries and testes
    c. emotional maturity; hormone surges
    d. reproductive organs; nonreproductive traits

3. According to Piaget, the ability to think logically about abstractions indicates

    a. concrete operational thought.
    b. egocentrism.
    c. formal operational thought.
    d. conservation.

4. According to Kohlberg, preconventional morality focuses on _____; conventional morality is more concerned with _____.

    a. upholding laws and social rules; self-interest
    b. self-interest; basic ethical principles
    c. upholding laws and social rules; basic ethical principles
    d. self-interest; upholding laws and social rules

5. Erikson contended that each stage of life has its own special psychosocial task or challenge. The primary task during adolescence is to

    a. attain formal operations.
    b. forge an identity.
    c. develop a sense of intimacy with another person.
    d. live independent of parents.

6. Later independence and earlier sexual maturity have significantly extended the interlude between biological maturity and social independence. As a result, some developmental psychologists now refer to the time from age 18 to the mid-20s and beyond (up to the time of social independence) as

    a. emerging adulthood.
    b. adolescence.
    c. formal operations.
    d. young adulthood.

Answers: 1. b, 2. d, 3. c, 4. d, 5. b, 6. a.

>> Terms and Concepts to Remember

adolescence, p. 120
puberty, p. 120
primary sex characteristics, p. 120

secondary sex characteristics, p. 121
menarche [meh-NAR-key], p. 121

identity, p. 124
intimacy, p. 125

>> Test Yourself

1. How has the transition from childhood to adulthood changed in Western cultures in the last 100 years?

    (Answer in Appendix C.)

*Multiple-choice **self-tests** and more may be found at www.worthpublishers.com/myers.*

Adulthood

At one time, psychologists viewed the center-of-life years between adolescence and old age as one long plateau. No longer. Those who follow the unfolding of people's adult lives now believe our development continues.

It is more difficult to generalize about adulthood stages than about life's early years. If you know that James is a 1-year-old and Jamal is a 10-year-old, you could say a great deal about each child. Not so with adults who differ by a similar number of years. The boss may be 30 or 60; the marathon runner may be 20 or 50; a 19-year-old can be a parent who supports a child or a child who gets an allowance. Yet our life courses are in some ways similar. Physically, cognitively, and especially socially, we are at age 50 different from our 25-year-old selves.

Physical Development

Cognitive Development

Social Development

Rick Doyle/ Corbis

Adult abilities vary widely
Eighty-seven-year-olds: Don't try this. In 2002, George Blair became the world's oldest barefoot water skier, 18 days after his eighty-seventh birthday.

> "I am still learning."
>
> Michelangelo, 1560, at age 85

Physical Development

10-1 : How do our bodies change in middle and late adulthood?

Our physical abilities—muscular strength, reaction time, sensory keenness, and cardiac output—all crest by the mid-twenties. Like the declining daylight after the summer solstice, the decline of physical prowess begins imperceptibly. Athletes are often the first to notice. World-class sprinters and swimmers peak by their early twenties. Women, because they mature earlier than men, also peak earlier. But most of us—especially those of us whose daily lives do not require top physical performance—hardly perceive the early signs of decline.

Physical Changes in Middle Adulthood

Middle-aged (post-40) athletes know all too well that physical decline gradually accelerates (**FIGURE 10.1**). As a 63-year-old who regularly plays basketball, I now find myself occasionally wondering whether my team really needs me down court. But even diminished vigor is sufficient for normal activities. Moreover, during early and middle adulthood, physical vigor has less to do with age than with a person's health and exercise habits. Many of today's physically fit 50-year-olds run 4 miles with ease, while sedentary 25-year-olds find themselves huffing and puffing up two flights of stairs.

For women, aging means a gradual decline in fertility. Among women 35 to 39, a single act of intercourse is half as likely to produce a pregnancy as it would be for a woman 19 to 26 (Dunson & others, 2002). But women's foremost biological sign of aging is **menopause,** the ending of the menstrual cycle, usually beginning within a few

■ **menopause** the time of natural cessation of menstruation; also refers to the biological changes a woman experiences as her ability to reproduce declines.

© The New Yorker Collection, 1999, Tom Cheney from cartoonbank.com. All Rights Reserved.

"Happy fortieth. I'll take the muscle tone in your upper arms, the girlish timbre of your voice, your amazing tolerance for caffeine, and your ability to digest french fries. The rest of you can stay."

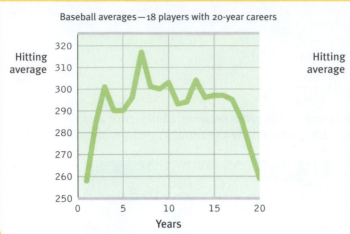

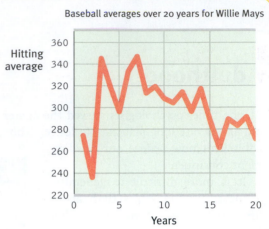

FIGURE 10.1

Gradually accelerating decline

An analysis of aging and batting averages of all twentieth-century major league baseball players revealed a gradual but accelerating decline in players' later years (Schall & Smith, 2000). The career performance record of the great Willie Mays is illustrative.

> "The things that stop you having sex with age are exactly the same as those that stop you riding a bicycle (bad health, thinking it looks silly, no bicycle)."
>
> Alex Comfort, *The Joy of Sex*, 2002

> "For some reason, possibly to save ink, the restaurants had started printing their menus in letters the height of bacteria."
>
> Dave Barry, *Dave Barry Turns Fifty*, 1998

Most stairway falls taken by older people occur on the top step, precisely where the person typically descends from a window-lit hallway into the darker stairwell (Fozard & Popkin, 1978). Our knowledge of aging could be used to design environments that would reduce such accidents (National Research Council, 1990).

years of age 50. Expectations and attitudes influence the emotional impact of menopause. Does a woman see it as a sign that she is losing her femininity and growing old? Or does she view it as liberation from menstrual periods and fears of pregnancy? In many cases, observes social psychologist Jacqueline Goodchilds (1987), "we'd have to diagnose [older women] as having P.M.F.—Post-Menstrual Freedom."

Men experience no equivalent to menopause—no cessation of fertility, no sharp drop in sex hormones. They do experience a more gradual decline in sperm count, testosterone level, and speed of erection and ejaculation. Some may also experience distress related to their perception of declining virility and physical capacities. But most age without such problems. After middle age, most men and women remain capable of satisfying sexual activity. When people over 60 were surveyed by the National Council on Aging, 39 percent expressed satisfaction with the amount of sex they were having and 39 percent said they wished for sex more frequently (Leary, 1998).

Physical Changes in Later Life

Is old age "more to be feared than death" (Juvenal, *Satires*)? Or is life "most delightful when it is on the downward slope" (Seneca, *Epistulae ad Lucilium*)? What is it like to grow old?

Sensory Abilities

Although physical decline begins in early adulthood, we are not usually acutely aware of it until later life. Visual sharpness diminishes, and adaptation to changes in light level slows. Muscle strength, reaction time, and stamina also diminish noticeably, as do hearing, distance perception, and the sense of smell (**FIGURE 10.2**). In later life, the stairs get steeper, the print gets smaller, and people seem to mumble more.

With age, the eye's pupil shrinks and its lens becomes less transparent, reducing the amount of light reaching the retina. In fact, a 65-year-old retina receives only about one-third as much light as its 20-year-old counterpart (Kline & Schieber, 1985). Thus, to see as well as a 20-year-old when reading or driving, a 65-year-old needs three times as much light—a reason for buying cars with untinted windshields. This also explains why older people sometimes ask younger people, "Don't you need better light for reading?"

Health

For those growing older, there is both bad and good news about health. The bad news: The body's disease-fighting immune system weakens, making the elderly more susceptible to life-threatening ailments such as cancer and pneumonia. The good news: Thanks partly to a lifetime's accumulation of antibodies, older people suffer fewer

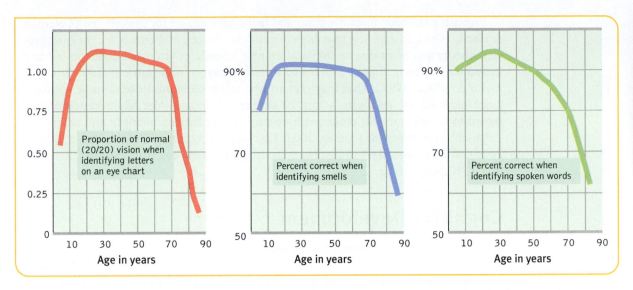

Michael Newman/PhotoEdit

FIGURE 10.2
The aging senses
Sight, smell, and hearing all are less acute among those over age 70. (From Doty & others, 1984.)

short-term ailments, such as common flu and cold viruses. For example, those over 65 are half as likely as 20-year-olds and one-fifth as likely as preschoolers to suffer upper respiratory flu each year (National Center for Health Statistics, 1990). This helps explain why older workers have lower absenteeism rates (Rhodes, 1983).

Aging levies a tax on the brain by slowing our neural processing. Up to the teen years, we process information with greater and greater speed (Fry & Hale, 1996; Kail, 1991). But compared with teens and young adults, older people take a bit more time to react, to solve perceptual puzzles, even to remember names (Bashore & others, 1997; Verhaeghen & Salthouse, 1997). The lag is greatest on complex tasks (Cerella, 1985; Poon, 1987). At video games, most 70-year-olds are no match for a 20-year-old. And, as **FIGURE 10.3** indicates, fatal accident rates per mile driven increase sharply after age 75. By age 85, they exceed the 16-year-old level. Nevertheless, because older people drive less, they account for less than 10 percent of crashes (Coughlin & others, 2004).

Brain regions important to memory begin to atrophy during aging (Schacter, 1996). In young adulthood, a small, gradual net loss of brain cells begins, contributing by age 80 to a brain-weight reduction of 5 percent or so. Aging may proceed more slowly in women. Not only do women worldwide live four years longer than men, their brains shrink more slowly than men's (Coffey & others, 1998).

How old does a person have to be before you think of him or her as old? The average 18- to 29-year-old says 67. The average person 60 and over says 76 (Yankelovich, 1995).

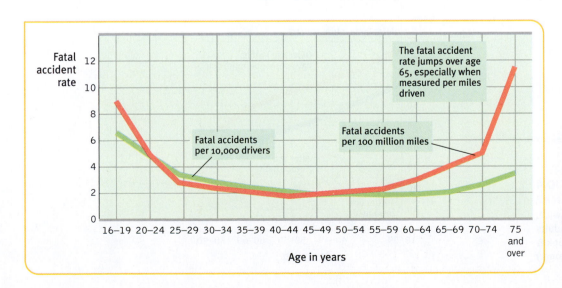

FIGURE 10.3
Age and driver fatalities
Slowing reactions contribute to increased accident risks among those 75 and older, and their greater fragility increases their risk of death when accidents happen (NHTSA, 2000). Would you favor driver exams based on performance, not age, to screen out those whose slow reactions or sensory impairments indicate accident risk?

Exercising the body feeds the brain and helps compensate for the cell loss (Coleman & Flood, 1986). In addition to enhancing muscles, bones, and energy and helping prevent obesity and heart disease, physical exercise stimulates brain cell development and neural connections, thanks perhaps to increased oxygen and nutrient flow (Kempermann & others, 1998). That may explain why active older adults tend to be mentally quick older adults, and why, across 20 studies, sedentary older adults randomly assigned to aerobic exercise programs have exhibited enhanced memory and sharpened judgment (Colcombe & Kramer, 2003; Colcombe & others, 2004; Weuve & others, 2004). We are more likely to rust from disuse than to wear out from overuse. "Use it or lose it" is sound advice.

Cognitive Development

10-2: In what ways do memory and intelligence change as we age?

Among the most controversial questions in the study of the human life span is whether adult cognitive abilities, such as memory, intelligence, and creativity, parallel the gradually accelerating decline of physical abilities.

Aging and Memory

As we age, we remember some things well. Looking back in later life, people asked to recall the one or two most important events over the last half-century tend to name events from their teens or twenties (Conway & others, 2005; Rubin & others, 1998). Whatever one experienced around this time of life—World War II, the civil rights movement, the Vietnam war, or the events of 9/11—becomes pivotal (Pillemer, 1998; Schuman & Scott, 1989). Our teens and twenties are also the time when we experience so many memorable "firsts"—first date, first job, first going to college, first meeting your parents-in-law.

For some types of learning and remembering, early adulthood is indeed a peak time. In one experiment, Thomas Crook and Robin West (1990) invited 1205 people to learn some names. Fourteen videotaped people said their names, using a common format: "Hi, I'm Larry." Then the same individuals reappeared and said, for example, "I'm from Philadelphia"—thus providing a visual and voice cue for remembering the person's name. As **FIGURE 10.4** shows, everyone remembered more names after a second and

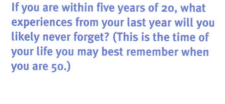
If you are within five years of 20, what experiences from your last year will you likely never forget? (This is the time of your life you may best remember when you are 50.)

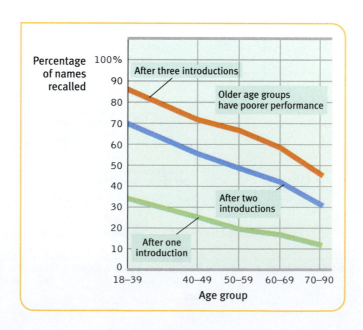

FIGURE 10.4
Tests of recall
Recalling new names introduced once, twice, or three times is easier for younger adults than for older ones. (Data from Crook & West, 1990.)

Chart: Percentage of names recalled (y-axis, 0–100%) by Age group (x-axis: 18–39, 40–49, 50–59, 60–69, 70–90)

After three introductions
Older age groups have poorer performance
After two introductions
After one introduction

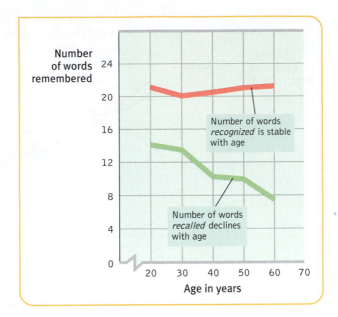

FIGURE 10.5
Recall and recognition in adulthood
In this experiment, the ability to *recall* new information declined during early and middle adulthood, but the ability to *recognize* new information did not. (From Schonfield & Robertson, 1966.)

third replay of the introductions, but younger adults consistently surpassed older adults on this task. Similar results appear in other studies. Within hours after Prime Minister Margaret Thatcher announced her resignation, young and old British people recalled how they heard the news. When asked again 11 months later, 90 percent of the younger group, but only 42 percent of the older group, told the same story (Cohen & others, 1994). Perhaps it is not surprising, then, that nearly two-thirds of people over age 40 say their memory is worse than it was 10 years ago (KRC, 2001).

But consider another experiment (Schonfield & Robertson, 1966), in which adults of various ages learned a list of 24 words. Without giving any clues, the researchers then asked some to *recall* as many words as they could from the list, and others simply to *recognize* words, using multiple-choice questions. Again, younger adults had better recall (**FIGURE 10.5**). No similar memory decline with age appeared on the recognition tests. Unless given a jolt of caffeine, older adults have better recognition memory early in the day rather than late (May & others, 1993; Ryan & others, 2002). So, how well older people remember depends: Are they being asked simply to *recognize* what they have tried to memorize (minimal decline) or to *recall* it without clues (greater decline)?

Remembering seems also to depend on the type of information you are trying to retrieve. If the information is meaningless—nonsense syllables or unimportant events—then the older you are, the more errors you are likely to make. But if the information is *meaningful,* older people's rich web of existing knowledge will help them to catch it, though they may take longer than younger adults to *produce* the words and things they know (Burke & Shafto, 2004). (Quick-thinking game show winners are usually younger to middle-aged adults.) Older people's capacity to learn and remember skills also declines less than their verbal recall (Graf, 1990; Labouvie-Vief & Schell, 1982; Perlmutter, 1983).

Aging and Intelligence

What happens to our broader intellectual powers as we age? Do they gradually decline, as does our ability to recall new material? Or do they remain constant, as does our ability to recognize meaningful material?

The answers depend on what we assess and how we assess it. **Crystallized intelligence**—one's accumulated knowledge as reflected in vocabulary and analogies tests—*increases* up to old age. **Fluid intelligence**—one's ability to reason speedily and abstractly, as when solving novel logic problems—*decreases* slowly up to age 75 or so,

■ **crystallized intelligence** one's accumulated knowledge and verbal skills; tends to increase with age.

■ **fluid intelligence** one's ability to reason speedily and abstractly; tends to decrease during late adulthood.

"In youth we learn, in age we understand."
Marie Von Ebner-Eschenbach, *Aphorisms*, 1883

FIGURE 10.6
The downs and ups of aging
Using a variety of reliable measures of processing capacity (such as speed of processing, working memory, and long-term memory) and world knowledge (such as vocabulary), Denise Park and her colleagues (2002) consistently illustrated that with age, our processing capacity declines but our vocabulary and general knowledge increase.

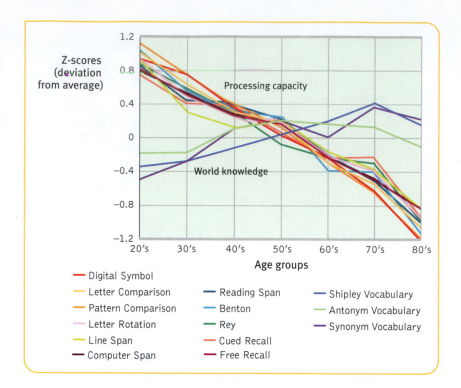

then more rapidly, especially after age 85 (Cattell, 1963; Horn, 1982). We can see this pattern in the intelligence scores of a national sample of adults. After adjustments for education, verbal scores (reflecting crystallized intelligence) held relatively steady from ages 20 to 74. Nonverbal, puzzle-solving intelligence declined. Thus, Denise Park and her colleagues (2002) confirm, with age we lose and we win (**FIGURE 10.6**). We lose recall memory and processing speed, but we gain vocabulary and knowledge.

These cognitive differences help explain why mathematicians and scientists produce much of their most creative work during their late twenties or early thirties, whereas those in literature, history, and philosophy tend to produce their best work in their forties, fifties, and beyond, after accumulating more knowledge (Simonton, 1988, 1990). For example, poets (who depend on fluid intelligence) reach their peak output earlier than prose authors (who need a deeper knowledge reservoir), a finding observed in every major literary tradition, for both living and dead languages.

Social Development

Many differences between younger and older adults are created not by the physical and cognitive changes that accompany aging but by significant life events. A new job means new relationships, new expectations, and new demands. Marriage brings the joy of intimacy and the stress of merging your life with another's. The birth of a child introduces responsibilities and significantly alters your life focus. The death of a loved one creates an irreplaceable loss and a need to reaffirm your own life. Do these normal events of adult life shape a predictable sequence of life changes?

Adulthood's Ages and Stages

10-3 : Is the journey from early adulthood to death marked by stages that serve as developmental milestones?

As people enter their forties, they undergo a transition to middle adulthood, a time when they realize that life will soon be mostly behind them instead of ahead of them. Some psychologists have argued that for many the midlife transition is a crisis, a time

"Midway in the journey of our life I found myself in a dark wood, for the straight way was lost."

Dante, *The Divine Comedy*, 1314

of great struggle, regret, or even feeling struck down by life. The popular image of the midlife crisis is an early-forties man who forsakes his family for a younger girlfriend and a hot sports car. But the fact—reported by large samples of people—is that unhappiness, job dissatisfaction, marital dissatisfaction, divorce, anxiety, and suicide do *not* surge during the early forties (Hunter & Sundel, 1989; Mroczek & Kolarz, 1998). Divorce, for example, is most common among those in their twenties, suicide among those in their seventies and eighties. One study of emotional instability in nearly 10,000 men and women found "not the slightest evidence" that distress peaks anywhere in the midlife age range (**FIGURE 10.7**). For the one in four adults who does report experiencing a life crisis, the trigger is not age, but a major event such as illness, divorce, or job loss (Lachman, 2004).

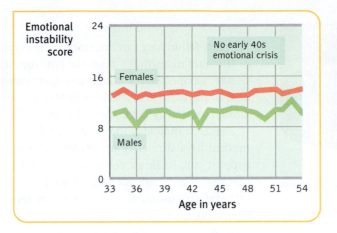

FIGURE 10.7
Early forties midlife crises? Among 10,000 people responding to a national health survey, there was no early forties increase in emotional instability ("neuroticism") scores. (From McCrae & Costa, 1990.)

For women and men, life events are triggering transitions to new life stages at increasingly unpredictable ages. The **social clock**—the definition of "the right time" to leave home, get a job, marry, have children, and retire—varies from era to era and culture to culture. In Jordan, 40 percent of brides are in their teens; in Hong Kong, only 3 percent are (United Nations, 1992). In Western Europe, fewer than 10 percent of men over 65 remain in the work force, as do 16 percent in the United States, 36 percent in Japan, and 69 percent in Mexico (Davies & others, 1991). And the once rigid sequence for Western women—of student to worker to wife to at-home mom to worker again—has loosened. Contemporary women occupy these roles in any order or all at once. The social clock still ticks, but people feel freer about being out of sync with it.

Even chance events can have lasting significance because they often deflect us down one road rather than another (Bandura, 1982). Romantic attraction, for example, is often influenced by chance encounters. Albert Bandura (2005) recalls the ironic true story of a book editor who came to one of his lectures on the "Psychology of Chance Encounters and Life Paths"—and ended up marrying the woman who happened to sit next to him.

Consider one study of identical twins and their spouses. Twins, especially identical twins, make similar choices of friends, clothes, vacations, jobs, and so on. So, if your identical twin became engaged to someone, wouldn't you (being in so many ways the same as your twin) expect to also feel attracted to this person? Surprisingly, only half the identical twins recalled really liking their co-twin's selection, and only 5 percent said, "I could have fallen for my twin's partner." Researchers David Lykken and Auke Tellegen (1993) surmise that romantic love is rather like ducklings' imprinting: Given repeated exposure to someone after childhood, you may form a bond (infatuation) with almost any available person who has a roughly similar background and level of attractiveness and who reciprocates your affections.

Adulthood's Commitments

10-4: What do psychologists view as adulthood's two primary commitments?

Two basic aspects of our lives do, however, dominate adulthood. Erik Erikson called them *intimacy* (forming close relationships) and *generativity* (being productive and supporting future generations). Researchers have chosen various terms—*affiliation* and *achievement, attachment* and *productivity, commitment* and *competence*. Sigmund Freud (1935) put it most simply: The healthy adult, he said, is one who can *love* and *work*.

> "The important events of a person's life are the products of chains of highly improbable occurrences."
> Joseph Traub, "Traub's Law," 2003

■ **social clock** the culturally preferred timing of social events such as marriage, parenthood, and retirement.

> "One can live magnificently in this world if one knows how to work and how to love."
> Leo Tolstoy, 1856

Love

Intimacy, attachment, commitment—love by whatever name—is central to healthy and happy adulthood.

Love

We flirt, fall in love, and commit—one person at a time. "Pair-bonding is a trademark of the human animal," observed anthropologist Helen Fisher (1993). From an evolutionary perspective, relatively monogamous pairing makes sense: Parents who cooperated to nurture their children to maturity were more likely to have their genes passed along to posterity than parents who didn't.

Research indicates that adult bonds of love are most satisfying and enduring when marked by a similarity of interests and values, a sharing of emotional and material support, and intimate self-disclosure. Marriage bonds are also likely to last when couples marry after age 20 and are well educated. Compared with their counterparts of 40 years ago, people in Western countries *are* better educated and marrying later. Yet, ironically, they are twice as likely to divorce. (Both Canada and the United States now have about one divorce for every two marriages [Bureau of the Census, 2004], and in Europe, divorce is only slightly less common.) The divorce rate partly reflects women's lessened economic dependence and men and women's rising expectations. We now hope not only for an enduring bond, but also for a mate who is a wage earner, caregiver, intimate friend, and warm and responsive lover.

Might test-driving life together in a "trial marriage" minimize divorce risk? In a 2001 Gallup survey of American twenty-somethings, 62 percent thought it would (Whitehead & Popenoe, 2001). In reality, in Europe, Canada, and the United States, those who cohabited before marriage had *higher* rates of divorce and marital dysfunction than those who had not (Dush & others, 2003; Popenoe & Whitehead, 2002). The risk appears greatest for those who cohabit prior to engagement (Kline & others, 2004). Cohabiters tend to be initially less committed to the ideal of enduring marriage, and they become even less marriage-supporting while cohabiting.

Nonetheless, the institution of marriage endures. Worldwide, reports the United Nations, 9 in 10 heterosexual adults marry. And marriage is a predictor of happiness, health, sexual satisfaction, and income. Surveys of more than 40,000 Americans since 1972 reveal that 40 percent of married adults, though only 23 percent of unmarried adults, report being "very happy." Lesbian couples, too, report greater well-being than those who are alone (Wayment & Peplau, 1995). Moreover, neighborhoods with high marriage rates typically have low rates of social pathologies such as crime, delinquency, and emotional disorders among children (Myers & Scanzoni, 2005).

Often, love bears children. For most people, this most enduring of life changes is a happy event. "I feel an overwhelming love for my children unlike anything I feel for anyone else," said 93 percent of American mothers in a national survey (Erickson & Aird, 2005). Many fathers feel the same. A few weeks after the birth of my first child I was suddenly struck by a realization: "So *this* is how my parents felt about me!"

When children begin to absorb time, money, and emotional energy, satisfaction with the marriage itself may decline. This is especially likely among employed women who, more than they expected, carry the traditional burden of doing the chores at home. Putting effort into creating an equitable relationship can thus pay double dividends: a more satisfying marriage, which breeds better parent-child relations (Erel & Burman, 1995).

Although love bears children, children eventually leave home. This departure is a significant and sometimes difficult event. For most people, however, an empty nest is a happy place (Adelmann & others, 1989; Glenn, 1975). Compared with middle-aged women with children at home, those living in an empty nest report greater happiness and greater enjoyment of their marriage. Many parents experience what sociologists Lynn White and John Edwards (1990) call a "postlaunch honeymoon," especially if they maintain close relationships with their children.

What do you think? Does marriage correlate with happiness because marital support and intimacy breed happiness, because happy people more often marry and stay married, or both?

If you have left home, did your parents suffer the "empty nest syndrome"—a feeling of distress focusing on a loss of purpose and relationship? Did they mourn the lost joy of listening for you in the wee hours of Saturday morning? Or did they seem to discover a new freedom, relaxation, and (if still married) renewed satisfaction with their own relationship?

Work

For many adults, the answer to "Who are you?" depends a great deal on the answer to "What do you do?" Was Freud right that work, including a career, contributes to self-fulfillment and life satisfaction? It does for those who enter the working world with a positive disposition that helps engender success which, over time, reinforces a positive approach to life. "Alienated and hostile adolescents," on the other hand, tend to have less satisfying work experiences that undermine their achieving a positive transition into the working world (Roberts & others, 2003).

Charles Harbutt/Actuality

LWA–Dann Tardif/ Corbis

Job satisfaction and life satisfaction
Work can provide us with a sense of identity and competence and opportunities for accomplishment. Perhaps this is why challenging and interesting occupations enhance people's happiness.

For women and men, choosing a career path is difficult, especially in today's changing work environment. During the first two years of college or university, few students can predict their later careers. Most shift from their initially intended majors, many find their postcollege employment in fields not directly related to their majors, and most will change careers (Rothstein, 1980). In the end, happiness is about having work that fits your interests and provides you with a sense of competence and accomplishment. And for those who choose to marry, it is having a partner who is a close, supportive companion and who sees you as special, and—for some—it includes having loving children whom you like and feel proud of.

Well-Being Across the Life Span

To live is to grow older. This moment marks the oldest you have ever been and the youngest you will henceforth be. That means we all can look back with satisfaction or regret, and forward with hope or dread. When people are asked what they would have done differently if they could relive their lives, their most common answer is "taken my education more seriously and worked harder at it" (Kinnier & Metha, 1989; Roese & Summerville, 2005). Other regrets—"I should have told my father I loved him," "I regret that I never went to Europe"—also focus less on mistakes made than on the things one *failed* to do (Gilovich & Medvec, 1995).

From early adulthood to midlife, people typically experience a strengthening sense of identity, confidence, and self-esteem (Miner-Rubino & others, 2004; Robins & Trzesniewski, 2005). In later life, challenges arise: Income shrinks, work is often taken away, the body deteriorates, recall fades, energy wanes, family members and friends die or move away, and the great enemy, death, looms ever closer. Small wonder many presume the over-65 years must be the worst of times. But they are not, as Ronald Inglehart (1990) discovered when he amassed interviews conducted

How will you look back on your life 10 years from now? Are you making choices that someday you will recollect with satisfaction?

FIGURE **10.8**
Age and life satisfaction
With the tasks of early adulthood behind them, many older adults have more time to pursue personal interests. No wonder their satisfaction with life remains high, and may even rise if they are healthy and active. As this graph based on multinational surveys shows, age differences in life satisfaction are trivial. (Data from Inglehart, 1990.)

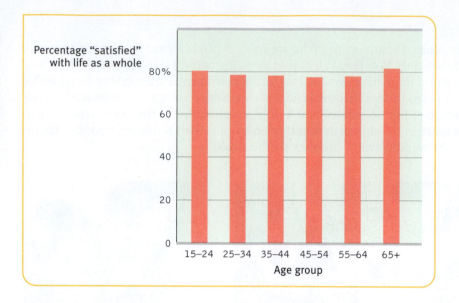

"The best thing about being 100 is *no peer pressure*."

Lewis W. Kuester, 2005, on turning 100

during the 1980s with representative samples of nearly 170,000 people in 16 nations. Older people report as much happiness and satisfaction with life as younger people do (**FIGURE 10.8**).

If anything, positive feelings grow after midlife and negative feelings subside (Charles & others, 2001; Mroczek, 2001). Older adults increasingly use words that convey positive emotions (Pennebaker & Stone, 2003). They attend less and less to negative information. For example, they are slower than younger adults to perceive negative faces (Mather & Carstensen, 2003). Their amygdala, a neural processing center for emotions, shows diminishing activity in response to negative events while maintaining its responsiveness to positive events (Mather & others, 2004). Moreover, the bad feelings we associate with negative events fade faster than do the good feelings we associate with positive events (Walker & others, 2003). This contributes to most older people's sense that life, on balance, has been mostly good. Given that growing older is an outcome of living (an outcome nearly all of us prefer to early dying), the positivity of later life is comforting (**FIGURE 10.9**). As the years go by, feelings mellow (Costa & others, 1987; Diener & others, 1986). Highs become less high, lows less low.

FIGURE **10.9**
Biopsychosocial influences on successful aging
Numerous biological, psychological, and social-cultural factors affect the way we age. With the right genes, we have a good chance of aging successfully if we maintain a positive outlook and stay mentally and physically active as well as connected to family and friends in the community.

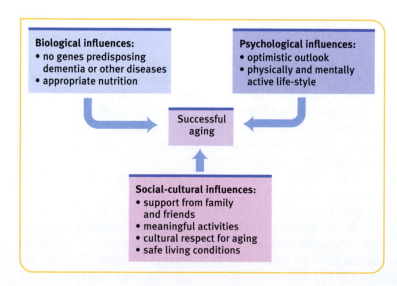

Death and Dying

Most of us will suffer and cope with the deaths of relatives and friends. Usually, the most difficult separation is from one's spouse—a loss suffered by five times more women than men. When, as usually happens, death comes at an expected late-life time, the grieving may be relatively short-lived. (**FIGURE 10.10** shows the typical emotions before and after a spouse's death.) Grief is especially severe when the death of a loved one comes suddenly and before its expected time on the social clock. The sudden illness that claims a 45-year-old life partner or the accidental death of a child may trigger a year or more of mourning flooded with memories, eventually subsiding to a mild depression that sometimes continues for several years (Lehman & others, 1987). For some, the loss is unbearable. One study, following more than 1 million Danes over the last half of the twentieth century, found that more than 17,000 people had suffered the death of a child under 18. In the five years following that death, their 3 percent rate of first psychiatric hospitalization was 67 percent higher than the rate recorded for parents who had not lost a child (Li & others, 2005).

The normal range of reactions to a loved one's death is wider than most suppose. Some cultures encourage public weeping and wailing; others hide grief. Within any culture, some individuals grieve more intensely and openly. Contrary to popular misconceptions, however,

- those who express the strongest grief immediately do not purge their grief more quickly (Bonanno & Kaltman, 1999; Wortman & Silver, 1989).
- for most people, bereavement therapy and self-help groups do little to enhance the healing power of time and supportive friends. Grieving spouses who talk often with others or who receive grief counseling adjust no better than those who grieve more privately (Bonanno, 2001, 2004; Genevro, 2003; Stroebe & others, 2001, 2002, 2005).
- terminally ill and bereaved people do not go through predictable stages, such as denial, anger, and so forth (Nolen-Hoeksema & Larson, 1999). Given similar losses, some people grieve hard and long, others more lightly and briefly.

We can be grateful for the waning of death-denying attitudes. Facing death with dignity and openness helps people complete the life cycle with a sense of life's meaningfulness and unity—the sense that their existence has been good and that life and death are parts of an ongoing cycle. Although death may be unwelcome, life itself can be affirmed even at death. This is especially so for people who review their lives not with despair but with what Erik Erikson called a sense of *integrity*—a feeling that one's life has been meaningful and worthwhile.

> "Love—why, I'll tell you what love is: It's you at 75 and her at 71, each of you listening for the other's step in the next room, each afraid that a sudden silence, a sudden cry, could mean a lifetime's talk is over."
>
> Brian Moore, *The Luck of Ginger Coffey*, 1960

> "Consider, friend, as you pass by, as you are now, so once was I. As I am now, you too shall be. Prepare, therefore, to follow me."
>
> Scottish tombstone epitaph

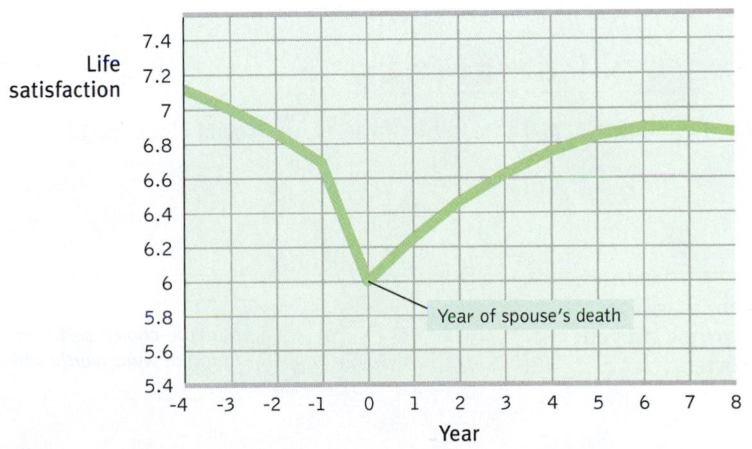

FIGURE 10.10

Life satisfaction before, during the year of, and after a spouse's death
Richard Lucas and his collaborators (2003) examined longitudinal annual surveys of more than 30,000 Germans. The researchers identified 513 married people who experienced the death of a spouse and did not remarry. They found that life satisfaction began to dip during the prewidowhood year, dropped significantly during the year of the spouse's death, and then eventually rebounded to nearly the earlier level. (*Source:* Richard Lucas.)

REVIEWING

>> MODULE REVIEW

10-1 : **How do our bodies change in middle and late adulthood?**
Muscular strength, reaction time, sensory abilities, and cardiac output begin to decline in the late twenties. Around age 50, *menopause* ends women's period of fertility, but they may continue to enjoy a satisfying sex life. Most women do not experience depression or other psychological problems with menopause. Men do not undergo a similar sharp drop in hormone levels or fertility.

10-2 : **In what ways do memory and intelligence change as we age?**
As the years pass, recall begins to decline, especially for meaningless information, but recognition memory remains strong. *Fluid intelligence* declines in later life but *crystallized intelligence* does not.

10-3 : **Is the journey from early adulthood to death marked by stages that serve as developmental milestones?**

Adults do not progress through an orderly sequence of age-related stages. More important are life events, and the loosening of strict dictates of the *social clock*—the culturally preferred timing of social events.

10-4 : **What do psychologists view as adulthood's two primary commitments?**
Adulthood's two major commitments are love (Erikson's intimacy—forming close relationships, especially with family) and work (productive activity, or what Erikson called generativity). Marriage seems more likely to last when people marry after age 20 and are well-educated, but Western couples who marry today are more than twice as likely to divorce as were those who married in 1960. Most people age gracefully, retaining a sense of well-being throughout life. Erikson's view of the crisis of late adulthood pits integrity against despair.

>> REHEARSE IT!

1. Some types of learning and remembering peak in early adulthood. By age 65, a person would be most likely to experience a decline in the ability to

   a. recall and list all the items in a chapter glossary.
   b. select the correct definition in a multiple-choice question.
   c. evaluate whether a statement is true or false.
   d. exercise sound judgment in answering an essay question.

2. Freud defined the healthy adult as one who is able to love and work. Erikson agreed, observing that the adult struggles to attain intimacy and

   a. affiliation.
   b. identity.
   c. competence.
   d. generativity.

3. Contrary to what many people assume,

   a. older people are much happier than adolescents.

   b. men in their forties express much greater dissatisfaction with life than do women of the same age.
   c. people of all ages report similar levels of happiness.
   d. those whose children have recently left home—the empty nesters—have the lowest level of happiness of all groups.

Answers: 1. a, 2. d, 3. c.

>> TERMS AND CONCEPTS TO REMEMBER

menopause, p. 129
crystallized intelligence, p. 133

fluid intelligence, p. 133

social clock, p. 135

>> TEST YOURSELF

1. Research has shown that living together before marriage predicts an increased likelihood of future divorce. Can you imagine two possible explanations for this correlation?

   (Answer in Appendix C.)

 *Multiple-choice **self-tests** and more may be found at www.worthpublishers.com/myers.*

Sensation and Perception

Sensation and Perception

Twenty-four hours a day, stimuli from the outside world bombard your body. Meanwhile, in a silent, cushioned, inner world, your brain floats in utter darkness. By itself, it sees nothing. It hears nothing. It feels nothing. This raises a question that predates psychology and helped inspire its beginnings: *How does the world out there get in?*

To modernize the question: How do we construct our representations of the external world? How do a campfire's flicker, crackle, and smoky scent activate neural connections? And how, from this living neurochemistry, do we create our conscious experience of the fire's motion and temperature, its aroma and beauty?

The feat begins when our sensory receptors detect physical energy from the environment and translate it into neural signals in a process traditionally called *sensation*. Sensory analysis at this level is *bottom-up processing*. But we must also select, organize, and interpret our sensations, a process traditionally called *perception*. Our mind interprets what our senses detect. Psychologists call this analysis, guided in part by our experience and expectations, *top-down processing*.

In our everyday experiences, sensory and perceptual processes form a continuum. In Modules 11 through 14, we slow down this process to study its parts, beginning with sensory detection (Modules 11 and 12) and working up to higher processing levels—perceptual organization and interpretation (Modules 13 and 14).

Failures occurring anywhere between sensory detection and perceptual interpretation can distort our view of the world, as happened to patient "E. H." After losing a temporal lobe area essential to recognizing faces, she suffers from a condition called *prosopagnosia*. She has complete sensation but incomplete perception. She can sense visual information—indeed may accurately report facial features—yet she is unable to recognize people. Shown an unfamiliar face, she does not react. Shown a familiar face, her autonomic nervous system responds with measurable perspiration. Still, she hasn't a clue who the person is. Shown her own face in a mirror, she is again stumped. Because of her brain damage, she cannot process top-down—she cannot relate her stored knowledge to the sensory input.

Introduction to Sensation and Perception: Vision

To construct the outside world inside our heads we must detect physical energy from the environment and then encode it as neural signals (a process traditionally called **sensation**). And we must also select, organize, and interpret our sensations (a process traditionally called **perception**). We not only sense raw sights and sounds, tastes and smells, we *perceive*. We hear not just a mix of pitches and rhythms but a child's cry, the traffic's hum, a symphony's crescendo. Our perceptions are affected by the biology of our sensory systems, but also by our previous experiences and cultural expectations. In transforming sensations into perceptions, we create the meaning.

Our sensory and perceptual processes work together to help us sort out the complex images in the **FIGURE 11.1** painting. Through **bottom-up processing,** which begins with our sensory receptors, we detect the lines, angles, and colors that form the horses, rider, and surroundings. But we also apply **top-down processing,** drawing on our experience and expectations, when we consider the painting's title, notice the apprehensive expressions, and then direct our attention to aspects of the painting that will give our observations meaning. (Did you notice the hidden faces?)

We begin our introduction to sensation and perception with a look at some basic principles, and then consider vision—for humans, the major sense.

Sensing the World: Some Basic Principles

Vision

■ **sensation** the process by which our sensory receptors and nervous system receive and represent stimulus energies from our environment.

■ **perception** the process of organizing and interpreting sensory information, enabling us to recognize meaningful objects and events.

■ **bottom-up processing** analysis that begins with the sensory receptors and works up to the brain's integration of sensory information.

■ **top-down processing** information processing guided by higher-level mental processes, as when we construct perceptions drawing on our experience and expectations.

Detail, *The Forest Has Eyes* by Bev Doolittle © The Greenwich Workshop, Inc., Trumbull, CT.

FIGURE 11.1
Top-down and bottom-up processing: *The Forest Has Eyes.* With top-down processing, you may, with this nudge, see some hidden faces.

Sensing the World: Some Basic Principles

Nature's sensory gifts suit each recipient's needs. They enable each organism to obtain the information it needs. Consider:

- A frog, which feeds on flying insects, has eyes with receptor cells that fire only in response to small, dark, moving objects. A frog could starve to death knee-deep in motionless flies. But let one zoom by and the frog's "bug detector" cells snap awake.

■ **psychophysics** the study of relationships between the physical characteristics of stimuli, such as their intensity, and our psychological experience of them.

■ **absolute threshold** the minimum stimulation needed to detect a particular stimulus 50 percent of the time.

■ **subliminal** below one's absolute threshold for conscious awareness.

■ **priming** the activation, often unconsciously, of certain associations, thus predisposing one's perception, memory, or response.

■ **difference threshold** the minimum difference between two stimuli required for detection 50 percent of the time. We experience the difference threshold as a *just noticeable difference* (or *jnd*).

■ **Weber's law** the principle that, to be perceived as different, two stimuli must differ by a constant minimum percentage (rather than a constant amount).

- A male silkworm moth has receptors so sensitive to the female sex-attractant odor that a single female need release only a billionth of an ounce per second to attract every male silkworm moth within a mile. That is why there continue to be silkworms.
- We are similarly designed to detect the important features of our environment. Our ears are most sensitive to sound frequencies that include human voice consonants and a baby's cry.

We begin our exploration of those sensory gifts with a question that cuts across all our sensory systems: What stimuli cross our threshold for conscious awareness?

Thresholds

We exist in a sea of energy. At this moment, you and I are being struck by x-rays and radio waves, ultraviolet and infrared light, and sound waves of very high and very low frequencies. To all of these we are blind and deaf. Other animals detect a world that lies beyond human experience (Hughes, 1999). Birds stay on course using a magnetic compass. Bats and dolphins locate prey with sonar (bouncing echoing sound off objects). On a cloudy day, bees navigate by detecting polarized light from an invisible (to us) sun.

The shades on our own senses are open just a crack, allowing us only a restricted awareness of this vast sea of energy. Let's see what **psychophysics** has discovered about the physical energy we can detect and its effect on our psychological experience.

Absolute Thresholds

11-1 : What is an absolute threshold, and are we influenced by stimuli below it?

To some kinds of stimuli we are exquisitely sensitive. Standing atop a mountain on an utterly dark, clear night, most of us could see a candle flame atop another mountain 30 miles away. We could feel the wing of a bee falling on our cheek. We could even smell a single drop of perfume in a three-room apartment (Galanter, 1962).

Our awareness of these faint stimuli illustrates our **absolute thresholds**—the minimum stimulation necessary to detect a particular light, sound, pressure, taste, or odor 50 percent of the time. To test your absolute threshold for sounds, a hearing specialist would expose each of your ears to varying sound levels. For each tone, the test would define where half the time you correctly detect the sound and half the time you do not. For each of your senses, that 50-50 recognition point defines your absolute threshold.

Subliminal Stimulation

Hoping to penetrate our unconscious, entrepreneurs offer audiotapes to help us lose weight, stop smoking, or improve our memories. Masked by soothing ocean sounds, unheard messages ("I am thin," "Smoke tastes bad," or "I do well on tests. I have total recall of information") attempt to influence our behavior. Such claims make two assumptions: We can unconsciously sense **subliminal** (literally, "below threshold") stimuli (**FIGURE 11.2**), and without our awareness, these stimuli have extraordinary suggestive powers. Can we? Do they?

Can we be affected by stimuli so weak as to be unnoticed? Under certain conditions, the answer is yes. An invisible image or word can briefly **prime** your response to a later question. In a typical experiment, the image or word is quickly flashed, then replaced by a *masking stimulus* that interrupts the brain's processing before conscious perception. For example, one experiment subliminally flashed either emotionally positive scenes (kittens, a romantic couple) or negative scenes (a werewolf, a dead body) an instant before participants viewed slides of people (Krosnick & others, 1992). Although consciously perceiving either scene as only a flash of light, the participants gave more positive ratings to people paired with positive images. People somehow looked nicer if their photo immediately followed unperceived kittens rather than an unperceived werewolf.

Subliminal persuasion?

Although subliminally presented stimuli *can* subtly influence people, experiments discount attempts at subliminal advertising and self-improvement. (The playful message here is not actually subliminal—because you can easily perceive it.)

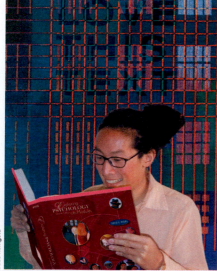

Babs Reingold

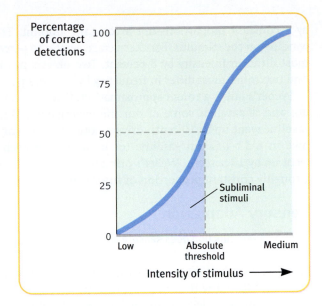

FIGURE 11.2
Absolute threshold
Do I taste it or not? When stimuli are detectable less than 50 percent of the time, they are "subliminal." *Absolute threshold* is the intensity at which we can detect a stimulus half the time.

This experiment illustrates an intriguing phenomenon: Sometimes we *feel* what we do not know and cannot describe. An imperceptibly brief stimulus often triggers a weak response that *can* be detected by brain scanning (Blankenburg & others, 2003). That small brain response may evoke a feeling, though not a conscious awareness of the stimulus. The conclusion (turn up the volume here): *Much of our information processing occurs automatically, out of sight, off the radar screen of our conscious mind.*

But does the fact of subliminal *sensation* verify entrepreneurial claims of subliminal *persuasion?* Can advertisers really manipulate us with "hidden persuasion"? The near-consensus among researchers is no. Their verdict is similar to that of astronomers who say of astrologers, yes, they are right that stars and planets are out there, but no, the celestial bodies don't directly affect us. The laboratory research reveals a *subtle, fleeting* effect. Priming thirsty people with the subliminal word *thirst* might therefore, for a brief interval, make a thirst-quenching beverage ad more persuasive (Strahan & others, 2002). But the subliminal tape hucksters claim something different: a *powerful, enduring* effect on *behavior.*

When Anthony Greenwald and his colleagues (1991, 1992) tested that claim in 16 experiments evaluating subliminal self-help tapes, his results were uniform: None had any therapeutic effect beyond that of a placebo (the effect of one's belief in them). His conclusion: "Subliminal procedures offer little or nothing of value to the marketing practitioner" (Pratkanis & Greenwald, 1988).

Difference Thresholds

11-2: How does the magnitude of a stimulus influence our threshold for detecting differences?

To function effectively, we need absolute thresholds low enough to allow us to detect important sights, sounds, textures, tastes, and smells. We also need to detect small differences among stimuli. A musician must detect minute discrepancies in an instrument's tuning. Parents must detect the sound of their own child's voice amid other children's voices.

The **difference threshold** (also called the *just noticeable difference,* or *jnd*) is the minimum difference a person can detect between any two stimuli half the time. That detectable difference increases with the size of the stimulus. Thus, if you add 1 ounce to a 10-ounce weight, you will detect the difference; add 1 ounce to a 100-ounce weight and you will not. More than a century ago, Ernst Weber noted something so simple and so widely applicable that we still refer to it as **Weber's law:** for their difference to be perceptible, two stimuli must differ

"The heart has its reasons which reason does not know."

Pascal, *Pensées,* 1670

The difference threshold
In this computer-generated copy of the Twenty-third Psalm, each line of the typeface changes imperceptibly. How many lines are required for you to experience a just noticeable difference?

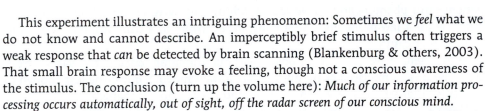

The LORD is my shepherd;
    I shall not want.
He maketh me to lie down
        in green pastures:
    he leadeth me
        beside the still waters.
He restoreth my soul:
    he leadeth me
        in the paths of righteousness
            for his name's sake.
Yea, though I walk through the valley
        of the shadow of death,
    I will fear no evil;
for thou art with me;
    thy rod and thy staff
        they comfort me.
Thou preparest a table before me
        in the presence of mine enemies:
    thou anointest my head with oil,
        my cup runneth over.
Surely goodness and mercy
        shall follow me
    all the days of my life:
and I will dwell
        in the house of the LORD
            for ever.

■ **sensory adaptation** diminished sensitivity as a consequence of constant stimulation.

by a constant proportion—not a constant amount. The exact proportion varies, depending on the stimulus. For the average person to perceive their differences, two lights must differ in intensity by 8 percent. Two objects must differ in weight by 2 percent. And two tones must differ in frequency by only 0.3 percent (Teghtsoonian, 1971).

Weber's law is a rough approximation. It works well for nonextreme sensory stimuli, and it parallels some of our life experiences. When the price of a $1-a-gallon gasoline went up by 10 cents, drivers noticed the change; it might take a 30-cent price hike in a $3-a-gallon gasoline to similarly raise eyebrows. In both cases, the price went up by 10 percent. Weber's principle: Our thresholds for detecting differences are a roughly constant proportion of the size of the original stimulus.

Sensory Adaptation

11-3 : What function does sensory adaptation serve?

Entering your neighbors' living room, you smell a musty odor. You wonder how they can stand it, but within minutes you no longer notice it. **Sensory adaptation**—our diminishing sensitivity to an unchanging stimulus—has come to your rescue. (To experience this phenomenon, move your watch up your wrist an inch: You will feel it—but only for a few moments.) After constant exposure to a stimulus, our nerve cells fire less frequently.

Why, then, if we stare at an object without flinching, does it not vanish from sight? Because, unnoticed by us, our eyes are always moving, quivering just enough to guarantee that stimulation on the eyes' receptors continually changes.

What if we actually could stop our eyes from moving? Would sights seem to vanish, as odors do? To find out, psychologists have devised ingenious instruments for maintaining a constant image on the eye's inner surface. Imagine that we have fitted a volunteer, Mary, with one of these instruments—a miniature projector mounted on a contact lens (**FIGURE 11.3a**). When Mary's eye moves, the image from the projector moves as well. So everywhere that Mary looks, the scene is sure to go.

If we project the profile of a face through such an instrument, what will Mary see? At first, she will see the complete profile. But within a few seconds, as her sensory system begins to fatigue, things get weird. Bit by bit, the image vanishes, only later to reappear and then disappear—in recognizable fragments or as a whole (**FIGURE 11.3b**).

Although sensory adaptation reduces our sensitivity, it offers an important benefit: Freedom to focus on *informative* changes in our environment without being distracted by the constant chatter of uninformative background stimulation. Our sensory receptors are alert to novelty; bore them with repetition and they free our attention for more important things. This reinforces a fundamental lesson: *We perceive the world not exactly as it is, but as it is useful for us to perceive it.*

Our sensitivity to changing stimulation helps explain television's attention-getting power. Cuts, edits, zooms, pans, and sudden noises demand attention. Even television

> "We need above all to know about changes; no one wants or needs to be reminded 16 hours a day that his shoes are on."
>
> Neuroscientist David Hubel (1979)

For 9 in 10 people—but, curiously, for only 1 in 3 of those with schizophrenia—this eye flutter turns off when the eye is following a moving target (Holzman & Matthyss, 1990).

> "My suspicion is that the universe is not only queerer than we suppose, but queerer than we can suppose."
>
> J. B. S. Haldane, *Possible Worlds*, 1927

FIGURE 11.3

Sensory adaptation: Now you see it, now you don't!

(a) A projector mounted on a contact lens makes the projected image move with the eye. (b) Initially the person sees the stabilized image, but soon she sees fragments fading and reappearing. (From "Stabilized images on the retina" by R. M. Pritchard. Copyright © 1961 Scientific American, Inc. All Rights Reserved.)

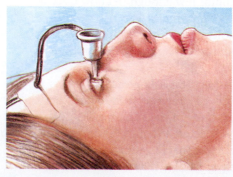

(a)

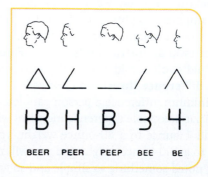

BEER   PEER   PEEP   BEE   BE

(b)

researchers marvel at TV's attention-grabbing power. During interesting conversations, notes researcher Percy Tannenbaum (2002), "I cannot for the life of me stop from periodically glancing over to the screen."

Sensory thresholds and adaptation are only two of the commonalities shared by the senses. All our senses receive sensory stimulation, transform it into neural information, and deliver that information to the brain. Let's look more closely at this process in vision, the sense we humans prize the most.

Vision

Every second of every day, your sensory systems perform an amazing feat: They convert one sort of energy to another. Your eyes, for example, receive light energy and *transduce* (transform) it into neural messages that your brain then processes into what you consciously see. How does such a taken-for-granted yet remarkable thing happen?

The Stimulus Input: Light Energy

11-4 : What are the characteristics of the energy we see as visible light?

Scientifically speaking, what strikes our eyes is not color but pulses of electromagnetic energy that our visual system perceives as color. What we see as visible light is but a thin slice of the whole spectrum of electromagnetic radiation. As **FIGURE 11.4** illustrates, this *electromagnetic spectrum* ranges from imperceptibly short waves of gamma rays, to the narrow band we see as visible light, to the long waves of radio transmission. Other organisms are sensitive to differing portions of the spectrum. Bees, for instance, cannot see red but can see ultraviolet light.

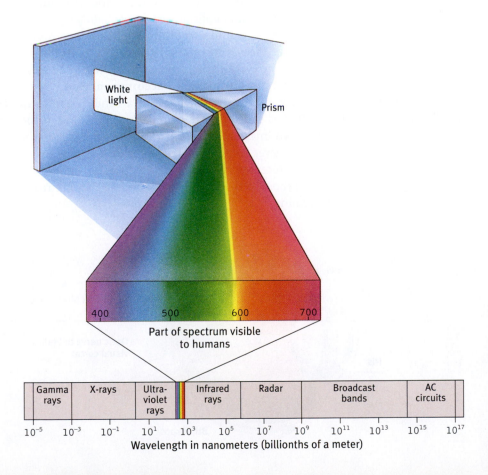

FIGURE 11.4

The spectrum of electromagnetic energy

This spectrum ranges from gamma rays as short as the diameter of an atom to radio waves over a mile long. The narrow band of wavelengths visible to the human eye (shown enlarged) extends from the shorter waves of blue-violet light to the longer waves of red light.

FIGURE 11.5
The physical properties of waves

(a) Waves vary in wavelength, the distance between successive peaks. Frequency, the number of complete wavelengths that can pass a point in a given time, depends on the wavelength. The shorter the wavelength, the higher the frequency. (b) Waves also vary in amplitude, the height from peak to trough. Wave amplitude determines the intensity of colors and sounds.

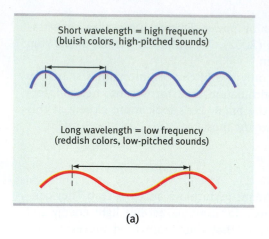

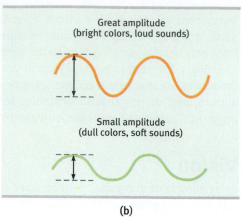

(a)   (b)

Two physical characteristics of light help determine our sensory experience of them. Light's **wavelength**—the distance from one wave peak to the next (**FIGURE 11.5a**)—determines its **hue** (the color we experience, such as blue or green). **Intensity,** the amount of energy in light waves (determined by a wave's amplitude, or height), influences brightness (**FIGURE 11.5b**). To understand how we transform physical energy into color and meaning, we first need to understand vision's window, the eye.

The Eye

11-5 : How does the eye transform light energy into neural messages?

Light enters the eye through the *cornea*, which protects the eye and bends light to provide focus (**FIGURE 11.6**). The light then passes through the *pupil*, a small adjustable opening surrounded by the *iris*, a colored muscle that adjusts light intake. The iris dilates or constricts in response to light intensity and even to inner emotions. (When we're feeling amorous, our telltale dilated pupils and dark eyes subtly signal our interest.) Each iris is so unique that an iris-scanning machine could confirm your identity.

Behind the pupil is a *lens* that focuses incoming light rays into an image on the **retina,** a multilayered tissue on the eyeball's sensitive inner surface. The lens focuses the rays by changing its curvature in a process called **accommodation.**

For centuries, scientists knew that when an image of a candle passes through a small opening, it casts an inverted mirror image on a dark wall behind. If the retina receives this sort of upside-down image as in Figure 11.6, how can we see the world right side up? Eventually, the answer became clear: The retina doesn't "see" a whole image. Rather, its millions of receptor cells convert particles of light energy into neural impulses and forwards those to the brain. *There,* the impulses are reassembled into a perceived, upright-seeming image.

■ **wavelength** the distance from the peak of one light or sound wave to the peak of the next. Electromagnetic wavelengths vary from the short blips of cosmic rays to the long pulses of radio transmission.

■ **hue** the dimension of color that is determined by the wavelength of light; what we know as the color names *blue, green,* and so forth.

■ **intensity** the amount of energy in a light or sound wave, which we perceive as brightness or loudness, as determined by the wave's amplitude.

■ **retina** the light-sensitive inner surface of the eye, containing the receptor rods and cones plus layers of neurons that begin the processing of visual information.

■ **accommodation** the process by which the eye's lens changes shape to focus near or far objects on the retina.

FIGURE 11.6
The eye

Light rays reflected from the candle pass through the cornea, pupil, and lens. The curvature and thickness of the lens change to bring either nearby or distant objects into focus on the retina. Rays from the top of the candle strike the bottom of the retina and those from the left side of the candle strike the right side of the retina. The candle's retinal image is thus upside-down and reversed.

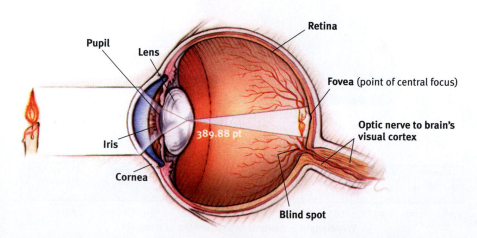

The Retina

If you followed a single light-energy particle into your eye, you would see that it first makes its way through the retina's outer layer of cells to its buried receptor cells, the **rods** and **cones**. Striking the rods and cones, the light energy would trigger chemical changes that generate neural signals (**FIGURE 11.7**). These signals activate the neighboring bipolar cells, which in turn activate the neighboring ganglion cells. The axons from the network of ganglion cells converge like the strands of a rope to form the **optic nerve** that carries information to your brain (where the thalamus receives and distributes the information). The optic nerve can send nearly 1 million messages at once through its nearly 1 million ganglion fibers. (The auditory nerve, which enables hearing, carries much less information through its mere 30,000 fibers.) Where the optic nerve leaves the eye there are no receptor cells—creating a **blind spot,** which you can experience by turning the page and following the directions in **FIGURE 11.8**.

Rods and cones differ in their geography and in the tasks they handle. Cones cluster around the **fovea,** the retina's area of central focus (see Figure 11.6). Many cones have their own hotline to the brain—bipolar cells that help relay the cone's individual message to the visual cortex, which devotes a large area to input from the fovea. These direct connections preserve the cones' precise information, making them better able to detect fine detail. Rods have no such hotline; they share bipolar cells with other rods, sending combined messages. To experience this difference in sensitivity to details, pick a word in this sentence and stare directly at it, focusing its image on the cones in your fovea. Notice that words a few inches off to the side appear blurred?

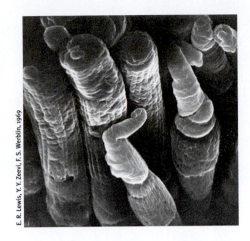

E. R. Lewis, Y. Y. Zeevi, F. S. Werblin, 1969

Rod-shaped rods and cone-shaped cones

As the scanning electron microscope shows, rods and cones are well named. The rods are more sensitive to light than are the color-sensitive cones, which is why the world looks colorless at night. Some nocturnal animals, such as toads, mice, rats, and bats, have retinas made up almost entirely of rods, allowing them to function well in dim light. These creatures probably have very poor color vision.

■ **rods** retinal receptors that detect black, white, and gray; necessary for peripheral and twilight vision, when cones don't respond.

■ **cones** retinal receptor cells that are concentrated near the center of the retina and that function in daylight or in well-lit conditions. The cones detect fine detail and give rise to color sensations.

■ **optic nerve** the nerve that carries neural impulses from the eye to the brain.

■ **blind spot** the point at which the optic nerve leaves the eye, creating a "blind" spot because no receptor cells are located there.

■ **fovea** the central focal point in the retina, around which the eye's cones cluster.

2. Chemical reaction in turn activates bipolar cells.

1. Light entering eye triggers photochemical reaction in rods and cones at back of retina.

Light

Cross section of retina

Light

Ganglion cell

Bipolar cell

Cone

Neural impulse

Rod

To visual cortex via the thalamus

Optic nerve

3. Bipolar cells then activate the ganglion cells, the axons of which converge to form the optic nerve. This nerve transmits information to the visual cortex (via the thalamus) in the brain's occipital lobe.

FIGURE 11.7
The retina's reaction to light

FIGURE 11.8
The blind spot

There are no receptor cells where the optic nerve leaves the eye (see Figure 11.6). This creates a blind spot in our vision. To demonstrate, close your left eye, look at the spot, and move the page to a distance from your face (about a foot) at which the car disappears. The blind spot does not normally impair your vision, because your eyes are moving and because one eye catches what the other misses.

TABLE 11.1

RECEPTORS IN THE HUMAN EYE

	Cones	Rods
Number	6 million	120 million
Location in retina	Center	Periphery
Sensitivity in dim light	Low	High
Color sensitive?	Yes	No
Detail sensitive?	Yes	No

Their image is striking the more peripheral region of your retina, where rods predominate (**TABLE 11.1**).

Cones also enable you to see color. But in dim light, they become ineffectual, which is why you then see no colors. This is when rods, which enable black-and-white vision, take the lead. Rods remain sensitive in dim light, and several will funnel their faint energy output onto a single bipolar cell. Thus, cones and rods each provide a special sensitivity—cones to detail and color, and rods to faint light.

When you enter a darkened theater or turn off the light at night, your pupils dilate to allow more light to reach your retina. It typically takes 20 minutes or more before your eyes fully adapt. You can demonstrate dark adaptation by closing or covering one eye for up to 20 minutes. Then make the light in the room not quite bright enough to read this book with your open eye. Now open the dark-adapted eye and read (easily). This period of dark adaptation is yet another instance of the remarkable flexibility of our sensory systems, for it parallels the average natural twilight transition between the sun's setting and darkness.

Knowing just this much about the eye, can you imagine why a cat sees so much better at night than you do?[1]

Visual Information Processing

11-6: How is visual information processed in the brain?

Visual information percolates through progressively more abstract levels. At the entry level, the retina processes information before routing it via the thalamus to the brain's cortex. The retina's neural layers—which are actually brain tissue that migrates to the eye during early fetal development—don't just pass along electrical impulses; they also help to encode and analyze the sensory information. The third neural layer in a frog's eye, for example, contains the "bug detector" cells that fire only in response to moving flylike stimuli.

After processing by the retina's nearly 130 million receptor rods and cones, information travels to the million or so ganglion cells, whose axons make up the optic nerve, which shoots the information to the brain. Any given retinal area relays its information to a corresponding location in the occipital lobe—the visual cortex in the back of your brain (**FIGURE 11.9**).

[1]There are at least two reasons: A cat's pupils can open much wider than yours, letting in more light; and a cat has a higher proportion of light-sensitive rods (Moser, 1987). But there is a trade-off: With fewer cones, a cat sees neither details nor color as well as you do.

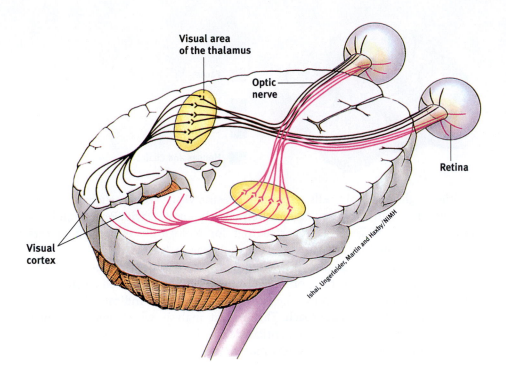

FIGURE 11.9

Pathway from the eyes to the visual cortex

Ganglion axons forming the optic nerve run to the thalamus, where they synapse with neurons that run to the visual cortex.

Feature Detection

Nobel prize winners David Hubel and Torsten Wiesel (1979) demonstrated that the occipital lobe's visual cortex has **feature detector** neurons that receive information from individual ganglion cells in the retina (**FIGURE 11.10**). They derive their name from their ability to respond to a scene's specific features—to particular edges, lines, angles, and movements. For example, one visual cortex cell might respond maximally to a bar flashed at a 1 o'clock tilt. If the bar is tilted further—say, to a 12 o'clock or 10 o'clock position—the cell quiets down.

Feature detectors in the visual cortex pass such information to other cortical areas where teams of cells *(supercell clusters)* respond to more complex patterns. One temporal lobe area just behind your right ear, for example, enables you to perceive faces. If this region were damaged, you might recognize other forms and objects, but not familiar faces. Functional MRI (fMRI) scans show other brain areas lighting up when people view other object categories (Downing & others, 2001), and amazingly specific combinations of activity may appear (**FIGURE 11.11**). "We can tell if a person is looking at a shoe, a chair, or a face, based on the pattern of their brain activity," notes researcher James Haxby (2001).

■ **feature detectors** nerve cells in the brain that respond to specific features of the stimulus, such as shape, angle, or movement.

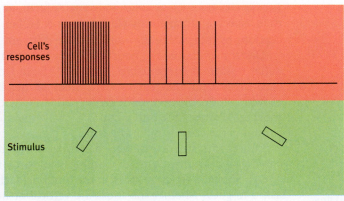

FIGURE 11.10

Electrodes record how individual cells in this monkey's visual cortex respond to different visual stimuli

Hubel and Wiesel won a Nobel prize for their discovery that most cells in the visual cortex respond only to particular features—for example, to the edge of a surface or to a bar at a 30-degree angle in the upper right part of the field of vision. Other cells integrate information from these simpler ones.

FIGURE 11.11
The telltale brain
Looking at faces, houses, and chairs activates different brain areas in this right-facing brain.

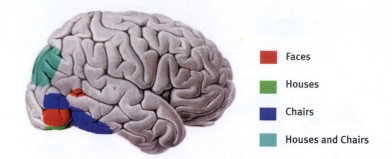

Faces

Houses

Chairs

Houses and Chairs

Other high-level brain cells respond to specific visual scenes, such as a face or an arm movement in a particular direction. Psychologist David Perrett and his colleagues (1988, 1992, 1994) reported that for biologically important objects and events, monkey brains (and surely ours as well) have a "vast visual encyclopedia" distributed as cells that specialize in responding to one type of stimulus—such as a specific gaze, head angle, posture, or body movement. Other supercell clusters integrate this information and fire only when the cues collectively indicate the direction of someone's attention and approach. This instant analysis, which aided our ancestors' survival, also helps a soccer goalie anticipate the direction of an impending kick and a driver anticipate a pedestrian's next movement.

Well-developed supercells
In this 2004 World Cup qualifying match, Brazil's Luiz Ronaldo (in yellow) instantly processed visual information about the positions and movements of Argentina's defenders and goalie and somehow managed to get the ball around them all—heading it into the net.

Parallel Processing

Unlike most computers, which do step-by-step serial processing, our brain engages in **parallel processing:** doing many things at once. The brain divides a visual scene into subdimensions such as color, movement, form, and depth (**FIGURE 11.12**) and works on each aspect simultaneously (Livingstone & Hubel, 1988). We then construct our perceptions by integrating the work of these different visual teams, working in parallel.

Destroy or disable the neural workstation for a visual subtask, and something peculiar results, as happened to "Mrs. M." (from Hoffman, 1998). Since a stroke damaged areas near the rear of both sides of her brain, she can no longer perceive movement. People in a room seem "suddenly here or there but I have not seen them moving." Pouring tea into a cup is a challenge because the fluid appears frozen—she cannot perceive it rising in the cup.

Others with stroke or surgery damage to their brain's visual cortex have experienced *blindsight,* a localized area of blindness in part of their field of vision (Weiskrantz, 1986). Shown a series of sticks in the blind field, they report seeing nothing. Yet when asked to guess whether the sticks are vertical or horizontal, they unerringly offer the correct response. When told, "You got them all right," they are astounded. There is, it seems, a second "mind"—a parallel processing system—operating unseen.

■ **parallel processing** the processing of many aspects of a problem simultaneously; the brain's natural mode of information processing for many functions, including vision. Contrasts with the step-by-step (serial) processing of most computers and of conscious problem solving.

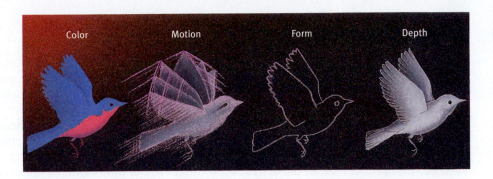

FIGURE 11.12
Parallel processing
Studies of patients with brain damage suggest that the brain delegates the work of processing color, motion, form, and depth to different areas. After taking a scene apart, how does the brain integrate these subdimensions into the perceived image? The answer to this question is the Holy Grail of vision research.

Indeed, "sight unseen" is how University of Durham psychologist David Milner (2003) describes the brain's two visual systems—"one that gives us our conscious perceptions, and one that guides our actions." The second he calls "the zombie within." Milner describes a woman with brain damage who can see fine details—the hairs on the back of a hand—without being able to recognize the hand. Asked to use her thumb and forefinger to estimate an object's size, she can't do it. Yet when reaching for the object, her thumb and forefinger are appropriately placed. She knows more than she is aware of.

Other senses process information with similar speed and intricacy. A scientific understanding of sensory information processing left neuropsychologist Roger Sperry awestruck (1985): The "insights of science give added, not lessened, reasons for awe, respect, and reverence." Think about it: As you look at someone, visual information is transduced and sent to your brain as millions of neural impulses, then constructed into its component features, and finally, in some as yet mysterious way, composed into a meaningful perceived image, which you compare with previously stored images and recognize as, for example, your grandmother. The whole process (**FIGURE 11.13**) is more complex than taking apart a car, piece by piece, transporting it to a different location, then having specialized workers reconstruct it. That all of this happens instantly, effortlessly, and continuously is indeed awesome.

> "I am fearfully and wonderfully made."
> King David, Psalms 139:14

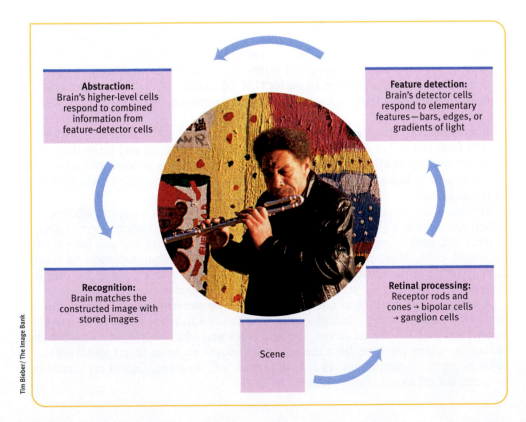

Abstraction:
Brain's higher-level cells respond to combined information from feature-detector cells

Feature detection:
Brain's detector cells respond to elementary features—bars, edges, or gradients of light

Recognition:
Brain matches the constructed image with stored images

Retinal processing:
Receptor rods and cones → bipolar cells → ganglion cells

Scene

Tim Bieber / The Image Bank

FIGURE 11.13
A simplified summary of visual information processing

Color Vision

11-7 : What theories contribute to our understanding of color vision?

We talk as though objects possess color: "A tomato is red." Perhaps you have pondered the old question, "If a tree falls in the forest and no one hears it, does it make a sound?" We can ask the same of color: If no one sees the tomato, is it red?

The answer is no. First, the tomato is everything *but* red, because it *rejects* (reflects) the long wavelengths of red. Second, the tomato's color is our mental construction. As Isaac Newton (1704) noted, "The [light] rays are not colored." Color, like all aspects of vision, resides not in the object but in the theater of our brains, as evidenced by our dreaming in color.

In the study of vision, one of the most basic and intriguing mysteries is how we see the world in color. How, from the light energy striking the retina, does the brain manufacture our experience of color—and of such a multitude of colors? Our difference threshold for colors is so low that we can discriminate some 7 million different color variations (Geldard, 1972).

At least most of us can. For about 1 person in 50, vision is color-deficient—and that person is usually male, because the defect is genetically sex-linked. To understand why some people's vision is color-deficient, it will help to first understand how normal color vision works.

Modern detective work on the mystery of color vision began in the nineteenth century when Hermann von Helmholtz built on the insights of an English physicist, Thomas Young. Knowing that any color can be created by combining the light waves of three primary colors—red, green, and blue—Young and von Helmholtz inferred that the eye must have three corresponding types of color receptors. Years later, researchers measured the response of various cones to different color stimuli and confirmed the **Young-Helmholtz trichromatic (three-color) theory,** which simply states that the retina has three types of color receptors, each especially sensitive to one of three colors. And surprise! Those colors are, indeed, red, green, and blue. When we stimulate combinations of these cones, we see other colors. For example, there are no receptors especially sensitive to yellow. Yet when both red-sensitive and green-sensitive cones are stimulated, we see yellow.

Most color-deficient people are not actually "colorblind." They simply lack functioning red- or green-sensitive cones, or sometimes both. Their vision—perhaps unknown to them, because their lifelong vision *seems* normal—is monochromatic (one-color) or dichromatic (two-color) instead of trichromatic, making it impossible to distinguish the red and green in **FIGURE 11.14** (Boynton, 1979). Dogs, too, lack receptors for the wavelengths of red, giving them only limited, dichromatic color vision (Neitz & others, 1989).

But trichromatic theory cannot solve all parts of the color vision mystery, as Ewald Hering soon noted. For example, we see yellow when mixing red and green light. But how is it that those blind to red and green can often still see yellow? And why does yellow appear to be a pure color and not a mixture of red and green, the way purple is of red and blue?

Hering, a physiologist, found a clue in the well-known occurrence of *afterimages.* When you stare at a green square for a while and then look at a white sheet of paper, you see red, green's *opponent color.* Stare at a yellow square and you will later see its opponent color, blue, on the white paper (as in the flag demonstration in **FIGURE 11.15**). Hering surmised that there must be two additional color processes, one responsible for red-versus-green perception, and one for blue-versus-yellow.

A century later, researchers confirmed Hering's **opponent-process theory.** As visual information leaves the receptor cells, we analyze it in terms of the opponent colors red and green, blue and yellow, and also black and white. In the retina and in the thalamus (where impulses from the retina are relayed en route to the visual cortex), some neurons are turned "on" by red but turned "off" by green. Others are turned on by green but off by red (DeValois & DeValois, 1975).

> "Only mind has sight and hearing; all things else are deaf and blind."
>
> Epicharmus, *Fragments*, 550 B.C.

■ **Young-Helmholtz trichromatic (three-color) theory** the theory that the retina contains three different color receptors—one most sensitive to red, one to green, one to blue—which when stimulated in combination can produce the perception of any color.

■ **opponent-process theory** the theory that opposing retinal processes (red-green, yellow-blue, white-black) enable color vision. For example, some cells are stimulated by green and inhibited by red; others are stimulated by red and inhibited by green.

FIGURE 11.14
Color-deficient vision
People who suffer red-green deficiency have trouble perceiving the number within the design.

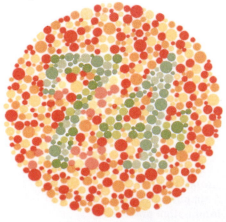

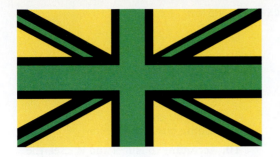

FIGURE 11.15
Afterimage effect
Stare at the center of the flag for a minute and then shift your eyes to the dot in the white space beside it. What do you see? (After tiring your neural response to black, green, and yellow, you should see their opponent colors.) Stare at a white wall and note how the size of the flag grows with the projection distance!

Opponent processes explain afterimages, such as in the flag demonstration, in which we tire our green response by staring at green. When we then stare at white (which contains all colors, including red), only the red part of the green-red pairing will fire normally.

The present solution to the mystery of color vision is therefore roughly this: Color processing occurs in two stages. The retina's red, green, and blue cones respond in varying degrees to different color stimuli, as the Young-Helmholtz trichromatic theory suggested. Their signals are then processed by the nervous system's opponent-process cells, en route to the visual cortex.

REVIEWING

>> MODULE REVIEW

Sensation—receiving and representing stimulus energies from our environment—involves *bottom-up processing*. *Perception*—the process of selecting, organizing, and interpreting sensory information—involves *top-down processing*. *Psychophysics* is the study of how sensations are perceived.

11-1 : **What is an absolute threshold, and are we influenced by stimuli below it?**
We sense only a portion of the sea of energy that surrounds us. Our *absolute threshold* for any stimulus is the minimum stimulation necessary for us to be consciously aware of it 50 percent of the time. We can process some information from stimuli too weak to recognize, but the effect is too restricted to enable unscrupulous opportunists to exploit us with *subliminal* messages.

11-2 : **How does the magnitude of a stimulus influence our threshold for detecting differences?**
The *difference threshold* (also called *just noticeable difference*, or *JND*) is the barely noticeable difference we discern between two stimuli 50 percent of the time. In humans, a difference threshold increases in proportion to the stimulus—a principle known as *Weber's law*.

11-3 : **What function does sensory adaptation serve?**
Sensory adaptation, our diminished sensitivity to constant or routine odors, sounds, and touches, helps to focus our attention on informative changes in stimulation, rather than on unchanging aspects of the environment.

11-4 : **What are the characteristics of the energy that we see as visible light?**
Each sense receives stimulation, transforms it into neural signals, and sends these neural messages to the brain. In vision, we convert light energy into these neural impulses. The energies we experience as visible light are a thin slice from the broad spectrum of electromagnetic radiation. The *hue* (blue, green, and so on) and brightness we perceive in a light depend on the *wavelength* and *intensity*.

11-5 : **How does the eye transform light energy into neural messages?**
After entering the eye and being focused by a cameralike lens (through the process of *accommodation*), light waves strike the *retina*, the inner surface of the eye. The retina's light-sensitive *rods* and color-sensitive *cones* convert the light energy into neural impulses, which travel along the *optic nerve* to the brain. The point at which the optic nerve leaves the eye is the *blind spot*.

11-6 : **How is visual information processed in the brain?**
In the visual cortex, *feature detectors* respond to specific features of the visual stimulus. Higher-level supercells integrate this pool of data for processing in other cortical areas. Subdimensions of vision (color, movement, depth, and form) are processed separately and simultaneously, illustrating the brain's capacity for *parallel processing*. The visual pathway faithfully represents retinal stimulation, but the brain's representation incorporates our assumptions, interests, and expectations.

11-7 : **What theories contribute to our understanding of color vision?**
The *Young-Helmholtz trichromatic (three-color) theory* proposed that the retina contains three types of color receptors, which we now know are cones. Each is most sensitive to the wavelengths of one of the three primary colors of light (red, green, or blue). Hering's *opponent-process theory* proposed two additional color processes (red-versus-green and blue-versus-yellow) plus a third black-versus-white process. This theory is also confirmed in current research, by the phenomenon of afterimages and by measuring opponent processes within visual neurons of the thalamus.

>> REHEARSE IT!

1. To construct meaning out of our external environment, we select, organize, and interpret sensory information. This is the process of
   a. sensation.
   b. sensory adaptation.
   c. encoding.
   d. perception.

2. Sensation is to _____ as perception is to _____ .
   a. absolute threshold; difference threshold
   b. bottom-up processing; top-down processing
   c. interpretation; detection
   d. conscious awareness; persuasion

3. The difference threshold is the minimum difference between two stimuli for required detection 50 percent of the time. Another term for this concept is
   a. just noticeable difference.
   b. sensory adaptation.
   c. absolute threshold.
   d. subliminal stimulation.

4. People wonder whether subliminal stimuli, such as undetectably faint sights or sounds, influence us. Subliminal stimuli are
   a. too weak to be processed by the brain in any way.
   b. consciously perceived more than 50 percent of the time.
   c. always strong enough to affect our behavior.
   d. below the absolute threshold for conscious awareness.

5. To be perceived as different, two lights must differ in intensity by at least 8 percent. This illustrates the principle called Weber's law, which states that for a difference to be perceived, two stimuli must differ by
   a. a fixed or constant energy amount.
   b. a constant minimum percentage.
   c. a constantly changing amount.
   d. more than 7 percent.

6. Sensory adaptation, which reduces our sensitivity to some stimuli in the environment (such as unpleasant smells), has survival benefits. It helps us focus on
   a. visual stimuli.
   b. feature detectors.
   c. constant features of the environment.
   d. important changes in the environment.

7. Two physical characteristics of light help determine our sensory experience of it. The characteristic that determines the color we experience, such as blue or green, is
   a. intensity.
   b. wavelength.
   c. amplitude.
   d. hue.

8. You have a blind spot in your retina. It's located in the area where
   a. there are rods but no cones.
   b. there are cones but no rods.
   c. the optic nerve leaves the eye.
   d. the bipolar cells meet the ganglion cells.

9. Rods and cones are the eye's receptor cells. Cones are especially sensitive to _____ light and are responsible for our _____ vision.

   a. bright; black-and-white
   b. dim; color
   c. bright; color
   d. dim; black-and-white

10. According to Hubel and Wiesel, the brain includes cells that respond maximally to certain bars, edges, and angles. These cells are called
    a. rods and cones.
    b. feature detectors.
    c. bug detectors.
    d. ganglion cells.

11. Unlike most computers, the brain is capable of simultaneously processing many aspects of an object or problem. We call this ability
    a. parallel processing.
    b. serial processing.
    c. opponent processing.
    d. accommodation.

12. Researchers today believe that the Young-Helmholtz and Hering theories together account for color vision. The Young-Helmholtz theory shows that the eye contains _____ , and the Hering theory accounts for the nervous system's having _____ .
    a. opposing retinal processes; three pairs of color receptors
    b. opponent-process cells; three types of color receptors
    c. three pairs of color receptors; opposing retinal processes
    d. three types of color receptors; opponent-process cells

Answers: 1. d, 2. b, 3. a, 4. d, 5. b, 6. d, 7. b, 8. c, 9. c, 10. b, 11. a, 12. d.

>> TERMS AND CONCEPTS TO REMEMBER

sensation, p. 143
perception, p. 143
bottom-up processing, p. 143
top-down processing, p. 143
psychophysics, p. 144
absolute threshold, p. 144
subliminal, p. 144
priming, p. 144
difference threshold, p. 145

Weber's law, p. 145
sensory adaptation, p. 146
wavelength, p. 148
hue, p. 148
intensity, p. 148
retina, p. 148
accommodation, p. 148
rods, p. 149
cones, p. 149

optic nerve, p. 149
blind spot, p. 149
fovea, p. 149
feature detectors, p. 151
parallel processing, p. 152
Young-Helmholtz trichromatic (three-color) theory, p. 154
opponent-process theory, p. 154

>> TEST YOURSELF

1. What is the rough distinction between sensation and perception?

2. What is the rapid sequence of events that occurs when you see and recognize someone you know?

(Answers in Appendix C.)

The Other Senses

For humans, vision is the major sense. More of our brain cortex is devoted to vision than to any other sense. Yet without our senses of hearing, touch, taste, smell, and body motion and position, our capacities for experiencing the world would be vastly diminished.

Hearing

Like our other senses, our hearing, or **audition,** is highly adaptive. We hear a wide range of sounds, but we hear best those sounds with frequencies in a range corresponding to that of the human voice. We also are remarkably sensitive to faint sounds, an obvious boon for our ancestors' survival when hunting or being hunted, or for detecting a child's whimper. (If our ears were much more sensitive, we would hear a constant hiss from the movement of air molecules.) We are also acutely sensitive to differences in sounds. We easily detect differences among thousands of human voices: Answering the phone, we recognize a friend calling from the moment she says "Hi." A fraction of a second after such events stimulate receptors in the ear, millions of neurons have simultaneously coordinated in extracting the essential features, comparing them with past experience, and identifying the stimulus (Freeman, 1991). For hearing as for the other senses, the fundamental question is, How do we do it?

■ **audition** the sense or act of hearing.

The Stimulus Input: Sound Waves

12-1: What are the characteristics of the air pressure waves that we hear as meaningful sounds?

Hit a piano key and the resulting stimulus energy is sound waves—jostling molecules of air, each bumping into the next, like a shove transmitted through a concert hall's crowded exit tunnel. The resulting waves of compressed and expanded air are like the ripples on a pond circling out from where a stone has been tossed. As we swim in our ocean of moving air molecules, our ears detect these brief air pressure changes. Exposed to a loud, low bass sound—perhaps from a bass guitar—we can also *feel* the vibration, and we hear by both air and bone conduction.

The ears then transform the vibrating air into nerve impulses, which our brain decodes as sounds. The strength, or *amplitude*, of sound waves (**FIGURE 12.1**) determines

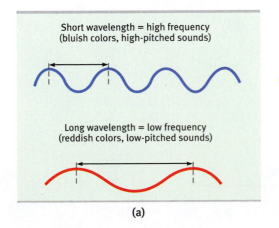

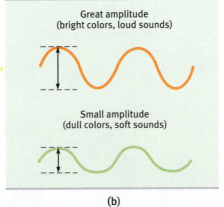

(a)   (b)

FIGURE 12.1

The physical properties of waves

(a) Waves vary in wavelength, the distance between successive peaks. Frequency, the number of complete wavelengths that can pass a point in a given time, depends on the wavelength. The shorter the wavelength, the higher the frequency. (b) Waves also vary in amplitude, the height from peak to trough. Wave amplitude determines the intensity of colors and sounds.

The sounds of music
A violin's short, fast waves create a high pitch, a cello's longer, slower waves a lower pitch. Differences in the waves' height, or amplitude, also create differing degrees of loudness.

Janine Wiedel Photolibrary/Alamy

■ **frequency** the number of complete wavelengths that pass a point in a given time (for example, per second).

■ **pitch** a tone's experienced highness or lowness; depends on frequency.

their *loudness*. Waves also vary in length, and therefore in **frequency.** Their frequency determines the **pitch** we experience: Long waves have low frequency—and low pitch. Short waves have high frequency—and high pitch. A piccolo produces much shorter, faster sound waves than does a bass guitar.

We measure sounds in *decibels*. The absolute threshold for hearing is arbitrarily defined as zero decibels. Every 10 decibels correspond to a tenfold increase in sound intensity. Thus, normal conversation (60 decibels) is 10,000 times more intense than a 20-decibel whisper. And a tolerable 100-decibel passing subway train is 10 billion times more intense than the faintest detectable sound. Prolonged exposure to sounds above 85 decibels—as happens in venues from frenzied sports arenas to bagpipe bands—can produce hearing loss (**FIGURE 12.2**).

FIGURE 12.2
The intensity of some common sounds
At close range, the thunder that follows lightning has 120-decibel intensity.

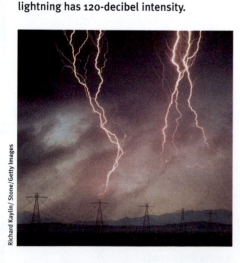

Richard Kaylin/ Stone/Getty Images

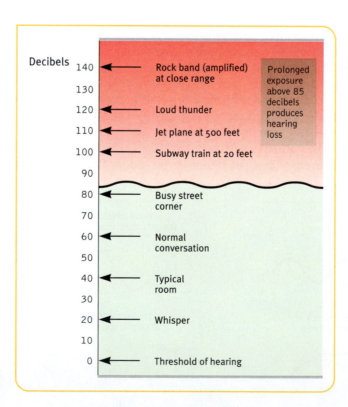

The Ear

12-2 : How does the ear transform sound energy into neural messages?

To hear, we must somehow convert sound waves into neural activity. But how? The human ear accomplishes this feat through an intricate mechanical chain reaction (**FIGURE 12.3**). First, the visible outer ear channels the sound waves through the auditory canal to the eardrum, a tight membrane that vibrates with the waves. The **middle ear** then transmits the eardrum's vibrations through a piston made of three tiny bones (the hammer, anvil, and stirrup) to the **cochlea,** a snail-shaped tube in the **inner ear.** The incoming vibrations cause the cochlea's membrane (the oval window) to vibrate, jostling the fluid that fills the tube. This motion causes ripples in the basilar membrane, bending the hair cells lining its surface, not unlike the wind bending a wheat field. The movement of the hair cells triggers impulses in the adjacent nerve cells, whose axons converge to form the auditory nerve, which sends neural messages (via the thalamus) to the temporal lobe's auditory cortex. From vibrating air to moving piston to fluid waves to electrical impulses to the brain: Voila! We hear.

My vote for the most magical part of the hearing process is the hair cells. A 1997 Howard Hughes Medical Institute report on these "quivering bundles that let us hear" marvels at their "extreme sensitivity and extreme speed." A cochlea has 16,000 of them, which sounds like a lot until we compare that with an eye's 130 million or so photoreceptors. But consider their responsiveness. Deflect the tiny bundles of cilia on the tip of a hair cell by the width of an atom—the equivalent of displacing the top of the Eiffel Tower by half an inch—and the alert hair cell, thanks to a special protein at its tip, triggers a neural response (Corey & others, 2004).

- **middle ear** the chamber between the eardrum and cochlea containing three tiny bones (hammer, anvil, and stirrup) that concentrate the vibrations of the eardrum on the cochlea's oval window.

- **cochlea** [KOHK-lee-uh] a coiled, bony, fluid-filled tube in the inner ear through which sound waves trigger nerve impulses.

- **inner ear** the innermost part of the ear, containing the cochlea, semicircular canals, and vestibular sacs.

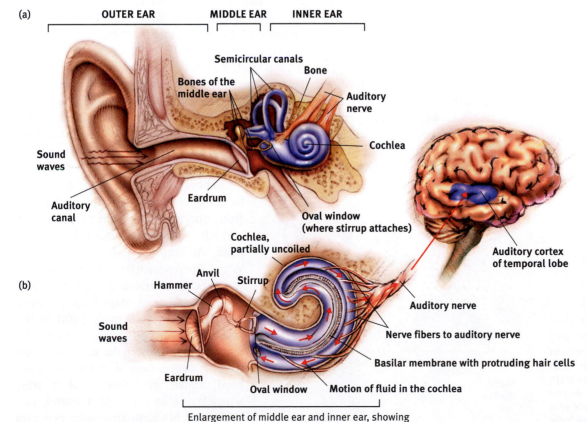

(a)   **OUTER EAR**   **MIDDLE EAR**   **INNER EAR**

Semicircular canals
Bones of the middle ear
Bone
Auditory nerve
Sound waves
Cochlea
Eardrum
Auditory canal
Oval window (where stirrup attaches)
Cochlea, partially uncoiled
Auditory cortex of temporal lobe
(b)
Anvil
Hammer
Stirrup
Sound waves
Auditory nerve
Nerve fibers to auditory nerve
Basilar membrane with protruding hair cells
Eardrum
Oval window
Motion of fluid in the cochlea

Enlargement of middle ear and inner ear, showing cochlea partially uncoiled for clarity

FIGURE 12.3

Hear here: How we transform sound waves into nerve impulses that our brain interprets

(a) The outer ear funnels sound waves to the eardrum. The bones of the middle ear amplify and relay the eardrum's vibrations through the oval window into the fluid-filled cochlea. (b) As shown in this detail of the middle and inner ear, the resulting pressure changes in the cochlear fluid cause the basilar membrane to ripple, bending the hair cells on the surface. Hair cell movements trigger impulses at the base of the nerve cells, whose fibers converge to form the auditory nerve, which sends neural messages to the thalamus and on to the auditory cortex.

Be kind to your inner ear's hair cells
When vibrating in response to sound, the hair cells shown here lining the cochlea produce an electrical signal.

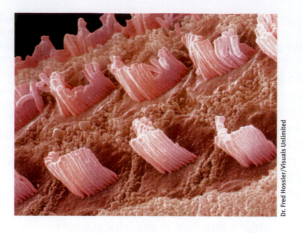

Dr. Fred Hossler/Visuals Unlimited

At the highest perceived frequency, hair cells can turn neural current on and off a thousand times per second! As you might expect of something so sensitive, they are, however, delicate and fragile. Blast them with hunting rifle shots or headset sounds and the hair cells' cilia will begin to wither or fuse.

Damage to hair cells accounts for most hearing loss. They have been likened to shag carpet fibers. Walk around on them and they will spring back with a quick vacuuming. But leave a heavy piece of furniture on them for a long time and they may never rebound. As a general rule, if we cannot talk over a noise, it is potentially harmful, especially if prolonged and repeated (Roesser, 1998). And if we experience ringing of the ears after exposure to loud machinery or music, we have been bad to our unhappy hair cells. As pain alerts us to possible bodily harm, ringing of the ears alerts us to possible hearing damage. It is hearing's equivalent of bleeding. People who spend many hours behind a power mower, above a jackhammer, or in a loud nightclub should wear earplugs. "Condoms or, safer yet, abstinence," say sex educators. "Earplugs or walk away," say hearing educators.

How Do We Locate Sounds?

Why don't we have one big ear—perhaps above our one nose? The better to hear you, as the wolf said to Red Riding Hood. As the placement of our eyes allows us to sense visual depth, so the placement of our two ears allows us to enjoy stereophonic ("three-dimensional") hearing. The slightly different messages sensed by two stereo recording microphones mimic the slightly different messages from our two ears.

Two ears are better than one for at least two reasons: If a car to the right honks, your right ear receives a more *intense* sound, and it receives sound slightly *sooner* than your left ear (**FIGURE 12.4**). Because sound travels 750 miles per hour and our ears are but 6 inches apart, the intensity difference and the time lag are extremely small. However, our supersensitive auditory system can detect such minute differences (Brown & Deffenbacher, 1979; Middlebrooks & Green, 1991). A just noticeable difference in the direction of two sound sources corresponds to a time difference of just 0.000027 second!

FIGURE 12.4
How we locate sounds
Sound waves strike one ear sooner and more intensely than the other. From this information, our nimble brain computes the sound's location. As you might therefore expect, people who lose all hearing in one ear often have difficulty locating sounds.

Air

Sound shadow

So how well do you suppose we do at locating a sound that is equidistant from our two ears, such as those that come from directly ahead, behind, overhead, or beneath us? Not very well. Why? Because such sounds strike the two ears simultaneously. Sit with closed eyes while a friend snaps fingers around your head. You will easily point to the sound when it comes from either side, but you will likely make some mistakes when it comes from directly ahead, behind, above, or below. That is why, when trying to pinpoint a sound, you cock your head, so that your two ears will receive slightly different messages.

Touch

12-3 : How do we sense touch and feel pain?

If you had to lose one sense, which would you prefer it to be? If you could have only one, which would you want?

Although not the first sense to come to mind, touch could be our priority sense. Right from the start, touch is essential to our development. Infant rats deprived of their mothers' grooming produce less growth hormone and have a lower metabolic rate—a good way to keep alive until the mother returns, but a reaction that stunts growth if prolonged. Infant monkeys allowed to see, hear, and smell—but not touch—their mothers become desperately unhappy; those separated by a screen with holes that allow touching are much less miserable. Premature babies gain weight faster and go home sooner if they are stimulated by hand massage. As lovers, we yearn to touch—to kiss, to stroke, to snuggle.

Humorist Dave Barry may be right to jest that your skin "keeps people from seeing the inside of your body, which is repulsive, and it prevents your organs from falling onto the ground." But skin does much more. Our "sense of touch" is actually a mix of at least four distinct skin senses—pressure, warmth, cold, and pain. Within the skin are different types of specialized nerve endings. Touching various spots on the skin with a soft hair, a warm or cool wire, and the point of a pin reveals that some spots are especially sensitive to pressure, others to warmth, others to cold, still others to pain.

Surprisingly, there is no simple relationship between what we feel at a given spot and the type of specialized nerve ending found there. Only pressure has identifiable receptors. Other skin sensations are variations of the basic four (pressure, warmth, cold, and pain):

- Stroking adjacent pressure spots creates a tickle.
- Repeated gentle stroking of a pain spot creates an itching sensation.
- Touching adjacent cold and pressure spots triggers a sense of wetness, which you can experience by touching dry, cold metal.

Touch sensations involve more than tactile stimulation, however. A self-produced tickle produces less somatosensory cortex activation than the same tickle would from something or someone else (Blakemore & others, 1998). (The brain is wise enough to be most sensitive to unexpected stimulation.) This top-down influence on touch sensation also appears in the rubber-hand illusion. Imagine yourself looking at a realistic rubber hand while your own hand is hidden (**FIGURE 12.5**). If an experimenter simultaneously touches your fake and real hands, you likely will perceive the rubber hand as your own and sense it being touched.

The precious sense of touch
As William James wrote in his *Principles of Psychology* (1890), "Touch is both the alpha and omega of affection."

FIGURE 12.5
The rubber-hand illusion
When Dublin researcher Deirdre Desmond simultaneously touches a volunteer's real and fake hands, the volunteer feels as though the seen fake hand is her own.

A pain-free, problematic life
Ashlyn Blocker (right), shown here with her mother and sister, has a rare genetic disorder. Unable to feel pain or extreme hot and cold, Ashlyn must frequently be checked for accidentally self-inflicted injuries. "Some people would say [that feeling no pain is] a good thing," says her mother. "But no, it's not. Pain's there for a reason. It lets your body know something's wrong and it needs to be fixed. I'd give anything for her to feel pain" (quoted by Bynum, 2004).

Pain

Be thankful for occasional pain. Pain is your body's way of telling you something has gone wrong. When drawing your attention to a burn, a break, or a rupture, pain tells you to change your behavior immediately. The rare people born without the ability to feel pain may experience severe injury or even die before early adulthood. Without the discomfort that makes us occasionally shift position, their joints fail from excess strain, and without the warnings of pain, the effects of unchecked infections and injuries accumulate (Neese, 1991).

More numerous are those who live with chronic pain, which is rather like an alarm that won't shut off. For those with illness-related *hyperalgesia*, an extreme sensitivity to something others would find only mildly painful, the sensory receptors and brain work together to make life miserable (Brune & Handwerker, 2004; Wiertelak & others, 1994). The suffering of such people, and of those with persistent or recurring backaches, arthritis, headaches, and cancer-related pain, prompts two questions: What is pain? How might we control it?

Biological, Psychological, and Social-Cultural Influences on Pain

Our pain experiences vary widely, depending on our physiology, our experiences and attention, and our surrounding culture (**FIGURE 12.6**). Pain is not only a bottom-up property of the senses—of the region where we feel it—but also a top-down product of our brain and our expectations. Carrie Armel and Vilayanur Ramachandran (2003) cleverly illustrated this point when they bent a finger slightly backward on the unseen hands of 16 volunteers, while simultaneously "hurting" (severely bending) a finger on a fake rubber hand. The volunteers felt as if their real finger were being twisted, and they responded with increased skin perspiration.

With pain, as with sights and sounds, the brain can misinterpret the spontaneous central nervous system activity that occurs in the absence of normal sensory input.

FIGURE 12.6
Biopsychosocial approach to pain
Our experience of pain is much more than neural messages sent to the brain.

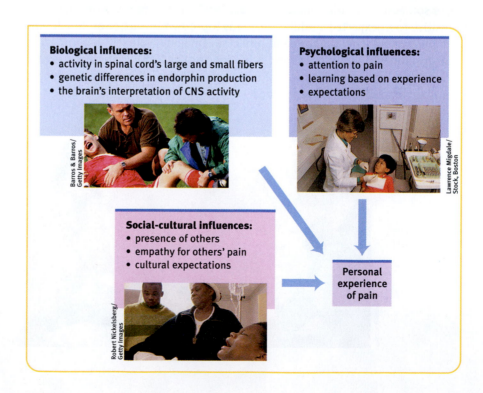

Biological influences:
• activity in spinal cord's large and small fibers
• genetic differences in endorphin production
• the brain's interpretation of CNS activity

Psychological influences:
• attention to pain
• learning based on experience
• expectations

Social-cultural influences:
• presence of others
• empathy for others' pain
• cultural expectations

Personal experience of pain

Consider people's experiences of *phantom limb sensations*. As the dreamer may see with eyes closed and the listener may hear a ringing during utter silence, so some 7 in 10 amputees may feel pain or movement in nonexistent limbs, notes psychologist Robert Melzack (1992, 1993). (An amputee may also try to step off a bed onto a phantom limb or to lift a cup with a phantom hand.) Even those born without a limb sometimes perceive sensations from the absent arm or leg. The brain, Melzack (1998) surmises, comes prepared to anticipate "that it will be getting information from a body that has limbs."

A similar phenomenon occurs with other senses. People with hearing loss often experience the sound of silence: phantom sounds—a ringing-in-the-ears sensation known as *tinnitus*. Those who lose vision to glaucoma, cataracts, diabetes, or macular degeneration may experience phantom sights—nonthreatening hallucinations (Ramachandran & Blakeslee, 1998). Nerve damage in the taste system can similarly produce taste phantoms, such as ice water seeming sickeningly sweet (Goode, 1999). Others have experienced phantom smells, such as nonexistent rotten food. The moral: *We see, hear, taste, smell, and feel with our brain*, which can sense even without functioning senses. Pain-producing brain activity may be triggered with or without sensory input, says Melzack (1999). A brain in a jar could conceivably experience pain and other sensory experiences. No brain, no pain.

Unlike vision, however, the pain system is not located in a simple neural cord running from a sensing device to a definable area in the brain. Moreover, there is no one type of stimulus that triggers pain (as light triggers vision), and there are no special receptors (like the retina's rods and cones) for pain. In fact, at low intensities, the stimuli that produce pain also cause other sensations, including warmth or coolness, smoothness or roughness.

Although no theory of pain explains all available findings, Melzack and biologist Patrick Wall's (1965, 1983) classic **gate-control theory** still provides a useful model. The spinal cord contains small nerve fibers that conduct most pain signals, and larger fibers that conduct most other sensory signals. Melzack and Wall theorized that the spinal cord contains a neurological "gate." When tissue is injured, the small fibers activate and open the gate, and you feel pain. Large-fiber activity closes the gate, blocking pain signals and preventing them from reaching the brain.

Thus, one way to treat chronic pain is to stimulate (by massage, by electric stimulation, or by acupuncture) "gate-closing" activity in the large neural fibers (Wall, 2000). Rubbing the area around your stubbed toe will create competing stimulation that will block some pain messages. Some people with arthritis wear a small, portable electrical stimulation unit next to a painful area. When the unit stimulates nerves in the area, the person feels a vibrating sensation rather than pain (Murphy, 1982).

Melzack and Wall noted that brain-to-spinal-cord messages can also close the gate, helping to explain some striking psychological influences on pain. When we are distracted from pain and soothed by the release of endorphins, our experience of pain may be greatly diminished. Sports injuries may go unnoticed until the after-game shower. During a 1989 basketball game, Ohio State University player Jay Burson broke his neck—and kept playing. People who carry a gene that boosts the availability of the body's natural painkillers, the endorphins, are less bothered by pain, and their brains are less responsive to it (Zubieta & others, 2003).

There is also more to our *memories* of pain than the pain we experienced. In experiments, and after medical procedures, people overlook a pain's duration. Their memory snapshots instead record its peak moment and how much pain they felt at the end. Daniel Kahneman and his co-researchers (1993) discovered this when they asked people to immerse one hand in painfully cold water for 60 seconds, and then the other hand in the same painfully cold water for 60 seconds followed by a slightly less painful 30 seconds more. Curiously, when asked which trial they would prefer to repeat, most preferred the longer trial, with more net pain—but less pain at the end. A physician used this principle with patients undergoing colon exams—lengthening the discomfort by a minute, but lessening its intensity (Kahneman, 1999). Although the extended milder discomfort added to their net

> "When belly with bad pains doth swell, It matters naught what else goes well."
> Sadi, *The Gulistan*, 1258

> "Pain is increased by attending to it."
> Charles Darwin, *Expression of Emotions in Man and Animals*, 1872

■ **gate-control theory** the theory that the spinal cord contains a neurological "gate" that blocks pain signals or allows them to pass on to the brain. The "gate" is opened by the activity of pain signals traveling up small nerve fibers and is closed by activity in larger fibers or by information coming from the brain.

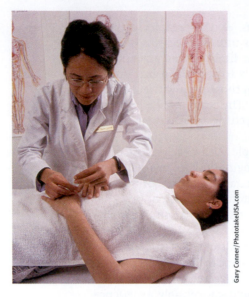

Seeking relief
This acupuncturist is attempting to help this woman gain relief from back pain by using needles on points of the patient's hand.

Gary Conner/PhototakeUSA.com

pain experience, patients experiencing this taper-down treatment later recalled the exam as less painful than those whose pain ended abruptly. In a parallel phenomenon, people rate an imagined terrible life with a moderately bad year added on as better than a terrible life that ends abruptly without the moderately bad year. And they rate an imagined wonderful life that ends abruptly as better than one with added mildly pleasant years (Diener & others, 2001).

Pain Control

If pain is where body meets mind—if it is indeed a physical and a psychological phenomenon—then it should be treatable both physically and psychologically. Depending on the type of symptoms, pain control clinics select one or more therapies from a list that includes drugs, surgery, acupuncture, electrical stimulation, massage, exercise, hypnosis, relaxation training, and thought distraction. Even an inert placebo can help, by dampening the brain's responses to painful experiences—mimicking analgesic drugs (Wager & others, 2004).

Distracting people with pleasant images ("Think of a warm, comfortable environment") or drawing their attention away from the painful stimulation ("Count backward by 3's") is an especially effective way to increase pain tolerance (Fernandez & Turk, 1989; McCaul & Malott, 1984). A well-trained nurse may distract needle-shy patients by chatting with them and asking them to look away when inserting the needle. For burn victims receiving excruciating wound care, an even more effective distraction comes from immersion in a computer-generated 3-D world (**FIGURE 12.7**). Functional MRI (fMRI) scans reveal that playing in the virtual reality reduces the brain's pain-related activity (Hoffman, 2004). Because pain is in the brain, diverting the brain's attention may bring relief.

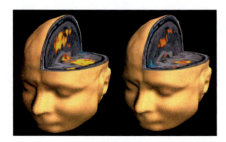

FIGURE 12.7
Virtual-reality pain control
For burn victims undergoing painful skin repair, an escape into virtual reality can powerfully distract attention, thus reducing pain and the brain's response to painful stimulation, as shown in the above fMRI scans.

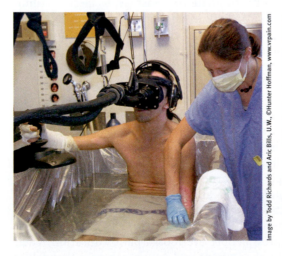

Image by Todd Richards and Aric Bills, U.W., ©Hunter Hoffman, www.vrpain.com

Taste

12-4 : How do we experience taste?

Like touch, our sense of taste involves several basic sensations. Until recently, taste's sensations were thought to be sweet, sour, salty, and bitter (McBurney & Gent, 1979), with all others stemming from mixtures of these four. Then, as investigators searched for specialized nerve fibers for the four taste sensations, they encountered a receptor for what we now know is a fifth—the meaty taste of *umami,* best experienced as the flavor enhancer monosodium glutamate (Chaudhari & others, 2000; Nelson & others, 2001; Smith & Margolskee, 2001).

Taste exists for more than our pleasure. Pleasureful tastes attracted our ancestors to energy-rich foods that enabled their survival. Aversive tastes deterred them from new foods that might be toxic. We see the inheritance of this biological wisdom in today's 2- to 6-year-olds, who are typically fussy eaters, especially when offered new meats or bitter-tasting vegetables, such as spinach and brussels sprouts (Cooke & others, 2003). Meat and plant toxins were both potentially dangerous sources of food poisoning for our ancestors, especially for children. Given repeated small tastes of disliked new foods, children will, however, typically begin to accept them (Wardle & others, 2003).

Taste is a chemical sense. Inside each little bump on the top and sides of your tongue are 200 or more taste buds, each containing a pore that catches food chemicals. Food molecules are sensed by 50 to 100 taste receptor cells that project antennalike hairs into the taste bud pore. Some of these receptors respond mostly to sweet-tasting molecules, others to salty- , sour-, umami-, or bitter-tasting ones. It doesn't take much to trigger a response that alerts the temporal lobe. If a stream of water is pumped across your tongue, the addition of a concentrated salty or sweet taste for but one-tenth of a second will get your attention (Kelling & Halpern, 1983). When a friend asks for "just a taste" of your soft drink, you can squeeze off the straw after a mere fraction of a second.

Taste receptors reproduce themselves every week or two, so if you burn your tongue with hot food it hardly matters. However, as you grow older, the number of taste buds decreases, as does taste sensitivity (Cowart, 1981). (No wonder adults enjoy strong-tasting foods that children resist.) Smoking and alcohol use accelerate the decline in taste buds and sensitivities.

Essential as taste buds are, there's more to taste than meets the tongue. Hold your nose, close your eyes, and have someone feed you various foods. A slice of apple may be indistinguishable from a chunk of raw potato; a piece of steak may taste like cardboard; without their smells, a cold cup of coffee may be hard to distinguish from a glass of red wine. To savor a taste, we normally breathe the aroma through our nose— which is why eating is not much fun when you have a bad cold. Smell can also change our perception of taste: A drink's strawberry odor enhances our perception of its sweetness. This is **sensory interaction** at work—the principle that one sense may influence another. Smell plus texture plus taste equals flavor.

Sensory interaction similarly influences what we hear. If I (as a person with hearing loss) watch a video with simultaneous captioning, I have no trouble hearing the words I am seeing (and may therefore think I don't need the captioning). If I then turn off the captioning, I suddenly realize I need it. But what do you suppose happens if we *see* a speaker saying one syllable while *hearing* another? Surprise: We may perceive a third syllable that blends both inputs. Seeing the mouth movements for *ga* while hearing *ba* we may perceive *da*—a phenomenon known as the *McGurk effect,* after its discoverers, psychologist Harry McGurk and his assistant John MacDonald (1976).

Much the same is true with vision and touch. Sensory interaction underlies the rubber hand illusion, where vision influences the sense of touch. In detecting events, the brain can combine simultaneous visual and touch signals, thanks to neurons projecting from the somatosensory cortex back to the visual cortex (Macaluso & others, 2000).

So, the senses interact: Seeing, hearing, touching, tasting, and smelling are not totally separate channels. In interpreting the world, the brain blends their inputs.

■ **sensory interaction** the principle that one sense may influence another, as when the smell of food influences its taste.

Sensory interaction
When a hard-of-hearing listener sees an animated face forming words being spoken at the other end of a phone line, the words become easier to understand (Knight, 2004).

Courtesy of RNID www.rnid.org.uk

Smell

12-5: How does our sense of smell work?

Inhale, exhale. Inhale, exhale. Breaths come in pairs—except at two moments: birth and death. Between those two moments, you will daily inhale and exhale nearly 20,000 breaths of life-sustaining air, bathing your nostrils in a stream of scent-laden molecules. The resulting experiences of smell (*olfaction*) are strikingly intimate: You inhale something of whatever or whoever it is you smell.

Like taste, smell is a chemical sense. We smell something when molecules of a substance carried in the air reach a tiny cluster of 5 million or more receptor cells at the top of each nasal cavity (**FIGURE 12.8**). These olfactory receptor cells, waving like sea anemones on a reef, respond selectively—to the aroma of a cake baking, to a wisp of smoke, to a friend's fragrance. Instantly they alert the brain through their axon fibers.

Even nursing infants and their mothers have a literal chemistry to their relationship. They quickly learn to recognize each other's scents (McCarthy, 1986). Aided by smell, a mother fur seal returning to a beach crowded with pups will find her own. Our own sense of smell is less impressive than the acuteness of our seeing and hearing. Looking out across a garden, we see its forms and colors in exquisite detail and hear a variety of birds singing, yet we smell little of it without sticking our nose into the blossoms.

> Impress your friends with your new word for the day: People unable to see are said to experience blindness. People unable to hear experience deafness. People unable to smell experience *anosmia*.

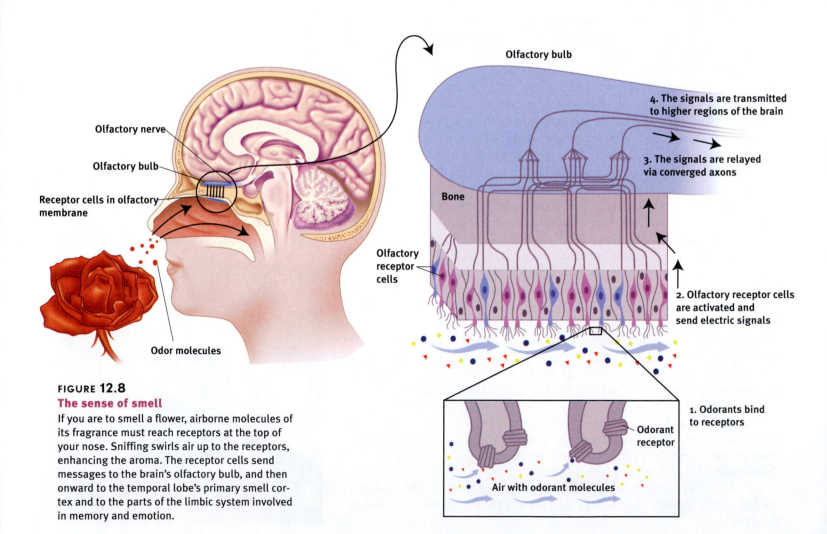

FIGURE 12.8

The sense of smell

If you are to smell a flower, airborne molecules of its fragrance must reach receptors at the top of your nose. Sniffing swirls air up to the receptors, enhancing the aroma. The receptor cells send messages to the brain's olfactory bulb, and then onward to the temporal lobe's primary smell cortex and to the parts of the limbic system involved in memory and emotion.

Odor molecules come in many shapes and sizes—so many, in fact, that it takes many different receptors to detect them. A large family of genes designs the 350 or so receptor proteins that recognize particular odor molecules (Miller, 2004). Richard Axel and Linda Buck (1991) discovered (in work for which they received a 2004 Nobel prize) that these receptor proteins are embedded on the surface of nasal cavity neurons. As a key slips into a lock, so odor molecules slip into these receptors. Yet we seem not to have a distinct receptor for each detectable odor. This suggests that some odors trigger a combination of receptors, whose activity the olfactory cortex interprets. As the alphabet's 26 letters can combine to form many words, so odor molecules bind to different receptor arrays, producing the 10,000 odors we can detect (Malnic & others, 1999). It is the combinations of olfactory receptors that allow us to distinguish the aromas of fresh-brewed and hours-old coffee.

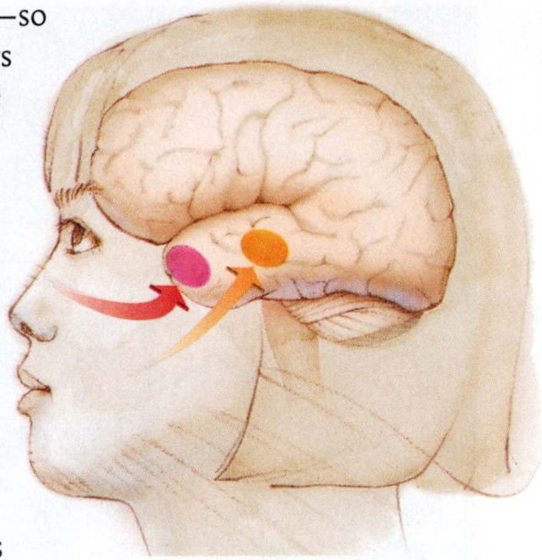

Odors can evoke unpleasant emotions. Rachel Herz and her colleagues (2004) frustrated Brown University students with a rigged computer game in a scented room. Later, if exposed to the same odor while working on a verbal task, their frustration was rekindled and they gave up sooner than students exposed to a different odor or no odor. The brain's circuitry helps explain this power to evoke memories and feelings (**FIGURE 12.9**). A hotline runs between the brain area that receives information from the nose and the brain's ancient limbic centers associated with memory and emotion. Smell is primitive. Eons before the elaborate analytical areas of our cerebral cortex had fully evolved, our mammalian ancestors sniffed for food—and for predators.

Though it's difficult to recall odors by name, we have a remarkable capacity to recognize long-forgotten odors and their associated personal episodes (Engen, 1987; Schab, 1991). Pleasant odors can evoke pleasant memories (Ehrlichman & Halpern, 1988). The smell of the sea, the scent of a perfume, or an aroma of a favorite relative's kitchen can bring to mind a happy time. It's a phenomenon understood by the British travel agent chain Lunn Poly. To evoke memories of lounging on sunny, warm beaches, the company has piped the aroma of coconut suntan oil into its shops (Fracassini, 2000).

Body Position and Movement

12-6 : How do our senses monitor our body's position and movement?

With only the five familiar senses of vision, hearing, touch, taste, and smell, we could not put food in our mouths, stand up, or reach out and touch someone. We would be helpless. To know just how to move your arms to grasp someone's hand, you need a sixth sense. You need to know the current position of your arms and hands and then be aware of their changing positions as you move them. For you to take just one step requires feedback from, and instructions to, some 200 muscles. The computations your brain must perform for sensorimotor coordination dwarf even those involved in reasoning. You come equipped with millions of position and motion sensors. They are all over your body—in the muscles, tendons, and joints—and they are continually providing information to your brain. If you twist your wrist one degree, the sensors immediately report it. This sense of your body parts' position and movement is **kinesthesis.**

FIGURE 12.9
The olfactory brain
Information from the taste buds (orange arrow) travels to an area of the temporal lobe not far from where the brain receives olfactory information, which interacts with taste. The brain's circuitry for smell (red arrow) also connects with areas involved in memory storage, which helps explain why a smell can trigger a memory explosion.

Humans have 10 to 20 million olfactory receptors. A bloodhound has some 200 million (Herz, 2001).

"The smell and taste of things bears unfaltering, in the tiny and almost impalpable drop of their essence, the vast structure of recollection."

French novelist Marcel Proust, in *Remembrance of Things Past* (1913), describing how the aroma and flavor of a bit of cake soaked in tea resurrected long-forgotten memories of the old family house.

■ **kinesthesis** [kin-ehs-THEE-sehs] the system for sensing the position and movement of individual body parts.

The intricate vestibular sense
Thank your inner ears for the information that enables your brain to monitor your body's position.

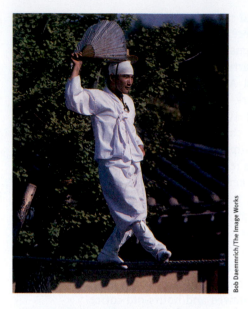

Bob Daemmrich/The Image Works

One can momentarily imagine being blind or deaf. Close your eyes, plug your ears, and experience the dark stillness. But what would it be like to live without touch or kinesthesis—without, therefore, being able to sense the positions of your limbs when you wake during the night? Ian Waterman of Hampshire, England, knows. In 1972, at age 19, Waterman contracted a rare viral infection that de-stroyed the nerves that enabled his sense of light touch and of body position and movement. People with this condition re-port feeling disembodied, as though their body is dead, not real, not theirs (Sacks, 1985). With prolonged practice Water-man has learned to walk and eat—by visu-ally focusing on his limbs and directing them accordingly. But if the lights go out, he crumples to the floor (Azar, 1998). Even for the rest of us, vision interacts with kinesthesis. Stand with your right heel in front of your left toes. Easy. Now close your eyes and you will probably wobble.

A companion **vestibular sense** monitors your head's (and thus your body's) posi-tion and movement. The biological gyroscopes for this sense of equilibrium are in the inner ear. The *semicircular canals,* which look like a three-dimensional pretzel (**FIGURE 12.10**), and the *vestibular sacs,* which connect the canals with the cochlea, contain fluid that moves when your head rotates or tilts. This movement stimulates hairlike receptors, which send messages to the cerebellum at the back of the brain, thus en-abling you to sense your body position and to maintain your balance.

FIGURE 12.10
Semicircular canals in the inner ear

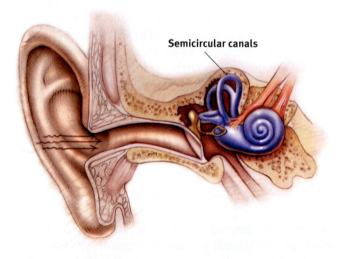

Semicircular canals

If you twirl around and then come to an abrupt halt, neither the fluid in your semicircular canals nor your kinesthetic receptors will immediately return to their neutral state. The aftereffect fools your dizzy brain with the sensation that you're still spinning. This illustrates a principle underlying perceptual illusions: *Mechanisms that normally give us an accurate experience of the world can, under special conditions, fool us.* Understanding how we get fooled provides clues to how our perceptual system works.

■ **vestibular sense** the sense of body movement and position, including the sense of balance.

>> Module Review

Although vision tends to dominate our other senses, our other senses, including hearing (*audition*), are highly adaptive.

12-1: **What are the characteristics of the air pressure waves that we hear as meaningful sounds?**

The bands of compressed and expanded air that we experience as sound vary in *frequency* and in amplitude, which we perceive as differences in *pitch* (a tone's highness or lowness) and loudness. Sound energy is measured in decibels. Prolonged exposure to sounds above 85 decibels can produce hearing loss.

12-2: **How does the ear transform sound energy into neural messages?**

Through a mechanical chain of events, sound waves traveling through the auditory canal cause tiny vibrations in the eardrum, which the bones of the *middle ear* amplify and relay to the fluid-filled *cochlea*. These vibrations create movement in tiny hair cells on the basilar membrane, triggering neural messages to the brain's auditory cortex. Minute differences in the loudness and timing of the sounds received by each ear allow us to localize sounds.

12-3: **How do we sense touch and feel pain?**

Our sense of touch is actually four senses—pressure, warmth, cold, and pain—that combine to produce other sensations, such as a tickle. One theory of pain is that a "*gate*" in the spinal cord either opens to permit pain signals traveling up small nerve fibers to reach the brain, or closes to prevent their passage. The biopsychosocial approach views pain as the sum of three sets of forces: biological influences, such as nerve fibers sending messages to

the brain; psychological influences, such as the situation and our past experiences; and social-cultural influences, such as cultural expectations and the presence of observers. Treatments to control pain often combine physiological and psychological elements.

12-4: **How do we experience taste?**

Taste, a chemical sense, is a composite of five basic sensations—sweet, sour, salty, bitter, and umami—and of the aromas that interact with information from the taste buds. Taste receptors are located in the taste buds on the tongue and in the back and roof of the mouth. The influence of smell on our sense of taste is an example of *sensory interaction*.

12-5: **How does our sense of smell work?**

Smell is a chemical sense, but there are no basic sensations for smell, as there are for touch and taste. Airborne molecules activate receptor cells located at the top of each nasal cavity. These receptors and their associated proteins recognize individual odor molecules. The receptors send messages to the brain's olfactory bulb, then to the temporal lobe, and to parts of the limbic system. Some odors trigger a combination of receptors. Odors can spontaneously evoke memories and their associated emotions.

12-6: **How do our senses monitor our body's position and movement?**

By means of millions of position and motion sensors all over the body, our *kinesthetic sense* monitors the position and movement of individual body parts. Our *vestibular sense* monitors the position and movement of the whole body. Receptors for the vestibular sense are located in the inner ear.

>> Rehearse it!

1. The amplitude of a light wave determines our perception of brightness. The amplitude of a sound wave determines our perception of
   a. loudness.
   b. pitch.
   c. audition.
   d. frequency.

2. The frequency of sound waves determines their pitch. The _____ the waves are, the lower their frequency is and the _____ their pitch.
   a. shorter; higher
   b. longer; lower
   c. lower; longer
   d. higher; shorter

3. Sound waves pass through the auditory canal to the eardrum, whose vibrations are transmitted to a snail-shaped tube in the inner ear. This tube, where the waves are converted into neural activity, is called the

   a. anvil.
   b. basilar membrane.
   c. cochlea.
   d. oval window.

4. At least four skin senses—pressure, warmth, cold, and pain—make up our sense of touch. Of all the skin senses, only _____ has its own identifiable receptor cells.
   a. pressure
   b. warmth
   c. cold
   d. pain

5. Although no theory fully explains our experience of pain, the gate-control theory helps. This theory notes that
   a. special pain receptors send signals directly to the brain.
   b. pain is a property of the senses, not of the brain.
   c. small spinal cord nerve fibers conduct most pain signals.

   d. the stimuli that produce pain are unrelated to other sensations.

6. The taste of the food we eat is greatly enhanced by its smell or aroma. This influence of one sense on another is an example of
   a. sensory adaptation.
   b. chemical sensation.
   c. gate-control theory.
   d. sensory interaction.

7. Our vestibular sense monitors our body's position and movement by tracking movements of the head. The receptors for the vestibular sense are in the
   a. skin.
   b. brain.
   c. inner ear.
   d. skeletal muscles.

Answers: 1. a, 2. b, 3. c, 4. a, 5. c, 6. d, 7. c.

>> Terms and Concepts to Remember

audition, p. 157
frequency, p. 158
pitch, p. 158
middle ear, p. 159

cochlea [KOHK-lee-uh], p. 159
inner ear, p. 159
gate-control theory, p. 163

sensory interaction, p. 165
kinesthesis [kin-ehs-THEE-sehs], p. 167
vestibular sense, p. 168

>> Test Yourself

1. In a nutshell, how do we transform sound waves into perceived sound?

2. What does the biopsychosocial approach to pain teach us?

3. How does our system for sensing smell differ from our sensory systems for touch and taste?

(Answers in Appendix C.)

*Multiple-choice **self-tests** and more may be found at www.worthpublishers.com/myers.*

Perceptual Organization

13-1: What did the Gestalt psychologists contribute to our understanding of how the brain organizes sensations into perceptions?

We sense sights and sounds, tastes and smells, touch and movement. Yet how do we see not just shapes and colors, but a rose in bloom, a familiar face, a sunset? How do we hear not just a mix of pitches and rhythms, but a child's cry of pain, the hum of distant traffic, a symphony? In short, how do we organize and interpret our sensations so that they become meaningful perceptions?

Early in the twentieth century, a group of German psychologists noticed that when given a cluster of sensations, people tend to organize them into a **gestalt,** a German word meaning a "form" or a "whole." For example, look at **FIGURE 13.1.** Note that the individual elements of the figure are really nothing but eight blue circles, each containing three converging white lines. When we view them all together, however, we see a *whole,* a form, a Necker cube.

Over the years, the Gestalt psychologists provided compelling demonstrations and described principles by which we organize our sensations into perceptions. As you read further about these principles, keep in mind the fundamental truth they illustrate: *Our brain does more than merely register information about the world.* Perception is not just opening a shutter and letting a picture print itself on the brain. We constantly filter sensory information and infer perceptions in ways that make sense to us. Mind matters.

- **gestalt** an organized whole. Gestalt psychologists emphasized our tendency to integrate pieces of information into meaningful wholes.

- **figure-ground** the organization of the visual field into objects (the *figures*) that stand out from their surroundings (the *ground*).

FIGURE 13.1
A Necker cube
What do you see: circles with white lines, or a cube? If you stare at the cube, you may notice that it reverses location, moving the tiny X in the center from the front edge to the back. At times the cube may seem to float in front of the page, with circles behind it; other times the circles may become holes in the page through which the cube appears, as though it were floating behind the page. There is far more to perception than meets the eye. (From Bradley & others, 1976.)

Form Perception

13-2: How do the principles of figure-ground and grouping contribute to our perception of form?

Imagine designing a video/computer system that, like your eye/brain system, could recognize faces at a glance. What abilities would it need?

Figure and Ground

To start with, the system would need to recognize faces as distinct from their backgrounds. Likewise, our first perceptual task is to perceive any object (the figure) as distinct from its surroundings (the ground). Among the voices you hear at a party, the one you attend to becomes the figure; all others, part of the ground. As you read, the words are the figure; the white paper, the ground. In **FIGURE 13.2,** the **figure-ground** relationship continually reverses—but always we organize the stimulus into a figure seen against a ground. Such reversible figure-and-ground illustrations demonstrate again that the same stimulus can trigger more than one perception.

FIGURE 13.2
Reversible figure and ground

Time Saving Suggestion, © 2003 Roger Shepherd.

■ **grouping** the perceptual tendency to organize stimuli into coherent groups.

■ **depth perception** the ability to see objects in three dimensions although the images that strike the retina are two-dimensional; allows us to judge distance.

■ **visual cliff** a laboratory device for testing depth perception in infants and young animals.

Grouping

Having discriminated figure from ground, we (and our video/computer system) now have to organize the figure into a meaningful form. Some basic features of a scene—such as color, movement, and light/dark contrast—we process instantly and automatically (Treisman, 1987). To bring order and form to these basic sensations, our minds follow certain rules for **grouping** stimuli together (**FIGURE 13.3**). These rules, identified by the Gestalt psychologists and applied even by infants, illustrate the idea that the perceived whole differs from the sum of its parts (Quinn & others, 2002; Rock & Palmer, 1990):

> *Proximity* We group nearby figures together. We see not six separate lines, but three sets of two lines.
>
> *Similarity* We group similar figures together. We see the triangles and circles as vertical columns of similar shapes, not as horizontal rows of dissimilar shapes.

Continuity We perceive smooth, continuous patterns rather than discontinuous ones. This pattern could be a series of alternating semicircles, but we perceive it as two continuous lines—one wavy, one straight.

Connectedness Because they are uniform and linked, we perceive the two dots and the line between them as a single unit.

Closure We fill in gaps to create a complete, whole object. Thus we assume that the circles (below, left) are complete but partially blocked by the (illusory) triangle. Add nothing more than little line segments that close off the circles and now your brain stops constructing a triangle.

Usually, these and other grouping principles help us construct reality. Sometimes, however, they lead us astray, as when we look at the doghouse in **FIGURE 13.4.**

FIGURE 13.3
Organizing stimuli into groups
We could perceive the stimuli shown here in many ways, yet people everywhere see them similarly. The Gestalt psychologists believed this shows that the brain follows rules to order sensory information into wholes.

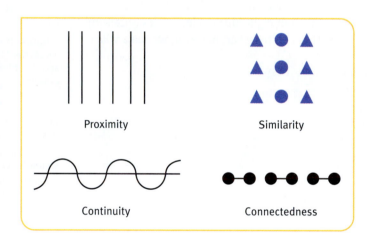

Proximity

Similarity

Continuity

Connectedness

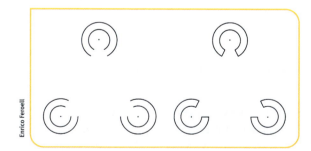

Enrico Feroelt

Photo by Walter Wick. Reprinted from GAMES Magazine. © 1983 PCS Games Limited Partnership.

FIGURE **13.4**

What's the secret to this impossible doghouse?
You probably perceive this doghouse as a gestalt—a whole (though impossible) structure. Actually, your brain imposes this sense of wholeness on the picture. As the photo on this module's final page shows, Gestalt grouping principles are at work here.

Depth Perception

13-3 : How do we see the world in three dimensions?

Two-dimensional images fall on our retinas, yet we somehow organize three-dimensional perceptions. **Depth perception,** seeing objects in three dimensions, enables us to estimate their distance from us. At a glance, we estimate the distance of an oncoming car or the height of a house. This ability is partly innate. Eleanor Gibson and Richard Walk (1960) discovered this using a miniature cliff with a drop-off covered by sturdy glass. Gibson's inspiration for these experiments occurred while she was picnicking on the rim of the Grand Canyon. She wondered: Would a toddler peering over the rim perceive the dangerous drop-off and draw back?

Back in their Cornell University laboratory, Gibson and Walk placed 6- to 14-month-old infants on the edge of a safe canyon—a **visual cliff** (FIGURE **13.5**). Their mothers then coaxed them to crawl out onto the glass. Most refused to do so, indicating that they could perceive depth. Perhaps by crawling age the infants had *learned* to perceive depth. Yet newborn animals with virtually no visual experience—including young kittens, a day-old goat, and newly hatched chicks—respond similarly.

Innervisions

FIGURE **13.5**
Visual cliff
Eleanor Gibson and Richard Walk devised this miniature cliff with a glass-covered drop-off to determine whether crawling infants and newborn animals can perceive depth. Even when coaxed, infants are reluctant to venture onto the glass over the cliff.

■ **binocular cues** depth cues, such as retinal disparity, that depend on the use of two eyes.

■ **retinal disparity** a binocular cue for perceiving depth: By comparing images from the two eyeballs, the brain computes distance—the greater the disparity (difference) between the two images, the closer the object.

■ **monocular cues** depth cues, such as interposition and linear perspective, available to either eye alone.

Each species, by the time it is mobile, has the perceptual abilities it needs. But if biological maturation predisposes our wariness of heights, experience amplifies it. Infants' wariness increases with their experiences of crawling, no matter when they begin to crawl.

How do we do it? How do we transform two differing two-dimensional retinal images into a single three-dimensional perception? The process begins with depth cues, some that depend on the use of two eyes, and others that are available to each eye separately.

Binocular Cues

Try this: With both eyes open, hold two pens or pencils in front of you and touch their tips together. Now do so with one eye closed. With one eye, the task becomes noticeably more difficult, demonstrating the importance of **binocular cues** in judging the distance of nearby objects. Two eyes are better than one.

Because our eyes are about 2½ inches apart, our retinas receive slightly different images of the world. When the brain compares these two images, the difference between them—their **retinal disparity**—provides an important cue to the relative distance of different objects. When you hold your finger directly in front of your nose, your retinas receive quite different views. (You can see this if you close one eye and then the other, or create a finger sausage as in **FIGURE 13.6.**) At a greater distance—say, when you hold your finger at arm's length—the disparity is smaller.

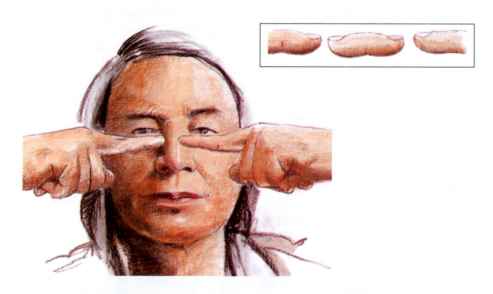

FIGURE 13.6
The floating finger sausage
Hold your two index fingers about 5 inches in front of your eyes, with their tips half an inch apart. Now look beyond them and note the weird result. Move your fingers out farther and the retinal disparity—and the finger sausage—will shrink.

The creators of three-dimensional (3-D) movies simulate or exaggerate retinal disparity by photographing a scene with two cameras placed a few inches apart (a feature we might want to build into our seeing computer). When we view the movie through spectacles that allow the left eye to see only the image from the left camera and the right eye only the image from the right camera, the 3-D effect mimics normal retinal disparity. Similarly, twin cameras in airplanes can take photos of terrain for integration into 3-D maps.

Monocular Cues

How do we judge whether a person is 10 or 100 meters away? In both cases, retinal disparity while looking straight ahead is slight. At such distances we depend on **monocular cues** (available to each eye separately), such as those in **FIGURE 13.7.**

FIGURE 13.7
Monocular depth cues

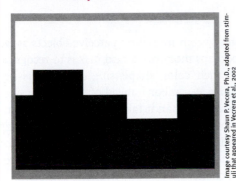

Image courtesy Shaun P. Vecera, Ph.D., adapted from stimuli that appeared in Vecera et al., 2002

Relative height

We perceive objects higher in our field of vision as farther away. Because we perceive the lower part of a figure-ground illustration as closer, we perceive it as figure (Vecera & others, 2002). Invert the illustration above and the black becomes ground, like a night sky.

Relative size

If we assume two objects are similar in size, *most* people perceive the one that casts the smaller retinal image as farther away.

Rene Magritte, *The Blank Signature*, oil on canvas, National Gallery of Art, Washington. Collection of Mr. and Mrs. Paul Mellon. Photo by Richard Carafelli.

Interposition

If one object partially blocks our view of another, we perceive it as closer. The depth cues provided by interposition make this an impossible scene.

Relative motion

As we move, objects that are actually stable may appear to move. If while riding on a bus you fix your gaze on some object—say, a house—the objects beyond the fixation point appear to move with you; objects in front of the fixation point appear to move backward. The farther those objects are from the fixation point, the faster they seem to move.

Direction of passenger's motion ➡️

Linear perspective

Parallel lines, such as railroad tracks, appear to converge with distance. The more they converge, the greater their perceived distance.

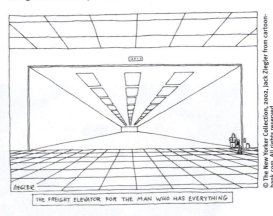

© The New Yorker Collection, 2002, Jack Ziegler from cartoonbank.com. All rights reserved.

Light and shadow

Nearby objects reflect more light to our eyes. Thus, given two identical objects, the dimmer one seems farther away. Shading, too, produces a sense of depth consistent with our assumption that light comes from above. Invert the illustration below and the hollow becomes a hill.

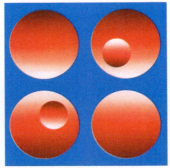

From "Perceiving Shape From Shading" by Vilayanur S. Ramachandran. Copyright © 1988 by Scientific American, Inc. All rights reserved.

■ **perceptual constancy** perceiving objects as unchanging (having consistent color, shape, size, or lightness) even as illumination and retinal images change.

■ **color constancy** perceiving familiar objects as having consistent color, even if changing illumination alters the wavelengths reflected by the object.

Perceptual Constancy

13-4 : How do perceptual constancies help us to organize our sensations into meaningful perceptions?

So far, we have noted that our video/computer system must first perceive objects as we do—as having a distinct form, location, and perhaps motion. Its next task is to recognize objects without being deceived by changes in their color, shape, size, or lightness—an ability we call **perceptual constancy.** You glance at someone ahead of you on the sidewalk and instantly recognize a classmate. In less time than it takes to draw a breath, information reaching your eyes has been sent to your brain and work teams comprising millions of neurons have extracted the essential features, compared them with stored images, and identified the person. This human perceptual feat, which has intrigued researchers for decades, provides a monumental challenge for our perceiving computer.

Color Constancy

Our experience of color depends on something more than the wavelength information received by the receptor cells in our retinas and transmitted by other cells to our brain.

That something more is the surrounding context. If you view only part of a tomato, its color will seem to change as the light changes. But if you see the whole tomato as one item in a bowl of fresh vegetables, its color will remain roughly constant as the lighting and wavelengths shift—a phenomenon known as **color constancy.** Dorothea Jameson (1985) noted that a chip colored blue under indoor lighting matches the wavelengths reflected by a gold chip in sunlight. Yet bring a bluebird indoors and it won't look like a goldfinch. Likewise, a green leaf hanging from a brown branch may, when the illumination changes, reflect the same light energy that formerly came from the brown branch. Yet to us the leaf stays greenish and the branch stays brownish.

Though we take color constancy for granted, the phenomenon is truly remarkable. It demonstrates that our experience of color comes not just from the object—the color is not in the isolated leaf. You and I see color thanks to our brains' computations of the light reflected by any object *relative to its surrounding objects.* But only if we grew up with normal light, it seems. Monkeys raised under a restricted range of wavelengths later have great difficulty recognizing the same color when illumination varies (Sugita, 2004).

In a context that does not vary, we maintain color constancy. But what if we change the context? Because the brain computes the color of an object relative to its context, the perceived color changes (as is dramatically apparent in **FIGURE 13.8**). Artists and decorators remember: Your perception of that brushstroke of paint will be determined not just by the paint in the can but by the surrounding colors. The take-home lesson: Comparisons govern our perceptions.

"From there to here, from here to there, funny things are everywhere."
Dr. Seuss, *One Fish, Two Fish, Red Fish, Blue Fish*, 1960

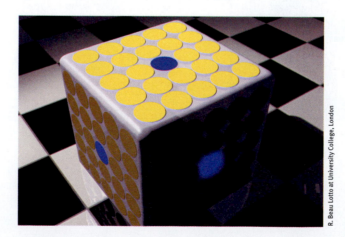

FIGURE 13.8
Color depends on context Believe it or not, these three blue disks are identical in color.

R. Beau Lotto at University College, London

Shape and Size Constancies

Sometimes an object whose actual shape cannot change *seems* to change shape with the angle of our view (**FIGURE 13.9**). More often, thanks to *shape constancy*, we perceive the form of familiar objects, like the door in **FIGURE 13.10**, as constant even while our retinal images of them change.

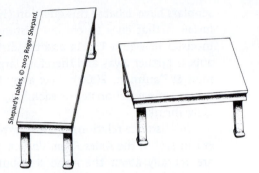

Thanks to *size constancy* we perceive objects as having a constant size, even while our distance from them varies. We assume a car is large enough to carry people, even when we see its tiny image from two blocks away. This illustrates the close connection between perceived *distance* and perceived *size*. Perceiving an object's distance gives us cues to its size. Likewise, knowing its general size—that the object is, say, a car—provides us with cues to its distance.

FIGURE 13.9
Perceiving shape
Do the tops of these tables have different dimensions? They appear to. But—believe it or not—they are identical. (Measure and see.) With both tables we adjust our perceptions relative to our viewing angle.

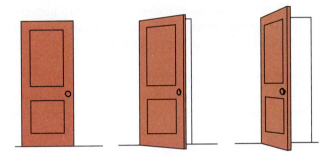

FIGURE 13.10
Shape constancy
A door casts an increasingly trapezoidal image on our retinas as it opens, yet we still perceive it as rectangular.

Size-Distance Relationship

It is a marvel how effortlessly size perception occurs. Given an object's perceived distance and the size of its image on our retinas, we instantly and unconsciously infer the object's size. Although the monsters in **FIGURE 13.11a** cast the same retinal images, the linear perspective tells our brain that the monster in pursuit is farther away. We therefore perceive it as larger.

This interplay between perceived size and perceived distance helps explain several well-known illusions. For example, can you imagine why the Moon looks up to 50 percent larger near the horizon than when high in the sky? For at least 22 centuries,

(a)   (b)

FIGURE 13.11
The interplay between perceived size and distance
(a) The monocular cues for distance (such as linear perspective and relative height) make the pursuing monster look larger than the pursued. It isn't.
(b) This visual trick, called the Ponzo illusion, is based on the same principle as the fleeing monsters. The two red bars cast identical-sized images on our retinas. But experience tells us that a more distant object can create the same-sized image as a nearer one only if it is actually larger. As a result, we perceive the bar that seems farther away as larger.

scholars have debated this question (Hershenson, 1989). One reason for the *Moon illusion* is that cues to objects' distances make the horizon Moon—like the distant monster in Figure 13.11a and the distant bar in the *Ponzo illusion* in **FIGURE 13.11b**—appear farther away and therefore larger than the Moon high in the night sky (Kaufman & Kaufman, 2000). Take away these distance cues—by looking at the horizon Moon (or each monster or each bar) through a paper tube—and the object immediately shrinks.

Size-distance relationships also explain why the two same-age girls seem so different in size in the *Ames Room illusion* (**FIGURE 13.12**). As the diagram reveals, the girls are actually about the same size, but the room is distorted. Viewed with one eye through a peephole, its trapezoidal walls produce the same images as those of a normal rectangular room viewed with both eyes. Presented with the camera's one-eyed view, the brain makes the reasonable assumption that the room *is* normal and each girl is therefore the same distance from us. And given the different sizes of the images on the retina, our brain ends up calculating that the girls are very different in size.

Our occasional misperceptions reveal the workings of our normally effective perceptual processes. The perceived relationship between distance and size is generally valid, but under special circumstances it can lead us astray—as when helping to create the Moon illusion and the Ames Room illusion.

Lightness Constancy

White paper reflects 90 percent of the light falling on it; black paper, only 10 percent. In sunlight a black paper may reflect 100 times more light than does a white paper viewed indoors, but it still looks black (McBurney & Collings, 1984). This illustrates *lightness constancy* (also called *brightness constancy*); we perceive an object as having a constant lightness even while its illumination varies. Perceived lightness depends on *relative luminance*—the amount of light an object reflects relative to its surroundings. If you view sunlit black paper through a narrow tube so nothing else is visible, it may look gray, because in bright sunshine it reflects a fair amount of light. View it without the tube and it is again black, because it reflects much less light than the objects around it. The phenomenon is similar to that of *color constancy*. As light changes, a red apple in a fruit bowl retains its redness, because our brain computes the light reflected by any object relative to its surrounding objects.

FIGURE 13.12

The illusion of the shrinking and growing girls

This distorted room, designed by Adelbert Ames, appears to have a normal rectangular shape when viewed through a peephole with one eye. The girl in the near corner appears disproportionately large because we judge her size based on the false assumption that she is the same distance away as the girl in the far corner.

S. Schwartzenberg/The Exploratorium

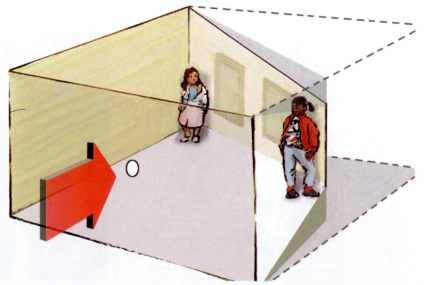

Perceived lightness stays roughly constant, given an unchanging context. But what happens when the surrounding context changes? As **FIGURE 13.13** shows, the visual system computes brightness and color relative to surrounding objects. Thus, perceived lightness changes with context.

Form perception, depth perception, motion perception, and perceptual constancy illuminate how we organize our visual experiences. Perceptual organization applies to other senses, too. It explains why we perceive a clock's steady tick not as a tick-tick-tick but as grouped sounds, say, TICK-tick, TICK-tick. Listening to an unfamiliar language, we have trouble hearing where one word stops and the next one begins. Listening to our own language, we automatically hear distinct words. This, too, is a form of perceptual organization. But it is more, for we even organize a string of letters—THEDOGATEMEAT—into words that make an intelligible phrase, more likely "The dog ate meat" than "The do gate me at" (McBurney & Collings, 1984). This process involves not only organization but interpretation—discerning meaning in what we perceive.

FIGURE 13.13
Brightness contrast
Squares A and B are identical in color, believe it or not. (If you don't believe me, photocopy the illustration, cut out the squares, and compare.) But we perceive B as lighter.

REVIEWING

>> MODULE REVIEW

13-1 : **What did the Gestalt psychologists contribute to our understanding of how the brain organizes sensations into perceptions?**
Gestalt psychologists searched for rules by which the brain organizes fragments of sensory data into *gestalts*, or meaningful forms. They showed that we constantly filter information and infer perceptions in ways that make sense to us.

13-2 : **How do the principles of figure-ground and grouping contribute to our perception of form?**
To recognize an object, we must first perceive it (see it as a *figure*) as distinct from its surroundings (the *ground*). We bring order and form to stimuli by organizing them into meaningful *groups*, following the rules of proximity, similarity, continuity, connectedness, and closure.

13-3 : **How do we see the world in three dimensions?**
Research on the *visual cliff* reveals that many species perceive the world in three dimensions at, or very soon after, birth. We transform two-dimensional retinal images into three-dimensional *depth perceptions* by use of *binocular cues* (such as *retinal disparity*) and *monocular cues* (such as relative size, interposition, relative height, relative motion, linear perspective, and light and shadow).

13-4 : **How do perceptual constancies help us to organize our sensations into meaningful perceptions?**
Perceptual constancy, the ability to recognize an object regardless of its changing angle, distance, or illumination, lets us perceive objects as unchanging despite the changing images they cast on our retina. Perceptual constancies help explain several well-known visual illusions, such as the Moon and the Ames Room illusions. *Color constancy*, our ability to perceive consistent color under varying illumination, shows that our brains construct our experience of color through comparisons with surrounding objects.

>> REHEARSE IT!

1. Gestalt psychologists identified the principles by which we organize our perceptions. Our tendencies to fill in the gaps and to perceive a pattern as continuous are two different examples of the organizing principle called

   a. the Ames illusion.
   b. depth perception.
   c. shape constancy.
   d. grouping.

2. In their experiments, Gibson and Walk used a visual cliff to test depth perception in infants and young animals. Their results suggest that

   a. infants have not yet developed depth perception.
   b. crawling infants perceive depth.
   c. we have no way of knowing whether infants can perceive depth.
   d. humans differ significantly from animals in being able to perceive depth in infancy.

3. The images that fall on our retinas are two-dimensional, or flat. Yet we perceive the world as having three-dimensional depth. Depth perception underlies our ability to

   a. group similar items in a gestalt.
   b. perceive objects as having a constant shape or form.
   c. judge distances.
   d. fill in the gaps in a figure.

4. In estimating distances, we use both binocular cues, which depend on both eyes, and monocular cues, which are available to either eye alone. Examples of monocular cues are interposition and

a. closure.
b. retinal disparity.
c. linear perspective.
d. brightness contrast.

5. Form perception and perceptual constancy are organizing principles that apply to hearing as well as vision. For example, in listening to a concerto, you follow the solo instrument and perceive the orchestra as accompaniment; this illustrates the organizing principle of

a. figure-ground.
b. shape constancy.
c. grouping.
d. depth or distance perception.

6. We perceive tomatoes as consistently red, despite shifting illumination. This phenomenon is known as

a. an afterimage.
b. color constancy.
c. color deficiency.
d. feature detection.

Answers: 1. d, 2. b, 3. c, 4. c, 5. a, 6. b.

>> TERMS AND CONCEPTS TO REMEMBER

gestalt, p. 171
figure-ground, p. 171
grouping, p. 172
depth perception, p. 173

visual cliff, p. 173
binocular cues, p. 174
retinal disparity, p. 174

monocular cues, p. 174
perceptual constancy, p. 176
color constancy, p. 176

>> TEST YOURSELF

1. What do we mean when we say that, in perception, the whole is greater than the sum of its parts?

(Answer in Appendix C.)

Multiple-choice **self-tests** and more may be found at www.worthpublishers.com/myers.

>> ANSWERS TO QUESTIONS WITHIN THE MODULE

Q. What's the secret to this impossible doghouse?

A. Another view of the impossible doghouse in Figure 13.4 reveals the secrets of this illusion. From the photo angle in Figure 13.4, the grouping principle of closure leads us to perceive the boards as continuous.

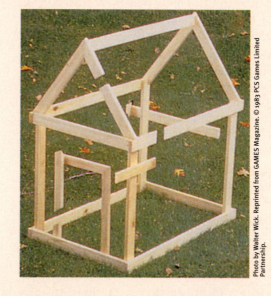

Photo by Walter Wick. Reprinted from GAMES Magazine. © 1983 PCS Games Limited Partnership.

Perceptual Interpretation

Philosophers have debated whether our perceptual abilities should be credited to our nature or our nurture. To what extent do we *learn* to perceive? German philosopher Immanuel Kant (1724–1804) maintained that knowledge comes from our *inborn* ways of organizing sensory experiences. Indeed, we come equipped to process sensory information. But British philosopher John Locke (1632–1704) argued that through our experiences we also *learn* to perceive the world. Indeed, we learn to link an object's distance with its size. So, just how important is experience? How radically does it shape our perceptual interpretations?

Sensory Deprivation and Restored Vision

14-1 : What does research on sensory restriction and restored vision reveal about the effects of experience on perception?

Writing to John Locke, William Molyneux wondered whether "a man *born* blind, and now adult, taught by his *touch* to distinguish between a cube and a sphere" could, if made to see, visually distinguish the two. Locke's answer was no, because the man would never have *learned* to see the difference.

Molyneux' hypothetical case has since been put to the test with a few dozen adults who, though blind from birth, have gained sight (Gregory, 1978; von Senden, 1932). Most had been born with cataracts—clouded lenses that allowed them to see only diffused light, rather as you or I might see a diffuse fog through a Ping-Pong ball sliced in half. After cataract surgery, the patients could distinguish figure from ground and could sense colors—suggesting that these aspects of perception are innate. But much as Locke supposed, they often could not recognize by sight objects that were familiar by touch.

Experience also influences our perception of faces. You and I perceive and recognize individual faces as a whole. Show us the same top half of a face paired with two different bottom halves (as in **FIGURE 14.1**), and the identical top halves will seem different. People deprived of visual experience during infancy surpass the rest of us at recognizing that the top halves are the same, because they didn't learn to process faces as a whole (Le Grand & others, 2004). For example, one 43-year-old man, whose sight was recently restored after 40 years of blindness, could associate people with distinct features ("Mary's the one with red hair") but could not instantly recognize a face. He also lacked perceptual constancy: As people walk away from him they seem to be shrinking in size (Bower, 2003). Vision, such cases make clear, is partly an acquired sense.

Seeking to gain more control than is provided by clinical cases, researchers have conducted Molyneux' imaginary experiment

> "Let us then suppose the mind to be, as we say, white paper void of all characters, without any ideas: How comes it to be furnished? . . . To this I answer, in one word, from EXPERIENCE."
>
> John Locke, *An Essay Concerning Human Understanding*, 1690

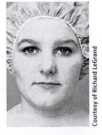

Courtesy of Richard LeGrand

FIGURE 14.1

Perceiving composite faces

To most people, the top halves of the two faces on the far left, created by Richard Le Grand and his colleagues (2004), look different. Actually, they are the same, though paired with two different lower face halves (near left). People deprived of visual experience early in life have more difficulty perceiving whole faces, which ironically enables their superiority at recognizing that the top halves of these faces are identical.

Learning to see
At age 3, Mike May lost his vision in an explosion. On March 7, 2000, after a new cornea restored vision to his right eye, he got his first look at his wife and children. Alas, although signals were reaching his long-dormant visual cortex, it lacked the experience to interpret them. Faces, apart from features such as hair, were not recognizable. Expressions eluded him. Yet he can see an object in motion and is gradually learning to navigate his world and to marvel at such things as dust floating in sunlight (Abrams, 2002).

Mike May, Allison Aliano Photography

with infant kittens and monkeys. In one experiment, they outfitted them with goggles through which the animals could see only diffuse, unpatterned light (Wiesel, 1982). After infancy, when their goggles were removed, these animals exhibited perceptual limitations much like those of humans born with cataracts. Their eyes had not degenerated; their retinas still relayed signals to their visual cortex. But lacking stimulation, the cortical cells had not developed normal connections. Thus, the animals remained functionally blind to shape. Experience guides, sustains, and maintains the brain's neural organization.

In both humans and animals, a similar period of sensory restriction does no permanent harm if it occurs later in life. Cover the eye of an animal for several months during adulthood, and its vision will be unaffected after the eye patch is removed. Remove cataracts that develop after early childhood, and a human, too, will enjoy normal vision.

The effects of visual experiences during infancy in cats, monkeys, and humans suggest there is a *critical period* shortly after birth—an optimal time when certain events must take place—for normal sensory and perceptual development. Human infants born today with an opaque lens (cataract) typically have corrective surgery within a few months. The brain network responsible for the corrected eye then rapidly develops, enabling improved visual acuity with as little as one hour's visual experience (Maurer & others, 1999). Congenitally deaf kittens and human infants given cochlear implants exhibit a similar "awakening" of the pertinent brain area (Klinke & others, 1999; Sirenteanu, 1999). Nurture sculpts what nature has endowed.

Perceptual adaptation
"Oops, missed," thinks researcher Hubert Dolezal as he views the world through inverting goggles. Yet, believe it or not, kittens, monkeys, and humans can adapt to an inverted world.

Courtesy of Hubert Dolezal

Perceptual Adaptation

14-2: How adaptable is our ability to perceive the world around us?

Given a new pair of glasses, we may feel slightly disoriented, even dizzy. Within a day or two, we adjust. Our **perceptual adaptation** to changed visual input makes the world seem normal again. But imagine a far more dramatic new pair of glasses—one that shifts the apparent location of objects 40 degrees to the left. When you first put them on and toss a ball to a friend, it sails off to the left. Walking forward to shake hands with the person, you veer to the left.

Could you adapt to this distorted world? Chicks cannot. When fitted with such lenses, they continue to peck where food grains *seem* to be (Hess, 1956; Rossi, 1968). But we humans adapt to distorting lenses quickly. Within a few minutes your throws would again be accurate, your stride on target. Remove the lenses and you would experience an aftereffect: At first your throws would err in the *opposite* direction, sailing off to the right; but again, within minutes you would readapt.

Indeed, given an even more radical pair of glasses—one that literally turns the world upside down—you could still adapt. Psychologist George Stratton (1896) experienced this when he invented, and for eight days wore, optical headgear that flipped left to right *and* up to down, making him the first person to experience a right-side-up retinal image while standing upright. The ground was up, the sky was down.

At first, Stratton felt disoriented. When he wanted to walk, he found himself searching for his feet, which were now "up." Eating was nearly impossible. He became nauseated and depressed. But Stratton persisted, and by the eighth day he could comfortably reach for something in the right direction and walk without bumping into things. When Stratton finally removed the headgear, he readapted quickly.

Later experiments replicated Stratton's experience (Dolezal, 1982; Kohler, 1962). After a period of adjustment, people wearing the optical gear have even been able to ride a motorcycle, ski the Alps, and fly an airplane. Did they adjust by perceptually converting their strange worlds to "normal" views? No. Actually, the world around them still seemed above their heads or on the wrong side. But by actively moving about in these topsy-turvy worlds, they adapted to the context and learned to coordinate their movements.

Perceptual Set

14-3: How do our assumptions, expectations, and contexts affect our perceptions?

As everyone knows, to see is to believe. As we also know, but less fully appreciate, to believe is to see. Our experiences, assumptions, and expectations may give us a **perceptual set,** or mental predisposition, that greatly influences (top-down) what we perceive. People perceive an adult-child pair as looking more alike when told they are parent and child (Bressan & Dal Martello, 2002). And consider: Is the image in the center picture of **FIGURE 14.2** a man playing a saxophone or a woman's face? What we see in such a drawing can be influenced by first looking at either of the two unambiguous versions (Boring, 1930).

Everyday examples of perceptual set abound. In 1972, a British newspaper published genuine, unretouched photographs of a "monster" in Scotland's Loch Ness—"the most amazing pictures ever taken," stated the paper. If this information creates in you the same perceptual set it did in most of the paper's readers, you, too, will see the monster in the photo reproduced in **FIGURE 14.3a.** But when Steuart Campbell (1986) approached the photos with a different perceptual set, he saw a curved tree trunk—as had others the day the photo was shot. With this different perceptual set,

■ **perceptual adaptation** in vision, the ability to adjust to an artificially displaced or even inverted visual field.

■ **perceptual set** a mental predisposition to perceive one thing and not another.

© The New Yorker Collection, 2002, Leo Cullum from cartoonbank.com. All rights reserved.

"The temptation to form premature theories upon insufficient data is the bane of our profession."

Sherlock Holmes, in Arthur Conan Doyle's *The Valley of Fear*, 1914

FIGURE 14.2
Perceptual set

What do you see in the center picture: a male saxophonist or a woman's face? Glancing first at one of the two unambiguous versions of the picture is likely to influence your interpretation.

Frank Searle, photo Adams/Corbis-Sygma

Dick Ruhl

FIGURE 14.3
Believing is seeing
What do you perceive in these photos? (a) Is this Nessie, the Loch Ness monster, or a log? (b) Are these flying saucers or clouds? We often perceive what we expect to see.

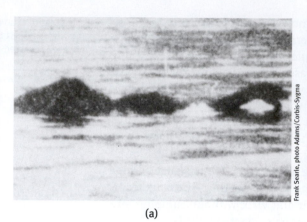

(a)

(b)

you may now notice that the object is floating motionless, without any rippling water or wake around it—hardly what we would expect of a lively monster. Apparently aided by perceptual set, thousands of others have marveled at a face on the Moon, Mother Teresa on a cinnamon bun, and Jesus on a pancake.

Perceptual set can similarly influence what we hear. Consider the kindly airline pilot who, on a takeoff run, looked over at his depressed co-pilot and said, "Cheer up." The co-pilot heard the usual "Gear up" and promptly raised the wheels—before they left the ground (Reason & Mycielska, 1982). Clearly, much of what we perceive comes not just from the world "out there" but also from what's behind our eyes and between our ears.

What determines our perceptual set? Our preexisting schemas for male saxophonists and women's faces, for monsters and tree trunks, for clouds and UFOs all influence how we interpret ambiguous sensations with top-down processing.

Context Effects

A given stimulus may trigger radically different perceptions, partly because of our differing set, but also because of the immediate context. An example: Imagine hearing a noise interrupted by the words "eel is on the wagon." Likely, you would actually perceive the first word as *wheel*. Given "eel is on the orange," you would hear *peel*. This curious phenomenon, discovered by Richard Warren, suggests that the brain can work backward in time to allow a later stimulus to determine how we perceive an earlier one. The context creates an expectation that, top-down, influences our perception as we match our bottom-up signal against it (Grossberg, 1995).

Even hearing sad rather than happy music can predispose people to perceive a sad meaning in spoken homophonic words—*mourning* rather than *morning*, *die* rather than *dye*, *pain* rather than *pane* (Halberstadt & others, 1995).

Emotional contexts also color our social perceptions. Spouses who feel loved and appreciated perceive less threat in stressful marital events—"He's just having a bad day" (Murray & others, 2003). Professional referees, if told a soccer team has a history of aggressive behavior, will assign more penalty cards after watching videotaped fouls (Jones & others, 2002). Lee Ross invites us to recall our own perceptions in different contexts: "Ever notice that when you're driving you hate pedestrians, the way they saunter through the crosswalk, almost daring you to hit them, but when you're walking you hate drivers?" (Jaffe, 2004).

The effects of perceptual set and context show how experience helps us construct perception. In everyday life, for example, stereotypes about gender (another instance of perceptual set) can color the perception. Without the obvious cues of pink or blue, people will struggle over whether to call the new baby "he" or "she." But told an infant is "David," people (especially children) may perceive "him" as bigger and stronger

When shown the phrase:
 Mary had a
 a little lamb
many people perceive what they expect, and miss the repeated word. Did you?

❝Have you ever noticed that anyone driving slower than you is an idiot, and anyone going faster is a maniac?❞
George Carlin, *George Carlin on Campus*, 1984

Culture and context effects
What is above the woman's head? In one study, nearly all the East Africans who were questioned said the woman was balancing a metal box or can on her head and that the family was sitting under a tree. Westerners, for whom corners and boxlike architecture are more common, were more likely to perceive the family as being indoors, with the woman sitting under a window. (Adapted from Gregory & Gombrich, 1973.)

than if the same infant is called "Diana" (Stern & Karraker, 1989). Some differences, it seems, exist merely in the eyes of their beholders.

To return to the question "Is perception innate or learned?" we can answer: It's both. The river of perception is fed by two streams: sensation and cognition. And that is why we need multiple levels of analysis (**FIGURE 14.4**). "Simple" perceptions are the brain's creative products.

If we accept the statement that perception is the product of sensation and cognition, what can we say about *extrasensory perception* (ESP), which claims that perception can occur apart from sensory input? For more on that question, turn the page to see Thinking Critically About: Extrasensory Perception.

> "We hear and apprehend only what we already half know."
>
> Henry David Thoreau, *Journal*, 1860

Biological influences:
- entry-level sensory analysis
- unlearned visual phenomena
- critical period for sensory development

Psychological influences:
- selective attention
- learned schemas
- Gestalt principles
- emotional context effects
- perceptual set

Perception: Our version of reality

Social-cultural influences:
- cultural assumptions and expectations
- physical context effects

FIGURE 14.4
Perception is a biopsychosocial phenomenon
Psychologists study how we perceive with different levels of analysis, from the biological to the social-cultural.

Perception and the Human Factor

14-4 : How do human factors psychologists help create user-friendly technology?

I love my new bedside clock-radio, though I struggle to remember which buttons are Snooze, Alarm Off, and Radio On. Our stove is also wonderful, except for the moments I spend puzzling over which control works which burner. The push-bar doors

THINKING CRITICALLY ABOUT:

EXTRASENSORY PERCEPTION

Can we perceive only what we sense? Or, without sensory input, are we capable of **extrasensory perception (ESP)**? Are there indeed people—any people—who can read minds, see through walls, or foretell the future? Many research psychologists and scientists—including 96 percent of the scientists in the U.S. National Academy of Sciences—are skeptical (McConnell, 1991). If ESP is real, we would need to overturn the scientific understanding that we are creatures whose minds are tied to our physical brains and whose perceptual experiences of the world are built of sensations. Sometimes new evidence does overturn our scientific preconceptions. Science, as we will see throughout this book, offers us various surprises—about the extent of the unconscious mind, about the effects of emotion on health, about what heals and what doesn't, and much more. Before we evaluate claims of ESP, let's review them.

Claims of ESP

Claims of paranormal phenomena include astrological predictions, psychic healing, communication with the dead, and out-of-body experiences. But the most testable and (for our discussion and perception) most relevant claims are for three varieties of ESP:

Telepathy, or mind-to-mind communication—one person sending thoughts to another or perceiving another's thoughts.

Clairvoyance, or perceiving remote events, such as sensing that a friend's house is on fire.

■ **extrasensory perception (ESP)** the controversial claim that perception can occur apart from sensory input. Said to include *telepathy, clairvoyance,* and *precognition.*

■ **parapsychology** the study of paranormal phenomena, including ESP and psychokinesis.

BIZARRO   By DAN PIRARO

Which supposed psychic ability does Psychic Pizza claim?

Precognition, or perceiving future events, such as a political leader's death or a sporting event's outcome.

Separate but closely linked with these are claims of *psychokinesis*, or "mind over matter," such as levitating a table or influencing the roll of a die. (The claim is illustrated by the wry request, "Will all those who believe in psychokinesis please raise my hand?")

Premonitions or Pretensions?

Can psychics see into the future? The tallied forecasts of "leading psychics" reveal meager accuracy. No greedy—or charitable—psychic has been able to predict the outcome of a lottery jackpot, or to make billions on the stock market. During the 1990s, tabloid psychics were all wrong in predicting surprising events. (Madonna did not become a gospel singer, the Statue of Liberty did not lose both its arms in a terrorist blast, Queen Elizabeth did not abdicate her throne to enter a convent.) And the new-century psychics missed the big-news events such as the horror of 9/11. Gene Emery (2004), who has tracked annual psychic forecasts for 26 years, reports that almost never have unusual predictions come true and virtually never have psychics anticipated any of the year's headline events.

Analyses reveal the hundreds of visions offered by psychics working with the police are no more accurate than guesses made by others (Reiser, 1982). Their sheer volume does increase the odds of an occasional correct guess, however, which psychics can then report to the media. Moreover, vague predictions can later be interpreted ("retrofitted") to match events that provide a perceptual set for interpreting them. Nostradamus, a sixteenth-century French psychic, explained in an unguarded moment that his ambiguous prophecies "could not possibly be understood till they were interpreted after the event and by it."

"A person who talks a lot is sometimes right."

Spanish proverb

Police departments are wise to all this. When Jane Ayers Sweat and Mark Durm (1993) asked the police departments of America's 50 largest cities whether they ever had used psychics, 65 percent said no. Of those that had, not one had found it helpful.

Are the spontaneous "visions" of everyday people any more accurate? Consider our dreams. Do they foretell the future, or do they only seem to do so because we are more likely to recall or reconstruct dreams that seem to have come true? Two Harvard psychologists (Murray & Wheeler, 1937) tested the prophetic power of dreams after aviator Charles Lindbergh's baby son was kidnapped and murdered in 1932, but before the body was discovered. When the researchers invited the public to report their dreams about the child, 1300 visionaries submitted dream reports. How many accurately envisioned the child dead? Five percent. And how many also correctly anticipated the body's location—buried among trees? Only 4 of the 1300. Although this number was surely no better than chance, to those 4 dreamers the accuracy of their *apparent* precognitions must have seemed uncanny.

Given the billions of events in the world each day, and given enough days, some stunning coincidences are sure to occur. By one careful estimate, chance alone would predict that more than a thousand times a day someone on Earth will think of someone and then within the ensuing five minutes will learn of the person's death (Charpak & Broch, 2004). With enough time or people, the improbable becomes inevitable.

That has been the experience of comics writer John Byrne (2003). Six months after his Spider-Man story about a New York blackout appeared, New York suffered its massive blackout. A subsequent Spider-Man storyline involved a major earthquake in Japan, "and again," he recalls, "the real thing happened in the month the issue hit the stands." Later, when working on a Superman comic book, he "had the Man of Steel fly to the rescue when disaster beset the NASA space shuttle. The *Challenger* tragedy happened almost immediately thereafter" (with time for the issue to be redrawn). "Most recently, and chilling, came when I was writing and drawing Wonder Woman and did a story in which the title character was killed as a prelude to her becoming a goddess." The issue cover "was done as a newspaper front page, with the headline 'Princess Diana Dies.' (Diana is Wonder Woman's real name.) That issue went on sale on a Thursday. The following Saturday . . . I don't have to tell you, do I?"

Putting ESP to Experimental Test
When faced with claims of mind reading or out-of-body travel or communication with the dead—how can we separate bizarre ideas from

Courtesy of Claire Cole

Testing psychic powers in the British population
Hertfordshire University psychologist Richard Wiseman created a "mind machine" to see if people can influence or predict a coin toss. Using a touch-sensitive screen, visitors to festivals around the country were given four attempts to call heads or tails. Using a random-number generator, a computer then decided the outcome. When the experiment concluded in January 2000, nearly 28,000 people had predicted 110,972 tosses—with 49.8 percent correct.

those that sound bizarre but are true? At the heart of science is a simple answer: *Test them to see if they work.* If they do, so much the better for the ideas. If they don't, so much the better for our skepticism.

This scientific attitude has led both believers and skeptics to agree that what **parapsychology** needs to give it credibility is a reproducible phenomenon and a theory to explain it. How might we test ESP claims in a controlled experiment? An experiment differs from a staged demonstration. In the laboratory, the experimenter controls what the "psychic" sees and hears. On stage, the psychic controls what the audi-

---

"A psychic is an actor playing the role of a psychic."

Psychologist magician Daryl Bem (1984)

---

ence sees and hears—often with mind-blowing performances in which they appear to communicate with the spirits of the dead, read minds, or levitate objects—only to have it revealed that these acts were nothing more than the illusions of stage magicians.

The search for a valid and reliable test of ESP has resulted in thousands of experiments. One controlled procedure has invited "senders" to telepathically transmit one of four visual images to "receivers" deprived of sensation in a nearby chamber (Bem & Honorton, 1994). The result? A reported 32 percent accurate response rate, surpassing the chance rate of 25 percent. But follow-up studies have (depending on who was summarizing the results) failed to replicate the phenomenon or produced mixed results (Bem & others, 2001; Milton & Wiseman, 2002; Storm, 2000, 2003).

One skeptic, magician James Randi, has a longstanding offer—now U.S. $1 million—"to anyone who proves a genuine psychic power under proper observing conditions" (Randi, 1999). French, Australian, and Indian groups have parallel offers of up to 200,000 euros to anyone with demonstrable paranormal abilities (CFI, 2003). And $50 million was available for information leading to Osama bin Laden's capture. Large as these sums are, the scientific seal of approval would be worth far more to anyone whose claims could be authenticated. To refute those who say there is no ESP, one need only produce a single person who can demonstrate a single, reproducible ESP phenomenon. (To refute those who say pigs can't talk would take but one talking pig.) So far, no such person has emerged. Randi's offer has been publicized for three decades and dozens of people have been tested, sometimes under the scrutiny of an independent panel of judges. Still, nothing.

on our campus buildings are sturdy, though occasionally frustrating when I push the wrong end. The extra buttons on my phone are handy, though when transferring a call I still must look up which buttons to press.

Human factors psychologists study such puzzles to understand how people and machines interact. Psychologist Donald Norman (1988) suggests how simple design changes could reduce some of our frustrations. For example, by exploiting *natural mapping,* we could design stove controls that require no labels (**FIGURE 14.5**). ATM machines are internally more complex than VCRs ever were, yet, thanks to human factors psychologists working with engineers, ATMs are easier to operate. TiVo has solved the TV recording problem with a simple point-and-click menu system ("record that one").

Norman (2001), who hosts a Web site (jnd.org) on designing equipment to fit people, bemoaned the complexity of assembling his new high-definition TV, receiver, speakers, digital recorder, DVD player, VCR, and seven remotes into a usable home theater system. "I was VP of Advanced Technology at Apple," says Norman, an MIT alumnus with a Ph.D. "I can program dozens of computers in dozens of languages. I understand television, really, I do. . . . It doesn't matter: I am overwhelmed." If only the makers of home entertainment equipment would minimize cords and cables by bundling audio, visual, control, and power lines into a single cable. If only a single control could operate a point-and-click menu. If only engineers would routinely work with human factors psychologists to test their designs and instructions on real people.

Technology developers often suffer the *curse of knowledge,* which leads them to mistakenly assume that others share their expertise—that what's clear to them will similarly be clear to others (Camerer & others, 1989; Nickerson, 1999). When you know a thing, it's hard to mentally simulate what it's like not to know.

Understanding human factors can do more than enable us to design for reduced frustration; it can help avoid disaster. Two-thirds of commercial air accidents, for example, have been caused by human error (Nickerson, 1998). After beginning commercial flights in the late 1960s, the Boeing 727 was involved in several landing accidents caused by pilot error. Psychologist Conrad Kraft (1978) noted a common setting for these accidents: All took place at night, and all involved landing short of the runway after crossing a dark stretch of water or unilluminated ground. Kraft reasoned that, beyond the runway, city lights would project a larger retinal image if on a rising terrain. This would make the ground seem farther away than it was. By re-creating these conditions in flight simulations, Kraft discovered that pilots were deceived into thinking they were flying higher than their actual altitudes (**FIGURE 14.6**). Aided by Kraft's finding, the airlines began requiring the co-pilot to monitor the altimeter—calling out altitudes during the descent—and the accidents diminished.

Later Boeing psychologists worked on other human factors problems (Murray, 1998): How should airlines best train and manage mechanics to reduce the maintenance errors

FIGURE 14.5
Natural mapping
(a) With traditionally positioned stove controls, a person must read the labels to figure out which knob works which burner. (b) By positioning the controls in a natural map, which the brain understands at a glance, we can eliminate the need to ponder written instructions just to boil water.

(a)

(b)

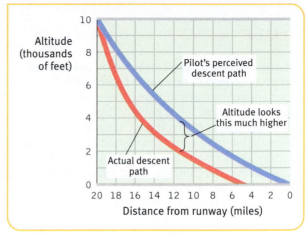

FIGURE **14.6**

The human factor in misperception

Lacking distance cues when approaching a runway from over a dark surface, pilots simulating a night landing tended to fly too low. (From Kraft, 1978.)

that underlie about 50 percent of flight delays and 15 percent of accidents? What illumination and typeface would make on-screen flight data easiest to read? How would warning messages be most effectively worded—as an action statement ("Pull Up") rather than a problem statement ("Ground Proximity")?

In studying human factors issues, psychologists' most powerful tool is research. If an organization wonders what sort of Web design (emphasizing content? speed? graphics?) would most effectively draw in visitors and entice them to return, the psychologist will want to test responses to several alternatives. If NASA (National Aeronautics and Space Administration) wonders what sort of spacecraft design would best facilitate sleeping, work, and morale, their human factors psychologists will want to test the alternatives (**FIGURE 14.7**).

Consider, finally, the available "assistive listening" technologies in various auditoriums, places of worship, and theaters. One technology, commonly available in the United States, requires people with hearing loss to use a headset attached to a pocket-sized receiver that detects infrared or FM signals from the room's sound system. The well-meaning people who design, purchase, and install these systems correctly understand that the technology puts sound directly into the user's ears. Alas, few people with hearing loss undergo the hassle and embarrassment of locating, requesting, wearing, and returning a conspicuous headset. Most such units therefore sit in closets. Britain, the Scandinavian countries, and Australia have instead installed "loop systems" that broadcast customized sound directly through a person's own hearing aid. When suitably equipped, a discrete touch of a switch can transform hearing aids into in-the-ear loudspeakers. A loop system (a special amplifier attached to a wire encircling an audience) can also work in homes, enabling TV sound or phone conversation to broadcast directly through hearing aids (see www.hearingloop.org). When offered convenient, inconspicuous, personalized sound, many more people elect to use assistive listening.

The point to remember: Designers and engineers should consider the human factor, by designing things to fit people, being mindful of the curse of knowledge, and user-testing their inventions before production and distribution.

To feel awe and to gain a deep reverence for life, we need look no further than our own sensation-based perception and its capacity for organizing formless nerve impulses into colorful sights, vivid sounds, and evocative smells. As Shakespeare's Hamlet recognized, "There are more things in Heaven and Earth, Horatio, than are dreamt of in your philosophy." Within our ordinary perceptual experiences lies much that is truly extraordinary—surely much more than has so far been dreamt of in our psychology. A century of research has revealed many of the secrets of sensation and perception, yet for future generations of researchers there remain profound and genuine mysteries to solve.

> " **So,** how does the mind work? I don't know. You don't know. Pinker doesn't know. And, I rather suspect, such is the current state of the art, that if God were to tell us, we wouldn't understand."
>
> Jerry Fodor, "Reply to Steven Pinker," 2005

FIGURE **14.7**

How not to go mad while going to Mars

Future astronauts headed to Mars will be confined in conditions of monotony, stress, and weightlessness for months on end. To help design and evaluate a workable human environment, such as for this Transit Habitation (Transhab) Module, NASA engages human factors psychologists (Weed, 2001; Wichman, 1992).

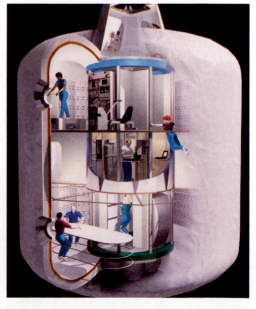

Courtesy of NASA

>> MODULE REVIEW

14-1: **What does research on sensory restriction and restored vision reveal about the effects of experience on perception?**

If visual perception were entirely innate, people who were born blind but regained sight after surgery should have normal visual perception. But they don't. After cataract surgery, for example, people who were blind from birth can distinguish figure from ground and can perceive colors, but they lack the experience to recognize shapes, forms, and complete faces. Animals reared with severely restricted visual input also suffer enduring visual handicaps when returned to a normal visual environment. A critical period exists for some aspects of sensory and perceptual development. Without early visual experience, the brain does not develop normally.

14-2: **How adaptable is our ability to perceive the world around us?**

Human vision is remarkably adaptable. Given glasses that shift the world slightly to the left or right, turn it upside down, or reverse it, people manage to *adapt* their movements and, with practice, to move about with ease.

14-3: **How do our assumptions, expectations, and contexts affect our perceptions?**

Perception is influenced by our learned assumptions and beliefs as well as by sensory input, as demonstrated by research on *perceptual set* and context effects. The ideas we have stored in memory help us to interpret otherwise ambiguous stimuli, which helps explain why some of us "see" monsters, faces, and UFOs that others do not. Our expectations also influence our views on *ESP*. Most psychologists remain skeptical of ESP claims because they do not believe the brain is capable of perception without sensation, and because researchers have not been able to replicate (reproduce) ESP effects under controlled conditions.

14-4: **How do human factors psychologists help create user-friendly technology?**

Human factors psychologists study how people perceive and use machines, and how machines and physical environments can be better suited to that use. Such studies have improved aircraft safety and have made many machines and technological devices less frustrating and easier to use.

>> REHEARSE IT!

1. John Locke believed that our perception of the world is learned through experience. Support for his view can be found in
   a. the writings of Immanuel Kant.
   b. research on critical periods.
   c. research on perceptual set and context.
   d. studies of extrasensory perception.

2. In some cases, surgeons have restored vision to patients who have been blind from birth. The newly sighted individuals were able to sense colors but had difficulty
   a. recognizing objects by touch.
   b. recognizing objects by sight.
   c. distinguishing figure from ground.
   d. distinguishing between bright and dim light.

3. Experiments in which volunteers wear glasses that displace or invert their visual fields show that, after a period of disorientation, people learn to function quite well. This ability is called
   a. context effect.
   b. perceptual set.
   c. sensory interaction.
   d. perceptual adaptation.

4. Our perceptual set influences what we perceive. This mental predisposition reflects our
   a. experiences, assumptions, and expectations.
   b. perceptual adaptation.
   c. skill at extrasensory perception.
   d. perceptual constancy.

5. Human factors psychologists explore ways that machines and physical environments can be adapted to human behaviors to reduce users' frustration and to avoid accidents. One tendency these psychologists watch carefully is the curse of knowledge, which is
   a. the idea that a little bit of knowledge is dangerous for the user.
   b. users' tendencies to override machines and resort to familiar habits.
   c. engineers' and designers' tendencies to assume that users are idiots and need overly detailed instructions.
   d. engineers' and designers' tendencies to assume that others share their knowledge.

Answers: 1. c, 2. b, 3. d, 4. a, 5. d.

>> TERMS AND CONCEPTS TO REMEMBER

perceptual adaptation, p. 182
perceptual set, p. 183

extrasensory perception (ESP), p. 186

parapsychology, p. 187

>> TEST YOURSELF

1. What type of evidence shows that, indeed, "there is more to perception than meets the senses"?

   (Answer in Appendix C.)

*Multiple-choice **self-tests** and more may be found at www.worthpublishers.com/myers.*

States of Consciousness

States of Consciousness

Now playing at an inner theater near you: the premiere showing of a sleeping person's vivid dream. This never-before-seen mental movie features captivating characters wrapped in a plot so original and unlikely, yet so intricate and so seemingly real, that the viewer later marvels at its creation.

Waking from a troubling dream, wrenched by its emotions, who among us has not wondered about this weird state of consciousness? How can our brain so creatively, colorfully, and completely construct this alternative, conscious world? In the shadowland between our dreaming and waking consciousness, we may even wonder for a moment which is real. And what shall we make of other altered states of consciousness, such as hypnosis and drug-altered hallucinations?

But first questions first: What is *consciousness*? Every science has concepts so fundamental they are nearly impossible to define. Biologists agree on what is alive but not on precisely what life is. In physics, *matter* and *energy* elude simple definition. To psychologists, consciousness is similarly a fundamental yet slippery concept.

> "Neither [psychologist] Steve Pinker nor I can explain human subjective consciousness. . . . We don't understand it."
>
> Evolutionary biologist Richard Dawkins (1999)

In Module 15 through 17, we consider what research tells us about consciousness during our normal waking and (sometimes disturbed) sleep cycles (Module 15), in the hypnotic state (Module 16), and under the influence of psychoactive—*consciousness-altering*—drugs (Module 17).

Waking and Sleeping Rhythms

Psychologists have long explored consciousness, at first eagerly, then warily, and now with renewed vigor. At its beginning, *psychology* was "the description and explanation of states of consciousness" (Ladd, 1887). But during the first half of the twentieth century, the difficulty of scientifically studying consciousness led many psychologists—including those in the emerging school of *behaviorism*—to turn to direct observations of behavior. By the 1960s, psychology had nearly lost consciousness and was defining itself as the science of behavior. Consciousness was likened to a car's speedometer: "It doesn't make the car go, it just reflects what's happening" (Seligman, 1991, p. 24).

After 1960, mental concepts began to reemerge. Advances in neuroscience made it possible to relate brain activity to sleeping, dreaming, and other mental states. Researchers began studying consciousness altered by hypnosis and drugs. Psychologists of all persuasions were affirming the importance of *cognition*, or mental processes. Psychology was regaining consciousness.

> "Psychology must discard all reference to consciousness."
>
> Behaviorist John B. Watson (1913)

Waking Consciousness

15-1 : What is consciousness, and how does it function?

For most psychologists today, **consciousness** is our awareness of ourselves and our environment. Consciousness assembles information from various sources, enabling us to reflect on our past and plan for our future. And it focuses our attention when we learn a complex concept or behavior—say, driving a car—making us aware of the car and the traffic. With practice, driving no longer requires our undivided attention, freeing us to focus our attentional spotlight on other things. This illustrates an important principle: Our conscious attention is *selective*.

States of consciousness
In addition to normal, waking awareness, consciousness comes to us in altered states, including daydreaming, sleeping, meditating, and drug-induced hallucinating.

Selective Attention

Through **selective attention,** our awareness focuses, like a flashlight beam, on a very limited aspect of all that we experience. By one estimate, our five senses take in 11,000,000 bits of information per second, of which we consciously process about 40 (Wilson, 2002). Yet we intuitively make great use of the other 10,999,960 bits. Until reading this sentence, you have been unaware that your shoes are pressing against your feet or that your nose is in your line of vision. Now, suddenly, your attentional spotlight shifts. Your feet feel encased, your nose stubbornly intrudes on the page before you. While attending to these words, you've also been blocking from awareness information coming from your peripheral vision. You can change that. As you stare at the X below, notice what surrounds the book (the edges of the page, your desktop, and so on).

X

■ **consciousness** our awareness of ourselves and our environment.

■ **selective attention** the focusing of conscious awareness on a particular stimulus.

Driven to distraction

In one driving-simulation experiment, students whose attention was diverted by cell-phone conversation (rather than merely listening to a radio) missed twice as many traffic signals as did those not talking on the phone.

SALLY FORTH

RESEARCH SHOWS EFFICIENCY IS CUT IN HALF WHEN YOU DO TWO THINGS AT ONCE.

I CAN DRIVE AND USE A CELL PHONE WITHOUT A PROBLEM.

BESIDES, I'M WIRED FOR MULTI-TASKING.

WELL, IT'S HARDER TO FOCUS ATTENTION THAN IT IS TO DIVIDE IT.

WHAT? SAY THAT AGAIN. NO, NOT YOU. I'M TALKING TO SALLY.

©2001 by King Features Syndicate, Inc. World rights reserved.

■ **inattentional blindness** failing to see visible objects when our attention is directed elsewhere.

At the level of conscious awareness, our attention is divided. Talk while driving and your attention will shift back and forth from the road to the phone. But when a demanding situation requires your full attention, you'll probably stop talking. This process of switching attentional gears, especially when shifting to complex tasks, can entail a slight delay in coping (Rubenstein & others, 2001). In University of Utah driving-simulation experiments, students conversing on cellphones were slower to detect and respond to traffic signals, billboards, and other cars (Strayer & Johnston, 2001; Strayer & others, 2003). Focused listening comes at a cost.

We similarly process only a tiny sliver of the immense array of visual stimuli constantly before us. Ulric Neisser (1979) and Robert Becklen and Daniel Cervone (1983) demonstrated this dramatically by showing people a one-minute videotape in which images of three black-shirted men tossing a basketball were superimposed over the images of three white-shirted players. The viewers' supposed task was to press a key every time a black-shirted player passed the ball. Most focused their attention so completely on the game that they failed to notice a young woman carrying an umbrella saunter across the screen midway through the tape. When researchers replayed the tape, viewers were astonished to see her. Their attention directed elsewhere, they exhibited **inattentional blindness.** In a recent repeat of the experiment, smart-aleck researchers Daniel Simons and Christopher Chabris (1999) sent a gorilla-suited assistant through the swirl of players (**FIGURE 15.1**). During its 5- to 9-second cameo appearance, the gorilla paused to thump its chest. Still, half the conscientious pass-counting participants failed to see it.

In other experiments, people have also exhibited *change blindness*. After a brief visual interruption, a big Coke bottle may disappear, a railing may rise, clothing color may change, but, more often than not, viewers won't notice (Resnick & others, 1997; Simons, 1996; Simons & Ambinder, 2005). (Similarly, two thirds of the people giving directions to a construction worker failed to notice when he was replaced by another worker [**FIGURE 15.2**].) Out of sight, out of mind.

FIGURE 15.1
Gorillas in our midst

When attending to one task (counting basketball passes by one of the three-person teams), about half the viewers display inattentional blindness by failing to notice a clearly visible gorilla passing through.

Daniel Simons, University of Illinois

An equally astonishing form of inattention is the *choice blindness* discovered by a Swedish research team. Petter Johansson and his colleagues (2005) showed 120 volunteers two female faces for 2 to 5 or more seconds and asked them which face was more attractive. The researchers then put the photos face down and handed viewers the one they had chosen, inviting them to explain their choice. But on 3 of 15 occasions, the tricky researchers used sleight-of-hand to switch the photos—showing viewers the face they had *not* chosen. Not only did the people seldom notice the deception (on only 13 percent of the switches), they readily explained why they preferred the face they had actually rejected. "I chose her because she smiled," said one person (after picking the solemn-faced one). Asked later whether they would notice such a switch in a "hypothetical experiment," 84 percent insisted they would. They exhibited a blindness the researchers call (can you see the twinkle in their eyes?) *choice-blindness blindness*.

© 1998 Psychonomic Society, Inc. Image provided courtesy of Daniel J. Simons.

FIGURE 15.2
Change blindness
While a man (white hair) provides directions to a construction worker, two experimenters rudely pass between them carrying a door. During this interruption, the original worker switches places with another person wearing different colored clothing. Most people, focused on their direction giving, do not notice the switch.

Some stimuli, however, are so powerful, so strikingly distinct, that we experience *pop-out*, as with the only smiling face in **FIGURE 15.3**. We don't *choose* to attend to these stimuli; they draw our eye and demand our attention.

Levels of Information Processing

Consciousness, our relatively slow and limited-capacity ability, enables us to exert voluntary control and to communicate our mental states to others, yet it is but the tip of the information-processing iceberg. We register and react to a vast number of stimuli we do not consciously perceive, performing well-learned tasks automatically and changing our attitudes and reconstructing our memories with no awareness of doing so. When we meet people, for example, we instantly and unconsciously react to their gender, age, and appearance, and *then* become aware of our response.

All of this unconscious information processing occurs simultaneously on multiple parallel tracks. Traveling a familiar route, your hands and feet do the driving while your mind is elsewhere. Running on automatic pilot allows consciousness—the mind's CEO—to monitor the whole system and deal with new challenges, while many assistants automatically take care of routine business.

Serial conscious processing, though slower, is skilled at solving new problems, which require our focused attention. Try this: If you are right-handed, you can move your right foot in a smooth counterclockwise circle, and you can write the number 3 repeatedly with your right hand—but probably not at the same time. (If you are musically inclined, try something equally difficult: Tap a steady three times with your left hand while tapping four times with your right hand.) Both tasks require conscious attention, which can be in only one place at a time. If time is nature's way of keeping everything from happening at once, then consciousness is nature's way of keeping us from thinking and doing everything at once.

© The New Yorker Collection, Charles Addams, from cartoonbank.com. All rights reserved.

FIGURE 15.3
The pop-out phenomenon

Sleep and Dreams

Sleep—the irresistible tempter to whom we inevitably succumb. Sleep—the equalizer of presidents and peasants. Sleep—sweet, renewing, mysterious sleep. Sleep's mysteries have intrigued scientists for centuries.

Now, in laboratories throughout the world, some of these mysteries are being solved as thousands sleep, attached to recording devices, while others observe. By recording brain waves and muscle movements, and by observing and waking sleepers from time to time, researchers are glimpsing things that a thousand years of common sense never told us. Perhaps you can anticipate some of their discoveries. Are the following statements true or false?

1. When people dream of performing some activity, their limbs often move in concert with the dream.

> " I love to sleep. Do you? Isn't it great? It really is the best of both worlds. You get to be alive and unconscious."
> Comedian Rita Rudner, 1993

Dolphins sleep with half their brain at a time and one eye closed.

■ **circadian** [ser-KAY-dee-an] **rhythm** the biological clock; regular bodily rhythms (for example, of temperature and wakefulness) that occur on a 24-hour cycle.

2. Sleepwalkers are acting out their dreams.
3. Sleep experts recommend treating insomnia with an occasional sleeping pill.
4. Some people dream every night; others seldom dream.

All these statements (adapted from Palladino & Carducci, 1983) are false. To see why, read on.

Biological Rhythms and Sleep

15-2 : How do our biological rhythms influence our daily functioning and our sleep and dreams?

Like the ocean, life has its rhythmic tides. Over varying time periods, our bodies fluctuate, and with them, our minds. Let's look more closely at two of those biological rhythms—our 24-hour biological clock and our 90-minute sleep cycle.

Circadian Rhythm

The rhythm of the day parallels the rhythm of life—from our waking to a new day's birth to our nightly return to what Shakespeare called "death's counterfeit." Our bodies roughly synchronize with the 24-hour cycle of day and night through a biological clock called the **circadian rhythm** (from the Latin *circa,* "about," and *diem,* "day"). Body temperature rises as morning approaches, peaks during the day, dips for a time in early afternoon (when many people take siestas), and then begins to drop again before we go to sleep. Thinking is sharpest and memory most accurate when we are at our daily peak in circadian arousal. Pulling an all-nighter, we feel groggiest about 4:00 A.M., and then we get a second wind after our normal wake-up time arrives.

Bright light in the morning tweaks the circadian clock by activating light-sensitive retinal proteins. These proteins trigger signals to the brain's *suprachiasmatic nucleus* (SCN)—a pair of pinhead-sized clusters of 20,000 cells in the hypothalamus that control the circadian clock (Foster, 2004). The SCN does so partly by causing the brain's pineal gland to decrease (in the morning) or increase (in the evening) its production of the sleep-inducing hormone *melatonin* (**FIGURE 15.4**).

Bright light at night thus helps delay sleep (Oren & Terman, 1998), which explains how we can unwittingly reset our biological clocks by staying up late and sleeping in on weekends. Sleep often eludes those who sleep till noon on Sunday and then go to bed just 11 hours later in preparation for the new workweek. They are like New Yorkers whose biology is on California time. But what about those Californians who find themselves on New York time, because they are awake when their circadian rhythm cries "Sleep!"? As studies in the laboratory and with shift workers have

At about age 20 (slightly earlier for women), we begin to shift from being evening-energized "owls" to being morning-loving "larks" (Roenneberg & others, 2004). Most university students are owls, with performance improving across the day (May & Hasher, 1998). Most older adults are larks, with performance declining as the day wears on. Retirement homes are typically quiet by mid-evening.

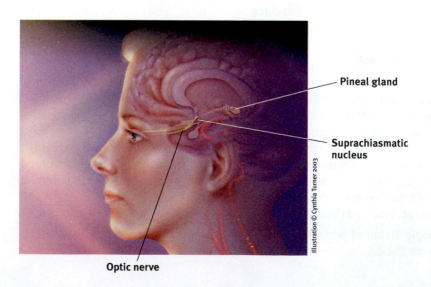

FIGURE 15.4
The biological clock
Light striking the retina causes the suprachiasmatic nucleus (a tiny neural center in the hypothalamus) to alter the production of biologically active substances, such as melatonin production by the pineal gland.

Pineal gland

Suprachiasmatic nucleus

Optic nerve

Illustration © Cynthia Turner 2003

shown, bright light—in this case, spending the next day outdoors—can help reset their biological clocks (Czeisler & others, 1986, 1989; Eastman & others, 1995).

Curiously—given that our ancestors' body clocks were attuned to the rising and setting sun of the 24-hour day—many of today's young adults adopt something closer to a 25-hour day, by staying up too late to get 8 hours of sleep. For this, we can thank (or blame) Thomas Edison, inventor of the light bulb. Being bathed in light disrupts our 24-hour biological clock (Czeisler & others, 1999; Dement, 1999). This helps explain why until our later years we must discipline ourselves to go to bed on time and force ourselves to get up. Most animals, too, when placed under unnatural constant illumination will exceed a 24-hour day. Artificial light delays sleep.

Sleep Stages

15-3 : What is the biological rhythm of our sleep?

As sleep overtakes us and different parts of our brain's cortex stop communicating, consciousness fades (Massimini & others, 2005). But the still-active sleeping brain does not emit a constant dial tone, for sleep has its own biological rhythm. About every 90 minutes, we pass through a cycle of five distinct sleep stages. This elementary fact apparently was unknown until 8-year-old Armond Aserinsky went to bed one night in 1952. His father, Eugene, a University of Chicago graduate student, needed to test an electroencephalograph he had been repairing that day (Aserinsky, 1988; Seligman & Yellen, 1987). Placing electrodes near Armond's eyes to record the rolling eye movements then believed to occur during sleep, Aserinsky watched the machine go wild, tracing deep zigzags on the graph paper. Could the machine still be broken? As the night proceeded and the activity periodically recurred, Aserinsky finally realized that the fast, jerky eye movements were accompanied by energetic brain activity. Awakened during one such episode, Armond reported having a dream. Aserinsky had discovered what we now know as **REM sleep** (rapid *eye* *m*ovement sleep).

To find out if similar cycles occur during adult sleep, Nathaniel Kleitman (1960) and Aserinsky pioneered procedures that have now been used with thousands of volunteers. To appreciate both their methods and findings, imagine yourself as a participant. As the hour grows late, you begin to fight sleepiness and yawn in response to reduced brain metabolism. (Yawning, which can be socially contagious, stretches your neck muscles and increases your heart rate, which increases your alertness [Moorcroft, 2003]). When you are ready for bed, the researcher tapes electrodes to your scalp (to detect your brain waves), just outside the corners of your eyes (to detect eye movements), and on your chin (to detect muscle tension) (**FIGURE 15.5**). Other devices allow the researcher to record your heart rate, your respiration rate, and the degree of your genital arousal.

> If our natural circadian rhythm were attuned to a 23-hour cycle, would we instead need to discipline ourselves to stay up later at night and sleep in longer in the morning?

> ■ **REM sleep** rapid eye movement sleep, a recurring sleep stage during which vivid dreams commonly occur. Also known as *paradoxical sleep*, because the muscles are relaxed (except for minor twitches) but other body systems are active.

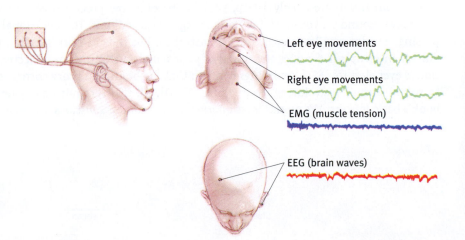

Left eye movements

Right eye movements

EMG (muscle tension)

EEG (brain waves)

FIGURE 15.5

Measuring sleep activity

Sleep researchers measure brain-wave activity, eye movements, and muscle tension by electrodes that pick up weak electrical signals from the brain, eyes, and facial muscles. (From Dement, 1978.)

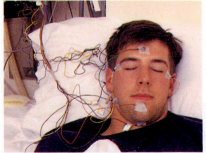

Hank Morgan/Rainbow

FIGURE 15.6
Brain waves and sleep stages

The regular alpha waves of an awake, relaxed state are quite different from the slower, larger delta waves of deep Stage 4 sleep. Although the rapid REM sleep waves resemble the near-waking Stage 1 sleep waves, the body is more aroused during REM sleep than during Stage 1 sleep. (From Dement, 1978.)

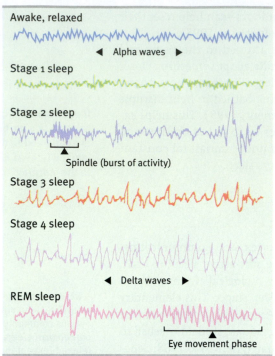

■ **alpha waves** the relatively slow brain waves of a relaxed, awake state.

■ **sleep** periodic, natural, reversible loss of consciousness—as distinct from unconsciousness resulting from a coma, general anesthesia, or hibernation. (Adapted from Dement, 1999.)

■ **hallucinations** false sensory experiences, such as seeing something in the absence of an external visual stimulus.

■ **delta waves** the large, slow brain waves associated with deep sleep.

When you are in bed with your eyes closed, the researcher in the next room sees on the EEG the relatively slow **alpha waves** of your awake but relaxed state (**FIGURE 15.6**). As you adapt to all this equipment, you grow tired and, in an unremembered moment, slip into **sleep.** The transition is marked by the slowed breathing and the irregular brain waves of Stage 1 (**FIGURE 15.7**).

In one of his 15,000 sleep research participants, William Dement (1999) observed the moment the perceptual door between the brain and outside world slammed shut. Dement asked this sleep-deprived young man, lying on his back with eyelids taped open, to press a button every time a strobe light flashed in his eyes (averaging about every 6 seconds). After a few minutes the young man missed one. Asked why, he said, "Because there was no flash." But there was a flash—which he missed because (as his brain activity revealed) he had fallen asleep for 2 seconds. Unaware that he had done so, he had missed not only the flash 6 inches from his nose but also the abrupt moment of his entry into sleep.

During this brief Stage 1 sleep you may experience fantastic images, resembling **hallucinations**—sensory experiences that occur without a sensory stimulus. You may have a sensation of falling (at which moment your body may suddenly jerk) or of floating weightlessly. Such *hypnagogic* sensations may later be incorporated into memories. People who claim to have been abducted by aliens—often shortly after getting into bed—commonly recall being floated off their beds.

You then relax more deeply and begin about 20 minutes of Stage 2 sleep, characterized by the periodic appearance of *sleep spindles*—bursts of rapid, rhythmic brainwave activity (see Figure 15.6). Although you can still be awakened without too much difficulty, you are now clearly asleep. Sleeptalking—usually garbled or nonsensical—can occur during Stage 2 or any other sleep stage (Mahowald & Ettinger, 1990).

Then for the next few minutes you go through the transitional Stage 3 to the deep sleep of Stage 4. First in Stage 3, and increasingly in Stage 4, your brain emits large, slow **delta waves.** These two slow-wave sleep stages last for about 30 minutes, during which you are hard to awaken. Curiously, it is at the end of the deep sleep of Stage 4 that children may wet the bed or begin sleepwalking. About 20 percent of 3- to 12-year-olds have at least one episode of sleepwalking, usually lasting 2 to 10 minutes; some 5 percent have repeated episodes (Giles & others, 1994).

Even when you are deeply asleep, your brain somehow processes certain stimuli. You move around on your bed, but you manage not to fall out. The occasional roar of passing vehicles may leave deep sleep undisturbed, but the cry from a baby's nursery quickly interrupts it. So does the sound of your name—a stimulus our selective attention is ever alert for. EEG recordings confirm that the brain's auditory cortex responds to sound stimuli even during sleep (Kutas, 1990). All this reminds us of one of this book's basic lessons: *We process most information outside our conscious awareness.*

FIGURE 15.7
The moment of sleep
We seem unaware of the moment we fall into sleep, but someone eavesdropping on our brain waves could tell. (From Dement, 1999.)

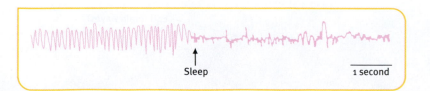

REM Sleep

About an hour after you first fall asleep, a strange thing happens. Rather than continuing in deep slumber, you ascend from your initial sleep dive. Returning through Stage 3 and Stage 2 (where you spend about half your night), you enter the most intriguing sleep phase of all—REM sleep (**FIGURE 15.8**). For about 10 minutes, your brain waves become rapid and saw-toothed, more like those of the nearly awake Stage 1 sleep. But unlike Stage 1 sleep, during REM sleep your heart rate rises, your breathing becomes rapid and irregular, and every half-minute or so your eyes dart around in a momentary burst of activity behind closed lids. Because anyone watching a sleeper's eyes can notice these REM bursts, it is amazing that science was ignorant of REM sleep until 1952.

Except during very scary dreams, your genitals become aroused during REM sleep, and you have an erection or increased vaginal lubrication and clitoral engorgement, regardless of whether the dream's content is sexual (Karacan & others, 1966). Men's common "morning erection" stems from the night's last REM period, often just before waking. In young men, sleep-related erections outlast REM periods, lasting 30 to 45 minutes on average (Karacan & others, 1983; Schiavi & Schreiner-Engel, 1988). A typical 25-year-old man therefore has an erection during nearly half his night's sleep, a 65-year-old man for one-quarter. Many men troubled by *erectile dysfunction* (impotence) have sleep-related erections, suggesting the problem is not between their legs.

Although your brain's motor cortex is active during REM sleep, your brainstem blocks its messages, leaving muscles relaxed—so relaxed that, except for an occasional finger, toe, or facial twitch, you are essentially paralyzed. Moreover, you cannot easily be awakened. Thus, REM sleep is sometimes called *paradoxical* sleep; the body is internally aroused and externally calm.

More intriguing than the paradoxical nature of REM sleep is what the rapid eye movements announce: the beginning of a dream. Even those who claim they never dream will, more than 80 percent of the time, recall a dream after being awakened during REM sleep. Unlike the fleeting images of Stage 1 sleep ("I was thinking about my exam today," or "I was trying to borrow something from someone"), REM sleep dreams are often emotional, usually storylike, and more richly hallucinatory:

> My husband and I were at some friends' house, but our friends weren't there. Their TV had been left on, but otherwise it was very quiet. After we wandered around for a while, their dogs finally noticed us and barked and growled loudly, with bared teeth.

"Boy are my eyes tired! I had REM sleep all night long."

Horses, which spend 92 percent of each day standing and can sleep standing, must lie down for REM sleep (Morrison, 2003).

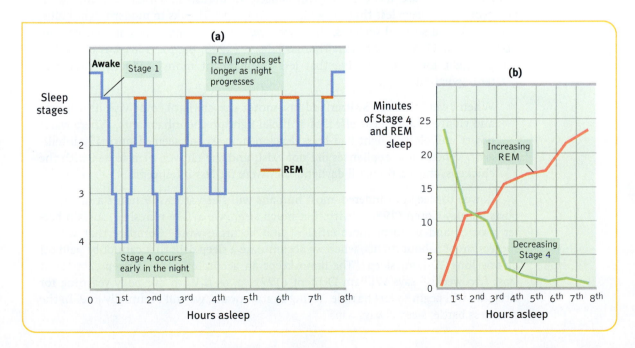

FIGURE 15.8

The stages in a typical night's sleep

Most people pass through the five-stage sleep cycle (graph a) several times, with the periods of Stage 4 sleep and then Stage 3 sleep diminishing and REM sleep periods increasing in duration. Graph b plots this increasing REM sleep and decreasing deep sleep based on data from 30 young adults. (From Cartwright, 1978; Webb, 1992.)

Some sleep deeply, some not
The fluctuating sleep cycle enables safe sleep for these soldiers on the battlefield. One benefit of communal sleeping is that someone will probably be awake or easily roused in the event of a threat during the night.

Luc Delahaye/Magnum Photos

People rarely snore during dreams. When REM starts, snoring stops.

Gallup poll:
"Usually, how many hours sleep do you get at night?"

5 or less	16%
6	27%
7	28%
8	28%
2001 average = 6.7 hours	
1942 average = 7.6 hours	

The sleep cycle repeats itself about every 90 minutes. As the night wears on, deep Stage 4 sleep gets progressively briefer and then disappears. The REM sleep period gets longer (see Figure 15.8b). By morning, 20 to 25 percent of our average night's sleep—some 100 minutes—has been REM sleep. Thirty-seven percent of people report rarely or never having dreams "that you can remember the next morning" (Moore, 2004). Unknown to those people, they spend about 600 hours a year experiencing some 1500 dreams, or more than 100,000 dreams over a typical lifetime—dreams swallowed by the night but never acted out, thanks to REM's protective paralysis.

Why Do We Sleep?

15-4 : How does sleep loss affect us? What is sleep's function?

The idea that "everyone needs 8 hours of sleep" is untrue. Newborns spend nearly two-thirds of their day asleep, most adults no more than one-third. Age-related differences in average sleeping time are rivaled by sleep differences among individuals at any age. Some people thrive with fewer than 6 hours per night; others regularly rack up 9 hours or more. Such sleep patterns may be genetically influenced. When Wilse Webb and Scott Campbell (1983) checked the pattern and duration of sleep among fraternal and identical twins, only the identical twins were strikingly similar.

Sleep patterns are also culturally influenced. In industrialized nations, for example, people now sleep less than they did a century ago. Thanks to modern light bulbs, shift work, and social diversions, those who would have gone to bed at 9:00 P.M. are now up until 11:00 P.M. or later. Thomas Edison (1948, pp. 52, 178) was pleased to accept credit for this, believing that less sleep meant more productive time and greater opportunities:

> When I went through Switzerland in a motor-car, so that I could visit little towns and villages, I noted the effect of artificial light on the inhabitants. Where water power and electric light had been developed, everyone seemed normally intelligent. When these appliances did not exist, and the natives went to bed with the chickens, staying there till daylight, they were far less intelligent.

Allowed to sleep unhindered, most humans will sleep at least 9 hours a night, reports Stanley Coren (1996). With that much sleep, we awake refreshed, sustain better moods, and perform more efficient and accurate work. Compare that with a succession of 5-hour nights, when we accumulate a sleep debt that cannot be paid off by one long 10-hour sleep. "The brain keeps an accurate count of sleep debt for at least two weeks," says William Dement (1999, p. 64). With our body yearning for sleep, we will begin to feel terrible. Trying to stay awake, we will eventually lose. In the tiredness battle, sleep always wins.

Obviously, then, we need sleep. Sleep commands roughly one-third of our lives—some 25 years, on average. But why? It seems an easy question to answer: Just keep people awake for several days and note how they deteriorate. If you were a volunteer in such an experiment, how do you think it would affect your body and mind? You would, of course, become terribly drowsy—especially during the hours when your biological clock programs you to sleep. But could the lack of sleep physically damage you? Would it noticeably alter your biochemistry or body organs? Would you become emotionally disturbed? Mentally disoriented?

The Effects of Sleep Loss

Good news! Psychologists have discovered a treatment that strengthens memory, increases concentration, boosts mood, moderates hunger and obesity, fortifies the disease-fighting immune system, and lessens the risk of fatal accidents. Moreover, while supplies last, it's available free!

Even better news: The treatment feels good, it can be self-administered, and the supplies are limitless. If you are a typical university-age student, often going to bed near 2:00 A.M. and dragged out of bed six hours later by the dreaded alarm, the treatment is simple: Each night just add an hour to your sleep.

People today more than ever suffer from patterns that not only leave them sleepy but also thwart their having an energized feeling of well-being (Mikulincer & others, 1989). Teenagers who typically need 8 or 9 hours of sleep now average less than 7 hours—nearly 2 hours less each night than did their counterparts of 80 years ago (Holden, 1993; Maas, 1999). Many fill this need by using their first class for an early siesta and after-lunch study hall for a slumber party. When the going gets boring, the students start snoring. Even when awake, students often function below their peak. And they know it: Four in five American teens and three in five 18- to 29-year-olds wish they could get more sleep on weekdays (Mason, 2003, 2005). Yet that teen who staggers glumly out of bed in response to an unwelcome alarm, yawns through morning classes, and feels half-depressed much of the day may be energized at 11 P.M. and mindless of the next day's looming sleepiness (Carskadon, 2002).

Sleep researcher William Dement (1997) reports that at Stanford University, 80 percent of students are "dangerously sleep deprived. . . . Sleep deprivation [entails] difficulty studying, diminished productivity, tendency to make mistakes, irritability, fatigue." A large sleep debt "makes you stupid," says Dement (1999, p. 231). (Are *you* a sleep-deprived student? Find out by taking the test in **TABLE 15.1**.)

But let's put this positively: To manage your life with enough sleep to awaken naturally and well rested is to be more alert, productive, healthy, and happy. The U.S. Navy and the National Institutes of Health have demonstrated this in experiments in which volunteers spent 14 hours daily in bed for at least a week. For the first few days, the volunteers averaged 12 hours sleep a day or more, apparently paying off a sleep debt that averaged 25 to 30 hours. That accomplished, they then settled back to 7.5 to 9 hours nightly and, with no sleep debt, felt energized and happier. In one Gallup survey (Mason, 2005), 63 percent of adults who reported getting the sleep they need also reported being "very satisfied" with their personal life (as did only 36 percent of those needing more sleep). "Millions of us are living a less than optimal life and performing at a less than optimal level, impaired by an amount of sleep debt that we're not even aware we carry," reflected Dement (1999, p. 72).

That impairment can include suppression of immune cells that fight off viral infections and cancer (Beardsley, 1996; Irwin & others, 1994). This may help explain why people who sleep 7 to 8 hours a night tend to outlive those who are chronically sleep deprived, and why older adults who have no difficulty falling or staying asleep tend to live longer than their sleep-deprived agemates (Dement, 1999; Dew & others, 2003). When infections do set in, we typically sleep more, boosting our immune cells.

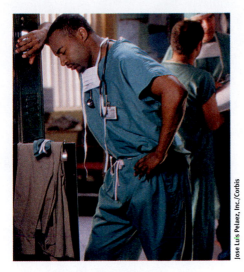

Jose Luis Pelaez, Inc./Corbis

Sleepless and suffering
This fatigued, sleep-deprived person may also experience a depressed immune system, impaired concentration, and greater vulnerability to accidents.

"Tiger Woods said that one of the best things about his choice to leave Stanford for the professional golf circuit was that he could now get enough sleep."
Stanford sleep researcher William Dement, 1997

In a 2001 Gallup poll, 61 percent of men, but only 47 percent of women, said they got enough sleep.

TABLE 15.1

ARE YOU SLEEP DEPRIVED?

Cornell University psychologist James Maas reports that most college students suffer the consequences of sleeping less than they should. To see if you are in that group, answer the following true-false questions:

True	False	
—	—	1. I need an alarm clock in order to wake up at the appropriate time.
—	—	2. It's a struggle for me to get out of bed in the morning.
—	—	3. Weekday mornings I hit the snooze bar several times to get more sleep.
—	—	4. I feel tired, irritable, and stressed out during the week.
—	—	5. I have trouble concentrating and remembering.
—	—	6. I feel slow with critical thinking, problem solving, and being creative.
—	—	7. I often fall asleep watching TV.
—	—	8. I often fall asleep in boring meetings or lectures or in warm rooms.
—	—	9. I often fall asleep after heavy meals or after a low dose of alcohol.
—	—	10. I often fall asleep while relaxing after dinner.
—	—	11. I often fall asleep within five minutes of getting into bed.
—	—	12. I often feel drowsy while driving.
—	—	13. I often sleep extra hours on weekend mornings.
—	—	14. I often need a nap to get through the day.
—	—	15. I have dark circles around my eyes.

If you answered "true" to three or more items, you probably are not getting enough sleep. To determine your sleep needs, Maas recommends that you "go to bed 15 minutes earlier than usual every night for the next week—and continue this practice by adding 15 more minutes each week—until you wake without an alarm clock and feel alert all day." (Quiz reprinted with permission from James B. Maas, *Power sleep: The revolutionary program that prepares your mind and body for peak performance* [New York: HarperCollins, 1999].)

Chronic sleep debt also alters metabolic and hormonal functioning in ways that mimic aging and are conducive to obesity, hypertension, and memory impairment (Spiegel & others, 1999; Taheri, 2004). Other effects include irritability, slowed performance, and impaired creativity, concentration, and communication (Harrison & Horne, 2000).

As a demonstration of the costs of sleep deprivation, Stanley Coren capitalized on what is, for many North Americans, a semi-annual sleep-manipulation experiment—the "spring forward" to "daylight savings" time and "fall backward" to "standard" time. Searching millions of records, Coren found that in both Canada and the United States, accidents increase immediately after the time change that shortens sleep. In Canada, for example, traffic accidents during 1991 and 1992 were 7 percent higher on the Monday after the spring time change than on the Monday before, and they were 7 percent *lower* on the Monday following the extra sleep bestowed by the fall time change (**FIGURE 15.9**).

Experiments reveal some effects of fatigue and sleep deprivation. Reaction times slow and errors increase on visual tasks similar to those involved in airport baggage screening, performing surgery, and reading X-rays (Horowitz & others, 2003). And sleep deprivation can be devastating for driving and piloting. Driver fatigue contributes to an estimated 20 percent of American traffic accidents (Brody, 2002), and to some 30 percent of Australian highway deaths (Maas, 1999). "Rest. That's what I need is rest," said Eastern Airlines Captain James Reeves to the control tower on a September 1974 morning—30 minutes before crashing his airliner at low altitude, killing the crew and all 68 passengers (Moorcroft, 1993). Consider also the timing of

In 1989, Michael Doucette was named America's Safest Driving Teen. In 1990, while driving home from college, he fell asleep at the wheel and collided with an oncoming car, killing both himself and the other driver. Michael's driving instructor later acknowledged never having mentioned sleep deprivation and drowsy driving (Dement, 1999).

"Drowsiness is red alert!"
William Dement, *The Promise of Sleep*, 1999

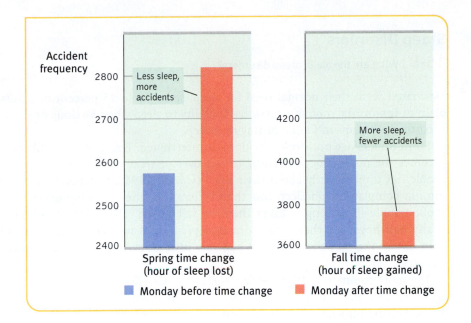

Accident frequency

Spring time change (hour of sleep lost)

Less sleep, more accidents

Fall time change (hour of sleep gained)

More sleep, fewer accidents

■ Monday before time change   ■ Monday after time change

FIGURE 15.9
Canadian traffic accidents, 1991 and 1992
On the Monday after the spring time change, when people lose one hour of sleep, accidents increased as compared with the Monday before. In the fall, traffic accidents normally increase because of greater snow, ice, and darkness, but they diminished after the time change. (Adapted from Coren, 1996.)

the 1989 *Exxon Valdez* oil spill; Union Carbide's 1984 Bhopal, India, disaster; and the 1979 Three Mile Island and 1986 Chernobyl nuclear accidents—all occurred after midnight, when operators in charge were likely to be drowsiest and unresponsive to signals that require an alert response. When sleepy frontal lobes confront an unexpected situation, misfortune often results.

Sleep Theories

So, nature charges us for our sleep debt. But why do we have this need for sleep?

We have very few answers, but sleep may have evolved for four reasons: First, *sleep protects*. When darkness precluded our distant ancestors' hunting and food gathering and made travel treacherous, they were better off asleep in a cave, out of harm's way. Those who didn't try to navigate around rocks and cliffs at night were more likely to leave descendants. This fits a broader principle: A species' sleep pattern tends to suit its ecological niche. Animals with the most need to graze and the least ability to hide tend to sleep less. Elephants and horses sleep 3 to 4 hours a day, gorillas 12 hours, and cats 14 hours. For bats and eastern chipmunks, both of which sleep 20 hours, to live is hardly more than to eat and to sleep (Moorcroft, 2003).

Second, *sleep helps us recuperate*. It helps restore and repair brain tissue. Bats and other animals with high waking metabolism burn a lot of calories, producing a lot of *free radicals*, molecules that are toxic to neurons. Sleeping a lot gives resting neurons time to repair themselves, while allowing unused connections to weaken (Siegel, 2003). Think of it this way: When consciousness leaves your house, brain construction workers come in for a makeover.

But sleep is not just for keeping us safe and for repairing our brain. New research reveals that *sleep is also for remembering*, for restoring and rebuilding our fading memories of the day's experiences. People trained to perform tasks recall them better after a night's sleep than after several hours awake (Fenn & others, 2003). And in both humans and rats, neural activity during slow-wave sleep reenacts and promotes recall of prior novel experiences (Peigneux & others, 2004; Ribeiro & others, 2004). Sleep also feeds creative thinking. After working on a task, then sleeping on it, people solve problems more insightfully than do those who stay awake (Wagner & others, 2004).

Finally, *sleep may play a role in the growth process*. During deep sleep, the pituitary gland releases a growth hormone. As we age, we release less of this hormone and spend less time in deep sleep (Pekkanen, 1982). Such discoveries are beginning to solve the ongoing riddle of sleep.

"Sleep faster, we need the pillows."
Yiddish proverb

"Corduroy pillows make headlines."
Anonymous

"The lion and the lamb shall lie down together, but the lamb will not be very sleepy."
Woody Allen, in the movie *Love and Death*, 1975

■ **insomnia** recurring problems in falling or staying asleep.

Sleep Disorders

15-5 : What are the major sleep disorders?

No matter what their normal need for sleep, some 10 to 15 percent of adults complain of **insomnia**—not an occasional inability to sleep when anxious or excited, but persistent problems in falling or staying asleep.

From middle age on, sleep is seldom uninterrupted. Being occasionally awakened becomes the norm, not something to fret over or treat with medication. But some people fret unnecessarily about their sleep (Coren, 1996). In laboratory studies, insomnia complainers do sleep less than others, but they typically overestimate—by about double—how long it takes them to fall asleep. They also underestimate by nearly half how long they actually have slept. Even if we have been awake only an hour or two, we may *think* we have had very little sleep, because it's the waking part we remember.

The most common quick fixes for true insomnia—sleeping pills and alcohol—can aggravate the problem, reducing REM sleep and leaving the person with next-day blahs. Relying on such aids, the person may need increasing doses to get an effect. Then, when the drug is discontinued, the insomnia can worsen.

Scientists are searching for natural chemicals that are abundant during sleep, hoping they might be synthesized as a sleep aid without side effects. In the meantime, sleep experts offer other natural alternatives:

- Exercise regularly but not in the late evening. (Late afternoon is best.)
- Avoid caffeine (this includes chocolate) after late afternoon, and avoid rich foods before bedtime. Instead, try a glass of milk, which provides raw materials for the manufacture of serotonin, a neurotransmitter that facilitates sleep.
- Relax before bedtime, using dimmer light.
- Sleep on a regular schedule (rise at the same time even after a restless night) and avoid naps. Sticking to a schedule boosts daytime alertness, too, as shown in an experiment in which University of Arizona students averaged 7.5 hours of sleep a night on either a varying or consistent schedule (Manber & others, 1996).
- Hide the clock face so you aren't tempted to check it repeatedly.
- Reassure yourself that a temporary loss of sleep causes no great harm.
- For any stressed organism, being vigilant is natural and adaptive. A personal conflict during the day often means a fitful sleep that night (Brissette & Cohen, 2002).
- If all else fails, settle for less sleep, either going to bed later or getting up earlier.

> "Sleep is like love or happiness. If you pursue it too ardently it will elude you."
>
> Wilse Webb, 1992 (p. 170)

> "In 1757 Benjamin Franklin gave us the axiom, 'Early to bed, early to rise, makes a man healthy, wealthy, and wise.' It would be more accurate to say 'consistently to bed and consistently to rise . . .'"
>
> James B. Maas, *Power Sleep*, 1999

Stress robs sleep
Urban police officers, especially those under stress, report poorer sleep quality and less sleep than average (Neylan & others, 2002).

Dwayne Newton/PhotoEdit

Rarer but also more troublesome than insomnia are the sleep disorders *narcolepsy*, *sleep apnea*, *night terrors*, and *sleepwalking* and *sleeptalking*.

Narcolepsy (from *narco*, "numbness," and *lepsy*, "seizure") sufferers experience periodic, overwhelming sleepiness. Attacks usually last less than 5 minutes but sometimes occur at the most inopportune times, perhaps just after taking a terrific swing at a softball or when laughing loudly, shouting angrily, or having sex (Dement, 1978, 1999). In severe cases, the person may collapse directly into a brief period of REM sleep, with its accompanying loss of muscular tension. People with narcolepsy—1 in 2000 of us, estimates the Stanford University Center for Narcolepsy (2002)—must therefore live with extra caution. As a traffic menace, "snoozing is second only to boozing," says the American Sleep Disorders Association, and those with narcolepsy are especially at risk (Aldrich, 1989).

Sleep apnea also puts millions of people at increased risk of traffic accidents (Teran-Santos & others, 1999). Although 1 in 20 of us has this disorder, it was unknown before modern sleep research. *Apnea* means "with no breath," and people with this condition intermittently stop breathing during sleep. After an airless minute or so, decreased blood oxygen arouses them and they wake up enough to snort in air for a few seconds, in a process that repeats hundreds of times each night, depriving them of slow-wave sleep. Apart from complaints of sleepiness and irritability during the day—and their mates' complaints about their loud "snoring"—apnea sufferers are often unaware of their disorder. (The next morning they have no recall of these episodes.)

Sleep apnea is associated with obesity, and as the number of obese people in the United States has increased, so has this disorder, particularly among overweight men. Anyone who snores at night, feels tired during the day, and possibly has high blood pressure as well (increasing the risk of a stroke or heart attack) should be checked for apnea (Dement, 1999). A physician may prescribe a masklike device with an air pump that keeps the sleeper's airway open and breathing regular. If one doesn't mind looking a little goofy in the dark (imagine a snorkeler at a slumber party), the treatment can be effective.

Unlike sleep apnea, **night terrors** target mostly children, who may sit up or walk around, talk incoherently, experience a doubling of heart and breathing rates, and appear terrified (Hartmann, 1981). They seldom wake up fully during an episode and recall little or nothing the next morning—at most, a fleeting, frightening image. Night terrors are not nightmares (which, like other dreams, typically occur during early morning REM sleep); night terrors usually occur during the first few hours of Stage 4.

Children also are most prone to *sleepwalking*—another Stage 4 sleep disorder—and to *sleeptalking*, conditions that run in families. Finnish twin studies reveal that occasional childhood sleepwalking occurs for about one-third of those with a sleepwalking fraternal twin and half of those with a sleepwalking identical twin. The same is true for sleeptalking (Hublin & others, 1997, 1998). Sleepwalking is usually harmless and unrecalled the next morning. Sleepwalkers typically return to bed on their own or are guided there by a family member. Young children, who have the deepest and lengthiest Stage 4 sleep, are the most likely to experience both night terrors and sleepwalking. As we grow older and deep Stage 4 sleep diminishes, so do night terrors and sleepwalking. After age 40, sleepwalking is rare.

Dreams

Discovering the link between REM sleep and dreaming opened a new era in dream research. Instead of relying on someone's hazy recall hours or days after having a dream, researchers could catch dreams as they happened. They could awaken people during or within 3 minutes after a REM sleep period and hear a vivid account.

Imagine observing a person with narcolepsy in medieval times. Might such symptoms and their associated hallucinations have seemed like demon possession?

■ **narcolepsy** a sleep disorder characterized by uncontrollable sleep attacks. The sufferer may lapse directly into REM sleep, often at inopportune times.

■ **sleep apnea** a sleep disorder characterized by temporary cessations of breathing during sleep and repeated momentary awakenings.

■ **night terrors** a sleep disorder characterized by high arousal and an appearance of being terrified; unlike nightmares, night terrors occur during Stage 4 sleep, within two or three hours of falling asleep, and are seldom remembered.

Did Brahms need his own lullabies?
Cranky, overweight, and nap-prone, Johannes Brahms exhibited common symptoms of sleep apnea (Margolis, 2000).

Archivo Iconografico, S.A./Corbis

"I do not believe that I am now dreaming, but I cannot prove that I am not."

Philosopher Bertrand Russell (1872–1970)

"For what one has dwelt on by day, these things are seen in visions of the night."

Menander of Athens (342–292 B.C.), *Fragments*

A popular sleep myth: If you dream you are falling and hit the ground (or if you dream of dying), you die. (Unfortunately, those who could confirm these ideas are not around to do so. Some people, however, have had such dreams and are alive to report them.)

■ **dream** a sequence of images, emotions, and thoughts passing through a sleeping person's mind. Dreams are notable for their hallucinatory imagery, discontinuities, and incongruities, and for the dreamer's delusional acceptance of the content and later difficulties remembering it.

■ **manifest content** according to Freud, the remembered story line of a dream (as distinct from its latent, or hidden, content).

What We Dream

15-6 : What do we dream?

REM **dreams**—"hallucinations of the sleeping mind"—are vivid, emotional, and bizarre. They are unlike daydreams, which tend to involve the familiar details of our life—perhaps picturing ourselves explaining to an instructor why a paper will be late, or replaying in our minds personal encounters we relish or regret. The dreams of REM sleep are so vivid we may confuse them with reality. Awakening from a nightmare, a 4-year-old may complain of a bear in the house.

We spend six years of our life in dreams, many of which are anything but sweet. For both women and men, 8 in 10 dreams are marked by negative emotions (Domhoff, 1999). People commonly dream of repeatedly failing in an attempt to do something; of being attacked, pursued, or rejected; or of experiencing misfortune (Hall & others, 1982). Dreams with sexual imagery occur less often than you might think. In one study, only 1 in 10 dreams among young men and 1 in 30 among young women had sexual overtones (Domhoff, 1996). More commonly, the story line of our dreams— what Sigmund Freud called their **manifest content**—incorporates traces of previous days' nonsexual experiences and preoccupations (De Koninck, 2000):

- After suffering a trauma, people commonly report nightmares.
- Robert Stickgold and his colleagues (2000) had people play the computer game "Tetris" for seven hours and then repeatedly awakened them during their first hour of sleep; three-fourths reported experiencing images of the game's falling blocks.
- People in hunter-gatherer societies often dream of animals; urban Japanese rarely do (Mestel, 1997).

Sensory stimuli in our sleeping environment may also intrude. A particular odor or the telephone's ringing may be instantly and ingeniously woven into the dream story. In a classic experiment, William Dement and Edward Wolpert (1958) lightly sprayed cold water on dreamers' faces. Compared with sleepers who did not get the cold-water treatment, these people were more likely to dream about a waterfall, a leaky roof, or even about being sprayed by someone. Even while in REM sleep, focused on internal stimuli, we maintain some awareness of changes in our external environment.

So, could we learn a foreign language by listening to tapes while we sleep? If only it were so easy. While sleeping we can learn to associate a sound with a mild electric shock (and to react to the sound accordingly). But we do not remember taped information played while we are soundly asleep (Eich, 1990; Wyatt & Bootzin, 1994). In fact, anything that happens during the 5 minutes just before we fall asleep is typically lost from memory (Roth & others, 1988). This explains why sleep apnea patients, who

MAXINE

repeatedly awaken with a gasp and then immediately fall back to sleep, do not recall the episodes. It also explains why dreams that momentarily awaken us are mostly forgotten by morning. To remember a dream, get up and stay awake for a few minutes.

Why We Dream

15-7: What is the function of dreams?

Dream theorists have proposed several explanations of why we dream, including these:

To satisfy our own wishes. In his landmark book *The Interpretation of Dreams*, published in 1900, Freud offered what he thought was "the most valuable of all the discoveries it has been my good fortune to make": Dreams provide a psychic safety valve that discharges otherwise unacceptable feelings. According to Freud, a dream's *manifest* (apparent) content is a censored, symbolic version of its **latent content,** which consists of unconscious drives and wishes that would be threatening if expressed directly. Although most dreams have no overt sexual imagery, Freud nevertheless believed that most adult dreams can be "traced back by analysis to erotic wishes." Thus, a gun might be a disguised representation of a penis.

Freud considered dreams the key to understanding our inner conflicts. However, his critics say it is time to wake up from Freud's dream theory, which is a scientific nightmare. Based on the accumulated science, "there is no reason to believe any of Freud's specific claims about dreams and their purposes," notes dream researcher William Domhoff (2000). Some contend that even if dreams are symbolic, they could be interpreted any way one wished. Others maintain that dreams hide nothing. A dream about a gun is a dream about a gun. Legend has it that even Freud, who loved to smoke cigars, remarked that "sometimes, a cigar is just a cigar." Freud's wish-fulfillment theory of dreams has in large part given way to other theories.

To file away memories. Researchers who see dreams as *information processing* believe that dreams may help sift, sort, and fix the day's experiences in our memory. People tested the next day generally improve on a learned task after a night of memory consolidation. But even after two nights of recovery sleep, those deprived of both slow-wave and REM sleep don't do as well as those who sleep undisturbed on their new learning (Stickgold & others, 2000, 2001). Not surprising, perhaps, since we have known for decades that REM sleep facilitates memory (McGrath & Cohen, 1978). People who hear unusual phrases or learn to find hidden visual images before bedtime remember less the next morning if awakened every time they begin REM sleep than they do if awakened during other sleep stages (Empson & Clarke, 1970; Karni & Sagi, 1994).

Brain scans confirm the link between REM sleep and memory. The brain regions that buzz as rats learn to navigate a maze, or as people learn to perform a visual-discrimination task, buzz again later during REM sleep (Louie & Wilson, 2001; Maquet, 2001). So precise are these activity patterns that scientists can tell where in the maze the rat would be if awake.

So, a night of solid sleep (and dreaming) has an important place in our lives: To sleep, perchance to remember. This is important news for teens and college students, many of whom, researcher Robert Stickgold (2000) believes, suffer from a kind of sleep bulimia, binge-sleeping on the weekend. "But if you don't get good sleep and enough sleep after you learn new stuff, you won't integrate it effectively into your memories," he warns. That may help explain why high-achieving secondary students with top grades average 25 minutes more sleep a night and go to bed 40 minutes earlier than their lower-achieving classmates (Wolfson & Carskadon, 1998).

To develop and preserve neural pathways. Dreams may also serve a *physiological function.* Perhaps dreams—or the associated brain activity of REM sleep—provide the sleeping brain with periodic stimulation. We know that stimulating experiences develop and preserve the brain's neural pathways. Infants, whose neural networks are fast developing, spend much of their abundant sleep time in REM sleep.

Would you suppose that people dream if blind from birth? Studies of blind people in France, Hungary, Egypt, and the United States all found them dreaming of using their nonvisual senses—hearing, touching, smelling, tasting (Buquet, 1988; Taha, 1972; Vekassy, 1977). Yet even congenitally blind people can experience visual images in dreams (Bértolo & others, 2003).

■ **latent content** according to Freud, the underlying meaning of a dream (as distinct from its manifest content).

"When people interpret [a dream] as if it were meaningful and then sell those interpretations, it's quackery."

Sleep researcher J. Allan Hobson (1995)

Rapid eye movements also stir the liquid behind the cornea; this delivers fresh oxygen to corneal cells, preventing their suffocation.

Question: Does eating spicy foods cause one to dream more?
Answer: Any food that causes you to awaken more increases your chance of recalling a dream (Moorcroft, 2003).

■ **REM rebound** the tendency for REM sleep to increase following REM sleep deprivation (created by repeated awakenings during REM sleep).

To make sense of neural static. Other theories propose that dreams erupt from neural activity spreading upward from the brainstem (Antrobus, 1991; Hobson, 2003, 2004). According to one version—the *activation-synthesis* theory—this neural activity is random, and dreams are the brain's attempt to make sense of it. Much as a neurosurgeon can produce hallucinations by stimulating different parts of a patient's cortex, so can stimulation originating within the brain. These internal stimuli activate brain areas that process visual images, but not the visual cortex area, which receives raw input from the eyes. As Freud might have expected, PET scans of sleeping people also reveal increased activity in the emotion-related limbic system (in the amygdala) during REM sleep. In contrast, frontal lobe regions responsible for inhibition and logical thinking seem to idle, which may explain why our dreams are less inhibited than we are (Maquet & others, 1996). Add the limbic system's emotional tone to the brain's visual bursts and—voila!—we dream. Damage either the limbic system or the visual centers active during dreaming, and dreaming itself may be impaired (Domhoff, 2003).

To reflect cognitive development. Some dream researchers dispute both the Freudian and activation-synthesis theories, preferring instead to see dreams as part of brain maturation and cognitive development (Domhoff, 2003; Foulkes, 1999). For example, prior to age 9, children's dreams seem more like a slide show and less like an active story in which the dreamer is an actor. Dreams overlap with waking cognition and feature coherent speech. They draw on our concepts and knowledge. **TABLE 15.2** compares major dream theories.

There is one thing dream theorists agree on: We need REM sleep. Deprived of it by repeatedly being awakened, people return more and more quickly to the REM stage after falling back to sleep. When finally allowed to sleep undisturbed, they literally sleep like babies—with increased REM sleep, a phenomenon called **REM rebound.** Withdrawing REM-suppressing sleeping medications also increases REM sleep, but with accompanying nightmares.

Most other mammals also experience REM rebound, suggesting that the causes and functions of REM sleep are deeply biological. That REM sleep occurs in mammals—and not in animals such as fish, whose behavior is less influenced by learning—also fits the information-processing theory of dreams.

So does this mean that because dreams serve physiological functions and extend normal cognition, they are psychologically meaningless? Not necessarily. Every psychologically meaningful experience involves an active brain. We are once again reminded of a basic principle: *Biological and psychological explanations of behavior are partners, not competitors.* Dreams may be akin to abstract art—open to more than one meaningful interpretation.

TABLE 15.2

DREAM THEORIES

Theory	Explanation	Critical Considerations
Freud's wish-fulfillment	Dreams provide a "psychic safety valve"—expressing otherwise unacceptable feelings; contain manifest (remembered) content and a deeper layer of latent content—a hidden meaning.	Lacks any scientific support; dreams may be interpreted in many different ways.
Information-processing	Dreams help us sort out the day's events and consolidate our memories.	But why do we sometimes dream about things we have not experienced?
Physiological function	Regular brain stimulation from REM sleep may help develop and preserve neural pathways.	This may be true, but it does not explain why we experience *meaningful* dreams.
Activation-synthesis	REM sleep triggers neural activity that evokes random visual memories, which our sleeping brain weaves into stories.	The individual's brain is weaving the stories, which still tells us something about the dreamer.
Cognitive	Dream content reflects dreamers' cognitive development—their knowledge and understanding.	Does not address the neuroscience of dreams.

REVIEWING

>> MODULE REVIEW

15-1: **What is consciousness, and how does it function?**

Psychology, which began as the study of *consciousness*, is again focusing on our awareness of ourselves and our environment. At any moment our *selective attention* makes us aware of only a very limited portion of the world around us, and we display *inattentional blindness* to other stimuli. We consciously process voluntary and novel tasks relatively slowly, attending to each one (serial processing). We automatically and unconsciously process familiar tasks, and our sensory systems and neural pathways register stimuli rapidly and simultaneously on multiple tracks (parallel processing).

15-2: **How do our biological rhythms influence our daily functioning and our sleep and dreams?**

Our internal "biological clocks" create periodic physiological fluctuations. The *circadian rhythm's* 24-hour cycle regulates our daily schedule of sleeping and waking. This cycle is in part a response to light striking the retina, triggering alterations in the level of sleep-inducing melatonin and other biochemical substances. Time changes, long flights, shifts in sleep schedules, and exposure to bright light can reset our biological clock.

15-3: **What is the biological rhythm of our sleep?**

We cycle through five *sleep* stages in about 90 minutes. Leaving the *alpha waves* of the awake, relaxed stage, we descend into transitional Stage 1 sleep, often with the sensation of falling or floating. Stage 2 sleep (in which we spend the most time) follows about 20 minutes later, with its characteristic sleep spindles. Then follow Stages 3 and 4, together lasting about 30 minutes, with large, slow *delta waves*. Reversing course, we retrace our path through these stages—with one difference: About an hour after falling asleep, we begin approximately 10 minutes of *REM (rapid eye movement) sleep*, in which most dreaming occurs. In this fifth stage (also known as paradoxical sleep), we are internally aroused but outwardly paralyzed. During a normal night's sleep, periods of Stage 4 and then Stage 3 sleep shorten and REM sleep lengthens.

15-4: **How does sleep loss affect us? What is sleep's function?**

Sleep deprivation puts people at risk not only for fatigue, but also for a depressed immune system; impaired concentration, creativity, and communication; irritability; and slowed performance (with greater vulnerability to accidents). Chronic sleep deprivation may contribute to obesity, hypertension, and memory impairment.

Some psychologists believe sleep played a protective role in human evolution by keeping people safe during potentially dangerous periods. Sleep also gives the brain time to restore and repair damaged neurons. During sleep, we restore and rebuild memories of the day's experiences, and a good night's sleep promotes insightful problem-solving the next day. Sleep encourages growth; the pituitary gland secretes a growth hormone in Stage 4 sleep.

15-5: **What are the major sleep disorders?**

The disorders of sleep include *insomnia* (recurring wakefulness), *narcolepsy* (sudden uncontrollable sleepiness or lapsing into REM sleep), *sleep apnea* (the stopping of breathing while asleep), *night terrors* (high arousal and the appearance of being terrified), sleepwalking, and sleeptalking. Overweight men are most prone to sleep apnea; children are most prone to night terrors, sleepwalking, and sleeptalking.

15-6: **What do we dream?**

We usually *dream* of ordinary events and everyday experiences, 80 percent of them involving some anxiety or misfortune. Fewer than 10 percent (and less among women) of dreams have any sexual content. Most dreams occur during REM sleep; those that happen during non-REM sleep tend to be vague fleeting images.

15-7: **What is the function of dreams?**

There are five major views of the function of dreams. (1) Freud believed dreams provide a safety valve, with their *manifest content* (or story line) acting as a censored version of their *latent content* (some underlying meaning that gratifies our unconscious wishes). (2) The information-processing perspective proposes that dreams help us sort out the day's experiences and fix them in memory. (3) Other physiological perspectives hold that REM-induced regular brain stimulation helps develop and preserve neural pathways in the brain. (4) The activation-synthesis explanation proposes that REM sleep triggers impulses in the visual cortex, evoking random visual images that our brain tries to weave into a story line. (5) The brain-maturation/cognitive-development perspective believes dreams represent the dreamer's level of development, knowledge, and understanding. Despite their differences, most sleep theorists agree that REM sleep and its associated dreams serve an important function, as shown by the *REM rebound* that occurs following REM deprivation.

>> REHEARSE IT!

1. Consciousness is our awareness of ourselves and our environment. Failure to see visible objects when our attention is occupied elsewhere is called

   a. parallel processing.
   b. awareness unconsciousness.
   c. inattentional blindness.
   d. subconscious processing.

2. We process most information outside of conscious awareness. We register and react to stimuli outside of our awareness by means of _____ processing. When we devote full conscious attention to stimuli, we use _____ processing.

   a. parallel; serial
   b. serial; parallel
   c. selective; complete
   d. complete; selective

3. Our body temperature tends to rise and fall in sync with a biological clock, which is referred to as

a. the circadian rhythm.
b. narcolepsy.
c. REM sleep.
d. hypnagogic sensations.

4. Stage 1 sleep is a twilight zone of light sleep. During Stage 1 sleep, a person is most likely to experience

a. sleep spindles.
b. hallucinations.
c. night terrors or nightmares.
d. rapid eye movements.

5. In the deepest stage of sleep—surprisingly, the stage when people sleepwalk—the brain emits large, slow delta waves. This deep stage of sleep is called

a. Stage 2.
b. Stage 4.
c. REM sleep.
d. paradoxical sleep.

6. An electroencephalograph shows that during sleep we pass through a cycle of five stages, each with characteristic brain waves. As the night progresses, the REM stage

a. gradually disappears.
b. becomes briefer and briefer.

c. remains about the same.
d. becomes progressively longer.

7. Various theories have been proposed to explain why we need sleep. They include all but which of the following?

a. Sleep has survival value.
b. Sleep helps us recuperate.
c. Sleep rests the eyes.
d. Sleep plays a role in the growth process.

8. Two relatively rare sleep disorders are narcolepsy and sleep apnea. With narcolepsy, the person _____; with sleep apnea, the person _____.

a. has persistent problems falling asleep; experiences a doubling of heart and breathing rates
b. experiences a doubling of heart and breathing rates; has persistent problems falling asleep
c. intermittently stops breathing; suffers periodic, overwhelming sleepiness
d. suffers periodic, overwhelming sleepiness; intermittently stops breathing

9. According to Sigmund Freud, dreams are the key to understanding our inner conflicts. In interpreting

dreams, Freud was most interested in their

a. information-processing function.
b. physiological function.
c. manifest content, or story line.
d. latent content, or symbolic meaning.

10. Some theories of dreaming propose that dreams serve a physiological purpose. One such theory suggests that dreams

a. are the brain's attempt to make sense of random neural activity.
b. provide a rest period for overworked brains.
c. serve as a safety valve for unfulfilled desires.
d. prevent the brain from being disturbed by periodic stimulations.

11. The tendency for REM sleep to increase following REM sleep deprivation is referred to as

a. paradoxical sleep.
b. deep sleep.
c. REM rebound.
d. slow-wave sleep.

Answers: 1. c, 2. a, 3. a, 4. b, 5. b, 6. d, 7. c, 8. d, 9. d, 10. a, 11. c.

>> Terms and Concepts to Remember

consciousness, p. 193
selective attention, p. 193
inattentional blindness, p. 194
circadian [ser-KAY-dee-an] rhythm, p. 196
REM (rapid eye movement) sleep, p. 197
alpha waves, p. 198

sleep, p. 198
hallucinations, p. 198
delta waves, p. 198
insomnia, p. 204
narcolepsy, p. 205
sleep apnea, p. 205

night terrors, p. 205
dream, p. 206
manifest content, p. 206
latent content, p. 207
REM rebound, p. 208

>> Test Yourself

1. During psychology's history, what were the ups and downs of "consciousness"?

2. Are you getting enough sleep? What might you ask yourself to answer this question?

(Answers in Appendix C.)

Multiple-choice **self-tests** and more may be found at www.worthpublishers.com/myers.

Hypnosis

Imagine you are about to be hypnotized. The hypnotist invites you to sit back, fix your gaze on a spot high on the wall, and relax. In a quiet, low voice the hypnotist suggests, "Your eyes are growing tired. . . . Your eyelids are becoming heavy . . . now heavier and heavier. . . . They are beginning to close. . . . You are becoming more deeply relaxed. . . . Your breathing is now deep and regular. . . . Your muscles are becoming more and more relaxed. Your whole body is beginning to feel like lead."

After a few minutes of this *hypnotic induction*, you may experience **hypnosis.** When the hypnotist suggests, "Your eyelids are shutting so tight that you cannot open them even if you try," it may indeed seem beyond your control to open your eyelids. Told to forget the number 6, you may be puzzled when you count 11 fingers on your hands. Invited to smell a sensuous perfume that is actually ammonia, you may linger delightedly over its pungent odor. Told that you cannot see a certain object, such as a chair, you may indeed report that it is not there, although you manage to avoid the chair when walking around.

Before considering whether the hypnotic state is actually an *altered* state of consciousness, let's consider some areas of general agreement.

Facts and Falsehoods

16-1: What powers does a hypnotist have over a hypnotized subject?

Those who study hypnosis agree that its power resides not in the hypnotist but in the subject's openness to suggestion (Bowers, 1984). Hypnotists have no magical mind-control power; they merely engage people's ability to focus on certain images or behaviors. But how open to suggestions are we?

Can Anyone Experience Hypnosis?

To some extent, we are all susceptible to suggestion. When people standing upright with their eyes closed are told repeatedly that they are swaying back and forth, most will indeed sway a little. In fact, postural sway is one of the items assessed on the Stanford Hypnotic Susceptibility Scale. People who respond to such suggestions without hypnosis are the same people who respond with hypnosis (Kirsch & Braffman, 2001).

After giving a brief hypnotic induction, a hypnotist suggests a series of experiences ranging from easy (one's outstretched arms will move together) to difficult (with eyes open, one will see a nonexistent person). Highly hypnotizable people—say, the 20 percent who can carry out a suggestion not to smell or react to a bottle of ammonia held under the nose—frequently become deeply absorbed in imaginative activities (Barnier & McConkey, 2004; Silva & Kirsch, 1992). Typically, these individuals have rich fantasy lives and easily become absorbed in the imaginary events of a novel or movie. (Perhaps you can recall being riveted by a movie into a trancelike state, oblivious to people or noise surrounding you.) Many researchers refer to hypnotic "susceptibility" as hypnotic *ability*—the ability to focus attention totally on a task, to become imaginatively absorbed in it, to entertain fanciful possibilities.

Can Hypnosis Enhance Recall of Forgotten Events?

Can hypnotic procedures enable people to recall kindergarten classmates? To retrieve forgotten or suppressed details of a crime? Should testimony obtained under hypnosis be admissible in court?

■ **hypnosis** a social interaction in which one person (the hypnotist) suggests to another (the subject) that certain perceptions, feelings, thoughts, or behaviors will spontaneously occur.

"Hypnosis is not a psychological truth serum and to regard it as such has been a source of considerable mischief."

Researcher Kenneth Bowers (1987)

Most people wrongly believe that our experiences are all "in there," recorded in our brain and available for recall if only we can break through our own defenses (Loftus, 1980). (In fact, memory research indicates that we do not encode everything that occurs around us, that we permanently store only some of our experiences, and that we may be unable to retrieve some memories we have stored.) In one community survey, 3 in 4 people agreed with the inaccurate statement that hypnosis enables people to "recover accurate memories as far back as birth" (Johnson & Hauck, 1999). But 60 years of research dispute such claims. "Hypnotically refreshed" memories combine fact with fiction. Without either person being aware of what is going on, a hypnotist's hints—"Did you hear loud noises?"—can plant ideas that become the subject's pseudomemory. Thus, American, Australian, and British courts increasingly ban testimony from witnesses who have been hypnotized (Druckman & Bjork, 1994; Gibson, 1995; McConkey, 1995).

Other striking examples of memories created under hypnosis come from the thousands of people who since 1980 have reported being abducted by UFOs. Most such reports have come from people who are predisposed to believe in aliens, are highly hypnotizable, and have undergone hypnosis (Newman & Baumeister, 1996; Nickell, 1996).

Can Hypnosis Force People to Act Against Their Will?

Researchers have induced hypnotized people to perform an apparently dangerous act: plunging one hand briefly into fuming "acid," then throwing the "acid" in a researcher's face (Orne & Evans, 1965). Interviewed a day later, these people exhibited no memory of their acts and emphatically denied they would ever follow such orders.

Had hypnosis given the hypnotist a special power to control others against their will? To find out, researchers Martin Orne and Frederich Evans unleashed that enemy of so many illusory beliefs—the control group: Orne asked other individuals to *pretend* they were hypnotized. Laboratory assistants, unaware that those in the experiment's control group had not been hypnotized, treated both groups the same. The result? All the *unhypnotized* participants (perhaps believing that the laboratory context assured safety) performed the same acts as those who were hypnotized.

"It wasn't what I expected. But facts are facts, and if one is proved to be wrong, one must just be humble about it and start again."

Agatha Christie's Miss Marple

Such studies illustrate a principle that social psychologist Stanley Milgram demonstrated: *An authoritative person in a legitimate context can induce people—hypnotized or not—to perform some unlikely acts.* Hypnosis researcher Nicholas Spanos (1982) put it directly: "The overt behaviors of hypnotic subjects are well within normal limits."

Can Hypnosis Be Therapeutic?

Hypnotherapists try to help patients harness their own healing powers (Baker, 1987). **Posthypnotic suggestions** have helped alleviate headaches, asthma, and stress-related skin disorders. One woman, who for more than 20 years suffered from open sores all over her body, was asked to imagine herself swimming in shimmering, sunlit liquids that would cleanse her skin, and to experience her skin as smooth and unblemished. Within three months her sores had disappeared (Bowers, 1984).

In one statistical digest of 18 studies, the average client whose therapy was supplemented with hypnosis showed greater improvement than 70 percent of other therapy patients (Kirsch & others, 1995, 1996). Hypnosis seemed especially helpful for treatment of obesity. However, drug, alcohol, and smoking addictions do not respond well to hypnosis (Nash, 2001). In controlled studies, hypnosis speeds the disappearance of warts, but so do the same positive suggestions given without hypnosis (Spanos, 1991, 1996).

Can Hypnosis Alleviate Pain?

Yes, hypnosis *can* relieve pain (Druckman & Bjork, 1994; Patterson, 2004). When unhypnotized people put their arms in an ice bath, they feel intense pain within 25 seconds. When hypnotized people do the same after being given suggestions to feel no

■ **posthypnotic suggestion** a suggestion, made during a hypnosis session, to be carried out after the subject is no longer hypnotized; used by some clinicians to help control undesired symptoms and behaviors.

■ **dissociation** a split in consciousness, which allows some thoughts and behaviors to occur simultaneously with others.

pain, they indeed report feeling little pain. As some dentists know, even light hypnosis can reduce fear, and thus hypersensitivity to pain. And nearly 10 percent of us can become so deeply hypnotized that even major surgery can be performed without anesthesia. Half of us can gain at least some pain relief from hypnosis. In surgical experiments, hypnotized patients have required less medication, recovered sooner, and left the hospital earlier than unhypnotized controls, thanks to the inhibition of pain-related brain activity (Lang & others, 2000; Patterson & Jensen, 2003).

How can this be? One theory of hypnotic pain relief finds the answer in **dissociation,** a split between different levels of consciousness. Hypnosis, it suggests, dissociates the sensation of the pain stimulus (of which the subject is still aware) from the emotional suffering that defines our experience of pain. The ice water therefore feels cold—very cold—but not painful.

Another theory proposes that hypnotic pain relief results from *selective attention*, as when an injured athlete, caught up in the competition, feels little or no pain until the game ends. Support for this view comes from PET scans showing that hypnosis reduces brain activity in a region that processes painful stimuli, but not in the sensory cortex, which receives the raw sensory input (Rainville & others, 1997). Hypnosis does *not* block sensory input, but it may block our *attention* to those stimuli.

The unanswered question of how hypnosis relieves pain—by *dissociating* the pain sensation from conscious awareness, or merely by focusing *attention* on other things—brings us to the basic issue: Is hypnosis a unique psychological state?

Explaining the Hypnotized State

16-2: Is hypnosis an extension of normal consciousness or an altered state of consciousness?

We have seen that hypnosis involves heightened suggestibility. We have also seen that hypnotic procedures do not endow a person with special powers. But they can sometimes help a person overcome stress-related ailments or cope with pain. So, just what *is* hypnosis?

Hypnosis as a Social Phenomenon

Those who believe that hypnotic phenomena reflect the workings of normal consciousness and the power of social influence (Lynn & others, 1990; Spanos & Coe, 1992) point out how powerfully our interpretations and attentional spotlight influence our ordinary perceptions.

Does this mean that people are consciously faking hypnosis? No—like actors caught up in their roles, subjects begin to feel and behave in ways appropriate for "good hypnotic subjects." The more they like and trust the hypnotist, the more they allow that person to direct their attention and fantasies (Gfeller & others, 1987). "The hypnotist's ideas become the subject's thoughts," explained Theodore Barber (2000), "and the subject's thoughts produce the hypnotic experiences and behaviors." If told to scratch their ear later when they hear the word *psychology*, subjects will likely do so only if they think the experiment is still under way (and scratching is therefore expected). If an experimenter eliminates their motivation for acting hypnotized—by stating that hypnosis reveals their "gullibility"—subjects become unresponsive.

Based on such findings, advocates of the *social influence theory* contend that hypnotic phenomena—like the behaviors associated with other supposed altered states, such as dissociative identity disorder (multiple personalities) and spirit or demon possession—are an extension of everyday social behavior, not something unique to hypnosis (Spanos, 1994, 1996).

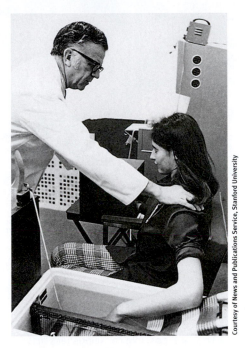

Dissociation or role-playing?
This hypnotized woman tested by Ernest Hilgard exhibited no pain when her arm was placed in an ice bath. But asked to press a key if some part of her felt the pain, she did so. To Hilgard, this was evidence of dissociation, or divided consciousness. Proponents of social influence theory, however, maintain that people responding this way are caught up in playing the role of "good subject."

Courtesy of News and Publications Service, Stanford University

Hypnosis as Divided Consciousness

Most hypnosis researchers grant that normal social and cognitive processes play a part in hypnosis, but they nevertheless believe hypnosis is more than inducing someone to play the role of "good subject." For one thing, hypnotized subjects will *sometimes* carry out suggested behaviors on cue, even when they believe no one is watching (Perugini & others, 1998). Moreover, these researchers cite studies in which distinctive brain activity accompanied hypnosis. In one experiment, when deeply hypnotized people were asked to imagine a color, areas of their brain lit up as if they were really seeing the color. What would be mere imagination in an unhypnotized state had become—to the hypnotized person's brain—a compelling hallucination (Kosslyn & others, 2000).

This would not have surprised famed researcher Ernest Hilgard (1986, 1992), who believed hypnosis involves not only social influence but also a special state of dissociated (divided) consciousness (**FIGURE 16.1**). Hilgard viewed hypnotic dissociation as a vivid form of everyday mind splits—similar to doodling while listening to a lecture or keying in the end of a sentence while starting a conversation.

Although the divided-consciousness theory of hypnosis is controversial, this much seems clear: There is, without doubt, much more to thinking and acting than we are conscious of. Our information processing, which starts with selective attention, *is* divided into simultaneous conscious and subconscious realms. In hypnosis as in life, *much of our behavior occurs on autopilot.*

Yet, there is also little doubt that social influences do play an important role in hypnosis. So, might the two views—social influence and divided consciousness—be bridged? Researchers John Kihlstrom and Kevin McConkey (1990) believe there is no contradiction between the two approaches, which are converging toward a "unified account of hypnosis." Hypnosis, they suggest, is an extension *both* of normal principles of social influence *and* of everyday dissociations between our conscious awareness and our automatic behaviors. So, when today's researchers refer to a "hypnotic state," they merely refer to the subjective experience of hypnosis, not to a unique trance state (Kirsch & Lynn, 1995, 1998a,b). Hypnosis researchers are moving beyond the "hypnosis is social influence" *versus* "hypnosis is divided consciousness" debate (Killeen & Nash, 2003; Woody & McConkey, 2003), and instead are exploring how brain activity, attention, and social influences combine to affect hypnotic phenomena.

> "The total possible consciousness may be split into parts which co-exist but mutually ignore each other."
>
> William James, *Principles of Psychology*, 1890

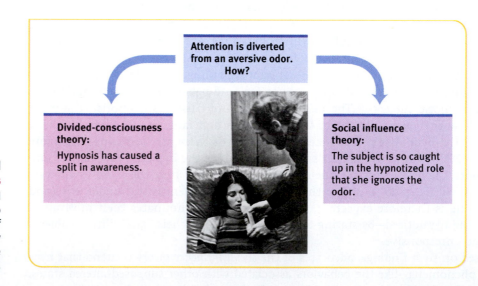

FIGURE 16.1
Explaining hypnosis
How did she do it? How was this hypnotized young woman in Ernest Hilgard's lab able to show no reaction to the terrible smell of ammonia? Divided-consciousness theory and social influence theory offer possible explanations.

Attention is diverted from an aversive odor. How?

Divided-consciousness theory:
Hypnosis has caused a split in awareness.

Social influence theory:
The subject is so caught up in the hypnotized role that she ignores the odor.

>> MODULE REVIEW

16-1: **What powers does a hypnotist have over a hypnotized subject?**

Psychologists now agree that *hypnosis* is a state of heightened suggestibility. People are suggestible in varying degrees. Hypnotized people are no more vulnerable to acting against their will than unhypnotized people are, and hypnosis does not enhance recall of forgotten events (it may even evoke false memories). Hypnotized people, like unhypnotized people, may perform unlikely acts when told to do so by an authoritative person. *Posthypnotic suggestions* have helped people harness their own healing powers to reduce headaches and some other disorders but have not been effective in treating addiction. Hypnosis can help relieve pain.

16-2: **Is hypnosis an extension of normal consciousness or an altered state of consciousness?**

Many psychologists believe that hypnosis is an extension of normal consciousness and that hypnotized people are unknowingly acting out the role of "good subject." Others believe hypnosis produces a *dissociation*—a split—between normal sensations and conscious awareness. Many contemporary researchers avoid this debate and focus instead on how brain activity, attention, and social influences interact to create hypnotic phenomena.

>> REHEARSE IT!

1. Hypnosis is a social interaction in which a hypnotist suggests to a subject that certain perceptions, feelings, thoughts, or behaviors will spontaneously occur. Subjects who are hypnotizable and will carry out a hypnotic suggestion typically

   a. have rich fantasy lives.
   b. have low self-esteem.
   c. are consciously faking their responses.
   d. are in a unique trance state.

2. Experts differ in their understandings of hypnosis, but most agree that hypnosis can be effectively used to

   a. elicit testimony about a "forgotten" event.
   b. re-create childhood experiences.
   c. relieve pain.
   d. alter personality.

3. Ernest Hilgard believed hypnosis is not merely an extension of normal social influence but involves dissociation, or

   a. nonconformity to social pressure.
   b. heightened suggestibility.
   c. a state of divided consciousness.
   d. conscious enactment of a hypnotic role.

Answers: 1. a, 2. c, 3. c.

>> TERMS AND CONCEPTS TO REMEMBER

hypnosis, p. 211

posthypnotic suggestion, p. 212

dissociation, p. 213

>> TEST YOURSELF

1. When is the use of hypnosis potentially harmful, and when can hypnosis be used to help?

   (Answer in Appendix C.)

Multiple-choice **self-tests** and more may be found at www.worthpublishers.com/myers.

Drugs and Consciousness

There is little dispute that drugs alter consciousness. **Psychoactive drugs** are chemicals that change perceptions and moods. Let's imagine a day in the life of a legal-drug user. It begins with a wake-up latté. By midday, several cigarettes have calmed frazzled nerves before an appointment at the plastic surgeon's office for Botox injections to smooth wrinkles. A diet pill before dinner helps stem the appetite, and its stimulating effects can later be partially offset with a glass of wine and two Tylenol PMs. And if performance needs enhancing, there are beta blockers for onstage performers, Viagra for middle-aged men, hormone-delivering "libido patches" for middle-aged women, and Adderall for students hoping to focus their concentration. Before drifting off into REM-depressed sleep, our hypothetical drug user is dismayed by a news report of "rising drug abuse."

Dependence and Addiction

17-1: What are dependence and addiction? Can substance abusers overcome their addictions?

Why might a person who rarely drinks alcohol get tipsy on one can of beer, but an experienced drinker show few effects until the second six-pack? Continued use of alcohol and other psychoactive drugs produces **tolerance:** The user experiences *neuroadaptation* (the brain adapts its chemistry to offset the drug effect). Thus, the user requires larger and larger doses to experience the drug's effect (**FIGURE 17.1**). Ironically, despite the connotations of alcohol "tolerance," alcoholics' brains, hearts, and livers suffer damage from the excessive alcohol they are "tolerating."

Users who stop taking psychoactive drugs may experience the undesirable side effects of **withdrawal.** As the body responds to the drug's absence, the user may feel physical pain and intense cravings, indicating **physical dependence.** People can also develop **psychological dependence,** particularly for stress-relieving drugs. Although not physically addictive, such drugs may nevertheless become an important part of the user's life, often as a way of relieving negative emotions. With either physical or psychological dependence, the user's primary focus may be obtaining and using the drug.

© 1992 by Sidney Harris.

"Just tell me where you kids got the idea to take so many drugs."

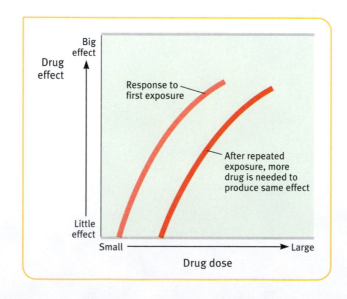

FIGURE 17.1
Drug tolerance
With repeated exposure to a psychoactive drug, the drug's effect lessens. Thus, it takes larger doses to get the desired effect.

Misconceptions About Addiction

An **addiction** is a craving for a substance despite adverse consequences and often with physical symptoms such as aches, nausea, and distress following sudden withdrawal. In recent pop psychology, the supposedly irresistible seduction of addiction has been extended to cover many behaviors formerly considered bad habits or even sins. Has the concept been stretched too far? Are addictions as irresistible as commonly believed? Many drug researchers believe the following three myths about addiction are *false*:

1. ***Addictive drugs quickly corrupt; for example, morphine taken to control pain is powerfully addictive and often leads to heroin abuse.*** People typically do not become addicted when using drugs medically. Those given morphine to control pain rarely develop the cravings of the addict who uses morphine as a mood-altering drug (Melzack, 1990). But after taking a psychoactive drug, some people—perhaps 10 percent—do indeed have a hard time using it in moderation or stopping altogether. Even so, controlled, occasional users far outnumber addicts of drugs such as alcohol and marijuana (Gazzaniga, 1988; Siegel, 1990). "Even for a very addictive drug like cocaine, only 15 to 16 percent of people become addicted within 10 years of first use," report Terry Robinson and Kent Berridge (2003). Much the same is true for rats, only some of which become compulsively addicted to cocaine (Deroche-Garmonet & others, 2004).

2. ***Addictions cannot be overcome voluntarily; therapy is required.*** Some addicts do benefit from treatment programs. Alcoholics Anonymous, for example, has supported many people in overcoming their alcohol dependence. But the recovery rates of treated and untreated groups differ less than one might suppose. Helpful as therapy or group support may be, people often recover on their own.

   Moreover, viewing addiction as a disease, as diabetes is a disease, can undermine self-confidence and the will to change cravings that, without treatment, "one cannot fight." And that, critics say, would be unfortunate, for many people do voluntarily stop using addictive drugs, without treatment. Most of America's 41 million ex-smokers kicked the habit on their own, usually after prior failed efforts or treatments.

3. ***We can extend the concept of addiction to cover not just drug dependencies, but a whole spectrum of repetitive, pleasure-seeking behaviors.*** We can, and we have, but should we? The addiction-as-disease-needing-treatment idea has been suggested for a host of driven behaviors, including overeating, shopping, exercise, sex, gambling, and work. Initially, we may use the term metaphorically ("I'm a science fiction addict"), but if we begin taking the metaphor as reality, addiction can become an all-purpose excuse. Those who embezzle to feed their "gambling addiction," surf the Web half the night to satisfy their "Internet addiction," or abuse or betray to indulge their "sex addiction" can then explain away their behavior as an illness.

Sometimes, though, behaviors such as gambling or cybersex do become compulsive and dysfunctional, much like abusive drug taking (Griffiths, 2001). Is there justification for stretching the addiction concept to cover certain social behaviors? Debates over the addiction-as-disease model continue.

Psychoactive Drugs

There are at least three categories of psychoactive drugs: *depressants, stimulants,* and *hallucinogens.* Drugs in all three categories do their work at the brain's synapses, by stimulating, inhibiting, or mimicking the activity of neurotransmitters (the brain's chemical messengers). But our expectations also play a role in the way these drugs affect us.

The odds of getting hooked after trying various drugs:

Marijuana:	9 percent
Alcohol:	15 percent
Cocaine:	17 percent
Heroin:	23 percent
Tobacco:	32 percent

Source: National Academy of Science, Institute of Medicine (Brody, 2003).

■ **psychoactive drug** a chemical substance that alters perceptions and mood.

■ **tolerance** the diminishing effect with regular use of the same dose of a drug, requiring the user to take larger and larger doses before experiencing the drug's effect.

■ **withdrawal** the discomfort and distress that follow discontinuing the use of an addictive drug.

■ **physical dependence** a physiological need for a drug, marked by unpleasant withdrawal symptoms when the drug is discontinued.

■ **psychological dependence** a psychological need to use a drug, such as to relieve negative emotions.

■ **addiction** compulsive drug craving and use.

" About 70 percent of Americans have tried illicit drugs, but . . . only a few percent have done so in the last month. . . . Past age 35, the casual use of illegal drugs virtually ceases." Having sampled the pleasures and their aftereffects, "most people eventually walk away."

Neuropsychologist Michael Gazzaniga (1997)

© The New Yorker Collection 1998. Leo Cullum from cartoonbank.com. All Rights Reserved.

"That is not one of the seven habits of highly effective people."

■ **depressants** drugs (such as alcohol, barbiturates, and opiates) that reduce neural activity and slow body functions.

Depressants

17-2 : What are depressants, and what are their effects?

Depressants are drugs such as alcohol, barbiturates (tranquilizers), and opiates that calm neural activity and slow body functions.

Alcohol

True or false? In large amounts, alcohol is a depressant; in small amounts, it is a stimulant.

False. Low doses of alcohol may, indeed, enliven a drinker, but they do so by slowing brain activity that controls judgment and inhibitions. Alcohol is an equal-opportunity drug: It increases harmful tendencies—as when sexually coercive college men lower their dates' sexual inhibitions by getting them to drink (Abbey, 1991; Mosher & Anderson, 1986). And it increases helpful tendencies—as when tipsy restaurant patrons leave extravagant tips (M. Lynn, 1988). *The urges you would feel if sober are the ones you will more likely act upon when intoxicated.*

Low doses of alcohol relax the drinker by slowing sympathetic nervous system activity. In larger doses, alcohol can become a staggering problem: Reactions slow, speech slurs, skilled performance deteriorates. Paired with sleep deprivation, alcohol is a potent sedative. (Although either sleep deprivation or drinking can put a driver at risk, their combination is deadlier yet.) These physical effects, combined with lowered inhibitions, contribute to alcohol's worst consequences—the several hundred thousand lives claimed worldwide each year in alcohol-related accidents and violent crime. Car accidents occur despite most drinkers' belief (when sober) that driving under the influence of alcohol is wrong and despite their insisting that they would not do so. Yet as blood-alcohol level rises and moral judgments become less mature, people's qualms about drinking and driving lessen—and virtually all will drive home from a bar, even if given a breathalyzer test and told they are intoxicated (Denton & Krebs, 1990; MacDonald & others, 1995).

Alcohol also disrupts the processing of recent experiences into long-term memories. Thus, heavy drinkers may not recall people they met the night before or what they said or did while intoxicated. These blackouts result partly from the way alcohol suppresses REM sleep, which helps fix the day's experiences into permanent memories. MRI scans show that prolonged and excessive drinking can also affect cognition by shrinking the brain, especially in women (**FIGURE 17.2**), who have less of a stomach enzyme that digests alcohol (Wuethrich, 2001). Girls and young women can also become addicted to alcohol more quickly than boys and young men do, and they suffer lung, brain, and liver damage at lower consumption levels (CASA, 2003).

Alcohol not only impairs judgment and memory, it also reduces self-awareness (Hull & others, 1986). Compared with people who feel good about themselves, those who want to suppress their awareness of failures or shortcomings are more likely to drink. Losing a business deal, a game, or a romance sometimes elicits a drinking binge. By focusing attention on the immediate situation and away from any future consequences, alcohol also lessens impulse control (Steele & Josephs, 1990). In surveys of rapists, more than half acknowledge drinking before committing their offense (Seto & Barbaree, 1995).

College campuses are not immune to alcohol's effect. Intoxicated and sexually active university students are less likely to use condoms in a sexually stimulating context (MacDonald & others, 1996, 2000). University women under alcohol's influence find an attractive but sexually promiscuous man a more appealing potential date than they do when sober. It seems, surmise Sheila Murphy and her colleagues (1998), "that when people have been drinking, the restraining forces of reason may weaken and yield under the pressure of their desires."

A University of Illinois campus survey showed that before sexual assaults, 80 percent of the male assailants and 70 percent of the female victims had been drinking (Camper, 1990). Another survey of 89,874 American collegians found alcohol or drugs involved in 79 percent of unwanted sexual intercourse experiences (Presley & others, 1997).

Facts: College and university students drink more alcohol than their nonstudent peers, and they spend more on alcohol than on books and other beverages combined. Fraternity and sorority members drink three times as much as other students (Atwell, 1986; Malloy, 1994; Slutske, 2005). Although few university students believe they have an alcohol problem, many meet the criteria for alcohol abuse (Marlatt, 1991). As students mature with age, they drink less.

FIGURE 17.2
Alcoholism shrinks the brain
MRI scans show brain shrinkage in women with alcoholism (left) compared with women in a control group (right).

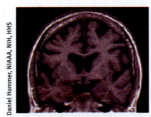 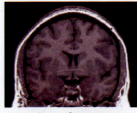

Scan of woman   Scan of woman
with alcoholism   without alcoholism

Daniel Hommer, NIAAA, NIH, HHS

Ray Ng/Time & Life Pictures/Getty Images

Dangerous disinhibition
Alcohol consumption leads to feelings of invincibility, which become especially dangerous behind the wheel of a car, such as this one totaled by a teenage drunk driver. This Colorado University Alcohol Awareness Week exhibit prompted many students to post their own anti-drinking pledges (white flags).

As with other psychoactive drugs, alcohol's behavioral effects stem not only from its alteration of brain chemistry but also from the user's expectations. Many studies have found that when people *believe* that alcohol affects social behavior in certain ways, and *believe,* rightly or wrongly, that they have been drinking alcohol, they will behave accordingly (Leigh, 1989).

Consider one such experiment by David Abrams and Terence Wilson (1983). They gave Rutgers University men who volunteered for a study on "alcohol and sexual stimulation" either an alcoholic or a nonalcoholic drink. (Both had strong tastes that masked any alcohol.) In each group, half the participants thought they were drinking alcohol and half thought they were not. After watching an erotic movie clip, the men who *thought* they had consumed alcohol were more likely to report having strong sexual fantasies and feeling guilt-free. Being able to *attribute* their sexual responses to alcohol released their inhibitions—whether they actually had drunk alcohol or not. If, as commonly believed, liquor is the quicker pick-her-upper, the effect lies partly in that powerful sex organ, the mind.

This research illustrates how different levels of analysis explain behavior: A drug's overall effect depends not only on its biological effects, but also on the psychology of the user's expectations, which vary with culture (Ward, 1994). If one culture assumes that a particular drug produces euphoria (or aggression or sexual arousal) and another does not, each culture may find its expectations fulfilled.

Barbiturates

The **barbiturate** drugs, or *tranquilizers,* mimic the effects of alcohol. Because they depress nervous system activity, barbiturates such as Nembutal, Seconal, and Amytal are sometimes prescribed to induce sleep or reduce anxiety. In larger doses, they can lead to impaired memory and judgment or even death. If combined with alcohol—as sometimes happens when people take a sleeping pill after an evening of heavy drinking—the total depressive effect on body functions can be lethal.

Opiates

The **opiates**—opium and its derivatives, morphine and heroin—also depress neural functioning. Pupils constrict, breathing slows, and lethargy sets in, as blissful pleasure replaces pain and anxiety. But for this short-term pleasure one may pay a long-term price: a gnawing craving for another fix, a need for progressively larger doses, and the extreme discomfort of withdrawal. When repeatedly flooded with an artificial opiate, the brain eventually stops producing its own opiates, the endorphins. If the artificial opiate is then withdrawn, the brain lacks the normal level of these painkilling neurotransmitters. Those who cannot or choose not to tolerate this state may pay an ultimate price—death by overdose.

Fact: **In a Harvard School of Public Health survey of 18,000 students at 140 colleges and universities, almost 9 in 10 students reported abuse by intoxicated peers, including sleep and study interruption, insults, sexual advances, and property damage (Wechsler & others, 1994). In a follow-up survey, 44 percent of students admitted binge drinking within the previous two weeks (Wechsler & others, 2002).**

Fact: **Drinking contributes to 1400 annual U.S. college student deaths, 70,000 sexual assaults, and 500,000 injuries (Hingson & others, 2002).**

■ **barbiturates** drugs that depress the activity of the central nervous system, reducing anxiety but impairing memory and judgment.

■ **opiates** opium and its derivatives, such as morphine and heroin; they depress neural activity, temporarily lessening pain and anxiety.

■ **stimulants** drugs (such as caffeine, nicotine, and the more powerful amphetamines, methamphetamine, cocaine, and Ecstasy) that excite neural activity and speed up body functions.

■ **amphetamines** drugs that stimulate neural activity, causing speeded-up body functions and associated energy and mood changes.

■ **methamphetamine** a powerfully addictive drug that stimulates the central nervous system, with speeded-up body functions and associated energy and mood changes; over time, appears to reduce baseline dopamine levels.

> "There is an overwhelming medical and scientific consensus that cigarette smoking causes lung cancer, heart disease, emphysema, and other serious diseases in smokers. Smokers are far more likely to develop serious diseases, like lung cancer, than nonsmokers."
>
> Philip Morris Companies Inc., 1999

Smoke a cigarette and nature will charge you 12 minutes—ironically, just about the length of time you spend smoking it (Discover, 1996).

Nic-a-teen

Aware that virtually all smokers start as teenagers—and that sales would plummet if no teens were enticed to smoke—cigarette companies target teens. By portraying tough, appealing, socially adept smokers, they entice teens to imitate. They are supported by the resurgence of Hollywood's modeling of smoking. With such stars as Vanessa Williams, Gwyneth Paltrow, Sharon Stone, Julia Roberts, Brad Pitt, Jim Carrey, Bruce Willis, and Arnold Schwarzenegger all looking cool or rebellious while dragging on a cigarette or cigar, teens in the mid-1990s were getting the message and becoming addicted in increasing numbers.

Stimulants

17-3 : What are stimulants, and what are their effects?

Stimulants temporarily excite neural activity and arouse body functions. People use these substances to stay awake, lose weight, or boost mood or athletic performance. Caffeine and nicotine are widely used stimulants. This category of drugs also includes **amphetamines,** and the even more powerful cocaine, Ecstasy, and **methamphetamine** ("speed") (NIDA, 2002, 2005). All strong stimulants increase heart and breathing rates and cause pupils to dilate, appetite to diminish (because blood sugar increases), and energy and self-confidence to rise. But methamphetamine has even greater effects, which can include eight hours or so of heightened energy and euphoria. The drug triggers the release of the neurotransmitter dopamine, which stimulates brain cells that enhance energy and mood.

As with other drugs, the benefits of stimulants come with a price. Stimulants—including coffee and caffeinated sodas—can be addictive and may induce an aftermath crash into fatigue, headaches, irritability, and depression (Silverman & others, 1992). Methamphetamine is highly addictive, and its aftereffects may include irritability, insomnia, hypertension, seizures, periods of disorientation, and occasional violent behavior. Over time, methamphetamine also appears to reduce baseline dopamine levels, leaving the user with permanently depressed functioning.

Nicotine

Imagine that cigarettes were harmless—except, once in every 25,000 packs, an occasional innocent-looking one is filled with dynamite instead of tobacco. Not such a bad risk of having your head blown off. But with 250 million packs a day consumed worldwide, we could expect more than 10,000 gruesome daily deaths (more than three times the 9/11 fatalities each and every day)—surely enough to have cigarettes banned everywhere.[1]

The lost lives from these dynamite-loaded cigarettes approximate those from today's actual cigarettes. Each year throughout the world, tobacco kills nearly 5 million of its 1.3 billion customers, reports the World Health Organization ([WHO] 2005). (Imagine the outrage if terrorists took down an equivalent of 25 loaded jumbo jets today, let alone tomorrow and every day thereafter.) And that number will soon double, according to WHO predictions. That means that half a billion (say that number slowly) people alive today will be killed by tobacco (Lopez, 1999).

Russel Einhorn/The Gamma Liaison Network

A teen-to-the-grave smoker has a 50 percent chance of dying from the habit, and the death is often agonizing and premature, as the Philip Morris company acknowledged in 2001. Responding to Czech Republic complaints about the health-care costs of tobacco, Philip Morris reassured the Czechs that there was actually a net "health-care cost savings due to early mortality" and the resulting savings on pensions and elderly housing (Herbert, 2001).

Eliminating smoking would increase life expectancy more than any other preventive measure. Why, then, do so many people smoke?

---

[1] This analogy, adapted here with world-based numbers, was suggested by mathematician Sam Saunders, as reported by K. C. Cole (1998).

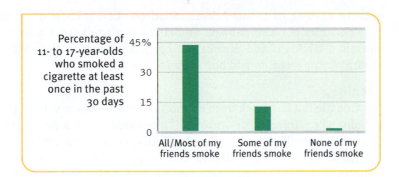

FIGURE 17.3

Peer influence
Kids don't smoke if their friends don't (Philip Morris, 2003). A correlation–causation question: Does the close link between teen smoking and friends' smoking reflect peer influence? Teens seeking similar friends? Or both? Asked "If you had to do it all over again, would you start smoking?" more than 85 percent of adult smokers answer No (Slovic & others, 2002).

Smoking usually begins during early adolescence. (If you are in college or university, and if by now the cigarette manufacturers haven't attracted your business, they almost surely never will.) Adolescents, self-conscious and often thinking the world is watching their every move, are vulnerable to smoking's allure. They may first light up to imitate cool models (often glamorous celebrities featured in popular films), to get the social reward of being accepted by other smokers, and to project a mature image (Covington & Omelich, 1988). Cigarette companies, mindful of these tendencies, have effectively modeled smoking with themes that appeal to youths: independence, adventure-seeking, social approval, sophistication. Typically, teens who start smoking also have friends who smoke, who suggest its pleasures, and who offer them cigarettes (Eiser, 1985; Evans & others, 1988; Rose & others, 1999). Among teens whose parents and best friends are nonsmokers, the smoking rate is close to zero (Moss & others, 1992, and see **FIGURE 17.3**).

Those addicted to nicotine find it very hard to quit; tobacco products are as addictive as heroin and cocaine. As with other addictions, a smoker becomes *dependent*; each year fewer than one of every seven smokers who want to quit will do so. A smoker also develops *tolerance*, eventually needing larger and larger doses to get the same effect. Quitting causes *nicotine-withdrawal* symptoms, including craving, insomnia, anxiety, and irritability. And all it takes to relieve these aversive states is a cigarette—a portable nicotine dispenser.

Nicotine, like other addictive drugs, is not only compulsive and mood-altering, it is also reinforcing. Smoking delivers its hit of nicotine within 7 seconds, triggering the release of epinephrine and norepinephrine, which in turn diminish appetite and boost alertness and mental efficiency (**FIGURE 17.4**). At the same time, nicotine stimulates the central nervous system to release neurotransmitters that calm anxiety and reduce sensitivity to pain. For example, nicotine stimulates the release of dopamine and (like heroin and morphine) opioids (Nowak, 1994; Scott & others, 2004). These rewards keep people smoking even when they wish they could stop—indeed, even when they know they are committing slow-motion suicide (Saad, 2002).

Nevertheless, half of all Americans who have ever smoked have quit, and more than 90 percent did so on their own, often after repeated attempts. For those who endure, the acute craving and withdrawal symptoms gradually dissipate

> "Humorist Dave Barry (1995) recalling why he smoked his first cigarette the summer he turned 15: "Arguments against smoking: 'It's a repulsive addiction that slowly but surely turns you into a gasping, gray-skinned, tumor-ridden invalid, hacking up brownish gobs of toxic waste from your one remaining lung.' Arguments for smoking: 'Other teen-agers are doing it.' Case closed! Let's light up!"

> "A cigarette in the hands of a Hollywood star on screen is a gun aimed at a 12- or 14-year-old."
>
> Screenwriter Joe Eszterhas, 2002

1. Arouses the brain to a state of increased alertness

2. Increases heart rate and blood pressure

3. At high levels, relaxes muscles and triggers the release of neurotransmitters that may reduce stress

4. Reduces circulation to extremities

5. Suppresses appetite for carbohydrates

FIGURE 17.4

Where there's smoke . . . : The physiological effects of nicotine
Nicotine reaches the brain within 7 seconds, twice as fast as intravenous heroin. Within minutes, the amount in the blood soars.

> "To cease smoking is the easiest thing I ever did; I ought to know because I've done it a thousand times."
>
> Mark Twain, 1835–1910

The recipe for Coca-Cola originally included an extract of the coca plant, creating a cocaine tonic for tired elderly people. Between 1896 and 1905, Coke was indeed "the real thing."

> "Cocaine makes you a new man. And the first thing that new man wants is more cocaine."
>
> Comedian George Carlin

over the ensuing six months (Ward & others, 1997). These nonsmokers may live not only healthier but also happier. Smoking correlates with higher rates of depression, chronic disabilities, and divorce (Doherty & Doherty, 1998; Vita & others, 1998). Healthy living seems to add both years to life and life to years.

Cocaine

Cocaine use is a fast track from euphoria to crash. When sniffed ("snorted"), and especially when injected or smoked ("free-based"), cocaine enters the bloodstream quickly. The result: a "rush" of euphoria that depletes the brain's supply of the neurotransmitters dopamine, serotonin, and norepinephrine (**FIGURE 17.5**). Within 15 to 30 minutes, a crash of agitated depression follows as the drug's effect wears off.

In national surveys, 5 percent of U.S. high school seniors and 5 percent of British 18- to 24-year olds reported having tried cocaine during the past year (Home Office, 2003; Johnston & others, 2005). Nearly half of the drug-using seniors had smoked *crack*, a crystallized form of cocaine. This faster-working, potent form of the drug produces a briefer but more intense high, a more intense crash, and a craving for more, which wanes after several hours only to return several days later (Gawin, 1991).

Cocaine-addicted monkeys have pressed levers more than 12,000 times to gain one cocaine injection (Siegel, 1990). Many regular cocaine users, animal and human, do become addicted. In situations that trigger aggression, ingesting cocaine may heighten reactions. Caged rats fight when given foot shocks, and they fight even more when given cocaine and foot shocks. Likewise, humans ingesting high doses of cocaine in laboratory experiments impose higher shock levels on a presumed opponent than do those receiving a placebo (Licata & others, 1993). Cocaine use may also lead to emotional disturbances, suspiciousness, convulsions, cardiac arrest, or respiratory failure.

As with all psychoactive drugs, cocaine's psychological effects depend not only on the dosage and form consumed but also on the situation and the user's expectations and personality. Given a placebo, cocaine users who *think* they are taking cocaine often have a cocainelike experience (Van Dyke & Byck, 1982).

FIGURE 17.5
Cocaine euphoria and crash

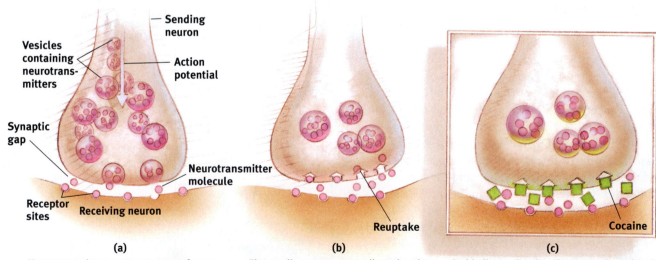

(a)
Neurotransmitters carry a message from a sending neuron across a synapse to receptor sites on a receiving neuron.

(b)
The sending neuron normally reabsorbs excess neurotransmitter molecules, a process called reuptake.

(c)
By binding to the sites that normally reabsorb neurotransmitter molecules, cocaine blocks reuptake of dopamine, norepinephrine, and serotonin (Ray & Ksir, 1990). The extra neurotransmitter molecules therefore remain in the synapse, intensifying their normal mood-altering effects and producing a euphoric rush. When the cocaine level drops, the absence of these neurotransmitters produces a crash.

Ecstasy

Ecstasy, a street name for MDMA (methylene-dioxymethamphetamine), is both a stimulant and a mild hallucinogen. As an amphetamine derivative, it triggers the release of the neurotransmitter dopamine. But its major effect is releasing stored serotonin and blocking its reabsorption, thus prolonging serotonin's feel-good flood (Braun, 2001). About a half-hour after taking an Ecstasy pill, users enter a three- to four-hour period of feelings of emotional elevation and, given a social context, connectedness with those around them ("I love everyone").

During the late 1990s, Ecstasy's popularity soared as a "club drug" taken at night clubs and all-night raves (Landry, 2002). There are, however, reasons not to be ecstatic about Ecstasy. One is its dehydrating effect, which—when combined with prolonged dancing—can lead to severe overheating, increased blood pressure, and death. Another is that long-term, repeated leeching of brain serotonin can damage serotonin-producing neurons, leading to decreased output and increased risk of permanently depressed mood (Croft & others, 2001; McCann & others, 2001; Roiser & others, 2005). Ecstasy also interferes with serotonin's control of the circadian clock (explaining the drug's disruption of sleep), suppresses the disease-fighting immune system, and impairs memory and other cognitive functions (Biello & Dafters, 2001; Pacifici & others, 2001; Reneman & others, 2001). Ecstasy delights for the night but dispirits the morrow.

AP Photo/Dale Sparks

Ecstasy
In the late 1990s, MDMA, know as Ecstasy, became popular as a "club drug." MDMA produces a euphoric high and feelings of intimacy. But its dehydrating effects, when combined with prolonged dancing, can be lethal. Repeated use also destroys serotonin-producing neurons and may permanently deflate mood and impair memory.

Hallucinogens

17-4 : What are hallucinogens, and what are their effects?

Hallucinogens distort perceptions and evoke sensory images in the absence of sensory input (which is why these drugs are also called psychedelics, meaning "mind-manifesting"). Some, such as the mild hallucinogen marijuana, are natural substances. Others are synthetic, the best known of which are LSD and MDMA (Ecstasy).

LSD

In 1943, Albert Hofmann reported perceiving "an uninterrupted stream of fantastic pictures, extraordinary shapes with intense, kaleidoscopic play of colors" (Siegel, 1984). Hofmann, a chemist, had created and accidentally ingested **LSD** (lysergic acid diethylamide). LSD and other powerful hallucinogens are chemically similar to (and therefore block the actions of) a subtype of the neurotransmitter serotonin (Jacobs, 1987).

The emotions of an LSD trip vary from euphoria to detachment to panic. As with all drug use, a person's current mood and expectations color the emotional experience, but the perceptual distortions and hallucinations have some commonalities. Psychologist Ronald Siegel (1982) reports that whether you provoke your brain to hallucinate by drugs, loss of oxygen, or extreme sensory deprivation, "it will hallucinate in basically the same way." The experience typically begins with simple geometric forms, such as a lattice, a cobweb, or a spiral. The next phase consists of more meaningful images; some may be superimposed on a tunnel or funnel, others may be replays of past emotional experiences. As the hallucination peaks, people frequently feel separated from their bodies and experience dreamlike scenes so real that they may become panic-stricken or harm themselves.

These sensations are strikingly similar to the **near-death experience,** an altered state of consciousness reported by about one-third of those who survive a brush with

■ **Ecstasy (MDMA)** a synthetic stimulant and mild hallucinogen. Produces euphoria and social intimacy, but with short-term health risks and longer-term harm to serotonin-producing neurons and to mood and cognition.

■ **hallucinogens** psychedelic ("mind-manifesting") drugs, such as LSD, that distort perceptions and evoke sensory images in the absence of sensory input.

■ **LSD** a powerful hallucinogenic drug; also known as *acid* (*lysergic acid diethyl-amide*).

■ **near-death experience** an altered state of consciousness reported after a close brush with death (such as through cardiac arrest); often similar to drug-induced hallucinations.

The Far Side® by Gary Larson © 1992 FarWorks, Inc. All Rights Reserved/Dist. by Creators Syndicate. Used with permission.

FIGURE 17.6
Near-death vision or hallucination?
Psychologist Ronald Siegel (1977) reported that people under the influence of hallucinogenic drugs often see "a bright light in the center of the field of vision. . . . The location of this point of light create[s] a tunnel-like perspective."

THE FAR SIDE®   BY GARY LARSON

death, as when revived from cardiac arrest (Moody, 1976; Ring, 1980; Schnaper, 1980). Many experience visions of tunnels (**FIGURE 17.6**), bright lights or beings of light, a replay of old memories, and out-of-body sensations (Siegel, 1980). Given that oxygen deprivation and other insults to the brain are known to produce hallucinations, it is difficult to resist wondering whether a brain under stress manufactures the near-death experience. Patients who have experienced temporal lobe seizures have reported similarly profound mystical experiences, as have solitary sailors and polar explorers while enduring monotony, isolation, and cold (Suedfeld & Mocellin, 1987).

Marijuana

Marijuana consists of the leaves and flowers of the hemp plant, which for 5000 years has been cultivated for its fiber. Whether smoked or eaten, marijuana's major active ingredient, **THC** (delta-9-tetrahydrocannabinol), produces a mix of effects that makes the drug difficult to classify. (Smoking gets the drug into the brain in about 7 seconds, producing a greater effect than does eating the drug, which causes its peak concentration to be reached at a slower, unpredictable rate.) Like alcohol, marijuana relaxes, disinhibits, and may produce a euphoric high. But marijuana is also a mild hallucinogen, amplifying sensitivity to colors, sounds, tastes, and smells. And unlike alcohol, which the body eliminates within hours, THC and its by-products linger in the body for a month or more. Thus, contrary to the usual tolerance phenomenon, regular users may achieve a high with smaller amounts of the drug than occasional users would need to get the same effect.

A user's experience can vary with the situation. If the person feels anxious or depressed, using marijuana may intensify these feelings. And the more one uses it, the greater one's risk of anxiety, depression, or possibly schizophrenia, even after controlling for other drug use and personal traits (Arseneault & others, 2002; Patton & others, 2002; Zammit & others, 2002). Daily use bodes worse than infrequent use.

The National Academy of Sciences (1982, 1999) and National Institute on Drug Abuse (2004) have identified other marijuana consequences. Like alcohol, marijuana impairs the motor coordination, perceptual skills, and reaction time necessary for safely operating an automobile or other machine. "THC causes animals to misjudge events," reports Ronald Siegel (1990, p. 163). "Pigeons wait too long to respond to buzzers or lights that tell them food is available for brief periods; and rats turn the wrong way in mazes." Marijuana also disrupts memory formation and interferes with immediate recall of information learned only a few minutes before. Such cognitive effects outlast the period of smoking (Pope & Yurgelun-Todd, 1996; Smith, 1995).

Scientists have shed light on marijuana's cognitive, mood, and motor effects with the discovery of concentrations of THC-sensitive receptors in the brain's frontal lobes, limbic system, and motor cortex (Iversen, 2000). As the 1970s discovery of receptors for morphine put researchers on the trail of morphine-like neurotransmitters (the endorphins), so the recent discovery of "cannabinoid receptors" has led to a successful hunt for naturally occurring THC-like molecules that bind with cannabinoid receptors. These molecules may naturally control pain. If so, this may help explain why marijuana can be therapeutic for those who suffer the pain, nausea, and severe

■ **THC** the major active ingredient in marijuana; triggers a variety of effects, including mild hallucinations.

TABLE 17.1

A GUIDE TO SELECTED PSYCHOACTIVE DRUGS

Drug	Type	Pleasurable Effects	Adverse Effects
Alcohol	Depressant	Initial high followed by relaxation and disinhibition	Depression, memory loss, organ damage, impaired reactions
Heroin	Depressant	Rush of euphoria, relief from pain	Depressed physiology, agonizing withdrawal
Caffeine	Stimulant	Increased alertness and wakefulness	Anxiety, restlessness, and insomnia in high doses; uncomfortable withdrawal
Methamphetamine	Stimulant	Euphoria, alertness, energy	Irritability, insomnia, hypertension, seizures
Cocaine	Stimulant	Rush of euphoria, confidence, energy	Cardiovascular stress, suspiciousness, depressive crash
Nicotine	Stimulant	Arousal and relaxation, sense of well-being	Heart disease, cancer
Ecstasy (MDMA)	Stimulant; mild hallucinogen	Emotional elevation, disinhibition	Dehydration, overheating, depressed mood, impaired cognitive and immune functioning
Marijuana	Mild hallucinogen	Enhanced sensation, relief of pain, distortion of time, relaxation	Impaired learning and memory, increased risk of psychological disorders, lung damage from smoke

weight loss associated with AIDS (Watson & others, 2000). Uses such as this have motivated legislation in some states to make the drug legally available for medical purposes. To avoid the toxicity of marijuana smoke—which, like cigarette smoke, can cause cancer, lung damage, and pregnancy complications—the Institute of Medicine recommends medical inhalers to deliver the THC.

Despite their differences, the psychoactive drugs summarized in **TABLE 17.1** share a common feature: They trigger negative aftereffects that offset their immediate positive effects and grow stronger with repetition. And that helps explain both tolerance and withdrawal. As the opposing, negative aftereffects grow stronger, it takes larger and larger doses to produce the desired high (tolerance), causing the aftereffects to worsen in the drug's absence (withdrawal). This in turn creates a need to switch off the withdrawal symptoms by taking yet more of the drug.

Influences on Drug Use

17-5: Why do some people become regular users of consciousness-altering drugs?

Drug use by North American youth increased during the 1970s. Then, with increased drug education and a more realistic and deglamorized media depiction of taking drugs, drug use declined sharply. After the early 1990s, the cultural antidrug voice softened, and drugs for a time were again glamorized in some music and films. Consider some marijuana-related trends:

- In the University of Michigan's annual survey of 15,000 U.S. high school seniors, the proportion who believe there is "great risk" in regular marijuana use rose from 35 percent in 1978 to 79 percent in 1991, then retreated to 55 percent in 2004 (Johnston & others, 2005).
- After peaking in 1978, marijuana use by U.S. high school seniors declined through 1992, then rose, but has recently been tapering off (**FIGURE 17.7**).
- In the UCLA/American Council on Education annual survey of new college and university students, support for the legalization of marijuana dropped from 53 percent in 1977 to 17 percent in 1989; support rebounded to 43 percent in 2005 (Astin & others, 1997; Pryor & others, 2005).

> "How strange would appear to be this thing that men call pleasure! And how curiously it is related to what is thought to be its opposite, pain! . . . Wherever the one is found, the other follows up behind."
>
> Plato, *Phaedo*, fourth century B.C.

FIGURE 17.7
Trends in drug use
The percentage of U.S. high school seniors who report having used alcohol, marijuana, or cocaine during the past 30 days declined from the late 1970s to 1992, when it partially rebounded for a few years. (From Johnston & others, 2005.)

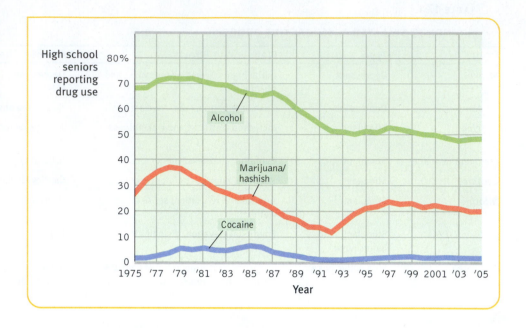

Similar ups and downs in attitude and usage since the late 1970s appear in Canadian and British surveys (Conner & McMillan, 1999; Smart & others, 1991). A 2003 survey of 100,000 teens in 35 European countries found that marijuana use in the prior 30 days ranged from zero to 1 percent in Romania and Sweden to 20 to 22 percent in Britain, Switzerland, and France (ESPAD, 2003).

For some adolescents, occasional drug use represents thrill seeking. Why, though, do other adolescents become regular drug users? In search of answers, researchers have engaged biological, psychological, and cultural levels of analysis.

Biological Influences

Some people may be biologically vulnerable to particular drugs. For example, evidence accumulates that heredity influences some aspects of alcohol abuse problems, especially those appearing by early adulthood (Crabbe, 2002):

- Adopted individuals are more susceptible to alcoholism if one or both biological parents have a history of it.
- Having an identical rather than fraternal twin with alcoholism puts one at increased risk for alcohol problems (Kendler & others, 2002). (In marijuana use also, identical twins more closely resemble one another than do fraternal twins.)
- Boys who at age 6 are excitable, impulsive, and fearless (genetically influenced traits) are more likely as teens to smoke, drink, and use other drugs (Masse & Tremblay, 1997).
- Researchers have bred rats and mice that prefer alcoholic drinks to water. One such strain has reduced levels of the brain chemical NPY; mice engineered to overproduce NPY are very sensitive to alcohol's sedating effect and drink little (Thiele & others, 1998).
- Researchers have also identified genes that are more common among people and animals predisposed to alcoholism. These genes may, for example, produce deficiencies in the brain's natural dopamine reward system.

Psychological and Social-Cultural Influences

Psychological and social-cultural influences also contribute to drug use (**FIGURE 17.8**). In their studies of youth and young adults, Michael Newcomb and L. L. Harlow (1986) found that one psychological factor is the feeling that one's life is meaningless

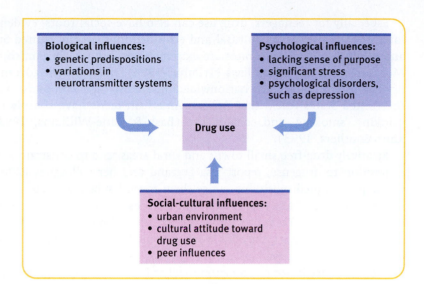

FIGURE **17.8**
Levels of analysis for drug use
The biopsychosocial approach enables researchers to investigate drug use from complementary perspectives.

and directionless, a common feeling among school dropouts who subsist without job skills, without privilege, and with little hope. When young unmarried adults leave home, alcohol and other drug use increases; when they marry and have children, it decreases (Bachman & others, 1997). Yet the ups and downs of marijuana usage over time seem due not to youth becoming more rebellious (which they have not). What predicts usage is instead the ups and downs in young people's perceptions of the degree of risk involved in regular marijuana use (**FIGURE 17.9**).

Heavy users of alcohol, marijuana, and cocaine often display other psychological influences. Many have experienced significant stress or failure and are depressed. Girls with a history of depression, eating disorders, or sexual or physical abuse are at risk for substance addiction, as are those undergoing school or neighborhood transitions (CASA, 2003; Logan & others, 2002). Monkeys, too, develop a taste for alcohol when stressed by permanent separation from their mothers at birth (Small, 2002). By temporarily dulling the pain of self-awareness, alcohol may offer a way to avoid coping with depression, anger, anxiety, or insomnia. The relief may be temporary, but behavior is often controlled more by its immediate consequences than by its later ones.

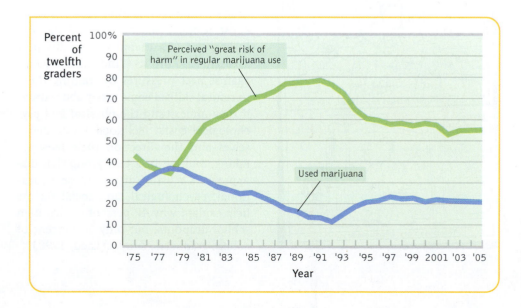

FIGURE **17.9**
Perceived marijuana risk and actual use
As the percentage of U.S. twelfth graders perceiving a "great risk" in regular marijuana use increases, the percentage having used it in the previous 30 days decreases. (Data from Johnston & others, 2005.)

Warning signs of alcoholism
- **Drinking binges**
- **Regretting things done or said when drunk**
- **Feeling low or guilty after drinking**
- **Failing to honor a resolve to drink less**
- **Drinking to alleviate depression or anxiety**
- **Avoiding family or friends when drinking**

Especially for teenagers, drug use can also have social roots, evident in differing rates of drug use across cultural and ethnic groups. In the United States, alcohol and other drug addiction rates are extremely low among the Amish, Mennonites, Mormons, and Orthodox Jews (Trimble, 1994). Independent government studies of drug use in households nationwide and among high schoolers in all regions of the United States reveal that African-American teens have sharply lower rates of drinking, smoking, and cocaine use (Bass & Kane-Williams, 1993; ISR, 2003; Kann & others, 1993).

Relatively drug-free small towns and rural areas tend to constrain any genetic predisposition to drug use, report Lisa Legrand and her colleagues (2005). For those whose genetic predispositions nudge them toward substance use, "cities offer more opportunities" and less supervision. But in cities or rural areas, peers influence attitudes about drugs. They also throw the parties and provide the drugs. If an adolescent's friends use drugs, the odds are that he or she will, too. If the friends do not, the opportunity may not even arise.

Peer influence is not just a matter of what friends do and say but also of what adolescents *believe* friends are doing and favoring. In one survey of sixth graders in 22 U.S. states, 14 percent believed their friends had smoked marijuana, though only 4 percent acknowledged doing so (Wren, 1999). When the drug is alcohol, young adolescents consume more after overestimating their friends' use (Aas & Klepp, 1992; Graham & others, 1991). University students are not immune to such misperceptions: Drinking dominates social occasions partly because students overestimate their fellow students' enthusiasm for alcohol and underestimate their views of its risks (Prentice & Miller, 1993; Self, 1994).

People whose beginning use was influenced by their peers are more likely to stop using drugs when friends stop or the social network changes (Kandel & Raveis, 1989). Most soldiers who became drug-addicted while in Vietnam ceased their drug use after returning home (Robins & others, 1974). Teenagers who come from happy families and do well in school tend not to use drugs, largely because they rarely associate with those who do (Oetting & Beauvais, 1987, 1990). As always with correlations, the traffic between friends' drug use and one's own may be two-way: Our friends influence us, but we also select as friends those who share our likes and dislikes.

SNAPSHOTS

Once upon a time, peer pressure caused Bob to start smoking.

RESTAURANT

Twenty years later, it forces him to quit.

© Jason Love

(c) Love A[4]

The findings suggest three possible channels of influence for drug prevention and treatment programs: (1) education about the long-term costs of a drug's temporary pleasures, (2) efforts to boost people's self-esteem and purpose in life, and (3) attempts to modify peer associations or to "inoculate" youth against peer pressures by training them in refusal skills. People rarely abuse drugs if they understand the physical and psychological costs, feel good about themselves and the direction their lives are taking, and are in a peer group that disapproves of using drugs. These educational, psychological, and social factors help explain why 42 percent of U.S. high school dropouts, but only 15 percent of college graduates, smoke (Ladd, 1998).

>> MODULE REVIEW

17-1: What are dependence and addiction? Can substance abusers overcome their addictions?

Depressants, stimulants, and hallucinogens are the three main categories of *psychoactive drugs* (substances that alter perceptions and mood); all interfere with the activity of chemical messengers (neurotransmitters) at synapses in the brain. Their effects also depend on the user's expectations. Continued use of psychoactive drugs produces *tolerance* (requiring larger doses to achieve the same effect) and may lead to *physical* or *psychological dependence*. *Addiction* is compulsive drug craving and use. Users who are physically dependent will experience *withdrawal*. Nevertheless, many people overcome addiction, some without the help of therapists.

17-2: What are depressants, and what are their effects?

Depressants, such as alcohol, *barbiturates*, and the *opiates*, dampen neural activity and slow body functions. Alcohol tends to disinhibit—it increases the likelihood that we will act on our impulses, whether harmful or helpful. It also slows nervous system activity, impairs judgment, reduces self-awareness, and disrupts memory processes by suppressing REM sleep. User expectations strongly influence alcohol's behavioral effects.

17-3: What are stimulants, and what are their effects?

Stimulants—caffeine, nicotine, the *amphetamines*, cocaine, and *Ecstasy*—excite neural activity and speed up body functions. All are highly addictive. Nicotine's effects make smoking a difficult habit to kick, but the percentage of Americans who smoke is nevertheless decreasing. Continued use of *methamphetamine* may permanently reduce dopamine production. Cocaine gives users a 15- to 30-minute high, followed by a crash. Its risks include cardiovascular stress and suspiciousness. Ecstasy is a combined stimulant and mild hallucinogen that produces a euphoric high and feelings of intimacy. Its users risk immune system suppression, permanent damage to mood and memory, and (if taken during physical activity) dehydration and escalating body temperatures.

17-4: What are hallucinogens, and what are their effects?

Hallucinogens—such as *LSD* and marijuana—distort perceptions and evoke hallucinations—sensory images in the absence of sensory input. The user's mood and expectations influence the effects of LSD, but common experiences are hallucinations and emotions varying from euphoria to panic. Marijuana's main ingredient, *THC*, may trigger feelings of disinhibition, euphoria, relaxation, relief from pain, and intense sensitivity to sensory stimuli. It may also increase feelings of depression or anxiety, impair motor coordination and reaction time, disrupt memory formation, and damage lung tissue (because of the inhaled smoke). People who have experienced a *near-death experience* during a life-threatening illness or accident have reported sensations that closely parallel drug-induced hallucinations, possibly reflecting a brain under stress.

17-5: Why do some people become regular users of consciousness-altering drugs?

Psychological factors (such as stress, depression, and hopelessness) and social factors (such as peer pressure) combine to lead many people to experiment with—and sometimes become dependent on—drugs. Cultural and ethnic groups have differing rates of drug use. Some people may be biologically more likely to become dependent on drugs such as alcohol. Each type of influence—biological, psychological, and social-cultural—offers a possible path for drug prevention and treatment programs.

>> REHEARSE IT!

1. Continued use of a psychoactive drug produces tolerance. This usually means that the user will

    a. feel physical pain and intense craving.
    b. be irreversibly addicted to the substance.
    c. need to take larger doses to get the desired effect.
    d. be able to take smaller doses to get the desired effect.

2. Depressants are drugs that reduce neural activity and slow down body functions. The depressants include alcohol, barbiturates,

    a. and opiates.
    b. cocaine, and morphine.

    c. caffeine, nicotine, and marijuana.
    d. and amphetamines.

3. Alcohol is a depressant that, in significant doses, powerfully affects behavior. Because alcohol _____, it may make a person more helpful or more aggressive.

    a. causes alcoholic blackouts
    b. destroys REM sleep
    c. produces hallucinations
    d. lowers inhibitions

4. Nicotine and cocaine stimulate neural activity, speed up body functions, and

    a. induce sensory hallucinations.
    b. interfere with memory.

    c. induce a temporary sense of well-being.
    d. lead to heroin use.

5. Ecstasy, which produces euphoria and social intimacy, is both a stimulant and a mild hallucinogen. Its long-term use can

    a. depress sympathetic nervous system activity.
    b. increase the brain's supply of dopamine.
    c. deplete the brain's supply of dopamine.
    d. destroy serotonin-producing neurons.

6. About one-third of those who have survived a brush with death report near-death experiences, which are strikingly similar to the hallucinations evoked by

   a. heroin.
   b. cocaine.
   c. LSD.
   d. alcohol.

7. Smoking marijuana can relieve certain kinds of pain and nausea. It also

   a. impairs motor coordination, perception, reaction time, and memory.
   b. inhibits people's emotions.
   c. leads to dehydration and overheating.
   d. stimulates brain cell development.

8. Social explanations for drug use often focus on the social effect of peer influence. An important *psychological* contributor to drug use is

   a. inflated self-esteem.
   b. the feeling that life is meaningless and directionless.
   c. genetic predispositions.
   d. overprotective parents.

Answers: 1. c, 2. a, 3. d, 4. c, 5. d, 6. c, 7. a, 8. b.

>> Terms and Concepts to Remember

psychoactive drug, p. 216
tolerance, p. 216
withdrawal, p. 216
physical dependence, p. 216
psychological dependence, p. 216
addiction, p. 217

depressants, p. 218
barbiturates, p. 219
opiates, p. 219
stimulants, p. 220
amphetamines, p. 220
metamphetamine, p. 220

Ecstasy (MDMA), p. 223
hallucinogens, p. 223
LSD, p. 223
near-death experience, p. 223
THC, p. 224

>> Test Yourself

1. A U.S. government survey of 27,616 current or former alcohol drinkers found that 40 percent of those who began drinking before age 15 grew dependent on alcohol. The same was true of only 10 percent of those who first imbibed at ages 21 or 22 (Grant & Dawson, 1998). What possible explanations might there be for this correlation between early use and later abuse?

2. In what ways are near-death experiences similar to drug-induced hallucinations?

(Answers in Appendix C.)

Multiple-choice **self-tests** and more may be found at www.worthpublishers.com/myers.

Learning

Learning

18-1 : What is learning?

When a chinook salmon first emerges from its egg in a stream's gravel bed, its genes provide most of the behavioral instructions it needs for life. It knows instinctively how and where to swim, what to eat, and how to protect itself from predators. Following a built-in plan, the young salmon soon begins its trek to the sea. After some four years in the ocean, the mature salmon returns to its birthplace. It navigates hundreds of miles to the mouth of its home river and then, guided by the scent of its home stream, begins an upstream odyssey to its ancestral spawning ground. Once there, the salmon seeks out the exact conditions of temperature, gravel, and water flow that will facilitate its breeding. It then mates and, its life mission accomplished, dies.

Unlike salmon, we are not born with a genetic blueprint for life. Much of what we do we learn from experience. Although we struggle to find the life direction a salmon is born with, our learning gives us more flexibility. We can learn how to build grass huts or snow shelters, submarines or space stations, and thereby adapt to almost any environment. Indeed, nature's most important gift to us may be our *adaptability*—our capacity to learn new behaviors that enable us to cope with changing circumstances.

No topic is closer to the heart of psychology than *learning, a relatively permanent change in an organism's behavior due to experience*. Psychologists study the learning of visual perceptions, of moral ideas, of a drug's expected effect. They also study how learning shapes our thought and language, our motivations and emotions, our personalities and attitudes. Modules 18 through 20 examine some of the processes of learning.

> "Learning is the eye of the mind."
> Thomas Drake, *Bibliotheca Scholastica Instructissima*, 1633

Learning breeds hope. What is learnable we can potentially teach—a fact that encourages parents, educators, coaches, and animal trainers. What has been learned we can potentially change by new learning—an assumption that underlies counseling, psychotherapy, and rehabilitation programs. No matter how unhappy, unsuccessful, or unloving we are, that need not be the end of our story.

By definition, experience is key to learning. More than 200 years ago, philosophers such as John Locke and David Hume echoed Aristotle's conclusion from 2000 years earlier: We learn by *association*. Our minds naturally connect events that occur in sequence. If, after seeing and smelling freshly baked bread, you eat some and find it satisfying, then the next time you see and smell fresh bread, your experience will lead you to expect that eating it will be satisfying again. And if you associate a sound with a frightening consequence, then your fear may be aroused by the sound itself. As one 4-year-old exclaimed after watching a TV character get mugged, "If I had heard that music,

"Actually, sex just isn't that important to me."

© 1984 by Sidney Harris, *American Scientist Magazine*.

I wouldn't have gone around the corner!" (Wells, 1981).

Most of us would be unable to name the order of the songs on our favorite CD. Yet hearing the end of one piece cues (by association) an anticipation of the next. Likewise, when singing your national anthem, you associate the end of each line with the beginning of the next. (Pick a line out of the middle and notice how much harder it is to recall the *previous* line.)

Other animals also learn by association. Disturbed by a squirt of water, the sea slug *Aplysia* protectively withdraws its gill. If the squirts continue, as happens naturally in choppy water, the withdrawal response diminishes. (The slug's response *habituates*.) But if the sea slug repeatedly receives an electric shock just after being squirted, its withdrawal response to the squirt instead grows stronger. The animal relates the squirt to the impending shock. Complex animals can learn to relate outcomes with their own responses. Seals in an aquarium will repeat behaviors, such as slapping and barking, that prompt people to toss them a herring.

By linking two events that occur close together, both the sea slug and the seals exhibit *associative learning*. The sea slug associates the squirt with impending shock; the seals associate slapping and barking with receiving a herring. In both cases, the animals learned something important to their survival: to predict the immediate future.

The significance of an animal's learning is illustrated by the challenges captive-bred animals face when introduced to the wild. After being bred and raised in captivity, 11 Mexican gray wolves—extinct in the United States since 1977—were released in Arizona's Apache National Forest in 1998. Eight months later, a lone survivor was recaptured. The pen-reared wolves had

Nature without appropriate nurture
Keiko—the killer whale of *Free Willy* fame—had all the right genes for being dropped right back into his Icelandic home waters. But lacking life experience, he required caregivers to his life's end in a Norwegian fjord.

Jouanneau Thomas / CORBIS SYGMA

learned how to hunt—and to move 100 feet away from people—but had not learned to run from a human with a gun. Their story is not unusual. Twentieth-century records document 145 reintroductions of 115 species. Of those, only 11 percent produced self-sustaining populations in the wild. Successful adaptation requires both nature (the needed genetic predispositions) and nurture (a history of appropriate learning).

Conditioning is the process of learning associations. In *classical conditioning,* the topic of Module 18, we learn to associate two stimuli and thus to anticipate events. We learn that a flash of lightning signals an impending crack of thunder, and so we start to brace ourselves when lightning flashes nearby (**FIGURE 1**).

In *operant conditioning,* Module 19's focus, we learn to associate a response (our behavior) and its consequence and

FIGURE 1
Classical conditioning

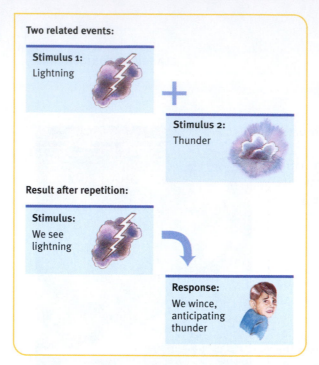

Two related events:

Stimulus 1:
Lightning

+

Stimulus 2:
Thunder

Result after repetition:

Stimulus:
We see
lightning

Response:
We wince,
anticipating
thunder

The concept of association by conditioning provokes questions: What principles influence the learning and the loss of associations? How can these principles be applied? And what really are the associations: Does the beep on a steer's pager evoke a mental representation of food, to which the steer responds by coming to the trough? Or does it make little sense to explain conditioned associations in terms of cognitive processes? (These questions are among the many being studied by researchers exploring how the brain stores and retrieves learning.)

Conditioning is not the only form of learning. As Module 20 explains, we also learn from others' experiences and examples through *observational learning*. Complex animals, such as chimpanzees, sometimes learn behaviors merely by observing others perform them. If one animal watches another learn to solve a puzzle that gains a food reward, the observing animal may perform the trick more quickly.

thus to repeat acts followed by good results (**FIGURE 2**) and avoid acts followed by bad results.

To simplify, we will consider these two types of associative learning separately in Modules 18 and 19, but you should be aware that they often occur together, as on one Japanese cattle ranch, where the clever rancher has outfitted his herd with electronic pagers, which he calls from his cellphone. After a week of training, the animals learn to associate two stimuli—the beep on their pager and the arrival of food (classical conditioning). But they also learn to associate their hustling to the food trough with the pleasure of eating (operant conditioning).

By conditioning and by observation we humans learn and adapt to our environments. We learn to expect and prepare for significant events such as food or pain (*classical conditioning*). We also learn to repeat acts that bring good results and to avoid acts that bring bad results (*operant conditioning*). By watching others we learn new behaviors (*observational learning*). And through language we also learn things we have neither experienced nor observed.

FIGURE 2
Operant conditioning

(a) Response: balancing a ball

(b) Consequence: receiving food

(c) Behavior strengthened

Classical Conditioning

18-2: How does classical conditioning demonstrate learning by association?

Pavlov's Experiments

Extending Pavlov's
    Understanding

Pavlov's Legacy

Although the idea of **associative learning**—learning that particular events occur to-gether—had long generated philosophical discussion, only in the early twentieth cen-tury did psychology's most famous research verify it. For many people, the name Ivan Pavlov (1849–1936) rings a bell. His experiments are classics, and the phenomenon he explored we justly call **classical conditioning.**

Pavlov's work also laid the foundation for many of psychologist John B. Watson's ideas. In searching for laws underlying **learning,** the relatively permanent behavioral changes that result from experience with the environment, Watson (1913) urged his colleagues to discard reference to inner thoughts, feelings, and motives. The science of psychology should instead study how organisms respond to stimuli in their environ-ments, said Watson. "Its theoretical goal is the prediction and control of behavior. In-trospection forms no essential part of its methods." Simply said, psychology should be an objective science based on observable behavior. This view, which influenced North American psychology during the first half of the twentieth century, Watson called **behaviorism.** Watson and Pavlov shared both a disdain for "mentalistic" concepts (such as consciousness) and a belief that the basic laws of learning were the same for all animals—whether dogs or humans. Few researchers today propose that psychology should ignore mental processes, but most now agree that classical conditioning is a basic form of learning by which all organisms adapt to their environment.

■ **associative learning** learning that two events (two stimuli, in classical condition-ing) occur together.

■ **classical conditioning** a type of learning in which an organism comes to associate stimuli. A neutral stimulus that signals an unconditioned stimulus (US) begins to pro-duce a response that anticipates and pre-pares for the unconditioned stimulus. Also called *Pavlovian* or *respondent conditioning*.

■ **learning** a relatively permanent change in an organism's behavior due to experience.

■ **behaviorism** the view that psychology (1) should be an objective science that (2) studies behavior without reference to mental processes. Most research psycholo-gists today agree with (1) but not with (2).

Pavlov's Experiments

18-3: How does a neutral stimulus become a CS, and what are the processes of acquisition, extinction, spontaneous recovery, generalization, and discrimination in classical conditioning?

Pavlov was driven by a lifelong passion for research. After setting aside his initial plan to follow his father into the Russian Orthodox priesthood, Pavlov received a medical degree at age 33 and spent the next two decades studying the digestive system. This work earned him Russia's first Nobel prize in 1904. But it was his novel experiments on learning, to which he devoted the last three decades of his life, that earned this feisty scientist his place in history.

Pavlov's new direction came when his cre-ative mind seized on a finding incidental to his work on the digestive system: When he put food in a dog's mouth the animal invariably salivated. Moreover, the dog began salivating to stimuli as-sociated with food—the mere sight of the food, the food dish, the presence of the person who regularly brought the food, or even the sound of that person's approaching footsteps. Initially, Pavlov considered these "psychic secretions" an annoyance—until he realized they pointed to a simple but important form of learning. From that time on, he studied learning, in the hope of better understanding the brain's workings.

Sovfoto

Ivan Pavlov
"Experimental investigation . . . should lay a solid foundation for a future true science of psychology" (1927).

■ **unconditioned response (UR)** in classical conditioning, the unlearned, naturally occurring response to the unconditioned stimulus (US), such as salivation when food is in the mouth.

■ **unconditioned stimulus (US)** in classical conditioning, a stimulus that unconditionally (naturally and automatically) triggers a response.

■ **conditioned response (CR)** in classical conditioning, the learned response to a previously neutral (but now conditioned) stimulus (CS).

■ **conditioned stimulus (CS)** in classical conditioning, an originally irrelevant stimulus that, after association with an unconditioned stimulus (US), comes to trigger a conditioned response.

At first, Pavlov and his assistants tried to imagine what the dog was thinking and feeling as it drooled in anticipation of the food. This only led them into fruitless debates. So to explore the phenomenon more objectively, they experimented. To eliminate the effect of other possible influences, they isolated the dog in a small room, secured it in a harness, and attached a device to divert its saliva to a measuring instrument. From an adjacent room they could present food—at first by sliding in a food bowl, later by blowing meat powder into the dog's mouth at a precise moment. They then paired various neutral stimuli—something the dog could see or hear—with food in the dog's mouth. If a neutral stimulus regularly signaled the arrival of food, would the dog associate the two stimuli? If so, would it begin salivating to the neutral stimulus in anticipation of the food?

The answers proved to be yes and yes. Just before placing food in the dog's mouth to produce salivation, Pavlov sounded a tone. After several pairings of tone and food, the dog, anticipating the meat powder, began salivating to the tone alone—and in later experiments, to a buzzer, a light, a touch on the leg, even the sight of a circle. (This procedure works with people, too. When Jay Gottfried and his colleagues [2003] showed some hungry young Londoners abstract figures before exposing them to the aroma of peanut butter or vanilla, their brains soon were responding in anticipation to the abstract images alone.)

Because salivation in response to food in the mouth was unlearned, Pavlov called it an **unconditioned response (UR).** Food in the mouth automatically, *unconditionally,* triggers a dog's salivary reflex (**FIGURE 18.1**). Thus, Pavlov called the food stimulus an **unconditioned stimulus (US).**

Salivation in response to the tone was *conditional* upon the dog's learning the association between the tone and the food. Today we call this learned response the **conditioned response (CR).** The previously irrelevant tone stimulus that now triggered the conditional salivation we call the **conditioned stimulus (CS).** Distinguishing these two kinds of stimuli and responses is easy. Just remember: conditioned = learned; *un*conditioned = *un*learned.

FIGURE 18.1

Pavlov's classic experiment

Pavlov presented a neutral stimulus (a tone) just before an unconditioned stimulus (food in mouth). The neutral stimulus then became a conditioned stimulus, producing a conditioned response.

BEFORE CONDITIONING

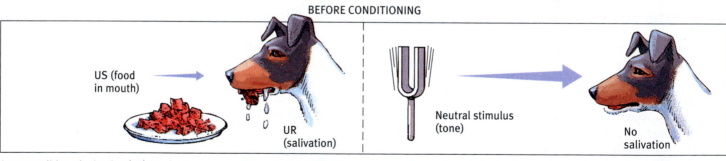

An unconditioned stimulus (US) produces an unconditioned response (UR).   A neutral stimulus produces no salivation response.

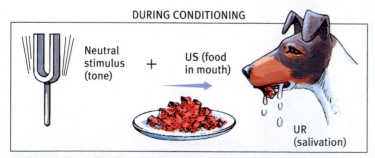

The unconditioned stimulus is repeatedly presented just after the neutral stimulus. The unconditioned stimulus continues to produce an unconditioned response.

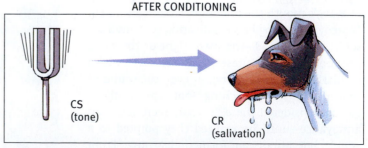

The neutral stimulus alone now produces a conditioned response (CR), thereby becoming a conditioned stimulus (CS).

PEANUTS

PEANUTS reprinted by permission of United Feature Syndicate, Inc.

A second example, drawn from more recent experiments, may help. An experimenter sounds a tone just before delivering an air puff to your eye. After several repetitions, you blink to the tone alone. What is the US? The UR? The CS? The CR?[1]

If Pavlov's demonstration of associative learning was so simple, what did he do for the next three decades? What discoveries did his research factory publish in his 532 papers on salivary conditioning (Windholz, 1997)? He and his associates explored the causes and effects of classical conditioning. Their experiments identified five major conditioning processes: *acquisition, extinction, spontaneous recovery, generalization,* and *discrimination.*

Acquisition

To understand the **acquisition,** or initial learning, of the stimulus-response relationship, Pavlov and his associates first had to confront the question of timing: How much time should elapse between presenting the neutral stimulus (the tone, the light, the touch) and the unconditioned stimulus? In most cases, the answer was "not much." With many species and procedures, half a second works well. What do you suppose would happen if the food (US) appeared before the tone (CS) rather than after? Would conditioning occur?

Not likely. Although there are exceptions, conditioning seldom occurs when the CS follows the US. Thus, classical conditioning is biologically adaptive, because it helps organisms *prepare* for good or bad events. Pavlov's tone (CS) signals an important biological event—the arrival of food (US). To a deer in the forest, the sound of a snapping twig (CS) may signal a predator's approach (US). If the good or bad event had already occurred, the CS would not likely signal anything significant.

Michael Domjan (1992, 1994, 2005) showed how the CS signals an important biological event by conditioning the sexual arousal of male Japanese quail. Just before presenting an approachable female, the researchers turned on a red light. Over time, with the red light continuing to herald a female's impending arrival, it caused the male quail to become excited. They developed a preference for their cage's red-light district, and when a female appeared, they copulated with her more quickly and released more semen and sperm (Domjan & others, 1998). All in all, the quail's capacity for classical conditioning gives it a reproductive edge. Again we see the larger lesson: Conditioning helps an animal survive and reproduce—by responding to cues that help it gain food, avoid dangers, defeat rivals, locate mates, and produce offspring (Hollis, 1997).

Objects, smells, and sights associated with sexual pleasure—even a geometric figure in one experiment—can become conditioned stimuli for sexual arousal in humans, too (Byrne, 1982). Psychologist Michael Tirrell (1990) recalls: "My first girlfriend loved

Question: If the aroma of cake baking sets your mouth to watering, what is the US? The CS? The CR? (See this module's final page for the answer.)

Remember:
US = *U*nconditioned *S*timulus
UR = *U*nconditioned *R*esponse
CS = *C*onditioned *S*timulus
CR = *C*onditioned *R*esponse

■ **acquisition** the initial stage in classical conditioning; the phase associating a neutral stimulus with an unconditioned stimulus so that the neutral stimulus comes to elicit a conditioned response.

[1]US = air puff; UR = blink to air puff; CS = tone; CR = blink to tone

FIGURE **18.2**
An unexpected CS
Onion breath does not usually produce sexual arousal. But when repeatedly paired with a passionate kiss, it can become a CS and do just that.

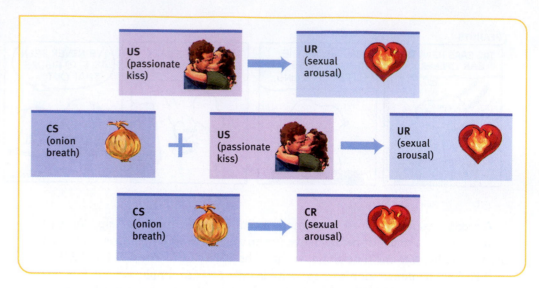

onions, so I came to associate onion breath with kissing. Before long, onion breath sent tingles up and down my spine. Oh what a feeling!" (*Questions:* What is the unconditioned stimulus here? What is the conditioned response? See **FIGURE 18.2**.)

Extinction and Spontaneous Recovery

After conditioning, what happens if the CS occurs repeatedly without the US? Will the CS continue to elicit the CR? Pavlov found that when he sounded the tone again and again without presenting food, the dogs salivated less and less. Their declining salivation illustrates **extinction,** the diminished responding that occurs when the CS (tone) no longer signals an impending US (food).

Pavlov found, however, that if he allowed several hours to elapse before sounding the tone again, the salivation to the tone would reappear spontaneously (**FIGURE 18.3**). This **spontaneous recovery**—the reappearance of a (weakened) CR after a pause—suggested to Pavlov that extinction was suppressing the CR rather than eliminating it.

After breaking up with his fire-breathing heartthrob, Tirrell also experienced extinction and spontaneous recovery. He recalls that "the smell of onion breath (CS), no longer paired with the kissing (US), lost its ability to shiver my timbers. Occasionally, though, after not sensing the aroma for a long while, smelling onion breath awakens a small version of the emotional response I once felt."

■ **extinction** the diminishing of a conditioned response; occurs in classical conditioning when an unconditioned stimulus (US) does not follow a conditioned stimulus (CS).

■ **spontaneous recovery** in classical conditioning, the reappearance, after a pause, of an extinguished conditioned response.

FIGURE **18.3**
Idealized curve of acquisition, extinction, and spontaneous recovery
The rising curve shows that the CR rapidly grows stronger as the CS and US are repeatedly paired (*acquisition*), then weakens as the CS is presented alone (*extinction*). After a pause, the CR reappears (*spontaneous recovery*).

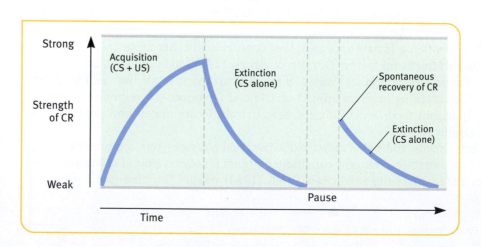

Generalization

Pavlov and his students noticed that a dog conditioned to the sound of one tone also responded somewhat to the sound of a different tone that had never been paired with food. Likewise, a dog conditioned to salivate when rubbed would also salivate somewhat when scratched (Windholz, 1989) or when stimulated on a different body part. This tendency to respond to stimuli similar to the CS is called **generalization.**

Generalization can be adaptive, as when toddlers taught to fear moving cars in the street respond similarly to trucks and motorcycles. So automatic is generalization that one Argentine writer who underwent torture still recoils with fear when he sees black shoes—his first glimpse of his torturers when they approached his cell. Generalization has been brought to the laboratory in studies comparing abused with nonabused children. Shown an angry face on a computer screen, abused children's brain-wave responses are dramatically stronger and longer lasting (Pollak & others, 1998).

Because of generalization, stimuli that are similar to naturally disgusting or appealing objects will, by association, evoke some disgust or liking. Normally desirable foods, such as fudge, are unappealing when presented in a disgusting form, as when shaped to resemble dog feces (Rozin & others, 1986). We perceive adults with childlike facial features (round face, large forehead, small chin, large eyes) as having childlike warmth, submissiveness, and naiveté (Berry & McArthur, 1986). In both cases, people's emotional reactions to one stimulus generalize to similar stimuli.

© UW-Madison News & Public Affairs. Photo by Jeff Miller

Discrimination

Pavlov's dogs also learned to respond to the sound of a particular tone and *not* to other tones. **Discrimination** is the learned ability to *distinguish* between a conditioned stimulus (which predicts the US) and other irrelevant stimuli. Being able to recognize differences is adaptive. Slightly different stimuli can be followed by vastly different consequences. Confronted by a pit bull, your heart may race; confronted by a golden retriever, it probably will not.

Extending Pavlov's Understanding

18-4 : Do cognitive processes and biological constraints affect classical conditioning?

Pavlov's and Watson's disdain for "mentalistic" concepts such as consciousness has given way to a growing realization that they underestimated the importance of *cognitive processes* (thoughts, perceptions, expectations) and *biological constraints* on an organism's learning capacity.

Cognitive Processes

The early behaviorists believed that various organisms' learned behaviors could be reduced to mindless mechanisms, so there was no need to consider cognition in rats and dogs. No longer. Robert Rescorla and Allan Wagner (1972) showed that an animal can learn the *predictability* of an event. If, for example, a shock always is preceded by a tone, and then sometimes also by a light that accompanies the tone, a rat will react with fear to the tone but not to the light. Although the light is always followed

© The New Yorker Collection, 1998, Sam Gross from cartoonbank.com. All Rights Reserved.

Stimulus generalization

"I don't care if she's a tape dispenser. I love her."

Why child abuse puts children at risk

Seth Pollak (University of Wisconsin-Madison) reports that abused children's sensitized brains react more strongly to angry faces. This generalized anxiety response may help explain their greater risk of psychological disorder.

■ **generalization** in classical conditioning, the tendency, once a response has been conditioned, for stimuli similar to the conditioned stimulus to elicit similar responses.

■ **discrimination** in classical conditioning, the learned ability to distinguish between a conditioned stimulus and stimuli that do not signal an unconditioned stimulus.

"All brains are, in essence, anticipation machines."

Daniel C. Dennett, *Consciousness Explained*, 1991

by the shock, it adds no new information; the tone is a better predictor. The more predictable the association, the stronger the conditioned response. It's as if the animal learns an *expectancy*, an awareness of how likely it is that the US will occur.

Such experiments help explain why classical conditioning treatments that ignore cognition often have limited success. For example, people receiving therapy for alcoholism sometimes are given alcohol spiked with a nauseating drug. Will they then associate alcohol with sickness? If classical conditioning were merely a matter of "stamping in" stimulus associations, we might hope so, and to some extent this does occur. However, the awareness that the nausea is induced by the drug, not the alcohol, often weakens the association between drinking alcohol and feeling sick. So, even in classical conditioning, it is (especially with humans) not only the simple CS–US association but also the thought that counts.

Biological Predispositions

Ever since Charles Darwin, scientists have assumed that all animals share a common evolutionary history and resulting commonalities in their makeup and functioning. Pavlov and Watson, for example, believed the basic laws of learning were essentially similar in all animals. So it should make little difference whether one studied pigeons or people. Moreover, it seemed that any natural response could be conditioned to any neutral stimulus. As learning researcher Gregory Kimble proclaimed in 1956, "Just about any activity of which the organism is capable can be conditioned and . . . these responses can be conditioned to any stimulus that the organism can perceive" (p. 195).

Twenty-five years later, Kimble (1981) humbly acknowledged that "half a thousand" scientific reports had proven him wrong. More than the early behaviorists realized, an animal's capacity for conditioning is constrained by its biology. Each species' predispositions prepare it to learn the associations that enhance its survival. Environments are not the whole story.

John Garcia was among those who challenged the prevailing idea that all associations can be learned equally well. While researching the effects of radiation on laboratory animals, Garcia and Robert Koelling (1966) noticed that rats began to avoid drinking water from the plastic bottles in radiation chambers. Could classical conditioning be the culprit? Might the rats have linked the plastic-tasting water (a CS) to the sickness (UR) triggered by the radiation (US)?

To test their hunch, Garcia and Koelling gave the rats a particular taste, sight, or sound (CS) and later also gave them radiation or drugs (US) that led to nausea and vomiting (UR). Two startling findings emerged: First, even if sickened as late as several hours after tasting a particular novel flavor, the rats thereafter avoided that flavor. This appeared to violate the notion that for conditioning to occur, the US must immediately follow the CS.

Second, the sickened rats developed aversions to tastes but not to sights or sounds. This contradicted the behaviorists' idea that any perceivable stimulus could serve as a CS. But it made adaptive sense, because for rats the easiest way to identify tainted food is to taste it. (If sickened after sampling a new food, they thereafter avoid the food—which makes it difficult to eradicate a population of "bait-shy" rats by poisoning.) Humans, too, seem biologically prepared to learn some things rather than others. If you become violently ill four hours after eating contaminated mussels, you will probably develop an aversion to the taste of mussels but not to the sight of the associated restaurant, its plates, the people you were with, or the music you heard there.

Garcia and Koelling's provocative experiments are but one instance in which psychological research that began with the discomfort of some laboratory animals enhanced the welfare of many others. In one well-known study, coyotes and wolves that were tempted into eating sheep carcasses laced with a sickening poison developed an aversion to sheep meat (Gustavson & others, 1974, 1976). Two wolves later penned

John Garcia

As the laboring son of California farmworkers, Garcia attended school only in the off-season during his early childhood years. After entering junior college in his late twenties, and earning his Ph.D. in his late forties, he received the American Psychological Association's Distinguished Scientific Contribution Award "for his highly original, pioneering research in conditioning and learning." He was also elected to the National Academy of Sciences.

Courtesy of John Garcia

with a live sheep seemed actually to fear it. The taste-aversion research not only saved the sheep from their predators, but also saved the sheep-shunning coyotes and wolves from ranchers and farmers who grew less adamant about destroying them. The research also stimulated later experiments that showed that conditioned taste aversion could successfully prevent baboons from raiding African gardens, raccoons from attacking chickens, and ravens and crows from feeding on crane eggs—all while preserving predators who occupy an important ecological niche (Garcia & Gustavson, 1997).

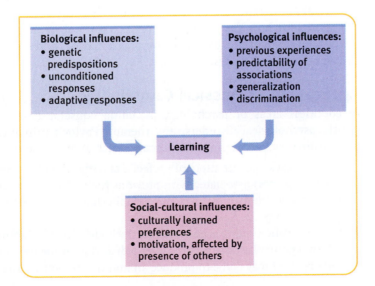

Colin Young-Wolff / Photo Edit Inc.

All these cases support Darwin's principle that natural selection favors traits that aid survival. Nature prepares the members of each species to learn those things crucial to their survival. Our ancestors who readily learned taste aversions were unlikely to eat the same toxic food again and were more likely to survive and leave descendants. Nausea, like anxiety, pain, and other bad feelings, serves a good purpose. Like a low-oil warning on a car dashboard, each alerts the body to a threat (Neese, 1991).

The discovery of biological constraints affirms the value of different levels of analysis, including the biological and cognitive (**FIGURE 18.4**), when we seek to understand phenomena such as learning. And once again, we see an important principle at work: *Learning enables animals to adapt to their environments.* Responding to stimuli that announce significant events, such as food or pain, is adaptive. So is a genetic predisposition to associate a CS with a US that follows predictably and immediately: Causes often immediately precede effects.

Often, but not always, as we saw in the taste-aversion findings. Adaptation also sheds light on this exception. The ability to discern that effect need not follow cause immediately—that poisoned food can cause sickness quite a while after it has been eaten—gives animals an adaptive advantage. Occasionally, however, our predispositions trick us. When chemotherapy triggers nausea and vomiting more than an hour following treatment, cancer patients may over time develop classically conditioned nausea (and sometimes anxiety) to the sights, sounds, and smells associated

Taste aversion

If you became violently ill after eating mussels, you probably would have a hard time eating them again. Their smell and taste would have become a CS for nausea. This learning occurs readily because our biology prepares us to learn taste aversions to toxic foods.

"Once bitten, twice shy."

G. F. Northall, *Folk-Phrases*, 1894

Biological influences:
• genetic predispositions
• unconditioned responses
• adaptive responses

Psychological influences:
• previous experiences
• predictability of associations
• generalization
• discrimination

Learning

Social-cultural influences:
• culturally learned preferences
• motivation, affected by presence of others

FIGURE 18.4
Biopsychosocial influences on learning
Today's learning theorists recognize that our learning results not only from environmental experiences, but also from cognitive and biological influences.

FIGURE **18.5**
Nausea conditioning in cancer patients

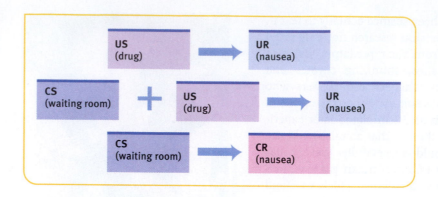

with the clinic (**FIGURE 18.5**) (Hall, 1997). Merely returning to the clinic's waiting room or seeing the nurses can provoke these conditioned feelings (Burish & Carey, 1986; Davey, 1992). Under normal circumstances, such revulsion to sickening stimuli would be adaptive.

Pavlov's Legacy

18-5: Why is Pavlov's work important?

What, then, remains of Pavlov's ideas about conditioning? A great deal. All the researchers we have met so far in this module agree that classical conditioning is a basic form of learning. Judged by today's knowledge of cognitive processes and biological predispositions, Pavlov's ideas were incomplete. But if we see further than Pavlov did, it is because we stand on his shoulders.

Why does Pavlov's work remain so important? If he had taught us only that old dogs can learn new tricks, his experiments would long ago have been forgotten. Why should we care that dogs can be conditioned to salivate at the sound of a tone? The importance lies first in this finding: *Many other responses to many other stimuli can be classically conditioned in many other organisms*—in fact, in every species tested, from earthworms to fish to dogs to monkeys to people (Schwartz, 1984). Thus, classical conditioning is one way that virtually all organisms learn to adapt to their environment.

Second, *Pavlov showed us how a process such as learning can be studied objectively*. He was proud that his methods involved virtually no subjective judgments or guesses about what went on in a dog's mind. The salivary response is an overt behavior measurable in cubic centimeters of saliva. Pavlov's success therefore suggested a scientific model for how the young discipline of psychology might proceed—by isolating the elementary building blocks of complex behaviors and studying them with objective laboratory procedures.

Applications of Classical Conditioning

In countless areas of psychology, including consciousness, motivation, emotion, health, psychological disorders, and therapy, Pavlov's principles of classical conditioning are now used to improve human health and well-being. Two examples:

- Former crack cocaine users often feel a craving when they again encounter cues (people, places) associated with previous highs. Thus, drug counselors advise addicts to steer clear of settings and paraphernalia associated with the euphoria of previous drug use.
- Classical conditioning even works on the body's disease-fighting immune system. When a particular taste accompanies a drug that influences immune responses, the taste by itself may come to produce an immune response (Ader & Cohen, 1985).

> "[Psychology's] factual and theoretical developments in this century—which have changed the study of mind and behavior as radically as genetics changed the study of heredity—have all been the product of objective analysis—that is to say, behavioristic analysis."
>
> Psychologist Donald Hebb (1980)

Pavlov's work also provided a basis for John Watson's (1913) idea that human emotions and behavior, though biologically influenced, are mainly a bundle of conditioned responses. In one famous study, Watson and Rosalie Rayner (1920; Harris, 1979) showed how specific fears might be conditioned. Their subject was an 11-month-old infant named Albert. Like most infants, "Little Albert" feared loud noises but not white rats. Watson and Rayner presented him with a white rat and, as he reached to touch it, struck a hammer against a steel bar just behind his head. After seven repetitions of seeing the rat and then hearing the frightening noise, Albert burst into tears at the mere sight of the rat (an ethically troublesome study by today's standards). What is more, five days later Albert showed generalization of his conditioned response by reacting with fear to a rabbit, a dog, and a sealskin coat, but not to dissimilar objects such as toys.

Brown Brothers

John B. Watson
Watson (1924) admitted to "going beyond my facts" when offering his famous boast: "Give me a dozen healthy infants, well-formed, and my own specified world to bring them up in and I'll guarantee to take any one at random and train him to become any type of specialist I might select—doctor, lawyer, artist, merchant-chief, and, yes, even beggar-man and thief, regardless of his talents, penchants, tendencies, abilities, vocations, and race of his ancestors."

Although Little Albert's fate is unknown, Watson's is not. After losing his professorship at Johns Hopkins University over an affair with Rayner (whom he later married), he became the J. Walter Thompson advertising agency's resident psychologist. There he used his knowledge of associative learning to conceive many successful campaigns, including one for Maxwell House that helped make the "coffee break" an American custom (Hunt, 1993).

Some psychologists, noting that Albert's fear wasn't learned quickly, had difficulty repeating Watson and Rayner's findings with other children. Nevertheless, Little Albert's case has had legendary significance for many psychologists. Some have wondered if each of us might not be a walking repository of conditioned emotions. Might our worst emotions be controlled by the application of extinction procedures or by conditioning new responses to emotion-arousing stimuli? One therapist told a patient, who for 30 years had feared going into an elevator alone, to force himself to enter 20 elevators a day. Within 10 days, his fear had nearly vanished (Ellis & Becker, 1982). This dramatic turnaround is but one example of how psychologists use behavioral techniques to treat emotional disorders.

Question: In Watson and Rayner's experiment, what was the US? The UR? The CS? The CR? (See this module's final page.)

>> MODULE REVIEW

18-1: What is learning?

Learning is a relatively permanent change in an organism's environment. Learning helps all animals, especially humans, adapt to their environments. In *associative learning*, we learn to associate two stimuli (as in classical conditioning) or a response and its consequences (as in operant conditioning). In observational learning, we learn by watching others' experiences and examples.

18-2: How does classical conditioning demonstrate learning by association?

Classical conditioning is a type of learning in which an organism comes to associate stimuli. Pavlov's work on classical conditioning laid the foundation for *behaviorism*, the view that psychology should be an objective science that studies behavior without reference to mental processes.

18-3: How does a neutral stimulus become a CS, and what are the processes of acquisition, extinction, spontaneous recovery, generalization, and discrimination in classical conditioning?

In classical conditioning, a *UR* is an event that occurs naturally (such as salivation), in response to some stimulus. A *US* is something that naturally and automatically (without learning) triggers the unlearned response (as food in the mouth triggers salivation). A *CS* is an originally neutral stimulus (such as a tone) that, through learning, comes to be associated with some unlearned response (salivating). A *CR* is the learned response (salivating) to the originally neutral but now conditioned stimulus. Classical conditioning occurs most readily when a CS is presented just before a US, preparing the organism for the upcoming event. This finding supports the view that classical conditioning

is biologically adaptive. The first stage in response learning involves the association of a CS with the US (*acquisition*). Responses are subsequently weakened if they are not reinforced (*extinction*), but they may reappear after a rest pause (*spontaneous recovery*). Responses may be triggered by stimuli similar to the conditioned stimulus (*generalization*) but not by dissimilar stimuli (*discrimination*).

18-4: Do cognitive processes and biological constraints affect classical conditioning?

The behaviorists' optimism that learning principles would generalize from one response to another and from one species to another has been tempered. Conditioning principles, we now know, are cognitively and biologically constrained. In classical conditioning, animals learn when to expect a US, and they may be aware of the link between stimuli and responses. Moreover, biological predispositions make learning some associations easier than learning others. For example, rats are biologically disposed to learn associations between, say, a peculiar taste and a sickness-producing drink, which they will then avoid. But they don't learn to avoid a sickening drink announced by a noise.

18-5: Why is Pavlov's work important?

Pavlov taught us that significant psychological phenomena can be studied objectively, and that conditioning principles have important applications, as in treating learned fears. He also demonstrated that principles of learning apply across species, although later research modified this finding somewhat to reflect the influence of cognition and biological predispositions.

>> REHEARSE IT!

1. *Learning* is defined as "a relatively permanent change in an organism's behavior due to
   a. instinct."
   b. mental processes."
   c. experience."
   d. formal education."

2. In associative learning, we learn that certain events occur together. Two forms of associative learning are classical conditioning, in which the organism associates _____, and operant conditioning, in which the organism associates _____.
   a. two responses; a response and a consequence
   b. two stimuli; two responses
   c. two stimuli; a response and a consequence
   d. two responses; two stimuli

3. After Pavlov paired a tone or other neutral stimulus with food in the mouth, dogs began salivating to the neutral stimulus alone. Salivation in response to a tone must be learned; the tone is therefore a/an
   a. conditioned stimulus.
   b. unconditioned stimulus.
   c. conditioned response.
   d. unconditioned response.

4. Dogs can learn to respond to one kind of stimulus and not to another—for example, to salivate at the sight of a circle (the CS) but not a square. Distinguishing between a CS and an irrelevant stimulus is
   a. generalization.
   b. discrimination.
   c. acquisition.
   d. spontaneous recovery.

5. Early behaviorists believed that for conditioning to occur, the unconditioned stimulus (US) must immediately follow the conditioned stimulus (CS). _____ demonstrated this was not always so.
   a. The Little Albert experiment
   b. Pavlov's experiments with dogs
   c. Watson's behaviorism theory
   d. Garcia and Koelling's taste-aversion studies

6. Taste-aversion research showed that animals develop aversions to certain tastes but not to sights or sounds. This finding supports
   a. Pavlov's demonstration of generalization.
   b. Darwin's principle that natural selection favors traits that aid survival.

c. Watson's view that study should be limited to observable behavior.

d. the early behaviorists' view that organisms can be conditioned to any stimulus.

7. After Watson and Rayner classically conditioned a small child named Albert to fear a white rat, the child later showed fear in response to a rabbit, a dog, and a sealskin coat. Little Albert's fear of objects resembling the rat illustrates

a. extinction.

b. generalization of the conditioned response.

c. spontaneous recovery.

d. discrimination between two stimuli.

Answers: 1. c, 2. c, 3. a, 4. b, 5. d, 6. b, 7. b.

>> TERMS AND CONCEPTS TO REMEMBER

associative learning, p. 235
classical conditioning, p. 235
learning, p. 235
behaviorism, p. 235
unconditioned response (UR), p. 236

unconditioned stimulus (US), p. 236
conditioned response (CR), p. 236
conditioned stimulus (CS), p. 236
acquisition, p. 237

extinction, p. 238
spontaneous recovery, p. 238
generalization, p. 239
discrimination, p. 239

>> TEST YOURSELF

1. As we develop, we learn cues that lead us to expect and prepare for good and bad events. We learn to repeat behaviors that bring rewards. And we watch others and learn. What do psychologists call these three types of learning?

2. In slasher movies, sexually arousing images of women are sometimes paired with violence against women. Based on classical conditioning principles, what might be an effect of this pairing?

(Answers in Appendix C.)

Multiple-choice **self-tests** and more may be found at www.worthpublishers.com/myers.

>> ANSWERS TO QUESTIONS WITHIN THE MODULE

Q. If the aroma of cake baking sets your mouth to watering, what is the US? The CS? The CR?

A. The cake (and its taste) is the US. The associated aroma is the CS. Salivation to the aroma is the CR.

Q. In Watson and Rayner's experiment, what was the US? The UR? The CS? The CR?

A. The US was the loud noise. The UR was the startled fear response. The CS was the rat. The CR was fear.

Operant Conditioning

19-1: What is operant conditioning, and how does it differ from classical conditioning?

It's one thing to classically condition an animal to salivate at the sound of a tone, or a child to fear cars in the street. In each case, the organism associates stimuli it does not control. It's something else to teach an elephant to walk on its hind legs or a child to say *please*. Another type of associative learning—*operant conditioning*—explains and trains such behaviors.

Classical and operant conditioning are both forms of **associative learning,** yet their difference is straightforward:

- Classical conditioning forms associations between stimuli (a CS and the US it signals). It also involves **respondent behavior**—behavior that occurs as an automatic response to some stimulus (such as salivating in response to meat powder and later in response to a tone).

- In **operant conditioning,** organisms associate their own actions with consequences. Actions followed by reinforcers increase; those followed by punishers decrease. Behavior that *operates* on the environment to *produce* rewarding or punishing stimuli is called **operant behavior.**

We can therefore distinguish classical from operant conditioning by asking: *Is the organism learning associations between events it does not control* (classical conditioning)? *Or is it learning associations between its behavior and resulting events* (operant conditioning)?

Skinner's Experiments

B. F. Skinner (1904–1990) was a college English major and an aspiring writer who, seeking a new direction, entered graduate school in psychology. He went on to become modern behaviorism's most influential and controversial figure. Skinner's work elaborated what psychologist Edward L. Thorndike (1874–1949) called the *law of effect:* Rewarded behavior is likely to recur. Using Thorndike's law of effect as a starting point, Skinner developed a *behavioral technology* that revealed principles of behavior control. These principles also enabled him to teach pigeons such unpigeonlike behaviors as walking in a figure 8, playing Ping-Pong, and keeping a missile on course by pecking at a target on a screen.

■ **associative learning** learning that certain events (a response and its consequences in operant conditioning) occur together.

■ **respondent behavior** behavior that occurs as an automatic response to some stimulus.

■ **operant conditioning** a type of learning in which behavior is strengthened if followed by a reinforcer or diminished if followed by a punisher.

■ **operant behavior** behavior that operates on the environment, producing consequences.

The law of effect at Stingray City
At this Cayman Island site, both stingrays and humans show that rewarded behaviors recur. For 35 years, fishing crews cleaned conch over this barrier reef. Stingrays began congregating to receive these yummy treats, and divers began hand-feeding the increasingly friendly rays. Today, tourists can do the same and can even pet the rays as they graze past them.

Charlotte van Oyen Witvliet

FIGURE 19.1
A Skinner box
Inside the box, the rat presses a bar (lever) for a food reward. Outside, a measuring device (not shown here) records the animal's accumulated responses.

For his pioneering studies, Skinner designed an **operant chamber,** popularly known as a Skinner box (**FIGURE 19.1**). The box has a bar or key that an animal presses or pecks to release a reward of food or water, and a device that records these responses. Operant conditioning experiments have done far more than teach us how to pull habits out of a rat. They have explored the precise conditions that foster efficient and enduring **learning.**

Shaping Behavior

In his experiments, Skinner used **shaping,** a procedure in which reinforcers, such as food, gradually guide an animal's actions toward a desired behavior. Imagine that you wanted to condition a hungry rat to press a bar. After observing how the animal naturally behaves before training, you would build on its existing behaviors. You might give the rat a food reward each time it approaches the bar. Once the rat is approaching regularly, you would require it to move closer before rewarding it, then closer still. Finally, you would require it to touch the bar before you gave it the food. With this method of successive approximations, you reward responses that are ever-closer to the final desired behavior, and you ignore all other responses. By making rewards contingent on desired behaviors, researchers and animal trainers gradually shape complex behaviors.

By shaping nonverbal organisms to discriminate between stimuli, a psychologist can also determine what they perceive. Can a dog distinguish colors? Can a baby discriminate sounds? If we can shape them to respond to one stimulus and not to another, then obviously they can perceive the difference. Experiments show that some animals are remarkably capable of forming concepts; they demonstrate this by discriminating between classes of events or objects. If an experimenter reinforces a pigeon for pecking after seeing a human face, but not after seeing other images, the pigeon will learn to recognize human faces (Herrnstein & Loveland, 1964). In this experiment, a face is a *discriminative stimulus;* like a green traffic light, it signals that a response will be reinforced. After being trained to discriminate among flowers, people, cars, and chairs, pigeons can usually identify in which of these categories a new pictured object belongs (Bhatt & others, 1988; Wasserman, 1993). They have even been trained to discriminate between Bach's music and Stravinsky's (Porter & Neuringer, 1984).

■ **operant chamber** a chamber also known as a *Skinner box,* containing a bar or key that an animal can manipulate to obtain a food or water reinforcer, with attached devices to record the animal's rate of bar pressing or key pecking. Used in operant conditioning research.

■ **learning** a relatively permanent change in an organism's behavior due to experience.

■ **shaping** an operant conditioning procedure in which reinforcers guide behavior toward closer and closer approximations of the desired behavior.

Shaping rats to save lives
A Gambian giant pouched rat, having been shaped to sniff out land mines, receives a bite of banana after successfully locating a mine during training in Mozambique.

Fred Bavendam/Peter Arnold, Inc.

A discriminating creature
University of Windsor psychologist Dale Woodyard uses a food reward to train this manatee to discriminate between objects of different shapes, colors, and sizes. Manatees remember such responses for a year or more.

In everyday life, we continually reward and shape the behavior of others, said Skinner, but we often do so unintentionally. Billy's whining, for example, annoys his mystified parents, but look how they typically deal with Billy:

Billy: *Could you tie my shoes?*
Father: *(Continues reading paper.)*
Billy: *Dad, I need my shoes tied.*
Father: *Uh, yeah, just a minute.*
Billy: *DAAAAD! TIE MY SHOES!*
Father: *How many times have I told you not to whine? Now, which shoe do we do first?*

Billy's whining is reinforced, because he gets something desirable—his dad's attention. Dad's response is reinforced because it gets rid of something aversive—Billy's whining.

HI AND LOIS

Reprinted with special permission of King Features Syndicate.

Or consider a teacher who pastes gold stars on a wall chart after the names of children scoring 100 percent on spelling tests. As everyone can then see, some children consistently get 100 percent. The others, who take the same test and may have worked harder than the academic all-stars, get no stars. The teacher would be better advised to apply the principles of operant conditioning—to reinforce all spellers for gradual improvements (successive approximations toward perfect spelling of words they find challenging).

Types of Reinforcers

19-2: What are the basic types of reinforcers?

People often refer rather loosely to the power of "rewards." This idea gains a more precise meaning in Skinner's concept of **reinforcement:** any event that strengthens (increases the frequency of) a preceding response. A reinforcer may be a tangible reward, such as food or money. It may be praise or attention—even being yelled at, for a

---

■ **reinforcer** in operant conditioning, any event that *strengthens* the behavior it follows.

■ **positive reinforcement** increasing behaviors by presenting positive stimuli, such as food. A positive reinforcer is any stimulus that, when *presented* after a response, strengthens the response.

■ **negative reinforcement** increasing behaviors by stopping or reducing negative stimuli, such as shock. A negative reinforcer is any stimulus that, when *removed* after a response, strengthens the response. (Note: negative reinforcement is *not* punishment.)

■ **primary reinforcer** an innately reinforcing stimulus, such as one that satisfies a biological need.

■ **conditioned reinforcer** a stimulus that gains its reinforcing power through its association with a primary reinforcer; also known as *secondary reinforcer.*

child hungry for attention. Or it may be an activity—borrowing the family car after doing the dishes, or taking a break after an hour of study.

Although anything that serves to increase behavior is a reinforcer, reinforcers vary with circumstances. What's reinforcing to one person (rock concert tickets) may not be to another. What's reinforcing in one situation (food when hungry) may not be in another.

Up to now, we've really been discussing **positive reinforcement,** which strengthens a response by *presenting* a typically pleasurable stimulus after a response. But there are *two* basic kinds of reinforcement (**TABLE 19.1**). The other type (**negative reinforcement**) strengthens a response by *reducing or removing* something undesirable or unpleasant. Taking aspirin may relieve your headache. Pushing the snooze button silences your annoying alarm. These consequences provide negative reinforcement and increase the likelihood that you will repeat these behaviors. When Billy stopped whining, that was a negative reinforcer for his dad. For drug addicts, the negative reinforcement of escaping withdrawal pangs can be a compelling reason to resume using (Baker & others, 2004). Note that contrary to popular usage, negative reinforcement is *not punishment;* rather, it *removes* a punishing (aversive) event.

Reuters / CORBIS

Positive reinforcement
A heat lamp positively reinforces this Taronga Zoo meerkat's behavior during a cold snap in Sydney, Australia.

TABLE 19.1

WAYS TO INCREASE BEHAVIOR

Operant Conditioning Term	Description	Examples
Positive reinforcement	*Add* a desirable stimulus	Getting a hug; receiving a paycheck
Negative reinforcement	*Remove* an aversive stimulus	Fastening seatbelt to turn off beeping

Sometimes negative and positive reinforcement coincide. Imagine a worried student who, after goofing off and getting a bad exam grade, studies harder for the next exam. This increased effort may be negatively reinforced by reduced anxiety, and positively reinforced by a better grade. Whether it works by reducing something aversive, or by giving something desirable, *reinforcement is any consequence that strengthens behavior.*

Question: In the whining Billy example, which behavior was positively reinforced and which was negatively reinforced? See this module's final page for the answer.

Primary and Conditioned Reinforcers

Primary reinforcers—getting food when hungry or having a painful headache go away—are innately satisfying. **Conditioned reinforcers,** also called *secondary reinforcers,* are learned. They get their power through their association with primary reinforcers. If a rat in a Skinner box learns that a light reliably signals that food is coming, the rat will work to turn on the light. The light has become a secondary reinforcer associated with food. Our lives are filled with secondary reinforcers—money, good grades, a pleasant tone of voice—each of which has been linked with more basic rewards. Secondary reinforcers greatly enhance our ability to influence one another.

Immediate and Delayed Reinforcers

Let's return to the imaginary shaping experiment in which you were conditioning a rat to press a bar. Before performing this "wanted" behavior, the hungry rat will engage in a sequence of "unwanted" behaviors—scratching, sniffing, and moving around. If you present food immediately after any one of these behaviors, the rat will likely repeat that rewarded behavior. But what if the rat presses the bar and you are distracted, and you delay giving the reinforcer? If the delay lasts longer than 30 seconds, the rat will not learn to press the bar. Other incidental behaviors—more sniffing and moving—will intervene and be reinforced.

Unlike rats, humans do respond to delayed reinforcers: the paycheck at the end of the week, the good grade at the end of the semester, the trophy at the end of the season.

© The New Yorker Collection, 1993, Tom Cheney from cartoonbank.com. All Rights Reserved.

"Oh, not bad. The light comes on, I press the bar, they write me a check. How about you?"

■ **continuous reinforcement** reinforcing the desired response every time it occurs.

■ **partial (intermittent) reinforcement** reinforcing a response only part of the time; results in slower acquisition of a response but much greater resistance to extinction than does continuous reinforcement.

■ **fixed-ratio schedule** in operant conditioning, a reinforcement schedule that reinforces a response only after a specified number of responses.

■ **variable-ratio schedule** in operant conditioning, a reinforcement schedule that reinforces a response after an unpredictable number of responses.

■ **fixed-interval schedule** in operant conditioning, a reinforcement schedule that reinforces a response only after a specified time has elapsed.

■ **variable-interval schedule** in operant conditioning, a reinforcement schedule that reinforces a response at unpredictable time intervals.

■ **punishment** an event that *decreases* the behavior that it follows.

> "The charm of fishing is that it is the pursuit of what is elusive but attainable, a perpetual series of occasions for hope."
> Scottish author John Buchan (1875–1940)

Indeed, to function effectively we must learn to delay gratification. In laboratory testing, some 4-year-olds show this ability. In choosing a candy, they prefer having a big reward tomorrow to munching on a small one right now. Such children tend to become socially competent and high-achieving adults (Mischel & others, 1989). A big step toward maturity—and toward gaining the most satisfying life—is learning to delay gratification, to control one's impulses in order to achieve more valued rewards (Logue, 1998a,b).

But to our detriment, small but immediate consequences (the enjoyment of watching late-night TV, for example) are sometimes more alluring than big but delayed consequences (tomorrow's sluggishness). For many teens, the immediate gratification of risky, unprotected sex in passionate moments prevails over the delayed gratifications of safe sex or saved sex (Loewenstein & Furstenberg, 1991). And for too many of us, the immediate rewards of today's gas-guzzling vehicles prevail over the bigger consequences of looming global warming, rising seas, and extreme weather.

Reinforcement Schedules

19-3 : How do different reinforcement schedules affect behavior?

So far, most of our examples have assumed **continuous reinforcement:** Reinforcing the desired response every time it occurs. Under such conditions, learning occurs rapidly, which makes continuous reinforcement preferable until a behavior is mastered. But extinction also occurs rapidly. When the reinforcement stops—when we stop presenting the food after the rat presses the bar—the behavior soon stops. If a normally dependable candy machine fails to deliver a chocolate bar twice in a row, we stop putting money into it (although a week later we may exhibit *spontaneous recovery* by trying again).

Real life rarely provides continuous reinforcement. Salespeople do not make a sale with every pitch, nor do anglers get a bite with every cast. But they persist because their efforts have occasionally been rewarded. This persistence is typical with **partial (intermittent) reinforcement** schedules, in which responses are sometimes reinforced, sometimes not (Nevin, 1988). Although initial learning is slower, intermittent reinforcement produces greater *resistance to extinction* than is found with continuous reinforcement. Imagine a pigeon that has learned to peck a key to obtain food. When the experimenter gradually phases out the delivery of food until it occurs only rarely and unpredictably, pigeons may peck 150,000 times without a reward (Skinner, 1953). With intermittent reinforcement, hope springs eternal.

Corresponding human examples come readily to mind:

- New York City's computer-controlled traffic lights made most of the city's 3250 pedestrian traffic-signal buttons at intersections obsolete. Yet occasionally, usually coincidentally, pedestrians are reinforced with a "Walk" light soon after pressing the button. So the mostly futile button pressing continues.
- Slot machines reward gamblers occasionally and unpredictably. This intermittent reinforcement affects them much as it affects pigeons: They keep trying, sometimes interminably.
- *Occasionally* giving in to children's tantrums for the sake of peace and quiet intermittently reinforces the tantrums. Lesson for parents: This is the very best procedure for making a behavior persist.

Skinner (1961) and his collaborators compared four schedules of partial reinforcement. Some are rigidly fixed, some unpredictably variable.

Fixed-ratio schedules reinforce behavior after a set number of responses. Just as coffee shops reward us with a free drink after every 10 purchased, laboratory animals may be reinforced on a fixed ratio of, say, one reinforcer for every 30 responses. Once conditioned, the animal will pause only briefly after a reinforcer and will then return to a high rate of responding (**FIGURE 19.2**).

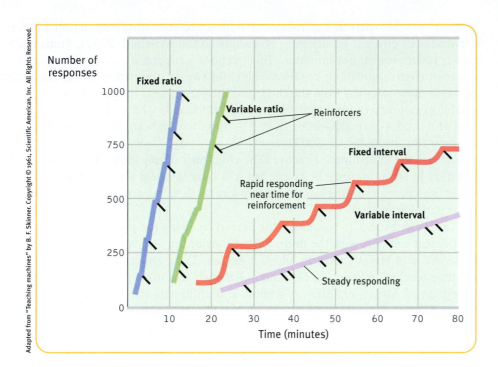

Adapted from "Teaching machines" by B. F. Skinner. Copyright © 1961, Scientific American, Inc. All Rights Reserved.

FIGURE 19.2

Intermittent reinforcement schedules
Skinner's laboratory pigeons produced these response patterns to each of four reinforcement schedules. (Reinforcers are indicated by diagonal marks.) For people, as for pigeons, reinforcement linked to number of responses (a ratio schedule) produces a higher response rate than reinforcement linked to amount of time elapsed (an interval schedule). But the predictability of the reward also matters. An unpredictable (variable) schedule produces more consistent responding than does a predictable (fixed) schedule.

Variable-ratio schedules provide reinforcers after an unpredictable number of responses. This is what slot-machine players and fly-casting anglers experience—unpredictable reinforcement—and what makes gambling and fly fishing so hard to extinguish. Like the fixed-ratio schedule, the variable-ratio schedule produces high rates of responding, because reinforcers increase as the number of responses increases.

Fixed-interval schedules reinforce the first response after a fixed time period. Just as people check more frequently for the mail as the delivery time approaches, or check to see if the Jell-O is set, pigeons on a fixed-interval schedule peck a key more frequently as the anticipated time for reward draws near, producing a choppy stop-start pattern (see Figure 19.2) rather than a steady rate of response.

Variable-interval schedules reinforce the first response after *varying* time intervals. Like the "You've got mail" that finally rewards persistence in rechecking for e-mail, variable-interval schedules tend to produce slow, steady responding. This makes sense, because there is no knowing when the waiting will be over.

Animal behaviors differ, yet Skinner (1956) contended that the reinforcement principles of operant conditioning are universal. It matters little, he said, what response, what reinforcer, or what species you use. The effect of a given reinforcement schedule is pretty much the same: "Pigeon, rat, monkey, which is which? It doesn't matter. . . . Behavior shows astonishingly similar properties."

Question: Door-to-door salespeople are reinforced by which schedule? People checking the oven to see if the cookies are done are on which schedule? Airline frequent-flyer programs that offer a free flight after every 25,000 miles of travel use which reinforcement schedule? (See this module's final page.)

Punishment

19-4 : How does punishment affect behavior?

Reinforcement increases a behavior; **punishment** does the opposite. A punisher is any consequence that *decreases* the frequency of a preceding behavior.

Swift and sure punishers can powerfully restrain unwanted behavior. The rat that is shocked after touching a forbidden object and the child who loses a treat after running into the street will learn not to repeat the behavior. Some punishments, though unintentional, are nevertheless quite effective: A dog that has learned to come running at the sound of the electric can opener will stop coming if its master starts running the machine to attract the dog and banish it to the basement.

Children see, children do?
Children who often experience physical punishment tend to display more aggression.

■ **cognitive map** a mental representation of the layout of one's environment. For example, after exploring a maze, rats act as if they have learned a cognitive map of it.

■ **latent learning** learning that occurs but is not apparent until there is an incentive to demonstrate it.

■ **intrinsic motivation** a desire to perform a behavior for its own sake.

■ **extrinsic motivation** a desire to perform a behavior due to promised rewards or threats of punishment.

Many psychologists and advocates of nonviolent parenting have pointed out the drawbacks of physical punishment (Gershoff, 2002; Marshall, 2002). Punished behavior is suppressed, not forgotten. This temporary suppression may (negatively) reinforce parents' punishing behavior. The child swears, the parent swats, the parent hears no more swearing from the child, and the parent feels the punishment was successful in stopping the behavior. No wonder spanking is a hit with so many U.S. parents of 3- and 4-year-olds—more than 9 in 10 of whom acknowledge spanking their children (Kazdin & Benjet, 2003).

But was the punishment effective? The child may simply learn discrimination: It's not okay to swear around the house, but it is okay to swear elsewhere. Similarly, the driver who gets a speeding ticket may buy a radar detector and speed freely when no radar patrol is around.

Punishment can also teach fear; the person receiving the punishment may associate the fear not only with the undesirable behavior but also with the person who administers it or the situation in which it occurs. Thus, children may come to fear a punitive teacher and try to avoid school. For such reasons, most European countries have banned hitting children in schools and child-care institutions (Leach, 1993, 1994). Eleven countries, including those in Scandinavia, have further outlawed hitting by parents, thereby extending to children the same legal protection given to spouses (EPOCH, 2000).

Finally, physical punishment may increase aggressiveness by modeling aggression as a way to cope with problems. This helps explain why so many aggressive delinquents and abusive parents come from abusive families (Straus & Gelles, 1980; Straus & others, 1997). Robert Larzelere (1996, 2000, 2004), however, notes a problem with studies that find that spanked children are at increased risk for aggression, depression, and low self-esteem. Well, yes, says Larzelere, just as people who have undergone psychotherapy are more likely to suffer depression—because they had preexisting problems that triggered the treatments. Which is the chicken and which is the egg? The correlations don't hand us an answer.

If one adjusts for preexisting antisocial behavior, then an occasional single swat or two to misbehaving 2- to 6-year-olds looks more effective, note Larzelere and Diana Baumrind and her co-authors (2002). That is especially so if the swat is used only as a backup to enhance the effectiveness of milder disciplinary tactics such as reasoning and time-out, and if it is combined with a generous dose of reassuring and reinforcing parenting. Punishment tells you what *not* to do; reinforcement tells you what *to* do. Thus, the combination is usually more effective than punishment alone. This approach has been used to change self-destructive behaviors by children who bite themselves or bang their heads. They may be mildly punished (say, with a squirt of water in the face) whenever they bite themselves, but also rewarded with positive attention and food when they behave well. The approach also works in the classroom. The teacher whose feedback on a paper says "No, but try this . . ." and "Yes, that's it!" reduces unwanted behavior by reinforcing alternative behaviors.

Parents of delinquent youth often lack this awareness of how to reinforce desirable behavior without screaming or hitting (Patterson & others, 1982). Training programs can help reframe contingencies from dire threats to positive incentives—from "You clean up your room this minute or no dinner!" to "You're welcome at the dinner table after you get your room cleaned up." When you stop to think about it, many threats of punishment are just as forceful, and perhaps more effective, if rephrased positively. Thus, "If you don't get your homework done, there'll be no car" would better be phrased as . . .

What punishment often teaches, said Skinner, is how to avoid it. Most psychologists now favor an emphasis on reinforcement: Notice people doing something right and affirm them for it.

Extending Skinner's Understanding

Skinner granted the existence of private thought processes and the biological underpinnings of behavior. Nevertheless, many psychologists criticized him for discounting the importance of these processes and predispositions.

Cognition and Operant Conditioning

19-5: Do cognitive processes and biological constraints affect operant conditioning?

A mere eight days before dying of leukemia, Skinner (1990) stood before the American Psychological Association convention for one final critique of "cognitive science," which he viewed as a throwback to early twentieth-century introspectionism. Skinner died resisting the growing belief that cognitive processes—thoughts, perceptions, expectations—have a necessary place in the science of psychology and even in our understanding of conditioning. (He regarded thoughts and emotions as behaviors that follow the same laws as other behaviors.) Yet we have seen several hints that cognitive processes might be at work in operant learning. For example, animals on a fixed-interval reinforcement schedule respond more and more frequently as the time approaches when a response will produce a reinforcer. Although a strict behaviorist would object to talk of "expectations," the animals behave as if they expected that repeating the response would soon produce the reward.

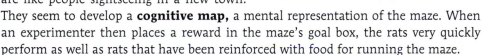
Will and Deni McIntyre/Photo Researchers

Evidence of cognitive processes has also come from studying rats in mazes. Rats exploring a maze, with no obvious reward, are like people sightseeing in a new town. They seem to develop a **cognitive map,** a mental representation of the maze. When an experimenter then places a reward in the maze's goal box, the rats very quickly perform as well as rats that have been reinforced with food for running the maze.

During their explorations, the rats seemingly experience **latent learning**—learning that becomes apparent only when there is some incentive to demonstrate it. Children, too, may learn from watching a parent, but demonstrate the learning much later when needed. The conclusion: There is more to learning than associating a response with a consequence. There is also cognition, and psychologists have provided some striking evidence of animals' cognitive abilities in solving problems and using aspects of language.

Intrinsic Motivation

The cognitive perspective has also led to an important qualification concerning the power of rewards: Promising people a reward for a task they already enjoy can backfire. Many think that offering tangible rewards will boost anyone's interest in an activity (Boggiano & others, 1987). Actually, in experiments, children promised a payoff for playing with an interesting puzzle or toy later play with the toy less than do their unpaid counterparts (Deci & others, 1999; Tang & Hall, 1995). It is as if the children think, "If I have to be bribed into doing this, it must not be worth doing for its own sake."

Excessive rewards can undermine **intrinsic motivation**—the desire to perform a behavior effectively and for its own sake. **Extrinsic motivation** is the desire to behave in certain ways to receive external rewards or avoid threatened punishment.

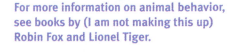
For more information on animal behavior, see books by (I am not making this up) **Robin Fox and Lionel Tiger.**

Latent learning
Animals, like people, can learn from experience, with or without reinforcement. After exploring a maze for 10 days, rats received a food reward at the end of the maze. They quickly demonstrated their prior learning of the maze—by immediately doing as well as (and even better than) rats that had been reinforced for running the maze. (From Tolman & Honzik, 1930.)

© The New Yorker Collection, 2000, Pat Byrnes, from cartoonbank.com. All Rights Reserved.

"Bathroom? Sure, it's just down the hall to the left, jog right, left, another left, straight past two more lefts, then right, and it's at the end of the third corridor on your right."

Tiger Woods' intrinsic motivation "I remember a daily ritual that we had: I would call Pop at work to ask if I could practice with him. He would always pause a second or two, keeping me in suspense, but he'd always say yes. . . . In his own way, he was teaching me initiative. You see, he never pushed me to play" (quoted in *USA Weekend,* 1997). Woods (shown here being consoled by his caddy, Steve Williams) reacted with strong emotion to his first tournament win after his father's death.

"Never try to teach a pig to sing. It wastes your time and annoys the pig."

Mark Twain (1835–1910)

To sense the difference, you might reflect on your own current experience. Are you feeling pressured to get this reading finished before a deadline? Worried about your course grade? Eager for rewards that depend on your doing well? If yes, then you are extrinsically motivated (as, to some extent, almost all students must be). Are you also finding the course material interesting? Does learning it make you feel more competent? If there were no grade at stake, might you be curious enough to want to learn the material for its own sake? If yes, intrinsic motivation also fuels your efforts. Intrinsically motivated people work and play in search of enjoyment, interest, self-expression, or challenge.

If youth sports coaches aim to promote enduring interest in an activity, and not just to pressure players into winning, they should focus on the intrinsic joy of play and reaching one's potential, note motivation researchers Edward Deci and Richard Ryan (1985, 1992, 2000). But a person's interest can survive if rewards are used neither to bribe nor to control but to signal a job well done, as in "most improved player" awards (Boggiano & others, 1985). If a reward boosts your feeling of competence after doing good work, your enjoyment of the task may increase. Rewards, rightly administered, can motivate high performance and creativity (Eisenberger & Rhoades, 2001; Henderlong & Lepper, 2002). And extrinsic rewards (such as the admissions scholarships and jobs that often follow good grades) are here to stay.

Biological Predispositions

As with classical conditioning, an animal's natural predispositions constrain its capacity for operant conditioning. Using food as a reinforcer, you can easily condition a hamster to dig or to rear up, because these are among the animal's natural food-searching behaviors. But you won't be so successful if you use food as a reinforcer to shape other hamster behaviors, such as face washing, that aren't normally associated with food or hunger (Shettleworth, 1973). Similarly, you could easily teach pigeons to flap their wings to avoid being shocked, and to peck to obtain food, because fleeing with their wings and eating with their beaks are natural pigeon behaviors. However, they would have a hard time learning to peck to avoid a shock, or to flap their wings to obtain food (Foree & LoLordo, 1973). The principle: *Biological constraints predispose organisms to learn associations that are naturally adaptive.*

Skinner's former associates Keller Breland and Marian Breland (1961) observed biological predispositions while training animals for circuses, TV shows, and movies. Like many behaviorists of the time, the Brelands assumed that operant principles would work on almost any response any animal could make. But after training 6000 animals of 38 different species, from chickens to whales, they concluded that biological

Natural athletes
Animals can most easily learn and retain behaviors that draw on their biological predispositions, such as cats' inborn tendency to leap high and land on their feet.

predispositions were more important than they had supposed. In one act, pigs trained to pick up large wooden "dollars" and deposit them in a piggy bank began to drift back to their natural ways. They would drop the coin, push it with their snouts as pigs are prone to do, pick it up again, and then repeat the sequence—delaying their food reinforcer. This *instinctive drift* occurred as the animals reverted to their biologically predisposed patterns.

Skinner's Legacy

B. F. Skinner was one of the most controversial intellectual figures of the late twentieth century. He stirred a hornet's nest by repeatedly insisting that external influences (not internal thoughts and feelings) shape behavior and by urging the use of operant principles to influence people's behavior at school, work, and home. Recognizing that behavior is shaped by its consequences, we should, he argued, administer rewards in ways that promote more desirable behavior.

Skinner's critics objected, saying that he dehumanized people by neglecting their personal freedom and by seeking to control their actions. Skinner's reply: External consequences already haphazardly control people's behavior, so why not administer those consequences for human betterment? Would not reinforcers be more humanitarian than the punishments used in homes, schools, and prisons? And if it is humbling to think that we are shaped by our histories, doesn't this very idea also give us hope that we can shape our future?

B. F. Skinner

"I am sometimes asked, 'Do you think of yourself as you think of the organisms you study?' The answer is yes. So far as I know, my behavior at any given moment has been nothing more than the product of my genetic endowment, my personal history, and the current setting" (1983).

Applications of Operant Conditioning

19-6: How might educators, business managers, and other individuals apply operant conditioning?

Psychologists are applying operant conditioning principles to help people moderate high blood pressure or gain social skills. Reinforcement technologies are also at work in schools, workplaces, and homes (Flora, 2004).

At School

A generation ago, Skinner and others advocated the use of teaching machines and textbooks that would shape learning in small steps and provide immediate reinforcement for correct responses. Such machines and texts, they said, would revolutionize education and free teachers to concentrate on their students' special needs.

To envision Skinner's idea, imagine two math teachers, each with a class of academically diverse students. Teacher A gives the whole class the same math lesson, knowing that some students will readily understand the concepts and that others will be frustrated. With so many different children, how can one teacher guide them individually?

Computer-assisted learning

Computers have helped realize Skinner's goal of individually paced instruction with immediate feedback.

The whiz kids breeze through unchallenged; the slower learners experience failure. Faced with a similar class, Teacher B paces the material according to each student's rate of learning and provides prompt feedback with positive reinforcement to both slow and fast learners. Does the individualized instruction of Teacher B seem unrealistic?

Although the predicted education revolution has not occurred, to the end of his life Skinner (1986, 1988, 1989) believed the ideal was achievable. "Good instruction demands two things," he said. "Students must be told immediately whether what they do is right or wrong and, when right, they must be directed to the step to be taken next." Computers were his final hope. For reading and math drills, the computer could be Teacher B—pacing material according to the student's rate of learning, quizzing the student to find gaps in understanding, providing immediate feedback, and keeping flawless records for the supervising teacher. Today's interactive student software, Web-based learning, and on-line testing bring us closer than ever before to achieving Skinner's ideal.

At Work

Armed with the knowledge that reinforcers influence productivity, many businesses have capitalized on psychological research, inviting employees to share profits and participate in company ownership. When workers' productivity boosts rewards for everyone, their motivation, morale, and cooperative spirit often increase (Deutsch, 1991). Reinforcement for a job well done is especially effective in boosting productivity when the desired performance is well-defined and achievable. The message for managers? *Reward specific achievable behaviors, not vaguely defined merit.* Even criticism triggers the least resentment and the greatest performance boost when specific and considerate (Baron, 1988).

© The New Yorker Collection, 1989, Ziegler from cartoonbank.com. All Rights Reserved.

It is also wise to make the reinforcement *immediate*. When IBM legend Thomas Watson observed an achievement, he would write the employee a check on the spot (Peters & Waterman, 1982). But rewards need not be material, or lavish. An effective manager may simply walk the floor and sincerely affirm people for good work, or write notes of appreciation for a completed project. As Skinner said, "How much richer would the whole world be if the reinforcers in daily life were more effectively contingent on productive work?"

At Home

Parents can take helpful advantage of operant conditioning. Parent-training researchers Michelle Wierson and Rex Forehand (1994) remind us that when parents say "Get ready for bed" but cave in to protests or defiance, they reinforce such behaviors. Eventually, exasperated, they may yell or gesture menacingly at their child, eliciting fearful compliance that in turn reinforces the parents' angry behavior. Over time, a destructive parent-child relationship develops. To disrupt this cycle, Wierson and Forehand suggest giving children attention and other reinforcers when they are behaving *well*. Target a specific behavior, reward it, and watch it increase. When children misbehave or are defiant, do not yell at or hit them. Simply explain the misbehavior and give them a time-out—for a specific time remove them from any reinforcing surroundings.

CLOSE-UP

TRAINING OUR MATES

By Amy Sutherland

For a book I was writing about a school for exotic animal trainers, I started commuting from Maine to California, where I spent my days watching students do the seemingly impossible: teaching hyenas to pirouette on command, cougars to offer their paws for a nail clipping, and baboons to skateboard.

I listened, rapt, as professional trainers explained how they taught dolphins to flip and elephants to paint. Eventually it hit me that the same techniques might work on that stubborn but lovable species, the American husband.

The central lesson I learned from exotic animal trainers is that I should reward behavior I like and ignore behavior I don't. After all, you don't get a sea lion to balance a ball on the end of its nose by nagging. The same goes for the American husband.

Back in Maine, I began thanking Scott if he threw one dirty shirt into the hamper. If he threw in two, I'd kiss him. Meanwhile, I would step over any soiled clothes on the floor without one sharp word, though I did sometimes kick them under the bed. But as he basked in my appreciation, the piles became smaller.

I was using what trainers call "approximations," rewarding the small steps toward learning a whole new behavior. . . . Once I started thinking this way, I couldn't stop. At the school in California, I'd be scribbling notes on how to walk an emu or have a wolf accept you as a pack member, but I'd be thinking, "I can't wait to try this on Scott." . . .

After two years of exotic animal training, my marriage is far smoother, my husband much easier to love. I used to take his faults personally; his dirty clothes on the floor were an affront, a symbol of how he didn't care enough about me. But thinking of my husband as an exotic species gave me the distance I needed to consider our differences more objectively.

Excerpted with permission from Sutherland, A. (2006, June 25). What Shamu Taught Me About A Happy Marriage. *New York Times*.

Finally, we can use operant conditioning in our own lives (see Close-Up: Training Our Mates). To reinforce your own desired behaviors and extinguish the undesired ones, psychologists suggest taking these steps:

1. *State your goal*—to stop smoking, eat less, or study or exercise more—in measurable terms, and make your intention public. You might, for example, aim to boost your study time by an hour a day and announce that goal to some supportive friends.

2. *Monitor* how often you engage in the behavior you wish to promote. You might log your current study time, noting under what conditions you do and don't study. (When I began writing textbooks, I logged how I spent my time throughout each day and was astonished to discover how much time I was wasting.)

3. *Reinforce* the desired behavior. To increase your study time, allow yourself a snack (or some other reinforcing activity) only after specified periods of study. Agree with your friends that you will join them for weekend activities only if you have met your realistic weekly studying goal.

4. *Reduce the incentives* gradually, as your new behaviors become more habitual, while giving yourself a mental pat on the back.

"I wrote another five hundred words. Can I have another cookie?"

© The New Yorker Collection, 2001, Mick Stevens from cartoonbank.com. All Rights Reserved.

Contrasting Classical and Operant Conditioning

Both classical and operant conditioning are forms of associative learning, and both involve acquisition, extinction, spontaneous recovery, generalization, and discrimination. The similarities are sufficient to make some researchers wonder if a single stimulus-response learning process might explain them both (Donahoe & Vegas, 2004). Their procedural difference is this: Through classical (Pavlovian) conditioning,

"O! This learning, what a thing it is."
William Shakespeare,
The Taming of the Shrew, 1597

TABLE 19.2

COMPARISON OF CLASSICAL AND OPERANT CONDITIONING

	Classical Conditioning	Operant Conditioning
Basic idea	Organism learns associations between events it doesn't control.	Organism learns associations between its behavior and resulting events.
Response	Involuntary, automatic.	Voluntary, operates on environment.
Acquisition	Associating events; CS announces US.	Associating response with a consequence (reinforcer or punisher).
Extinction	CR decreases when CS is repeatedly presented alone.	Responding decreases when reinforcement stops.
Spontaneous recovery	The reappearance, after a rest period, of an extinguished CR.	The reappearance, after a rest period, of an extinguished response.
Generalization	The tendency to respond to stimuli similar to the CS.	Organism's response to similar stimuli is also reinforced.
Discrimination	The learned ability to distinguish between a CS and other stimuli that do not signal a US.	Organism learns that certain responses, but not others, will be reinforced.
Cognitive processes	Organisms develop expectation that CS signals the arrival of US.	Organisms develop expectation that a response will be reinforced or punished; they also exhibit latent learning, without reinforcement.
Biological predispositions	Natural predispositions constrain what stimuli and responses can easily be associated.	Organisms best learn behaviors similar to their natural behaviors; unnatural behaviors instinctively drift back toward natural ones.

an organism associates different stimuli that it does not control and responds automatically (respondent behaviors) (**TABLE 19.2**). Through operant conditioning, an organism associates its operant behaviors—those that act on its environment to produce rewarding or punishing stimuli—with their consequences. Cognitive processes and biological predispositions influence both classical and operant conditioning.

REVIEWING

>> MODULE REVIEW

19-1: **What is operant conditioning, and how does it differ from classical conditioning?**

In *operant conditioning*, an organism learns associations between its own behavior and resulting events; this form of conditioning involves *operant behavior* (behavior that operates on the environment, producing consequences). In classical conditioning, the organism forms associations between behaviors it does not control; this form of conditioning involves *respondent behavior* (automatic response to some stimulus).

Expanding on Edward Thorndike's law of effect, B. F. Skinner and other researchers found that the behavior of rats or pigeons placed in an *operant chamber* (Skinner box) can be *shaped* by rewarding closer and closer approximations of the desired behavior.

19-2: **What are the basic types of reinforcers?**

Reinforcers can be *positive* (when presented after a response) or *negative* (when they cause an aversive stimulus to be withdrawn);

primary (unlearned) or *conditioned* (learned through association with primary reinforcers); and immediate or delayed. Regardless of type, all reinforcers strengthen the behaviors they follow.

19-3: **How do different reinforcement schedules affect behavior?**

Partial reinforcement schedules (*fixed-interval, fixed-ratio, variable-interval,* and *variable-ratio*) produce slower acquisition of the target behavior than does *continuous reinforcement*. They also produce greater resistance to extinction.

19-4: **How does punishment affect behavior?**

Punishment involves administering an undesirable consequence (such as spanking) or withdrawing something desirable (such as taking away a favorite toy), and attempts to decrease the frequency of a behavior (a child's disobedience). Punishment can have undesirable side effects, including suppressing rather than changing unwanted behaviors, teaching aggression, creating fear, encouraging discrimination (so that the undesirable behavior appears when the punisher is not present).

19-5: Do cognitive processes and biological constraints affect operant conditioning?

Skinner underestimated the importance of cognitive and biological constraints. Research on *cognitive mapping* and *latent learning* points to the importance of cognitive processes in *learning*. Training that attempts to override biological constraints will probably not endure, because the animals will revert to their predisposed patterns. Research also shows the limits of rewards: Excess rewards can undermine *intrinsic motivation* by leading people to attribute their behavior to outside rewards.

19-6: How might educators, business managers, and other individuals apply operant conditioning?

In school, teachers can use shaping techniques to guide students' behaviors, and interactive software and Web sites to provide immediate feedback to students. At work, managers can boost productivity and morale by rewarding well-defined and achievable behaviors. At home, parents can reward behaviors they consider desirable, but not those that are undesirable. Individually, we can use these principles to reinforce our own desired behaviors and extinguish undesirable ones.

>> Rehearse it!

1. Salivating in response to a tone paired with food is a (an) _____; pressing a bar to obtain food is a (an) _____.
   a. primary reinforcer; secondary reinforcer
   b. secondary reinforcer; primary reinforcer
   c. operant behavior; respondent behavior
   d. respondent behavior; operant behavior

2. Thorndike's law of effect states that "rewarded behavior is likely to recur." This law became the basis for operant conditioning and the "behavioral technology" developed by
   a. Ivan Pavlov.
   b. John Garcia.
   c. B. F. Skinner.
   d. John B. Watson

3. B. F. Skinner taught rats to press a bar to obtain a food pellet. To guide the rat's natural behavior toward the desired behavior, he used
   a. shaping.
   b. punishment.

   c. taste aversion.
   d. classical conditioning.

4. A reinforcer is anything presented after a response that increases the frequency of that response. If you clap your hands to stop your dog from barking, which you find irritating, the stopping of the barking is for you the termination of an aversive stimulus, or a
   a. positive reinforcer.
   b. negative reinforcer.
   c. punishment.
   d. secondary reinforcer.

5. Partial reinforcement is reinforcing a desired response only some of the times it occurs. The partial reinforcement schedule that reinforces a response at *unpredictable times* is a
   a. fixed-interval schedule.
   b. variable-interval schedule.
   c. fixed-ratio schedule.
   d. variable-ratio schedule.

6. A medieval proverb notes that "a burnt child dreads the fire." In behavioral terms, the burning is an example of a

   a. primary reinforcer.
   b. negative reinforcer.
   c. punisher.
   d. positive reinforcer.

7. Most researchers now believe that cognitive processes (thoughts, perceptions, and expectations) play an important role in learning. Evidence for the effect of these processes comes from studies in which rats
   a. spontaneously recover previously learned behavior.
   b. develop cognitive maps.
   c. exhibit respondent behavior.
   d. generalize responses.

8. Rats were carried passively through a maze and given no reward. In later trials involving food rewards, they immediately did as well as rats that had been reinforced for running the maze. The rats that had learned without reinforcement demonstrate
   a. modeling.
   b. biological predisposition.
   c. shaping.
   d. latent learning.

Answers: 1. d, 2. c, 3. a, 4. b, 5. b, 6. c, 7. b, 8. d.

>> Terms and Concepts to Remember

associative learning, p. 246
respondent behavior, p. 246
operant conditioning, p. 246
operant behavior, p. 246
operant chamber, p. 247
learning, p. 247
shaping, p. 247
reinforcer, p. 248

positive reinforcement, p 249
negative reinforcement, p. 249
primary reinforcer, p. 249
conditioned reinforcer, p. 249
continuous reinforcement, p. 250
partial (intermittent) reinforcement, p. 250
fixed-ratio schedule, p. 250

variable-ratio schedule, p. 251
fixed-interval schedule, p. 251
variable-interval schedule, p. 251
punishment, p. 251
cognitive map, p. 253
latent learning, p. 253
intrinsic motivation, p. 253
extrinsic motivation, p. 253

>> TEST YOURSELF

1. *Positive reinforcement,* *negative reinforcement,* and *punishment* are tricky concepts for many students. Can you fit the right term in the four boxes in this table? I'll do the first one (positive reinforcement) for you.

(Answer in Appendix C.)

Type of Stimulus	Give It	Take It Away
Desired (for example, a compliment):	Positive reinforcement	
Undesired/aversive (for example, an insult):		

*Multiple-choice **self-tests** and more may be found at www.worthpublishers.com/myers.*

>> ANSWERS TO QUESTIONS WITHIN THE MODULE

Q. In the "whining Billy" example, which behavior was positively reinforced and which was negatively reinforced?

A. Billy's whining was *positively* reinforced, because Billy got something desirable—his father's attention. His dad's response to the whining (doing what Billy wanted) was *negatively* reinforced, because it got rid of Billy's annoying whining.

Q. Door-to-door salespeople are reinforced by which schedule? People checking the oven to see if the cookies are done are on which schedule? Airline frequent-flyer programs that offer a free flight after every 25,000 miles of travel use which reinforcement schedule?

A. Door-to-door salespeople are reinforced on a variable-ratio schedule (after varying numbers of rings). Cookie checkers are reinforced on a fixed-interval schedule. Frequent-flyer programs use a fixed-ratio schedule.

Learning by Observation

20-1 : What is observational learning?

From drooling dogs, running rats, and pecking pigeons we have learned much about the basic processes of **learning.** But conditioning principles alone do not tell us the whole story. Among higher animals, especially humans, learning need not occur through direct experience. **Observational learning,** in which we observe and imitate others, also plays a big part. A child who sees his sister burn her fingers learns not to touch the hot stove. And a monkey watching another selecting certain pictures to gain treats learns to imitate that behavior (**FIGURE 20.1**). This process of observing and imitating a specific behavior is often called **modeling.** We learn all kinds of social behaviors by observing and imitating models. Lord Chesterfield (1694–1773) had the idea: "We are, in truth, more than half what we are by imitation."

Bandura's Experiments

Applications of Observational Learning

FIGURE 20.1
Cognitive imitation
When Monkey A (below left) sees Monkey B touch four pictures on a display screen in a certain order to gain a banana, Monkey A learns to imitate that order, even when shown a different configuration (Subiaul & others, 2004).

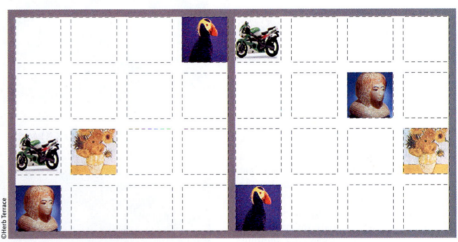

Monkey A's screen   Monkey B's screen

Neuroscientists have discovered **mirror neurons** (in a frontal-lobe area adjacent to the brain's motor cortex) that provide a neural basis for observational learning. When a monkey performs a task such as grasping, holding, or tearing, these neurons fire (Rizzolatti & others, 2002). But they also fire when the monkey observes another monkey performing the same task. When one monkey sees, these neurons mirror what another monkey does.

It's not just monkey business. PET scans reveal that humans, too, have mirror neurons in this brain area. Mirror neurons help give rise to children's empathy and to their ability to infer another's mental state (an ability known as *theory of mind*). As adults, we often feel what another feels, and we find it harder to frown when viewing a smile than when viewing a frown (Dimberg & others, 2000, 2002). Seeing a loved one's pain, it's not just our faces that mirror their emotion, but also our brains. As

■ **learning** a relatively permanent change in an organism's behavior due to experience.

■ **observational learning** learning by observing others.

■ **modeling** the process of observing and imitating a specific behavior.

■ **mirror neurons** frontal lobe neurons that fire when performing certain actions or when observing another doing so. The brain's mirroring of another's action may enable imitation and empathy.

> "Children need models more than they need critics."
>
> Joseph Joubert, *Pensées*, 1842

FIGURE 20.2 shows, the pain imagined by an empathic romantic partner triggers some of the same brain activity experienced by the one actually having the pain (Singer & others, 2004).

FIGURE 20.2
Experienced and imagined pain in the brain

Brain activity related to actual pain (left) is mirrored in the brain of an observing loved one. Empathy in the brain shows up in emotional brain areas, but not in the somatosensory cortex, which receives the physical pain input.

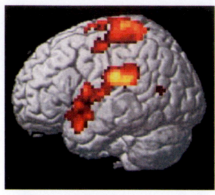

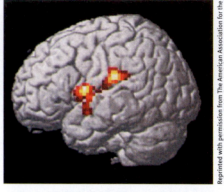

Pain   Empathy

Reprinted with permission from The American Association for the Advancement of Science, Subiaul et al., *Science* 305:407-410 (2004) ©2004 AAAS.

FIGURE 20.3
Learning from observation

This 14-month-old boy in Andrew Meltzoff's laboratory is imitating behavior he has seen on TV. In the top photo the infant leans forward and carefully watches the adult pull apart a toy. In the middle photo he has been given the toy. In the bottom photo he pulls the toy apart, imitating what he has seen the adult do.

Meltzoff, A. N. (1988). Imitation of televised models by infants. *Child Development*, 59, 1221–1229. Photos courtesy of A. N. Meltzoff and M. Hanuk.

The imitation of models shapes even very young children's behavior. Shortly after birth, an infant may imitate an adult who sticks out his tongue. By 9 months, infants will imitate novel play behaviors. And by age 14 months (FIGURE 20.3), children will imitate acts modeled on television (Meltzoff, 1988; Meltzoff & Moore, 1989, 1997). Children see, children do.

Bandura's Experiments

Picture this scene from a famous experiment by Albert Bandura, the pioneering researcher of observational learning (Bandura & others, 1961). A preschool child works on a drawing. An adult in another part of the room is building with Tinkertoys. The adult then gets up and for nearly 10 minutes pounds, kicks, and throws around the room a large inflated Bobo doll, yelling such remarks as, "Sock him in the nose. . . . Hit him down. . . . Kick him."

After observing this outburst, the child is taken to another room filled with appealing toys. Soon the experimenter interrupts the child's play and explains that she has decided to save these good toys "for the other children." She now takes the frustrated child to an adjacent room containing a few toys, including a Bobo doll. Left alone, what does the child do?

Compared with children not exposed to the adult model, those who viewed the model's actions were much more likely to lash out at the doll. Apparently, observing the aggressive outburst lowered their inhibitions. But something more than lowered inhibitions was at work, for the children also imitated the very acts they had observed and used the very words they had heard.

What determines whether we will imitate a model? Bandura believes part of the answer is reinforcements and punishments—those received by the model as well as by the imitator. By watching, we learn to anticipate a behavior's consequences in situations like those we are observing. We are especially likely to imitate people we perceive as similar to ourselves, as successful, or as admirable.

Applications of Observational Learning

The big news from Bandura's studies is that we look and we learn. Models—in one's family or neighborhood, or on TV—may have effects—good or bad.

Positive Observational Learning

The good news is that **prosocial** (positive, helpful) models can have prosocial effects. To encourage children to read, read to them and surround them with books and people who read. To increase the odds that your children will practice your religion, worship and attend religious activities with them. People who exemplify nonviolent, helpful behavior can prompt similar behavior in others. India's Mahatma Gandhi and America's Martin Luther King, Jr., both drew on the power of modeling, making nonviolent action a powerful force for social change in both countries. Parents are also powerful models. European Christians who risked their lives to rescue Jews from the Nazis usually had a close relationship with at least one parent who modeled a strong moral or humanitarian concern; this was also true for U.S. civil rights activists in the 1960s (London, 1970; Oliner & Oliner, 1988). The observational learning of morality begins early. Socially responsive toddlers who readily imitate their parents tend to become preschoolers with a strong internalized conscience (Forman & others, 2004).

Models are most effective when their actions and words are consistent. Sometimes, however, models say one thing and do another. Many parents seem to operate according to the principle "Do as I *say,* not as I do." Experiments suggest that children learn to do both (Rice & Grusec, 1975; Rushton, 1975). Exposed to a hypocrite, they tend to imitate the hypocrisy by doing what the model did and saying what the model said.

Negative Observational Learning

The bad news is that observational learning may have *antisocial effects*. This helps us understand how abusive parents might have aggressive children, and why many men who beat their wives had wife-battering fathers (Stith & others, 2000). Critics note that the intergenerational transmission of abuse could be genetic. But with monkeys we know it can be environmental. In study after study, young monkeys that received high levels of aggression when reared apart from their mothers grew up to be perpetrators of aggression (Chamove, 1980). The lessons we learn as children are not easily unlearned as adults, and they are sometimes visited on future generations.

Courtesy of Albert Bandura, Stanford University

Albert Bandura
"The Bobo doll follows me wherever I go. The photographs are published in every introductory psychology text and virtually every undergraduate takes introductory psychology. I recently checked into a Washington hotel. The clerk at the desk asked, 'Aren't you the psychologist who did the Bobo doll experiment?' I answered, 'I am afraid that will be my legacy.' He replied, 'That deserves an upgrade. I will put you in a suite in the quiet part of the hotel' " (2005).

Bob Daemmrich/The Image Works

A model grandma
This boy is learning to cook by observing his grandmother. As the sixteenth-century proverb states, "Example is better than precept."

■ **prosocial behavior** positive, constructive, helpful behavior. The opposite of antisocial behavior.

"The problem with television is that the people must sit and keep their eyes glued to a screen: The average American family hasn't time for it. Therefore the showmen are convinced that . . . television will never be a serious competitor of [radio] broadcasting."

New York Times, 1939

TV's greatest effect may stem from what it displaces. Children and adults who spend four hours a day watching TV spend four fewer hours in active pursuits—talking, studying, playing, reading, or socializing with friends. What would you have done with your extra time if you had never watched TV, and how might you therefore be different?

"Thirty seconds worth of glorification of a soap bar sells soap. Twenty-five minutes worth of glorification of violence sells violence."

U.S. Senator Paul Simon, Remarks to the Communitarian Network, 1993

Gallup surveys asked American teens (Mazzuca, 2002): "Do you feel there is too much violence in the movies, or not?" 1977: 42 percent said yes. 1999: 23 percent said yes.

TV is a powerful source of observational learning. By watching TV programs, children may "learn" that physical intimidation is an effective way to control others, that free and easy sex brings pleasure without later misery or disease, or that men are supposed to be tough and women gentle. And they have ample time to learn such lessons. During their first 18 years, most children in developed countries spend more time watching TV than they spend in school. In the United States, where 9 in 10 teens watch TV daily, someone who lives to 75 will have spent 9 years staring at the tube (Gallup, 2002; Kubey & Csikszentmihalyi, 2002). With more than a billion TV sets now in homes worldwide, CNN reaching 150 countries, and MTV broadcasting in 17 languages, television has created a global pop culture (Gunderson, 2001; Lippman, 1992).

Television viewers are learning about life from a rather peculiar storyteller, one who reflects the culture's mythology but not its reality. During the late twentieth century, the average child viewed some 8000 TV murders and 100,000 other acts of violence before finishing elementary school (Huston & others, 1992). If one includes cable programming and video rentals, the violence numbers escalate. (Popular rental films like *Die Hard 1,* with its 264 deaths, are much more violent than major network programs.) An analysis (Donnerstein, 1998) of more than 3000 network and cable programs aired during 1996–1997 revealed that nearly 6 in 10 featured violence, that 74 percent of the violence went unpunished, that 58 percent did not show the victims' pain, that nearly half the incidents involved "justified" violence, and that nearly half involved an attractive perpetrator.

Do you think viewing televised aggression influences some people to commit aggression? Was the judge who in 1993 tried two British 10-year-olds for their murder of a 2-year-old right to suspect that one possible influence was the aggressors' exposure to "violent video films"? Were the American media right to think that the teen assassins who killed 13 of their Columbine High School classmates had been influenced by repeated viewings of *Natural Born Killers* and by frequently playing splatter games such as *Doom?* To answer similar questions, researchers have conducted both correlational and experimental studies (Anderson & others, 2003).

Correlational studies do link violence viewing with violent behavior.

- In the United States and Canada, homicide rates doubled between 1957 and 1974, coinciding with the introduction and spread of TV. Moreover, census regions that were late in acquiring TV service had their homicide rate jump correspondingly later.
- White South Africans were first introduced to TV in 1975. A similar near-doubling of the homicide rate began after 1975 (Centerwall, 1989).
- Elementary school children who have a high exposure to media violence (via television, videos, and video games) also tend to be involved in more fights themselves (**FIGURE 20.4**).

"There is absolutely no doubt," concluded the 1993 American Psychological Association Commission on Violence and Youth, "that higher levels of viewing violence on television are correlated with increased acceptance of aggressive attitudes and increased aggressive behavior."

But remember: *Correlation does not imply causation,* so these correlational studies do not prove that viewing violence *causes* aggression (Freedman, 1988; McGuire, 1986). Maybe aggressive children prefer violent programs. Maybe children of neglectful or abusive parents are both more aggressive and more often left in front of the TV. Maybe violent programs simply reflect, rather than affect, violent trends.

To pin down causation, experimenters have randomly assigned some viewers to view violence and others to view entertaining nonviolence. Does viewing cruelty prepare people, when irritated, to react more cruelly? To some extent, it does. "The consensus among most of the research community," reported the National Institute of Mental Health (1982), "is that violence on television does lead to aggressive behavior by children and teenagers who watch the programs." This is especially so when an attractive

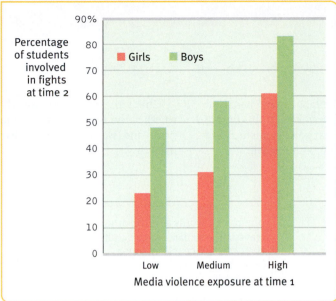

Ron Chapple / Taxi / Getty Images

FIGURE 20.4

Media violence viewing predicts future aggressive behavior

Douglas Gentile and his colleagues (2004) studied more than 400 third to fifth graders. After controlling for existing differences in hostility and aggression, the researchers reported increased aggression in those heavily exposed to violent television, videos, and video games.

person commits seemingly justified, realistic violence that goes unpunished and causes no visible pain or harm (Donnerstein, 1998).

The violence effect seems to stem from a combination of factors including *imitation* (Geen & Thomas, 1986). As we noted earlier, children as young as 14 months will imitate acts they observe on TV. One research team observed a sevenfold increase in violent play immediately after children viewed the "Power Rangers" (Boyatzis & others, 1995). Boys often precisely imitated the characters' flying karate kicks and other violent acts. Imitation may also have played a role in the first eight days after the 1999 Columbine High School massacre, when every U.S. state except Vermont had to deal with copycat threats or incidents. Pennsylvania alone had 60 threats of school violence (Cooper, 1999).

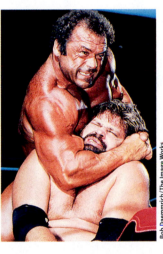

Bob Daemmrich/The Image Works

Glassman/The Image Works

Violence viewing leads to violent play

Research has shown that viewing media violence does lead to increased expression of aggression in the viewers, as with these boys imitating pro wrestlers.

But prolonged exposure to violence also *desensitizes* viewers; they become more indifferent to it when later viewing a brawl, whether on TV or in real life (Rule & Ferguson, 1986). While spending three evenings watching sexually violent movies, male viewers in one experiment became progressively less bothered by the rapes and slashings. Compared with research participants who did not watch these films, they later expressed less sympathy for domestic violence victims, and they rated the victims' injuries as less severe (Mullin & Linz, 1995).

Indeed, suggested Edward Donnerstein and his co-researchers (1987), an evil psychologist could hardly imagine a better way to make people indifferent to brutality than to expose them to a graded series of scenes, from fights to killings to the mutilations in slasher movies. Watching cruelty fosters indifference.

Albert Bandura's work—like that of Ivan Pavlov, John Watson, B. F. Skinner, and thousands of others who advanced our knowledge of learning principles—illustrates the impact that can result from single-minded devotion to a few well-defined problems and ideas. All these researchers defined the issues and impressed on us the importance of learning. As their legacy demonstrates, intellectual history is often made by people who risk going to extremes in pushing ideas to their limits (Simonton, 2000).

© The New Yorker Collection, 2000, J. Day from cartoonbank.com. All Rights Reserved.

"Don't you understand? This is life, this is what is happening. We can't switch to another channel."

REVIEWING

>> MODULE REVIEW

20-1 : What is observational learning?

In *observational learning*, we watch and imitate others' behavior. *Mirror neurons* in the frontal lobes may be involved in this type of *learning*. We are likely to imitate actions that go unpunished, and models we perceive to be like us, successful, or admirable.

Children tend to imitate what a model both does and says, whether the behavior is *prosocial* or antisocial. If a model's actions and words are inconsistent, children may imitate that hypocrisy.

>> REHEARSE IT!

1. Children learn many social behaviors by imitating parents and other models. This type of learning is called

   a. observational learning.
   b. reinforced learning.
   c. operant conditioning.
   d. classical conditioning.

2. Parents are powerful models of behavior. They are most effective in getting their children to imitate them if

   a. their words and actions are consistent.
   b. they have outgoing personalities.

   c. one parent works and the other stays home to care for the children.
   d. they carefully explain why a behavior is acceptable in adults but not in children.

3. Bandura believes that modeling is not automatic. Whether a child will imitate a model depends in part on the

   a. child's family connections to the model.
   b. child's ability to distinguish right from wrong.
   c. rewards and punishments received by the model.

   d. child's age in relation to that of the model.

4. There is considerable controversy about the effects of heavy exposure to television programs showing violence. However, most experts agree that repeated viewing of TV violence

   a. makes all viewers significantly more aggressive.
   b. has little effect on viewers.
   c. dulls the viewer's sensitivity to violence.
   d. makes viewers angry and frustrated.

Answers: 1. a, 2. a, 3. c, 4. c.

>> TERMS AND CONCEPTS TO REMEMBER

learning, p. 261
observational learning, p. 261

modeling, p. 261
mirror neurons, p. 261

prosocial behavior, p. 263

>> TEST YOURSELF

1. Jason's parents and older friends all smoke, but they advise him not to. Juan's parents and friends don't smoke, but they say nothing to deter him from doing so. Will Jason or Juan be more likely to start smoking?

   (Answer in Appendix C.)

> *Multiple-choice **self-tests** and more may be found at www.worthpublishers.com/myers.*

Memory

Memory

Be thankful for memory. We take it for granted, except when it malfunctions. But it is our memory, notes Rebecca Rupp (1998, p. xvii), that "allows us to recognize friends, neighbors, and acquaintances and call them by their names; to knit, type, drive, and play the piano; to speak English, Spanish, or Mandarin Chinese." It is our memory that accounts for time and defines our life. It is our memory that enables us to sing our national anthem, find our way home, and locate the food and water we need for survival. It is our shared memories that bind us together as Irish or Aussies, as Serbs or Albanians. And it is our memories that occasionally pit us against those whose offenses we cannot forget.

In large part, you are what you remember. Without memory, your storehouse of accumulated learning, there would be no savoring of past joys, no guilt or anger over painful recollections. You would instead live in an enduring present, each moment fresh. But each person would be a stranger, every language foreign, every task—dressing, cooking, biking—a new challenge. You would even be a stranger to yourself, lacking that continuous sense of self that extends from your distant past to your momentary present. Memory researcher James McGaugh (2003) suggested, "If you lose the ability to recall your old memories

"Waiter, I'd like to order, unless I've eaten, in which case bring me the check."

© The New Yorker Collection, 1992, Robert Mankoff from cartoonbank.com. All Rights Reserved.

then you have no life. You might as well be a rutabaga or a cabbage."

To think about memory, we first need a model of how it works. Module 21 introduces a modified version of Richard Atkinson and Richard Shiffrin's classic and influential three-stage model of memory. In that module, we also examine sensory memory, short-term/working memory, and long-term memory—thus reviewing how we move information into our memories, retain it, and later retrieve it. Module 22 looks at what happens when our memories fail us (as when we forget information, misremember it, or create false memories). That module concludes with some tips on how you can apply memory researchers' findings to your own education.

Information Processing

The Phenomenon of Memory

To a psychologist, **memory** is learning that has persisted over time, information that has been stored and can be retrieved.

Research on memory's extremes has helped us understand how memory works. At age 92, my father suffered a small stroke that had but one peculiar effect. His genial personality was intact. He was as mobile as before. He knew us and while poring over family photo albums could reminisce in detail about his past. But he had lost most of his ability to lay down new memories of conversations and everyday episodes. He could not tell me what day of the week it was. Told repeatedly of his brother-in-law's death, he expressed surprise each time he heard the news.

At the other extreme are people who would be medal winners in a memory Olympics, such as Russian journalist Shereshevskii, or S, who had merely to listen while other reporters scribbled notes (Luria, 1968). Where you and I could parrot back a string of about 7—maybe even 9—digits, S could repeat up to 70, provided they were read about 3 seconds apart in an otherwise silent room. Moreover, he could recall digits or words backward as easily as forward. His accuracy was unerring, even when recalling a list as much as 15 years later, after having memorized hundreds of others. "Yes, yes," he might recall. "This was a series you gave me once when we were in your apartment. . . . You were sitting at the table and I in the rocking chair. . . . You were wearing a gray suit and you looked at me like this. . . ."

Amazing? Yes, but consider your own pretty staggering capacity for remembering countless voices, sounds, and songs; tastes, smells, and textures; faces, places, and happenings. Imagine viewing more than 2500 slides of faces and places, for only 10 seconds each. Later you see 280 of these slides, paired with others not previously seen. If you are like the participants in this experiment by Ralph Haber (1970), you would recognize 90 percent of those you had seen before.

How do we accomplish such memory feats? How can we remember things we have not thought about for years, yet forget the name of someone we met a minute ago? How are memories stored in our brains? How can two people's memories of the same event be so different? Why will you be likely later in this module to misrecall this sentence: *"The angry rioter threw the rock at the window"*? How can we improve our memories? These will be among the questions we consider as we review more than a century of research on memory.

© The New Yorker Collection, 1987, W. Miller from cartoonbank.com. All Rights Reserved.

Studying Memory: Information-Processing Models

21-1 : How do psychologists describe the human memory system?

A model of how memory works can help us think about how we form and retrieve memories. Building a memory is somewhat like my information processing in creating this book. For each edition, I first glimpse countless items of information, including some 100,000 journal article titles. Most of it I ignore, but some things merit

■ **memory** the persistence of learning over time through the storage and retrieval of information.

■ **encoding** the processing of information into the memory system—for example, by extracting meaning.

■ **storage** the retention of encoded information over time.

■ **retrieval** the process of getting information out of memory storage.

■ **sensory memory** the immediate, very brief recording of sensory information in the memory system.

■ **short-term memory** activated memory that holds a few items briefly, such as the seven digits of a phone number while dialing, before the information is stored or forgotten.

■ **long-term memory** the relatively permanent and limitless storehouse of the memory system. Includes knowledge, skills, and experiences.

FIGURE 21.1

A modified three-stage processing model of memory

Today's researchers recognize other ways long-term memories form. For example, as we will see, some information slips into long-term memory via a "back door," without our having consciously attended to it. And we have learned that short-term memory is more than passive rehearsal; it is better termed *working memory* to recognize the active processing that occurs there.

temporary storage in my briefcase for more detailed processing later. Most of these items I eventually discard. The rest—typically about 3000 articles and news items—gets organized and filed for long-term storage. Later, I retrieve this information and draw from it as I spin the story of today's psychology. You, too, must select, process, store, and retrieve information, not only in researching and writing your term papers, but also in learning skills and processing countless daily events.

In some ways, our memory is like a computer's information-processing system. To remember any event, we must *get information into our brain* (**encoding**), *retain* that information (**storage**), and later *get it back out* (**retrieval**). Consider how a computer *encodes, stores,* and *retrieves* information. First, it translates input (keystrokes) into an electronic language, much as the brain encodes sensory information into a neural language. The computer permanently stores vast amounts of information on a disk, from which it can later be retrieved.

Like all analogies, the computer model has its limits. Our memories are less literal and more fragile than a computer's. Moreover, most computers process information speedily but sequentially, even while alternating between tasks. The brain is slower but does many things at once—in parallel.

Psychologists have proposed several information-processing models of memory. One modern model, *connectionism,* views memories as emerging from interconnected neural networks. Specific memories arise from particular activation patterns within these networks. In an older but easier-to-picture model, Richard Atkinson and Richard Shiffrin (1968) proposed that we form memories through three stages:

1. We first record to-be-remembered information as a fleeting **sensory memory.**
2. From there, we process information into a **short-term memory** bin, where we encode it through rehearsal.
3. Finally, information moves into **long-term memory** for later retrieval.

Although historically important and helpfully simple, this three-step process is limited and fallible. In this module, we use a *modified version of the three-stage processing model of memory* (**FIGURE 21.1**). This updated model accommodates two important new concepts:

• Some information, as we will see, skips Atkinson and Shiffrin's first two stages and is processed directly and automatically into long-term memory, without our conscious awareness.

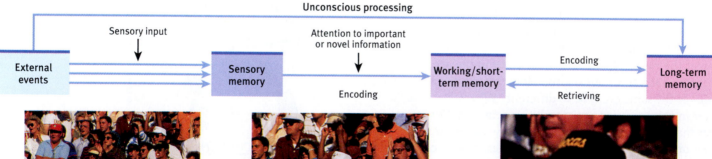

Unconscious processing

Sensory input

Attention to important or novel information

External events → Sensory memory → Working/short-term memory → Long-term memory

Encoding

Encoding

Retrieving

Sensory memory registers incoming information, allowing your brain to capture for a fleeting moment a sea of faces.

We pay attention to and encode important or novel stimuli—in this case an angry face in the crowd.

If we stare at the face long enough (rehearsal), or if we're sufficiently disturbed by it (it's deemed "important"), we will encode it for long-term storage, and we may, an hour later, be able to call up an image of the face.

- **Working memory,** a newer understanding of Atkinson and Shiffrin's second stage, concentrates on the active processing of information in this intermediate stage. Because we cannot possibly focus on all the information bombarding our senses at once, we shine the flashlight beam of our attention on certain incoming stimuli— often those that are novel or important. These incoming stimuli, along with information we retrieve from long-term memory, become conscious short-term memories in a temporary work site where we actively associate new and old information and solve problems (Engle, 2002). But unlike brick-and-mortar work sites, the content of our working memory quickly fades unless we keep using it or rehearsing it.

Let's use this model now to look more closely at how we encode, store, and retrieve information.

Encoding: Getting Information In

21-2: How do automatic and effortful processing help us encode sights, sounds, and other sensations and transfer them into our memory system?

How We Encode

Some information, such as the route you walked to your last class, you process with great ease, freeing your memory system to focus on less familiar events. But to retain novel information, such as a friend's new cellphone number, you need to pay attention and try hard.

Automatic Processing

With little or no effort, you absorb an enormous amount of information. For example, without conscious effort you **automatically process** information about

- *space.* While studying, you often encode the place on a page where certain material appears; later, when struggling to recall that information, you may visualize its location.
- *time.* While going about your day, you unintentionally note the sequence of the day's events. Later, when you realize you've left your coat somewhere, you re-create that sequence and retrace your steps.
- *frequency.* You effortlessly keep track of how many times things happen, thus enabling you to realize "this is the third time I've run into her today."

Thanks to our brain's capacity for parallel processing, all this multitasking and more goes on without our conscious attention. Automatic processing is so effortless that it is difficult to shut off. When you see words in your native language, perhaps on the side of a delivery truck, you cannot help but register their meanings.

This was not always so easy, of course. When you first learned to read, you sounded out individual letters to figure out what words they made. With effort, you plodded slowly through a mere 20 to 50 words on a page. Reading, like some other forms of information processing, initially requires attention and effort, but with experience and practice becomes automatic. Imagine now learning to read reversed sentences like this:

.citamotua emoceb nac gnissecorp luftroffE

At first, this requires effort, but after enough practice, you would also perform this task much more automatically. We have developed many of our skills in this way: learning to drive, rollerblade, or find our way around town.

Effortful Processing

21-3: How much does rehearsal aid in forming memories?

We encode and retain vast amounts of information automatically, but we remember other types of information, such as this module's concepts, only with effort and attention (**FIGURE 21.2** on the next page). **Effortful processing** often produces durable and accessible memories.

■ **working memory** a newer understanding of short-term memory that involves conscious, active processing of incoming auditory and visual-spatial information, and of information retrieved from long-term memory.

■ **automatic processing** unconscious encoding of incidental information, such as space, time, and frequency, and of well-learned information, such as word meanings.

■ **effortful processing** encoding that requires attention and conscious effort.

FIGURE 21.2

Automatic versus effortful processing
Some information, such as where you ate dinner yesterday, you process automatically. Other information, such as this module's concepts, requires effort to encode and remember.

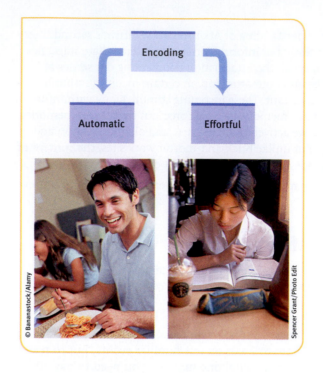

When learning novel information such as names, we can boost our memory through **rehearsal,** or conscious repetition. The pioneering researcher of verbal memory, German philosopher Hermann Ebbinghaus (1850–1909), showed this long ago. Impatient with philosophical speculations about memory, Ebbinghaus decided he would scientifically study his own learning and forgetting of novel verbal materials.

To create novel verbal material for learning, Ebbinghaus formed a list of all possible nonsense syllables by sandwiching one vowel between two consonants. Then, for a particular experiment, he would randomly select a sample of the syllables, practice them, and test himself. To get a feel for his experiments, rapidly read aloud, eight times over, the following list (from Baddeley, 1982). Then try to recall the items:

> JIH, BAZ, FUB, YOX, SUJ, XIR, DAX, LEQ, VUM, PID, KEL, WAV, TUV, ZOF, GEK, HIW.

The day after learning such a list, Ebbinghaus could recall few of the syllables. But were they entirely forgotten? As **FIGURE 21.3** portrays, the more frequently he repeated the list aloud on day 1, the fewer repetitions he required to relearn the list on day 2. Here, then, was a simple beginning principle: *The amount remembered depends on the time spent learning.* Even after we learn material, additional rehearsal (*overlearning*) increases retention. *The point to remember:* For novel verbal information, practice—effortful processing—does indeed make perfect.

Later memory research revealed other interesting aspects of the link between rehearsal and memory. Among them are the spacing effect and the serial position effect.

To paraphrase Ebbinghaus (1885), those who learn quickly also forget quickly. We retain information better when our rehearsal is distributed over time (as when learning classmates' names), a phenomenon called the **spacing effect** (Bjork, 1999; Dempster, 1988). In a 9-year experiment, Harry Bahrick and three of his family members (1993) practiced foreign language word translations for a given number of times, at intervals ranging from 14 to 56 days. Their consistent finding: The longer the space between practice sessions, the better their retention up to 5 years later. The practical implication? Spreading out learning—over a semester or a year, rather than over a shorter term—should help you not only on comprehensive final exams, but also in retaining the information for a lifetime. So here is another point to remember: *Spaced study beats cramming.*

> "He should test his memory by reciting the verses."
>
> Abdur-Rahman Abdul Khaliq, "Memorizing the Quran"

> "The mind is slow in unlearning what it has been long in learning."
>
> Roman philosopher Seneca (4 B.C.–65 A.D.)

c. an increase in a synapse's firing potential after brief, rapid stimulation.

d. aging people's potential for learning.

10. A person with amnesia following hippocampus damage will typically be unable to learn new facts or recall recent events. However, the person may be able to learn new skills, such as riding a bicycle, which is an

a. explicit memory.
b. implicit memory.
c. iconic memory.
d. echoic memory.

11. Research suggests that the hippocampus, a neural center in the limbic system of the brain, plays an important role in some types of learning. The hippocampus seems to function as a

a. temporary processing site for explicit memories.

b. temporary processing site for implicit memories.

c. permanent storage area for emotion-based memories.

d. permanent storage area for iconic and echoic memories.

12. To measure long-term memory, psychologists test people's ability to recall information, to recognize what they have learned, and to relearn previously learned material. A psychologist who asks you to write down as many objects as you can remember having seen a few minutes earlier is testing your

a. recall.
b. recognition.
c. recall and recognition.
d. relearning.

13. To gain access to a memory, we activate associations leading to that memory. The associations may be specific odors, visual images, or emotions, which are all examples of

a. relearning.
b. déjà vu.
c. declarative memories.
d. retrieval cues.

14. In some cases, retrieval may be enhanced by being in a context similar to one you have already experienced. The resulting feeling that "you've been there before" is known as

a. déjà vu.
b. mood-congruent memory.
c. relearning.
d. an explicit memory.

15. When happy, we tend to recall happy times. When depressed, we more often recall depressing events. This tendency to recall experiences consistent with our current emotions is called

a. mnemonics.
b. chunking.
c. repression.
d. mood-congruent memory.

Answers: 1. b, 2. a, 3. b, 4. a, 5. d, 6. c, 7. b, 8. c, 9. c, 10. b, 11. a, 12. a, 13. d, 14. a, 15. d.

>> TERMS AND CONCEPTS TO REMEMBER

memory, p. 269
encoding, p. 270
storage, p. 270
retrieval, p. 270
sensory memory, p. 270
short-term memory, p. 270
long-term memory, p. 270
working memory, p. 271
automatic processing, p. 271
effortful processing, p. 271

rehearsal, p. 272
spacing effect, p. 272
serial position effect, p. 273
imagery, p. 275
mnemonics [nih-MON-iks], p. 275
chunking, p. 276
iconic memory, p. 277
echoic memory, p. 277
long-term potentiation (LTP), p. 280
flashbulb memory, p. 281

amnesia, p. 281
implicit memory, p. 282
explicit memory, p. 282
hippocampus, p. 282
recall, p. 283
recognition, p. 283
relearning, p. 283
priming, p. 285
déjà vu, p. 286
mood-congruent memory, p. 287

>> TEST YOURSELF

1. Memory includes (in alphabetical order) long-term memory, sensory memory, and working/short-term memory. What's the correct order of these three memory stores?

2. What would be the most effective strategy to learn and retain a list of names of key historical figures for a week? For a year?

3. Your friend tells you that her father experienced brain damage in an accident. She wonders if psychology can explain why he can still play checkers very well but has a hard time holding a sensible conversation. What can you tell her?

4. What is priming?

(Answers in Appendix C.)

>> ANSWERS TO QUESTION WITHIN THE MODULE

Q. How many Fs are in the following sentence?
FINISHED FILES ARE THE RESULTS OF YEARS OF SCIENTIFIC STUDY COMBINED WITH THE EXPERIENCE OF YEARS.

A. Partly because your initial processing of the letters was primarily acoustic rather than visual, you probably missed some of the six Fs, especially those that sound like a *V* rather than an *F*.

Q. Multiple-choice questions test our
a. recall.
b. recognition.
c. relearning

Fill-in-the blank questions test our _____.

A. Multiple-choice questions test recognition. Fill-in-the blank questions test recall.

MODULE 22

Forgetting, Memory Construction, and Improving Memory

Forgetting

22-1: Why do we forget? At what points in the memory system can our memory fail us?

Amid all the applause for memory—all the efforts to understand it, all the books on how to improve it—have any voices been heard in praise of forgetting? William James (1890, p. 680) was such a voice: "If we remembered everything, we should on most occasions be as ill off as if we remembered nothing." To discard the clutter of useless or out-of-date information—where we parked the car yesterday, a friend's old phone number, restaurant orders already cooked and served—is surely a blessing. The Russian journalist and memory whiz Shereshevskii accumulated a junk heap of memories that haunted him. They dominated his consciousness. He had difficulty thinking abstractly—generalizing, organizing, evaluating. A good memory is helpful, but so is the ability to forget. If a memory-enhancing pill becomes available, it had better not be too effective.

More often, however, our memory dismays and frustrates us. Memories are quirky. My own memory can easily call up such episodes as that wonderful first kiss with the woman I love or trivial facts like the air mileage from London to Detroit. Then it abandons me when I'm trying to recall that new colleague's name or where I left my sunglasses, and I discover I have failed to encode, store, or retrieve the information. Memory researcher Daniel Schacter (1999) enumerates seven ways our memories fail us—the seven sins of memory, he calls them:

Three sins of forgetting:

- *Absent-mindedness*—inattention to details leads to encoding failure (our mind is elsewhere as we lay down the car keys).
- *Transience*—storage decay over time (after we part ways with former classmates, unused information fades).
- *Blocking*—inaccessibility of stored information (seeing an actor in an old movie, we feel the name on the tip of our tongue but experience retrieval failure—we cannot get it out).

Three sins of distortion:

- *Misattribution*—confusing the source of information (putting words in someone else's mouth or remembering a dream as an actual happening).
- *Suggestibility*—the lingering effects of misinformation (a leading question—"Did Mr. Jones touch your private parts?"—later becomes a young child's false memory).
- *Bias*—belief-colored recollections (current feelings toward a friend may color our recalled initial feelings).

One sin of intrusion:

- *Persistence*—unwanted memories (being haunted by images of a sexual assault).

Let's first consider the sins of forgetting, then those of distortion and intrusion. We end the module with some tips on how to apply what we know about memory to minimize the sins of forgetting.

> "Happiness is nothing more than health and a poor memory."
> Physician Albert Schweitzer (1875–1965)

Cellist Yo-Yo Ma forgot his 266-year-old, $2.5 million cello in a New York taxi. (He later recovered it.)

> "Amnesia seeps into the crevices of our brains, and amnesia heals."
> Joyce Carol Oates, "Words Fail, Memory Blurs, Life Wins," 2001

Encoding Failure

Much of what we sense we never notice, and what we fail to encode, we will never remember (**FIGURE 22.1**). Age can affect encoding efficiency. The brain areas that jump into action when young adults encode new information are less responsive in older adults. This slower encoding helps explain age-related memory decline (Grady & others, 1995). (Although, older people tend to recall less than younger adults do, they usually remember as well as younger people when given reminders or a recognition test.)

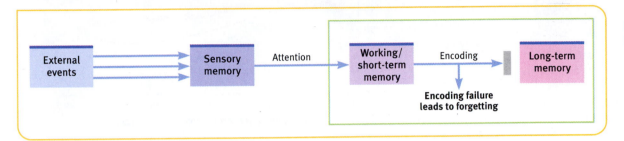

FIGURE 22.1
Forgetting as encoding failure
We cannot remember what we have not encoded.

But no matter how young we are, we selectively attend to few of the myriad sights and sounds continually bombarding us. Consider something you have looked at countless times: What letters accompany the number 5 on your telephone? For most of us, the question is surprisingly difficult. This detail is not personally meaningful, and few of us have made the effort to encode it. We encode some information—where we had dinner yesterday—automatically; other types of information—like the concepts in this module—require effort and attention. Without this effortful processing, many memories never form.

Storage Decay

Even after encoding something well, we sometimes later forget it. To study the durability of stored memories, Hermann Ebbinghaus (1885) learned lists of nonsense syllables and measured how much he retained when relearning each list, from 20 minutes to 30 days later. The result was his famous *forgetting curve* (**FIGURE 22.2**), confirmed by later experiments: The course of forgetting is initially rapid, then levels

> "Each of us finds that in [our] own life every moment of time is completely filled. [We are] bombarded every second by sensations, emotions, thoughts . . . nine-tenths of which [we] must simply ignore. The past [is] a roaring cataract of billions upon billions of such moments: Any one of them too complex to grasp in its entirety, and the aggregate beyond all imagination. . . . At every tick of the clock, in every inhabited part of the world, an unimaginable richness and variety of 'history' falls off the world into total oblivion."
>
> English novelist-critic C. S. Lewis (1967)

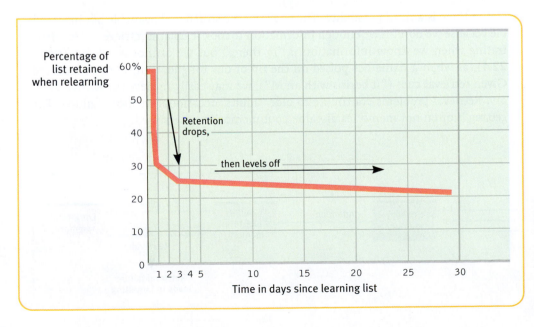

FIGURE 22.2
Ebbinghaus' forgetting curve
After learning lists of nonsense syllables, Ebbinghaus studied how much he retained up to 30 days later. He found that memory for novel information fades quickly, then levels out. (Adapted from Ebbinghaus, 1885.)

Andrew Holbrooke/Corbis

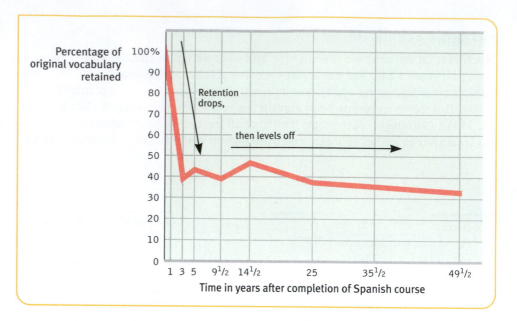

FIGURE 22.3
The forgetting curve for Spanish learned in school
Compared with people just completing a Spanish course, those 3 years out of the course remembered much less. Compared with the 3-year group, however, those who studied Spanish even longer ago did not forget much more. (Adapted from Bahrick, 1984.)

off with time (Wixted & Ebbesen, 1991). One such experiment was Harry Bahrick's (1984) study of the forgetting curve for Spanish vocabulary learned in school. Compared with those just completing a high school or college Spanish course, people 3 years out of school had forgotten much of what they had learned (**FIGURE 22.3**). However, what people remembered then, they still remembered 25 and more years later. Their forgetting had leveled off.

One explanation for these forgetting curves is a gradual fading of the physical *memory trace*. Cognitive neuroscientists are getting closer to solving the mystery of the physical storage of memory and are increasing our understanding of how memory storage could decay. But memories fade for other reasons, including the accumulation of learning that disrupts our retrieval.

Retrieval Failure

We have seen that forgotten events are like books you can't find in your campus library—some because they were never acquired (not encoded), others because they were discarded (stored memories decay).

But there is a third possibility: The book may be stored and available but inaccessible because we don't have enough information to look it up and retrieve it. How frustrating when we know information is "in there," but we cannot get it out (**FIGURE 22.4**), as when a name lies poised on the tip of our tongue, waiting to be retrieved. Given retrieval cues ("It begins with an M"), we may easily retrieve the elusive memory. Retrieval problems contribute to older adults' occasional memory failures. Forgetting is often not memories discarded but memories unretrieved.

Deaf persons fluent in sign language experience a parallel "tip of the fingers" phenomenon (Thompson & others, 2005).

FIGURE 22.4
Retrieval failure
We store in long-term memory what's important to us or what we've rehearsed. But sometimes even stored information cannot be accessed, which leads to forgetting.

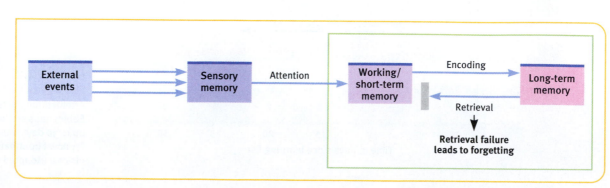

CLOSE-UP

RETRIEVING PASSWORDS

There's something that you need lots of, and that your grandparents at your age didn't: passwords. To log into your e-mail, retrieve your voice mail, draw cash from a machine, access your phone card, use the copy machine, or persuade the keypad to open the building door, you need to remember your password. A typical introductory psychology student faces eight demands for passwords, report Alan Brown and his colleagues (2004).

With so many passwords needed, what's a person to do? As **FIGURE 22.5** illustrates, we are plagued by proactive interference from irrelevant old information and by retroactive interference from other newly learned information.

Memory researcher Henry Roediger takes a simple approach to storing all the important phone, PIN, and code numbers in his life: "I have a sheet in my shirt pocket with all the numbers I need," says Roediger (2001), adding that he can't mentally store them all, so why bother?

Other strategies may help those who do not want to lose their PINs in the wash. First, duplicate. The average student uses four different passwords to meet those eight needs. Second, harness retrieval cues. Surveys in Britain and the United States reveal that about half of our passwords harness a familiar name or date. Others often involve familiar phone or identification numbers.

For on-line banking or other situations where security is essential, use a mix of letters and numbers, advise Brown and his colleagues. After composing such a password, rehearse it, then rehearse it a day later, and continue rehearsing at increasing intervals. In such ways, long-term memories will form and be retrievable at the cash and copy machines.

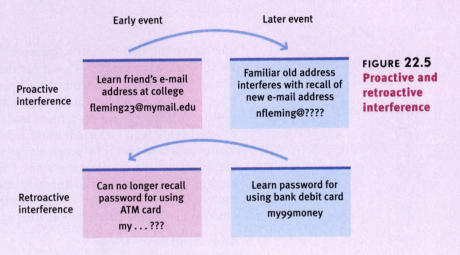

FIGURE 22.5 Proactive and retroactive interference

Interference

Learning some items may interfere with retrieving others, especially when the items are similar. If someone gives you a phone number, you may be able to recall it later. But if two more people give you their numbers, each successive number will be more difficult to recall. Likewise, if you buy a new combination lock or get a new phone number, your memory of the old one may interfere. Such **proactive** (*forward-acting*) **interference** occurs when something you learned earlier disrupts your recall of something you experience later. As you collect more and more information, your mental attic never fills, but it certainly gets cluttered.

Retroactive (*backward-acting*) **interference** occurs when new information makes it harder to recall something you learned earlier. It is rather like a second stone tossed in a pond, disrupting the waves rippling out from a first. (See Close-Up: Retrieving Passwords.)

Information presented in the hour before sleep is protected from retroactive interference, because the opportunity for interfering events is minimized. Researchers John Jenkins and Karl Dallenbach (1924) discovered this in a now-classic experiment. Day after day, two people each learned some nonsense syllables, then tried to recall them after up to eight hours of being awake or asleep at night. Forgetting occurred more rapidly after being awake and involved with other activities (see **FIGURE 22.6** on the next page). The investigators surmised that "forgetting is not so much a matter of the decay of old impressions and associations as it is a matter of interference, inhibition, or obliteration of the old by the new" (1924, p. 612). Later experiments have confirmed the benefits of sleep and found that the hour before a night's sleep is a good

■ **proactive interference** the disruptive effect of prior learning on the recall of new information.

■ **retroactive interference** the disruptive effect of new learning on the recall of old information.

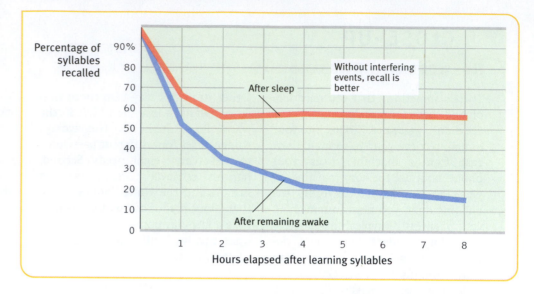

FIGURE 22.6
Retroactive interference
More forgetting occurred when a person stayed awake and experienced other new material. (From Jenkins & Dallenbach, 1924.)

time to commit information to memory (Benson & Feinberg, 1977; Fowler & others, 1973; Nesca & Koulack, 1994). But not the seconds just before sleep; information presented then is seldom remembered (Wyatt & Bootzin, 1994). Nor do we remember taped information played during sleep, although our ears register it (Wood & others, 1992). Without opportunity for rehearsal, most learning doesn't occur.

Interference is an important cause of forgetting, and it may explain why ads viewed during violent or sexual TV programs are so forgettable (Bushman & Bonacci, 2002). But we should not overstate the point. Sometimes old information can facilitate our learning of new information. Knowing Latin may help us to learn French—a phenomenon called *positive transfer*. It is when old and new information compete with each other, as in learning Spanish soon after learning French, that interference occurs.

Motivated Forgetting

To remember our past is often to revise it. Years ago, the huge cookie jar in our kitchen was jammed with freshly baked chocolate chip cookies. Still more were cooling across racks on the counter. Twenty-four hours later, not a crumb was left. Who had taken them? During that time, my wife, three children, and I were the only people in the house. So while memories were still fresh, I conducted a little memory test. Andy acknowledged wolfing down as many as 20. Peter admitted eating 15. Laura guessed she had stuffed her then-6-year-old body with 15 cookies. My wife, Carol, recalled eating 6, and I remembered consuming 15 and taking 18 more to the office. We sheepishly accepted responsibility for 89 cookies. Still, we had not come close; there had been 160.

This would not have surprised Michael Ross and his colleagues (1981), who time and again showed that people unknowingly revise their own histories. One group of people, told the benefits of frequent tooth-brushing, then recalled (more than others did) having frequently brushed their teeth in the preceding two weeks. A group of students, having taken a highly touted study skills course, later inflated their estimates of self-improvement. By *de*flating their evaluations of their previous study habits, they convinced themselves they had really benefited (Conway & Ross, 1984).

Why do our memories fail us? Why did my family and I not remember the number of cookies each of us had eaten? As **FIGURE 22.7** reminds us, we automatically encode sensory information in amazing detail. So was it an encoding problem? Or a storage problem—might our memories of cookies, like Ebbinghaus' memory of nonsense syllables, have vanished almost as fast as the cookies themselves? Or was the information still intact but irretrievable because it would be embarrassing to remember?[1]

"[It is] necessary to remember that events happened in the desired manner. And if it is necessary to rearrange one's memories . . . then it is necessary to forget that one has done so. The trick of doing this can be learned like any other mental technique. . . . It is called doublethink."
George Orwell, *Nineteen Eighty-Four*, 1948

---

[1]One of my cookie-scarfing sons, on reading this in his father's textbook years later, confessed he had fibbed "a little."

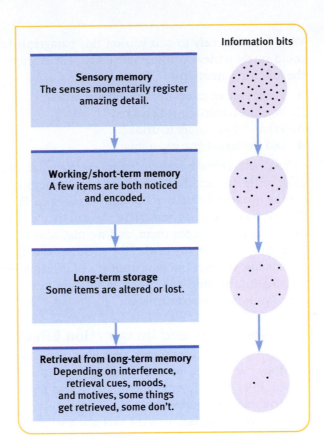

Information bits

Sensory memory
The senses momentarily register amazing detail.

Working/short-term memory
A few items are both noticed and encoded.

Long-term storage
Some items are altered or lost.

Retrieval from long-term memory
Depending on interference, retrieval cues, moods, and motives, some things get retrieved, some don't.

FIGURE 22.7
When do we forget?
Forgetting can occur at any memory stage. As we process information, we filter, alter, or lose much of it.

Sigmund Freud might have argued that our memory systems self-censored this information. He proposed that we **repress** painful memories to protect our self-concept and to minimize anxiety. But the submerged memory will linger, he believed, to be retrieved by some later cue or during therapy. Here is a sample case. A woman had an intense, unexplained fear of running water. One day her aunt whispered, "I have never told." Like relighting a blown-out candle, these words cued the woman's memory of an incident when, as a disobedient young child, she had wandered away from a family picnic and become trapped under a waterfall—until being rescued by her aunt, who promised not to tell her parents (Kihlstrom, 1990). Repression was central to Freud's psychology, and it has become part of psychology's lore. Most everyone, including 9 in 10 university students, believes that "memories for painful experiences are sometimes pushed into unconsciousness" (Brown & others, 1996). Therapists often assume it. Yet increasing numbers of memory researchers think repression rarely, if ever, occurs. More typically, it seems, we have trouble forgetting traumatic experiences. Let's look at some of the evidence.

Memory Construction

22-2 : How accurate are our memories?

Picture yourself having this experience:

You go to a fancy restaurant for dinner. You are seated at a table with a white tablecloth. You study the menu. You tell the server you want broiled salmon, a baked potato with sour cream, and a salad with blue cheese dressing. You also order some red wine from the wine list. A few minutes later the server returns with your salad. Later the rest of the meal arrives. You enjoy it all, except the salmon is a bit overdone.

■ **repression** in psychoanalytic theory, the basic defense mechanism that banishes from consciousness anxiety-arousing thoughts, feelings, and memories.

■ misinformation effect incorporating misleading information into one's memory of an event.

Were I immediately to quiz you on this paragraph (adapted from Hyde, 1983), you could surely retrieve considerable detail. For example, without looking back, answer the following questions:

1. What kind of salad dressing did you order?
2. Was the tablecloth red checked?
3. What did you order to drink?
4. Did the server give you a menu?

You were probably able to recall exactly what you ordered, and maybe even the color of the tablecloth. We do have an enormous capacity for storing and reproducing the incidental details of our daily experience. But did the server give you a menu? Not in the paragraph given. Nevertheless, many answer yes. We often construct our memories as we encode them, and we may also alter our memories as we withdraw them from our memory bank. Like scientists who infer a dinosaur's appearance from its remains, we infer our past from stored information plus what we now assume. By filtering information and filling in missing pieces, your concept of restaurants directed your memory construction.

Misinformation and Imagination Effects

In more than 200 experiments, involving more than 20,000 people, Elizabeth Loftus has shown how eyewitnesses similarly reconstruct their memories when later questioned. In one classic experiment, Loftus and John Palmer showed a film of a traffic accident and then quizzed people about what they had seen (Loftus & Palmer, 1974). Those asked, "How fast were the cars going when they *smashed* into each other?" gave higher speed estimates than those asked, "How fast were the cars going when they *hit* each other?" A week later, the researchers asked both groups if they recalled seeing any broken glass. Those who had heard *smashed* were more than twice as likely to report seeing glass fragments (**FIGURE 22.8**). In fact, the film showed no broken glass.

In many follow-up experiments around the world, people have witnessed an event, received or not received misleading information about it, and then taken a memory test. The repeated result is a **misinformation effect:** After exposure to subtle misinformation, many people misremember. They have misrecalled a yield sign as a stop sign, hammers as screwdrivers, Coke cans as peanut cans, *Vogue* magazine as *Mademoiselle,* "Dr. Henderson" as "Dr. Davidson," breakfast cereal as eggs, and a clean-shaven man as a man with a mustache (Loftus & others, 1992). As memories fade with time, misinformation becomes easier to inject (Loftus, 1992).

So unwitting is the misinformation effect that we may later find it nearly impossible to discriminate between our memories of real and suggested events (Schooler & others, 1986). Perhaps you can recall recounting an experience, and filling in memory gaps with plausible guesses and assumptions. We all do it, and after more

FIGURE 22.8
Memory construction
When people who had seen the film of a car accident were later asked a leading question, they recalled a more serious accident than they had witnessed. (From Loftus, 1979.)

Depiction of actual accident

Leading question:
"About how fast were the cars going when they *smashed* into each other?"

Memory construction

DOONESBURY

By Garry Trudeau DOONESBURY © 1994 G. B. Trudeau. Reprinted with permission of UNIVERSAL PRESS SYNDICATE.

retellings, we may recall the guessed details—now absorbed into our memories—as if we had actually observed them (Roediger & others, 1993). Others' vivid retelling of an event may also implant false memories.

Even repeatedly *imagining* nonexistent actions and events can create false memories. Students who repeatedly imagined simple acts such as breaking a toothpick or picking up a stapler later experienced this *imagination inflation*; they were more likely than others to think they had actually done such things during the experiment's first phase (Goff & Roediger, 1998). Similarly, one in four American and British university students asked to imagine certain childhood events, such as breaking a window with their hand or having a skin sample removed from a finger, later recalled the imagined event as something that had really happened (Garry & others, 1996; Mazzoni & Memon, 2003). Imagination inflation occurs partly because visualizing something and actually perceiving it activate similar brain areas (Gonsalves & others, 2004).

Imagined events later seem more familiar, and familiar things seem more real. Thus, the more vividly we can imagine things, the more likely we are to inflate them into memories (Loftus, 2001; Porter & others, 2000). People who believe aliens transported them to spaceships for medical exams tend to have powerful imaginations and, in memory tests, to be more susceptible to false memories (Clancy & others, 2002). Those who believe they have recovered memories of childhood sexual abuse likewise tend to have vivid imaginations and to score high on false memory tests (Clancy & others, 2000; McNally, 2003).

To see how far the mind's search for a fact will go in creating a fiction, Richard Wiseman and his University of Hertfordshire colleagues (1999) staged eight seances, each attended by 25 curious people. During each session, the medium—actually a professional actor and magician—urged everyone to concentrate on the moving table. Although it never moved, he suggested it had: "That's good. Lift the table up. That's good. Keep concentrating. Keep the table in the air." When questioned two weeks later, one in three participants recalled actually having seen the table levitate.

Memory construction helps explain why "hypnotically refreshed" memories of crimes so easily incorporate errors, some of which originate with the hypnotist's leading questions ("Did you hear loud noises?"). It explains why dating partners who fall in love *over*estimate their first impressions of one another ("It was love at first sight"), while those who break up *under*estimate their earlier liking ("We never really clicked") (McFarland & Ross, 1987). And it explains why people asked how they felt

> "Memory is insubstantial. Things keep replacing it. Your batch of snapshots will both fix and ruin your memory. . . . You can't remember anything from your trip except the wretched collection of snapshots."
> Annie Dillard, "To Fashion a Text," 1988

> "Memory isn't like reading a book; it's more like writing a book from fragmentary notes."
> Psychologist John F. Kihlstrom (1994)

"It isn't so astonishing, the number of things I can remember, as the number of things I can remember that aren't so."

Mark Twain (1835–1910)

10 years ago about marijuana or gender issues recall attitudes closer to their current views than to the views they had actually reported a decade earlier (Markus, 1986). As George Vaillant (1977, p. 197) noted after following adult lives through time, "It is all too common for caterpillars to become butterflies and then to maintain that in their youth they had been little butterflies. Maturation makes liars of us all."

Source Amnesia

Among the frailest parts of a memory is its source. Thus, we may recognize someone but have no idea where we have seen the person. Or we may dream an event and later be unsure whether it really happened. Or we may hear something and later recall seeing it (Henkel & others, 2000). In all these cases, we retain the memory of the event, but not of the context in which we acquired it.

Australian psychologist Donald Thompson became part of his own research on memory distortion when authorities brought him in for questioning about a rape. Although he was a near-perfect match to the victim's memory of the rapist, Thompson had an airtight alibi: Just before the rape occurred, he was being interviewed on live TV and could not possibly have made it to the crime scene. Then it came to light that the victim had been watching the interview—ironically about face recognition—and had experienced **source amnesia**, confusing her memories of Thompson with those of the rapist (Schacter, 1996).

Debra Poole and Stephen Lindsay (1995, 2001, 2002) demonstrated source amnesia (also called *source misattribution*) in a group of preschoolers. They had the children interact with "Mr. Science," who engaged them in activities such as blowing up a balloon with baking soda and vinegar. Three months later, their parents on three successive days read them a story describing some things they had experienced with Mr. Science and some they had not. When a new interviewer asked what Mr. Science had done with them—"Did Mr. Science have a machine with ropes to pull?"—4 in 10 children spontaneously recalled him doing things that happened only in the story.

Children's Eyewitness Recall

Because memory is reconstruction as well as reproduction, we can't be sure whether a memory is real by how real it feels. Much as perceptual illusions may seem like real perceptions, unreal memories *feel* like real memories. If memories can be sincere, yet sincerely wrong, might children's recollections of sexual abuse be prone to error?

Stephen Ceci (1993) thinks "it would be truly awful to ever lose sight of the enormity of child abuse." Yet, as we have seen, interviewers who ask leading questions can plant false memories. Ceci and Maggie Bruck's (1993, 1995) studies of children's memories have sensitized them to children's suggestibility. For example, they asked 3-year-olds to show on anatomically correct dolls where a pediatrician had touched them. Fifty-five percent of the children who had not received genital examinations pointed to either genital or anal areas. And when they used suggestive interviewing techniques, the researchers found that most preschoolers and many older children could be induced to report false events, such as seeing a thief steal food in their day-care center (Bruck & Ceci, 1999, 2004).

In one study, Ceci and Bruck had a child choose a card from a deck of possible happenings and an adult then read from the card. For example, "Think real hard, and tell me if this ever happened to you. Can you remember going to the hospital with a mousetrap on your finger?" After 10 weekly interviews, with the same adult repeatedly asking children to think about several real and fictitious events, a new adult asked the same question. The stunning result: 58 percent of preschoolers produced false (often vivid) stories regarding one or more events they had never experienced, as the little boy in the following story did (Ceci & others, 1994):

Authors and songwriters sometimes suffer source amnesia. They think an idea came from their own creative imagination, when in fact they are unintentionally plagiarizing something they earlier read or heard.

■ **source amnesia** attributing to the wrong source an event we have experienced, heard about, read about, or imagined. (Also called *source misattribution*.) Source amnesia, along with the misinformation effect, is at the heart of many false memories.

My brother Colin was trying to get Blowtorch [an action figure] from me, and I wouldn't let him take it from me, so he pushed me into the wood pile where the mousetrap was. And then my finger got caught in it. And then we went to the hospital, and my mommy, daddy, and Colin drove me there, to the hospital in our van, because it was far away. And the doctor put a bandage on this finger.

Given such detailed stories, professional psychologists who specialize in interviewing children were often fooled. They could not reliably separate real memories from false ones. Nor could the children themselves. The above child, reminded that his parents had told him several times that the mousetrap incident never happened—that he had imagined it—protested, "But it really did happen. I remember it!"

Does this then mean that children can never be accurate eyewitnesses? No. If questioned about their experiences in neutral words they understand, children often accurately recall what happened and who did it (Goodman & others, 1990; Howe, 1997; Pipe, 1996). When interviewers use less suggestive, more effective techniques, even 4- to 5-year-old children produce more accurate recall (Holliday & Albon, 2004; Pipe & others, 2004). Children are especially accurate when they have not talked with involved adults prior to the interview and when their disclosure is made in a first interview with a neutral person who asks nonleading questions.

Repressed or Constructed Memories of Abuse?

What then shall we say about clinicians who have guided people in "recovering" memories of childhood abuse? Are they triggering false memories that damage innocent adults, or are they uncovering the truth?

In one American survey, the average therapist estimated that 11 percent of the population—some 34 million people—have repressed memories of childhood sexual abuse (Kamena, 1998). In another survey, of British and American doctoral-level therapists, 7 in 10 said they had used techniques such as hypnosis or drugs to help clients recover suspected repressed memories of childhood sexual abuse (Poole & others, 1995).

Some have reasoned with patients that "people who've been abused often have your symptoms, so you probably were abused. Let's see if, aided by hypnosis or drugs, or helped to dig back and visualize your trauma, you can recover it." As we might expect from the research on source amnesia and the misinformation effect, patients exposed to such techniques may form an image of a threatening person. With further visualization, the image grows more vivid, leaving the patient stunned, angry, and ready to confront or sue the equally stunned and devastated parent, relative, or clergy member, who then vigorously denies the accusation. After 32 therapy sessions, one woman recalled her father abusing her when she was 15 months old.

Without questioning the professionalism of most therapists, some scientific critics charged that clinicians who use "memory work" techniques such as "guided imagery," hypnosis, and dream analysis to recover memories "are nothing more than merchants of mental chaos, and, in fact, constitute a blight on the entire field of psychotherapy" (Loftus & others, 1995). Irate clinicians countered that those who dispute recovered memories of abuse add to abused people's trauma and play into the hands of child molesters.

In an effort to find a sensible common ground that might resolve this ideological battle—psychology's "memory war"—study panels have been convened and public statements made by the American Medical, American Psychological, and American Psychiatric Associations; the Australian Psychological Society; the British Psychological Society; and the Canadian Psychiatric Association. Those committed to protecting abused children and those committed to protecting wrongly accused adults agree on several points.

> "[The] research leads me to worry about the possibility of false allegations. It is not a tribute to one's scientific integrity to walk down the middle of the road if the data are more to one side."
>
> Stephen Ceci (1993)

© The New Yorker Collection, 1993, Lorenz from cartoonbank.com. All Rights Reserved.

TODAY'S SPECIAL GUEST

BRUNDAGE MORNALD, OF BATTLE CREEK, MONTANA UNDER HYPNOSIS, MR. MORNALD RECOVERED LONG-BURIED MEMORIES OF A PERFECTLY NORMAL, HAPPY CHILDHOOD.

- **Injustice happens.** Some innocent people have been falsely convicted. Some guilty people have evaded responsibility by casting doubt on their truth-telling accusers.
- **Incest and other sexual abuse happen.** And they happen more often than we once supposed. There is no characteristic "survivor syndrome" (Kendall-Tackett & others, 1993). However, sexual abuse can leave its victims predisposed to problems ranging from sexual dysfunction to depression.
- **Forgetting happens.** Many of the abused were either very young when abused or may not have understood the meaning of their experience—circumstances under which forgetting is "utterly common." Forgetting isolated past events, both negative and positive, is an ordinary part of everyday life.
- **Recovered memories are commonplace.** Cued by a remark or an experience, we recover memories of long-forgotten events, both pleasant and unpleasant. What is debated is whether the unconscious mind sometimes *forcibly represses* painful experiences and, if so, whether these can be retrieved by certain therapist-aided techniques.
- **Memories of things happening before age 3 are unreliable.** People do not reliably recall happenings of any sort from their first three years—a phenomenon called *infantile amnesia*. Most psychologists—including most clinical and counseling psychologists—therefore are skeptical of "recovered" memories of abuse during infancy (Gore-Felton & others, 2000; Knapp & Vande Creek, 2000). The older a child's age when suffering sexual abuse, and the more severe it was, the more likely it is to be remembered (Goodman & others, 2003).
- **Memories "recovered" under hypnosis or the influence of drugs are especially unreliable.** "Age-regressed" hypnotized subjects incorporate suggestions into their memories, even memories of "past lives."
- **Memories, whether real or false, can be emotionally upsetting.** Both the accuser and the accused may suffer when what was born of mere suggestion becomes, like an actual trauma, a stinging memory that drives bodily stress (McNally, 2003). People knocked unconscious in unremembered accidents have later developed stress disorders after being haunted by memories they constructed from photos, news reports, and friends' accounts (Bryant, 2001).

To more closely approximate therapist-aided recall, Elizabeth Loftus and her colleagues (1996) have experimentally implanted false memories of childhood traumas. In one study, she had a trusted family member recall for a teenager three real childhood experiences and a false one—a vivid account of the child's being lost for an extended time in a shopping mall at age 5 until being rescued by an elderly person. Two days later, one participant, Chris, said, "That day I was so scared that I would never see my family again." Two days after that, he began to visualize the flannel shirt, bald head, and glasses of the old man who supposedly had found him. Told the story was made up, Chris was incredulous: "I thought I remembered being lost . . . and looking around for the guys. I do remember that, and then crying, and Mom coming up and saying, 'Where were you? Don't you . . . ever do that again.'" In other experiments, a third of participants have become wrongly convinced that they almost drowned as a child, and about half were led to falsely recall an awful experience, such as a vicious animal attack (Heaps & Nash, 2001; Porter & others, 1999).

Such is the memory construction process by which people can recall being abducted by UFOs, victimized by a satanic cult, molested in a crib, or living a past life. Thousands of reasonable, normally

> "When memories are 'recovered' after long periods of amnesia, particularly when extraordinary means were used to secure the recovery of memory, there is a high probability that the memories are false."
>
> Royal College of Psychiatrists Working Group on Reported Recovered Memories of Child Sexual Abuse (Brandon & others, 1998)

Elizabeth Loftus

"The research findings for which I am being honored now generated a level of hostility and opposition I could never have foreseen. People wrote threatening letters, warning me that my reputation and even my safety were in jeopardy if I continued along these lines. At some universities, armed guards were provided to accompany me during speeches."
Elizabeth Loftus, on receiving the Association for Psychological Science's William James Fellow Award, 2001

Don Shrubshell

functioning human beings, notes Loftus, "speak in terror-stricken voices about their experience aboard flying saucers. They *remember,* clearly and vividly, being abducted by aliens" (Loftus & Ketcham, 1994, p. 66).

Loftus knows firsthand the phenomenon she studies. At a family reunion, an uncle told her that at age 14, she found her mother's drowned body. Shocked, she denied it. But the uncle was adamant, and over the next three days she began to wonder if *she* had a repressed memory. "Maybe that's why I'm so obsessed with this topic." As the now-upset Loftus pondered her uncle's suggestion, she "recovered" an image of her mother lying in the pool, face down, and of herself finding the body. "I started putting everything into place. Maybe that's why I'm such a workaholic. Maybe that's why I'm so emotional when I think about her even though she died in 1959."

Then her brother called. Their uncle now remembered what other relatives also confirmed. Aunt Pearl, not Loftus, had found the body (Loftus & Ketcham, 1994; Monaghan, 1992).

Loftus also knows firsthand the reality of sexual abuse. A male baby-sitter molested her when she was 6 years old. She has not forgotten. And that makes her wary of those whom she sees as trivializing real abuse by suggesting and seeking out uncorroborated traumatic experiences, then accepting them uncritically as fact. The enemies of the truly victimized are not only those who prey and those who deny, she says, but those whose writings and allegations "are bound to lead to an increased likelihood that society in general will disbelieve the genuine cases of childhood sexual abuse that truly deserve our sustained attention" (Loftus, 1993).

So, does repression of threatening memories ever occur? Psychologists continue to have heated debates on this topic, which is a recurring theme in so much popular psychology. But this much now appears certain: The most common response to a traumatic experience (witnessing a parent's murder, experiencing the horrors of a Nazi death camp, being terrorized by a hijacker or a rapist, escaping the collapsing World Trade Center towers, surviving the Asian tsunami) is not banishment of the experience into the unconscious. Rather, such experiences are typically etched on the mind as vivid, persistent, haunting memories. Playwright Eugene O'Neill understood. As one of the characters in his *Strange Interlude* (1928) exclaimed, "The devil! . . . what beastly incidents our memories insist on cherishing!"

Although scorned by some trauma therapists, Loftus has been elected president of the science-oriented Association for Psychological Science, awarded psychology's biggest prize ($200,000), and elected to the U.S. National Academy of Sciences and the Royal Society of Edinburgh.

> "Horror sears memory, leaving . . . the consuming memories of atrocity."
>
> Robert Kraft, *Memory Perceived: Recalling the Holocaust,* 2002

Improving Memory

22-3 : How might we apply memory principles to everyday situations, such as remembering a person's name or even the material of this module?

Now and then we are dismayed at our forgetfulness—at our embarrassing inability to recall someone's name, at forgetting to bring up a point in conversation, at forgetting to bring along something important, at finding ourselves standing in a room unable to recall why we are there (Herrmann, 1982). Is there anything we can do to minimize such misdeeds of our memory system? Much as biology benefits medicine and botany benefits agriculture, so can the psychology of memory benefit education. Here for easy reference is a summary of concrete suggestions for improving memory. The SQ3R—Survey, Question, Read, Rehearse, Review—study technique used in this text incorporates several of these strategies.

> **Study repeatedly to boost long-term recall.** Overlearn. To learn a name, say it to yourself after being introduced; wait a few seconds and say it again; wait longer and say it again. To learn a concept, provide yourself with many separate study sessions: Take advantage of life's little intervals—riding on the bus, walking across campus, waiting for class to start.

Thinking and memory
Most of what we know is not the result of efforts to memorize. We learn because we're curious and because we spend time thinking about our experiences. Actively thinking as we read, by rehearsing and relating ideas, yields the best retention.

> "I have discovered that it is of some use when you lie in bed at night and gaze into the darkness to repeat in your mind the things you have been studying. Not only does it help the understanding, but also the memory."
>
> Leonardo da Vinci (1452–1519)

> "Knit each new thing on to some acquisition already there."
>
> William James, *Principles of Psychology*, 1890

Spend more time rehearsing or actively thinking about the material. To memorize specific facts or figures, for example, Thomas Landauer (2001) suggests: "rehearse the name or number you are trying to memorize, wait a few seconds, rehearse again, wait a little longer, rehearse again, then wait longer still and rehearse yet again. The waits should be as long as possible without losing the information." New memories are weak; exercise them and they will strengthen. Speed-reading (skimming) complex material—with minimal rehearsal—yields little retention. Rehearsal and critical reflection help more. It pays to study actively!

Make the material personally meaningful. To build a network of retrieval cues, take thorough text and class notes in your own words. Mindlessly repeating someone else's words is relatively ineffective. To apply the concepts to your own life, form images, understand and organize information, relate the material to what you already know or have experienced, and put it in your own words. Increase retrieval cues by forming as many associations as possible. Without such cues, you may find yourself stuck when a question uses phrasing different from the rote forms you memorized.

To remember a list of unfamiliar items, use mnemonic devices. Make up a story to associate items with memorable images or jingles. Vivid images or words in familiar rhymes can act as pegs on which you can "hang" items. Chunk information into acronyms.

Refresh your memory by activating retrieval cues. Mentally re-create the situation and the mood in which your original learning occurred. Return to the same location. Jog your memory by allowing one thought to cue the next.

Minimize interference. Study before sleeping. Do not schedule back-to-back study times for topics that are likely to interfere with each other, such as Spanish and French.

Test your own knowledge, both to rehearse it and to help determine what you do not yet know. Don't be lulled into overconfidence by your ability to recognize information. Test your recall using the Preview Questions. Outline sections on a blank page. Define the terms and concepts listed at each module's end before turning back to their definitions. Take practice tests (see the Rehearse It and Test Yourself questions on the final page of each module). The printed study guide that accompanies this text, and the companion Web site (www.worthpublishers.com/myers), are both good sources for such tests.

REVIEWING

>> Module Review

22-1: **Why do we forget? At what points in the memory system can our memory fail us?**

One explanation of forgetting is that we fail to encode information for entry into our memory system. Without effortful processing, we never notice or process much of what we sense. Memories may also fade after storage—rapidly at first, and then leveling off. This trend is known as the forgetting curve. Forgetting also results from retrieval failure, often when old and new material compete for retrieval, or when we don't have adequate retrieval cues, or even, said Freud, by motivated forgetting, or *repression*. In *proactive interference*, something learned in the past (a friend's old phone number) interferes with our ability to recall something recently learned (the friend's new number). In *retroactive interference*, something recently learned (vocabulary in this semester's Spanish course) interferes with something learned in the past (vocabulary in last year's French course).

22-2: **How accurate are our memories?**

Memories are not stored as exact copies, and they certainly are not retrieved as such. Rather, we construct our memories, using both stored and new information. Memory is thus best understood not only as a cognitive and a biological phenomenon, but also as a social-cultural phenomenon (see **FIGURE 22.9**).

If children or adults are exposed to misinformation after an event, they may incorporate the misleading details into their memory of the event. This *misinformation effect* is one of the two main components of false memories. The other is *source amnesia*, in which we attribute something heard, read, or imagined to a wrong source. Memory researchers and psychologists motivated to protect abused children and wrongly accused adults agree that incest and abuse happen, more than we once supposed. But unless the victim was a child too young to remember any early experiences, such traumas are usually remembered vividly, not banished into an active but inaccessible unconscious. Nevertheless, constructed memories can be very destructive for accusers and those who are falsely accused.

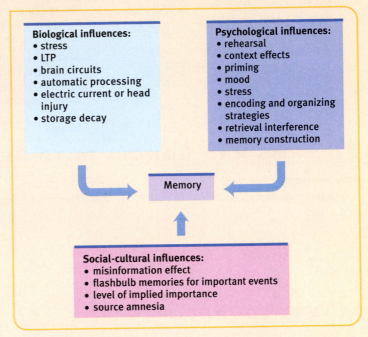

FIGURE 22.9

Levels of analysis for the study of memory
As with other psychological phenomena, memory is fruitfully studied at biological, psychological, and social-cultural levels.

22-3: **How might we apply memory principles to everyday situations, such as remembering a person's name or even the material of this module?**

The psychology of memory suggests concrete strategies for improving memory. These include scheduling spaced study times; actively rehearsing information to be learned; aiding encoding by making well-organized, vivid, and personally meaningful associations; using mnemonic techniques; returning to contexts and moods that are rich with association; minimizing interference; and self-testing to rehearse information and find gaps in your memory.

>> Rehearse it!

1. In some cases, forgetting may be due to encoding failure. That is, meaningless information may not be transferred from

a. the environment into sensory memory.

b. sensory memory into long-term memory.

c. long-term memory into short-term memory.

d. short-term memory into long-term memory.

2. Ebbinghaus found that about three days after a session of learning nonsense syllables, he had forgotten much of what he had learned. Ebbinghaus' "forgetting curve" shows that after this initial decline, one's memory for novel information tends to

a. increase slightly.

b. decrease noticeably.

c. decrease greatly.

d. level out.

3. Experiments show that the hour before sleep is a good time to memorize information because this minimizes the disrupting effects of all the other new events that might claim our attention. Going to sleep after learning new material minimizes

a. the misinformation effect.

b. amnesia.

c. retroactive interference.

d. proactive interference.

4. People unknowingly revise or re-arrange their memories of events. According to Sigmund Freud, painful or unacceptable memories are self-censored, or blocked from consciousness, through a mechanism called
   a. repression.
   b. proactive interference.
   c. the misinformation effect.
   d. physical decay of the memory trace.

5. Because we often alter information as we encode it and because we tend to fill in memory gaps with our assumptions about events, our memories are generally not exact reproductions of events. One reason for this memory reconstruction is
   a. proactive interference.
   b. the misinformation effect.
   c. retroactive interference.
   d. the eyewitness recall effect.

6. Aspects of our memories are distributed to different parts of the brain. Thus, while we may recognize a face in the crowd, we may not be able to recall where we know the person from. This is called
   a. the misinformation effect.
   b. proactive interference.
   c. source amnesia.
   d. repression.

Answers: 1. d, 2. d, 3. c, 4. a, 5. b, 6. c.

>> TERMS AND CONCEPTS TO REMEMBER

proactive interference, p. 293
retroactive interference, p. 293

repression, p. 295
misinformation effect, p. 296

source amnesia, p. 298

Multiple-choice **self-tests** and more may be found at www.worthpublishers.com/myers.

>> TEST YOURSELF

1. Can you offer an example of proactive interference?

2. What—given the commonality of source amnesia—might life be like if we remembered all our waking experiences and all our dreams?

3. What are the recommended memory strategies you just read about? (One advised rehearsing to-be-remembered material. What were the others?)

(Answers in Appendix C.)

Thinking, Language, and Intelligence

Thinking, Language, and Intelligence

Throughout history, we humans have both deplored our foolishness and celebrated our wisdom. The poet T. S. Eliot was struck by "the hollow men . . . Headpiece filled with straw." But Shakespeare's Hamlet extolled the human species as "noble in reason! . . . infinite in faculties! . . . in apprehension how like a god!" Psychologists, too, have marveled at both our abilities and our errors.

We have studied the human brain—3 pounds of wet tissue the size of a small cabbage, yet containing circuitry more complex than the planet's telephone networks. We have appreciated the competence of newborn infants. We have relished the human sensory system, which disassembles visual stimuli into millions of nerve impulses, distributes them for parallel processing, and then reassembles them into clear and colorful perceived images. We have pondered our memory's seemingly limitless capacity and the ease with which we process information, consciously and unconsciously. Little wonder that our species has had the collective genius to invent the camera, the car, and the computer; to unlock the atom and crack the genetic code; to travel out to space and into the oceans' depths.

Yet we have also seen that our species is kin to the other animals, influenced by the same principles that produce learning in rats and pigeons. As one pundit said, echoing Pavlov, "How like a dog!" We have noted that we assimilate reality into our preconceptions and succumb to perceptual illusions. We have seen how easily we deceive ourselves about pseudopsychic claims, hypnotic feats, and false memories.

In Modules 23 through 25, we encounter further instances of these two images of the human condition—the rational and the irrational. We will consider how we form concepts, solve problems, and make judgments (Module 23). We will look at our flair for language and ask whether our species alone has this capability (Module 24). And in Module 25, we will focus on an ongoing debate in which psychologists and others pick sides on two major questions: (1) Does each of us have an inborn, general mental capacity? and (2) Can we quantify this capacity as a meaningful number?

Thinking

Thinking, or **cognition,** refers to all the mental activities associated with processing, understanding, remembering, and communicating. *Cognitive psychologists* study these activities, including the logical and sometimes illogical ways in which we create concepts, solve problems, make decisions, and form judgments. Their research helps us to think smart—to appreciate the powers and the limits of our intuition, and to reason more effectively.

We begin with the building blocks of thinking: concepts. As you read this discussion and others in this module, join me in reflecting on how deserving we are of our name, *Homo sapiens*—wise human.

Concepts

23-1: What are the functions of concepts?

To think about the countless events, objects, and people in our world, we simplify things. We form **concepts**—mental groupings of similar objects, events, and people. The concept *chair* includes many items—a baby's high chair, a reclining chair, the chairs around a dinner table, a dentist's chair—all of which are for sitting. Chairs vary, but it is their common features that define the concept of *chair.*

Imagine life without concepts. We would need a different name for every object and idea. We could not ask a child to "throw the ball" because there would be no concept of *ball* (or *throw*). Instead of saying, "They were angry," we would have to describe facial expressions, vocal intensities, gestures, and words. Such concepts as *ball* and *angry* provide us with much information without much cognitive effort.

To simplify things further, we organize concepts into category *hierarchies.* Cab drivers organize their cities into geographical sectors, which subdivide into neighborhoods and again into blocks. Once our categories exist, we use them efficiently. Shown a bird, car, or food, people need no more time to identify an item's category than to perceive that something is there. "As soon as you know it is there, you know what it is," report Kalanit Grill-Spector and Nancy Kanwisher (2005).

We form some concepts by *definition.* Told that a triangle has three sides, we thereafter classify all three-sided geometric forms as triangles. More often, however, we form our concepts by developing **prototypes**—a mental image or best example that incorporates all the features we associate with a category (Rosch, 1978). The more closely something matches our prototype of a concept, the more readily we recognize it as an example of the concept. A robin and a penguin both satisfy our definition of *bird:* a two-footed animal that has wings and feathers and hatches from an egg. Yet people agree more quickly that "a robin is a bird" than that "a penguin is a bird." For most of us, the robin is the birdier bird; it more closely resembles our bird prototype.

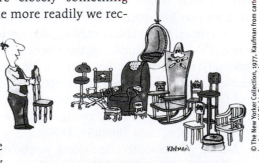

"Attention, everyone! I'd like to introduce the newest member of our family."

■ **cognition** the mental activities associated with thinking, knowing, remembering, and communicating.

■ **concept** a mental grouping of similar objects, events, ideas, or people.

■ **prototype** a mental image or best example of a category. Matching new items to the prototype provides a quick and easy method for including items in a category (as when comparing feathered creatures to a prototypical bird, such as a robin).

© The New Yorker Collection, 1977, Kaufman from cartoonbank.com. All Rights Reserved.

Daniel J. Cox/Liaison/Getty Images

J. Messerschmidt/The Picture Cube

A bird and a . . . ?
If asked to imagine a bird, most people quickly come up with a mental picture that is something like this American robin. It takes them a bit longer to conceptualize a penguin as a bird because it doesn't match their prototype of a small, feathered, flying creature.

Move away from our prototypes, and category boundaries may blur. Is a tomato a fruit? Is a 17-year-old female a girl or a woman? Is a whale a mammal? Because this marine animal fails to match our prototype, we are slower to recognize it as a mammal. Similarly, we are slow to perceive an illness when our symptoms don't fit one of our disease prototypes (Bishop, 1991). People whose heart attack symptoms (shortness of breath, exhaustion, a dull weight in the chest) don't match their prototype of a heart attack (sharp chest pain) may not seek help. And when discrimination doesn't fit our prejudice prototypes—of White against Black, male against female, young against old—we often fail to notice it. People more easily detect male prejudice against females than female against males or female against females (Inman & Baron, 1996; Marti & others, 2000). So, concepts speed and guide our thinking, but they don't always make us wise.

Solving Problems

23-2 : What strategies do we use to solve problems, and what obstacles hinder our problem solving?

One tribute to our rationality is our problem-solving skill in coping with novel situations. What's the best route around this traffic jam? How shall we respond to a friend's criticism? How can we get into the house when we've lost our keys?

Some problems we solve through trial and error. Thomas Edison tried thousands of light bulb filaments before stumbling upon one that worked. For other problems, we use **algorithms,** step-by-step procedures that guarantee a solution. But step-by-step algorithms can be laborious and exasperating. For example, to find another word using all the letters in *SPLOYOCHYG*, we could try each letter in each position, but we would need to generate and examine the 907,200 resulting permutations. In such cases, we often resort to simpler strategies called **heuristics.** Thus, we might reduce the number of options in our *SPLOYOCHYG* example by excluding rare letter combinations, such as two Y's together. By using heuristics and then applying trial and error, we may hit upon the answer (see this module's final page).

Sometimes, the problem-solving strategy seems to be no strategy at all. We puzzle over a problem, and suddenly, the pieces fall together as we perceive the solution in a sudden flash of **insight.** Ten-year-old Johnny Appleton displayed insight in solving a problem that had stumped construction workers: how to rescue a young robin that had fallen into a narrow 30-inch-deep hole in a cement-block wall. Johnny's solution: to slowly pour in sand, giving the bird enough time to keep its feet on top of the constantly rising sand (Ruchlis, 1990).

A team of researchers, including psychologists Mark Jung-Beeman, John Kounios, and Edward Bowden (2004), have identified brain activity associated with sudden flashes of insight. They gave people a problem: Think of a word that will form a compound word or phrase with each of three words in a set (such as *pine, crab,* and *sauce*),

Heuristic searching To search for guava juice you could search every supermarket aisle (an algorithm) or check the bottled beverage, natural foods, and produce sections (heuristics). The heuristic approach is often speedier, but an algorithmic search guarantees you will find it eventually.

B₂M Productions/Digital Vision/Getty Images

and press a button to sound a bell when you know the answer. (Did you guess *apple?*) As the bell sounded, the researchers mapped the problem-solver's brain activity, using functional MRIs or EEGs. About half the solutions were by a sudden Aha! insight, accompanied by a burst of activity in the right temporal lobe, just above the ear (**FIGURE 23.1**). And preceding the button pressing, by about 0.3 seconds, was a type of activity that seemed to correspond with unconscious processing popping into a conscious insight.

Insight gives us a sense of satisfaction, a feeling of happiness. The joy of a joke may similarly lie in our sudden comprehension of an unexpected ending or a double meaning. See for yourself, with these two jokes rated funniest (among 2 million ratings of 40,000 submitted jokes) in an Internet humor study co-sponsored by Richard Wiseman (2002) and the British Association for the Advancement of Science. First, the runner-up:

> Sherlock Holmes and Dr. Watson are going camping. They pitch their tent under the stars and go to sleep. Sometime in the middle of the night Holmes wakes Watson up.
>
> **Holmes:** "Watson, look up at the stars, and tell me what you deduce."
> **Watson:** "I see millions of stars and even if a few of those have planets, it's quite likely there are some planets like Earth, and if there are a few planets like Earth out there, there might also be life. What does it tell you, Holmes?"
> **Holmes:** "Watson, you idiot, somebody has stolen our tent!"

And roll the drums for the winner:

> A couple of New Jersey hunters are out in the woods when one of them falls to the ground. He doesn't seem to be breathing, his eyes are rolled back in his head. The other guy whips out his cellphone and calls the emergency services. He gasps to the operator: "My friend is dead! What can I do?" The operator, in a calm, soothing voice says: "Just take it easy. I can help. First, let's make sure he's dead." There is a silence, then a shot is heard. The guy's voice comes back on the line: "OK, now what?"

Obstacles to Problem Solving

Inventive as we can be in solving problems, the correct answer may elude us. Two cognitive tendencies—*confirmation bias* and *fixation*—often lead us astray.

Confirmation Bias

We seek evidence verifying our ideas more eagerly than we seek evidence that might refute them (Klayman & Ha, 1987; Skov & Sherman, 1986). This tendency, known as **confirmation bias,** is a major obstacle to problem solving. Peter Wason (1960) demonstrated the confirmation bias by giving British university students the three-number sequence 2-4-6 and asking them to guess the rule he had used to devise the series. (The rule was simple: any three ascending numbers.) Before submitting answers, students generated their own sets of three numbers, and Wason told them whether their sets conformed to his rule. Once they felt certain they had the rule, they were to announce it. The result? Seldom right but never in doubt. Most of Wason's students formed a wrong idea ("Maybe it's counting by twos") and then searched only for evidence confirming the wrong rule (by testing 6-8-10, 100-102-104, and so forth).

"Ordinary people," said Wason (1981), "evade facts, become inconsistent, or systematically defend themselves against the threat of new information relevant to the issue." The results are sometimes momentous. The United States launched its war against Iraq on the assumption that Saddam Hussein possessed weapons of mass destruction (WMD) that posed an immediate threat. When that assumption turned out to be false, flaws in the judgment process identified by the bipartisan U.S. Senate

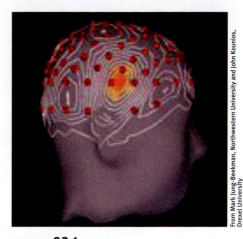

FIGURE 23.1
The Aha! moment
A burst of right temporal lobe activity accompanies insight solutions to word problems.

■ **algorithm** a methodical, logical rule or procedure that guarantees solving a particular problem. Contrasts with the usually speedier—but also more error-prone—use of *heuristics*.

■ **heuristic** a simple thinking strategy that often allows us to make judgments and solve problems efficiently; usually speedier but also more error-prone than *algorithms*.

■ **insight** a sudden and often novel realization of the solution to a problem; it contrasts with strategy-based solutions.

■ **confirmation bias** a tendency to search for information that confirms one's preconceptions.

❝ The human understanding, when any proposition has been once laid down . . . forces everything else to add fresh support and confirmation."

Francis Bacon, *Novum Organum*, 1620

From "Problem Solving" by M. Scheerer. Copyright © 1963 by Scientific American, Inc. All Rights Reserved.

FIGURE 23.2
The matchstick problem
How would you arrange six matches
to form four equilateral triangles?

(From "Problem Solving" by M. Scheerer. Copyright © 1963 by Scientific American, Inc. All Rights Reserved.)

FIGURE 23.3
The candle-mounting problem
Using these materials, how would you
mount the candle on a bulletin board?
(From Duncker, 1945.)

Select Committee on Intelligence (2004) included confirmation bias. Administration analysts "had a tendency to accept information which supported [their presumptions] . . . more readily than information which contradicted" them. Sources denying such weapons were deemed "either lying or not knowledgeable about Iraq's problems, while those sources who reported ongoing WMD activities were seen as having provided valuable information."

Fixation

Fixation—the inability to see a problem from a fresh perspective—is a true impediment to problem solving. Once we incorrectly represent a problem, it's hard to restructure how we approach it. If the solution to the matchstick problem in **FIGURE 23.2** eludes you, you may be experiencing fixation.

Another type of fixation—our tendency to think of only the familiar functions for objects, without imagining alternative uses—goes by the awkward but appropriate label **functional fixedness.** A person may ransack the house for a screwdriver when a dime would have turned the screw. As an example, try the candle-mounting problem in **FIGURE 23.3**. Did you experience functional fixedness?

If you had trouble solving the matchstick and candle-mounting problems, turn the next page to see the solutions in **FIGURES 23.4** and **23.5.** Perceiving and relating familiar things in new ways is part of creativity.

Making Decisions and Forming Judgments

23-3 : How do heuristics, overconfidence, and framing influence our decisions and judgments?

When making each day's hundreds of judgments and decisions—Is it worth the bother to take an umbrella? Can I trust this person? Should I shoot the basketball or pass to the player who's hot?—we seldom take the time and effort to reason systematically. We just follow our intuition. After interviewing policymakers in government, business, and education, social psychologist Irving Janis (1986) concluded that they "often do not use a reflective problem-solving approach. How do they usually arrive at their decisions? If you ask, they are likely to tell you . . . they do it mostly by *the seat of their pants.*"

Using and Misusing Heuristics

When we need to act quickly, those mental shortcuts we call heuristics often do help us overcome analysis paralysis. Thanks to the mind's automatic information processing, intuitive judgments are instantaneous. But the price we sometimes pay for this efficiency—quick but bad judgments—can be costly. Research by cognitive psychologists Amos Tversky and Daniel Kahneman (1974) on the *representativeness* and *availability heuristics* showed how these shortcuts can lead even the smartest people into dumb decisions.

> "In creating these problems, we didn't set out to fool people. All our problems fooled us, too."
>
> Amos Tversky (1985)

> "Intuitive thinking [is] fine most of the time. . . . But sometimes that habit of mind gets us in trouble."
>
> Nobel laureate Daniel Kahneman (2005)

Amos Tversky, 1937–1996

Courtesy of Greymayer Award, University of Louisville and the Tversky family

Daniel Kahneman

Courtesy of Greymayer Award, University of Louisville and Daniel Kahneman

The Representativeness Heuristic

To judge the likelihood of things in terms of how well they represent particular proto-types is to use the **representativeness heuristic.** To illustrate, consider:

> A stranger tells you about a person who is short, slim, and likes to read po-etry, and then asks you to guess whether this person is more likely to be a professor of classics at an Ivy League university or a truck driver (adapted from Nisbett & Ross, 1980). Which would be the better guess?

Did you answer "professor"? Many people do, because the description seems more *representative* of Ivy League scholars than of truck drivers. The representativeness heuristic enabled you to make a snap judgment. But it also led you to ignore other rel-evant information. When I help people think through this question, the conversation goes something like this:

Question:	First, let's figure out how many professors fit the description. How many Ivy League universities do you suppose there are?
Answer:	Oh, about 10, I suppose.
Question:	How many classics professors would you guess there are at each?
Answer:	Maybe 4.
Question:	Okay, that's 40 Ivy League classics professors. What fraction of these are short and slim?
Answer:	Let's say half.
Question:	And, of these 20, how many like to read poetry?
Answer:	I'd say half—10 professors.
Question:	Okay, now let's figure how many truck drivers fit the description. How many truck drivers do you suppose there are?
Answer:	Maybe 400,000.
Question:	What fraction are short and slim?
Answer:	Not many—perhaps 1 in 8.
Question:	Of these 50,000, what percentage like to read poetry?
Answer:	Truck drivers who like poetry? Maybe 1 in 100—oh, oh, I get it—that leaves 500 short, slim, poetry-reading truck drivers.
Comment:	Yup. So, even if we accept your stereotype that the description is more representative of classics professors than of truck drivers, the odds are 50 to 1 that this person is a truck driver.

The representativeness heuristic influences many of our daily decisions. To judge the likelihood of something, we intuitively compare it with our mental representation of that category—of, say, what truck drivers are like. If the two match, that fact usually overrides other considerations of statistics or logic.

The Availability Heuristic

The **availability heuristic** operates when we base our judgments on how mentally available information is. If instances of an event come to mind quickly and with little effort, we presume such events are common. The faster people can remember an in-stance of some event ("a broken promise"), the more they expect it to recur (MacLeod & Campbell, 1992). Cognitively available events *are* more likely to recur—but not always. To see this, make a guess: Does the letter *k* appear more often as the first or third letter in English usage?

Because words beginning with *k* come to mind more easily than words having *k* as their third letter, most people guess that *k* occurs more frequently as the first letter. Actually, *k* is much more likely to appear as the third letter. So far in this module, words such as *know, kingdom,* and *kin* are outnumbered 37 to 8 by words such as *make, likely, asked,* and *acknowledged.*

Why does the availability heuristic lead us astray? Anything that enables informa-tion to "pop into mind"—how recently we heard about an event, how vivid and con-crete it was, or how distinctive—can increase its perceived availability. If someone from a particular ethnic group commits a terrorist act, our readily available memory

■ **fixation** the inability to see a problem from a new perspective; an impediment to problem solving.

■ **functional fixedness** the tendency to think of things only in terms of their usual functions; an impediment to problem solving.

■ **representativeness heuristic** judging the likelihood of things in terms of how well they seem to represent, or match, particular prototypes; may lead one to ignore other relevant information.

■ **availability heuristic** estimating the likelihood of events based on their avail-ability in memory; if instances come readily to mind (perhaps because of their vivid-ness), we presume such events are common.

"The problem is I can't tell the difference between a deeply wise, intuitive nudge from the Universe and one of my own bone-headed ideas!"

"The information-processing shortcuts—called heuristics—which are normally both highly efficient and immensely time-saving in day-to-day situations, work systematically against us in the marketplace. . . . The tendency to underestimate or altogether ignore past probabilities in making a decision is undoubtedly the most significant problem of intuitive predictions."

David Dreman, *Contrarian Investment Strategy: The Psychology of Stock Market Success*, 1979

FIGURE 23.4
Solution to the matchstick problem
To solve this problem, you must view it from a new perspective, breaking the fixation of limiting solutions to two dimensions.

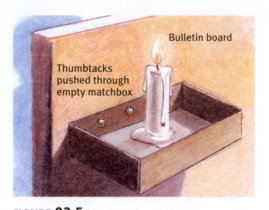

FIGURE 23.5
Solution to the candle-mounting problem
Solving this problem requires recognizing that a matchbox can have other functions besides holding matches. (From Duncker, 1945.)

of the dramatic event may shape our impression of the whole group. When statistical reality is pitted against a single vivid case, the memorable case often wins. (For more on the power of vivid cases, see Thinking Critically About: The Fear Factor.)

Overconfidence

Our use of intuitive heuristics when forming judgments, our eagerness to confirm the beliefs we already hold, and our knack for explaining away failures combine to create **overconfidence,** a tendency to overestimate the accuracy of our knowledge and judgments. Across various tasks, people overestimate what their performance was, is, or will be (Metcalfe, 1998).

People are also more confident than correct when answering such questions as, "Is absinthe a liqueur or a precious stone?" (It's a licorice-flavored liqueur.) On questions where only 60 percent of people answer correctly, respondents typically feel 75 percent confident. Even those who feel 100 percent certain err about 15 percent of the time (Fischhoff & others, 1977).

Overconfidence plagues decisions outside the laboratory, too. It was an overconfident Hitler who invaded Russia, an overconfident Lyndon Johnson who waged war with North Vietnam, an overconfident George W. Bush who marched into Iraq to eliminate supposed weapons of mass destruction. On a smaller scale, overconfidence drives stockbrokers and investment managers to market their ability to outperform stock market averages, despite overwhelming evidence to the contrary (Malkiel, 2004). A purchase of stock X, recommended by a broker who judges this to be the time to buy, is usually balanced by a sale made by someone who judges this to be the time to sell. Despite their confidence, buyer and seller cannot both be right.

Students, too, are routinely overconfident about how quickly they can do assignments and write papers (Buehler & others, 1994), typically expecting to finish ahead of schedule. In fact, the projects generally take about twice the number of days predicted. Despite our painful underestimates, we remain overly confident of our next prediction. Moreover, anticipating how much we will accomplish, we then overestimate our future free time (Zauberman & Lynch, 2005). Knowing we will have more free time next month than we do today, we happily accept invitations, only to discover we're just as busy when the day rolls around.

Failing to appreciate our potential for error can have serious consequences, but overconfidence does have adaptive value. People who err on the side of overconfidence live more happily, find it easier to make tough decisions, and seem more credible than those who lack self-confidence (Baumeister, 1989; Taylor, 1989). Moreover,

"Don't believe everything you think."

Bumper sticker

Predict your own behavior
When will you finish reading this module?

Worth Publishers photo by Nicole Villamora

given prompt and clear feedback—as weather forecasters receive after each day's predictions—we can learn to be more realistic about the accuracy of our judgments (Fischhoff, 1982). The wisdom to know when we know a thing and when we do not is born of experience.

The Effects of Framing

A further test of rationality is whether the same issue, presented in two different but logically equivalent ways, will elicit the same answer. For example, one surgeon tells someone that 10 percent of people die while undergoing a particular surgery. Another tells someone that 90 percent survive. The information is the same. The effect is not. To both patients and physicians, the risk seems greater when hearing that 10 percent will die (Marteau, 1989; McNeil & others, 1988; Rothman & Salovey, 1997).

The effects of **framing,** the way we present an issue, are sometimes striking. Nine in 10 college students rate a condom as effective if it has a supposed "95 percent success rate" in stopping the AIDS virus; only 4 in 10 think it successful when given a "5 percent failure rate" (Linville & others, 1992). And people express more surprise when a "1 in 20" event happens than when an equivalent "10 in 200" event happens (Denes-Raj & others, 1995). To scare people, frame risks as numbers, not percentages. People told that a chemical exposure is projected to kill 10 of every 10 million people (imagine 10 dead people!) feel more frightened than if told the fatality risk is an infinitesimal .000001 (Kraus & others, 1992).

Consider how the framing effect influences economic and business decisions. Merchants mark up their "regular prices" to appear to offer huge savings on "sale prices." A $100 coat marked down from $150 by Store X can seem like a better deal than the same coat priced regularly at $100 by Store Y (Urbany & others, 1988). Similarly, consumers respond more positively to ground beef described as "75 percent lean" rather than "25 percent fat" (Levin & Gaeth, 1988; Sanford & others, 2002). Likewise, a price difference for paying by credit card versus cash feels better if framed as a "cash discount."

The point to remember: Those who understand the power of framing can use it to influence our decisions—for example, by framing survey questions to support or reject their particular viewpoint.

The Belief Perseverance Phenomenon

23-4 : How do our preexisting beliefs influence our decision making?

That our judgments can flip-flop dramatically is startling. Equally startling is our tendency to cling to our beliefs in the face of contrary evidence. **Belief perseverance** often fuels social conflict, as it did in one study of people with opposing views of capital punishment (Lord and his colleagues, 1979). Those on both sides studied two supposedly new research findings, one supporting and the other refuting the claim that the death penalty deters crime. Each side was more impressed by the study supporting its own beliefs, and each readily disputed the other study. Thus, showing the pro- and anti–capital-punishment groups the same mixed evidence actually *increased* their disagreement.

If you want to rein in the belief perseverance phenomenon, a simple remedy exists: *Consider the opposite.* When Charles Lord and his colleagues (1984) repeated the capital-punishment study, they asked some participants to be "as *objective* and *unbiased* as possible." The plea did nothing to reduce biased evaluations of evidence. They asked another group to consider "whether you would have made the same high or low evaluations had exactly the same study produced results on the *other* side of the issue." Having imagined and pondered *opposite* findings, these people became much less biased in their evaluations of the evidence.

"When you know a thing, to hold that you know it; and when you do not know a thing, to allow that you do not know it; this is knowledge."

Confucius (551–479 B.C.), *Analects*

© The New Yorker Collection, 1989, Weber from cartoonbank.com. All Rights Reserved.

"This CD player costs less than players selling for twice as much."

■ **overconfidence** the tendency to be more confident than correct—to overestimate the accuracy of one's beliefs and judgments.

■ **framing** the way an issue is posed; how an issue is framed can significantly affect decisions and judgments.

■ **belief perseverance** clinging to one's initial conceptions after the basis on which they were formed has been discredited.

"Once you have a belief, it influences how you perceive all other relevant information. Once you see a country as hostile, you are likely to interpret ambiguous actions on their part as signifying their hostility."

Political scientist Robert Jervis (1985)

"To begin with, it was only tentatively that I put forward the views I have developed . . . but in the course of time they have gained such a hold upon me that I can no longer think in any other way."

Sigmund Freud,
Civilization and Its Discontents, 1930

THINKING CRITICALLY ABOUT :

THE FEAR FACTOR—DO WE FEAR THE RIGHT THINGS?

"Most people reason dramatically, not quantitatively," said Oliver Wendell Holmes. After 9/11, many people feared flying more than driving, even though Americans were—mile for mile—39.5 times more likely to die in an automobile crash than on a commercial flight in the months between 2000 and 2002 (National Safety Council, 2005). In a late-2001 essay, I calculated that if—because of 9/11—we flew 20 percent less and instead drove half those unflown miles, about 800 more people would die in traffic accidents in the year after 9/11 (Myers, 2001). In checking this estimate against accident data (why didn't I think of that?), German psychologist Gerd Gigerenzer (2004) found that the last three months of 2001 did indeed produce significantly more U.S. traffic fatalities than the three-month average in the previous five years (**FIGURE 23.6**). Long after 9/11, the dead terrorists were still killing Americans. As air travel gradually recovered during 2002, 2003, and 2004, U.S. commercial flights carried nearly 2 billion passengers, with only 34 deaths—none on a major airline big jet (Miller, 2005). Meanwhile, 128,000 Americans died in traffic accidents.

Why do we fear the wrong things? Why do we judge terrorism to be a greater risk than accidents—which kill nearly as many per *week* in just the United States as did terrorism (2527 deaths worldwide) in all of the 1990s (Johnson, 2001)? Even with the horror of 9/11, more Americans in 2001 died of food poisoning (which scares few) than of

FIGURE 23.6
Still killing Americans
Images of 9/11 etched a sharper image in our minds than did the millions of fatality-free flights on U.S. airlines during 2002 and after. Such dramatic events, being readily available to memory, shape our perceptions of risk. In the three months after 2001, those faulty perceptions led more people to travel, and some to die, by car. (Adapted from Gigerenzer, 2004.)

AP/Wide World Photos

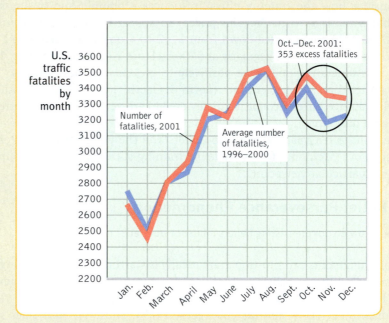

Oct.–Dec. 2001: 353 excess fatalities

Number of fatalities, 2001

Average number of fatalities, 1996–2000

U.S. traffic fatalities by month

"I'm happy to say that my final judgment of a case is almost always consistent with my prejudgment of the case."

© The New Yorker Collection, 1973, Fradon from cartoonbank.com. All Rights Reserved.

The more we come to appreciate why our beliefs might be true, the more tightly we cling to them. Once people have explained to themselves why they believe a child is "gifted" or "learning disabled," or why candidate X or Y will be more likely to preserve peace, or why stock in company Z is worth owning, they tend to ignore evidence undermining that belief. Prejudice persists. Once beliefs form and get justified, it takes more compelling evidence to change them than it did to create them.

terrorism (which scares many). Psychological science has identified four influences on our intuitions about risk.

First, we fear *what our ancestral history has prepared us to fear*. Human emotions were road tested in the Stone Age. Yesterday's risks prepare us to fear snakes, lizards, and spiders (which combined now kill virtually no one in developed countries). And they prepare us to fear confinement and heights, and therefore flying.

Second, we fear *what we cannot control*. Driving we control, flying we do not.

Third, we fear *what is immediate*. Threats related to flying are mostly telescoped into the moments of takeoff and landing, while the dangers of driving are diffused across many moments to come, each trivially dangerous. Similarly, many smokers (whose habit shortens their lives, on average, by about five years) fret openly before flying (which, averaged across people, shortens life by one day). Smoking's toxicity kills in the distant future.

Fourth, we fear *what is most readily available in memory*. Powerful, available memories—like the image of United Flight 175 slicing into the World Trade Center—serve as our measuring rods as we intuitively judge risks. Thousands of safe car trips have extinguished our anxieties about driving.

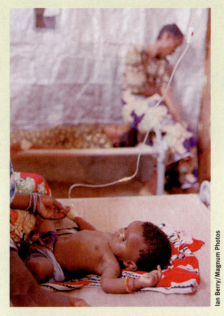

Dramatic deaths in bunches breed concern and fear
The memorable South Asian tsunami that killed some 300,000 people stirred an outpouring of concern and new tsunami-warning technology. Meanwhile, a "silent tsunami" of poverty-related malaria was killing about that many of the world's children every couple months, noted Jeffrey Sachs, the head of a United Nations project aiming to cut extreme poverty in half by 2015 (Dugger, 2005).

Ian Berry/Magnum Photos

Vivid events also distort our comprehension of risks and probable outcomes. We comprehend disasters that have killed people dramatically, in bunches. But we fear too little those threats that will claim lives undramatically, one by one, and in the distant future. As Bill Gates has noted, each year a half-million children worldwide—the equivalent of four 747s full of children every day—die quietly, one by one, from rotavirus, and we hear nothing of it (Glass, 2004). Dramatic outcomes capture our attention; probabilities we hardly grasp.

Nevertheless, we must "learn to protect ourselves and our families against future terrorist attacks," warns a U.S. Department of Homeland Security ad that has appeared periodically in my local newspapers. We must buy and store the food supplies, duct tape, and battery-powered radios we'll need if "there's a terrorist attack on your city." With 4 in 10 Americans being at least somewhat worried "that you or someone in your family will become a victim of terrorism," the "Be afraid!" message—be afraid not just of a terrorist attack on somebody somewhere, but of one on you and your place—has been heard (Carroll, 2005).

The point to remember: It is perfectly normal to fear purposeful violence from those who hate us. When terrorists strike again, we will all recoil in horror. But smart thinkers will remember this: *Check your fears against the facts and resist those who serve their own purposes by cultivating a culture of fear.* By so doing, we can take away the terrorists' most omnipresent weapon: exaggerated fear.

The Perils and Powers of Intuition

We have seen how our irrational thinking can plague our efforts to solve problems, make wise decisions, form valid judgments, and reason logically. Moreover, these perils of intuition appear even when people are offered extra pay for thinking smart, even when they are asked to justify their answers, and even when they are expert physicians or clinicians (Shafir & LeBoeuf, 2002). From this we might conclude that our heads are indeed filled with straw.

But we must not abandon hope for human rationality. Today's cognitive scientists are also revealing intuition's powers, as you have seen throughout this book. For the most part, our cognition's instant, intuitive reactions enable us to react quickly and *usually* adaptively.

Chick sexing
When acquired expertise becomes an automatic habit, as it is for experienced chick sexers, it feels like intuition. At a glance, they just know.

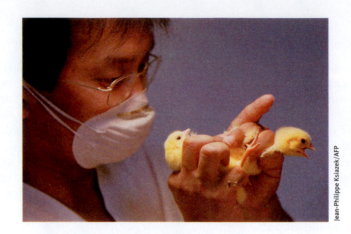

Jean-Philippe Ksiazek/AFP

In showing how everyday heuristics usually make us smart (and only sometimes make us dumb), Gerd Gigerenzer (2004) asked both American and German university students, "Which city has more inhabitants: San Diego or San Antonio?" After thinking a moment, 62 percent of the Americans guessed right: San Diego. But German students, many of whom had not heard of San Antonio (apologies to our Texas friends), used a fast and frugal intuitive heuristic: Pick the one you recognize. With less knowledge but an adaptive heuristic, 100 percent of the German respondents answered correctly.

Intuition is huge. More than we realize, thinking occurs off-screen, with the results occasionally displayed on-screen. Intuition is adaptive. It feeds our expertise, our creativity, our love, and our spirituality. And intuition, smart intuition, is born of experience. Chess masters can look at a board and intuitively know the right move. Playing "blitz chess," where every move is made after barely more than a glance, they display a hardly diminished skill (Burns, 2004). Experienced chicken sexers can tell you a chick's sex at a glance, yet cannot tell you how they do it. In each case, the immediate insight describes acquired, speedy expertise that feels like instant intuition. Experienced nurses, firefighters, art critics, car mechanics, hockey players, and you, for anything in which you develop a deep and special knowledge, learn to size up many a situation in an eyeblink. Intuition is recognition, observed Nobel laureate psychologist-economist Herbert Simon (2001). It is analysis "frozen into habit."

Mindful of intuition's perils and powers, we can think smarter, knowing our gut intuitions are terrific at some things, such as instantly reading emotions in others' faces, but not so good at others, such as assessing risks. Wisdom comes with knowing the difference.

In the discussion of decision making and overconfidence, I asked you to predict when you would finish this module. What time is it now? Did you underestimate or overestimate how quickly you would finish?

Let's pause to consider the question posed on the first page of this module—how deserving are we of our name *Homo sapiens?* If we were being graded on decision making and judgment, our error-prone species might rate a C+. On problem solving, where humans are inventive yet vulnerable to fixation, we would probably receive better marks, perhaps a B. On cognitive efficiency, our fallible but quick heuristics earn us an A.

>> MODULE REVIEW

23-1: What are the functions of concepts?

Cognition is a term covering all the mental activities associated with thinking, knowing, remembering, and communicating. We use *concepts* to simplify and order the world around us. We divide clusters of objects, events, ideas, or people into categories based on their similarities. In creating hierarchies, we subdivide these categories into smaller and more detailed units. We form other concepts, such as triangles, by definition (three-sided objects). But we form most concepts around *prototypes,* or best examples of a category. Matching objects and ideas against prototypes is an efficient way of making snap judgments about what belongs in a specific category.

23-2: What strategies do we use to solve problems, and what obstacles hinder our problem solving?

Problem solving often involves algorithms and heuristics. An *algorithm* is a time-consuming but thorough set of rules or procedures (such as a recipe for cookies, or a step-by-step description for evacuating a building during a fire) that guarantees a solution to a problem. A *heuristic* is a simpler thinking strategy (such as running for an exit if you smell heavy smoke) that may allow us to solve problems quickly, but sometimes leads us to incorrect solutions. *Insight* differs from both because it is not a strategy-based solution, but rather an Aha! reaction—a sudden flash of inspiration that solves a problem.

We do, however, face certain obstacles to successful problem solving. The *confirmation bias* predisposes us to verify rather than challenge our hypotheses. And *fixations,* such as *functional fixedness,* may prevent our taking a needed fresh perspective on a problem.

23-3: How do heuristics, overconfidence, and framing influence our decisions and judgments?

The *representativeness heuristic* leads us to judge the likelihood of things in terms of how well they represent our prototype for a group of items. The *availability heuristic* leads us to judge the likelihood of things based on how vivid they are or how readily they come to mind. These shortcuts can cause us to ignore important information or to underestimate the chances of something happening. Heuristics can also blind us to our vulnerability to error, a phenomenon known as *overconfidence.* The way someone poses, or *frames,* a question affects our responses.

23-4: How do our preexisting beliefs influence our decision making?

One way our preexisting beliefs influence our decisions is *belief perseverance,* clinging to our ideas because the explanation we once accepted as valid lingers in our mind even after it has been discredited. The best remedy for belief perseverance is to consider the opposite. Despite our capacity for error and our susceptibility to bias, human intuition can be efficient and adaptive, as when we gain expertise in a field and grow adept at making quick, shrewd judgments.

>> REHEARSE IT!

1. We use the concept *bird* to think and talk about a variety of creatures, all having wings and feathers. A concept is
   a. a mental grouping of similar things.
   b. an example of insight.
   c. a fixation on certain characteristics.
   d. a hierarchy.

2. Sometimes we solve problems through trial and error, trying hundreds or even thousands of solutions before finding one that works. At other times we are more methodical or systematic. The most systematic procedure for solving a problem is a(n)
   a. heuristic.
   b. algorithm.
   c. insight.
   d. intuition.

3. A major obstacle to problem solving is the *confirmation bias,* the tendency to search for information that confirms our preconceptions while ignoring information that might prove us wrong. Another obstacle to problem solving is *fixation,* which is a(n)
   a. tendency to base our judgments on vivid memories.
   b. art of framing the same question in two different ways.
   c. inability to view a problem from a new perspective.
   d. rule of thumb for judging the likelihood of an event in terms of our mental image of it.

4. You move into a new neighborhood and notice that your next-door neighbor is very neatly dressed, wears glasses, and is reading a Greek play. Given a choice between her being a librarian and a store clerk, you incorrectly guess that she is a librarian. You were probably led astray by
   a. the availability heuristic.
   b. confirmation bias.
   c. overconfidence.
   d. the representativeness heuristic.

5. After the 9/11 attacks by foreign-born terrorists, some observers initially assumed that the 2003 East Coast blackout was probably also the work of foreign-born terrorists. This assumption illustrates
   a. belief perseverance.
   b. the availability heuristic.
   c. functional fixedness.
   d. confirmation bias.

6. The way an issue is posed can affect our decisions and judgments. When consumers respond more positively to ground beef described as "75 percent lean" than to the same product labeled "25 percent fat," they have been influenced by
   a. belief perseverance.
   b. fixation.
   c. confirmation bias.
   d. framing.

Answers: 1. a, 2. b, 3. c, 4. d, 5. b, 6. d.

>> TERMS AND CONCEPTS TO REMEMBER

cognition, p. 307

concept, p. 307

prototype, p. 307

algorithm, p. 308

heuristic, p. 308

insight, p. 308

confirmation bias, p. 309

fixation, p. 310

functional fixedness, p. 310

representativeness heuristic, p. 311

availability heuristic, p. 311

overconfidence, p. 312

framing, p. 313

belief perseverance, p. 313

>> TEST YOURSELF

1. The availability heuristic is a quick-and-easy but sometimes misleading guide to judging reality. What is the availability heuristic?

   (Answer in Appendix C.)

   *Multiple-choice **self-tests** and more may be found at www.worthpublishers.com/myers.*

>> ANSWER TO QUESTION WITHIN THE MODULE

Q. Can you find another word using all the letters of *SPLOYOCHYG?*

A. Psychology

Language and Thought

M O D U L E

The most tangible indication of our thinking power is **language**—our spoken, written, or signed words and the ways we combine them as we think and communicate. Humans have long and proudly proclaimed that language sets us above all other animals. "When we study human language," asserted linguist Noam Chomsky (1972), "we are approaching what some might call the 'human essence,' the qualities of mind that are, so far as we know, unique" to humans. To cognitive scientist Steven Pinker (1990), language is "the jewel in the crown of cognition."

Imagine an alien species that could pass thoughts from one head to another merely by pulsating air molecules in the space between them. Perhaps these weird creatures could inhabit a future Spielberg movie? Actually, we are those creatures! When we speak, our brain and voice box conjure up air pressure waves that we send banging against another's ear drum—enabling us to transfer thoughts from our brain into theirs. As Pinker (1998) notes, we sometimes sit for hours "listening to other people make noise as they exhale, because those hisses and squeaks contain *information*." And thanks to all those funny sounds created in our heads from the air pressure waves we send out, adds Bernard Guerin (2003), we get people's attention, we get them to do things, and we maintain relationships.

When the human vocal tract evolved the ability to utter vowels, our capacity for language exploded, catapulting our species forward (Diamond, 1989). Whether spoken, written, or signed, language enables us not only to communicate but to transmit civilization's accumulated knowledge across generations. Monkeys mostly know what they see. Thanks to language, we know much that we've never seen.

Language Development

24-1 : When do children acquire language, and how do they master this complex task?

Make a quick guess: How many words did you learn during the years between your first birthday and your high school graduation? Ready? The answer is about 60,000 (Bloom, 2000). That averages (after age 1) to nearly 3500 words each year, or 10 each day! How you did it—how the 3500 words a year you learned could so far outnumber the roughly 200 words a year that your schoolteachers consciously taught you—is one of the great human wonders.

Before you were able to add 2 + 2, you were creating your own original and grammatically appropriate sentences. Most of us would have trouble stating the rules of *syntax*—correctly stringing words together to form sentences. Yet as preschoolers, you comprehended and spoke with a facility that puts to shame your fellow college students now struggling to learn a foreign language. We humans have an astonishing facility for language. With remarkable efficiency, we selectively sample tens of thousands of words in memory, effortlessly combine them on the fly with near-perfect syntax, and spew them out three words a second (Vigliocco & Hartsuiker, 2002). We also adapt our language to our social and cultural context, following rules for speaking (How far apart should we stand?) and listening (Is it OK to interrupt?). It is amazing, given how many ways there are to mess up, that we effortlessly master this social dance. So, when and how does it happen?

Although you probably know between 60,000 and 80,000 words, you use only 150 words for about half of what you say.

■ **language** our spoken, written, or signed words and the ways we combine them to communicate meaning.

TABLE 24.1

SUMMARY OF LANGUAGE DEVELOPMENT

Month (approximate)	Stage
4	Babbles many speech sounds.
10	Babbling resembles household language.
12	One-word stage.
24	Two-word, telegraphic speech.
24+	Language develops rapidly into complete sentences.

When Do We Learn Language?

Children's language development moves from simplicity to complexity. Infants start without language (*in fantis* means "not speaking"). Yet by 4 months of age, babies can read lips and discriminate speech sounds. They prefer to look at a face that matches a sound, so we know they can recognize that *ah* comes from wide open lips and *ee* from a mouth with corners pulled back (Kuhl & Meltzoff, 1982). This marks the beginning of the development of babies' *receptive language,* their ability to comprehend speech. Babies' receptive language abilities begin to mature before their *productive language,* their ability to produce words.

Around 4 months of age, babies enter a **babbling stage** (TABLE 24.1) in which they spontaneously utter a variety of sounds, such as *ah-goo.* Babbling is not an imitation of adult speech, for it includes sounds from various languages, even those not spoken in the household. From this early babbling, a listener could not identify an infant as being, say, French, Korean, or Ethiopian. Deaf infants who observe their Deaf parents signing begin to babble more with their hands (Petitto & Marentette, 1991). Even before nurture molds our speech, nature enables a wide range of possible sounds. Many of these natural babbling sounds are consonant-vowel pairs formed by simply bunching the tongue in front of the mouth (*da-da, na-na, ta-ta*) or by opening and closing the lips (*ma-ma*), both of which babies do naturally for feeding (MacNeilage & Davis, 2000).

By the time infants are about 10 months old, their babbling has changed so that a trained ear can identify the language of the household (de Boysson-Bardies & others, 1989). Sounds and intonations outside that language begin to disappear. Without exposure to other languages, they become functionally deaf to speech sounds outside their native language (Pallier & others, 2001). Thus, by adulthood those who speak only English cannot discriminate certain Japanese sounds within speech. Nor can Japanese adults with no training in English distinguish between the English *r* and *l.* Thus (believe it or not), *la-la-ra-ra* may sound like the same repeated syllable to a Japanese adult. This makes life challenging for the Japanese tourist who is told the train station is "just after the next light." The next what? After the street veering right, or farther down, after the traffic light?

Around the first birthday (the exact age varies from child to child), most children enter the **one-word stage.** They have already learned that sounds carry meanings, and if repeatedly trained to associate, say, *fish* with a picture of a fish, one-year-olds will look at a fish when a researcher says "Fish, fish! Look at the fish!" (Schafer, 2005). Not surprisingly, they now begin to use sounds—usually only one barely recognizable syllable, such as *ma* or *da*—to communicate meaning. But family members quickly learn to understand, and gradually the infant's language conforms more to the family's language. At this one-word stage, an inflected word may equal a sentence. "Doggy!" may mean "Look at the dog out there!"

At about 18 months, children's word learning explodes from about a word per week to a word per day. By their second birthday, most have entered the **two-word stage.** They start uttering two-word sentences in **telegraphic speech:** Like telegrams (TERMS ACCEPTED. SEND MONEY), this early form of speech contains mostly nouns and verbs (*Want juice*). Also like telegrams, it follows rules of syntax; the words are in a sensible order. English-speaking children typically place adjectives before nouns—*big doggy* rather than *doggy big.*

Once children move out of the two-word stage, they quickly begin uttering longer phrases (Fromkin & Rodman, 1983). By early elementary school, they understand complex sentences and begin to enjoy the humor conveyed by double meanings: "You never starve in the desert because of all the sand-which-is there."

"Got idea. Talk better. Combine words. Make sentences."

© 1994 by Sidney Harris.

Explaining Language Development

Attempts to explain how we acquire language have sparked a spirited intellectual controversy. The nature-nurture debate surfaces again and, here as elsewhere, appreciation for innate predisposition and the nature-nature interaction has grown.

Skinner: Operant Learning

Behaviorist B. F. Skinner (1957) believed we can explain language development with familiar learning principles, such as association (of the sights of things with the sounds of words); imitation (of the words and syntax modeled by others); and reinforcement (with success, smiles, and hugs when the child says something right). Thus, Skinner (1985) argued, babies learn to talk in many of the same ways that animals learn to peck keys and press bars: "Verbal behavior evidently came into existence when, through a critical step in the evolution of the human species, the vocal musculature became susceptible to operant conditioning."

Chomsky: Inborn Universal Grammar

Linguist Noam Chomsky (1959, 1987) thinks Skinner's ideas were naive. He (1987) likened the behaviorist view of how language develops to filling a bottle with water, but developing language is not just being "filled up" with the right kinds of experiences. He maintains that children acquire untaught words and grammar at a rate too extraordinary to be explained solely by learning principles. They generate all sorts of sentences they have never heard, sometimes with novel errors. (No parent teaches the sentence, "I hate you, Daddy.") Chomsky instead has viewed language development much like "helping a flower to grow in its own way." Language will naturally occur, given adequate nurture; it just "happens to the child." And the reason it happens is that we come prewired with a sort of switch box—a *language acquisition device*—already in place. It is as if the switches need to be turned either "on" or "off" for us to understand and produce language. As we hear language, the switches get set for the language we are to learn.

Underlying human language, Chomsky says, is a *universal grammar*. Thus, all human languages have the same grammatical building blocks, such as nouns and verbs, subjects and objects, negations and questions. As Steven Pinker (2002) points out, there are no other conceivable ways to power a communication system.

Contemporary psychologists view language development from multiple perspectives, and they believe we benefit from both Skinner's and Chomsky's views. Children's genes design complex brain wiring that prepares them to learn language as they interact with their caregivers. Skinner's emphasis on learning helps explain how infants acquire their language as they interact with others. Chomsky's emphasis on our built-in readiness to learn grammar rules helps explain why preschoolers acquire language so readily and use grammar so well. Once again, we see biology and experience working together (**FIGURE 24.1**).

Thus, we learn readily the specific grammar of whatever language we experience, whether spoken or signed (Bavelier & others, 2003). And no matter what that language is, we start speaking mostly in nouns *(kitty, da-da)* rather than verbs and adjectives (Bornstein & others, 2004). It happens so naturally—as naturally as birds learning to fly—that training hardly helps.

Childhood seems to represent a *critical period* for mastering certain aspects of language. Deaf children who gain hearing with cochlear implants by age 2 develop better oral speech than do those who receive implants after age 4 (Greers, 2004). For deaf or hearing children, later-than-usual exposure to language (at age 2 or 3) unleashes their brain's idle language capacity, producing a rush of language. But children who have not been exposed to either a spoken or a signed language during their early years (by about age 7) gradually lose their ability to master *any* language. Natively deaf children who learn sign language after age 9 never learn it as well as those who become deaf at age 9 after learning English. They also never learn English as well as other natively deaf children who learned sign in infancy (Mayberry & others, 2002). The striking conclusion: When a young brain does not learn *any* language, its language-learning capacity never fully develops.

■ **babbling stage** beginning at about 4 months, the stage of speech development in which the infant spontaneously utters various sounds at first unrelated to the household language.

■ **one-word stage** the stage in speech development, from about age 1 to 2, during which a child speaks mostly in single words.

■ **two-word stage** beginning about age 2, the stage in speech development during which a child speaks mostly two-word statements.

■ **telegraphic speech** early speech stage in which a child speaks like a telegram—"go car"—using mostly nouns and verbs and omitting auxiliary words.

Slightly more than half the world's 6000 languages are spoken by fewer than 10,000 people. And slightly more than half the world's population speaks one of the top 20 languages (Gibbs, 2002).

Creating a language

Brought together as if on a desert island (actually a school), Nicaragua's young deaf children over time drew upon sign gestures from their own home to create their own Nicaraguan Sign Language, complete with words and intricate grammar. Our biological predisposition for language does not create language in a vacuum. But activated by a social context, nature and nurture work creatively together (Osborne, 1999; Sandler & others, 2005; Senghas & Coppola, 2001).

Susan Meiselas/Magnum Photos

FIGURE **24.1**
Levels of understanding language development
Genes help design the mechanisms for a language, and experience modifies the brain. Grow up in Paris and you will speak French (environment matters), but not if you are a cat (genes matter).

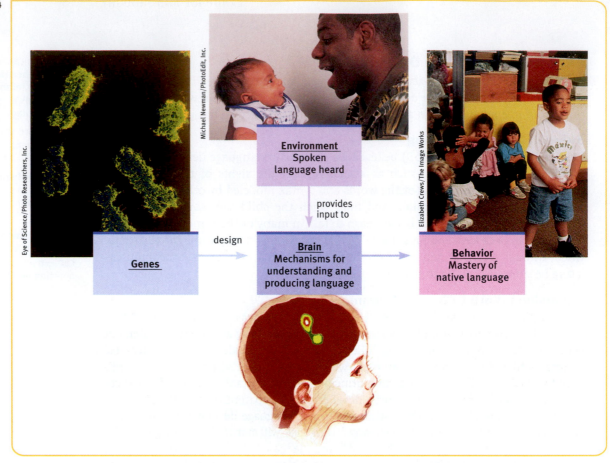

Environment
Spoken language heard

provides input to

Genes

design

Brain
Mechanisms for understanding and producing language

Behavior
Mastery of native language

After the window for learning language closes, even learning a second language seems more difficult. People who learn a second language as adults usually speak it with the accent of their first. Grammar learning is similarly more difficult. Jacqueline Johnson and Elissa Newport (1991) asked Korean and Chinese immigrants to identify whether each of 276 English sentences ("Yesterday the hunter shoots a deer") was grammatically correct or incorrect. Some test-takers had arrived in the United States in early childhood, others as adults, but all had been in the country for approximately 10 years. Nevertheless, as **FIGURE 24.2** reveals, those who learned their second language early learned it best. The older the age at which one emigrates to a new country, the harder it is to learn its language (Hakuta & others, 2003).

"Childhood is the time for language, no doubt about it. Young children, the younger the better, are good at it; it is child's play. It is a onetime gift to the species."

Lewis Thomas, *The Fragile Species*, 1992

FIGURE **24.2**
New language learning gets harder with age
Young children have a readiness to learn language. Ten years after coming to the United States, Asian immigrants took a grammar test. Those who arrived before age 8 understood American English grammar as well as native speakers did. Although there is no sharply defined critical period for second language learning, those who arrived later did not. (From Johnson & Newport, 1991.)

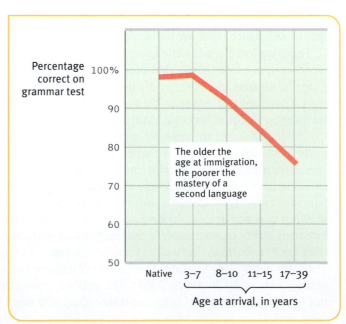

Percentage correct on grammar test

100%

90

80

The older the age at immigration, the poorer the mastery of a second language

70

60

50

Native   3–7   8–10   11–15   17–39

Age at arrival, in years

Copyright © Don Smetzer/Photo Edit—All rights reserved.

The impact of early experiences is also evident in language learning in the 90+ percent of deaf children born to hearing-nonsigning parents. These children typically do not experience language during their early years. Compared with children exposed to sign language from birth, those who learn to sign as teens or adults are like immigrants who learn English after childhood. They can master the basic words and learn to order them, but they never become as fluent as native signers in producing and comprehending subtle grammatical differences (Newport, 1990). Moreover, the late-learners show less brain activity in right hemisphere regions that are active as native signers read sign language (Newman & others, 2002). As a flower's growth will be stunted without nourishment, so, too, will children become linguistically stunted if isolated from language during the critical period for its acquisition.

Thinking and Language

24-2: What is the relationship between thinking and language?

Thinking and language intricately intertwine. Asking which comes first is one of psychology's chicken-and-egg questions. Do our ideas come first and we wait for words to name them? Or are our thoughts conceived in words and therefore unthinkable without them?

Language Influences Thinking

Linguist Benjamin Lee Whorf contended that language determines the way we think. According to Whorf's (1956) **linguistic determinism** hypothesis, different languages impose different conceptions of reality: "Language itself shapes a man's basic ideas." The Hopi, Whorf noted, have no past tense for their verbs. Therefore, he contended, a Hopi could not so readily *think* about the past.

To say that language *determines* the way we think is much too strong. But to those who speak two dissimilar languages, such as English and Japanese, it seems obvious that a person may think differently in different languages (Brown, 1986). Unlike English, which has a rich vocabulary for self-focused emotions such as anger, Japanese has more words for interpersonal emotions such as sympathy (Markus & Kitayama, 1991). Many bilinguals report that they have different senses of self, depending on which language they are using (Matsumoto, 1994). They may even reveal different personality profiles when taking the same test in their two languages (Dinges & Hull, 1992).

Michael Ross, Elaine Xun, and Anne Wilson (2002) demonstrated this by inviting China-born, bilingual University of Waterloo students to describe themselves in English or Chinese. English-language versions of self-descriptions fit typical Canadian profiles: Students expressed mostly positive self-statements and moods. Responding in Chinese, students gave typically Chinese self-descriptions: They reported more agreement with Chinese values and roughly equal positive and negative self-statements and moods. Their language use seemed to shape how they thought of themselves.

So our words may not determine what we think, but they do *influence* our thinking (Hardin & Banaji, 1993; Özgen, 2004). We use our language in forming categories. In Brazil, the isolated Piraha tribespeople have words for the numbers "1" and "2," but numbers above that are simply "many." Thus if shown seven nuts in a row, they find it very difficult to lay out the same number from their own pile (Gordon, 2004). And whether we live in New Mexico, New South Wales, or New Guinea, we also use our native language to classify and remember colors (Davidoff, 2004; Roberson & others, 2004). If that language is English, you might view three colors and call two of them "yellow" and one of them "blue." Later you would likely see and recall the yellows as being more similar. But if you were a member of Papua New Guinea's Berinmo tribe, which has words for two different shades of yellow, you would better recall the distinctions between the two yellows.

George Ancona

No means no—no matter how you say it!
Deaf children of deaf-signing parents and hearing children of hearing parents have much in common. They develop language skills at about the same rate, and they are equally effective at opposing parental wishes and demanding their way.

" **Language is not a straightjacket."**
Psychologist Lila Gleitman, American Association for the Advancement of Science Convention, 2002

Before reading on, use a pen or pencil to sketch this idea: "The girl pushes the boy." I'll ask you about this later.

Learn a language and you learn about a culture. When a language becomes extinct—the likely fate of most of the world's 6000 remaining languages—the world loses the culture and thinking that hang on that language.

■ **linguistic determinism** Whorf's hypothesis that language determines the way we think.

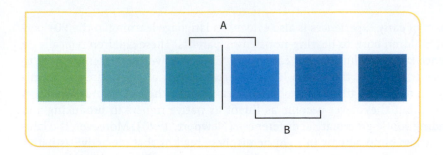

FIGURE 24.3
Language and perception
Emre Özgen (2004) reports that when people view blocks of equally different colors, they perceive those with different names as more different. Thus the "green" and "blue" in contrast A may appear to differ more than the two similarly different blues in contrast B.

"All words are pegs to hang ideas on."
Henry Ward Beecher, *Proverbs from Plymouth Pulpit*, 1887

Many native English speakers, including most Americans, are monolingual. Most humans are bilingual or multilingual. Does monolingualism limit people's ability to comprehend the thinking of other cultures?

A safe sign
We have outfielder William Hoy to thank for baseball sign language. The first deaf player to join the major leagues (1892), he invented hand signals for "Strike!" "Safe!" (shown here) and "Yerr Out!" (Pollard, 1992). Such gestures worked so well that referees in all sports now use invented signs, and fans are fluent in sports sign language.

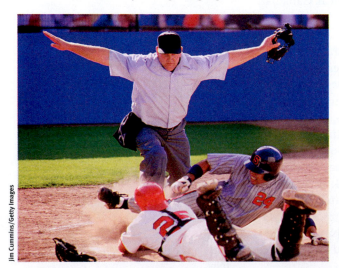
Jim Cummins/Getty Images

Perceived differences grow when we assign different names to colors. On the color spectrum, blue blends into green—until we draw a dividing line between the portions we call "blue" and "green." Although equally different on the color spectrum (**FIGURE 24.3**), two different "blues" (or two different "greens") that share the same name are harder to distinguish than two items named "blue" and "green" (Özgen, 2004).

Given words' subtle influence on thinking, we do well to choose our words carefully. Does it make any difference whether I write, "A child learns language as *he* interacts with *his* caregivers" or "Children learn language as *they* interact with *their* caregivers"? Many studies have found that it does. When hearing the generic *he* (as in "the artist and his work") people are more likely to picture a male (Henley, 1989; Ng, 1990). If *he* and *his* were truly gender-free, we shouldn't skip a beat when hearing that "man, like other mammals, nurses his young."

To expand language is to expand the ability to think. Young children's thinking develops hand in hand with their language (Gopnik & Meltzoff, 1986). Indeed, it is very difficult to think about or conceptualize certain abstract ideas (commitment, freedom, or rhyming) without language! And what is true for preschoolers is true for everyone: *It pays to increase your word power.* That's why most textbooks, including this one, introduce new words—to teach new ideas and new ways of thinking.

Increased word power helps explain what McGill University researcher Wallace Lambert (1992; Lambert & others, 1993) calls the *bilingual advantage*. Bilingual children, who learn to inhibit one language while using the other, are also better able to inhibit their attention to irrelevant information. If asked to say whether a sentence ("Why is the cat barking so loudly?") is grammatically correct, they can more efficiently focus on the grammar alone (Bialystok, 2001).

Lambert helped devise a Canadian program that immerses English-speaking children in French. (From 1981 to 1999, the number of non-Quebec Canadian children immersed in French rose from 65,000 to 280,000 [Commissioner, 1999].) For most of their first three years in school, the English-speaking children are taught entirely in French, and thereafter gradually shift by the end of their schooling to classes mostly in English. Not surprisingly, the children attain a natural French fluency unrivaled by other methods of language teaching. Moreover, compared with similarly capable children in control groups, they do so without detriment to their English fluency, and with increased aptitude scores, math scores, and appreciation for French-Canadian culture (Genesee & Gándara, 1999).

Stop now, and look at how you sketched "the girl pushes the boy," which I asked you to do earlier. Anne Maass and Aurore Russo (2003) report that people whose language reads from left to right mostly position the pushing girl on the left. Those who speak Arabic, a language that reads from right to left, mostly place her on the right. Whether we are deaf or hearing, minority or majority, language transforms experience and links us to one another. Language also connects us to the past and the future. "To destroy a people, destroy their language," observed poet Joy Harjo.

Thinking in Images

When you are alone, do you talk to yourself? Is "thinking" simply conversing with yourself? Without a doubt, words convey ideas. But aren't there times when ideas precede words? To turn on the cold water in your bathroom, in which direction do you turn the handle? To answer this question, you probably thought not in words but with *nondeclarative (procedural) memory*—a mental picture of how you do it.

Indeed, we often think in images. Artists think in images. So do composers, poets, mathematicians, athletes, and scientists. Albert Einstein reported that he achieved some of his greatest insights through visual images and later put them into words. Pianist Liu Chi Kung showed the value of thinking in images. One year after placing second in the 1958 Tchaikovsky piano competition, Liu was imprisoned during China's cultural revolution. Soon after his release, after seven years without touching a piano, he was back on tour, the critics judging his musicianship better than ever. How did he continue to develop without practice? "I did practice," said Liu, "every day. I rehearsed every piece I had ever played, note by note, in my mind" (Garfield, 1986).

For someone who has learned a skill, such as ballet dancing, even *watching* the activity will activate the brain's internal simulation of it, reports one British research team after collecting functional MRI scans (fMRIs) as people watched videos (Calvo-Merino & others, 2004). So will imagining an activity. **FIGURE 24.4** shows an fMRI of a person imagining the experience of pain, activating neural networks that are active during actual pain (Grèzes & Decety, 2001).

Small wonder, then, that "mental practice has become a standard part of training" for Olympic athletes (Suinn, 1997). One experiment on mental practice and basketball foul shooting tracked the University of Tennessee women's team over 35 games (Savoy & Beitel, 1996). During that time, the team's free-throw shooting increased from approximately 52 percent in games following standard physical practice to some 65 percent after mental practice. Players had repeatedly imagined making foul shots under various conditions, including being "trash-talked" by their opposition. In a dramatic conclusion, Tennessee won the national championship game in overtime, thanks in part to their foul shooting.

Mental rehearsal can also help you achieve an academic goal, as Shelley Taylor and her UCLA colleagues (1998) demonstrated with two groups of introductory psychology students facing a midterm exam one week later. (Scores of other students formed a control group, not engaging in any mental simulation.) The first group was told to spend five minutes each day visualizing themselves scanning the posted grade list, seeing their A, beaming with joy, and feeling proud. This daily *outcome simulation* had little effect, adding only 2 points to their exam-scores average. Another group spent five minutes each day visualizing themselves effectively studying—reading the chapters, going over notes, eliminating distractions, declining an offer to go out. This daily *process simulation* paid off—this second group began studying sooner, spent more time at it, and beat the others' average by 8 points. *The point to remember:* It's better to spend your fantasy time planning how to get somewhere than to dwell on the imagined destination.

A thoughtful art
Playing the piano engages thinking without language. In the absence of a piano, mental practice can sustain one's skill.

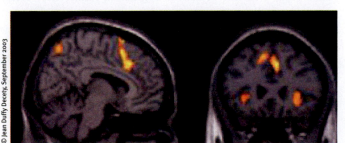

FIGURE 24.4
The power of imagination
Imagining a physical activity triggers action in the same brain areas that are triggered when actually performing that activity. These fMRIs show a person imagining the experience of pain, which activates some of the same areas in the brain as the actual experience of pain.

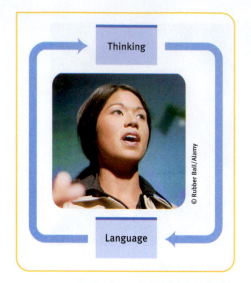

FIGURE 24.5

The interplay of thought and language

The traffic runs both ways between thinking and language. Thinking affects our language, which affects our thought.

Experiments on thinking without language bring us back to a now-familiar principle: Much of our information processing occurs outside of consciousness and beyond language. Inside our ever-active brain, many streams of activity flow in parallel, function automatically, are remembered implicitly, and only occasionally surface as conscious words.

What, then, should we say about the relationship between thinking and language? As we have seen, language does influence our thinking. But if thinking did not also affect language, there would never be any new words. And new words and new combinations of old words express new ideas. The basketball term *slam dunk* was coined after the act itself had become fairly common. So, let us say that *thinking affects our language, which then affects our thought* (**FIGURE 24.5**).

Psychological research on thinking and language demonstrates that the human mind is simultaneously capable of striking intellectual failures and of striking intellectual power. Misjudgments are common and can have disastrous consequences. So we do well to appreciate our capacity for error. Yet our efficient heuristics—our snap-judgment strategies—often serve us well. Moreover, our ingenuity at problem solving and our extraordinary power of language mark humankind as almost "infinite in faculties."

Animal Thinking and Language

24-3: Do animals—in some sense we can identify with—think? Do they even exhibit language?

If in our use of language we humans are, as the psalmist long ago rhapsodized, "little lower than God," where do other animals fit in the scheme of things? Are they "little lower than human"? Let's see what the research on animal thinking and language can tell us.

Do Animals Think?

Animals, especially the great apes, display remarkable capacities for thinking. They can, for example, *form concepts.* After monkeys learn to classify cats and dogs, certain frontal lobe neurons in their brains fire in response to new "catlike" images, others to new "doglike" images (Freedman & others, 2001). Even pigeons—mere birdbrains—can sort objects (pictures of cars, cats, chairs, flowers) according to their similarity. Shown a picture of a never-before-seen chair, the pigeon will reliably peck a key that represents the category "chairs" (Wasserman, 1995).

We also are not the only creatures to *display insight,* as psychologist Wolfgang Köhler (1925) demonstrated in an experiment with Sultan, a chimpanzee. Köhler placed a piece of fruit and a long stick well beyond Sultan's reach, and a short stick inside his cage. Spying the short stick, Sultan grabbed it and tried to reach the fruit. After several unsuccessful attempts, Sultan dropped the stick and seemed to survey the situation. Then suddenly, as if thinking "Aha!" he jumped up, seized the short stick again, and used it to pull in the longer stick—which he then used to reach the fruit. Clear evidence of animal cognition, said Köhler, showed there is more to learning than conditioning.

But chimpanzees, like humans, are *shaped by reinforcement* when they solve problems. Forest-dwelling chimpanzees have become natural tool users (Boesch-Achermann & Boesch, 1993). They break off a reed or a stick, strip the twigs and leaves, carry it to a termite mound, fish for termites by twisting it just so, and then carefully remove it without scraping off many termites. They even select different tools for different purposes—a heavy stick to puncture holes, a light, flexible stick for fishing (Sanz & others, 2004). One anthropologist, trying to mimic the chimpanzee's deft termite fishing, failed miserably.

(a)

(b)

FIGURE 24.6
Cultural transmission
(a) On the western bank of one Ivory Coast river, a youngster watches as its mother uses a stone hammer to open a nut. On the river's other side, a few miles away, chimpanzees do not follow this custom.
(b) This bottlenose dolphin in Shark Bay, Western Australia, is a member of a small group that uses marine sponges as a protective glove when probing the sea floor for fish.

Researchers have found at least 39 local customs related to chimp tool use, grooming, and courtship (Whiten & Boesch, 2001). One group may slurp ants directly from the stick, while another group plucks them off individually. One group may break nuts with a stone hammer, another with a wooden hammer. Such group differences, along with differing dialects and hunting styles, seem not to be genetic. Rather, they are the chimpanzee equivalent of cultural diversity. Like humans, chimpanzees invent behaviors and *transmit cultural patterns* to their peers and offspring (**FIGURE 24.6a**). So do orangutans (van Schaik & others, 2003). And so do some Australian dolphins (**FIGURE 24.6b**), which have learned to break off sponges and wear them on their snouts while probing the sea floor for fish (Krützen & others, 2005).

Do Animals Exhibit Language?

Without doubt, animals communicate. Vervet monkeys have different alarm cries for different predators: a barking call for a leopard, a cough for an eagle, and a chuttering for a snake. Hearing the leopard alarm, other vervets climb the nearest tree. Hearing the eagle alarm, they rush into the bushes. Hearing the snake chutter, they stand up and scan the ground (Byrne, 1991). Whales also communicate, with clicks and wails. Honeybees do a dance that informs other bees of the direction and distance of the food source. And what shall we say of dogs' ability to interact with us? Take Rico the border collie, who knows and can fetch 200 items by name. Moreover, reports a team of psychologists at Leipzig's Max Planck Institute, if asked to retrieve a novel toy with a name he has never heard, Rico will pick out the novel item from among a group of familiar items (Kaminski & others, 2004). Hearing that novel word for the second time four weeks later, he as often as not retrieves the object. Without question, such feats show animals' comprehension and communication. But is this language?

Comprehending canine
Rico, a border collie with a 200-word vocabulary, can infer that an unfamiliar sound refers to a novel object.

The Case of the Apes

The greatest challenge to our claim to be the only language-using species has come from our closest genetic relatives, the chimpanzees. Psychologists Allen Gardner and Beatrix Gardner (1969) aroused enormous scientific and public interest when they taught sign language to the chimpanzee Washoe. After four years, Washoe could use 132 signs; by age 32, Washoe was using 181 signs (Sanz & others, 1998). One *New York Times* reporter, having learned sign language from his deaf parents, visited Washoe and exclaimed, "Suddenly I realized I was conversing with a member of another species in my native tongue."

Further evidence of gestured "ape language" surfaced during the 1970s. Usually apes sign just single words such as "that" or "gimme" (Bowman, 2003). But sometimes they string signs together to form intelligible sentences. Washoe signed, "You

Seeing a doll floating in her water, Washoe signed, "Baby in my drink."

Paul Fusco/Magnum Photos

But is this language?
Chimpanzees' ability to express themselves in American Sign Language (ASL) raises questions about the very nature of language. Here, the trainer is asking, "What is this?" The sign in response is "Baby." Does the response constitute language?

> [Our] view that [we are] unique from all other forms of animal life is being jarred to the core."
>
> Duane Rumbaugh and Sue Savage-Rumbaugh (1978)

me go out, please." Apes even appeared to combine words creatively. Washoe designated a swan as a "water bird." Koko, a gorilla trained by Francine Patterson (1978), reportedly described a long-nosed Pinocchio doll as an "elephant baby." Lana, a "talking" chimpanzee that punches a crude computer keyboard which translates her entries into English, wanted her trainer's orange. She had no word for *orange*, but she did know her colors and the word for *apple*, so she improvised: "?Tim give apple which-is orange" (Rumbaugh, 1977).

Granted, these vocabularies and sentences are simple, rather like those of a 2-year-old child. Yet as reports of ape language accumulated, it seemed that they might indeed be "little lower than human."

But Can Apes Really Talk?

By the late 1970s, fascination with "talking apes" turned toward cynicism: Were the chimps language champs or were the researchers chumps? The ape language researchers were making monkeys of themselves, said the skeptics, who raised the following arguments:

- Unlike speaking or signing children, who effortlessly soak up dozens of new words a week, apes gain their limited vocabularies only with great difficulty (Wynne, 2004). Saying that apes can learn language because they can sign words is like saying humans can fly because they can jump.
- Chimpanzees can make signs or push buttons in sequence to get a reward, but pigeons, too, can peck a sequence of keys to get grain (Straub & others, 1979). After training a chimpanzee he named Nim Chimsky, Herbert Terrace (1979) concluded that much of apes' signing is nothing more than aping their trainers' signs and learning that certain arm movements produce rewards.
- Presented with ambiguous information, people, thanks to their *perceptual set*, tend to see what they want or expect to see. Interpreting chimpanzee signs as language may be little more than the trainers' wishful thinking, claimed Terrace. (When Washoe signed *water bird,* she perhaps was separately naming *water* and *bird.*)
- "Give orange me give eat orange me eat orange . . ." is a far cry from the exquisite syntax of a 3-year-old (Anderson, 2004; Pinker, 1995). To the child, "you tickle" and "tickle you" communicate different ideas. A chimpanzee, lacking human syntax, might sign the phrases interchangeably.

In science as in politics, controversy can stimulate progress. Despite skeptics' reactions, further evidence of chimpanzees' abilities to think and communicate were reported. One surprising finding was of Washoe's training her adopted son in the signs she had learned. After her second infant died, Washoe became withdrawn when told, "Baby dead, baby gone, baby finished." Two weeks later, caretaker-researcher Roger Fouts (1992, 1997) signed better news: "I have baby for you." Washoe reacted with instant excitement, hair on end, swaggering and panting while signing over and again, "Baby, my baby." It took several hours for Washoe and the foster infant, Loulis, to warm to each other, whereupon she broke the ice by signing, "Come baby" and cuddling Loulis.

In the months that followed, Loulis picked up 68 signs simply by observing Washoe and three other language-trained chimps. They now sign spontaneously, asking one another to *chase, tickle, hug, come,* or *groom.* People who sign are in near-perfect agreement about what the chimps are saying, 90 percent of which pertains to social interaction, reassurance, or play (Fouts & Bodamer, 1987). The chimps are even modestly bilingual; they can translate spoken English words into signs (Shaw, 1989–1990).

Even more stunning was the report by Sue Savage-Rumbaugh and her colleagues (1993) of pygmy chimpanzees learning to *comprehend syntax* in English spoken to them. Kanzi, a pygmy chimpanzee with the seeming grammatical abilities of a human 2-year-old, happened onto language while observing his adoptive mother during language training. Kanzi has behaved intelligently whether asked, "Can you show me the light?" or "Can you bring me the [flash]light?" or "Can you turn the light on?" Kanzi also knows the spoken words *snake, bite,* and *dog.* Given stuffed animals and asked—for the first time—to "make the dog bite the snake," he put the snake to the dog's mouth. For chimpanzees as for humans, early life is a critical time for learning language. Without early exposure to speech or word symbols, adults will not gain language competence (Rumbaugh & Savage-Rumbaugh, 1994).

The provocative claims that "apes share our capacity for language" and the skeptical counterclaims that "apes no use language" (as Washoe might have put it) have moved psychologists toward a greater appreciation of both apes' remarkable abilities and our own (Friend, 2004; Rumbaugh & Washburn, 2003). Most now agree that humans alone possess language, if by the term we mean verbal or signed expression of complex grammar. If we mean, more simply, an ability to communicate through a meaningful sequence of symbols, then apes are indeed capable of language.

Believing that animals could not think, Descartes and other philosophers argued that they were living robots without any moral rights. Animals, it has been said at one time or another, cannot plan, conceptualize, count, use tools, show compassion, or use language (Thorpe, 1974). Today, we know better. Animal researchers have shown us that primates exhibit insight, show family loyalty, communicate with one another, display altruism, transmit cultural patterns across generations, and comprehend the syntax of human speech. Accepting and working out the moral implications of all this is an unfinished task for our own thinking species.

"Although humans make sounds with their mouths and occasionally look at each other, there is no solid evidence that they actually communicate with each other."

© 1979 by Sidney Harris/American Scientist magazine.

"Chimps do not develop language. But that is no shame on them; humans would surely do no better if trained to hoot and shriek like chimps, to perform the waggle-dance of the bee, or any of the other wonderful feats in nature's talent show."

Steve Pinker (1995)

>> MODULE REVIEW

24-1 : When do children acquire language, and how do they master this complex task?

At about 4 months of age, infants *babble,* making a wide range of sounds found in *languages* all over the world. By about 10 months, their babbling contains only the sounds of their household language. By about 12 months, babies speak in *single words,* followed by *two-word* (*telegraphic*) utterances before their second birthday. Shortly after, children begin speaking in full sentences. The timing of these stages may vary, but all children follow this sequence.

Behaviorist B. F. Skinner proposed that we learn language by the familiar principles of association, imitation, and reinforcement. Challenging this claim, linguist Noam Chomsky argued that children are biologically prepared to learn words and use grammar. Psychologists today believe we do have a predisposition to learn language, but the particular language we learn is the result of our experience. Childhood is a critical period for learning language.

24-2 : What is the relationship between thinking and language?

Benjamin Whorf proposed that *language determines* thought. Contemporary psychologists believe it is more accurate to say that language influences thought. Research on bilingual people demonstrates that different languages embody different ways of

thinking. Subtle prejudices can be conveyed by the words we choose to express our everyday thoughts.

When we think in images we use procedural memory—our unconscious memory system for motor and cognitive skills and conditioned associations. Thinking in images is especially useful for mentally practicing upcoming events and can actually increase our skills.

24-3 : Do animals—in some sense we can identify with—think? Do they even exhibit language?

Evidence accumulates that primates form concepts, display insight, use and create tools, and transmit cultural innovations. Animals obviously communicate, but a vigorously debated issue is whether language is a uniquely human ability. Several species of apes have learned to communicate with humans by using sign language or by pushing buttons wired to a computer. These apes have developed vocabularies of hundreds of words, have communicated by stringing words togeter, and have taught their skills to younger animals. But research reveals important differences between apes' and humans' facilities with language, especially in their respective abilities to order words grammatically.

>> REHEARSE IT!

1. Children progress from babbling to one-word communications and then to sentences of two words. The one-word stage of speech development is usually reached at about

   a. 4 months.
   b. 6 months.
   c. 1 year.
   d. 2 years.

2. B. F. Skinner believed that we learn language the same way we learn other behaviors—through association, imitation, and reinforcement. Skinner's behaviorist view is most helpful in explaining

   a. the onset of babbling.
   b. the speech behavior of deaf infants.
   c. the seemingly effortless mastery of grammatical rules by very young children.
   d. why children learn their household's language.

3. According to Noam Chomsky, we are biologically prepared to acquire language and are born with a readiness to learn the grammatical rules of the language we hear or see. He believes all we need to acquire language is

   a. instruction in grammar.
   b. exposure to language in early childhood.
   c. reinforcement for babbling and other early verbal behaviors.
   d. imitation and drill.

4. Benjamin Lee Whorf proposed that our language determines the way we perceive and think about the world. Although we now know that language influences, rather than determines, our thinking, Whorf's hypothesis does help explain why

   a. a person who learns a second language thinks differently in that language.
   b. children have a built-in readiness to learn grammatical rules.
   c. children's babbling contains sounds not found in the languages spoken in their homes.
   d. artists, athletes, and others are able to think in visual images.

5. *Insight* is defined as a sudden and often novel realization of a problem's solution. Of the examples discussed in this section, the problem-solving behavior that most closely resembled insight was

   a. Loulis the chimpanzee's ability to learn signs by observing Washoe.
   b. Sultan the chimpanzee's use of a short stick to pull in a long stick.
   c. Kanzi the chimpanzee's ability to understand subtle grammatical differences in English sentences.
   d. Washoe the chimpanzee's use of sign language to request her baby.

6. There is much controversy over whether apes can be taught to use language in the way that humans do. However, most researchers agree that apes can

   a. communicate through symbols.
   b. reproduce most human speech sounds.
   c. master language in adulthood.
   d. surpass a human 3-year-old in language skills.

Answers: 1. c, 2. d, 3. b, 4. a, 5. b, 6. a.

>> TERMS AND CONCEPTS TO REMEMBER

language, p. 319
babbling stage, p. 320

one-word stage, p. 320
two-word stage, p. 320

telegraphic speech, p. 320
linguistic determinism, p. 323

>> TEST YOURSELF

1. If children are not yet speaking, is there any reason to think they would benefit from parents and other caregivers reading to them?

2. To say that "words are the mother of ideas" assumes the truth of what concept?

3. If your dog barks at a stranger at the front door, does this qualify as language? What if the dog yips in a telltale way to let you know she needs to go out?

   (Answers in Appendix C.)

*Multiple-choice **self-tests** and more may be found at www.worthpublishers.com/myers.*

M O D U L E

Intelligence

Do you believe that we humans differ from one another in our intellectual capacities? No controversy in psychology has been more heated than the question of whether there exists in each person a general intellectual capacity that can be measured and quantified as a number. School boards, courts, and scientists debate the usefulness and fairness of intelligence and other aptitude tests. Is it discriminatory to use such tests to rank individuals and determine whether to admit them to a particular educational program, university, or job? Do group differences reflect nature (heredity) or nurture (environment)? Let's consider findings from a century of research.

What Is Intelligence?

25-1: Is intelligence a single general ability or several distinct abilities?

Intelligence is a socially constructed concept. Cultures deem "intelligent" whatever attributes enable success in those cultures (Sternberg & Kaufman, 1998). In the Amazon rain forest, intelligence may be understanding the medicinal qualities of local plants; in a Minnesota high school, it may be superior performance on cognitive tasks. In each context, **intelligence** is the ability to learn from experience, solve problems, and use knowledge to adapt to new situations. In research studies, *intelligence* is whatever intelligence tests measure, which historically, as we will see, has tended to be school smarts.

© Maya Goded/Magnum Photos

Despite this general agreement, controversy remains, which you may be able to relate to your own experiences. You probably know some people with talents in science, others who excel at the humanities, and still others gifted in athletics, art, music, or dance. You may also know a talented artist who is dumbfounded by the simplest mathematical problems, or a brilliant math student with little aptitude for literary discussion. Are all of these people intelligent? Could you rate their intelligence on a single scale? Or would you need several different scales? The answer depends in part on how you answer another question: Is intelligence a single overall ability or several specific abilities?

Theories of Intelligence

Charles Spearman (1863–1945) believed we have one **general intelligence** (often shortened to **g**). He granted that people often have special abilities that stand out. Spearman had helped develop *factor analysis,* a statistical procedure that identifies clusters of related items. He had noted that those who score high in one area, such as verbal intelligence, typically score higher than average in other areas, such as spatial or reasoning ability. Spearman believed this common gift or skill set, the *g factor,* underlies all of our intelligent behavior, from navigating the sea to excelling in school.

Hands-on healing
The socially constructed concept of intelligence varies from culture to culture. This folk healer in Peru displays his intelligence in his knowledge about his medicinal plants and understanding of the needs of the people he is helping.

■ **intelligence** mental quality consisting of the ability to learn from experience, solve problems, and use knowledge to adapt to new situations.

■ **general intelligence (g)** a general intelligence factor that, according to Spearman and others, underlies specific mental abilities and is therefore measured by every task on an intelligence test.

New York Times interviewer Deborah Solomon, 2004: *"What is your IQ?"* Physicist Stephen Hawking: *"I have no idea. People who boast about their IQ are losers."*

❝ *g* is one of the most reliable and valid measures in the behavioral domain . . . and it predicts important social outcomes such as educational and occupational levels far better than any other trait."

Behavior geneticist Robert Plomin (1999)

Islands of genius: Savant syndrome
(left) Matt Savage, a 13-year-old with autism, is also an award-winning jazz pianist. Matt has his own band—the Matt Savage Trio. (middle) Kim Peek, the inspiration for the character Raymond Babbit in the movie *Rain Man,* depends on his father for many of his daily needs. Yet Peek knows more than 7600 books by heart, as well as all U.S. area codes, Zip codes, and TV stations. (right) Alonzo Clemons, despite a developmental disability, can create perfect replicas of any animal he briefly sees. His bronze figures have earned him a national reputation.

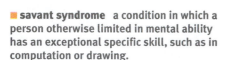

■ **savant syndrome** a condition in which a person otherwise limited in mental ability has an exceptional specific skill, such as in computation or drawing.

> "You have to be careful, if you're good at something, to make sure you don't think you're good at other things that you aren't necessarily so good at. . . . Because I've been very successful at [software development] people come in and expect that I have wisdom about topics that I don't."
>
> Bill Gates (1998)

Not so, say other psychologists. Howard Gardner (1983, 1999) views intelligence as multiple abilities that come in packages. Gardner finds evidence for this view in studies of people with diminished or exceptional abilities. Brain damage, for example, may destroy one ability but leave others intact. And consider people with **savant syndrome,** who often score low on intelligence tests but have an island of brilliance (Treffert & Wallace, 2002). Some have virtually no language ability, yet are able to compute numbers as quickly and accurately as an electronic calculator, or identify almost instantly the day of the week that corresponds to any given date in history, or render incredible works of art or musical performances (Miller, 1999). About four in five people with savant syndrome are males, and many also have *autism,* a developmental disorder.

Using such evidence, Gardner argues that we do not have *an* intelligence, but rather *multiple, relatively independent intelligences*. He identifies a total of eight (**TABLE 25.1**), including the verbal and mathematical aptitudes assessed by standard tests. Thus, the computer programmer, the poet, the street-smart adolescent who becomes a crafty executive, and the point guard on the basketball team exhibit different kinds of intelligence (Gardner, 1998). He notes,

> If a person is strong (or weak) in telling stories, solving mathematical proofs, navigating around unfamiliar terrain, learning an unfamiliar song, mastering a new game that entails dexterity, understanding others, or understanding himself, one simply does not know whether comparable strengths (or weaknesses) will be found in other areas.

A general intelligence score is therefore like the overall rating of a city—which doesn't give you much specific information about its schools, streets, or nightlife.

Wouldn't it be wonderful if the world were so just, responds intelligence researcher Sandra Scarr (1989), that being weak in one area would be compensated by genius in some other area? Alas, the world is not just. People with mental disadvantages, for example, often have lesser physical abilities as well—Special Olympics gives them and others a chance to enjoy fair competition. General intelligence scores predict performance on various complex tasks and in various jobs; g matters (Gottfredson, 2002a,b, 2003a,b; Reeve & Hakel, 2002). In one digest of 127 studies, an academic intelligence score that predicted graduate school success also predicted later job success (Kuncel & others, 2004).

Other researchers point out that high intelligence does more to get you into a profession (via the schools and training programs that take you there) than it does to make you successful once there. The recipe for success combines talent with grit: Those who become highly successful are also conscientious, well-connected, and doggedly energetic.

TABLE 25.1

GARDNER'S EIGHT INTELLIGENCES

Aptitude	Exemplar
1. Linguistic	T. S. Eliot, poet
2. Logical-mathematical	Albert Einstein, scientist
3. Musical	Igor Stravinsky, composer
4. Spatial	Pablo Picasso, artist
5. Bodily-kinesthetic	Martha Graham, dancer
6. Intrapersonal (self)	Sigmund Freud, psychiatrist
7. Interpersonal (other people)	Mahatma Gandhi, leader
8. Naturalist	Charles Darwin, naturalist

Courtesy of Cameras on Wheels

Spatial intelligence genius
In 1998, World Checkers Champion Ron "Suki" King of Barbados set a new record by simultaneously playing 385 players in 3 hours and 44 minutes. Thus, while his opponents often had hours to plot their game moves, King could only devote about 35 seconds to each game. Yet he still managed to win all 385 games!

Anders Ericsson (2002; Ericsson & Lehmann, 1996) reports that a common ingredient of expert performance in chess, dancing, sports, computer programming, music, and medicine is "about 10 years of intense, daily practice."

Robert Sternberg (1985, 1999, 2003) sees value in many of these ideas. He agrees that there is more to success than traditional intelligence. And he agrees with Gardner's idea of multiple intelligences. But Sternberg's *triarchic theory* distinguishes three, not eight, intelligences:

- *Analytical (academic problem-solving) intelligence*—assessed by intelligence tests, which present well-defined problems having a single right answer. Such tests predict school grades reasonably well but predict vocational success more modestly.
- *Creative intelligence*—demonstrated in reacting adaptively to novel situations and generating novel ideas.
- *Practical intelligence*—required for everyday tasks, which may be ill-defined, with multiple solutions. Managerial success, for example, depends less on academic problem-solving skills than on a shrewd ability to manage oneself, one's tasks, and other people. Sternberg and Richard Wagner's (1993, 1995) test of practical managerial intelligence measures skill at writing effective memos, motivating people, delegating tasks and responsibilities, reading people, and promoting one's own career. Business executives who score high on this test tend to earn higher salaries and receive better performance ratings than do those who score low.

Although Sternberg (1998, 1999) and Gardner (1998) differ on specific points, they agree that multiple abilities can contribute to life success. (Neither candidate in the 2000 U.S. presidential election had scored exceptionally high on college entrance aptitude tests, notes Sternberg [2000], yet both, after college, have been successful.) They also agree that the differing varieties of giftedness add spice to life and challenges for education. Under Gardner's or Sternberg's influence, many teachers have been trained to appreciate the varieties of ability and to apply multiple intelligence theory in their classrooms. However we define *intelligence,* one thing is clear: Academic intelligence does not always equal creativity.

Intelligence and Creativity

25-2: What is creativity, and what fosters this ability?

Pierre de Fermat, a seventeenth-century mischievous genius, challenged mathematicians of his day to match his solutions to various number theory problems. His most famous challenge—his so-called last theorem, proposed after mathematicians solved all the others—baffled the greatest mathematical minds, even after a $2 million prize (in today's dollars) was offered in 1908 to whoever first created a proof.

Street smarts

This child selling candy on the streets of Manaus, Brazil, is developing practical intelligence at a very young age.

David R. Frazier Photolibrary, Inc. / Alamy

Like countless others, Princeton mathematician Andrew Wiles had pondered the problem for more than 30 years and had come to the brink of a solution. Then, one morning, out of the blue, the final "incredible revelation" struck him. "It was so indescribably beautiful; it was so simple and so elegant. I couldn't understand how I'd missed it and I just stared at it in disbelief for 20 minutes. Then during the day I walked around the department, and I'd keep coming back to my desk looking to see if it was still there. It was still there. I couldn't contain myself, I was so excited. It was the most important moment of my working life" (Singh, 1997, p. 25).

Wiles' incredible moment illustrates **creativity**—the ability to produce ideas that are both novel and valuable. Studies suggest that a certain level of aptitude—a score of about 120 on a standard intelligence test—is necessary but not sufficient for creativity. Exceptionally creative architects, mathematicians, scientists, and engineers usually score no higher on intelligence tests than do their less creative peers (MacKinnon & Hall, 1972; Simonton, 2000). So, clearly there is more to creativity than what intelligence tests reveal. Indeed, the two kinds of thinking engage different brain areas. Intelligence tests, which demand a single correct answer, require *convergent thinking*. Creativity tests (How many uses can you think of for a brick?) require *divergent thinking*. Injury to the left parietal lobe damages the convergent thinking required by intelligence test scores and for school success. Injury to certain areas of the frontal lobes can leave reading, writing, and arithmetic skills intact but destroy imagination (Kolb & Whishaw, 2006).

As noted earlier, Robert Sternberg views creative intelligence as separate from academic problem-solving intelligence. Studies of creative people suggest five components of creativity beyond a minimal level of aptitude (Sternberg, 1988; Sternberg & Lubart, 1991, 1992):

1. **Expertise,** a well-developed base of knowledge, furnishes the ideas, images, and phrases we use as mental building blocks. "Chance favors only the prepared mind," observed Louis Pasteur. The more blocks we have, the more chances we have to combine them in novel ways. Wiles' well-developed base of knowledge put the needed theorems and methods at his disposal.

2. **Imaginative thinking skills** provide the ability to see things in novel ways, to recognize patterns, to make connections. Having mastered a problem's basic elements, we redefine or explore it in a new way. Copernicus first developed expertise regarding the solar system and its planets and then creatively defined the system as revolving around the Sun, not the Earth. Wiles' imaginative solution combined two important but incomplete solutions.

3. **A venturesome personality** seeks new experiences rather than following the pack, tolerates ambiguity and risk, and perseveres in overcoming obstacles. Inventor Thomas Edison tried countless substances before finding the right one for his lightbulb filament. Wiles said he labored in near-isolation from the mathematics community partly to stay focused and avoid distraction.

4. **Intrinsic motivation,** linked to our most creative moments, is feeling "motivated primarily by the interest, enjoyment, satisfaction, and challenge of the work itself—rather than by external pressures," point out Teresa Amabile and Beth Hennessey

After picking up a Nobel prize in Stockholm, physicist Richard Feynman stopped in Queens, New York, to look at his high school record. "My grades were not as good as I remembered," he reported, "and my IQ was [a good, though unexceptional] 124" (Faber, 1987).

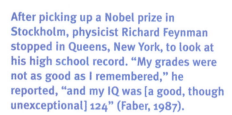

"If you would allow me any talent, it's simply this: I can, for whatever reason, reach down into my own brain, feel around in all the mush, find and extract something from my persona, and then graft it onto an idea."

Cartoonist Gary Larson,
The Complete Far Side, 2003

FURIOUS GEORGE

Everyone held up their crackers as David threw the cheese log into the ceiling fan.

Imaginative thinking
Cartoonists often display creativity as they see things in new ways or make unusual connections.

(1992). Creative people focus not so much on extrinsic motivators—meeting deadlines, impressing people, or making money—as on the pleasure and challenge of the work itself. Asked how he solved such difficult scientific problems, Isaac Newton reportedly answered, "By thinking about them all the time." Wiles concurred: "I was so obsessed by this problem that for eight years I was thinking about it all the time—when I woke up in the morning to when I went to sleep at night" (Singh & Riber, 1997).

5. *A creative environment* sparks, supports, and refines creative ideas. After studying the careers of 2026 prominent scientists and inventors, Dean Keith Simonton (1992) noted that the most eminent among them were mentored, challenged, and supported by their relationships with colleagues. Many have the *emotional intelligence* needed to network effectively with peers. Even Wiles stood on the shoulders of others and wrestled his problem with the collaboration of a former student.

■ **creativity** the ability to produce novel and valuable ideas.

■ **emotional intelligence** the ability to perceive, understand, manage, and use emotions.

Emotional Intelligence

25-3: Is our ability to manage our own emotions and to empathize with others a form of intelligence?

Also distinct from academic intelligence is what Nancy Cantor and John Kihlstrom (1987) first called *social intelligence*—the know-how involved in comprehending social situations and managing oneself successfully. More recently, researchers (Salovey & Mayer, 1990; Salovey & Grewal, 2005) have focused on a critical part of social intelligence, **emotional intelligence.** John Mayer, Peter Salovey, and David Caruso (2002; Grewal & Salovey, 2005) have developed an emotional intelligence test to assess both overall emotional intelligence and its four components, the abilities to

- *perceive* emotions (to recognize them in faces, music, and stories).
- *understand* emotions (to predict them and how they change and blend).
- *manage* emotions (to know how to express them in varied situations).
- *use* emotions to enable adaptive or creative thinking.

Emotionally intelligent people are self-aware. In both the United States and Germany, those scoring high on managing emotions enjoy higher-quality interactions with friends of both sexes (Lopes & others, 2004). They avoid being hijacked by overwhelming depression, anxiety, or anger. They can read others' emotions and know what to say to soothe a grieving friend, encourage a colleague, and manage a conflict. These findings may help explain why those scoring high in emotional intelligence across 69 studies in many countries also exhibit modestly better job performance (Van Rooy & Viswesvaran, 2004). They can delay gratification in pursuit of long-range rewards, rather than being overtaken by immediate impulses. Simply said, they are emotionally smart, and thus they often succeed in career, marriage, and parenting situations where academically smarter (but emotionally less intelligent) people fail.

"You're wise, but you lack tree smarts."

■ **intelligence test** a method for assessing an individual's mental aptitudes and comparing them with those of others, using numerical scores.

■ **mental age** measure of intelligence test performance devised by Binet; the chronological age that most typically corresponds to a given level of performance. Thus, a child who does as well as the average 8-year-old is said to have a mental age of 8.

■ **Stanford-Binet** the widely used American revision (by Terman at Stanford University) of Binet's original intelligence test.

■ **intelligence quotient (IQ)** defined originally as the ratio of mental age (*ma*) to chronological age (*ca*) multiplied by 100 (thus, IQ = *ma/ca* x 100). On contemporary intelligence tests, the average performance for a given age is assigned a score of 100.

■ **Wechsler Adult Intelligence Scale (WAIS)** the WAIS is the most widely used intelligence test; contains verbal and performance (nonverbal) subtests.

> "I worry about [intelligence] definitions that collapse assessments of our cognitive powers with statements about the kind of human beings we favor."
>
> Howard Gardner, "Rethinking the Concept of Intelligence," 2000

Brain damage reports have provided extreme examples of the results of diminished emotional intelligence even though general intelligence is intact. University of Iowa neuroscientist Antonio Damasio (1994) tells of Elliot, who had a brain tumor removed: "I never saw a tinge of emotion in my many hours of conversation with him, no sadness, no impatience, no frustration." Shown disturbing pictures of injured people, destroyed communities, and natural disasters, Elliot shows—and realizes he feels—no emotion. Like Data, the human-appearing android of *Star Trek: The Next Generation,* he knows but he cannot feel. Unable to intuitively adjust his behavior in response to others' feelings, Elliot lost his job. He went bankrupt. His marriage collapsed. He remarried and divorced again. At last report, he was dependent on custodial care from a sibling and a disability check.

Some scholars, however, are concerned that emotional intelligence stretches the concept of intelligence too far. Multiple-intelligence man Howard Gardner (1999) suggests that it is wise to stretch the concept beyond our processing of words, numbers, and logic, and into the realms of space, music, and information about ourselves and others. But let us also, he says, respect emotional sensitivity, creativity, and motivation as important but different. Stretch a word to include everything we prize and it will lose its meaning.

Perhaps, then, we can liken mental abilities to physical abilities. Athleticism is not one thing but many. The ability to run fast is distinct from the strength needed for power lifting, which is distinct from the eye-hand coordination required to throw a ball on target. A champion weightlifter rarely has the potential to be a skilled ice skater. Yet there remains some tendency for good things to come packaged together—for running speed and throwing accuracy to correlate, thanks to general athletic ability. Similarly, intelligence involves several distinct abilities, which correlate enough to define a small general intelligence factor. Let's turn, then, to how psychologists have designed tests to assess mental abilities.

Assessing Intelligence

How do we assess intelligence? Movie hero Forrest Gump's answer, "Stupid is as stupid does," catches the spirit of psychology's simplest answer: Intelligent is as intelligent does on an IQ test. In other words, *intelligence* is whatever **intelligence tests** measure. So, what are these tests, and what makes a test credible? Answering those questions begins with a look at why psychologists created tests of mental abilities and how they have used those tests.

The Origins of Intelligence Testing

25-4 : When and why were intelligence tests created?

Alfred Binet: Predicting School Achievement

The modern intelligence-testing movement began at the turn of the twentieth century when France passed a law requiring that all children attend school. Some children, including many newcomers to Paris, seemed incapable of benefiting from the regular school curriculum and in need of special classes. But how could the schools objectively identify children with special needs?

The French government hesitated to trust teachers' subjective judgments of children's learning potential. Academic slowness might merely reflect inadequate prior education. Also, teachers might prejudge children on the basis of their social backgrounds. To minimize bias, France's minister of public education in 1904 commissioned Alfred Binet (1857–1911) and others to study the problem.

Binet and his collaborator, Théodore Simon, began by assuming that all children follow the same course of intellectual development but that some develop more rapidly. On tests, therefore, a "dull" child should perform as does a typical younger

Alfred Binet

"The scale, properly speaking, does not permit the measure of intelligence, because intellectual qualities . . . cannot be measured as linear surfaces are measured" (Binet & Simon, 1905).

National Library of Medicine

child, and a "bright" child as does a typical older child. Thus, their goal became measuring each child's **mental age,** the level of performance typically associated with a certain chronological age. The average 9-year-old, for example, has a mental age of 9. Children with below-average mental ages, such as 9-year-olds who perform at the level of a typical 7-year-old, would struggle with schoolwork considered normal for their age.

After testing a variety of reasoning and problem-solving questions on Binet's two daughters, and then on "bright" and "backward" Parisian schoolchildren, Binet and Simon succeeded. They had developed items that would predict how well French children would handle their schoolwork. Binet hoped the test would be used to improve children's education, but he also feared it would be used to label children and limit their opportunities (Gould, 1981).

Lewis Terman: The Innate IQ

Those fears were realized soon after Binet's death in 1911, when others adapted his tests for use as a numerical measure of inherited intelligence. This began with Stanford University professor Lewis Terman (1877–1956), who attempted to use Binet's test with California schoolchildren but found that the Paris-developed age norms worked poorly. Adapting some of Binet's original items, adding others, and establishing new age norms, Terman extended the upper end of the test's range from teenagers to "superior adults." He also gave his revision the name it retains today—the **Stanford-Binet.**

From such tests, German psychologist William Stern derived the famous **intelligence quotient,** or **IQ.** The IQ was simply a person's mental age divided by chronological age and multiplied by 100 to get rid of the decimal point:

$$IQ = \frac{\text{mental age}}{\text{chronological age}} \times 100$$

Thus, an average child, whose mental and chronological ages are the same, has an IQ of 100. But an 8-year-old who answers questions as would a typical 10-year-old has an IQ of 125.

The original IQ formula worked fairly well for children but not for adults. (Should a 40-year-old who does as well on the test as an average 20-year-old be assigned an IQ of only 50?) Most current intelligence tests, including the Stanford-Binet, no longer compute an IQ (though the term "IQ" still lingers in everyday vocabulary as a shorthand expression for "intelligence test score"). Instead, they represent the test-taker's performance *relative* to the *average performance of others the same age.* This average performance is arbitrarily assigned a score of 100, and about two-thirds of all test-takers fall between 85 and 115.

Psychologist David Wechsler created what is now the most widely used intelligence test, the **Wechsler Adult Intelligence Scale (WAIS),** with a version for school-age children (the *Wechsler Intelligence Scale for Children [WISC]*), and another for preschool children. The WAIS yields not only an overall intelligence score, as does the Stanford-Binet, but also separate scores for verbal comprehension, perceptual organization, working memory, and processing speed. These scores are derived from the WAIS' 11 subtests, broken into verbal and

" The IQ test was invented to predict academic performance, nothing else. If we wanted something that would predict life success, we'd have to invent another test completely."

Social psychologist Robert Zajonc (1984b)

Mrs. Randolph takes mother's pride too far.

Matching patterns
Block design puzzles test the ability to analyze patterns. Wechsler's individually administered intelligence test comes in forms suited for adults (WAIS) and children (WISC).

VERBAL

General Information
What day of the year is Independence Day?

Similarities
In what way are *wool* and *cotton* alike?

Arithmetic Reasoning
If eggs cost 60 cents a dozen, what does 1 egg cost?

Vocabulary
Tell me the meaning of corrupt.

Comprehension
Why do people buy fire insurance?

Digit Span
Listen carefully, and when I am through, say the numbers right after me.

7   3   4   1   8   6

Now I am going to say some more numbers, but I want you to say them backward.

3   8   4   1   6

PERFORMANCE

Picture Completion
I am going to show you a picture with an important part missing. Tell me what is missing.

'85

SUN	MON	TUE	WED	THU	FRI	SAT
1	2	3	4	5	6	7
8	9	10	11	12	13	14
15	16	17	18	19	20	21
22	23	24	25	26	27	28
29	30					

Picture Arrangement
The pictures below tell a story. Put them in the right order to tell the story.

Block Design
Using the four blocks, make one just like this.

Object Assembly
If these pieces are put together correctly, they will make something. Go ahead and put them together as quickly as you can.

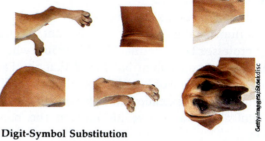

Getty Images/iStockdisc

Digit-Symbol Substitution

Code

△	○	⧄	✕	◇
1	2	3	4	5

Test

1	5	4	2	1	3	5	4	1	5

Thorndike et al., Measurement and evaluation in psychology and education, 5e, © 1990. Published by Prentice Hall.

FIGURE 25.1

Sample items from the Wechsler Adult Intelligence Scale (WAIS) subtests
(Adapted from Thorndike & Hagen, 1977.)

performance areas, as illustrated in **FIGURE 25.1**. Striking differences among the scores can provide clues to cognitive strengths or weaknesses that teachers or therapists can build upon. For example, a low verbal comprehension score combined with high scores on other subtests could indicate a reading or language disability. Other comparisons can help a psychologist or psychiatrist establish a rehabilitation plan for a stroke patient. Such uses are possible, of course, only when people trust the test results.

Principles of Test Construction

25-5: By what criteria can we judge intelligence tests?

To be widely accepted, psychological tests—whether **aptitude** (the capacity to learn) or **achievement** (what has already been learned)—must meet three criteria: They must be *standardized*, *reliable*, and *valid*. The Stanford-Binet and Wechsler tests meet these requirements.

Standardization

The number of questions you answer correctly on an intelligence test would tell us almost nothing. To evaluate your performance, we need a basis for comparing it with others' performance. To enable meaningful comparisons, test-makers first give the test to a representative sample of people. When you later take the test following the same procedures, your scores can be compared with the sample's scores to determine your position relative to others. This process of defining meaningful scores relative to a pretested group is called **standardization**.

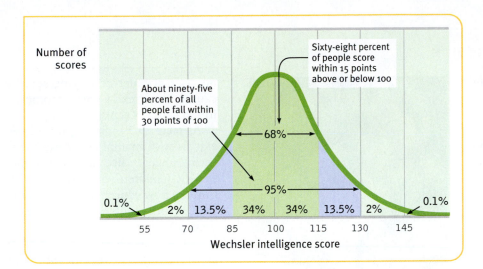

FIGURE **25.2**
The normal curve
Scores on aptitude tests tend to form a normal, or bell-shaped, curve around an average score. For the Wechsler scale, for example, the average score is 100.

Group members' scores typically form a *normal distribution,* a bell-shaped pattern that forms the **normal curve** (FIGURE **25.2**). No matter what we measure—heights, weights, or mental aptitudes—people's scores tend to form this roughly symmetrical shape. On an intelligence test, we call the midpoint, the average score, 100. Moving out from the average, toward either extreme, we find fewer and fewer people. For the Stanford-Binet and the Wechsler tests, a person's score indicates whether that person's performance fell above or below the average. A performance higher than all but 2 percent of all scores earns an intelligence score of 130. A performance lower than 98 percent of all scores earns an intelligence score of 70.

Reliability

Knowing where you stand in comparison to the standardizing group still won't tell us much about your intelligence unless the test has **reliability**—unless it yields dependably consistent scores. To check a test's reliability, researchers retest people. They may use the same test or they may split the test in half and see whether odd-question scores and even-question scores agree. If the two scores generally agree, or *correlate,* the test is reliable. The higher the correlation between the *test-retest* or the *split-half* scores, the higher the test's reliability. The tests we have considered so far—the Stanford-Binet, the WAIS, and the WISC—all have reliabilities of about +.9, which is very high. When retested, people's scores generally match their first score closely.

Validity

High reliability does not ensure a test's **validity**—the extent to which the test actually measures or predicts what it promises. If you use an inaccurate tape measure to measure people's heights, your height report would have high reliability (consistency) but low validity. It is enough for some tests that they have **content validity,** meaning the test taps the pertinent behavior. The road test for a driver's license has content validity because it samples the tasks a driver routinely faces. Course exams have content validity if they assess one's mastery of a representative sample of course material. But we expect intelligence tests to have **predictive validity:** They should predict future performance and to some extent, they do. (Turn the page to see Close-Up: Extremes of Intelligence.)

Are general aptitude tests as predictive as they are reliable? As critics are fond of noting, the answer is plainly no. The predictive power of aptitude tests is fairly strong in the early school years, but later it weakens. Past grades, which reflect both aptitude and motivation, are better predictors of future achievements.

■ **aptitude test** a test designed to predict a person's future performance; *aptitude* is the capacity to learn.

■ **achievement test** a test designed to assess what a person has learned.

■ **standardization** defining meaningful scores by comparison with the performance of a pretested standardization group.

■ **normal curve** the symmetrical bell-shaped curve that describes the distribution of many physical and psychological attributes. Most scores fall near the average, and fewer and fewer scores lie near the extremes.

■ **reliability** the extent to which a test yields consistent results, as assessed by the consistency of scores on two halves of the test, on alternate forms of the test, or on retesting.

■ **validity** the extent to which a test measures or predicts what it is supposed to. (See also *content validity* and *predictive validity*.)

■ **content validity** the extent to which a test samples the behavior that is of interest (such as a driving test that samples driving tasks).

■ **predictive validity** the success with which a test predicts the behavior it is designed to predict; it is assessed by computing the correlation between test scores and the criterion behavior. (Also called *criterion-related validity*.)

CLOSE-UP

EXTREMES OF INTELLIGENCE

One way to glimpse the validity and significance of any test is to compare people who score at the two extremes of the normal curve. The two groups should differ noticeably, and they do.

In one famous project begun in 1921, Lewis Terman studied more than 1500 California schoolchildren with IQ scores over 135. Contrary to the popular notion that intellectually gifted children are frequently maladjusted because they are "in a different world" from their nongifted peers, Terman's high-scoring children, like those in later studies, were healthy, well-adjusted, and unusually successful academically (Lubinski & Benbow, 2000; Stanley, 1997). When restudied over the next seven decades, most people in Terman's group had attained high levels of education (Austin & others, 2002; Holahan & Sears, 1995). They included many doctors, lawyers, professors, scientists, and writers, but no Nobel prize winners. (Terman did test one future Nobel laureate in physics but excluded him from the gifted sample because his measured IQ wasn't high enough [Cassandro & Simonton, 2003].) Children with extraordinary academic gifts are sometimes

"Joining Mensa means that you are a genius. . . . I worried about the arbitrary 132 cutoff point, until I met someone with an IQ of 131 and, honestly, he was a bit slow on the uptake."

Steve Martin, 1997

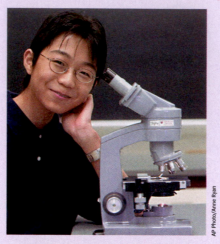

The extremes of intelligence

Sho Yano was playing Mozart by age 4, aced the SAT at age 8, and graduated *summa cum laude* from Loyola University at age 12, at which age he began combined Ph.D.–M.D. studies at the University of Chicago.

more isolated, introverted, and in their own worlds (Winner, 2000). But most thrive.

Another extreme of the normal curve are those whose intelligence test scores fall at 70 or below. To be labeled as having **mental retardation,** a child must have both a low test score and difficulty adapting to the normal demands of independent living. Only about 1 percent of the population meets both criteria, with males outnumbering females by 50 percent (American Psychiatric Association, 1994). Mental retardation sometimes has a known physical cause. **Down syndrome,** for example, is a disorder of varying severity caused by an extra chromosome 21 in the person's genetic makeup.

As **TABLE 25.2** indicates, most individuals with mental retardation can, with support, live in mainstream society. Children with mild retardation are now educated in less restrictive environments than they were even 50 years ago. Many are integrated, or *mainstreamed,* into regular classrooms. Most grow up with their own families, then move into a protected living arrangement, such as a group home. The hope, and often the reality, is a happy and dignified life.

These improvements partly reflect opinion changes about the best way to care for people with mental retardation. But there may be another reason why people who score just below 70 on an intelligence test can live independently today. What if people who score near 70 are getting smarter?

In fact, overall intelligence test performance has been improving over the past decade. This worldwide phenomenon is called the *Flynn effect* in honor of New Zealand researcher James Flynn (1987, 1999), who first calculated its magnitude. As **FIGURE 25.3** indicates, the average person's intelligence test score 80 years ago was—by today's standard—only a 76! Such rising performance has been observed in 20 countries, from Canada to rural Australia (Daley & others, 2003).

The Flynn effect's cause is a mystery (Neisser, 1997, 1998). Does it result

Genetic and Environmental Influences on Intelligence

25-6: Is intellect influenced more by heredity or by environment?

Intelligence runs in families. But why? Are our intellectual abilities mostly inherited? Or are they molded by our environment?

Few issues arouse such passion or have such serious political implications. Consider: If we mainly inherit our differing mental abilities, and if success reflects those

TABLE 25.2

DEGREES OF MENTAL RETARDATION

Level	Approximate Intelligence Scores	Percentage of Persons with Retardation	Adaptation to Demands of Life
Mild	50–70	85%	May learn academic skills up to sixth-grade level. Adults may, with assistance, achieve self-supporting social and vocational skills.
Moderate	35–50	10%	May progress to second-grade level academically. Adults may contribute to their own support by laboring in sheltered workshops.
Severe	20–35	3–4%	May learn to talk and to perform simple work tasks under close supervision but are generally unable to profit from vocational training.
Profound	Below 20	1–2%	Require constant aid and supervision.

Source: Reprinted with permission from the *Diagnostic and Statistical Manual of Mental Disorders,* Fourth Edition, text revision. Copyright 2000 American Psychiatric Association.

■ **mental retardation** a condition of limited mental ability, indicated by an intelligence score of 70 or below and difficulty in adapting to the demands of life; varies from mild to profound.

■ **Down syndrome** a condition of retardation and associated physical disorders caused by an extra chromosome in one's genetic makeup.

from greater test sophistication? Better nutrition? More education? More stimulating environments? Less childhood disease? Smaller families and more parental investment? Whatever its cause, one thing is certain: Thanks to the Flynn effect, intelligence tests have been periodically restandardized. When that has happened, individuals who scored near 70 on earlier tests suddenly lose about 6 IQ points, and the number of people diagnosed with retardation suddenly jumps (Kanaya & others, 2003). With the new norms, more people suddenly become eligible for special education and for Social Security payments (for those with a mental disability), and fewer for execution. (The U.S. Supreme Court ruled in 2002 that the execution of people with mental retardation is "cruel and unusual punishment.") For people near that score of 70, intelligence testing can be high stakes.

FIGURE 25.3
Getting smarter?

In every country studied, intelligence test performance rose during the twentieth century, as shown here with American Wechsler and Stanford-Binet test performance between 1918 and 1989. In Britain, test scores have risen 27 points since 1942. (From Hogan, 1995.)

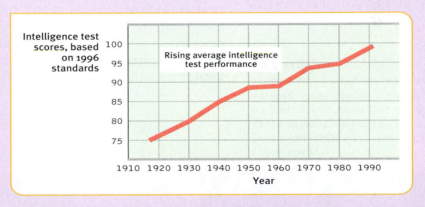

abilities, then people's socioeconomic standing will correspond to their inborn differences. This could lead to those on top believing their intellectual birthright justifies their social positions.

But if mental abilities are primarily nurtured by the environments that raise and inform us, then children from disadvantaged environments can expect to lead disadvantaged lives. In this case, people's standing will result from their unequal opportunities.

For now, as best we can, let us set aside such political implications and examine the evidence.

© The New Yorker Collection, 1999, Donald Reilly from cartoonbank.com. All Rights Reserved.

"I told my parents that if grades were so important they should have paid for a smarter egg donor."

Twin and Adoption Studies

Do people who share the same genes also share comparable mental abilities? As you can see from **FIGURE 25.4,** which summarizes many studies, the answer is clearly yes. In support of the genetic contribution to intelligence, researchers cite three sets of findings:

- The intelligence test scores of identical twins reared together are virtually as similar as those of the same person taking the same test twice (Lykken, 1999; Plomin, 2001). (The scores of fraternal twins, who typically share only half their genes, are much less similar.) Likewise, the test scores of identical twins reared separately are similar enough to lead twin researcher Thomas Bouchard (1996a) to estimate that "about 70 percent" of intelligence score variation "can be attributed to genetic variation." Other estimates range from 50 to 75 percent (Devlin & others, 1997; Neisser & others, 1996; Plomin, 2003).
- Brain scans reveal that identical twins have very similar gray matter volume, and that their brains (unlike those of fraternal twins) are virtually the same in areas associated with verbal and spatial intelligence (Thompson & others, 2001).
- Are there genes for genius? Researchers are trying to identify genes that contribute to human cognitive ability, but progress has been slow (Plomin, 2003). By inserting an extra gene into fertilized mouse eggs, however, researchers have produced smarter mice—mice that excel at learning and remembering the location of a hidden underwater platform or at recognizing cues that signal impending shock (Tsien, 2000). The gene helps create a neural receptor involved in memory.

But other evidence points to the effects of environment. We know that adoption enhances children's intelligence scores (van Ijzendoorn & Juffer, 2005). And fraternal twins, who are genetically no more alike than any other siblings—but who are treated more alike because they are the same age—tend to score more alike than other siblings. So if shared environment matters, do children in adoptive families share similar aptitudes?

Seeking to disentangle genes and environment, researchers have compared the intelligence test scores of adopted children with those of their adoptive siblings and with those of (a) their biological parents, the providers of their genes, and (b) their adoptive parents, the providers of their home environment. During childhood, the intelligence test scores of adoptive siblings correlate modestly. Over time, adopted children accumulate experience in their differing adoptive families. So would you expect the family environment effect to grow with age and the genetic legacy effect to shrink?

FIGURE 25.4

Intelligence: Nature and nurture

The most genetically similar people have the most similar intelligence scores. Note: 1.0 indicates a perfect correlation; zero indicates no correlation at all. (Data from McGue & others, 1993.)

photo credit here

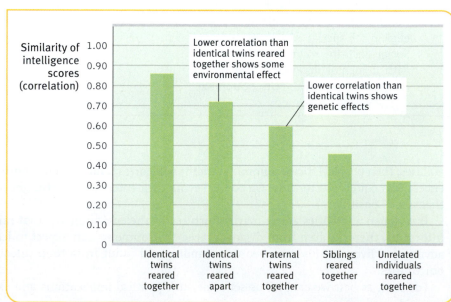

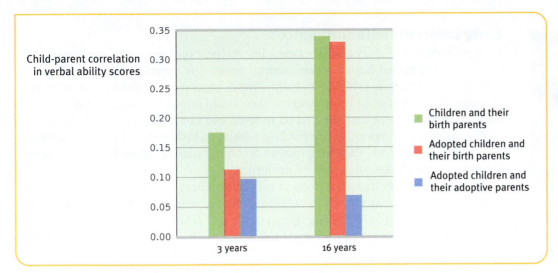

Child-parent correlation in verbal ability scores

- Children and their birth parents
- Adopted children and their birth parents
- Adopted children and their adoptive parents

3 years   16 years

FIGURE 25.5

Who do adopted children resemble?

As the years went by in their adoptive families, children's verbal ability scores became modestly more like their *biological* parents' scores. (Adapted from Plomin & DeFries, 1998.)

If you would, behavior geneticists have a surprise for you. Mental similarities between adopted children and their adoptive families wane with age, until the correlation is roughly zero by adulthood (McGue & others, 1993). Genetic influences—not environmental ones—become more apparent as we accumulate life experience (Bouchard, 1995, 1996b). Identical twins' similarities, for example, continue or increase into their eighties (McClearn & others, 1997; Plomin & others, 1997). Similarly, adopted children's intelligence scores over time become more like those of their biological parents (**FIGURE 25.5**).

Heritability

Estimates of the **heritability** of intelligence—the variation in intelligence test scores attributable to genetic factors—put it at about 50 percent or a tad more. Does this mean your genes are responsible for 50 percent of your intelligence and your environment for the rest? No. It means we credit heredity with 50 percent of the *variation* in intelligence among people being studied. This point is so often misunderstood that I repeat: Heritability never pertains to an *individual,* only to why people differ from one another.

Heritability differences among people due to genes can vary from study to study. Where environments vary widely, as they do among children of less-educated parents, environmental differences are more predictive of intelligence scores (Rowe & others, 1999). To see why, consider humorist Mark Twain's proposal to raise boys in barrels to age 12, feeding them through a hole. Given the boys' equal environments, differences in their individual intelligence test scores at age 12 could be explained only by their heredity. Thus, heritability for their differences would be nearly 100 percent. But if we raise people with similar heredities in drastically different environments (barrels versus advantaged homes), the environment effect will be greater, and heritability will therefore be lower. In a world of clones, heritability would be zero.

Genes and environment work together. If you try out for a basketball team and are just slightly taller and quicker than others, notes James Flynn (2003), you will more likely be picked, play more, and get more coaching. The same would be true for your separated identical twin—who might, *not just for genetic reasons,* also come to excel at basketball. Likewise, if you have a natural aptitude for academics, you will more likely stay in school, read books, and ask questions—all of which will amplify your cognitive brain power. Thanks to such gene-environment correlation, modest genetic advantages can be socially multiplied into big performance advantages. Our genes shape the experiences that shape us.

■ **heritability** the proportion of variation among individuals that we can attribute to genes. The heritability of a trait may vary, depending on the range of populations and environments studied.

Question: Check your understanding of heritability: If environments become more equal, the heritability of intelligence would
a. increase.
b. decrease.
c. be unchanged.
(See this module's final page.)

© The New Yorker Collection, 2000, Leo Cullum from cartoonbank.com. All Rights Reserved.

"Selective breeding has given me an aptitude for the law, but I still love fetching a dead duck out of freezing water."

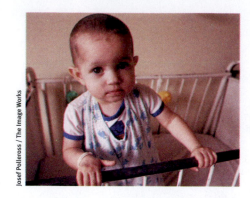

Devastating neglect
Romanian orphans who had minimal interaction with caregivers, such as this child in the Lagunul Pentro Copii orphanage in 1990, suffered delayed development.

"There is a large body of evidence indicating that there is little if anything to be gained by exposing middle-class children to early education."

Developmental psychologist
Edward F. Zigler (1987)

Early Environmental Influences

We have seen that biology and experience intertwine. Nowhere is this more apparent than in impoverished human environments. Severe life experiences can leave footprints on the brain, as J. McVicker Hunt (1982) observed in a destitute Iranian orphanage. The typical child Hunt observed there could not sit up unassisted at age 2 or walk at age 4. The little care the infants received was not in response to their crying, cooing, or other behaviors, so the children developed little sense of personal control over their environment. They were instead becoming passive "glum lumps." Extreme deprivation was bludgeoning native intelligence.

Aware of both the dramatic effects of early experiences and the impact of early intervention, Hunt began a program of "tutored human enrichment." He trained caregivers to play language-fostering games with 11 infants, imitating the babies' babbling, then engaging them in vocal follow-the-leader, and finally teaching them sounds from the Persian language. The results were dramatic. By 22 months of age, the infants could name more than 50 objects and body parts, and they so charmed visitors that most were adopted—an unprecedented success for the orphanage.

Hunt's findings are an extreme case of a more general finding: Among the poor, environmental conditions can override genetic differences, depressing cognitive development. Unlike children of affluence, siblings within impoverished families have more similar intelligence scores (Turkheimer & others, 2003). Schools with lots of poverty-level children often have less-qualified teachers, as one study of 1450 Virginia schools found. And even after controlling for poverty, less-qualified teachers predicted lower achievement scores (Tuerk, 2005). Malnutrition also plays a role. Relieve infant malnutrition with nutritional supplements, and poverty's effect on physical and cognitive development lessens (Brown & Pollitt, 1996).

Do studies of such early interventions indicate that providing an "enriched" environment can "give your child a superior intellect," as some popular books claim? Most experts are doubtful (Bruer, 1999). Malnutrition, sensory deprivation, and social isolation can retard normal brain development, but there is no environmental recipe for fast-forwarding a normal infant into a genius. All babies should have normal exposure to sights, sounds, and speech. Beyond that, Sandra Scarr's (1984) verdict still is widely shared: "Parents who are very concerned about providing special educational lessons for their babies are wasting their time."

Schooling and Intelligence

Later in childhood, schooling is one intervention that pays dividends reflected in intelligence scores. Schooling and intelligence interact, and both enhance later income (Ceci & Williams, 1997). Hunt was a strong believer in the ability of education to boost children's chances for success by developing their cognitive and social skills. Indeed, his 1961 book, *Intelligence and Experience,* helped launch Project Head Start in 1965. Head Start, a U.S. government-funded preschool program, serves more than 900,000 children, most of whom come from families below the poverty level (Head Start, 2005).

Does it succeed? Researchers study Head Start and other preschool programs by comparing children who experience the program with their counterparts who don't. Quality programs, offering individual attention, increase children's school readiness, which decreases their likelihood of repeating a grade or being placed in special education. Generally, the aptitude benefits dissipate over time (reminding us that life experience *after* Head Start matters, too). Psychologist Edward Zigler, the program's first director, nevertheless believes there are long-term benefits (Ripple & Zigler, 2003; Zigler & Styfco, 2001). High-quality preschool programs can provide at least a small boost to emotional intelligence—creating better attitudes toward learning and reducing school dropouts and criminality (Reynolds & others, 2001).

Jacques Chenet/Woodfin Camp & Associates

AP Photo/Paul Sakuma

As the years go by, intelligence and education continue to interact (Ceci & Williams, 1997), with intelligence scores rising during the school year and dropping over the summer months and when schooling is discontinued. Completing high school elevates intelligence scores over those obtained by comparable children who leave school early.

Getting a head start
To increase readiness for schoolwork and expand children's notions of where school might lead them, Project Head Start offers educational activities. Here children in a classroom learn about colors, and children on a field trip prepare for the annual Head Start parade in Boston.

Group Differences in Intelligence Test Scores

25-7: How, and why, do ethnic and gender groups differ in aptitude test performance?

If there were no group differences in aptitude scores, psychologists could politely debate hereditary and environmental influences in their ivory towers. But there are group differences. What are they? And what shall we make of them?

Ethnic Similarities and Differences

Fueling this discussion are two disturbing but agreed-upon facts:

- Racial groups differ in their average scores on intelligence tests.
- High-scoring people (and groups) are more likely to attain high levels of education and income.

A statement by 52 intelligence researchers explained: "The bell curve for Whites is centered roughly around IQ 100; the bell curve for American Blacks roughly around 85; and those for different subgroups of Hispanics roughly midway between those for Whites and Blacks" (Avery & others, 1994). Comparable results come from other academic aptitude tests. In recent years, the Black-White difference has diminished somewhat, and among children has dropped to 10 points in some studies (Neisser & others, 1996). Yet the test score gap stubbornly persists.

There are differences among other groups as well. European New Zealanders outscore native Maori New Zealanders. Israeli Jews outscore Israeli Arabs. Most Japanese outscore the stigmatized Japanese minority, the Burakumin. And those who can hear outscore those born deaf (Braden, 1994; Steele, 1990; Zeidner, 1990).

Everyone further agrees that such *group* differences provide little basis for judging individuals. Women outlive men by six years, but knowing someone's sex doesn't tell us with any precision how long that person will live. Even Charles Murray and Richard Herrnstein (1994), whose writings drew attention to Black-White differences, reminded us that "millions of Blacks have higher IQs than the average White."

Swedes and Bantus differ in complexion and language. That first factor is genetic, the second environmental. So what about intelligence scores?

Since 1850, the average Dutch man has grown from 5 feet 4 inches to today's 5 feet 10 inches (Bogin, 1998).

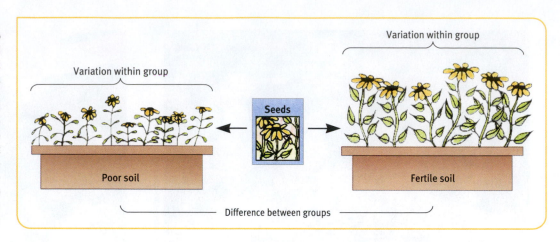

FIGURE 25.6
Group differences and environmental impact
Even if the variation between members within a group reflects genetic differences, the average difference between groups may be wholly due to the environment. Imagine that seeds from the same mixture are sown in different soils. Although height differences *within* each window box will be genetic, the height difference *between* the two groups will be environmental. (From Lewontin, 1976.)

In prosperous country X everyone eats all they want. In country Y the rich are well fed, but the semistarved poor are often thin. In which country will the heritability of body weight be greater? (See this module's final page.)

Nature's own morphing
Nature draws no sharp boundaries between races, which blend gradually one into the next around the Earth. Thanks to the human urge to classify, however, people socially define themselves in racial categories, which become catch-all labels for physical features, social identity, and nationality.
© Paul Almasy/Corbis; © Rob Howard/ Corbis; © Barbara Bannister; Gallo Images/ Corbis; © David Turnley/Corbis; © Dave Bartruff/Corbis; © Haruyoshi Yamaguchi/Corbis; © Richard T. Nowitz/Corbis; © Owen Franken/Corbis; © Paul Almasy/Corbis; © John-Francis Bourke/zefa/Corbis

As we have seen, heredity contributes to individual differences in intelligence. Does that mean it also contributes to group differences? Some psychologists believe it does, perhaps because of the world's differing climates and survival challenges (Herrnstein & Murray, 1994; Lynn, 1991, 2001; Rushton, 1998, 2003).

But we have also seen that group differences in a heritable trait may be entirely environmental, as in our earlier barrel-versus-home–reared boys example. Consider one of nature's experiments: Allow some children to grow up hearing their culture's dominant language, while others, born deaf, do not. Then give both groups an intelligence test rooted in the dominant language, and (no surprise) those with expertise in that language will score highest. Although individual performance differences may be substantially genetic, the group difference is not (**FIGURE 25.6**).

Or consider this: If each identical twin were exactly as tall as his or her co-twin, heritability would be 100 percent. Imagine that we then separated some young twins and gave only half of them a nutritious diet, and that the well-nourished twins all grew to be exactly 3 inches taller than their counterparts—an environmental effect comparable to that actually observed in both Britain and America, where adolescents are several inches taller than their counterparts were a half-century ago (Angoff, 1987; Lynn, 1987). What would the heritability of height now be for our well-nourished twins? Still 100 percent, because the variation in height within the group would remain entirely predictable from the heights of their malnourished identical siblings. So even perfect heritability within groups would not eliminate the possibility of a strong environmental impact on the group differences.

Might the racial gap be similarly environmental? Think about it:

Genetics research reveals that under the skin, the races are remarkably alike (Cavalli-Sforza & others, 1994; Lewontin, 1982). Individual differences within a race are much greater than differences between races. The average genetic difference between two Icelandic villagers or between two Kenyans greatly exceeds the group difference between Icelanders and Kenyans. Moreover, looks can deceive. Light-skinned Europeans and dark-skinned Africans are genetically closer than are dark-skinned Africans and dark-skinned Aboriginal Australians.

Race is not a neatly defined biological category. Some scholars argue that there is a reality to race, noting that there are genetic markers for race and that medical risks (such as skin cancer or high blood pressure) vary by race. Behavioral traits may also vary by race. "No runner of Asian or European descent—a majority of the world's population—has broken 10 seconds in the 100-meter dash, but dozens of runners of West African descent have done so," observes psychologist David Rowe (2005). Many more social scientists, though, see race primarily as a social construction without well-defined physical boundaries (Helms & others, 2005; Smedley & Smedley, 2005; Sternberg & others, 2005). People with varying ancestry may categorize themselves in the same race. Moreover, with increasingly mixed ancestries, more and more people defy neat racial categorization. (What race is Tiger Woods?)

Asian students outperform North American students on math achievement and aptitude tests. But this difference appears to be a recent phenomenon and may reflect conscientiousness more than competence. Asian students also attend school 30 percent more days per year and spend much more time in and out of school studying math (Geary & others, 1996; Larson & Verma, 1999; Stevenson, 1992).

The intelligence test performance of today's better-fed, better-educated, and more test-prepared population exceeds that of the 1930s population—by the same margin that the intelligence test score of the average White today exceeds that of the average Black. No one attributes the generational group difference to genetics.

White and black infants have scored equally well on an infant intelligence measure (preference for looking at novel stimuli—a crude predictor of future intelligence scores [Fagan, 1992]).

In different eras, different ethnic groups have experienced golden ages—periods of remarkable achievement. Twenty-five-hundred years ago it was the Greeks and the Egyptians, then the Romans; in the eighth and ninth centuries, genius seemed to reside in the Arab world; 500 years ago it was the Aztec Indians and the peoples of Northern Europe. Today, people marvel at Asians' technological genius. Cultures rise and fall over centuries; genes do not. That fact makes it difficult to attribute a natural superiority to any race.

The culture of scholarship
The children of Indochinese refugee families studied by Nathan Caplan, Marcella Choy, and James Whitmore (1992) typically excel in school. On weekday nights after dinner, the family clears the table and begins homework. Family cooperation is valued, and older siblings help younger ones.

Gender Similarities and Differences

In science, as in everyday life, differences, not similarities, excite interest. Compared with the anatomical and physiological similarities between men and women, our sex differences are relatively minor. Yet it is the differences we find exciting. Similarly, in the psychological domain, gender similarities vastly outnumber gender differences, but most people find differences more newsworthy.

Spelling Girls are better spellers: At the end of high school in the United States, only 30 percent of males spell better than the average female (Lubinski & Benbow, 1992). Through 2004, of the 80 U.S. national spelling bee champions, 42 were girls.

Verbal ability Girls excel at verbal fluency and remembering words. And, year after year, among nearly 200,000 students taking Germany's Test for Medical Studies, young women surpass men in remembering facts from short medical cases (Stumpf & Jackson, 1994). (My wife, who remembers many of my experiences for me, tells me that if she died I'd be a man without a past.)

Nonverbal memory Girls have an edge in locating objects (Halpern, 2000). In studies of more than 100,000 American adolescents, girls also modestly surpassed boys in memory for picture associations (Hedges & Nowell, 1995).

Sensation Girls are more sensitive to touch, taste, and odor.

Emotion-detecting ability Women are better emotion detectors than men are. Robert Rosenthal, Judith Hall, and their colleagues (1979; McClure, 2000) discovered this while studying sensitivity to emotional cues (an aspect of emotional intelligence). They showed hundreds of people brief film clips of portions of a person's emotionally expressive face or body, sometimes with a garbled voice added. For example, after showing a 2-second scene revealing only the face of an upset woman, the researchers asked people to guess whether the woman was criticizing someone for being late or was talking about her divorce. Rosenthal and Hall found that some people, many of them women, are much better emotion detectors than others. Such skills may explain women's somewhat greater responsiveness in both positive and negative emotional situations.

> "Do not obtain your slaves from Britain, because they are so stupid and so utterly incapable of being taught."
>
> Cicero, 106–43 B.C.

Despite the gender equivalence in intelligence test scores, males are more likely than females to overestimate their own test scores. Both males and females tend to rate their father's scores higher than their mother's, their brothers' scores higher than their sisters', and their sons' scores higher than their daughters' (Furnham, 2001; Furnham & others, 2002a,b, 2004a,b,c).

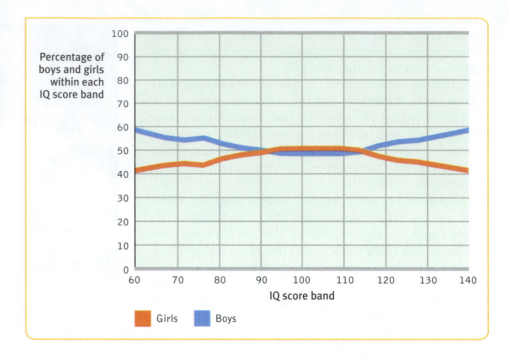

FIGURE 25.7
Gender and variability
When nearly 80,000 Scottish 11-year-olds were administered an intelligence test in 1932, the average IQ scores for girls (100.6) and boys (100.5) were virtually identical. But boys were modestly overrepresented at the low and high extremes. (Adapted from Deary & others, 2003.)

In the first 56 years of the college Putnam Mathematical Competition, all of the nearly 300 awardees were men (Arenson, 1997). In 1997, a woman broke the male grip by joining 5 men in the winner's circle. In 1998, Melanie Wood became the first female member of a U.S. math Olympics team (Shulman, 2000). Her training began at an early age: When mall-shopping with her then-4-year-old daughter, Melanie's mother would alleviate her child's boredom by giving her linear equations to solve.

Could this ability also have helped our ancestral mothers read emotions in their infants and would-be lovers, in turn fueling cultural tendencies to encourage women's empathic skills? Some evolutionary psychologists believe so.

Underachievement Boys outnumber girls at the low extremes and therefore in special education classes (Kleinfeld, 1998; **FIGURE 25.7**). They also tend to talk later and to stutter more often.

Math and spatial aptitudes On math tests given to more than 3 million representatively sampled people in 100 independent studies, males and females obtained nearly identical average scores (Hyde & others, 1990). But again—despite greater diversity within the genders than between them—group differences make the news. In 20 of 21 countries, females displayed an edge in math computation, but males scored higher in math problem solving (Bronner, 1998; Hedges & Nowell, 1995). In Western countries, virtually all math prodigies participating in the International Mathematics Olympiad have been males. (More female math prodigies have, however, reached the top levels in non-Western countries such as China [Halpern, 1991]).

The score differences are sharpest at the extremes. Among 12- to 14-year-olds scoring extremely high on Scholastic Assessment Test math, boys have outnumbered

World math Olympics champs
After outscoring 350,000 of their U.S. peers, these boys all had perfect scores in competition with math whizzes from 68 other countries.

Courtesy Robert Allen Strawn

Which two circles contain a configuration of blocks identical
to the one in the circle at the left?

Standard   Responses

FIGURE 25.8
The mental rotation test
This is a test of spatial abilities. Which two
responses show a different view of the
standard? (From Vandenberg & Kuse, 1978.)
(See this module's final page for answers.)

girls 13 to 1, and within that precocious group, the boys more often went on to earn
a degree in the inorganic sciences and engineering (Benbow & others, 2000). In the
United States, males also have an edge in the annual physics and computer science
Advanced Placement exams (Stumpf & Stanley, 1998).

The average male edge seems most reliable in spatial ability tests like the one
shown in **FIGURE 25.8**, which involves speedily rotating three-dimensional objects in
one's mind (Collins & Kimura, 1997; Halpern, 2000). Exposure to high levels of
male sex hormones during the prenatal period does enhance spatial abilities (Berenbaum & others, 1995). Such skills help when fitting suitcases into a car trunk, playing chess, or doing certain types of geometry problems.

From an evolutionary perspective (Geary, 1995, 1996; Silverman & others, 1992,
1998), those same skills helped our ancestral fathers track prey and make their way
home. The survival of our ancestral mothers may have benefited more from a keen
memory for the location of edible plants—a legacy that lives today in women's superior memory for objects and their location.

Evolutionary psychologist Steven Pinker (2005) argues that biological as well as
social influences appear to affect gender differences in life priorities (women's greater
interest in people versus men's in money and things), in risk-taking (with men more
reckless), and in math reasoning and spatial abilities. Such differences are, he notes,
observed across cultures, stable over time, observed in genetic boys raised as girls, and
influenced by prenatal hormones.

Elizabeth Spelke (2005), however, urges caution in charting male-female intellectual worlds. It oversimplifies to say that women have more "verbal ability" and
men more "math ability." Women excel at verbal fluency, men at verbal analogies.
Women excel at rapid math calculations, men at rapid math reasoning. Women
excel at remembering objects' spatial positions, men at remembering geometric
layouts. Other critics urge us to remember that social expectations and divergent
opportunities shape boys' and girls' interests and abilities (Crawford & others,

AP Photo/Paul Sakuma

Nature or nurture?
At this 2005 Google Inc.-sponsored
computer coding competition, programmers
competed for cash prizes and possible jobs.
What do you think accounted for the fact that
only one of the 100 finalists was female?

■ **stereotype threat** a self-confirming concern that one will be evaluated based on a negative stereotype.

1995; Eccles & others, 1990). The male edge in math problem solving is detectable only after elementary school. Traditionally, math and science have been considered masculine subjects, but as more parents encourage their daughters to develop their abilities in math and science, the gender gap is narrowing (Nowell & Hedges, 1998). In some fields, including psychology, women now earn most of the Ph.D.s. Yet, notes Diane Halpern (2005) with a twinkle in her eye, "no one has asked if men have the innate ability to succeed in those academic disciplines where they are underrepresented."

The Question of Bias

25-8: Are intelligence tests biased and discriminatory?

Knowing there are group differences in intelligence test scores leads us to wonder whether intelligence tests are biased. The answer depends on which of two very different definitions of bias are used, and on an understanding of stereotypes.

A test may be considered biased if it detects not only innate differences in intelligence but also performance differences caused by cultural experiences. This in fact happened to Eastern European immigrants in the early 1900s. Lacking the experience to answer questions about their new culture, many were classified as feeble-minded. David Wechsler, who entered the United States as a 6-year-old Romanian just before this group, designed the WAIS. In this popular sense, intelligence tests are biased. They measure your developed abilities, which reflect, in part, your education and experiences.

The *scientific* meaning of bias is different. It hinges on the test's validity—on whether it predicts future behavior only for some groups of test-takers. For example, if the U.S. SAT accurately predicted the college achievement of women but not that of men, then the test would be biased. The near-consensus among psychologists, as summarized by the U.S. National Research Council's Committee on Ability Testing and the American Psychological Association's Task Force on Intelligence, is that the major U.S. aptitude tests are *not* biased in this statistical meaning of the term (Neisser & others, 1996; Wigdor & Garner, 1982). Their predictive validity is roughly the same for women and men, for Blacks and Whites, and for rich and poor. If an intelligence test score of 95 predicts slightly below average grades, that rough prediction usually applies equally to both genders and all ethnic and economic groups.

Test-Takers' Expectations

Throughout this text, we have seen that our expectations and attitudes can influence our perceptions and behaviors. Once again, we find this effect in intelligence testing. When Steven Spencer and his colleagues (1997) gave a difficult math test to equally capable men and women, women did not perform as well as men—except when they had been led to expect that women usually do as well as men on the test. Otherwise, the women apparently felt apprehensive, and it affected their performance. With Claude Steele and Joshua Aronson, Spencer (2002) also observed this self-fulfilling **stereotype threat** when black students, taking verbal aptitude tests under conditions designed to make them feel threatened, performed at a lower level. Stereotype threat helps explain why women have scored higher on math tests when no male test-takers were in the group, and why Blacks have scored higher when tested by Blacks than when tested by Whites (Danso & Esses, 2001; Inzlicht & Ben-Zeev, 2000).

Steele (1995, 1997) concluded that telling students they probably won't succeed (as remedial "minority support" programs often do) functions as a stereotype that can erode test and school performance. Over time, such students may detach their

"Math class is tough!"
"Teen talk" talking Barbie doll (introduced February 1992, recalled October 1992)

self-esteem from academics and look for recognition elsewhere. Indeed, as African-American boys progress from eighth to twelfth grade, they tend to underachieve relative to their abilities, and the disconnect between their grades and their self-esteem becomes pronounced (Osborne, 1997). Minority students in university programs that challenge them to believe in their potential have produced markedly higher grades and had lower dropout rates.

What then can we realistically conclude about aptitude tests and bias? The tests do seem biased (appropriately so, some would say) in one sense—sensitivity to performance differences caused by cultural experience. But they are not biased in the scientific sense of making valid statistical predictions for different groups.

Bottom line: Are the tests discriminatory? Again, the answer can be yes or no. In one sense, yes, their purpose is to discriminate—to distinguish among individuals. In another sense, their purpose is to reduce discrimination by reducing reliance on subjective criteria for school and job placement—who you know, how you dress, or whether you are the "right kind of person." Civil service aptitude tests, for example, were devised to discriminate more fairly and objectively, by reducing the political, racial, and ethnic discrimination that preceded their use. Banning aptitude tests would lead those who decide on jobs and admissions to rely more on other considerations, such as their personal opinions.

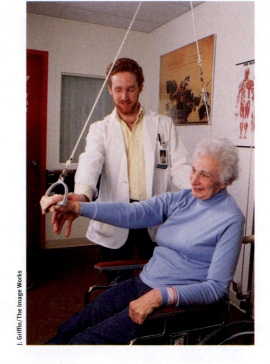

J. Griffin/The Image Works

Perhaps, then, our goals for tests of mental abilities should be threefold. First, we should realize the benefits Alfred Binet foresaw—to enable schools to recognize who might profit most from early intervention. Second, we must remain alert to Binet's fear that intelligence test scores may be misinterpreted as literal measures of a person's worth and fixed potential. And finally, we must remember that the competence that general intelligence tests sample is important; it helps enable success in some life paths. But it reflects only one aspect of personal competence. Our practical intelligence and emotional intelligence matter, too, as do other forms of creativity, talent, and character. The carpenter's spatial ability differs from the programmer's logical ability, which differs from the poet's verbal ability. Because there are many ways of being successful, our differences are variations of human adaptability.

Untestable compassion
Intelligence test scores are only one part of the picture of a whole person. They don't measure the abilities, talent, and commitment of, for example, people who devote their lives to helping others.

"Almost all the joyful things of life are outside the measure of IQ tests."
Madeleine L'Engle, *A Circle of Quiet*, 1972

>> MODULE REVIEW

25-1: Is intelligence a single general ability or several distinct abilities?

Most psychologists now define *intelligence* as the ability to learn from experience, solve problems, and adapt to new situations. And most psychologists agree that people have specific abilities, such as verbal and mathematical aptitudes. However, they debate whether a *general intelligence* (*g*) factor runs through all aptitudes. Studies of special conditions, such as the *savant syndrome,* and of impairments following brain injuries, have identified clusters of mental aptitudes, supporting the idea of multiple intelligences. Howard Gardner proposes eight such intelligences (linguistic, logical-mathematical, musical, spatial, bodily kinesthetic, intrapersonal, interpersonal, and naturalist). Robert Sternberg specifies three components of intelligence (analytical, creative, and practical).

25-2: What is creativity, and what fosters this ability?

Creativity correlates somewhat with intelligence, but beyond an intelligence test score of about 120, that link disappears. Creativity also correlates with a developed expertise, imaginative thinking skills, a venturesome personality, intrinsic motivation, and the support offered by a creative environment.

25-3: Is our ability to manage our own emotions and to empathize with others a form of intelligence?

Emotional intelligence has been described as the ability to perceive, understand, manage, and use emotions. Critics question whether this concept stretches the idea of intelligence too far.

25-4: When and why were intelligence tests created?

An *intelligence test* is a method for assessing an individual's mental aptitudes and comparing them with those of others, using numerical scores.

In the early 1900s, French psychologist Alfred Binet and his colleague Théodore Simon developed questions in an attempt to measure *mental age* and thus to help predict children's future progress in the Paris school system. Lewis Terman of Stanford University adapted Binet's test and offered his *Stanford-Binet* for use with adults in the United States. William Stern derived the *intelligence quotient* (*IQ*) to define performance on Terman's test. The most widely used intelligence test is the *Wechsler Adult Intelligence Scale* (*WAIS*).

25-5: By what criteria can we judge intelligence tests?

All good tests—whether *aptitude tests* (designed to predict ability to learn a particular skill) or *achievement tests* (designed to assess current competence)—must be *standardized,* to establish a basis for meaningful comparisons of scores. They must also be *reliable,* so they yield dependably consistent scores. And they must be *valid,* so they measure what they are supposed to measure (*content validity*) or predict, on the basis of a specified criterion, what they are supposed to predict (*predictive validity*).

Test scores usually fall into a bell-shaped distribution, the *normal curve.* The average score is assigned an arbitrary number (such as 100 on an intelligence test). At the extremes of the bell curve are the gifted and those with *mental retardation.* One cause of mental retardation is *Down syndrome.*

25-6: Is intellect influenced more by heredity or by environment?

Studies of twins, family members, and adopted children support the idea that there is a significant genetic contribution to intelligence scores. *Heritability,* the variation in a trait that can be attributed to genes, pertains only to variation of a characteristic within a group, not to the origin of a characteristic in any individual. Heritability of intelligence increases as environmental differences decrease.

Studies of children reared in extremely impoverished, enriched, or culturally different environments indicate the influence of life experiences on intelligence test performance.

25-7: How, and why, do ethnic and gender groups differ in aptitude test performance?

Like individuals, groups vary in intelligence test scores. Hereditary variation within a group need not signify a hereditary explanation of between-group differences. In the case of the racial gaps in test scores, the evidence suggests that environmental differences are largely, perhaps entirely, responsible.

Girls tend to score higher on spelling tests; verbal ability; nonverbal memory; sensitivity to touch, taste, and odor; and on reading others' emotions. Boys tend to score higher on math and spatial relations tests. Psychologists debate evolutionary and cultural explanations of gender differences in specific abilities.

25-8: Are intelligence tests biased and discriminatory?

Aptitude tests aim to predict how well a test-taker will perform in a given situation. So they are necessarily "biased" in the sense that they are sensitive to performance differences caused by cultural experience.

But bias can also mean what psychologists commonly mean by the term—that a biased test predicts less accurately for one group than for another. In this sense of the term, most experts do not consider the major aptitude tests to be significantly biased.

>> REHEARSE IT!

1. Savant syndrome is retardation combined with incredible ability in one specific area. The existence of savant syndrome seems to support
   a. Sternberg's distinction among three aspects of intelligence.
   b. Spearman's notion of general intelligence, or *g* factor.
   c. Gardner's theory of multiple intelligences.
   d. Binet's concept of mental age.

2. Intelligence tests predict school grades reasonably well but are less successful at predicting achievement in other areas. Robert Sternberg has therefore identified three aspects of intelligence, which are
   a. spatial, academic, and artistic intelligence.
   b. musical, athletic, and academic intelligence.
   c. academic, practical, and creative intelligence.
   d. emotional, practical, and spatial intelligence.

3. Emotional intelligence is the ability to perceive, understand, and regulate emotions. Emotionally intelligent people are characterized by
   a. the tendency to seek immediate gratification.
   b. the ability to understand their own emotions but not those of others.
   c. high practical intelligence.
   d. self-awareness.

4. Creativity is the ability to produce novel and valuable ideas. Which of the following is *not* a characteristic of a creative person?
   a. expertise
   b. extrinsic motivation
   c. a venturesome personality
   d. imaginative thinking skills

5. The Wechsler Adult Intelligence Scale (WAIS) yields an overall intelligence score as well as separate verbal and performance (nonverbal) scores. The WAIS is best able to tell us
   a. what part of an individual's intelligence is determined by genetic inheritance.
   b. whether the test-taker will succeed in a job.
   c. how the test-taker compares with other adults in vocabulary and arithmetic reasoning.
   d. whether the test-taker has specific skills for music and the performing arts.

6. The Stanford-Binet, the Wechsler Adult Intelligence Scale, and the Wechsler Intelligence Scale for Children are known to have very high reliability (about +.9). This means that
   a. a pretest has been given to a representative sample.
   b. the test yields consistent results, for example on retesting.
   c. the test measures what it is supposed to measure.
   d. the results of the test will predict future behavior, such as college grades or success in business.

7. Intelligence quotient, or IQ, was originally defined as mental age divided by chronological age and multiplied by 100. By this definition, a 6-year-old child with a measured mental age of 6 would have an IQ of 100. Likewise, the IQ of a 6-year-old with a mental age of 9 would be
   a. 67.
   b. 133.
   c. 86.
   d. 150.

8. About 50 percent of intelligence score variation among individuals can be attributed to heredity. The strongest support for heredity's influence on intelligence is the finding that
   a. identical twins, but not other siblings, have nearly identical intelligence test scores.
   b. the correlation between intelligence test scores of fraternal twins is lower than that for other siblings.
   c. separated fraternal twins living in different environments tend to have similar intelligence test scores.
   d. children whose birthdays just make the cutoff point for school entrance temporarily have higher intelligence test scores than those born only slightly later.

9. The heritability of a trait may vary, depending on the range of populations and environments studied. To say that the heritability of intelligence is about 50 percent means that 50 percent of
   a. an individual's intelligence is due to genetic factors.
   b. the similarities between men and women are attributable to genes.
   c. the variation in intelligence within a group of people is attributable to genetic factors.
   d. intelligence is due to the mother's genes and the rest is due to the father's genes.

10. Within the limits set by heredity, experiences help shape intelligence. The experience that has the clearest, most profound effect on intellectual development is
    a. being enrolled in a Head Start program.
    b. growing up in an economically disadvantaged home or neighborhood.
    c. being raised in a very neglectful home or institution.
    d. being exposed to very stimulating toys and lessons in infancy.

Answers:
1. c, 2. c, 3. d, 4. b, 5. c, 6. b, 7. d, 8. a, 9. c, 10. c.

>> TERMS AND CONCEPTS TO REMEMBER

intelligence, p. 331
general intelligence (*g*), p. 331
savant syndrome, p. 332
creativity, p. 334
emotional intelligence, p. 335
intelligence test, p. 336
mental age, p. 337
Stanford-Binet, p. 337

intelligence quotient (IQ), p. 337
Wechsler Adult Intelligence Scale (WAIS),
   p. 337
aptitude test, p. 338
achievement test, p. 338
standardization, p. 338
normal curve, p. 339
reliability, p. 339

validity, p. 339
content validity, p. 339
predictive validity, p. 339
mental retardation, p. 340
Down syndrome, p. 340
heritability, p. 343
stereotype threat, p. 350

>> TEST YOURSELF

1. Joseph is a straight-A student at Harvard Law School, writes a small column for the *Harvard Law Review,* and will be working for a Supreme Court justice next year. Judith is very proud of her grandson and says he is way more intelligent than she ever was. But Joseph is also very proud of his grandmother, who had been imprisoned by the Nazis. When the war ended, she walked out of Germany, contacted a relief agency, traveled to the United States, and began a new life. According to the definition of intelligence in this module, is Joseph the only intelligent person in this story? Why or why not?

2. What was the purpose of Binet's pioneering intelligence test?

3. The Smiths have enrolled their 2-year-old son in a special program that promises to assess his IQ and, if he places in the top 5 percent of test-takers, to create a plan that will guarantee his admission to a top university at age 18. Is this a good plan?

4. As society succeeds in creating equality of opportunity, it will also increase the heritability of ability. The heritability of intelligence scores will be greater in a society marked by equal opportunity than in a society of peasants and aristocrats. Why?

(Answers in Appendix C.)

 *Multiple-choice **self-tests** and more may be found at www.worthpublishers.com/myers.*

>> ANSWERS TO QUESTIONS WITHIN THE MODULE

Q. If environments became more equal, the heritability of intelligence would
  a. increase
  b. decrease.
  c. be unchanged.

A. Heritability—variation explained by genetic influences—will *increase* as environmental variation decreases.

Q. In prosperous country X everyone eats all they want. In country Y the rich are well fed, but the semistarved poor are often thin. In which country will the heritability of body weight be greater?

A. Heritability—differences due to genes—will be greater in country X, where environmental differences in nutrition are minimal.

Q. Which two responses in Figure 25.8 (repeated below) show a different view of the standard? (From Vandenberg & Kuse, 1978.)

Standard   **Responses**

A. The first and fourth alternatives are different views of the standard.

Motivation

Motivation

"What's my motivation?" the actor asks the director. In our everyday conversation, "What motivated you to do *that?*" is a way of asking "What *caused* your behavior?" To psychologists, a *motivation* is a need or desire that *energizes* behavior and *directs* it toward a goal. Experienced mountaineer Aron Ralston understands the extent to which motivation can energize and direct behavior. Having bagged nearly all of Colorado's tallest peaks, many of them solo and in winter, Ralston, on a Saturday spring morning in 2003, ventured to do some solo canyon hiking that seemed so risk-free he did not bother to tell anyone where he was going. In Utah's narrow Bluejohn Canyon, just 150 yards above his final rappel, he was climbing over an 800-pound rock when it shifted and pinned his right wrist and arm. He was, as the title of his recent book says, caught *Between a Rock and a Hard Place.*

Realizing no one would be rescuing him, Ralston tried with all his might to dislodge the rock. Then, with his dull pocket knife, he tried chipping away at the rock. When that, too, failed, he rigged up ropes to lift the rock. Alas, nothing worked. Hour after hour, then cold night after cold night, he was stuck. By Tuesday, he had run out of food and water. On Wednesday, as thirst and hunger gnawed, he began saving and sipping his own urine. Using his video recorder, he said his good-byes to family and friends, for whom he now felt intense love: "So again love to everyone. Bring love and peace and happiness and beautiful lives into the world in my honor. Thank you. Love you."

On Thursday, surprised to find himself still alive, Ralston had a seemingly divine insight into his reproductive future, a vision of a preschool boy being scooped up by a one-armed man. With this inspiration, he summoned his remaining strength and his enormous will to live and, over the next hour, willfully broke his bones and

AP Photo/ Rocky Mountain News, Judy Walgren

Motivation personified
Aron Ralston's motivation to live and belong energized and directed his sacrificing half of his arm.

then proceeded to use that dull knife to cut off his arm. The moment after putting on a tourniquet, chopping the last piece of skin, and breaking free—and before rappelling with his bleeding half-arm down a 65-foot cliff and hiking 5 miles until finding someone—he was, in his own words, "just reeling with this euphoria . . . having been dead and standing in my grave, leaving my last will and testament, etching 'Rest in peace' on the wall, all of that, gone and then replaced with having my life again. It was undoubtedly the sweetest moment that I will ever experience" (Ralston, 2004).

Aron Ralston's thirst and hunger, his sense of belonging to others, and his underlying will to live and become a father highlight motivation's energizing and directing power. In Modules 26 through 28, we explore how four motives—hunger, sex, the need to belong, and achievement at work—arise from the interplay between nature (the physiological "push") and nurture (the cognitive and cultural "pulls"). We begin, in Module 26, with a look at how psychologists approach the study of motivation.

Introduction to Motivation: Hunger

26

A **motivation** is a need or desire that *energizes* behavior and *directs* it toward a goal. In this module we'll be focusing on the *hunger* motive. But first, let's step back and see how psychologists have understood motivation.

Motivational Concepts

Four perspectives have been useful in psychology's attempt to understand motivated behaviors. These include *instinct theory* (now replaced by the evolutionary perspective), *drive-reduction theory* (emphasizing the interaction between inner pushes and external pulls), and *arousal theory* (emphasizing the urge for an optimum level of stimulation). The fourth perspective, Abraham Maslow's *hierarchy of needs,* describes how some motives are, if unsatisfied, more basic and compelling than others.

Instincts and Evolutionary Psychology

26-1 : What underlying assumption is shared by instinct theory and evolutionary psychology?

Early in the twentieth century, as the influence of Charles Darwin's evolutionary theory grew, it became fashionable to classify all sorts of behaviors as instincts. If people criticized themselves, it was because of their "self-abasement instinct." If they boasted, it reflected their "self-assertion instinct." After scanning 500 books, one sociologist compiled a list of 5759 supposed human instincts! Before long, this fad for naming instincts collapsed under its own weight. Rather than *explaining* human behaviors, the early instinct theorists were simply *naming* them. It was like "explaining" a bright child's low grades by labeling the child an "underachiever." To name a behavior is *not* to explain it.

To qualify as an **instinct,** a complex behavior must have a fixed pattern throughout a species and be unlearned (Tinbergen, 1951). Such behaviors are common in other species. Newly hatched ducks and geese form attachments to the first moving

"What do you think . . . should we get started on that motivation research or not?"

© The New Yorker Collection, 2000, Bob Zahn from cartoonbank.com. All Rights Reserved.

■ **motivation** a need or desire that energizes and directs behavior.

■ **instinct** a complex behavior that is rigidly patterned throughout a species and is unlearned.

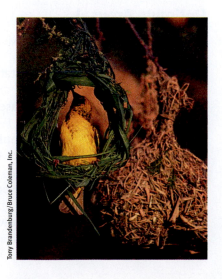

Same motive, different wiring

The more complex the nervous system, the more adaptable the organism. Both the woman and the weaverbird satisfy their need for shelter in ways that reflect their inherited capacities. The woman's behavior is flexible; she can learn whatever skills she needs to build a house. The bird's behavior pattern is fixed; it can build only this kind of nest.

thing they see. And mature salmon swim hundreds of miles upstream to mate and then die in the place they were born. Human behavior, too, exhibits certain un-learned fixed patterns, including infants' innate reflexes for rooting and sucking. Most psychologists, though, view human behavior as directed by physiological needs and by psychological wants.

Although instinct theory failed to explain human motives, the underlying assumption that genes predispose species-typical behavior remains as strong as ever. Psychologists may apply this perspective, for example, to explanations of our human similarities; to animals' biological predispositions to learn certain behaviors; and to the influence of evolution on our persistent fears, our helping behaviors, and our romantic attractions.

Drives and Incentives

26-2: How does drive-reduction theory help us understand the forces that energize and direct some of our behavior?

When the original instinct theory of motivation collapsed, it was replaced by **drive-reduction theory**—the idea that a physiological need creates an aroused state that drives the organism to reduce the need by, say, eating or drinking. With few exceptions, when a physiological need increases, so does a psychological *drive*—an aroused, motivated state.

The physiological aim of drive reduction is **homeostasis**—the maintenance of a steady internal state. An example of homeostasis (literally "staying the same") is the body's temperature-regulation system, which works like a thermostat. Both systems operate through feedback loops. Sensors feed room temperature to a control device. If the room temperature cools, the control device switches on the furnace. Likewise, if our body temperature cools, blood vessels constrict to conserve warmth, and we feel driven to put on more clothes or seek a warmer environment.

Not only are we *pushed* by our "need" to reduce drives, we also are *pulled* by **incentives**—positive or negative stimuli that lure or repel us. This is one way our individual learning histories influence our motives. Depending on our learning, the aroma of good food, whether fresh roasted peanuts or toasted ants, can motivate our behavior. So can the sight of those we find attractive or threatening.

When there is both a need and an incentive, we feel strongly driven. The food-deprived person who smells baking bread feels a strong hunger drive. In the presence of that drive, the baking bread becomes a compelling incentive. *For each motive, we can therefore ask, "How is it pushed by our inborn physiological needs and pulled by incentives in the environment?"*

Optimum Arousal

26-3: What type of motivated behavior does arousal theory attempt to explain?

We are much more than homeostatic systems, however. Some motivated behaviors actually *increase* arousal. Well-fed animals will leave their shelter to explore, seemingly in the absence of any need-based drive. From taking such risks, animals gain information and resources (Renner, 1992).

Curiosity drives monkeys to monkey around trying to figure out how to unlock a latch that opens nothing (**FIGURE 26.1**) or how to open a window that allows them to see outside their room (Butler, 1954). It drives the 9-month-old infant who investigates every accessible corner of the house. It drives the scientists whose work this text discusses. And it drives explorers and adventurers. Asked why he wanted to climb Mount Everest, George Mallory answered, "Because it is there." Those who, like Mallory, enjoy high arousal are most likely to enjoy intense music, novel foods, and risky behaviors (Zuckerman, 1979).

■ **drive-reduction theory** the idea that a physiological need creates an aroused tension state (a drive) that motivates an organism to satisfy the need.

■ **homeostasis** a tendency to maintain a balanced or constant internal state; the regulation of any aspect of body chemistry, such as blood glucose, around a particular level.

■ **incentive** a positive or negative environmental stimulus that motivates behavior.

■ **hierarchy of needs** Maslow's pyramid of human needs, beginning at the base with physiological needs that must first be satisfied before higher-level safety needs and then psychological needs become active.

Harlow Primate Laboratory, University of Wisconsin

Glenn Swier

FIGURE 26.1
Driven by curiosity
Baby monkeys and young children are fascinated by things they've never handled before. Their drive to explore the relatively unfamiliar is one of several motives that do not fill any immediate physiological need.

So, human motivation aims not to eliminate arousal but to seek optimum levels of arousal. Having all our biological needs satisfied, we feel driven to experience stimulation. Lacking stimulation, we feel bored and look for a way to increase arousal to some optimum level. However, with too much stimulation comes stress, and we then look for a way to decrease arousal.

A Hierarchy of Motives

26-4 : What is the basic idea behind Maslow's hierarchy of needs?

Some needs take priority over others. At this moment, with your needs for air and water satisfied, other motives—such as your desire to achieve—are energizing and directing your behavior. Let your need for water go unsatisfied and your thirst will preoccupy you. But if you were deprived of air, your thirst would disappear.

Abraham Maslow (1970) described these priorities as a **hierarchy of needs** (**FIGURE 26.2**). At the base of this pyramid are our physiological needs, such as those for food and water. Only if these needs are met are we prompted to meet our need for safety, and then to satisfy the uniquely human needs to give and receive love and to enjoy self-esteem. Beyond this, said Maslow (1971), lies the highest of human needs: to actualize one's full potential.

> "Hunger is the most urgent form of poverty."
>
> Alliance to End Hunger, 2002

FIGURE 26.2
Maslow's hierarchy of needs
Once our lower-level needs are met, we are prompted to satisfy our higher-level needs. While struggling to meet their basic needs for water, food, safe shelter, and medical attention, the survivors of the 2005 New Orleans hurricane were probably not immediately concerned with the higher-level needs on Maslow's hierarchy, such as esteem and self-actualization. (From Maslow, 1970.)

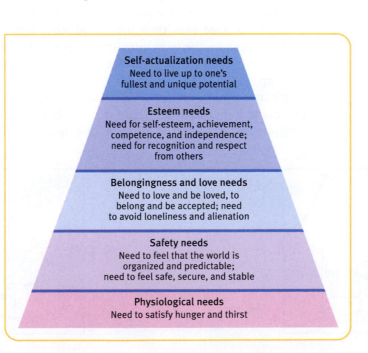

Self-actualization needs
Need to live up to one's fullest and unique potential

Esteem needs
Need for self-esteem, achievement, competence, and independence; need for recognition and respect from others

Belongingness and love needs
Need to love and be loved, to belong and be accepted; need to avoid loneliness and alienation

Safety needs
Need to feel that the world is organized and predictable; need to feel safe, secure, and stable

Physiological needs
Need to satisfy hunger and thirst

Joe Skipper/Reuters/Corbis

■ **glucose** the form of sugar that circulates in the blood and provides the major source of energy for body tissues. When its level is low, we feel hunger.

Maslow's hierarchy is somewhat arbitrary; the order of such needs is not universally fixed. People have starved themselves to make a political statement. Nevertheless, the simple idea that some motives are more compelling than others provides a framework for thinking about motivation, and life-satisfaction surveys in 39 nations support this basic idea (Oishi & others, 1999). In poorer nations that lack easy access to money and the food and shelter it buys, financial satisfaction more strongly predicts subjective well-being. In wealthy nations, where most are able to meet basic needs, home-life satisfaction is a better predictor. Self-esteem matters most in individualist nations, whose citizens tend to focus more on personal achievements than on family and community identity. So what motives preoccupy you depend on your situation.

Let's now consider hunger, a motive at the most basic physiological level, and see how environmental factors interact with what is physiologically given.

The Physiology of Hunger

26-5: What physiological factors cause us to feel hungry?

A vivid demonstration of the supremacy of physiological needs came from starvation experiences in World War II prison camps. David Mandel (1983), a Nazi concentration camp survivor, recalled how a starving "father and son would fight over a piece of bread. Like dogs." One father, whose 20-year-old son stole his bread from under his pillow while he slept, went into a deep depression, asking over and over how his son could do such a thing. The next day the father died. "Hunger does something to you that's hard to describe," Mandel explained.

To learn more about the results of semistarvation, scientist Ancel Keys and his colleagues (1950) fed 36 male volunteers—all conscientious objectors to the war—just enough to maintain their initial weight. Then, for six months, they cut this food level in half. The effects soon became visible. Without thinking about it, the men began conserving energy; they appeared listless and apathetic. Their body weights dropped rapidly, eventually stabilizing at about 25 percent below their starting weights. But the psychological effects were especially dramatic. Consistent with Maslow's idea of a needs hierarchy, the men became obsessed with food. They talked food. They daydreamed food. They collected recipes, read cookbooks, and feasted their eyes on delectable forbidden foods. At the same time, they lost interest in sex and social activities. They became preoccupied with their unfulfilled basic need. As one participant reported, "If we see a show, the most interesting part of it is contained in scenes where people are eating. I couldn't laugh at the funniest picture in the world, and love scenes are completely dull."

Keys' semistarved volunteers felt their hunger in response to a homeostatic system designed to maintain normal body weight and an adequate nutrient supply. But what precisely triggers hunger? Is it the pangs of an empty stomach? That is how it feels.

> "Nobody wants to kiss when they are hungry."
>
> Dorothea Dix, 1801–1887

GARFIELD

GARFIELD 1986 PAWS, INC. Dist. by UNIVERSAL PRESS SYNDICATE. Reprinted with permission. All Rights Reserved.

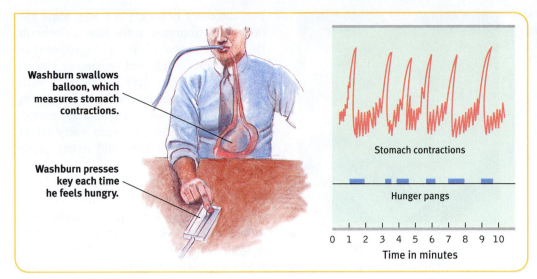

FIGURE 26.3
Monitoring stomach contractions
Using this procedure, Washburn showed that stomach contractions (transmitted by the stomach balloon) accompany our feelings of hunger (indicated by a key press). (From Cannon, 1929.)

Washburn swallows balloon, which measures stomach contractions.

Washburn presses key each time he feels hungry.

Stomach contractions

Hunger pangs

0 1 2 3 4 5 6 7 8 9 10
Time in minutes

And so it seemed after A. L. Washburn, working with Walter Cannon (Cannon & Washburn, 1912), intentionally swallowed a balloon. When inflated in his stomach, the balloon transmitted his stomach contractions to a recording device (**FIGURE 26.3**). While his stomach was being monitored, Washburn pressed a key each time he felt hungry. The discovery: Washburn was indeed having stomach contractions whenever he felt hungry.

Would hunger persist without stomach pangs? To answer that question, researchers removed some rats' stomachs and attached their esophagi to their small intestines (Tsang, 1938). Did the rats continue to eat? Indeed they did. Some hunger persists similarly in humans whose ulcerated or cancerous stomachs have been removed.

If the pangs of an empty stomach are not the only source of hunger, what else matters? Body chemicals and brain states offer some insights.

> "The full person does not understand the needs of the hungry."
>
> Irish proverb

Body Chemistry and the Brain

People and other animals automatically regulate their caloric intake to prevent energy deficits and maintain a stable body weight, suggesting that somehow, somewhere, the body is keeping tabs on its available resources. One such resource is the blood sugar **glucose.** Increases in the hormone *insulin* (secreted by the pancreas) diminish blood glucose, partly by converting it to stored fat. If your blood glucose level drops, you won't consciously feel this change. But, your brain, which is automatically monitoring your blood chemistry and your body's internal state, will trigger your hunger. Signals from your stomach, intestines, and liver (indicating whether glucose is being deposited or withdrawn) all signal your brain to motivate eating or not. But how does the brain integrate and respond to these messages? More than a half-century ago, researchers began unraveling this puzzle when they located hunger controls within the hypothalamus, a small but complex neural traffic intersection buried deep in the brain (**FIGURE 26.4**).

Two distinct hypothalamic centers help control eating. Activity along the sides of the hypothalamus (the *lateral hypothalamus*) brings on hunger. If electrically stimulated there, well-fed animals begin to eat; if the area is destroyed, even starving animals have no interest in food.

Activity in the second center—the lower mid-hypothalamus (the *ventromedial hypothalamus*)—depresses hunger. Stimulate this area and an animal will stop eating; destroy it and the animal's stomach and intestines will process food more rapidly, causing it to become extremely fat (Duggan & Booth, 1986; Hoebel & Teitelbaum, 1966).

FIGURE 26.4
The hypothalamus
The hypothalamus (colored red) performs various body maintenance functions, including control of hunger. Blood vessels supply the hypothalamus, enabling it to respond to our current blood chemistry as well as to incoming neural information about the body's state.

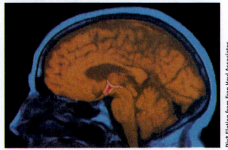

Pix* Elation from Fran Heyl Associates

Evidence for the brain's control of eating

A lesion near the middle (ventromedial) area of the hypothalamus caused this rat's weight to triple.

Richard Howard

■ **set point** the point at which an individual's "weight thermostat" is supposedly set. When the body weight falls below this level, an increase in hunger and a lowered metabolic rate may act to restore the lost weight.

■ **basal metabolic rate** the body's resting rate of energy expenditure.

This discovery helps explain why some patients with tumors near the base of the brain (in what we now realize is the hypothalamus) eat excessively and become very overweight (Miller, 1995). Rats with mid-hypothalamus lesions eat more often, produce more fat, and use less fat for energy, rather like a miser who runs every bit of extra money to the bank and resists taking any out (Pinel, 1993).

The hypothalamus monitors levels of the body's appetite hormones. One of these is *ghrelin,* a hunger-arousing hormone secreted by an empty stomach. When people with severe obesity undergo bypass surgery that seals off part of the stomach, the remaining stomach then produces much less ghrelin, and their appetite lessens (Lemonick, 2002). Other appetite hormones include *leptin, orexin,* and *PYY* (**FIGURE 26.5**).

The complex interaction of appetite hormones and brain activity may help explain the body's apparent predisposition to maintain itself at a particular weight level. When semistarved rats fall below their normal weight, this "weight thermostat" signals the body to restore the lost weight: Hunger increases and energy expenditure decreases. If body weight rises—as happens when rats are force-fed—hunger decreases and energy expenditure increases. This stable weight toward which semistarved and overstuffed rats return is their **set point** (Keesey & Corbett, 1983). In rats and humans, heredity influences body type and set point.

Human bodies regulate weight through the control of food intake, energy output, and **basal metabolic rate**—the rate of energy expenditure for maintaining basic body functions when the body is at rest. By the end of their 24 weeks of semistarvation, the men who participated in Keys' experiment had stabilized at three-quarters of their normal weight, while taking in half of their previous calories. How did they manage this? By reducing their energy expenditure, partly through inactivity but partly because of a 29 percent drop in their basal metabolic rate.

Some researchers, however, doubt that our bodies have a preset tendency to maintain optimum weight (Assanand & others, 1998). They point out that slow, sustained changes in body weight can alter one's set point, and that psychological factors also sometimes drive our feelings of hunger. Given unlimited access to a wide variety of tasty foods, people and other animals tend to overeat and gain weight (Raynor & Epstein, 2001). For all these reasons, some researchers have abandoned the idea of a biologically fixed *set point.* They prefer the term *settling point* to indicate the level at which a person's weight settles in response to caloric intake and expenditure (which are influenced by environment as well as biology).

FIGURE 26.5
The appetite hormones

Insulin: Hormone secreted by pancreas; controls blood glucose.
Leptin: Protein secreted by fat cells; when abundant, causes brain to increase metabolism and decrease hunger.
Orexin: Hunger-triggering hormone secreted by hypothalamus.
Ghrelin: Hormone secreted by empty stomach; sends "I'm hungry" signals to the brain.
PYY: Digestive tract hormone; sends "I'm *not* hungry" signals to the brain.

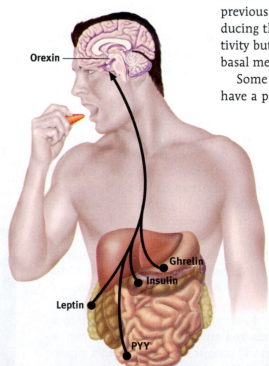

Orexin

Ghrelin

Insulin

Leptin

PYY

The Psychology of Hunger

26-6: What psychological influences affect our eating behavior and feelings of hunger?

Our eagerness to eat is indeed pushed by our physiological state—our body chemistry and hypothalamic activity. Yet there is more to hunger than meets the stomach. This was strikingly apparent when Paul Rozin and his trickster colleagues (1998) tested two patients with amnesia who had no memory for events occurring more than a minute ago. If, 20 minutes after eating a normal lunch, the patients were offered another, both readily consumed it . . . and usually a third meal offered 20 minutes after the second was finished. This suggests that part of knowing when to eat is our memory of our last meal. As time accumulates since we last ate, we anticipate eating again and start feeling hungry.

Psychological influences on eating behavior are strikingly evident when the desire to be thin overwhelms normal homeostatic pressures (see Close-Up: Eating Disorders on the next page).

Taste Preference: Biology or Culture?

Body chemistry and environmental factors together influence not only when we feel hunger, but also what we feel hungry for—our taste preference. When feeling tense or depressed, do you crave starchy, carbohydrate-laden foods? Carbohydrates help boost levels of the neurotransmitter serotonin, which has calming effects.

Our preferences for sweet and salty tastes are genetic and universal. Other taste preferences are conditioned, as when people given highly salted foods develop a liking for excess salt (Beauchamp, 1987), or when people develop an aversion to a food eaten before becoming violently ill. (The frequency of children's illnesses provides many chances for them to learn food aversions.)

Culture affects taste, too. Bedouins enjoy eating the eye of a camel, which most North Americans would find repulsive. Similarly, most North Americans and Europeans shun horse, dog, and rat meat, all of which are prized elsewhere.

Rats themselves tend to avoid unfamiliar foods (Sclafani, 1995). So do we, especially those that are animal-based. In experiments, people have tried novel fruit drinks or ethnic foods. With repeated exposure, their appreciation for the new taste typically increases; moreover, exposure to one set of novel foods increases our willingness to try another (Pliner, 1982; Pliner & others, 1993). This *neophobia* surely was adaptive for our ancestors, protecting them from potentially toxic substances.

© The New Yorker Collection, 2002, Alex Gregory from cartoonbank.com. All Rights Reserved.

"Never get a tattoo when you're drunk and hungry."

An acquired taste
For Alaska Natives (left), but not for most other North Americans, whale blubber is a tasty treat. For these Campa Indians in Peru (right), roasted ants are similarly delicious. People everywhere learn to enjoy the fatty, bitter, or spicy foods prescribed by their culture.

CLOSE-UP

EATING DISORDERS

Our bodies are naturally disposed to maintain a normal weight, including energy reserves in case food becomes unavailable for a time. Yet sometimes psychological influences may overwhelm this biological wisdom. This is strikingly evident in two disorders: anorexia and bulimia.

Anorexia nervosa always begins as a weight-loss diet. People with this disorder—usually adolescents and 9 out of 10 times females—drop significantly below normal weight (typically, by 15 percent or more). Yet even when emaciated, they feel fat and remain obsessed with losing weight.

Bulimia nervosa may also be triggered by a weight-loss diet, broken by gorging on forbidden foods. In a cycle of repeating episodes, overeating is followed by compensatory vomiting, laxative use, fasting, or excessive exercise. Binge-purge eaters—mostly women in their late teens or early twenties—eat the way some people with alcoholism drink—in spurts, sometimes influenced by friends who are bingeing (Crandall, 1988). Preoccupied with food (craving sweet and high-fat foods), and fearful of becoming overweight, they experience bouts of depression and anxiety, most severe during and following binges (Hinz & Williamson, 1987; Johnson & others, 2002). About half of those with anorexia also display

the binge-purge-depression symptoms of bulimia. Unlike anorexia, bulimia is marked by weight fluctuations within or above normal ranges, making the condition easy to hide.

Eating disorders do *not* provide (as some have speculated) a telltale sign of childhood sexual abuse (Smolak & Murnen, 2002; Stice, 2002). The family environment may provide a fertile ground for the growth of eating disorders in other ways, however.

- Mothers of girls with eating disorders tend to focus on their own weight and on their daughters' weight and appearance (Pike & Rodin, 1991).

- Families of bulimia patients have a higher-than-usual incidence of childhood obesity and negative self-evaluation (Jacobi & others, 2004).

- Families of anorexia patients tend to be competitive, high-achieving, and protective (Pate & others, 1992; Yates, 1989, 1990).

Anorexia sufferers often have low self-evaluations, set perfectionist standards, fret about falling short of expectations, and are intensely concerned with how others perceive them (Polivy & Herman, 2002; Striegel-Moore & others, 1993). Some of these factors also predict teen boys' pursuit

of unrealistic muscularity (Ricciardelli & McCabe, 2004).

But genetics may also influence susceptibility to eating disorders. Twins are somewhat more likely to share the disorder if they are identical rather than fraternal (Fairburn & others, 1999; Kaplan, 2004). Evolution may have predisposed such genes, suggests Shan Guisinger (2004). Faced with famine, our ancestors who denied their starvation and became hyperactive rather than listless and apathetic may have been more likely to search for food.

There are, however, cultural and gender components to these disorders. Body ideals vary across culture and time. In India, women students rate their ideals as close to their actual shape. In much of Africa—where plump means prosperous and thinness can signal poverty, AIDS, and hunger—bigger is better (Knickmeyer, 2001).

But bigger is not better in Western cultures, where, according to a recent analysis of 222 studies of 141,000 people (Feingold & Mazzella, 1998), the rise in eating disorders over the last 50 years has coincided with a dramatic increase in women having a poor body image. In one national survey, nearly one-half of all U.S. women reported feeling negative about their appearance and preoccupied with

Dying to be thin

Anorexia was identified and named in the 1870s, when it appeared among affluent adolescent girls (Brumberg, 2000). This 1930s photo illustrates the physical condition (left). Many modern-day celebrities have struggled publicly with eating disorders, including former teen actress Mary-Kate Olsen (right).

Reprinted by permission of *The New England Journal of Medicine,* 207, (Oct. 5, 1932), 613–617.

Lisa O'Connor/Zuma/Corbis

"Thanks, but we don't eat."

being or becoming overweight (Cash & Henry, 1995).

Gender differences in body image stood out clearly in a turn-of-the-century British survey of 3500 bank and university staff, in which men were more likely to *be* overweight and women were more likely to *perceive* themselves as overweight (Emslie & others, 2001).

Such differences appeared again in an experiment (Fredrickson & others, 1998) in which University of Michigan men and women donned either a sweater or a swimsuit and completed a math test while alone in a changing room. For the women but not the men, wearing the swimsuit triggered self-consciousness and shame that disrupted their math performance. And gender also sorted responses in an informal survey of 60,000 people, in which 9 in 10 women said they would rather have a perfect body than have a mate with a perfect body; 6 of 10 men preferred the reverse (Lever, 2003).

Part of the pressure on women is surely transmitted by the doctored images of unnaturally thin models

and celebrities that appear in the media (Tovee & others, 1997). Viewing such images, women often feel ashamed, depressed, and dissatisfied with their own bodies—the very attitudes that predispose eating disorders (Stice & Shaw, 1994; Posavac & others, 1998). Eric Stice and his colleagues (2001) tested this idea by giving some adolescent girls (but not others) a 15-month subscription to a teen fashion magazine (*Seventeen*). Compared with their counterparts who had not received the magazines, vulnerable girls (who were already dissatisfied, idealizing thinness, and lacking social support) exhibited increased body dissatisfaction and eating disorder tendencies. But even ultra-thin models do not reflect the impossible standard of the classic Barbie doll. Adjusted to a height of 5 feet 7 inches, her 32–16–29 figure (in centimeters, 82–41–73) defines a body shape approximated by fewer than 1 in 100,000 women (Norton & others, 1996).

Should it surprise us, then, that cultures without a thin-ideal for women are also cultures without eating disorders? Ghanaians, for example, idealize a larger body size than do Americans—and experience fewer eating disorders (Cogan & others, 1996). The same is true of African-American women compared with

"Why do women have such low self-esteem? There are many complex psychological and societal reasons, by which I mean Barbie."

Dave Barry, 1999

European-American women (Parker & others, 1995). And should we be surprised that those most vulnerable to eating disorders are also those (usually women) who most idealize thinness and have the greatest body dissatisfaction (Stice, 2002; Thompson & Stice, 2001; Vohs & others, 2001)? It seems clear that the sickness of today's eating disorders lies in part within our weight-obsessed culture—a culture that says, in countless ways, "Fat is bad," that motivates millions of women to be "always dieting," and that encourages eating binges by pressuring women to live in a constant state of semistarvation.

■ **anorexia nervosa** an eating disorder in which a normal-weight person (usually an adolescent female) diets and becomes significantly (15 percent or more) underweight, yet, still feeling fat, continues to starve.

■ **bulimia nervosa** an eating disorder characterized by episodes of overeating, usually of high-calorie foods, followed by vomiting, laxative use, fasting, or excessive exercise.

"Diana remained throughout a very insecure person at heart, almost childlike in her desire to do good for others, so she could release herself from deep feelings of unworthiness, of which her eating disorders were merely a symptom."

Charles, Ninth Earl of Spencer, eulogizing his sister Princess Diana, 1997

"Gee, I had no idea you were married to a supermodel."

FIGURE 26.6

FIGURE 26.6

Hot cultures like hot spices
Countries with hot climates, in which food historically spoiled more quickly, feature recipes with more bacteria-inhibiting spices (Sherman & Flaxman, 2001). India averages nearly 10 spices per meat recipe, Finland 2 spices.

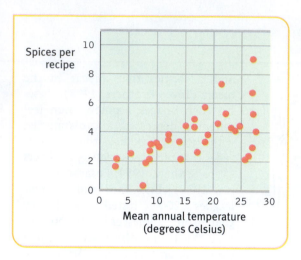

Other taste preferences are also adaptive. For example, the spices most commonly used in the recipes of hot climates, where food—especially meat—spoils more quickly, inhibit the growth of bacteria (**FIGURE 26.6**). Pregnancy-related nausea is another example of adaptive taste preferences. Food aversions stemming from this nausea peak about the tenth week, when the developing embryo is most vulnerable to toxins.

Obesity and Weight Control

26-7 : What factors predispose some people to become and remain obese?

Why do some people gain weight while others eat the same amount and seldom add a pound? And why do so few overweight people win the battle of the bulge? Is there weight-loss hope for the 65 percent of Americans who, according to the Centers for Disease Control, are overweight?

Our bodies store fat for good reasons. Fat is an ideal form of stored energy—a high-calorie fuel reserve to carry the body through periods when food is scarce—a common occurrence in the feast-or-famine existence of our prehistoric ancestors. (Think of that spare tire around the middle as an energy storehouse—biology's counterpart to a hiker's waist-borne snack pack.) No wonder that in most developing societies today, as in Europe in earlier centuries—in fact, wherever people face famine—obesity signals affluence and social status (Furnham & Baguma, 1994).

In those parts of the world where food and sweets are now abundantly available, the rule that once served our hungry distant ancestors (When you find energy-rich fat or sugar, eat it!) has become dysfunctional.

Pretty much everywhere this book is being read, obesity is on the rise. Worldwide, 60 percent of people are overweight, estimates the World Health Organization (Booth & Neufer, 2005). In the United States, the adult obesity rate has more than doubled in the last 40 years, to over 30 percent (CDC, 2004). Just since 1986, the number of obese Americans carrying more than 100 pounds of extra weight has quadrupled (Sturm, 2003). Australia, similar to Britain and America, classifies some 60 percent of its population as overweight or obese (Australian Bureau of Statistics, 1999; Halsey & Webb, 2000; Healey, 2004). In Canada, the proportion of people classified as overweight has increased by 60 percent since 1985 (Statistics Canada, 1999).

Being slightly overweight poses only modest health risks (Gibbs, 2005). Fitness matters more than being a little overweight. But significant obesity (**FIGURE 26.7**), especially among children, increases the risk of diabetes, high blood pressure, heart disease, gallstones, arthritis, and certain types of cancer, thus shortening life expectancy (Olshansky & others, 2005). The risks are greater for apple-shaped people who carry their weight in pot bellies than for pear-shaped people with ample hips and thighs (Greenwood, 1989). New research also has linked women's obesity to their risk of late-life Alzheimer's disease and brain tissue loss (Gustafson & others, 2003, 2004).

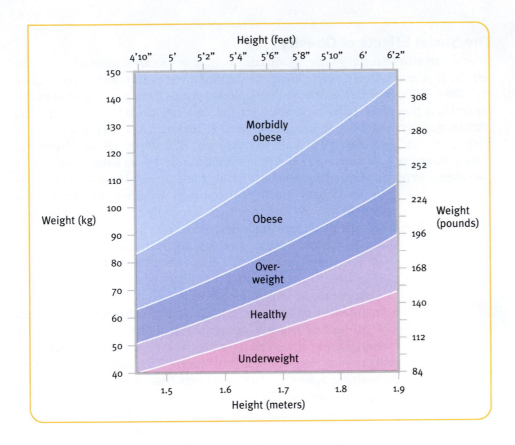

FIGURE 26.7

Obesity measured as body mass index (BMI)

U.S. government guidelines encourage a body mass index (BMI) under 25. The World Health Organization and many countries define *obesity* as a BMI of 30 or more. The shading in this graph is based on BMI measurements for these heights and weights. BMI is calculated by using the following formula:

$$\frac{\text{Weight in kg (pounds} \times .45)}{\text{Squared height in meters (inches} \div 39.4)^2} = \text{BMI}$$

Not surprisingly, then, one study (Calle & others, 1999) that followed more than 1 million Americans over 14 years revealed that being significantly overweight can cut life short (**FIGURE 26.8**). Those overweight at age 40 die three years earlier than their slim counterparts, reports another long-term study (Peeters & others, 2003). The death rate is especially high among very overweight men. Understandably, in 2004 the U.S. Medicare system began recognizing obesity as an illness.

Yearly health care expenditures per U.S. woman, ages 35 to 44, appear below (Wee & others, 2005). As economist Paul Krugman (2005) says, "Fat is a fiscal issue."

Normal weight:	$2127
BMIs 25 to 29.9:	$2358
BMIs 30 to 34.9:	$2873
BMIs 35 to 39.9:	$3058
BMIs 40 and up:	$3506

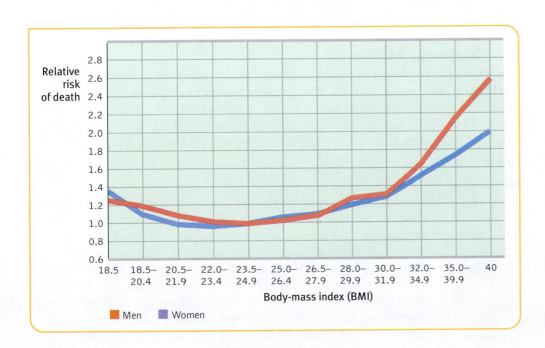

FIGURE 26.8

Obesity and mortality

Relative risk of death among healthy non-smokers rises with extremely high or low body mass index. (Data from 14-year study of 1.05 million Americans, Calle & others, 1999.)

"For fat students, the school experience is one of almost constant harassment."
Report on Size Discrimination, National Education Association, 1994

The Social Effects of Obesity

Obesity can also be socially toxic, by affecting both how you are treated and how you feel about yourself. Obese people know the stereotype: slow, lazy, and sloppy (Crandall, 1994, 1995; Ryckman & others, 1989). Widen people's images on a video monitor (making them look fatter) and observers suddenly rate them as less sincere, less friendly, meaner, and more obnoxious (Gardner & Tockerman, 1994). The social effects of obesity were clear in a study that followed 370 obese 16- to 24-year-old women (Gortmaker & others, 1993). When restudied seven years later, two-thirds of the women were still obese. They also were making less money—$7000 a year less—than an equally intelligent comparison group of some 5000 nonobese women. And they were less likely to be married. In personal ads, men often state their preference for, and women often advertise, slimness (Miller & others, 2000; Smith & others, 1990).

In one clever experiment, Regina Pingitore and her colleagues (1994) demonstrated weight discrimination. They videotaped mock job interviews in which professional actors appeared as either normal-weight or (wearing makeup and prostheses to make them look 30 pounds heavier) overweight applicants. When appearing overweight, the same person—using the same lines, intonation, and gestures—was rated less worthy of hiring. The weight bias was especially strong against women applicants (**FIGURE 26.9**). Other studies reveal that weight discrimination, though hardly discussed, is greater than race and gender discrimination. It occurs at every stage of the employment cycle—hiring, placement, promotion, compensation, discipline, and discharge (Roehling, 1999). Experiments show that anti-fat prejudice even extends to applicants who are *seen* with an obese person (Hebl & Mannix, 2003).

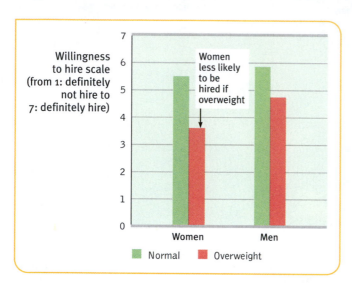

FIGURE 26.9
Gender and weight discrimination
When women applicants were made to look overweight, university students were less willing to think they would hire them. Among men applicants, weight mattered less. (Data from Pingitore & others, 1994.)

Weight discrimination takes its toll at home, too. In studies of patients especially unhappy with their weight—those who had lost an average of 100 pounds after short-cutting digestion with intestinal bypass surgery—4 in 5 said their children had asked them not to attend school functions. And 9 in 10 said they would rather have a leg amputated than be obese again (Rand & Macgregor, 1990, 1991).

Why don't obese people drop their excess baggage and free themselves of all this pain? The answer lies in the physiology of fat.

The Physiology of Obesity

Research on the physiology of obesity challenges the stereotype of severely overweight people being weak-willed gluttons. First, consider the arithmetic of weight gain: People get fat by consuming more calories than they expend. The energy equivalent of a pound of fat is 3500 calories; therefore, dieters have been told they will lose a pound for every 3500-calorie reduction in their diet. Surprise: This conclusion is false. Why? Read on.

Fat Cells

The immediate determinants of body fat are the size and number of fat cells. A typical adult has 30 to 40 billion of these miniature fuel tanks, half of which lie near the skin's surface. A fat cell can vary from relatively empty, like a deflated balloon, to overly full. In an obese person, fat cells may swell to two or three times their normal size and then divide or trigger nearby immature fat cells to divide—resulting in up to 75 billion fat cells (Hirsch, 2003). Once the number of fat cells increases—due to genetic predisposition, early childhood eating patterns, or adult overeating—it never decreases (**FIGURE 26.10**). On a diet, fat cells may shrink, but they never disappear (Sjöstrum, 1980).

FIGURE 26.10
Fat cells
We store energy in fat cells, which become larger and more numerous if we are obese, and smaller (but still more numerous) if we then lose weight. (Adapted from Jules Hirsch, 2003.)

Never obese   Obese   Reduced obese

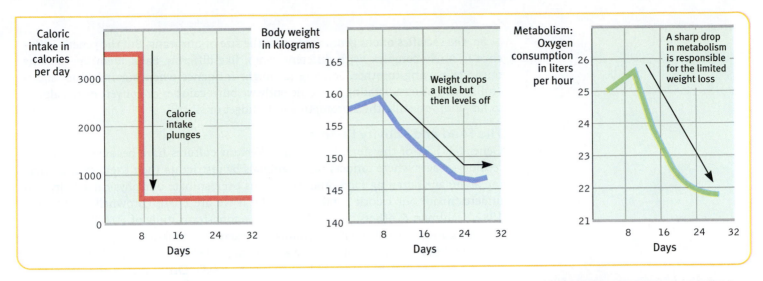

Set Point and Metabolism

Once we become fat, we require less food to maintain our weight than we did to attain it. Why? Because compared with other tissue, fat has a lower metabolic rate—it takes less food energy to maintain. An obese person's body has been maintaining body weight within a higher-than-average range. When weight drops below this range (called a *set point* or *settling point*), the person's hunger increases and metabolism decreases. Thus, the body adapts to starvation by burning off fewer calories, and to extra calories by burning off more.

In a classic month-long experiment (Bray, 1969), obese patients whose daily food intake was reduced from 3500 to 450 calories lost only 6 percent of their weight—partly because their bodies reacted as though they were being starved, and their metabolic rates dropped about 15 percent (**FIGURE 26.11**). That is why reducing your food intake by 3500 calories may not reduce your weight by 1 pound. That is also why further weight loss comes slowly following the rapid losses during the initial three weeks or so of a rigorous diet. And that is why amounts of food that worked to maintain weight before a diet began may increase it when a diet ends—the body is still conserving energy.

Thirty years after the Bray study, researchers performed a reverse experiment (Levine & others, 1999). They overfed volunteers 1000 calories a day for eight weeks. Those who gained the least weight tended to spend the extra caloric energy by fidgeting more. Lean people are naturally disposed to fidget and move about more (and burn more calories) than are energy-conserving overweight people who tend to sit still longer, report James Levine and his colleagues (2005). (The researchers outfitted people with undergarments that for 10 days monitored their movements every half second.) These individual differences in resting metabolism explain why two people of the same height, age, and activity level can maintain the same weight, even if one of them eats much less than the other does.

FIGURE 26.11

The effects of a severe diet on obese patients' body weight and metabolism

After seven days on a 3500-calorie diet, six obese patients were given only 450 calories a day for the next 24 days. Body weight declined only 6 percent and then leveled off, because metabolism dropped about 15 percent. (From Bray, 1969.)

The Genetic Factor

Do our genes predispose us to fidget or sit still? Possibly. Studies do reveal a genetic influence on body weight. Consider:

- Despite shared family meals, adoptive siblings' body weights are uncorrelated with one another or with those of their adoptive parents. Rather, people's weights resemble those of their biological parents (Grilo & Pogue-Geile, 1991).
- Identical twins have closely similar weights, even when reared apart (Plomin & others, 1997; Stunkard & others, 1990). Across studies, their weight correlates +.74. The much lower +.32 correlation among fraternal twins suggests that genes explain two-thirds of our varying body mass (Maes & others, 1997).
- Given an obese parent, a boy is three times, and a girl six times, more likely to be obese than their counterparts with normal-weight parents (Carrière, 2003).

So, the specifics of our genes predispose the size of our jeans. But the genetic influence is surely complex, with different genes, like differing band members, making music by playing together. Some genes might influence when our intestines signal "full," with others dictating how efficiently we burn calories or convert extra calories to fat, and, yes, still others prompting us to fidget or sit still.

The Food and Activity Factors

Genes tell part of the story, but not all. Western cultures have become like animal feedlots—places where farmers fatten animals by restricting their exercise and offering abundant fattening food. And most of us overestimate our physical activity and underestimate our caloric intake, especially if we are obese (Brownell & Wadden, 1992; Lichtman & others, 1992). In a massive long-term study of 50,000 nurses, researchers found—even after controlling for exercise, smoking, age, and diet—that each two-hour increase in daily TV watching predicted a 23 percent obesity increase and a 7 percent diabetes increase (Hu & others, 2003). Other studies show that people living in walking-dependent communities such as Manhattan tend to weigh less than more sedentary folks in car-dependent suburbs (Ewing & others, 2003). Among Ontario's Old Order Amish, where farming and gardening is labor intensive and pedometers reveal that men walk nine miles a day and women seven miles, the obesity rate is one-seventh the U.S. rate (Bassett & others, 2004).

Lack of exercise is compounded by high-calorie foods served in ever-larger sizes. Compared with our counterparts in the early 1900s, we are eating a higher-fat, higher-sugar diet, expending fewer calories, and suffering higher rates of diabetes at younger ages (Brody, 2003; Thompson, 1998). Today's women are eating 300 more calories a day and today's men nearly 200 more than the daily intake in 1971 (O'Connor, 2004). And just since 1971, they are eating three times as many meals in fast-food restaurants (Farley & Cohen, 2001). On most North American college campuses, yesterday's cafeteria line with limited choices has been replaced by today's food buffet, with multiple serving stations offering all-you-can-eat entrees and make-your-own waffles washed down with limitless soft drinks (Brody, 2003). For many, the understandable result is the "freshman 15." Small wonder that your parents and grandparents at age 30 likely weighed less than you did or will. Since 1960, the average adult American has grown one inch and gained 23 pounds (Ogden & others, 2004). Taken together, Big Macs, Double Whoppers, sugar-laden drinks, and inactivity form a weapon of mass destruction.

The "bottom" line: New stadiums, theaters, and subway cars are offering wider seats to accommodate this population growth (Hampson, 2000). The Washington State Ferries abandoned its 50-year-old standard of 18 inches per person. "Eighteen-inch butts are a thing of the past," explained a spokesperson (Shepherd, 1999). New York City, facing a large problem with Big Apple bottoms, has mostly replaced its 17.5-inch bucket-style subway seats with bucketless seats (Hampson, 2000). In the end, today's people need more room.

Note how these findings reinforce a familiar lesson: There can be high levels of *heritability* (genetic influence on individual differences) without heredity explaining group differences. Genes mostly determine why one person today is heavier than another. Environment mostly determines why people today are heavier than their counterparts 50 years ago. Our eating behavior also demonstrates the now familiar interaction among biological, psychological, and social-cultural factors (**FIGURE 26.12**).

Over the next 40 years you will eat about 20 tons of food. If during those years you increase your daily intake by just .01 ounce more than required for your energy needs, you will gain 24 pounds (Martin & others, 1991).

FIGURE 26.12
Levels of analysis for our hunger motivation

Clearly, we are biologically driven to eat, yet psychological and social-cultural factors strongly influence what, when, and how much we eat.

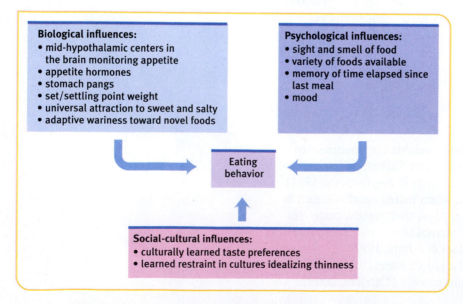

Biological influences:
• mid-hypothalamic centers in the brain monitoring appetite
• appetite hormones
• stomach pangs
• set/settling point weight
• universal attraction to sweet and salty
• adaptive wariness toward novel foods

Psychological influences:
• sight and smell of food
• variety of foods available
• memory of time elapsed since last meal
• mood

Eating behavior

Social-cultural influences:
• culturally learned taste preferences
• learned restraint in cultures idealizing thinness

Losing Weight

Perhaps you are shaking your head: "Slim chance we have of becoming and staying thin. If we lose weight on a diet, our metabolism slows and our hungry fat cells cry out, 'Feed me!' We're fated for fat!" Indeed, the condition of an obese person's body reduced to average weight is much like that of a semistarved body. Held under normal set point, each body "thinks" it is starving. Having lost weight, formerly obese people look normal, but their fat cells may be abnormally small, their metabolism slowed, and their minds obsessed with food.

The battle of the bulge rages on as intensely as ever, and it is most intense among those with two X chromosomes.

"It works as well as most other diet plans. . . . I've lost over $200 in less than three weeks."

For most people, the only long-term result of participating in a commercial weight-loss program is a thinner wallet.

© 1994, Tribune Media Services, Inc. All Rights Reserved.

Fighting obesity is an enormous business. Americans spend $40 billion a year on diet foods and drinks (Kolata, 2004). Two-thirds of women and half of men say they want to lose weight; about half of those women and men say they are "seriously trying" (Moore, 2003). Asked if they would rather "be five years younger or weigh 15 pounds less," 29 percent of men and 48 percent of women said they would prefer losing the weight (*Responsive Community,* 1996). So what are their chances?

With fat cells, settling points, metabolism, and genetic and environmental factors all tirelessly conspiring against shedding excess pounds, what advice can psychology offer? Perhaps the most important point is that permanent weight loss is not easy. Millions of people can vouch that it is possible to lose weight; they have done it lots of times. But short of drastic surgery to tie off part of the stomach and small intestine, most people who succeed on a weight-loss program eventually regain most of the weight (Garner & Wooley, 1991; Jeffery & others, 2000). Those who do manage to keep pounds off set realistic and moderate goals, undertaking programs that modify their life-style and ongoing eating behavior. They realize that being moderately heavy is less risky than being extremely thin (Ernsberger & Koletsky, 1999). They lose weight gradually: "A reasonable time line for a 10 percent reduction in body weight is six months," advises the National Institutes of Health (1998). And they exercise regularly. Lack of exercise helps explain why many fail to lose weight permanently. In a Centers for Disease Control study of 107,000 adults, only one in five of those trying to lose weight was following the government recommendation to both count calories and exercise 150 minutes weekly (Serdula & others, 1999). For other helpful hints, see Close-Up: For Those Who Want to Lose Weight, on the next page.

CLOSE-UP

FOR THOSE WHO WANT TO LOSE WEIGHT

People struggling with obesity are well advised to seek medical evaluation and guidance. For others who wish to take off a few pounds, researchers have offered these tips.

Begin only if you feel motivated and self-disciplined. For most people, permanent weight loss requires making a career of staying thin—a life-long change in eating habits combined with gradually increased exercise.

Minimize exposure to tempting food cues. Keep tempting foods out of the house or out of sight. Go to the supermarket only on a full stomach, and avoid the sweets and chips aisles. Eat simple meals, with only a few different foods; given more variety, people consume more.

Take steps to boost your metabolism. Inactive people are often overweight (**FIGURE 26.13**). In a 1980s study of 6671 young people 12 to 17 years old, and in a 1990s follow-up study of 4063 individuals 8 to 16 years old, obesity was more common among those who watched the most television (Andersen & others, 1998; Dietz & Gortmaker, 1985). Of course, overweight people may avoid activity, preferring to sit and watch

TV. But the association between TV watching and obesity remained when many other factors were controlled, suggesting that inactivity and snacking while watching TV do contribute to obesity. The good news is that one of the few predictors of successful long-term weight loss is exercise, both during and after changing your eating patterns (Jeffery & others, 2000; McGuire & others, 1999; Wadden & others, 1998). Exercise, such as brisk walking, running, and swimming, not only empties fat cells, builds muscle, and makes you feel better, it also temporarily speeds up metabolism and can help lower your settling point (Bennett, 1995; Kolata, 1987; Thompson & others, 1982). Even brief bouts of exercise—four 10-minute walks a day—provide benefits (Jakicic & others, 1999).

Eat healthy foods. Whole grains, fruits, vegetables, and healthy fats such as those found in olive oil and fish help regulate appetite and artery-clogging cholesterol (Taubes, 2001, 2002). Better crispy greens than Krispy Kremes.

Don't starve all day and eat one big meal at night. This eating pattern, common among overweight

"I looked at you and thought, I bet this man runs marathons."

© The New Yorker Collection, 1999, Edward Koren from cartoonbank.com. All Rights Reserved.

people, slows metabolism. Moreover, those who eat a balanced breakfast are, by late morning, more alert and less fatigued (Spring & others, 1992).

Beware of the binge. Among people who consciously restrain their eating, drinking alcohol or feeling anxious or depressed can unleash the urge to eat (Herman & Polivy, 1980). So can being distracted from monitoring your eating (Ward & Mann, 2000). (Ever notice that you eat more when out with friends?) Once the diet is broken, the person often thinks "what the heck" and then binges (Polivy & Herman, 1985, 1987). A lapse need not become a full collapse: Remember, most people occasionally lapse.

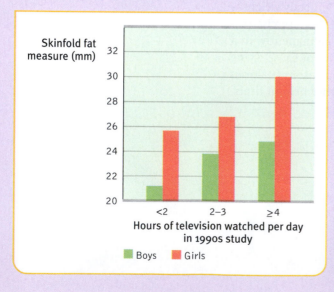

Skinfold fat measure (mm)

Hours of television watched per day in 1990s study

■ Boys   ■ Girls

Tony Freeman/PhotoEdit

FIGURE 26.13

American idle: Couch potatoes beware—TV watching correlates with obesity

As life-styles have become more sedentary and TV watching has increased, so has the percentage of overweight people in Britain, North America, and elsewhere. When California children were placed in a TV-reduction educational program, they watched less—and lost weight (Robinson, 1999).

REVIEWING

>> MODULE REVIEW

Motivation is the energizing and directing of our behavior. The instinct, drive-reduction, arousal, and hierarchy of needs perspectives offer insights into motivated behaviors.

26-1: **What underlying assumption is shared by instinct theory and evolutionary psychology?**

Under Darwin's influence, early theorists viewed behavior as controlled by biological forces, such as specific *instincts*. When it became clear that people were naming, not explaining, various behaviors by calling them instincts, this approach fell into disfavor. The underlying idea—that genes predispose species-typical behavior—is, however, still influential in evolutionary psychology.

26-2: **How does drive-reduction theory help us understand the forces that energize and direct some of our behavior?**

Drive-reduction theory proposes that physiological needs create aroused psychological states that drive us to reduce or satisfy those needs. The aim of drive reduction is internal stability, or *homeostasis.* We are most strongly driven when pushed by the need to reduce a drive and pulled by an external *incentive.* Depending on our personal and cultural experiences, we respond more to some stimuli than to others.

26-3: **What type of motivated behavior does arousal theory attempt to explain?**

Arousal theory helps explain the motivations for behaviors that do not reduce physiological needs or tension states. Curiosity-driven behaviors, for example, suggest that too little stimulation can motivate people to seek a higher level of arousal.

26-4: **What is the basic idea behind Maslow's hierarchy of needs?**

Maslow's *hierarchy of needs* proposes a pyramid-shaped sequence in which lower-level needs, such as hunger and thirst, are more compelling than higher-level needs, such as the need to love or to be respected.

26-5: **What physiological factors cause us to feel hungry?**

Hunger's inner push primarily originates not from the stomach's contractions but from variations in body chemistry, including hormones that heighten or reduce hunger. For example, we are likely to feel hungry when our blood *glucose* levels are low, or when the hormone ghrelin is secreted by the empty stomach. This information is integrated by the hypothalamus, which regulates the body's weight as it influences our feelings of hunger and fullness. To maintain weight, the body also adjusts its *basal metabolic rate* of energy expenditure.

26-6: **What psychological influences affect our eating behavior and feelings of hunger?**

Our hunger is influenced not only by our physical state but also by our memory of when we last ate and our expectation of when we should eat again. Humans prefer certain tastes (such as sweet and salty) but learn from family and culture to satisfy those preferences with specific foods. Some taste aversions (to new foods or foods that have made us ill) have survival value. A dramatic increase in poor body image has coincided with a rise in eating disorders among Western women. *Anorexia nervosa* and *bulimia nervosa* may have a genetic component, but cultural pressures, low self-esteem, and negative emotions seem to interact with stressful life experiences to produce these eating disorders.

26-7: **What factors predispose some people to become and remain obese?**

Fat is a concentrated fuel reserve stored in fat cells. Under genetic influence, the number and size of these cells determine one's body fat. Obese people find it difficult to lose weight permanently because the number of fat cells is not reduced by a diet, because fat cells require less energy expenditure than muscle cells to maintain themselves, and because the overall metabolic rate decreases when body weight drops below its *set point.* Those who nevertheless wish to diet should minimize exposure to food cues, boost energy expenditure through exercise, and make a lifelong change in eating patterns.

>> REHEARSE IT!

1. Although instinct theory fails to explain most human behavior, the existence of simple fixed patterns such as an infant's rooting and sucking suggests some innate tendencies in humans. Indeed, the underlying assumption of instinct theory—that _____—is as strong as ever.

   a. physiological needs arouse psychological states
   b. genes predispose species-typical behavior
   c. physiological needs increase arousal
   d. external needs energize and direct behavior

2. Drive-reduction theory proposes that a need, or deprivation (for example, a lack of water), leads to an aroused state or drive; this in turn motivates the organism to act to reduce this drive (drink a glass of water) and restore internal stability. The maintenance of a balanced internal state is called

   a. instinct.
   b. pursuit of stimulation.
   c. a hierarchy of needs.
   d. homeostasis.

3. Motivated behaviors satisfy a variety of needs. When feeling bored, we may look for ways to

   a. reduce physiological needs.
   b. search out respect from others.
   c. increase arousal.
   d. ensure stability.

4. Behavior is also influenced by incentives in the environment, as when the smell of baking bread triggers a desire to eat. To explain the effects of external incentives, we must refer to

   a. biological needs.
   b. instinct.
   c. individual learning histories.
   d. homeostasis.

5. According to Abraham Maslow, we are not prompted to satisfy psychological needs, such as the need to be accepted or loved, until we have satisfied more basic needs. The most basic needs are physiological needs, including the need for food, water, and oxygen; just above these are

   a. safety needs.
   b. self-esteem needs.
   c. belongingness needs.
   d. psychological needs.

6. The hypothalamus, a structure deep within the brain, controls feelings of hunger and fullness, in part by evaluating changes in blood chemistry. Hunger occurs in response to high blood insulin and

   a. high blood glucose and low levels of ghrelin.
   b. low blood glucose and high levels of ghrelin.
   c. a low basal metabolic rate.
   d. a high basal metabolic rate.

7. Set point theory proposes that our bodies tend to maintain themselves at a particular weight level. When our weight falls below the set point, we feel hungrier (and eat more) and lethargic (and reduce our energy expenditure). This "weight thermostat" is an example of

   a. homeostasis.
   b. an eating disorder.
   c. individual learning.
   d. binge-purge episodes.

8. Some of our responses to food and eating are learned; others are genetic and universal. Which of the following is a genetically disposed response to food?

   a. An aversion to eating cats and dogs
   b. An interest in novel foods
   c. A preference for sweet and salty foods
   d. An aversion to carbohydrates

9. Both anorexia nervosa and bulimia nervosa are eating disorders characterized by abnormal eating patterns. Which of the following is true of bulimia nervosa?

   a. People with bulimia continue to want to lose weight even when they are underweight.
   b. Bulimia is marked by weight fluctuations within or above normal ranges.
   c. Bulimia patients often come from middle-class families that are competitive, high-achieving, and protective.
   d. If one twin is diagnosed with bulimia, the chances of the other twin's sharing the disorder are greater if they are fraternal rather than identical twins.

10. Obese people find it very difficult to lose weight permanently. This is due to several factors, including the fact that

    a. with dieting, fat cells shrink and then disappear.
    b. the set point of obese people is lower than average.
    c. with dieting, basal metabolic rate increases.
    d. there is a genetic influence on body weight.

Answers: 1. b, 2. d, 3. c, 4. c, 5. a, 6. b, 7. a, 8. c, 9. b, 10. d.

>> TERMS AND CONCEPTS TO REMEMBER

motivation, p. 357
instinct, p. 357
drive-reduction theory, p. 358
homeostasis, p. 358

incentive, p. 358
hierarchy of needs, p. 359
glucose, p. 361
set point, p. 362

basal metabolic rate, p. 362
anorexia nervosa, p. 364
bulimia nervosa, p. 364

>> TEST YOURSELF

1. While on a long road trip, you consider pulling over to call a loved one. But it's getting late and you are hungry, so you drive on ahead to the next town. What motivational perspective would most easily explain this behavior and why?

2. You are traveling and have not eaten anything in eight hours. As your long-awaited favorite dish is placed in front of you, your mouth waters. Even imagining this may set your mouth to watering. What triggers this anticipatory drooling?

(Answers in Appendix C.)

*Multiple-choice **self-tests** and more may be found at www.worthpublishers.com/myers.*

Sexual Motivation

MODULE 27

Sex is part of life. Had this not been so for all your ancestors, you would not be reading this book. Sexual motivation is nature's clever way of making people procreate, thus enabling our species' survival. When two people feel attracted, they hardly stop to think of themselves as guided by their genes. As the pleasure we take in eating is nature's inventive method of getting our body nourishment, so the pleasure of sex is our genes' way of preserving and spreading themselves. Our human need to belong—to connect in close relationships—enhances our chances of leaving a genetic legacy.

The Physiology of Sex

Sexual arousal depends on the interplay of internal and external stimuli. To understand sexual motivation, we must consider both.

The Sexual Response Cycle

27-1: What are the stages of the human sexual response cycle?

In the 1960s, gynecologist-obstetrician William Masters and his collaborator Virginia Johnson (1966) made headlines by recording the physiological responses of volunteers who masturbated or had intercourse. With the help of 382 female and 312 male volunteers—a somewhat atypical sample, consisting only of people able and willing to display arousal and orgasm while being observed in a laboratory—Masters and Johnson monitored or filmed more than 10,000 sexual "cycles." Their description of the **sexual response cycle** identified four stages, similar in men and women. During the initial *excitement phase,* the genital areas become engorged with blood, a woman's vagina expands and secretes lubricant, and her breasts and nipples may enlarge.

In the *plateau phase,* excitement peaks as breathing, pulse, and blood pressure rates continue to increase. The penis becomes fully engorged and some fluid—frequently containing enough live sperm to enable conception—may appear at its tip. Vaginal secretion continues to increase, the clitoris retracts, and orgasm feels imminent.

Masters and Johnson observed muscle contractions all over the body during *orgasm;* these were accompanied by further increases in breathing, pulse, and blood pressure rates. A woman's arousal and orgasm facilitate conception by helping propel semen from the penis, positioning the uterus to receive sperm, and drawing the sperm further inward. A woman's orgasm therefore not only reinforces intercourse, which is essential to natural reproduction, it also increases retention of deposited sperm (Furlow & Thornhill, 1996). In the excitement of the moment, men and women are hardly aware of all this as their rhythmic genital contractions create a pleasurable feeling of sexual release.

The feeling apparently is much the same for both sexes. In one study, a panel of experts could not reliably distinguish between descriptions of orgasm written by men and those written by women (Vance & Wagner, 1976). University of Groningen neuroscientist Gerg Holstege and his colleagues (2003a,b) understand why. They discovered that when men and women undergo PET scans while having orgasms, the same subcortical brain regions glow. And when people who are passionately in love undergo functional MRI (fMRI) scans while viewing photos of their beloved or of a stranger, men's and women's brain responses to their partners are pretty similar (Fisher & others, 2002).

> "Maybe...it starts with a kiss."
> Prenatal photographer Lennart Nilsson, answering the question "When does life begin?"

"I love the idea of there being two sexes, don't you?"

A nonsmoking 50-year-old male has about a 1-in-a-million chance of a heart attack during any hour. This increases to merely 2-in-a-million during the hour following sex (with no increase for those who exercise regularly). Compared with risks associated with heavy exertion or anger, this risk seems not worth losing sleep (or sex) over (Muller & others, 1996).

■ **sexual response cycle** the four stages of sexual responding described by Masters and Johnson—excitement, plateau, orgasm, and resolution.

■ **refractory period** a resting period after orgasm, during which a man cannot achieve another orgasm.

■ **sexual disorder** a problem that consistently impairs sexual arousal or functioning.

■ **estrogen** a sex hormone, secreted in greater amounts by females than by males. In nonhuman female mammals, estrogen levels peak during ovulation, promoting sexual receptivity.

■ **testosterone** the most important of the male sex hormones. Both males and females have it, but the additional testosterone in males stimulates the growth of the male sex organs in the fetus and the development of the male sex characteristics during puberty.

After orgasm, the body gradually returns to its unaroused state as the engorged genital blood vessels release their accumulated blood—relatively quickly if orgasm has occurred, relatively slowly otherwise. (It's like the nasal tickle that goes away rapidly if you have sneezed, slowly otherwise.) During this *resolution phase,* the male enters a **refractory period,** lasting from a few minutes to a day or more, during which he is incapable of another orgasm. The female's much shorter refractory period may enable her to have another orgasm if restimulated during or soon after resolution.

Masters and Johnson sought not only to describe the human sexual response cycle but also to understand and treat the inability to complete it. **Sexual disorders** are problems that consistently impair sexual functioning. Some involve sexual motivation, especially lack of sexual energy and arousability. For men, others include *premature ejaculation* and *erectile dysfunction* (inability to have or maintain an erection). For women, the problem may be *orgasmic dysfunction* (infrequently or never experiencing orgasm). Most women who experience sexual distress relate it to their emotional relationship with the partner during sex, not to physical aspects of the activity (Bancroft & others, 2003).

Men or women with sexual disorders can often be helped by receiving therapy. In behaviorally oriented therapy, for example, men learn ways to control their urge to ejaculate, and women are trained to bring themselves to orgasm. Starting with the introduction of Viagra in 1998, erectile dysfunction has been routinely treated by taking a pill.

Hormones and Sexual Behavior

27-2 : How do sex hormones influence human sexual development and arousal?

Sex hormones have two effects: They direct the physical development of male and female sex characteristics, and (especially in nonhuman animals) they activate sexual behavior. In most mammals, nature neatly synchronizes sex with fertility. The female becomes sexually receptive ("in heat") when production of the female hormone **estrogen** peaks at ovulation. In experiments, researchers can stimulate receptivity by injecting female animals with estrogen. Male hormone levels are more constant, and researchers cannot so easily manipulate the sexual behavior of male animals with hormones (Feder, 1984). Nevertheless, castrated male rats—having lost their testes, which manufacture the male sex hormone **testosterone**—gradually lose much of their interest in receptive females. They gradually regain it if injected with testosterone.

In humans, hormones more loosely influence sexual behavior, although sexual desire rises slightly at ovulation among women with mates (Pillsworth & others, 2004). One study invited partnered women not at risk for pregnancy to keep a diary of their sexual activity. (These women were either using intrauterine devices or had undergone surgery to prevent pregnancy.) On the days around ovulation, intercourse was 24 percent more frequent (Wilcox & others, 2004). But women's sexuality also differs from that of other mammalian females in being more responsive to testosterone level than to estrogen level (Meston & Frohlich, 2000; Reichman, 1998). If a woman's natural testosterone level drops, as happens with removal of the ovaries or adrenal glands, her sexual interest may wane. But testosterone-replacement therapy can often restore diminished sexual appetite, as it did for 549 naturally menopausal women who found that a testosterone-replacement patch restored sexual activity, arousal, and pleasure more than did a placebo (Davis & others, 2003; Kroll & others, 2004).

In men, normal fluctuations in testosterone levels, from man to man and hour to hour, have little effect on sexual drive (Byrne,

© The New Yorker Collection, 1993, Robert Mankoff from cartoonbank.com. All Rights Reserved.

"Fill'er up with testosterone."

1982). Indeed, fluctuations in male hormones are partly a *response* to sexual stimulation. When James Dabbs and his colleagues (1987, 2000) had heterosexual male collegians converse separately with another male student and with a female student, the men's testosterone levels rose with the social arousal, but especially after talking with the female. Thus, sexual arousal can be a cause as well as a consequence of increased testosterone levels.

Although normal short-term hormonal changes have little effect on men's and women's desire, large hormonal shifts over the life span have a greater effect. A person's interest in dating and sexual stimulation usually increases with the pubertal surge in sex hormones, as happens with male testosterone levels during puberty.

If the hormonal surge is precluded—as it was during the 1600s and 1700s for prepubertal boys who were castrated to preserve their soprano voices for Italian opera—the normal development of sex characteristics and sexual desire does not occur (Peschel & Peschel, 1987). When adult men are castrated, sex drive typically falls as testosterone levels decline (Hucker & Bain, 1990). Male sex offenders taking a drug that reduces testosterone level to that of a prepubertal boy similarly lose much of their sexual urge (Money & others, 1983). In later life, as sex hormone levels decline, the frequency of sexual fantasies and intercourse declines as well (Leitenberg & Henning, 1995). For men with abnormally low testosterone levels, testosterone-replacement therapy often increases sexual desire and also energy and vitality (Yates, 2000).

To summarize: We might compare human sex hormones, especially testosterone, to the fuel in a car. Without fuel, a car will not run. But if the fuel level is minimally adequate, adding more fuel to the gas tank won't change how the car runs. The analogy is imperfect, because hormones and sexual motivation interact. However, the analogy correctly suggests that biology is a necessary but not sufficient explanation of human sexual behavior. The hormonal fuel is essential, but so are the psychological stimuli that turn on the engine, keep it running, and shift it into high gear.

The Psychology of Sex

27-3: How do internal and external stimuli contribute to sexual arousal?

Hunger and sex are different sorts of motivations. Hunger responds to a *need*. If we do not eat, we die. Sex is not in this sense a need. If we do not have sex, we may feel like dying, but we do not. Nevertheless, there are similarities between hunger and sexual motivation. Both depend on internal physiological factors. And both are influenced by external and imagined stimuli, as well as cultural expectations (**FIGURE 27.1**).

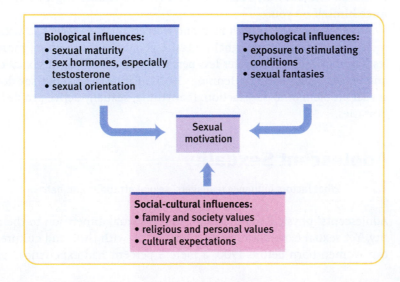

Biological influences:
• sexual maturity
• sex hormones, especially testosterone
• sexual orientation

Psychological influences:
• exposure to stimulating conditions
• sexual fantasies

Sexual motivation

Social-cultural influences:
• family and society values
• religious and personal values
• cultural expectations

FIGURE 27.1

Levels of analysis for sexual motivation

Compared with our motivation for eating, our sexual motivation is less influenced by biological factors. Psychological and social-cultural factors play a bigger role.

Sotographs/The Gamma-Liaison Network/Getty Images

Sexually explicit TV programs also divert attention from TV ads, making the ads more forgettable. Ads embedded in nonsexual and nonviolent programs more often produce memory for the products (Bushman & Bonacci, 2002).

"There is no difference between being raped and being run over by a truck except that afterward men ask if you enjoyed it."
Marge Piercy, "Rape Poem," 1976

External Stimuli

Many studies confirm that men become aroused when they see, hear, or read erotic material. Surprising to many (because sexually explicit materials are sold mostly to men) is that most women—at least the less-inhibited women who volunteer to participate in such studies—report or exhibit nearly as much arousal to the same stimuli (Heiman, 1975; Stockton & Murnen, 1992). (Their brains do, however, respond differently, with fMRI scans revealing a more active amygdala in men viewing erotica [Hamann & others, 2004].)

People may find such arousal either pleasing or disturbing. (Those who find it disturbing often limit their exposure to such materials, just as those wishing to control hunger limit their exposure to tempting cues.) With repeated exposure, the emotional response to any erotic stimulus often *habituates* (lessens). During the 1920s, when Western women's hemlines first reached the knee, an exposed leg was a mildly erotic stimulus, as were modest (by today's standards) two-piece swimsuits and movie scenes of a mere kiss.

Can sexually explicit material have adverse effects? Research indicates that it can. Depictions of women being sexually coerced—and enjoying it—tend to increase viewers' acceptance of the false idea that women enjoy rape and tend to increase male viewers' willingness to hurt women (Malamuth & Check, 1981; Zillmann, 1989). Images of sexually attractive women and men may also lead people to devalue their own partners and relationships. After male collegians watch TV or magazine depictions of sexually attractive women, they often find an average woman, or their own girlfriends or wives, less attractive (Kenrick & Gutierres, 1980; Kenrick & others, 1989; Weaver & others, 1984). Viewing X-rated sex films similarly tends to diminish people's satisfaction with their own sexual partners (Zillmann, 1989). Some sex researchers suspect that reading or watching erotica may create expectations that few men and women can fulfill.

Imagined Stimuli

The brain, it has been said, is our most significant sex organ. The stimuli inside our heads—our imagination—can influence sexual arousal and desire. People who, because of a spinal cord injury, have no genital sensation, can still feel sexual desire (Willmuth, 1987).

Wide-awake people become sexually aroused not only by memories of prior sexual activities but also by fantasies. In one survey of masturbation-related fantasies (Hunt, 1974), 19 percent of women and 10 percent of men reported imagining being taken by someone overwhelmed with desire for them. Fantasy is not reality, however. To paraphrase Susan Brownmiller (1975), there's a big difference between fantasizing that Brad Pitt just won't take no for an answer and having a hostile stranger actually force himself on you.

About 95 percent of both men and women say they have had sexual fantasies. But men (whether gay or straight) fantasize about sex more often, more physically, and less romantically—and prefer less personal and faster-paced sexual content in books and videos (Leitenberg & Henning, 1995). Fantasizing about sex does *not* indicate a sexual problem or dissatisfaction. If anything, sexually active people have more sexual fantasies.

Adolescent Sexuality

27-4 : What factors influence teenagers' sexual attitudes and behaviors?

Adolescents' physical maturation fosters a sexual dimension to their emerging identity. Yet sexual expression varies dramatically with time and culture. Among American women born before 1900, a mere 3 percent had experienced premarital sex by age 18 (Smith, 1998). In the United States today, about half of ninth- to twelfth-graders report having had sexual intercourse, as do 42 percent of Canadian 16-year-olds (Boroditsky & others, 1995; CDC, 2004). Teen intercourse rates are higher in Western Europe but much lower in Arab and Asian countries and among North Americans of Asian descent (McLaughlin & others, 1997). In one survey, only 2.5 percent of 4688 unmarried Chinese students entering Hong Kong's six universities reported having had sexual intercourse (Meston & others, 1996).

Sex during the teen years is often unprotected, leading to risks of pregnancy and *sexually transmitted infections* (STIs, also called STDs, for *sexually transmitted diseases*).

Teen Pregnancy

Compared with European teens, American teens have lower rates of intercourse, but they also have lower rates of contraceptive use and thus higher rates of teen pregnancy and abortion (Call & others, 2002). (Only one-third of sexually active male teens use condoms consistently [Sonenstein, 1992]). Why?

Ignorance Half of sexually active Canadian teen girls have mistaken ideas about which birth control methods will protect them from pregnancy and STIs (Immen, 1995). Most teens also overestimate their peers' sexual activity, and that misperception may influence their own behavior (Child Trends, 2001).

Guilt related to sexual activity In one survey, 72 percent of sexually active 12- to 17-year-old American girls said they regretted having had sex (Reuters, 2000). Sexual inhibitions can reduce sexual activity, but they may also reduce attempts at birth control if passion overwhelms intentions (Gerrard & Luus, 1995).

Minimal communication about birth control Many teenagers are uncomfortable discussing contraception with their parents, partners, and peers (Kotva & Schneider, 1990; Milan & Kilmann, 1987). Teens who talk freely with friends or parents and are in an exclusive relationship with a partner with whom they communicate openly are more likely to use contraceptives.

Alcohol use Sexually active teens are typically alcohol-using teens (Albert & others, 2003; National Research Council, 1987), and those who use alcohol prior to sex are less likely to use condoms (Kotchick & others, 2001). By depressing the brain centers that control judgment, inhibition, and self-awareness, alcohol tends to break down normal restraints, a phenomenon well known to sexually coercive males.

Mass media norms of unprotected promiscuity An average hour of prime-time television on the three major U.S. networks contains approximately 15 sexual acts, words, and innuendos. The partners are usually unmarried, with no prior romantic relationship, and few communicate any concern for birth control or STIs (Brown & others, 2002; Kunkel, 2001; Sapolsky & Tabarlet, 1991). TV and movie portrayals of unsafe sex without consequence, contends Planned Parenthood, amounts to a campaign of sex disinformation.

Sexually Transmitted Infections

Unprotected sex has led to increased rates of sexually transmitted infections. Two-thirds of new infections occur in people under 25 (ASHA, 2003). Teenage girls, because of their less mature biological development and lower levels of protective antibodies, seem especially vulnerable to STIs (Guttmacher, 1994; Morell, 1995). To comprehend the mathematics of sexually transmitted infection, imagine this scenario: Over the course of a year, Pat has sex with 9 people, each of whom over the same period has sex with 9 other people, who in turn have sex with 9 others. How many "phantom" sex partners (past partners of partners) will Pat have? Laura Brannon and Timothy Brock (1994) report that the actual number—511—is more than five times the estimate given by the average student.

Given these odds, the rapid spread of STIs is not surprising. Condoms offer no protection against certain skin-to-skin STIs (Medical Institute, 1994; NIH, 2001).

"Will your child learn to multiply before she learns to subtract?"
Anti–teen-pregnancy poster, Children's Defense Fund

"All of us who make motion pictures are teachers, teachers with very loud voices."
Film producer George Lucas, Academy Award ceremonies, 1992

"Condoms should be used on every conceivable occasion."
Anonymous

■ **sexual orientation** an enduring sexual attraction toward members of either one's own sex (homosexual orientation) or the other sex (heterosexual orientation).

Condoms do, however, reduce tenfold the risk of contracting HIV (human immunodeficiency virus—the virus that causes AIDS) from an infected partner (Pinkerton & Abramson, 1997).

One response to these facts of life has been a greater emphasis on teen abstinence within some comprehensive sex education programs. A National Longitudinal Study of Adolescent Health among 12,000 teens found several predictors of sexual restraint:

High intelligence Teens with high rather than average intelligence test scores more often delay sex, evidently because they appreciate possible negative consequences and are more focused on future achievement than on here-and-now pleasures (Halpern & others, 2000).

Religiosity Actively religious teens and adults more often reserve sex for marital commitment (Rostosky & others, 2004; Smith, 1998).

Father presence In studies following hundreds of New Zealand and U.S. girls from age 5 to 18, a father's absence was linked to sexual activity before age 16 and teen pregnancy (Ellis & others, 2003). These associations held even after adjusting for other adverse influences, such as poverty.

Participation in service learning programs Several experiments have found lower pregnancy rates among teens volunteering as tutors or teachers' aides or participating in community projects, than found among comparable teens randomly assigned to control conditions (Kirby, 2002; O'Donnell & others, 2002). Researchers are unsure why. Does service learning promote a sense of personal competence, control, and responsibility? Does it encourage more future-oriented thinking? Or does it simply reduce opportunities for unprotected sex?

In recent history, the pendulum of sexual values has swung from the European eroticism of the early 1800s to the conservative Victorian era of the late 1800s, from the libertine flapper era of the 1920s to the family values period of the 1950s. The pendulum may have begun a new swing toward commitment in the twenty-first century, with declining teen birth rates since 1991, and virgins (54 percent in 2002) now outnumbering nonvirgins (46 percent) among U.S. 15- to 19-year-olds (CDC, 2004; Mohn & others, 2003).

Sexual Orientation

27-5 : What does current research tell us about why some people are attracted to members of their own sex and others are attracted to members of the other sex?

To motivate is to energize and direct behavior. So far, we have considered the energizing of sexual motivation but not its direction. We express the direction of our sexual interest in our **sexual orientation**—our enduring sexual attraction toward members of our own sex (*homosexual orientation*) or the other sex (*heterosexual orientation*). Cultures vary in their attitudes toward homosexuality. But as far as we know, all cultures in all times have been predominantly heterosexual (Bullough, 1990). Whether a culture condemns or accepts homosexuality, heterosexuality prevails and homosexuality survives.

Gay men and lesbians often recall childhood play preferences like those of the other sex (Bailey & Zucker, 1995). But most homosexual people report not becoming aware of same-sex attraction until during or shortly after puberty, and not thinking of themselves as gay or lesbian until around age 20 (Garnets & Kimmel, 1990).

Sexual Orientation Statistics

How many people are exclusively homosexual? About 10 percent, as the popular press has often assumed? A little more than 20 percent, as average Americans estimated in a 2002 Gallup survey (Robinson, 2002)? Not according to more than a dozen national surveys in the early 1990s, which explored sexual orientation in Europe and the United States, using methods that protected the respondent's anonymity. The most accurate figure seems to be about 3 or 4 percent of men and 1 or 2 percent of

In one British survey, of the 18,876 people contacted, 1 percent were reportedly asexual, having "never felt sexually attracted to anyone at all" (Bogaert, 2004).

women (Laumann & others, 1994; National Center for Health Statistics, 1991; Smith, 1998). Estimates derived from the sex of unmarried partners reported in the 2000 U.S. Census suggest that 2.5 percent of the population is gay or lesbian (Tarmann, 2002). Fewer than 1 percent of survey respondents—for example, 12 people out of 7076 Dutch adults in one recent survey (Sandfort & others, 2001)—reported being actively bisexual. A larger number of adults in that study reported having had an isolated homosexual experience. And most people report having had an occasional homosexual fantasy. Health experts find it helpful to know sexual statistics, but numbers do not decide issues of human rights.

What does it feel like to be homosexual in a heterosexual culture? If you are heterosexual, one way to understand is to imagine how you would feel if you were ostracized or fired for openly admitting or displaying your feelings toward someone of the other sex; if you overheard people making crude jokes about heterosexual people; if most movies, TV shows, and advertisements portrayed (or implied) homosexuality; and if your family members were pleading with you to change your heterosexual lifestyle and to enter into a homosexual marriage.

Facing such reactions, homosexual people often struggle with their sexual orientation. They may at first try to ignore or deny their desires, hoping they will go away. But they don't. Then they may try to change, through psychotherapy, willpower, or prayer. But the feelings typically persist, as do those of heterosexual people—who are similarly incapable of becoming homosexual (Haldeman, 1994, 2002; Myers & Scanzoni, 2005). Most of today's psychologists therefore view sexual orientation as neither willfully chosen nor willfully changed. Sexual orientation in some ways is like handedness: Most people are one way, some the other. A very few are truly ambidextrous. Regardless, the way one is endures.

Women's sexual orientation tends to be less strongly felt and potentially more fluid and changeable than men's (Diamond, 2000, 2003; Peplau & Garnets, 2000). Men's lesser sexual variability is apparent in many ways, notes Roy Baumeister (2000). Across time, across cultures, across situations, and across differing levels of education, religiosity, and peer influence, adult women's sexual drive and interests are more flexible and varying than are adult men's. Women, more than men, for example, prefer to alternate periods of high sexual activity with periods of almost none, and they are somewhat more likely than men to feel bisexual attractions. Baumeister calls this phenomenon the gender difference in *erotic plasticity*.

Gays and lesbians suffer elevated rates of depression and risk of suicide attempts, which researchers suspect result from their experiences with bullying, harassment, and discrimination (Sandfort & others, 2001; Warner & others, 2004). Most people, whether straight or gay, accept their orientation—by electing celibacy, by engaging in promiscuous sex (a choice more commonly made by gay men than by lesbian women), or by entering into a committed, long-term love relationship (a choice more often made by lesbians than by gays) (Kulkin & others, 2000; Peplau, 1982; Remafedi, 1999; Weinberg & Williams, 1974). Mental health professionals are now more accepting of clients' sexual orientation. The American Psychiatric Association dropped homosexuality from its list of "mental illnesses" in 1973, as did the World Health Organization in 1993, and Japan's and China's psychiatric associations in 1995 and 2001.

Origins of Sexual Orientation

If our sexual orientation is indeed something we do not choose and seemingly cannot change, then where do these preferences—heterosexual or homosexual—come from? See if you can anticipate the consensus that has emerged from hundreds of research studies by responding yes or no to the following questions:

1. Is homosexuality linked with problems in a child's relationships with parents, such as with a domineering mother and an ineffectual father, or a possessive mother and a hostile father?

Studies indicate that men who describe themselves as bisexual tend to respond like homosexual men; they typically have genital arousal to same-sex erotic stimuli (Rieger & others, 2005).

Personal values affect sexual orientation less than they affect sexual behavior. Compared with people who rarely attend religious services, for example, those who attend regularly are one-third as likely to have cohabited before marriage, and they report having had many fewer sex partners. But (if male) they are just as likely to be homosexual (Smith, 1998).

Note that the scientific question is not "What causes homosexuality?" (or "What causes heterosexuality?") but "What causes differing sexual orientations?" In pursuit of answers, psychological science compares the backgrounds and physiology of people whose sexual orientations *differ*.

2. Does homosexuality involve a fear or hatred of people of the other gender, leading individuals to direct their sexual desires toward members of their own sex?
3. Is sexual orientation linked with levels of sex hormones currently in the blood?
4. As children, were many homosexuals molested, seduced, or otherwise sexually victimized by an adult homosexual?

The answer to all these questions appears to be no (Storms, 1983). In interviews with nearly 1000 homosexuals and 500 heterosexuals, Kinsey Institute investigators assessed nearly every imaginable psychological cause of homosexuality—parental relationships, childhood sexual experiences, peer relationships, dating experiences (Bell & others, 1981; Hammersmith, 1982). Their findings: Homosexuals were no more likely than heterosexuals to have been smothered by maternal love, neglected by their father, or sexually abused. And consider this: If "distant fathers" were more likely to produce homosexual sons, then shouldn't boys growing up in father-absent homes more often be gay? (They are not.) And shouldn't the rising number of such homes have led to a noticeable increase in the gay population? (It has not.)

Homosexual people do, however, appear more often in certain populations. One study (Ludwig, 1995) of the biographies of 1004 eminent people found homosexual and bisexual people overrepresented (11 percent of the sample), especially among poets (24 percent), fiction writers (21 percent), and artists and musicians (15 percent). Men who have older brothers are also somewhat more likely to be gay, report Ray Blanchard (1997, 2001) and Anthony Bogaert (2003). Assuming the odds of homosexuality are roughly 3 percent among first sons, they rise to about 4 percent among second sons, 5 percent or a little more for third sons, and so on for each additional older brother. The reason for this curious phenomenon—the *fraternal birth-order effect*—is unclear. Blanchard suspects a defensive maternal immune response to foreign substances produced by male fetuses. The maternal antibodies may become stronger after each pregnancy with a male fetus and may prevent the fetus' brain from developing in a male-typical pattern. Women with older sisters, and women who were womb-mates of twin brothers, exhibit no such sibling effect (Rose & others, 2002).

So, what else might influence sexual orientation? One theory proposes that people develop same-sex erotic attachments if segregated by gender at the time their sex drive matures (Storms, 1981). Indeed, gay men tend to recall going through puberty somewhat earlier, when peers are more likely to be all males (Bogaert & others, 2002). But even in tribal cultures in which homosexual behavior is expected of all boys before marriage, heterosexuality prevails (Money, 1987). (As this illustrates, homosexual *behavior* does not always indicate a homosexual *orientation*.)

The bottom line from a half-century's theory and research: If there are environmental factors that influence sexual orientation, we do not yet know what they are. This reality has motivated researchers to consider more carefully the possible biological influences on orientation, including evidence of homosexuality in the animal world, and the influences of differing brain centers, genetics, and prenatal hormone exposure.

Same-Sex Attraction in Animals

At Coney Island's New York Aquarium, Wendell and Cass spent several years as devoted same-sex partners. The Central Park Zoo penguins Silo and Roy show similar devotion. Biologist Bruce Bagemihl (1999) identifies several hundred species in which at least occasional same-sex relations have been observed. Grizzlies, gorillas, monkeys, flamingos, and owls are all on the long list. Among rams, for example, some 6 to 10 percent—to sheep-breeding ranchers, the "duds"—display same-sex attraction by shunning ewes and seeking to mount other males (Perkins & Fitzgerald, 1997). Some degree of homosexuality seems to be a natural part of the animal world.

"Gay" penguins
New York Aquarium penguins Wendell and Cass have company in the animal kingdom.

David Hecker/AFP/Getty Images

The Brain and Sexual Orientation

Researcher Simon LeVay (1991) studied sections of the hypothalamus taken from deceased heterosexual and homosexual people. As a gay scientist, LeVay wanted to do "something connected with my gay identity." He knew he had to avoid biasing the results, so he did the study *blind,* without knowing which donors were gay. For nine months he peered through his microscope at a cell cluster he thought might be important. Then one morning, he broke the codes: One cell cluster was reliably larger in heterosexual men than in women and homosexual men. "I was almost in a state of shock," LeVay said (1994). "I took a walk by myself on the cliffs over the ocean. I sat for half an hour just thinking what this might mean."

It should not surprise us that brains differ with sexual orientation. Remember our maxim: *Everything psychological is simultaneously biological.* But when did the brain difference begin? At conception? In the womb? During childhood or adolescence? Did experience produce the difference? Or did genes or prenatal hormones (or genes via prenatal hormones)?

LeVay does not view this neural center as a sexual orientation center; rather, he sees it as an important part of the neural pathway engaged in sexual behavior. He acknowledges that sexual behavior patterns may influence the brain's anatomy. In fish, birds, rats, and humans, brain structures vary with experience—including sexual experience, reports sex researcher Marc Breedlove (1997). But LeVay believes it more likely that brain anatomy influences sexual orientation. His hunch seems confirmed by the discovery of a similar hypothalamic difference between the 6 to 10 percent of male sheep that display same-sex attraction and the 90+ percent attracted to females (Larkin & others, 2002; Roselli & others, 2002). Moreover, report University of London psychologists Qazi Rahman and Glenn Wilson (2003), "The neuroanatomical correlates of male homosexuality differentiate very early postnatally, if not prenatally."

Responses to hormone-derived sexual scents also point to a brain difference (Savic & others, 2005). When straight women are given a whiff of a scent derived from men's sweat, their hypothalamus lights up in an area governing sexual arousal. Gay men's brains respond similarly to the men's scent. But straight men's brains show the arousal response only to a female hormone derivative. Gays and lesbians similarly differed from their straight counterparts in another study of preferences for sex-related sweat odors (Martins & others, 2005).

Laura Allen and Roger Gorski (1992) also concluded that brain anatomy influences sexual orientation after discovering that a section of the anterior commissure (the fibers that, like the corpus callosum, connect right and left hemispheres) is one-third larger in homosexual men than in heterosexual men. "The emerging neuroanatomical picture," noted Brian Gladue (1994), "is that, in some brain areas, homosexual men are more likely to have female-typical neuroanatomy than are heterosexual men."

Genes and Sexual Orientation

There is evidence to suggest a genetic influence on sexual orientation. "First, homosexuality does appear to run in families," note Brian Mustanski and Michael Bailey (2003). "Second, twin studies have established that genes play a substantial role in explaining individual differences in sexual orientation." Identical twins are somewhat more likely than fraternal twins to share a homosexual orientation. However, because sexual orientations differ in many identical twin pairs (especially female twins), we know that other factors besides genes are at work. And third, experimenters have, by genetic manipulations, created female fruit flies that during courtship act like males (pursuing other females) and males that act like females (Demir & Dickson, 2005). "We have shown that a single gene in the fruit fly is sufficient to determine all aspects of the flies' sexual orientation and behavior," explained Barry Dickson (2005).

"Studies indicate that male homosexuality is more likely to be transmitted from the mother's side of the family."
Robert Plomin, John DeFries, Gerald McClearn, and Michael Rutter, *Behavioral Genetics,* 1997

Researchers have speculated about possible reasons why "gay genes" might exist. Given that same-sex couples cannot naturally reproduce, how could such genes have survived in the human gene pool? One possible answer is kin selection. Evolutionary psychologists remind us that many of our genes also reside in our biological relatives. Perhaps, then, gay people's genes live on through their supporting the survival and reproductive success of their nieces, nephews, and other relatives (who also carry many of the same genes). Or perhaps maternal genetics is at work. A recent Italian study (Camperio-Ciani & others, 2004) confirms what others have found—that homosexual men have more homosexual relatives on their mother's side than on their father's. It also finds that, compared with the maternal relatives of heterosexual men, the maternal relatives of homosexual men produce more offspring. Perhaps, surmised the researchers, genes that convey a reproductive advantage in mothers and aunts somehow influence the sexual orientation of their sons and nephews.

Prenatal Hormones and Sexual Orientation

Elevated rates of homosexual orientation in identical *and* fraternal twins suggest that not just shared genetics but also a shared prenatal environment may be a factor. In animals and some exceptional human cases, abnormal prenatal hormone conditions have altered a fetus' sexual orientation. German researcher Gunter Dorner (1976, 1988) pioneered this research by manipulating a fetal rat's exposure to male hormones, thereby "inverting" its sexual orientation. Similarly, when pregnant sheep are injected with testosterone during a critical period of fetal development, their female offspring will later show homosexual behavior (Money, 1987).

In humans, a critical period for the brain's neural-hormonal control system may exist between the middle of the second and fifth months after conception (Ellis & Ames, 1987; Gladue, 1990; Meyer-Bahlburg, 1995). Exposure to the hormone levels typically experienced by female fetuses during this time appears to predispose the person (whether female or male) to be attracted to males in later life.

On several traits, homosexual individuals of both sexes appear to fall midway between heterosexual females and males (**TABLE 27.1**). For example, most people have

Genetic study of sexual orientation: Are you in (or do you know of) a family with two or more gay brothers? If so, a nationwide study being conducted by a Chicago-area university research team welcomes your visit to www.gaybros.com.

TABLE 27.1

BIOLOGICAL CORRELATES OF SEXUAL ORIENTATION

On average (the evidence is strongest for males), various biological and behavioral traits of gays and lesbians fall between those of straight men and straight women. Tentative findings—some in need of replication—include these:

Brain differences
- One hypothalamic cell cluster is larger in straight men than in women and gay men; same difference is found in male sheep displaying other-sex versus same-sex attraction.
- Anterior commissure is larger in gay men than in women or straight men.
- Gay men's hypothalamus reacts as does a woman's to the smell of sex-related hormones.

Genetic influences
- Shared sexual orientation is higher among identical twins than among fraternal twins.
- Sexual attraction in fruit flies can be genetically manipulated.

Prenatal hormonal influences
- Altered prenatal hormone exposure may lead to homosexuality in humans and other animals.
- Men with several older brothers are more likely to be gay.

These brain differences and genetic and prenatal influences may contribute to observed gay-straight differences in
- spatial abilities.
- fingerprint ridge counts.
- auditory system development.
- handedness.
- occupational preferences.
- relative finger lengths.
- gender nonconformity.
- age of onset of puberty in males.
- male body size.
- sleep length.
- physical aggression.

more fingerprint ridges on their right hand than on their left, but some studies find that this difference is greater for heterosexual males than for females and gay males (Hall & Kimura, 1994; Mustanski & others, 2002; Sanders & others, 2002). Given that fingerprint ridges are complete by the sixteenth fetal week, this difference may be due to prenatal hormones. Prenatal hormones also are a possible explanation for why data from 20 studies revealed that "homosexual participants had 39 percent greater odds of being non–right-handed" (Lalumière & others, 2000).

Lesbians likewise have some male-typical traits. For example, their cochlea and hearing system develop in a way that is intermediate between those of heterosexual females and heterosexual males, and which seems attributable to prenatal hormonal influence (McFadden, 2002).

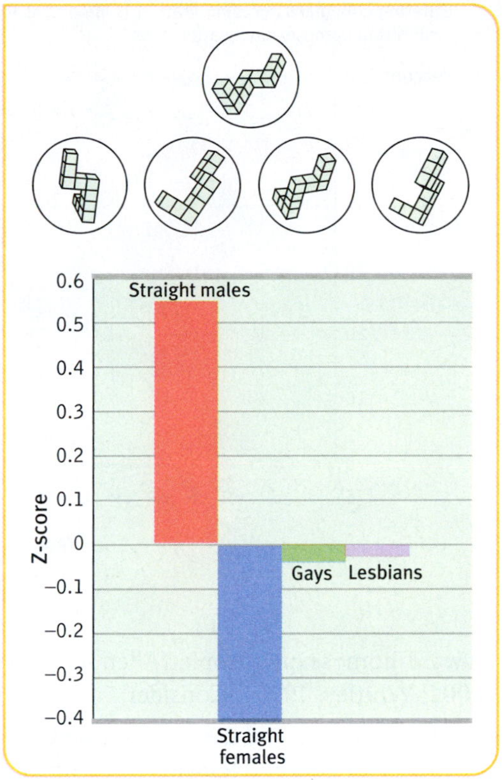

FIGURE 27.2

Spatial abilities and sexual orientation

Which of the four figures can be rotated to match the target figure at the top? Straight males tend to find this an easier task than do straight females, with gays and lesbians intermediate. (From Rahman, Wilson, & Abrahams, 2003, with 60 people tested in each group.)

Another striking illustration of gay-straight differences appears in studies showing that homosexual men's spatial abilities resemble those typical of heterosexual women (Cohen, 2002; Gladue, 1994; McCormick & Witelson, 1991; Sanders & Wright, 1997). On mental rotation tasks such as the one illustrated in **FIGURE 27.2**, for example, heterosexual men tend to outscore women. A study by Qazi Rahman and colleagues (2003) found that, as on a number of other measures, the scores of both homosexual males and females fall between those of heterosexual males and heterosexual females.

Because the physiological evidence is preliminary and controversial, some scientists remain skeptical. Rather than specifying sexual orientation, they suggest, biological factors may predispose a *temperament* that influences sexuality "in the context of individual learning and experience" (Byne & Parsons, 1993). Daryl Bem (1996, 1998, 2000) has theorized that genes code for prenatal hormones and brain anatomy, which predispose temperaments that lead children to prefer gender-typical or gender-atypical activities and friends. These preferences may later lead children to feel attracted to whichever sex feels different from their own. The dissimilar-seeming sex (whether or not it conforms to one's own anatomy) becomes associated with anxiety and other forms of arousal, which are eventually transformed into romantic arousal. The exotic becomes erotic.

Regardless of the process, the consistency of the genetic, prenatal, and brain findings has swung the pendulum toward a biological explanation of sexual orientation (Rahman & Wilson, 2003). Nature more than nurture, most psychiatrists now believe, predisposes orientation (Vreeland & others, 1995). This helps explain why sexual orientation is so difficult to change.

Still, some people wonder: Should the cause of sexual orientation matter? Perhaps it shouldn't, but people's assumptions matter. Those who believe, as do 40 percent of Americans (up from 13 percent in 1977 [Gallup, 2002]) and most gays and lesbians, that sexual orientation is biologically disposed, express more accepting attitudes

Gay more than straight men express interest in occupations that attract many women, such as decorator, florist, and flight attendant (Lippa, 2002). (Given that some 96 percent of men are not gay, most men in such occupations may nevertheless be straight.)

"Modern scientific research indicates that sexual orientation is . . . partly determined by genetics, but more specifically by hormonal activity in the womb."

Glenn Wilson and Qazi Rahman, *Born Gay: The Psychobiology of Sex Orientation*, 2005

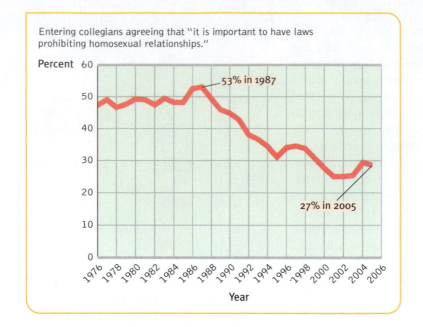

Entering collegians agreeing that "it is important to have laws prohibiting homosexual relationships."

53% in 1987

27% in 2005

toward homosexual people (Allen & others, 1996; Furnham & Taylor, 1990; Kaiser, 2001; Whitley, 1990). Consider:

- Between 1977 and 2002, American Gallup surveys found that support for equal job rights for gays and lesbians rose from 56 to 85 percent. They also found that agreement that "homosexuality should be an acceptable alternative life-style" rose from 34 to 52 percent.
- In Canadian Gallup surveys between 1992 and 2001, support for same-sex marriages nearly doubled—from 24 to 46 percent (Mazzuca, 2002), and will likely rise further, now that Canada has begun allowing same-sex marriage.
- Among entering collegians, support for laws prohibiting homosexual relationships has plummeted since 1987 (**FIGURE 27.3**).

These dramatic attitude shifts do not represent a liberalization of all sex-related attitudes. For example, in periodic U.S. national surveys, agreement that extramarital sex is "always wrong" *increased* from 69.6 percent in 1973 to 79.4 percent in 2000 (NORC, 2002).

To gay and lesbian activists, the new biological research is a double-edged sword (Diamond, 1993). If sexual orientation, like skin color and sex, is genetically influenced, that offers a further rationale for civil rights protection. Moreover, it may alleviate parents' concerns about their children being unduly influenced by gay teachers and role models. At the same time, this biological research raises the troubling possibility that genetic markers of sexual orientation could someday be identified through fetal testing, and a fetus could be aborted simply for being predisposed to an unwanted orientation.

Sex and Human Values

27-6: Is scientific research on sexual motivation value-free?

Recognizing that values are both personal and cultural, most sex researchers and educators strive to keep their writings on sexual behavior and its motivation value-free. But the very words we use to describe behavior can reflect our personal values. Whether we label certain sexual behaviors as "perversions" or as part of an "alternative sexual life-style" depends on our attitude toward the behaviors. Labels describe, but they also evaluate.

A sharing of love
For most adults, a sexual relationship fulfills not only a biological motive, but also a social need for intimacy.

Andreanna Seymore/Getty Images

Sex education separated from the context of human values may also give some students the idea that sexual intercourse is simply a recreational activity. Diana Baumrind (1982), a University of California child-rearing expert, has observed that an implication that adults are neutral about adolescent sexual activity is unfortunate, because "promiscuous recreational sex poses certain psychological, social, health, and moral problems that must be faced realistically."

Perhaps we can agree that the knowledge provided by sex research is preferable to ignorance, and yet also agree that researchers' values should be stated openly, enabling us to debate them and to reflect on our own values. We should remember that scientific research on sexual motivation does not aim to define the personal meaning of sex in our own lives. You could know every available fact about sex—that the initial spasms of male and female orgasm come at 0.8-second intervals, that the female nipples expand 10 millimeters at the peak of sexual arousal, that systolic blood pressure rises some 60 points and the respiration rate to 40 breaths per minute—but fail to understand the human significance of sexual intimacy.

Surely one significance of sexual intimacy is its expression of our profoundly social nature. Sex is a socially significant act. Men and women can achieve orgasm alone, yet most people find greater satisfaction while embracing their loved one. There is a yearning for closeness in sexual motivation. Sex at its human best is life-uniting and love-renewing.

The Need to Belong

27-7 : Why do some psychologists believe we have a need to belong— to affiliate with others?

Separated from friends or family—isolated in prison, alone at a new school, living in a foreign land—most people feel keenly their lost connections with important others. We are what Aristotle called *the social animal.* "Without friends," wrote Aristotle in his *Nichomachean Ethics,* "no one would choose to live, though he had all other goods." We have a need to affiliate with others, even to become strongly attached to certain others in enduring, close relationships. Human beings, contended the personality theorist Alfred Adler, have an "urge to community" (Ferguson, 1989). Roy Baumeister and Mark Leary (1995) have assembled evidence for this deep *need to belong.*

Aiding Survival

Social bonds boosted our ancestors' survival rate. By keeping children close to their caregivers, attachments served as a powerful survival impulse. As adults, those who formed attachments were more likely to come together to reproduce and to stay together to nurture their offspring to maturity. To be "wretched" literally means, in its Middle English origin (*wrecche*), to be without kin nearby.

Cooperation in groups also enhanced survival. In solo combat, our ancestors were not the toughest predators. But as hunters, they learned that six hands were better than two. And as foragers, they gained protection from predators and enemies by traveling in groups. Those who felt a need to belong survived and reproduced most successfully, and their genes now predominate. We are innately social creatures. People in every society on Earth belong to groups and prefer and favor "us" over "them." With the need to belong satisfied by close, supportive relationships, people indeed are generally happier and healthier.

Wanting to Belong

The need to belong colors our thoughts and emotions. We spend a great deal of time thinking about actual and hoped-for relationships. When relationships form, we often feel joy. Falling in mutual love, people have been known to feel their cheeks

Separation amplifies the felt need to belong

In the film *Cast Away,* Chuck Noland (played by Tom Hanks) combats social starvation by talking with his girlfriend's snapshot and a volleyball he named Wilson.

20TH Century Fox/Dreamworks/The Kobal Collection

ache from their irrepressible grins. Asked, "What is necessary for your happiness?" or "What is it that makes your life meaningful?" most people mention—before anything else—close, satisfying relationships with family, friends, or romantic partners (Berscheid, 1985). Happiness hits close to home.

Pause a moment to consider: What was your most satisfying moment in the past week? Kennon Sheldon and his colleagues (2001) asked that question of American and South Korean collegians, then asked them to rate how much this peak experience had satisfied various needs. In both countries, the satisfaction of self-esteem and relatedness-belonging needs were the top two contributors to the peak moment. Another study found that *very* happy university students are not distinguished by their money but by their "rich and satisfying close relationships" (Diener & Seligman, 2002). The need to belong runs deeper, it seems, than any need to be rich.

South Africans have a word for these human bonds that define us all. *Ubuntu* (oo-BOON-too), explains Desmond Tutu (1999), expresses the fact that "my humanity is caught up, is inextricably bound up, in yours." A Zulu maxim captures the idea: *Umuntu ngumuntu ngabantu*—"a person is a person through other persons."

Acting to Increase Social Acceptance

When we feel included, accepted, and loved by those important to us, our self-esteem rides high. Indeed, say Mark Leary and his colleagues (1998), self-esteem is a gauge of how valued and accepted we feel. Much of our social behavior therefore aims to increase our belonging—our social acceptance and inclusion. To avoid rejection, we generally conform to group standards and seek to make favorable impressions. To win friendship and esteem, we monitor our behavior, hoping to create the right impressions. Seeking love and belonging, we spend billions on clothes, cosmetics, and diet and fitness aids—all motivated by our quest for acceptance.

Like sexual motivation, which feeds both love and exploitation, the need to belong feeds both deep attachments and menacing threats. Out of our need to define a "we" come loving families, faithful friendships, and team spirit, but also teen gangs, ethnic rivalries, and fanatic nationalism.

Maintaining Relationships

For most of us, familiarity breeds liking, not contempt. Thrown together in groups at school, at summer camp, on a vacation cruise, we later resist breaking those social bonds—we promise to call, to write, to come back for reunions. Parting, we feel distress. Attachments can keep people in abusive relationships when the fear of being alone seems worse than the pain of emotional or physical abuse. Even when bad relationships break, people suffer. In one 16-nation survey, separated and divorced people were only half as likely as married people to say they were "very happy"

The need to connect
Six days a week, women from the Philippines work as "domestic helpers" in 154,000 Hong Kong households. On Sundays, they throng to the central business district to picnic, dance, sing, talk, and laugh. "Humanity could stage no greater display of happiness," reported one observer (*Economist*, 2001).

(Inglehart, 1990). After such separations, feelings of loneliness and anger—and sometimes even a strange desire to be near the former partner—linger.

Our fear of being alone has some basis in reality. Children who move through a series of foster homes, with repeated disruption of budding attachments, may come to have difficulty forming deep attachments. And children reared in institutions without a sense of belonging to anyone, or locked away at home under extreme neglect, become pathetic creatures—withdrawn, frightened, speechless.

When something threatens or dissolves our social ties, negative emotions—anxiety, loneliness, jealousy, guilt—overwhelm us. The bereaved often feel life is empty, pointless. Even the first weeks living on a college campus away from home can be distressing. For immigrants and refugees moving alone to new places, the stress and loneliness can be depressing. But if feelings of acceptance and connection build, so do self-esteem, positive feelings, and desires to help rather than hurt others (Buckley & Leary, 2001). After years of placing individual refugee and immigrant families in isolated communities, U.S. policies today encourage *chain migration* (Pipher, 2002). The second refugee Sudanese family settling in a town generally has an easier adjustment than the first.

The Pain of Ostracism

Sometimes, though, the need to belong is denied. Perhaps you can recall such a time, when you felt excluded or ignored or shunned. Perhaps you received the silent treatment. Perhaps others avoided you, or averted their eyes in your presence, or even mocked you behind your back.

Social psychologist Kipling Williams (2002) and his colleagues have studied such experiences of *ostracism*—of social exclusion—in both natural and laboratory settings. Worldwide, humans use the punishing effects of various forms of ostracism—exile, imprisonment, solitary confinement—to control social behavior. For children, even a brief time-out in isolation can be punishing. To be shunned—given the cold shoulder or the silent treatment, with others' eyes avoiding yours—is to have one's need to belong threatened, observe Kipling Williams and Lisa Zadro (2001). "It's the meanest thing you can do to someone, especially if you know they can't fight back. I never should have been born," said Lea, a lifelong victim of the silent treatment by her mother and grandmother. Like Lea, people often respond to ostracism with depressed moods, initial efforts to restore their acceptance, and then withdrawal. After two years of silent treatment by his employer, Richard reported, "I came home every night and cried. I lost 25 pounds, had no self-esteem and felt that I wasn't worthy."

Rejected and unable to remedy the situation, people may turn nasty. In a series of experiments, Jean Twenge and her collaborators (2001, 2002; Baumeister & others, 2002) told some students (who had taken a personality test) that they were "the type likely to end up alone later in life" or that people they had met didn't want them in a group that was forming. They told other students that they would have "rewarding relationships throughout life" or that "everyone chose you as someone they'd like to work with." Those excluded became much more likely to engage in self-defeating behaviors and underperform on aptitude tests. They also were more likely to act in disparaging or aggressive ways against those who had excluded them (blasting them with noise, for example). "If intelligent, well-adjusted, successful university students can turn aggressive in response to a small laboratory experience of social exclusion," noted the research team, "it is disturbing to imagine the aggressive tendencies that might arise from a series of important rejections or chronic exclusion from desired groups in actual social life."

Surveying evidence from decades of research, Roy Baumeister and Mark Leary (1995) conclude that "human beings are fundamentally and pervasively motivated by a need to belong."

A violent response to social exclusion
Most socially excluded teens do not commit violence, but some do. Charles "Andy" Williams, described by a classmate as someone his peers derided as "freak, dork, nerd, stuff like that," went on a shooting spree at his suburban California high school, killing 2 and wounding 13 (Bowles & Kasindorf, 2001).

AP/Wide World Photos

REVIEWING

>> MODULE REVIEW

27-1 : What are the stages of the human sexual response cycle?
Physiologically, the human *sexual response cycle* normally follows a pattern of excitement, plateau, orgasm, and resolution. During the resolution phase, males enter a *refractory period,* a resting period in which renewed arousal and orgasm are impossible. Some *sexual disorders* respond well to behavioral treatment, which assumes that people can learn to modify their sexual responses.

27-2 : How do sex hormones influence human sexual development and arousal?
The sex hormones *testosterone* and *estrogen* are present in both males and females, but males have a higher level of testosterone and females a higher level of estrogen. These hormones help our bodies develop and function as either male or female. In nonhuman animals, they also help stimulate sexual activity. In women with mates, desire does rise slightly at ovulation, but women's sexuality is more responsive to testosterone level than to estrogen level. Short-term shifts in testosterone level are normal in men.

27-3 : How do internal and external stimuli contribute to sexual arousal?
Erotic material and other external stimuli can trigger sexual arousal in both men and women. Sexually explicit materials may lead people to perceive their partners as comparatively less appealing and to devalue their relationships. Sexually coercive material tends to increase viewers' acceptance of rape and violence toward women. In combination with the internal hormonal push and the external pull of sexual stimuli, imagined stimuli (fantasies) help trigger sexual arousal.

27-4 : What factors influence teenagers' sexual attitudes and behaviors?
Adolescents' physical maturation fosters a sexual dimension to their emerging identity. But culture is a big influence, too, as is apparent from varying rates of teen intercourse and pregnancy. A near-epidemic of sexually transmitted infections has triggered new research and educational programs pertinent to adolescent sexuality.

27-5 : What does current research tell us about why some people are attracted to members of their own sex and others are attracted to members of the other sex?
Studies indicate that about 3 or 4 percent of men and 1 or 2 percent of women are homosexual, and that *sexual orientation* is enduring. Research does not support cause-effect links between homosexuality and a child's relationships with parents, father-absent homes, fear or hatred of people of the other gender, childhood sexual experiences, peer relationships, or dating experiences. The likelihood of a biological component of homosexuality is indicated by the existence of same-sex behavior in several hundred species; straight-gay differences in body and brain characteristics; genetic studies of family members and twins; and the effect of exposure to certain hormones during critical periods of development. The increasing public perception that sexual orientation is biologically influenced is reflected in increasing acceptance of gays and lesbians and their relationships.

27-6 : Is scientific research on sexual motivation value-free?
Sex research and sex education are not value-free, and some believe researchers and educators should openly acknowledge their sex-related values.

27-7 : Why do some psychologists believe we have a need to belong—to affiliate with others?
Our need to affiliate—to feel connected and identified with others—boosted our ancestors' chances for survival, which may explain why humans in every society live in groups. When ostracized (excluded or shunned by others), people suffer from stress and depression and may engage in self-defeating or antisocial behavior. Those who are socially secure in their relationships tend to be healthier and happier.

>> REHEARSE IT!

1. In describing the sexual response cycle, Masters and Johnson noted that
   a. a plateau phase followed orgasm.
   b. men experience a refractory period during which they cannot experience orgasm.
   c. the feeling that accompanies orgasm is stronger in men than in women.
   d. testosterone is released in the female as well as in the male.

2. Daily and monthly fluctuations in hormone levels do not greatly affect sexual desire in humans, but hormonal changes over the life span can have significant effects. A striking effect of hormonal changes on human sexual behavior is the
   a. arousing influence of erotic materials.
   b. sharp rise in sexual interest at puberty.
   c. decrease in women's sexual desire at the time of ovulation.
   d. increase in testosterone levels in castrated males.

3. Sexual behavior is motivated by internal biological factors, by external stimuli, and by imagined stimuli. An example of an external stimulus that might influence sexual behavior is
   a. blood level of testosterone.
   b. the onset of puberty.
   c. a sexually explicit film.
   d. an erotic fantasy or dream.

4. More than half of all sexually active teens either do not use contraceptives or do not use them regularly. Factors contributing to teen

pregnancies include ignorance about reproduction and contraception, guilt about sexual behavior, mass media norms of promiscuity, insufficient communication about contraception, and

a. the "just say no" attitude.
b. the unavailability of abortion.
c. the decreased rates of sexually transmitted diseases.
d. alcohol use.

5. Sexual orientation refers to our enduring sexual attraction to members of a particular gender. Current research suggests several possible contributors to sexual orientation.

Which of the following is NOT one of those contributors?

a. Certain cell clusters in the hypothalamus
b. A domineering mother and ineffectual father
c. A section of fibers connecting the right and left hemispheres of the brain
d. Exposure to hormone levels typically experienced by female fetuses

6. Some researchers contend that humans are strongly motivated by a need to belong. Which of the following is NOT part of the evidence presented to support this view?

a. Students who rated themselves as "very happy" also tended to have satisfying close relationships.
b. Social exclusion—such as exile or solitary confinement—is considered a severe form of punishment.
c. As adults, adopted children tend to resemble their biological parents and to yearn for an affiliation with them.
d. Children who are extremely neglected become withdrawn, frightened, and speechless.

Answers: 1. b, 2. b, 3. c, 4. d, 5. b, 6. c.

>> Terms and Concepts to Remember

sexual response cycle, p. 375
refractory period, p. 376

sexual disorder, p. 376
estrogen, p. 376

testosterone, p. 376
sexual orientation, p. 380

>> Test Yourself

1. How might the evolutionary psychology perspective explain sexual motivation and our need to affiliate?

(Answer in Appendix C.)

*Multiple-choice **self-tests** and more may be found at www.worthpublishers.com/myers.*

28 Motivation at Work

Personnel Psychology

Organizational Psychology: Motivating Achievement

Sometimes, notes Gene Weingarten (2002), a humor writer knows "when to just get out of the way." Here are some sample job titles from the U.S. Department of Labor *Dictionary of Occupational Titles:* Animal impersonator, human projectile, banana ripening-room supervisor, impregnator, impregnator helper, dope sprayer, finger waver, rug scratcher, egg smeller, bottom buffer, cookie breaker, brain picker, hand pouncer, bosom presser, mother repairer, and breaker repairer.

Have you ever noticed that when you are immersed in an activity, time flies? And that when you are watching the clock, it seems to move more slowly? French researchers have confirmed that the more we attend to an event's duration, the longer it seems to last (Couli & others, 2004).

The healthy life, said Sigmund Freud, is filled by love and by work. For most of us, work is life's biggest single waking activity. To live is to work. Work helps satisfy several levels of need. Work supports us. Work connects us. Work defines us. Meeting someone for the first time, and wondering "Who are you?" we may ask, "So, what do you do?"

If we feel dissatisfied with our work-related pay, relationships, or identity, we may change where or for whom we work. Most people therefore have neither a single vocation nor a predictable career path. Two decades from now, most of you reading this book will be doing work you cannot now imagine. To prepare you and others for this unknown future, many colleges and universities focus less on training your job skills and more on enlarging your capacities for understanding, thinking, and communicating in any work environment.

Amy Wrzesniewski and her colleagues (1997, 2001) have identified person-to-person variations in people's attitudes toward their work. Across various occupations, some people view their work as a *job,* a necessary way to make money but not a positive and fulfilling activity. Others view their work as a *career,* an opportunity to advance from one position to a better position. The rest—those who view their work as a *calling*, a fulfilling and socially useful activity—report the highest satisfaction with their work and their lives.

This finding would not surprise Mihaly Csikszentmihalyi (1990, 1999), who has observed that people's quality of life increases when they are purposefully engaged. Between the anxiety of being overwhelmed and stressed, and the apathy of being underwhelmed and bored, lies a zone in which people experience **flow.** Csikszentmihalyi (chick-SENT-me-hi) formulated the flow concept after studying artists who spent hour after hour painting or sculpting with enormous concentration. Immersed in a project, they worked as if nothing else mattered, and then promptly forgot about it once they finished. The artists seemed driven less by the external rewards of producing art—money, praise, promotion—than by the intrinsic rewards of creating the work. Recognizing that e-mail and other Internet-related distractions can disrupt such flow, Microsoft is developing an *attentional user interface* that aims to "detect when users are available for communication, or when the user is in a state of flow" (Ullman, 2005).

Csikszentmihalyi's later observations—of dancers, chess players, surgeons, writers, parents, mountain climbers, sailors, and farmers; of Australians, North Americans, Koreans, Japanese, and Italians; of people from their teens to their golden years—confirmed an overriding principle: It's exhilarating to flow with an activity that fully engages our skills. Flow experiences boost our sense of self-esteem, competence, and well-being. When researchers beeped people at random intervals and asked them to report what they were doing and how much they were enjoying themselves, those who were vegetating usually reported little sense of flow and little satisfaction. People reported more positive feelings when interrupted while doing something active, something that engaged their skills, be it play or work. And other research (Inglehart, 1990) indicates that in almost every industrialized nation, people have reported markedly lower well-being if unemployed (**FIGURE 28.1**). Idleness may sound like bliss, but purposeful work enriches our lives.

In industrialized nations, work has been changing, from farming to manufacturing to "knowledge work." More and more work is *outsourced* to temporary employees and consultants who communicate electronically from virtual workplaces in remote

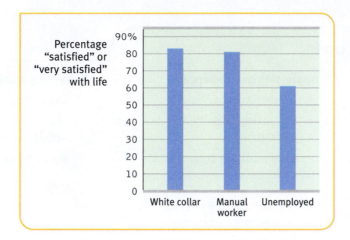

FIGURE 28.1
The bane of unemployment
To want work but not have it is to feel less satisfied with life. Data from 169,776 adults in 16 nations (Inglehart, 1990).

■ **flow** a completely involved, focused state of consciousness, with diminished awareness of self and time, resulting from optimal engagement of one's skills.

■ **industrial-organizational (I/O) psychology** the application of psychological concepts and methods to optimizing human behavior in workplaces.

■ **personnel psychology** a subfield of I/O psychology that focuses on employee recruitment, selection, placement, training, appraisal, and development.

■ **organizational psychology** a subfield of I/O psychology that examines organizational influences on worker satisfaction and productivity and facilitates organizational change.

locations. (This book and its teaching package are developed and produced by a team of people in a dozen cities, from Alaska to Florida.) As work changes, will our attitudes toward our work also change? Will our satisfaction with work increase or decrease? Will the *psychological contract*—the subjective sense of mutual obligations between workers and employers—become more or less trusting and secure? These are among the questions that fascinate psychologists who study work-related behavior.

Industrial-organizational (I/O) psychology is a fast-growing profession that applies psychology's principles to the workplace. (Turn the page to see Close-Up: I/O Psychology at Work.) One subfield, *human factors psychology,* explores how machines and environments can be optimally designed to fit human abilities and expectations. Here we consider two other subfields:

- **Personnel psychology,** which applies psychology's methods and principles to selecting and evaluating workers. Personnel psychologists match people with jobs, by identifying and placing well-suited candidates.
- **Organizational psychology,** which considers how work environments and management styles influence worker motivation, satisfaction, and productivity. Organizational psychologists modify jobs and supervision in ways that boost morale and productivity.

Personnel Psychology

28-1: What tools and techniques do personnel psychologists use to marry the individual's strengths with the organization's needs?

Psychologists can assist organizations at various stages of selecting and assessing employees. They may help identify needed job skills, decide upon selection methods, recruit and evaluate applicants, introduce and train new employees, and appraise their performance.

Harnessing Strengths

As a new AT&T human resource executive, psychologist Mary Tenopyr (1997) was assigned to solve a problem: Customer service representatives were failing at a high rate. After concluding that many of the hires were ill-matched to the demands of their new job, Tenopyr developed a new selection instrument:

1. She asked new applicants to respond to various questions (without as yet making any use of their responses).
2. She followed up later to assess which of the applicants excelled on the job.
3. She identified the individual items on the earlier test that best predicted who would succeed.

Artistic strengths

At age 21, Henri Matisse was a sickly and often depressed lawyer's clerk. When his mother gave him a box of paints to cheer him up one day, he felt the darkness lift and his energy surge. He began to fill his days with painting and drawing and went on to art school and a life as one of the world's great painters. For Matisse, doing art felt like "a comfortable armchair." That is how exercising our strengths often feels.

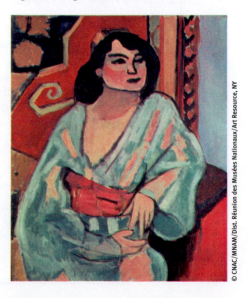

© CNAC/MNAM/Dist. Réunion des Musées Nationaux/Art Resource, NY

CLOSE-UP

I/O PSYCHOLOGY AT WORK

As scientists, consultants, and management professionals, industrial-organizational psychologists are found working in varied areas:

PERSONNEL PSYCHOLOGY
Selecting and placing employees

- Developing and validating assessment tools for selecting, placing, and promoting workers
- Analyzing job content
- Optimizing worker placement

Training and developing employees

- Identifying needs
- Designing training programs
- Evaluating training programs

Appraising performance

- Developing criteria
- Measuring individual performance
- Measuring organizational performance

ORGANIZATIONAL PSYCHOLOGY
Developing organizations

- Analyzing organizational structures
- Maximizing worker satisfaction and productivity
- Facilitating organizational change

Enhancing quality of worklife

- Expanding individual productivity
- Identifying elements of satisfaction
- Redesigning jobs

HUMAN FACTORS (ENGINEERING) PSYCHOLOGY

- Designing optimum work environments
- Optimizing person-machine interactions
- Developing systems technologies

Adapted from the Society of Industrial and Organizational Psychology (siop.org)

The happy result of her data-driven work was a new test that enabled AT&T to identify likely-to-succeed customer representatives.

As this illustrates, personnel selection aims to match people's strengths with work that enables them and their organizations to flourish. Marry the strengths of people with the tasks of organizations and the result is often prosperity and profit.

Your strengths are any enduring qualities that can be productively applied. Are you naturally curious? Persuasive? Charming? Persistent? Competitive? Analytical? Empathic? Organized? Articulate? Neat? Mechanical? Any such trait, if matched with suitable work, can function as a strength. (See Close-Up: Discovering Your Strengths.)

CLOSE-UP

DISCOVERING YOUR STRENGTHS

You can use some of the techniques personnel psychologists have developed to identify your own strengths and pinpoint types of work that will likely prove satisfying and successful. Buckingham and Clifton (2001) have suggested asking yourself:

- What activities give me pleasure? (Bringing order out of chaos? Playing host? Helping others? Challenging sloppy thinking?)
- What activities leave me wondering, "When can I do this again?" (Rather than "When will this be over?")

- What sort of challenges do I relish? (And which do I dread?)
- What sorts of tasks do I learn easily? (And which do I struggle with?)

Satisfied and successful people devote far less time to correcting their deficiencies than to accentuating their strengths. Top performers are "rarely well rounded," Buckingham and Clifton found (p. 26). Instead, they have sharpened their existing skills. Given the persistence of our traits and temperaments, we should focus not on our deficiencies, but

rather on identifying and employing our talents. Better to recognize the activities we quickly learn and become absorbed in—and to further develop those strengths—than to sign up for assertiveness training if shy, for public speaking courses if nervous and soft-spoken, or for drawing classes if we express our artistic side in stick figures.

As Robert Louis Stevenson said in *Of Men and Books* (1882), "To be what we are, and to become what we are capable of becoming, is the only end of life."

Marcus Buckingham and Donald Clifton (2001) argue that the first step to a stronger organization is instituting a *strengths-based selection system*. Thus, as a manager, you would first identify a group of the most effective people in any role—the ones you would want to hire more of—and compare their strengths with those of a group of the least effective people in that role. In defining these groups, you would try to measure performance as objectively as possible. In one Gallup study of more than 5000 telecommunications customer-service representatives, those evaluated most favorably by their managers were strong in "harmony" and "responsibility," while those actually rated most effective by customers were strong in energy, assertiveness, and eagerness to learn. So, for example, if you needed a new software developer, and you had discovered that your best software developers are analytical, disciplined, and eager to learn, you would focus employment ads less on experience than on the identified strengths: "Do you take a logical and systematic approach to problem solving [*analytical*]? Are you a perfectionist who strives for timely completion of your projects [*disciplined*]? Do you want to learn to use Java, C++, and PHP [*eager to learn*]? If you can say yes to these questions, then please call. . . ."

To identify people's strengths and pair them to jobs, personnel managers use various tools, including ability tests, personality tests, and behavioral observations in *assessment centers* that simulate job tasks. Here we focus on job interviews.

Do Interviews Predict Performance?

Interviewers tend to feel confident in their ability to predict long-term job performance from an unstructured, get-acquainted interview. Most would be shocked to find out that, whether predicting job or graduate school success, interviewers' judgments are error-prone. In reviewing 85 years of personnel-selection research, I/O psychologists Frank Schmidt and John Hunter (1998; Schmidt, 2002) determined that for all but less-skilled jobs, general mental ability best predicts on-the-job performance. Subjective overall evaluations from informal interviews are more useful than handwriting analysis (which is worthless), but less informative than aptitude tests, work samples, job knowledge tests, and past job performance. If there's a contest between what our gut tells us about someone and what test scores, work samples, and past performance tell us, we should distrust our gut.

The Interviewer Illusion

Interviewers often overrate their discernment, a phenomenon psychologist Richard Nisbett (1987) has labeled the *interviewer illusion*. "I have excellent interviewing skills, and so don't need reference checking as much as someone who doesn't have my ability to read people," is a comment sometimes heard by I/O consultants. Four factors explain this gap between interviewers' intuition and the resulting reality:

> "Between the idea and reality . . . falls the shadow."
>
> T. S. Eliot, *The Hollow Men*, 1925

- *Interviews disclose the interviewee's good intentions, which are less revealing than habitual behaviors* (Ouellette & Wood, 1998). Intentions matter. People can change. But the best predictor of the person we will be is the person we have been. Wherever we go, we take ourselves along.
- *Interviewers more often follow the successful careers of those they have hired than the successful careers of those they have rejected and lost track of.* This missing feedback prevents interviewers from getting a reality check on their hiring ability.
- *Interviewers presume that people are what they seem to be in the interview situation.* When meeting others, we discount the enormous influence of varying situations and mistakenly presume that what we see is what we will get. But mountains of research on everything from chattiness to conscientiousness reveals that how we behave reflects not only our enduring traits, but also the details of the particular situation (wanting to impress an interviewer).
- *Interviewers' preconceptions and moods color how they perceive interviewees' responses* (Cable & Gilovich, 1998; Macan & Dipboye, 1994). If interviewers

instantly like a person who perhaps is similar to themselves, they may interpret the person's assertiveness as indicating "confidence" rather than "arrogance." If told certain applicants have been prescreened, interviewers are disposed to judge them more favorably.

An unstructured interview does provide a sense of someone's personality—their expressiveness, warmth, and verbal ability, for example. But if we let our intuitions bias the hiring process, notes Malcolm Gladwell (2000), then "all we will have done is replace the old-boy network, where you hired your nephew, with the new-boy network, where you hire whoever impressed you most when you shook his hand. Social progress, unless we're careful, can merely be the means by which we replace the obviously arbitrary with the not so obviously arbitrary."

Structured Interviews

Hoping to improve prediction and selection, personnel psychologists have put people in simulated work situations, scoured sources for information on past performance, aggregated evaluations from multiple interviews, administered tests, and developed job-specific interviews. Unlike casual conversation aimed at getting a feel for someone, **structured interviews** offer a disciplined method of collecting information. A personnel psychologist may analyze a job, script questions, and train interviewers. The interviewers then put the same questions, in the same order, to all applicants, and rate each applicant on established scales.

In an *unstructured* interview, someone might ask, "How organized are you?" "How well do you get along with people?" or "How do you handle stress?" Street-smart applicants know how to score high: "Although I sometimes drive myself too hard, I handle stress by prioritizing and delegating, and by making sure I leave time for sleep and exercise."

By contrast, structured interviews pinpoint strengths (attitudes, behaviors, knowledge, and skills) that distinguish high performers in a particular line of work. The process includes describing job-specific situations and asking candidates to explain how they would handle them, and how they handled similar situations in their prior employment. "Tell me about a time when you were caught between conflicting demands, without time to accomplish both. How did you handle that?"

To reduce memory distortions and bias, the interviewer takes notes and makes ratings as the interview proceeds, and avoids irrelevant and follow-up questions. The structured interview therefore feels less warm, but that can be explained to the applicant: "This conversation won't typify how we relate to each other in this organization."

A review of 150 findings revealed that structured interviews had double the predictive accuracy of unstructured seat-of-the-pants interviews (Schmidt & Hunter, 1998; Wiesner & Cronshaw, 1988). Thanks partly to its greater reliability and partly to its job-analysis focus, the predictive power of one structured interview is roughly equal to that of the average judgment from three or four unstructured interviews (Huffcutt & others, 2001; Schmidt & Zimmerman, 2004).

Appraising Performance

Performance appraisal serves organizational purposes: It helps decide who to retain, how to appropriately reward and pay people, and how to better harness employee strengths, sometimes with job shifts or promotions. Performance appraisal also serves individual purposes: Feedback affirms workers' strengths and helps motivate needed improvements.

Performance appraisal methods include

- *checklists* on which supervisors simply check behaviors that describe the worker ("always attends to customers' needs," "takes long breaks").

■ **structured interviews** interview process that asks the same job-relevant questions of all applicants, each of whom is rated on established scales.

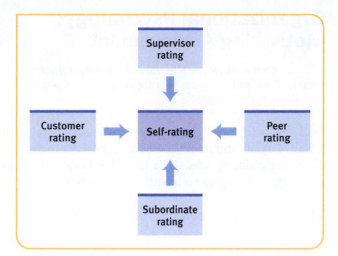

FIGURE 28.2
360-degree feedback
With multisource 360-degree feedback, one's knowledge, skills, and behaviors are rated by self and surrounding others. Professors, for example, may be rated by their department chairs, their students, and their colleagues. After receiving all these ratings, professors discuss the 360-degree feedback with their department chair.

- *graphic rating scales* on which a supervisor checks the extent to which a worker is dependable, productive, and so forth.
- *behavior rating scales* on which a supervisor checks behaviors that best describe a worker's performance. If rating the extent to which a worker "follows procedures," the supervisor might mark the employee somewhere between "often takes shortcuts" and "always follows established procedures" (Levy, 2003).

In some organizations, performance feedback comes not only from supervisors but also from all organizational levels. If you join an organization that practices *360-degree feedback* (**FIGURE 28.2**), you will rate yourself, your manager, and your other colleagues, and you will be rated by your manager, other colleagues, and customers (Green, 2002). The net result is often more open communication and more complete appraisal.

By encouraging multiple raters and developing objective, job-relevant performance measures, personnel psychologists seek to support their organizations while also helping employees perceive the appraisal process as fair.

To recap, personnel psychologists assist organizations in analyzing jobs, recruiting well-suited applicants, selecting and placing employees, and appraising their performance (**FIGURE 28.3**).

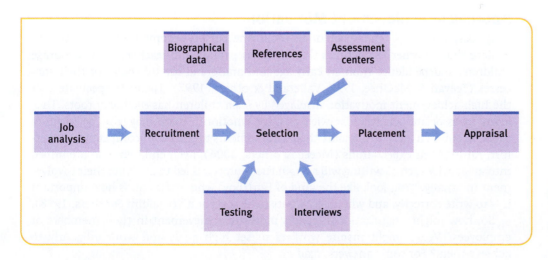

FIGURE 28.3
Personnel psychologists' tasks
Personnel psychologists consult in human resource activities, from job definition to employee appraisal.

McClelland, D. C., et al. (1953). The achievement motive. New York: Appleton-Century Crofts. Reprinted by permission of Irvington Publishers, New York.

FIGURE 28.4

What is this boy daydreaming about?

By analyzing responses to ambiguous photos like this, motivation researchers have sought clues to people's level of achievement motivation.

■ **achievement motivation** a desire for significant accomplishment: for mastery of things, people, or ideas; for attaining a high standard.

What is your greatest achievement to date? What is your greatest future ambition—to attain fame? Fortune? Creative accomplishment? Security? Love? Power? Wisdom? Spiritual wholeness?

"They can because they think they can."

Virgil, Aeneid, 19 B.C.

Organizational Psychology: Motivating Achievement

28-2: What does research reveal about achievement motivations? How do organizational psychologists help organizations to energize and direct people's behavior in the workplace?

Both the matching of talents to work and the appraisal of work matter. So does motivation. Organizational psychologists seek ways to engage and motivate ordinary people doing ordinary jobs. Let's consider first some general aspects of achievement motivation that apply both within and outside the workplace.

Identifying Achievement Motivation

Think of someone you know who strives to succeed by excelling at any task where evaluation is possible. Now think of someone who is less driven. Psychologist Henry Murray (1938) defined the first person's high need for achievement, or **achievement motivation,** as a desire for significant accomplishment, for mastering skills or ideas, for control, and for rapidly attaining a high standard.

How might we measure such a motive? Murray and investigators David McClelland and John Atkinson presumed that people's fantasies would reflect their concern for achievement. So they asked research participants to invent stories about ambiguous pictures. If a person who was shown the daydreaming boy in **FIGURE 28.4** said the boy was preoccupied with pursuit of a goal, that he imagined himself performing a heroic act, or that he was feeling pride about some success, the researchers scored the response as indicating achievement concerns. If people's stories consistently included such themes, McClelland and Atkinson regarded them as having a high need for achievement.

Would you expect people whose stories express high achievement to prefer tasks that are easy, moderately challenging, or very difficult? People whose stories suggest low achievement motivation tend to choose either very easy or very difficult tasks, where failure is either unlikely or not embarrassing (Geen, 1984). Those whose stories express high achievement motivation tend to prefer moderately difficult tasks, where success is attainable yet attributable to their skill and effort. In a ring-toss game they often stand at an intermediate distance from the stake, enabling some successes while providing a suitable challenge. When things get difficult, people with a strong need to achieve do persist more (Cooper, 1983). By contrast, high school underachievers persist less in completing college degrees, holding on to jobs, and maintaining their marriages (McCall, 1994).

Sources of Achievement Motivation

Why, despite having similar potentials, does one person become more motivated to achieve than another? Sometimes the answer is parents and teachers who encourage children's independence from an early age and praise and reward them for their successes (Teevan & McGhee, 1972; Vallerand & others, 1997). Theorists speculate that the high achievement motivation displayed by such children has *emotional* roots. They learn to associate achievement with positive emotions. There may also be *cognitive* roots, as children learn to attribute their achievements to their own competence and effort, raising their expectations (Meece & others, 2006). Even children who are bribed into an activity such as writing will sustain their interest if led to attribute their involvement internally: "You look like the kind of [girl/boy] who understands how important it is to write correctly, and who really wants to be good at it" (Cialdini & others, 1998).

So, how might organizational leaders motivate achievement in their members or employees? What might inspire workers to set high goals and work diligently to achieve them? For some answers, read on.

Satisfaction and Engagement

I/O psychologists understand that satisfaction with work feeds satisfaction with life and that decreased job stress feeds improved health. Does employee satisfaction also contribute to successful organizations? Positive moods at work do contribute to creativity, persistence, and helpfulness (Brief & Weiss, 2002). But are engaged, happy workers also less often absent? Less likely to quit? Less prone to theft? More punctual? More productive? Conclusive evidence of satisfaction's benefits is, some have said, the holy grail of I/O psychology. Statistical digests of prior research have found a modest positive correlation between individual job satisfaction and performance (Judge & others, 2001; Parker & others, 2003). In one recent analysis of 4500 employees at 42 British manufacturing companies, the most productive workers tended to be those in satisfying work environments (Patterson & others, 2004).

In the United States, the *Fortune* "100 Best Companies to Work For" have also produced markedly higher-than-average returns for their investors (Fulmer & others, 2003). Other positive data come from the biggest-ever study, a recent analysis of Gallup data from more than 198,000 employees (TABLE 28.1) in nearly 8000 business units of 36 large companies (including some 1100 bank branches, 1200 stores, and 4200 teams or departments). James Harter, Frank Schmidt, and Theodore Hayes (2002) explored correlations between various measures of organizational success and *employee engagement*—the extent of workers' involvement, satisfaction, and enthusiasm. They found that engaged workers know what's expected of them, have what they need to do their work, feel fulfilled in their work, have regular opportunities to do what they do best, perceive that they are part of something significant, and have opportunities to learn and develop. They also found that business units with engaged employees have more loyal customers, less turnover, higher productivity, and greater

Capital-Journal/David Eulitt/AP/Wide World Photos

Engaged employees facilitate organizational success

Best Buy's 400 electronic goods stores have nearly identical product layout and operations manuals. Yet some stores have much more engaged employees—and more profitable performance. The store with the highest worker-engagement scores is in the top tenth of stores in having profits beyond budget. And the store with the least-engaged employees is in the bottom tenth (Buckingham, 2001).

TABLE **28.1**

THE GALLUP WORKPLACE AUDIT

Overall satisfaction—On a 5-point scale, where 5 is extremely satisfied and 1 is extremely dissatisfied, how satisfied are you with (name of company) as a place to work? _____
On a scale of 1 to 5, where 1 is strongly disagree and 5 is strongly agree, please indicate your agreement with the following items.

1. I know what is expected from me at work.

2. I have the materials and equipment I need to do my work right.

3. At work, I have the opportunity to do what I do best every day.

4. In the last seven days, I have received recognition or praise for doing good work.

5. My supervisor, or someone at work, seems to care about me as a person.

6. There is someone at work who encourages my development.

7. At work, my opinions seem to count.

8. The mission/purpose of my company makes me feel my job is important.

9. My associates (fellow employees) are committed to doing quality work.

10. I have a best friend at work.

11. In the last six months, someone at work has talked to me about my progress.

12. This last year, I have had opportunities at work to learn and grow.

Note: These statements are proprietary and copyrighted by The Gallup Organization. They may not be printed or reproduced in any manner without the written consent of The Gallup Organization. Reprinted here by permission.

Three types of employees (Crabtree, 2005):

Engaged: working with passion and feeling a profound connection to their company or organization.

Not-engaged: putting in the time, but investing little passion or energy into their work.

Actively disengaged: unhappy workers undermining what their colleagues accomplish.

profits: "Business units above the median on employee engagement had a 70 percent higher success rate than those below the median." Business units in the top quarter on employee engagement averaged about $100,000 more in monthly revenue. A separate analysis for a company with 275 retail stores found that annual turnover was 55 percent among stores whose employee engagement was in the top quarter, and 75 percent among stores with employees in the bottom quarter (Harter, 2000).

Managing Well

Every leader dreams of managing in ways that enhance people's satisfaction, engagement, and productivity and their organization's success. Effective leaders harness job-relevant strengths, set goals, and choose an appropriate leadership style.

Harnessing Job-Relevant Strengths

"The major challenge for CEOs over the next 20 years will be the effective deployment of human assets," observes Marcus Buckingham (2001). That challenge is "about psychology. It's about getting [individuals] to be more productive, more focused, more fulfilled than [they were] yesterday." To do so, he and others maintain, effective leaders want first to select the right people. Then, they aim to discern their employees' natural talents, adjust their work roles to suit their talents, and develop those talents into great strengths (**FIGURE 28.5**). For example, should every college professor at a given school be expected to teach the same load, advise the same number of students, serve on the same number of committees, and engage in the same amount of research? Or should each job description be tailored to harness a specific person's unique strengths?

FIGURE 28.5
On the right path
The Gallup Organization path to organizational success (adapted from Fleming, 2001).

Loyal customers, growth, profits

Identify strengths → Match to work → Positive managing → Engaged employees

Positive coaching

Larry Brown, an adviser to "The Positive Coaching Alliance," has been observed during practices to offer his players 4 to 5 positive comments for every negative comment (Insana, 2005). In 2004, his underdog Detroit Pistons won the National Basketball Association championship.

Ezra Shaw/Getty Images

Managers who excel spend less time trying to instill talents that are not there and more time developing and drawing out what is there. Kenneth Tucker (2002) notes that great managers

- start by helping people identify and measure their talents.
- match tasks to talents and then give people freedom to do what they do best.
- care how their people feel about their work.
- reinforce positive behaviors through recognition and reward.

Thus, rather than focusing on weaknesses and packing people off to training seminars to fix those problems, good managers focus training time on educating people about their strengths and building upon them (which means not promoting people into roles ill-suited to their strengths).

Celebrating engaged and productive employees in every organizational role builds upon a basic principle of operant conditioning: *To teach a behavior, catch a person doing something right and reinforce it.* This principle also applies to reinforcing employees. It sounds simple, but many managers are like parents who, when a child returns home with perfect scores, except for that one troublesome biology class, focus on the biology score and ignore the rest. "Sixty-five percent of Americans received NO praise or recognition in the workplace last year," reported the Gallup Organization (2004).

Setting Specific, Challenging Goals

In study after study, people merely asked to do their best do not do so. But more specific, challenging goals do motivate higher achievement, especially when combined with progress reports (Locke & Latham, 2002). Specific, measurable objectives, such as "finish gathering information for the history paper by Friday," serve to direct attention, promote effort, motivate persistence, and stimulate creative strategies. When people share in setting a goal and find the goal challenging yet attainable, reaching it boosts their self-evaluation (White & others, 1995). Moreover, when people state not only goals but also implementation intentions—action plans that specify when, where, and how they will march toward achieving those goals—they become more focused in their work and on-time completion becomes more likely (Burgess & others, 2004; Koestner & others, 2002; Koole & Spijker, 2000). (Before beginning each new edition of this book, my editor, my associates, and I manage by objectives—we agree on target dates for the completion of each module draft.) So, to motivate high productivity, effective leaders work with people to define explicit goals, elicit commitments to implementation plans, and provide feedback on progress.

Choosing an Appropriate Leadership Style

Leadership varies from a boss-focused directive style to a democratic style that empowers workers in setting goals and strategies. Which works best may depend on the situation and the leader. The best leadership style for leading a discussion may not be the best style for leading troops on a charge (Fiedler, 1981). Moreover, different leaders are suited to different styles. Some excel at **task leadership**—setting standards, organizing work, and focusing attention on goals. Being goal-oriented, task leaders are good at keeping a group centered on its mission. Typically, they have a directive style, which can work well if the leader is bright enough to give good orders (Fiedler, 1987).

Other managers excel at **social leadership**—mediating conflicts and building high-achieving teams (Evans & Dion, 1991). Social leaders often have a democratic style: They delegate authority and welcome the participation of team members. Many experiments show that social leadership is good for morale. Subordinates usually feel more satisfied and motivated when they can participate in decision making (Burger, 1987; Spector, 1986).

Because effective leadership styles vary with the situation and the person, the once-popular *great person theory of leadership*—that all great leaders share certain traits—now

■ **task leadership** goal-oriented leadership that sets standards, organizes work, and focuses attention on goals.

■ **social leadership** group-oriented leadership that builds teamwork, mediates conflict, and offers support.

> " Good leaders don't ask more than their constituents can give, but they often ask—and get—more than their constituents intended to give or thought it was possible to give."
>
> John W. Gardner, *Excellence*, 1984

© The New Yorker Collection, 1988, Anthony Taber from cartoonbank.com. All Rights Reserved.

seems overstated. But a leader's personality does matter. Effective leaders of laboratory groups, work teams, and large corporations tend to exude a self-confident *charisma* (House & Singh, 1987; Shamir & others, 1993). Their charisma is a mix of a *vision* of some goal, an ability to *communicate* it clearly and simply, and enough optimism and faith in their group to *inspire* others to follow. In one study of 50 Dutch companies, the highest morale was at those firms with chief executives who most inspired their colleagues "to transcend their own self-interests for the sake of the collective" (de Hoogh & others, 2004). Leadership of this kind—*transformational leadership*—motivates others to identify with and commit themselves to the group's mission. Transformational leaders, many of whom are natural extraverts, articulate high standards, inspire people to share their vision, and offer personal attention (Bono & Judge, 2004). The frequent result is more engaged, trusting, and effective workers (Turner & others, 2002).

Peter Smith and Monir Tayeb (1989) compiled data from studies in India, Taiwan, and Iran indicating that effective managers—whether in coal mines, banks, or government offices—often exhibit a high degree of *both* task and social leadership. As achievement-minded people, effective managers certainly care about how well work is done, yet at the same time they are sensitive to their subordinates' needs. In one national survey of American workers, those in family-friendly organizations offering flexible-time hours reported feeling greater loyalty to their employers (Roehling & others, 2001).

Many successful businesses have also increased employee participation in making decisions, a management style common in Sweden and Japan and increasingly elsewhere (Naylor, 1990; Sundstrom & others, 1990). Although managers often think better of work they have directly supervised, studies reveal a *voice effect:* If given a chance to voice their opinion during a decision-making process, people will respond more positively to the decision (van den Bos & Spruijt, 2002). And as we noted earlier, positive engaged employees are a mark of thriving organizations.

Sharing vision and decisions
As CEO, Jeffrey Bleustein helped Harley-Davidson thrive, in part by replacing the organization's command-and-control management style with one based on companywide consensus planning and decision making.

The rags-to-riches Harley-Davidson story illustrates the potential of inviting workers to participate in decision making (Teerlink & Ozley, 2000). In 1987, the struggling company began transforming its *command-and-control* management process to a *joint-vision process.* The aim: "To push decision-making, planning, and strategizing from a handful of people at the top, down throughout the organization. We wanted all the employees to think every day about how to improve the company," reported CEO Jeffrey Bleustein (2002). In the mid-1990s, Harley signed a cooperative agreement with its unions that included them "in decision-making in virtually every aspect of the business." Consensus decision-making can take longer, but "when the decision is made, it gets implemented quickly and the commitment is by the group," says Bleustein. The result has been more engaged workers and also more satisfied stockholders. Every $1 of Harley-Davidson stock purchased at the beginning of 1988 was worth $125 by mid-2005.

Identifiable physiological mechanisms drive some motives, such as hunger (though learned tastes and cultural expectations matter, too). Achievement at work is more obviously driven by psychological factors, such as an intrinsic quest for mastery and the external rewards of recognition. But what unifies these and all other motives is their common effect: The energizing and directing of behavior.

REVIEWING

>> MODULE REVIEW

For most people, work is a huge part of life. At its best, when work puts us in *flow*, work can be satisfying and enriching. What, then, enables worker motivation, productivity, and satisfaction? *I/O psychology* studies behavior in the workplace through its primary subfields: *personnel psychology, organizational psychology,* and *human factors psychology.*

28-1: What tools and techniques do personnel psychologists use to marry the individual's strengths with the organization's needs?

Personnel psychologists aim to identify people's strengths and to match them with organizational tasks. Subjective interviews lead to quickly formed impressions, but they also frequently foster an illusory overconfidence in one's ability to predict employee success. *Structured interviews,* pinpointing job-relevant strengths, enhance interview reliability and validity. Personnel psychologists also assist organizations in appraisal that fosters organizational goals, motivates individuals, and is welcomed as fair.

28-2: What does research reveal about achievement motivation? How do organizational psychologists help organizations to energize and direct people's behavior in the workplace?

Achievement motivation may stem from a person's social needs for competence and independence. People with a high need to achieve tend to prefer moderately challenging tasks and tend to persist in accomplishing them. When parents and teachers encourage and affirm their children's independent achievement, children may learn to associate achievement with positive emotions and to attribute their success to their own competence. Organizational psychologists can help management motivate employees to achieve, which contributes to an engaged, committed, satisfied workforce. Effective leaders build on people's strengths, work with them to set specific and challenging goals, and adapt their *leadership style* (*task* or *social*) to the situation.

>> REHEARSE IT!

1. People who view their work as a calling report the highest satisfaction with their work and with their lives. When engaged in their work, these people often experience _____, a focused state of consciousness, with diminished awareness of themselves and of time.

   a. stress
   b. apathy
   c. flow
   d. facilitation

2. Industrial/organizational psychologists apply psychology's concepts and methods to optimizing human behavior in the workplace. The three main divisions within I/O psychology are _____, _____, and _____ psychology.

   a. motivational; management; small group
   b. personnel; organizational; human factors
   c. motivational; personnel; human factors
   d. personnel; management; small group

3. After analyzing the tasks and responsibilities for the job of creative director in a Web design firm, a personnel psychologist scripted a set of questions to ask all applicants. Then the firm's interviewers were trained to ask these questions, take notes, rate applicants' responses, and avoid irrelevant follow-up questions. This technique is known as a(n)

   a. structured interview.
   b. unstructured interview.
   c. performance appraisal checklist.
   d. behavior rating scale.

4. Performance appraisal helps organizations retain and reward workers, and gives feedback to employees on their performance. If you rate your own performance and your manager's, and your manager, your peers, and your customers rate your performance and your manager's, your organization is using

   a. flow procedure.
   b. graphic feedback.
   c. structured interviews.
   d. 360-degree feedback.

5. Psychologists know that achievements are not distributed in a bell curve, as intelligence scores are. Achievement therefore must be more than just raw ability. Studies of highly motivated children have found that

   a. their parents and teachers tend to encourage their independence and praise and reward their successes.
   b. their teachers and caregivers use primarily material rewards, such as cash and prizes.
   c. these children are aggressive, antisocial, and self-absorbed.
   d. these children are distinguished by extraordinary natural talent.

6. Task leadership is goal-oriented, whereas social leadership is group-oriented. Research indicates that effective managers exhibit

   a. only task leadership.
   b. only social leadership.
   c. both task and social leadership, depending on the situation and the person.
   d. task leadership for building teams and social leadership for setting standards.

Answers: 1. b, 2. b, 3. a, 4. d, 5. a, 6. c.

>> TERMS AND CONCEPTS TO REMEMBER

flow, p. 392

industrial-organizational (I/O) psychology, p. 393

personnel psychology, p. 393

organizational psychology, p. 393

structured interviews, p. 396

achievement motivation, p. 398

task leadership, p. 401

social leadership, p. 401

>> TEST YOURSELF

1. Given a choice of tasks, high achievers usually select one that is moderately challenging, but low achievers tend to choose very easy or very difficult tasks. What would explain this difference?

   (Answer in Appendix C.)

> *Multiple-choice **self-tests** and more may be found at www.worthpublishers.com/myers.*

Emotions, Stress, and Health

Emotions, Stress, and Health

No one needs to tell you that feelings add color to your life, or that in times of stress they can disrupt your life or save it. Of all the species, we seem the most emotional (Hebb, 1980). More often than any other creature, we express fear, anger, sadness, joy, and love, and these psychological states often entail physical reactions. Nervous about an important encounter, we feel stomach butterflies. Anxious over speaking in public, we frequent the bathroom. Smoldering over a conflict with a family member, we get a splitting headache.

You can surely recall a time when you were overcome with emotion. I retain a flashbulb memory for the day I went to a huge store to drop off film and brought along Peter, my toddler first-born child. As I set Peter down on his feet and prepared to complete the paperwork, a passerby warned, "You'd better be careful or you'll lose that boy!" Not more than a few breaths later, after dropping the film in the slot, I turned and found no Peter beside me.

With mild anxiety, I peered around one end of the counter. No Peter in sight. With slightly more anxiety, I peered around the other end. No Peter there, either. Now, with my heart accelerating, I circled the neighboring counters. Still no Peter anywhere. As anxiety turned to panic, I began racing up and down the store aisles. He was nowhere to be found.

Apprised of my alarm, the store manager used the public-address system to ask customers to assist in looking for a missing child. Soon after, I passed the customer who had warned me. "I told you that you were going to lose him!" he said scornfully. With visions of kidnapping (strangers routinely adored that beautiful child), I braced for the possibility that my negligence had caused me to lose what I loved above all else, and—dread of all dreads—that I might have to return home and face my wife without our only child.

But then, as I passed the customer service counter yet again, there he was, having been found and returned by some obliging customer! In an instant, the arousal of dread spilled into ecstasy. Clutching my son, with tears suddenly flowing, I found myself unable to speak my thanks and stumbled out of the store awash in grateful joy.

What do we know about emotions? How do our emotional responses affect our well-being? The research findings on the three components of emotion—the physiological response to stimuli, the expressive behaviors, and the conscious experience of the emotion—are the topics of Modules 29 and 30. Then in Modules 31 and 32 we consider what stress is, how it affects our health, and what we can do to cope with life's stresses and promote good health.

Theories and Physiology of Emotion

Theories of Emotion

29-1: What are the components of an emotion?

Where do emotions come from? Why do we have them? What are they made of? Emotions are our body's adaptive response. They exist not to give us interesting experiences but to enhance our survival. When we face challenges, emotions focus our attention and energize our action. Our heart races. Our pace quickens. All our senses go on high alert. Receiving unexpected good news, we may find our eyes tearing. We raise our hands triumphantly. We feel exuberance and a newfound confidence.

Emotions are a mix of (1) physiological arousal (heart pounding), (2) expressive behaviors (quickened pace), and (3) conscious experience, including thoughts (I lose my child in a store—is this a kidnapping?) and feelings (a sense of fear, and later—on finding the child—joy). The puzzle for psychologists has been figuring out how these three pieces fit together.

There are two controversies over the interplay of our physiology, expressions, and experience in emotions. The first, a chicken-and-egg debate, is old: Does physiological arousal precede or follow the emotional experience? (Did I first notice my heart racing and my faster step, and then feel anxious dread about losing my son, Peter? Or did my sense of fear come first, stirring my heart and legs to respond?) The second controversy concerns the interaction between thinking and feeling: Does cognition always precede emotion? (Was I required to make a conscious appraisal of the kidnapping threat before I could react emotionally?)

Common sense tells most of us that we cry because we are sad, lash out because we are angry, tremble because we are afraid. First comes conscious awareness, then the physiological trimmings. But to pioneering psychologist William James, this commonsense view of emotion was 180 degrees out of line. According to James, "We feel sorry because we cry, angry because we strike, afraid because we tremble" (1890, p. 1066). Perhaps you can recall a time when your car skidded on slick pavement. As it careened crazily you counter-steered and regained control. Just after the fishtail ended, you noticed your racing heart and *then*, shaking with fright, you felt the whoosh of emotion. Your feeling of fear *followed* your body's response. James' idea, also proposed by Danish physiologist Carl Lange, is called the **James-Lange theory.**

The James-Lange theory struck U.S. physiologist Walter Cannon (1871–1943) as implausible. Cannon thought the body's responses were not distinct enough to evoke the different emotions. Does a racing heart signal fear, anger, or love? Also, changes in heart rate, perspiration, and body temperature seemed too slow to trigger sudden emotion. Cannon, and later another physiologist, Philip Bard, concluded that physiological arousal and our emotional experience occur *simultaneously*: The emotion-triggering stimulus is routed simultaneously to the brain's cortex, causing the subjective awareness of emotion, and to the sympathetic nervous system, causing the body's arousal. This **Cannon-Bard theory** implies that your heart begins pounding *as* you experience fear; one does not cause the other.

Let's check your understanding of the James-Lange and Cannon-Bard theories. Imagine that your brain could not sense your heart pounding or your stomach churning. According to each theory, how would this affect your experienced emotions?

- **emotion** a response of the whole organism, involving (1) physiological arousal, (2) expressive behaviors, and (3) conscious experience.

- **James-Lange theory** the theory that our experience of emotion is our awareness of our physiological responses to emotion-arousing stimuli.

- **Cannon-Bard theory** the theory that an emotion-arousing stimulus simultaneously triggers (1) physiological responses and (2) the subjective experience of emotion.

The joys of friendship

According to the James-Lange theory, we don't just smile because we share a friend's joy. We also share the joy because we are smiling with them.

Digital Vision/Getty Images

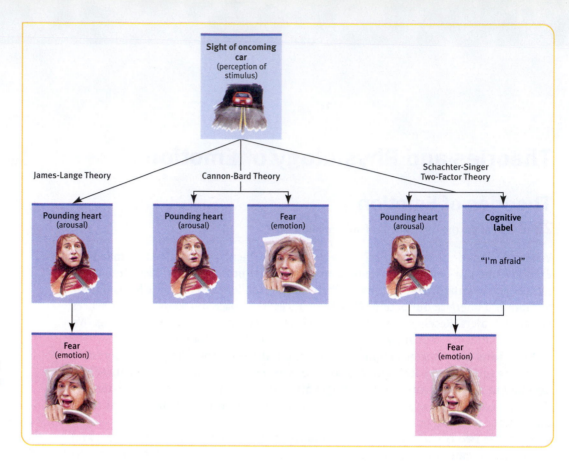

FIGURE **29.1**
Theories of emotion

Cannon and Bard would have expected you to experience emotions normally, because they believed emotions occur separately from (though simultaneously with) the body's arousal. James and Lange would have expected greatly diminished emotions because they believed that to experience emotion you must first perceive your body's arousal.

The James-Lange theory finds support in observations of people with severed spinal cords. Psychologist George Hohmann (1966) interviewed 25 soldiers who suffered such injuries in World War II. He asked them to recall emotion-arousing incidents that occurred before and after their spinal injuries. Those with lower-spine injuries, who had lost sensation only in their legs, reported little change in their emotions. Those who could feel nothing below the neck reported a considerable decrease in emotional intensity (as James and Lange would have expected). The anger, as one man confessed, "just doesn't have the heat to it that it used to. It's a mental kind of anger." But emotions expressed mostly in body areas above the neck are felt more intensely by those with high spinal-cord injury. Virtually all the men Hohmann interviewed reported increases in weeping, lumps in the throat, and getting choked up when saying good-bye, worshipping, or watching a touching movie. Such evidence has led some researchers to view feelings as "mostly shadows" of our bodily responses and behaviors (Damasio, 2003).

Most researchers agree with Cannon and Bard that our experienced emotions also involve cognition (Averill, 1993). Whether we fear the man behind us on the dark street depends entirely on whether we interpret his actions as threatening or friendly. So, with James and Lange we can say that our body's reactions are an important ingredient of emotion. And with Cannon and Bard we can say that there is more to the experience of emotion than reading our body's responses.

Stanley Schachter and Jerome Singer (1962) proposed a third theory: that our physiology and our cognitions—perceptions, memories, and interpretations—together create emotion. In their **two-factor theory,** emotions therefore have two ingredients: physical arousal and a cognitive label (**FIGURE 29.1**). Like James and Lange,

■ **two-factor theory** Schachter-Singer's theory that to experience emotion one must (1) be physically aroused and (2) cognitively label the arousal.

Schachter and Singer presumed that our experience of emotion grows from our awareness of our body's arousal. Yet like Cannon and Bard, Schachter and Singer also believed that emotions are physiologically similar. Thus, in their view, an emotional experience requires a conscious interpretation of the arousal.

To assess the James-Lange, Cannon-Bard, and two factor theories, we'll consider in the next section the answers researchers have gleaned to three questions:

- Does physiological arousal always precede emotional experience?
- Are different emotions marked by distinct physiological responses?
- What is the connection between what we *think* and how we *feel*?

> Not only emotion, but most psychological phenomena (vision, sleep, memory, sex, and so forth) can be approached these three ways—physiologically, behaviorally, and cognitively.

Embodied Emotion

Whether you are eagerly anticipating a long-awaited vacation, falling in love, or grieving the death of a loved one, you need little convincing that emotions involve the body. Feeling without a body is like breathing without lungs. Some physical responses are easy to notice, others—many taking place at the level of neurons in your brain—happen without your awareness. As you hear a motorcycle slowing down behind you on a dark street, your muscles tense, your stomach develops butterflies, your mouth becomes dry.

Emotions and the Autonomic Nervous System

29-2 : What physiological changes accompany emotions?

In a crisis it is your *autonomic nervous system (ANS)* that mobilizes your body for action (**FIGURE 29.2**). To provide energy, your liver pours extra sugar into your bloodstream. To help burn the sugar, your respiration increases to supply needed oxygen. Your digestion slows, diverting blood from your internal organs to your muscles. With blood sugar driven into the large muscles, running becomes easier. Your pupils dilate, letting in more light. To cool your stirred-up body, you perspire. If wounded, your blood would clot more quickly. After your next crisis, think of this: Without any conscious effort, your body's response to danger was wonderfully coordinated and adaptive—preparing you to fight or flee.

> " Fear lends wings to his feet."
> Virgil, *Aeneid*, 19 B.C.

Autonomic Nervous System Controls Physiological Arousal		
Sympathetic division (arousing)		Parasympathetic division (calming)
Pupils dilate	EYES	Pupils contract
Decreases	SALIVATION	Increases
Perspires	SKIN	Dries
Increases	RESPIRATION	Decreases
Accelerates	HEART	Slows
Inhibits	DIGESTION	Activates
Secrete stress hormones	ADRENAL GLANDS	Decrease secretion of stress hormones
Reduced	IMMUNE SYSTEM FUNCTIONING	Enhanced

FIGURE 29.2
Emotional arousal
Emotional arousal involves autonomic nervous system activation.

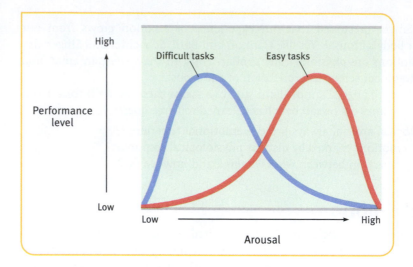

FIGURE 29.3
Arousal and performance
Performance peaks at lower levels of arousal for difficult tasks, and at higher levels for easy or well-learned tasks. Facing a difficult exam, high anxiety may disrupt performance. Teaching anxious students how to relax before an exam can therefore enable them to perform better (Hembree, 1988).

One explanation of sudden death caused by a voodoo "curse" is that the terrified person's parasympathetic nervous system, which calms the body, overreacts to the extreme arousal by slowing the heart to a stop (Seligman, 1974).

The *sympathetic division* of the ANS directs the adrenal glands atop the kidneys to release the stress hormones epinephrine (adrenaline) and norepinephrine (noradrenaline). This hormonal surge increases heart rate, blood pressure, and blood sugar levels. When the crisis passes, the parasympathetic neural centers become active, calming the body. Even after the *parasympathetic division* inhibits further release of stress hormones, those already in the bloodstream linger awhile, so arousal diminishes gradually.

Prolonged physical arousal, produced by sustained stress, taxes the body, yet in many situations, arousal is adaptive. Too little arousal (say, sleepiness) can be as disruptive as extremely high levels. When you're taking an exam, it pays to be moderately aroused—alert but not trembling with nervousness (**FIGURE 29.3**).

Physiological Similarities Among Specific Emotions

29-3 : Do different emotions activate different physiological responses?

Imagine conducting an experiment measuring the physiological responses of emotions. In each of four rooms, you have someone watching a movie: In the first, the person is viewing a horror show; in the second, an anger-provoking film; in the third, a sexually arousing film; in the fourth, an utterly boring movie. From the control center you monitor each person's physiological responses, measuring perspiration, breathing, and heart rates. Do you think you could tell who is frightened? Who is angry? Who is sexually aroused? Who is bored?

With training, you could probably pick out the bored viewer. But discerning physiological differences among fear, anger, and sexual arousal would be much more difficult (Cacioppo & others, 1997; Zillmann, 1986).

To you and me, sexual arousal, fear, and anger nevertheless *feel* different. If sexually stimulated, you will experience a genital response. If afraid, you may feel a clutching, sinking sensation in your chest and a knot in your stomach. If angry, you may feel "hot under the collar" and experience a pressing inner tension. And, despite similar arousal, fear and anger not only feel different, they also *look* different. People may appear "paralyzed with fear" or "ready to explode." So, does research pinpoint any distinct physiological or brain pattern indicators of each emotion? Sometimes. Read on.

Physiological Differences Among Specific Emotions

The finger temperatures and hormone secretions that accompany fear and rage do sometimes differ (Ax, 1953; Levenson, 1992). And, though fear and joy can prompt similar increased heart rate, they stimulate different facial muscles. During fear, brow muscles tense. During joy, muscles in the cheek and under the eye pull into a smile (Witvliet & Vrana, 1995).

"No one ever told me that grief felt so much like fear. I am not afraid, but the sensation is like being afraid. The same fluttering in the stomach, the same restlessness, the yawning. I keep on swallowing."
C. S. Lewis, *A Grief Observed*, 1961

Emotional arousal
Elated excitement and panicky fear involve similar physiological arousal. That allows us to flip rapidly between the two emotions.

M. Grecco/Stock, Boston

Emotions differ much more in the brain circuits they use (Kalin, 1993; Panksepp, 1982). Observers watching (and subtly mimicking) fearful faces show more amygdala brain activity than do those watching angry faces (Whalen & others, 2001). The power of the amygdala is also apparent in other research. Stimulate one area of a cat's amygdala, and it will pull back in terror at the sight of a mouse. Stimulate another amygdala area and the cat will look enraged—pupils dilated, fur and tail erect, claws out, hissing furiously.

Emotions also activate different areas of the brain's cortex. Experiencing negative emotions such as disgust, people show more activity in the right prefrontal cortex than in the left. Depression-prone people, and those with generally negative personalities, also show more right frontal activity (Harmon-Jones, Abramson, & others, 2002). One man, having lost part of his right frontal lobe in brain surgery, became (his not-unhappy wife reported) less irritable and more affectionate (Goleman, 1995). My father, after a right-hemisphere stroke at age 92, lived the last two years of his life with happy gratitude and nary a complaint or negative emotion.

When people experience positive moods—when they are enthusiastic, energized, and happy—brain scans and EEG recordings reveal more left frontal lobe activity. People with positive personalities—exuberant infants and alert, energetic, and persistently goal-directed adults—also show more activity in the left frontal lobe than in the right (Davidson, 2000, 2003; Urry & others, 2004). Indeed, the more a person's baseline frontal lobe activity tilts left, the more upbeat the person typically is. When you're happy and you know it, your brain will surely show it. (Given the physical indicators of emotion, might we, like Pinocchio, give some telltale sign whenever we lie? Turn the page to see Thinking Critically About Lie Detection.)

Cognition and Emotion

29-4 : To experience emotions, must we consciously interpret and label them?

What is the connection between what we *think* and how we *feel?* Which is the chicken and which the egg? Can we experience emotion apart from thinking? Or do we become what we think?

Cognition Can Define Emotion

Sometimes our arousal response to one event spills over into our response to the next event. Imagine arriving home after an invigorating run and finding a message that you got a longed-for job. With arousal lingering from the run, would you feel more elated than if you received this news after awakening from a nap?

To find out whether this *spillover effect* exists, Stanley Schachter and Jerome Singer (1962) aroused college men with injections of the hormone epinephrine. Picture yourself as one of their participants: After receiving the injection, you go to a waiting room, where you find yourself with another person (actually an accomplice of the experimenters) who is acting either euphoric or irritated. As you observe this person, you begin to feel your heart race, your body flush, and your breathing become more rapid. If told to expect these effects from the injection, what would you feel? Schachter and Singer's volunteers felt little emotion—because they attributed their arousal to the drug. But if told the injection would produce no effects, what would you feel? Perhaps you would react, as another group of participants did, by "catching" the apparent emotion of the person you are with—becoming happy if the accomplice is acting euphoric, and testy if the accomplice is acting irritated.

This discovery—that a stirred-up state can be experienced as one emotion or another very different one, depending on how we interpret and label it—has been replicated in dozens of experiments. Insult people who have just been aroused by pedaling an exercise bike or watching rock videos and they will find it easy to misattribute their arousal to the provocation. Their feelings of anger will be greater than those of people who were similarly provoked but not previously aroused. Likewise,

In 1966, a young man named Charles Whitman killed his wife and mother and then climbed to the top of a tower at the University of Texas and shot 38 people. An autopsy later revealed a tumor pressing against his amygdala, which may have contributed to his violence.

THINKING CRITICALLY ABOUT :

LIE DETECTION

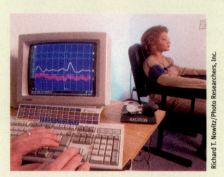

Can polygraph tests like this identify liars?
To learn more, read on.

The creators and users of the *lie detector,* or **polygraph,** have believed that our physical indicators of emotion can provide a telltale equivalent of Pinocchio's nose. Actually, polygraphs do not literally detect lies, and their accuracy has been increasingly questioned as our understanding of physiological measures of emotion has grown.

Rather, they measure several physical responses that accompany emotion, such as changes in breathing, cardiovascular activity, and perspiration. While you try to relax, an examiner monitors these responses as you answer questions. Some items, called control questions, aim to make anyone a little nervous. If asked, "In the last 20 years, have you ever taken something that didn't belong to you?" many people will tell a white lie and say no, causing arousal the polygraph will detect. If your physiological reactions to critical questions ("Did you ever steal anything from your previous employer?") are weaker than to control questions, the examiner infers you are telling the truth. The assumption has been that only a thief becomes agitated when denying a theft.

But there are two problems: First, as you have seen, our physiological arousal is much the same from one emotion to another—anxiety, irritation, and guilt all prompt similar physiological reactivity. Second, these tests err about one-third of the time, especially when innocent people respond with heightened tension to the accusations implied by the relevant questions (**FIGURE 29.4**). Many rape victims, for example, "fail" lie detector tests when reacting emotionally while telling the truth about their assailant (Lykken, 1991). Good advice, then, would be never to take a lie detector test if you are innocent.

A 2002 U.S. National Academy of Sciences report noted that "no spy has ever been caught [by] using the polygraph." It is not for lack of trying. The FBI, CIA, and Departments of Defense and Energy in the United States have spent millions of dollars testing tens of thousands of employees. Meanwhile Aldrich Ames, who enjoyed an unexplained lavish lifestyle as a Russian spy within the CIA, went undetected. Ames "took scores of polygraph tests and passed them all," notes Robert Park (1999). "Nobody thought to investigate the source of his sudden wealth—after all, he was passing the lie detector tests." The truth is, lie detectors can lie.

A more effective approach to lie detection uses the *guilty knowledge test,* which assesses a suspect's physiological responses to crime-scene details known only to the police and the guilty person (Ben-Shakhar & Elaad, 2003). If a camera and computer had been stolen, for example, presumably only one guilty of the crime would react strongly to the specific brand name of these items. Given enough such specific probes, an innocent person will seldom be wrongly accused.

■ **polygraph** a machine, commonly used in attempts to detect lies, that measures several of the physiological responses accompanying emotion (such as perspiration and cardiovascular and breathing changes).

FIGURE 29.4
How often do lie detectors lie?
Benjamin Kleinmuntz and Julian Szucko (1984) had polygraph experts study the polygraph data of 50 theft suspects who later confessed to being guilty and 50 suspects whose innocence was later established by someone's confession. Had the polygraph experts been the judges, more than one-third of the innocent would have been declared guilty, and almost one-fourth of the guilty would have been declared innocent.

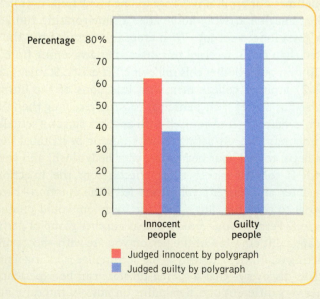

Reuters/Corbis

AP Photo/Nati Harnik

The spillover effect
Arousal from a soccer match (left photo) or a political protest (right photo) can fuel anger, which can descend into rioting or other violent confrontations.

sexually aroused people react with more hostility in anger-provoking situations. And, vice versa—the arousal that lingers after an intense argument or a frightening experience may intensify sexual passion (Palace, 1995). Just as the Schachter-Singer two-factor theory predicts, arousal + label = emotion. As we have seen, emotional arousal is not as undifferentiated as Schachter and Singer believed. But arousal—from emotions as diverse as anger, fear, and sexual excitement—can indeed spill from one emotion to another (Reisenzein, 1983; Sinclair & others, 1994; Zillmann, 1986). *The point to remember:* Arousal fuels emotion; cognition channels it.

Cognition Does Not Always Precede Emotion

To experience an emotion, must we first label our arousal? Sometimes we experience unlabeled emotion. Imagine receiving some unsettling news. There's a deadline you've forgotten about, or you discover that you've hurt someone's feelings. As the ongoing conversation distracts your attention, you lose awareness of the bad news. Yet as its bodily effects linger, the now-unlabeled feeling still churns. You feel a little bad. You know there's a reason. But for the moment you can't put your finger on it. Robert Zajonc (pronounced ZI-yence; 1980, 1984a) has contended that we actually have many emotional reactions apart from, or even before, our interpretations of a situation. For example, when people repeatedly view stimuli flashed too briefly for them to perceive and recall, they nevertheless come to prefer those stimuli. Without being consciously aware of having seen the stimuli, they rather like them. A subliminally flashed smiling or angry face can also prime us to feel better or worse about a follow-up stimulus (Murphy & others, 1995). In one set of experiments, thirsty people drank about 50 percent more fruit-flavored drink after viewing a subliminally flashed (thus unperceived) happy rather than neutral face (Berridge & Winkielman, 2003). If flashed an angry face, they drank substantially less.

Research on neurological processes shows how we can experience emotion unconsciously, before cognition. Like speedy reflexes that operate apart from the brain's thinking cortex, some emotions take what Joseph LeDoux (2004) calls the "low road," via neural pathways that bypass the cortex (site of the "high road" pathway). One low-road pathway runs from the eye or ear via the thalamus to the *amygdala*, an emotional control center (**FIGURE 29.5**). This amygdala shortcut, bypassing the cortex, enables our greased-lightning emotional response before

Can you recall liking something or someone immediately, without knowing why?

FIGURE 29.5
The brain's shortcut for emotions
Sensory input may be routed (a) directly to the amygdala (via the thalamus) for an instant emotional reaction and (b) to the cortex for analysis.

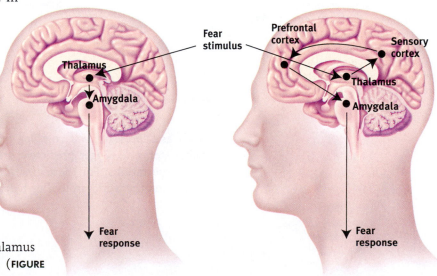

(a) The speedy low road   (b) The thinking high road

Courtesy of Paul J. Whalen, PhD, Dartmouth College, www.whalenlab.info

FIGURE 29.6
The brain's sensitivity to threats
Even when fearful eyes (left) were flashed too briefly for people to consciously perceive them, fMRI scans revealed that their hypervigilant amygdala was alerted (Whalen & others, 2004).

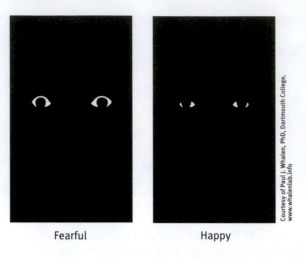

Fearful   Happy

our intellect intervenes. So speedy is the amygdala response that we may be unaware of what's transpired (Dimberg & others, 2000). In one fascinating experiment, Paul Whalen and his colleagues (2004) used fMRI scans to observe the amygdala's response to subliminally presented fearful eyes (**FIGURE 29.6**). Compared with a control condition that presented the whites of happy eyes, the fearful eyes triggered increased amygdala activity (despite no one's being aware of seeing them).

The amygdala sends more neural projections up to the cortex than it receives back. This makes it easier for our feelings to hijack our thinking than for our thinking to rule our feelings, note LeDoux and Jorge Armony (1999). In the forest, we jump at the sound of rustling bushes nearby, leaving the cortex to decide later whether the sound was made by a predator or just the wind. Such an experience supports Zajonc's belief that *some* of our emotional reactions involve no deliberate thinking and that cognition is not always necessary for emotion. The heart is not always subject to the mind.

Emotion researcher Richard Lazarus (1991, 1998) conceded that our brains process and react to vast amounts of information without our conscious awareness, and he willingly granted that some emotional responses do not require *conscious* thinking. But, he noted, even instantaneously felt emotions require some sort of cognitive appraisal of the situation; otherwise, how would we *know* what we are reacting to? The appraisal may be effortless and we may not be conscious of it, but it is still a mental function. Emotions arise when we *appraise* an event as beneficial or harmful to our well-being, whether we truly know it is or not. We appraise the sound of the rustling bushes as the presence of a threat. Later, we learn that it was "just the wind."

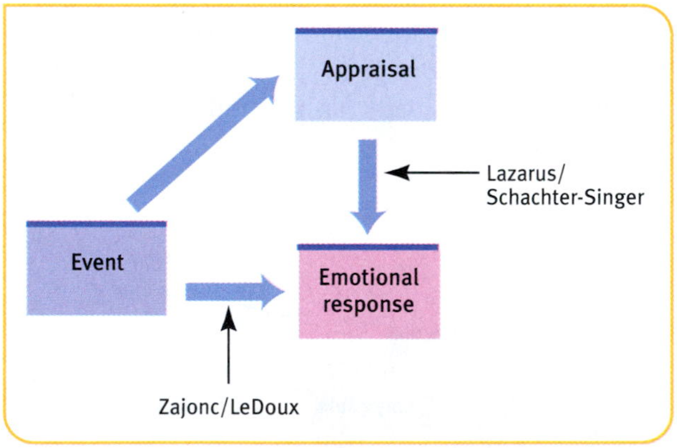

To sum up, as Zajonc and LeDoux have demonstrated, some emotional responses—especially simple likes, dislikes, and fears—involve no conscious thinking (**FIGURE 29.7**). We may fear a spider, even if we "know" it is harmless. Such responses are difficult to alter by changing our thinking.

Other emotions—including moods such as depression and complex feelings such as hatred and love—are, as Lazarus, Schachter, and Singer predicted, greatly affected by our interpretations, memories, and expectations. For these emotions, learning to *think* more positively about ourselves and the world around us helps us *feel* better.

FIGURE 29.7
Two routes to emotion
Zajonc and LeDoux emphasize that some emotional responses are immediate, before any conscious appraisal. Lazarus, Schachter, and Singer emphasized that our appraisal and labeling of events also determine our emotional responses.

Appraisal

Event

Lazarus/
Schachter-Singer

Emotional
response

Zajonc/LeDoux

REVIEWING

>> MODULE REVIEW

29-1: What are the components of an emotion?

Emotions are psychological responses of the whole organism that involve an interplay among (1) physiological arousal, (2) expressive behaviors, and (3) conscious experience.

Three theories support different combinations of these responses. The *James-Lange theory* maintains that our emotional feelings follow our body's response to the emotion-inducing stimuli. The *Cannon-Bard theory* implies that our body responds to emotion at the same time we experience that emotion (one does not cause the other). The *two-factor theory* holds that our emotions have two ingredients: physical arousal and a cognitive label.

29-2: What physiological changes accompany emotions?

Emotions are both psychological and physiological. Much of the physiological activity is controlled by the autonomic nervous system's sympathetic (arousing) and parasympathetic (calming) divisions. Our performance on a task is usually best when arousal is moderate, though this varies with the difficulty of the task.

29-3: Do different emotions activate different physiological responses?

When two emotions are similarly arousing, the physiological responses that accompany them are nearly indistinguishable to an untrained observer. However, scientists have discovered subtle differences in activity in the brain's cortical areas, in use of brain pathways, and in secretion of hormones associated with different emotions.

Polygraphs measure several physiological indicators of emotion. Although they detect lies at a rate better than chance, they are not accurate enough to justify their widespread use in business and government. The use of guilty knowledge questions may increase the accuracy of these tests.

29-4: To experience emotions, must we consciously interpret and label them?

Stanley Schachter's two-factor theory of emotion contends that the cognitive labels we put on our states of arousal are an essential ingredient of emotion. Richard Lazarus agreed that cognition is essential: Many important emotions arise from our interpretations or inferences. Robert Zajonc and Joseph LeDoux, however, believe that some simple emotional responses occur instantly, not only outside our conscious awareness but before any cognitive processing occurs. The issue has practical implications: To the degree that emotions are rooted in thinking, we can hope to change them by changing our thinking.

>> REHEARSE IT!

1. Two important theories of emotion are the James-Lange theory and the Cannon-Bard theory. The James-Lange theory states that our experience of an emotion is a consequence of our physiological response to a stimulus; we are afraid because our heart pounds. The Cannon-Bard theory proposes that the physiological response (like heart pounding) and the subjective experience of, say, fear

   a. are unrelated.
   b. occur simultaneously.
   c. occur in the opposite order (with feelings of fear first).
   d. are regulated by the thalamus.

2. Assume that after spending an hour on a treadmill, you receive a letter saying that your scholarship request has been approved. The two-factor theory of emotion would predict that your physical arousal will

   a. weaken your happiness.
   b. intensify your happiness.
   c. transform your happiness into relief.

   d. have no particular effect on your happiness.

3. Research suggests that we can experience an aroused state as one of several different emotions, depending on how we interpret and label the arousal. If physically aroused by swimming, then heckled by an onlooker, we may interpret our arousal as anger and

   a. become less physically aroused.
   b. feel angrier than usual.
   c. feel less angry than usual.
   d. act euphoric.

4. Emotions such as fear and anger involve a general autonomic arousal orchestrated by the sympathetic nervous system. In many situations, arousal is adaptive. For example, with a challenging task, such as taking an exam, performance is likely to be disrupted when arousal is

   a. very high.
   b. moderate.
   c. low.
   d. diminishing.

5. Feelings of fear and anger involve a similar general autonomic arousal, but they activate different brain areas. For example, stimulate one area of a cat's _____ and the cat draws back in terror; stimulate another area of that structure and the cat hisses with rage.

   a. cortex
   b. hypothalamus
   c. reticular formation
   d. amygdala

6. Robert Zajonc and Joseph LeDoux maintain that some of our emotional reactions occur before we have had the chance to label or interpret them. Richard Lazarus disagreed. These psychologists differ about whether emotional responses occur in the absence of

   a. physical arousal.
   b. the hormone epinephrine.
   c. cognitive processing.
   d. learning.

Answers: 1. b, 2. b, 3. b, 4. a, 5. d, 6. c.

>> TERMS AND CONCEPTS TO REMEMBER

emotion, p. 407

James-Lange theory, p. 407

Cannon-Bard theory, p. 407

two-factor theory, p. 408

polygraph, p. 412

>> TEST YOURSELF

1. Christine is holding her 8-month-old baby when a fierce dog appears out of nowhere and, with teeth bared, leaps for the baby's face. Christine immediately ducks for cover to protect the baby, screams at the dog, then notices that her heart is banging in her chest and she's broken out in a cold sweat. How would the James-Lange, Cannon-Bard, and two-factor theories explain Christine's emotional reaction?

2. How do the two divisions of the autonomic nervous system help us respond to and recover from a crisis, and why is this relevant to the study of emotions?

(Answers in Appendix C.)

Multiple-choice **self-tests** and more may be found at www.worthpublishers.com/myers.

Expressing and Experiencing Emotion

Expressed Emotion

30-1: How do we communicate nonverbally?

There is a simple method of deciphering people's emotions: We read their bodies, listen to their tone of voice, and study their faces. People's expressive behavior reveals their emotion. Does this nonverbal language vary with culture, or is it universal? And do our expressions influence our experienced emotions?

Detecting Emotion

All of us communicate nonverbally as well as verbally. To Westerners, a firm handshake immediately conveys an outgoing, expressive personality (Chaplin & others, 2000). With a gaze, an averted glance, or a stare we can communicate intimacy, submission, or dominance (Kleinke, 1986). Among those passionately in love, gazing into one another's eyes is typically prolonged and mutual (Rubin, 1970). Joan Kellerman, James Lewis, and James Laird (1989) wondered if intimate gazes would stir such feelings between strangers. To find out, they asked unacquainted male-female pairs to gaze intently for two minutes either at one another's hands or into one another's eyes. After separating, the eye-gazers reported feeling a tingle of attraction and affection.

Most of us are good enough at reading nonverbal cues to decipher the emotions in an old silent film. We are especially good at detecting nonverbal threats. When hearing emotions conveyed in another language, people most readily detect anger (Scherer & others, 2001). When viewing subliminally flashed words, we more often sense the presence of a negative word, such as *snake* or *bomb* (Dijksterhuis & Aarts, 2003). In a crowd of faces, a single angry face will "pop out" faster than a single happy one (Fox & others, 2000; Hansen & Hansen, 1988; Öhman & others, 2001).

By exposing different parts of emotion-laden faces, Robert Kestenbaum (1992) discovered that we read fear and anger mostly from the eyes, and happiness from the mouth. Some of us are more sensitive than others to such cues. Robert Rosenthal, Judith Hall, and their colleagues (1979) discovered this by showing hundreds of people brief film clips of portions of a person's emotionally expressive face or body, sometimes accompanied by a garbled voice. For example, after a 2-second scene revealing only the face of an upset woman, the researchers would ask whether the woman was criticizing someone for being late or was talking about her divorce. Rosenthal and Hall reported that, given such "thin slices," some people are much better than others at detecting emotion. Introverts tend to excel at reading others' emotions, although extraverts are themselves easier to read (Ambady & others, 1995).

Experience can sensitize us to particular emotions. Shown a series of faces that morphed from sadness or fear to anger, physically abused children are much quicker than other children to see anger (see **FIGURE 30.1** on the next page). Shown a face that is 60 percent fear and 40 percent anger, they are as likely to perceive anger as fear. Their perceptions become sensitively attuned to glimmers of danger signals that nonabused children miss.

"Your face, my thane, is a book where men may read strange matters."
Lady Macbeth to her husband, in William Shakespeare's *Macbeth*

Injected as part of the war on wrinkles, Botox paralyzes facial muscles that create wrinkles, allowing the overlying skin to relax and smooth. By erasing the subtle expressions of frown lines or twinkling eyes, might this cosmetic procedure hide subtle emotions?

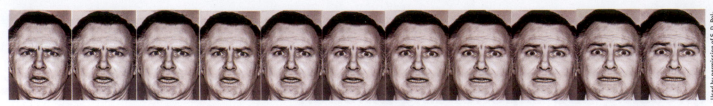

Used by permission of S. D. Pollack, D. J. Kistler and the National Academy of Sciences

FIGURE **30.1**

Experience influences how we perceive emotions

Viewing the morphed middle face, evenly mixing anger with fear (shown here) or sadness, physically abused children were more likely than nonabused children to perceive the face as angry (Pollak & Kistler, 2002; Pollak & Tolley-Schell, 2003).

Hard-to-control facial muscles reveal signs of emotions you may be trying to conceal. Lifting just the inner part of your eyebrows, which few people do consciously, reveals distress or worry. Eyebrows raised and pulled together signal fear. Activated muscles under the eyes and raised cheeks suggest a natural smile. A feigned smile, such as one we make for a photographer, often continues for more than 4 or 5 seconds. Most authentic expressions have faded by that time. Feigned smiles are also switched on and off more abruptly than is a genuine happy smile (Bugental, 1986).

Dr. Paul Ekman, University of California at San Francisco

Which of Paul Ekman's smiles is feigned, which natural?

The smile on the right engages the facial muscles of a natural smile.

Our brains are rather amazing detectors of subtle expressions. Elisha Babad, Frank Bernieri, and Robert Rosenthal (1991) discovered just *how* amazing after videotaping teachers talking to unseen schoolchildren. A mere 10-second clip of either the teacher's voice or face provided enough clues for both young and old viewers to determine whether the teacher liked and admired the child he or she was addressing.

Specific interpretations of postures and gestures are risky, however. Fidgeting, for example, may reveal anxiety *or* boredom. Either a cold stare *or* the avoidance of eye contact may signify hostility. Folded arms may convey either irritation *or* relaxation.

A silent language of emotion

Hindu classic dance uses the face and body to effectively convey 10 different emotions (Hejmadi & others, 2000).

Network Photographers/Alamy

Such gestures, facial expressions, and tones of voice are all absent in computer-based communication. E-mail communications sometimes include sideways *emoticons,* such as ;-) for a knowing wink and :-(for a frown. But e-mail letters and Internet discussions otherwise lack nonverbal cues to status, personality, and age. Nobody knows what you look or sound like, or anything about your background; you are judged solely on your words. When first meeting an e-mail pen pal face to face, people are often surprised at the person they encounter.

It's also easy to misread e-mailed communications, where the absence of expressive e-motion can make for ambiguous emotion. So can the absence of those vocal nuances by which we signal that a statement is serious, kidding, or sarcastic. Research by Justin Kruger and his colleagues (1999) shows that communicators often think their "just kidding" intent is equally clear, whether e-mailed or spoken. But they commonly exhibit egocentrism by not foreseeing misinterpretations in the absence of nonverbal cues.

Gender, Emotion, and Nonverbal Behavior

Is women's intuition, as so many believe, superior to men's? Consider: As Jackie Larsen left her Grand Marais, Minnesota, church prayer group one April 2001 morning, she encountered Christopher Bono, a clean-cut, well-mannered youth. Bono's car had broken down, and he said he was looking for a ride to meet friends in Thunder Bay. When Bono later appeared in Larsen's shop, where she had promised to help him phone his friends, she felt a pain in her stomach. Intuitively sensing that something was very wrong with this young man, she insisted that they talk outside on the sidewalk. "I said, 'I am a mother and I have to talk to you like a mother. . . . I can tell by your manners that you have a nice mother.'" At the mention of his mother, Bono's eyes fixed on her. "I don't know where my mother is," he said.

As the conversation ended, Larsen directed Bono back to the church to meet the pastor. She also called the police and suggested that they trace his license plates. The car was registered to his mother in southern Illinois. When police went to her apartment, they found blood all over and Lucia Bono dead in the bathtub. Christopher Bono, 16, was charged with first-degree murder (Biggs, 2001).

Was it a coincidence that Larsen, who saw through Bono's calm exterior, was a woman? Some psychologists would say no. In her analysis of 125 studies of sensitivity to nonverbal cues, Judith Hall (1984, 1987) discerned that, when given "thin slices," women generally surpass men at reading people's emotional cues. Women's nonverbal sensitivity also gives them an edge in spotting lies (DePaulo, 1994). And women have surpassed men in discerning whether a male-female couple is a genuine romantic couple or a posed phony couple, and in discerning which of two people in a photo is the other's supervisor (Barnes & Sternberg, 1989).

Women's nonverbal sensitivity helps explain their greater emotional literacy. Invited by Lisa Feldman Barrett and her colleagues (2000) to describe how they would feel in certain situations, men described simpler emotional reactions. You might like to try this yourself: Ask some people how they might feel when saying good-bye to friends after graduation. Barrett's work suggests you are more likely to hear men say, simply, "I'll feel bad," and to hear women express more complex emotions: "It will be bittersweet; I'll feel both happy and sad."

Women's skill at decoding others' emotions may also contribute to their greater emotional responsiveness in both positive and negative situations (Grossman & Wood, 1993; Sprecher & Sedikides, 1993; Stoppard & Gruchy, 1993). In studies of 23,000 people from 26 cultures around the world, women more than men reported themselves open to feelings (Costa & others, 2001). That helps explain the extremely strong perception that emotionality is "more true of women"—a perception expressed by nearly 100 percent of 18- to 29-year-old Americans (Newport, 2001).

When surveyed, women are also far more likely than men to describe themselves as empathic. If you have *empathy,* you identify with others and imagine what it must be like to walk in their shoes. You rejoice with those who rejoice and weep with those who weep. Physiological measures of empathy, such as one's heart rate while seeing another's distress, reveal a much smaller gender gap than is reported in surveys (Eisenberg & Lennon, 1983). Nevertheless, females are more likely to *express* empathy—to cry and to report distress when observing someone in distress. Ann Kring and Albert Gordon (1998) observed this gender difference in videotapes of men and women students watching film clips that were sad (children with a dying parent), happy (slapstick comedy), or frightening (a man nearly falling off the ledge of a tall building). As **FIGURE 30.2** shows, the women reacted more visibly to each film

FIGURE 30.2

Gender and expressiveness

Although male and female students did not differ dramatically in self-reported emotions or physiological responses while viewing emotional films, the women's faces *showed* much more emotion. (From Kring & Gordon, 1998.)

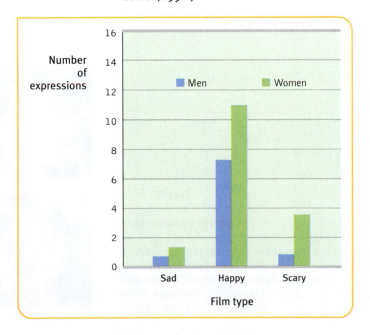

type. Women also tend to experience emotional events (such as viewing pictures of mutilation) more deeply—with more brain activation in areas sensitive to emotion—and then to remember the scenes better three weeks later (Canli & others, 2002).

In another exploration of gender and facial expression, Harold Hill and Alan Johnston (2001) animated an image of an average head with expressions (smirks, head tosses, raised eyebrows) that had been digitally captured from the faces of London University students as they read a joke. Despite having no anatomical clues to gender, observers could usually detect gender in the telltale expressions.

Culture and Emotional Expression

30-2 : Are nonverbal expressions of emotion universally understood?

The meaning of gestures varies with the culture. Some years ago, psychologist Otto Klineberg (1938) observed that in Chinese literature people clapped their hands to express worry or disappointment, laughed a great "Ho-Ho" to express anger, and stuck out their tongues to show surprise. Similarly, the North American "thumbs up" and "A-OK" signs are considered insults in certain other cultures. (When former U.S. President Richard Nixon made the latter sign in Brazil, he didn't realize he was saying "Let's have sex.") Just how important cultural definitions of gestures can be was demonstrated in 1968, when North Korea publicized photos of supposedly happy officers from a captured U.S. Navy spy ship. In the photo, three of the men raised their middle fingers; they had told captors it was a "Hawaiian good luck sign" (Fleming & Scott, 1991).

Do facial expressions also have different meanings in different cultures? To find out, two investigative teams—one led by Paul Ekman, Wallace Friesen, and others (1975, 1987, 1994), the other by Carroll Izard (1977, 1994)—showed photographs of different facial expressions to people in different parts of the world and asked them to guess the emotion. You can try this matching task yourself by pairing the six emotions with the six faces of **FIGURE 30.3**.

Regardless of your cultural background, you probably did pretty well. A smile's a smile the world around. Ditto for anger, and to a lesser extent the other basic expressions (Elfenbein & Ambady, 1999). (There is no culture where people frown when they are happy.) Despite some differences, cultures and languages share many similarities in the ways they categorize emotions—as anger, fear, and so on.

Do people from different cultures share these similarities because they share experiences, such as American movies, the BBC, and CNN? Apparently not. Ekman and his team asked isolated people in New Guinea to display various emotions in

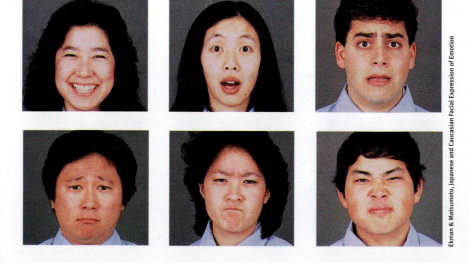

FIGURE 30.3
Culture-specific or culturally universal expressions?
As people of differing cultures and races, do our faces speak differing languages? Which face expresses disgust? Anger? Fear? Happiness? Sadness? Surprise? The answers are on this module's final page. (From Matsumoto and Ekman, 1989.)

Ekman & Matsumoto, Japanese and Caucasian Facial Expression of Emotion response to such statements as, "Pretend your child has died." When the researchers showed videotapes of the New Guineans' facial reactions to North American collegians, the students read them easily.

Facial expressions do contain some nonverbal accents that provide clues to one's culture (Marsh & others, 2003). So it is not surprising that data from 182 studies show slightly enhanced accuracy when people judge emotions from their own culture (Elfenbein & Ambady, 2002, 2003a,b). Still, the telltale signs of emotion generally cross cultures.

Children's facial expressions—even those of blind children who have never seen a face—are also universal (Eibl-Eibesfeldt, 1971). People blind from birth spontaneously exhibit the common facial expressions associated with such emotions as joy, sadness, fear, and anger (Galati & others, 1997). The world over, children cry when distressed, shake their heads when defiant, and smile when they are happy.

The discovery that facial muscles speak a fairly universal language would not have surprised pioneering emotion researcher Charles Darwin (1809–1882). He speculated that in prehistoric times, before our ancestors communicated in words, their ability to convey threats, greetings, and submission with facial expressions helped them survive. That shared heritage, he believed, is why all humans express the basic emotions with similar facial expressions. A sneer, for example, retains elements of an animal's baring its teeth in a snarl. Emotional expressions may enhance our survival in other ways, too. Surprise raises the eyebrows and widens the eyes, enabling us to take in more information. Disgust wrinkles the nose, closing it from foul odors.

Smiles, too, are social phenomena as well as emotional reflexes. Bowlers don't smile when they score a strike—they smile when they turn to face their companions (Jones & others, 1991; Kraut & Johnston, 1979). Even euphoric winners of Olympic gold medals typically don't smile when they are awaiting their ceremony but do when interacting with officials and facing the crowd and cameras (Fernández-Dols & Ruiz-Belda, 1995).

It has also been adaptive for us to interpret faces in particular contexts. People judge an angry face set in a frightening situation as afraid. They judge a fearful face set in a painful situation as pained (Carroll & Russell, 1996). Movie directors harness this phenomenon by creating contexts and soundtracks that amplify our perceptions of particular emotions.

Although cultures share a universal facial language for basic emotions, they differ in how much emotion they express. In cultures that encourage individuality, as in Western Europe, Australia, New Zealand, and North America, emotional displays often are intense and prolonged. People focus on their own goals and attitudes and express themselves accordingly. Watching a film of someone's hand being cut, Americans grimace (whether alone or with other viewers). Japanese viewers hide their emotions when in the presence of others (Triandis, 1994). Cultural differences exist both between and within nations. The Irish and their Irish-American descendants tend to be more expressive than Scandinavians and their Scandinavian-American descendants (Tsai & Chentsova-Dutton, 2003). And that reminds us of a familiar lesson: Like most psychological events, emotion is best understood not only as a biological and cognitive phenomenon, but also as a social-cultural phenomenon.

The Effects of Facial Expressions

30-3: Do our facial expressions influence our feelings?

As William James struggled with feelings of depression and grief, he came to believe that we can control emotions by going "through the outward movements" of any emotion we want to experience. "To feel cheerful," he advised, "sit up cheerfully, look around cheerfully, and act as if cheerfulness were already there."

> " For news of the heart, ask the face."
> Guinean proverb

While weightless, astronauts' fluids move toward their upper body and their faces become puffy. This makes nonverbal communication more difficult, increasing the risks of misunderstanding, especially among multinational crews (Gelman, 1989).

> "Whenever I feel afraid
> I hold my head erect
> And whistle a happy tune."
>
> Richard Rodgers and Oscar Hammerstein,
> *The King and I*, 1958

> "Refuse to express a passion and it
> dies. . . . If we wish to conquer undesirable
> emotional tendencies in ourselves, we
> must . . . go through the outward
> movements of those contrary dispositions
> which we prefer to cultivate."
>
> William James, *Principles of Psychology*, 1890

Recent findings concerning the emotional effects of facial expressions are precisely what James might have predicted. Expressions not only communicate emotion, they also amplify and regulate it. In his 1872 book, *The Expression of the Emotions in Man and Animals,* Darwin contended that "the free expression by outward signs of an emotion intensifies it. . . . He who gives way to violent gestures will increase his rage."

Was Darwin right? Let's test Darwin's hypothesis: Fake a big grin. Now scowl. Can you feel the "smile therapy" difference? Participants in dozens of experiments have felt a difference. For example, James Laird and his colleagues (1974, 1984, 1989) subtly induced students to make a frowning expression by asking them to "contract these muscles" and "pull your brows together" (supposedly to help the researchers attach facial electrodes). The results? The students reported feeling a little angry. Students similarly induced to smile felt happier, found cartoons funnier, and recalled happier memories than did the frowners. People instructed to mold their faces in ways that express other basic emotions also experienced those emotions. For example, they reported feeling more fear than anger, disgust, or sadness when made to construct a fearful expression: "Raise your eyebrows. And open your eyes wide. Move your whole head back, so that your chin is tucked in a little bit, and let your mouth relax and hang open a little" (Duclos & others, 1989). The face is more than a billboard that displays our feelings; it also feeds our feelings.

In the absence of competing emotions, this *facial feedback* effect is subtle yet detectable (**FIGURE 30.4**). Just activating one of the smiling muscles by holding a pen in the teeth (rather than with the lips, which activates a frowning muscle) is enough to make cartoons seem more amusing (Strack & others, 1988). A heartier smile—made not just with the mouth but with raised cheeks that crinkle the eyes—enhances positive feelings even more when you are reacting to something pleasant or funny (Soussignan, 2001). Smile warmly on the outside and you feel better on the inside. Scowl and the whole world seems to scowl back.

FIGURE 30.4
How to make people frown without telling them to frown
Randy Larsen, Margaret Kasimatis, and Kurt Frey's (1992) solution: Attach two golf tees above the eyebrows and ask people to make the tee tips touch. Research participants felt sad while viewing scenes of war, sickness, and starvation, and even sadder with their "sad face" muscles activated.

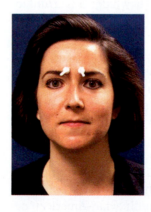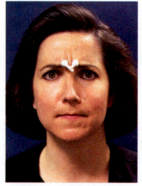

Courtesy of Louis Schakel/Michael Kausman/The New York Times Pictures

A request from your author: Smile often as you read this book.

Sara Snodgrass and her associates (1986) observed the *behavior feedback* phenomenon with walking. You can duplicate the participants' experience: Walk for a few minutes with short, shuffling steps, keeping your eyes downcast. Now walk around taking long strides, with your arms swinging and your eyes looking straight ahead. Can you feel your mood shift? Going through the motions awakens the emotions.

One small way to become more empathic—to feel what others feel—is to let your own face mimic another person's expression (Vaughn & Lanzetta, 1981). Acting as another acts helps us feel what another feels. Indeed, natural mimicry of others' emotions helps explain why emotions are contagious (Dimberg & others, 2000; Neumann & Strack, 2000).

Experienced Emotion

How many distinct emotions are there? Carroll Izard (1977) isolated 10 such basic emotions (joy, interest-excitement, surprise, sadness, anger, disgust, contempt, fear, shame, and guilt), most of which are present in infancy (**FIGURE 30.5**). Jessica Tracey and Richard Robins (2004) believe that pride is also a distinct emotion, signaled by a small smile, head slightly tilted back, and an open posture. And Phillip Shaver and his colleagues (1996) believe that love, too, may be a basic emotion. But Izard has argued that other emotions are combinations of these 10. Love, he says, is a mixture of joy and interest-excitement.

Let's take a closer look at two of these emotions: anger and happiness. What functions do they serve? What influences our experience of each?

(a) Joy (mouth forming smile, cheeks lifted, twinkle in eye)

(b) Anger (brows drawn together and downward, eyes fixed, mouth squarish)

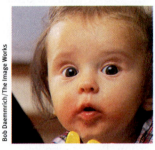
(c) Interest (brows raised or knitted, mouth softly rounded, lips may be pursed)

FIGURE 30.5
Infants' naturally occurring emotions
To identify the emotions present from birth, Carroll Izard analyzed the facial expressions of very young infants.

(d) Disgust (nose wrinkled, upper lip raised, tongue pushed outward)

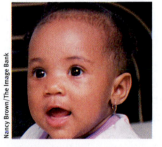
(e) Surprise (brows raised, eyes widened, mouth rounded in oval shape)

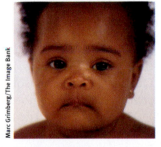
(f) Sadness (brow's inner corner raised, mouth corners drawn down)

(g) Fear (brows level, drawn in and up, eyelids lifted, mouth corners retracted)

Anger

30-4 : What are the causes and consequences of anger?

Anger, the sages have said, is "a short madness" (Horace, 65–8 B.C.) that "carries the mind away" (Virgil, 70–19 B.C.) and can be "many times more hurtful than the injury that caused it" (Thomas Fuller, 1654-1734). But they have also said, "noble anger" (William Shakespeare, 1564-1616) "makes any coward brave" (Cato, 234-149 B.C.) and "brings back . . . strength" (Virgil).

What makes us angry? To find out, James Averill (1983) asked people to recall or keep careful records of their experiences with anger. Most reported becoming at least mildly angry several times a week, some several times a day. The anger was often a response to friends' or loved ones' perceived misdeeds and was especially common when another person's act seemed willful, unjustified, and avoidable. But blameless annoyances—foul odors, high temperatures, a traffic jam, aches and pains—also have the power to make us angry (Berkowitz, 1990).

"I thought it would be nice if we had a forum where we could get together and have screaming tantrums."

> "Anger will never disappear so long as thoughts of resentment are cherished in the mind."
>
> The Buddha, 500 B.C.

What do we do with our anger? And what *should* we do with our anger? In a Gallup survey of teens, boys more than girls reported walking away from the situation or working it off with exercise; girls more often reported talking with a friend, listening to music, or writing (Ray, 2005).

When anger fuels physically or verbally aggressive acts we later regret, it becomes maladaptive. Anger also primes prejudice; after 9/11, Americans who responded with anger more than fear displayed intolerance for immigrants and Muslims (DeSteno & others, 2004; Skitka & others, 2004). And anger can harm us—chronic hostility is linked to heart disease (Smith & Ruiz, 2002; Williams, 1993). But controlled expressions of anger are more adaptive than either hostile outbursts or pent-up, angry feelings. Participants in Averill's research recalled that when they were angry they often reacted assertively rather than hurtfully. Their anger frequently led them to talk things over with the offender, thereby lessening the aggravation.

Popular books and articles on aggression at times advise that even releasing angry feelings as hostile outbursts can be better than internalizing them. When irritated, should we lash out at the offender? Was Ann Landers (1969) right that "youngsters should be taught to vent their anger"? Are "recovery" therapists right in encouraging us to rage at our dead parents, imaginatively curse the boss, or confront our childhood abuser?

Such encouragement to vent our rage is typical in individualized cultures, but it would seldom be heard in cultures where people's identity is centered more on the group. People who keenly sense their *inter*dependence see anger as a threat to group harmony (Markus & Kitayama, 1991). In Tahiti, for instance, people learn to be considerate and gentle. In Japan, from infancy on, angry expressions are less common than in Western cultures.

The Western "vent your anger" advice presumes that through aggressive action or fantasy we can achieve emotional release, or **catharsis.** Experimenters report that *sometimes* when people retaliate against a provoker, they may indeed calm down. But this tends to be true only *if* their counterattack is directed against the provoker, *if* their retaliation seems justifiable, and *if* their target is not intimidating (Geen & Quanty, 1977; Hokanson & Edelman, 1966). In short, expressing anger can be *temporarily* calming *if* it does not leave us feeling guilty or anxious.

However, despite the afterglow—people sometimes feel better afterward—catharsis usually fails to cleanse one's rage. More often, expressing anger breeds more anger. For one thing, it may provoke further retaliation, thus escalating a minor conflict into a major confrontation. For another, expressing anger can magnify anger. Ebbe Ebbesen and his colleagues (1975) saw this when they interviewed 100 frustrated engineers and technicians just laid off by an aerospace company. They asked some of the workers questions that released hostility, such as, "What instances can you think of where the company has not been fair with you?" When these people later filled out a questionnaire that assessed their attitudes toward the company, did this opportunity to "drain off" their hostility reduce it? Quite the contrary. Compared with those who had not vented their anger, those who had let it all out exhibited *more* hostility. Even when provoked people hit a punching bag *believing* it will be cathartic, the effect is the opposite—leading them to exhibit *more* cruelty (Bushman & others, 1999). And when they wallop a punching bag while ruminating about the person who angered them, they become even more aggressive when given a chance for revenge. "Venting to reduce anger is like using gasoline to put out a fire," concluded the researcher, Brad Bushman (2002).

Ironically, when angry outbursts do temporarily calm us, they may be reinforcing and therefore habit forming. If stressed managers find they can drain off some of their tension by berating an employee, then the next time they feel irritated and tense they may be more likely to explode again. Think about it: The next time you are angry you are likely to do whatever has relieved your anger in the past.

SIX CHIX

The catharsis myth: Is it true?

■ **catharsis** emotional release. In psychology, the catharsis hypothesis maintains that "releasing" aggressive energy (through action or fantasy) relieves aggressive urges.

What, then, is the best way to handle our anger? Experts offer two suggestions. First, wait. You can bring down the level of physiological arousal of anger by waiting. "It is true of the body as of arrows," noted Carol Tavris (1982), "what goes up must come down. Any emotional arousal will simmer down if you just wait long enough." Second, deal with anger in a way that involves neither being chronically angry over every little annoyance nor passively sulking, merely rehearsing your reasons for your anger. Ruminating inwardly about the causes of your anger serves only to increase it (Rusting & Nolen-Hoeksema, 1998). Don't join those who stifle their feelings over a series of provocations and then suddenly overreact to a single incident (Baumeister & others, 1990). Calm yourself in other ways, such as by exercising, playing an instrument, or talking it through with a friend.

Anger does communicate strength and competence (Tiedens, 2001). It can benefit a relationship when it expresses a grievance in ways that promote reconciliation rather than retaliation. Civility means not only keeping silent about trivial irritations but also communicating important ones clearly and assertively. A nonaccusing statement of feeling—perhaps letting one's housemate know that "I get irritated when you leave your dirty dishes for me to clean up"—can help resolve the conflicts that cause anger.

What if someone else's behavior really hurts you? Research suggests that the age-old response of forgiveness may be what the doctor ordered. Without letting the offender off the hook or inviting further harm, forgiveness releases anger and can calm the body. To explore the bodily effects of forgiveness, Charlotte Witvliet and her co-researchers (2001) invited college students to recall an incident where someone had hurt them. As the students mentally rehearsed forgiveness, their negative feelings—and their perspiration, blood pressure, heart rate, and facial tension—all were lower than when they rehearsed their grudges.

Wolfgang Kaehler

A cool culture
Domestic violence is rare in Micronesia. This photo of community life on Pulap Island suggests one possible reason: Family life takes place in the open on this island. Relatives and neighbors who witness angry outbursts can step in before the emotion escalates into child, spouse, or elder abuse.

Happiness

30-5 : What are the causes and consequences of happiness?

"How to gain, how to keep, how to recover happiness is in fact for most men at all times the secret motive for all they do," observed William James (1902, p. 76). People everywhere—in 48 countries on six continents in one study—also desire happiness for their children (Diener & Lucas, 2004). Understandably so, for one's state of happiness or unhappiness colors everything. People who are happy perceive the world as safer, make decisions more easily, rate job applicants more favorably, are more cooperative, and live healthier and more energized and satisfied lives (Lyubomirsky & others, 2005; Myers, 1993). When your mood is gloomy and your thinking preoccupied, life as a whole seems depressing. Let your mood brighten and your thinking broadens and becomes more playful and creative (Fredrickson, 2002, 2003). Your relationships, your self-image, and your hopes for the future also seem more promising. Positive emotions fuel upward spirals.

Moreover—and this is one of psychology's most consistent findings—when we feel happy we are more willing to help others. In study after study, a mood-boosting experience (finding money, succeeding on a challenging task, recalling a happy event) has made people more likely to give money, pick up someone's dropped papers, volunteer time, and do other good deeds. Psychologists call it the **feel-good, do-good phenomenon** (Salovey, 1990). Happiness doesn't just feel good, it does good. (Doing good also promotes good feeling, a phenomenon harnessed by some happiness coaches and instructors as they assign people to perform a daily "random act of kindness" and to record the results.)

■ **feel-good, do-good phenomenon** people's tendency to be helpful when already in a good mood.

■ **subjective well-being** self-perceived happiness or satisfaction with life. Used along with measures of objective well-being (for example, physical and economic indicators) to evaluate people's quality of life.

Despite the significance of happiness, psychology throughout its history has more often focused on negative emotions. Since 1887, *Psychological Abstracts* (a guide to psychology's literature) has included, as of this writing, 13,995 articles mentioning anger, 88,451 mentioning anxiety, and 112,556 mentioning depression. For every 17 articles on these topics, only one dealt with the positive emotions of joy (1639), life satisfaction (5696), or happiness (5251). There is, of course, good reason to focus on negative emotions; they can make our lives miserable and drive us to seek help. But researchers are becoming increasingly interested in **subjective well-being,** assessed either as feelings of happiness (sometimes defined as a high ratio of positive to negative feelings) or as a sense of satisfaction with life. A new *positive psychology* is on the rise.

The Short Life of Emotional Ups and Downs

In their happiness research, psychologists have studied influences on both our temporary moods and our long-term life satisfaction. When studying people's hour-by-hour moods, David Watson (2000) and Daniel Kahneman and his colleagues (2004) discovered that positive emotion rises over the early to middle part of most days (**FIGURE 30.6**). Studying people's reports of day-to-day moods confirms that stressful events—an argument, a sick child, a car problem—trigger bad moods. No surprise there. But by the next day, the gloom nearly always lifts (Affleck & others, 1994; Bolger & others, 1989; Stone & Neale, 1984). If anything, people tend to rebound from bad days to a *better*-than-usual good mood the following day. When in a bad mood, can you usually depend on rebounding within a day or two? Are your times of elation similarly hard to sustain? Over the long run, our emotional ups and downs tend to balance.

> "Weeping may tarry for the night, but joy comes with the morning."
>
> Psalms 30:5

Apart from prolonged grief over the loss of a loved one or lingering anxiety after a trauma (such as child abuse, rape, or the terrors of war), even tragedy is not permanently depressing. Learning that one is HIV-positive is devastating. But after five weeks of adapting to the grim news, those who tested positive felt less emotionally distraught than they had expected (Sieff & others, 1999). Kidney dialysis patients recognize that their health is relatively poor, yet in their moment-to-moment experiences they report being just as happy as healthy nonpatients (Riis & others, 2005). People who become blind or paralyzed also usually recover near-normal levels of day-to-day happiness (Gerhart & others, 1994; Myers, 1993). "If you are a paraplegic," explains Daniel Kahneman (2005), "you will gradually start thinking of other things, and the more time you spend thinking of other things the less miserable you are going to be." A major disability does often leave people less happy than the average person (Lucas, 2005). Yet they reportedly express considerably more happiness than able-bodied people with depression (Kübler & others, 2005; Schwartz & Estrin, 2004). Even patients "locked-in" a motionless body "rarely want to die," report Eimar Smith and Mark Delargy (2005), which "counters a popular misconception that such patients would have been better off dead."

FIGURE 30.6
Moods across the day
When psychologist David Watson (2000) sampled nearly 4500 mood reports from 150 people, he found this pattern of variation from the average levels of positive and negative emotions.

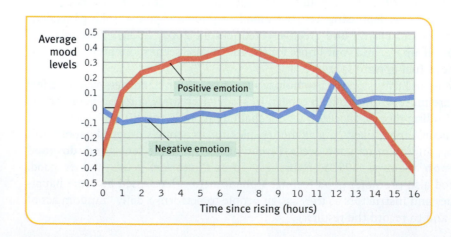

Courtesy of Anna Putt

Human resilience

Seven weeks after her 1994 wedding, Anna Putt of South Midlands, England, shown here with her husband, Des, suffered a brain-stem stroke that left her "locked-in." For months afterward, she recalls, "I was paralyzed from the neck down and was unable to communicate. These were VERY frightening times. But with encouragement from family, friends, faith, and medical staff, I tried to keep positive." In the ensuing three years, she became able to "talk" (by nodding at letters), to steer an electric wheelchair with her head, and to use a computer (by nodding while wearing spectacles that guide a cursor). Despite her paralysis, she reports that "I enjoy going out in the fresh air. My motto is 'Don't look back, move forward.' God would not want me to stop trying and I have no intention of doing so. Life is what you make of it!"

In less life-threatening contexts, the pattern continues. Faculty members up for tenure expect their lives would be deflated by a negative decision. Actually, 5 to 10 years later, those denied are not noticeably less happy than those who were awarded tenure, report Daniel Gilbert and colleagues (1998). The same is true of romantic breakups, which feel devastating. The surprising reality: *We overestimate the duration of emotions and underestimate our capacity to adapt.*

Wealth and Well-Being

The emotional impact of dramatically positive events also dissipates sooner than we might expect. Once their rush of euphoria wears off, state lottery winners typically find their overall happiness unchanged (Brickman & others, 1978). Other research confirms that there is much more to well-being than being well-off. Many people (including most German citizens, and most new American collegians, as **FIGURE 30.7** suggests) believe they would be happier if they had more money (Csikszentmihalyi, 1999).

They probably would be—temporarily. Yet in the long run, increased affluence hardly affects happiness. Even in Calcutta slums, people "are more satisfied than one might expect" (Biswas-Diener & Diener, 2001; Suhail & Chaudry, 2004). Wealth is like health: Its utter absence can breed misery, yet having it is no guarantee of happiness. Growing up poor puts one at risk for certain problems, but so does growing up rich. Children of affluence are at greater-than-normal risk for substance abuse, anxiety, and depression (Luthar & Latendresse, 2005).

During the last four decades, the average U.S. citizen's buying power more than doubled. Did this greater wealth—enabling twice as many cars per person, not to mention iPods, laptops, and camera cellphones—also buy more happiness? As **FIGURE 30.8** (see next page) shows, the average American, though certainly richer, is not happier. In 1957, some 35 percent said they were "very happy," as did slightly fewer—34 percent—in 2004.

> "I have a 'fortune cookie maxim' that I'm very proud of: Nothing in life is quite as important as you think it is while you are thinking about it. So, nothing will ever make you as happy as you think it will."
>
> Nobel Laureate psychologist Daniel Kahneman, Gallup interview, "What Were They Thinking?" 2005

> "Australians are three times richer than their parents and grandparents were in the 1950s, but they are not happier."
>
> *A Manifesto for Well-Being*, 2005

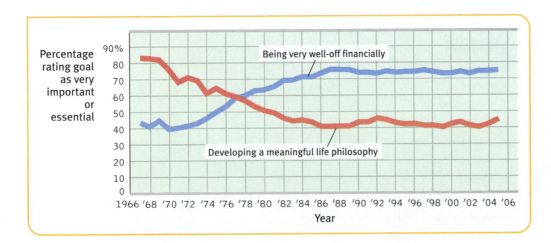

FIGURE 30.7

The changing materialism of entering college students

Surveys of more than 200,000 entering U.S. college students per year have revealed an increasing desire for wealth after 1970. (From *The American Freshman* surveys, UCLA, 1966 to 2005.)

FIGURE 30.8
Does money buy happiness?

It surely helps us to avoid certain types of pain. Yet, though buying power has almost tripled since the 1950s, the average American's reported happiness has remained almost unchanged. (Happiness data from National Opinion Research Center surveys; income data from *Historical Statistics of the United States* and *Economic Indicators*.)

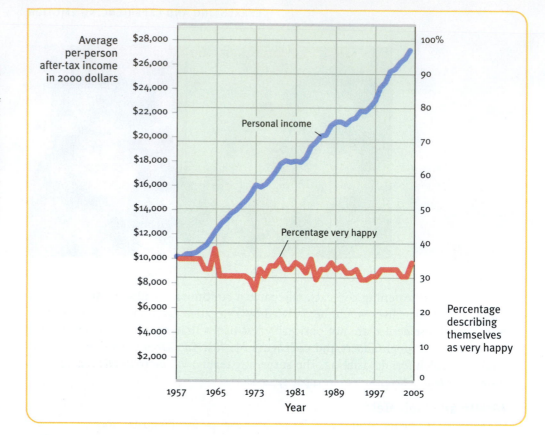

"Money won't make you happy, Waldron. So instead of a raise, I'm giving a Prozac."

> "Americans say that money doesn't bring happiness. But it helps you to live with misery in comfort."
>
> Farah Pahlavi, exiled widow of the wealthy Shah of Iran, 2004

Indeed, if we can judge from statistics—including doubled divorce and teen suicide rates, and mushrooming depression—contemporary Americans seem to be more often miserable. Much the same has been true of the European countries, Australia, and Japan: In these countries, people enjoy better nutrition, health care, education, and science, and they are somewhat happier than those in very poor countries (Diener & Biswas-Diener, 2002; Eckersley, 2000). Yet their increasing real incomes have *not* produced increasing happiness. And in the latest World Values Surveys of well-being in 82 countries, the happiest two—Puerto Rico and Mexico—were far from the richest (though the unhappiest, mostly in Eastern Europe, were economically stressed—see **TABLE 30.1**). Such findings lob a bombshell at modern materialism: *Economic growth in affluent countries has provided no apparent boost to morale or social well-being.*

"But on the positive side, money can't buy happiness—so who cares?"

TABLE 30.1

SUBJECTIVE WELL-BEING (COMBINED HAPPINESS AND SATISFACTION) IN 82 SOCIETIES

The Top 10	The Bottom 10
1. Puerto Rico	73. Bulgaria
2. Mexico	74. Belarus
3. Denmark	75. Georgia
4. Ireland	76. Romania
5. Iceland	77. Moldova
6. Switzerland	78. Russia
7. Northern Ireland	79. Armenia
8. Colombia	80. Ukraine
9. Netherlands	81. Zimbabwe
10. Canada	82. Indonesia

(The United States and Australia were in a virtual tie for fifteenth place.)

Source: Ronald Inglehart and others (2004)

What matters more than money (assuming one can afford life's necessities with a sense of security) is how you feel about what you have. Those who live with a sense of gratitude—or who cultivate their gratitude by each day writing down what they are grateful for—enjoy greater happiness (McCullough & others, 2004; Watkins, 2004).

Equally interesting are studies showing that individuals who strive hardest for wealth tend to live with lower well-being, a finding that "comes through very strongly in every culture I've looked at," reports Richard Ryan (1999). This is especially so for those seeking money to prove themselves, gain power, or show off rather than support their families (Srivastava & others, 2001). Ryan's collaborator, Tim Kasser (2000, 2002), concludes from their studies that those who instead strive for "intimacy, personal growth, and contribution to the community" experience a higher quality of life. A similar correlation appears among 7167 college students surveyed in 41 countries. Those who value love more than money report much higher satisfaction with life than do their money-hungry peers (**FIGURE 30.9**).

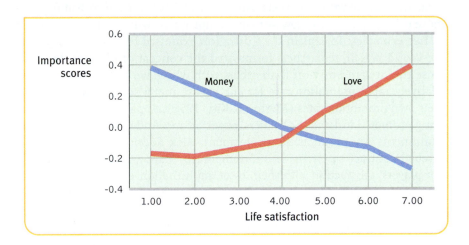

FIGURE 30.9

Values and life satisfaction

Among college and university students worldwide, those who report high life satisfaction give priority to love over money. (From Diener & Oishi, 2000.)

Two Psychological Phenomena: Adaptation and Comparison

Two psychological principles explain why, for all but the very poor, more money buys no more than a temporary surge of happiness and why our emotions seem attached to elastic bands that pull us back from highs or lows. In its own way, each principle suggests that happiness is relative.

Happiness and Prior Experience   The **adaptation-level phenomenon** describes our tendency to judge various stimuli relative to those we have previously experienced. As psychologist Harry Helson (1898–1977) explained, we adjust our *neutral* levels—the points at which sounds seem neither loud nor soft, temperatures neither hot nor cold, events neither pleasant nor unpleasant—based on our experience. We then notice and react to variations up or down from these levels.

So, could we ever create a permanent social paradise? Social psychologist Donald Campbell (1975) answered no: If you woke up tomorrow to your utopia—perhaps a

> "No happiness lasts for long."
>
> Seneca, *Agamemnon*, A.D. 60

> "Continued pleasures wear off. . . . Pleasure is always contingent upon change and disappears with continuous satisfaction."
>
> Dutch psychologist Nico Frijda (1988)

HI & LOIS

© 2001 by King Features Syndicate, Inc. World rights reserved.© H. L. Schwadron

■ **adaptation-level phenomenon** our tendency to form judgments (of sounds, of lights, of income) relative to a neutral level defined by our prior experience.

© *The New Yorker* Collection, 1999, William Hamilton from cartoonbank.com. All Rights Reserved.

"Shortly after I realized I had plenty, I realized there was plenty more."

world with no bills, no ills, perfect scores, someone who loves you unreservedly—you would feel euphoric, for a time. But then you would gradually recalibrate your adaptation level. Before long you would again sometimes feel gratified (when achievements surpass expectations), sometimes feel deprived (when they fall below), and sometimes feel neutral. *The point to remember:* Satisfaction and dissatisfaction, success and failure—all are relative to our recent experience. Satisfaction, as Ryan (1999) says, "has a short half-life."

■ **relative deprivation** the perception that one is worse off relative to those with whom one compares oneself.

> I have also learned why people work so hard to succeed: It is because they envy the things their neighbors have. But it is useless. It is like chasing the wind. . . . It is better to have only a little, with peace of mind, than be busy all the time with both hands, trying to catch the wind."
>
> Ecclesiastes 4:4

> Our poverty became a reality. Not because of our having less, but by our neighbors having more."
>
> Will Campbell, *Brother to a Dragonfly*, 1977

The effect of comparison with others helps explain why students of a given level of academic ability tend to have a higher academic self-concept if they attend a school where most other students are not exceptionally able (Marsh & Parker, 1984). If you were near the top of your high school class, you might feel inferior upon entering a college where everyone was near the top of their class.

Happiness and Others' Attainments Happiness is relative not only to our past experience but also to our comparisons with others (Lyubomirsky, 2001). We are always comparing ourselves with others. And whether we feel good or bad depends on who those others are. We are slow-witted or clumsy only when others are smart or agile.

Two examples: To explain the frustration expressed by U.S. Air Corps soldiers during World War II, researchers formulated the concept of **relative deprivation**—the sense that we are worse off than others with whom we compare ourselves. Despite a relatively rapid promotion rate for the group, many soldiers were frustrated about their own promotion rates (Merton & Kitt, 1950). Apparently, seeing so many others being promoted inflated the soldiers' expectations. And when expectations soar above attainments, the result is disappointment. Alex Rodriguez's 10-year, $252 million baseball contract surely made him temporarily happy, but it also diminished other star players' satisfaction with their lesser, multimillion-dollar contracts. Likewise, the economic surge that has made some urban Chinese newly affluent may have fueled among others a sense of relative deprivation (Burkholder, 2005a,b).

Such comparisons help us understand why the middle- and upper-income people in a given country, who can compare themselves with the relatively poor, tend to be slightly more satisfied with life than their less fortunate compatriots. Nevertheless, once people reach a moderate income level, further increases do little to increase their happiness. Why? Because as people climb the ladder of success they mostly compare themselves with peers who are at or above their current level (Gruder, 1977; Suls & Tesch, 1978). "Beggars do not envy millionaires, though of course they will envy other beggars who are more successful," noted Bertrand Russell (1930, p. 90). Thus, "Napoleon envied Caesar, Caesar envied Alexander, and Alexander, I daresay, envied Hercules, who never existed. You cannot, therefore, get away from envy by means of success alone, for there will always be in history or legend some person even more successful than you are" (pp. 68–69).

Just as comparing ourselves with those who are better off creates envy, so counting our blessings as we compare ourselves with those less well off boosts our contentment. Marshall Dermer and his colleagues (1979) demonstrated this by asking University of Wisconsin-Milwaukee women to study others' deprivation and suffering. After viewing vivid depictions of how grim life was in Milwaukee in 1900, or after imagining and then writing about various personal tragedies, such as being burned and disfigured, the women expressed greater satisfaction with their own lives. Similarly, when mildly depressed people read about someone who is even more depressed, they feel somewhat better (Gibbons, 1986). "I cried because I had no shoes," states a Persian saying, "until I met a man who had no feet."

Predictors of Happiness

If, as the adaptation-level phenomenon implies, our emotions tend to balance around normal, why do some people seem so filled with joy and others so gloomy day after day? What makes one person normally happy and another less so? The answers

TABLE 30.2

HAPPINESS IS . . .

Researchers Have Found That Happy People Tend To	However, Happiness Seems Not Much Related to Other Factors, Such As
Have high self-esteem (in individualistic countries).	Age.
Be optimistic, outgoing, and agreeable.	Gender (women are more often depressed, but also more often joyful).
Have close friendships or a satisfying marriage.	Education level.
Have work and leisure that engage their skills.	Parenthood (having children or not).
Have a meaningful religious faith.	Physical attractiveness.
Sleep well and exercise.	

Source: Summarized from DeNeve & Cooper (1998), Diener & others (2003), Lucas & others (2004), Myers (1993, 2000), and Myers & Diener (1995, 1996).

The New Yorker Collection, 2001, Pat Byrnes from cartoonbank.com. All Rights Reserved.

P. BYRNES

"Researchers say I'm not happier for being richer, but do you know how much researchers make?"

vary somewhat by culture. Self-esteem matters more to individualistic Westerners, social acceptance matters more to those in communal cultures (Diener & others, 2003). But across many countries, research does reveal several predictors of happiness (**TABLE 30.2**).

Although tasks and relationships affect our happiness, genes matter, too. From their study of 254 identical and fraternal twins, David Lykken and Auke Tellegen (1996) estimated that 50 percent of the difference among people's happiness ratings is heritable. Even identical twins raised apart are often similarly happy. Depending on our outlook and recent experiences, our happiness seems to fluctuate around our "happiness set point," which disposes some people to be ever upbeat and others more negative. But when researchers have followed thousands of lives over two decades, they observe that people's satisfaction with life is not fixed (Fujita & Diener, 2005; Mroczek & Spiro, 2005). Satisfaction may rise or fall, and happiness can be influenced by factors that are under our control. (See Close-Up: How to Be Happier.)

Our studies of happiness, regardless of their source and duration, remind us that emotions combine physiological activation (left hemisphere especially), expressive behaviors (huge smile), and conscious experience, including thoughts (I was so ready for that test) and feelings (pride, satisfaction). Anger, happiness, and so much else have this in common: They are biopsychosocial phenomena (**FIGURE 30.10**). Our genetic predispositions, brain activity, outlooks, experiences, relationships, and cultures jointly form us.

Studies of chimpanzees in zoos reveal that happiness in chimpanzees, as rated by 200 employees, is also genetically influenced (Weiss & others, 2000, 2002).

© *The New Yorker* Collection, 1996, J. B. Handelsman from cartoonbank.com. All Rights Reserved.

Handelsman

"I could cry when I think of the years I wasted accumulating money, only to learn that my cheerful disposition is genetic."

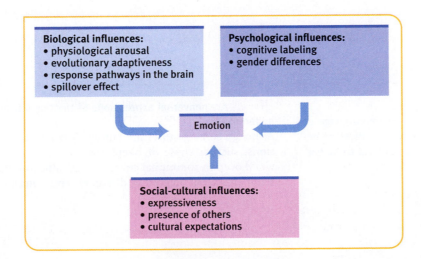

Biological influences:
- physiological arousal
- evolutionary adaptiveness
- response pathways in the brain
- spillover effect

Psychological influences:
- cognitive labeling
- gender differences

Emotion

Social-cultural influences:
- expressiveness
- presence of others
- cultural expectations

FIGURE 30.10

Levels of analysis for the study of emotion

As with other psychological phenomena, researchers explore emotion at biological, psychological, and social-cultural levels.

HOW TO BE HAPPIER

Happiness, like cholesterol level, is a genetically influenced trait. Yet as cholesterol is also influenced by diet and exercise, so our happiness is to some extent under our personal control. Here are some research-based suggestions for improving your mood and increasing your satisfaction with life.

1. *Realize that enduring happiness doesn't come from financial success.* People adapt to changing circumstances—even to wealth or a disability. Thus wealth is like health: Its utter absence breeds misery, but having it (or any circumstance we long for) doesn't guarantee happiness.

2. *Take control of your time.* Happy people feel in control of their lives, often aided by mastering their use of time. It helps to set goals and break them into daily aims. Although we often overestimate how much we will accomplish in any given day (leaving us frustrated), we generally underestimate how much we can accomplish in a year, given just a little progress every day.

3. *Act happy.* We can sometimes act ourselves into a frame of mind. Manipulated into a smiling expression, people feel better; when they scowl, the whole world seems to scowl back. So put on a happy face. Talk as if you feel positive self-esteem, are optimistic, and are outgoing. Going through the motions can trigger the emotions.

4. *Seek work and leisure that engage your skills.* Happy people often are in a zone called flow—absorbed in a task that challenges them without overwhelming them. The most expensive forms of leisure (sitting on a yacht) often provide less flow experience than gardening, socializing, or craft work.

5. *Join the "movement" movement.* An avalanche of research reveals that aerobic exercise not only promotes health and energy, it also is an antidote for mild depression and anxiety. Sound minds reside in sound bodies. Off your duffs, couch potatoes.

6. *Give your body the sleep it wants.* Happy people live active vigorous lives yet reserve time for renewing sleep and solitude. Many people suffer from sleep debt, with resulting fatigue, diminished alertness, and gloomy moods.

7. *Give priority to close relationships.* Intimate friendships with those who care deeply about you can help you weather difficult times. Confiding is good for soul and body. Resolve to nurture your closest relationships: to not take those closest to you for granted, to display to them the sort of kindness that you display to others, to affirm them, to play together and share together.

8. *Focus beyond self.* Reach out to those in need. Happiness increases helpfulness (those who feel good do good). But doing good also makes one feel good.

9. *Be grateful.* People who keep a gratitude journal—who pause each day to reflect on some positive aspect of their lives (their health, friends, family, freedom, education, senses, natural surroundings, and so on) experience heightened well-being.

10. *Nurture your spiritual self.* For many people, faith provides a support community, a reason to focus beyond self, and a sense of purpose and hope. That helps explain why people active in faith communities report greater-than-average happiness and often cope well with crisis.

Digested from David G. Myers, *The Pursuit of Happiness* (Avon Books).

REVIEWING

>> MODULE REVIEW

30-1: **How do we communicate nonverbally?**
Much of our communication is through the silent language of the body. Even very thin (seconds-long) videotaped slices of behavior can reveal feelings. Women and introverts tend to be better at reading people's emotional cues.

30-2: **Are nonverbal expressions of emotion universally understood?**
Although some gestures are culturally determined, facial expressions, such as those of happiness and anger, are common the world over. In communal cultures that value interdependence, intense displays of potentially disruptive emotions are infrequent.

30-3 : **Do our facial expressions influence our feelings?**
Expressions do more than communicate emotion to others. They also amplify the felt emotion and signal the body to respond accordingly. Emotions arise from the interplay of cognition, physiology, and expressive behaviors (**FIGURE 30.11**).

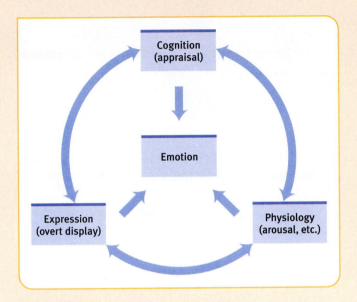

FIGURE 30.11
The ingredients of emotion
From the interplay of physiology, expression, and cognition comes emotion.

30-4 : **What are the causes and consequences of anger?**
Anger is most often evoked by events that not only are frustrating or insulting but also are interpreted as willful, unjustified, and avoidable. Blowing off steam (*catharsis*) may be temporarily calming, but in the long run it does not reduce anger. Expressing anger can actually make us angrier.

30-5 : **What are the causes and consequences of happiness?**
A good mood boosts people's perceptions of the world and their willingness to help others (the *feel-good, do-good phenomenon*). The moods triggered by the day's good or bad events seldom last beyond that day. Even significant good events, such as a substantial rise in income, seldom increase happiness for long. We can explain the relativity of happiness with the *adaptation-level phenomenon* and the *relative deprivation* principle. Nevertheless, some people are usually happier than others, and researchers have identified factors that predict such happiness.

>> REHEARSE IT!

1. Some nonverbal behaviors—threats and smiles, for example—are universally understood; others are not. People in different cultures are most likely to differ in their interpretations of
   a. adults' facial expressions.
   b. children's facial expressions.
   c. frowns.
   d. postures and gestures.

2. When people are induced to assume fearful expressions, they often report feeling a little fearful. This result is known as the _____ effect.
   a. facial feedback
   b. culture-specific
   c. natural mimicry
   d. emotional contagion

3. In some situations, venting anger— "blowing up"—seems to calm a person temporarily. More often, acting angry increases hostility. Experts suggest that to bring down anger, a good first step is to

   a. retaliate verbally or physically.
   b. wait or "simmer down."
   c. express anger in action or fantasy.
   d. review the grievance silently.

4. After graduating from college, you get a job and move into a large metropolitan city. At first, you find the street noise irritatingly loud, but after a while, it no longer bothers you, thus illustrating the

   a. relative deprivation principle.
   b. adaptation-level principle.
   c. feel-good, do-good phenomenon.
   d. catharsis principle.

5. A philosopher notes that one cannot escape envy by means of success alone: There will always be someone more successful, more accomplished, or richer with whom to compare oneself. In psychology, this observation is embodied in the

   a. relative deprivation principle.
   b. adaptation-level principle.
   c. need to belong.
   d. feel-good, do-good phenomenon.

6. When comparing happy and unhappy people, researchers find that happy people are optimistic, outgoing, and likely to have satisfying close relationships. One of the most consistent findings of psychological research is that happy people are also

   a. more likely to express anger.
   b. generally luckier than others.
   c. concentrated in the wealthier nations.
   d. more likely to help others.

7. Age, race, and gender seem not to be predictably related to subjective feelings of happiness or well-being. However, researchers have found that happy people tend to

   a. have children.
   b. score high on intelligence tests.
   c. have a meaningful religious faith.
   d. complete high school and some college education.

Answers: 1. d, 2. a, 3. b, 4. b, 5. a, 6. d, 7. c.

>> TERMS AND CONCEPTS TO REMEMBER

catharsis, p. 424

feel-good, do-good phenomenon, p. 425

subjective well-being, p. 426

adaptation-level phenomenon, p. 429

relative deprivation, p. 430

>> TEST YOURSELF

1. Who tends to express more emotion—men or women? How do we know the answer to that question?

2. What things do (and do not) predict self-reported happiness?

(Answers in Appendix C.)

>> ANSWER TO QUESTION WITHIN THE MODULE

Q. Which of the faces in Figure 30.3 expresses disgust? Anger? Fear? Happiness? Sadness? Surprise?

A. The photos in Figure 30.3 from left to right and top to bottom, express happiness, surprise, fear, sadness, anger, and disgust.

*Multiple-choice **self-tests** and more may be found at www.worthpublishers.com/myers.*

Stress and Illness

What happens when our emotional experiences are both negative and prolonged? How does the resulting *stress* affect our bodies?

Stress and Stressors

31-1 : What is stress?

Walking along the path toward his mountain campsite, Karl hears a rustle at his feet. As he glimpses a rattlesnake, his body mobilizes: His muscles tense, his adrenaline flows, his heart pounds, and he flees, racing to the security of camp. Once there, Karl's muscles gradually relax and his heart rate and breathing ease.

At about the same time, Karen leaves her suburban apartment and, delayed by road construction, arrives at the parking lot of the commuter train station just in time to see the 8:05 pull away. Catching the next train, she arrives in the city late and elbows her way through crowds of rush-hour pedestrians. Once at her bank office, she apologizes to her first client, who wonders where Karen has been and why his quarterly investment report is not ready. Karen does her best to mollify the client. Afterward, she notices her tense muscles, clenched teeth, and churning stomach.

Karl's response to stress saved his life; Karen's, if chronic, could increase her risk of serious illness or stress-linked health problems. Moreover, feeling under pressure, she might sleep and exercise less and smoke and drink more, further endangering her long-term health.

Four in 10 people frequently report experiencing stress (Saad, 2001). What are they talking about? Stress is a slippery concept. It sometimes describes threats or challenges ("Karen was under a lot of stress"), other times our responses ("When Karl saw the rattler, he experienced acute stress"). Karen's missed train was a *stressor,* Karl's physical and emotional responses were a *stress reaction,* and the process by which Karen and Karl related to their environments was *stress.*

Thus, **stress** is not just a stimulus or a response. It is the process by which we appraise and cope with environmental threats and challenges (**FIGURE 31.1**). Stress arises less from events themselves than from how we appraise them (Lazarus, 1998). One person, alone in a house, dismisses its creaking sounds and experiences no stress; someone else suspects an intruder and becomes alarmed. One person regards a new job as a welcome challenge; someone else appraises it as risking failure.

■ **stress** the process by which we perceive and respond to certain events, called stressors, that we appraise as threatening or challenging.

FIGURE 31.1
Stress appraisal
The events of our lives flow through a psychological filter. How we appraise an event influences how much stress we experience and how effectively we respond.

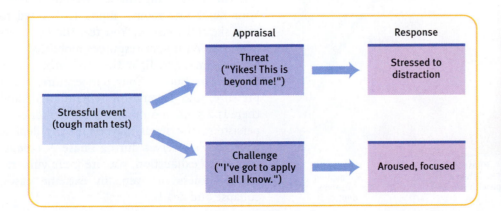

Appraisal

Response

Threat ("Yikes! This is beyond me!")

Stressed to distraction

Stressful event (tough math test)

Challenge ("I've got to apply all I know.")

Aroused, focused

Bob Daemmrich/The Image Works

When short-lived, or when perceived as challenges, stressors can have positive effects. A momentary stress can mobilize the immune system for fending off infections and healing wounds (Segerstrom & Miller, 2004). Stress also arouses and motivates us to conquer problems. Championship athletes, successful entertainers, and great teachers and leaders all thrive and excel when aroused by a challenge (Blascovich & others, 2004). Having conquered cancer or rebounded from a lost job, some people emerge with stronger self-esteem and a deepened spirituality and sense of purpose. Indeed, some stress early in life is conducive to later emotional resilience (Landauer & Whiting, 1979). Adversity can beget growth.

But stressors can also threaten us. And experiencing severe or prolonged stress may harm us. Children's physiological responses to severe child abuse put them at later risk of chronic disease (Repetti & others, 2002). Those who had post-traumatic stress reactions to heavy combat in the Vietnam War went on to suffer greatly elevated rates of circulatory, digestive, respiratory, and infectious diseases (Boscarino, 1997).

The Stress Response System

Medical interest in stress dates back to Hippocrates (460–377 B.C.). But it was not until the 1920s that Walter Cannon (1929) confirmed that the stress response is part of a unified mind-body system. He observed that extreme cold, lack of oxygen, and emotion-arousing incidents all trigger an outpouring of the stress hormones epinephrine and norepinephrine from the adrenal glands. This is but one part of the sympathetic nervous system's response. When alerted by any of a number of brain pathways, the sympathetic nervous system increases heart rate and respiration, diverts blood from digestion to the skeletal muscles, dulls pain, and releases sugar and fat from the body's stores—all to prepare the body for the wonderfully adaptive response that Cannon called *fight or flight*.

There are alternatives to fight-or-flight. One is a common response to the stress of a loved one's death: Withdraw. Pull back. Conserve energy. Another, especially common among women, report Shelley Taylor and her colleagues (2000), is to seek and give support: "Tend and befriend."

Canadian scientist Hans Selye's (1936, 1976) 40 years of research on stress extended Cannon's findings and helped make stress a major concept in both psychology and medicine. Selye studied animals' reactions to various stressors, such as electric shock, surgical trauma, and immobilizing restraint. He discovered that the body's adaptive response to stress was so general—like a single burglar alarm that sounds no matter what intrudes—that he called it the **general adaptation syndrome (GAS).**

Selye saw the GAS as having three phases (**FIGURE 31.2**). Let's say you suffer a physical or emotional trauma. In Phase 1, you experience an *alarm reaction* due to the sudden activation of your sympathetic nervous system. Your heart rate zooms. Blood is diverted to your skeletal muscles. You feel the faintness of shock. With your resources mobilized, you are now ready to fight the challenge during Phase 2, *resistance*. Your temperature, blood pressure, and respiration remain high, and there is a sudden outpouring of hormones. If persistent, the stress may eventually deplete your body's reserves during Phase 3, *exhaustion*. With exhaustion, you are more vulnerable to illness or even, in extreme cases, collapse and death.

FIGURE 31.2
Selye's general adaptation syndrome
This girl being carried to freedom and medical attention managed to escape her terrorist captors in a 2004, three-day Chechnya school holdup. After such a trauma, the body enters an alarm phase of temporary shock. From this it rebounds, as stress resistance rises. If the stress is prolonged, as it was for the 400 school hostages and their waiting loved ones, wear and tear may lead to exhaustion.

EPA/Yuri Kochetkov/Landow

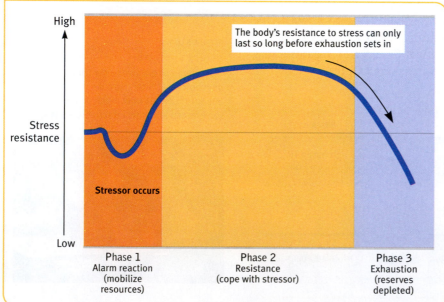

The body's resistance to stress can only last so long before exhaustion sets in

Stressor occurs

High

Stress resistance

Low

Phase 1	Phase 2	Phase 3
Alarm reaction (mobilize resources)	Resistance (cope with stressor)	Exhaustion (reserves depleted)

Few medical experts today quarrel with Selye's basic point: Although the human body comes designed to cope with temporary stress, prolonged stress can produce physical deterioration. Even fearful, easily stressed rats have been found to die sooner (after about 600 days) than their more confident siblings, which average 700-day life spans (Cavigelli & McClintock, 2004). Such findings serve as further incentives to today's health psychologists, as they ask, What causes stress? And how does stress affect us?

Stressful Life Events

31-2 : What events provoke stress responses?

Research has focused on our responses to three types of stressors: catastrophes, significant life changes, and daily hassles.

Catastrophes

Catastrophes are unpredictable large-scale events, such as war and natural disasters, that nearly everyone appraises as threatening. Although people often provide one another with aid as well as comfort after such events, the health consequences can be significant. In the three weeks after the 9/11 terrorist attacks, two-thirds of Americans surveyed by University of Michigan researchers said they were having some trouble concentrating and sleeping (Wahlberg, 2001). In another national survey, New Yorkers were especially likely to report such symptoms (NSF, 2001). Sleeping pill prescriptions rose by a reported 28 percent in the New York area (HMHL, 2002).

Do other community disasters usually produce effects this great? After digesting data from 52 studies of catastrophic floods, hurricanes, and fires, Anthony Rubonis and Leonard Bickman (1991) found the typical effect more modest but nonetheless genuine. In disaster's wake, rates of psychological disorders such as depression and anxiety rose an average 17 percent. Refugees fleeing their homeland also suffer increased rates of psychological disorder. Their stress stems from the trauma of uprooting and family separation, and from the challenges of adjusting to a foreign culture's new language, ethnicity, climate, and social norms (Pipher, 2002; Williams & Berry, 1991).

Significant Life Changes

The second type of life-event stressor is a significant personal life change—leaving home, the death of a loved one, the loss of a job, a marriage, a divorce. Life transitions and insecurities are often keenly felt during young adulthood. That helps explain why, when 15,000 Canadian adults were asked whether "You are trying to take on too many things at once," responses indicated highest stress levels among the youngest adults. The same is true of Americans: Half of adults under age 50 report "frequent" stress, as do fewer than 30 percent of those over 50 (Saad, 2001).

Some psychologists study the health effects of life changes by following people over time to see if such events precede illnesses. Others compare the life changes recalled by those who have or have not suffered a specific health problem, such as a heart attack. A review of these studies commissioned by the U.S. National Academy of Sciences revealed that people recently widowed, fired, or divorced are more vulnerable to disease (Dohrenwend & others, 1982). A Finnish study of 96,000 widowed people confirmed the phenomenon: Their risk of death doubled in the week following their partner's death (Kaprio & others, 1987). Experiencing a cluster of crises puts one even more at risk.

■ **general adaptation syndrome (GAS)** Selye's concept of the body's adaptive response to stress in three states—alarm, resistance, exhaustion.

Les Stone/Corbis

Toxic stress
On the day of its 1994 earthquake, Los Angeles experienced a fivefold increase in sudden-death heart attacks—especially in the first two hours after the quake and near its epicenter. Physical exertion (running, lifting debris) was a factor in only 13 percent of the deaths, leaving stress as the likely trigger for the others (Muller & Verrier, 1996).

"It's not the large things that send a man to the madhouse . . . no, it's the continuing series of small tragedies . . . not the death of his love but the shoelace that snaps with no time left."

Charles Bukowski, cited by Lazarus in Wallis, 1983

■ **coronary heart disease** the clogging of the vessels that nourish the heart muscle; the leading cause of death in many developed countries.

■ **Type A** Friedman and Rosenman's term for competitive, hard-driving, impatient, verbally aggressive, and anger-prone people.

■ **Type B** Friedman and Rosenman's term for easygoing, relaxed people.

In both India and America, Type A bus drivers are literally hard-driving: They brake, pass, and honk their horns more often than their more easygoing Type B colleagues (Evans & others, 1987).

Daily Hassles

Our happiness stems less from enduring good fortune than from our response to daily events—a perfect exam score, a gratifying e-mail, your team winning the big game. This principle works for negative events, too. Everyday annoyances—rush-hour traffic, aggravating housemates, long lines at the store, too many things to do, e-mail spam, and obnoxious cellphone talkers—may be the most significant sources of stress (Kohn & Macdonald, 1992; Lazarus, 1990; Ruffin, 1993). Although some people can simply shrug off such hassles, others are "driven up the wall" by them.

Over time, these little stressors can add up and take a toll on our health and well-being. Hypertension (high blood pressure) rates are high among residents of urban ghettos, where the stresses that accompany poverty, unemployment, solo parenting, and overcrowding are part of daily life for many people. And these daily pressures may be compounded by racism, which—like other stressors—can have both psychological and physical consequences. Thinking that some of the people you encounter each day will distrust you, dislike you, or doubt your abilities makes daily life stressful. Rodney Clark and his colleagues (1999) found that this stress took a toll on the health of many African-Americans, driving up blood pressure levels.

Stress and the Heart

31-3 : Why are some of us more prone than others to coronary heart disease?

Elevated blood pressure is just one of the factors that increase the risk of **coronary heart disease,** the closing of the vessels that nourish the heart muscle. Although infrequent before 1900, this condition became by the 1950s North America's leading cause of death, and it remains so today. In addition to hypertension and a family history of the disease, many behavioral and physiological factors—smoking, obesity, a high-fat diet, physical inactivity, and an elevated cholesterol level—increase the risk of heart disease. The psychological factors of stress and personality also play a big role.

In 1956, cardiologists Meyer Friedman, Ray Rosenman, and their colleagues stumbled upon an indication of how big that role is (Friedman & Ulmer, 1984). While studying the eating behavior of San Francisco women and their husbands, Friedman and Rosenman discovered that the women consumed as much cholesterol and fat as their husbands did, yet they were far less susceptible to heart disease. Was it because of their female sex hormones? No, the researchers surmised, because African-American women—with the same sex hormones but facing more *stress* than the white women—were as prone to heart disease as their husbands.

To test the idea that stress increases vulnerability to heart disease, Friedman and Rosenman measured the blood cholesterol level and clotting speed of 40 tax accountants. From January through March, both of these coronary warning indicators were completely normal. Then, as the accountants began scrambling to finish their clients' tax returns before the April 15 filing deadline, their cholesterol and clotting measures rose to dangerous levels. In May and June, with the deadline past, the measures returned to normal. The researchers' hunch had paid off: Stress predicted heart attack risk.

The stage was set for Friedman and Rosenman's classic nine-year study of more than 3000 healthy men aged 35 to 59. At the start of the study, they interviewed each man for 15 minutes about his work and eating habits. During the interview, they noted the man's manner of talking and other behavioral patterns. Those who seemed the most reactive, competitive, hard-driving, impatient, time-conscious, supermotivated, verbally aggressive, and easily angered they called **Type A.** The roughly equal number who were more easygoing they called **Type B.** Which group do you suppose turned out to be the most coronary-prone?

By the time the study was complete, 257 men had suffered heart attacks; 69 percent of them were Type A. Moreover, not one of the "pure" Type Bs—the most mellow and laid-back of their group—had suffered a heart attack.

As often happens in science, this exciting discovery provoked enormous public interest. But after the honeymoon period, in which the finding seemed definitive and revolutionary, other researchers began asking: Is the finding reliable? If so, what is the toxic component of the Type A profile: Time-consciousness? Competitiveness? Anger?

More recent research has revealed that Type A's toxic core is negative emotions—especially the anger associated with an aggressively reactive temperament (Smith & Ruiz, 2002; Williams, 1993). Type A individuals are more often "combat ready." When harassed or challenged, their active sympathetic nervous system redistributes bloodflow to the muscles and away from internal organs such as the liver, which removes cholesterol and fat from the blood. Thus, their blood may contain excess cholesterol and fat that later get deposited around the heart. Further stress—sometimes conflicts brought on by their own abrasiveness—may trigger the altered heart rhythms that, in those with weakened hearts, can cause sudden death (Kamarck & Jennings, 1991). In important ways, the hearts and minds of people interact.

The effect of an anger-prone personality appears most noticeably in studies in which interviewers assess verbal assertiveness and emotional intensity. (If you pause in the middle of a sentence, an intense, anger-prone person may jump in and finish it for you.) Among young and middle-aged adults, those who react with anger over little things are the most coronary-prone. One study followed 13,000 middle-aged people for five years. Among those with normal blood pressure, people who had scored high on anger were three times more likely to have had heart attacks, even after researchers controlled for smoking and weight (Williams & others, 2000). Another study followed 1055 male medical students over an average of 36 years. Those who had reported being hot-tempered were five times more likely to have had a heart attack by age 55 (Chang & others, 2002). As Charles Spielberger and Perry London (1982) put it, rage "seems to lash back and strike us in the heart muscle."

Pessimism seems to be similarly toxic. Laura Kubzansky and her colleagues (2001) studied 1306 initially healthy men who a decade earlier had scored as optimists, pessimists, or neither. Over the decade, pessimists were more than twice as likely as optimists to develop heart disease, even after other risk factors such as smoking had been ruled out (FIGURE 31.3).

Depression, too, can be lethal. The accumulated evidence from 57 studies suggests that "depression substantially increases the risk of death, especially death by unnatural causes and cardiovascular disease" (Wulsin & others, 1999). One study of 7406 women age 67 or older found that among those with no depressive symptoms, 7 percent died within six years, as did 24 percent of those with six or more depressive symptoms (Whooley & Browner, 1998). In the years following a heart attack, people with high scores for depression are four times more likely than their low-scoring counterparts to develop further heart problems (Frasure-Smith & Lesperance, 2005). Depression is disheartening.

> "The fire you kindle for your enemy often burns you more than him."
>
> Chinese proverb

> "A cheerful heart is a good medicine, but a downcast spirit dries up the bones."
>
> Proverbs 17:22

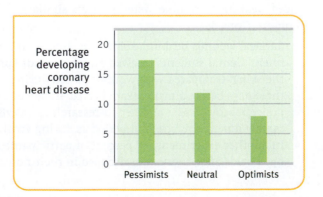

FIGURE 31.3

Pessimism and heart disease

A Harvard School of Public Health team found pessimistic adult men at doubled risk of developing heart disease over a 10-year period. (From Kubzansky & others, 2001.)

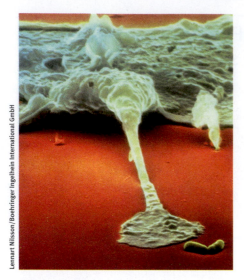

FIGURE 31.4
The immune system in action
A large macrophage (at top) is about to trap and ingest a tiny bacterium (lower right). Macrophages constantly patrol our bodies in search of invaders—such as this *Escherichia coli* bacterium—and debris, such as worn-out red blood cells.

> " In the eyes of God or biology or what have you, it is just very important to have women."
>
> Immunologist Normal Talal (1995)

■ **psychophysiological illness** literally, "mind-body" illness; any stress-related physical illness, such as hypertension and some headaches.

■ **psychoneuroimmunology (PNI)** the study of how psychological, neural, and endocrine processes together affect the immune system and resulting health.

■ **lymphocytes** the two types of white blood cells that are part of the body's immune system: *B lymphocytes* form in the bone marrow and release antibodies that fight bacterial infections; *T lymphocytes* form in the thymus and other lymphatic tissue and attack cancer cells, viruses, and foreign substances.

> " When the heart is at ease, the body is healthy."
>
> Chinese proverb

Stress and Susceptibility to Disease

31-4 : How does stress make us more vulnerable to disease?

Not so long ago, the term *psychosomatic* described psychologically caused physical symptoms. To laypeople, the term implied that the symptoms were unreal—"merely" psychosomatic. To avoid such connotations and to better describe the genuine physiological effects of psychological states, most experts today refer instead to stress-related **psychophysiological illnesses,** such as hypertension and some headaches. Stress also affects our resistance to disease, and this understanding has led to the burgeoning development of the field of **psychoneuroimmunology (PNI).** PNI studies how *psychological, neural,* and endocrine processes affect our *immune* system (psycho-neuro-immunology), and how all these factors influence our health and wellness.

Psychoneuroimmunology

Hundreds of new experiments reveal the nervous and endocrine systems' influence on the immune system (Sternberg, 2001). Your immune system is a complex surveillance system that defends your body by isolating and destroying bacteria, viruses, and other foreign substances. This system includes two types of white blood cells, called **lymphocytes.** *B lymphocytes* form in the bone marrow and release antibodies that fight bacterial infections. *T lymphocytes* form in the thymus and other lymphatic tissue and attack cancer cells, viruses, and foreign substances—even "good" ones, such as transplanted organs. Two other important agents of the immune system are the *macrophage* ("big eater"), which identifies, pursues, and ingests harmful invaders and worn-out cells (**FIGURE 31.4**), and the *natural killer cells* (NK cells), which pursue diseased cells (such as those infected by viruses or cancer). Age, nutrition, genetics, body temperature, and stress all influence the immune system's activity.

Your immune system can err in two directions. Responding too strongly, it may attack the body's own tissues, causing arthritis or an allergic reaction. Underreacting, it may allow a dormant herpes virus to erupt or cancer cells to multiply. Women are immunologically stronger than men (Morell, 1995), making them less susceptible to infections. But this very strength also makes them more susceptible to self-attacking diseases, such as lupus and multiple sclerosis.

Your immune system is not a headless horseman. The brain regulates the secretion of stress hormones, which suppress the disease-fighting lymphocytes. Thus, when animals are physically restrained, given unavoidable electric shocks, or subjected to noise, crowding, cold water, social defeat, or maternal separation, their immune systems become less active (Maier & others, 1994). One study monitored immune responses in 43 monkeys over six months (Cohen & others, 1992). Twenty-one were stressed by being housed with new roommates—three or four new monkeys—each month. (To empathize with the monkeys, recall the stress of leaving home to attend school or summer camp, and imagine having to repeat this experience monthly.) Compared with monkeys left in stable groups, the socially disrupted monkeys experienced weakened immune systems. Stress similarly depresses the immune system of humans. Consider:

- Surgical wounds heal more slowly in stressed animals and humans. In one experiment, dental students received punch wounds (precise small holes punched in the skin). Compared with wounds placed during summer vacation, those placed three days before a major exam healed 40 percent more slowly. In fact, report Janice Kiecolt-Glaser and her co-researchers (1998), "no student healed as rapidly during this stressful period as during vacation."
- In another experiment, 47 percent of participants living stress-filled lives developed colds after a virus was dropped in their noses, as did only 27 percent of

those living relatively free of stress (**FIGURE 31.5**). In follow-up research, the happiest and most relaxed people were likewise markedly less vulnerable to an experimentally delivered cold virus (Cohen & others, 2003).

- Managing stress may be life-sustaining. The one personality trait shared by 169 centenarians (people over 100) is their ability to manage stress well (Perls & others, 1999).

The stress effect on immunity makes physiological sense (Maier & others, 1994). It takes energy to fight infections, produce inflammations, and maintain fevers. Thus, when diseased, our bodies reduce muscular energy output by inactivity and increased sleep. But stress creates a competing energy need. Stress triggers an aroused fight-or-flight response, diverting energy from the disease-fighting immune system to the muscles and brain, rendering us more vulnerable to illness. *The bottom line:* Stress does not make us sick, but it does restrain our immune functioning, making us more vulnerable to foreign invaders.

Stress and AIDS

AIDS has become the world's fourth leading cause of death and the number one killer in Africa. AIDS, as its name tells us, is an immune disorder—an *acquired immune deficiency syndrome* caused by the *human immunodeficiency virus (HIV)*, which is spread by the exchange of bodily fluids, primarily semen and blood. If a disease spread by human contact kills slowly, as does HIV, it ironically can be lethal to more people: Those who carry the disease have time to spread it, often without realizing they are infected. When the HIV infection manifests itself as AIDS, some years after the initial infection, the person has difficulty fighting off other diseases, such as pneumonia. Worldwide, reports the United Nations, more than 25 million people have died of AIDS, including 3.1 million in 2005 (UNAIDS, 2005). (In the United States, where "only" a half-million of these fatalities have occurred, AIDS has killed more people than did combat in all the twentieth-century wars.) In 2005, worldwide some 40 million—half of them women—were infected with HIV, often without their awareness (UNAIDS, 2005). In Africa, UNAIDS (2005) warns, more than 80 million AIDS deaths are possible by 2025.

So if stress serves to suppress immune functioning, could it also exacerbate the course of AIDS? Researchers have found that stress and negative emotions do correlate with a progression from HIV infection to AIDS and with the speed of decline in those infected (Bower & others, 1998; Kiecolt-Glaser & Glaser, 1995; Leserman & others, 1999). HIV-infected men faced with stressful life circumstances, such as the loss of a partner, exhibit somewhat greater immune suppression and a faster disease progression.

Would efforts to reduce stress help control the disease? Although the benefits are small compared with available drug treatments, the answer appears again to be yes. Educational initiatives, bereavement support groups, cognitive therapy, and exercise programs that reduce distress have all had positive consequences for HIV-positive individuals (Baum & Posluszny, 1999; Schneiderman, 1999). Better yet is preventing HIV infection, which is the focus of many educational programs, such as the ABC (abstinence, being faithful, condom use) program used in many countries, with notable success in Uganda (Altman, 2004; USAID, 2004).

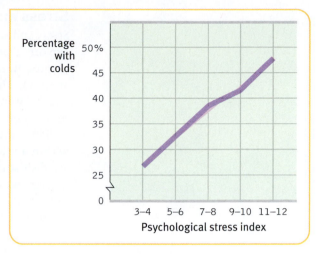

Percentage with colds (y-axis: 0, 25, 30, 35, 40, 45, 50%)
Psychological stress index (x-axis: 3–4, 5–6, 7–8, 9–10, 11–12)

FIGURE 31.5
Stress and colds

In an experiment by Sheldon Cohen and colleagues (1991), people with the highest life stress scores were also most vulnerable when exposed to an experimentally delivered cold virus.

In North America and Western Europe, 75 percent of people with AIDS are men. In Sub-Saharan Africa, 60 percent of people with AIDS are women (and among 15- to 24-year-olds, 75% are women). Girls' thin layer of cervical cells makes them especially vulnerable (Altman, 2004; UNAIDS, 2005).

Africa is ground zero for AIDS

In Lesotho and elsewhere, the "ABC" Campaign—Abstinence, Be Faithful, and use Condoms—forms part of prevention efforts.

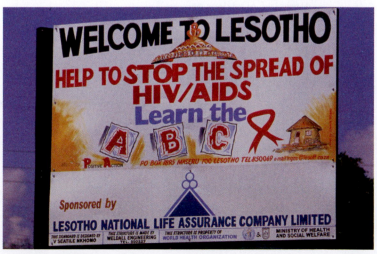
UNAIDS/G. Pirozzi

Stress and Cancer

Stress and negative emotions have also been linked to cancer's rate of progression. To explore a possible connection between stress and cancer, experimenters have implanted tumor cells into rodents or given them *carcinogens* (cancer-producing substances). Those rodents also exposed to uncontrollable stress, such as inescapable shocks, were more prone to cancer (Sklar & Anisman, 1981). In rodents with immune systems weakened by stress, tumors developed sooner and grew larger.

Some investigators have reported that people are at increased risk for cancer within a year after experiencing depression, helplessness, or bereavement. One large Swedish study revealed that people with a history of workplace stress had 5.5 times greater risk of colon cancer than those who reported no such problems, a difference not attributable to differing age, smoking, drinking, or physical characteristics (Courtney & others, 1993). Other researchers have found no link between stress and human cancer (Edelman & Kidman, 1997; Fox, 1998; Petticrew & others, 1999, 2002). Concentration camp survivors and former prisoners of war, for example, have not exhibited elevated cancer rates.

One danger in hyping reports on attitudes and cancer is that some patients may be led to blame themselves for their illness—"If only I had been more expressive, relaxed, and hopeful." A corollary danger is a "wellness macho" among the healthy, who take credit for their "healthy character" and lay a guilt trip on the ill: "She has cancer? That's what you get for holding your feelings in and being so nice." Dying thus becomes the ultimate failure.

The emerging view seems to be that stress does not create cancer cells. At worst, it may affect their growth by weakening the body's natural defenses against proliferating, malignant cells. Although a relaxed, hopeful state may enhance these defenses, we should be aware of the thin line that divides science from wishful thinking. The powerful biological processes at work in advanced cancer or AIDS are not likely to be completely derailed by avoiding stress or maintaining a relaxed but determined spirit (Anderson, 2002; Kessler & others, 1991).

We can view the stress effect on our disease resistance as a price we pay for the benefits of stress (**FIGURE 31.6**). Stress invigorates our lives by arousing and motivating us. An unstressed life would hardly be challenging or productive. Moreover, it pays to spend our resources in fighting or fleeing an external threat. But we do so at the cost of diminished resources for fighting internal threats to health. When the stress is momentary, the cost is negligible. When uncontrollable aggravations persist, the cost may become considerable.

> "I didn't give myself cancer."
>
> Mayor Barbara Boggs Sigmund, 1939–1990, Princeton, New Jersey

When organic causes of illness are unknown, it is tempting to invent psychological explanations. Before the germ that causes tuberculosis was discovered, personality explanations of TB were popular (Sontag, 1978).

FIGURE 31.6

Stress can have a variety of health-related consequences
This is especially so when experienced by "disease-prone" angry, depressed, or anxious persons.

Kathleen Finlay/Masterfile

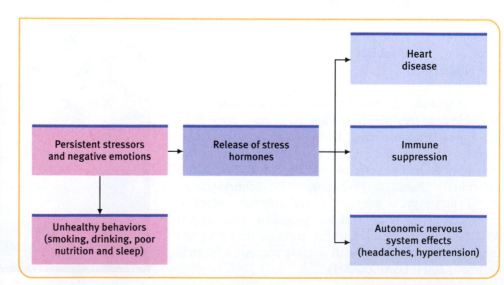

This *behavioral medicine* research, integrating behavioral and medical knowledge, provides yet another reminder of one of contemporary psychology's overriding themes: *Mind and body interact; everything psychological is simultaneously physiological.* Psychological states are physiological events that influence other parts of our physiological system. Just pausing to *think* about biting into an orange section—the sweet, tangy juice from the pulpy fruit flooding across your tongue—can trigger salivation. As the Indian sage Santi Parva recognized more than 4000 years ago, "Mental disorders arise from physical causes, and likewise physical disorders arise from mental causes." There is an interplay between our heads and our health. We are biopsychosocial systems.

REVIEWING

>> MODULE REVIEW

31-1: What is stress?

Walter Cannon viewed *stress,* the process by which we appraise and respond to events that challenge or threaten us, as a "fight-or-flight" system. Hans Selye saw it as a three-stage (alarm-resistance-exhaustion) *general adaptation syndrome (GAS).*

31-2: What events provoke stress responses?

Modern research on stress assesses the health consequences of catastrophic events, significant life changes, and daily hassles. The events that tend to provoke stress responses are those that we perceive as both negative and uncontrollable.

31-3: Why are some of us more prone than others to coronary heart disease?

Coronary heart disease, North America's number one cause of death, has been linked with the competitive, hard-driving, impatient, and (especially) anger-prone *Type A* personality. Under stress, the body of a reactive, hostile person secretes more of the hormones that accelerate the buildup of plaque on the heart's artery walls. *Type B* personalities are more relaxed and easygoing.

31-4: How does stress make us more vulnerable to disease?

Stress diverts energy from the immune system, inhibiting the activities of its B and T *lymphocytes,* macrophages, and NK cells. Although stress does not cause diseases such as cancer, it may influence the disease's progression.

>> REHEARSE IT!

1. The physiologist Walter Cannon described the role of the sympathetic nervous system in preparing the body for fight or flight. Hans Selye extended Cannon's findings by describing the body's adaptive response to stress in general. Selye's general adaptation syndrome (GAS) consists of an alarm reaction followed by

   a. fight or flight.
   b. resistance then exhaustion.
   c. challenge then recovery.
   d. stressful life events.

2. In the months following a catastrophe, such as an earthquake or hurricane, there is a higher-than-usual number of short-term illnesses and stress-related psychological disorders. Following widowhood, there is an increased risk of illness and death. These findings suggest that

   a. daily hassles have adverse health consequences.
   b. experiencing a very stressful event increases one's vulnerability to illness and death.
   c. the amount of stress felt is directly related to the number of stressors involved.
   d. having a negative outlook has an adverse effect on recovery from illness.

3. Stressors are events that we appraise as challenging or threatening. Research suggests that the most significant sources of stress are

   a. catastrophes.
   b. traumatic events, such as the loss of a loved one.
   c. daily hassles.
   d. threatening events that we witness.

4. Cardiologists Meyer Friedman, Ray Rosenman, and their colleagues observed that heart attacks were more frequent in Type A men—in those who appeared to be hard-driving, verbally aggressive, and anger-prone. The component of Type A behavior linked most closely to coronary heart disease is

   a. living a fast-paced life-style.
   b. working in a competitive area.
   c. meeting deadlines and challenges.
   d. feeling angry and negative much of the time.

5. Stress hormones suppress the lymphocytes, which ordinarily attack bacteria, viruses, cancer cells, and other foreign substances. The stress hormones are released mainly in response to a signal from the

a. lymphocytes and macrophages.
b. brain.
c. upper respiratory tract.
d. adrenal glands.

6. Research has shown that people are at increased risk for cancer a year or so after experiencing depression, helplessness, or bereavement. In describing this link between emotions

and cancer, researchers are quick to point out that

a. accumulated stress causes cancer.
b. anger is the negative emotion most closely linked to cancer.
c. stress does not create cancer cells, but it weakens the body's natural defenses against them.

d. feeling optimistic about chances of survival ensures that a cancer patient will get well.

Answers: 1. b, 2. b, 3. c, 4. d, 5. b, 6. c.

>> TERMS AND CONCEPTS TO REMEMBER

stress, p. 435
general adaptation syndrome (GAS), p. 436
coronary heart disease, p. 438

Type A, p. 438
Type B, p. 438
psychophysiological illness, p. 440

psychoneuroimmunology, p. 440
lymphocytes, p. 440

>> TEST YOURSELF

1. What are the basic links in our stress response system?

   (Answer in Appendix C.)

*Multiple-choice **self-tests** and more may be found at www.worthpublishers.com/myers.*

Promoting Health

Promoting health begins with implementing strategies that prevent illness and enhance wellness. Traditionally, people have thought about their health only when something goes wrong—visiting a physician for diagnosis and treatment. That, say health psychologists, is like ignoring a car's maintenance and going to a mechanic only when the car breaks down. Now that we realize that our attitudes and behaviors affect our health, we are turning our attention to health maintenance—ways of coping with stress, preventing illness, and promoting well-being.

Coping With Stress

32-1: What factors affect our ability to cope with stress?

Stressors are unavoidable. This fact, coupled with the growing awareness that persistent stress correlates with heart disease, lowered immunity, and other bodily ailments, gives us a clear message. We need to learn to cope with the stress in our lives by finding emotional, cognitive, or behavioral ways to alleviate it. We address some stressors directly, with *problem-focused coping*. For example, if our impatience leads to a family fight, we may go directly to that family member to work things out. If, despite our best efforts, we cannot get along with that family member, we may also incorporate an emotion-focused coping, such as reaching out to friends to help address our own emotional needs.

We tend to use problem-focused strategies when we feel a sense of control over a situation and think we can change the circumstances, or at least change ourselves to more capably deal with the circumstances. We turn to *emotion-focused* strategies when we cannot—or *believe* we cannot—change a situation. Sometimes these strategies are movements toward better long-term health, as when we attempt to gain emotional distance from a damaging, discontinued relationship or keep busy with active hobbies to avoid thinking about an old addiction. Emotion-focused strategies can be nonadaptive, however, as when students worried about not keeping up with the reading in class go out to party to get it off their mind. Sometimes a problem-focused strategy (catching up with the reading) more effectively reduces stress and promotes long-term health and satisfaction.

Several factors affect our ability to cope successfully, including our feelings of personal control, our explanatory style, and our supportive connections.

Perceived Control

If two rats receive simultaneous shocks, but one can turn a wheel to stop the shocks, the helpless rat, but not the wheel-turner, becomes more susceptible to ulcers and lowered immunity to disease (Laudenslager & Reite, 1984). In humans, too, uncontrollable threats trigger the strongest stress responses (Dickerson & Kemeny, 2004). For example, a bacterial infection often combines with uncontrollable stress to produce the most severe ulcers (Overmier & Murison, 1997). To cure the ulcer, kill the bug with antibiotics and control the stomach's acid secretions with reduced stress.

Perceiving a loss of control, we become vulnerable to ill health. Elderly nursing home residents who have little perceived control over their activities tend to decline faster and die sooner than do those given more control over their activities (Rodin,

1986). Workers given control over their work environment—by being able to adjust office furnishings and control interruptions and distractions—also experience less stress (O'Neill, 1993). This helps explain why British civil service workers at the executive grades outlive those at clerical or laboring grades, and why Finnish workers with low job stress are less than half as likely to die of cardiovascular disease (strokes or heart disease) as those with a demanding job and little control. The more control workers have, the longer they live (Bosma & others, 1997, 1998; Kivimaki & others, 2002; Marmot & others, 1997).

Control may also help explain a well-established link between economic status and longevity. In one study of 843 grave markers in an old graveyard in Glasgow, Scotland, those with the costliest, highest pillars (indicating the most affluence) tended to have lived the longest (Carroll & others, 1994). Likewise, Scottish regions with the least overcrowding and unemployment have the greatest longevity. There and elsewhere, high economic status predicts a lower risk of heart and respiratory diseases (Sapolsky, 2005). Wealthy predicts healthy among children, too (Chen, 2004). With higher economic status comes reduced risks of infant mortality, low birth weight, smoking, and violence. Even among other primates, those at the bottom of the social pecking order are more likely than their higher-status companions to become sick when exposed to a coldlike virus (Cohen & others, 1997). But for those high-status baboons and monkeys who frequently have to physically defend their dominant position, high status also entails stress (Sapolsky, 2005).

Why does perceived loss of control predict health problems? Animal studies show—and human studies confirm—that losing control provokes an outpouring of stress hormones. When rats cannot control shock or when primates or humans feel unable to control their environment, stress hormone levels rise, blood pressure increases, and immune responses drop (Rodin, 1986; Sapolsky, 2005). Captive animals therefore experience more stress and are more vulnerable to disease than are wild animals (Roberts, 1988). The crowding that occurs in high-density neighborhoods, prisons, and college dorms is another source of diminished feelings of control—and of elevated levels of stress hormones and blood pressure (Fleming & others, 1987; Ostfeld & others, 1987).

Laughter among friends is good medicine

Laughter arouses us, massages muscles, and then leaves us feeling relaxed (Robinson, 1983). Humor (though not hostile sarcasm) may defuse stress and strengthen immune activity (Berk & others, 2001; Kimata, 2001). People who laugh a lot also have exhibited a lower incidence of heart disease (Clark & others, 2001).

Explanatory Style

Another influence on our ability to cope with stress is whether our basic outlook is optimistic or pessimistic. Psychologists Michael Scheier and Charles Carver (1992) report that optimists—people who agree with statements such as, "In uncertain times, I usually expect the best"—perceive more control, cope better with stressful events, and enjoy better health. During the last month of a semester, students previously identified as optimistic report less fatigue and fewer coughs, aches, and pains. And during the stressful first few weeks of law school, those who are optimistic ("It's unlikely that I will fail") enjoy better moods and stronger infection-thwarting immune systems (Segerstrom & others, 1998). Optimists also respond to stress with smaller increases in blood pressure, and they recover more quickly from heart bypass surgery.

One study that followed 2428 middle-aged Finnish men for up to 10 years discovered that the number of deaths among men with a bleak, hopeless outlook was more than double that found among their optimistic counterparts. Another study asked 795 Americans aged 64 to 79 years if they were "hopeful about the future." When the researchers checked up on these folks about five years later, 29 percent of those answering "no" had died—more than double the 11 percent of deaths among those who said "yes" (Stern & others, 2001). Mayo Clinic research similarly finds that optimists tend to outlive pessimists (Maruta & others, 2002). That was also so among 180 Catholic nuns who at about 22 years of age wrote brief autobiographies. Despite living thereafter with similar life-styles and status, those who had expressed happiness, love, and other positive feelings lived an average seven years longer than their more dour counterparts (Danner & others, 2001). By age 80, some 54 percent of those expressing few positive emotions had died, as had only 24 percent of the most positive-spirited.

Social Support

Social support also matters. Consider Linda and Emily. When interviewed for a study conducted by UCLA social psychologist Shelley Taylor (1989), both Los Angeles women had married, raised three children, suffered comparable breast tumors, and recovered from surgery and six months of chemotherapy. But there was a difference. Linda, a widow in her early fifties, was living alone, her children scattered in Atlanta, Boston, and Europe. "She had become odd in ways that people sometimes do when they are isolated," reported Taylor. "Having no one with whom to share her thoughts on a daily basis, she unloaded them somewhat inappropriately with strangers, including our interviewer."

Interviewing Emily was difficult in a different way. Phone calls interrupted. Her children, all living nearby, were in and out of the house, dropping things off with a quick kiss. Her husband called from his office for a brief chat. Two dogs roamed the house, greeting visitors enthusiastically. All in all, Emily "seemed a serene and contented person, basking in the warmth of her family."

Three years later, the researchers tried to reinterview the women. Linda, they learned, had died two years before. Emily was still lovingly supported by her family and friends and was as happy and healthy as ever.

No two cancers are identical, so we cannot be certain that different social situations led to Linda's and Emily's fates. But they do illustrate a conclusion drawn from several large studies: Social support—feeling liked, affirmed, and encouraged by intimate friends and family—promotes not only happiness, but also health.

Relationships can sometimes be stressful, especially in crowded living conditions lacking privacy (Evans & others, 1989). "Hell is others," wrote Jean-Paul Sartre. Peter Warr and Roy Payne (1982) asked a representative sample of British adults what, if anything, had emotionally strained them the day before. Their most frequent answer? "Family."

But asked what prompted yesterday's times of pleasure, the same British sample, by an even larger margin, again answered, "Family." For most of us, family relationships provide not only our greatest heartaches (even when well-meaning, family intrusions can be stressful) but also our greatest comfort and joy. Moreover, seven massive investigations, each following thousands of people for several years, revealed that close relationships predict health. Compared with those having few social ties, people are less likely to die prematurely if supported by close relationships with friends, family, fellow workers, members of a faith community, or other support groups (Cohen, 1988; House & others, 1988; Nelson, 1988).

Carefully controlled studies indicate that married people live longer, healthier lives than the unmarried (Murray, 2000; Wilson & Oswald, 2002). The National Center for Health Statistics (2004) reports that regardless of people's age, sex, race, and income, they tend to be healthier if married. A seven-decades-long Harvard study found that a good marriage at age 50 predicts healthy aging better than does a low cholesterol level at 50 (Vaillant, 2002). But marital functioning also matters. Conflict-laden marriages are not conducive to health; positive, happy, supportive ones are (Kiecolt-Glaser & Newton, 2001).

Environments that support our need to belong foster stronger immune functioning. Given ample social support, spouses of cancer patients exhibit stronger immune functioning (Baron & others, 1990). Social ties and positive sociability even confer

> "Woe to one who is alone and falls and does not have another to help."
>
> Ecclesiastes 4:10

CLOSE-UP

PETS ARE FRIENDS, TOO

Jonathan Cavendish /Corbis

Have you ever wished for a friend who would love you just as you are, who is nonjudgmental, and who is always there for you, no matter your mood? For many tens of millions of people that friend exists, and it is a loyal dog or a friendly cat.

Many people describe their pet as a cherished family member who helps them feel calm, happy, and valued. Can pets also help people handle stress? If so, might pets have healing power? From her review of research, Karen Allen (2003) reports that, yes, pets have been found to increase the odds of survival after a heart attack, to relieve depression among AIDS patients, and to lower the level of blood lipids that contribute to cardiovascular risk. As nursing pioneer Florence Nightingale (1860) foresaw, "A small pet animal is often an excellent companion for the sick." Allen reports from her own research that women's blood pressure rises as they struggle with challenging math problems in the presence of a best friend or even a spouse, but much less so when accompanied by their dog.

So would pets be good medicine for people who do not have pets? To find out, Allen studied a group of stockbrokers who lived alone, described their work as stressful, and had high blood pressure. She randomly selected half to adopt an animal shelter cat or dog. When later facing stress, these new pet owners exhibited less than half the blood pressure increase of their counterparts without pets. The effect was greatest for those with few social contacts or friends. Her conclusion: For lowering blood pressure, pets are no substitute for effective drugs and exercise. But they are, for those who enjoy animals and especially for those who live alone, a healthy pleasure.

resistance to cold viruses. Sheldon Cohen and his colleagues (1997, 2004) demonstrated this by putting 276 healthy volunteers in quarantine for five days after administering nasal drops laden with a cold virus, and then repeating the experiment with 334 more volunteers. (In both experiments, the volunteers were paid $800 each to endure this experience.) The cold fact is that the effect of social ties is nothing to sneeze at. Age, race, sex, smoking, and other health habits being equal, those with the most social ties were least likely to catch a cold, and if they caught one, they produced less mucus. More sociability meant less susceptibility. More than 50 studies further reveal that social support calms the cardiovascular system, lowering blood pressure and stress hormones (Uchino & others, 1996, 1999). Humans aren't the only source of stress-buffering comfort. After stressful events, Medicare patients who have a dog or other companionable pet are less likely to visit their doctor (Siegel, 1990). (See Close-Up: Pets Are Friends, Too.)

Close relationships also provide the opportunity to *confide* painful feelings, a social support component that has now been extensively studied. In one study, health psychologists James Pennebaker and Robin O'Heeron (1984) contacted the surviving spouses of people who had committed suicide or died in car accidents. Those who bore their grief alone had more health problems than those who could express it openly. Talking about our troubles can be "open heart therapy."

Suppressing emotions is sometimes detrimental to our physical health. When Pennebaker surveyed more than 700 undergraduate women, he found that about 1 in 12 reported a traumatic sexual experience in childhood. Compared with women who had experienced nonsexual traumas, such as parental death or divorce, the sexually abused women—especially those who had kept their secret to themselves—reported more headaches and stomach ailments. Another study, of 437 Australian ambulance drivers, confirmed the ill effects of suppressing one's emotions after witnessing traumas (Wastell, 2002).

Writing about personal traumas in a diary can help (Hemenover, 2003; Lyubomirsky & others, 2006). When volunteers in one experiment did this, they had fewer health problems during the ensuing four to six months (Pennebaker, 1990). As one participant explained, "Although I have not talked with anyone about what I wrote, I was finally able to deal with it, work through the pain instead of trying to block it out. Now it doesn't hurt to think about it."

Pennebaker and his colleagues (1989) also invited 33 Holocaust survivors to spend two hours recalling their experiences. Many did so in intimate detail never before disclosed. In the weeks following, most watched a videotape of their recollections and showed it to family and friends. Those who were most self-disclosing had the most improved health 14 months later. Talking about a stressful event can temporarily arouse people, but in the long run it calms them (Mendolia & Kleck, 1993). Confiding is good for the soul.

Managing Stress Effects

31-2: What tactics can we use to manage stress and reduce stress-related ailments?

Having a sense of control, developing a more optimistic explanatory style, and building our base of social support can help us *experience* less stress and thus improve our health. But sometimes we cannot alleviate stress and simply need to *manage* our stress in a healthful way. Aerobic exercise, biofeedback, relaxation, meditation, and spirituality may help us gather inner strength and lessen the effects of stress.

Aerobic Exercise

Aerobic exercise is sustained exercise that increases heart and lung fitness. Jogging, swimming, and biking are common examples. Such exercise strengthens the body. Does it also boost the spirit?

Exercise and Mood

Many studies suggest that aerobic exercise can reduce stress, depression, and anxiety. For example, 3 in 10 American and Canadian people, and 2 in 10 British people who do aerobic exercise three times a week or more also manage stressful events better, exhibit more self-confidence, feel more vigor, and feel depressed and fatigued less often than those who exercise less (McMurray, 2004). In a 2002 Gallup survey, nonexercisers were twice as likely as exercisers to report being "not too happy" (Brooks, 2002). But if we state this observation the other way around—that stressed and depressed people exercise less—cause and effect become unclear.

Experiments have resolved this ambiguity by randomly assigning stressed, depressed, or anxious people either to aerobic exercise or to other treatments. In one such experiment, Lisa McCann and David Holmes (1984) assigned one third of a group of mildly depressed female college students to a program of aerobic exercise and another third to a treatment of relaxation exercises; the remaining third, a control group, received no treatment. As **FIGURE 32.1** shows, 10 weeks later the women in the aerobic exercise program reported the greatest decrease in depression. Many of them had, quite literally, run away from their troubles. Vigorous exercise provides a "substantial" immediate mood boost, reports David Watson (2000) from his monitoring of university students. Even a 10-minute walk stimulates two hours of increased well-being by raising energy levels and lowering tension (Thayer, 1987, 1993).

■ **aerobic exercise** sustained exercise that increases heart and lung fitness; may also alleviate depression and anxiety.

© The New Yorker Collection, 1993, Edward Koren from cartoonbank.com. All Rights Reserved.

"Is there anyone here who specializes in stress management?"

FIGURE **32.1**
Aerobic exercise and depression
Mildly depressed college women who participated in an aerobic exercise program showed markedly reduced depression, compared with those who did relaxation exercises or received no treatment. (From McCann & Holmes, 1984).

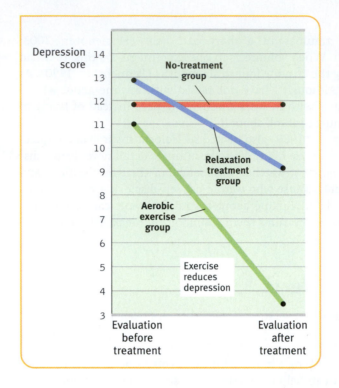

The mood boost
When one's energy or spirits are sagging, few things reboot the day better than exercising (as I can vouch from my daily noontime basketball). Aerobic exercise appears to counteract depression partly by increasing arousal (replacing depression's low-arousal state) and by doing naturally what Prozac does—increasing the brain's serotonin activity.

More than 150 other studies confirm that exercise reduces depression and anxiety and is therefore a useful adjunct to antidepressant drugs and psychotherapy (Arent & others, 2000; Berger & Motl, 2000; Dunn & others, 2005). Not only is exercise about as effective as drugs, some research suggests it better prevents symptom recurrence (Babyak & others, 2000; Salmon, 2001). Researchers are now wondering *why* aerobic exercise alleviates negative emotions. They know that exercise

- orders up mood-boosting chemicals from our body's internal pharmacy—neurotransmitters such as norepinephrine, serotonin, and the endorphins (Jacobs, 1994; Salmon, 2001).
- modestly enhances cognitive abilities, such as memory (Etnier & others, 1997).
- promotes the growth of new brain cells in mice exercising daily on a running-wheel regimen (Kempermann & Gage, 1999).

Perhaps the emotional benefits of exercise are also a side effect of increased warmth and body arousal (counteracting depression's low-arousal state), or of the muscle relaxation and sounder sleep that occur afterward. Or perhaps a sense of accomplishment and an improved physique enhance one's emotional state.

Exercise and Health

Other research reveals that exercise not only boosts our mood, but also strengthens the heart, increases blood flow, keeps blood vessels open, and lowers both blood pressure and the blood pressure reaction to stress (Ford, 2002; Manson, 2002). And being physically healthy may make us stronger and better able to manage our stress. Compared with inactive adults, people who exercise suffer half as many heart attacks (Powell & others, 1987). Exercise makes the muscles hungry for the "bad fats" that, if not used by the muscles, contribute to clogged arteries (Barinaga, 1997). One study following adult Finnish twins for nearly 20 years revealed that, other things being equal, occasional exercise reduced the risk of death by 29 percent, compared with no exercise. Daily conditioning exercise reduced death risk by 43 percent (Kujala & others, 1998).

By one estimate, moderate exercise adds not only quality of life (more energy and better mood) but also quantity of life—two additional years, on average. "Perhaps God does not subtract the time spent exercising from your allotted time on Earth," jested Martin Seligman (1994, p. 193).

Biofeedback, Relaxation, and Meditation

Knowing the damaging effects of stress, could we train people to counteract stress, bringing their heart rate and blood pressure under conscious control? When a few psychologists started experimenting with this idea, many of their colleagues thought them foolish. After all, these functions are controlled by the autonomic ("involuntary") nervous system. Then, in the late 1960s, experiments by respected psychologists made the skeptics wonder. Neal Miller, for one, found that rats could modify their heartbeat if given pleasurable brain stimulation when their heartbeat increased or decreased. Later research revealed that some paralyzed humans could also learn to control their blood pressure (Miller & Brucker, 1979).

Miller was experimenting with **biofeedback,** a system of recording, amplifying, and feeding back information about subtle physiological responses. Biofeedback instruments mirror the results of a person's own efforts, thereby allowing the person to learn techniques for controlling a particular physiological response (**FIGURE 32.2**).

After a decade of study, however, researchers decided the initial claims for biofeedback were overblown and oversold (Miller, 1985). A 1995 National Institutes of Health panel declared that biofeedback works best on tension headaches. Many have since turned to alternative medicine (see Thinking Critically About: Complementary and Alternative Medicine) in search of quick relief from stress and illnesses, but simple methods of relaxation, which require no expensive equipment, produce many of the same results biofeedback once promised.

Sixty studies find that relaxation procedures can help alleviate headaches, hypertension, anxiety, and insomnia (Stetter & Kupper, 2002). Such findings would not surprise Meyer Friedman and his colleagues. To find out whether teaching Type A heart attack victims (Type A people are, by definition, competitive, hard-driving, impatient, and anger-prone) to relax might reduce their risk of another attack, the researchers randomly assigned hundreds of middle-aged, male heart-attack survivors to one of two groups. The first group received standard advice from cardiologists concerning medications, diet, and exercise habits. The second group received similar advice plus continuing counseling on modifying their life-styles—how to slow down and relax by walking, talking, and eating more slowly; by smiling at others and laughing at themselves; by admitting mistakes; by taking time to enjoy life; and by renewing their religious faith. As **FIGURE 32.3** indicates, during the ensuing three years, the second group experienced half as many repeat heart attacks as the first group. This, wrote the exuberant Friedman, was an unprecedented, spectacular reduction in heart-attack recurrence. A smaller-scale British study similarly divided heart-attack–prone people into

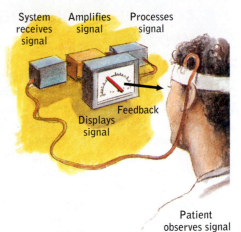

FIGURE 32.2
Biofeedback systems

Biofeedback systems—such as this one, which records tension in the forehead muscle of a headache sufferer—allow people to monitor their subtle physiological responses. As this man relaxes his forehead muscle, the pointer on the display screen (or a tone) may go lower.

■ **biofeedback** a system for electronically recording, amplifying, and feeding back information regarding a subtle physiological state, such as blood pressure or muscle tension.

FIGURE 32.3
Recurrent heart attacks and life-style modification

The San Francisco Recurrent Coronary Prevention Project offered counseling from a cardiologist to survivors of heart attacks. Those who were also guided in modifying their Type A life-style suffered fewer repeat heart attacks. (From Friedman & Ulmer, 1984.)

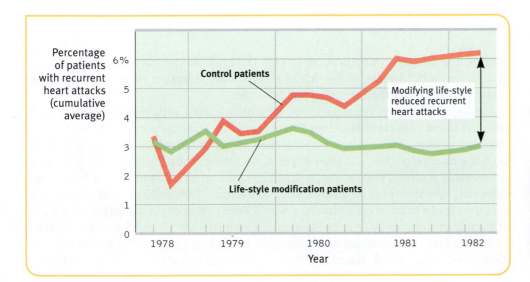

Percentage of patients with recurrent heart attacks (cumulative average)

Control patients

Life-style modification patients

Modifying life-style reduced recurrent heart attacks

Year

THINKING CRITICALLY ABOUT:

COMPLEMENTARY AND ALTERNATIVE MEDICINE

One health care growth market is **complementary and alternative medicine (CAM),** which encompasses some of the methods we've discussed, including relaxation, as well as acupuncture, massage therapy, homeopathy, spiritual healing, herbal remedies, chiropractic, and aromatherapy. In Germany, herbal remedies and homeopathy are enormously popular. In China, herbal therapies have long flourished, as have acupuncture and acupressure therapies that claim to correct "imbalances of energy flow" (called Qi or Chi) at identifiable points close to the skin. Andrew Weil's many books on alternative medicine have sold millions of copies, putting him on the cover of *Time* magazine. Facing political pressure to explore these techniques, the U.S. National Institutes of Health (NIH) established the National Center for Complementary

■ **complementary and alternative medicine (CAM)** as yet unproven health care treatments intended to supplement (complement) or serve as alternatives to conventional medicine, and which typically are not widely taught in medical schools, used in hospitals, or reimbursed by insurance companies. When research shows a therapy to be safe and effective, it usually then becomes part of accepted medical practice.

and Alternative Medicine, which the center defines as health care treatments not taught widely in medical schools, not usually reimbursed by insurance companies, and not used in hospitals (**TABLE 32.1**).

So what shall we make of CAM? Some aspects, such as life-style changes and stress management, have acknowledged validity, and certain techniques have proved useful for specific ailments, such as acupuncture, massage therapy, and aromatherapy for pain relief in cancer patients (Fellowes & others, 2004). Do the other aspects offer, as some believe, a new medical paradigm? Or do they represent, as others maintain, a retreat from rationality and science?

Critics point out that people consult physicians for diagnosable, curable diseases and turn to CAM techniques either for incurable illnesses or when well but feeling subpar. Thus, an otherwise healthy person with a cold may try an herbal remedy and then credit the subsequent return to good health to CAM, rather than to the body's natural return to normal. (Of course, the same may happen when people take traditional medicine for a cold.) CAM will seem especially

effective with cyclical diseases, such as arthritis and allergies, as people seek therapy during the downturn and presume its effectiveness during the ensuing upturn. Add to this the healing power of belief—the placebo effect—plus the natural disappearance (*spontaneous remission*) of many diseases, and CAM practices are bound to seem effective, whether they are or not. One study of 302 migraine headache patients in Germany found that 51 percent of those receiving acupuncture treatment found relief, as did only 15 percent of those in a waiting list control group. But among a third group that received "sham acupuncture" (needles inserted at nonacupuncture points), 53 percent enjoyed relief. Such results, the investigators suspected, may indicate "a powerful placebo effect" (Linde & others, 2005).

In November 1998, the *Journal of the American Medical Association* published seven new CAM research studies. Three explored treatments that proved useless (chiropractic manipulation for tension headaches, a popular herb for weight loss, and acupuncture to control nerve pain caused by HIV). Four other treatments, however—an herb mixture

control and life-style modification groups (Eysenck & Grossarth-Maticek, 1991). During the next 13 years, it also found a 50 percent reduction in death rate among those trained to alter their thinking and life-style.

Cardiologist Herbert Benson (1996) became intrigued with meditative relaxation when he found that experienced meditators could decrease their blood pressure, heart rate, and oxygen consumption and raise their fingertip temperature. You can experience the essence of this *relaxation response,* as Benson calls it, right now: Assume a comfortable position, breathe deeply, and relax your muscles from foot to face. Now, close your eyes and focus on a single word or a phrase. (About 80 percent of Benson's patients choose to focus on a favorite prayer.) When other thoughts intrude, let them drift away as you silently repeat your phrase continually for 10 to 20 minutes. Tibetan Buddhists deep in meditation and Franciscan nuns deep in centering prayer report a diminished sense of self, space, and time. Brain scans reveal the neural footprints of

Meditation is a modern phenomenon with a long history: "Sit down alone and in silence. Lower your head, shut your eyes, breathe out gently, and imagine yourself looking into your own heart. . . . As you breathe out, say 'Lord Jesus Christ, have mercy on me.' . . . Try to put all other thoughts aside. Be calm, be patient, and repeat the process very frequently" (Gregory of Sinai, died 1346).

TABLE 32.1

FIVE DOMAINS OF COMPLEMENTARY AND ALTERNATIVE MEDICINE

Alternative medical systems	Therapies used in place of conventional medicine, including homeopathy in Western cultures and traditional Chinese medicine and Ayurveda in non-Western cultures.
Mind-body interventions	Techniques designed to enhance the mind's capacity to affect bodily function and symptoms, including meditation, prayer, mental healing, and therapies that use creative outlets such as art, music, or dance.
Biologically based therapies	Therapies using natural substances such as herbs, foods, and vitamins.
Manipulative and body-based methods	Based on manipulation and/or movement of one or more parts of the body, including chiropractic or osteopathic manipulation, and massage.
Energy therapies	Use presumed energy fields. Biofield therapies, such as qi gong, Reiki, and therapeutic touch, are intended to affect energy fields that purportedly surround and penetrate the human body. Bioelectromagnetic-based therapies involve the unconventional use of electromagnetic fields, such as pulsed or magnetic fields.

Source: Adapted from the National Center for Complementary and Alternative Medicine, NIH http://nccam.nih.gov/health/whatiscam/

Much of today's mainstream medicine began as yesterday's alternative medicine. Natural botanical life has given us digitalis (from purple foxglove), morphine (from the opium poppy), and penicillin (from penicillium mold). In each case, the active ingredient was verified in controlled trials. We have medical and public health science to thank for the antibiotics, vaccines, surgical procedures, sanitation, and emergency medicine that helped lengthen our life expectancy by three decades during the last century.

"CAM changes continually," notes the National Center for Complementary and Alternative Medicine (2006), "as those therapies that are proven to be safe and effective become adopted into conventional health care." Indeed, said *New England Journal of Medicine* editors Marcia Angell and Jerome Kassirer (1998), "There cannot be two kinds of medicine—conventional and alternative. There is only medicine that has been adequately tested and medicine that has not, medicine that works and medicine that may or may not work. Once a treatment has been tested rigorously, it no longer matters whether it was considered alternative at the outset."

for inflammatory bowel syndrome, an herbal remedy for bladder problems, yoga for carpal tunnel syndrome pain, and a Chinese method for inducing fetuses in the breech position to turn—showed some benefits. As always, the way to discern what works and what does not is to experiment: Randomly assign patients to receive the therapy or a placebo control. Then ask the critical question: When neither the therapist nor the patient knows who is getting the real therapy, is the real therapy effective?

"In God we trust. All others must have data."
George Lundberg, Editor, Journal of the American Medical Association, 1998

such spiritual feelings during these mystical experiences: A part of the parietal lobe that tracks where we are in space is less active than usual, and a frontal lobe area involved in focused attention is more active (Newberg & D'Aquili, 2001).

Psychologist Richard Davidson reports that Buddhist monks who are experienced in meditation display elevated levels of the left frontal lobe activity associated with positive emotions. To explore whether such activity is a *result* of meditation, Davidson and his colleagues (2003) ran baseline brain scans of volunteers who were *not* experienced meditators, and then randomly assigned them either to a control group or to an eight-week course in "mindfulness meditation." Compared with both the control group and their own baseline, the meditation participants exhibited noticeably more left-hemisphere activity, and also improved immune functioning after the training. Such effects may help explain the astonishing results of a study that randomly assigned 73 residents of homes for the elderly either to daily meditation or to none. After three years, one-fourth of the nonmeditators had died, but all the meditators were still alive (Alexander & others, 1989). A more recent study found that hypertension patients assigned to meditation training had (compared with other treatment groups) a 30 percent lower cardiovascular death rate over the ensuing 19-year study period (Schneider & others, 2005).

Spirituality and Faith Communities

As humans suffered ills and sought healing throughout history, two healing traditions—religion and medicine—have joined hands in caring for them. Often those hands belonged to the same person—the spiritual leader was also the healer. Maimonides was a twelfth-century rabbi and a renowned physician. Hospitals, which were first established in monasteries and then spread by missionaries, often carry the names of saints or faith communities.

As medical science matured, healing and religion diverged. Rather than asking God to spare their children from smallpox, people were able to vaccinate them. Rather than seeking a spiritual healer when burning with bacterial fever, they were able to use antibiotics. Recently, however, religion and healing are converging once again. In 1992, 4 percent of American medical schools offered spirituality and health courses; in 2005, 75 percent did (Koenig, 2002; Puchalski, 2005).

More than a thousand studies have sought to correlate the *faith factor* with health and healing. For example, Jeremy Kark and his colleagues (1996) compared the death rates for 3900 Israelis either in one of 11 religiously orthodox or in one of 11 matched, nonreligious collective settlements (kibbutz communities). The researchers reported that over a 16-year period, "belonging to a religious collective was associated with a strong protective effect" not explained by age or economic differences. In every age group, religious community members were about half as likely to have died as were their nonreligious counterparts. This is roughly comparable to the gender difference in mortality.

In response to such findings, Richard Sloan and his skeptical colleagues (1999, 2000, 2002, 2005) remind us that mere correlations can leave many factors uncontrolled. Consider one obvious possibility: Women are more religiously active than men, and women outlive men. So perhaps religious involvement is merely an expression of the gender effect on longevity.

However, several new studies find the religiosity-longevity correlation among men alone, and even more strongly among women (McCullough & others, 2000, 2005). One study that followed 5286 Californians over 28 years found that, after controlling for age, gender, ethnicity, and education, frequent religious attenders were 36 percent less likely to have died in any year (**FIGURE 32.4**).

FIGURE 32.4

Predictors of mortality: not smoking, frequent exercise, and regular religious attendance

Epidemiologist William Strawbridge and his co-workers (1997, 1999; Oman & others, 2002) followed 5286 Alameda, California, adults over 28 years. After adjusting for age and education, the researchers found that not smoking, regular exercise, and religious attendance all predicted a lowered risk of death in any given year. Women attending weekly religious services, for example, were only 54 percent as likely to die in a typical study year as were nonattenders.

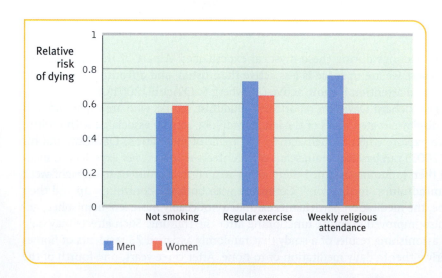

A U.S. National Health Interview Survey (Hummer & others, 1999) followed 21,204 people over 8 years. After controlling for age, sex, race, and region, researchers found that nonattenders were 1.87 times more likely to have died than were those attending more than weekly. This translated into a life expectancy at age 20 of 83 years for frequent attenders and 75 years for infrequent attenders (**FIGURE 32.5**).

These correlational findings do not indicate that nonattenders who start attending services and change nothing else will live 8 years longer. But they do indicate that as a *predictor* of health and longevity, religious involvement rivals nonsmoking and exercise effects. Such findings demand explanation. Can you imagine what intervening variables might account for the correlation?

First, religiously active people have healthier life-styles; for example, they smoke and drink less (Lyons, 2002; Strawbridge & others, 2001). Health-oriented, vegetarian Seventh Day Adventists have a longer-than-usual life expectancy (Berkel & de Waard, 1983). Religiously orthodox Israelis eat less fat than do their nonreligious compatriots. But such differences are not great enough to explain the dramatically reduced mortality in the religious kibbutzim, argued the Israeli researchers. In the recent American studies, too, about 75 percent of the longevity difference remains after controlling for unhealthy behaviors such as inactivity and smoking (Musick & others, 1999).

Social support is another variable that helps explain the faith factor (George & others, 2002). For Judaism, Christianity, and Islam, faith is not solo spirituality but a communal experience that helps satisfy the need to belong. The more than 350,000 faith communities in North America and the millions more elsewhere provide support networks for their active participants—people who are there for one another when misfortune strikes. Moreover, religion encourages another predictor of health and longevity—marriage. In the religious kibbutzim, for example, divorce has been almost nonexistent.

But even after controlling for gender, unhealthy behaviors, social ties, and preexisting health problems, the mortality studies find much of the mortality reduction remaining (George & others, 2000; Powell & others, 2003). Researchers therefore speculate that a third set of intervening variables is the stress protection and enhanced well-being associated with a coherent worldview, a sense of hope for the long-term future, feelings of ultimate acceptance, and the relaxed meditation of prayer or Sabbath observance (**FIGURE 32.6**). These variables might also help to explain other recent findings among the religiously active, such as healthier immune functioning and fewer hospital admissions and, for AIDS patients, fewer stress hormones and longer survival (Ironson & others, 2002; Koenig & Larson, 1998; Lutgendorf & others, 2004).

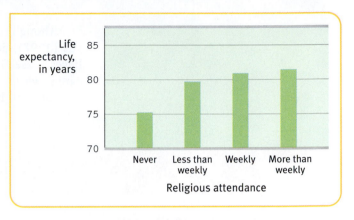

FIGURE 32.5

Religious attendance and life expectancy

In a national health survey financed by the U.S. Centers for Disease Control and Prevention, religiously active people had longer life expectancies. (Data from Hummer & others, 1999.)

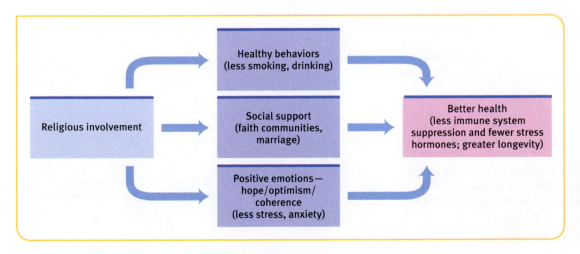

FIGURE 32.6

Possible explanations for the correlation between religious involvement and health/longevity

Although the religion-health correlation is yet to be fully explained, Harold Pincus (1997), deputy medical director of the American Psychiatric Association, believes these findings "have made clear that anyone involved in providing health care services . . . cannot ignore . . . the important connections between spirituality, religion, and health."

REVIEWING

>> MODULE REVIEW

32-1: **What factors affect our ability to cope with stress?**
Having a sense of control, developing a more optimistic explanatory style, and building our base of social support can help us reduce stress. Direct, problem-focused coping strategies are usually best, but emotion-focused coping can also be beneficial. Optimists seem to cope more successfully with stress and enjoy better health.

32-2: **What tactics can we use to manage stress and reduce stress-related ailments?**
Among the components of stress-management programs are *aerobic exercise, biofeedback,* and relaxation. Counseling Type A heart attack survivors to slow down and relax has helped lower rates of recurring attacks. Social support also helps people cope, partly by buffering the impact of stress. Researchers are investigating the active components of the religion-health correlation.

>> REHEARSE IT!

1. The stress we experience depends on how we perceive the events of our lives. A person (or animal) is most likely to find an event stressful and to suffer reduced immunity and other adverse health effects if the event seems
   a. painful or harmful.
   b. predictable and negative.
   c. uncontrollable and negative.
   d. both repellent and attractive.

2. A number of studies reveal that aerobic exercise raises energy levels and helps alleviate depression and anxiety. One explanation for these emotional effects of exercise is that exercise triggers the release of mood-boosting neurotransmitters such as norepinephrine, serotonin, and the
   a. placebos.
   b. endorphins.
   c. B lymphocytes.
   d. T lymphocytes.

3. Long-term studies of thousands of people indicate that people who have close relationships—a strong social support system—are less likely to die prematurely than those who do not. These studies support the idea that
   a. social ties can be a source of stress.
   b. gender influences longevity.
   c. Type A behavior is responsible for many premature deaths.
   d. social support has a beneficial effect on health.

Answers: 1. c, 2. b, 3. d.

>> TERMS AND CONCEPTS TO REMEMBER

aerobic exercise, p. 449
biofeedback, p. 451

complementary and alternative medicine (CAM), p. 452

>> TEST YOURSELF

1. Those who frequently attend religious services live longer than those who attend infrequently or not at all. What type of research finding is this, and what explanations might it have?

   (Answer in Appendix C.)

*Multiple-choice **self-tests** and more may be found at www.worthpublishers.com/myers.*

Personality

Personality

33-1: What is personality?

Lord of the Rings hobbit-hero Frodo Baggins knew that throughout his harrowing journey there was one who would never fail him—his loyal and ever-cheerful companion, Sam Gamgee. Even before they left their beloved hometown, Frodo warned Sam that the journey would not be easy:

> "It is going to be very dangerous, Sam. It is already dangerous. Most likely neither of us will come back."
> "If you don't come back, sir, then I shan't, that's certain," said Sam. "[The Elves told me] 'Don't you leave him!' Leave him! I said. I never mean to. I am going with him, if he climbs to the Moon; and if any of those Black Riders try to stop him, they'll have Sam Gamgee to reckon with." (Tolkien, *The Fellowship of the Ring,* p. 96)

And so they did! Later in the story, when it became clear that Frodo had to venture into the dreaded land of Mordor without the rest of the company, it was Sam who insisted he would accompany Frodo, come what may. It was Sam who lifted Frodo's flagging spirits with songs and stories from their boyhood, and Sam upon whom Frodo leaned when he could barely take another step. When Frodo was overcome by the evil of the ring he bore, it was Sam who saved Frodo from completely succumbing to it. And in the end, it was Sam who enabled Frodo to successfully reach the end of his journey. Sam Gamgee—the cheerful, conscientious, emotionally stable optimist—never faltered in his faithfulness or his belief that they could overcome the threatening darkness.

J. R. R. Tolkien's character Sam Gamgee, as he appears and reappears throughout the trilogy, exhibits the distinctiveness and consistency that define **personality**—an individual's characteristic pattern of thinking, feeling, and acting. Other mod-

> "There is no man who is not, at each moment, what he has been and what he will be."
> Oscar Wilde, 1854–1900

ules in this book emphasize our similarity—how we all develop, perceive, learn, remember, think, and feel. Modules 33 through 35 emphasize our individuality.

Actually, much of psychology deals with personality. Across the field, psychologists study biological influences on personality; personality development across the life span; personality-related aspects of learning, motivation, emotion, and health; disorders of personality; and social influences on personality.

We begin with two grand theories that have become part of our cultural legacy. These historically significant perspectives helped establish the field of personality psychology, and they raised key issues still being addressed in today's research and clinical work.

- Sigmund Freud's *psychoanalytic* theory (Module 33) proposed that childhood sexuality and unconscious motivations influence personality.
- The *humanistic* approach (Module 34) focused on our inner capacities for growth and self-fulfillment.

These historic theories, which offer sweeping perspectives on human nature, are complemented by what Module 35 goes on to explore: today's more focused and down-to-earth scientific research on specific aspects of personality.

Today's personality researchers study the basic dimensions of personality, the biological roots of these basic dimensions, and the interaction of persons and environments. They also study self-esteem, self-serving bias, and cultural influences on one's sense of self. And they study the unconscious mind—with findings that probably would have surprised Freud himself.

■ **personality** an individual's characteristic pattern of thinking, feeling, and acting.

The Psychoanalytic Perspective

"Sigmund Freud has left an important—and I believe indelible—mark on human self-understanding," observes Drew Westen (1998). Others disagree, noting that Freud's current influence in psychological science has diminished (Robins & others, 1999). But love him or hate him, Freud has profoundly influenced Western culture. Ask 100 people on the street to name a notable deceased psychologist, suggests Keith Stanovich (1996, p. 1), and "Freud would be the winner hands down." In the popular mind, he is to psychology's history what Elvis is to rock music's history. Freud's influence lingers in literary and film interpretation, psychiatry, and clinical psychology. So, who was this early **personality** theorist, and what did he teach?

Long before entering the University of Vienna in 1873, a youthful Sigmund Freud showed signs of independence and brilliance. He had a prodigious memory and so loved reading plays, poetry, and philosophy that he once ran up a bookstore debt beyond his means. As a teen he often took his evening meal in his tiny bedroom in order to lose no time from his studies.

Freud went to medical school and after graduation set up a private practice, specializing in nervous disorders. Before long, however, he faced patients whose disorders made no neurological sense. For example, a patient might have lost all feeling in a hand—yet there is no sensory nerve that, if damaged, would numb the entire hand and nothing else. Freud's search for a cause for such disorders set his mind running in a direction destined to change human self-understanding.

Exploring the Unconscious

33-2 : What was Freud's view of human personality and its development and dynamics?

Might some neurological disorders have psychological rather than physiological causes? Observing patients led Freud to his "discovery" of the unconscious. He decided that the peculiar loss of feeling in one's hand might be caused by a fear of touching one's genitals; that unexplained blindness or deafness might be caused by not wanting to see or hear something that aroused intense anxiety. Initially, Freud thought hypnosis might unlock the door to the unconscious, but patients displayed an uneven capacity for hypnosis. He then turned to **free association,** in which he merely told the patient to relax and say whatever came to mind, no matter how embarrassing or trivial. Freud assumed that a line of mental dominoes had fallen from his patients' distant past to their troubled present. Free association, he believed, allowed him to retrace that line, following a chain of thought leading into the patient's unconscious, where painful unconscious memories, often from childhood, could be retrieved and released. Freud called his theory of personality and the associated treatment techniques **psychoanalysis.**

Basic to Freud's theory was his belief that the mind is mostly hidden (see **FIGURE 33.1** on the next page). Our conscious awareness is like the part of an iceberg that floats above the surface. Below the surface is the much larger, **unconscious** region containing thoughts, wishes, feelings, and memories, of which we are unaware. Some of these thoughts we store temporarily in a *preconscious* area, from which we can retrieve them into conscious awareness. Of greater interest to Freud was the mass of unacceptable passions and thoughts that he believed we *repress*, or forcibly block from our

Sigmund Freud, 1856–1939
"I was the only worker in a new field."

Culver Pictures

■ **free association** in psychoanalysis, a method of exploring the unconscious in which the person relaxes and says whatever comes to mind, no matter how trivial or embarrassing.

■ **psychoanalysis** Freud's theory of personality that attributes thoughts and actions to unconscious motives and conflicts; the techniques used in treating psychological disorders by seeking to expose and interpret unconscious tensions.

■ **unconscious** according to Freud, a reservoir of mostly unacceptable thoughts, wishes, feelings, and memories. According to contemporary psychologists, information processing of which we are unaware.

459

© The New Yorker Collection, 1983, Dana Fradon from cartoonbank.com. All Rights Reserved.

FIGURE 33.1

Freud's idea of the mind's structure

Psychologists have used an iceberg image to illustrate Freud's idea that the mind is mostly hidden beneath the conscious surface. Note that the id is totally unconscious, but ego and superego operate both consciously and unconsciously. Unlike the parts of a frozen iceberg, however, the id, ego, and superego interact.

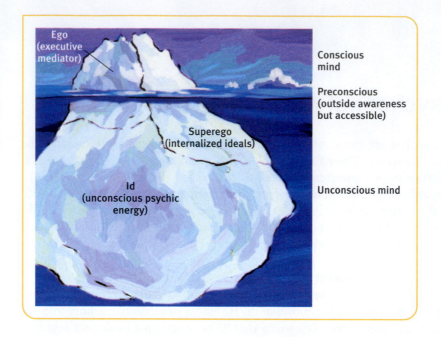

"Good morning, beheaded—uh, I mean beloved."

consciousness because they would be too unsettling to acknowledge. Freud believed that, although we are not consciously aware of them, these troublesome feelings and ideas powerfully influence us, sometimes gaining expression in disguised forms—the work we choose, the beliefs we hold, our daily habits, our troubling symptoms.

For Freud the determinist, nothing was ever accidental. He believed he could glimpse the unconscious seeping not only into people's free associations, beliefs, habits, and symptoms but also into slips of the tongue and pen. He illustrated with a financially stressed patient who, not wanting any large pills, said, "Please do not give me any bills, because I cannot swallow them." Similarly, Freud viewed jokes as expressions of repressed sexual and aggressive tendencies, and dreams as the "royal road to the unconscious." The remembered content of dreams (their *manifest content*) he believed to be a censored expression of the dreamer's unconscious wishes (the dream's *latent content*). In his analysis of dreams, Freud searched for the nature of patients' inner conflicts and their release from inner tensions.

Personality Structure

In Freud's view, human personality—including its emotions and strivings—arises from a conflict between our aggressive, pleasure-seeking biological impulses and the internalized social restraints against them. Freud believed personality is the result of our efforts to resolve this basic conflict—to express these impulses in ways that bring satisfaction without also bringing guilt or punishment. To understand the mind's dynamics during this conflict, Freud proposed three interacting systems: the *id, ego,* and *superego* (Figure 33.1).

The **id** has a reservoir of unconscious psychic energy constantly striving to satisfy basic drives to survive, reproduce, and aggress. The id operates on the *pleasure principle:* If not constrained by reality, it seeks immediate gratification. To envision an id-dominated person, think of newborn infants, crying out for satisfaction the moment they feel a need, caring nothing for the outside world's conditions and demands. Or think of people with a present rather than future time perspective—those who often use tobacco, alcohol, and other drugs, and would sooner party now than sacrifice today's pleasure for future success and happiness (Keough & others, 1999).

As the **ego** develops, the young child learns to cope with the real world. The ego, operating on the *reality principle,* seeks to gratify the id's impulses in realistic ways that will bring long-term pleasure rather than pain or destruction. (Imagine what would happen if, lacking an ego, we expressed our unrestrained sexual or aggressive impulses whenever we felt them.) The ego contains our partly conscious perceptions, thoughts, judgments, and memories.

Beginning around age 4 or 5, Freud theorized, a child's ego recognizes the demands of the newly emerging **superego,** the voice of our moral compass (conscience) that forces the ego to consider not only the real but the ideal, and that focuses solely on how one *ought* to behave. The superego strives for perfection, judging actions and producing positive feelings of pride or negative feelings of guilt. Someone with an exceptionally strong superego may be virtuous yet, ironically, guilt-ridden; another with a weak superego may be wantonly self-indulgent and remorseless.

Because the superego's demands often oppose the id's, the ego struggles to reconcile the two. It is the personality "executive," mediating the impulsive demands of the id, the restraining demands of the superego, and the real-life demands of the external world. If chaste Jane feels sexually attracted to John, she may satisfy both id and superego by joining a volunteer organization to which John belongs.

Personality Development

Analysis of his patients' histories convinced Freud that personality forms during life's first few years. Again and again his patients' symptoms seemed rooted in unresolved conflicts from early childhood. He concluded that children pass through a series of **psychosexual stages,** during which the id's pleasure-seeking energies focus on distinct pleasure-sensitive areas of the body called *erogenous zones* (**TABLE 33.1**).

"Fifty is plenty."   "Hundred and fifty."

The ego struggles to reconcile the demands of superego and id, said Freud.

Freud believed that during the *phallic stage* boys seek genital stimulation, and they develop both unconscious sexual desires for their mother and jealousy and hatred for their father, whom they consider a rival. Given these feelings, boys supposedly also feel guilt and a lurking fear of punishment, perhaps by castration, from their father. Freud called this collection of feelings the **Oedipus complex** after the Greek legend of Oedipus, who unknowingly killed his father and married his mother. Some psychoanalysts in Freud's era believed that girls experienced a parallel *Electra complex.* Freud's own thinking seemed to vary on this issue.

Children eventually cope with threatening feelings, said Freud, by repressing them and by identifying with (trying to become like) the rival parent. It's as though something inside the child decides, "If you can't beat 'em [the parent of the same sex],

Identification
Freud believed that children cope with threatening feelings of competition with their same-sex parent by identifying with that parent.

■ **id** contains a reservoir of unconscious psychic energy that, according to Freud, strives to satisfy basic sexual and aggressive drives. The id operates on the *pleasure principle,* demanding immediate gratification.

■ **ego** the largely conscious, "executive" part of personality that, according to Freud, mediates among the demands of the id, superego, and reality. The ego operates on the *reality principle,* satisfying the id's desires in ways that will realistically bring pleasure rather than pain.

■ **superego** the part of personality that, according to Freud, represents internalized ideals and provides standards for judgment (the conscience) and for future aspirations.

■ **psychosexual stages** the childhood stages of development (oral, anal, phallic, latency, genital) during which, according to Freud, the id's pleasure-seeking energies focus on distinct erogenous zones.

■ **Oedipus** [ED-uh-puss] **complex** according to Freud, a boy's sexual desires toward his mother and feelings of jealousy and hatred for the rival father.

TABLE 33.1

FREUD'S PSYCHOSEXUAL STAGES

Stage	Focus
Oral (0–18 months)	Pleasure centers on the mouth—sucking, biting, chewing
Anal (18–36 months)	Pleasure focuses on bowel and bladder elimination; coping with demands for control
Phallic (3–6 years)	Pleasure zone is the genitals; coping with incestuous sexual feelings
Latency (6 to puberty)	Dormant sexual feelings
Genital (puberty on)	Maturation of sexual interests

© The New Yorker Collection, 1983, Dana Fradon from cartoonbank.com. All Rights Reserved.

"Oh, for goodness' sake! Smoke!"

join 'em." Through this **identification** process, children's superegos gain strength as they incorporate many of their parents' values. Freud believed that identification with the same-sex parent provides what psychologists now call our *gender identity*— our sense of being male or female. Freud presumed that our early childhood relations with parents, caregivers, and everything else influences our developing identity, personality, and frailties.

In Freud's view, conflicts unresolved during earlier psychosexual stages could surface as maladaptive behavior in the adult years. At any point in the oral, anal, or phallic stages, strong conflict could lock, or **fixate,** the person's pleasure-seeking energies in that stage. A person who had been either orally overindulged or deprived (perhaps by abrupt, early weaning) might fixate at the oral stage, for example. This orally fixated adult could exhibit either passive dependence (like that of a nursing infant) or an exaggerated denial of this dependence—perhaps by acting tough and uttering biting sarcasm. Or the person might continue to seek oral gratification by smoking and eating excessively. In such ways, Freud suggested, the twig of personality is bent at an early age.

Defense Mechanisms

33-3: How did Freud think people defended themselves against anxiety?

Anxiety, said Freud, is the price we pay for civilization. As members of social groups, we must control our sexual and aggressive impulses, not act them out. But sometimes the ego fears losing control of this inner war between the demands of the id and the superego, and the result is a dark cloud of unfocused anxiety, which leaves us feeling unsettled but unsure why.

Freud proposed that the ego protects itself with **defense mechanisms,** tactics that reduce or redirect anxiety by distorting reality. Here are six examples.

- **Repression** banishes anxiety-arousing thoughts and feelings from consciousness. According to Freud, *repression underlies all the other defense mechanisms,* each of which disguises threatening impulses and keeps them from reaching consciousness. Freud believed that repression explains why we do not remember our childhood lust for our parent of the other sex. However, he also believed that repression is often incomplete, that repressed urges seep out in dream symbols and slips of the tongue.

- **Regression** allows us to retreat to an earlier, more infantile stage of development. Facing the anxious first days of school, a child may regress to the oral comfort of thumb-sucking. Juvenile monkeys, when anxious, retreat to infantile clinging to their mothers or to one another (Suomi, 1987). Even homesick new college students may long for the security and comfort of home.

- In **reaction formation,** the ego unconsciously makes unacceptable impulses look like their opposites. En route to consciousness, the unacceptable proposition "I hate him" becomes "I love him." Timidity becomes daring. Feelings of inadequacy become bravado.

- **Projection** disguises threatening impulses by attributing them to others. Thus, "He doesn't trust me" may be a projection of the actual feeling "I don't trust him" or "I don't trust myself." An El Salvadoran saying captures the idea: "The thief thinks everyone else is a thief."

- **Rationalization** occurs when we unconsciously generate self-justifying explanations to hide from ourselves the real reasons for our actions. Thus, habitual drinkers may say they drink with their friends "just to be sociable." Students who fail to study may rationalize, "All work and no play makes Jack [or Jill] a dull person."

- **Displacement** diverts sexual or aggressive impulses toward an object or person that is psychologically more acceptable than the one that aroused the feelings.

> "For seven and a half years I've worked alongside President Reagan. We've had triumphs. Made some mistakes. We've had some sex . . . uh . . . setbacks."
> George H. W. Bush, 1988

> "The lady doth protest too much, methinks."
> William Shakespeare, *Hamlet,* 1600

Regression
Faced with a mild stressor, children and young monkeys will regress, retreating to the comfort of earlier behaviors.

Children who fear expressing anger against their parents may displace it by kicking the family pet. Students upset over an exam may snap at a roommate.

Note that all these defense mechanisms function indirectly and unconsciously. They reduce anxiety by disguising our threatening impulses. Just as the body unconsciously defends itself against disease, so also, believed Freud, does the ego unconsciously defend itself against anxiety.

The Neo-Freudian and Psychodynamic Theorists

33-4 : Which of Freud's ideas did his followers accept or reject? How do Freud's ideas hold up today?

Freud's writings were controversial, but they soon attracted followers, mostly young, ambitious physicians who formed an inner circle around their strong-minded leader. These pioneering psychoanalysts and others, whom we now call *neo-Freudians,* accepted Freud's basic ideas: the personality structures of id, ego, and superego; the importance of the unconscious; the shaping of personality in childhood; and the dynamics of anxiety and the defense mechanisms. But they veered away from Freud in two important ways. First, they placed more emphasis on the conscious mind's role in interpreting experience and in coping with the environment. And second, they doubted that sex and aggression were all-consuming motivations. Instead, they tended to emphasize loftier motives and social interactions. The following examples illustrate.

Alfred Adler and Karen Horney [HORN-eye] agreed with Freud that childhood is important. But they believed that childhood *social,* not sexual, tensions are crucial for personality formation. Adler (who had proposed the still-popular idea of the *inferiority complex*) himself struggled to overcome childhood illnesses and accidents, and he believed that much of our behavior is driven by efforts to conquer childhood feelings of inferiority, feelings that trigger our strivings for superiority and power. Horney said childhood anxiety, caused by the dependent child's sense of helplessness, triggers our desire for love and security. Horney countered Freud's assumptions that women have weak superegos and suffer "penis envy," and she attempted to balance the bias she detected in this masculine view of psychology.

Unlike other neo-Freudians, Carl Jung—Freud's disciple-turned-dissenter—placed less emphasis on social factors and agreed with Freud that the unconscious exerts a powerful influence. But to Jung (pronounced Yoong), the unconscious contains more than our repressed thoughts and feelings. He believed we also have a **collective unconscious,** a common reservoir of images derived from our species' universal

■ **identification** the process by which, according to Freud, children incorporate their parents' values into their developing superegos.

■ **fixation** according to Freud, a lingering focus of pleasure-seeking energies at an earlier psychosexual stage, in which conflicts were unresolved.

■ **defense mechanisms** in psychoanalytic theory, the ego's protective methods of reducing anxiety by unconsciously distorting reality.

■ **repression** in psychoanalytic theory, the basic defense mechanism that banishes anxiety-arousing thoughts, feelings, and memories from consciousness.

■ **regression** psychoanalytic defense mechanism in which an individual faced with anxiety retreats to a more infantile psychosexual stage, where some psychic energy remains fixated.

■ **reaction formation** psychoanalytic defense mechanism by which the ego unconsciously switches unacceptable impulses into their opposites. Thus, people may express feelings that are the opposite of their anxiety-arousing unconscious feelings.

■ **projection** psychoanalytic defense mechanism by which people disguise their own threatening impulses by attributing them to others.

■ **rationalization** defense mechanism that offers self-justifying explanations in place of the real, more threatening, unconscious reasons for one's actions.

■ **displacement** psychoanalytic defense mechanism that shifts sexual or aggressive impulses toward a more acceptable or less threatening object or person, as when redirecting anger toward a safer outlet.

■ **collective unconscious** Carl Jung's concept of a shared, inherited reservoir of memory traces from our species' history.

Alfred Adler

"The individual feels at home in life and feels his existence to be worthwhile just so far as he is useful to others and is overcoming feelings of inferiority" (*Problems of Neurosis*, 1964).

Karen Horney

"The view that women are infantile and emotional creatures, and as such, incapable of responsibility and independence is the work of the masculine tendency to lower women's self-respect" (*Feminine Psychology*, 1932).

Carl Jung

"We can keep from a child all knowledge of earlier myths, but we cannot take from him the need for mythology" (*Symbols of Transformation*, 1912).

experiences. Jung said that the collective unconscious explains why, for many people, spiritual concerns are deeply rooted and why people in different cultures share certain myths and images, such as mother as a symbol of nurturance. (Today's psychologists discount the idea of inherited experiences. But many do believe that our shared evolutionary history shaped some universal dispositions.)

Freud died in 1939. Since then, some of his ideas have been incorporated into *psychodynamic theory.* "Most contemporary dynamic theorists and therapists are not wedded to the idea that sex is the basis of personality," notes Drew Westen (1996). They "do not talk about ids and egos, and do not go around classifying their patients as oral, anal, or phallic characters." What they do assume, with Freud, is that much of our mental life is unconscious, that we often struggle with inner conflicts among our wishes, fears, and values, and that childhood shapes our personalities and ways of becoming attached to others.

Assessing Unconscious Processes

33-5: What are projective tests, and what do clinicians in the Freudian tradition hope to learn from them?

Those who study personality or provide therapy need ways to evaluate personality characteristics. Methods of assessment differ because they are tailored to different personality theories. So what might be the tool of choice for clinicians working in the Freudian tradition?

Evaluating personality from this perspective would require a road into the unconscious mind, which contains residues from early childhood experiences. (Recall that Freud believed free association and dream interpretation could reveal the unconscious.) Objective assessment tools, such as agree-disagree or true-false questionnaires would be inadequate because they would merely tap the conscious surface. The tool of choice would be a sort of psychological x-ray—a test that sees through our surface pretensions and reveals our hidden conflicts and impulses.

Projective tests aim to provide such a view by presenting an ambiguous stimulus and then asking test-takers to describe it or tell a story about it. The stimulus has no inherent significance, so any meaning people read into it presumably is a projection of their interests and conflicts.

"We don't see things as they are; we see things as we are."

The Talmud

FIGURE 33.2
The TAT
This clinician presumes that the hopes, fears, and interests expressed in this boy's descriptions of a series of ambiguous pictures in the Thematic Apperception Test (TAT) are projections of his inner feelings.

Lew Merrim/Photo Researchers, Inc.

FIGURE 33.3
The Rorschach test
In this projective test, people tell what they see in a series of symmetrical inkblots. Some who use this test are confident that the interpretation of ambiguous stimuli will reveal unconscious aspects of the test-taker's personality. Others use it as an icebreaker or to supplement other information.

Andy Warhol Foundation/Corbis

In the 1930s, Henry Murray introduced the **Thematic Apperception Test (TAT),** in which people view ambiguous pictures and then make up stories about them (**FIGURE 33.2**). One use of storytelling has been to assess achievement motivation. Shown a daydreaming boy, those who imagine he is fantasizing about an achievement are presumed to be projecting their own goals.

The most widely used projective test is the famous **Rorschach inkblot test,** introduced in 1921 by Swiss psychiatrist Hermann Rorschach [ROAR-shock]. The test assumes that what we see in its 10 inkblots reflects our inner feelings and conflicts (**FIGURE 33.3**). If we see predatory animals or weapons, the examiner may infer we have aggressive tendencies.

Is this a reasonable assumption? If so, can a psychologist use the Rorschach to understand one's personality and diagnose an emotional disorder? Applying the two primary criteria of a good test—*reliability* (consistency of results) and *validity* (predicting what it's supposed to)—how good is the Rorschach?

Critics point out that no universally accepted system exists for scoring and interpreting the Rorschach tests (Sechrest & others, 1998). Two raters who have been trained in different scoring systems display only minimal agreement on the results of a given test. The test is also not very successful at predicting behavior or at discriminating between groups (for example, identifying who is suicidal and who is not). The Rorschach is not an emotional MRI.

Nonetheless, clinicians—82 percent of whom report administering it at least occasionally—often cherish the Rorschach (Lilienfeld & others, 2000; Watkins & others, 1995). Some offer Rorschach-based assessments of criminals' violence potential to judges. Other clinicians view it as a diagnostic tool, a source of suggestive leads, or an icebreaker and a revealing interview technique. There is now a research-based, computer-aided coding and interpretation tool that aims to improve agreement among raters and enhance the test's validity (Erdberg, 1990; Exner, 2003).

But the evidence is insufficient to its revilers, who note that inkblot assessments diagnose many normal adults as pathological (Wood & others, 2003, 2006). They argue that only a few of the many Rorschach-derived scores, such as ones for hostility and anxiety, have demonstrated validity. Alternative projective assessment techniques fare little better, conclude Scott Lilienfeld, James Wood, and Howard Garb (2001). "Even seasoned professionals," they warn, "can be fooled by their intuitions and their faith in tools that lack strong evidence of effectiveness. When a substantial body of research demonstrates that old intuitions are wrong, it is time to adopt new ways of thinking." Freud himself probably would have been uncomfortable with trying to diagnose patients based on tests and would have been more interested in the therapist-patient interactions that take place during the test.

■ **projective test** a personality test, such as the Rorschach or TAT, that provides ambiguous stimuli designed to trigger projection of one's inner dynamics.

■ **Thematic Apperception Test (TAT)** a projective test in which people express their inner feelings and interests through the stories they make up about ambiguous scenes.

■ **Rorschach inkblot test** the most widely used projective test, a set of 10 inkblots, designed by Hermann Rorschach; seeks to identify people's inner feelings by analyzing their interpretations of the blots.

©1983 by Sidney Harris; American Scientist Magazine.

"The forward thrust of the antlers shows a determined personality, yet the small sun indicates a lack of self-confidence...."

❝The Rorschach Inkblot Test has been resoundingly discredited . . . I call it the Dracula of psychological tests, because no one has been able to drive a stake through the cursed thing's heart."
Carol Tavris, "Mind Games: Psychological Warfare Between Therapists and Scientists," 2003

"Many aspects of Freudian theory are indeed out of date, and they should be: Freud died in 1939, and he has been slow to undertake further revisions."

Psychologist Drew Westen (1998)

Evaluating the Psychoanalytic Perspective

Contradictory Evidence from Modern Research

We critique Freud from an early twenty-first-century perspective, a perspective that itself will be subject to revision. Freud did not have access to neurotransmitter or DNA studies, or to all that we have since learned about human development, thinking, and emotion. To criticize his theory by comparing it with current concepts, some say, is like comparing Henry Ford's Model T with today's Explorer.

But Freud's admirers and his critics agree that recent research contradicts many of his specific ideas. Today's developmental psychologists see our development as lifelong, not fixed in childhood. They doubt that infants' neural networks are mature enough to sustain as much emotional trauma as Freud assumed. Some think Freud overestimated parental influence and underestimated peer influence (and abuse). They also doubt that conscience and gender identity form as the child resolves the Oedipus complex at age 5 or 6. We gain our gender identity earlier and become strongly masculine or feminine even without a same-sex parent present. And they note that Freud's ideas about childhood sexuality arose from his skepticism of stories of childhood sexual abuse told by his female patients—stories that some scholars believe he attributed to their own childhood sexual wishes and conflicts (Esterson, 2001; Powell & Boer, 1994). Today, we understand how Freud's questioning might have created false memories of abuse, but we also know that childhood sexual abuse does happen.

New ideas about why we dream dispute Freud's belief that dreams disguise and fulfill wishes. And slips of the tongue can be explained as competition between similar verbal choices in our memory network. Someone who says "I don't want to do that—it's a lot of brothel" may simply be blending *bother* and *trouble* (Foss & Hakes, 1978). Researchers find little support for Freud's idea that defense mechanisms disguise sexual and aggressive impulses (though our cognitive gymnastics do indeed work to protect our self-esteem). History also has failed to support another of Freud's ideas—that suppressed sexuality causes psychological disorders. From Freud's time to ours, sexual inhibition has diminished; psychological disorders have not.

"I remember your name perfectly but I just can't think of your face."

Oxford professor W. A. Spooner, 1844–1930, famous for his linguistic flip-flops (*spoonerisms*). Spooner rebuked one student for "fighting a liar in the quadrangle" and another who "hissed my mystery lecture," adding "You have tasted two worms."

Is Repression a Myth?

Freud's entire psychoanalytic theory rests on his assumption that the human mind often *represses* painful experiences, banishing them into the unconscious until they resurface, like long-lost books in a dusty attic. Recover and resolve the painful repressed memories of our childhood and emotional healing will follow. Under Freud's influence, repression became a widely accepted concept, used to explain hypnotic phenomena, psychological disorders, and apparent lost and recovered memories of childhood traumas (Cheit, 1998). In one survey, 88 percent of university students believed that painful experiences commonly get pushed out of awareness and into the unconscious (Garry & others, 1994).

Actually, contend many of today's researchers, repression, if it ever occurs, is a rare mental response to terrible trauma. "Repression folklore is . . . partly refuted, partly untested, and partly untestable," says Elizabeth Loftus (1995). Even those who have witnessed a parent's murder or survived Nazi death camps retain their unrepressed memories of the horror (Helmreich, 1992, 1994; Malmquist, 1986; Pennebaker, 1990).

There are exceptions—one death camp survivor reportedly forgot for more than 30 years the snatching and shooting of her infant son (Kraft, 1996). Some researchers believe that extreme, prolonged stress, such as the stress some severely abused children experience, might disrupt memory by damaging the hippocampus (Schacter, 1996). But the far more common reality is that high stress (and associated stress hormones) enhances memory. Indeed, traumatic events, such as rape and torture, haunt survivors, who experience unwanted flashbacks. They are seared onto the soul. "You see the babies," said Holocaust survivor Sally H. (1979). "You see the screaming mothers. You see hanging people. You sit and you see that face there. It's something you don't forget."

"During the Holocaust, many children . . . were forced to endure the unendurable. For those who continue to suffer [the] pain is still present, many years later, as real as it was on the day it occurred."

Eric Zillmer, Molly Harrower, Barry Ritzler, and Robert Archer, *The Quest for the Nazi Personality*, 1995

The Modern Unconscious Mind

33-6 : How do contemporary psychologists view the unconscious?

Freud was right about at least one thing: We indeed have limited access to all that goes on in our minds (Erdelyi, 1985, 1988; Kihlstrom, 1990). Research confirms the reality of unconscious *implicit learning* (Fletcher & others, 2005; Frensch & Rünger, 2003). Experiments point to a vast realm of out-of-sight information.

Nevertheless, the "iceberg" notion held by today's research psychologists differs from Freud's—so much so, argues Anthony Greenwald (1992), that it is time to abandon Freud's view of the unconscious. Many psychologists now think of the unconscious not as seething passions and repressive censoring but as cooler information processing that occurs without our awareness. To these researchers, the unconscious also involves

- the schemas that automatically control our perceptions and interpretations.
- the right-hemisphere activity that enables the split-brain patient's left hand to carry out an instruction the patient cannot verbalize.
- the parallel processing of different aspects of vision and thinking.
- the implicit memories that operate without conscious recall, and even among those with amnesia.
- the emotions that activate instantly, before conscious analysis.
- the self-concept and stereotypes that automatically and unconsciously influence how we process information about ourselves and others.

More than we realize, we fly on autopilot. Our lives are guided by off-screen, out-of-sight, unconscious information processing. The unconscious mind is huge. This understanding of unconscious information processing is more like the pre-Freudian view of an underground stream of thought from which spontaneous creative ideas surface.

Recent research has also provided some support for Freud's idea of defense mechanisms (even if they don't work exactly as Freud supposed). For example, Roy Baumeister and his colleagues (1998) found that people tend to see their foibles and attitudes in others, a phenomenon that Freud called projection and that today's researchers call the *false consensus effect,* the tendency to overestimate the extent to which others share our beliefs and behaviors. People who cheat on their taxes or break speed limits tend to think many others do likewise. Supportive evidence is meager for other defenses, such as displacement, that are tied to instinctual energy. More evidence exists for defenses, such as reaction formation, that defend self-esteem. Defense mechanisms, Baumeister concludes, are motivated less by the seething impulses that Freud presumed than by our need to protect our self-image.

Freud's Ideas as Scientific Theory

Psychologists also criticize Freud's theory for its scientific shortcomings, for falling short of the standard that good scientific theories explain observations and offer testable hypotheses. Freud's theory rests on few objective observations, and parts of it offer few hypotheses to verify or reject. (For Freud, his own recollections and interpretations of patients' free associations, dreams, and slips were evidence enough.)

What is the most serious problem with Freud's theory? It offers after-the-fact explanations of any characteristic (of one person's smoking, another's fear of horses, another's sexual orientation) yet fails to *predict* such behaviors and traits. If you feel angry at your mother's death, you illustrate his theory because "your unresolved childhood dependency needs are threatened." If you do not feel angry, you again illustrate his theory because "you are repressing your anger." That, said Calvin Hall and Gardner Lindzey (1978, p. 68), "is like betting on a horse after the race has been run." A good theory makes testable predictions.

> Two passengers leaned against the ship's rail and stared at the sea. 'There sure is a lot of water in the ocean,' said one. 'Yes,' answered his friend, 'we've only seen the top of it.'"
>
> Psychologist George A. Miller (1962)

> We are arguing like a man who should say, 'If there were an invisible cat in that chair, the chair would look empty; but the chair does look empty; therefore there is an invisible cat in it.'"
>
> C. S. Lewis, *Four Loves*, 1958

For such reasons, some of Freud's critics offer harsh words. They see a decaying Freudian edifice built on the swamplands of childhood sexuality, repression, dream analysis, and after-the-fact speculation. "When we stand on [Freud's] shoulders, we only discover that we're looking further in the wrong direction," says John Kihlstrom (1997). To Freud's most searing critic, Frederick Crews (1998), what is original about Freud's ideas is not good, and what is good is not original (the unconscious mind is an idea that dates back to Plato).

So, should psychology post a "Do Not Resuscitate" order on this old theory? Freud's supporters object. To criticize Freudian theory for not making testable predictions is, they say, like criticizing baseball for not being an aerobic exercise, something it was never intended to be. Freud never claimed that psychoanalysis was predictive science. He merely claimed that, looking back, psychoanalysts could find meaning in our state of mind (Rieff, 1979).

Freud's supporters also note that some of his ideas *are* enduring. It was Freud who drew our attention to the unconscious and the irrational, to our self-protective defenses, to the importance of human sexuality, and to the tension between our biological impulses and our social well-being. It was Freud who challenged our self-righteousness, punctured our pretensions, and reminded us of our potential for evil.

In science, Charles Darwin's legacy lives while Freud's is waning (Bornstein, 2001). In the popular culture, Freud's legacy lives on. Some ideas that many people assume to be true—that childhood experiences mold personality, that dreams have meaning, that many behaviors have disguised motives—are part of that legacy. His early-twentieth-century concepts penetrate our twenty-first-century language. Without realizing their source, we may speak of *ego, repression, projection, complex* (as in "inferiority complex"), *sibling rivalry, Freudian slips,* and *fixation.* "Freud's premises may have undergone a steady decline in currency within academia for many years," noted Martin Seligman (1994), "but Hollywood, the talk shows, many therapists, and the general public still love them."

REVIEWING

>> MODULE REVIEW

33-1: What is personality?

To psychologists, *personality* is one's distinctive and consistent pattern of thinking, feeling, and acting.

33-2: What was Freud's view of human personality and its development and dynamics?

Sigmund Freud's treatment of emotional disorders led him to believe that they spring from unconscious dynamics, which he sought to analyze through *free associations* and dreams. He referred to his theory and techniques as *psychoanalysis*. He saw personality as composed of pleasure-seeking psychic impulses (the *id*), a reality-oriented executive (the *ego*), and an internalized set of ideals (the *superego*).

Freud believed that children develop through *psychosexual stages*—the oral, anal, phallic, latency, and genital stages. He suggested that our personalities are influenced by how we have resolved conflicts associated with these stages and whether we have remained *fixated* at any stage.

33-3: How did Freud think people defended themselves against anxiety?

Tensions between the demands of id and superego cause anxiety. The ego copes by using *defense mechanisms,* such as *repression.*

33-4: Which of Freud's ideas did his followers accept or reject? How do Freud's ideas hold up today?

Neo-Freudians Alfred Adler and Karen Horney accepted many of Freud's ideas, as did Carl Jung. But they also argued that we have motives other than sex and aggression, and that the ego's conscious control is greater than Freud supposed.

Today's research psychologists find some of Freud's specific ideas implausible, unvalidated, or contradicted by new research, and they note that his theory offers only after-the-fact explanations.

Many researchers believe that repression rarely, if ever, occurs. Nevertheless, Freud drew psychology's attention to the unconscious, to the struggle to cope with anxiety and sexuality, and to the conflict between biological impulses and social restraints. His cultural impact has been enormous.

33-5: What are projective tests, and what do clinicians in the Freudian tradition hope to learn from them?

Projective tests attempt to assess personality by presenting ambiguous stimuli designed to reveal the unconscious. Although projective tests, such as the *Rorschach inkblots,* have questionable reliability and validity, many clinicians continue to use them.

33-6: How do contemporary psychologists view the unconscious?

Freud's view of the *unconscious*—a reservoir of repressed and mostly unacceptable thoughts, wishes, feelings, and memories—has not survived empirical scrutiny. But current information-processing research confirms that our access to all that goes on in our mind is very limited. The current view of the unconscious is that it consists of schemas that control our perceptions; parallel processing (as in vision) that occurs without our conscious knowledge; implicit memories of learned skills; instantly activated emotions; and self-concepts and stereotypes that filter information about ourselves and others.

Psychology's false consensus effect (the tendency to overestimate the effect to which others share our beliefs and behaviors) bears a resemblance to Freud's *projection* defense mechanism. *Reaction formation* also seems to happen. But current theorists believe that the motivation triggering defense mechanisms is a need to protect our self-image, not a well of instinctual energy or impulses.

>> REHEARSE IT!

1. According to Freud, we block from consciousness unacceptable or unbearably painful thoughts, wishes, feelings, and memories. The blocked material surfaces in disguised forms—for example, in physical symptoms, dreams, or slips of the tongue. This unconscious blocking of unacceptable thoughts is
   a. free association.
   b. repression.
   c. anxiety.
   d. reaction formation.

2. According to Freud's view of personality structure, the "executive" system, the ————, seeks to gratify the impulses of the ———— in more acceptable ways.

   a. id; ego
   b. ego; superego
   c. ego; id
   d. id; superego

3. Freud proposed that children incorporate parental values through a process called *identification.* Closely associated with this process is the development of the "voice of conscience," the part of the personality that internalizes ideals and that Freud called the
   a. ego.
   b. superego.
   c. reality principle.
   d. sublimation.

4. According to the psychoanalytic view of development, we all pass through a series of psychosexual stages, such as the oral, anal, and phallic stages. Conflicts unresolved at any of these stages may lead to

   a. dormant sexual feelings.
   b. fixation in that stage.
   c. preconscious blocking of impulses.
   d. a distorted gender identity.

5. Freud identified many defense mechanisms, including regression (coping with anxiety by retreating to an earlier developmental stage) and projection (disguising threatening impulses by attributing them to others). All defense mechanisms distort or disguise reality, and all are

   a. conscious.
   b. unconscious.
   c. preconscious.
   d. rationalizations.

6. Projective tests ask test-takers to respond to an ambiguous stimulus, for example, by describing it or telling a story about it. One well-known projective test, which uses inkblots as stimuli, was created by

   a. Alfred Adler.
   b. Karen Horney.
   c. Sigmund Freud.
   d. Hermann Rorschach.

7. In general, neo-Freudians such as Alfred Adler and Karen Horney accepted many of Freud's views but placed more emphasis on

   a. development throughout the life span.

   b. the collective unconscious.
   c. the role of the id.
   d. social interactions.

8. Psychodynamic theorists and therapists tend to reject Freud's view that sex is the basis of personality. But they would agree with Freud about

   a. the existence of unconscious mental processes.
   b. the Oedipus and Electra complexes.
   c. the predictive value of Freudian theory.
   d. the superego's role as the executive part of personality.

9. Sigmund Freud viewed the unconscious as a reservoir of repressed and mostly unacceptable thoughts, wishes, feelings, and memories. Which of the following is *not* part of the contemporary view of the unconscious?

   a. Repressed memories of anxiety-provoking events.
   b. Schemas that influence our perceptions and interpretations.
   c. Parallel processing that occurs without our conscious knowledge.
   d. Instantly activated emotions and implicit memories of learned skills.

Answers: 1. b, 2. c, 3. a, 4. b, 5. b, 6. d, 7. d, 8. a, 9. a.

>> TERMS AND CONCEPTS TO REMEMBER

personality, p. 458
free association, p. 459
psychoanalysis, p. 459
unconscious, p. 459
id, p. 460
ego, p. 460
superego, p. 461
psychosexual stages, p. 461

Oedipus [ED-uh-puss] complex, p. 461
identification, p. 462
fixation, p. 462
defense mechanisms, p. 462
repression, p. 462
regression, p. 462
reaction formation, p. 462

projection, p. 462
rationalization, p. 462
displacement, p. 462
collective unconscious, p. 463
projective test, p. 464
Thematic Apperception Test (TAT), p. 465
Rorschach inkblot test, p. 465

>> TEST YOURSELF

1. What, according to Freud, were some of the important defense mechanisms, and what do they defend against? How many of these find support in modern research?

   (Answer in Appendix C.)

> *Multiple-choice **self-tests** and more may be found at www.worthpublishers.com/myers.*

The Humanistic Perspective

34-1: What did humanistic psychologists view as the central feature of personality, and what was their goal in studying personality?

By the 1960s, some personality psychologists had become discontented with the negativism of Sigmund Freud's psychoanalytic theory and the mechanistic psychology of B. F. Skinner's behaviorism. In contrast to Freud's study of the base motives of "sick" people, these *humanistic psychologists* focused on the ways "healthy" people strive for self-determination and self-realization. In contrast to behaviorism's scientific objectivity, they studied people through their own self-reported experiences and feelings.

Two pioneering theorists—Abraham Maslow (1908–1970) and Carl Rogers (1902–1987)—offered a *third-force perspective* that emphasized human potential and seeing the world through the person's (not the researcher's) eyes.

Abraham Maslow's Self-Actualizing Person

Maslow proposed that we are motivated by a *hierarchy of needs.* If our physiological needs are met, we become concerned with personal safety; if we achieve a sense of security, we then seek to love, to be loved, and to love ourselves; with our love needs satisfied, we seek self-esteem. Having achieved self-esteem, we ultimately seek **self-actualization,** the process of fulfilling our potential.

Maslow (1970) developed his ideas by studying healthy, creative people rather than troubled clinical cases. He based his description of self-actualization on a study of those who seemed notable for their rich and productive lives—among them, Abraham Lincoln, Thomas Jefferson, and Eleanor Roosevelt. Maslow reported that these people shared certain characteristics: They were self-aware and self-accepting, open and spontaneous, loving and caring, and not paralyzed by others' opinions. Secure in their sense of who they were, their interests were problem-centered rather than self-centered. They focused their energies on a particular task, one they often regarded as their mission in life. Most enjoyed a few deep relationships rather than many superficial ones. Many had been moved by spiritual or personal *peak experiences* that surpassed ordinary consciousness.

These, said Maslow, are mature adult qualities, ones found in those who have learned enough about life to be compassionate, to have outgrown their mixed feelings toward their parents, to have found their calling, to have "acquired enough courage to be unpopular, to be unashamed about being openly virtuous, etc." Maslow's work with college students led him to speculate that those likely to become self-actualizing adults were likable, caring, "privately affectionate to those of their elders who deserve it," and "secretly uneasy about the cruelty, meanness, and mob spirit so often found in young people."

Carl Rogers' Person-Centered Perspective

Fellow humanistic psychologist Carl Rogers agreed with much of Maslow's thinking. Rogers believed that people are basically good and are endowed with self-actualizing tendencies. Unless thwarted by an environment that inhibits growth, each of us is like an acorn, primed for growth and fulfillment. Rogers (1980) believed that a growth-promoting climate required three conditions—genuineness, acceptance, and empathy.

Ted Polumbaum/Time Pix/Getty Images

Abraham Maslow
"Any theory of motivation that is worthy of attention must deal with the highest capacities of the healthy and strong person as well as with the defensive maneuvers of crippled spirits" (*Motivation and Personality,* 1970).

■ **self-actualization** according to Maslow, the ultimate psychological need that arises after basic physical and psychological needs are met and self-esteem is achieved; the motivation to fulfill one's potential.

The picture of empathy
Being open and sharing confidences is easier when the listener shows real understanding. Within such relationships people can relax and fully express their true selves.

According to Rogers, people nurture our growth by being *genuine*—by being open with their own feelings, dropping their facades, and being transparent and self-disclosing.

People also nurture our growth by being *accepting*—by offering us what Rogers called **unconditional positive regard.** This is an attitude of grace, an attitude that values us even knowing our failings. It is a profound relief to drop our pretenses, confess our worst feelings, and discover that we are still accepted. In a good marriage, a close family, or an intimate friendship, we are free to be spontaneous without fearing the loss of others' esteem.

Finally, people nurture our growth by being *empathic*—by sharing and mirroring our feelings and reflecting our meanings. "Rarely do we listen with real understanding, true empathy," said Rogers. "Yet listening, of this very special kind, is one of the most potent forces for change that I know."

Genuineness, acceptance, and empathy are the water, sun, and nutrients that enable people to grow like vigorous oak trees, according to Rogers. For "as persons are accepted and prized, they tend to develop a more caring attitude toward themselves" (Rogers, 1980, p. 116). As persons are empathically heard, "it becomes possible for them to listen more accurately to the flow of inner experiencings."

Rogers believed that genuineness, acceptance, and empathy nurture growth not only in the relationship between therapist and client but also between parent and child, leader and group, teacher and student, administrator and staff member—in fact, between any two human beings.

For Maslow, and even more for Rogers, a central feature of personality is one's **self-concept**—all the thoughts and feelings we have in response to the question, "Who am I?" If our self-concept is positive, we tend to act and perceive the world positively. If it is negative—if in our own eyes we fall far short of our *ideal self*—said Rogers, we feel dissatisfied and unhappy. A worthwhile goal for therapists, parents, teachers, and friends is therefore, he said, to help others know, accept, and be true to themselves.

Assessing the Self

34-2: How did humanistic psychologists assess a person's sense of self?

Humanistic psychologists sometimes assessed personality by asking people to fill out questionnaires that would evaluate self-concept. One questionnaire, inspired by Carl Rogers, asked people to describe themselves both as they would *ideally* like to be and as they *actually* are. When the ideal and the actual selves are nearly alike, said Rogers, the self-concept is positive. Assessing his clients' personal growth during therapy, he looked for successively closer ratings of actual and ideal selves.

Some humanistic psychologists believed that any standardized assessment of personality, even a questionnaire, is depersonalizing. Rather than forcing the person to respond to narrow categories, these humanistic psychologists presumed that interviews and intimate conversations would provide a better understanding of each person's unique experiences.

Evaluating the Humanistic Perspective

34-3: How has the humanistic perspective on personality influenced psychology? What criticisms have been leveled against this perspective?

One thing said of Freud can also be said of the humanistic psychologists: Their impact has been pervasive. Their ideas have influenced counseling, education, child-rearing, and management.

■ **unconditional positive regard** according to Rogers, an attitude of total acceptance toward another person.

■ **self-concept** all our thoughts and feelings about ourselves, in answer to the question, "Who am I?"

They have also influenced—sometimes in ways they did not intend—much of today's popular psychology. Many people have absorbed Maslow's and Rogers' ideas—that a positive self-concept is the key to happiness and success, that acceptance and empathy help nurture positive feelings about oneself, and that people are basically good and capable of self-improvement. One study found that, by a four-to-one margin, Americans believe "human nature is basically good" rather than "fundamentally perverse and corrupt" (NORC, 1985). Humanistic psychologists can also take satisfaction in the changed response to one item on the most widely used personality test: Among those in the 1930s normal standardization sample, only 9 percent agreed that "I am an important person"; by the mid-1980s, more than half agreed (Holden, 1986). Responding to a 1989 Gallup poll, 85 percent of Americans rated "having a good self-image or self-respect" as *very* important; 0 percent rated it unimportant. And 89 percent of people responding to a 1992 *Newsweek* Gallup poll rated self-esteem as very important for "motivating a person to work hard and succeed." Humanistic psychology's message has been heard.

Perhaps one reason that message has been so well received is that its emphasis on the individual self reflects and reinforces Western cultural values. Movie plots feature rugged individualists who, true to themselves, buck social convention or take the law into their own hands. Popular songs have proclaimed "I Did It My Way" and reminded us that to love yourself is "The Greatest Love of All" (Schoeneman, 1994).

The prominence of the humanistic perspective set off a backlash of criticism. First, said the critics, its concepts are vague and subjective. Consider the description of self-actualizing people as open, spontaneous, loving, self-accepting, and productive. Is this a scientific description? Isn't it merely a description of Maslow's personal values and ideals? Maslow, noted M. Brewster Smith (1978), offered impressions of his own personal heroes. Imagine another theorist who began with a different set of heroes—perhaps Napoleon, Alexander the Great, and John D. Rockefeller, Sr. This theorist would likely describe self-actualizing people as "undeterred by the needs of others," "motivated to achieve," and "obsessed with power."

Critics also objected to the idea that, as Rogers put it, "The only question which matters is, 'Am I living in a way which is deeply satisfying to me, and which truly expresses me?'" (quoted by Wallach & Wallach, 1985). The individualism encouraged by humanistic psychology—trusting and acting on one's feelings, being true to oneself, fulfilling oneself—can, the critics have said, lead to self-indulgence, selfishness, and an erosion of moral restraints (Campbell & Specht, 1985; Wallach & Wallach, 1983). Indeed, it is those who focus beyond themselves who are most likely to experience social support, to enjoy life, and to cope effectively with stress (Crandall, 1984).

Humanistic psychologists have countered that a secure, nondefensive self-acceptance is actually the first step toward loving others. Indeed, people who feel intrinsically liked and accepted—for who they are, not just for their achievements—exhibit less-defensive attitudes (Schimel & others, 2001).

A final accusation leveled against humanistic psychology is that it fails to appreciate the reality of our human capacity for evil. Faced with global warming, overpopulation, terrorism, and the spread of nuclear weapons, we may become apathetic from either of two rationalizations. One is a naive optimism that denies the threat ("People are basically good; everything will work out"). The other is a dark despair ("It's hopeless; why try?"). Action requires enough realism to fuel concern and enough optimism to provide hope. Humanistic psychology, say the critics, encourages the needed hope but not the equally necessary realism about evil.

A father *not* offering unconditional positive regard.

© The New Yorker Collection, 2001, Pat Byrnes from cartoonbank.com. All Rights Reserved

P. BYRNES.

"Just remember, son, it doesn't matter whether you win or lose—unless you want Daddy's love."

© The New Yorker Collection, 1979, Dana Fradon from cartoonbank.com. All Rights Reserved.

"We do pretty well when you stop to think that people are basically good."

REVIEWING

>> MODULE REVIEW

34-1: **What did humanistic psychologists view as the central feature of personality, and what was their goal in studying personality?**

Humanistic psychologists sought to turn psychology's attention toward the growth potential of healthy people. Abraham Maslow believed that if basic human needs are fulfilled, people will strive toward *self-actualization*. To nurture growth in others, Carl Rogers advised being genuine, accepting, and empathic. In this climate of *unconditional positive regard*, he believed, people can develop a deeper self-awareness and a more realistic and positive *self-concept*.

34-2: **How did humanistic psychologists assess a person's sense of self?**

Humanistic psychologists assessed personality through question-naires on which people reported their self-concept and in therapy by seeking to understand others' subjective personal experiences.

34-3: **How has the humanistic perspective on personality influenced psychology? What criticisms have been leveled against this perspective?**

Humanistic psychology helped to renew psychology's interest in the concept of self. Nevertheless, humanistic psychology's critics complained that its concepts were vague and subjective, its values Western and self-centered, and its assumptions naively optimistic.

>> REHEARSE IT!

1. Abraham Maslow's hierarchy of needs proposes that we first satisfy basic physiological and psychological needs, and then we become moti-vated to fulfill our potential through self-actualization. Maslow based his ideas on

   a. Freudian theory.
   b. his experiences with patients.
   c. a series of laboratory experiments.
   d. his study of healthy, creative people.

2. According to Carl Rogers, a growth-promoting environment is one that

   offers genuineness, acceptance, and empathy. The total acceptance Rogers advocated is called

   a. self-concept.
   b. unconditional positive regard.
   c. self-actualization.
   d. the "ideal self."

3. The humanistic perspective, which focused on the potential for human growth and self-fulfillment, has in-fluenced counseling, education, child-rearing, and popular psychol-ogy. The humanistic perspective has

   been so well received because

   a. it emphasizes the group and our social nature.
   b. it has a sound basis in scientific studies.
   c. it has predictive value as a testing instrument.
   d. its emphasis on the individual self reflects and reinforces Western cultural values.

   Answers: 1. d, 2. b, 3. d.

>> TERMS AND CONCEPTS TO REMEMBER

self-actualization, p. 471   unconditional positive regard, p. 472   self-concept, p. 472

>> TEST YOURSELF

1. What does it mean to be "empathic"? To be "self-actualized"?

   (Answer in Appendix C.)

*Multiple-choice **self-tests** and more may be found at www.worthpublishers.com/myers.*

Contemporary Research on Personality

35

The Trait Perspective

Trait researchers attempt to define personality in terms of stable and enduring behavior patterns, such as Sam Gamgee's loyalty and optimism. The trait perspective can be traced in part to a remarkable meeting in 1919, when Gordon Allport, a curious 22-year-old psychology student, interviewed Sigmund Freud in Vienna. Allport soon discovered just how preoccupied the founder of psychoanalysis was with finding hidden motives, even in Allport's own behavior during the interview. That experience ultimately led Allport to do what Freud did not do—to describe personality in terms of fundamental **traits**—people's characteristic behaviors and conscious motives (such as the professional curiosity that actually motivated Allport to see Freud). Meeting Freud, said Allport, "taught me that [psychoanalysis], for all its merits, may plunge too deep, and that psychologists would do well to give full recognition to manifest motives before probing the unconscious." Allport came to define personality in terms of identifiable behavior patterns. He was concerned less with *explaining* individual traits than with *describing* them.

Isabel Briggs Myers (1987) and her mother, Kathleen Briggs, attempted to sort people according to Carl Jung's personality types, based on their responses to 126 questions. The *Myers-Briggs Type Indicator,* which has been taken by 2.5 million Americans a year and used by 89 of the 100 largest corporations, is quite simple (Gladwell, 2004). It offers choices, such as "Do you usually value sentiment more than logic, or value logic more than sentiment?" Then it counts the test-taker's preferences, labels them as indicating, say, a "feeling" or "thinking" type, and feeds them back to the person in complimentary terms. Feeling types, for example, are told they are sensitive to values and "sympathetic, appreciative, and tactful"; thinking types are told they "prefer an objective standard of truth" and are "good at analyzing." (Every type has its strengths, so everyone gets flattered.)

Most people agree with their announced type profile. It mirrors their declared preferences and leaves them feeling good. They may also accept their label as a basis for being matched with work partners and tasks that supposedly suit their temperaments. A National Research Council report noted, however, that despite the test's popularity in business and career counseling, its initial use outran research on its value as a predictor of job performance, and "the popularity of this instrument in the absence of proven scientific worth is troublesome" (Druckman & Bjork, 1991, p. 101; see also Pittenger, 1993). Since those cautionary words, research on the Myers-Briggs has been accumulating, thanks to periodicals such as the *Journal of Psychological Type.*

Exploring Traits

35-1: How do psychologists use traits to describe personality?

Classifying people as one or another distinct personality type fails to capture their full individuality. We are each a unique complex of multiple traits. So how else could we describe our personalities? We might describe an apple by placing it along several trait dimensions—relatively large or small, red or yellow, sweet or sour. By placing people on several trait dimensions simultaneously, psychologists can describe countless individual personality variations, much as researchers can describe thousands of colors in terms of their variations on just three color dimensions—hue, saturation, and brightness.

■ **trait** a characteristic pattern of behavior or a disposition to feel and act, as assessed by self-report inventories and peer reports.

Chris Rock: the extravert

Trait labels such as *extraversion* can describe our temperament and typical behaviors.

What trait dimensions describe personality? If you had an upcoming blind date, what personality traits might give you an accurate sense of the person? Allport and his associate H. S. Odbert (1936) counted all the words in an unabridged dictionary with which one could describe people. How many were there? Almost 18,000! How, then, could psychologists condense the list to a manageable number of basic traits?

Factor Analysis

One way has been to propose traits, such as anxiety, that some theory regards as basic. A newer technique is *factor analysis,* a statistical procedure that has been used to identify clusters of related test items. Imagine that people who describe themselves as outgoing also tend to say that they like excitement and practical jokes and dislike quiet reading. Such a statistically correlated cluster of behaviors reflects a basic factor, or trait—in this case, *extraversion.*

British psychologists Hans Eysenck and Sybil Eysenck [EYE-zink] believed that we can reduce many of our normal individual variations to two or three dimensions, including *extraversion-introversion* and *emotional stability-instability* (**FIGURE 35.1**). People in 35 countries around the world, from China to Uganda to Russia, have taken the *Eysenck Personality Questionnaire,* and when their answers were analyzed, the extraversion and emotionality factors inevitably emerged as basic personality dimensions (Eysenck, 1990, 1992). The Eysencks believed that these factors are genetically influenced, and recent research supports this belief.

Biology and Personality

Brain-activity scans of extraverts add to the growing list of traits and mental states that have been explored with brain-imaging procedures. (That list includes intelligence, impulsivity, addictive cravings, sexual attraction, aggressiveness, empathy, spiritual experience, and even racial and political attitudes [Olson, 2005]). Such studies indicate that extraverts seek stimulation because their normal *brain arousal* is relatively low. For example, PET scans show that a frontal lobe area involved in behavior inhibition is less active in extraverts than in introverts (Johnson & others, 1999).

Our biology influences our personality in other ways as well. Our *genes* have much to say about the temperament and behavioral style that help define our personality. Jerome Kagan, for example, attributes differences in children's shyness and inhibition to their *autonomic nervous system reactivity.* Given a reactive autonomic nervous system, we respond to stress with greater anxiety and inhibition. The fearless, curious child may become the rock-climbing or fast-driving adult.

Samuel Gosling and his colleagues (2003) report that personality differences among dogs (in energy, affection, reactivity, and curious intelligence) are as evident, and as consistently judged, as personality differences among humans. Even birds have

FIGURE 35.1

Two personality factors

Mapmakers can tell us a lot by using two axes (north-south and east-west). Hans Eysenck and Sybil Eysenck use two primary personality factors— extraversion–introversion and stability–instability— as axes for describing personality variation. Varying combinations define other, more specific traits. (From Eysenck & Eysenck, 1963.)

UNSTABLE

Moody	Touchy
Anxious	Restless
Rigid	Aggressive
Sober	Excitable
Pessimistic	Changeable
Reserved	Impulsive
Unsociable	Optimistic
Quiet	Active
INTROVERTED	**EXTRAVERTED**
Passive	Sociable
Careful	Outgoing
Thoughtful	Talkative
Peaceful	Responsive
Controlled	Easygoing
Reliable	Lively
Even-tempered	Carefree
Calm	Leadership

STABLE

stable personalities. Among a European relative of the chickadee, bold birds more quickly inspect new objects and explore trees (Groothuis & Carere, 2005; Verbeek & others, 1994). By selective breeding, researchers can produce bold or shy birds. Both have their place in natural history. In lean years, bold birds are more likely to find food; in abundant years, shy birds feed with less risk.

Assessing Traits

35-2: What are personality inventories, and what are their strengths and weaknesses as trait-assessment tools?

If stable and enduring traits guide our actions, can we devise valid and reliable tests of them? Several trait assessment techniques exist. Some profile a person's behavior patterns—often providing quick assessments of a single trait, such as extraversion, anxiety, or self-esteem. **Personality inventories**—longer questionnaires covering a wide range of feelings and behaviors—are designed to assess several traits at once.

The most extensively researched personality inventory is the **Minnesota Multiphasic Personality Inventory (MMPI).** Although it assesses "abnormal" personality tendencies rather than normal personality traits, the MMPI illustrates a good way of developing a personality inventory. One of its creators, Starke Hathaway (1960), compared his effort to that of Alfred Binet, who developed the first intelligence test by selecting items that discriminated children who would have trouble progressing normally in French schools. The MMPI items, too, were **empirically derived.** That is, from a large pool of items, Hathaway and his colleagues selected those on which particular diagnostic groups differed. They then grouped the questions into 10 clinical scales.

Hathaway and others initially gave hundreds of true-false statements ("No one seems to understand me"; "I get all the sympathy I should"; "I like poetry") to groups of psychologically disordered patients and to "normal" people. They retained any statement—no matter how silly it sounded—on which the patient group's answer differed from that of the normal group. "Nothing in the newspaper interests me except the comics" may seem senseless, but it just so happened that depressed people were more likely to answer "true." (Nevertheless, people have had fun spoofing the MMPI with their own mock items: "Weeping brings tears to my eyes," "Frantic screams make me nervous," and "I stay in the bathtub until I look like a raisin" [Frankel & others, 1983].) Today's MMPI-2 also has scales assessing, for instance, work attitudes, family problems, and anger.

In contrast to the subjectivity of most projective tests, personality inventories are scored objectively—so objectively that a computer can administer and score them. (The computer can also provide descriptions of people who previously responded similarly.) Objectivity does not, however, guarantee validity. For example, individuals taking the MMPI for employment purposes can give socially desirable answers to create a good impression. But in so doing they may also score high on a "lie scale" that assesses faking (as when people respond "false" to a universally true statement such as "I get angry sometimes"). The objectivity of the MMPI has contributed to its popularity and to its translation into more than 100 languages.

The Big Five Factors

35-3: Which traits seem to provide the most useful information about personality variation?

Today's trait researchers believe that earlier trait dimensions, such as the Eysencks' introverted–extraverted and unstable–stable dimensions, are important, but they do not tell the whole story. A slightly expanded set of factors—dubbed the *Big Five*—does a better job (John & Srivastava, 1999; McCrae & Costa, 1999). If a test specifies where you are on the five dimensions (conscientiousness, agreeableness, neuroticism, openness,

■ **personality inventory** a questionnaire (often with true-false or agree-disagree items) on which people respond to items designed to gauge a wide range of feelings and behaviors; used to assess selected personality traits.

■ **Minnesota Multiphasic Personality Inventory (MMPI)** the most widely researched and clinically used of all personality tests. Originally developed to identify emotional disorders (still considered its most appropriate use), this test is now used for many other screening purposes.

■ **empirically derived test** a test (such as the MMPI) developed by testing a pool of items and then selecting those that discriminate between groups.

TABLE **35.1**

THE "BIG FIVE" PERSONALITY FACTORS

(*Memory tip:* Picturing a **CANOE** will help you recall these.)

Trait Dimension	Endpoints of the Dimension		
Conscientiousness	Organized Careful Disciplined	⟷ ⟷ ⟷	Disorganized Careless Impulsive
Agreeableness	Soft-hearted Trusting Helpful	⟷ ⟷ ⟷	Ruthless Suspicious Uncooperative
Neuroticism (emotional stability vs. instability)	Calm Secure Self-satisfied	⟷ ⟷ ⟷	Anxious Insecure Self-pitying
Openness	Imaginative Preference for variety Independent	⟷ ⟷ ⟷	Practical Preference for routine Conforming
Extraversion	Sociable Fun-loving Affectionate	⟷ ⟷ ⟷	Retiring Sober Reserved

Source: Adapted from McCrae & Costa (1986, p. 1002).

and extraversion; see **TABLE 35.1**), it has said much of what there is to say about your personality. Around the world, people describe others in terms roughly consistent with this list. The Big Five may not have the last word, but for now the winning number in the personality lottery is five. The Big Five—today's "common currency for personality psychology" (Funder, 2001)—has been the most active personality research topic since the early 1990s and is currently our best approximation of the basic trait dimensions (Endler & Speer, 1998). This recent wave of research explores various questions:

- *How stable are these traits?* In adulthood, the Big Five traits are quite stable, with some tendencies (emotional instability [neuroticism], extraversion, and openness) waning a bit during early and middle adulthood, and others (agreeableness and conscientiousness) rising (McCrae & others, 1999; Vaidya & others, 2002). Conscientiousness increases the most during people's twenties, as people mature and learn to manage their jobs and relationships. Agreeableness increases the most during people's thirties and continues to increase through their sixties (Srivastava & others, 2003).

- *How heritable are they?* Heritability of individual differences varies with the diversity of people studied, but it generally runs 50 percent or a tad more for each dimension (Loehlin & others, 1998).

- *How well do they apply to various cultures?* The Big Five dimensions describe personality in various cultures reasonably well (McCrae, 2001; Paunonen & others, 2000). "Features of personality traits are common to all human groups," infer Robert McCrae and 79 co-researchers (2005) from their recent 50-culture study.

By exploring such questions, Big Five research has sustained trait psychology and renewed appreciation for the importance of personality.

Evaluating the Trait Perspective

35-4 : Does research support the consistency of personality traits over time and across situations?

Are our personality traits stable and enduring? Or does our behavior depend on where and with whom we find ourselves? J. R. R. Tolkien created characters, like the loyal Sam Gamgee, whose personality traits were consistent across various times and places. The Italian playwright Luigi Pirandello had a different view. For him, personality was ever-changing, tailored to the particular role or situation. In one of Pirandello's plays, Lamberto Laudisi describes himself: "I am really what you take me to be; though, my dear madam, that does not prevent me from also being really what your husband, my sister, my niece, and Signora Cini take me to be—because they also are absolutely right!" To which Signora Sirelli responds, "In other words you are a different person for each of us."

The Person-Situation Controversy

Who, then, typifies human personality, Tolkien's consistent Sam Gamgee or Pirandello's inconsistent Laudisi? Both. Our behavior is influenced by the interaction of our inner disposition with our environment. Still, the question lingers: Which is *more* important? Are we *more* as Tolkien or as Pirandello imagined us to be?

When we explore this *person-situation controversy,* we look for genuine personality traits that persist over time *and* across situations. Are some people dependably conscientious and others unreliable, some cheerful and others dour, some friendly and outgoing and others shy? If we are to consider friendliness a trait, friendly people must act friendly at different times and places. Do they? In considering research that has followed lives through time, some scholars (especially those who study infants) are impressed with personality change; others are struck by personality stability during adulthood. As **FIGURE 35.2** illustrates, data from 152 long-term studies reveal that personality trait scores are positively correlated with scores obtained seven years later, and that as people grow older their personality stabilizes. Interests may change—the avid collector of tropical fish may become the avid gardener. Careers may change—the determined salesperson may become a determined social worker. Relationships may change—the hostile spouse may start over with a new partner. But most people recognize their traits as their own, note Robert McCrae and Paul Costa (1994), "and it is well that they do. A person's recognition of the inevitability of his or her one and only personality is . . . the culminating wisdom of a lifetime." So most people—including most psychologists—would probably side with Tolkien's assumption of stability of personality traits.

But the consistency of specific *behaviors* from one situation to the next is another matter. As Walter Mischel (1968, 1984, 2004) has pointed out, people do not act with predictable consistency. Mischel's studies of college students' conscientiousness revealed but a modest relationship between a student's being conscientious on one occasion (say, showing up for class on time) and being similarly conscientious on another occasion (say, turning in assignments on time). Pirandello would not have been surprised. If you've noticed how outgoing you are in some situations and how reserved you are in others, perhaps you're not surprised either (though for certain traits, Mischel reports, you may accurately assess yourself as more consistent).

> "There is as much difference between us and ourselves, as between us and others."
> Michel de Montaigne, *Essays,* 1588

Roughly speaking, the temporary, external influences on behavior are the focus of social psychology, and the enduring, inner influences are the focus of personality psychology. In actuality, behavior always depends on the interaction of persons with situations.

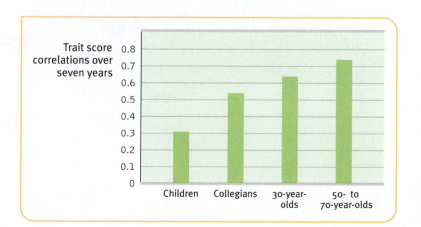

FIGURE 35.2
Personality stability
With age, personality traits become more stable, as reflected in the correlation of trait scores with follow-up scores seven years later. (Data from Roberts & DelVecchio, 2000).

HOW TO BE A "SUCCESSFUL" ASTROLOGER OR PALM READER

Can we discern people's traits from the alignment of the stars and planets at the time of their birth? From their handwriting? From lines on their palms?

Astronomers scoff at the naiveté of astrology—the constellations have shifted in the millennia since astrologers formulated their predictions (Kelly, 1997, 1998). Humorists mock it: "No offense," writes Dave Barry, "but if you take the horoscope seriously your frontal lobes are the size of Raisinets." Psychologists instead ask questions: Does it work? Can astrologers surpass chance when given someone's birth date and asked to identify the person from a short lineup of different personality descriptions? Can people pick out their own horoscopes from a lineup of horoscopes?

The consistent answers have been: No, no, and no (British Psychological Society, 1993; Carlson, 1985; Kelly, 1997). Graphologists, who make predictions from handwriting samples, have similarly been found to do no better than chance when trying to discern people's occupations from examining several pages of their handwriting (Beyerstein & Beyerstein, 1992; Dean & others, 1992). Nevertheless, graphologists—and introductory psychology students—will often *perceive* correlations between personality and handwriting even where there are none (King & Koehler, 2000).

If all these perceived correlations evaporate under close scrutiny, how do astrologers and the like persuade thousands of newspapers and millions of people worldwide to buy their advice? Ray Hyman (1981), palm reader turned research psychologist, has revealed the suckering methods of astrologers, palm readers, and crystal-ball gazers.

Their first technique, the "stock spiel," builds on the observation that each of us is in some ways like no one else and in other ways just like everyone. That some things are true of us all enables the "seer" to offer statements that seem impressively accurate: "I sense that you worry about things more than you let on, even to your best friends." A number of such generally true statements can be combined into a personality description. Imagine that you take a personality test and then receive the following character sketch:

> You have a strong need for other people to like and to admire you. You have a tendency to be critical of yourself. . . . You pride yourself on being an independent thinker and do not accept other opinions without satisfactory proof. You have found it unwise to be too frank in revealing yourself to others. At times you are extraverted, affable, sociable; at other times you are introverted, wary, and reserved. Some of your aspirations tend to be pretty unrealistic (Davies, 1997; Forer, 1949).

In experiments, college students have received stock assessments like this one, drawn from statements in a newsstand astrology book. When they think the bogus, generic feedback was prepared just for them and when it is favorable, they nearly al-

ways rate the description as either "good" or "excellent" (Davies, 1997). Even skeptics of astrology, when given a flattering description attributed to an astrologer, begin to think that "maybe there's something to this astrology stuff after all" (Glick & others, 1989). An astrologer, it has been said, is someone "prepared to tell you what you think of yourself" (Jones, 2000).

French psychologist Michael Gauguelin had similar results when he placed an ad in a Paris newspaper offering a free personal horoscope. Ninety-four percent of those receiving the horoscope praised the description as accurate. Whose horoscope had they all actually received? That of France's Dr. Petiot, a notorious mass murderer (Kurtz, 1983). This acceptance of stock, positive descriptions is called the *Barnum effect,* named in honor of master showman P. T. Barnum's dictum, "There's a sucker born every minute."

A second technique used by seers is to "read" our clothing, physical features, nonverbal gestures, and reactions to what they are saying. Imagine yourself as the character reader visited by a young woman in her late twenties or early thirties. Hyman described the woman as "wearing expensive jewelry, a wedding band, and a black dress of cheap material. The observant reader noted that she was wearing shoes which were advertised for people with foot trouble." Do these clues suggest anything?

Drawing on these observations, the character reader proceeded to amaze his client with his insights.

He assumed the woman had come to see him, as did most of his female customers, because of a love or financial problem. The black dress and the wedding band led him to reason that her husband had died recently. The expensive jewelry suggested she had been financially comfortable during the marriage, but the cheap dress suggested her husband's death had left her impoverished. The therapeutic shoes signified she was now on her feet more than she had been used to, implying that she had been working to support herself since her husband's death. Based on these insights, the reader correctly guessed that the woman was wondering if she should remarry in hope of ending her economic hardship. No wonder, say the skeptics, that when mediums cannot see the person who has come to them, their clients cannot recognize the reading that was meant for them from among other readings (O'Keeffe & Wiseman, 2005).

If you are not as shrewd as this character reader, Hyman says it hardly matters. If people seek you out for a reading, start with some safe sympathy: "I sense you're having some problems lately. You seem unsure what to do. I get the feeling another person is involved." Then tell them what they want to hear. Memorize some Barnum statements from astrology and fortune-telling manuals and use them liberally. Tell people it is their responsibility to cooperate by relating your message to their specific experiences. Later they will recall that you predicted those specific details. Phrase statements as questions, and when you detect a positive response assert the statement strongly. Finally, be a good listener, and later, in different words, reveal to people what they earlier revealed to you. If you dupe them, they will come.

Better yet, beware of those who, by exploiting people with these techniques, are fortune takers rather than fortune tellers.

© The New Yorker Collection, Leo Cullum from cartoonbank.com. All Rights Reserved.

"Madame Zelinski can provide an even more accurate reading with your date of birth and Social Security number."

© The New Yorker Collection, 1984, W. Miller from cartoonbank.com. All Rights Reserved.

"Mr. Coughlin over there was the founder of one of the first motorcycle gangs."

This inconsistency in behaviors also makes personality test scores weak predictors of behaviors. People's scores on an extraversion test, for example, do not neatly predict how sociable they actually will be on any given occasion. If we remember such results, says Mischel, we will be more cautious about labeling and pigeonholing individuals. We will be more restrained when asked to predict whether someone is likely to violate parole, commit suicide, or be an effective employee. Years in advance, science can tell us the phase of the moon for any given date. A day in advance, meteorologists can often predict the weather. But we are much further from being able to predict how *you* will feel and act tomorrow.

However, people's *average* outgoingness, happiness, or carelessness over *many* situations is predictable (Epstein, 1983a,b). In ratings of someone's shyness or agreeableness, this consistency enables people who know someone well to agree on their ratings (Kenrick & Funder, 1988). As our best friends can verify, we *do* have personality traits—genetically influenced traits, we now know.

Moreover, our traits are socially significant. They influence our health, our thinking, and our job performance (Deary & Matthews, 1993; Hogan, 1998). Our traits even lurk, report Samuel Gosling and his colleagues in a series of studies, in our

- *music preferences.* Classical, jazz, blues, and folk music lovers tend to be open to experience and verbally intelligent; country, pop, and religious music lovers tend to be cheerful, outgoing, and conscientious (Rentfrow & Gosling, 2003).
- *dorm rooms and offices.* Our personal spaces display our identity and leave a behavioral residue (in our scattered laundry or neat desktop). And that helps explain why just a few minutes' inspection of our living and working spaces can enable someone to assess with reasonable accuracy our conscientiousness, our openness to new experiences, and even our emotional stability (Gosling & others, 2002).
- *personal Web sites.* Is a personal Web site also a canvas for self-expression? Or is it an opportunity for people to present themselves in false or misleading ways? It's more the former, report Simine Vazire and Gosling (2004). Visitors to personal Web sites quickly gain important clues to the owner's extraversion, conscientiousness, and openness to experience.

In unfamiliar, formal situations—perhaps as a guest in the home of a person from another culture—our traits may remain hidden as we attend carefully to social cues. In familiar, informal situations—just hanging out with friends—we feel less constrained, allowing our traits to emerge (Buss, 1989). In these informal situations, our expressive styles—our animation, manner of speaking, and gestures—are impressively consistent. That's why even very "thin slices" of someone's behavior—such as observing three 2-second clips of a teacher—can be revealing (Ambady & Rosenthal, 1992, 1993).

Our spaces express our personalities
Even at "zero acquaintance," people can discern something of others' personality from glimpsing their Web site, dorm room, or office. So, what is your read on University of Texas researcher Samuel Gosling?

John Langford Photography

To sum up, we can say that at any moment the immediate situation powerfully influences a person's behavior, especially when the situation makes clear demands. We can better predict drivers' behavior at traffic lights from knowing the color of the lights than from knowing the drivers' personalities. Averaging our behavior across many occasions does, however, reveal distinct personality traits. Traits exist. We differ. And our differences matter.

The Social-Cognitive Perspective

35-5: In the view of social-cognitive psychologists, what mutual influences shape an individual's personality?

Today's psychological science views persons as biopsychosocial organisms. The **social-cognitive perspective** on personality proposed by Albert Bandura (1986, 2001, 2005) emphasizes the interaction of our biologically influenced psychological traits with our situations. Much as nature and nurture always work together, so do persons and their situations.

Like learning theorists, social-cognitive theorists believe we learn many of our behaviors either through conditioning or by observing others and modeling our behavior after theirs. (That is the "social" part.) They also emphasize the importance of mental processes: What we *think* about our situations affects our behavior. (That is the "cognitive" part.) Instead of focusing solely on how our environment *controls* us (behaviorism), social-cognitive theorists focus on how we and our environment *interact:* How do we interpret and respond to external events? How do our schemas, our memories, and our expectations influence our behavior patterns?

Reciprocal Influences

Bandura (1986) called the process of interacting with our environment **reciprocal determinism.** "Behavior, internal personal factors, and environmental influences," he said, "all operate as interlocking determinants of each other" (**FIGURE 35.3**). For example, children's TV-viewing habits (past behavior) influence their viewing preferences (internal factor), which influence how television (environmental factor) affects their current behavior. The influences are mutual.

■ **social-cognitive perspective** views behavior as influenced by the interaction between persons (and their thinking) and their social context.

■ **reciprocal determinism** the interacting influences between personality and environmental factors.

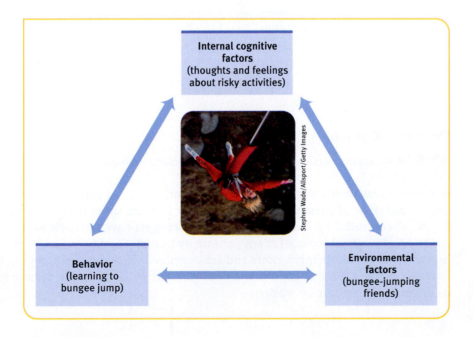

FIGURE 35.3
Reciprocal determinism
The social-cognitive perspective proposes that our personalities are shaped by the interaction of personal/cognitive factors (our feelings and thoughts), our environment, and our behaviors.

Consider three specific ways in which individuals and environments interact:

1. *Different people choose different environments.* The school you attend, the reading you do, the television programs you watch, the music you listen to, the friends you associate with—all are part of an environment you have chosen, based partly on your dispositions (Ickes & others, 1997). You choose your environment and it then shapes you.

2. *Our personalities shape how we interpret and react to events.* Anxious people, for example, are attuned to potentially threatening events (Eysenck & others, 1987). Thus, they perceive the world as threatening, and they react accordingly.

3. *Our personalities help create situations to which we react.* Many experiments reveal that how we view and treat people influences how they in turn treat us. If we expect someone to be angry with us, we may give the person a cold shoulder, touching off the very anger we expect. If we have an easygoing, positive disposition, we will likely enjoy close, supportive friendships (Donnellan & others, 2005; Kendler, 1997).

In such ways, we are both the products and the architects of our environments.

If all this has a familiar ring, it may be because it parallels and reinforces a pervasive theme in psychology and in this book: *Behavior emerges from the interplay of external and internal influences.* Boiling water turns an egg hard and a potato soft. A threatening environment turns one person into a hero, another into a scoundrel. *At every moment,* our behavior is influenced by our biology, our social experiences, and our cognition and personality (**FIGURE 35.4**).

FIGURE 35.4
The biopsychosocial approach to the study of personality
As with other psychological phenomena, personality is fruitfully studied at multiple levels.

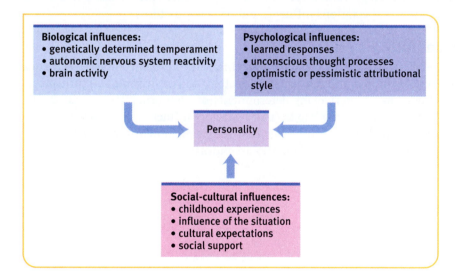

Personal Control

35-6: What are the causes and consequences of personal control?

In studying how we interact with our environment, social-cognitive psychologists emphasize our sense of **personal control**—whether we learn to see ourselves as controlling, or as controlled by, our environment. Psychologists have two basic ways to study the effect of personal control (or any personality factor). One: *Correlate* people's feelings of control with their behaviors and achievements. Two: *Experiment,* by raising or lowering people's sense of control and noting the effects. Both methods have helped us understand that control matters.

Internal Versus External Locus of Control

Consider your own feelings of control. Do you believe that your life is beyond your control? That the world is run by a few powerful people? That getting a good job depends mainly on being in the right place at the right time? Or do you more strongly believe that what happens to you is your own doing? That the average person can influence government decisions? That being a success is a matter of hard work, not luck?

Hundreds of studies have compared people who differ in their perceptions of control. On the one side are those who have what psychologist Julian Rotter called an **external locus of control**—the perception that chance or outside forces determine their fate. On the other are those who perceive an **internal locus of control** and believe that to a great extent they control their own destiny. In study after study, "internals" achieve more in school, act more independently, enjoy better health, and feel less depressed than do "externals" (Lachman & Weaver, 1998; Lefcourt, 1982; Presson & Benassi, 1996). Moreover, they are better able to delay gratification and cope with various stressors, including marital problems (Miller & others, 1986).

Self-control—the ability to control impulses and delay gratification—in turn predicts good adjustment, better grades, and social success, report June Tangney and her colleagues (2004). Students who plan their day's activities and then live out their day as planned are also at low risk for depression (Nezlek, 2001).

None of us experiences unvarying self-control. Self-control requires attention and energy. Like a muscle, self-control temporarily weakens after an exertion, replenishes with rest, and becomes stronger with exercise, report Roy Baumeister and Julia Exline (2000). Exercising willpower depletes mental energy. In one experiment, hungry people's resisting temptations to eat chocolate chip cookies led to their giving up sooner on a tedious task.

Learned Helplessness Versus Personal Control

People who feel helpless and oppressed often perceive control as external. This perception may then deepen their feelings of resignation. In fact, this is precisely what researcher Martin Seligman (1975, 1991) and others found in experiments with both animals and people. Dogs strapped in a harness and given repeated shocks, with no opportunity to avoid them, learned a sense of helplessness. Later placed in another situation where they *could* escape the punishment by simply leaping a hurdle, the dogs cowered as if without hope. People, too, when repeatedly faced with traumatic events over which they have no control, come to feel helpless, hopeless, and depressed. Psychologists call this passive resignation **learned helplessness** (FIGURE 35.5). In contrast, animals able to escape the shocks in Seligman's first situation learn personal control and easily escape the shocks in the new situation.

■ **personal control** our sense of controlling our environment rather than feeling helpless.

■ **external locus of control** the perception that chance or outside forces beyond one's personal control determine one's fate.

■ **internal locus of control** the perception that one controls one's own fate.

■ **learned helplessness** the hopelessness and passive resignation an animal or human learns when unable to avoid repeated aversive events.

RUBES

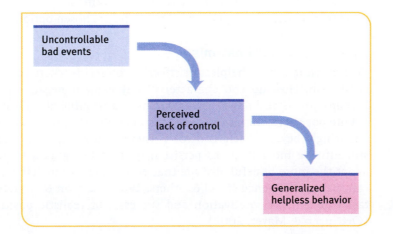

FIGURE 35.5
Learned helplessness
When animals and people experience no control over repeated bad events, they often learn helplessness.

Part of the shock we feel in an unfamiliar culture comes from a diminished sense of control when unsure how people in the new environment will respond (Triandis, 1994). Similarly, people given little control over their world in prisons, factories, colleges, and nursing homes experience lower morale and increased stress. Measures that increase control—allowing prisoners to move chairs and control room lights and the TV, having workers participate in decision making, offering nursing home patients choices about their environment—noticeably improve health and morale (Miller & Monge, 1986; Ruback & others, 1986; Wener & others, 1987). In one famous study of nursing home patients, 93 percent of those encouraged to exert more control became more alert, active, and happy (Rodin, 1986). As researcher Ellen Langer (1983, p. 291) concluded, "perceived control is basic to human functioning." She recommended that "for the young and old alike," it is important that we create environments that enhance our sense of control and personal efficacy. No wonder so many people like their iPods and TiVos, which give them control of the content and timing of their entertainment.

The verdict of these studies is reassuring: Under conditions of personal freedom and empowerment, people thrive. Small wonder that the citizens of stable democracies report higher levels of happiness (Inglehart, 1990). Shortly before the democratic revolution in the former East Germany, psychologists Gabriele Oettingen and Martin Seligman (1990) studied the telltale body language of working-class men in East and West Berlin bars. Compared with their counterparts on the other side of the Wall, the empowered West Berliners much more often laughed, sat upright rather than slumped, and had upward- rather than downward-turned mouths.

Happy are those who choose their own path
These happy East Berliners, crossing over to West Berlin after the wall came down in 1989, seem to personify this sentiment, from the Roman philosopher Seneca.

Peter Turnley/Corbis

Some freedom and control is better than none, notes Barry Schwartz (2000, 2004). But does ever-increasing choice breed ever-happier lives? Apparently not. Schwartz notes that the "excess of freedom" in today's Western cultures contributes to decreasing life satisfaction, increased depression, and sometimes paralysis. (One reason I haven't replaced my rusty 12-year-old car is my dread of sorting through all the choices.) Increased consumer choices have not been an unmixed blessing. After choosing among 30 brands of jam or chocolate, people express less satisfaction than those choosing among a half-dozen options (Iyengar & Lepper, 2000). This *tyranny of choice* brings information overload and a greater likelihood that we will feel regret over some of the unchosen options.

Optimism Versus Pessimism

One measure of how helpless or effective you feel is where you stand on optimism-pessimism. How do you characteristically explain negative and positive events? Perhaps you have known students whose *attributional style* is negative—who attribute poor performance to their lack of ability ("I can't do this") or to situations enduringly beyond their control ("There is nothing I can do about it"). Such students are more likely to persist in getting low grades than are students who adopt the more hopeful attitude that effort, good study habits, and self-discipline can make a difference (Noel & others, 1987; Peterson & Barrett, 1987). Mere fantasies do not fuel motivation and success, but realistic positive expectations do (Oettingen & Mayer, 2002).

CLOSE-UP

TOWARD A MORE POSITIVE PSYCHOLOGY

During its first century, psychology understandably focused much of its attention on understanding and alleviating negative states. We have studied abuse and anxiety, depression and disease, prejudice and poverty. Since 1887, articles on selected negative emotions have outnumbered those on positive emotions by 17 to 1.

In ages past, notes 1998 American Psychological Association president Martin Seligman (2002), times of relative peace and prosperity have enabled cultures to turn their attention from repairing weakness and damage to promoting "the highest qualities of life." Prosperous fifth-century Athens nurtured philosophy and democracy. Flourishing fifteenth-century Florence nurtured great art. Victorian England, flush with the bounty of the British empire, nurtured honor, discipline, and duty. In this millennium, Seligman believes, thriving Western cultures have a parallel opportunity to create, as a "humane, scientific monument," a more **positive psychology**—a psychology concerned not only with weakness and damage but also with strength and virtue. Thanks to his own leadership and to some $30 million in new funding, the new positive psychology movement is gaining strength (Seligman, 2004).

Positive psychology shares with humanistic psychology an interest in advancing human fulfillment, but its methodology is scientific. From these roots have grown not only the new

Courtesy of Martin E.P. Seligman, Ph.D. Director, Positive Psychology Center/University of Pennsylvania

Martin E. P. Seligman

"The main purpose of a positive psychology is to measure, understand, and then build the human strengths and the civic virtues."

studies of happiness and health, but also the shift in emphasis from learned helplessness and depression to optimism and thriving. "Positive psychology," say Seligman and colleagues (2005) "is an umbrella term for the study of positive emotions, positive character traits, and enabling institutions."

Taken together, satisfaction with the past, happiness with the present, and optimism about the future define the movement's first pillar: *positive emotions.* Happiness, Seligman argues, is a by-product of a pleasant, engaged, and meaningful life.

■ **positive psychology** the scientific study of optimal human functioning; aims to discover and promote strengths and virtues that enable individuals and communities to thrive.

Positive psychology is about building not just a pleasant life, says Seligman, but also a *good life* that engages one's skills, and a *meaningful life* that points beyond oneself. Thus, the second pillar, *positive character,* focuses on exploring and enhancing virtues such as creativity, courage, compassion, integrity, self-control, leadership, wisdom, and spirituality. Current research examines the roots and fruits of such virtues, sometimes by studying individuals who exemplify them in extraordinary ways.

The third pillar, *positive groups, communities, and cultures,* seeks to foster a positive social ecology, including healthy families, communal neighborhoods, effective schools, socially responsible media, and civil dialogue.

Will psychology have a more positive mission in this century? Without slighting the need to repair damage and cure disease, positive psychology's proponents hope so. With *American Psychologist* and *British Psychologist* special issues devoted to positive psychology, with new books (*Authentic Happiness,* 2002; *A Psychology of Human Strengths,* 2003; *Character Strengths and Virtues,* 2004), with 150 networked scientists worldwide working in 50 research groups, and with prizes, research awards, summer institutes, and a new graduate program promoting positive psychology scholarship, these psychologists have reason to be positive.

Health, too, benefits from a basic optimism. A depressed hopelessness dampens the body's disease-fighting immune system. In repeated studies, optimists have outlived pessimists or lived with fewer illnesses. Such studies helped point Seligman toward proposing a more positive psychology (see Close-Up: Toward a More Positive Psychology).

If positive thinking in the face of adversity pays dividends, so, too, can a dash of realism (Schneider, 2001). Self-disparaging explanations of past failures can depress ambition, but realistic anxiety over possible *future* failures can fuel energetic efforts to avoid the dreaded fate (Goodhart, 1986; Norem, 2001; Showers, 1992). Students concerned about failing the upcoming exam may study thoroughly and outperform their equally able but more confident peers. Edward Chang (2001) reports that, compared with European-American students, Asian-American students express somewhat greater pessimism—which he suspects helps explain their impressive academic achievements. Success requires enough optimism to provide hope and enough pessimism to prevent complacency.

Excessive optimism can blind us to real risks. Neil Weinstein (1980, 1982, 1996) has shown how our natural positive-thinking bias can promote "an unrealistic optimism about future life events." Most college students perceive themselves as less likely than their average classmate to develop drinking problems, drop out of school, or have a heart attack by age 40. Most late adolescents see themselves as much less vulnerable than their peers to the AIDS virus (Abrams, 1991). Those who optimistically venture into ill-fated relationships, deny the effects of smoking, or engage in unprotected sex remind us that, like pride, blind optimism may go before a fall.

Ironically, people often are most overconfident when most incompetent. That's because it often takes competence to recognize competence, note Justin Kruger and David Dunning (1999). They found that most students scoring at the low end of tests of grammar and logic believed they had scored in the top half. If you do not know what good grammar is, you may be unaware that your grammar is poor. This "ignorance of one's own incompetence" phenomenon has a parallel, as I can vouch, in hard-of-hearing persons' difficulty recognizing their own hearing loss. We're not so much "in denial" as we are simply unaware of what we don't hear. If I fail to hear my friend calling my name, the friend notices my inattention. But for me it's a nonevent. I hear what I hear—which, to me, seems pretty normal.

The difficulty in recognizing one's own incompetence helps explain why so many low-scoring students are dumbfounded after doing badly on an exam. If you don't know all the Scrabble word possibilities you've overlooked, you may feel pretty smart—until someone points them out. As Deanna Caputo and Dunning (2005) demonstrate in experiments that re-create this phenomenon, our ignorance of what we don't know helps sustain our confidence in our own abilities.

> "O God, give us grace to accept with serenity the things that cannot be changed, courage to change the things which should be changed, and the wisdom to distinguish the one from the other."
>
> Reinhold Niebuhr, "The Serenity Prayer," 1943

> "I didn't think it could happen to me."
>
> Earvin "Magic" Johnson, *My Life*, 1993 (after contracting HIV)

> "Ignorance more freely begets confidence than does knowledge."
>
> Charles Darwin, *The Descent of Man*, 1871

> "The living-room [Scrabble] player is lucky. . . . He has no idea how miserably he fails with almost every turn, how many possible words or optimal plays slip by unnoticed."
>
> Stefan Fatsis, *Word Freak*, 2001

DOONESBURY

© 1986 by G. B. Trudeau. Distributed by Universal Press Syndicate.

Assessing Behavior in Situations

35-7: What underlying principle guides social-cognitive psychologists in their assessment of people's behavior and beliefs?

Social-cognitive psychologists explore how people interact with situations. To predict behavior, they often observe behavior in realistic situations.

The idea, though effective, is not new. One ambitious example was the U.S. Army's World War II strategy for assessing candidates for spy missions. Rather than using paper-and-pencil tests, army psychologists subjected the candidates to simulated undercover conditions. They tested their ability to handle stress, solve problems, maintain leadership, and withstand intense interrogation without blowing their covers. Although time-consuming and expensive, this assessment of behavior in a realistic situation helped predict later success on actual spy missions (OSS Assessment Staff, 1948).

© NBC / Courtesy Everett Collection

Assessing behavior in situations
Reality TV shows have taken "show me" job interviews to the extreme, but they do illustrate a valid point. Seeing how a potential employee behaves in a job-relevant situation helps predict job performance.

Military and educational organizations and many Fortune 500 companies are adopting similar strategies in their evaluations of hundreds of thousands of people each year in assessment centers (Bray & others, 1991, 1997; Spychalski & others, 1997). AT&T has observed prospective managers doing simulated managerial work. Many colleges assess potential faculty members' teaching abilities by observing them teach, and assess graduate students' potentials via internships and student teaching. Armies assess their soldiers by observing them during military exercises. Most American cities with populations of 50,000 or more use assessment centers in evaluating police and fire officers (Lowry, 1997).

These procedures exploit the principle that the best means of predicting future behavior is neither a personality test nor an interviewer's intuition. Rather, it is the person's past behavior patterns in similar situations (Mischel, 1981; Ouellette & Wood, 1998; Schmidt & Hunter, 1998). As long as the situation and the person remain much the same, the best predictor of future job performance is past job performance; the best predictor of future grades is past grades; the best predictor of future aggressiveness is past aggressiveness; the best predictor of drug use in young adulthood is drug use in high school. If you can't check the person's past behavior, the next-best thing is to create an assessment situation that simulates the task so you can see how the person handles it.

A *New York Times* analysis of 100 rampage murders over the last half-century revealed that 55 of the killers had regularly exploded in anger and 63 had threatened violence (Goodstein & Glaberson, 2000). Most didn't, out of the blue, "just snap."

Evaluating the Social-Cognitive Perspective

35-8: What has the social-cognitive perspective contributed to the study of personality, and what criticisms have been leveled against it?

The social-cognitive perspective on personality sensitizes researchers to how situations affect, and are affected by, individuals. More than other perspectives, it builds from psychological research on learning and cognition.

Critics charge that the social-cognitive perspective focuses so much on the situation that it fails to appreciate the person's inner traits. Where is the person in this view of personality, ask the dissenters (Carlson, 1984), and where are human emotions? True, the situation does guide our behavior. But, say the critics, in many instances our unconscious motives, our emotions, and our pervasive traits shine through. Personality traits have been shown to predict behavior at work, love, and play. Our biologically influenced traits really do matter. Consider Percy Ray Pridgen and Charles Gill. Each faced the same situation: They had jointly won a $90 million lottery jackpot (Harriston, 1993). When Pridgen learned of the winning numbers, he began trembling uncontrollably, huddled with a friend behind a bathroom door while confirming the win, then sobbed. When Gill heard the news, he told his wife and then went to sleep.

Exploring the Self

Psychology's concern with people's sense of self dates back at least to William James, who devoted more than 100 pages of his 1890 *Principles of Psychology* to the topic. By 1943, Gordon Allport lamented that the self had become "lost to view." Although humanistic psychology's emphasis on the self did not instigate much scientific research, it did help renew the concept of self and keep it alive. Now, more than a century after James, the self is one of Western psychology's most vigorously researched topics. Every year, new studies galore appear on self-esteem, self-disclosure, self-awareness, self-schemas, self-monitoring, and so forth—more than 220,000 articles in all since 1967. Underlying this research is an assumption that the self, as organizer of our thoughts, feelings, and actions, is a pivotal center of personality.

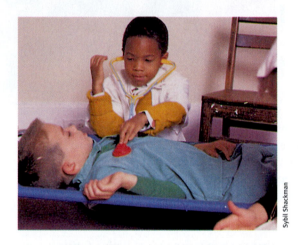

Possible selves
By giving them a chance to try out many possible selves, pretend games offer children important opportunities to grow emotionally, socially, and cognitively. This young boy may or may not grow up to be a physician, but playing adult roles will certainly bear fruit in terms of an expanded vision of what he might become.

Sybil Shackman

One example of thinking about self is the concept of *possible selves* put forth by Hazel Markus and her colleagues (Cross & Markus, 1991; Markus & Nurius, 1986). Your possible selves include your visions of the self you dream of becoming—the rich self, the successful self, the loved and admired self. They also include the self you fear becoming—the unemployed self, the lonely self, the academically failed self. Such possible selves motivate us by laying out specific goals and calling forth the energy to work toward them. University of Michigan students in a combined undergraduate/medical school program earn higher grades if they undergo the program with a clear vision of themselves as successful doctors. Dreams do often give birth to achievements.

"The first step to better times is to imagine them."
Chinese fortune cookie

■ **spotlight effect** overestimating others' noticing and evaluating our appearance, performance, and blunders (as if we presume a spotlight shines on us).

Our self-focused perspective may motivate us, but it can also lead us to presume too readily that others are noticing and evaluating us. Thomas Gilovich (1996) demonstrated this **spotlight effect** by having individual Cornell University students don Barry Manilow T-shirts before entering a room with other students. Feeling self-conscious, the T-shirt wearers guessed that nearly half of their peers would take note of the shirt as they walked in. In reality, only 23 percent did. This absence of attention applies not only to our dorky clothes and bad hair but also to our nervousness, irritation, or attraction: Fewer people notice than we presume (Gilovich & Savitsky, 1999). Others are also less aware than we suppose of the variability—the ups and downs—of our appearance and performance (Gilovich & others, 2002). Even after a blunder (setting off a library alarm, showing up in the wrong clothes), we stick out like a sore thumb less than we imagine (Savitsky & others, 2001). Knowing about the spotlight effect can be empowering. Help public speakers to understand that their natural nervousness is not so apparent to their audience and their speaking performance improves (Savitsky & Gilovich, 2003).

■ **self-esteem** one's feelings of high or low self-worth.

The Benefits of Self-Esteem

35-9: Are we helped or hindered by high self-esteem?

How we feel about ourselves is also important. High **self-esteem**—a feeling of self-worth—pays dividends. People who feel good about themselves (who strongly agree with self-affirming questionnaire statements) have fewer sleepless nights, succumb less easily to pressures to conform, are more persistent at difficult tasks, are less shy and lonely, and are just plain happier (Crocker & Wolfe, 1999; Leary, 1999; Murray & others, 2002; Watson & others, 2002).

Psychologists Roy Baumeister and colleagues (2003, 2005), William Damon (1995), Robyn Dawes (1994), Mark Leary (1999), and Martin Seligman (1994, 2002) nevertheless doubt that high self-esteem is really "the armor that protects kids" from life's problems. Maybe self-esteem simply reflects reality. Maybe feeling good *follows* doing well. Maybe it's a side effect of meeting challenges and surmounting difficulties. Maybe self-esteem is a gauge that reads out the state of our relationships with others. If so, isn't pushing the gauge artificially higher akin to forcing a car's low fuel gauge to display "full"? And if problems and failures cause low self-esteem, won't the best boost therefore come not so much from our repeatedly telling children how wonderful they are as from their own effective coping and hard-won achievements?

However, experiments do reveal an *effect* of low self-esteem. Temporarily deflate people's self-image (say, by telling them they did poorly on an aptitude test or by disparaging their personality) and they will be more likely to disparage others or to express heightened racial prejudice (Ybarra, 1999). Those who are negative about themselves also tend to be thin-skinned and judgmental (Baumgardner & others, 1989; Pelham, 1993). Some "love their neighbors as themselves"; others loathe their neighbors as themselves. In experiments, those made to feel insecure often become excessively critical, as if to impress others with their own brilliance (Amabile, 1983). Such findings are consistent with humanistic psychologists Abraham Maslow's and Carl Rogers' presumptions that a healthy self-image pays dividends. Accept yourself and you'll find it easier to accept others. Disparage yourself and you will be prone to the floccinaucinihilipilification[1] of others. Said more simply, people who are down on themselves tend to be down on other things and people.

> "There's a lot of talk about self-esteem these days. It seems pretty basic to me. If you want to feel proud of yourself, you've got to do things you can be proud of."
>
> Oseola McCarty, Mississippi washerwoman, after donating $150,000 to the University of Southern Mississippi

Culture and Self-Esteem

Is it true, as so many assume, that ethnic minorities suffer impoverished self-esteem? The accumulated evidence says no. For example, comparisons of more than half a million people have actually revealed slightly *higher* self-esteem scores for black than

© The New Yorker Collection, 1996, Mike Twohy from cartoonbank.com. All Rights Reserved.

---

[1] I couldn't resist throwing that in. But don't worry, you won't be tested on floccinaucinihilipilification, which is the act of estimating something as worthless (and was the longest nontechnical word in the first edition of the *Oxford English Dictionary*).

PEANUTS

for white children, adolescents, and young adults (Gray-Little & Hafdahl, 2000; Twenge & Crocker, 2002).

Some people wonder: How can this be? Some members of stigmatized groups (people of color, those with disabilities, women) have faced discrimination and lower status, yet, according to Jennifer Crocker and Brenda Major (1989), they maintain their self-esteem in three ways:

- They value the things at which they excel.
- They attribute problems to prejudice.
- They do as everyone does—they compare themselves to those in their own group.

These findings help us understand why, despite the realities of prejudice, such groups report levels of happiness roughly comparable to others.

Self-Serving Bias

■ **self-serving bias** a readiness to perceive oneself favorably.

Carl Rogers (1958) once objected to the religious doctrine that humanity's problems arise from excessive self-love, or pride. He noted that most people he had known "despise themselves, regard themselves as worthless and unlovable." Mark Twain had a similar idea: "No man, deep down in the privacy of his heart, has any considerable respect for himself."

Actually, most of us have a good reputation with ourselves. In studies of self-esteem, even those who score low respond in the midrange of possible scores. (A low–self-esteem person responds to statements such as "I have good ideas" with qualifying adjectives such as *somewhat* or *sometimes*.) Moreover, one of psychology's most provocative and firmly established recent conclusions concerns our potent **self-serving bias**—our readiness to perceive ourselves favorably (Mezulis & others, 2004; Myers, 2005). Consider these findings:

People accept more responsibility for good deeds than for bad, and for successes than for failures. Athletes often privately credit their victories to their own prowess and their losses to bad breaks, lousy officiating, or the other team's exceptional performance. After receiving poor grades on an exam, most students in a half-dozen studies criticized the exam, not themselves. On insurance forms, drivers have explained accidents in such words as: "An invisible car came out of nowhere, struck my car, and vanished." "As I reached an intersection, a hedge sprang up, obscuring my vision, and I did not see the other car." "A pedestrian hit me and went under my car." The question "What have I done to deserve this?" is one we usually ask of our troubles, not our successes—those, we assume we deserve.

Most people see themselves as better than average. This is true for nearly any subjective and socially desirable dimension. In national surveys, most business executives say they are more ethical than their average counterpart. In several studies, 90 percent of business managers and more than 90 percent of college professors rated their performance as superior to that of their average peer. In Australia, 86 percent of people rate their job performance as above average, and only 1

"To love oneself is the beginning of a life-long romance."
Oscar Wilde, *An Ideal Husband*, 1895

percent as below average. The phenomenon, which reflects the overestimation of self rather than the underestimation of others (Epley & Dunning, 2000), is less striking in Asia, where people value modesty. Yet self-serving biases have been observed worldwide: among Dutch, Australian, and Chinese students; Japanese drivers; Indian Hindus; and French people of most walks of life. Ironically, people even see themselves as more immune than others to self-serving bias (Pronin & others, 2002). The world, it seems, is Garrison Keillor's Lake Wobegon writ large—a place where "all the women are strong, all the men are good-looking, and all the children are above average."

Self-serving bias flies in the face of pop psychology. "All of us have inferiority complexes," wrote John Powell (1989, p. 15). "Those who seem not to have such a complex are only pretending." But additional findings remove any doubts (Myers, 2005):

- We remember and justify our past actions in self-enhancing ways.
- We exhibit an inflated confidence in our beliefs and judgments.
- We overestimate how desirably *we* would act in situations where most people behave less than admirably.
- We often seek out favorable, self-enhancing information.
- We are quicker to believe flattering descriptions of ourselves than unflattering ones, and we are impressed with psychological tests that make us look good.
- We exhibit group pride—a tendency to see our group (our school, our country, our race) as superior.

Moreover, pride does often go before a fall. Self-serving perceptions underlie conflicts ranging from blaming one's spouse for marital discord to arrogantly promoting one's own ethnic superiority. "Aryan pride" fueled Nazi atrocities. No wonder religion and literature so often warn against the perils of excessive pride.

Finding their self-esteem threatened, people with large egos may do more than put others down; they may react violently. Among children, the recipe for frequent fighting mixes high self-esteem with social rejection. The most aggressive children tend to have high self-regard that gets punctured by other kids' dislike (van Boxtel & others, 2004). An adolescent or adult with a swelled head that gets deflated by insult is potentially dangerous. Brad Bushman and Roy Baumeister (1998) experimented with this "dark side of high self-esteem." They had 540 undergraduate volunteers write a paragraph, in response to which another supposed student gave them either praise ("Great essay!") or stinging criticism ("One of the worst essays I have read!"). Then the essay writers played a reaction-time game against the other student. After wins, they could assault their opponent with noise of any intensity for any duration.

Can you anticipate the result? After criticism, those with unrealistically high self-esteem were "exceptionally aggressive." They delivered three times the auditory torture of those with normal self-esteem. Threatened egotism, more than low self-esteem, it seems, predisposes aggression. "Encouraging people to feel good about themselves when they haven't earned it" poses problems, Baumeister (2001) concludes. "Conceited, self-important individuals turn nasty toward those who puncture their bubbles of self-love."

Despite the demonstrated perils of pride, many people reject the idea of self-serving bias, insisting it overlooks those who feel worthless and unlovable and seem to despise themselves. If self-serving bias prevails, why do so many people disparage themselves? For three reasons: Sometimes self-directed put-downs are *subtly strategic:* They elicit reassuring strokes. Saying "No one likes me" may at least elicit "But not everyone has met you!" Other times, such as before a game or an exam, self-disparaging comments *prepare us for possible failure.* The coach who

Three in four pet owners believe their pet is smarter than average (Nier, 2004).

"The [self-]portraits that we actually believe, when we are given freedom to voice them, are dramatically more positive than reality can sustain."
Shelley Taylor, *Positive Illusions*, 1989

"The enthusiastic claims of the self-esteem movement mostly range from fantasy to hogwash. The effects of self-esteem are small, limited, and not all good."
Roy Baumeister (1996)

extols the superior strength of the upcoming opponent makes a loss understandable, a victory noteworthy. And finally, self-disparagement also frequently pertains to one's *old self*. People are much more critical of their distant past selves than of their current selves—even when they have not changed (Wilson & Ross, 2001). "At 18, I was a jerk; today I'm more sensitive." In their own eyes, chumps yesterday, champs today.

Even so, it's true: All of us some of the time, and some of us much of the time, *do* feel inferior—especially when we compare ourselves with those who are a step or two higher on the ladder of status, looks, income, or ability. The deeper and more frequently we have such feelings, the more unhappy, even depressed, we are. But for most people, thinking has a naturally positive bias.

While recognizing the dark side of self-serving bias and self-esteem, some researchers prefer isolating the effects of two types of self-esteem—defensive and secure (Jordan & others, 2003; Kernis, 2003; Ryan & Deci, 2004). *Defensive self-esteem* is fragile. It focuses on sustaining itself, which makes failures and criticism feel threatening. Such egotism exposes one to perceived threats, which feed anger and disorder, note Jennifer Crocker and Lora Park (2004). Thus, like low self-esteem, defensive self-esteem correlates with aggressive and antisocial behavior (Donnellan & others, 2005). *Secure self-esteem* is less fragile, because it is less contingent on external evaluations. To feel accepted for who we are, and not for our looks, wealth, or acclaim, relieves pressures to succeed and enables us to focus beyond ourselves. By losing ourselves in relationships and purposes larger than self, Crocker and Park add, we may achieve a more secure self-esteem and greater quality of life.

Recognizing both the perils of self-righteousness and the dividends of secure self-esteem, psychologists Baumeister (1989), Jonathan Brown (1991), and Shelley Taylor (1989; Taylor & others, 2003) have all suggested that humans function best with modest self-enhancing illusions. Like the Japanese and European magnetic levitation trains, Brown notes, we function optimally when riding just off the rails—not so high that we gyrate and crash, yet not so in touch that we grind to a halt.

> "If you compare yourself with others, you may become vain and bitter; for always there will be greater and lesser persons than yourself."
>
> Max Ehrmann, "Desiderata," 1927

REVIEWING

>> MODULE REVIEW

35-1 : **How do psychologists use traits to describe personality?**
Rather than explain the hidden aspects of personality, *trait* theorists describe the predispositions that underlie our actions. For example, through factor analysis, researchers have isolated important dimensions of personality. Genetic predispositions influence many traits.

35-2 : **What are personality inventories, and what are their strengths and weaknesses as trait-assessment tools?**
Personality inventories (like the *MMPI*) are questionnaires on which people respond to items designed to gauge a wide range of feelings and behaviors. Items on the test are *empirically derived,* and the tests are objectively scored. But people can fake their answers to create a good impression, and the ease of computerized testing may lead to misuse of these tests.

35-3 : **Which traits seem to provide the most useful information about personality variation?**
The Big Five personality dimensions—conscientiousness, agreeableness, neuroticism, openness, and extraversion—offer a reasonably comprehensive picture of personality.

35-4 : **Does research support the consistency of personality traits over time and across situations?**
Critics of trait theory question the consistency with which traits are expressed. Although people's traits persist over time, human behavior varies widely from situation to situation. Despite these variations, a person's average behavior across different situations tends to be fairly consistent.

35-5 : **In the view of social-cognitive psychologists, what mutual influences shape an individual's personality?**
The *social-cognitive perspective* applies principles of learning, cognition, and social behavior to personality, with particular emphasis on the ways in which our personality influences and is influenced by our interaction with the environment. It assumes *reciprocal determinism*—that personal-cognitive factors interact with the environment to influence people's behavior.

35-6 : **What are the causes and consequences of personal control?**
By studying how people vary in their perceived *locus of control* and in their experiences of *learned helplessness*, researchers have found that a sense of *personal control* helps people to cope with life. Research on learned helplessness has evolved into research on optimism and now into a broader *positive psychology* movement.

35-7 : **What underlying principle guides social-cognitive psychologists in their assessment of people's behavior and beliefs?**
Social-cognitive researchers study how people's behaviors and beliefs both affect and are affected by their situations. The underlying principle for much of this work is that the best way to predict someone's behavior in a given situation is to observe that person's behavior in similar situations.

35-8 : **What has the social-cognitive perspective contributed to the study of personality, and what criticisms have been leveled against it?**
Though faulted for underemphasizing the importance of unconscious dynamics, emotions, and inner traits, the social-cognitive perspective builds on psychology's well-established concepts of learning and cognition and reminds us of the power of social situations.

35-9 : **Are we helped or hindered by high self-esteem?**
Research confirms the importance of high *self-esteem*. But it also warns of the dangers of unrealistically high self-esteem. The *self-serving bias*, for example, leads us to perceive ourselves favorably, often causing us to overestimate our abilities and underestimate our faults.

>> REHEARSE IT!

1. Trait theory describes personality in terms of characteristic behaviors, or traits, such as agreeableness or extraversion. A pioneering trait theorist was
   a. Sigmund Freud.
   b. Alfred Adler.
   c. Gordon Allport.
   d. Carl Rogers.

2. Trait theorists assess personality by developing a profile of a person's traits. For example, they administer personality inventories—long questionnaires that ask people to report their characteristic feelings and behaviors. The most widely used of all personality inventories is the
   a. extraversion-introversion scale.
   b. Person-Situation Inventory.
   c. MMPI.
   d. Positive Psychology Self-Sort.

3. Hans Eysenck and Sybil Eysenck defined personality in terms of two primary factors—extraversion-introversion and stability-instability. Most researchers today believe that the Eysenck dimensions are too limiting and prefer the so-called Big Five personality factors. Which of the following is not one of the Big Five?
   a. Conscientiousness
   b. Anxiety
   c. Extraversion
   d. Agreeableness

4. People's scores on personality tests are only mildly predictive of their behavior. Such tests best predict
   a. a person's behavior on a specific occasion.
   b. a person's average behavior across many situations.
   c. behavior involving a single trait, such as conscientiousness.
   d. behavior that depends on the situation or context.

5. Albert Bandura, a social-cognitive theorist, believes that interacting with our environment involves reciprocal determinism, or mutual influences among personal factors, environmental factors, and behavior. An example of an environmental factor is

   a. the presence of books in a home.
   b. a preference for outdoor play.
   c. the ability to read at a fourth-grade level.
   d. the fear of violent action on television.

6. When elderly patients take an active part in managing their own care and surroundings, their morale and health tend to improve. Such findings indicate that people do better when they experience

   a. learned helplessness.
   b. an external locus of control.
   c. an internal locus of control.
   d. reciprocal determinism.

7. Working with animals and people, Martin Seligman studied an attitude of passive resignation, which he called learned helplessness. He found, for example, that a dog will respond with learned helplessness if it has received repeated shocks and has had

   a. the opportunity to escape.
   b. no control over the shocks.
   c. pain or discomfort.
   d. no food or water prior to the shocks.

8. A goal of many personality theories is to be able to predict a person's behavior in a particular situation. _____ theory is very sensitive to the way people affect, and are affected by, particular situations, but it says little about enduring traits.

   a. Psychoanalytic
   b. Humanistic
   c. Trait
   d. Social-cognitive

9. Psychologist Thomas Gilovich demonstrated the spotlight effect by having students wear Barry Manilow T-shirts into a room where other students were gathered. The spotlight effect is our tendency to

   a. perceive ourselves favorably and perceive others unfavorably.
   b. try out many possible selves.
   c. become excessively critical when made to feel insecure.
   d. overestimate others' attention to and evaluation of our appearance, performance, and blunders.

10. Researchers have found that high self-esteem is beneficial (people who feel good about themselves have fewer sleepless nights, for example, and are less likely to use drugs). Low self-esteem tends to be linked with life problems. How should this link between low self-esteem and life problems be interpreted?

    a. Life problems cause low self-esteem.
    b. The answer isn't clear because the link is correlational and does not indicate cause and effect.
    c. Low self-esteem leads to life problems.
    d. Because of the self-serving bias, we must assume that external factors cause low self-esteem.

11. Research indicates that people tend to accept responsibility for their successes or good qualities and blame circumstances or luck for their failures. This is an example of

    a. low self-esteem.
    b. self-actualization.
    c. self-serving bias.
    d. empathy.

Answers:
1. c, 2. c, 3. b, 4. b, 5. a, 6. c, 7. b, 8. d, 9. d, 10. b, 11. c.

>> Terms and Concepts to Remember

trait, p. 475
personality inventory, p. 477
Minnesota Multiphasic Personality
   Inventory (MMPI), p. 477
empirically derived test, p. 477

social-cognitive perspective, p. 483
reciprocal determinism, p. 483
personal control, p. 484
external locus of control, p. 485
internal locus of control, p. 485

learned helplessness, p. 485
positive psychology, p. 487
spotlight effect, p. 490
self-esteem, p. 491
self-serving bias, p. 492

>> Test Yourself

1. How many trait dimensions are currently used to describe personality, and what are those dimensions?

2. How do learned helplessness and optimism influence behavior?

3. In a 1997 Gallup poll, white Americans estimated 44 per-cent of their fellow white Americans to be high in prejudice (scoring them 5 or higher on a 10-point scale). How many rated themselves similarly high in prejudice? Just 14 percent. What phenomenon does this illustrate? Explain.

(Answers in Appendix C.)

Multiple-choice **self-tests** and more may be found at www.worthpublishers.com/myers.

Psychological Disorders

Psychological Disorders

I felt the need to clean my room at home in Indianapolis every Sunday and would spend four to five hours at it. I would take every book out of the bookcase, dust and put it back. At the time I loved doing it. Then I didn't want to do it anymore, but I couldn't stop. The clothes in my closet hung exactly two fingers apart. . . . I made a ritual of touching the wall in my bedroom before I went out because something bad would happen if I didn't do it the right way. I had a constant anxiety about it as a kid, and it made me think for the first time that I might be nuts.

Marc, diagnosed with obsessive-compulsive disorder (from Summers, 1996)

Whenever I get depressed it's because I've lost a sense of self. I can't find reasons to like myself. I think I'm ugly. I think no one likes me. . . . I become grumpy and short-tempered. Nobody wants to be around me. I'm left alone. Being alone confirms that I am ugly and not worth being with. I think I'm responsible for everything that goes wrong.

Greta, diagnosed with depression (from Thorne, 1993, p. 21)

Voices, like the roar of a crowd, came. I felt like Jesus; I was being crucified. It was dark. I just continued to huddle under the blanket, feeling weak, laid bare and defenseless in a cruel world I could no longer understand.

Stuart, diagnosed with schizophrenia (from Emmons & others, 1997)

People are fascinated by the exceptional, the unusual, the abnormal. "The sun shines and warms and lights us and we have no curiosity to know why this is so," observed Ralph Waldo Emerson, "but we ask the reason of all evil, of pain, and hunger, and [unusual] people." But why such fascination with disturbed people? Do we see in them something of our- selves? At various moments, all of us feel, think, or act the way disturbed people do much of the time. We, too, get anxious, depressed, withdrawn, suspicious, or de- luded, just less intensely and more briefly. It's no wonder, then, that studying psy- chological disorders may at times evoke an eerie sense of self-recognition, one that il- luminates the dynamics of our own per- sonality. "To study the abnormal is the best way of understanding the normal," proposed William James (1842–1910).

Another reason for our curiosity is that so many of us have felt, either personally or through friends or family, the bewilder- ment and pain of a psychological disorder that may bring unexplained physical symptoms, irrational fears, or a feeling that life is not worth living. Indeed, as members of the human family, most of us will at some point encounter a psychologi- cally disturbed person.

Module 36 introduces psychological disorders, explaining the major perspec- tives and categories, the risks of labeling, and the prevalence of the various disor- ders. Module 37 describes three types of disorders: *anxiety disorders,* which are characterized by persistent distressing anx- iety or maladaptive behaviors that reduce anxiety; the rare and controversial *disso- ciative disorders;* and the problematic *per- sonality disorders,* which impair social functioning. Module 38 examines the emotional extremes of *mood disorders* in depth. And Module 39 outlines the symp- toms and characteristics of those suffering from *schizophrenia,* a frightening split from reality.

Introduction to Psychological Disorders

36-1 : Where should we draw the line between normality and disorder?

Most people would agree that someone who is too depressed to get out of bed for weeks at a time has a psychological disorder. But what about those who, having experienced a loss, are unable to resume their usual social activities? Where should we draw the line between sadness and depression? Between zany creativity and bizarre irrationality? Between normality and abnormality? Let's start with these questions:

- How should we *define* psychological disorders?
- How should we *understand* disorders—as sicknesses that need to be diagnosed and cured, or as natural responses to a troubling environment?
- How should we *classify* psychological disorders? And can we do so in a way that allows us to help people without stigmatizing them with *labels?*
- How *prevalent* are these disorders, and who is likely to experience them?

Defining Psychological Disorders

Mental health workers view **psychological disorders** as persistently harmful thoughts, feelings, and actions. When behavior is *deviant, distressful,* and *dysfunctional,* psychiatrists and psychologists label it disordered (Comer, 2004).

Being different (*deviant*) from most other people in one's culture is *part* of what it takes to define a psychological disorder. As the reclusive poet Emily Dickinson observed in 1862,

> *Assent—and you are sane—*
> *Demur—you're straightaway dangerous—*
> *and handled with a Chain.*

Standards for deviant behavior vary by context and by culture. In one context—wartime—mass killing may be viewed as normal and even heroic. And in cultures practicing ancestor worship, people may claim to talk with the dead and not be seen as disordered because other people find them rational (Friedrich, 1987).

■ **psychological disorder** deviant, distressful, and dysfunctional behavior patterns.

Culture and normality
Men of the West African Wodaabe tribe put on elaborate makeup and costumes to attract women. In Western society, the same behavior would break behavioral norms and might be judged abnormal.

Carol Beckwith

"Who in the rainbow can draw the line where the violet tint ends and the orange tint begins? Distinctly we see the difference of the colors, but where exactly does the one first blendingly enter into the other? So with sanity and insanity?"

Herman Melville, *Billy Budd, Sailor*, 1924

Standards for deviance also vary with time. From 1952 through December 9, 1973, homosexuality was classified as an illness. By day's end on December 10, it was not. The American Psychiatric Association had dropped homosexuality as a disorder because more and more of its members no longer viewed it as a psychological problem. (Later research has revealed that the stigma and stresses associated with being homosexual do, however, increase the risk of mental health problems [Meyer, 2003].) In this new century, controversy swirls over the frequent diagnosing of children with *attention-deficit hyperactivity disorder* (see Thinking Critically About: ADHD—Normal High Energy or Genuine Disorder?).

But there is more to a disorder than being deviant. Olympic gold medalists deviate from the norm in their physical abilities, and society honors them. To be considered disordered, deviant behavior must also cause the person *distress*.

Deviant and distressful behaviors are more likely to be considered disordered when also judged *dysfunctional*. By this measuring stick, even typical behaviors, such as the occasional despondency many college students feel, may signal a psychological disorder *if* they become disabling. Dysfunction is key to defining a disorder: An intense fear of spiders may be deviant, but if it doesn't impair your life it is not a disorder.

Disordered behavior may also be dangerous. If depression deepens and people develop suicidal thoughts, they may be considered a danger to themselves.

Understanding Psychological Disorders

36-2 : What theoretical models or perspectives can help us understand psychological disorders?

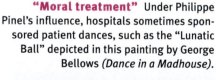

■ **medical model** the concept that diseases, in this case psychological disorders, have physical causes that can be *diagnosed*, *treated*, and, in most cases, *cured*, often through treatment in a hospital.

To explain puzzling behavior, people in earlier times often presumed that strange forces—the movements of the stars, godlike powers, or evil spirits—were at work. "The devil made him do it," you might have said had you lived during the Middle Ages, and you might have approved of a cure to get rid of the evil force by exorcising the demon. Until the last two centuries, "mad" people were sometimes caged in zoolike conditions or given "therapies" appropriate to a demon: beatings, burning, or castration. In other times, therapy might have included pulling teeth, removing lengths of intestines, cauterizing the clitoris, or giving transfusions of animal blood (Farina, 1982).

The Medical Model

"Moral treatment" Under Philippe Pinel's influence, hospitals sometimes sponsored patient dances, such as the "Lunatic Ball" depicted in this painting by George Bellows (*Dance in a Madhouse*).

In opposition to this brutal treatment, reformers such as Philippe Pinel (1745–1826) in France insisted that madness was not demon possession but a sickness of the mind caused by severe stresses and inhumane conditions. For Pinel and other reformers, "moral treatment" included boosting patients' morale by unchaining them and talking with them, and by replacing brutality with gentleness, isolation with activity, and filth with clean air and sunshine.

George Wesley Bellows, *Dance in a Madhouse*, 1907, © 1997 The Art Institute of Chicago

By the 1800s, the discovery that syphilis infects the brain and distorts the mind provided the impetus for further reform. Hospitals replaced asylums, and the medical world began searching for physical causes of mental disorders and for treatments that would cure them. Today, this **medical model** is recognizable in the terminology of the mental *health* movement: A mental *illness* (also called a psycho*pathology*) needs to be *diagnosed* on the basis of its *symptoms* and *cured* through *therapy*, which may include *treatment* in a psychiatric *hospital*.

The medical perspective has gained credibility from recent discoveries that genetically influenced abnormalities in brain structure and biochemistry contribute to a number of disorders. But psychological factors, such as traumatic stress, also play an important role.

THINKING CRITICALLY ABOUT :

ADHD—NORMAL HIGH ENERGY OR GENUINE DISORDER?

Eight-year-old Todd has always been energetic. At home, he chatters away and darts from one activity to the next, rarely settling down to read a book or focus on a game. At play, he is reckless and overreacts when playmates bump into him or take one of his toys. At school, his exasperated teacher complains that fidgety Todd doesn't listen, follow instructions, or stay in his seat and do his lessons.

If taken for a psychological evaluation, Todd may be diagnosed with **attention-deficit hyperactivity disorder (ADHD)**, as are some 4 percent of children who display at least one of its key symptoms (*inattention, hyperactivity,* and *impulsivity*) (NIMH, 2003).

To skeptics, being distractible, fidgety, and impulsive sounds like a "disorder" caused by a single genetic variation: a Y chromosome. And sure enough, ADHD is diagnosed two to three times more often in boys than in girls. Does energetic child + boring school = ADHD overdiagnosis? Is the label being applied to healthy schoolchildren who, in more natural outdoor environments, would seem perfectly normal?

Skeptics think so. In the decade after 1987, they note, the proportion of American children being treated for ADHD nearly quadrupled (Olfson & others, 2003). By 2005, a Gallup survey showed that 10 percent of American 13- to 17-year-olds were being medicated for ADHD (Mason, 2005). How commonplace the diagnosis is depends in part on teacher referrals. Some teachers refer lots of kids for ADHD assessment, others none. ADHD rates have varied by a factor of 10 in different counties of New York State (Carlson, 2000).

On the other side of the debate are those who argue that the more frequent diagnosis of ADHD today reflects increased awareness of the disorder, especially in those areas where rates are highest. They acknowledge that diagnoses can be subjective and that they are sometimes inconsistent—ADHD is not as objectively defined as is a broken arm. Nevertheless, declared the World Federation for Mental Health (2005), "there is strong agreement among the international scientific community that ADHD is a real neurobiological disorder whose existence should no longer be debated." ADHD is marked in neuroimaging studies by telltale brain activity, notes a consensus statement by 75 researchers (Barkley & others, 2002).

What, then, is known about ADHD's causes? It is not caused by too much sugar or poor schools. (Researchers have found, however, that toddlers who watch lots of TV are, at age 7, more likely than average to display ADHD symptoms [Christakis & others, 2004].) It often coexists with a learning disorder or with defiant and temper-prone behavior. The National Institute of Mental Health (1999, 2003) believes ADHD is heritable. It is treatable with nonaddictive medications such as Ritalin and Adderall, which are stimulants but help calm the hyperactivity and increase a person's ability to sit and focus on a task. Psychological therapies, such as those focused on shaping behaviors in the classroom and at home, have also helped address the distress of ADHD.

New research is seeking not only more information on causes but also a more objective assessment of ADHD. Possibilities include a physical measure of fidgeting, an eye-tracking device that gauges ability to focus on and follow spots of light, and more detailed brain imaging (Ashtari & others, 2004; Pavlidis, 2005; Teicher, 2002).

Other research is targeting effects of long-term use of stimulant drugs. About 80 percent of children medicated for ADHD still require medication as teens, as do 50 percent or more as adults. People appear to tolerate long-term use with no increased risk of substance abuse (Biederman & others, 1999), but other possible effects are being investigated. In one study, rats were given prolonged exposure to Ritalin early in life, at a dosage comparable to that commonly prescribed for children. When the drug was withdrawn later in life, the rats (compared with others in a control group) were more prone to depressive symptoms and to giving up quickly when facing challenging tasks (Carlezon & others, 2003).

The bottom line: Extreme inattention, hyperactivity, and impulsivity can derail social, academic, and vocational achievements, and these symptoms can be addressed with medication and other treatment. But the debate continues over whether normal rambunctiousness is too often diagnosed as a psychiatric disorder, and whether there is a cost to the long-term use of stimulant drugs in treating ADHD.

■ **attention-deficit hyperactivity disorder (ADHD)** a psychological disorder marked by the appearance by age 7 of one or more of three key symptoms: extreme inattention, hyperactivity, and impulsivity.

FIGURE **36.1**
The biopsychosocial approach to psychological disorders
Today's psychology studies how biological, psychological, and social-cultural factors interact to produce specific psychological disorders.

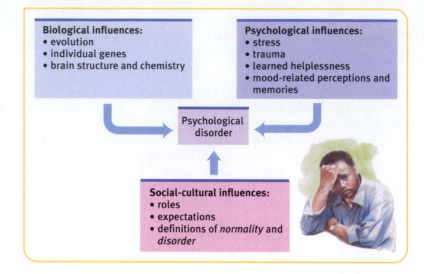

> "It's no measure of health to be well adjusted to a profoundly sick society."
>
> Krishnamurti, 1895–1986

The Biopsychosocial Approach

Today's psychologists contend that *all* behavior, whether called normal or disordered, arises from the interaction of nature (genetic and physiological factors) and nurture (past and present experiences). To presume that a person is "mentally ill," they say, attributes the condition to a "sickness" that must be found and cured. But maybe instead there is a difficulty in the person's environment, in the person's current interpretations of events, or in the person's bad habits and poor social skills.

Evidence of such effects comes from links between specific disorders and cultures (Beardsley, 1994; Castillo, 1997). Cultures differ in their sources of stress, and they produce different ways of coping. The eating disorders anorexia nervosa and bulimia nervosa, for example, occur mostly in Western cultures. Latin America lays claim to *susto,* a condition marked by severe anxiety, restlessness, and a fear of black magic. *Taijin-kyofusho,* social anxiety about one's appearance combined with a readiness to blush and a fear of eye contact, appears in Japan. Such disorders may share an underlying dynamic (such as anxiety) while differing in the symptoms (an eating problem or a type of fear) manifested in a particular culture. But not all disorders are culturebound. Depression and schizophrenia occur worldwide. From Asia to Africa and across the Americas, schizophrenia's symptoms often include irrationality and incoherent speech (Brislin, 1993; Draguns, 1990b).

To assess the whole set of influences—genetic predispositions and physiological states; inner psychological dynamics; and social and cultural circumstances—we need to use a biopsychosocial model (**FIGURE 36.1**). This approach recognizes that mind and body are inseparable. Negative emotions contribute to physical illness, and physical abnormalities contribute to emotional malaise. We are mind embodied.

Classifying Psychological Disorders

36-3 : How and why do clinicians classify psychological disorders?

In biology and the other sciences, classification creates order. To classify an animal as a "mammal" says a great deal—that it is warm-blooded, has hair or fur, and nourishes its young with milk. In psychiatry and psychology, too, classification orders and describes symptoms. To classify a person's disorder as "schizophrenia" suggests that the person talks incoherently, hallucinates or has delusions (bizarre beliefs), shows either little emotion or inappropriate emotion, or is socially withdrawn. "Schizophrenia" provides a handy shorthand for describing a complex disorder.

In psychiatry and psychology, diagnostic classification aims not only to describe a disorder but also to predict its future course, imply appropriate treatment, and stimulate research into its causes. Indeed, to study a disorder we must first name and describe it. A current authoritative scheme for classifying psychological disorders is the American Psychiatric Association's *Diagnostic and Statistical Manual of Mental Disorders* (Fourth Edition), nicknamed **DSM-IV.** This 1994 volume, now updated as a 2000 "text revision" (DSM-IV-TR), will be more substantially revised as DSM-V, to appear about 2011. (A set of case illustrations accompanying DSM-IV provides several of this book's case examples.) DSM-IV was developed in coordination with the tenth edition of the World Health Organization's *International Classification of Diseases* (ICD-10), which covers both medical and psychological disorders.

Despite its medical terminology ("diagnosing," "symptoms," "illness"), most practitioners find the DSM-IV a helpful and practical tool. It is also financially necessary: North American health insurance companies usually require an ICD diagnosis before they pay for therapy.

Without presuming to explain their causes, the DSM-IV describes various disorders and lists their prevalence. To be helpful and useful, the categories and diagnostic guidelines must be reliable, and to a reasonable extent they are. If one psychiatrist or psychologist diagnoses someone as having, say, catatonic schizophrenia, the chances are good that another mental health worker will independently give the same diagnosis. Following these guidelines, clinicians answer a series of objective questions about observable behaviors, such as, "Is the person afraid to leave home?" In one study, 16 psychologists used this structured-interview procedure to diagnose 75 psychiatric patients as suffering from (1) depression, (2) generalized anxiety, or (3) some other disorder (Riskind & others, 1987). Without knowing the first psychologist's diagnosis, another psychologist viewed a videotape of each interview and offered a second opinion. For 83 percent of the patients, the two opinions agreed.

Some critics have faulted the manual for casting too wide a net and bringing "almost any kind of behavior within the compass of psychiatry" (Eysenck & others, 1983). Others note that as the number of disorder categories has swelled (from 60 in the 1950s DSM to 400 in today's), so has the number of adults who meet the criteria for at least one of them—nearly 30 percent in one recent year, according to a U.S. survey (Regier & others, 1998). As a complement to the DSM, some psychologists are offering a manual of human strengths and virtues (see Close-Up: The "un-DSM": A Diagnostic Manual of Human Strengths on the next page).

Labeling Psychological Disorders

36-4 : Why do some psychologists criticize the use of diagnostic labels?

The DSM has other critics who register a more fundamental complaint—that these labels are at best arbitrary and at worst value judgments masquerading as science. Once we label a person, we view that person differently (Farina, 1982). Labels create preconceptions that guide our perceptions and our interpretations.

In a now-classic study of the biasing power of labels, David Rosenhan (1973) and seven others went to hospital admissions offices, complaining of "hearing voices" saying "empty," "hollow," and "thud." Apart from this complaint and giving false names and occupations, they answered questions truthfully. All eight normal people were misdiagnosed with disorders.

Should we be surprised? As one psychiatrist noted, if someone swallowed blood, went to an emergency room, and spat it up, would we fault the doctor for diagnosing a bleeding ulcer? Perhaps not. But what followed the diagnosis *was* startling. Until being released (an average of 19 days later), the "patients" exhibited no further symptoms.

■ **DSM-IV** the American Psychiatric Association's *Diagnostic and Statistical Manual of Mental Disorders* (Fourth Edition), a widely used system for classifying psychological disorders. Presently distributed in an updated "text revision" (DSM-IV-TR).

"I'm always like this, and my family was wondering if you could prescribe a mild depressant."

"One of the unpardonable sins, in the eyes of most people, is for a man to go about unlabeled. The world regards such a person as the police do an unmuzzled dog, not under proper control."

T. H. Huxley, *Evolution and Ethics*, 1893

CLOSE-UP

The "un-DSM": A Diagnostic Manual of Human Strengths

Psychologists Christopher Peterson and Martin Seligman (2004) have noted the usefulness of the DSM-IV in ordering and defining harmful dysfunctions. Would it not also be useful, these researchers ask, to have a companion catalog of human strengths—the thinking-feeling-action tendencies that contribute to the *good* life, for self and others?

The result, *The Values in Action Classification of Strengths*, resembles the DSM-IV in proposing a research-based common vocabulary. Assessment strategies and questionnaires aid researchers in assessing six clusters of 24 strengths:

Building strengths
In their work for Habitat for Humanity, former U.S. President Jimmy Carter and First Lady Rosalynn Carter model strengths related to love and justice.

- **Wisdom and knowledge**— curiosity; love of learning; critical judgment and open-mindedness; creativity; and perspective (wisdom)

- **Courage (overcoming opposition)**—bravery/valor; industry and perseverance; integrity and honesty; and vitality (zest and enthusiasm)

- **Love**—kindness; intimate attachment; and social intelligence

- **Justice**—citizenship and teamwork; fairness and equity; and leadership

- **Temperance**—humility; self-control; prudence and caution; and forgiveness and mercy

- **Transcendence**—appreciation of beauty, awe/wonder; gratitude; hope and optimism; playfulness and humor; and spirituality and purpose

This classification of human strengths is another expression of the positive psychology movement. Psychological science seeks to understand and help alleviate human ills and evils, agree positive psychology advocates, but also to understand and promote human strengths and virtues.

Yet after analyzing the (quite normal) life histories, clinicians were able to "discover" the causes of their disorders, such as reacting to mixed emotions about a parent. Even the routine behavior of taking notes was misinterpreted as a symptom.

Labels matter. When people watched videotaped interviews, those told the interviewees were job applicants perceived them as normal (Langer & others, 1974, 1980). Those who thought they were watching psychiatric or cancer patients perceived them as "different from most people." Therapists who thought an interviewee was a psychiatric patient perceived him as "frightened of his own aggressive impulses," a "passive, dependent type," and so forth. A label can, as Rosenhan discovered, have "a life and an influence of its own." (See Thinking Critically About: Insanity and Responsibility).

Surveys in North America (Page, 1977) and Europe have demonstrated the stigmatizing power of labels. Getting a job or finding a place to rent can be a challenge for those known to be just released from prison—or a mental hospital. But as we are coming to understand that many psychological disorders are diseases of the brain, not failures of character, the stigma seems to be lifting (Solomon, 1996). Public figures are feeling freer to "come out" and speak with candor about their struggles with disorders such as depression. And the more contact people have with individuals with disorders, the more accepting their attitudes are (Kolodziej & Johnson, 1996).

Nevertheless, stereotypes linger in media portrayals of psychological disorders. Some are reasonably accurate and sympathetic. But too often they stereotype people with a disorder as objects of humor or ridicule (*As Good as It Gets*), as homicidal maniacs (Hannibal Lecter in *Silence of the Lambs*), or as freaks (Hyler & others,

INSANITY AND RESPONSIBILITY

My brain . . . my genes . . . my bad upbringing made me do it. Such defenses were anticipated by Shakespeare's *Hamlet*. If I wrong someone when not myself, he explained, "then Hamlet does it not, Hamlet denies it. Who does it then? His madness." Such is the essence of a legal insanity defense, created in 1843 after a deluded Scotsman tried to shoot the prime minister (who he thought was persecuting him) but killed an assistant by mistake. Like U.S. President Ronald Reagan's near-assassin, John Hinckley, Scotsman Daniel M'Naughten was sent to a mental hospital rather than to prison.

In both cases, the public was outraged. "Hinckley Insane, Public Mad," declared one headline. And they were mad again when a deranged Jeffrey Dahmer in 1991 admitted murdering 15 young men and eating parts of their bodies. They were mad in 1998 when 15-year-old Kip Kinkel, driven by "those voices in my head," killed his parents and 2 fellow Springfield, Oregon, students and wounded 25 others. All of these people were sent to jails, not hospitals, following their arrests. As was Andrea Yates in her first trial in Texas in 2002, when—after being taken off

Jail or hospital?

Two weeks after being taken off antipsychotic medication by her psychiatrist, Andrea Yates drowned her five children, ages 7, 5, 3, 2, and 6 months, in her bathtub, apparently believing she was sparing them "the fires of hell." Although she was psychotic, one jury rejected the insanity defense, believing that she still could have discerned right from wrong. On retrial, a second jury found her not guilty by reason of insanity.

her antipsychotic medication—she drowned her five children. But in 2006, at Yates' second trial (after the first was set aside for technical reasons), the public wasn't so sure, and she was instead hospitalized.

Most people with psychological disorders are not violent. But what

should society do with those who are? A 1999 U.S. Justice Department study found that about 16 percent of U.S. jail and prison inmates had severe mental disorders. This is roughly 100,000 more than the 183,000 psychiatric inpatients in all types of U.S. hospitals (Bureau of the Census, 2004; Butterfield, 1999). Many people who have been executed or are now on death row have been limited by mental retardation or motivated by delusional voices. The State of Arkansas forcibly medicated one murderer with schizophrenia, Charles Singleton, with antipsychotic drugs—in order to make him mentally competent, so that he could then be put to death.

Which of Yates' two juries made the right decision? The first, which decided that people who commit such rare but terrible crimes should be held responsible? Or the second, which decided to blame the "madness" that clouds their vision? This much seems likely: If some superpsychologist were to understand the biological and environmental basis for everything—from generosity to vandalism—society would still wish to hold people responsible for their actions.

1991; Wahl, 1992). In real life, people with disorders are more likely to be the victims of violence, rather than the perpetrators (Marley & Bulia, 2001). Indeed, reports the U.S. Surgeon General's Office (1999, p. 7), "There is very little risk of violence or harm to a stranger from casual contact with an individual who has a mental disorder."

Not only can labels bias perceptions, they can also change reality. When teachers are told certain students are "gifted," when students expect someone to be "hostile," or when interviewers check to see whether someone is "extraverted," they may act in ways that elicit the very behavior expected (Snyder, 1984). Someone who was led to think you are nasty may treat you coldly, leading you to respond as a mean-spirited person would. Labels can serve as self-fulfilling prophecies.

But let us remember the benefits of diagnostic labels. Mental health professionals use labels to communicate about their cases, to comprehend the underlying causes, and to discern effective treatment programs.

Rates of Psychological Disorders

36-5 : How many people suffer, or have suffered, from a psychological disorder?

The World Health Organization (WHO, 2004) reports that, worldwide, some 450 million people suffer psychological disorders. These disorders account for 15.4 percent of the years of life lost due to death or disability—scoring slightly below cardiovascular conditions and slightly above cancer (Murray & Lopez, 1996). Rates and symptoms of psychological disorders vary by culture, but no known society is free of two terrible maladies: depression and schizophrenia (Castillo, 1997; Draguns, 1990a,b, 1997).

So who is most vulnerable to psychological disorders? At what times of life? To answer such questions, various countries have conducted lengthy, structured interviews with representative samples of thousands of their citizens. After asking hundreds of questions that probed for symptoms—"Has there ever been a period of two weeks or more when you felt like you wanted to die?"—the researchers have estimated the current, prior-year, and lifetime prevalence of various disorders.

How many people have, or have had, a psychological disorder? More than most of us suppose:

- Summarizing a U.S. National Institute of Mental Health interview study and a follow-up survey, William Narrow and his colleagues (2002) estimated that 1 in 7 Americans had suffered a clinically significant psychological disorder during the prior year (**TABLE 36.1**).
- Britain's Office of National Statistics (2002) has reported a similar disorder rate, as have Australian government surveys (Andrews & others, 1999; Sawyer & others, 2000).
- A twenty-first-century World Health Organization (2004) study—based on 90-minute interviews of 60,463 people—estimated the number of prior-year mental disorders in 20 countries. As **FIGURE 36.2** displays, the lowest rate of reported mental disorders was in Shanghai, the highest rate in the United States. Moreover, when people immigrate to the United States from Mexico and elsewhere, their mental health and their children's decline as they assimilate over time. For example, compared with people who have recently immigrated from Mexico, Mexican-Americans born in the United States are at greater risk of mental disorder (Grant & others, 2004; Vega & others, 1998).

TABLE 36.1

PRIOR-YEAR PREVALENCE OF SELECTED DISORDERS IN UNITED STATES

Psychological Disorder	Percentage
Alcohol abuse	5.2
Generalized anxiety	4.0
Phobias	7.8
Obsessive-compulsive disorder	2.1
Mood disorder	5.1
Schizophrenia	1.0
Antisocial personality	1.5
Any mental disorder	14.9

(Some people experience two or more of these disorders, such as depression and alcohol abuse, simultaneously.)

Source: Data from Narrow & others, 2002.

Who is most vulnerable to mental disorders? The answer varies with the disorder. One predictor of mental disorder, poverty, crosses ethnic and gender lines. The incidence of serious psychological disorders is doubly high among those below the poverty line (Centers for Disease Control, 1992). Like so many other correlations, the poverty-disorder association raises a chicken-and-egg question: Does poverty cause disorders? Or do disorders cause poverty? It is both, though the answer varies with the disorder. Schizophrenia understandably leads to poverty. Yet the stresses and demoralization of poverty can also precipitate disorders, especially depression in women and substance abuse in men (Dohrenwend & others, 1992). In one natural experiment on the poverty-pathology link, researchers tracked rates of behavior problems in North Carolina Native American children as economic development enabled a dramatic reduction in their community's poverty rate. As the study began, children of poverty exhibited more deviant and aggressive behaviors. After four years, children whose families had moved above the poverty line exhibited a 40 percent decrease in the behavior problems, while those who continued in their previous positions below or above the poverty line exhibited no change (Costello & others, 2003).

At what times of life do disorders strike? Usually by early adulthood. "Over 75 percent of our sample with any disorder had experienced its first symptoms by age 24," reported Lee Robins and Darrel Regier (1991, p. 331). The symptoms of antisocial personality disorder and of phobias are among the earliest to appear, at a median age of 8 and 10, respectively. Symptoms of alcohol abuse, obsessive-compulsive disorder, bipolar disorder, and schizophrenia appear at a median age near 20. Major depression often hits somewhat later, at a median age of 25. Such findings make clear the need for research and treatment to help the growing number of people, especially teenagers and young adults, who suffer the bewilderment and pain of a psychological disorder.

Although mindful of the pain, we can also be encouraged by the many successful people—including Leonardo da Vinci, Isaac Newton, and Leo Tolstoy—who pursued brilliant careers while enduring psychological difficulties. The bewilderment, fear, and sorrow caused by psychological disorders are real. But hope, too, is real, as our understanding of these disorders continues to grow.

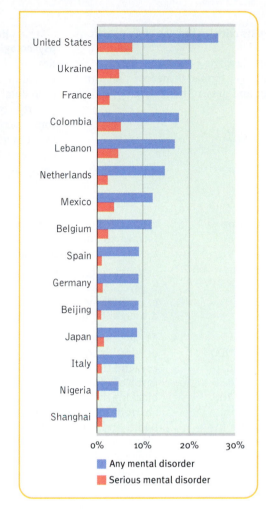

FIGURE 36.2

Prior-year prevalence of disorders in selected countries

From World Health Organization (2004) interviews in 20 countries.

REVIEWING

>> MODULE REVIEW

36-1: Where should we draw the line between normality and disorder?

Psychologists and psychiatrists consider behavior disordered when it is deviant, distressful, and dysfunctional. The definition of "deviant" varies with context and culture. It also varies with time; for example, some children who might have been judged rambunctious a few decades ago now are being diagnosed with *attention-deficit hyperactivity disorder*.

36-2: What theoretical models or perspectives can help us understand psychological disorders?

The *medical model* assumes that *psychological disorders* are mental illnesses that can be diagnosed on the basis of their symptoms and cured through therapy, sometimes in a hospital. The biopsychosocial approach assumes that disordered behavior, like other behavior, arises from genetic predispositions and physiological states; inner psychological dynamics; and social-cultural circumstances.

36-3: How and why do clinicians classify psychological disorders?

Many psychiatrists and psychologists use the American Psychiatric Association's *Diagnostic and Statistical Manual of Mental Disorders (DSM-IV)* for naming and describing psychological disorders in treatment and research. Diagnostic labels aid mental health professionals by providing a common language and shared concepts for communications and research. Most U.S. health insurance organizations require DSM-IV diagnoses before they will pay for therapy.

36-4 : Why do some psychologists criticize the use of diagnostic labels?

We pay a price for the benefits of classifying disorders: Labels can create preconceptions that unfairly stigmatize people and can bias our perceptions of their past and present behavior.

36-5 : How many people suffer, or have suffered, from a psychological disorder?

Research indicates that 1 in 7 U.S. adults has or has had a psychological disorder, usually by early adulthood. Poverty is a predictor of mental illness. Conditions and experiences associated with poverty contribute to the development of mental disorders, but some mental disorders, such as schizophrenia, can drive people into poverty. Among Americans who have ever experienced a psychological disorder, the three most common were phobias, alcohol abuse, and mood disorder.

>> REHEARSE IT!

1. Although some psychological disorders are culture-bound, others are universal. For example, in every known culture some people have

    a. bulimia nervosa.
    b. anorexia nervosa.
    c. schizophrenia.
    d. susto.

2. A physician may wash her hands 100 times a day, and few people would think her behavior was disordered. But if a lawyer washes his hands 100 times a day for no apparent reason and has no time left to meet with his clients, the hand washing will probably be labeled disordered because it is, among other things,

    a. distressing and dysfunctional.
    b. not explained by the medical model.
    c. harmful to others.
    d. untreatable.

3. Some therapists adhere to the idea that psychological disorders are sicknesses and that people with these disorders should be referred to hospitals, where they can be treated as patients. This approach is called the

    a. social-cultural perspective.
    b. psychological model.
    c. medical model.
    d. diagnostic model.

4. Many psychologists reject the "disorders-as-illness" view and instead contend that other factors may be involved—for example, a growth-blocking difficulty in the person's environment or the person's bad habits and poor social skills. Psychologists who take this approach to psychological disorders are said to be advocates of the _____ approach.

    a. medical
    b. positive psychology
    c. biopsychosocial
    d. diagnostic labels

5. The American Psychiatric Association's system of classifying psychological disorders is found in the *Diagnostic and Statistical Manual of Mental Disorders (Fourth Edition, Revised)*, or DSM-IV-TR. One study found that psychologists using DSM-IV agreed on a diagnosis for more than 80 percent of patients. The DSM-IV's reliability stems in part from its reliance on

    a. structured-interview procedures.
    b. in-depth histories of the patients.
    c. input from patients' family and friends.
    d. the theories of Peterson, Seligman, and others.

6. Researchers note that 1 in 7 American adults are suffering or have suffered a psychiatric disorder. One predictor that crosses ethnic and gender lines and is closely correlated with serious psychological disorder is

    a. age.
    b. education.
    c. poverty.
    d. religious faith.

Answers: 1. c, 2. a, 3. c, 4. c, 5. a, 6. c.

>> TERMS AND CONCEPTS TO REMEMBER

psychological disorder, p. 499
medical model, p. 500

attention-deficit hyperactivity disorder (ADHD), p. 501

DSM-IV, p. 503

>> TEST YOURSELF

1. What is the biopsychosocial approach, and why is it important in our understanding of psychological disorders?

2. Does poverty cause psychological disorders? Explain.

    (Answers in Appendix C.)

Multiple-choice **self-tests** and more may be found at www.worthpublishers.com/myers.

Anxiety, Dissociative, and Personality Disorders

Anxiety Disorders

37-1: What are anxiety disorders, and how do they differ from the ordinary worries and fears we all experience?

Anxiety is part of life. Speaking in front of a class, peering down from a ledge, or waiting to play in a big game, any one of us might feel anxious. At times we may feel enough anxiety to avoid making eye contact or talking with someone—"shyness," we call it. Fortunately for most of us, our uneasiness is not intense and persistent. If it becomes so, we may have one of the **anxiety disorders,** marked by distressing, persistent anxiety or maladaptive behaviors that reduce anxiety. In this section we focus on five anxiety disorders:

- *Generalized anxiety disorder,* in which a person is unexplainably and continually tense and uneasy
- *Panic disorder,* in which a person experiences sudden episodes of intense dread
- *Phobias,* in which a person feels irrationally and intensely afraid of a specific object or situation
- *Obsessive-compulsive disorder,* in which a person is troubled by repetitive thoughts or actions
- *Post-traumatic stress disorder*, in which a person has lingering memories, nightmares, and other symptoms for weeks after a severely threatening, uncontrollable event

Anxiety Disorders

Dissociative Disorders

Personality Disorders

Generalized Anxiety Disorder

For the past two years, Tom, a 27-year-old electrician, has had periods of dizziness, sweating palms, heart palpitations, and ringing in his ears. He feels edgy and sometimes finds himself shaking. With reasonable success he hides his symptoms from his family and co-workers. But he allows himself few other social contacts, and occasionally he has to leave work. His family doctor and a neurologist can find no physical problem.

■ **anxiety disorders** psychological disorders characterized by distressing, persistent anxiety or maladaptive behaviors that reduce anxiety.

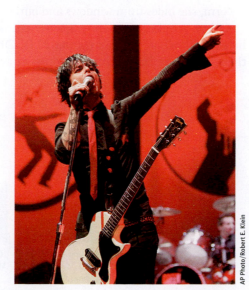

Coping with disorder
"The only way I knew how to deal with it was to write a song about it," musician Billy Joe Armstrong of Green Day explained, referring to his song "Basket Case," which chronicles a personal struggle with anxiety disorders.

AP Photo/Robert E. Klein

Gender and anxiety: Eight months after 9/11, more U.S. women (34 percent) than men (19 percent) told Gallup (2002) they were still less willing than before 9/11 to go into skyscrapers or fly on planes. In early 2003, more women (57 percent) than men (36 percent) were "somewhat worried" about becoming a terrorist victim (Jones, 2003).

Tom's unfocused, out-of-control, negative feelings suggest **generalized anxiety disorder.** The symptoms of this disorder are commonplace; their persistence is not. People with this condition (two-thirds are women) worry continually, and they are often jittery, agitated, and sleep-deprived. Concentration is difficult, as attention switches from worry to worry, and their tension and apprehension may leak out through furrowed brows, twitching eyelids, trembling, perspiration, or fidgeting. One of the worst characteristics of this disorder is that the person cannot identify, and therefore cannot deal with or avoid, its cause. To use Sigmund Freud's term, the anxiety is *free-floating*. Generalized anxiety disorder is often accompanied by depressed mood, but even without depression it tends to be disabling (Hunt & others, 2004). Moreover, it may lead to physical problems, such as ulcers and high blood pressure.

Panic Disorder

Panic disorder is to anxiety what a tornado is to a windy day. It strikes suddenly, wreaks havoc, and disappears. For the 1 person in 75 with this disorder, anxiety suddenly escalates into a terrifying *panic attack*—a minutes-long episode of intense fear that something horrible is about to happen. Heart palpitations, shortness of breath, choking sensations, trembling, or dizziness typically accompany the panic, which may be misperceived as a heart attack or other serious physical ailment. Smokers have a two- to fourfold risk of a first-time panic attack (Breslau & Klein, 1999; Goodwin & Hamilton, 2002; Isensee & others, 2003). Because nicotine is a stimulant, lighting up doesn't lighten up.

One woman recalled suddenly feeling "hot and as though I couldn't breathe. My heart was racing and I started to sweat and tremble and I was sure I was going to faint. Then my fingers started to feel numb and tingly and things seemed unreal. It was so bad I wondered if I was dying and asked my husband to take me to the emergency room. By the time we got there (about 10 minutes) the worst of the attack was over and I just felt washed out" (Greist & others, 1986).

Phobias

Phobias are anxiety disorders in which an irrational fear causes the person to avoid some specific object, activity, or situation. Many people accept their phobias and live with them, but others are incapacitated by their efforts to avoid the feared situation. Marilyn, an otherwise healthy and happy 28-year-old, so fears thunderstorms that she feels anxious as soon as a weather forecaster mentions possible storms later in the week. If her husband is away and a storm is forecast, she may stay with a close relative. During a storm, she hides from windows and buries her head to avoid seeing the lightning.

Other people suffer from *specific phobias* focused on specific animals, insects, heights, blood, or tunnels (**FIGURE 37.1**). Often they avoid the stimulus that arouses the fear, hiding during thunderstorms or avoiding high places.

FIGURE 37.1
Some common and uncommon specific fears
This national interview study identified the commonality of various specific fears. A strong fear becomes a phobia if it provokes a compelling but irrational desire to avoid the dreaded object or situation. (From Curtis & others, 1998.)

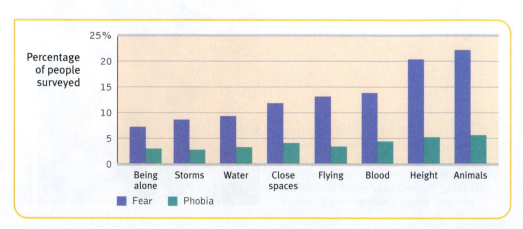

Not all phobias are so specific. *Social phobia* is shyness taken to an extreme. Those with a social phobia, an intense fear of being scrutinized by others, avoid potentially embarrassing social situations, such as speaking up, eating out, or going to parties—or will sweat, tremble, or have diarrhea when doing so.

People who have experienced several panic attacks may come to fear the fear itself and avoid situations where the panic has struck before. If the fear is intense enough, it may become *agoraphobia,* fear or avoidance of situations in which escape might be difficult or help unavailable when panic strikes. Given such fear, people may avoid being outside the home, in a crowd, on a bus, or even on an elevator. After spending five years sailing the world, Charles Darwin began suffering panic disorder at age 28. Because of the attacks, he moved to the country, avoided social gatherings, and traveled only in his wife's company. But the relative seclusion did free him to focus on developing his evolutionary theory. "Even ill health," he reflected, "has saved me from the distraction of society and its amusements" (quoted in Ma, 1997).

Obsessive-Compulsive Disorder

As with generalized anxiety and phobias, we can see aspects of our own behavior in **obsessive-compulsive disorder (OCD).** We may at times be obsessed with senseless or offensive thoughts that will not go away. Or we may engage in compulsive behaviors, rigidly checking, ordering, and cleaning before guests arrive, or lining up books and pencils "just so" before studying.

Obsessive thoughts and compulsive behaviors cross the fine line between normality and disorder when they become so persistent that they interfere with everyday living and cause the person distress. Checking to see you locked the door is normal; checking 10 times is not. Washing your hands is normal; washing so often that your skin becomes raw is not. (**TABLE 37.1** offers more examples.) At some time during their lives, often during their late teens or twenties, 2 to 3 percent of people cross that line from normal preoccupations and fussiness to debilitating disorder (Karno & others, 1988). The obsessive thoughts become so haunting, the compulsive rituals so senselessly time-consuming, that effective functioning becomes impossible.

■ **generalized anxiety disorder** an anxiety disorder in which a person is continually tense, apprehensive, and in a state of autonomic nervous system arousal.

■ **panic disorder** an anxiety disorder marked by unpredictable minutes-long episodes of intense dread in which a person experiences terror and accompanying chest pain, choking, or other frightening sensations.

■ **phobia** an anxiety disorder marked by a persistent, irrational fear and avoidance of a specific object or situation.

■ **obsessive-compulsive disorder (OCD)** an anxiety disorder characterized by unwanted repetitive thoughts (obsessions) and/or actions (compulsions).

TABLE 37.1

COMMON OBSESSIONS AND COMPULSIONS AMONG CHILDREN AND ADOLESCENTS WITH OBSESSIVE-COMPULSIVE DISORDER

Thought or Behavior	Percentage Reporting Symptom
Obsessions *(repetitive thoughts)*	
Concern with dirt, germs, or toxins	40
Something terrible happening (fire, death, illness)	24
Symmetry, order, or exactness	17
Compulsions *(repetitive behaviors)*	
Excessive hand washing, bathing, tooth brushing, or grooming	85
Repeating rituals (in/out of a door, up/down from a chair)	51
Checking doors, locks, appliances, car brake, homework	46

Source: Adapted from Rapoport, 1989.

OCD is more common among teens and young adults than among older people (Samuels & Nestadt, 1997). A 40-year follow-up study of 144 Swedish people diagnosed with the disorder found that, for most, the obsessions and compulsions had gradually lessened, though only 1 in 5 had completely recovered (Skoog & Skoog, 1999).

Snapshots

Obsessing about obsessive-compulsive disorder.

■ **post-traumatic stress disorder (PTSD)**
an anxiety disorder characterized by haunting memories, nightmares, social withdrawal, jumpy anxiety, and/or insomnia that lingers for four weeks or more after a traumatic experience.

Post-Traumatic Stress Disorder

During the 1991 Persian Gulf conflict, Jack's platoon was repeatedly under fire. In one ambush, his closest friend was killed while Jack stood a few feet away. Jack himself killed someone in an assault. Years later, images of these events intrude on him as flashbacks and nightmares. He still jumps at the sound of a firecracker or the backfire of a car. When annoyed, he lashes out in ways he seldom did before being in combat. To calm his continuing anxiety, he drinks more than he should.

Jack's complaints—recurring haunting memories and nightmares, a numbed social withdrawal, jumpy anxiety, and insomnia—are typical of **post-traumatic stress disorder (PTSD)** (Kessler, 2000).

Jack is not alone. One in six U.S. combat infantry has reported symptoms of PTSD, depression, or severe anxiety in the months after returning home from the Iraq war (Hoge & others, 2004). PTSD symptoms have also been reported by survivors of accidents, disasters, and violent and sexual assaults (including an estimated two-thirds of prostitutes) (Brewin & others, 1999; Farley & others, 1998; Taylor & others, 1998).

A month after the 9/11 terrorist attacks, a survey of Manhattan residents indicated that 8.5 percent were suffering PTSD, most as a result of the attack (Galea & others, 2002). Among those living near the World Trade Center, 20 percent reported such telltale signs as nightmares, severe anxiety, and fear of public places (Susser & others, 2002).

To pin down the frequency of this disorder, the U.S. Centers for Disease Control (1988) compared 7000 Vietnam combat veterans with 7000 noncombat veterans who served during the same years. On average, according to a recent reanalysis, 19 percent of all Vietnam veterans reported PTSD symptoms, but the rate was 10 percent among those who had never seen combat and 32 percent among those who had experienced heavy combat (Dohrenwend & others, 2006). Similar variations in rates have been found among those who have experienced a natural disaster, or who have been kidnapped, held captive, tortured, or raped (Brewin & others, 2000; Brody, 2000; Kessler, 2000).

So what determines whether a person gets PTSD after a traumatic event? Research indicates that the greater one's emotional distress during a trauma, the higher the risk for post-traumatic symptoms (Ozer & others, 2003). And the more frequent and severe the assault experiences, the more adverse the long-term outcomes tend to be (Golding, 1999). A sensitive limbic system also seems to increase vulnerability, by flooding the body with stress hormones (Ozer & Weiss, 2004).

Toxic trauma
Many veterans, such as this U.S. Army Reserve sergeant at a Veteran's Administration Hospital, have recently been treated for post-traumatic stress disorder.

AP Photo/Lawrence Journal-World, Thad Allender

Researchers also point to the impressive *survivor resiliency* most people display (Bonanno, 2004, 2005). About half of adults experience at least one traumatic event in their lifetime, but only about 1 in 10 women and 1 in 20 men develop PTSD (Ozer & Weiss, 2004). More than 9 in 10 New Yorkers, although stunned and grief-stricken by 9/11, did *not* respond pathologically, and by the following January the stress symptoms of the rest had mostly subsided (Galea & others, 2002). Similarly, most combat-stressed veterans and most political dissidents who survive dozens of episodes of torture do *not* later exhibit PTSD (Mineka & Zinbarg, 1996). Psychologist Peter Suedfeld (1998, 2000), who as a boy survived the Holocaust under conditions of privation while his mother died in Auschwitz, has documented the resilience of Holocaust survivors, most of whom have lived productive lives. "It is not always true that 'What doesn't kill you makes you stronger,' but it is often true," he reports. And "what doesn't kill you may reveal to you just how strong you really are."

Indeed, suffering can lead to what Richard Tedeschi and Lawrence Calhoun (2004) call *post-traumatic growth*. Tedeschi and Calhoun have found that the struggle with challenging crises, such as facing cancer, often leads people later to report an increased appreciation for life, more meaningful relationships, increased personal strength, changed priorities, and a richer spiritual life. This idea—that suffering has transformative power—is also found in Judaism, Christianity, Hinduism, Buddhism, and Islam.

Some psychologists believe that PTSD has been overdiagnosed, due partly to a broadening definition of *trauma* (which originally meant direct exposure to serious threat, such as combat or rape [McNally, 2003]). PTSD is actually infrequent, say the critics, and well-intentioned attempts to have people relive the trauma may exacerbate their emotions and pathologize normal stress reactions (Wakefield & Spitzer, 2002). "Debriefing" survivors right after a trauma by getting them to revisit the experience and vent emotions has actually proven generally ineffective and sometimes harmful (McNally & others, 2003; Rose & others, 2003).

Explaining Anxiety Disorders

37-2: What are the sources of the anxious feelings and thoughts that characterize anxiety disorders?

Anxiety is both a feeling and a cognition—a doubt-laden appraisal of one's safety or social skill. How do these anxious feelings and cognitions arise? Freud's psychoanalytic theory proposed that, beginning in childhood, people repress intolerable impulses, ideas, and feelings and that this submerged mental energy sometimes produces mystifying symptoms such as anxiety. Many of today's psychologists have turned to two contemporary perspectives—learning and biological—for a more complete understanding.

The Learning Perspective

Fear Conditioning When bad events happen unpredictably and uncontrollably, anxiety often develops (Chorpita & Barlow, 1998). Decades of research on conditioning show that dogs learn to fear neutral stimuli associated with shock, and infants come to fear objects associated with frightening noises. Using classical conditioning, researchers have also created chronically anxious, ulcer-prone rats by giving them unpredictable electric shocks (Schwartz, 1984). Like assault victims who report feeling anxious when returning to the scene of the crime, the rats become apprehensive in their lab environment. This link between conditioned fear and general anxiety may help explain why anxious people are hyperattentive to possible threats, and how panic-prone people come to associate anxiety with certain cues (Bouton & others, 2001; Mineka & Zinbarg, 1996). In one survey, 58 percent of those with social phobia experienced their disorder after a traumatic event (Ost & Hugdahl, 1981).

Conditioned fears may remain long after we have forgotten the experiences that produced them (Jacobs & Nadel, 1985). As newly mobile infants, we experience many falls and near-falls, and we gradually learn an adaptive fear of heights (Campos & others, 1992).

Through such conditioning, the short list of naturally painful and frightening events can multiply into a long list of human fears. My car was once struck by another whose driver missed a stop sign. For months afterward, I felt a twinge of unease when any car approached from a side street. Marilyn's phobia may have been similarly conditioned during a terrifying or painful experience associated with a thunderstorm. Two specific learning processes that can contribute to such anxiety are stimulus generalization and reinforcement.

Stimulus generalization occurs, for example, when a person fears heights after a fall and later develops a fear of flying in an airplane without ever having flown. Once phobias and compulsions arise, *reinforcement* helps maintain them. Avoiding or escaping the feared situation reduces anxiety, thus reinforcing the phobic behavior. Feeling anxious or fearing a panic attack, a person may go inside and be reinforced by feeling calmer (Antony & others, 1992). Compulsive behaviors operate similarly. If washing your hands relieves your feelings of anxiety, you may wash your hands again when those feelings return.

An emotional high

Although we humans seem biologically predisposed to fear heights—certainly an adaptive response—this construction worker seems fearless. The biological perspective helps us understand why most people would be terrified in this situation.

John Coletti/Stock, Boston

Observational Learning We may also learn fear through observational learning—by observing others' fears. As Susan Mineka (1985) demonstrated, wild monkeys transmit their fear of snakes to their watchful offspring. Human parents similarly transmit fears to their children. Moreover, just observing someone receiving a mild electric shock after a conditioned stimulus produces fear learning similar to that produced by direct experience (Olsson & Phelps, 2004).

The Biological Perspective

There is, however, more to anxiety than simple conditioning or observational learning, as evident from how few people develop lasting phobias after suffering traumas. The biological perspective can help us understand why we learn some fears more readily and why some individuals are more vulnerable.

Natural Selection We humans seem biologically prepared to fear threats faced by our ancestors. Most of our phobias focus on such objects: spiders, snakes, and other animals; closed spaces and heights; storms and darkness. (Those fearless about these occasional threats were less likely to survive and leave descendants.) It is easy to condition but hard to extinguish fears of such stimuli (Davey, 1995; Öhman, 1986). Many of our modern fears may also have an evolutionary explanation. For example, a fear of flying may also come from our biological past, which predisposes us to fear confinement and heights.

Moreover, consider what people tend *not* to learn to fear. World War II air raids produced remarkably few lasting phobias. As the air blitzes continued, the British, Japanese, and German populations became not more panicked, but rather more indifferent to planes outside of their immediate neighborhood (Mineka & Zinbarg, 1996). Evolution has not prepared us to fear bombs dropping from the sky.

Just as our phobias focus on dangers faced by our ancestors, our compulsive acts typically exaggerate behaviors that contributed to our species' survival. Grooming gone wild becomes hair pulling. Washing up becomes ritual hand washing. Checking territorial boundaries becomes checking and rechecking an already locked door (Rapoport, 1989).

Genes Some people more than others seem predisposed to anxiety. Genes matter. Pair a traumatic event with a sensitive, high-strung temperament and the result may be a new phobia. Among monkeys, fearfulness runs in families. Individual monkeys react more strongly to stress if their close biological relatives are anxiously reactive (Suomi, 1986). In humans, vulnerability to anxiety disorder rises when the afflicted relative is an identical twin (Barlow, 1988; Hettema & others, 2001; Kendler & others, 1992, 1999, 2002a,b). Identical twins also may develop similar phobias, even when raised separately (Carey, 1990; Eckert & others, 1981). One pair of 35-year-old female identical twins independently became so afraid of water that each would wade in the ocean backward and only up to the knees.

The Brain Generalized anxiety, panic attacks, and even obsessions and compulsions are biologically measurable as an overarousal of brain areas involved in impulse control and habitual behaviors. When the disordered brain detects that something is amiss, it seems to generate a mental hiccup of repeating thoughts or actions (Gehring & others, 2000). Brain scans of people with OCD reveal elevated activity in specific brain areas during behaviors such as compulsive hand washing, checking, ordering, or hoarding (Mataix-Cols & others, 2004, 2005). As **FIGURE 37.2** shows, the *anterior cingulate cortex,* a brain region that monitors our actions and checks for errors, seems especially likely to be hyperactive in those with OCD (Ursu & others, 2003). Fear-learning experiences that traumatize the brain can also create fear circuits within the amygdala (Armony & others, 1998). Some antidepressant drugs dampen this fear-circuit activity and its associated obsessive-compulsive behavior.

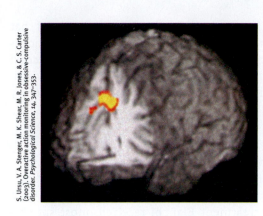

S. Ursu, V. A. Stenger, M. K. Shear, M. R. Jones, & C. S. Carter (2003). Overactive action monitoring in obsessive-compulsive disorder. *Psychological Science, 14*, 347–353.

FIGURE 37.2

An obsessive-compulsive brain

Neuroscientist Stefan Ursu and his colleagues (2003) used functional magnetic resonance imaging (fMRI) scans to compare the brains of those with and without OCD as they engaged in a challenging cognitive task. The fMRI scans showed elevated activity in the anterior cingulate cortex of those with OCD.

The biological perspective cannot explain all aspects of anxiety disorders, such as the sharp increase in the anxiety levels of both children and college students over the last half-century, which appears to be related to fraying social support accompanying family breakup (Twenge, 2000). It is nevertheless clear that biology is an important part of anxiety.

Dissociative Disorders

37-3 : What are dissociative disorders, and why are they controversial?

Among the most bewildering disorders are the rare **dissociative disorders.** These are disorders of consciousness, in which a person appears to experience a sudden loss of memory or change in identity, often in response to an overwhelmingly stressful situation. Their conscious awareness is said to dissociate (become separated from) painful memories, thoughts, and feelings. (Note that this explanation presumes the existence of repressed memories, which have recently been questioned.)

Dissociation itself is not so rare. Now and then, many people may have a sense of being unreal, of being separated from their body, of watching themselves as if in a movie. Sometimes we may say, "I was not myself at the time." Perhaps you can recall getting in your car and driving to some unintended location while your mind was preoccupied elsewhere. Facing trauma, such detachment may actually protect a person from being overwhelmed by emotion. Only when such experiences are severe and prolonged do they suggest a dissociative disorder.

Dissociative Identity Disorder

A massive dissociation of self from ordinary consciousness characterizes those with **dissociative identity disorder (DID),** in which two or more distinct identities are said to alternately control the person's behavior. Each personality has its own voice and mannerisms. Thus the person may be prim and proper one moment, loud and flirtatious the next. Typically, the original personality denies any awareness of the other(s).

People diagnosed with DID are usually not violent, but cases have been reported of dissociations into a "good" and a "bad" (or aggressive) personality—a modest version of the Dr. Jekyll/Mr. Hyde split immortalized in Robert Louis Stevenson's story. One unusual case involved Kenneth Bianchi, accused in the "Hillside Strangler" rapes and murders of 10 California women. During a hypnosis session with Bianchi, psychologist John Watkins (1984) "called forth" a hidden personality: "I've talked a bit to Ken, but I think that perhaps there might be another part of Ken that . . . maybe feels somewhat differently from the part that I've talked to. . . . Would you talk with me, Part, by saying, 'I'm here'?" Bianchi answered "Yes" and then claimed to be "Steve."

■ **dissociative disorders** disorders in which conscious awareness becomes separated (dissociated) from previous memories, thoughts, and feelings.

■ **dissociative identity disorder (DID)** a rare dissociative disorder in which a person exhibits two or more distinct and alternating personalities. Also called *multiple personality disorder*.

Multiple personalities

Chris Sizemore's story, *The Three Faces of Eve,* gave early visibility to what is now called *dissociative identity disorder.*

Lois Bernstein/Gamma Liaison

APP/Wide World Photos

The "Hillside Strangler"
Kenneth Bianchi is shown here at his trial.

"Pretense may become reality."
—Chinese proverb

Speaking as Steve, Bianchi stated that he hated Ken because Ken was nice and that he (Steve), aided by a cousin, had murdered women. He also claimed Ken knew nothing about Steve's existence and was innocent of the murders. Was Bianchi's second personality a ruse, simply a way of disavowing responsibility for his actions? Indeed, Bianchi—a practiced liar who had read about multiple personality in psychology books—was later convicted.

Understanding Dissociative Identity Disorder

Skeptics question whether DID is a genuine disorder or an extension of our normal capacity for personality shifts. Nicholas Spanos (1986, 1994, 1996) asked college students to pretend they were accused murderers being examined by a psychiatrist. Given the same hypnotic treatment Bianchi received, most spontaneously expressed a second personality. This discovery made Spanos wonder: Are dissociative identities simply a more extreme version of our capacity to vary the "selves" we present—as when we display a goofy, loud self while hanging out with friends, and a subdued, respectful self around grandparents? Are clinicians who discover multiple personalities merely triggering role-playing by fantasy-prone people? Do they, like actors who commonly report "losing themselves" in their roles, then convince themselves of the authenticity of their own role enactments? Spanos was no stranger to this line of thinking. In a related research area, he had also raised these questions about the hypnotic state. Given that most DID patients are highly hypnotizable, whatever explains one condition—dissociation or role-playing—may help explain the other.

Skeptics also find it suspicious that the disorder is so localized in time and space. Between 1930 and 1960, the number of DID diagnoses in North America was 2 per decade. In the 1980s, when the DSM contained the first formal code for this disorder, the number of reported cases had exploded to more than 20,000 (McHugh, 1995a). The average number of displayed personalities also mushroomed—from 3 to 12 per patient (Goff & Simms, 1993). And outside North America, the disorder is much less prevalent, although in other cultures some people are said to be "possessed" by an alien spirit (Aldridge-Morris, 1989; Kluft, 1991). In Britain, DID—which some consider "a wacky American fad" (Cohen, 1995)—is rare. In India and Japan, it is essentially nonexistent.

Such findings, skeptics say, point to a cultural phenomenon—a disorder created by therapists in a particular social context (Merskey, 1992). Patients do not enter therapy saying "Allow me to introduce myselves." Rather, note skeptics, some therapists—often practitioners of hypnosis (Goff, 1993; Piper, 1998)—go fishing for multiple personalities: "Have you ever felt like another part of you does things you can't control? Does this part of you have a name? Can I talk to the angry part of you?" Once patients permit a therapist to talk, by name, "to the part of you that says those angry things" they have begun acting out the fantasy. The result may be a real phenomenon, which vulnerable patients may experience as another self. Others disagree, finding support for DID as a genuine disorder in the distinct brain and body states associated with differing personalities (Putnam, 1991). Handedness, too, sometimes switches with personality (Henninger, 1992). Ophthalmologists have also detected shifting visual acuity and eye-muscle balance as patients switched personalities, changes that did not occur among control group members trying to simulate DID (Miller & others, 1991).

Researchers and clinicians have interpreted DID symptoms from psychoanalytic and learning perspectives. Both views agree that the symptoms are ways of dealing with anxiety. Psychoanalysts see them as defenses against the anxiety caused by the eruption of unacceptable impulses; a wanton second personality enables the discharge of forbidden impulses. Learning theorists see dissociative disorders as behaviors reinforced by anxiety reduction.

© The New Yorker Collection, 2001, Leo Cullum from cartoonbank.com. All Rights Reserved.

"Would it be possible to speak with the personality that pays the bills?"

Others include dissociative disorders under the umbrella of post-traumatic disorders—a natural, protective response to "histories of childhood trauma" (Putnam, 1995). Many DID patients have suffered physical, sexual, or emotional abuse as children (Gleaves, 1996; Kihlstrom, 2005; Lilienfeld & others, 1999). In one study of 12 murderers diagnosed with DID, 11 had suffered severe, torturous child abuse (Lewis & others, 1997). One was set afire by his parents. Another was used in child pornography and was scarred from being made to sit on a stove burner.

So the debate continues. On one side are those who believe multiple personalities are the desperate efforts of the traumatized to detach from a horrific existence. On the other are the skeptics who think DID is a condition contrived by fantasy-prone, emotionally vulnerable people, and constructed out of the therapist-patient interaction. If the skeptics' view wins, predicts psychiatrist Paul McHugh (1995b), "this epidemic will end in the way that the witch craze ended in Salem. The [multiple personality phenomenon] will be seen as manufactured."

Personality Disorders

37-4: What characteristics are typical of personality disorders?

Some maladaptive behavior patterns impair people's social functioning without depression or delusions. Among them are **personality disorders,** disruptive, inflexible, and enduring behavior patterns that impair one's social functioning. One cluster of disorders expresses anxiety, such as a fearful sensitivity to rejection that predisposes the withdrawn *avoidant personality disorder*. A second cluster expresses eccentric behaviors, such as the emotionless disengagement of the *schizoid personality disorder*. A third cluster exhibits dramatic or impulsive behaviors.

Antisocial Personality Disorder

The most troubling and heavily researched personality disorder is the **antisocial personality disorder.** The person (formerly called a *sociopath* or a *psychopath*) is typically a male whose lack of conscience becomes plain before age 15, as he begins to lie, steal, fight, or display unrestrained sexual behavior (Cale & Lilienfeld, 2002). About half of such children become antisocial adults—unable to keep a job, irresponsible as a spouse and parent, and assaultive or otherwise criminal (Farrington, 1991). When the antisocial personality combines a keen intelligence with amorality, the result may be a charming and clever con artist—or worse.

Despite their antisocial behavior, most criminals do not fit the description of antisocial personality disorder. Why? Because most criminals actually show responsible concern for their friends and family members. Antisocial personalities feel and fear little, and in extreme cases, the results can be horrifyingly tragic. Henry Lee Lucas confessed that during his 32 years of crime, he had bludgeoned, suffocated, stabbed, shot, or mutilated some 360 women, men, and children—the first (a woman) at age 13. During the last 6 years of his reign of terror, Lucas teamed with Elwood Toole, who reportedly slaughtered about 50 people he "didn't think was worth living anyhow." It ended when Lucas confessed to stabbing and dismembering his 15-year-old common-law wife, who was Toole's niece.

The antisocial personality expresses little regret over violating others' rights. "Once I've done a crime, I just forget it," said Lucas. Toole was equally matter-of-fact: "I think of killing like smoking a cigarette, like another habit" (Darrach & Norris, 1984).

Understanding Antisocial Personality Disorder

Antisocial personality disorder is woven of both biological and psychological strands. No single gene codes for a complex behavior such as crime, but twin and adoption studies reveal that biological relatives of those with antisocial and unemotional tendencies are

■ **personality disorders** psychological disorders characterized by inflexible and enduring behavior patterns that impair social functioning.

■ **antisocial personality disorder** a personality disorder in which the person (usually a man) exhibits a lack of conscience for wrongdoing, even toward friends and family members. May be aggressive and ruthless or a clever con artist.

> "Though this be madness, yet there is method in 't."
> —William Shakespeare, *Hamlet*, 1600

Antisocial personality?
Dennis Rader, known as the "BTK killer" in Kansas, was convicted in 2005 of killing 10 people over a 30-year span. Rader exhibited the extreme lack of conscience that marks antisocial personality disorder.

EPA/Jeff Tuttle/Landov

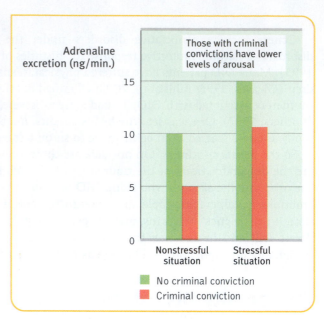

FIGURE **37.3**
Cold-blooded arousability and risk of crime
Levels of the stress hormone adrenaline were measured in two groups of 13-year-old Swedish boys. In both stressful and nonstressful situations, those later convicted of a crime (as 18- to 26-year-olds) showed relatively low arousal. (From Magnusson, 1990.)

at increased risk for antisocial behavior (Rhee & Waldman, 2002; Viding & others, 2005). Their genetic vulnerability appears as a fearless approach to life. Awaiting aversive events, such as electric shocks or loud noises, they show little autonomic nervous system arousal (Hare, 1975). Even as youngsters, before committing any crime, they react with lower levels of stress hormones than do others their age (**FIGURE 37.3**).

Some studies have detected the early signs of antisocial behavior in children as young as ages 3 to 6 (Caspi & others, 1996; Tremblay & others, 1994). Boys who later became aggressive or antisocial adolescents tended, as young children, to have been impulsive, uninhibited, unconcerned with social rewards, and low in anxiety. If channeled in more productive directions, such fearlessness may lead to courageous heroism, adventurism, or star-level athleticism (Poulton & Milne, 2002). Lacking a sense of social responsibility, the same disposition may produce a cool con artist or killer (Lykken, 1995).

Genetic influences help wire the brain. Adrian Raine (1999) compared PET scans of 41 murderers' brains with those from people of similar age and sex. Raine found reduced activity in the murderers' frontal lobes, an area of the cortex that helps control impulses (**FIGURE 37.4**). This reduction was especially apparent in those who murdered impulsively. In a follow-up study, Raine and his team (2000) found that violent repeat offenders had 11 percent less frontal lobe tissue than normal. This helps explain why people with antisocial personality disorder exhibit marked deficits in frontal lobe cognitive functions, such as planning, organization, and inhibition (Morgan & Lilienfeld, 2000).

FIGURE **37.4**
Murderous minds
PET scans illustrate reduced activation (less red and yellow) in a murderer's frontal cortex—a brain area that helps brake impulsive, aggressive behavior. (From Raine, 1999.)

Genetics alone is hardly the whole story of antisocial crime, however. Relative to 1960, the average American in 1995 (before the late 1990s crime decline) was twice as likely to be murdered, four times as likely to report being raped, four times as likely to report being robbed, and five times as likely to report being assaulted (FBI, *Uniform Crime Reports*). Violent crime was also surging in other Western nations. Yet the human gene pool had hardly changed. Or consider the British social experiment begun in 1787, exiling 160,000 criminals to Australia. The descendants of these exiles, carrying their ancestors' supposed "criminal genes," have helped create a civilized democracy whose crime rate is similar to Britain's. Genetic predispositions do put some individuals more at risk for antisocial conduct than others; biological as well as environmental influences explain why 5 to 6 percent of offenders commit 50 to 60 percent of crimes (Lyman, 1996). But we must look to sociocultural factors to explain the modern epidemic of violence.

Courtesy of Adrian Raine, University of Southern California

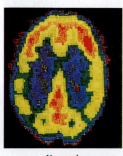
Normal

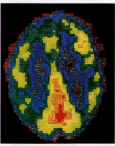
Murderer

REVIEWING

>> MODULE REVIEW

37-1: **What are anxiety disorders, and how do they differ from the ordinary worries and fears we all experience?**

Anxiety is part of our everyday experience. It is classified as a psychological disorder only when it becomes distressing or persistent, or is characterized by maladaptive behaviors intended to reduce the anxiety.

People with *generalized anxiety disorder* (two-thirds of whom are women) feel persistently and uncontrollably tense and apprehensive, for no apparent reason. In the more extreme *panic disorder,* anxiety escalates into periodic episodes of intense dread. Those with a *phobia* may be irrationally afraid of a specific object or situation. Persistent and repetitive thoughts (obsessions) and actions (compulsions) characterize *obsessive-compulsive disorder.* Symptoms of *post-traumatic stress disorder* include four or more weeks of haunting memories, nightmares, social withdrawal, jumpy anxiety, and sleep problems following some traumatic and uncontrollable event.

37-2: **What are the sources of the anxious feelings and thoughts that characterize anxiety disorders?**

The psychoanalytic perspective viewed *anxiety disorders* as the discharging of repressed impulses. Psychologists working from the learning perspective view anxiety disorders as a product of fear conditioning, stimulus generalization, reinforcement of fearful behaviors, and observational learning of others' fear. Those working from the biological perspective consider the evolutionary survival value of fears of life-threatening animals, objects, or situations; inherited predispositions; and abnormal responses in the brain.

37-3: **What are dissociative disorders, and why are they controversial?**

Dissociative disorders are conditions in which conscious awareness seems to become separated from previous memories, thoughts, and feelings. Skeptics note that *dissociative identity disorder,* formerly called multiple personality disorder, increased dramatically in the late twentieth century, that it is rarely found outside North America, and that it may reflect role-playing by people who are vulnerable to therapists' suggestions.

37-4: **What characteristics are typical of personality disorders?**

Personality disorders are enduring, maladaptive patterns of behavior that impair social functioning. *Antisocial personality disorder* is characterized by a lack of conscience and, sometimes, aggressive and fearless behavior. Genetic predispositions may interact with environment to produce this disorder.

>> REHEARSE IT!

1. When anxiety is so distressing, uncontrollable, or persistent that it results in maladaptive behavior, the person is said to have an anxiety disorder. If that anxiety takes the form of an irrational fear of a specific object or situation, the disorder is called
   a. a phobia.
   b. a panic attack.
   c. generalized anxiety.
   d. an obsessive-compulsive disorder.

2. The experience of anxiety often involves physical symptoms, such as trembling, dizziness, chest pains, or choking sensations. An episode of intense dread, typically accompanied by such symptoms and by feelings of terror, is called
   a. a specific phobia.
   b. compulsion.
   c. a panic attack.
   d. an obsessive fear.

3. Marina's mother never had to remind her to clean her room. When Marina became consumed with the need to clean the entire house and refused to participate in any other activities, her family consulted a therapist, who diagnosed her as having
   a. obsessive-compulsive disorder.
   b. generalized anxiety disorder.
   c. a phobia.
   d. a panic attack.

4. Rats subjected to unpredictable shocks in the laboratory become chronically anxious. To the learning researcher this suggests that anxiety is a response to
   a. a phobia.
   b. biological factors.
   c. a genetic predisposition.
   d. fear conditioning.

5. Some psychologists believe our biological predispositions to fear certain stimuli may play a role in the development of phobias. But psychologists of the learning perspective propose that phobias are
   a. the result of individual genetic makeup.
   b. a way of repressing unacceptable impulses.
   c. conditioned fears.
   d. a symptom of having been abused as a child.

6. Dissociative identity disorder is relatively rare. This disorder is controversial because
   a. criminals have used it as a defense.
   b. it was reported frequently in the 1920s but rarely today.
   c. it is almost never reported outside North America.
   d. its symptoms are nearly identical to those of obsessive-compulsive disorder.

7. Unlike other psychological disorders, personality disorders need not involve any apparent depression or loss of contact with reality. A personality disorder, such as antisocial personality, is characterized by
   a. the presence of multiple personalities.
   b. disorganized thinking.
   c. enduring and maladaptive personality traits.
   d. elevated level of autonomic nervous system arousal.

Answers: 1. a, 2. c, 3. a, 4. d, 5. c, 6. c, 7. c.

>> TERMS AND CONCEPTS TO REMEMBER

anxiety disorders, p. 509

generalized anxiety disorder, p. 510

panic disorder, p. 510

phobia, p. 510

obsessive-compulsive disorder (OCD), p. 511

post-traumatic stress disorder (PTSD), p. 512

dissociative disorders, p. 515

dissociative identity disorder, p. 515

personality disorders, p. 517

antisocial personality disorder, p. 517

>> TEST YOURSELF

1. How do generalized anxiety disorder, phobias, and obsessive-compulsive disorder differ?

2. Is antisocial personality disorder an inherited condition?

   (Answers in Appendix C.)

> *Multiple-choice **self-tests** and more may be found at www.worthpublishers.com/myers.*

Mood Disorders

38-1 : What are mood disorders, and what forms do they take?

The emotional extremes of **mood disorders** come in two principal forms: (1) *major depressive disorder,* in which the person experiences prolonged hopelessness and lethargy until usually rebounding to normality, and (2) *bipolar disorder* (formerly called *manic-depressive disorder*), in which the person alternates between depression and mania, an overexcited, hyperactive state.

Major Depressive Disorder

If you are like most college students, at some time during this year—more likely the dark months of winter than the bright days of summer—you will probably experience a few of the symptoms of depression. You may feel deeply discouraged about the future, dissatisfied with your life, or isolated from others. You may lack the energy to get things done or even to force yourself out of bed; be unable to concentrate, eat, or sleep normally; or even wonder if you would be better off dead. Perhaps academic success came easily to you in high school, and now you find that disappointing grades jeopardize your goals. Maybe social stresses, such as feeling you don't belong or the breakup of a romance, have plunged you into despair. And maybe brooding has at times only worsened your self-torment.

You are not alone. Depression is the "common cold" of psychological disorders—an expression that effectively describes its pervasiveness but not its seriousness. Although phobias are more common, depression is the number one reason people seek mental health services. Moreover, it is the leading cause of disability worldwide (WHO, 2002). In any given year a depressive episode plagues 5.8 percent of men and 9.5 percent of women, reports the World Health Organization.

As anxiety is a response to the threat of future loss, depressed mood is often a response to past and current loss. To feel bad in reaction to profoundly sad events (such as the death of a loved one) is to be in touch with reality. In such times, depression is like a car's low–oil-pressure light—a signal that warns us to stop and take protective measures. Biologically speaking, life's purpose is not happiness but survival and reproduction, and to this end, coughing, vomiting, and various forms of pain protect the body from dangerous toxins. Similarly, depression is a sort of psychic hibernation: It slows us down, defuses aggression, and restrains risk taking (Allen & Badcock, 2003). To grind temporarily to a halt and ruminate, as depressed people do, is to reassess one's life when feeling threatened, and to redirect energy in more promising ways. From this perspective, there is sense to suffering.

But when does this response become seriously maladaptive? Joy, contentment, sadness, and despair are different points on a continuum, points at which any of us may be found at any given moment. But the difference between a blue mood after bad news and a mood disorder is like the difference between gasping for breath for a few minutes after a hard run and being chronically short of breath.

Major depressive disorder occurs when at least five signs of depression (including lethargy, feelings of worthlessness, or loss of interest in family, friends, and activities) last two or more weeks and are not caused by drugs or a medical condition. To sense what major depression feels like, suggest some clinicians, imagine combining the anguish of grief with the sluggishness of jet lag.

For some people, recurring depression during winter's dark months constitutes a "seasonal affective disorder." For others, winter darkness means more blue moods. When asked "Have you cried today?" Americans answered "yes" more often in the winter:

	Percentage answering yes	
	Men	Women
August	4%	7%
December	8%	21%

Source: Time/CNN survey, 1994

> " My life had come to a sudden stop. I was able to breathe, to eat, to drink, to sleep. I could not, indeed, help doing so; but there was no real life in me."
>
> Leo Tolstoy, *My Confession*, 1887

■ **mood disorders** psychological disorders characterized by emotional extremes. See *major depressive disorder*, *mania*, and *bipolar disorder*.

■ **major depressive disorder** a mood disorder in which a person experiences, in the absence of drugs or a medical condition, two or more weeks of significantly depressed moods, feelings of worthlessness, and diminished interest or pleasure in most activities.

Creativity and bipolar disorders
History has given us many creative artists, composers, and writers with bipolar disorder, including (left to right) Walt Whitman, Virginia Woolf, Samuel Clemens (Mark Twain), and Ernest Hemingway.

Bipolar Disorder

With or without therapy, episodes of major depression usually end, and people temporarily or permanently return to their previous behavior patterns. However, some people rebound to, or sometimes start with, the opposite emotional extreme—the euphoric, hyperactive, wildly optimistic state of **mania.** If depression is living in slow motion, mania is fast forward. Alternating between depression and mania signals **bipolar disorder.** During the manic phase of bipolar disorder, the person is typically overtalkative, overactive, and elated (though easily irritated if crossed); has little need for sleep; and shows fewer sexual inhibitions. Speech is loud, flighty, and hard to interrupt.

One of mania's maladaptive symptoms is grandiose optimism and self-esteem. People in this state find advice irritating, but they need protection from their own poor judgment, which may lead to reckless spending or unsafe sex. In milder forms, mania's energy and free-flowing thinking can fuel creativity. George Frideric Handel (1685–1759), who many believe suffered a mild form of bipolar disorder, composed his nearly four-hour-long *Messiah* during three weeks of intense, creative energy (Keynes, 1980). Robert Schumann composed 51 musical works during two years of mania (1840 and 1849) and none during 1844, when he was severely depressed (Slater & Meyer, 1959). Those who rely on precision and logic, such as architects, designers, and journalists, suffer bipolar disorder less often than do those who rely on emotional expression and vivid imagery, reports Arnold Ludwig (1995). Composers, artists, poets, novelists, and entertainers seem especially prone (Jamison, 1993, 1995; Kaufman & Baer, 2002; Ludwig, 1995).

It is as true of emotions as of everything else: What goes up comes down. Before long, the elated mood either returns to normal or plunges into a depression. Though as maladaptive as major depressive disorder, bipolar disorder is much less common. It also afflicts as many men as women.

> "All the people in history, literature, art, whom I most admire: Mozart, Shakespeare, Homer, El Greco, St. John, Chekhov, Gregory of Nyssa, Dostoevsky, Emily Brontë: not one of them would qualify for a mental-health certificate."
>
> Madeleine L'Engle, *A Circle of Quiet,* 1972

Explaining Mood Disorders

38-2 : What causes mood disorders, and what might explain the Western world's rising incidence of depression among youth and young adults?

In thousands of studies, psychologists have been accumulating evidence to help explain mood disorders and suggest more effective ways to treat and prevent them. Researcher Peter Lewinsohn and his colleagues (1985, 1998) have summarized the facts that any theory of depression must explain, including the following:

- *Many behavioral and cognitive changes accompany depression.* People trapped in a depressed mood are inactive and feel unmotivated. They are sensitive to negative happenings, more often recall negative information, and expect negative outcomes (my team will lose, my grades will fall, my love will fail). When the mood lifts, these behavioral and cognitive accompaniments disappear. Nearly half the time, people exhibit symptoms of another disorder, such as anxiety or substance abuse, in addition to depression.

■ **mania** a mood disorder marked by a hyperactive, wildly optimistic state.

■ **bipolar disorder** a mood disorder in which the person alternates between the hopelessness and lethargy of depression and the overexcited state of mania. (Formerly called manic-depressive disorder.)

- *Depression is widespread.* Its commonality suggests that its causes, too, must be common.
- *Compared with men, women are nearly twice as vulnerable to major depression* (FIGURE **38.1**). In general, women are most vulnerable to disorders involving internalized states, such as depression, anxiety, and inhibited sexual desire. Men's disorders tend to be more external—alcohol abuse, antisocial conduct, lack of impulse control. When women get sad, they often get sadder than men do. When men get mad, they often get madder than women do.
- *Most major depressive episodes self-terminate.* Therapy tends to speed recovery, yet most people suffering major depression eventually return to normal even without professional help. The plague of depression comes and, a few weeks or months later, it usually goes, though it sometimes recurs later.

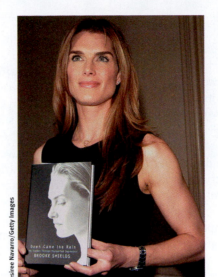

Desiree Navarro/Getty Images

Down Came the Rain
Actress Brooke Shields chronicled her disabling postpartum depression in this 2005 book.

- *Stressful events related to work, marriage, and close relationships often precede depression.* A family member's death, a job loss, a marital crisis, or a physical assault increase one's risk of depression. If stress-related anxiety is a "crackling, menacing brushfire," notes biologist Robert Sapolsky (2003), "depression is a suffocating heavy blanket thrown on top of it." One long-term study (Kendler, 1998) tracked rates of depression in 2000 people. The risk of depression ranged from less than 1 percent among those who had experienced no stressful life event in the preceding month to 24 percent among those who had experienced three such events in that month. The early loss of a parent due to death or separation also increases later vulnerability to depression (Agid & others, 1999).
- *With each new generation, depression is striking earlier (now often in the late teens) and affecting more people.* This is true in Canada, the United States, Germany, Italy, France, Lebanon, New Zealand, Taiwan, and Puerto Rico (Cross-National Collaborative Group, 1992). In one study (Sawyer & others, 2000), 12 percent of Australian adolescents reported symptoms of depression. Most hid it from their parents; almost 90 percent of their parents perceived their depressed teen as *not* suffering depression. In North America, today's young adults are three times more likely than their grandparents to report having recently—or ever—suffered depression (despite the grandparents' many more years of being at risk). Asked "Have you ever felt that you were going to have a nervous breakdown?" 17 percent of Americans said "yes" in 1957, as did 24 percent in 1996 (Swindle & others, 2000). The increase appears partly authentic, but may also reflect today's young adults' greater willingness to disclose depression, as well as our tendency to forget many negative experiences over time.

About 50 percent of those who recover from depression will suffer another episode within two years. Recovery is more likely to be permanent the later the first episode strikes, the longer the person stays well, the fewer the previous episodes, the less stress experienced, and the more social support received (Belsher & Costello, 1988; Fergusson & Woodward, 2002; Kendler & others, 2001).

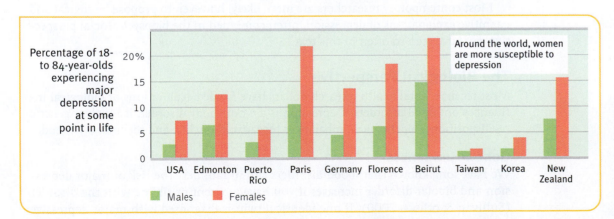

FIGURE **38.1**
Gender and major depression
Interviews with 38,000 adults in 10 countries confirm what many smaller studies have found: Women's risk of major depression is nearly double that of men's. Lifetime risk of depression also varies by culture—from 1.5 percent in Taiwan to 19 percent in Beirut. (Data from Weissman & others, 1996.)

CLOSE-UP

SUICIDE

"But life, being weary of these worldly bars,
Never lacks power to dismiss itself."
—William Shakespeare, *Julius Caesar*, 1599

Each year some 1 million despairing people worldwide will elect a permanent solution to what might have been a temporary problem (Mann, 2003; WHO, 2004). Comparing the suicide rates of different groups, researchers have found

- **national differences:** England's, Italy's, and Spain's suicide rates are little more than half those of Canada, Australia, and the United States. Austria's and Finland's are about double (WHO, 2002a). Within Europe, the most suicide-prone people (Lithuanians) have been 15 times more likely to kill themselves than the least (Portuguese).

- **racial differences:** Within the United States, Whites are nearly twice as likely as Blacks to kill themselves (NIMH, 2002).

- **gender differences:** Women are much more likely than men to attempt suicide; in China, they account for most suicides (WHO, 2002c). But (except in China) men are two to four times more likely (depending on the country) to succeed (**FIGURE 38.2**). Men use more lethal methods, such as firing a bullet into the head, the method of choice in 6 of 10 U.S. suicides.

- **age differences and trends:** In late adulthood, rates increase, dramatically so among men (Figure 38.2). Since 1960, suicide rates have also surged among older teens, especially males (Eckersley & Dear, 2002). In America, Australia, Great Britain, Canada, and New Zealand, for example, rates for 15- to 25-year-olds doubled or more than doubled in the 30 years after 1960. That surge was almost entirely among males in both the United States and Australia (Hassan & Carr, 1989). Late-teen and early-twenties

anxiety and depression rates also increased during this time.

- **other group differences:** Suicide rates are much higher among the rich, the nonreligious, and those who are single, widowed, or divorced (Hoyer & Lund, 1993; Stack, 1992; Stengel, 1981). Gay and lesbian youth much more often suffer distress and attempt suicide than do their heterosexual peers (Goldfried, 2001).

The risk of suicide is at least five times greater for those who have been depressed than for the general population (Bostwick & Pankratz, 2000). People seldom commit suicide while in the depths of depression, when energy and initiative are lacking. It is when they begin to rebound and become capable of following through that the risk increases. Compared with people who suffer no disorder, those addicted to alcohol are roughly 100 times more likely to commit suicide; some 3 percent of them do (Murphy & Wetzel, 1990). Even among people

Researchers may accept all these facts without agreeing on a theory that will best explain them. For example, proponents of Sigmund Freud's psychoanalytic theory (or the more modern psychodynamic approach) have an idea: Depression often occurs when significant losses, such as the breakup of a current romantic relationship, evoke feelings associated with losses experienced in childhood (the intimate relationship with one's mother, for example). Alternatively, these theorists may view depression as unresolved anger toward one's parents, turned inward against oneself.

Most contemporary researchers are more likely, however, to propose biological and cognitive explanations of depression, often combined in the biopsychosocial perspective you have seen so often in this text.

The Biological Perspective

Most recent mental health research dollars have funded explorations of biological influences on mood disorders. Depression is a whole-body disorder. It involves genetic predispositions, biochemical imbalances, negative thoughts, and melancholy mood.

Genetic Influences

We have long known that mood disorders run in families. The risk of major depression and bipolar disorder increases if you have a parent or sibling with the disorder (Sullivan & others, 2000). If one identical twin is diagnosed with major depressive

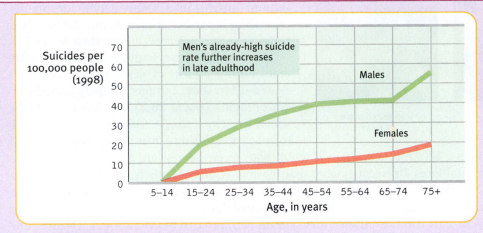

Suicides per 100,000 people (1998)

Men's already-high suicide rate further increases in late adulthood

Males

Females

Age, in years

FIGURE 38.2

Suicide rates by gender and age

Worldwide suicide rates are higher among males than among females. The highest rates of all are found among older men. (From WHO, 2002a.)

way of switching off unendurable pain and relieving the perceived burden on family members (Joiner & others, 2002; Shneidman, 1987).

In retrospect, families and friends may recall signs that they believe should have forewarned them—verbal hints, giving possessions away, or withdrawal and preoccupation with death. But few who talk of suicide or think suicidal thoughts (a number that includes one-third of all adolescents and college students) actually attempt suicide, and few of those who attempt it complete the act (Yip, 1998). U.S. hospital emergency rooms, for example, log a half-million visits as a result of attempted suicides each year (Surgeon General, 1999). But about 30,000 do succeed, one-third of whom have tried to kill themselves previously. Most discussed it beforehand. So, if a friend talks suicide to you, it's important to listen and to direct the person to professional help. Anyone who threatens suicide is at least sending a signal of feeling desperate or despondent.

who have attempted suicide, those who abuse alcohol are five times more likely than others to kill themselves eventually (Beck & Steer, 1989). Teenage suicides are often linked with drug and alcohol abuse; the final act may follow a traumatic event, such as a romantic breakup or a guilt-provoking antisocial act (Fowler & others, 1986; Kolata, 1986).

Social suggestion may trigger suicide. Following highly publicized suicides and TV programs featuring suicide, known suicides increase. So do fatal auto "accidents" and private airplane crashes.

Suicide is not necessarily an act of hostility or revenge. The elderly sometimes choose death as an alternative to current or future suffering. In people of all ages, suicide may be a

disorder, the chances are about 1 in 2 that at some time the other twin will be, too. If one identical twin has bipolar disorder, the chances are 7 in 10 that the other twin will at some point be diagnosed similarly. Among fraternal twins, the corresponding odds are just under 2 in 10 (Tsuang & Faraone, 1990). The greater similarity among identical twins holds even among twins reared apart (DiLalla & others, 1996). Moreover, adopted people who suffer a mood disorder often have close biological relatives who suffer mood disorders, become dependent on alcohol, or commit suicide (Wender & others, 1986). (Close-Up: Suicide reports other research findings on suicide.)

To tease out the genes that put people at risk for depression, some researchers have turned to *linkage analysis*. After finding families in which the disorder appears across several generations, geneticists examine DNA from affected and unaffected family members, looking for differences. Linkage analysis points us to a chromosome neighborhood, note behavior genetics researchers Robert Plomin and Peter McGuffin (2003); "a house-to-house search is then needed to find the culprit gene." Such studies are reinforcing the view that depression is a complex condition. Many genes probably work together, producing a mosaic of small effects that interact with other factors to put some people at greater risk.

Gene-hunters' pursuit of bipolar-DNA links

Linkage studies seek to identify aberrant genes in family members suffering a disorder. These Pennsylvania Amish family members—an isolated population sharing a common lifestyle and some vulnerability to bipolar disorder—have volunteered for such studies.

Jerry Irwin Photography

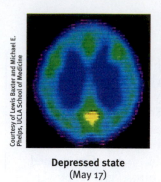 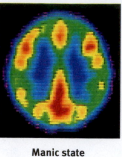 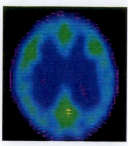

Depressed state
(May 17)

Manic state
(May 18)

Depressed state
(May 27)

FIGURE 38.3

The ups and downs of bipolar disorder

PET scans show that brain energy consumption rises and falls with the patient's emotional switches. Red areas are where the brain rapidly consumes glucose.

The Depressed Brain

Using modern technology, researchers are also gaining insight into brain activity during depressed and manic states, and into the effects of certain neurotransmitters during these states.

Many studies have found less activity in the brain during periods of depression, indicating a slowed-down state, and more activity during periods of mania (**FIGURE 38.3**). The left frontal lobe, which is active during positive emotions, is likely to be inactive during depressed states (Davidson & others, 2002). In one study of people with severe depression, MRI scans found their frontal lobes 7 percent smaller than normal (Coffey & others, 1993). Other studies show that the *hippocampus,* a memory-processing center linked with the brain's emotional circuitry, is vulnerable to stress-related damage.

At least two neurotransmitter systems play a role in mood disorders. (Neurotransmitters are messenger molecules that shuttle signals between nerve cells.) The first, *norepinephrine,* which increases arousal and boosts mood, is scarce during depression and overabundant during mania. (Drugs that alleviate mania reduce norepinephrine.) Most people with a history of depression also have a history of habitual smoking. This may indicate an attempt to self-medicate with inhaled nicotine, which can temporarily increase norepinephrine and boost mood (HMHL, 2002). The second neurotransmitter, *serotonin,* is also scarce during depression. Some genes now under scrutiny provide codes for a protein that controls serotonin activity (Plomin & McGuffin, 2003). The effects of one such gene were clear in a large study of New Zealand young adults who had experienced several major stresses (such as a relationship breakup or a family death). These stressed individuals were much more likely to suffer depression *if* they carried a variation of the serotonin-controlling gene (Caspi & others, 2003). This study's recipe for depression included two necessary ingredients: significant stress and the gene, interacting. As we have seen so often throughout this book, genes and environments—nature and nurture—together form us.

Drugs that relieve depression tend to increase norepinephrine or serotonin supplies by blocking either their reuptake (as Prozac, Zoloft, and Paxil do with serotonin) or their chemical breakdown. Repetitive physical exercise, such as jogging, reduces depression as it increases serotonin (Jacobs, 1994). One way boosting serotonin may promote recovery from depression is by stimulating hippocampus neuron growth (Jacobs & others, 2000).

The Social-Cognitive Perspective

Biological influences contribute to depression, but they don't fully explain it. The social-cognitive perspective focuses attention on the roles of thinking and acting.

Depressed people view life through dark glasses. Their intensely negative assumptions about themselves, their situation, and their future lead them to magnify bad experiences and minimize good ones. Listen to Norman, a Canadian college professor, recalling his depression:

> I [despaired] of ever being human again. I honestly felt subhuman, lower than the lowest vermin. Furthermore, I was self-deprecatory and could not understand why anyone would want to associate with me, let alone love me. . . . I was positive that I was a fraud and a phony and that I didn't deserve my Ph.D. I didn't deserve to have tenure; I didn't deserve to be a Full Professor. . . . I didn't deserve the research grants I had been awarded; I couldn't understand how I had written books and journal articles. . . . I must have conned a lot of people. (Endler, 1982, pp. 45–49)

Research reveals how self-defeating beliefs and a negative explanatory style feed depression's vicious cycle.

Courtesy of Lewis Baxter and Michael E. Phelps, UCLA School of Medicine

Negative Thoughts and Negative Moods Interact

Self-defeating beliefs may arise from *learned helplessness*. Both dogs and humans act depressed, passive, and withdrawn after experiencing uncontrollable painful events (Seligman, 1975, 1991). Learned helplessness is more common in women than in men, and they may respond more strongly to stress (Hankin & Abramson, 2001; Mazure & others, 2002; Nolen-Hoeksema, 2001, 2003). Thirty-six percent of women and 16 percent of men entering American colleges feel "frequently overwhelmed by all I have to do" (Sax & others, 2004). (Men report spending more of their time in "light anxiety" activities such as sports, TV watching, and partying, possibly avoiding activities that might make them feel overwhelmed.) This may help explain why, beginning in their early teens, women are nearly twice as vulnerable to depression (Kessler, 2001). Susan Nolen-Hoeksema (2003) believes women's higher risk of depression may relate to what she describes as their tendency to *overthink,* to ruminate. Women often have vivid recall for both wonderful and horrid experiences; men more vaguely recall such experiences (Seidlitz & Diener, 1998). This gender difference in emotional memory may feed women's greater rumination over negative events and explain why fewer men than women report being frequently overwhelmed on entering college.

But why do life's unavoidable failures lead some people—women or men—and not others to become depressed? The answer lies partly in their *explanatory style*—who or what they blame for their failures. Think how you might feel if you failed a test. If you can externalize the blame (What an unfair test!), you are more likely to feel angry. But if you blame yourself, you probably will feel stupid and depressed.

So it is with depressed people, who tend to explain bad events in terms that are *stable* ("It's going to last forever"), *global* ("It's going to affect everything I do"), and *internal* ("It's all my fault") (**FIGURE 38.4**). Depression-prone people respond to bad events in an especially self-focused, self-blaming way (Mor & Winquist, 2002; Pyszczynski & others, 1991; Wood & others, 1990a,b). Their self-esteem fluctuates more rapidly up with boosts and down with threats (Butler & others, 1994).

Michael Marsland

Susan Nolen-Hoeksema

"This epidemic of morbid meditation is a disease that women suffer much more than men. Women can ruminate about anything and everything—our appearance, our families, our career, our health." (*Women Who Think Too Much: How to Break Free of Overthinking and Reclaim Your Life*, 2003)

"I have learned to accept my mistakes by referring them to a personal history which was not of my making."

B. F. Skinner (1983)

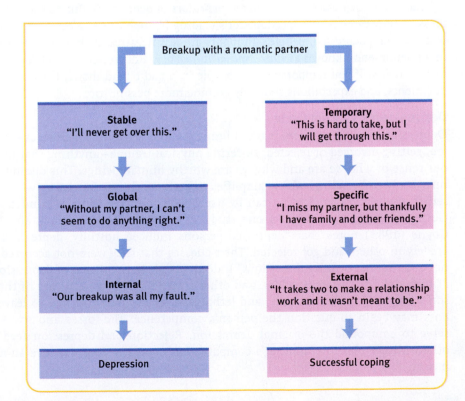

FIGURE 38.4
Explanatory style and depression

PEANUTS

Might Charlie Brown be helped by an optimism-training program?

The result of these pessimistic, overgeneralized, self-blaming attributions may be a depressing sense of hopelessness (Abramson & others, 1989). As Martin Seligman notes, "A recipe for severe depression is preexisting pessimism encountering failure" (1991, p. 78). What then might we expect of new college students who are not depressed but do exhibit a pessimistic explanatory style? Lauren Alloy and her collaborators (1999) monitored Temple University and University of Wisconsin students every 6 weeks for 2.5 years. Among those identified as having pessimistic thinking styles, 17 percent had a first episode of major depression, as did only 1 percent of those who began college with optimistic thinking styles. Follow-up research has found that students who exhibit optimism as they begin college develop more social support, which contributes to a lowered risk of depression (Brissette & others, 2002).

Seligman (1991, 1995) contends that depression is common among young Westerners because the rise of individualism and the decline of commitment to religion and family force young people to take personal responsibility for failure or rejection. In non-Western cultures, where close-knit relationships and cooperation are the norm, major depression is less common and less tied to self-blame over personal failure. In Japan, for example, depressed people instead tend to report feeling shame over letting others down (Draguns, 1990a).

There is, however, a chicken-and-egg problem with the social-cognitive explanation of depression. Self-defeating beliefs, negative attributions, and self-blame surely do support depression. Peter Barnett and Ian Gotlib (1988) note that such cognitions *coincide* with a depressed mood and are *indicators* of depression. But do they *cause* depression, any more than a speedometer's reading 70 mph causes a car's speed? Before or after being depressed, people's thoughts are less negative. Perhaps this is because, in a phenomenon known as *state-dependent memory,* a depressed mood triggers negative thoughts. If you temporarily put people in a bad or sad mood, their memories, judgments, and expectations suddenly become more pessimistic.

Depression's Vicious Cycle

Depression, as we have seen, is often brought on by stressful experiences—losing a job, getting divorced or rejected, suffering physical trauma—anything that disrupts our sense of who we are and why we are worthy human beings. This disruption in turn leads to brooding, which amplifies negative feelings. But being withdrawn, self-focused, and complaining can by itself elicit rejection (Furr & Funder, 1998; Gotlib & Hammen, 1992). In one study, researchers Stephen Strack and James Coyne (1983) noted that "depressed persons induced hostility, depression, and anxiety in others and got rejected. Their guesses that they were not accepted were not a matter of cognitive distortion." Indeed, people in the throes of depression are at high risk for divorce, job loss, and other stressful life events. Weary of the person's fatigue, hopeless attitude, and lethargy, a spouse may threaten to leave or a boss may begin to question the person's competence. The losses and stress only serve to compound the original depression. Rejection and depression feed each other. Misery may love another's company, but company does not love another's misery.

"Man never reasons so much and becomes so introspective as when he suffers, since he is anxious to get at the cause of his sufferings."

Luigi Pirandello, *Six Characters in Search of an Author*, 1922

We can now assemble some of the pieces of the depression puzzle (FIGURE 38.5): (1) Negative, stressful events interpreted through (2) a ruminating, pessimistic explanatory style create (3) a hopeless, depressed state that (4) hampers the way the person thinks and acts. This, in turn, fuels (1) negative experiences such as rejection.

It is a cycle we can all recognize. Bad moods feed on themselves: When we *feel* down, we *think* negatively and remember bad experiences. On the brighter side, we can break the cycle of depression at any of these points—by moving to a different environment, by reversing our self-blame and negative attributions, by turning our attention outward, or by engaging in more pleasant activities and more competent behavior.

Winston Churchill called depression a "black dog" that periodically hounded him. Poet Emily Dickinson was so afraid of bursting into tears in public that she spent much of her adult life in seclusion (Patterson, 1951). Abraham Lincoln was so withdrawn and brooding as a young man that his friends feared he might take his own life (Kline, 1974). As each of these lives reminds us, people can and do struggle through depression. Most regain their capacity to love, to work, and even to succeed at the highest levels.

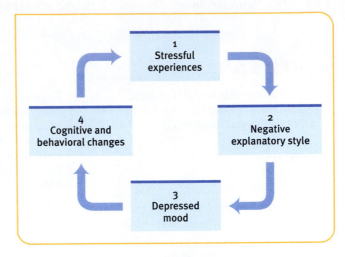

FIGURE 38.5
The vicious cycle of depressed thinking
Cognitive therapists attempt to break this cycle by changing the way depressed people process events. Psychiatrists attempt to alter with medication the biological roots of persistently depressed moods.

>> MODULE REVIEW

38-1: What are mood disorders, and what forms do they take?

Mood disorders are characterized by emotional extremes. A person with *major depressive disorder* experiences two or more weeks of seriously depressed moods and feelings of worthlessness, takes little interest in most activities, and derives little pleasure from them. These feelings are not caused by drugs or a medical condition. People with the less common condition of *bipolar disorder* experience not only depression but also *mania,* episodes of hyperactive and wildly optimistic impulsive behavior.

38-2: What causes mood disorders, and what might explain the Western world's rising incidence of depression among youth and young adults?

Depression researchers are exploring two sets of influences. One focuses on genetic predispositions and on abnormalities in brain structures and functions (including those found in neurotransmitter systems). The second, the social-cognitive perspective, examines the influence of cyclic self-defeating beliefs, learned helplessness, negative attributions, and stressful experiences. The biopsychosocial approach considers influences on many levels (FIGURE 38.6). Increased rates of depression among young Westerners may be due to the rise of individualism and the decline of commitment to religion and family, but this is a correlational finding, so the cause-effect relationship is not yet clear.

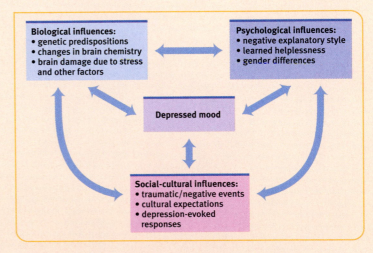

FIGURE 38.6
Biopsychosocial approach to depression
Seriously depressed moods result from a combination of interacting factors. Altering any one component can alter the others.

>> REHEARSE IT!

1. The disorder that is so common it has been called the "common cold" of psychological disorders is

   a. amnesia.
   b. depression.
   c. bipolar disorder.
   d. schizophrenia.

2. A person with bipolar disorder may alternate between the lethargy of depression and the overexcited state of mania. Although bipolar disorder is as maladaptive as depression, it is much less common and it affects

   a. more women than men.
   b. more men than women.
   c. women and men equally.
   d. primarily scientists and doctors.

3. Depression affects many people, often following a stressful event, such as divorce or job change. In a depressive episode, a person tends to be inactive and unmotivated and overly sensitive to negative happenings. Since the mid-twentieth century, the rate of depression has been

   a. increasing among young people.
   b. decreasing among young people.
   c. increasing among elderly women.
   d. decreasing among elderly women.

4. Twin and adoption studies show that depression tends to run in families. It can often be alleviated by drugs that block the reuptake of neurotransmitters, such as

   a. norepinephrine and dopamine.
   b. epinephrine and dopamine.
   c. endorphins and serotonin.
   d. norepinephrine and serotonin.

5. Psychologists who emphasize the importance of negative perceptions, beliefs, and thoughts in depression are working within the _____ perspective.

   a. psychoanalytic
   b. biological
   c. behavioral
   d. social-cognitive

Answers: 1. b, 2. c, 3. a, 4. d, 5. d.

>> TERMS AND CONCEPTS TO REMEMBER

mood disorders, p. 521
major depressive disorder, p. 521

mania, p. 522

bipolar disorder, p. 522

>> TEST YOURSELF

1. What does it mean to say that "depression is the common cold of psychological disorders"?

   (Answer in Appendix C.)

*Multiple-choice **self-tests** and more may be found at www.worthpublishers.com/myers.*

Schizophrenia

If depression is the disabling but common cold of psychological disorders, chronic schizophrenia is the cancer. Literally translated, **schizophrenia** means "split mind." It refers not to a multiple-personality split but rather to a split from reality that shows itself in disorganized thinking, disturbed perceptions, and inappropriate emotions and actions.

For convenience, we may discuss schizophrenia as if it were a single disorder. Actually, it is a cluster of disorders that share some features and differ in others.

Symptoms of Schizophrenia

39-1: What patterns of thinking, perceiving, feeling, and behaving characterize schizophrenia?

People with schizophrenia may have *positive symptoms* (the *presence* of inappropriate behaviors) or *negative symptoms* (the *absence* of appropriate behaviors). Those with positive symptoms may experience hallucinations, talk in disorganized and deluded ways, and exhibit inappropriate laughter, tears, or rage. Those with negative symptoms have toneless voices, expressionless faces, or mute and rigid bodies. Because schizophrenia is a cluster of disorders, these varied symptoms could have more than one cause.

Disorganized Thinking

Imagine trying to communicate with Maxine, a young woman whose thoughts spill out in no logical order. Her biographer, Susan Sheehan (1982, p. 25), observed her saying aloud to no one in particular, "This morning, when I was at Hillside [Hospital], I was making a movie. I was surrounded by movie stars. . . . I'm Mary Poppins. Is this room painted blue to get me upset? My grandmother died four weeks after my eighteenth birthday."

As this strange monologue illustrates, the thinking of a person with schizophrenia is fragmented, bizarre, and distorted by false beliefs called **delusions** ("I'm Mary Poppins"). Those with *paranoid* tendencies are particularly prone to delusions of persecution. Even within sentences, jumbled ideas may create what is called *word salad*. One young man begged for "a little more allegro in the treatment," and suggested that "liberationary movement with a view to the widening of the horizon" will "ergo extort some wit in lectures."

Disorganized thoughts may result from a breakdown in *selective attention*. We normally have a remarkable capacity for giving our undivided attention to one set of sensory stimuli while filtering out others. Those with schizophrenia cannot do this. Thus, irrelevant, minute stimuli, such as the grooves on a brick or the inflections of a voice, may distract their attention from a bigger event or a speaker's meaning. As one former patient recalled, "What had happened to me . . . was a breakdown in the filter, and a hodge-podge of unrelated stimuli were distracting me from things which should have had my undivided attention" (MacDonald, 1960, p. 218). This selective-attention difficulty is but one of dozens of cognitive differences associated with schizophrenia.

■ **schizophrenia** a group of severe disorders characterized by disorganized and delusional thinking, disturbed perceptions, and inappropriate emotions and actions.

■ **delusions** false beliefs, often of persecution or grandeur, that may accompany schizophrenia and other disorders.

Art by people diagnosed with schizophrenia
Commenting on the kind of art work shown here, poet and art critic John Ashbery wrote: "The lure of the work is strong, but so is the terror of the unanswerable riddles it proposes."

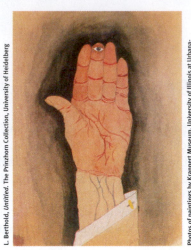

> "When someone asks me to explain schizophrenia I tell them, you know how sometimes in your dreams you are in them yourself and some of them feel like real nightmares? My schizophrenia was like I was walking through a dream. But everything around me was real. At times, today's world seems so boring and I wonder if I would like to step back into the schizophrenic dream, but then I remember all the scary and horrifying experiences."
>
> Stuart Emmons, with Craig Geisler, Kalman J. Kaplan, and Martin Harrow, *Living With Schizophrenia*, 1997

Disturbed Perceptions

A person with schizophrenia may have *hallucinations* (sensory experiences without sensory stimulation), seeing, feeling, tasting, or smelling things that are not there. Most often, however, the hallucinations are auditory, voices that may make insulting remarks or issue orders, perhaps telling the patient that she is bad or that she must burn herself with a cigarette lighter. Imagine your own reaction if a dream broke into your waking consciousness. When the unreal seems real, the resulting perceptions are at best bizarre, at worst terrifying.

Inappropriate Emotions and Actions

The emotions of schizophrenia are often utterly inappropriate, split off from reality. Maxine laughed after recalling her grandmother's death. On other occasions, she cried when others laughed, or became angry for no apparent reason. A person with schizophrenia may also lapse into an emotionless *flat affect,* a zombielike state of apparent apathy.

Motor behavior may also be inappropriate. Some perform senseless, compulsive acts, such as continually rocking or rubbing an arm. Others, who exhibit *catatonia,* may remain motionless for hours and then become agitated.

As you can imagine, such disorganized thinking, disturbed perceptions, and inappropriate emotions and actions profoundly disrupt social relationships and make it difficult to hold a job. During their most severe periods, those with schizophrenia live in a private inner world, preoccupied with illogical ideas and unreal images. Given a supportive environment, some eventually recover to enjoy a normal life or experience bouts of schizophrenia only intermittently. Others remain socially withdrawn and isolated throughout much of their lives.

Onset and Development of Schizophrenia

39-2: What forms does schizophrenia take?

Nearly 1 in 100 people will develop schizophrenia this year, joining the estimated 24 million worldwide who suffer this dreaded disorder (WHO, 2002d). It typically strikes as young people are maturing into adulthood, it knows no national boundaries, and it affects both males and females—though men tend to be struck earlier, more severely, and slightly more often (Aleman & others, 2003).

For some, schizophrenia will appear suddenly, seemingly as a reaction to stress. For others, as was the case with Maxine, schizophrenia develops gradually, emerging from a long history of social inadequacy (which helps explain why those predisposed to schizophrenia often end up in the lower socioeconomic levels, or even homeless). One rule holds true around the world (World Health Organization, 1979): When schizophrenia is a slow-developing process (called *chronic,* or *process,* schizophrenia), recovery is doubtful. Those with chronic schizophrenia often exhibit the negative symptom of withdrawal. Men, whose schizophrenia develops on average four years earlier than women's, more often exhibit negative symptoms and chronic schizophrenia (Räsänen & others, 2000). When a previously well-adjusted person develops schizophrenia rapidly (called *acute,* or *reactive,* schizophrenia) following particular life stresses, recovery is much more likely. They more often have the positive symptoms that respond to drug therapy (Fenton & McGlashan, 1991, 1994; Fowles, 1992).

Understanding Schizophrenia

39-3 : What causes schizophrenia?

Schizophrenia is not only the most dreaded psychological disorder but also one of the most heavily researched. Most of the new research studies link it with brain abnormalities and genetic predispositions. Schizophrenia is a disease of the brain exhibited in symptoms of the mind.

Brain Abnormalities

Might imbalances in brain chemistry underlie schizophrenia? Scientists have long known that strange behavior can have strange chemical causes. The saying "mad as a hatter" refers to the psychological deterioration of British hatmakers whose brains, it was later discovered, were slowly poisoned as they moistened the brims of mercury-laden felt hats with their lips (Smith, 1983). Scientists are clarifying the mechanism by which chemicals such as LSD produce hallucinations. These discoveries hint that schizophrenia symptoms might have a biochemical key.

Dopamine Overactivity

Researchers discovered one such key when they examined schizophrenia patients' brains after death, and found an excess of receptors for *dopamine*—a sixfold excess for the so-called D4 dopamine receptor (Seeman & others, 1993; Wong & others, 1986). They speculate that such a high level may intensify brain signals in schizophrenia, creating positive symptoms such as hallucinations and paranoia. As we might therefore expect, drugs that block dopamine receptors often lessen these symptoms; drugs that increase dopamine levels, such as amphetamines and cocaine, sometimes intensify them (Swerdlow & Koob, 1987). Dopamine overactivity may underlie patients' overreactions to irrelevant external and internal stimuli.

Abnormal Brain Activity and Anatomy

Modern brain-scanning techniques reveal that many people with chronic schizophrenia have abnormal activity in multiple brain areas. Some have abnormally low brain activity in the frontal lobes, which are critical for reasoning, planning, and problem solving (Morey & others, 2005; Pettegrew & others, 1993; Resnick, 1992). People diagnosed with schizophrenia also display a noticeable decline in the brain waves that reflect synchronized neural firing in the frontal lobes (Spencer & others, 2004; Symond & others, 2005). Out-of-sync neurons may disrupt the integrated functioning of neural networks, possibly contributing to schizophrenia symptoms.

About 60 percent of schizophrenia patients smoke, often heavily. Nicotine apparently stimulates certain brain receptors, which helps focus attention (Javitt & Coyle, 2004).

Chris Usher

Studying the neurophysiology of schizophrenia

Psychiatrist E. Fuller Torrey is collecting the brains of hundreds of those who died as young adults and suffered disorders such as schizophrenia and bipolar disorder. Torrey is making tissue samples available to researchers worldwide.

One study took PET scans of brain activity while people were hallucinating (Silbersweig & others, 1995). When participants heard a voice or saw something, their brains became vigorously active in several core regions, including the thalamus, a structure deep in the brain that filters incoming sensory signals and transmits them to the cortex. Another PET scan study of people with paranoia found increased activity in a fear-processing center, the amygdala (Epstein & others, 1998).

Many studies have found enlarged, fluid-filled areas and a corresponding shrinkage of cerebral tissue in people with schizophrenia (Wright & others, 2000), and one study even found such abnormalities in the brains of people who would *later* develop this disorder (Pantelis & others, 2002). The greater the shrinkage, the more severe the thought disorder (Collinson & others, 2003; Nelson & others, 1998; Shenton, 1992). One smaller-than-normal area is the cortex. Another is the thalamus, which may explain why people with schizophrenia have difficulty filtering sensory input and focusing attention (Andreasen & others, 1994). The bottom line of various studies, reports Nancy Andreasen (1997, 2001), is that schizophrenia involves not one isolated brain abnormality but problems with several brain regions and their interconnections.

Naturally, scientists wonder what causes these abnormalities. Some suspect a mishap during prenatal development or delivery. Two known risk factors for schizophrenia are low birth weight and oxygen deprivation during delivery (Buka & others, 1999; Zornberg & others, 2000). Famine may also increase risks. People conceived during the peak of the Dutch wartime famine later displayed a doubled rate of schizophrenia, as did those conceived during the famine of 1959 to 1961 in eastern China (St. Clair & others, 2005; Susser & others, 1996).

Maternal Virus During Midpregnancy

Consider another possible culprit: a midpregnancy viral infection that impairs fetal brain development. Can you imagine some ways to test this fetal-virus idea? Scientists have asked the following:

- *Are people at increased risk of schizophrenia if, during the middle of their fetal development, their country experienced a flu epidemic?* The repeated answer is yes (Mednick & others, 1994; Murray & others, 1992; Wright & others, 1995).

- *Are people born in densely populated areas, where viral diseases spread more readily, at greater risk for schizophrenia?* The answer, confirmed in a study of 1.75 million Danes, is yes (Jablensky, 1999; Mortensen, 1999).

- *Are those born during the winter and spring months—after the fall-winter flu season—also at increased risk?* The answer is again yes, at 5 to 8 percent increased risk (Torrey & others, 1997, 2002).

- *In the Southern Hemisphere, where the seasons are the reverse of the Northern Hemisphere, are the months of above-average schizophrenia births similarly reversed?* Again, the answer is yes, though somewhat less so. In Australia, for example, people born between August and October are at greater risk—unless they migrated from the Northern Hemisphere, in which case their risk is greater if they were born between January and March (McGrath & others, 1995, 1999).

- *Are mothers who report being sick with influenza during pregnancy more likely to bear children who develop schizophrenia?* In one study of nearly 8000 women, the answer was yes. The schizophrenia risk increased from the customary 1 percent to about 2 percent—but only when infections occurred during the second trimester (Brown & others, 2000).

- *Does blood drawn from pregnant women whose offspring develop schizophrenia show higher-than-normal levels of antibodies that suggest a viral infection?* In one study of 27 women whose children later developed schizophrenia, the answer was yes (Buka & others, 2001). And the answer was again yes in a huge California study, which collected blood samples from some 20,000 pregnant women during the 1950s and 1960s. Some children born of those pregnancies were later diagnosed with schizophrenia. When antibodies in the mother's blood indicated she had been exposed to influenza during the first half of the pregnancy, the child's risk of developing schizophrenia tripled. Flu during the second half of the pregnancy produced no such increase (Brown & others, 2004).

These converging lines of evidence suggest that prenatal viral infections play a contributing role in the development of schizophrenia. They also strengthen the recommendation that "women who will be more than three months pregnant during the flu season" have a flu shot (CDC, 2003).

Why might a second-trimester maternal flu bout put fetuses at risk? Is it the virus itself? The mother's immune response to it? Medications taken? (Wyatt & others, 2001). Does the infection weaken the brain's supportive glial cells, leading to reduced synaptic connections (Moises & others, 2002)? In time, answers may become available.

Genetic Factors

Prenatal viruses do appear to increase the odds that a child will develop schizophrenia. But this theory cannot tell us why some 98 percent of women who catch the flu during their second trimester of pregnancy bear children who do *not* develop schizophrenia. Might people also inherit a predisposition to this disorder? The evidence strongly suggests that, yes, some do. The nearly 1-in-100 odds of any person's being diagnosed with schizophrenia become about 1 in 10 among those whose sibling or parent has the disorder, and close to 1 in 2 if the affected sibling is an identical twin (**FIGURE 39.1**). And, although only a dozen or so such cases are on record, the co-twin of an identical twin with schizophrenia retains that 1-in-2 chance when the twins are reared apart (Plomin & others, 1997).

Remember, though, that identical twins also share a prenatal environment. About two-thirds also share a placenta and the blood it supplies. Other sets of identical twins have two single placentas. If an identical twin has schizophrenia, the co-twin's chances of being similarly afflicted are 6 in 10 if they shared a placenta. If they had separate placentas, the chances are only 1 in 10 (Davis & others, 1995a,b; Phelps & others, 1997). Twins who share a placenta are more likely to experience the same prenatal viruses. So it is possible that shared germs as well as shared genes produce identical twin similarities.

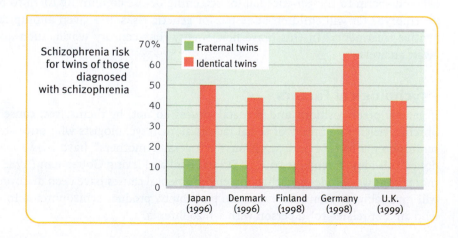

FIGURE 39.1
Risk of developing schizophrenia
The lifetime risk of developing schizophrenia varies with one's genetic relatedness to someone having this disorder. Across countries, barely more than 1 in 10 fraternal twins, but some 5 in 10 identical twins, share a schizophrenia diagnosis. (Adapted from Gottesman, 2001.)

Schizophrenia in identical twins
When twins differ, only the one afflicted with schizophrenia typically has enlarged, fluid-filled cranial cavities (right) (Suddath & others, 1990). The difference between the twins implies some nongenetic factor, such as a virus, is also at work, helping to "turn on" genes that predispose some people to schizophrenia.

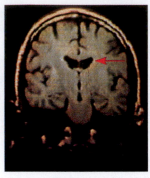
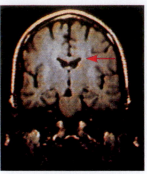

No schizophrenia   Schizophrenia

Adoption studies, however, confirm that the genetic link is real (Gottesman, 1991). Children adopted by someone who develops schizophrenia seldom "catch" the disorder. Rather, adopted children have an elevated risk if a biological parent is diagnosed with schizophrenia.

With the genetic factor established, researchers are now sleuthing specific genes that, in some combination, might predispose schizophrenia-inducing brain abnormalities (Callicott & others, 2005; Egan & others, 2004). (It is not our genes but our brains that directly control our behavior.) Some of these genes influence the effects of dopamine and other neurotransmitters in the brain. Others affect the production of *myelin,* a fatty substance that coats the axons of nerve cells and lets impulses travel at high speed through neural networks. Despite tantalizing findings, the culprit genes have proven elusive. The genetic contribution to schizophrenia is beyond question. But the genetic formula is not as straightforward as the inheritance of eye color. A complex disorder such as schizophrenia is surely influenced by multiple genes with small effects. And even within this context, other factors—such as the prenatal viral infections, nutritional deprivation, and oxygen deprivation at birth mentioned earlier—may somehow help to "turn on" the genes that predispose some of us to this disease.

Our knowledge of human genetics and of genetic influences on maladies such as schizophrenia is exploding, thanks partly to millions of new National Institute of Mental Health dollars focused on solving the schizophrenia riddle. So, can scientists develop genetic tests that reveal who is at risk? If so, will people in the future subject their embryos to genetic testing (and gene repair or abortion) if they are at risk for this or some other psychological or physical malady? Might they take their egg and sperm to the genetics lab for screening before combining them to produce an embryo? Or will children be tested for genetic risks and given appropriate preventive treatments? In this brave new twenty-first–century world, such questions await answers.

Psychological Factors

If genetic predispositions and prenatal viruses do not, by themselves, cause schizophrenia, neither do family or social factors alone. Psychologists who once attributed schizophrenia to cold and capricious "refrigerator mothers" have long since abandoned this idea. It remains true, as Susan Nicol and Irving Gottesman (1983) noted more than two decades ago, that "no environmental causes have been discovered that will invariably, or even with moderate probability, produce schizophrenia in persons who are not related to" a person with schizophrenia.

Courtesy of Genain family

The Genain quadruplets
The odds of any four people picked at random all being diagnosed with schizophrenia are 1 in 100 million. But genetically identical sisters Nora, Iris, Myra, and Hester Genain all have the disease. Two of the sisters have more severe forms of the disorder than the others, suggesting the influence of environmental as well as biological factors.

Few of us can easily relate to the strange thoughts, perceptions, and behaviors of schizophrenia. Sometimes our thoughts do jump around, but we do not talk nonsensically. Occasionally we feel unjustly suspicious of someone, but we do not fear that the world is plotting against us. Often our perceptions err, but rarely do we see or hear things that are not there. We have felt regret after laughing at someone's misfortune, but we rarely giggle in response to bad news. At times we just want to be alone, but we do not live in social isolation. However, millions of people around the world do talk strangely, suffer delusions, hear nonexistent voices, see things that are not there, laugh or cry at inappropriate times, or withdraw into private imaginary worlds. The quest to solve the cruel puzzle of schizophrenia therefore continues, and more vigorously than ever.

REVIEWING

>> MODULE REVIEW

39-1: **What patterns of thinking, perceiving, feeling, and behaving characterize schizophrenia?**
Schizophrenia is a group of disorders that typically strike during late adolescence, affect men very slightly more than women, and seem to occur in all cultures. Symptoms of schizophrenia are disorganized and delusional thinking (which may stem from a breakdown of selective attention), disturbed perceptions, and inappropriate emotions and actions. *Delusions* are false beliefs; hallucinations are sensory experiences without sensory stimulation.

39-2: **What forms does schizophrenia take?**
Schizophrenia may emerge gradually from a chronic history of social inadequacy (in which case the outlook is dim) or suddenly in reaction to stress (in which case the prospects for recovery are brighter). Positive symptoms are defined as the presence of inappropriate behaviors; negative symptoms, as the absence of appropriate behaviors.

39-3: **What causes schizophrenia?**
People with schizophrenia have increased receptors for the neurotransmitter dopamine, which may intensify the positive symptoms of schizophrenia. Brain abnormalities associated with schizophrenia include enlarged, fluid-filled cerebral cavities and corresponding decreases in the cortex. Brain scans reveal abnormal activity in the frontal lobes, thalamus, and amygdala. Malfunctions in multiple brain regions and their connections apparently interact to produce the symptoms of schizophrenia. Research support is mounting for the causal effects of a virus suffered in mid-pregnancy. Twin and adoption studies also point to a genetic predisposition that interacts with environmental factors to produce schizophrenia.

>> Rehearse it!

1. People with schizophrenia may speak illogically and hear voices urging self-destruction. Hearing voices in the absence of any auditory stimulation is an example of a(n)

   a. flat emotion.
   b. inappropriate emotion.
   c. word salad.
   d. hallucination.

2. Schizophrenia is actually a cluster of disorders characterized by positive or negative symptoms. A person with positive symptoms is most likely to experience

   a. catatonia.
   b. delusions.
   c. withdrawal.
   d. flat emotion.

3. Stressful events and inherited abnormalities in brain chemistry and structure are possible factors in the development of schizophrenia. Chances for recovery are best when

   a. onset is sudden, in response to stress.
   b. deterioration occurs gradually, during childhood.
   c. no environmental causes can be identified.
   d. there is a detectable brain abnormality.

Answers: 1. d, 2. b, 3. a.

>> Terms and Concepts to Remember

schizophrenia, p. 531   delusions, p. 531

>> Test Yourself

1. What do we know about the causes of schizophrenia?

   (Answer in Appendix C.)

*Multiple-choice **self-tests** and more may be found at www.worthpublishers.com/myers.*

Therapy

Therapy

We have treated psychological disorders with a bewildering array of harsh and gentle methods: by cutting holes in the head, and by giving warm baths and massages; by restraining, bleeding, or "beating the devil" out of people, and by placing them in sunny, serene environments; by administering drugs and electric shocks, and by talking—talking about childhood experiences, about current feelings, about maladaptive thoughts and behaviors.

The transition from brutal to gentler treatments occurred thanks to the efforts of reformers such as Philippe Pinel in France and Dorothea Dix in the United States, Canada, and Scotland. Both advocated constructing mental hospitals to offer more humane methods of treatment. Since the mid-1950s, however, the introduction of therapeutic drugs and community-based treatment programs has largely emptied mental health hospitals.

Today's mental health therapies can be classified into two main categories: the *psychological therapies (psychotherapy)* (Modules 40 and 41) and the *biomedical therapies* (Module 42). The favored treatment depends on both the disorder and the therapist's viewpoint.

Culver Pictures

Dorothea Dix (1802–1887)
"I . . . call your attention to the state of the Insane Persons confined within this Commonwealth, in cages."

The history of treatment

As William Hogarth's (1697–1764) engraving (right) of London's St. Mary of Bethlehem hospital (commonly called Bedlam) depicts, eighteenth-century visitors to mental hospitals paid to gawk at patients, as though they were viewing zoo animals. Benjamin Rush (1746–1813), a founder of the movement for more humane treatment of the mentally ill, designed the chair below "for the benefit of maniacal patients." He believed the restraints would help them regain their sensibilities.

The Granger Collection

The Granger Collection

The Psychological Therapies

40

Psychological therapy, or **psychotherapy,** is an interaction in which a trained therapist uses psychological techniques to assist someone seeking to overcome difficulties or achieve personal growth. It is often the preferred treatment for learning-related disorders, such as phobias.

Depending on the client and the problem, some therapists—particularly the many using a biopsychosocial approach—draw from a variety of techniques. Some are interested in counteracting unhealthy social conditions. Children of poverty, for example, are at risk for conduct disorder; children of affluence are at risk for eating disorders. Others—indeed, half of all psychotherapists—describe themselves as taking an **eclectic approach,** using a blend of therapies (Beitman & others, 1989; Castonguay & Goldfried, 1994). Closely related to eclecticism is *psychotherapy integration.* Rather than picking and choosing methods, integration advocates aim to combine them into a single, coherent system.

Among the dozens of types of psychotherapy, we will look at only the most influential. Each is built on one or more of psychology's major theories: psychoanalytic, humanistic, behavioral, and cognitive. Most of these techniques can be used one-on-one or in groups.

Psychoanalysis

40-1: What are the aims and methods of psychoanalysis, and how have they been adapted in psychodynamic therapy?

Sigmund Freud's **psychoanalysis** was the first of the psychological therapies, and its terminology has crept into our modern vocabulary. Few clinicians today practice therapy as Freud did, but some of his techniques and assumptions survive, especially in the *psychodynamic therapies.*

Aims

Because Freud assumed that many psychological problems are fueled by childhood's residue of repressed impulses and conflicts, he and his students tried to bring these repressed feelings into patients' conscious awareness. By gaining insight into the origins of the disorder—by excavating their childhood's past and fulfilling the ancient imperative to "know thyself" in a deep way—patients then work through the buried feelings and take responsibility for their own growth. Psychoanalytic theory presumes that healthier, less anxious living becomes possible when people release the energy they had previously devoted to id-ego-superego conflicts.

■ **psychotherapy** treatment involving psychological techniques; consists of interactions between a trained therapist and someone seeking to overcome psychological difficulties or achieve personal growth.

■ **eclectic approach** an approach to psychotherapy that, depending on the client's problems, uses techniques from various forms of therapy.

■ **psychoanalysis** Sigmund Freud's therapeutic technique. Freud believed the patient's free associations, resistances, dreams, and transferences—and the therapist's interpretations of them—released previously repressed feelings, allowing the patient to gain self-insight.

Freud's consulting room
Freud's office was rich with antiquities from around the world, including artwork related to his ideas about unconscious motives. His famous couch, piled high with pillows, placed patients in a comfortable reclining position facing away from him to help them focus inward.

© The New Yorker Collection, 1983, W. Miller from cartoonbank.com. All Rights Reserved.

Methods

Psychoanalysis is historical reconstruction. Psychoanalytic theory emphasizes the formative power of childhood experiences, and analysis aims to unearth the past in hope of unmasking the present. But how?

After trying hypnosis and discarding it as unreliable, Freud turned to *free association*. Imagine yourself as a patient using free association. First, you relax, perhaps by lying on a couch. To help you focus on your own thoughts and feelings, the psychoanalyst may sit out of your line of vision. You say aloud whatever comes to your mind, at one moment a childhood memory, at another a dream or recent experience. It sounds easy, but soon you notice how often you edit your thoughts as you speak, omitting what seems trivial, irrelevant, or shameful. Even in the safe presence of the analyst, you may pause momentarily before uttering an embarrassing thought. You may joke or change the subject to something less threatening. Sometimes your mind goes blank or you find yourself unable to remember important details.

To the psychoanalyst, these blocks in the flow of your free associations indicate **resistance.** They hint that anxiety lurks and you are defending against sensitive material. The analyst will want to make you aware of your resistances and then **interpret** their meaning, providing *insight* into your underlying wishes, feelings, and conflicts. If offered at the right moment, this interpretation—of, say, your not wanting to talk about your mother—may illuminate what you are avoiding and demonstrate how this resistance fits with other pieces of your psychological puzzle.

Freud believed that another clue to unconscious conflicts is your dreams' *latent content*—their underlying but censored meaning. Thus, after inviting you to report a dream, the analyst may offer a dream analysis, suggesting its meaning.

During many such sessions you will probably disclose to your analyst more of yourself than you have ever revealed to anyone else, much of it pertaining to your earliest memories. You may find yourself experiencing strong positive or negative feelings for your analyst, who may suggest you are **transferring** to your analyst feelings you experienced in earlier relationships with family members or other important people. By exposing feelings you have previously defended against, such as dependency or mingled love and anger, transference will give you a belated chance to work through them, with your analyst's help. Examining your feelings may also give you insight into your current relationships, not just those of your past childhood.

Psychoanalysts acknowledge the criticism that their interpretations are hard to refute because they cannot be proven or disproven. But they insist that interpretations often are a great help to patients. Psychoanalysis, they say, is therapy, not science.

> "I haven't seen my analyst in 200 years. He was a strict Freudian. If I'd been going all this time, I'd probably almost be cured by now."
>
> Woody Allen, after awakening from suspended animation in the movie *Sleeper*

Traditional psychoanalysis takes time, up to several years of several sessions a week, and it is expensive. (Three times a week for just two years at more than $100 per hour comes to at least $30,000.) Outside of France, Germany, Quebec, and New York City, relatively few therapists offer it (Goode, 2003). This is not surprising, given that U.S. managed health care limits the types and length of insured mental health services.

© The New Yorker Collection, 2002, Gregory from cartoonbank.com. All Rights Reserved.

"In the mental-health profession, we try to avoid negative labels, like 'a hundred and fifty bucks an hour—that's *crazy*!' or 'three fifty-minute sessions a week—that's *insane*!'"

Psychodynamic Therapy

Influenced by Freud, *psychodynamic* therapists try to understand a patient's current symptoms by focusing on themes across important relationships, including childhood experiences and the therapist relationship. They also help the person explore and gain perspective on defended-against thoughts and feelings. But these therapists may talk to the patient face to face (rather than out of the line of vision), once a week (rather than several times weekly), and for only a few weeks or months (rather than several years).

No brief excerpt can exemplify the way psychodynamic therapy interprets a patient's conflict. But the following interaction between therapist David Malan and a depressed patient does illustrate the goal of enabling insight by looking for common, recurring themes, especially in relationships. Note how Malan interprets the woman's earlier remarks (when she did most of the talking) and suggests that her relationship with him reveals a characteristic pattern of behavior (1978, pp. 133–134).

Malan: I get the feeling that you're the sort of person who needs to keep active. If you don't keep active, then something goes wrong. Is that true?

Patient: Yes.

Malan: I get a second feeling about you and that is that you must, underneath all this, have an awful lot of very strong and upsetting feelings. Somehow they're there but you aren't really quite in touch with them. Isn't this right? I feel you've been like that as long as you can remember.

Patient: For quite a few years, whenever I really sat down and thought about it I got depressed, so I tried not to think about it.

Malan: You see, you've established a pattern, haven't you? You're even like that here with me, because in spite of the fact that you're in some trouble and you feel that the bottom is falling out of your world, the way you're telling me this is just as if there wasn't anything wrong.

Interpersonal psychotherapy, a brief (12- to 16-session) variation of psychodynamic therapy, has been effective in treating depression (Weissman, 1999). Interpersonal psychotherapy aims to help people gain insight into the roots of their difficulties, but its goal is symptom relief in the here and now, not overall personality change. Rather than focusing mostly on undoing past hurts and offering interpretations, the therapist focuses primarily on current relationships and on helping people improve their relationship skills.

"You say, 'Off with her head' but what I'm hearing is, 'I feel neglected.'"

Humanistic Therapies

40-2: What are the basic themes of humanistic therapy, such as Rogers' client-centered approach?

The humanistic perspective has emphasized people's inherent potential for self-fulfillment. Not surprisingly, humanistic therapists aim to boost self-fulfillment by helping people grow in self-awareness and self-acceptance. Like psychoanalytic therapies, humanistic therapies attempt to reduce the conflicts that are impeding natural developmental growth. But humanistic therapists differ in focusing on

- the *present* and *future* more than the past. They explore feelings as they occur, rather than achieving insights into the childhood origins of the feelings.
- *conscious thoughts* rather than unconscious.
- taking immediate *responsibility* for one's feelings and actions, rather than uncovering hidden determinants.
- *promoting growth* instead of curing illness. Thus, those in therapy became "clients" rather than "patients" (a change many therapists have adopted).

Carl Rogers (1961, 1980) developed the widely used humanistic technique he called **client-centered therapy,** which focuses on the person's conscious self-perceptions. In this *nondirective therapy*, the therapist listens, without judging or interpreting, and refrains from directing the client toward certain insights.

Believing that most people already possess the resources for growth, Rogers encouraged therapists to exhibit *genuineness, acceptance,* and *empathy.* When therapists drop their facades and genuinely express their true feelings, when they enable their clients to feel unconditionally accepted, and when they empathically sense

■ **resistance** in psychoanalysis, the blocking from consciousness of anxiety-laden material.

■ **interpretation** in psychoanalysis, the analyst's noting supposed dream meanings, resistances, and other significant behaviors and events in order to promote insight.

■ **transference** in psychoanalysis, the patient's transfer to the analyst of emotions linked with other relationships (such as love or hatred for a parent).

■ **client-centered therapy** a humanistic therapy, developed by Carl Rogers, in which the therapist uses techniques such as active listening within a genuine, accepting, empathic environment to facilitate clients' growth. (Also called *person-centered therapy*.)

Active listening

Carl Rogers (right) empathized with a client during this group therapy session.

and reflect their clients' feelings, the clients may deepen their self-understanding and self-acceptance (Hill & Nakayama, 2000). As Rogers (1980, p. 10) explained,

> Hearing has consequences. When I truly hear a person and the meanings that are important to him at that moment, hearing not simply his words, but him, and when I let him know that I have heard his own private personal meanings, many things happen. There is first of all a grateful look. He feels released. He wants to tell me more about his world. He surges forth in a new sense of freedom. He becomes more open to the process of change.
>
> I have often noticed that the more deeply I hear the meanings of the person, the more there is that happens. Almost always, when a person realizes he has been deeply heard, his eyes moisten. I think in some real sense he is weeping for joy. It is as though he were saying, "Thank God, somebody heard me. Someone knows what it's like to be me."

"We have two ears and one mouth that we may listen the more and talk the less."

Zeno, 335–263 B.C., *Diogenes Laertius*

■ **active listening** empathic listening in which the listener echoes, restates, and clarifies. A feature of Rogers' client-centered therapy.

"Hearing" refers to Rogers' technique of **active listening**—echoing, restating, and seeking clarification of what the person expresses (verbally or nonverbally) and acknowledging the expressed feelings. Active listening is now an accepted part of therapeutic counseling practices in many schools, colleges, and clinics. The counselor listens attentively and interrupts only to restate and confirm feelings, to accept what is being expressed, or to seek clarification. The following brief excerpt between Rogers and a male client illustrates how he sought to provide a psychological mirror that would help clients see themselves more clearly.

Rogers: Feeling that now, hm? That you're just no good to yourself, no good to anybody. Never will be any good to anybody. Just that you're completely worthless, huh?—Those really are lousy feelings. Just feel that you're no good at all, hm?

Client: Yeah. *(Muttering in low, discouraged voice)* That's what this guy I went to town with just the other day told me.

Rogers: This guy that you went to town with really told you that you were no good? Is that what you're saying? Did I get that right?

Client: M-hm.

Rogers: I guess the meaning of that if I get it right is that here's somebody that—meant something to you and what does he think of you? Why, he's told you that he thinks you're no good at all. And that just really knocks the props out from under you. *(Client weeps quietly.)* It just brings the tears. *(Silence of 20 seconds)*

Client: *(Rather defiantly)* I don't care though.

Rogers: You tell yourself you don't care at all, but somehow I guess some part of you cares because some part of you weeps over it. *(Meador & Rogers, 1984, p. 167)*

Can a therapist be a perfect mirror, without selecting and interpreting what is reflected? Rogers conceded that one cannot be *totally* nondirective. Nevertheless, he believed that the therapist's most important contribution is to accept and understand the client. Given a nonjudgmental, grace-filled environment that provides *unconditional positive regard,* people may accept even their worst traits and feel valued and whole.

If you want to listen more actively in your own relationships, three hints may help:

1. *Paraphrase.* Check your understandings by summarizing the speaker's words in your own words.
2. *Invite clarification.* "What might be an example of that?" may encourage the speaker to say more.
3. *Reflect feelings.* "It sounds frustrating" might mirror what you're sensing from the speaker's body language and intensity.

Behavior Therapies

40-3 : What are the assumptions and techniques of the behavior therapies?

The therapies we have considered so far assume that many psychological problems diminish as self-awareness grows. Traditional psychoanalysts expect problems to subside as people gain insight into their unresolved and unconscious tensions. Humanistic therapists expect problems to abate as people get in touch with their feelings. Proponents of **behavior therapy,** however, doubt the healing power of self-awareness. (You can become aware of why you are highly anxious during exams and still be anxious.) They assume that problem behaviors *are* the problems, and the application of learning principles can eliminate them. Rather than delving deeply below the surface looking for inner causes, behavior therapists view maladaptive symptoms—such as phobias or sexual disorders—as learned behaviors that can be replaced by constructive behaviors.

■ **behavior therapy** therapy that applies learning principles to the elimination of unwanted behaviors.

■ **counterconditioning** a behavior therapy procedure that conditions new responses to stimuli that trigger unwanted behaviors; based on classical conditioning. Includes *exposure therapies* and *aversive conditioning.*

Classical Conditioning Techniques

One cluster of behavior therapies derives from principles developed in Ivan Pavlov's early-twentieth-century conditioning experiments. As Pavlov and others showed, we learn various behaviors and emotions through classical conditioning. Could maladaptive symptoms be examples of conditioned responses? If so, might reconditioning be a solution? Learning theorist O. H. Mowrer thought so, when he developed a successful conditioning therapy for chronic bed-wetters. The child sleeps on a liquid-sensitive pad connected to an alarm. Moisture on the pad triggers the alarm, waking the child. With sufficient repetition, this association of urinary relaxation with waking up stops the bed-wetting. In three out of four cases the treatment is effective, and the success provides a boost to the child's self-image (Christophersen & Edwards, 1992; Houts & others, 1994).

Another example: If a claustrophobic fear of elevators is a learned aversion to the stimulus of being in a confined space, then might one unlearn the fear by counter-conditioning the fear response? **Counterconditioning** pairs the trigger stimulus (in this case, the enclosed space of the elevator) with a new response (relaxation) that is incompatible with fear. And indeed, behavior therapists have successfully counter-conditioned people with this fear. Two specific counterconditioning techniques—*exposure therapy* and *aversive conditioning*—may be used to replace unwanted responses.

What might a psychoanalyst say about Mowrer's therapy for bed-wetting? How might a behavior therapist reply?

Exposure Therapies

Picture this scene reported in 1924 by behaviorist psychologist Mary Cover Jones: Three-year-old Peter is petrified of rabbits and other furry objects. Jones plans to replace Peter's fear of rabbits with a conditioned response incompatible with fear. Her

THE FAR SIDE® BY GARY LARSON

The Far Side © 1986 FARWORKS. © 1986 FarWorks, Inc. All Rights Reserved. Reprinted with permission./Dist. by Creators Syndicate

Professor Gallagher and his controversial technique of simultaneously confronting the fear of heights, snakes, and the dark.

strategy is to associate the fear-evoking rabbit with the pleasurable, relaxed response associated with eating.

As Peter begins his midafternoon snack, Jones introduces a caged rabbit on the other side of the huge room. Peter, eagerly munching away on his crackers and drinking his milk, hardly notices. On succeeding days, she gradually moves the rabbit closer and closer. Within two months, Peter is tolerating the rabbit in his lap, even stroking it while he eats. Moreover, his fear of other furry objects subsides as well, having been "countered," or replaced, by a relaxed state that cannot coexist with fear (Fisher, 1984; Jones, 1924).

Unfortunately for those who might have been helped by her counterconditioning procedures, Jones' story of Peter and the rabbit did not immediately become part of psychology's lore. It was more than 30 years later that psychiatrist Joseph Wolpe (1958; Wolpe & Plaud, 1997) refined Jones' technique into what have become the most widely used types of behavior therapy: **exposure therapies,** which expose people to what they normally avoid. As people can habituate to the sound of a train passing their new apartment, so, with repeated exposure, can they become less anxiously responsive to things that once petrified them (Deacon & Abramowitz, 2004).

One widely used exposure therapy is **systematic desensitization.** Wolpe assumed, as did Jones, that you cannot be simultaneously anxious and relaxed. Therefore, if you can repeatedly relax when facing anxiety-provoking stimuli, you can gradually eliminate your anxiety. The trick is to proceed gradually. Let's see how this might work with a common phobia. Imagine yourself afraid of public speaking. A behavior therapist might first ask for your help in constructing a hierarchy of anxiety-triggering speaking situations. Yours might range from mildly anxiety-provoking situations, perhaps speaking up in a small group of friends, to panic-provoking situations, such as having to address a large audience.

Next, using *progressive relaxation,* the therapist would train you to relax one muscle group after another, until you achieve a drowsy state of complete relaxation and comfort. Then the therapist asks you to imagine, with your eyes closed, a mildly anxiety-arousing situation: You are having coffee with a group of friends and are trying to decide whether to speak up. If imagining the scene causes you to feel any anxiety, you signal your tension by raising your finger, and the therapist instructs you to switch off the mental image and go back to deep relaxation. This imagined scene is repeatedly paired with relaxation until you feel no trace of anxiety.

The therapist progresses up the constructed anxiety hierarchy, using the relaxed state to desensitize you to each imagined situation. After several sessions, you practice what you had imagined in actual situations, beginning with relatively easy tasks and gradually moving to more anxiety-filled ones. Conquering your anxiety in an actual situation, not just in your imagination, raises your self-confidence (Foa & Kozak, 1986; Williams, 1987). Eventually, you may even become a confident public speaker.

When an anxiety-arousing situation is too expensive, difficult, or embarrassing to re-create, **virtual reality exposure therapy** offers an efficient middle ground. Wearing a head-mounted display unit that projects a three-dimensional virtual world, you would view a lifelike series of scenes. As your head turns, motion sensors adjust the scene. Experiments led by several research teams have treated people who

Virtual reality exposure therapy
Within the confines of a room, virtual reality technology exposes people to vivid simulations of feared stimuli, such as a plane's takeoff.

Bob Mahoney / The Image Works

Bob Mahoney The Image Works

fear flying, fear heights, fear particular animals, and fear public speaking (Gershon & others, 2002; Rothbaum & others, 2002). People who fear flying, for example, can peer out a virtual window of a simulated plane, feel vibrations, and hear the engine roar as the plane taxis down the runway and takes off. In initial experiments, those experiencing virtual reality exposure therapy have had greater relief from their fears—in real life—than have those in control groups (Hoffman, 2004; Krijn & others, 2004).

Aversive Conditioning

In systematic desensitization, the goal is substituting a positive (relaxed) response for a negative (fearful) response to a *harmless* stimulus. In **aversive conditioning,** the goal is substituting a negative (aversive) response for a positive response to a *harmful* stimulus (such as alcohol). Thus, aversive conditioning is the reverse of systematic desensitization—it seeks to condition an aversion to something the client *should* avoid.

The procedure is simple: It associates the unwanted behavior with unpleasant feelings. To treat nail biting, one can paint the fingernails with a yucky-tasting nail polish (Baskind, 1997). To treat alcoholism, an aversion therapist offers the client appealing drinks laced with a drug that produces severe nausea. By linking alcohol with violent nausea, the therapist seeks to transform the person's reaction to alcohol from positive to negative (**FIGURE 40.1**).

Does aversive conditioning work? In the short run it may. Arthur Wiens and Carol Menustik (1983) studied 685 patients with alcoholism who completed an aversion therapy program at a Portland, Oregon, hospital. One year later, after returning for several booster treatments of alcohol-sickness pairings, 63 percent were still successfully abstaining. But after three years, only 33 percent had remained abstinent.

The problem is that in therapy, as in research, cognition influences conditioning. People know that outside the therapist's office they can drink without fear of nausea. Their ability to discriminate between the aversive conditioning situation and all other situations can limit the treatment's effectiveness. Thus, aversive conditioning is often used in combination with other treatments.

■ **exposure therapies** behavioral techniques, such as systematic desensitization, that treat anxieties by exposing people (in imagination or actuality) to the things they fear and avoid.

■ **systematic desensitization** a type of exposure therapy that associates a pleasant relaxed state with gradually increasing anxiety-triggering stimuli. Commonly used to treat phobias.

■ **virtual reality exposure therapy** An anxiety treatment that progressively exposes people to simulations of their greatest fears, such as airplane flying, spiders, or public speaking.

■ **aversive conditioning** a type of counterconditioning that associates an unpleasant state (such as nausea) with an unwanted behavior (such as drinking alcohol).

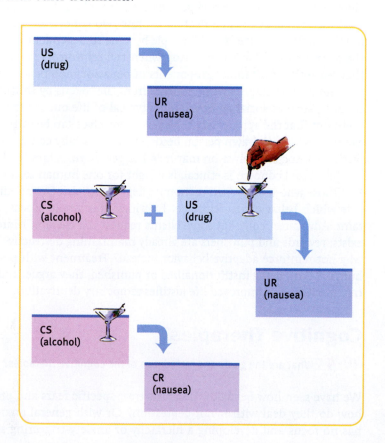

FIGURE 40.1

Aversion therapy for alcoholism

After repeatedly imbibing an alcoholic drink mixed with a drug that produces severe nausea, some people with a history of alcohol abuse develop at least a temporary conditioned aversion to alcohol.

Operant Conditioning

A basic concept in operant conditioning is that voluntary behaviors are strongly influenced by their consequences. Knowing this, behavior therapists can practice *behavior modification*—reinforcing desired behaviors and withholding reinforcement for undesired behaviors or punishing them. Using operant conditioning to solve specific behavior problems has raised hopes for some cases thought to be hopeless. Children with mental retardation have been taught to care for themselves. Socially withdrawn children with autism have learned to interact. People with schizophrenia have been helped to behave more rationally in their hospital ward. In such cases, therapists use positive reinforcers to shape behavior in a step-by-step manner, rewarding closer and closer approximations of the desired behavior.

In extreme cases, treatment must be intensive. In one study, 19 withdrawn, uncommunicative 3-year-olds with autism participated in a 2-year program in which their parents spent 40 hours each week attempting to shape their behavior (Lovaas, 1987). The combination of positively reinforcing desired behaviors and ignoring or punishing aggressive and self-abusive behaviors worked wonders for some. By first grade, 9 of the 19 children were functioning successfully in school and exhibiting normal intelligence. In a group of 40 comparable children who did not undergo this treatment, only one showed similar improvement.

Rewards used to modify behavior vary. For some people, the reinforcing power of attention or praise is sufficient. Others require concrete rewards, such as food. In institutional settings, therapists may create a **token economy.** When people display appropriate behavior, such as getting out of bed, washing, dressing, eating, talking coherently, cleaning up their rooms, or playing cooperatively, they receive a token or plastic coin as a positive reinforcer. Later, they can exchange their accumulated tokens for various rewards, such as candy, TV time, trips to town, or better living quarters. Token economies have been successfully applied in various settings (homes, classrooms, hospitals, institutions for the delinquent) and among members of various populations (including disturbed children and people with schizophrenia and other mental disabilities).

Critics of behavior modification express two concerns. The first is practical: How durable are the behaviors? Will people become so dependent on extrinsic rewards that the appropriate behaviors will stop when the reinforcers stop, as may happen when they leave the institution? Proponents of behavior modification believe the behaviors will endure if therapists wean patients from the tokens by shifting them toward other rewards, such as social approval, more typical of life outside the institution. They also point out that the appropriate behaviors themselves can be intrinsically rewarding. For example, as a withdrawn person becomes more socially competent, the intrinsic satisfactions of social interaction may help the person maintain the behavior.

The second concern is ethical: Is it right for one human to control another's behavior? Those who set up token economies deprive people of something they desire and decide which behaviors to reinforce. To critics, this whole process has an authoritarian taint. Advocates reply that some clients request the therapy. Moreover, control already exists; rewards and punishers are already maintaining destructive behavior patterns. So why not reinforce adaptive behavior instead? Treatment with positive rewards is more humane than being institutionalized or punished, they argue, and the right to effective treatment and an improved life justifies temporary deprivation.

Cognitive Therapies

40-4 : What are the goals and techniques of the cognitive therapies?

We have seen how behavior therapists treat specific fears and problem behaviors. But how do they deal with major depression? Or with general anxiety, in which anxiety has no focus and developing a hierarchy of anxiety-triggering situations is difficult?

■ **token economy** an operant conditioning procedure in which people earn a token of some sort for exhibiting a desired behavior and can later exchange the tokens for various privileges or treats.

■ **cognitive therapy** therapy that teaches people new, more adaptive ways of thinking and acting; based on the assumption that thoughts intervene between events and our emotional reactions.

Lara Jo Regan/Gamma Liaison

Cognitive therapy for eating disorders aided by journaling
Cognitive therapists guide people toward new ways of explaining their good and bad experiences. By recording each day's positive events, and how one enabled them, for example, people may become more mindful of their self-control.

Behavior therapists treating these less clearly defined psychological problems have had help from the same *cognitive revolution* that has profoundly changed other areas of psychology during the last five decades.

The **cognitive therapies** assume that our thinking colors our feelings (**FIGURE 40.2**), that between the event and our response lies the mind. Self-blaming and overgeneralized explanations of bad events are often an integral part of the vicious cycle of depression. The depressed person interprets a suggestion as criticism, disagreement as dislike, praise as flattery, friendliness as pity. Ruminating on such thoughts sustains the bad mood. If such thinking patterns can be learned, then surely they can be replaced. Cognitive therapists therefore try in various ways to teach people new, more constructive ways of thinking. If people are miserable, they can be helped to change their minds.

> "Life does not consist mainly, or even largely, of facts and happenings. It consists mainly of the storm of thoughts that are forever blowing through one's mind."
>
> Mark Twain, 1835–1910

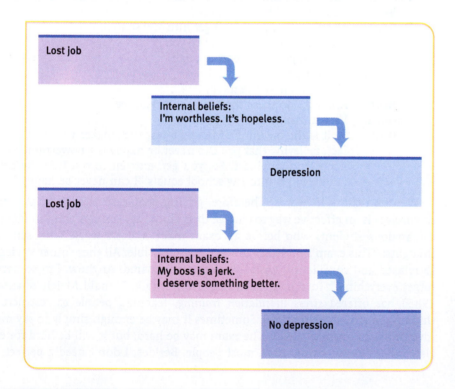

FIGURE 40.2
A cognitive perspective on psychological disorders
The person's emotional reactions are produced not directly by the event but by the person's thoughts in response to the event.

Beck's Therapy for Depression

Cognitive therapist Aaron Beck was originally trained in Freudian techniques. As Beck analyzed the dreams of depressed people, he found recurring negative themes of loss, rejection, and abandonment that extended into their waking thoughts. Such negativity even extends into therapy, as clients recall and rehearse their failings and worst impulses (Kelly, 2000). With cognitive therapy, Beck and his colleagues (1979) have sought to reverse clients' catastrophizing beliefs about themselves, their situations, and their futures. With gentle questioning intended to reveal irrational thinking, they persuade depressed people to take off the dark glasses through which they view life (Beck & others, 1979, pp. 145–146):

Patient: I agree with the descriptions of me but I guess I don't agree that the way I think makes me depressed.

Beck: How do you understand it?

Patient: I get depressed when things go wrong. Like when I fail a test.

Beck: How can failing a test make you depressed?

Patient: Well, if I fail I'll never get into law school.

Beck: So failing the test means a lot to you. But if failing a test could drive people into clinical depression, wouldn't you expect everyone who failed the test to have a depression? . . . Did everyone who failed get depressed enough to require treatment?

Patient: No, but it depends on how important the test was to the person.

Beck: Right, and who decides the importance?

Patient: I do.

Beck: And so, what we have to examine is your way of viewing the test (or the way that you think about the test) and how it affects your chances of getting into law school. Do you agree?

Patient: Right.

Beck: Do you agree that the way you interpret the results of the test will affect you? You might feel depressed, you might have trouble sleeping, not feel like eating, and you might even wonder if you should drop out of the course.

Patient: I have been thinking that I wasn't going to make it. Yes, I agree.

Beck: Now what did failing mean?

Patient: *(tearful)* That I couldn't get into law school.

Beck: And what does that mean to you?

Patient: That I'm just not smart enough.

Beck: Anything else?

Patient: That I can never be happy.

Beck: And how do these thoughts make you feel?

Patient: Very unhappy.

Beck: So it is the meaning of failing a test that makes you very unhappy. In fact, believing that you can never be happy is a powerful factor in producing unhappiness. So, you get yourself into a trap—by definition, failure to get into law school equals "I can never be happy."

We often think in words. Therefore, getting people to change what they say to themselves is an effective way to change their thinking. Perhaps you can identify with the anxious students who before an exam make matters worse with self-defeating thoughts: "This exam's probably going to be impossible. All these other students seem so relaxed and confident. I wish I were better prepared. Anyhow, I'm so nervous I'll forget everything." To change such negative self-talk, Donald Meichenbaum (1977, 1985) has offered *stress inoculation training,* teaching people to restructure their thinking in stressful situations. Sometimes it may be enough simply to say more positive things to oneself: "Relax. The exam may be hard, but it will be hard for everyone else, too. I studied harder than most people. Besides, I don't need a perfect score to

PEANUTS

get a good grade." In experiments, depression-prone children and college students exhibit a halved rate of future depression after being trained to dispute their negative thoughts (Seligman, 2002). To a great extent, it *is* the thought that counts.

Cognitive-Behavior Therapy

Cognitive-behavior therapy aims not only to alter the way people think (cognitive therapy), but also to alter the way they act (behavior therapy). It seeks to make people aware of their irrational negative thinking, to replace it with new ways of thinking, *and* to practice the more positive approach in everyday settings.

In one study, for example, people with obsessive-compulsive behaviors learned to relabel their compulsive thoughts (Schwartz & others, 1996). Feeling the urge to wash their hands again, they would tell themselves, "I'm having a compulsive urge," and attribute it to their brain's abnormal activity, as previously viewed in PET scans. Instead of giving in to the urge, they would then spend 15 minutes in an enjoyable, alternative behavior, such as practicing an instrument, taking a walk, or gardening. This helped "unstick" the brain by shifting attention and engaging other parts of the brain. For two or three months, the weekly therapy sessions continued, with relabeling and refocusing practice at home. By the study's end, most participants' symptoms had diminished and their PET scans revealed normalized brain activity.

Group and Family Therapies

40-5 : What are the benefits of group therapy?

Except for traditional psychoanalysis, most therapies may also occur in small groups. Group therapy does not provide the same degree of therapist involvement with each client; however, it saves therapists' time and clients' money—and it often is no less effective than individual therapy (Fuhriman & Burlingame, 1994). Therapists frequently suggest group therapy for people experiencing family conflicts or those whose behavior is distressing to others. For up to 90 minutes a week, the therapist guides the interactions of 6 to 10 people as they engage issues and react to one another.

Group sessions also offer a unique benefit: The social context allows people both to discover that others have problems similar to their own and to receive feedback as they try out new ways of behaving. It can be a relief to find that you are not alone—to learn that others, despite their apparent composure, share your problems and your troublesome feelings. It can also be reassuring to hear that you yourself look poised even though you feel anxious and self-conscious.

One special type of group interaction, **family therapy,** assumes that no person is an island, that we live and grow in relation to others, especially our families. We struggle to differentiate ourselves from our families, but we also need to connect with them emotionally. Some of our problem behaviors arise from the tension between these two tendencies, which can create family stress. Therapists tend to view families as systems, in which each person's actions trigger reactions from others. To break that pattern, the therapist often attempts to guide family members toward positive relationships and improved communication.

■ **cognitive-behavior therapy** a popular integrated therapy that combines cognitive therapy (changing self-defeating thinking) with behavior therapy (changing behavior).

■ **family therapy** therapy that treats the family as a system. Views an individual's unwanted behaviors as influenced by or directed at other family members.

>> MODULE REVIEW

Psychotherapy is an emotionally charged, confiding interaction between a therapist and a person experiencing psychological difficulties. The major psychotherapies derive from the familiar psychoanalytic, humanistic, behavioral, and cognitive perspectives on psychology. Today, many therapists combine aspects of these perspectives in an *eclectic approach* or psychotherapy integration.

40-1: What are the aims and methods of psychoanalysis, and how have they been adapted in psychodynamic therapy?

Through *psychoanalysis*, Sigmund Freud and his students aimed to help people gain insight into the unconscious origins of their disorders, to work through the accompanying feelings, and to take responsibility for their own growth. Techniques included free association, dream analysis, and *interpretation* of *resistances* and *transference* to the therapist of long-repressed feelings. Traditional psychoanalysis is no longer practiced widely. Contemporary psychodynamic therapy has been influenced by traditional psychoanalysis, but is briefer and less expensive. It focuses on a patient's current conflicts and defenses by searching for themes common to many past and present important relationships, including (but not limited to) childhood experiences and interactions with the therapist. Interpersonal therapy (a brief 12- to 16-session form of psychodynamic therapy) deals primarily with current symptoms (such as depression) rather than the origins of unconscious conflicts.

40-2: What are the basic themes of humanistic therapy, such as Rogers' client-centered approach?

Humanistic therapists focus on clients' current conscious feelings and on their taking responsibility for their own growth. Carl Rogers' *client-centered therapy* proposed that therapists' most im-

portant contributions are to function as a psychological mirror through *active listening* and to provide a growth-fostering environment of unconditional positive regard, characterized by genuineness, acceptance, and empathy.

40-3: What are the assumptions and techniques of the behavior therapies?

Behavior therapists do not attempt to explain the origin of problems or to promote self-awareness. Instead, they attempt to modify the problem behaviors themselves. Thus, they may *countercondition* behaviors through *exposure therapies* such as *systematic desensitization* or *aversive conditioning*. Or they may apply operant conditioning principles with behavior modification techniques, such as *token economies*.

40-4: What are the goals and techniques of the cognitive therapies?

The *cognitive therapies*, such as Aaron Beck's cognitive therapy for depression, aim to change self-defeating thinking by training people to look at themselves in new, more positive ways. *Cognitive-behavior therapy* also helps clients to regularly practice new ways of thinking and talking.

40-5: What are the benefits of group therapy?

Group therapy sessions can help more people and cost less per person than individual therapy would. Clients may benefit from knowing others have similar problems and from getting feedback and reassurance. *Family therapy* views a family as an interactive system and attempts to help members discover the roles they play and to learn to communicate more openly and directly.

>> REHEARSE IT!

1. All of the psychological therapies involve verbal interactions between a trained professional and a person with a problem. A therapist who encourages people to relate their dreams and searches for the unconscious roots of their problems is drawing from
   a. psychoanalysis.
   b. humanistic therapies.
   c. client-centered therapy.
   d. nondirective therapy.

2. According to psychoanalytic theory, a patient's emotional relationship with the therapist mirrors other important relationships in the patient's life—for example, an early relationship with a parent. Developing strong feelings for the analyst is an important part of the psychoanalytic process and is called

   a. transference.
   b. resistance.
   c. interpretation.
   d. empathy.

3. Humanistic therapists focus on present experience—on becoming aware of feelings as they arise and taking responsibility for them. Compared with psychoanalysts, humanistic therapists are more likely to emphasize
   a. hidden or repressed feelings.
   b. childhood experiences.
   c. psychological disorders.
   d. self-fulfillment and growth.

4. Especially important to Carl Rogers' client-centered therapy is the technique of active listening. The therapist who practices active listening
   a. engages in free association.

   b. exposes the patient's resistances.
   c. restates and clarifies the client's statements.
   d. directly challenges the client's self-perceptions.

5. Behavior therapists apply learning principles to the treatment of problems such as phobias and alcoholism. In such treatment, the goal is to
   a. identify and treat the underlying causes of the problem.
   b. improve learning and insight.
   c. eliminate the unwanted behavior.
   d. improve communication and social sensitivity.

6. Behavior therapists often use counterconditioning to produce new responses to old stimuli. Two counterconditioning techniques are systematic desensitization and

   a. resistance.
   b. aversive conditioning.
   c. transference.
   d. active listening.

7. The technique of systematic desensitization teaches people to relax in the presence of progressively more anxiety-provoking stimuli. Systematic desensitization has been found to be especially effective in the treatment of

   a. phobias.
   b. depression.
   c. alcoholism.
   d. bed-wetting.

8. In token economies, people who display a desired behavior or take a step in the right direction earn tokens, which they can later exchange for other rewards. Token economies are an application of

   a. classical conditioning.
   b. counterconditioning.
   c. cognitive therapy.
   d. operant conditioning.

9. Aaron Beck's form of cognitive therapy teaches people to stop attributing failures to personal inadequacy, and success to external circumstances. This form of cognitive therapy has been shown to be especially effective in treating

   a. mental retardation.
   b. phobias.
   c. alcoholism.
   d. depression.

10. Psychotherapy is in large part an individual process, although most therapies may occur in therapist-led small groups. The social context of this group therapy tells people that others have problems similar to theirs and allows them to act out alternative behaviors. In family therapy, the therapist assumes that

    a. only one family member needs to change.
    b. each person's actions trigger reactions from other family members.
    c. dysfunctional families must improve their interactions or give up their children.
    d. all of the above are true.

Answers: 1. a, 2. a, 3. d, 4. c, 5. c, 6. b, 7. a, 8. d, 9. d, 10. b.

>> TERMS AND CONCEPTS TO REMEMBER

psychotherapy, p. 541
eclectic approach, p. 541
psychoanalysis, p. 541
resistance, p. 542
interpretation, p. 542
transference, p. 542

client-centered therapy, p. 543
active listening, p. 544
behavior therapy, p. 545
counterconditioning, p. 545
exposure therapies, p. 546
systematic desensitization, p. 546

virtual reality exposure therapy, p. 546
aversive conditioning, p. 547
token economy, p. 548
cognitive therapy, p. 549
cognitive-behavior therapy, p. 551
family therapy, p. 551

>> TEST YOURSELF

1. What is the major distinction between the underlying assumption in psychoanalytic and humanistic therapies and the underlying assumption in behavior therapies?

   (Answer in Appendix C.)

Multiple-choice **self-tests** and more may be found at www.worthpublishers.com/myers.

Evaluating Psychotherapies

Advice columnist Ann Landers frequently urged her troubled letter writers to get professional help: "[Don't] give up. Hang in there until you find [a psychotherapist] who fills the bill. It's worth the effort." And to a second writer on the same day: "There are many excellent mental health facilities in your city. I urge you to make an appointment at once" (Farina & Fisher, 1982).

Therapists can verify that many Americans share this confidence in **psychotherapy's** effectiveness. Before 1950, psychiatrists were the primary providers of mental health care. Today, surging demands for psychotherapy also occupy the time and attention of clinical and counseling psychologists; clinical social workers; pastoral, marital, abuse, and school counselors; and psychiatric nurses. Thus, in addition to 55,000 clinical psychiatrists and 95,000 doctoral-level clinical psychologists in the United States, a quarter-million other therapists, many with social work training, are licensed to see clients (Glenn, 2003). Many work in community mental health programs, providing outpatient therapy, crisis phone lines, and halfway houses for those in transition from hospitalization to independent living.

With such an enormous outlay of time, money, effort, and hope, it is important to ask: Is the faith that millions of people worldwide place in these therapists justified? And was the *Wall Street Journal* (1999) therefore wrong to suppose that including psychotherapy in health insurance plans would lead to "endless payments for dubious benefits of apparently marginal problems"?

Is Psychotherapy Effective?

41-1 : Does psychotherapy work? Who decides?

The question, though simply put, is not simply answered. For one thing, measuring therapy's effectiveness is not like taking your body's temperature to see if your fever has gone away. If you and I were to undergo psychotherapy, how would we gauge its effectiveness? By how we feel about our progress? How our therapist feels about it? How our friends and family feel about it? How our behavior has changed?

Clients' Perceptions

If clients' testimonials were the only measuring stick, we could strongly affirm the effectiveness of psychotherapy. When 2900 *Consumer Reports* readers (1995; Kotkin & others, 1996; Seligman, 1995) related their experiences with mental health professionals, 89 percent said they were at least "fairly well satisfied." Among those who recalled feeling *fair* or *very poor* when beginning therapy, 9 in 10 now were feeling *very good, good,* or at least *so-so.* We have their word for it—and who should know better?

We should not dismiss these testimonials lightly. People enter therapy because they are suffering, and most leave feeling better about themselves. But there are several reasons why client testimonials do not persuade psychotherapy's skeptics:

- ***People often enter therapy in crisis.*** When, with the normal ebb and flow of events, the crisis passes, people may attribute their improvement to the therapy.
- ***Clients may need to believe the therapy was worth the effort.*** To admit investing time and money in something ineffective is like admitting to having one's car serviced repeatedly by a mechanic who never fixes it. Self-justification is a powerful human motive.

■ **psychotherapy** treatment involving psychological techniques; consists of interactions between a trained therapist and someone seeking to overcome psychological difficulties or achieve personal growth.

- ***Clients generally speak kindly of their therapists.*** Even if the problems remain, say the critics, clients "work hard to find something positive to say. The therapist had been very understanding, the client had gained a new perspective, he learned to communicate better, his mind was eased, anything at all so as not to have to say treatment was a failure" (Zilbergeld, 1983, p. 117).

Clinicians' Perceptions

If clinicians' perceptions accurately reflected therapeutic effectiveness, we would have even more reason to celebrate. Case studies of successful treatment abound. Furthermore, every therapist treasures compliments from clients as they say good-bye or later express their gratitude. The problem is that clients justify entering psychotherapy by emphasizing their unhappiness, justify leaving by emphasizing their well-being, and stay in touch only if satisfied. Therapists are most aware of the failures of *other* therapists—those whose clients, having experienced only temporary relief, are now seeking a new therapist for their recurring problems. Thus, the same person with the same recurring difficulty—the same old anxieties, depression, or marital difficulty—may be a "success" story in several therapists' files.

Because people enter therapy when they are extremely unhappy, and usually leave when they are less extremely unhappy, most therapists, like most clients, testify to therapy's success—regardless of the treatment. Although "treatments" have varied widely, from chains to counseling, every generation views its own approach as enlightened.

Outcome Research

How, then, can we objectively measure the effectiveness of psychotherapy? What types of people and problems are best helped, and by what type of psychotherapy? The questions have both academic and personal relevance. If you feel anxious or depressed, or someone close to you shows symptoms of some psychological disorder, the likelihood of psychotherapy's being of help will be crucial information.

In search of answers, psychologists have turned to controlled research studies. Similar research in the 1800s transformed medicine from concocted treatments (bleeding, purging, infusions of plant and metal substances) into a science. The transformation occurred when skeptical physicians began to realize that many patients got better on their own, that most of the fashionable treatments were doing no good, and that sorting fact from superstition required following illnesses closely—with and without a particular treatment. Typhoid fever patients, for example, often improved after being bled, convincing most physicians that the treatment worked. Not until a control group was given mere bed rest—and 70 percent were observed to improve after five weeks of fever—did physicians learn, to their shock, that this treatment was worthless (Thomas, 1992).

In psychology, the opening challenge to the effectiveness of psychotherapy was issued by British psychologist Hans Eysenck (1952). Launching a spirited debate, he summarized studies showing that two-thirds of those receiving psychotherapy for disorders such as depression and anxiety improved markedly. To this day, no one disputes that optimistic estimate.

Why, then, are we still debating psychotherapy's effectiveness? Because Eysenck also reported similar improvement among *untreated* persons, such as those who were on waiting lists. With or without psychotherapy, he said, roughly two-thirds improved noticeably. Time was a great healer.

The avalanche of criticism prompted by Eysenck's conclusions revealed shortcomings in his analyses. Also, in 1952 Eysenck could find only 24 studies of psychotherapy outcomes to analyze. Today, there are hundreds. The best of these *randomized clinical trials* randomly assign people on a waiting list to therapy or to no therapy. Afterward, researchers evaluate.

> "Fortunately, [psycho]analysis is not the only way to resolve inner conflicts. Life itself still remains a very effective therapist."
>
> Karen Horney, *Our Inner Conflicts*, 1945

In the first statistical digest of these studies, Mary Lee Smith and her colleagues (1980) combined the results of 475 investigations (**FIGURE 41.1**). Psychotherapists welcomed the result: The average therapy client ends up better off than 80 percent of the untreated individuals on waiting lists. The claim is more modest than it first appears—by definition, about 50 percent of untreated people also are better off than the average untreated person. Nevertheless, Smith and her collaborators exulted that "psychotherapy benefits people of all ages as reliably as schooling educates them, medicine cures them, or business turns a profit" (p. 183).

Newer research summaries confirm that psychotherapy works (Kopta & others, 1999; Shadish & others, 2000). In one ambitious study, the National Institute of Mental Health compared three depression treatments: cognitive therapy, interpersonal therapy, and a standard drug therapy. Twenty-eight experienced therapists at research sites in Norman, Oklahoma; Washington, DC; and Pittsburgh, Pennsylvania, were trained in one of the three methods and randomly assigned their share of the 239 participants suffering from depression. Clients in all three groups improved more than did those in a control group who received merely an inert medication and supportive attention, encouragement, and advice. Among those completing a full 16-week program, the depression lifted for slightly more than half in each of the three treatment groups—but for only 29 percent of those in the control group (Elkin & others, 1989). This verdict echoes the results of the earlier outcome studies: *Those not undergoing therapy often improve, but those undergoing therapy are more likely to improve.*

Is psychotherapy also cost-effective? Again, the answer is yes. Studies by health insurers show that mental health treatment can more than pay for itself with reduced medical costs (American Psychological Association, 1991). When people seek psychological treatment, their search for other medical treatment drops—by 16 percent in one digest of 91 studies (Chiles & others, 1999). Given the staggering annual cost of psychological disorders and substance abuse—including crime, accidents, lost work, and treatment—this is a good investment, much like money spent on prenatal and well-baby care. Both *reduce* long-term costs. Boosting employees' psychological well-being, for example, can lower medical costs, improve work efficiency, and diminish absenteeism.

But note that the claim—that psychotherapy, *on average*, is somewhat effective—refers to no one therapy in particular. It is like saying, "Surgery is somewhat effective," or reassuring lung-cancer patients that "on average," medical treatment of health problems is effective. What people want to know is not the average effectiveness of all therapy but the particular effectiveness of a treatment for their specific problems.

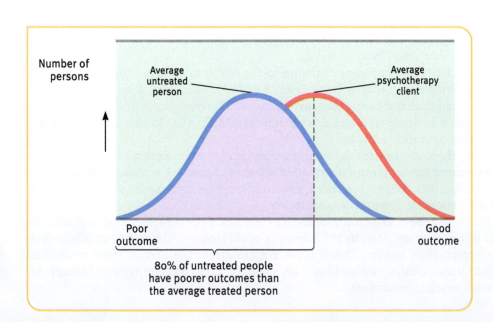

FIGURE 41.1
Treatment versus no treatment
These two normal distribution curves based on data from 475 studies show the improvement of untreated people and psychotherapy clients. The outcome for the average therapy client surpassed that for 80 percent of the untreated people. (Adapted from Smith & others, 1980.)

The Relative Effectiveness of Different Therapies

41-2: Are some therapies more effective than others?

So what can we tell people considering therapy, and those paying for it, about *which* psychotherapy will be most effective for their problem? Despite claims of superiority by advocates of different types of therapy, the statistical summaries and surveys revealed no one type of therapy as generally superior (Smith & others, 1977, 1980). Clients seemed equally satisfied, *Consumer Reports* concluded, whether treated by a psychiatrist, psychologist, or social worker; whether seen in a group or individual context; whether the therapist had extensive or relatively limited training and experience (Seligman, 1995). More than two decades after the early analyses, newer studies concur. There is little if any connection between clinicians' experience, training, supervision, and licensing and their clients' outcomes (Bickman, 1999; Luborsky & others, 2002). Was the dodo bird in *Alice in Wonderland* right: "Everyone has won and all must have prizes"?

Not quite. Some forms of therapy get prizes for particular problems. Behavioral conditioning therapies, for example, have achieved especially favorable results with specific behavior problems, such as bed-wetting, phobias, compulsions, marital problems, and sexual disorders (Bowers & Clum, 1988; Hunsley & DiGiulio, 2002; Shadish & Baldwin, 2005). And new studies confirm cognitive therapy's effectiveness in coping with depression and reducing suicide risk (Brown & others, 2005; DeRubeis & others, 2005; Hollon & others, 2005).

Moreover, we can say that therapy is most effective when the problem is clear-cut (Singer, 1981; Westen & Morrison, 2001). Those who experience phobias or panic, who are unassertive, or who are frustrated by sexual performance problems can hope for improvement. Those with less-focused problems, such as depression and anxiety, usually benefit in the short term but often relapse later. And those with chronic schizophrenia or a desire to change their entire personality are unlikely to benefit from psychotherapy alone (Zilbergeld, 1983). The more specific the problem, the greater the hope.

Meanwhile, controversy continues—some call it psychology's civil war—over the extent to which science should guide both clinical practice and the willingness of health care providers and insurers to pay for psychotherapy. On the one side are research psychologists using scientific methods to extend the list of well-defined and validated therapies for various disorders. On the other side are the nonscientist therapists who view their practices as more art than science, not something amenable to describing in a manual or testing in an experiment. People are too complex and therapy too intuitive for a cookie-cutter approach, they say. Between these two groups stand the science-oriented clinicians, who believe that by basing practice on evidence and making mental health professionals accountable for effectiveness, therapy stands to gain credibility. Moreover, the public will be protected from pseudotherapies, and therapists will be protected from accusations of sounding like snake-oil salesmen—"Trust me, I know it works, I've seen it work."

> "Whatever differences in treatment efficacy exist, they appear to be extremely small, at best."
> Bruce Wampold and colleagues (1997)

> "Different sores have different salves."
> English proverb

Evaluating Alternative Therapies

41-3: How do alternative therapies fare under scientific scrutiny?

The tendency of many abnormal states of mind to return to normal, combined with the *placebo effect,* creates fertile soil for pseudotherapies. Bolstered by anecdotes, heralded by the media, praised on the Internet, alternative therapies can spread like wildfire. In one national survey, 57 percent of those with a history of anxiety attacks and

54 percent of those with a history of depression had used alternative treatments such as herbal medicine, massage, and spiritual healing (Kessler & others, 2001).

What can we say of such therapies? Testimonials aside (every therapy, effective or not, will *seem* effective to some), what does the evidence say? This is a tough question, because there is no evidence for or against most alternative therapies. Their proponents and devotees often feel personal experience is evidence enough. But some therapies have been the subject of controlled research.

Let's now evaluate two alternative therapies—eye movement desensitization and reprocessing (EMDR) and light exposure therapy. As we do, remember that sifting sense from nonsense requires the scientific attitude: being skeptical but not cynical, open to surprises but not gullible.

Eye Movement Desensitization and Reprocessing

EMDR (eye movement desensitization and reprocessing) is a therapy that thousands adore, and thousands more dismiss as a sham—"an excellent vehicle for illustrating the differences between scientific and pseudoscientific therapy techniques," suggest James Herbert and seven others (2000). Francine Shapiro (1989) developed EMDR after walking in a park one day and observing that anxious thoughts vanished as her eyes spontaneously darted about. In her novel anxiety treatment, she had people imagine traumatic scenes while she triggered eye movements by waving her finger in front of their eyes, supposedly enabling them to unlock and reprocess previously frozen trauma memories. She tried this on 22 people haunted by old traumatic memories, and all reported marked reductions in their distress after just one therapeutic session. This extraordinary result evoked an enormous response from mental health professionals, 40,000 of whom from 52 countries have undergone training (EMDR, 2002). Not since the similarly charismatic Franz Anton Mesmer introduced *animal magnetism* (hypnosis) more than two centuries ago (also after feeling inspired by an outdoor experience) has a new therapy attracted so many devotees so quickly.

Does it work? For 84 to 100 percent of single-trauma victims participating in four recent studies, the answer is yes, reports Shapiro (1999, 2002). (When EMDR did not fare well in other trials, Shapiro argued that the therapists were not properly trained.) Moreover, the treatment need take no more than three 90-minute sessions. The Society of Clinical Psychology task force on empirically validated treatments acknowledges that the treatment is "probably efficacious" for the treatment of nonmilitary post-traumatic stress disorder (Chambless & others, 1997). Encouraged by their seeming successes, EMDR therapists are now applying the technique to other anxiety disorders, such as panic disorder, and, with Shapiro's (1995, 2002) encouragement, to a wide range of complaints, including pain, grief, paranoid schizophrenia, rage, and guilt.

Why, wonder the skeptics, should rapidly moving one's eyes while recalling traumas be therapeutic? Indeed, it seems eye movements are not the therapeutic ingredient. In trials in which people imagined traumatic scenes and tapped a finger, or just stared straight ahead while the therapist's finger wagged, the therapeutic results were the same (Devilly, 2003). The skeptics suspect that what is therapeutic is the combination of exposure therapy—repeatedly reliving traumatic memories in a safe and reassuring context—and a robust placebo effect. Had Mesmer's pseudotherapy been compared with no treatment at all, notes Richard McNally (1999), it, too (thanks to the healing power of positive belief), could have been found "probably efficacious."

> "Studies indicate that EMDR is just as effective with fixed eyes. If that conclusion is right, what's useful in the therapy (chiefly behavioral desensitization) is not new, and what's new is superfluous."
>
> *Harvard Mental Health Letter*, 2002

Light Exposure Therapy

Have you ever found yourself oversleeping, gaining weight, and feeling lethargic during the dark mornings and overcast days of winter? For some people, especially women and those living far from the equator, the wintertime blahs constitute a form of depression known as *seasonal affective disorder,* for which the appropriate acronym is SAD. To counteract these dark spirits, National Institute of Mental Health researchers in the early 1980s had an idea: Give SAD people a timed daily dose of intense light. Sure enough, people reported they felt better. Was this a bright idea, or a dim-witted example of the placebo effect, attributable to people's expectations? Recent studies shed light on this therapy. One exposed some people with SAD to 90 minutes of bright light and others to a sham placebo treatment—a hissing "negative ion generator" about which the staff expressed similar enthusiasm (but which, unknown to the participants, was not turned on). After four weeks of exposure, 61 percent of those exposed to morning light had greatly improved, as had 50 percent of those exposed to evening light and 32 percent of those exposed to the placebo treatment (Eastman & others, 1998). Two other studies found that 30 minutes of light exposure produced relief for more than half the people receiving morning light therapy and for one-third receiving evening light therapy (Terman & others, 1998, 2001). From 20 carefully controlled trials we have a verdict (Golden & others, 2005): For many people, morning bright light does indeed dim SAD symptoms.

Light therapy
To counteract winter depression, some people spend time each morning exposed to intense light that mimics natural outdoor light. Light boxes to counteract SAD are available from health supply and lighting stores.

Commonalities Among Psychotherapies

41-4: What three elements are shared by all forms of psychotherapy?

How might we explain the studies that found little correlation between therapists' training and experience and clients' outcomes? Jerome Frank (1982), Marvin Goldfried (Goldfried & Padawer, 1982), Hans Strupp (1986), and Bruce Wampold (2001) offer a hint. These researchers studied the common ingredients of various therapies and suggest they all offer at least three benefits: hope for demoralized people; a new perspective on oneself and the world; and an empathic, trusting, caring relationship. These nonspecific factors aren't all that therapy offers, but they are important (Barker & others, 1988; Jones & others, 1988; Roberts & others, 1993). They are part of what the growing numbers of self-help and support groups offer their members. And they have been part of what traditional healers offer (Jackson, 1992). Healers—special people to whom others disclose their suffering—have for centuries listened in order to understand and to empathize, reassure, advise, console, interpret, or explain. For those thinking about seeking therapy, Close-Up: A Consumer's Guide to Psychotherapists offers some tips on when to seek help and how to start searching for a therapist.

Hope for Demoralized People
People seeking therapy typically feel anxious, depressed, devoid of self-esteem, and incapable of turning things around. What any therapy offers is the expectation that, with commitment from the therapy seeker, things can and will get better. This belief, apart from any therapeutic technique, may function as a placebo, improving morale, creating feelings of self-efficacy, and diminishing symptoms (Prioleau & others, 1983). Similar effects have been found in therapy experiments in which the placebo treatment was listening to inspirational tapes or taking a fake pill.

Statistical analyses showing that improvement is greater for placebo-treated people than for untreated people (although not as great as for those receiving actual psychotherapy) suggests that one way therapies help is by offering hope. The therapy-seeker's attitude—the person's motivation, confidence, and commitment—affects the outcome. Thus, each therapy, in its individual way, may harness the person's own healing powers. And that, says psychiatrist Jerome Frank, helps us understand why all sorts of treatments—including some folk healing rites that are powerless apart from the participants' belief—may in their own time and place produce cures.

CLOSE-UP

A CONSUMER'S GUIDE TO PSYCHOTHERAPISTS

Life for everyone is marked by a mix of serenity and stress, blessing and bereavement, good moods and bad. So, when should a person seek the help of a mental health professional? When troubling thoughts and emotions interfere with your normal living, you might consider talking to a professional. The American Psychological Association offers these common trouble signals:

- Feelings of hopelessness
- Deep and lasting depression
- Self-destructive behavior, such as alcohol and drug abuse
- Disruptive fears
- Sudden mood shifts
- Thoughts of suicide
- Compulsive rituals, such as hand washing
- Sexual difficulties

In looking for a therapist, you may want to have a preliminary consultation with two or three. You can describe your problem and learn each therapist's treatment approach. You can ask questions about the therapist's values, credentials (TABLE 41.1), and fees. And, knowing the importance of the emotional bond between therapist and client, you can assess your own feelings about each of them.

TABLE 41.1

THERAPISTS AND THEIR TRAINING

Type	Description
Counselors	Marriage and family counselors specialize in problems arising from family relations. Pastoral counselors provide counseling to countless people. Abuse counselors work with substance abusers and with spouse and child abusers and their victims.
Clinical or psychiatric social workers	A two-year master of social work graduate program plus post-graduate supervision prepares some social workers to offer psychotherapy, mostly to people with everyday personal and family problems. About half have earned the National Association of Social Workers' designation of clinical social worker.
Clinical psychologists	Most are psychologists with a Ph.D. or Psy.D. and expertise in research, assessment, and therapy, supplemented by a supervised internship and, often, post-doctoral training. About half work in agencies and institutions, half in private practice.
Psychiatrists	Psychiatrists are physicians who specialize in the treatment of psychological disorders. Not all psychiatrists have had extensive training in psychotherapy, but as M.D.s they can prescribe medications. Thus, they tend to see those with the most serious problems. Many have their own private practice.

A New Perspective

Every therapy offers people a plausible explanation of their symptoms and an alternative way of looking at themselves or responding to their world. Therapy can offer new experiences as well, ones that help people change their behaviors and their views of themselves. Armed with a believable fresh perspective, they may approach life with a new attitude.

An Empathic, Trusting, Caring Relationship

To say that outcome is unrelated to training and experience is not to say all therapists are equally effective. No matter what therapeutic technique they use, effective therapists are empathic people who seek to understand another's experience; who communicate their care and concern to the client; and who earn the client's trust and respect through respectful listening, reassurance, and advice. Marvin Goldfried and his associates (1998) found these qualities in taped therapy sessions from 36 recognized master therapists. Some were cognitive-behavior therapists, others were psychodynamic-interpersonal therapists. Regardless, the striking finding was how *similar* they were during the parts of their sessions they considered most significant. At key moments, the empathic therapists of both persuasions would help clients evaluate themselves, link one aspect of their life with another, and gain insight into their interactions with others. Warmth and empathy are hallmarks of healers everywhere, whether psychiatrists, witch doctors, or shamans

© 1994 by Sidney Harris—"Stress Test," Rutgers University Press.

"I utilize the best from Freud, the best from Jung, and the best from my Uncle Marty, a very smart fellow."

(Torrey, 1986). The emotional bond between therapist and client—the *therapeutic alliance*—is a key aspect of effective therapy (Klein & others, 2003; Wampold, 2001). Indeed, one National Institute of Mental Health depression-treatment study found that the most effective therapists were those who were perceived as most empathic and caring and who established the closest therapeutic bonds with their clients (Blatt & others, 1996).

That all therapies offer *hope* through a *fresh perspective* offered by a *caring person* is supported by an analysis of 39 studies. Each study compared treatment offered by professional therapists with treatment offered by laypeople: friendly professors, people who had had a few hours' training in empathic listening skills, and college students supervised by a professional clinician. The result? The *paraprofessionals*, as these and other briefly trained people are called, typically proved as effective as the professionals (Christensen & Jacobson, 1994). Although most of the problems they treated were mild, the trained paraprofessionals were—believe it or not—as effective as professionals even when dealing with more disturbed adults, such as those diagnosed with serious depression.

To recap, people who seek help usually improve. So do many of those who do not undergo psychotherapy, and that is a tribute to our human resourcefulness and our capacity to care for one another. Nevertheless, though the therapist's orientation and experience appear not to matter much, people who receive some psychotherapy usually improve more than those who do not. People with clear-cut, specific problems tend to improve the most.

Part of what all therapies offer is hope, a fresh way of looking at life, and an empathic, caring relationship. That may explain why the empathy and friendly counsel of paraprofessionals are often as helpful as professional psychotherapy. And that may also explain why people who feel supported by close relationships—who enjoy the fellowship and friendship of caring people—are less likely to need or seek therapy (Frank, 1982; O'Connor & Brown, 1984).

A caring relationship
Effective therapists form a bond of trust with their patients.

Culture and Values in Psychotherapy

41-5: How do differences in culture and values influence the relationship between a therapist and a client?

All therapies offer hope, and nearly all therapists attempt to enhance their clients' sensitivity, openness, personal responsibility, and sense of purpose (Jensen & Bergin, 1988). But in matters of cultural and moral diversity, therapists differ from one another and may differ from their clients (Kelly, 1990).

These differences can become significant when a therapist from one culture meets a client from another. In North America, Europe, and Australia, for example, most therapists reflect their culture's individualism, which often gives priority to personal desires and identity. Clients who are immigrants from Asian countries, which expect people to be more mindful of others' expectations, may have trouble relating to therapies that require them to think only of their own well-being. Such differences help explain the reluctance of some minority populations to use mental health services (Sue, 2006). In one experiment, Asian-American clients matched with counselors who shared their cultural values (rather than mismatched with those who did not) perceived more counselor empathy and felt more alliance with the counselor (Kim & others, 2005). Recognizing that therapists and clients may differ in their values, communication styles, and language, many therapy training programs now provide training in cultural sensitivity and recruit members of underrepresented cultural groups. (For a social-cultural perspective on disorders and therapy, see the Close-Up: Preventing Psychological Disorders by Treating the Social Contexts That Breed Them.)

CLOSE-UP

PREVENTING PSYCHOLOGICAL DISORDERS BY TREATING THE SOCIAL CONTEXTS THAT BREED THEM

41-6 : What is the rationale for preventive mental health programs?

Psychotherapies and biomedical therapies tend to locate the cause of psychological disorders within the person with the disorder. We infer that people who act cruelly must be cruel and that people who act "crazy" must be "sick." We attach labels to such people, thereby distinguishing them from "normal" folks. It follows, then, that we try to treat "abnormal" people by giving them insight into their problems, by changing their thinking, and/or by helping them gain control with drugs.

There is an alternative viewpoint: We could interpret many psychological disorders as understandable responses to a disturbing and stressful society. According to this view, it is not just the person who needs treatment, but also the person's social context. Better to prevent a problem by reforming a sick situation and by developing people's coping competencies than to wait for a problem to arise and then treat it.

A story about the rescue of a drowning person from a rushing river

illustrates this viewpoint: Having successfully administered first aid to the first victim, the rescuer spots another struggling person and pulls her out, too. After a half-dozen repetitions, the rescuer suddenly turns and starts running away while the river sweeps yet another floundering person into view. "Aren't you going to rescue that fellow?" asks a bystander. "Heck no," the rescuer replies. "I'm going upstream to find out what's pushing all these people in."

Preventive mental health is upstream work. It seeks to prevent psychological casualties by identifying and alleviating the conditions that cause them. George Albee (1986) believes there is abundant evidence that poverty, meaningless work, constant criticism, unemployment, racism, and sexism undermine people's sense of competence, personal control, and self-esteem. Such stresses increase their risk of depression, alcoholism, and suicide.

Albee contends that we who care about preventing psychological casualties should therefore support programs that alleviate these demoralizing situations. We eliminated smallpox not by treating the afflicted but by inoculating the unafflicted. We conquered yellow fever by controlling mosquitoes. Preventing psychological problems means empowering those who have learned an attitude of helplessness, changing

environments that breed loneliness, renewing the disintegrating family, and bolstering parents' and teachers' skills at nurturing children's achievements and resulting self-esteem. Indeed, "Everything aimed at improving the human condition, at making life more fulfilling and meaningful, may be considered part of primary prevention of mental or emotional disturbance" (Kessler & Albee, 1975, p. 557).

There is, however, more to the story of psychological disorders than toxic environments and pessimism. Anxiety disorders, major depression, bipolar disorder, and schizophrenia are in part biological events. Yet Albee reminds us again of one of this book's themes: *A human being is an integrated biopsychosocial system.* For years we have trusted our bodies to physicians and our minds to psychiatrists and psychologists. That neat separation no longer seems valid. Stress affects body chemistry and health. And chemical imbalances, whatever their cause, can produce schizophrenia and depression. *"Mens sana in corpore sano,"* says an ancient Latin adage: "A healthy mind in a healthy body."

"It is better to prevent than to cure."
Peruvian folk wisdom

"Mental disorders arise from physical ones, and likewise physical disorders arise from mental ones."

The Mahabharata, c. A.D. 200

Another area of potential value conflict is religion. Highly religious people may prefer religiously similar therapists (Worthington & others, 1996), and they may have trouble establishing an emotional bond with a therapist who does not share their values.

Albert Ellis, a well-known therapist, and Allen Bergin, co-editor of the *Handbook of Psychotherapy and Behavior Change,* illustrated how sharply therapists can differ, and how those differences can affect their view of a healthy person. Ellis (1980) assumed that "no one and nothing is supreme," that "self-gratification" should be encouraged, and that "unequivocal love, commitment, service, and . . . fidelity to any interpersonal commitment, especially marriage, leads to harmful consequences."

Bergin (1980) assumed the opposite—that "because God is supreme, humility and the acceptance of divine authority are virtues," that "self-control and committed love and self-sacrifice are to be encouraged," and that "infidelity to any interpersonal commitment, especially marriage, leads to harmful consequences."

Bergin and Ellis disagreed more radically than most therapists on what values are healthiest. In so doing, however, they illustrated their agreement on a more general point: Psychotherapists' personal beliefs and values influence their practice. Because clients tend to adopt their therapists' values (Worthington & others, 1996), some psychologists believe therapists should divulge those values more openly.

REVIEWING

>> MODULE REVIEW

41-1 : Does psychotherapy work? Who decides?

Because the positive testimonials of clients and therapists cannot prove that therapy is actually effective, psychologists have conducted hundreds of outcome studies of *psychotherapy*. These studies of randomized clinical trials indicate that people who remain untreated often improve, but those who receive psychotherapy are more likely to improve, regardless of what kind of therapy they receive and for how long. Placebo treatments or the sympathy and friendly counsel of paraprofessionals also tend to produce more improvement than occurs when people receive no treatment.

41-2 : Are some therapies more effective than others?

Statistical studies indicate that no one type of psychotherapy is superior to all others. Therapy is most effective for those with clear-cut, specific problems. Some therapies seem to be well-suited to specific psychological disorders. Behavioral conditioning, for example, is effective in treating phobias and compulsions, and cognitive therapy is effective in reducing depression and suicide risk.

41-3 : How do alternative therapies fare under scientific scrutiny?

Controlled research has not supported the claims of eye movement and desensitization reprocessing (EMDR) therapy. Its apparent successes may be due to its exposure therapy component plus the placebo effect. In scientific testing, light exposure therapy does seem to relieve the symptoms of seasonal affective disorder (SAD).

41-4 : What three elements are shared by all forms of psychotherapy?

All psychotherapies offer new hope for demoralized people; a fresh perspective; and (if the therapist is effective) an empathic, trusting, and caring relationship.

41-5 : How do differences in culture and values influence the relationship between a therapist and a client?

Therapists differ in the values that influence their aims. These differences may create problems when therapists work with clients with different cultural or religious perspectives. A person seeking therapy may want to ask about the therapist's treatment approach, values, credentials, and fees.

41-6 : What is the rationale for preventive mental health programs?

Advocates of preventive mental health programs argue that many psychological disorders could be prevented. Their aim is to change oppressive, esteem-destroying environments into more benevolent, nurturing environments that foster individual growth and self-confidence. The biopsychosocial approach in therapy considers not just biological or individual influences, but also social and cultural considerations.

>> REHEARSE IT!

1. The question "Is psychotherapy effective?" has been the subject of hundreds of scientific studies and innumerable personal accounts. The most *enthusiastic or optimistic* view of psychotherapy comes from

   a. outcome research.
   b. psychologist Hans Eysenck.
   c. reports of clinicians and clients.
   d. a government study of treatment for depression.

2. On average, troubled people who undergo therapy are more likely to improve than those who do not, and therapy tends to be most effective when the problem is clear-cut and specific. Studies show that _____ therapy is most effective overall.

   a. behavior
   b. humanistic
   c. psychodynamic
   d. no one type of

3. People's belief that a treatment will help them is often sufficient to cause some improvement. Improved morale and diminished symptoms in response to a neutral treatment, such as an inert pill, is an example of a(n)

   a. placebo effect.
   b. preventive mental health.
   c. SAD response.
   d. EMDR therapy.

4. Those who offer or receive alternative therapies usually feel that testimonials are enough evidence of the success of the therapy. One alternative therapy that has passed the test of critical evaluation is

   a. psychoanalysis.
   b. light exposure therapy.

   c. eye movement desensitization and reprocessing.
   d. client-centered therapy.

5. Poverty, unemployment, racism, and sexism are conditions that put people at high risk for developing psychological disorders. An approach that seeks to identify and alleviate such conditions before they cause disorders is

   a. behavioral conditioning therapy.
   b. cognitive therapy.
   c. outcome research.
   d. preventive mental health.

Answers: 1, c, 2, d, 3, a, 4, b, 5, d

>> TERMS AND CONCEPTS TO REMEMBER

psychotherapy, p. 554

>> TEST YOURSELF

1. How does the placebo effect bias clients' appraisals of the effectiveness of psychotherapies?

   (Answer in Appendix C.)

Multiple-choice **self-tests** and more may be found at www.worthpublishers.com/myers.

The Biomedical Therapies

The therapy often used to treat serious disorders is **biomedical therapy**—physically changing the brain's functioning by altering its chemistry with drugs, or affecting its circuitry with electroconvulsive shock, magnetic impulses, or psychosurgery. Although psychologists can provide psychological therapies, only psychiatrists (as medical doctors) offer most biomedical therapies.

Drug Therapies

42-1: What are the most common forms of biomedical therapies? What criticisms have been leveled against drug therapies?

By far the most widely used biomedical treatments today are the drug therapies. Since the 1950s, discoveries in **psychopharmacology** (the study of drug effects on mind and behavior) have revolutionized the treatment of people with severe disorders, liberating hundreds of thousands from hospital confinement. Thanks to drug therapy—and to efforts to minimize involuntary hospitalization and to support people with community mental health programs—the resident population of U.S. state and county mental hospitals is a fraction of what it was a half-century ago (**FIGURE 42.1**).

Almost any new treatment, including drug therapy, is greeted by an initial wave of enthusiasm as many people apparently improve. But that enthusiasm often diminishes after researchers subtract the rates of (1) normal recovery among untreated persons and (2) recovery due to the *placebo effect,* which arises from the positive expectations of patients and mental health workers alike. So, to evaluate the effectiveness of any new drug, researchers give half the patients the drug, and the other half a similar-appearing placebo (an inert substance, such as a sugar pill). Because neither the staff nor the patients know who gets which, this is called a *double-blind technique.* The good news: In double-blind studies, several types of drugs have proven useful in treating psychological disorders.

■ **biomedical therapy** prescribed medications or medical procedures that act directly on the patient's nervous system.

■ **psychopharmacology** the study of the effects of drugs on mind and behavior.

FIGURE 42.1

The emptying of U.S. mental hospitals

After the widespread introduction of antipsychotic drugs, starting in about 1955, the number of residents in state and county mental hospitals declined sharply. But in the rush to deinstitutionalize the mentally ill, many people who were ill-equipped to care for themselves were left homeless on city streets. (Data from the U.S. National Institute of Mental Health and Bureau of the Census, 2004.)

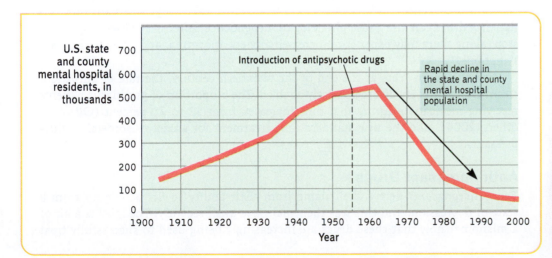

Les Snider/The Image Works

Antipsychotic Drugs

The revolution in drug therapy for psychological disorders began with the accidental discovery that certain drugs, used for other medical purposes, calmed psychotic patients. These *antipsychotic* drugs, such as chlorpromazine (sold as Thorazine), dampened responsiveness to irrelevant stimuli. Thus they provided the most help to schizophrenia patients experiencing positive symptoms, such as auditory hallucinations and paranoia (Lehman & others, 1998; Lenzenweger & others, 1989). Patients exhibiting negative symptoms, such as apathy and withdrawal, often do not respond well to these antipsychotic drugs. A newer drug, clozapine (marketed since 1989 as Clozaril), does sometimes enable "awakenings" in these individuals. It may also help those who have positive symptoms but have not responded to other drugs. Patients who take clozapine must have regular blood tests because in 1 percent of cases, it has a toxic effect on white blood cells.

The molecules of antipsychotic drugs are similar enough to molecules of the neurotransmitter dopamine to occupy its receptor sites and block its activity (Pickar & others, 1984; Taubes, 1994). (Clozapine blocks serotonin activity as well.) The finding that most antipsychotic drugs block dopamine receptors reinforces the idea that an overactive dopamine system contributes to schizophrenia.

Antipsychotics are powerful drugs. Some can produce sluggishness, tremors, and twitches similar to those of Parkinson's disease, which is marked by too little dopamine (Kaplan & Saddock, 1989). Long-term use of these medications can also produce *tardive dyskinesia,* with involuntary movements of the facial muscles (such as grimacing), tongue, and limbs. Many of the newer antipsychotics have fewer such side effects, but they may increase the risk of obesity and diabetes (Lieberman & others, 2005). Despite the drawbacks, these drugs, in the appropriate dosage, combined with life-skills programs and family support, have enabled hundreds of thousands of people with schizophrenia who had been consigned to the back wards of mental hospitals to return to work and to near-normal lives (Leucht & others, 2003).

Perhaps you can guess an occasional side effect of L-dopa, a drug that raises dopamine levels for Parkinson's patients: hallucinations.

Antianxiety Drugs

Like alcohol, *antianxiety* agents, such as Xanax or Ativan, depress central nervous system activity (and so should not be used in combination with alcohol). Antianxiety drugs are often used in combination with psychological therapy, calming anxiety as the person learns to cope with frightening situations and fear-triggering stimuli.

A criticism sometimes made of the behavior therapies—that they reduce symptoms without resolving underlying problems—is also made of antianxiety drugs. Unlike the behavior therapies, however, these substances may be used as an ongoing treatment. "Popping a Xanax" at the first sign of tension can produce psychological dependence; the immediate relief reinforces a person's tendency to take drugs when anxious. Antianxiety drugs can also cause physiological dependence. After heavy use, people who stop taking them may experience increased anxiety, insomnia, and other withdrawal symptoms.

Over the dozen years at the end of the twentieth century, the rate of outpatient treatment for anxiety disorders nearly doubled. The proportion of psychiatric patients receiving medication during that time increased from 52 to 70 percent (Olfson & others, 2004). And the new standard drug treatment for anxiety disorders? Antidepressants.

Antidepressant Drugs

The *antidepressants* derive their name from their ability to lift people up from a state of depression, and this was their main use until recently. The label is a bit of a misnomer now that these drugs are increasingly being used to successfully treat

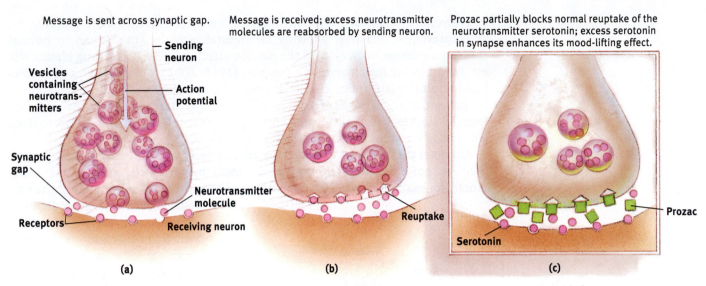

(a) Message is sent across synaptic gap.

Sending neuron

Vesicles containing neurotransmitters

Action potential

Synaptic gap

Receptors

Neurotransmitter molecule

Receiving neuron

(b) Message is received; excess neurotransmitter molecules are reabsorbed by sending neuron.

Reuptake

(c) Prozac partially blocks normal reuptake of the neurotransmitter serotonin; excess serotonin in synapse enhances its mood-lifting effect.

Prozac

Serotonin

FIGURE 42.2

Biology of antidepressants

Shown here is the action of Prozac, which partially blocks the reuptake of serotonin.

anxiety disorders such as obsessive-compulsive disorder. They work by increasing the availability of norepinephrine or serotonin, neurotransmitters that elevate arousal and mood and appear scarce during depression. Fluoxetine, which tens of millions of users worldwide have known as Prozac, partially blocks the reabsorption and removal of serotonin from synapses (**FIGURE 42.2**). Because they slow the synaptic vacuuming up of serotonin, Prozac, and its cousins Zoloft and Paxil, are called *selective-serotonin-reuptake-inhibitors (SSRIs)*. Other antidepressants work by blocking the reabsorption or breakdown of both norepinephrine and serotonin. Though effective, these dual-action drugs have more potential side effects, such as dry mouth, weight gain, hypertension, or dizzy spells (Anderson, 2000; Mulrow, 1999). Administering them by means of a patch, bypassing the intestines and liver, helps reduce such side effects (Bodkin & Amsterdam, 2002).

After the introduction of SSRI drugs, the percentage of patients receiving medication for depression jumped dramatically, from 70 percent in 1987, the year before SSRIs were introduced, to 89 percent in 2001 (Olfson & others, 2003; Stafford & others, 2001).

Be advised: Patients with depression who begin taking antidepressants do not wake up the next day singing "Oh, what a beautiful morning!" Although the drugs begin to influence neurotransmission within hours, their full psychological effect often requires four weeks. One possible reason for the delay is that increased serotonin seems to promote *neurogenesis*—the birth of new brain cells, perhaps reversing stress-induced loss of neurons (Jacobs, 2004; Santarelli & others, 2003).

Antidepressant drugs are not the only way to give the body a lift. Aerobic exercise, which helps calm people who feel anxious and energize those who feel depressed, does about as much good for some people with mild to moderate depression, and has additional positive side effects. Cognitive therapy, by helping people reverse their habitual negative thinking style, can boost the drug-aided relief from depression and reduce the post-treatment risk of relapse (Hollon & others, 2002; Keller & others, 2000). Better yet, some studies suggest, is to attack depression from both above and below (Goldapple & others, 2004; TADS, 2004). Use antidepressant drugs (which work, bottom-up, on the emotion-forming limbic system) in conjunction with cognitive behavior therapy (which works, top-down, starting with changed frontal lobe activity).

One side effect of SSRI drugs can be decreased sexual appetite, which has led to their occasional prescription to control sexual behavior (Slater, 2000).

On U.S. college campuses, the 9 percent of counseling center visitors taking psychiatric medication in 1994 nearly tripled, to 24.5 percent in 2004 (Duenwald, 2004).

"If this doesn't help you don't worry, it's a placebo."

© The New Yorker Collection, 2000, P. C. Vey from cartoonbank.com. All Rights Reserved.

Everyone agrees that people with depression often improve after a month on antidepressants. But after allowing for natural recovery (the return to normal called *spontaneous recovery*) and the placebo effect, how big is the drug effect? Not big, report Irving Kirsch and his colleagues (1998, 2002). Their analyses of double-blind clinical trials indicate that placebos produced improvement comparable to 75 percent or so of the active drug's effect. Another research team analyzed data from 45 studies. Given antidepressants, 41 percent of participants improved; given placebos, 31 percent improved (Khan & others, 2000).

Although the effects of drug therapy are less exciting than many TV ads suggest, they also are less frightening than other stories have warned. Some people taking Prozac, for example, have committed suicide, but their numbers seem fewer than we

© The New Yorker Collection, 2001, Barbara Smaller from cartoonbank.com. All Rights Reserved.

"I think the dosage needs adjusting. I'm not nearly as happy as the people in the ads."

would expect from the millions of depressed people now taking the medication. Prozac users who commit suicide are like cellphone users who get brain cancer. Given the millions of people taking Prozac and using cellphones, alarming anecdotes tell us nothing. The question critical thinkers want answered is this: Do these groups suffer an elevated *rate* of suicide and brain cancer? The answer in each case appears to be no (Grunebaum & others, 2004; Paulos, 1995; Tollefson & others, 1993, 1994).

Mood-Stabilizing Medications

In addition to antipsychotic, antianxiety, and antidepressant drugs, psychiatrists have *mood-stabilizing drugs* in their arsenal. The simple salt *lithium* can be an effective mood stabilizer for those suffering the emotional highs and lows of bipolar disorder. Australian physician John Cade discovered this in the 1940s when he administered lithium to a patient with severe mania. Although Cade's reasoning was misguided—he thought lithium had calmed excitable guinea pigs when actually it had made them sick—his patient became perfectly well in less than a week (Snyder, 1986). After suffering mood swings for years, about 7 in 10 people with bipolar disorder benefit from a long-term daily dose of this cheap salt (Solomon & others, 1995). Their risk of suicide is but one-sixth that of bipolar patients not taking lithium (Tondo & others, 1997). Although we do not fully understand why, lithium works. And so does Depakote, a drug originally used to treat epilepsy and more recently found effective in the control of manic episodes associated with bipolar disorder.

© The New Yorker Collection, 2000, P. C. Vey from cartoonbank.com. All Rights Reserved.

"First of all I think you should know that last quarter's sales figures are interfering with my mood-stabilizing drugs."

Brain Stimulation

Electroconvulsive Therapy

42-2 : What is electroconvulsive therapy? When is it used?

The medical use of electricity is an ancient practice. Physicians treated the Roman Emperor Claudius (10 B.C.–A.D. 54) for headaches by pressing electric eels to his temples.

A more controversial brain manipulation occurs through shock treatment, or **electroconvulsive therapy (ECT).** When ECT was first introduced in 1938, the wide-awake patient was strapped to a table and jolted with roughly 100 volts of electricity to the brain, producing racking convulsions and brief unconsciousness. ECT therefore gained a barbaric image, one that lingers still. Today, however, the patient receives a general anesthetic and a muscle relaxant (to prevent injury from convulsions) before a psychiatrist delivers a series of brief electrical pulses to the patient's brain. Within 30 minutes, the patient awakens and remembers nothing of the treatment or of the hours preceding it (**FIGURE 42.3**). After three such sessions each week for two to four weeks, 80 percent or more of people receiving ECT improve markedly, showing some memory loss for the treatment period but no discernible brain damage (Bergsholm & others, 1989; Coffey, 1993). Study after study confirms that ECT is an effective treatment for severe depression in patients who have not responded to drug therapy (Consensus Conference, 1985; UK ECT Review Group, 2003). By 2001, confidence in ECT had further increased, with a *JAMA* (*Journal of the American Medical Association*) editorial concluding that "the results of ECT in treating severe depression are among the most positive treatment effects in all of medicine" (Glass, 2001).

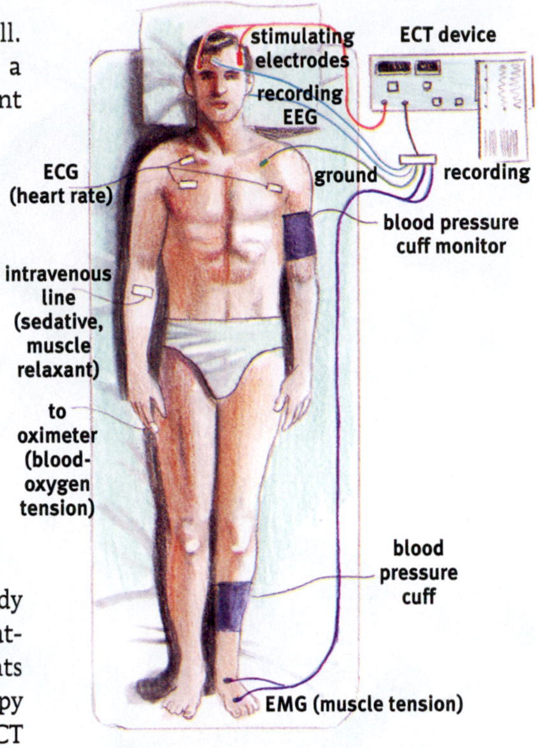

FIGURE 42.3
Electroconvulsive therapy
Although controversial, ECT is often an effective treatment for depression that does not respond to drug therapy.

How does ECT allieviate severe depression? After more than 50 years, no one knows for sure. One recipient likened ECT to the smallpox vaccine, which was saving lives before we knew how it worked. Perhaps the shock-induced seizures cause the brain to react by calming neural centers where overactivity produces depression.

ECT reduces suicidal thoughts and is credited with saving many from suicide (Kellner & others, 2005). It is now administered with briefer pulses that disrupt memory less (Fink, 1998; Kho & others, 2003). Yet its Frankensteinlike image continues. No matter how impressive the results, the idea of electrically shocking people into convulsions still strikes many as barbaric, especially given our ignorance about why ECT works. Moreover, ECT-treated patients, like other patients with a history of depression, are vulnerable to relapse. Nevertheless, ECT is, in the minds of many psychiatrists and patients, a lesser evil than severe depression's misery, anguish, and risk of suicide. "A miracle had happened in two weeks," reported noted research psychologist Norman Endler (1982) after ECT alleviated his deep depression.

Alternatives to ECT

Hopes are now rising for gentler alternatives for jump-starting the depressed brain. Some patients with chronic depression have found relief through a chest implant that intermittently stimulates the vagus nerve, which sends signals to the brain's mood-related limbic system (Marangell & others, 2002; Rush & others, 2005).

Depressed moods also seem to improve when repeated pulses surge through a magnetic coil held close to a person's skull (**FIGURE 42.4** on the next page). Unlike deep brain stimulation, the magnetic energy penetrates only to the brain's surface (though tests are under way with a higher energy field that penetrates more deeply). The painless procedure—called **repetitive transcranial magnetic stimulation (rTMS)**—is performed on wide-awake patients for 20 to 30 minutes for two to four weeks. Unlike ECT, the rTMS procedure produces no seizures, memory loss,

■ **electroconvulsive therapy (ECT)** a biomedical therapy for severely depressed patients in which a brief electric current is sent through the brain of an anesthetized patient.

■ **repetitive transcranial magnetic stimulation (rTMS)** the application of repeated pulses of magnetic energy to the brain; used to stimulate or suppress brain activity.

FIGURE **42.4**
Magnets for the mind
Repetitive transcranial magnetic stimulation (rTMS) sends a painless magnetic field through the skull to the cortical surface, where pulses can be used to stimulate or dampen activity in various areas. (From George, 2003.)

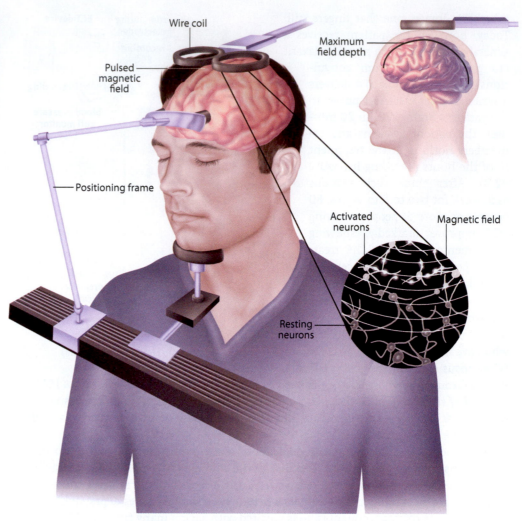

or other side effects. After studies confirmed the therapeutic effect, two large, multilocation rTMS clinical experiments began in 2005 (Cohen & others, 2005; Janicak, 2005; Martin & others, 2005). One possible explanation of this effect is that the stimulation energizes depressed patients' relatively inactive left frontal lobe (Helmuth, 2001). When repeatedly stimulated, nerve cells can form functioning circuits through a process called *long-term potentiation* (LTP). Conclusive data from the clinical experiments will indicate whether magnetic stimulation fulfills its promise as a valuable new treatment for depression.

Psychosurgery

42-3 : Under what conditions might psychosurgery be considered for changing behavior or moods?

■ **psychosurgery** surgery that removes or destroys brain tissue in an effort to change behavior.

■ **lobotomy** a now-rare psychosurgical procedure once used to calm uncontrollably emotional or violent patients. The procedure cut the nerves connecting the frontal lobes to the emotion-controlling centers of the inner brain.

Because its effects are irreversible, **psychosurgery**—surgery that removes or destroys brain tissue—is the most drastic and the least-used biomedical intervention for changing behavior. In the 1930s, Portuguese physician Egas Moniz developed what became the best-known psychosurgical operation: the **lobotomy.** Moniz found that cutting the nerves connecting the frontal lobes with the emotion-controlling centers of the inner brain calmed uncontrollably emotional and violent patients. In a crude but easy and inexpensive procedure that took only about 10 minutes, a neurosurgeon would shock the patient into a coma, hammer an icepick-like instrument through each eye socket into the brain, and then wiggle it to sever connections running up to the frontal lobes. Tens of thousands of severely disturbed people were "lobotomized" during the 1940s and 1950s, and Moniz was honored with a Nobel prize (Valenstein, 1986).

Although the intention was simply to disconnect emotion from thought, the effect was often more drastic: The lobotomy usually produced a permanently lethargic, immature, impulsive personality. During the 1950s, after some 35,000 people had been lobotomized in the United States alone, calming drugs became available and psychosurgery was largely abandoned. Today, lobotomies are history, and other psychosurgery is used only in extreme cases. For example, if a patient suffers uncontrollable seizures, surgeons can deactivate the specific nerve clusters that cause or transmit the convulsions. MRI-guided precision surgery is also occasionally done to cut the circuits involved in severe obsessive-compulsive disorder (Sachdev & Sachdev, 1997). Because these procedures are irreversible, however, neurosurgeons perform them only as a last resort.

The effectiveness of the biomedical therapies reminds us of a fundamental lesson: We find it convenient to talk of separate psychological and biological influences, but everything psychological is also biological (**FIGURE 42.5**). Every thought and feeling depends on the functioning brain. Every creative idea, every moment of joy or anger, every period of depression emerges from the electrochemical activity of the living brain. The influence is two-way: When psychotherapy relieves obsessive-compulsive behavior, PET scans reveal a calmer brain (Schwartz & others, 1996).

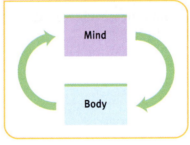

FIGURE 42.5
Mind-body interaction
The biomedical therapies assume that mind and body are a unit: Affect one and you will affect the other.

REVIEWING

>> MODULE REVIEW

42-1 : **What are the most common forms of biomedical therapies? What criticisms have been leveled against drug therapies?**
The *biomedical therapies* treat psychological disorders with medications or medical procedures that act directly on a patient's nervous system. Drug therapy is the most widely used biomedical therapy. The antipsychotic drugs, used in treating schizophrenia, block dopamine activity. Some can have serious side effects, including tardive dyskinesia (with involuntary movements of facial muscles, tongue, and limbs) or increased risk of obesity and diabetes. Antianxiety drugs, which depress central nervous system activity, are used to treat anxiety disorders. These drugs can be physically and psychologically addictive. Antidepressant drugs, which increase the availability of serotonin and norepinephrine, are used for depression and anxiety disorders. Lithium is a mood stabilizer prescribed for those with bipolar disorder.

42-2 : **What is electroconvulsive therapy? When is it used?**
In *electroconvulsive therapy (ECT)*, a brief electric current is sent through the brain of an anesthetized patient. Although researchers cannot explain how ECT works, it remains an effective, last-resort treatment for severely depressed people who have not responded to other therapy. Newer alternative treatments for depression include *repetitive transcranial magnetic stimulation (rTMS)* and implants that directly stimulate some nerves.

42-3 : **Under what conditions might psychosurgery be considered for changing behavior or moods?**
Radical *psychosurgical* procedures such as *lobotomy* were once popular, but neurosurgeons now rarely perform brain surgery to change behavior or moods. Brain surgery is a treatment of last resort because its effects are irreversible.

>> REHEARSE IT!

1. Antipsychotic drugs, used to calm schizophrenia patients, often bring relief from auditory hallucinations and other troubling symptoms. However, some of them can have unpleasant side effects, most notably

   a. hyperactivity.
   b. convulsions and momentary memory loss.
   c. sluggishness, tremors, and twitches.
   d. paranoia.

2. Xanax and Ativan, which depress central nervous system activity, are often used as ongoing treatment and can lead to dependency. These drugs are referred to as _____ drugs.

   a. antipsychotic
   b. antianxiety
   c. antidepressant
   d. antineurotic

3. One substance that often brings relief to patients suffering the highs and lows of bipolar disorder is

   a. rTMS.
   b. Xanax.
   c. lithium.
   d. clozapine.

4. Electroconvulsive therapy (ECT) and lobotomy (a type of psychosurgery) are biomedical treatments. Lobotomy, once used to treat uncontrollably violent patients, is no longer an accepted treatment. ECT, however, remains in use as a treatment for

   a. severe obsessive-compulsive disorder.
   b. severe depression.
   c. schizophrenia.
   d. anxiety disorders.

Answers: 1. c, 2. b, 3. c, 4. b.

>> TERMS AND CONCEPTS TO REMEMBER

biomedical therapy, p. 565
psychopharmacology, p. 565
electroconvulsive therapy (ECT), p. 568

repetitive transcranial magnetic stimulation (rTMS), p. 569

psychosurgery, p. 570
lobotomy, p. 570

>> TEST YOURSELF

1. How do researchers evaluate the effectiveness of particular drug therapies?

2. What are the influences to keep in mind for successful therapeutic intervention?

   (Answers in Appendix C.)

Multiple-choice **self-tests** and more may be found at www.worthpublishers.com/myers.

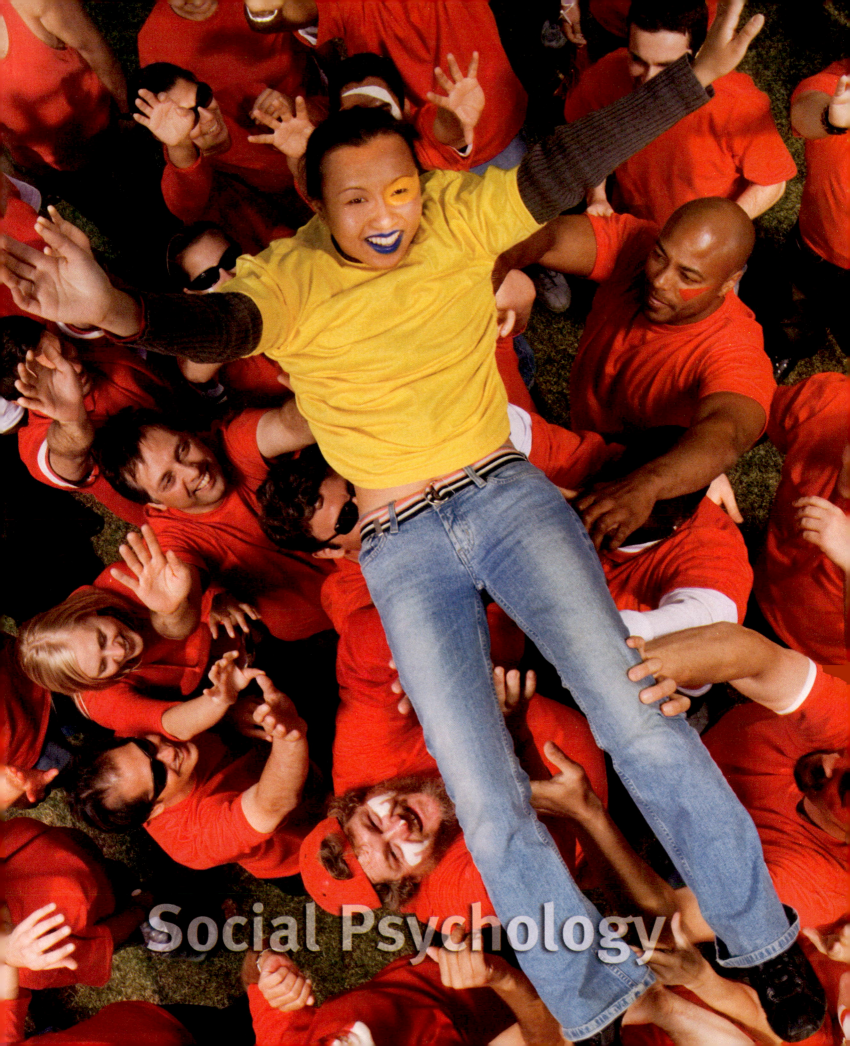

Social Psychology

Social Psychology

On September 11, 2001, shortly after terrorists flew hijacked planes into the World Trade Center, I spoke by phone with my daughter, Laura. She was on the street in her Manhattan neighborhood, describing the tumultuous scene, when suddenly she yelled, "Oh my gosh! Oh my gosh!" as the second massive tower collapsed before her eyes. By almost anyone's definition, this catastrophic violence—accomplished by a mere 19 men with box cutters—was an evil act, to which the communal response was fear mixed with anger. A bully's single kick that collapses a nearly finished sandcastle triggers both fright and outrage. Likewise, for millions of stunned Americans, 9/11 evoked anxiety about what might come next and a lust for revenge.

But the cataclysm also triggered an outpouring of love and compassion. From around the country and the world, money and countless truckloads of food, clothing, and teddy bears—more than New Yorkers could possibly use—poured in. People in Toledo, Fargo, and Stockholm wept for those who wept. There on 6th Avenue and 24th Street, strangers hugged and talked, trying to make sense of senseless destruction. Although few transfusions would be needed, willing donors formed long lines at blood banks. "Everywhere I go I see concern," Laura wrote that evening.

> I see compassion. I see people with many differences united. I don't see violence. I don't see impatience. I don't see cruelty. Except when I look at that cloud of smoke, a constant backdrop all day. People are helping each other. People are desperate to do whatever they can.

> In the midst of this nightmare, I am utterly filled with love for the people of this city. It is incredible to witness their response. I am covered in goose bumps. My faith in humanity rises over that cloud and I see goodness and respect.

We watch and we wonder: What drives people to feel such hatred and to destroy so many innocent lives? And what motivates the heroic altruism of those who died trying to save others and of the many more who reached out to those coping with loss?

As the 9/11 horror so compellingly demonstrates, we are social animals. Depending on who or what influences our thinking, we may assume the best or the worst in others. And depending on our attitudes, we may approach them with closed fists or open arms.

"We cannot live for ourselves alone," remarked the novelist Herman Melville. "Our lives are connected by a thousand invisible threads." Social psychologists explore these connections by scientifically studying how we *think about* one another (Module 43), *influence* one another (Module 44), and *relate to* one another (Module 45).

Social Thinking

Especially when the unexpected occurs, we analyze why people act as they do. Does her warmth reflect romantic interest, or is that how she relates to everyone? Does his absenteeism signify illness? Laziness? A stressful work atmosphere? Was the horror of 9/11 the work of crazed people, or of ordinary people corrupted by life events? Such questions intrigue social psychologists. Just as personality psychologists study the enduring, inner determinants of behavior that help to explain why different people act differently in a given situation, so **social psychologists** study the social influences that help explain why the same person acts differently in different situations.

Attributing Behavior to Persons or to Situations

Attitudes and Actions

Attributing Behavior to Persons or to Situations

43-1: How do we tend to explain others' behavior? How do we explain our own behavior?

After studying how people explain others' behavior, Fritz Heider (1958) proposed an **attribution theory.** Heider noted that people usually attribute others' behavior either to their internal dispositions or to their external situations. A teacher, for example, may wonder whether a child's hostility reflects an aggressive personality (*a dispositional attribution*) or a reaction to stress or abuse (*a situational attribution*).

In class, we notice that Juliette seldom talks; over coffee, Jack talks nonstop. Attributing their behaviors to their personal dispositions, we decide Juliette is shy and Jack is outgoing. Because people do have enduring personality traits, such attributions are sometimes valid. However, we often fall prey to the **fundamental attribution error,** by overestimating the influence of personality and underestimating the influence of situations. In class, Jack may be as quiet as Juliette. Catch Juliette at a party and you may hardly recognize your quiet classmate.

An experiment by David Napolitan and George Goethals (1979) illustrates the phenomenon. They had Williams College students talk, one at a time, with a young woman who acted either aloof and critical or warm and friendly. Beforehand, they told half the students the woman's behavior would be spontaneous. They told the other half the truth—that she had been instructed to *act* friendly (or unfriendly). What do you suppose was the effect of being told the truth?

There was no effect. The students disregarded the information. If the woman acted friendly, they inferred she really was a warm person. If she acted unfriendly, they inferred she really was a cold person. In other words, they attributed her behavior to her personal disposition *even when told that her behavior was situational*—that she was merely acting that way for the purposes of the experiment. Although the fundamental attribution error occurs in all cultures studied, this tendency to attribute behavior to people's dispositions runs especially strong in individualistic Western countries. In East Asian cultures, for example, people are more sensitive to the power of the situation (Masuda & Kitayama, 2004).

■ **social psychology** the scientific study of how we think about, influence, and relate to one another.

■ **attribution theory** suggests how we explain someone's behavior—by crediting either the situation or the person's disposition.

■ **fundamental attribution error** the tendency for observers, when analyzing another's behavior, to underestimate the impact of the situation and to overestimate the impact of personal disposition.

B. Busco/The Image Bank/Getty Images

The fundamental attribution error
If our new colleague at work acts grouchy, we may infer that she's a grouchy person, discounting her having lost sleep over a family worry, having a flat tire on the way to work, and being unable to find a parking place.

You have surely committed the fundamental attribution error. In judging whether your psychology instructor is shy or outgoing, you have perhaps by now inferred that he or she has an outgoing personality. But you know your instructor only from the classroom, a situation that demands outgoing behavior. Catch the instructor in a different situation and you might be surprised (as some of my students have been when confronting me in a pick-up basketball game). Outside their assigned roles, professors seem less professorial, presidents less presidential, servants less servile.

The instructor, on the other hand, observes his or her own behavior in many different situations—in the classroom, in meetings, at home—and so might say, "Me, outgoing? It all depends on the situation. In class or with good friends, yes, I'm outgoing. But at conventions I'm really rather shy." So, when explaining *our own* behavior, or the behavior of those we know well and see in varied situations, we are sensitive to how behavior changes with the situation (Idson & Mischel, 2001).

When explaining *others'* behavior, particularly the behavior of strangers we have observed in only one type of situation, we often commit the fundamental attribution error: We disregard the situation and leap to unwarranted conclusions about their personality traits. Many people initially assumed the 9/11 terrorists were obviously crazy, when actually they went unnoticed in their neighborhoods, health clubs, and favorite restaurants.

Researchers who have reversed the perspectives of actor and observer—by having each view a videotape replay of the situation from the other's perspective—have also reversed the attributions (Lassiter & Irvine, 1986; Storms, 1973). Seeing the world from the actor's perspective, the observers better appreciate the situation. Taking the observer's point of view, the actors better appreciate their own personal style.

> "Calling [9/11] *senseless, mindless, insane*, or the work of *madmen* is wrong . . . [it] fails to adopt the perspective of the perpetrators, as an act with a clearly defined purpose that we must understand in order to challenge it most effectively."
>
> Psychologist Philip G. Zimbardo, "Fighting Terrorism by Understanding Man's Capacity for Evil," September 16, 2001

The Effects of Attribution

In everyday life we often struggle to explain others' actions. A jury must decide whether a shooting was malicious or in self-defense. An interviewer must judge whether the applicant's geniality is genuine. When we make such judgments, our attributions—either to the person or to the situation—have important consequences (Fincham & Bradbury, 1993; Fletcher & others, 1990). Happily married couples attribute a spouse's tart-tongued remark to a temporary situation ("She must have had a bad day at work"). Unhappily married persons attribute the same remark to a mean disposition ("Why did I marry such a hostile person?").

Or consider the political effects of attribution: How do you explain poverty or unemployment? Researchers in Britain, India, Australia, and the United States (Furnham, 1982; Pandey & others, 1982; Wagstaff, 1982; Zucker & Weiner, 1993) report that political conservatives tend to attribute such social problems to the personal dispositions of the poor and unemployed themselves: "People generally get what they deserve. Those who don't work are often freeloaders. Anybody who takes the initiative can still get ahead." "Society is not to blame for crime, criminals are," said one conservative U.S. presidential candidate (Dole, 1996). Political liberals (and social scientists) are more likely to blame past and present situations: "If you or I had to live with the same poor education, lack of opportunity, and discrimination, would we be any better off?" To understand and prevent terrorism, they say, consider the situations that breed terrorists. Better to drain the swamps than swat the mosquitoes.

© The New Yorker Collection, 1980, J. B. Handelsman from cartoonbank.com. All Rights Reserved.

"Otis, shout at that man to pull himself together."

An attribution question
Some people blamed the New Orleans residents for not evacuating before the predicted Hurricane Katrina. Others attributed their inaction to the situation—to their not having cars or not being offered bus transportation.

Paul Buck/EPA/Landow

Managers also have to make attributions. In evaluating employees, they are likely to attribute poor performance to personal factors, such as limited ability or lack of motivation. But remember the actor's viewpoint: Workers doing poorly on a job recognize situational influences, such as inadequate supplies, poor working conditions, difficult co-workers, or impossible demands (Rice, 1985).

The point to remember: Our attributions—to individuals' dispositions or to their situations—should be made carefully. They have real consequences.

Attitudes and Actions

43-2 : Does what we think predict what we will do, or does what we do shape what we will think?

Attitudes are feelings, often based on our beliefs, that predispose our reactions to objects, people, and events. If we *believe* someone is mean, we may *feel* dislike for the person and *act* unfriendly.

Attitudes Can Affect Actions

Our attitudes predict our behavior imperfectly. Other factors, including the external situation, also influence behavior. Strong social pressures can weaken the attitude-behavior connection (Wallace & others, 2005). For example, the American public's overwhelming support for President George W. Bush's preparation to attack Iraq motivated Democratic leaders to vote to support Bush's war plan, despite their private reservations (Nagourney, 2002). Nevertheless, attitudes may indeed affect behavior when other influences are minimal, when the attitude is specific to the behavior, and when we are keenly aware of our attitudes.

Actions Can Affect Attitudes

Now consider a more surprising principle: Not only will people sometimes stand up for what they believe, they will also come to believe in what they have stood up for. Many streams of evidence confirm that *attitudes follow behavior* (**FIGURE 43.1**).

The Foot-in-the-Door Phenomenon

Convincing people to act against their beliefs can affect their attitude. During the Korean War, many captured U.S. soldiers were imprisoned in war camps run by Chinese communists. Without using brutality, the captors secured the collaboration of hundreds of their prisoners in various activities. Some merely ran errands or accepted favors. Others made radio appeals and false confessions. Still others informed on fellow prisoners and divulged military information. When the war ended, 21 prisoners chose to stay with the communists. More returned home "brainwashed"—convinced that communism was a good thing for Asia.

A key ingredient of the Chinese "thought-control" program was its effective use of the **foot-in-the-door phenomenon**—a tendency for people who agree to a small action to comply later with a larger one. The Chinese began with harmless requests but gradually escalated their demands on the prisoners (Schein, 1956). Having "trained" the prisoners to speak or write trivial statements, the communists then asked them to copy or create something more important, noting, perhaps, the flaws of capitalism. Then, perhaps to gain privileges, the prisoners participated in group discussions, wrote self-criticisms, or uttered public confessions. After doing so, they often adjusted their beliefs toward consistency with their public acts.

■ **attitude** feelings, often based on our beliefs, that predispose us to respond in a particular way to objects, people, and events.

■ **foot-in-the-door phenomenon** the tendency for people who have first agreed to a small request to comply later with a larger request.

FIGURE 43.1
Attitudes follow behavior
Cooperative actions, such as those performed by people on sports teams, feed mutual liking. Such attitudes, in turn, promote positive behavior.

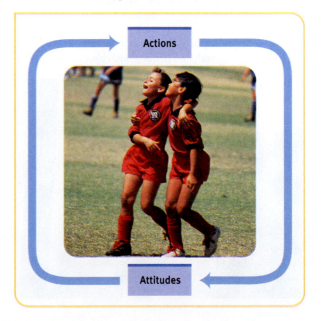

The point is simple, says Robert Cialdini (1993): To get people to agree to something big, "start small and build." And be wary of those who would exploit you with the tactic. This chicken-and-egg spiral, of actions-feeding-attitudes-feeding-actions, enables behavior to escalate. A trivial act makes the next act easier. Succumb to a temptation and you will find the next temptation harder to resist.

Dozens of experiments have simulated part of the war prisoners' experience by coaxing people into acting against their attitudes or violating their moral standards. The nearly inevitable result: Doing becomes believing. When people are induced to harm an innocent victim—by making nasty comments or delivering electric shocks—they then begin to disparage their victim. If induced to speak or write on behalf of a position they have qualms about, they begin to believe their own words.

Fortunately, the attitudes-follow-behavior principle works as well for good deeds as for bad. The foot-in-the-door tactic has helped boost charitable contributions, blood donations, and product sales. In one experiment, researchers posing as safe-driving volunteers asked Californians to permit the installation of a large, poorly lettered "Drive Carefully" sign in their front yards. Only 17 percent consented. They approached other home owners with a small request first: Would they display a 3-inch-high "Be a Safe Driver" sign? Nearly all readily agreed. When reapproached two weeks later to allow the large, ugly sign in their front yards, 76 percent consented (Freedman & Fraser, 1966).

Racial attitudes likewise follow behavior. In the years immediately following the introduction of school desegregation in the United States and the passage of the Civil Rights Act of 1964, white Americans expressed diminishing racial prejudice. And as Americans in different regions came to act more alike—thanks to more uniform national standards against discrimination—they began to think more alike. Experiments confirm the observation: Moral action strengthens moral convictions.

Role-Playing Affects Attitudes

■ **role** a set of explanations (norms) about a social position, defining how those in the position ought to behave.

When you adopt a new **role**—when you become a college student, marry, or begin a new job—you strive to follow the social prescriptions. At first, your behaviors may feel phony, because you are *acting* a role. The first weeks in the military feel artificial—as if one is pretending to be a soldier. The first weeks of a marriage may feel like "playing house." Before long, however, what began as play-acting in the theater of life becomes *you*.

Researchers have confirmed this effect by assessing people's attitudes before and after they adopt a new role, sometimes in laboratory situations, sometimes in everyday situations, such as before and after taking a job. In one well-known laboratory study, male college students volunteered to spend time in a simulated prison devised by psychologist Philip Zimbardo (1972). Some he randomly designated as guards; he gave them uniforms, billy clubs, and whistles and instructed them to enforce certain rules. The remainder became prisoners; they were locked in barren cells and forced to wear humiliating outfits. After a day or two in which the volunteers self-consciously "played" their roles, the simulation became real—too real. Most of the guards developed disparaging attitudes, and some devised cruel and degrading routines. One by one, the prisoners broke down, rebelled, or became passively resigned, causing Zimbardo to call off the study after only six days. More recently, similar situations have played themselves out in the real world—as in Iraq at the Abu Ghraib Prison (see Close-Up).

Greece's military junta during the early 1970s took advantage of the effects of role-playing to train men to become torturers (Staub, 1989). The men's indoctrination into their roles occurred in small steps. First, the trainee stood guard outside the interrogation cells—the "foot in the door." Next, he stood guard inside. Only then was he ready to become

The power of the situation
In Philip Zimbardo's Stanford Prison simulation, a toxic situation triggered degrading behaviors among those assigned to the guard role.

Philip G. Zimbardo, Inc.

CLOSE-UP

ABU GHRAIB PRISON: AN "ATROCITY-PRODUCING SITUATION"?

As the first photos emerged in 2004 from Iraq's Abu Ghraib Prison, the civilized world was shocked. The photos showed U.S. military guards stripping prisoners naked, placing hoods on them, stacking them in piles, prodding them with electricity, taunting them with attack dogs, and subjecting them to sleep deprivation, humiliation, and extreme stress. Was the problem, as so many people initially supposed, a few bad apples—irresponsible or even sadistic guards? That was the U.S. Army's seeming verdict when it court-martialed and imprisoned some of the guards, and then cleared four of the five top commanding officers responsible for Abu Ghraib's policies and operations. The lower-level military guards were "sick bastards," explained the defense attorney for one of the commanding officers (Tarbert, 2004).

Many social psychologists, however, reminded us that a toxic situation can make even good apples go bad

Originally published in the New Yorker

Bad apples or bad barrels?
Both the Stanford Prison Experiment in 1972 and the real-life Abu Ghraib Prison fiasco in 2004 were powerfully toxic situations, contends social psychologist Philip Zimbardo.

(Fiske & others, 2004). "When ordinary people are put in a novel, evil place, such as most prisons, Situations Win, People Lose," offered Philip Zimbardo (2004), adding, "That is true for the majority of people in all the relevant social psychological research done over the past 40 years."

Consider the situation, explains Zimbardo. The guards, some of them model soldier-reservists with no prior criminal or sadistic history, were exhausted from working 12-hour shifts, seven days a week, for more than a month at a time. They were dealing with an enemy, and their prejudices were heightened by fears of lethal attacks and by the violent deaths of many fellow soldiers. They were put in an understaffed guard role, given minimal training and oversight, and encouraged to "soften up" for interrogation detainees who had been denied access to the Red Cross. "When you put that set of horrendous work conditions and external factors together, it creates an evil barrel. You could put virtually anybody in it and you're going to get this kind of evil behavior" (Zimbardo, 2005).

---

actively involved in the questioning and torture. As the nineteenth-century writer Nathaniel Hawthorne noted, "No man, for any considerable period, can wear one face to himself and another to the multitude without finally getting bewildered as to which may be true." What we do, we gradually become.

Cognitive Dissonance: Relief From Tension

So far we have seen that actions can affect attitudes, sometimes turning prisoners into collaborators, doubters into believers, mere acquaintances into friends, and compliant guards into abusers. But why? One explanation is that when we become aware that our attitudes and actions don't coincide, we experience tension, or *cognitive dissonance*. To relieve this tension, according to the **cognitive dissonance theory** proposed by Leon Festinger, we often bring our attitudes into line with our actions. It is as if we rationalize, "If I chose to do it (or say it), I must believe in it." The less coerced and more responsible we feel for a troubling act, the more dissonance we feel. The more dissonance we feel, the more motivated we are to find consistency, such as changing our attitudes to help justify the act.

The U.S. invasion of Iraq was mainly premised on the presumed threat of Saddam Hussein's weapons of mass destruction (WMD). As the war began, only 38 percent of Americans surveyed said the war was justified even if Iraq did not have WMD (Gallup, 2003), and nearly 80 percent believed such weapons would be found (Duffy, 2003; Newport & others, 2003). When no WMD were found, many Americans felt

> "Fake it until you make it."
> Alcoholics Anonymous saying

■ **cognitive dissonance theory** the theory that we act to reduce the discomfort (dissonance) we feel when two of our thoughts (cognitions) are inconsistent. For example, when our awareness of our attitudes and of our actions clash, we can reduce the resulting dissonance by changing our attitudes.

© The New Yorker Collection, 2004, Robert Mankoff from cartoonbank.com. All Rights Reserved.

"Look, I have my misgivings, too, but what choice do we have except stay the course?"

dissonance, which was heightened by their awareness of the war's financial and human costs, by scenes of chaos in Iraq, and by inflamed anti-American and pro-terrorist sentiments in some parts of the world.

To reduce dissonance, some people revised their memories of the main rationale for going to war, which now became liberating an oppressed people and promoting democracy in the Middle East. Before long, the once-minority opinion became the majority view: 58 percent of Americans said they supported the war even if there were no WMD (Gallup, 2003). "Whether or not they find weapons of mass destruction doesn't matter," explained Republican pollster Frank Luntz (2003), "because the rationale for the war changed." It was not until late 2004, when hopes for a flourishing peace waned, that Americans' support for the war dropped below 50 percent.

Dozens of experiments have explored cognitive dissonance by making people feel responsible for behavior that is inconsistent with their attitudes and that has foreseeable consequences. As a subject in one of these experiments, you might agree for a measly $2 to help a researcher by writing an essay that supports something you don't believe in (perhaps a tuition increase). Feeling responsible for the statements (which are not consistent with your attitudes), you would probably feel dissonance, especially if you thought an administrator would be reading your essay. How could you reduce the uncomfortable dissonance? One way would be to start believing your phony words. Your pretense would become your reality.

The attitudes-follow-behavior principle has a heartening implication: Although we cannot directly control all our feelings, we can influence them by altering our behavior. Facial expressions and body postures affect our emotions. If we are down in the dumps, we can do as cognitive therapists advise and talk in more positive, self-accepting ways with fewer self–put-downs. If we are unloving, we can become more loving by behaving as if we were so—by doing thoughtful things, expressing affection, giving affirmation. "Assume a virtue, if you have it not," says Hamlet to his mother. "For use can almost change the stamp of nature." *The point to remember:* Cruel acts shape the self. But so do acts of good will. Act as though you like someone, and you soon will. Changing our behavior can change how we think about others and how we feel about ourselves.

> "Sit all day in a moping posture, sigh, and reply to everything with a dismal voice, and your melancholy lingers. . . . If we wish to conquer undesirable emotional tendencies in ourselves, we must . . . go through the outward movements of those contrary dispositions which we prefer to cultivate."
>
> William James, *Principles of Psychology*, 1890

REVIEWING

>> MODULE REVIEW

43-1: How do we tend to explain others' behavior? How do we explain our own behavior?

Social psychologists study how people think about, influence, and relate to one another. We generally explain people's behavior by *attributing* it either to internal dispositions or to external situations. In accounting for others' actions, we often underestimate the influence of the situation, thus committing the *fundamental attribution error*. When we explain our own behavior, however, we more often point to the situation and not to ourselves.

43-2: Does what we think predict what we will do, or does what we do shape what we will think?

Attitudes predict behavior only under certain conditions, as when other influences are minimized, when the attitude is specific to the behavior, and when people are aware of their attitudes.

Studies of the *foot-in-the-door phenomenon* and of *role*-playing reveal that our actions can also modify our attitudes, especially when we feel responsible for those actions. *Cognitive dissonance theorists* explain that behavior shapes attitudes because people feel discomfort when their actions go against their feelings and beliefs; they reduce the discomfort by bringing their attitudes more into line with what they have done.

>> REHEARSE IT!

1. In explaining a person's behavior, we tend to make the fundamental attribution error—we overestimate the impact of internal factors (such as disposition, or personality) and underestimate the impact of the situation in which the behavior occurs. Thus, if we encounter a person seemingly high on drugs, we might attribute the person's behavior to

   a. moral weakness or an addictive personality.
   b. peer pressure.
   c. the easy availability of the drug on city streets.
   d. society's acceptance of drug use.

2. During the Korean War, the Chinese "brainwashed" captured American soldiers to think that communism was a good thing for Asia. A key ingredient in this process was their use of people's tendency to more readily agree to a larger request if they have already agreed to a small request. This tendency is called

   a. the fundamental attribution error.
   b. the foot-in-the-door phenomenon.
   c. the behavior-follows-attitudes principle.
   d. role-playing.

3. When we are aware of a discrepancy between our attitudes and our behavior, cognitive dissonance theory predicts that we will act to reduce the discomfort or dissonance we feel. The theory explains why

   a. people who act against their attitudes tend to change their attitudes.
   b. attitudes predict actions when social pressures are minimized.
   c. changing an attitude—through persuasion—often fails to result in behavioral changes.
   d. people are hypocritical, talking one way and acting another.

Answers: 1. a, 2. b, 3. a.

>> TERMS AND CONCEPTS TO REMEMBER

social psychology, p. 575
attribution theory, p. 575
fundamental attribution error, p. 575

attitude, p. 577
foot-in-the-door phenomenon, p. 577

role, p. 578
cognitive dissonance theory, p. 579

>> TEST YOURSELF

1. Driving to school one wintry day, Marco narrowly misses a car that slides through a red light. "Slow down! What a terrible driver," he thinks to himself. Moments later, Marco himself slips through an intersection and yelps, "Wow! These roads are awful. The city snow plows need to get out here." What social psychology principle has Marco just demonstrated? Explain.

(Answer in Appendix C.)

Multiple-choice **self-tests** and more may be found at www.worthpublishers.com/myers.

MODULE

44

Social Influence

Social psychology's great lesson is the enormous power of social influence. This influence can be seen in our conformity, our compliance, and our group behavior. Suicides, bomb threats, airplane hijackings, and UFO sightings all have a curious tendency to come in clusters. On campus, jeans are the dress code; on New York's Wall Street or London's Bond Street, dress suits are the norm. When we know how to act, how to groom, how to talk, life functions smoothly. Armed with principles of social influence, advertisers, fund-raisers, and campaign workers aim to sway our decisions to buy, to donate, to vote. Isolated with others who share their grievances, dissenters may gradually become rebels, and rebels may become terrorists. Let's examine the pull of these social strings. How strong are they? How do they operate?

Conformity and Obedience

44-1: What do experiments on conformity and compliance reveal about the power of social influence?

Behavior is contagious.

- One person laughs, coughs, or yawns, and others in the group soon do the same. Chimps, too, are more likely to yawn after observing another chimp yawn (Anderson & others, 2004).
- A cluster of people stand gazing upward, and passersby pause to do likewise.
- Bartenders and street musicians know to "seed" their tip containers with money to suggest that others have given.
- "Sickness" can also be psychologically contagious. In the anxious 9/11 aftermath, more than two dozen elementary and middle schools had outbreaks of children reporting red rashes, sometimes causing parents to wonder whether biological terrorism was at work (Talbot, 2002). Some cases may have been stress-related, but mostly, said health experts, people were just noticing normal early acne, insect bites, eczema, and dry skin from overheated classrooms.

We are natural mimics—an effect Tanya Chartrand and John Bargh (1999) call the *chameleon effect*. Unconsciously mimicking others' expressions, postures, and voice tones helps us feel what they are feeling. This helps explain why we feel happier around happy people than around depressed ones, and why studies of groups of British nurses and accountants reveal *mood linkage*—sharing up and down moods (Totterdell & others, 1998). Just hearing someone reading a neutral text in either a happy- or sad-sounding voice creates "mood contagion" in listeners (Neumann & Strack, 2000).

Chartrand and Bargh demonstrated the chameleon effect when they had students work in a room alongside a confederate working for the experimenter. Sometimes the confederates rubbed their face; on other occasions, they shook their foot. Sure enough, participants tended to rub their own face when they were with the face-rubbing person and shake their own foot when they were with the foot-shaking person. Such automatic mimicry is part of empathy. The most empathic people mimic—and are liked—the most. And those most eager to fit in with a group seem intuitively to know this, for they are especially prone to unconscious mimicry (Lakin & Chartrand, 2003).

Niche conformity

Are these students asserting their individuality or identifying themselves with others of the same microculture?

Yuriko Nakao/Reuters/Corbis

NON SEQUITUR   by WILEY

BANKING on the YOUTH MARKET...

NON SEQUITER © 2000 Wiley. Dist. by Universal Press Syndicate Reprinted with permission.

■ **social psychology** the scientific study of how we think about, influence, and relate to one another.

■ **conformity** adjusting one's behavior or thinking to coincide with a group standard.

Sometimes the effects of suggestibility are more serious. In the eight days following the 1999 shooting rampage at Colorado's Columbine High School, every U.S. state except Vermont experienced threats of copycat violence. Pennsylvania alone recorded 60 such threats (Cooper, 1999). Sociologist David Phillips and his colleagues (1985, 1989) found that suicides, too, sometimes increase following a highly publicized suicide. In the wake of Marilyn Monroe's suicide on August 6, 1962, for example, the number of suicides in the United States exceeded the usual August count by 200.

What causes suicide clusters? Do people act similarly because of their influence on one another? Or because they are simultaneously exposed to the same events and conditions? Seeking answers, social psychologists have conducted experiments on group pressure and conformity.

Group Pressure and Conformity

Suggestibility is a subtle type of **conformity**—adjusting our behavior or thinking toward some group standard. To study conformity, Solomon Asch (1955) devised a simple test. As a participant in what you believe is a study of visual perception, you arrive at the experiment location in time to take a seat at a table where five people are already seated. The experimenter asks which of three comparison lines is identical to a standard line (**FIGURE 44.1**). You see clearly that the answer is Line 2 and await your turn to say so after the others. Your boredom with this experiment begins to show when the next set of lines proves equally easy.

Now comes the third trial, and the correct answer seems just as clear-cut, but the first person gives what strikes you as a wrong answer: "Line 3." When the second person and then the third and fourth give the same wrong answer, you sit up straight and squint. When the fifth person agrees with the first four, you feel your heart begin to pound. The experimenter then looks to you for your answer. Torn between the unanimity of your five fellow respondents and the evidence of your own eyes, you feel tense and much less sure of yourself than you were moments ago. You hesitate before answering, wondering whether you should suffer the discomfort of being the oddball. What answer do you give?

FIGURE 44.1

Asch's conformity experiments

Which of the three comparison lines is equal to the standard line? What do you suppose most people would say after hearing five others say, "Line 3"? In this photo from one of Asch's experiments, the student in the center shows the severe discomfort that comes from disagreeing with the responses of other group members (in this case, confederates of the experimenter).

William Vendivert/Scientific American

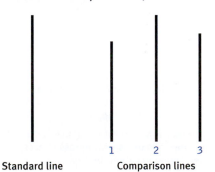

Standard line   Comparison lines

In the experiments conducted by Asch and others after him, thousands of college students have experienced this conflict. Answering such questions alone, they erred less than 1 percent of the time. But the odds were quite different when several others—confederates working for the experimenter—answered incorrectly. Asch reports that more than one-third of the time, these "intelligent and well-meaning" college-student participants were then "willing to call white black" by going along with the group.

Conditions That Strengthen Conformity

Asch's procedure became the model for later investigations. Although experiments have not always found so much conformity, they do reveal that conformity increases when

- one is made to feel incompetent or insecure.
- the group has at least three people.
- the group is unanimous. (The dissent of just one other person greatly increases social courage.)
- one admires the group's status and attractiveness.
- one has made no prior commitment to any response.
- others in the group observe one's behavior.
- one's culture strongly encourages respect for social standards.

Thus, we might predict the behavior of Austin, an enthusiastic but insecure new fraternity member: Noting that the 40 other members appear unanimous in their plans for a fund-raiser, Austin is unlikely to voice his dissent.

Reasons for Conforming

Fish swim in schools. Birds fly in flocks. And humans, too, tend to go with their group, to think what it thinks and do what it does. But why? Why do we clap when others clap, eat as others eat, believe what others believe, even see what others see? Frequently, it is to avoid rejection or to gain social approval. In such cases, we are responding to what social psychologists call **normative social influence.** We are sensitive to social *norms*—understood rules for accepted and expected behavior—because the price we pay for being different may be severe.

Respecting norms is not the only reason we conform: Groups may provide valuable information, and only an uncommonly stubborn person will never listen to others. When we accept others' opinions about reality, we are responding to **informational social influence.** "Those who never retract their opinions love themselves more than they love truth," observed the eighteenth-century French essayist Joseph Joubert.

Our view of social influence as bad or good depends on our values. When influence supports what we approve, we applaud those who are "open-minded" and "sensitive" enough to be "responsive." When influence supports what we disapprove, we scorn the "submissive conformity" of those who comply with others' wishes. Cultural values also affect our tendency to conform to others' views. Cultures vary in the extent to which they value individualism or collectivism. Western Europeans and people in most English-speaking countries tend to prize individualism more than conformity and obedience. These values are reflected in social influence experiments that have been conducted in 17 countries: In individualist cultures, conformity rates are lower (Bond & Smith, 1996).

Obedience

Social psychologist Stanley Milgram (1963, 1974), a student of Solomon Asch, knew that people often comply with social pressures. But how would they respond to outright commands? To find out, he undertook what have become social psychology's most famous and controversial experiments. Imagine yourself as one of the nearly 1000 participants in Milgram's 20 experiments.

> "Have you ever noticed how one example—good or bad—can prompt others to follow? How one illegally parked car can give permission for others to do likewise? How one racial joke can fuel another?"
>
> Marian Wright Edelman,
> *The Measure of Our Success*, 1992

■ **normative social influence** influence resulting from a person's desire to gain approval or avoid disapproval.

■ **informational social influence** influence resulting from one's willingness to accept others' opinions about reality.

Responding to an advertisement, you come to Yale University's psychology department to participate in an experiment. Professor Milgram's assistant explains that the study concerns the effect of punishment on learning. You and another person draw slips from a hat to see who will be the "teacher" (which your slip says) and who will be the "learner." The learner is then led to an adjoining room and strapped into a chair that is wired through the wall to an electric shock machine. You sit in front of the machine, which has switches labeled with voltages. Your task: to teach and then test the learner on a list of word pairs. You are to punish the learner for wrong answers by delivering brief electric shocks, beginning with a switch labeled "15 Volts—Slight Shock." After each of the learner's errors, you are to move up to the next higher voltage. With each flick of a switch, lights flash, relay switches click on, and an electric buzzing fills the air.

If you comply with the experimenter's instructions, you hear the learner grunt when you flick the third, fourth, and fifth switches. After you activate the eighth switch (labeled "120 Volts—Moderate Shock"), the learner shouts that the shocks are painful. After the tenth switch ("150 Volts—Strong Shock"), he cries, "Get me out of here! I won't be in the experiment anymore! I refuse to go on!" When you hear these pleas, you draw back. But the experimenter prods you: "Please continue—the experiment requires that you continue." If you still resist, he insists, "It is absolutely essential that you continue," or "You have no other choice, you *must* go on."

If you obey, you hear the learner's protests escalate to shrieks of agony as you continue to raise the shock level with each succeeding error. After the 330-volt level, the learner refuses to answer and falls silent. Still, the experimenter pushes you toward the final, 450-volt switch, ordering you to ask the questions and, if no correct answer is given, to administer the next shock level.

How far do you think you would follow the experimenter's commands? In a survey Milgram conducted before the experiment, most people declared they would stop playing such a sadistic-seeming role soon after the learner first indicated pain and certainly before he shrieked in agony. This also was the prediction made by each of 40 psychiatrists whom Milgram asked to guess the outcome. When Milgram actually conducted the experiment with men aged 20 to 50, he was astonished to find that 63 percent complied fully—right up to the last switch. Ten later studies that included women found women's compliance rates were similar to men's (Blass, 1999).

Did the "teachers" figure out the hoax—that no shock was being delivered? Did they correctly guess the learner was a confederate who only pretended to feel the shocks? Did they realize the experiment was really testing their willingness to comply with commands to inflict punishment? No, the teachers typically displayed genuine distress: They perspired, trembled, laughed nervously, and bit their lips.

Milgram's use of deception and stress triggered a debate over his research ethics. In his own defense, Milgram pointed out that, after the participants learned of the deception and actual research purposes, virtually none regretted taking part (though perhaps by then the participants had reduced their dissonance). When 40 of the "teachers" who had agonized most were later interviewed by a psychiatrist, none appeared to be suffering emotional aftereffects. All in all, said Milgram, the experiments provoked less enduring stress than university students experience when facing and failing big exams (Blass, 1996).

Wondering whether the participants obeyed because the learners' protests were not convincing, Milgram repeated the experiment with 40 new teachers. This time his confederate mentioned a "slight heart condition" while being strapped into the chair, and then he complained and screamed more intensely as the shocks became more punishing. Can you predict what happened?

Courtesy of CUNY Graduate School and University Center

Stanley Milgram (1933–1984)
This social psychologist's obedience experiments "belong to the self-understanding of literate people in our age" (Sabini, 1986).

"Drive off the cliff, James, I want to commit suicide."

Drawing by Mel Yauk.

© 1965 By Stanley Milgram, from the film *Obedience*, dist. by Penn State, Media Sales

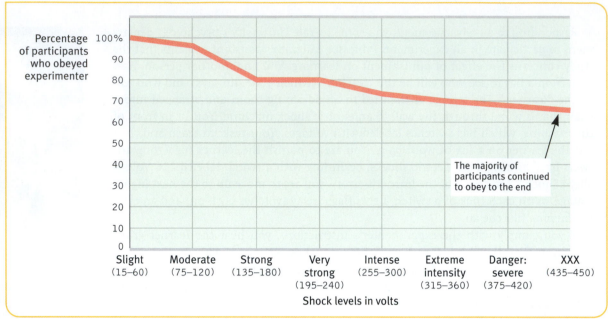

Percentage of participants who obeyed experimenter

The majority of participants continued to obey to the end

Slight (15–60) Moderate (75–120) Strong (135–180) Very strong (195–240) Intense (255–300) Extreme intensity (315–360) Danger: severe (375–420) XXX (435–450)

Shock levels in volts

FIGURE 44.2

Milgram's follow-up obedience experiment

In a repeat of the earlier experiment, 65 percent of the adult male "teachers" fully obeyed the experimenter's commands to continue. They did so despite the "learner's" earlier mention of a heart condition and despite hearing cries of protest after 150 volts and agonized protests after 330 volts. (Data from Milgram, 1974.)

In these follow-up experiments, 65 percent of the new teachers complied fully (**FIGURE 44.2**). Milgram later discovered that subtle details of a situation powerfully influence people. In repeat experiments that varied the social conditions, the proportion of fully compliant participants ranged from 0 to 93 percent. Obedience was highest when

- the person giving the orders was close at hand and was perceived to be a legitimate authority figure.
- the authority figure was supported by a prestigious institution. Compliance was somewhat lower when Milgram dissociated his experiments from Yale University.
- the victim was depersonalized or at a distance, even in another room. (Similarly, in combat with an enemy they can see, many soldiers either do not fire their rifles or do not aim them properly. Such refusals to kill are rare among those who operate the more distant weapons of artillery or aircraft [Padgett, 1989].)
- there were no role models for defiance; that is, no other participants were seen disobeying the experimenter.

The power of legitimate, close-at-hand authorities is dramatically apparent in stories of those who complied with orders to carry out the Holocaust atrocities, and those who didn't. Obedience alone does not explain the Holocaust; anti-Semitic ideology produced eager killers as well (Mastroianni, 2002). But obedience was a factor. In the summer of 1942 nearly 500 middle-aged German reserve police officers were dispatched to German-occupied Jozefow, Poland. On July 13, the group's visibly upset commander informed his recruits, mostly family men, that they had been ordered to round up the village's Jews, who were said to be aiding the enemy. Able-bodied men were to be sent to work camps, and all the rest were to be shot on the spot. Given a chance to refuse participation in the executions, only about a dozen immediately did so. Within 17 hours, the remaining 485 officers killed 1500 helpless women, children, and elderly by shooting them in the back of the head as they lay face down. Hearing the pleadings of the victims, and seeing the gruesome results, some 20 percent of the officers did eventually dissent, managing either to miss their victims or to wander away and hide until the slaughter was over (Browning, 1992). But in real life, as in Milgram's experiments, the disobedient were the minority.

Another story was being played out in the French village of Le Chambon, where French Jews destined for deportation to Germany were being sheltered by villagers who openly defied orders to cooperate with the "New Order." The villagers' ancestors had themselves been persecuted and their pastors had been teaching them to "resist whenever our adversaries will demand of us obedience contrary to the orders of the Gospel" (Rochat, 1993). Ordered by police to give a list of sheltered Jews, the head pastor modeled defiance: "I don't know of Jews, I only know of human beings." Without realizing how long and terrible the war would be, or how much punishment and poverty they would suffer, the resisters made an initial commitment to resist. Supported by their beliefs, their role models, their interaction with one another, and their own initial acts, they remained defiant to the war's end.

AP/Wide World Photos

Standing up for democracy
Some individuals—roughly one in three in Milgram's experiments—resist social coercion, as did this unarmed man in Beijing, by single-handedly challenging an advancing line of tanks the day after the 1989 Tiananmen Square student uprising was suppressed.

Lessons From the Conformity and Obedience Studies

What do the Asch and Milgram experiments teach us about ourselves? How does judging the length of a line or flicking a shock switch relate to everyday social behavior? This research, like all psychological experiments, aimed not to re-create the literal behaviors of everyday life but to capture and explore the underlying processes that shape those behaviors. Asch and Milgram devised experiments in which the participants had to choose between adhering to their own standards and being responsive to others, a dilemma we all face frequently.

In Milgram's experiments, participants were also torn between what they should respond to—the pleas of the victim or the orders of the experimenter. Their moral sense warned them not to harm another, yet it also prompted them to obey the experimenter and to be a good research participant. With kindness and obedience on a collision course, obedience usually won.

Such experiments demonstrate that strong social influences can make people conform to falsehoods or capitulate to cruelty. "The most fundamental lesson of our study," Milgram noted, is that "ordinary people, simply doing their jobs, and without any particular hostility on their part, can become agents in a terrible destructive process" (1974, p. 6). Milgram did not entrap his "teachers" by asking them first to zap "learners" with enough electricity to make their hair stand on end. Rather, he exploited the foot-in-the-door effect, beginning with a little tickle of electricity and escalating step by step. In the minds of those throwing the switches, the small action became justified, making the next act tolerable. In Jozefow, in Le Chambon, and in Milgram's experiments, those who resisted usually did so early. After the first acts of compliance or resistance, attitudes began to follow and justify behavior.

So it happens when people succumb, gradually, to evil. In any society, great evils sometimes grow out of people's compliance with lesser evils. The Nazi leaders suspected that most German civil servants would resist shooting or gassing Jews directly, but they found them surprisingly willing to handle the paperwork of the Holocaust (Silver & Geller, 1978). Likewise, when Milgram asked 40 men to administer the learning test while someone else did the shocking, 93 percent complied. Contrary to images of devilish villains, cruelty does not require monstrous characters; all it takes is ordinary people corrupted by an evil situation—ordinary soldiers who follow orders to torture prisoners, ordinary students who follow orders to haze initiates into their group, ordinary employees who follow orders to produce and market harmful products. Before leading the 9/11 attacks, Mohamed Atta reportedly was a sane, rational person who had been a "good boy" and an excellent student from a close-knit family—not someone who fits our image of a barbaric monster.

"I was only following orders."
Adolf Eichmann, Director of Nazi deportation of Jews to concentration camps

"The normal reaction to an abnormal situation is abnormal behavior."
James Waller, *Becoming Evil: How Ordinary People Commit Genocide and Mass Killing*, 2007

■ **social facilitation** stronger responses on simple or well-learned tasks in the presence of others.

Group Influence

44-2 : How does the mere presence of others influence our actions? How does our behavior change when we act as part of a group?

How do groups affect our behavior? To find out, social psychologists study the various influences that operate in the simplest of groups—one person in the presence of another—and those that operate in more complex groups, such as families, teams, and committees.

Individual Behavior in the Presence of Others

Appropriately, social psychology's first experiments focused on the simplest of all questions about social behavior: How are we influenced by people watching us or joining us in various activities?

Social Facilitation

Having noticed that cyclists' racing times were faster when they competed against each other than when they competed with a clock, Norman Triplett (1898) hypothesized that the presence of others boosts performance. To test his hypothesis, Triplett had adolescents wind a fishing reel as rapidly as possible. He discovered that they wound the reel faster in the presence of someone doing the same thing. This phenomenon of stronger performance in others' presence is called **social facilitation.** For example, after a light turns green, drivers take about 15 percent less time to travel the first 100 yards when another car is beside them at the intersection than when they are alone (Towler, 1986).

But on tougher tasks (learning nonsense syllables or solving complex multiplication problems), people perform *less* well when observers or others working on the same task are present. Further studies revealed why the presence of others sometimes helps and sometimes hinders performance (Guerin, 1986; Zajonc, 1965). When others observe us, we become aroused. This arousal strengthens the most *likely* response—the correct one on an easy task, an incorrect one on a difficult task. Thus, when we are being observed, we perform well-learned tasks more quickly and accurately, and unmastered tasks less quickly and accurately. James Michaels and his associates (1982) found that expert pool players who made 71 percent of their shots when alone made 80 percent when four people came to watch them. Poor shooters, who made 36 percent of their shots when alone, made only 25 percent when watched. The energizing effect of an enthusiastic audience probably contributes to the home advantage enjoyed by various sports teams. Studies of more than 80,000 college and professional athletic events in Canada, the United States, and England reveal that home teams win about 6 in 10 games (somewhat fewer for baseball and football, somewhat more for basketball and soccer—see **TABLE 44.1**).

The point to remember: What you do well, you are likely to do even better in front of an audience, especially a friendly audience; what you normally find difficult may seem all but impossible when you are being watched.

Social facilitation also helps explain a funny effect of crowding: Comedy records

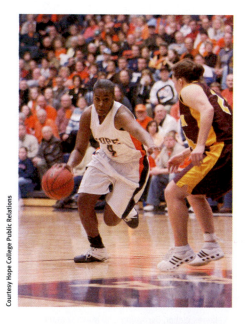

Courtesy Hope College Public Relations

Social facilitation
Skilled athletes often find they are "on" before an audience. What they do well, they do even better when people are watching.

TABLE 44.1

HOME ADVANTAGE IN MAJOR TEAM SPORTS

Sport	Games Studied	Home Team Winning Percentage
Baseball	23,034	53.5%
Football	2,592	57.3
Ice hockey	4,322	61.1
Basketball	13,596	64.4
Soccer	37,202	69.0

From Courneya & Carron (1992)

that are mildly amusing to people in an uncrowded room seem funnier in a densely packed room (Aiello & others, 1983; Freedman & Perlick, 1979). As comedians and actors know, a "good house" is a full one. The arousal triggered by crowding amplifies other reactions, too. If sitting close to one another, participants in experiments like a friendly person even more, an unfriendly person even less (Schiffenbauer & Schiavo, 1976; Storms & Thomas, 1977). The practical lesson: If choosing a room for a class or setting up chairs for a gathering, have barely enough seating.

Social Loafing

Social facilitation experiments test the effect of others' presence on performance on an individual task, such as shooting pool. But what happens to performance when people perform the task as a group? In a team tug-of-war, for example, do you suppose the effort a person puts forth would be more than, less than, or the same as the effort he or she would exert in a one-on-one tug-of-war? To find out, Alan Ingham and his fellow researchers (1974) asked blindfolded University of Massachusetts students to "pull as hard as you can" on a rope. When Ingham fooled the students into believing three others were also pulling behind them, they exerted only 82 percent as much effort as when they knew they were pulling alone.

To describe this diminished effort, Bibb Latané (1981; Jackson & Williams, 1988) coined the term **social loafing.** In 78 experiments conducted in the United States, India, Thailand, Japan, China, and Taiwan, social loafing occurred on various tasks, though it was especially common among men in individualistic cultures (Karau & Williams, 1993). In one of Latané's experiments, blindfolded people seated in a group clapped or shouted as loud as they could while listening through headphones to the sound of loud clapping or shouting. When told they were doing it with the others, the participants produced about one-third less noise than when they thought their individual efforts were identifiable.

Why this social loafing? First, people acting as part of a group feel less accountable and therefore worry less about what others think. Second, they may view their contribution as dispensable (Harkins & Szymanski, 1989; Kerr & Bruun, 1983). As many leaders of organizations know—and as you have perhaps observed on student group assignments—if group members share equally in the benefits regardless of how much they contribute, some may slack off. Unless highly motivated and identified with their group, they may free-ride on the other group members' efforts.

Deindividuation

So, the presence of others can arouse people (as in the social facilitation experiments) or can diminish their feelings of responsibility (as in the social loafing experiments). But sometimes the presence of others both arouses people *and* diminishes their sense of responsibility. The result can be uninhibited behavior ranging from a food fight in the dining hall or screaming at a basketball referee to vandalism or rioting. Abandoning normal restraints to the power of the group is termed **deindividuation.** To be deindividuated is to be less self-conscious and less restrained when in a group situation.

Deindividuation often occurs when group participation makes people feel aroused and anonymous. In one experiment, New York University women dressed in depersonalizing Ku Klux Klan-style hoods delivered twice as much electric shock to a victim as did identifiable women (Zimbardo, 1970). (As in all such experiments, the "victim" did not actually receive the shocks.) Similarly, tribal warriors who depersonalize themselves with face paints or masks are more likely than those with exposed faces to kill, torture, or mutilate captured enemies (Watson, 1973). Whether in a mob, at a rock concert, at a ballgame, or at worship, to lose self-consciousness (to become deindividuated) is to become more responsive to the group experience.

■ **social loafing** the tendency for people in a group to exert less effort when pooling their efforts toward attaining a common goal than when individually accountable.

■ **deindividuation** the loss of self-awareness and self-restraint occurring in group situations that foster arousal and anonymity.

■ **group polarization** the enhancement of a group's prevailing inclinations through discussion within the group.

Effects of Group Interaction

44-3 : What are group polarization and groupthink?

We have examined the conditions under which being in the presence of others can

- motivate people to exert themselves or tempt them to free-ride on the efforts of others.
- make easy tasks easier and difficult tasks harder.
- enhance humor or fuel mob violence.

Research shows that *interacting* with others can similarly have both bad and good effects.

Group Polarization

Educational researchers have noted that, over time, initial differences between groups of college students tend to grow. If the first-year students at College X tend to be more intellectually oriented than those at College Y, that difference will probably be amplified by the time they are seniors. Similarly, if the political conservatism of students who join fraternities and sororities is greater than that of students who do not, the gap in the political attitudes of the two groups will probably widen as they progress through college (Wilson & others, 1975). Likewise, notes Eleanor Maccoby (2002) from her decades of observing gender development, girls talk more intimately than boys do and play and fantasize less aggressively—and these gender differences widen over time as they interact mostly with their own gender.

This enhancement of a group's prevailing tendencies—called **group polarization**—occurs when people within a group discuss an idea that most of them either favor or oppose. Group polarization can have beneficial results, as when it amplifies a sought-after spiritual awareness, or reinforces the resolve of those in a self-help group, or strengthens feelings of tolerance in a low-prejudice group. But it can also have dire consequences. George Bishop and I discovered that when high-prejudice students discussed racial issues, they became *more* prejudiced (**FIGURE 44.3**). (Low-prejudice students became even more accepting.) The experiment's ideological separation and polarization finds a seeming parallel in the growing polarization of American politics. The percentage of landslide counties—voting 60 percent or more for one presidential candidate—increased from 26 percent in 1976 to 48 percent in 2004 (Bishop, 2004). More and more, people are living near and learning from others who think as they do.

The polarizing effect of interaction among the like-minded applies also to suicide terrorists. After analyzing terrorist organizations around the world, psychologists Clark McCauley and Mary Segal (1987; Mc-Cauley, 2002) noted that the terrorist mentality does not erupt suddenly. Rather, it usually arises among people who get together because of a grievance and then become more and more extreme as they interact in isolation from any moderating influences. Increasingly, group members (who may be isolated with other "brothers" and "sisters" in camps) categorize the world as "us" against "them" (Moghaddam, 2005; Qirko, 2004). Suicide terrorism is virtually never done on a personal whim, reports researcher Ariel Merari (2002).

The Internet provides a medium for group polarization. Its tens of thousands of virtual groups enable bereaved parents, peacemakers, and teachers to find solace and support from kindred spirits. But the Internet also enables people who share interests in government conspiracy, extraterrestrial visitors, white supremacy, or citizen militias to find one another and to find support for their shared suspicions (McKenna & Bargh, 1998).

FIGURE 44.3
Group polarization

If a group is like-minded, discussion strengthens its prevailing opinions. Talking over racial issues increased prejudice in a high-prejudice group of high school students and decreased it in a low-prejudice group (Myers & Bishop, 1970).

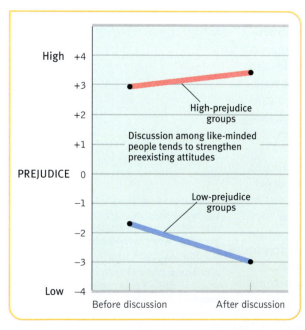

Groupthink

Does group interaction ever distort important decisions? Social psychologist Irving Janis began to think so as he read historian Arthur M. Schlesinger, Jr.'s account of how President John F. Kennedy and his advisers blundered into an ill-fated plan to invade Cuba with 1400 CIA-trained Cuban exiles. When the invaders were easily captured and soon linked to the U.S. government, Kennedy wondered in hindsight, "How could we have been so stupid?"

To find out, Janis (1982) studied the decision-making procedures that led to the fiasco. He discovered that the soaring morale of the recently elected president and his advisers fostered undue confidence in the plan. To preserve the good group feeling, any dissenting views were suppressed or self-censored, especially after President Kennedy voiced his enthusiasm for the scheme. Since no one spoke strongly against the idea, everyone assumed consensus support. To describe this harmonious but unrealistic group thinking, Janis coined the term **groupthink.**

Janis and others then examined other historical fiascos—the failure to anticipate the 1941 Japanese attack on Pearl Harbor, the escalation of the Vietnam War, the U.S. Watergate cover-up, the Chernobyl nuclear reactor accident (Reason, 1987), and the U.S. space shuttle *Challenger* explosion (Esser & Lindoerfer, 1989). They discovered that in these cases, too, groupthink was fed by overconfidence, conformity, self-justification, and group polarization.

Groupthink surfaced again, reported the bipartisan U.S. Senate Intelligence Committee (2004), when "personnel involved in the Iraq WMD issue demonstrated several aspects of groupthink: examining few alternatives, selective gathering of information, pressure to conform within the group or withhold criticism, and collective rationalization." This groupthink led analysts to "interpret ambiguous evidence as conclusively indicative of a WMD program as well as ignore or minimize evidence that Iraq did not have [WMD] programs."

Despite such fiascos and tragedies, two heads are better than one in solving some types of problems. Knowing this, Janis also studied instances in which U.S. presidents and their advisers collectively made good decisions, such as when the Truman administration formulated the Marshall Plan, which offered assistance to Europe after World War II, and when the Kennedy administration worked to keep the Soviets from installing missiles in Cuba. In such instances—and in the business world, too, Janis believed—groupthink is prevented when a leader welcomes various opinions, invites experts' critiques of developing plans, and assigns people to identify possible problems. Just as the suppression of dissent bends a group toward bad decisions, so open debate often shapes good ones. None of us is as smart as all of us.

The Power of Individuals

44-4: How much power do we have as individuals? Can a minority sway a majority?

In affirming the power of social influence, we must not overlook our power as individuals. *Social control* (the power of the situation) and *personal control* (the power of the individual) interact. People aren't billiard balls. When feeling pressured, we may react by doing the opposite of what is expected, thereby reasserting our sense of freedom (Brehm & Brehm, 1981).

Three individual soldiers asserted their personal control at Iraq's Abu Ghraib Prison (O'Connor, 2004), where U.S. military guards were mistreating prisoners. Lt. David Sutton put an end to one incident, which he reported to his commanders. Navy dog-handler William Kimbro refused pressure to participate in improper interrogations using his attack dogs. Specialist Joseph Darby brought visual images of the horrors into the light of day, providing incontestable evidence of the atrocities. Each risked ridicule or even court-martial for not following orders.

> "One's impulse to blow the whistle on this nonsense was simply undone by the circumstances of the discussion."
> Arthur M. Schlesinger, Jr., *A Thousand Days*, 1965

> "Truth springs from argument among friends."
> Philosopher David Hume, 1711–1776

■ **groupthink** the mode of thinking that occurs when the desire for harmony in a decision-making group overrides a realistic appraisal of alternatives.

Margaret Bourke-White/Life Magazine. © 1946 Time Warner, Inc.

Gandhi

As the life of Mahatma Gandhi powerfully testifies, a consistent and persistent minority voice can sometimes sway the majority. The nonviolent appeals and fasts of the Hindu nationalist and spiritual leader were instrumental in winning India's independence from Britain in 1947.

As these three soldiers discovered, committed individuals can sway the majority and make social history. Were this not so, communism would have remained an obscure theory, Christianity would be a small Middle Eastern sect, and Rosa Parks' refusal to sit at the back of the bus would not have ignited the U.S. civil rights movement. Technological history, too, is often made by innovative minorities who overcome the majority's resistance to change. To many, the railroad was a nonsensical idea; some farmers even feared that train noise would prevent hens from laying eggs. People derided Robert Fulton's steamboat as "Fulton's Folly." As Fulton later said, "Never did a single encouraging remark, a bright hope, a warm wish, cross my path." Much the same reaction greeted the printing press, the telegraph, the incandescent lamp, and the typewriter (Cantril & Bumstead, 1960).

European social psychologists have sought to better understand *minority influence*—the power of one or two individuals to sway majorities (Moscovici, 1985). They investigated groups in which one or two individuals consistently expressed a controversial attitude or an unusual perceptual judgment. They repeatedly found that a minority that unswervingly holds to its position is far more successful in swaying the majority than is a minority that waffles. Holding consistently to a minority opinion will not make you popular, but it may make you influential. This is especially so if your self-confidence stimulates others to consider why you react as you do. Although people often follow the majority view publicly, they may privately develop sympathy for the minority view. Even when a minority's influence is not yet visible, it may be persuading some members of the majority to rethink their views (Wood & others, 1994). The powers of social influence are enormous, but so are the powers of the committed individual.

REVIEWING

>> MODULE REVIEW

44-1: What do experiments on conformity and compliance reveal about the power of social influence?

As suggestibility studies demonstrate, when we are unsure about our judgments, we are likely to adjust them toward the group standard. Solomon Asch found that under certain conditions people will *conform* to a group's judgment even when it is clearly incorrect. We may conform either to gain social approval (*normative social influence*) or because we welcome the information that others provide (*informational social influence*). In Stanley Milgram's famous experiments, people torn between obeying an experimenter and responding to another's pleas to stop the shocks usually chose to obey orders, even though obedience appeared to mean harming another person.

44-2: How does the mere presence of others influence our actions? How does our behavior change when we act as part of a group?

Experiments on *social facilitation* reveal that the presence of either observers or co-actors can arouse individuals, boosting their performance on easy tasks but hindering it on difficult ones.

When people pool their efforts toward a group goal, *social loafing* may occur as individuals free-ride on others' efforts. When a group experience arouses people and makes them anonymous, they may become less self-aware and self-restrained, a psychological state known as *deindividuation*.

44-3: What are group polarization and groupthink?

Within groups, discussions among like-minded members often produce *group polarization,* an enhancement of the group's prevailing attitudes. This is one cause of *groupthink,* the tendency for harmony-seeking groups to make unrealistic decisions after suppressing unwelcome information.

44-4: How much power do we have as individuals? Can a minority sway a majority?

The power of the group is great, but so is the power of the individual. Even a small minority sometimes sways a group, especially when the minority expresses its views consistently.

>> REHEARSE IT!

1. Conformity involves adjusting our thinking and behavior toward others in the group. Researchers have found that a person is most likely to conform to a group if
   a. the group members have diverse opinions.
   b. the person feels competent and secure.
   c. the group consists of at least three people.
   d. other group members will not observe the person's behavior.

2. In a classic experiment on obedience, Stanley Milgram tested research participants' (the "teachers") willingness to comply with a command to deliver what they believed to be painful high-voltage shocks to another person. More than 60 percent complied with the commands to deliver even the strongest shocks. Milgram's later experiments showed that the rate of compliance was highest when
   a. the victim was at a distance from the "teacher."
   b. the victim was close at hand.
   c. other "teachers" refused to go along with the experimenter.
   d. the "teachers" believed the victim had a heart condition.

3. In the presence of others we become aroused: Professional sports teams play better before a crowd. Social facilitation—improved performance in the presence of others—occurs with
   a. any physical task.
   b. new learning.
   c. a well-learned task.
   d. competitive sports or activities only.

4. When people are part of a group working toward a common goal, their individual efforts are diminished. Bibb Latané and his colleagues called this
   a. minority influence.
   b. social facilitation.
   c. social loafing.
   d. group polarization.

5. In a group situation that fosters arousal and anonymity, a person sometimes loses self-consciousness and self-control. This phenomenon, called *deindividuation*, is best illustrated by
   a. improved performance in front of an audience.
   b. unrestrained behavior at a mass rally.
   c. evasion of responsibility in a group clean-up effort.
   d. denial of one's own perceptions in the face of an opposing consensus.

6. If a group is like-minded, discussion strengthens its prevailing opinion. This effect is called
   a. groupthink.
   b. minority influence.
   c. group polarization.
   d. social facilitation.

7. Group interaction has the potential to distort important group decisions. For example, when a group's desire for harmony overrides its realistic appraisal of alternatives, _____ has occurred.
   a. group polarization
   b. groupthink
   c. social facilitation
   d. deindividuation

Answers: 1. c, 2. a, 3. c, 4. c, 5. b, 6. c, 7. b.

>> TERMS AND CONCEPTS TO REMEMBER

social psychology, p. 582
conformity, p. 583
normative social influence, p. 584

informational social influence, p. 584
social facilitation, p. 588
social loafing, p. 589

deindividuation, p. 589
group polarization, p. 590
groupthink, p. 591

>> TEST YOURSELF

1. You are organizing a Town Hall–style meeting of fiercely competitive political candidates. To add to the fun, friends have suggested handing out masks of the candidates' faces for supporters to wear. What phenomenon might these masks engage?

(Answer in Appendix C.)

Multiple-choice **self-tests** and more may be found at www.worthpublishers.com/myers.

45

Social Relations

What does **social psychology** teach us about how we *relate* to one another? What causes us to harm or to help or to fall in love? How can we transform the closed fists of aggression into the open arms of compassion? We will ponder the bad and the good: from prejudice and aggression to attraction, altruism, and peacemaking.

Prejudice

Prejudice means "prejudgment." It is an unjustifiable and usually negative attitude toward a group—often a different cultural, ethnic, or gender group. Like all attitudes, **prejudice** is a mixture of *beliefs* (called **stereotypes**), *emotions* (hostility, envy, or fear), and predispositions to *action* (to discriminate). To *believe* that obese people are gluttonous, to *feel* antipathy for an obese person, and to be hesitant to hire or date an obese person is to be prejudiced. Prejudice is a negative *attitude;* **discrimination** is a negative *behavior.*

Like other forms of prejudgment, prejudices are schemas that influence how we notice and interpret events. In one 1970s study, most white participants perceived a white man shoving a black man as "horsing around." When they saw a black man shove a white man, they interpreted the act as "violent" (Duncan, 1976). Our preconceived ideas about people bias our impressions of their behavior. Prejudgments color perceptions.

How Prejudiced Are People?

To learn about levels of prejudice, we can assess what people say and what they do. To judge by what Americans say, gender and racial attitudes have changed dramatically in the last half-century. The one-third of Americans who in 1937 said they would vote for a qualified woman whom their party nominated for president soared to 87 percent in 2003 (Jones & Moore, 2003). Support for all forms of racial contact, including interracial marriage (**FIGURE 45.1**), has also dramatically increased. Nearly everyone agrees that children of all races should attend the same schools and that women and men should receive the same pay for the same job.

■ **social psychology** the scientific study of how we think about, influence, and relate to one another.

FIGURE 45.1
Prejudice over time
Americans' approval of interracial marriage has soared over the past half-century. (Gallup surveys reported by Ludwig, 2004.)

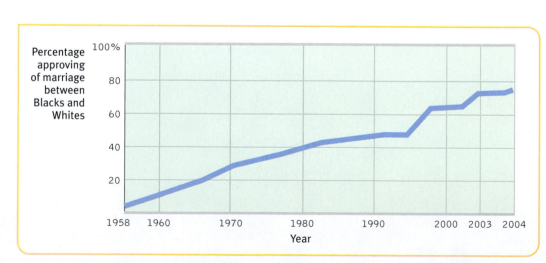

CLOSE-UP

AUTOMATIC PREJUDICE

As we have seen throughout this book, we process information on two levels: conscious and unconscious. To some extent, our thinking, our memories, and our attitudes are *explicit*—on the radar screen of our awareness. And to an even greater extent, today's researchers believe, they are *implicit*—below the radar, out-of-sight. Modern studies of implicit, automatic attitudes indicate that prejudice is often more of an unthinking knee-jerk response than a decision. Consider these findings on U.S. racial prejudice:

Implicit racial associations As Anthony Greenwald and his colleagues (1998) showed, even people who deny harboring racial prejudice may carry negative associations. For example, 9 in 10 white respondents took longer to identify pleasant words (such as *peace* and *paradise*) as "good" when presented with black-sounding names (such as Latisha and Darnell) rather than white-sounding names (such as Katie and Ian). Moreover, report Kurt Hugenberg and Galen Bodenhausen (2003), people who displayed the most implicit prejudice on this test also were the quickest to perceive anger and apparent threat in black faces.

Unconscious patronization Kent Harber (1998) asked white university women to evaluate a flawed essay said to be written by a black or a white fellow student. When they believed the writer was black, the women gave markedly higher ratings and never expressed the harsh criticisms they assigned to white-authored essays, such as "When I read college work this bad I just want to lay my head down on the table and cry." Did the evaluators calibrate their evaluations to their racial stereotypes, Harber wondered, leading them to patronize the black writers with less exacting standards? If used in real-world evaluations, such low expectations and the resulting "inflated praise and insufficient criticism" could hinder minority student achievement. (To preclude such bias, many teachers read essays while "blind" to their authors.)

Race-influenced perceptions Two research teams were curious about the shooting of an unarmed man in the doorway of his Bronx apartment building by officers who mistook his wallet for a gun. Each research team reenacted the situation, asking people to press buttons quickly to "shoot" or not shoot men who suddenly appeared on screen holding either a gun or a harmless object such as a flashlight or bottle (Correll & others, 2002; Greenwald & others, 2003). People (both Blacks and Whites, in one of the studies) more often mistakenly shot targets who were black.

Seeing black Several studies show that the more a person's features are perceived as typical of their racial category, the more likely they are to elicit race-based responding (Maddox, 2004). In one study of 182 police officers, Jennifer Eberhardt and her collaborators (2004) found that "black faces looked more criminal to police officers; the more black, the more criminal."

Reflexive bodily responses Today's biopsychosocial approach has stimulated neuroscience studies that measure people's instant responses to viewing white and black faces. These studies have detected implicit prejudice in people's facial-muscle responses and in the activation of their amygdala, an emotion-processing center (Cunningham & others, 2004; Eberhardt, 2005; Vanman & others, 2004). Even people who consciously express little prejudice may give off telltale signals as their body responds selectively to another's race.

If your own gut check sometimes reveals feelings you would rather not have about other people, be assured that you are not alone. It is what we do with our feelings that matters. By monitoring our feelings and actions, and by replacing old habits with new ones based on new friendships, we can free ourselves from prejudice.

Yet as overt prejudice wanes, subtle prejudice lingers. Despite increased verbal support for interracial marriage, many people admit that in socially intimate settings (dating, dancing, marrying) they would feel uncomfortable with someone of another race. And in Western Europe, where many "guest workers" and refugees settled at the end of the twentieth century, "modern prejudice"—rejecting immigrant minorities as job applicants for supposedly nonracial reasons—has been replacing blatant prejudice (Jackson & others, 2001; Pettigrew, 1998). A slew of recent experiments illustrate that prejudice can be not only subtle but also automatic and unconscious (see Close-Up: Automatic Prejudice).

But prejudice still surfaces in public settings. In a 2004 survey of Europeans, 6 in 10 people in both Britain and Germany said immigrants are a bad influence on their country (Lester, 2004). In most places in the world, gays and lesbians cannot comfortably acknowledge who they are and whom they love. In several U.S. states where

■ **prejudice** an unjustifiable (and usually negative) attitude toward a group and its members. Prejudice generally involves stereotyped beliefs, negative feelings, and a predisposition to discriminatory action.

■ **stereotype** a generalized (sometimes accurate but often overgeneralized) belief about a group of people.

■ **discrimination** unjustifiable negative behavior toward a group or its members.

"Unhappily the world has yet to learn how to live with diversity."
Pope John Paul II, Address to the United Nations, 1995

black motorists are a minority of the drivers and speeders on interstate highways, they have been the majority of those stopped and searched by state police (Lamberth, 1998; Staples, 1999a,b).

Gender prejudice and discrimination persist, too. Despite gender equality in intelligence scores, people tend to perceive their fathers as more intelligent than their mothers (Furnham & Rawles, 1995). In Saudi Arabia, women are not allowed to drive. In Western countries, we pay more to those (usually men) who drive machines that take care of our streets than to those (usually women) who take care of our children. Worldwide, women are more likely to live in poverty (Lipps, 1999), and their 69 percent literacy rate is well below men's 83 percent (PRB, 2002).

Female infants are no longer left out on a hillside to die of exposure, as was the practice in ancient Greece. Yet even today boys are often valued more than their sisters. With testing that enables sex-selective abortions, several south Asian countries, including certain regions of China and India, have experienced a shortfall in female births. Natural female mortality and the normal 105-to-100 male-to-female birth ratio hardly explains the world's estimated 101 million (say that number slowly) "missing women" (Sen, 2003). In 2005, China announced that the newborn sex ratio had reached 119 boys for every 100 girls (Yardley, 2005). With demographic predictions of 40 million Chinese bachelors unable to find mates, China has declared that sex-selective abortions—gender genocide—are now a criminal offense.

Suppose that you could only have one child. Would you prefer that it be a boy or a girl? When Gallup asked that question of Americans, two-thirds expressed a gender preference, and for two-thirds of those—in 2003 as in 1941—it was for a boy (Lyons, 2003). But the news isn't all bad for girls and women. Most people *feel* more positively about women in general than they do about men (Eagly, 1994; Haddock & Zanna, 1994). People worldwide see women as having some traits, such as nurturance, sensitivity, and less aggressiveness, that most people prefer (Glick & others, 2004; Swim, 1994). That may explain why women tend to like women more than men like men (Rudman & Goodwin, 2004). And perhaps that is also why people prefer slightly feminized computer-generated faces—men's and women's—to slightly masculinized faces. Researcher David Perrett and his colleagues (1998) speculate that a slightly feminized male face connotes kindness, cooperativeness, and other traits of a good father. When the British Broadcasting Company invited 18,000 women to guess which of the men in **FIGURE 45.2** was most likely to place a personal ad seeking a "special lady to love and cherish forever," 66 percent guessed the slightly feminized face (b).

Social Roots of Prejudice

45-1: What are the social and emotional roots of prejudice?

Why does prejudice arise? Inequalities, social divisions, and emotional scapegoating are partly responsible.

Social Inequalities

When some people have money, power, and prestige and others do not, the "haves" usually develop attitudes that justify things as they are. In the extreme case, slave owners perceived slaves as innately lazy, ignorant, and irresponsible—as having the very traits that "justified" enslaving them. More commonly, women are perceived as unassertive but sensitive and therefore suited for the caretaking tasks they have traditionally performed (Hoffman & Hurst, 1990). In short, prejudice rationalizes inequalities.

Discrimination also increases prejudice through the reactions it provokes in its victims. In his classic 1954 book, *The Nature of Prejudice*, Gordon Allport noted that being a victim of discrimination can produce either self-blame or anger. Both reactions may

FIGURE 45.2
Who do you like best?
Which one placed an ad seeking a special lady to love and cherish forever?

(a)

(b)

Professor Dave Perrett, St. Andrews University

Mike Hewitt/Getty Images

The ingroup

Scotland's famed "Tartan Army" soccer fans, shown here during a match against archrival England, share a social identity that defines "us" (the Scottish ingroup) and "them" (the English outgroup).

create new grounds for prejudice through the classic *blame-the-victim* dynamic. If the circumstances of poverty breed a higher crime rate, someone can then use the higher crime rate to justify continuing the discrimination against those who live in poverty.

Us and Them: Ingroup and Outgroup

Thanks to our ancestral need to belong, we are a group-bound species. We cheer for our groups, kill for them, die for them. Indeed, we define who we are—our identities—partly in terms of our groups. Australian psychologists John Turner (1987) and Michael Hogg (1996) note that through our *social identities* we associate ourselves with certain groups and contrast ourselves with others. When Ian identifies himself as a man, an Aussie, a Labourite, a University of Sydney student, a Catholic, and a MacGregor, he knows who he is, and so do we.

The social definition of who you are also implies who you are not. Mentally drawing a circle that defines "us" (the **ingroup**) excludes "them" (the **outgroup**). Such group identifications typically promote an **ingroup bias**—a favoring of one's own group. Even arbitrarily creating an us-them distinction—by grouping people with the toss of a coin—leads people to show favoritism to their own group when dividing any rewards (Tajfel, 1982; Wilder, 1981).

The urge to distinguish enemies from friends and to have one's group be dominant predisposes prejudice against strangers (Whitley, 1999). To Greeks of the classical era, all non-Greeks were "barbarians." Most children believe their own school is better than the other schools in town. Many high school students form cliques—jocks, goths, skaters, gangsters, freaks, geeks—and disparage those outside their group. Even chimpanzees have been seen to wipe clean the spot where they were touched by a chimp from another group (Goodall, 1986).

- **ingroup** "Us"—people with whom one shares a common identity.
- **outgroup** "Them"—those perceived as different or apart from one's ingroup.
- **ingroup bias** the tendency to favor one's own group.

> All good people agree,
> And all good people say
> All nice people, like Us, are We
> And everyone else is They.
> But if you cross over the sea
> Instead of over the way
> You may end by (think of it)
> Looking on We
> As only a sort of They."
> Rudyard Kipling, "We and They," 1926

Eric Travers/EPA/Landov

French fury

Members of France's marginalized ethnic groups reached the tipping point for tolerance in 2005, when they began destructive rioting.

Emotional Roots of Prejudice

Prejudice springs not only from the divisions of society but also from the passions of the heart. Facing the terror of death tends to heighten patriotism and produce loathing and aggression toward "them"—those who threaten one's world (Pyszczynski & others, 2002). Recalling such terror may alter attitudes, as happened to participants when Mark Landau and eight others (2004) reminded them of their own mortality or of the terror of 9/11. This terror reminder led to their expressing increased support for President Bush.

Prejudice may also express anger: When things go wrong, finding someone to blame can provide a target, a scapegoat, for one's anger. In the late 1600s, New England settlers, after suffering devastating losses at the hands of Native Americans and their French allies, lashed out by hanging people as supposed witches (Norton, 2002). Following 9/11, some outraged people lashed out at innocent Arab-Americans, about whom negative stereotypes blossomed. Calls to eliminate Saddam Hussein, whom Americans had been grudgingly tolerating, also increased. "Fear and anger create aggression, and aggression against citizens of different ethnicity or race creates racism and, in turn, new forms of terrorism," noted Philip Zimbardo (2001).

Evidence for this **scapegoat theory** of prejudice comes from high prejudice levels among economically frustrated people and from experiments in which a temporary frustration intensifies prejudice. In experiments, students who experience failure or are made to feel insecure will often restore their self-esteem by disparaging a rival school or another person (Cialdini & Richardson, 1980; Crocker & others, 1987). To boost our own sense of status, it helps to have others to denigrate. That is why a rival's misfortune sometimes provides a twinge of pleasure. By contrast, those made to feel loved and supported become more open to and accepting of others who differ (Mikulincer & Shaver, 2001).

Cognitive Roots of Prejudice

45-2: What are the cognitive roots of prejudice?

Prejudice springs from the divisions of society, the passions of the heart, and also from the mind's natural workings. Stereotyped beliefs are a by-product of how we cognitively simplify the world.

Categorization

One way we simplify our world is to categorize. A chemist categorizes molecules as organic and inorganic. A mental health professional categorizes psychological disorders by types. In categorizing people into groups, however, we often stereotype them, biasing our perceptions of their diversity. We recognize how greatly we differ from other individuals in our groups. But we overestimate the similarity of those within other groups. "They"—the members of some other group—seem to look and act alike, but "we" are diverse (Bothwell & others, 1989). To those in one ethnic group, members of another often seem more alike in appearance, personality, and attitudes than they are. With experience, however, people get better at recognizing individual faces from another group. For example, people of European descent more accurately identify individual African faces if they have watched a great deal of basketball on television, exposing them to many African-heritage faces (Li & others, 1996).

Vivid Cases

We often judge the frequency of events by instances that readily come to mind. In a classic experiment, Myron Rothbart and his colleagues (1978) demonstrated this ability to overgeneralize from vivid, memorable cases. They divided University of Oregon student volunteers into two groups, then showed them information about

"If the Tiber reaches the walls, if the Nile does not rise to the fields, if the sky doesn't move or the Earth does, if there is famine, if there is plague, the cry is at once: 'The Christians to the lion!'"

Tertullian, *Apologeticus*, A.D. 197

■ **scapegoat theory** the theory that prejudice offers an outlet for anger by providing someone to blame.

■ **just-world phenomenon** the tendency of people to believe the world is just and that people therefore get what they deserve and deserve what they get.

■ **aggression** any physical or verbal behavior intended to hurt or destroy.

50 men. The first group's list included 10 men arrested for nonviolent crimes, such as forgery. The second group's list included 10 men arrested for violent crimes, such as assault. Later, when both groups recalled how many men on their list had committed any sort of crime, the second group overestimated the number. Vivid (violent) cases are readily available to our memory and therefore influence our judgments of a group (**FIGURE 45.3**).

FIGURE 45.3
Vivid cases feed stereotypes
The 9/11 Muslim terrorists created, in many minds, an exaggerated stereotype of Muslims as terror-prone. Actually, reported a National Research Council panel on terrorism, when offering this inexact illustration, most terrorists are not Muslim and "the vast majority of Islamic people have no connection with and do not sympathize with terrorism" (Smelser & Mitchell, 2002).

Islam   Terrorism

The Just-World Phenomenon

As we noted earlier, people often justify their prejudice by blaming its victims. Bystanders, too, may blame victims by assuming the world is just and therefore "people get what they deserve." In experiments, merely observing someone receive painful shocks has led many people to think less of the victim (Lerner, 1980). This **just-world phenomenon** reflects an idea we commonly teach our children—that good is rewarded and evil is punished. From this it is but a short leap to assume that those who succeed must be good and those who suffer must be bad. Such reasoning enables the rich to see both their own wealth and the poor's misfortune as justly deserved. As one German civilian is said to have remarked when visiting the Bergen-Belsen concentration camp shortly after World War II, "What terrible criminals these prisoners must have been to receive such treatment."

Hindsight bias is also at work here (Carli & Leonard, 1989). Have you ever heard people say that rape victims, abused spouses, or people with AIDS got what they deserved? In some countries, women who have been raped have been sentenced to severe punishment for having violated a law against adultery (Mydans, 2002). An experiment by Ronnie Janoff-Bulman and her collaborators (1985) illustrates this phenomenon of blaming the victim. When given a detailed account of a date that ended with the woman being raped, people perceived the woman's behavior as at least partly to blame. In hindsight, they thought, "She should have known better." (Blaming the victim also serves to reassure people that it couldn't happen to them.) Others, given the same account with the rape ending deleted, did not perceive the woman's behavior as inviting rape.

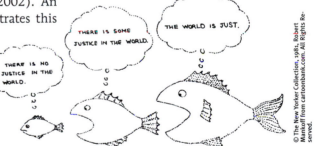

© The New Yorker Collection, 1981, Robert Mankoff from cartoonbank.com. All Rights Reserved.

Aggression

The most destructive force in our social relations is aggression. In psychology, *aggression* has a more precise meaning than it does in everyday usage. The assertive, persistent salesperson is not aggressive. Nor is the dentist who makes you wince with pain. But the person who passes along a vicious rumor about you, the person who verbally assaults you, and the attacker who mugs you are aggressive. In psychology, **aggression** is any physical or verbal behavior intended to hurt or destroy, whether done reactively out of hostility or proactively as a calculated means to an end. Thus, murders and assaults that occurred as hostile outbursts are aggression. So were the 110 million war-related deaths that took place during the last century, many of which were cool and calculated.

Aggression research affirms that behavior emerges from the interaction of biology and experience. For a gun to fire, the trigger must be pulled; with some people, as with hair-trigger guns, it doesn't take much to trip an explosion. Let us look first at biological factors that influence our thresholds for aggressive behavior, then at the psychological factors that pull the trigger.

In the last 25 years in the United States, guns caused some 800,000 suicidal, homicidal, and accidental deaths. Compared with people of the same sex, race, age, and neighborhood, those who keep a gun in the home (ironically, often for protection) are nearly three times more likely to be murdered in the home—nearly always by a family member or close acquaintance. For every self-defense use of a gun in the home, there are 4 unintentional shootings, 7 criminal assaults or homicides, and 11 attempted or completed suicides (Kellermann & others, 1993, 1997, 1998).

The Biology of Aggression

45-3: What biological factors make us more prone to hurt one another?

Aggression varies too widely from culture to culture, era to era, and person to person to be considered an unlearned instinct. But biology does *influence* aggression. Stimuli that trigger aggressive behavior operate through our biological system. We can look for biological influences at three levels—genetic, neural, and biochemical. Our genes engineer our individual nervous systems, which operate electrochemically.

Genetic Influences

Animals have been bred for aggressiveness—sometimes for sport, sometimes for research. Twin studies suggest that genes influence human aggression as well (Miles & Carey, 1997; Rowe & others, 1999). If one identical twin admits to "having a violent temper," the other twin will often independently admit the same. Fraternal twins are much less likely to respond similarly. Researchers are now searching for genetic markers found in those who commit the most violence. (One is already well known and is carried by half the human race: the Y chromosome.)

Neural Influences

Animal and human brains have neural systems that, when stimulated, either inhibit or produce aggressive behavior (Moyer, 1983). Consider:

- The domineering leader of a caged monkey colony had a radio-controlled electrode implanted in a brain area that, when stimulated, inhibits aggression. When researchers placed the button that activated the electrode in the colony's cage, one small monkey learned to push it every time the boss became threatening.
- A mild-mannered woman had an electrode implanted in her brain's limbic system (in the amygdala) by neurosurgeons seeking to diagnose a disorder. Because the brain has no sensory receptors, she was unable to feel the stimulation. But at the flick of a switch she snarled, "Take my blood pressure. Take it now," then stood up and began to strike the doctor.
- Intensive evaluation of 15 death-row inmates revealed that all 15 had suffered a severe head injury. Although most neurologically impaired people are not violent, researcher Dorothy Lewis and her colleagues (1986) inferred that unrecognized neurological disorders may be one ingredient in the violence recipe. Other studies of violent criminals have revealed diminished activity in the frontal lobes, which play an important role in controlling impulses (Amen & others, 1996; Davidson & others, 2000; Raine, 1999).

So, does the brain have a "violence center" that produces aggression when stimulated? Actually, no one spot in the brain controls aggression, because aggression is a complex behavior that occurs in particular contexts. Rather, the brain has neural systems that *facilitate* aggression, given provocation. And it has a frontal lobe system for inhibiting aggression, making aggression more likely if this system is damaged, inactive, disconnected, or not yet fully mature.

Biochemical Influences

Hormones, alcohol, and other substances in the blood influence the neural systems that control aggression. A raging bull will become a gentle Ferdinand when castration reduces its testosterone level. The same is true of castrated mice. When injected with testosterone, the castrated mice once again become aggressive.

Although humans are less sensitive to hormonal changes, violent criminals tend to be muscular young males with lower-than-average intelligence scores, low levels of the neurotransmitter serotonin, and higher-than-average testosterone levels (Dabbs & others, 2001a; Pendick, 1994). Drugs that sharply reduce their testosterone levels also subdue their aggressive tendencies. High testosterone correlates with irritability,

"It's a guy thing."

© The New Yorker Collection, 1995, D. Reilly from cartoonbank.com. All Rights Reserved.

Misuaki Iwago/Minden Pictures

A lean, mean fighting machine—the testosterone-laden female hyena
The hyena's unusual embryology pumps testosterone into female fetuses. The result is revved-up young female hyenas who seem born to fight.

low tolerance for frustration, assertiveness, and impulsiveness—qualities that predispose somewhat more aggressive responses to provocation (Dabbs & others, 2001b; Harris, 1999). Among both teenage boys and adult men, high testosterone levels correlate with delinquency, hard drug use, and aggressive-bullying responses to frustration (Berman & others, 1993; Dabbs & Morris, 1990; Olweus & others, 1988). With age, testosterone levels—and aggressiveness—diminish.

The traffic between hormones and behavior is two-way. Testosterone heightens dominance and aggressiveness. But dominating behavior also boosts testosterone levels (Mazur & Booth, 1998). One study measured testosterone levels in the saliva of male college basketball fans before and after a big game. Testosterone levels swelled among the victorious fans and sank among the dejected ones (Bernhardt & others, 1998).

For both biological and psychological reasons, alcohol unleashes aggressive responses to frustration (Bushman, 1993; Ito & others, 1996; Taylor & Chermack, 1993). (Just *thinking* you've imbibed alcohol has some effect; but so, too, does unknowingly ingesting alcohol slipped into a drink.) Police data and prison surveys reinforce conclusions drawn from experiments on alcohol and aggression: Aggression-prone people are more likely to drink and to become violent when intoxicated (White & others, 1993). People who have been drinking commit 4 in 10 violent crimes and 3 in 4 acts of spousal abuse (Greenfeld, 1998).

> " We could avoid two-thirds of all crime simply by putting all able-bodied young men in cryogenic sleep from the age of 12 through 28."
>
> David T. Lykken, *The Antisocial Personalities*, 1995

The Psychology of Aggression

45-4 : What psychological factors may trigger aggressive behavior?

Biological factors influence the ease with which aggression is triggered. But what psychological factors pull the trigger?

Aversive Events

Although suffering sometimes builds character, it may also bring out the worst in us. Studies in which animals or humans experience unpleasant events reveal that those made miserable often make others miserable (Berkowitz, 1983, 1989).

Being blocked short of a goal also increases people's readiness to aggress. This phenomenon is called the **frustration-aggression principle:** Frustration creates anger, which may in some people generate aggression, especially in the presence of an aggressive cue, such as a gun. Recall that organisms often respond to stress with a *fight-or-flight reaction*. After the frustration and stress of 9/11, Americans responded with a readiness to fight. Terrorism similarly may spring from a desire for revenge, sometimes after a friend or family member has been killed or injured.

■ **frustration-aggression principle** the principle that frustration—the blocking of an attempt to achieve some goal—creates anger, which can generate aggression.

FIGURE 45.4
Uncomfortably hot weather and aggressive reactions
Between 1980 and 1982 in Houston, murders and rapes were more common on days over 91 degrees Fahrenheit (33 degrees centigrade), as shown in the graph. This finding is consistent with those from laboratory experiments in which people working in a hot room react to provocations with greater hostility. (From Anderson & Anderson, 1984.)

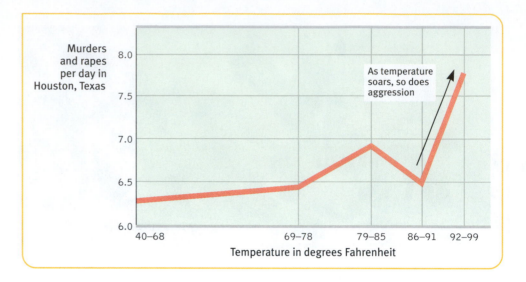

Like frustration, other aversive stimuli—physical pain, personal insults, foul odors, hot temperatures, cigarette smoke, and a host of others—can also evoke hostility. For example, violent crime and spousal abuse rates are higher during hotter years, seasons, months, and days (**FIGURE 45.4**). When people get overheated, they think, feel, and act more aggressively. From the available data, Craig Anderson and his colleagues (2000) project that, other things being equal, global warming of 4 degrees Fahrenheit (about 2 degrees centigrade) would induce more than 50,000 additional assaults and murders in the United States alone.

Ostracism can also be a real pain. In a series of studies, Jean Twenge and her collaborators (2001, 2002, 2003) told some people that others whom they had met didn't want them in their group, or that a personality test indicated they "were likely to end up alone later in life." Those led to feel socially excluded were later more likely to disparage or even deliver a blast of noise to someone who insulted them. This rejection-induced aggression brings to mind various North American and European school shootings, committed by youth who had been shunned and mocked by peers. Other studies confirm that rejection often intensifies aggression (Catanese & Tice, 2005; Gaertner & Iuzzini, 2005).

Learning That Aggression Is Rewarding

Aggression may be a natural response to aversive events, but learning can alter natural reactions. Animals naturally eat when they are hungry. But if appropriately rewarded or punished, they can be taught either to overeat or to starve.

Our reactions are more likely to be aggressive in situations where experience has taught us that aggression pays. Children whose aggression successfully intimidates other children may become more aggressive. Animals that have successfully fought to get food or mates become increasingly ferocious.

Different cultures model, reinforce, and evoke different tendencies toward violence. For example, crime rates are higher (and average happiness is lower) in countries marked by a great disparity between rich and poor (Triandis, 1994). Richard Nisbett and Dov Cohen (1996) show how violence can vary by culture within a country. They analyzed violence among white Americans in southern towns settled by Scots-Irish herders whose tradition emphasized "manly honor," the use of arms to protect one's flock, and a history of coercive slavery. Their cultural descendants have triple the homicide rates and are more supportive of physically punishing children, of warfare initiatives, and of uncontrolled gun ownership than are their white counterparts in New England towns settled by the more traditionally peaceful Puritan, Quaker, and Dutch farmer-artisans.

Social influence also appears in high violence rates among cultures and families that experience minimal father care (Triandis, 1994). For example, the U.S. Bureau of Justice Statistics has reported that 70 percent of imprisoned juveniles did not grow up with two parents (Beck & others, 1988). (An absent parent is usually a father.) A correlation between father absence and violence in the United States holds for all races, income levels, and locations (Myers, 2000).

It is important, however, to note how many people are leading gentle, even heroic, lives amid social stresses, reminding us again that individuals differ. The person matters. That people differ over time and place reminds us that environments also differ, and situations matter. Yesterday's plundering Vikings have become today's peace-promoting Scandinavians. Like all behavior, aggression arises from the interaction of persons and situations.

Once established, however, aggressive behavior patterns are difficult to change. To foster a kinder, gentler world we had best model and reward sensitivity and cooperation from an early age, perhaps by training parents to discipline without modeling violence. Modeling violence—screaming and hitting—is precisely what exasperated parents often do. Parents of delinquent youngsters typically discipline with beatings, thus modeling aggression as a method of dealing with problems (Patterson & others, 1982, 1992). They also frequently cave into (reward) their children's tears and temper tantrums.

Parent-training programs advise a more positive approach. They encourage parents to reinforce desirable behaviors and to frame statements positively ("When you finish loading the dishwasher you can go play," rather than "If you don't load the dishwasher, there'll be no playing"). One *aggression-replacement program* that brought down re-arrest rates of juvenile offenders and gang members taught the youths and their parents communication skills, trained them in how to control anger, and encouraged more thoughtful moral reasoning (Goldstein & others, 1998).

Observing Models of Aggression

Parents are hardly the only aggression models. Observing TV violence tends to desensitize people to cruelty and prime them to respond aggressively when provoked. Does this media effect extend to sexual violence? We do know that sexually coercive men typically are promiscuous and hostile in their relationships with women (**FIGURE 45.5**). Might sexually explicit media contribute to such tendencies?

Content analyses reveal that most X-rated films depict quick, casual sex between strangers, but that scenes of rape and sexual exploitation of women by men are also common (Cowan & others, 1988; NCTV, 1987; Yang & Linz, 1990). Rape scenes often portray the victim at first fleeing and resisting her attacker, but then becoming aroused and finally driven to ecstasy. In less graphic form, the same unrealistic script— she resists, he persists, she melts—is commonplace on TV and in romance novels. In *Gone With the Wind,* Scarlett O'Hara is carried to bed screaming and wakes up singing. Most rapists accept this *rape myth*—the idea that some women invite or enjoy rape and get "swept away" while being "taken" (Brinson, 1992). (In actuality, rape is traumatic, and it frequently harms women's reproductive and sexual health [Golding, 1996].)

Laboratory experiments reveal that repeatedly watching X-rated films (even if nonviolent) later makes one's own partner seem less attractive, makes a woman's friendliness seem more sexual, and makes sexual aggression seem less serious (Harris, 1994). In one such

> "Why do we kill people who kill people to show that killing people is wrong?"
>
> National Coalition to Abolish the Death Penalty, 1992

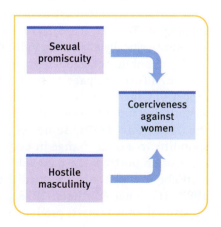

FIGURE 45.5

Men who sexually coerce women

The recipe for coercion against women combines an impersonal approach to sex with a hostile masculinity. (Adapted from Malamuth, 1996.)

In follow-up studies, Zillmann (1989) found that after massive exposure to X-rated sexual films, men and women became more accepting of extramarital sex, of women's sexual submission to men, and of a man's seducing a 12-year-old girl. As people heavily exposed to televised crime perceive the world as more dangerous, so people heavily exposed to pornography see the world as more sexual.

experiment, Dolf Zillmann and Jennings Bryant (1984) showed undergraduates six brief, sexually explicit films each week for six weeks. A control group viewed nonerotic films during the same six-week period. Three weeks later, both groups read a newspaper report about a man convicted but not yet sentenced for raping a hitch-hiker. When asked to suggest an appropriate prison term, those who had viewed sexually explicit films recommended sentences half as long as those recommended by the control group.

Experiments cannot elicit actual sexual violence, but they can assess a man's willingness to hurt a woman. Often the research gauges the effect of violent versus nonviolent erotic films on men's willingness to deliver supposed electric shocks to women who had earlier provoked the men. These experiments suggest that it's not the eroticism but rather the depictions of sexual *violence* (whether in R-rated slasher films or X-rated films) that most directly affect men's acceptance and performance of aggression against women. A conference of 21 social scientists, including many of the researchers who conducted these experiments, produced a consensus (Surgeon General, 1986): "Pornography that portrays sexual aggression as pleasurable for the victim increases the acceptance of the use of coercion in sexual relations." Contrary to much popular opinion, viewing such depictions does not provide an outlet for bottled-up impulses. Rather, "in laboratory studies measuring short-term effects, exposure to violent pornography increases punitive behavior toward women."

Acquiring Social Scripts

Significant behaviors, such as violence, usually have many determinants, making any single explanation an oversimplification. Asking what causes violence is therefore like asking what causes cancer. Those who study the effects of asbestos exposure on cancer rates may remind us that asbestos is indeed a cancer cause, albeit only one among many. Likewise, report Neil Malamuth and his colleagues (1991, 1995), several factors can create a predisposition to sexual violence. They include the media but also dominance motives, disinhibition by alcohol, and a history of child abuse. Still, if media depictions of violence can disinhibit and desensitize; if viewing sexual violence fosters hostile, domineering attitudes and behaviors; and if viewing pornography leads viewers to trivialize rape, devalue their partners, and engage in uncommitted sex, then media influence is not a minor issue.

Social psychologists attribute the media's influence partly to the *social scripts* (mental tapes for how to act, provided by our culture) they portray. When we find ourselves in new situations, uncertain how to act, we rely on social scripts. After so many action films, youngsters may acquire a script that gets played when they face real-life conflicts. Challenged, they may "act like a man" by intimidating or eliminating the threat. Likewise, after viewing the multiple sexual innuendoes and acts found in most prime-time TV hours—often involving impulsive or short-term relationships—youths may acquire sexual scripts they later enact in real-life relationships (Kunkel & others, 2001; Sapolsky & Tabarlet, 1991). (To see how video games can teach social scripts, see Thinking Critically About: Do Video Games Teach, or Release, Violence?)

Might public consciousness be raised by making people aware of such information? (Turn the page to see Close-Up: Parallels Between Smoking Effects and Media Violence Effects.) In the 1940s, movies often depicted African-Americans as childlike superstitious buffoons. Today, we would not tolerate such images. In the 1960s and 1970s, some rock music and movies glamorized drug use. Responding to a tidal change in cultural attitudes, the entertainment industry now more often portrays the dark side of drug use. In response to growing public concern about violence in the media, television violence levels declined in the early 1990s (Gerbner & others, 1993). The growing sensitivity to violence has raised hopes that entertainers, producers, and audiences might someday look back with

DO VIDEO GAMES TEACH, OR RELEASE, VIOLENCE?

Violent video games became an issue for public debate after teen assassins in Paducah, Kentucky; Littleton, Colorado; and more than a dozen other places seemed to mimic the carnage in the splatter games they had so often played (Anderson, 2004a). In 2002, two Grand Rapids, Michigan, teens and a man in his early twenties spent part of a night drinking beer and playing Grand Theft Auto III, using cars to run down simulated pedestrians, then beating them with fists, leaving a bloody body behind (Kolker, 2002). Then they went driving on a real drive, spotted a 38-year-old man on a bicycle, ran him down with their car, got out, stomped and punched him, and returned home to play the game some more. (The man, a father of three, died six days later.)

When youths play such games, do they learn social scripts? Interactive games transport the player into their own vivid reality. When youths play Grand Theft Auto: San Andreas, they can carjack vehicles; run down pedestrians; do drive-by shootings; pick up a prostitute, have sex with her, and then kill her. What scripts are being learned?

Most abused children don't become abusive adults. And most youths who spend hundreds of hours in these mass murder simulators won't become teen assassins. Still, we wonder: If passively viewing violence elevates aggressive responses to provocation and lowers sensitivity to cruelty, what will be the effect of actively role-playing aggression? Although very few will commit slaughter, how many will become desensitized to violence and more open to violent acts?

Thirty-eight recent studies of more than 7000 people offer some answers (Anderson & others, 2004). Mary Ballard and Rose Wiest (1998) observed a rising level of arousal and feelings of hostility in

Desensitizing people to violence

college men as they played Mortal Kombat. Other studies have found that video games can prime aggressive thoughts and increase aggression. Consider this report from Craig Anderson and Karen Dill (2000): University men who have spent the most hours playing violent video games tend to be the most physically aggressive (for example, to acknowledge having hit or attacked someone else). In one experiment, people randomly assigned to play a game involving bloody murders with groaning victims (rather than to play nonviolent Myst) became more hostile. On a follow-up task, they also were more likely to blast intense noise at a fellow student.

Studies of young adolescents by Douglas Gentile and his co-researchers (2004) further reveal that kids who play a lot of violent video games see the world as more hostile, get into more arguments and fights, and get worse grades (those hours aren't spent reading or studying). Ah, but is this merely because naturally hostile kids are

drawn to such games? No, says Gentile. Even among violent-game players who scored low in hostility, the 38 percent who had been in fights was nearly 10 times the 4 percent involved in fights among their nongaming counterparts. Moreover, over time, the nongamers become more likely to have fights only if they start playing the violent games. Anderson (2004a) believes that, due partly to the more repetitive and active participation of game play, violent video games have even greater effects "than the well-documented effects of exposure to violent television and movies."

Although much remains to be learned, these studies again disconfirm the *catharsis hypothesis*—the idea that we feel better if we "blow off steam" by venting our emotions. Playing violent video games increases aggressive thoughts, emotions, and behaviors. One video game company's CEO rationalizes that we are "violent by nature [and] need release valves." "It's a way to process violent feelings and anxieties through a fantasy medium," adds a prominent civil liberties lawyer in explaining her hunch that playing violent games calms violent tendencies (Heins, 2004). Actually, expressing anger breeds more anger, and practicing violence breeds more violence. Tomorrow's games may have even greater effects. Social psychologists Susan Persky and Jim Blascovich (2005) created a violent video game for students to play on either a desktop computer or by putting on a headset and stepping into a virtual reality. As they predicted, the virtual reality more dramatically heightened aggressive feelings and behavior during and after the play.

"We are what we repeatedly do."

Aristotle

Mark C. Burnett/Stock, Boston

CLOSE-UP

PARALLELS BETWEEN SMOKING EFFECTS AND MEDIA VIOLENCE EFFECTS

Researchers Brad Bushman and Craig Anderson (2001) note that the correlation between viewing violence and behaving aggressively nearly equals the correlation between smoking and lung cancer. They also note other parallels:

1. Not everyone who smokes gets lung cancer.

2. Smoking is only one cause of lung cancer, although an important one.

3. The first cigarette can nauseate, but the sickening effect lessens with repetition.

4. The short-term effect of one cigarette is minor and dissipates within an hour or so.

5. The long-term, cumulative effect of smoking can be severe.

6. Corporate interests have denied the smoking–lung cancer link.

1. Not everyone who watches violence becomes aggressive.

2. Viewing violence is only one cause of aggression, although an important one.

3. The first violence exposure can upset, but the upset lessens with repetition.

4. One violent TV program can prime aggressive thoughts and behaviors, but the effect dissipates within an hour or so.

5. The long-term, cumulative effect of viewing violence is increased likelihood of habitual aggression.

6. Corporate interests have denied the viewing violence–aggression link.

embarrassment on the days when movies "entertained" people with scenes of torture, mutilation, and sexual coercion.

To sum up, research reveals biological, psychological, and social influences on aggressive behavior. Like so much else, aggression is a biopsychosocial phenomenon (**FIGURE 45.6**).

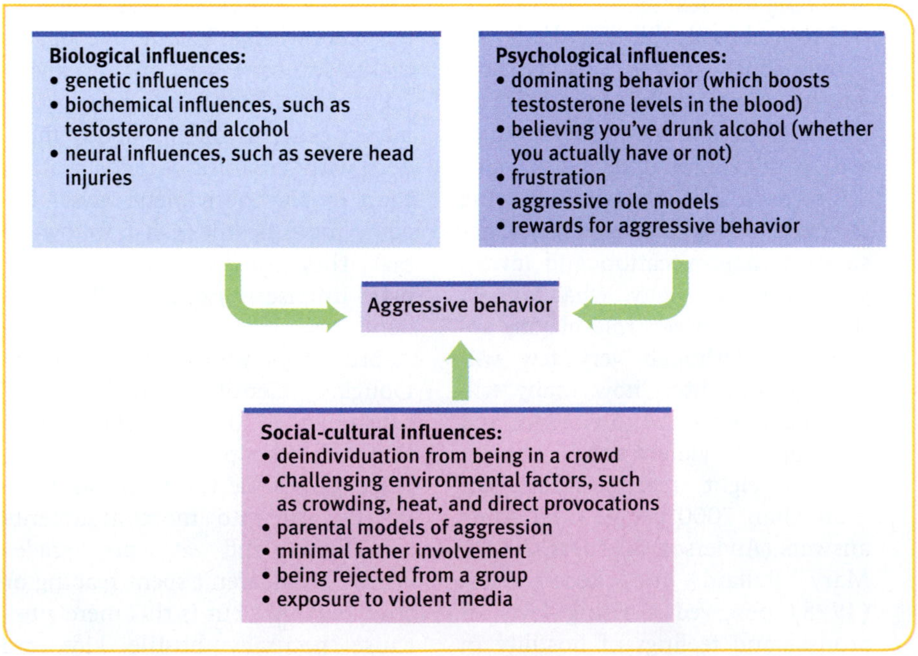

FIGURE 45.6
Biopsychosocial understanding of aggression
Many factors contribute to aggressive behavior, but there are many ways to combat these influences, including learning anger management and communication skills, and avoiding violent media and video games.

Biological influences:
• genetic influences
• biochemical influences, such as testosterone and alcohol
• neural influences, such as severe head injuries

Psychological influences:
• dominating behavior (which boosts testosterone levels in the blood)
• believing you've drunk alcohol (whether you actually have or not)
• frustration
• aggressive role models
• rewards for aggressive behavior

Aggressive behavior

Social-cultural influences:
• deindividuation from being in a crowd
• challenging environmental factors, such as crowding, heat, and direct provocations
• parental models of aggression
• minimal father involvement
• being rejected from a group
• exposure to violent media

Attraction

45-5: Why do we befriend or fall in love with some people but not with others?

Pause a moment and think about your relationships with two people—a close friend, and someone who stirs in you feelings of romantic love. What is the psychological chemistry that binds us together in these special sorts of attachments that help us cope with all other relationships? Social psychology suggests some answers.

The Psychology of Attraction

We endlessly wonder how we can win others' affection and what makes our own affections flourish or fade. Does familiarity breed contempt, or does it intensify our affection? Do birds of a feather flock together, or do opposites attract? Is beauty only skin deep, or does attractiveness matter greatly? Consider three ingredients of our liking for one another: proximity, physical attractiveness, and similarity.

Proximity

Before friendships become close, they must begin. *Proximity*—geographic nearness—is friendship's most powerful predictor. Proximity provides opportunities for aggression, but much more often it breeds liking. Study after study reveals that people are most inclined to like, and even to marry, those who live in the same neighborhood, who sit nearby in class, who work in the same office, who share the same parking lot, who eat in the same dining hall. Look around.

Why is proximity so conducive to liking? Obviously, part of the answer is the greater availability of those we often meet. But there is more to it than that. For one thing, repeated exposure to novel stimuli—be they nonsense syllables, musical selections, geometric figures, Chinese characters, human faces, or the letters of our own name—increases our liking for them (Moreland & Zajonc, 1982; Nuttin, 1987; Zajonc, 2001). People are even somewhat more likely to marry someone whose first or last name resembles their own (Jones & others, 2004).

This phenomenon, exploited by advertisers, we call the **mere exposure effect.** Within certain limits (Bornstein, 1989, 1999), familiarity breeds fondness. Richard Moreland and Scott Beach (1992) demonstrated this by having four equally attractive women silently attend a 200-student class for zero, 5, 10, or 15 class sessions. At the end of the course, students were shown slides of each woman and asked to rate each one's attractiveness. The most attractive? The ones they'd seen most often. The phenomenon will come as no surprise to the young Taiwanese man who wrote more than 700 letters to his girlfriend, urging her to marry him. She did marry—the mail carrier (Steinberg, 1993).

Familiarity breeds acceptance
When this rare white penguin was born in the Sydney, Australia, zoo, his tuxedoed peers ostracized him. Zookeepers thought they would need to dye him black to gain acceptance. But after three weeks of contact, the other penguins came to accept him.

■ **mere exposure effect** the phenomenon that repeated exposure to novel stimuli increases liking of them.

The mere exposure effect
The mere exposure effect applies even to ourselves. Because the human face is not perfectly symmetrical, the face we see in the mirror is not the same as the one our friends see. Most of us prefer the familiar mirror image, while our friends like the reverse (Mita & others, 1977). The Bill Gates known to us all is at left. The person he sees in the mirror each morning is shown at right, and that's the photo he would probably prefer.

© The New Yorker Collection, 2004, Mike Twohy from cartoonbank.com. All Rights Reserved.

"I'm going to have to recuse myself."

No face is more familiar than one's own. And that explains why, when Lisa De-Bruine (2002) had McMaster University students play a game with a supposed other player, they were more trusting and cooperative when the other person's image had some features of their own face morphed into it. In me I trust. In a follow-up study, DeBruine (2004) found that men also *liked* other men (and women liked other women) whose faces incorporated some morphed features of their own.

For our ancestors, the mere exposure phenomenon was adaptive. What was familiar was generally safe and approachable. What was unfamiliar was more often dangerous and threatening. Robert Zajonc (1998) concludes that evolution has hard-wired into us the tendency to bond with those who are familiar and to be wary of those who are unfamiliar. Gut-level prejudice against those culturally different may thus be a primitive, automatic emotional response (Devine, 1995).

Physical Attractiveness

Once proximity affords you contact, what most affects your first impressions: The person's sincerity? Intelligence? Personality? Hundreds of experiments reveal that it is something far more superficial: Appearance. For people taught that "beauty is only skin deep" and that "appearances can be deceiving," the power of physical attractiveness is unnerving. In one early study, Elaine Hatfield and her co-workers (Walster & others, 1966) randomly matched new University of Minnesota students for a Welcome Week dance. Before the dance, each student took a battery of personality and aptitude tests. On the night of the blind date, the couples danced and talked for more than two hours and then took a brief intermission to rate their dates. What determined whether they liked each other? As far as the researchers could determine, only one thing mattered: Physical attractiveness (which had been rated by the researchers beforehand). Both the men and the women liked good-looking dates best. Although women are more likely than men to *say* that another's looks don't affect them, a man's looks do affect women's behavior (Feingold, 1990; Sprecher, 1989; Woll, 1986).

People's physical attractiveness has wide-ranging effects. It predicts their frequency of dating, their feelings of popularity, and others' initial impressions of their personalities. We perceive attractive people to be healthier, happier, more sensitive, more successful, and more socially skilled, though not more honest or compassionate (Eagly & others, 1991; Feingold, 1992; Hatfield & Sprecher, 1986). Attractive, well-dressed people are more likely to make a favorable impression on potential employers and to enjoy occupational success (Cash & Janda, 1984; Langlois & others, 2000; Solomon, 1987). Income analyses show a penalty for plainness or obesity and a premium for beauty (Engemann & Owyang, 2005).

An analysis of 100 top-grossing films since 1940 found that attractive characters were portrayed as morally superior to unattractive characters (Smith & others, 1999).

> "Personal beauty is a greater recommendation than any letter of introduction."
>
> Aristotle, *Apothegems*, 330 B.C.

Percentage of Men and Women Who "Constantly Think About Their Looks"

	Men	Women
Canada	18%	20%
United States	17	27
Mexico	40	45
Venezuela	47	65

From Roper Starch survey, reported by McCool (1999).

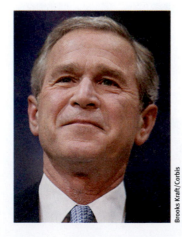

Brooks Kraft/Corbis

Good looks help people get good jobs
In the 2004 presidential election, many Americans found the face on the left more likeable and trustworthy.

But Hollywood modeling doesn't explain why, to judge from their gazing times, even babies prefer attractive over unattractive faces (Langlois & others, 1987). So do some blind people, discovered University of Birmingham professor John Hull (1990, p. 23) after going blind. A colleague's remarking on a woman's beauty would strangely affect his feelings. He finds this "deplorable . . . but I still feel it. . . . What can it matter to me what sighted men think of women . . . yet I do care what sighted men think, and I do not seem able to throw off this prejudice."

The importance of looks seems unfair and unenlightened. Why should it matter? Two thousand years ago the Roman statesman Cicero felt the same way: "The final good and the supreme duty of the wise person is to resist appearance." Cicero might be reassured by two other findings about attractiveness.

First, people's attractiveness is surprisingly unrelated to their self-esteem and happiness (Diener & others, 1995; Major & others, 1984). One reason may be that, except after comparing themselves with superattractive people, few people (thanks, perhaps, to the mere exposure effect) view themselves as unattractive (Thornton & Moore, 1993). Another reason is that strikingly attractive people are sometimes suspicious that praise for their work may simply be a reaction to their looks. When less attractive people are praised, they are more likely to accept it as sincere (Berscheid, 1981).

Cicero might also find comfort in knowing that attractiveness judgments are relative. The standards by which judges crown Miss Universe hardly apply to the whole planet. Rather, beauty is in the eye of the culture—beauty standards reflect one's place and time. Hoping to look attractive, people in different cultures have pierced their noses, lengthened their necks, bound their feet, and dyed or painted their skin and hair. They have gorged themselves to achieve a full figure or liposuctioned fat to achieve a slim one, applied chemicals hoping to rid themselves of unwanted hair or to regrow wanted hair, strapped on leather garments to make their breasts seem smaller or surgically filled their breasts with silicone and put on Wonder Bras to make them look bigger. In North America, the ultra-thin ideal of the Roaring Twenties gave way to the soft, voluptuous Marilyn Monroe ideal of the 1950s, only to be replaced by today's lean yet busty ideal. Americans now spend more on beauty supplies than on education and social services combined and, when still not satisfied, undergo millions of cosmetic medical treatments each year, including plastic surgery, Botox skin smoothing, teeth-capping or whitening, and laser hair removal (Wall, 2002). But the beauty race is like the arms race, with the result that since 1970 more and more women have become *un*happy with their appearance (Feingold & Mazella, 1998).

Some aspects of attractiveness, however, do cross place and time (Cunningham & others, 2005; Langlois & others, 2000). Men in 37 cultures, from Australia to Zambia, judge women as more attractive if they have a youthful appearance. Women feel attracted to healthy-looking men, but especially to those who seem mature, dominant, and affluent.

When Neanderthals fall in love.

© 1999 by Leigh Robin, Creators Syndicate, Inc.

New York Times columnist Maureen Dowd on liposuction (January 19, 2000): "Women in the 50's vacuumed. Women in the 00's *are* vacuumed. Our Hoovers have turned on us!"

© ABC TV. Courtesy: Everett Collection

Extreme makeover

In affluent, beauty-conscious cultures, increasing numbers of people, such as this woman from the American TV show *Extreme Makeover,* have turned to cosmetic surgery to improve their looks. If money were no concern, might you ever do the same?

Victor Englebert/Photo Researchers

Margaret Gowan/Tony Stone Worldwide

Nancy Brown/The Image Bank

In the eye of the beholder
Conceptions of attractiveness vary by culture. Moreover, the current concept of attractiveness in Morocco, Kenya, and Scandinavia may well change in the future.

Cultural standards aside, attractiveness also depends on our feelings about the person. In a Rodgers and Hammerstein musical, Prince Charming asks Cinderella, "Do I love you because you're beautiful, or are you beautiful because I love you?" Chances are it's both. As we see our loved ones again and again, their physical imperfections grow less noticeable and their attractiveness grows more apparent (Beaman & Klentz, 1983; Gross & Crofton, 1977). Shakespeare said it in *A Midsummer Night's Dream*: "Love looks not with the eyes, but with the mind." Come to love someone and watch beauty grow.

> "Love has ever in view the absolute loveliness of that which it beholds."
>
> George MacDonald, *Unspoken Sermons*, 1867

Similarity

Let's say that proximity has brought you into contact with someone and that your appearance has made a favorable first impression. What now influences whether acquaintances develop into friends? For example, as you get to know someone better, is the chemistry better if you are opposites or if you are alike?

It makes a good story—extremely different types living in harmonious union: Rat, Mole, and Badger in *The Wind in the Willows,* Frog and Toad in Arnold Lobel's books. The stories delight us by expressing what we seldom experience, for we tend not to like dissimilar people (Rosenbaum, 1986). In real life, opposites retract. Birds that flock together usually are of a feather. Friends and couples are far more likely to share common attitudes, beliefs, and interests (and, for that matter, age, religion, race, education, intelligence, smoking behavior, and economic status) than are randomly paired people. Much as you and I may dismiss such differences, seeing ourselves as one human family in a global village, we can't hang out with 6 billion people. Moreover, the more alike people are, the more their liking endures (Byrne, 1971). Journalist Walter Lippmann was right to suppose that love is best sustained "when the lovers love many things together, and not merely each other." That is also the assumption of one psychologist-founded Internet dating site, which claims to use the similarities that mark happy couples to match singles, some 10,000 of whom are known to have married (Carter & Snow, 2004; Warren, 2005). Similarity breeds content.

Proximity, attractiveness, and similarity are not the only determinants of attraction. We also like those who like us, especially when our self-image is low. When we believe someone likes us, we respond to them more warmly, which leads them to like us even more (Curtis & Miller, 1986). To be liked is powerfully rewarding.

Indeed, a simple *reward theory of attraction*—that we will like those whose behavior is rewarding to us and that we will continue relationships that offer more rewards than costs—can explain all the findings we have considered so far. When a person lives or works in close proximity with someone else, it costs less time and effort to develop the friendship and enjoy its benefits. Attractive people are aesthetically pleasing, and associating with them can be socially rewarding. Those with similar views reward us by validating our own.

© The New Yorker Collection, 2005, Paul Noth from cartoonbank.com. All Rights Reserved.

"I can't wait to see what you're like online."

HI & LOIS

Reprinted with special permission of King Features Syndicate.

Romantic Love

45-6: Does our love for a partner remain the same as time passes?

Occasionally, people move quickly from initial impressions, to friendship, to the more intense, complex, and mysterious state of romantic love. Elaine Hatfield (1988) distinguishes two types of love: temporary passionate love and a more enduring companionate love.

Passionate Love

Noting that arousal is a key ingredient of **passionate love,** Hatfield suggests that Stanley Schachter's two-factor theory of emotion can help us understand this intense positive absorption in another. The theory assumes that (1) emotions have two ingredients—physical arousal plus cognitive appraisal—and that (2) arousal from any source can enhance one emotion or another, depending on how we interpret and label the arousal.

In tests of this theory, college men have been aroused by fright, by running in place, by viewing erotic materials, or by listening to humorous or repulsive monologues. They were then introduced to an attractive woman and asked to rate her (or their girlfriend). Unlike unaroused men, those who were stirred up attributed some of their arousal to the woman or girlfriend and felt more attracted to her (Carducci & others, 1978; Dermer & Pyszczynski, 1978; White & Kight, 1984).

Outside the laboratory, Donald Dutton and Arthur Aron (1974, 1989) went to two bridges across British Columbia's rocky Capilano River. One, a swaying footbridge, was 230 feet above the rocks; the other was low and solid. An attractive young female accomplice intercepted men coming off each bridge, sought their help in filling out a short questionnaire, and then offered her phone number in case they wanted to hear more about her project. Far more of those who had just crossed the high bridge—which left their hearts pounding—accepted the number and later called the woman. To be revved up and to associate some of that arousal with a desirable person is to feel the pull of passion. Adrenaline makes the heart grow fonder.

Companionate Love

Although the spark of romantic love often endures, the intense absorption in the other, the thrill of the romance, the giddy "floating on a cloud" feeling typically fades. Does this mean the French are correct in saying that "love makes the time pass and time makes love pass"? Or can friendship and commitment keep a relationship going after the passion cools?

Hatfield reports that as love matures it becomes a steadier **companionate love**—a deep, affectionate attachment. There may be adaptive wisdom to this change from passion to affection. Passionate love often produces children, whose survival is aided by the parents' waning obsession with one another. Social psychologist Ellen Berscheid and her colleagues (1984) noted that the failure to appreciate passionate

> "When two people are under the influence of the most violent, most insane, most delusive, and most transient of passions, they are required to swear that they will remain in that excited, abnormal, and exhausting condition continuously until death do them part."
>
> George Bernard Shaw, "Getting Married," 1908

■ **passionate love** an aroused state of intense positive absorption in another, usually present at the beginning of a love relationship.

■ **companionate love** the deep affectionate attachment we feel for those with whom our lives are intertwined.

MATRIMONY

Sometimes passionate love becomes enduring companionate love, sometimes not *(invert the picture)*
What, in addition to similar attitudes and interests, predicts long-term loving attachment?

Courtship and Matrimony (From the collection of Werner Nekes)

COURTSHIP

> "When a match has equal partners then I fear not."
>
> Aeschylus, *Prometheus Bound*, 478 B.C.

love's limited half-life can doom a relationship: "If the inevitable odds against eternal passionate love in a relationship were better understood, more people might choose to be satisfied with the quieter feelings of satisfaction and contentment." Indeed, recognizing the short duration of passionate love, some societies have deemed such feelings an irrational reason for marrying. Better, such cultures say, to choose (or have someone choose for you) a partner with a compatible background and interests. Non-Western cultures, where people rate love less important for marriage, do have lower divorce rates (Levine & others, 1995).

One key to a gratifying and enduring relationship is **equity:** Both partners receive in proportion to what they give. When equity exists—when both partners freely give and receive, when they share decision making—their chances for sustained and satisfying companionate love are good (Gray-Little & Burks, 1983; Van Yperen & Buunk, 1990). Mutually sharing self and possessions, giving and getting emotional support, promoting and caring about one another's welfare are at the core of every type of loving relationship (Sternberg & Grajek, 1984). It's true for lovers, for parent and child, and for intimate friends.

Another vital ingredient of loving relationships is **self-disclosure,** the revealing of intimate details about ourselves—our likes and dislikes, our dreams and worries, our proud and shameful moments. "When I am with my friend," noted the Roman statesman Seneca, "me thinks I am alone, and as much at liberty to speak anything as to think it." Self-disclosure breeds liking, and liking breeds self-disclosure (Collins & Miller, 1994). As one person reveals a little, the other reciprocates, the first then reveals more, and on and on, as friends or lovers move to deeper intimacy. Each increase in intimacy rekindles passion (Baumeister & Bratslavsky, 1999).

One experiment marched pairs of volunteer students through 45 minutes of increasingly self-disclosing conversation—from "When did you last sing to yourself" to "When did you last cry in front of another person? By yourself?" By the experiment's end, those experiencing the escalating intimacy felt remarkably close to their conversation partner, much closer than others who had spent the time with small-talk questions, such as "What was your high school like?" (Aron & others, 1997). Given self-disclosing intimacy plus mutually supportive equality, the odds favor enduring companionate love.

■ **equity** a condition in which people receive from a relationship in proportion to what they give to it.

■ **self-disclosure** revealing intimate aspects of oneself to others.

Altruism

45-7: Why do we help others? When are we most—and least—likely to help?

Carl Wilkens, a Seventh Day Adventist missionary, was living with his family in Kigali, Rwanda, when Hutu militia began to slaughter the Tutsi in 1994. The U.S. government, church leaders, and friends all implored Wilkens to leave. He refused. After evacuating his family, and even after every other American had left Kigali, he alone stayed and contested the 800,000-person genocide. When the militia came to kill him and his Tutsi servants, his Hutu neighbors deterred them. Despite repeated death threats, he spent his days risking roadblocks to take food and water to orphanages and to negotiate, plead, and bully his way through the bloodshed, saving lives time and again. "It just seemed the right thing to do," he later explained (Kristof, 2004).

Elsewhere in Kigali, Paul Rusesabagina, a Hutu married to a Tutsi and the acting manager of a luxury hotel, was sheltering more than 1200 terrified Tutsis and moderate Hutus. When international peacemakers abandoned the city and hostile militia threatened his guests in the "Hotel Rwanda" (as it came to be called in a 2004 movie), the courageous Rusesabagina began cashing in past favors, bribing the militia, and telephoning influential persons abroad to bring pressure on local authorities, thereby sparing the lives of the hotel's occupants from the surrounding chaos.

Such unselfish regard for the welfare of others is **altruism,** which became a major concern of social psychologists after an especially vile act of sexual violence. On March 13, 1964, a stalker repeatedly stabbed Kitty Genovese, then raped her as she lay dying outside her Queens, New York, apartment at 3:30 A.M. "Oh, my God, he stabbed me!" Genovese screamed into the early morning stillness. "Please help me!" Windows opened and lights went on as neighbors—38, said an initial *New York Times* report, though the number was later contested—heard her screams. Her attacker fled and then returned to stab her eight more times and rape her again. Not until he had fled for good did anyone so much as call the police, at 3:50 A.M.

■ **altruism** unselfish regard for the welfare of others.

> "Probably no single incident has caused social psychologists to pay as much attention to an aspect of social behavior as Kitty Genovese's murder."
>
> R. Lance Shotland (1984)

Bystander Intervention

Reflecting on the Genovese murder and other such tragedies, most commentators were outraged by the bystanders' "apathy" and "indifference." Rather than blaming the onlookers, social psychologists John Darley and Bibb Latané (1968b) attributed their inaction to an important situational factor—the presence of others. Given certain circumstances, they suspected, most of us might behave similarly.

After staging emergencies under various conditions, Darley and Latané assembled their findings into a decision scheme: We will help only if the situation enables us first to notice the incident, then to interpret it as an emergency, and finally to assume responsibility for helping (**FIGURE 45.7**). At each step, the presence of other bystanders

FIGURE 45.7

The decision-making process for bystander intervention

Before helping, one must first notice an emergency, then correctly interpret it, and then feel responsible. (From Darley & Latané, 1968b.)

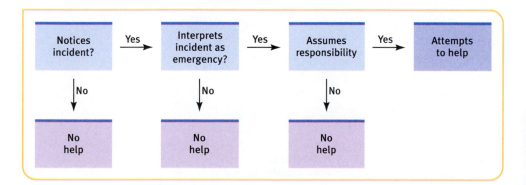

Notices incident? —Yes→ Interprets incident as emergency? —Yes→ Assumes responsibility —Yes→ Attempts to help

No ↓ No help   No ↓ No help   No ↓ No help

Akos Szilvasi/Stock, Boston

turns people away from the path that leads to helping. In the laboratory and on the street, people in a group of strangers are more likely than solitary individuals to keep their eyes focused on what they themselves are doing or where they are going. If they notice an unusual situation, they may infer from the blasé reactions of the other passersby that the situation is not an emergency. "The person lying on the sidewalk must be drunk," they think, and move on.

But sometimes, as with the Genovese murder, the emergency is unambiguous and people still fail to help. The witnesses looking out through their windows noticed the incident, correctly interpreted the emergency, and yet failed to assume responsibility. Why? To find out, Darley and Latané (1968a) simulated a physical emergency in their laboratory. University students participated in a discussion over an intercom. Each student was in a separate cubicle, and only the person whose microphone was switched on could be heard. One of the students was an accomplice of the experimenters. When his turn came, he made sounds as though he were having an epileptic seizure and called for help.

How did the other students react? As **FIGURE 45.8** shows, those who believed only they could hear the victim—and therefore thought they bore total responsibility for helping him—usually went to his aid. Those who thought others also could hear were more likely to react as did Kitty Genovese's neighbors. When more people shared responsibility for helping—when there was diffusion of responsibility—any single listener was less likely to help.

In hundreds of additional experiments, psychologists have studied the factors that influence bystanders' willingness to relay an emergency phone call, aid a stranded motorist, donate blood, pick up dropped books, contribute money, and give time. For example, Latané, James Dabbs (1975), and 145 collaborators took 1497 elevator rides in three cities and "accidentally" dropped coins or pencils in front of 4813 fellow passengers. The women coin droppers were more likely to receive help than were the men—a gender difference often reported by other researchers (Eagly & Crowley, 1986). But the major finding was the **bystander effect**—any particular bystander was less likely to give aid with other bystanders present. When alone with the person in need, 40 percent helped; in the presence of five other bystanders, only 20 percent helped.

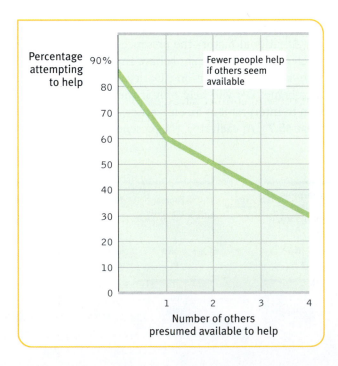

FIGURE 45.8

Responses to a simulated physical emergency

When people thought they alone heard the calls for help from a person they believed to be having an epileptic seizure, they usually helped. But when they thought four others were also hearing the calls, fewer than a third responded. (From Darley & Latané, 1968a.)

From their observations of behavior in tens of thousands of such situations, altruism researchers have discerned some additional patterns. The *best* odds of our helping someone occur when

- the person appears to need and deserve help.
- the person is in some way similar to us.
- we have just observed someone else being helpful.
- we are not in a hurry.
- we are in a small town or rural area.
- we are feeling guilty.
- we are focused on others and not preoccupied.
- we are in a good mood.

This last result, that happy people are helpful people, is one of the most consistent findings in all of psychology. No matter how people are cheered—whether by being made to feel successful and intelligent, by thinking happy thoughts, by finding money, or even by receiving a posthypnotic suggestion—they become more generous and more eager to help (Carlson & others, 1988).

> "Oh, make us happy and you make us good!"
>
> Robert Browning, *The Ring and the Book*, 1868

Conflict and Peacemaking

45-8 : What social processes fuel conflict?

We live in surprising times. With astonishing speed, late-twentieth-century democratic movements swept away totalitarian rule in Eastern European countries, and hopes for a new world order displaced the Cold War chill. And yet, the twenty-first century began with terrorist acts and war, and the world continued to spend $2 billion every day for arms and armies—money that could have been used for housing, nutrition, education, and health. Knowing that wars begin in human minds, psychologists have wondered: What in the human mind causes destructive conflict? How might the perceived threats of social diversity be replaced by a spirit of cooperation?

To a social psychologist, a **conflict** is a seeming incompatibility of actions, goals, or ideas. The elements of conflict are much the same at all levels, from nations at war, to cultural disputes within a society, to individuals in a marital dispute. In each situation, people become enmeshed in a potentially destructive social process that can produce results no one wants.

Enemy Perceptions

Psychologists have noticed that those in conflict have a curious tendency to form diabolical images of one another. These distorted images are ironically similar, so similar in fact that we call them *mirror-image perceptions:* As we see "them"—as untrustworthy and evil intentioned—so "they" see us. Each demonizes the other.

Mirror-image perceptions often feed a vicious cycle of hostility. If Juan believes Maria is annoyed with him, he may snub her, causing her to act in ways that justify his perception. As with individuals, so with countries. Perceptions can become self-fulfilling prophecies. They may confirm themselves by influencing the other country to react in ways that seem to justify them.

In the early twenty-first century, many Americans came to loathe Saddam Hussein. Like the "evil" Saddam Hussein, declared George W. Bush (2001), "some of today's tyrants are gripped by an implacable hatred of the United States of America. They hate our friends, they hate our values, they hate democracy and freedom and individual liberty. Many care little for the lives of their own people." Hussein (2002) reciprocated the perception, seeing the United States as "an evil tyrant" that, with Satan as its protector, lusted for oil and aggressively attacked those who "defend what is right."

■ **bystander effect** the tendency for any given bystander to be less likely to give aid if other bystanders are present.

■ **conflict** a perceived incompatibility of actions, goals, or ideas.

■ **superordinate goals** shared goals that override differences among people and require their cooperation.

The point is not that truth must lie midway between two such views (one may be more accurate). The point is that enemy perceptions often form mirror images. Moreover, as enemies change, so do perceptions. In American minds and media, the "bloodthirsty, cruel, treacherous" Japanese of World War II later became our "intelligent, hardworking, self-disciplined, resourceful allies" (Gallup, 1972).

How can we make peace? Can cooperation, communication, and conciliation transform the antagonisms fed by prejudice and conflicts into attitudes that promote peace? Research indicates that, in some cases, they can.

Cooperation

45-9: How can we transform feelings of prejudice, aggression, and conflict into attitudes that promote peace?

Does it help to put two conflicting parties into close contact? It depends. When such contact is noncompetitive and between parties with equal status, such as fellow store clerks, it may help. Initially prejudiced co-workers of different races have, in such circumstances, usually come to accept one another. Among North Americans and Europeans, friendly contact with ethnic minorities has led to less prejudice (Pettigrew, 1969, 2004). However, mere contact is not always enough. In most desegregated schools, ethnic groups resegregate themselves in the lunchrooms and on the school grounds (Clack & others, 2005; Schofield, 1986). People in each group often think that they would welcome more contact with the other group, but they assume the other group does not reciprocate the wish (Shelton & Richeson, 2005). "I don't reach out to them, because I don't want to be rebuffed; they don't reach out to me, because they're just not interested." When such mirror-image misperceptions are corrected, friendships may then form and prejudices melt.

> "You cannot shake hands with a clenched fist."
>
> Indira Gandhi, 1971

To see if enemies could overcome their differences, researcher Muzafer Sherif (1966) first instigated conflict. He placed 22 Oklahoma City boys in two separate areas of a Boy Scout camp. He then put the two groups through a series of competitive activities, with prizes going to the victors. Before long, each group became intensely proud of itself and hostile to the other group's "sneaky," "smart-alecky stinkers." Food wars broke out during meals. Cabins were ransacked. Fistfights had to be broken up by members of the camp staff. When Sherif brought the two groups together, they avoided one another, except to taunt and threaten.

Nevertheless, within a few days Sherif transformed these young enemies into jovial comrades. He gave them **superordinate goals**—shared goals that overrode their differences and that could be achieved only through cooperation. A planned disruption of the camp water supply necessitated that all 22 boys work together to

Superordinate goals override differences
Cooperative efforts to achieve shared goals are an effective way to break down social barriers.

Syracuse Newspapers / The Image Works

restore water. Renting a movie in those pre-DVD days required their pooled resources. A stalled truck needed the combined force of all the boys pulling and pushing together to get it moving. Having used isolation and competition to make strangers into enemies, Sherif used shared predicaments and goals to reconcile the enemies and make them friends. What reduced conflict was not mere contact, but *cooperative* contact.

A shared predicament—a fearsome external threat and a superordinate desire to overcome it—likewise had a powerfully unifying effect in the weeks after 9/11. Nothing breeds solidarity quite like a common enemy. As suicide attacks in Israel can unify partisan Jews, and as Israeli military attacks on Palestinians can unify diverse Muslims, so Americans immediately felt that "we" were under attack. Gallup-surveyed approval of "our President" shot up from 51 percent the week before the attack to a highest-ever level of 90 percent 10 days after, just surpassing the previous approval-rating record of 89 percent enjoyed by his father, George Bush, at the climax of the 1991 Persian Gulf War (Newport, 2002). In chat groups and everyday speech, even the word *we* (relative to *I*) surged in the immediate aftermath (Pennebaker, 2002).

John Dovidio and Samuel Gaertner (1999) report that cooperation has especially positive effects when it leads people to define a new, inclusive group that dissolves their former subgroups. Seat the members of two groups not on opposite sides, but alternately around the table. Give them a new, shared name. Have them work together. Such experiences change "us and them" into "we." Those once perceived as being in another group now are seen as part of one's own group. One 18-year-old New Jersey man would not be surprised. After 9/11, he explained a shift in his social identity: "I just thought of myself as black. But now I feel like I'm an American, more than ever" (Sengupta, 2001). In one experiment by Dovidio and his colleagues (2004), white Americans who read a newspaper article about a terrorist threat against all Americans subsequently expressed reduced prejudice against African-Americans.

During the 1970s, several teams of educational researchers simultaneously wondered: If cooperative contacts between members of rival groups encourage positive attitudes, could we apply this principle in multicultural schools? Could we promote interracial friendships by replacing competitive classroom situations with cooperative ones? And could cooperative learning maintain or even enhance student achievement? Many experiments confirm that in all three cases, the answer is yes (Johnson & Johnson, 1989, 1994; Slavin & others, 2003). Members of interracial groups who work together on projects and play together on athletic teams typically come to feel friendly toward those of the other race. So do those who engage in cooperative classroom learning. So encouraging are these results that thousands of teachers have introduced interracial cooperative learning into their classrooms. Working with fellow students in all their diversity sets the stage, declared the Carnegie Council on Adolescent Development (1989), for "adult work life and for citizenship in a multicultural society."

The power of cooperative activity to make friends of former enemies has led psychologists to urge increased international exchange and cooperation (Klineberg, 1984). As we engage in mutually beneficial trade, as we work to protect our common destiny on this fragile planet, and as we become more aware that our hopes and fears are shared, we can change misperceptions that lead to fragmentation and conflict into a solidarity based on common interests. As working toward shared goals reminds us, we are more alike than different.

Communication

When real-life conflicts become intense, a third-party mediator—a marriage counselor, labor mediator, diplomat, community volunteer—may facilitate much-needed communication (Rubin & others, 1994). Mediators help each party to voice its viewpoint and to understand the other's. By leading each side to think about the other's underlying needs and goals, the mediator aims to replace a competitive orientation with a cooperative orientation that aims at a mutually beneficial resolution. A classic

> "Most of us have overlapping identities which unite us with very different groups. We *can* love what we are, without hating what—and who—we are *not*. We can thrive in our own tradition, even as we learn from others."
>
> U.N. Secretary General Kofi Annan, Nobel Prize Lecture, 2001

> "I am prepared this day to declare myself a citizen of the world, and to invite everyone everywhere to embrace this broader vision of our interdependent world, our common quest for justice, and ultimately for Peace on Earth."
>
> Father Theodore Hesburgh, *The Human Imperative*, 1974

■ **GRIT** Graduated and Reciprocated Initiatives in Tension-Reduction—a strategy designed to decrease international tensions.

example: Two friends, after quarreling over an orange, agreed to split it. One squeezed his half for juice. The other used the peel from her half to make a cake. If only the two had understood each other's motives, they could have hit on the win-win solution of one having all the juice, the other all the peel.

Such understanding and cooperative resolution is most needed, yet least likely, in times of anger or crisis (Bodenhausen & others, 1994; Tetlock, 1988). When conflicts intensify, images become more stereotyped, communication more difficult, and judgments more rigid.

Conciliation

When tension and suspicion peak, cooperation and communication may become impossible. Each party is likely to threaten, coerce, or retaliate. In the weeks before the Persian Gulf War, President George Bush threatened, in the full glare of publicity, to "kick Saddam's ass." Saddam Hussein communicated in kind, threatening to make Americans "swim in their own blood."

Under such conditions, is there an alternative to war or surrender? Social psychologist Charles Osgood (1962, 1980) has advocated a strategy of "Graduated and Reciprocated Initiatives in Tension-Reduction," nicknamed **GRIT.** In applying GRIT, one side first announces its recognition of mutual interests and its intent to reduce tensions. It then initiates one or more small, conciliatory acts. Without weakening one's retaliatory capability, this modest beginning opens the door for reciprocation by the other party. Should the enemy respond with hostility, one reciprocates in kind. But so, too, with any conciliatory response. Thus, President Kennedy's gesture of stopping atmospheric nuclear tests began a series of reciprocated conciliatory acts that culminated in the 1993 atmospheric test-ban treaty.

In laboratory experiments, GRIT has been an effective strategy for increasing trust and cooperation (Lindskold & others, 1978, 1988). Even during intense personal conflict, when communication has been nonexistent, a small conciliatory gesture—a smile, a touch, a word of apology—may work wonders. Conciliations allow both parties to begin edging down the tension ladder to a safer rung where communication and mutual understanding can begin.

And how good that such can happen, for civilization advances not by cultural isolation—maintaining walls around ethnic enclaves—but by tapping the knowledge, the skills, and the arts that are each culture's legacy to the whole human race. Thomas Sowell (1991) observed that, thanks to cultural sharing, every modern society is enriched by a cultural mix. We have China to thank for paper and printing, and for the magnetic compass that opened the great explorations. We have Egypt to thank for trigonometry. We have the Islamic world and India's Hindus to thank for our Arabic numerals. While celebrating and claiming these diverse cultural legacies, we can also welcome the enrichment of today's social diversity. We can view ourselves as instruments in a human orchestra. And we can therefore affirm our own culture's heritage while building bridges of communication, understanding, and cooperation across cultural traditions as we think about, influence, and relate to one another.

© The New Yorker Collection, 1983, W. Miller from cartoonbank.com. All Rights Reserved.

"To begin with, I would like to express my sincere thanks and deep appreciation for the opportunity to meet with you. While there are still profound differences between us, I think the very fact of my presence here today is a major breakthrough."

>> MODULE REVIEW

45-1: What are the social and emotional roots of prejudice?

Prejudice is a mixture of beliefs (often *stereotypes*), emotions, and predispositions to action. It often arises as those who enjoy social and economic superiority attempt to justify the status quo. Even the temporary assignment of people to groups can cause an *ingroup bias*. Prejudice may also boost our self-esteem, and cause us, when frustrated, to focus anger on a *scapegoat*.

45-2: What are the cognitive roots of prejudice?

Research reveals how our ways of processing information—for example, by overestimating similarities when we categorize people or by noticing and remembering vivid cases—work to create stereotypes. In addition, favored social groups often rationalize their higher status with the *just-world phenomenon*.

45-3: What biological factors make us more prone to hurt one another?

Aggressive behavior, like all behavior, is a product of nature and nurture. Although psychologists dismiss the idea that *aggression* is instinctual, aggressiveness is genetically influenced. Moreover, certain areas of the brain, when stimulated, activate or inhibit aggression, and these neural areas are biochemically influenced.

45-4: What psychological factors may trigger aggressive behavior?

A variety of psychological factors, such as heat, crowding, and provocation, heighten people's hostility. Such stimuli are especially likely to trigger aggression in those rewarded for aggression, those who have learned aggression from role models, and those who have been influenced by media violence. Enacting violence in video games also heightens aggressive behavior. Such factors desensitize people to cruelty and prime them to behave aggressively when provoked. Media influences may also cultivate the rape myth (the idea that some women invite or enjoy rape) and make sexual aggression seem less terrible.

45-5: Why do we befriend or fall in love with some people but not with others?

Three factors are known to affect our liking for one another. Proximity—geographical nearness—is conducive to attraction, partly because *mere exposure* to novel stimuli enhances liking. Physical attractiveness influences social opportunities and the way one is perceived. As acquaintanceship moves toward friendship, similarity of attitudes and interests greatly increases liking.

45-6: Does our love for a partner remain the same as time passes?

We can view *passionate love* as an aroused state that we cognitively label as love. The strong affection of *companionate love*, which often emerges as a relationship matures, is enhanced by an *equitable* relationship and by intimate *self-disclosure*.

45-7: Why do we help others? When are we most—and least—likely to help?

Altruism is unselfish regard for the well-being of others. Any given bystander is less likely to help if others are present. The *bystander effect* is especially apparent in situations where the presence of others inhibits one's noticing the event, interpreting it as an emergency, or assuming responsibility for offering help. Many factors, including mood, also influence willingness to help someone in distress.

45-8: What social processes fuel conflict?

Conflicts between individuals and cultures often arise from destructive social processes. The spiral of conflict feeds and is fed by distorted mirror-image perceptions, in which each party views itself as moral and the other as untrustworthy and evil-intentioned.

45-9: How can we transform feelings of prejudice, aggression, and conflict into attitudes that promote peace?

Enemies sometimes become friends, especially when the circumstances favor cooperation to achieve *superordinate goals*, understanding through communication, and reciprocated conciliatory gestures.

>> REHEARSE IT!

1. Experiments show that when people are temporarily frustrated, they express more intense prejudice. When things go wrong, prejudice provides an outlet for our anger—and gives us someone to blame. This effect is best described by

   a. ingroup bias.
   b. scapegoat theory.
   c. mere exposure effect.
   d. the just-world phenomenon.

2. Stereotypes arise in part from our tendency to judge the frequency of events in terms of cases that come readily to mind. Thus, if several well-publicized murders are committed by members of a particular group, we tend to react with fear and suspicion toward all members of that group. In other words, we

   a. blame the victim.
   b. overgeneralize from vivid, memorable cases.
   c. create a scapegoat.
   d. rationalize inequality.

3. Aggression—physical or verbal behavior intended to hurt someone—is influenced by biology at the genetic, neural, and biochemical levels. Evidence of a biochemical influence on aggression is the finding that

   a. aggressive behavior varies widely from culture to culture.
   b. animals can be bred for aggressiveness.
   c. stimulation of an area of the brain's limbic system produces aggressive behavior.
   d. a higher-than-average level of the hormone testosterone is associated with violent behavior in males.

4. Studies show that parents of delinquent young people tend to use beatings to enforce discipline. This demonstrates that aggression can be

   a. learned through direct rewards.
   b. triggered by exposure to violent media.
   c. learned through observation of aggressive models.
   d. caused by hormone changes at puberty.

5. A 1986 conference of social scientists studying the effects of pornography unanimously agreed that violent pornography

   a. has little effect on most viewers.
   b. is the primary cause of reported and unreported rapes.
   c. leads viewers to be more accepting of coercion in sexual relations.
   d. has no effect, other than short-term arousal and entertainment.

6. There is considerable controversy about the effects of heavy exposure to television programs showing violence. However, most experts would agree that repeated viewing of television violence

   a. makes all viewers significantly more aggressive.
   b. has little effect on viewers.
   c. dulls the viewer's sensitivity to violence.
   d. makes viewers angry and frustrated.

7. Repeated exposure to a stimulus—including a new human face—increases our liking of the stimulus. This mere exposure effect helps explain why proximity is a powerful predictor of friendship and marriage, and why, for example, people tend to marry someone

   a. about as attractive as themselves.
   b. who lives or works nearby.
   c. of similar religious or ethnic background.
   d. who has similar attitudes and habits.

8. Male subjects who are aroused by various stimuli and then introduced to an attractive woman tend to attribute their arousal to the woman, and to report positive feelings toward her. This supports the two-factor theory of emotion, which assumes that emotions such as passionate love consist of physical arousal plus

   a. a reward.
   b. proximity.
   c. companionate love.
   d. our interpretation of that arousal.

9. Companionate love is described as a deep, affectionate attachment. _____ is/are vital to the maintenance of such loving relationships.

   a. Equity and self-disclosure
   b. Physical attraction
   c. Intense positive absorption
   d. Passionate love

10. Many factors determine whether a bystander will come to the aid of a stranger in an emergency. One is the bystander effect, which states that a particular bystander is less likely to give aid if

   a. the victim is similar to the bystander in appearance.
   b. no one else is present.
   c. other people are present.
   d. the incident occurs in a deserted or rural area.

11. Social psychologists have attempted to define the circumstances that facilitate conflict resolution. One way of fostering cooperation is by providing contentious groups with superordinate goals, which are

   a. the goals of friendly competition.
   b. shared goals that override differences.
   c. goals for winning at negotiations.
   d. goals for reducing conflict through increased contact.

Answers:
1. b, 2. b, 3. d, 4. c, 5. c, 6. c, 7. b, 8. d, 9. a, 10. c, 11. b.

>> Terms and Concepts to Remember

social psychology, p. 594
prejudice, p. 594
stereotype, p. 594
discrimination, p. 594
ingroup, p. 597
outgroup, p. 597
ingroup bias, p. 597

scapegoat theory, p. 598
just-world phenomenon, p. 599
aggression, p. 599
frustration-aggression principle, p. 601
mere exposure effect, p. 607
passionate love, p. 611
companionate love, p. 611

equity, p. 612
self-disclosure, p. 612
altruism, p. 613
bystander effect, p. 614
conflict, p. 615
superordinate goals, p. 616
GRIT, p. 618

>> Test Yourself

1. Why didn't anybody help Kitty Genovese? What social relations principle did this incident illustrate?

   (Answer in Appendix C.)

Multiple-choice **self-tests** and more may be found at www.worthpublishers.com/myers.

APPENDIX A

Statistical Reasoning in Everyday Life

Today's statistics are tools that help us see and interpret what the unaided eye might miss. To be an educated person today is to be able to apply simple statistical principles to everyday reasoning. One needn't remember complicated formulas to think more clearly and critically about data.

A-1: What is the first important point to remember when assessing studies that use statistical reasoning?

Top-of-the-head estimates often misread reality and then mislead the public. Someone throws out a big round number. Others echo it, and before long the big round number becomes public misinformation. A few examples:

- *One percent of Americans (2.7 million) are homeless.* Or is it 300,000, an earlier estimate by the federal government? Or 600,000, an estimate by the Urban Institute (Crossen, 1994)?
- *Ten percent of people are lesbians or gay men.* Or is it 2 to 3 percent, as suggested by various national surveys?
- *We ordinarily use but 10 percent of our brain.* Or is it closer to 100 percent? (Which 90 percent, or even 10 percent, would you be willing to sacrifice?)

The point to remember: Doubt big, round, undocumented numbers. Rather than swallow top-of-the-head estimates, focus on thinking smarter by applying simple statistical principles to everyday reasoning.

Describing Data

Once researchers have gathered their data, their first task is to *organize* them. One way is to use a simple *bar graph,* as in **FIGURE A.1** on the next page, which displays a distribution of trucks of different brands still on the road after a decade. When reading statistical graphs such as this, take care. As you can see, people can design a graph to make a difference look small or big, depending on what they want to emphasize.

The point to remember: Think smart. When viewing figures in magazines and on television, read the scale labels and note their range.

Measures of Central Tendency

A-2: What are the three measures of central tendency, and which is most affected by extreme scores?

The next step is to summarize the data using some measure of *central tendency,* a single score that represents a whole set of scores. The simplest measure is the **mode,** the most frequently occurring score or scores. The most commonly reported is the **mean,** or arithmetic average—the total sum of all the scores divided by the number of scores. On a divided highway, the median is the middle. So, too, with data: The **median** is the midpoint—the 50th percentile. If you arrange all the scores in order from the highest to the lowest, half will be above the median and half will be below it.

"Figures can be misleading—so I've written a song which I think expresses the real story of the firm's performance this quarter."

■ **mode** the most frequently occurring score(s) in a distribution.

■ **mean** the arithmetic average of a distribution, obtained by adding the scores and then dividing by the number of scores.

■ **median** the middle score in a distribution; half the scores are above it and half are below it.

FIGURE **A.1**
Read the scale labels
An American truck manufacturer offered graph (a)—with actual brand names included—to suggest the much greater durability of its trucks. Note, however, how the apparent difference shrinks as the vertical scale changes (graph b).

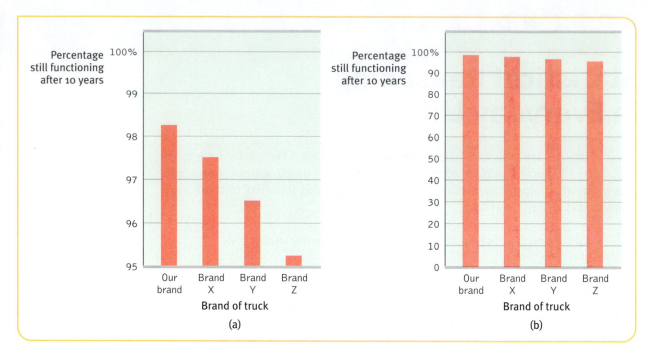

(a)

(b)

Measures of central tendency neatly summarize data. But consider what happens to the mean when a distribution is lopsided or *skewed*. With income data, for example, the mode, median, and mean often tell very different stories (**FIGURE A.2**). This happens because the mean is biased by a few extreme scores. When Microsoft co-founder Bill Gates sits down in an intimate cafe, its average (mean) patron instantly becomes a billionaire. Understanding this, you can see how a British newspaper could accurately run the headline "Income for 62% Is Below Average" (Waterhouse, 1993). Because the bottom *half* of British income earners receive only a *quarter* of the national income cake, most British people, like most people everywhere, make less than the mean.

In the United States, advocates and critics described the 2003 tax cut with different statistics, both true. The White House explained that "92 million Americans will receive an average tax cut of $1083." Critics agreed, but also noted that 50 million taxpayers got no cut, and half of the 92 million who did benefit received less than $100 (Krugman, 2003). Mean and median tell different true stories.

The point to remember: Always note which measure of central tendency is reported. Then, if it is a mean, consider whether a few atypical scores could be distorting it.

The average person has one ovary and one testicle.

FIGURE **A.2**
A skewed distribution
This graphic representation of the distribution of incomes illustrates the three measures of central tendency—mode, median, and mean. Note how just a few high incomes make the mean—the fulcrum point that balances the incomes above and below—deceptively high.

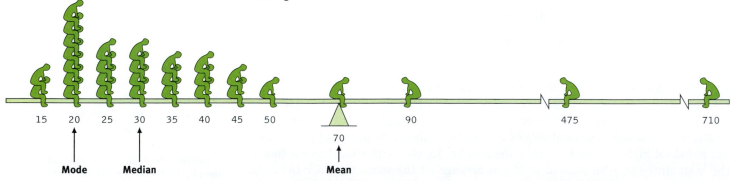

 One family   Income per family in thousands of dollars

Measures of Variation

A-3 : What is the most useful measure of variation in a set of data?

Knowing the value of an appropriate measure of central tendency can tell us a great deal. But it also helps to know something about the amount of *variation* in the data—how similar or diverse the scores are. Averages derived from scores with low variability are more reliable than averages based on scores with high variability. Consider a basketball player who scored between 13 and 17 points in each of her first 10 games in a season. Knowing this, we would be more confident that she would score near 15 points in her next game than if her scores had varied from 5 to 25 points.

The **range** of scores—the gap between the lowest and highest scores—provides only a crude estimate of variation because a couple of extreme scores in an otherwise uniform group, such as the $475,000 and $710,000 incomes in Figure A.2, will create a deceptively large range.

The more useful standard for measuring how much scores deviate from one another is the **standard deviation.** It better gauges whether scores are packed together or dispersed, because it uses information from each score (**TABLE A.1**). (The computation assembles information about how much individual scores differ from the mean.) If your college or university attracts students of a certain ability level, their intelligence scores will have a smaller standard deviation than the one found in the more diverse community population outside your school.

You can grasp the meaning of the standard deviation more easily if you consider how scores tend to be distributed in nature. Large numbers of data—heights, weights, intelligence scores, grades (though not incomes)—often form a roughly symmetrical, bell-shaped distribution. Most cases fall near the mean, and fewer cases fall near

■ **range** the difference between the highest and lowest scores in a distribution.

■ **standard deviation** a computed measure of how much scores vary around the mean score.

© The New Yorker Collection, 1988, Mirachi from cartoonbank.com. All Rights Reserved.

"The poor are getting poorer, but with the rich getting richer it all averages out in the long run."

TABLE A.1

STANDARD DEVIATION IS MUCH MORE INFORMATIVE THAN MEAN ALONE

Note that the test scores in Class A and Class B have the same mean (80), but very different standard deviations, which tell us more about how the students in each class are really faring.

Test Scores in Class A			Test Scores in Class B		
Score	Deviation from the Mean	Squared Deviation	Score	Deviation from the Mean	Squared Deviation
72	−8	64	60	−20	400
74	−6	36	60	−20	400
77	−3	9	70	−10	100
79	−1	1	70	−10	100
82	+2	4	90	+10	100
84	+4	16	90	+10	100
85	+5	25	100	+20	400
87	+7	49	100	+20	400
Total = 640		Sum of (deviations)² = 204	Total = 640		Sum of (deviations)² = 2000

Mean = 640 ÷ 8 = 80   Mean = 640 ÷ 8 = 80

Standard deviation =

$$\sqrt{\frac{\text{Sum of (deviations)}^2}{\text{Number of scores}}} = \sqrt{\frac{204}{8}} = 5.0$$

Standard deviation =

$$\sqrt{\frac{\text{Sum of (deviations)}^2}{\text{Number of scores}}} = \sqrt{\frac{2000}{8}} = 15.8$$

FIGURE A.3
The normal curve
Scores on aptitude tests tend to form a normal, or bell-shaped, curve. For example, the Wechsler intelligence test scale calls the average score 100.

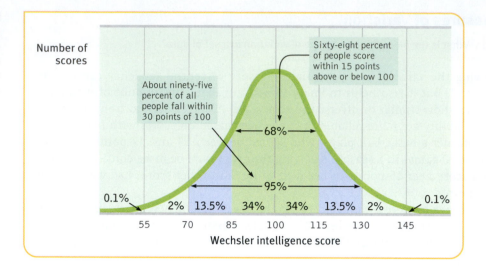

■ **normal curve** (normal distribution) a symmetrical, bell-shaped curve that describes the distribution of many types of data; most scores fall near the mean (68 percent fall within one standard deviation of it) and fewer and fewer near the extremes.

■ **correlation coefficient** a statistical measure of the extent to which two factors vary together, and thus of how well either factor predicts the other. Scores with a *positive correlation coefficient* go up and down together (as with high school and college GPAs). A *negative correlation coefficient* indicates that one score falls as the other rises (as in the relationship between self-esteem and depression).

■ **scatterplot** a graphed cluster of dots, each of which represents the values of two variables. The slope of the points suggests the direction of the relationship between the two variables. The amount of scatter suggests the strength of the correlation (little scatter indicates high correlation).

either extreme. This *bell-shaped* distribution is so typical that we call the curve it forms the **normal curve.**

As **FIGURE A.3** shows, a useful property of the normal curve is that roughly 68 percent of the cases fall within one standard deviation on either side of the mean. About 95 percent of cases fall within two standard deviations. With intelligence test scores, for example, about 68 percent of test-takers will score within ±15 points of 100. About 95 percent will score within ±30 points.

Correlation: A Measure of Relationships

A-4 : What does it mean when we say that two things are correlated?

Throughout this book we often ask how much two things relate: How closely related are the personality scores of identical twins? How well do intelligence test scores predict achievement? How often does stress lead to disease? Describing behavior is a first step toward predicting it. When surveys and naturalistic observations reveal that one trait or behavior accompanies another, we say the two *correlate*. A **correlation coefficient** is a statistical measure of relationship (written as *r*, as in **FIGURE A.4**). It reveals how closely two things vary together and thus how well either one *predicts* the other. Knowing how much the number of one's close friends *correlates* with happiness tells us how well friendships *predict* happiness. But they do not tell you which causes which. (Can you speculate possible explanations for a positive correlation?)

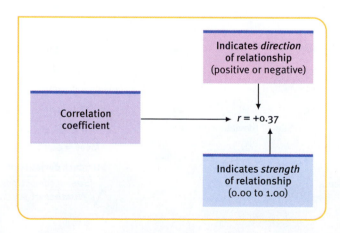

FIGURE A.4
How to read a correlation coefficient

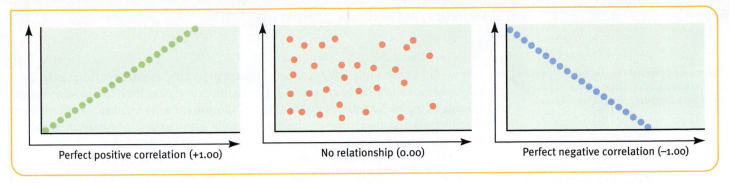

Perfect positive correlation (+1.00)	No relationship (0.00)	Perfect negative correlation (−1.00)

To get a feel for whether one set of scores relates to a second set, we can plot, or display, the data, as in the **scatterplots** in FIGURE A.5, which shows perfect positive and negative correlations. A correlation's possible range is as follows:

- +1.00, which means that one set of scores increases in direct proportion to the other's increase.
- 0.00, meaning that the scores are unrelated.
- −1.00, which means that one set of scores goes up precisely as the other goes down.

Note that a correlation's being negative has nothing to do with its strength or weakness; a negative correlation means two things relate inversely. (As toothbrushing goes up from zero, tooth decay goes down.) A weak correlation, indicating little or no relationship, is one that has a coefficient near zero.

Statistics can help us see what the naked eye sometimes misses. To demonstrate this for yourself, try an imaginary project. Wondering if tall people are more or less easygoing, you collect two sets of scores: men's heights and men's temperaments. You measure the heights of 20 men, and you have someone else independently assess their temperaments (from zero for extremely calm to 100 for highly reactive).

With all the relevant data (TABLE A.2) right in front of you, can you tell whether there is (1) a positive correlation between height and reactive temperament, (2) very little or no correlation, or (3) a negative correlation?

Comparing the columns in Table A.2, most people detect very little relationship between height and temperament. In fact, the correlation in this imaginary example is moderately positive, +0.63, as you could see if you plotted the data on a graph, as in FIGURE A.6. The upward slope of the cluster of points as one moves to the right shows that the two sets of scores (height and reactivity) tend to rise together.

FIGURE **A.5 Scatterplots, showing patterns of correlation** Correlations can range from +1.00 (scores on one measure increase in direct proportion to scores on another) to −1.00 (scores on one measure decrease precisely as scores rise on the other).

TABLE **A.2**

HEIGHT AND TEMPERAMENT OF 20 MEN

	Height in Inches	Temperament
1	80	75
2	63	66
3	61	60
4	79	90
5	74	60
6	69	42
7	62	42
8	75	60
9	77	81
10	60	39
11	64	48
12	76	69
13	71	72
14	66	57
15	73	63
16	70	75
17	63	30
18	71	57
19	68	84
20	70	39

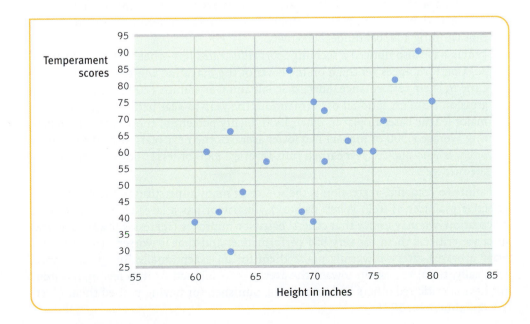

FIGURE **A.6 Scatterplot for height and temperament** This display of data from 20 imagined people (each represented by a data point) reveals an upward slope, indicating a positive correlation. The considerable scatter of the data indicates the correlation is much lower than +1.0.

■ **regression toward the mean** the tendency for extremes of unusual scores or events to fall back (regress) toward the average.

If we fail to see a relationship when data are presented as systematically as in Table A.2, how much less likely are we to notice them in everyday life? To see what is right in front of us, we sometimes need statistical illumination. We can easily see evidence of gender discrimination when given statistically summarized information about job level, seniority, performance, gender, and salary. But we often see no discrimination when the same information dribbles in, case by case (Twiss & others, 1989).

The point to remember: Although the correlation coefficient tells us nothing about cause and effect, it can help us see the world more clearly by revealing the actual extent to which two things relate.

A-5 : What is regression toward the mean?

Correlations not only make visible the relationships that we might otherwise miss, they also restrain our "seeing" nonexistent relationships. When we believe there is a relationship between two things, we are likely to notice and recall instances that confirm our belief. The result is an *illusory correlation.* If we believe that dreams are forecasts of actual events, we may notice and recall confirming instances more than disconfirming instances.

Illusory correlations feed an *illusion of control*—that chance events are subject to our personal control. Gamblers, remembering their lucky rolls, may come to believe they can influence the roll of the dice by again throwing gently for low numbers and hard for high numbers. The illusion that uncontrollable events correlate with our actions is also fed by a statistical phenomenon called **regression toward the mean.** Average results are more typical than extreme results. Thus, after an unusual event, things tend to return toward their average level; extraordinary happenings tend to be followed by more ordinary ones.

The point may seem obvious, yet we regularly miss it. Thus, we sometimes attribute what may be a normal statistical regression (the expected falling back to normal) to something we have done. Examples are abundant:

- Students who score much lower or higher on an exam than they usually do are likely, when retested, to return to their average.
- Unusual ESP subjects who defy chance when first tested nearly always lose their "psychic powers" when retested (a phenomenon parapsychologists have called the "decline effect").
- Scientists who win a Nobel prize—an extraordinary accomplishment—almost always experience diminished accomplishments thereafter, leading some to believe that winning a Nobel hinders creativity.
- People have also noticed a seeming *Sports Illustrated jinx*—that athletes whose peak performances get them on the cover of the magazine will then suffer a decline in their performance. Edward Schall and Gary Smith (2002) illustrated regression from exceptional performance in the year-to-year performance of all major league baseball players since 1900. Eighty percent of those with a high batting average (.300 or higher) had lower averages the next year. And 80 percent of pitchers who allowed few earned runs (average 3.00 or less) allowed more runs the next year.

Failure to recognize regression is the source of many superstitions and of some ineffective practices as well. When day-to-day behavior has a large element of chance fluctuation, we may notice that others' behavior improves (regresses toward average) after we criticize them for very bad performance, and that it worsens (regresses toward average) after we warmly praise them for an exceptionally fine performance. Ironically, then, regression toward the average can mislead us into feeling rewarded for having criticized others and into feeling punished for having praised them (Tversky & Kahneman, 1974).

The point to remember: When a fluctuating behavior returns to normal, there is no need to invent fancy explanations for why it does so. Regression toward the mean is probably at work.

Making Inferences

Data are "noisy." One group's average score could conceivably differ from another's not because of any real difference but merely because of chance fluctuations in the people sampled. How confidently, then, can we infer that an observed difference accurately estimates the true difference?

When Is a Difference Reliable?

A-6 : When can we safely generalize from a sample?

In deciding when it is safe to generalize from a sample, we should keep three principles in mind. Let's look at each in turn.

1. ***Representative samples are better than biased samples.*** The best basis for generalizing is not from the exceptional and memorable cases one finds at the extremes (remember Bill Gates' income?) but from a representative sample of cases. No research involves a representative sample of the whole human population. Thus, it pays to keep in mind what population a study has sampled. (To see how an unrepresentative sample can lead you astray, see Close-Up: Cross-Sectional and Longitudinal Studies.)

- **cross-sectional study** a study in which people of different ages are compared with one another.

- **longitudinal study** research in which the same people are restudied and retested over a long period of time.

CLOSE-UP

CROSS-SECTIONAL AND LONGITUDINAL STUDIES

A-7 : What are cross-sectional studies and longitudinal studies, and why is it important to know which method was used?

When interpreting research results, smart thinkers consider how researchers arrived at their conclusions. One way studies vary is in the time period for gathering data.

In **cross-sectional studies,** researchers compare different groups at the same time. For example, they might compare intelligence test scores among people in differing age groups. In those studies, older adults, on average, give fewer correct answers than do younger adults. This could suggest that mental ability declines with age, and indeed, that was the conclusion drawn from many early cross-sectional studies of intelligence.

In **longitudinal studies,** researchers study and restudy the same group at different times in their life span. After colleges began giving intelligence tests to entering students about 1920, several psychologists saw their chance to study intelligence longitudinally. What they expected to find was a decrease in intelligence after about age 30 (Schaie & Geiwitz, 1982). What they actually found was a surprise: Until late in life, intelligence remained stable. On some tests, it even increased.

Why did these new results differ from the earlier cross-sectional findings? In retrospect, researchers realized that cross-sectional studies that compared 70-year-olds and 30-year-olds were comparing people not only of two different ages but also of two different eras. They were comparing generally less-educated people (born,

say, in the early 1900s) with better-educated people (born after 1950); people raised in large families with people raised in smaller families; people from less-affluent families with people from more-affluent families.

Others have since pointed out that longitudinal studies have their own pitfalls. Participants who survive to the end of longitudinal studies may be the healthiest (and brightest) people. When researchers adjust for the loss of participants, as did one study following more than 2000 people over 75 in Cambridge, England, they find a steeper intelligence decline, especially as people age after 85 (Brayne & others, 1999).

The point to remember: When interpreting research results, pay attention to the methodology used, such as whether it was a longitudinal or cross-sectional study.

■ **statistical significance** a statistical statement of how likely it is that an obtained result occurred by chance.

2. *Less-variable observations are more reliable than those that are more variable.* As we noted in the example of the basketball player whose points scored were consistent, an average is more reliable when it comes from scores with low variability.

3. *More cases are better than fewer.* An eager prospective college student visits two campuses, each for a day. At the first, the student randomly attends two classes and discovers both instructors to be witty and engaging. At the next campus, the two sampled instructors seem dull and uninspiring. Returning home, the student (discounting the small sample size of only two teachers at each school) tells friends about the "great teachers" at the first, and the "bores" at the second. Again, we know it but we ignore it: *Averages based on many cases are more reliable* (less variable) than averages based on only a few cases.

The point to remember: Don't be overly impressed by a few anecdotes. Generalizations based on a few unrepresentative cases are unreliable.

When Is a Difference Significant?

A-8 : What do we mean when we say that an observed difference is significant?

Statistical tests also help us determine whether differences are meaningful. Here is the underlying logic: When *averages* from two samples are each *reliable* measures of their respective populations (as when each is based on many observations that have small variability), then their difference (sometimes even a very small difference) is likely to be reliable as well. (The less the variability in women's and in men's aggression scores, the more confidence we would have that any observed gender difference is reliable.) But when the *difference* between the sample averages is *large,* we have even more confidence that the difference between them reflects a real difference in their populations.

In short, when sample averages are reliable and the difference between them is relatively large, we say the difference has **statistical significance.** This simply means that the difference is probably not due to chance variation between the samples. In judging statistical significance, psychologists are conservative. They are like juries who must presume innocence until guilt is proven. For most psychologists, proof beyond a reasonable doubt means not making much of a finding unless the odds of its occurring by chance are less than 5 percent (an arbitrary criterion).

When reading about research, you should remember that, given large enough or homogeneous enough samples, a difference between them may be "statistically significant" yet have little practical significance. For example, comparisons of intelligence test scores among hundreds of thousands of first-born and later-born individuals indicate a highly significant tendency for first-born individuals to have higher average scores than their later-born siblings (Zajonc & Markus, 1975). But because the scores differ by only one or two points, the difference has little practical importance. Such findings have caused some psychologists to advocate alternatives to significance testing (Hunter, 1997). Better, they say, to use other ways to express a finding's "effect size"—its magnitude and reliability. *The point to remember:* Statistical significance indicates the likelihood that a result will happen by chance. It does not indicate the importance of the result.

REVIEWING

>> APPENDIX REVIEW

A-1 : **What is the first important point to remember when assessing studies that use statistical reasoning?**

Doubt big, round, undocumented numbers. Think smarter by applying simple statistical reasoning.

A-2 : **What are the three measures of central tendency, and which is most affected by extreme scores?**

Always note which measure of central tendency—the *mean* (the arithmetic average), *median* (the middle score), or *mode* (the most frequently occurring score) is reported. Then, if it is a mean, consider whether a few atypical scores could be distorting it.

A-3 : **What is the most useful measure of variation in a set of data?**

The *standard deviation* provides the most reliable measure of variation. Many types of data form a *normal curve*. When looking at statistical graphs in the media, think critically: Always read the scale labels and note their *range*.

A-4 : **What does it mean when we say that two things are correlated?**

A *correlation coefficient* tells us the extent to which two things relate. Correlation coefficients cannot tell cause and effect, but they do tell us how well one event predicts the other, and they also restrain us from seeing nonexistent relationships.

A-5 : **What is regression toward the mean?**

Fluctuating behaviors tend to return to normal. There is no need to invent fancy explanations for why they do so. *Regression toward the mean* is probably at work.

A-6 : **When can we safely generalize from a sample?**

To safely generalize from a sample, we would want it to be representative of the population we wish to study, to provide consistent (not highly variable) data, and to be large rather than small. Generalizations based on only a few cases are unreliable.

A-7 : **What are cross-sectional and longitudinal studies, and why is it important to know which method was used?**

Cross-sectional studies compare people of different ages at the same time; *longitudinal studies* retest the same people over time. The two methods give different perspectives. Cross-sectional studies show the effects of time and environment on many different individuals; longitudinal studies show those effects on the same people.

A-8 : **What do we mean when we say that an observed difference is significant?**

Statistical significance indicates the likelihood that a result will occur by chance. It does not indicate the importance of the result.

>> REHEARSE IT!

1. The three measures of central tendency are the mode, the mean, and the median. Which of these three measures is most easily distorted by a few very large or very small scores?

   a. The mode
   b. The mean
   c. The median
   d. They are all equally vulnerable to distortion from atypical scores.

2. The standard deviation is the most useful measure of variation in a set of data. The standard deviation tells us

   a. the difference between the highest and lowest scores in the set.

   b. the extent to which the sample being used deviates from the bigger population it represents.
   c. how much individual scores differ from the mode.
   d. how much individual scores differ from the mean.

3. A correlation coefficient is a statistical measure of the extent to which two factors, such as two sets of scores, vary together. In a _____ correlation, the scores would travel up and down together; in a(n) _____ correlation, one score would fall as the other rises.

   a. positive; negative
   b. positive; illusory

   c. negative; inverse
   d. strong; weak

4. Statistical significance is a measure of how likely it is that an observed difference is real and not due to chance alone. When sample averages are _____ and the difference between them is _____, we can say the difference has statistical significance.

   a. reliable; large
   b. reliable; small
   c. due to chance; large
   d. due to chance; small

   Answers: 1. b, 2. d, 3. a, 4. a.

>> TERMS AND CONCEPTS TO REMEMBER

mode, p. A-1
mean, p. A-1
median, p. A-1
range, p. A-3

standard deviation, p. A-3
normal curve, p. A-4
correlation coefficient, p. A-4
scatterplot, p. A-5

regression toward the mean, p. A-6
cross-sectional study, p. A-7
longitudinal study, p. A-7
statistical significance, p. A-8

Careers in Psychology

Jennifer Zwolinski

University of San Diego

What can you do with a degree in psychology? Lots!

As a psychology major, you will graduate with a scientific mindset and an awareness of basic principles of human behavior (biological mechanisms, development, cognition, psychological disorders, social interaction). This background will prepare you for success in many areas, including business, helping professions, health services, marketing, law, sales, and teaching. You may even go on to graduate school for specialized training to become a psychology professional. This appendix describes the various levels of psychology education and some jobs available at those levels; psychology's specialized subfields; and ways you can improve your chances of admission to graduate school.[1]

Preparing for a Career in Psychology

Psychology is the second most popular major in the United States, second only to business (*Princeton Review,* 2005). More than 70,000 psychology majors graduate from U.S. colleges and universities each year. An undergraduate degree in psychology can prepare you for a broad array of jobs after graduation. For other jobs, you will need a graduate degree.

The Bachelor's Degree

Psychology majors graduate with a valuable skill set that increases their marketability in many fields. About 42 percent of U.S. psychology majors go on to graduate school in psychology (Fogg & others, 2004). What happens to the rest? Most work in for-profit organizations after graduation, especially in management, sales, and administration. **TABLE B.1** on the next page shows the top 10 occupations that employ people with a bachelor's degree in psychology.

Clearly, psychology majors are marketable beyond the boundaries of psychology. Their sought-after skills and abilities include an ability to work and get along with others, a desire and willingness to learn new skills, adaptability to changing situations, and good critical-thinking and problem-solving skills (Landrum, 2001). There are some things that all psychology majors can do to maximize success in the job market. Employers that hire people with only a bachelor's degree tend to favor individuals with positive explanatory styles and practical experience as well as a good education (Cannon, 2005). Betsy Morgan and Ann Korschgen

---

[1]Although this text covers the world of psychology for students in many countries, this appendix draws primarily from available U.S. data. Its description of psychology's subfields and its suggestions for preparing to enter the profession are, however, also applicable in many other countries.

TABLE B.1

TOP 10 U.S. OCCUPATIONS THAT EMPLOY PEOPLE WITH A BACHELOR'S DEGREE IN PSYCHOLOGY

1. Top- and mid-level managers, executives, administrators
2. Sales occupations, including retail
3. Social workers
4. Other management-related occupations
5. Personnel, training, labor relations specialists
6. Other administrative (record clerks, telephone operators)
7. Insurance, securities, real estate, business services
8. Other marketing and sales occupations
9. Registered nurses, pharmacists, therapists, physician assistants
10. Accountants, auditors, other financial specialists

Source: Fogg & others (2004).

(1998) offer the following helpful tips for increasing your chances of getting a job after graduation:

1. Get to know your instructors.
2. Take courses that support your interests.
3. Familiarize yourself with available resources, such as campus career services and alumni.
4. Participate in at least one internship experience.
5. Volunteer some of your time and talent to campus or community organizations, such as Psi Chi (the national honor society in psychology) or your school's psychology club.

Postgraduate Degrees

A graduate degree in psychology will give you proficiency in an area of psychological specialization. According to the U.S. Bureau of Labor Statistics (2004), psychologists with advanced degrees held approximately 139,000 jobs in 2000. Such jobs are expected to increase 21 to 35 percent (depending on the subfield of psychology) through 2012 because of the need for psychological services in a variety of settings. The work settings for psychologists vary somewhat by type of graduate degree. As shown in FIGURE B.1, many psychologists with a doctorate work in universities and colleges; most people with a master's degree work in other educational institutions (such as elementary and middle schools) and in for-profit companies. Among those seeking advanced training in psychology in the United States, 29 percent earn a master's degree, 7 percent earn a doctoral degree, and 6 percent earn some other professional degree (e.g., law or health professions) (Fogg & others, 2004).

The Master's Degree

A master's degree in psychology requires at least two years of full-time graduate study in a specific subfield of psychology. In addition to specialized course work in psychology, requirements usually include practical experience in an applied setting and/or a master's thesis reporting on an original research project. You might acquire a master's degree to do specialized work in psychology. As a graduate with a master's degree, you might handle research and data collection and analysis in a university, government, or private industry setting. You might work under the supervision of a

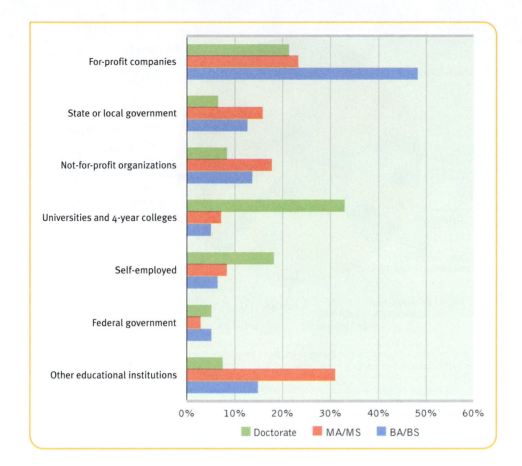

FIGURE B.1
Work settings for psychology-degree recipients
(Fogg & others, 2004).

psychologist with a doctorate, providing some clinical service such as therapy or testing. Or you might find a job in the health, government, industry, or education fields. You might also acquire a master's degree as a stepping stone for more advanced study in a doctoral program in psychology, which will considerably expand the number of employment opportunities available to you (Super & Super, 2001).

Doctoral Degrees

You will probably need five to seven years of graduate study in a specific subfield of psychology to get your doctoral degree. The *doctor of philosophy (Ph.D.)* in psychology culminates in a *dissertation* (an extensive research paper you will be required to defend orally) based on original research. Courses in quantitative research methods, which include the use of computer-based analysis, are an important part of graduate study and are necessary to complete the dissertation. The *doctor of psychology (Psy.D.)* may be based on clinical (therapeutic) work and examinations rather than a dissertation. If you pursue clinical and counseling psychology programs, you should expect at least a one-year internship in addition to the regular course work, clinical practice, and research.

FIGURE B.2 lists by subfield the Ph.D.s earned in the United States in a recent year. Clinical psychology is the most popular specialty area among holders of doctorates in psychology. The largest employment growth areas for doctoral graduates have been in the for-profit and self-employment sectors, including health services providers, industrial/organizational psychology, and educational psychology. About one-third of doctoral-level psychologists are employed in academic settings (Fogg & others, 2004).

In 2001, a total of 73 percent of new doctoral respondents and 55 percent of new master's respondents indicated that their primary occupational position was their

FIGURE **B.2**
U.S. Ph.D.s by subfield, 2001

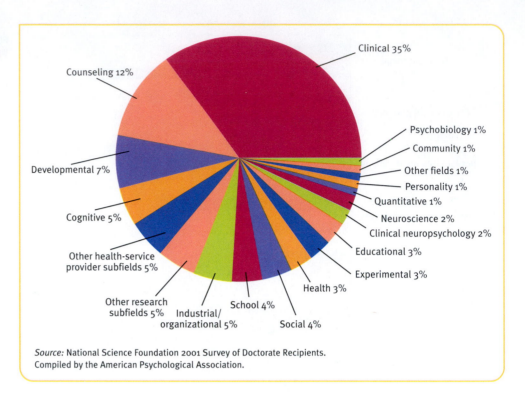

Clinical 35%

Counseling 12%

Psychobiology 1%

Community 1%

Other fields 1%

Personality 1%

Quantitative 1%

Neuroscience 2%

Clinical neuropsychology 2%

Educational 3%

Experimental 3%

Health 3%

Social 4%

School 4%

Industrial/organizational 5%

Other research subfields 5%

Other health-service provider subfields 5%

Cognitive 5%

Developmental 7%

Source: National Science Foundation 2001 Survey of Doctorate Recipients. Compiled by the American Psychological Association.

first choice. Most new graduates with a master's degree or a Ph.D. are fairly satisfied with their current positions overall in terms of salary, benefits, opportunities for personal development, supervisors, colleagues, and working conditions (Kohout & Wicherski, 2004; Singleton & others, 2003).

Subfields of Psychology

If you are like most psychology students, you may be unaware of the wide variety of specialties and work settings available in psychology (Terre & Stoddart, 2000). To date, the American Psychological Association (APA) has 54 divisions (**TABLE B.2**). The following paragraphs (arranged alphabetically) describe some careers in the main specialty areas of psychology, most of which require a graduate degree in psychology.

Clinical psychologists promote psychological health in individuals, groups, and organizations. Some clinical psychologists specialize in specific psychological disorders. Others treat a range of disorders, from adjustment difficulties to severe psychopathology. Clinical psychologists might engage in research, teaching, assessment, and consultation. Some hold workshops and lectures on psychological issues for other professionals or for the public. Clinical psychologists work in a variety of settings, including private practice, mental health service organizations, schools, universities, industries, legal systems, medical systems, counseling centers, government agencies, and military services.

To become a clinical psychologist, you will need to earn a doctorate from a clinical psychology program. The APA sets the standards for clinical psychology graduate programs, offering *accreditation* (official recognition) to those who meet their standards. Unlike practitioners in most other subfields of psychology, clinical psychologists must, in all U.S. states, obtain a license to offer services such as therapy and testing.

Cognitive psychologists primarily do research to add to psychology's store of knowledge. Cognitive psychologists study thought processes and focus on such topics as perception, language, attention, problem solving, memory, judgment and decision

Prescription privileges

Many psychologists would like the opportunity to prescribe therapeutic medicines in order to expand the scope of clinical practice and to meet the need for psychiatric services in many parts of the United States. Psychologists in the U.S. military and in the states of New Mexico and Louisiana currently have prescription privileges.

Tom Stewart/Corbis

TABLE **B.2**

APA DIVISIONS BY NUMBER AND NAME

1. Society for General Psychology	29. Psychotherapy
2. Society for the Teaching of Psychology	30. Society of Psychological Hypnosis
3. Experimental Psychology	31. State, Provincial, and Territorial Psychological Association Affairs
4. *There is no Division 4.*	32. Humanistic Psychology
5. Evaluation, Measurement, and Statistics	33. Mental Retardation and Developmental Disabilities
6. Behavioral Neuroscience and Comparative Psychology	34. Population and Environmental Psychology
7. Developmental Psychology	35. Society for the Psychology of Women
8. Society for Personality and Social Psychology	36. Psychology of Religion
9. Society for the Psychological Study of Social Issues (SPSSI)	37. Child, Youth, and Family Services
10. Society for the Psychology of Aesthetics, Creativity, and the Arts	38. Health Psychology
11. *There is no Division 11.*	39. Psychoanalysis
12. Society of Clinical Psychology	40. Clinical Neuropsychology
13. Society of Consulting Psychology	41. American Psychology-Law Society
14. Society for Industrial and Organizational Psychology	42. Psychologists in Independent Practice
15. Educational Psychology	43. Family Psychology
16. School Psychology	44. Society for the Psychological Study of Lesbian, Gay, and Bisexual Issues
17. Society of Counseling Psychology	45. Society for the Psychological Study of Ethnic Minority Issues
18. Psychologists in Public Service	46. Media Psychology
19. Society for Military Psychology	47. Exercise and Sport Psychology
20. Adult Development and Aging	48. Society for the Study of Peace, Conflict, and Violence: Peace Psychology Division
21. Applied Experimental and Engineering Psychology	49. Group Psychology and Group Psychotherapy
22. Rehabilitation Psychology	50. Addictions
23. Society for Consumer Psychology	51. Society for the Psychological Study of Men and Masculinity
24. Society for Theoretical and Philosophical Psychology	52. International Psychology
25. Behavior Analysis	53. Society of Clinical Child and Adolescent Psychology
26. Society for the History of Psychology	54. Society of Pediatric Psychology
27. Society for Community Research and Action: Division of Community Psychology	55. American Society for the Advancement of Pharmacotherapy
28. Psychopharmacology and Substance Abuse	56. Trauma Psychology

Source: American Psychological Association

making, forgetting, and intelligence. Recent areas of research interest include designing computer-based models of thought processes and identifying biological correlates of cognition. As a cognitive psychologist, you might work as a professor, industrial consultant, or human factors specialist in an educational or business setting.

Community psychologists move beyond focusing on specific individuals or families and deal with broad problems of mental health in community settings. These psychologists believe that human behavior is powerfully influenced by the interaction between people and their physical, social, political, and economic environments. They seek to improve individual functioning by enhancing environmental settings that promote psychological health. Community psychologists focus on prevention,

Karen Moskowitz/Getty Images

Cognitive consulting
Cognitive psychologists may advise businesses on how to operate more effectively by understanding the human factors involved.

promotion of positive mental health, and crisis intervention, with special attention to the problems of underserved groups and ethnic minorities. As a community psychologist, your work settings could include federal, state, and local departments of mental health, corrections, and welfare. You might conduct research or help evaluate research in health service settings, serve as an independent consultant for a private or government agency, or teach and consult as a college or university faculty member.

Counseling psychologists help people adjust to life transitions or make life-style changes. This field is very similar to clinical psychology, except that counseling psychologists typically help people with adjustment problems rather than severe psychopathology. Like clinical psychologists, counseling psychologists conduct therapy and provide assessments to individuals and groups. As a counseling psychologist, you would emphasize your clients' strengths, helping clients cope during a transitional time using their own skills, interests, and abilities. You might find yourself working in an academic setting as a faculty member or administrator or in a university counseling center, community mental health center, business, or private practice. As with clinical psychology, you will need to obtain a state license to provide counseling services to the public.

Developmental psychologists conduct research in age-related behavioral changes and apply their scientific knowledge to educational, child care, policy, and related settings. As a developmental psychologist, you would investigate change across a broad range of topics, including the biological, social, psychological, and cognitive aspects of development. Developmental psychology informs a number of applied fields, including educational psychology, school psychology, child psychopathology, and gerontology. You would probably specialize in behavior during infancy, childhood, adolescence, or middle or late adulthood. Your work setting could be an educational institution, day-care center, youth group program, or senior center.

Educational psychologists study the relationship between learning and our physical and social environments. They study the psychological processes involved in learning and develop strategies for enhancing the learning process. As an educational psychologist, you might work in a university—in a psychology department or a school of education. You might conduct basic research on topics related to learning or develop innovative methods of teaching to enhance the learning process. You might be employed by a school or government agency or charged with designing and implementing effective employee-training programs in a business setting.

Experimental or *research psychologists* are a diverse group of scientists who investigate a variety of basic behavioral processes in research involving humans and/or other animals. Prominent areas of study in experimental research include motivation, thought, attention, learning, memory, perception, and language. As an experimental psychologist, you would most likely work in an academic setting, teaching courses and supervising students' research in addition to conducting your own research. Or you might be employed by a research institution, business, industry affiliate, or government agency.

Health psychologists are researchers and practitioners concerned with psychology's contribution to promoting health and preventing disease. As applied psychologists or clinicians, they may help individuals lead healthier lives by designing, conducting, and evaluating programs to stop smoking, lose weight, improve sleep, or prevent the spread of sexually transmitted infections. As researchers and clinicians, they identify conditions and practices associated with health and illness to help create effective interventions. In public service, health psychologists study and work to improve government policies and health-care systems. As a health psychologist, you could be employed in a hospital, medical school, rehabilitation center, public health agency, college or university, or, if you are also a clinical psychologist, in private practice.

Forensic psychologists apply psychological principles to legal issues. They conduct research on the interface of law and psychology, help to create public policies related to mental health, and help law-enforcement agencies in criminal investigations. They also provide therapy and assessment to assist the legal community. Some forensic psychologists hold law degrees and provide clients with legal services as well. Although most forensic psychologists are clinical psychologists, they might have expertise in other areas of psychology, such as social or cognitive psychology. As a forensic psychologist, you might work in a university psychology department, law school, research organization, community mental health agency, law-enforcement agency, court, or correctional setting.

Industrial/organizational (I/O) psychologists study the relationship between people and their working environments. They may develop new ways to increase productivity, improve personnel selection, or promote job satisfaction in a business setting. Their interests include organizational structure and change, consumer behavior, and personnel selection and training. As an I/O psychologist, you might conduct workplace training or provide organizational analysis and development. You may find yourself working in business, industry, the government, or a college or university. Or you may be self-employed as a consultant or work for a management counseling firm.

Neuropsychologists investigate the relationship between neurological processes (structure and function of the brain) and behavior. As a neuropsychologist you might assess, diagnose, or treat disorders related to the central nervous system, such as Alzheimer's disease or stroke. If you are a *clinical neuropsychologist,* you might work in the neurology, neurosurgery, or psychiatric unit of a hospital. Neuropsychologists also work in academic settings, where they conduct research and teach.

Psychometric and *quantitative psychologists* study the methods and techniques used to acquire psychological knowledge. A psychometrician may update existing neurocognitive or personality tests or devise new tests for use in clinical and school settings or in business and industry. These psychologists also administer, score, and interpret such tests. Quantitative psychologists collaborate with researchers to design, analyze, and interpret the results of research programs. As a psychometric or quantitative psychologist, you will need to be well trained in research methods, statistics, and computer technology. You will most likely be employed by a university or college, testing company, private research firm, or government agency.

Rehabilitation psychologists are researchers and practitioners who work with people who have lost optimal functioning after an accident, illness, or other event. As a rehabilitation psychologist, you would probably work in a medical rehabilitation institution or hospital. You might also work in a medical school, university, state or federal vocational rehabilitation agency, or in private practice serving people with physical disabilities.

School psychologists are involved in the assessment of and intervention for children in educational settings. They diagnose and treat cognitive, social, and emotional problems that may negatively influence children's learning or overall functioning at school. As a school psychologist, you would collaborate with teachers, parents, and administrators, making recommendations to improve student learning. You would work in an academic setting, a mental health clinic, a federal or state government agency, a child guidance center, or a behavioral research laboratory.

Social psychologists are interested in our interactions with others. Social psychologists study how our beliefs, feelings, and behaviors are affected by and influence other people. They study topics such as attitudes, aggression, prejudice, interpersonal attraction, group behavior, and leadership. As a social psychologist, you might work in organizational consultation, marketing research, or other applied psychology fields.

AP Photo/Jennifer Graylock

Criminal profiling
On the popular TV show *Law and Order, Special Victims Unit,* Dr. George Huang (played by B. D. Wong) is an FBI agent and psychiatrist who uses his background in forensic psychology to conduct criminal investigations.

You would probably also be a college or university faculty member. Some social psychologists work for hospitals, federal agencies, or businesses performing applied research.

Sport psychologists are interested in how participation in sports and other physical activities can enhance personal development and well-being throughout the life span. As a sport psychologist, you would study the psychological factors that influence, and are influenced by, participation in sports and other physical activities, and you would apply this knowledge to everyday settings. You would most likely work as part of a team or organization, but you might also work in a private capacity.

Preparing Early for Graduate Study in Psychology

Competition for the openings for advanced degrees in psychology is keen. If you choose to go to graduate school, there a number of things you can do now to maximize your chances of gaining admission to the school of your choice.

If possible, begin preparing during your first year on campus to maximize opportunities and obtain the experience needed to gain admission to a competitive program. Kristy Arnold and Kelly Horrigan (2002) offer a number of suggestions to facilitate this process:

1. *Network.* Get to know faculty members and the psychology department by attending activities and meetings. Become involved in psychology clubs and in Psi Chi, the national honor society in psychology. These meetings connect students with similar interests and expose them to a broader study of the field.
2. *Become actively involved in research as early as possible.* Start by doing simple tasks such as data entry and data collection, and over time you will be prepared to conduct your own research project under the supervision of a research mentor.
3. *Volunteer or get a job in a psychology-related field.* Getting involved will show your willingness to apply psychological concepts to real-world settings. Further, it will showcase your ability to juggle a number of tasks successfully, such as work and school—an important skill for graduate school success.
4. *Maintain good grades.* Demonstrate the ability to do well in graduate school by demonstrating successful completion of challenging courses, especially those related to your interests in graduate school.

In your junior year, you should begin studying for the Graduate Record Exam (GRE), the standardized test that applicants to graduate school must complete. If you start preparing early, you will be ready for success in your graduate school application and study.

Membership benefits
Members of the Psi Chi Honor Society, such as those meeting here, enjoy educational and professional benefits. They may attend special Psi Chi sessions at psychological conventions, apply for research grants and awards, and read about research advances in the society's journal *Eye on Psi Chi.*

Stephen Simpson/Getty Images

So, the next time someone asks you what you will do with your psychology degree, tell them you have a lot of options. You might use your acquired skills and understanding to get a job and succeed in any number of fields, or you might pursue graduate school and then career opportunities in psychology or other associated professions. In any case, what you have learned about behavior and mental processes will surely enrich your life (Hammer, 2003).

For More Information

Actkinson, T. R. (2000). Master's and myth. *Eye on Psi Chi, 4,* 19–25.

American Psychological Association (2003). *Careers for the twenty-first century.* Washington, DC.

American Psychological Association (2005). *Graduate study in psychology.* Washington, DC.

Appleby, D. C. (2002). *The savvy psychology major.* Dubuque, IA: Kendall/Hunt.

Arnold, K., & Horrigan, K. (2002). Gaining admission into the graduate program of your choice. *Eye on Psi Chi,* 30–33.

Aubrecht, L. (2001). What can you do with a BA in psychology? *Eye on Psi Chi, 5,* 29–31.

Huss, M. (1996). Secrets to standing out from the pile: Getting into graduate school. *Psi Chi Newsletter,* 6–7.

Lammers, B. (2000). Quick tips for applying to graduate school in psychology. *Eye on Psi Chi, 4,* 40–42.

Landrum, E. (2001). I'm getting my bachelor's degree in psychology. What can I do with it? *Eye on Psi Chi, 6,* 22–24.

Morgan, B., & Korschgen, A. (2001). Psychology career exploration made easy. *Eye on Psi Chi,* 35–36.

Sternberg, R. (Ed.) (2002). *Career paths in psychology: Where your degree can take you.* Washington, DC: APA.

Answers to Test Yourself Questions

MODULE 1 · The History and Scope of Psychology

1. What events defined the founding of scientific psychology?

ANSWER: The most outstanding event defining the founding of scientific psychology was Wilhelm Wundt's opening of the University of Leipzig psychology laboratory in 1879. Wundt and others, including William James, used introspection—self-examination of one's own emotional states and mental processes—to explore the mind. James also wrote an important psychology textbook, completed in 1890.

2. What are psychology's major levels of analysis?

ANSWER: Psychology's three major levels of analysis are the biological, psychological, and social-cultural. The complementary insights of psychologists studying behavior and mental processes from the neuroscience, evolutionary, behavior genetics, psychodynamic, behavioral, cognitive, and social-cultural perspectives offer a richer understanding than could usually be gained from any one viewpoint alone.

MODULE 2 · Research Strategies: How Psychologists Ask and Answer Questions

1. What is the scientific attitude, and why is it important for critical thinking?

ANSWER: The scientific attitude combines *curiosity, skeptical* testing of various claims and ideas, and *humility* about one's own unexamined presumptions. Examining assumptions, searching for hidden values, evaluating evidence, and assessing conclusions are essential parts of critical thinking.

2. What are the strengths and weaknesses of the three different methods psychologists use to describe behavior—case studies, surveys, and naturalistic observation?

ANSWER: *Case studies* offer in-depth insights that may provide clues to what's true of others—or may, if the case is atypical, mislead. *Surveys* can accurately reveal the tendencies of large populations. But if the questions are leading, or if nonrandom samples are queried, the results can again mislead us. *Naturalistic observation* enables study of behavior undisturbed by researchers. But the lack of control may leave cause and effect ambiguous.

3. Here are some recently reported correlations, with interpretations drawn by journalists. Further research, often including experiments, has clarified cause and effect in each case. Knowing just these correlations, can you come up with other possible explanations for each of these?

a. *Alcohol use is associated with violence. (One interpretation: Drinking triggers or unleashes aggressive behavior.)* Perhaps anger triggers drinking, or perhaps the same genes or rearing predispose both drinking and aggression. (Here researchers have learned that drinking does indeed trigger aggressive behavior.)

b. *Educated people live longer, on average, than less-educated people. (One interpretation: Education lengthens life and enhances health.)* Perhaps richer people can afford more education *and* better health care. (Research supports *this* conclusion.)

c. *Teens engaged in team sports are less likely to use drugs, smoke, have sex, carry weapons, and eat junk food than are teens who do not engage in team sports. (One interpretation: Team sports encourage healthy living.)* Perhaps some third factor explains this correlation—teens who use drugs, smoke, have sex, carry weapons, and eat junk food may be "loners" who do not enjoy playing on any team.

d. *Adolescents who frequently see smoking in movies are more likely to smoke. (One interpretation: Movie stars' behavior influences impressionable teens.)* Perhaps adolescents who smoke and attend movies frequently have less parental supervision and more access to spending money than other adolescents.

4. **Why, when testing a new drug for blood pressure, would we learn more about its effectiveness from giving it to half of the participants in a group of 1000 than to all 1000 participants?**
ANSWER: To determine whether this drug is medically effective, we must compare its effect on those randomly assigned to receive it (the experimental group) with those who receive a placebo (the control group). The only difference between the groups is whether they received the actual drug. So, if blood pressure is lower in the experimental group, then we know that the drug itself has produced this effect, not just the participants' knowledge that they are being treated (placebo effect).

5. **How are human and animal research participants protected?**
ANSWER: Legislation, laboratory regulation and inspection, and local ethics committees serve to protect human and animal welfare.

MODULE 3 Neural and Hormonal Systems

1. **How do neurons communicate with one another?**
ANSWER: A neuron fires when excitatory inputs exceed inhibitory inputs by a sufficient threshold. When the resulting impulse reaches the axon's end, it triggers the release of chemical neurotransmitters. After crossing a tiny gap, these molecules activate receptor sites on neighboring neurons. So, the brief answer to how neurons communicate with one another is *chemically*.

2. **How does information flow through your nervous system as you pick up a fork? Can you summarize this process?**
ANSWER: Your central nervous system's hungry brain activates and guides the muscles of your arm and hand via your peripheral nervous system's motor neurons. As you pick up the fork, your brain processes the information from your sensory nervous system, enabling it to continue to guide the fork to your mouth. The functional circle starts with sensory input, continues with interneuron processing by the central nervous system, and finishes with motor output.

3. **Why is the pituitary gland called the "master gland"?**
ANSWER: The pituitary gland, responding to signals from the hypothalamus, releases hormones that act as triggers. In response, other endocrine glands release their own hormones, which in turn influence brain and behavior.

MODULE 4 The Brain

1. **Within what brain region would damage be most likely to disrupt your ability to skip rope? Your ability to sense tastes or sounds? In what brain region would damage perhaps leave you in a coma? Without the very breath and heartbeat of life?**
ANSWER: These regions are, respectively, the *cerebellum,* the *thalamus,* the *reticular formation,* and the *medulla.* These questions assess your understanding of the essential functions of the lower-level brain areas.

MODULE 5 Behavior Genetics and Evolutionary Psychology

1. What are the three main criticisms of the evolutionary explanation of human sexuality?
ANSWER: Critics of the evolutionary explanation of human sexuality point out that (1) it starts with an effect and works backward to propose an explanation; (2) unethical and immoral men could use such explanations to rationalize their behavior toward women; and (3) this explanation overlooks the effects of cultural expectations and socialization.

MODULE 6 Environmental Influences on Behavior

1. To predict whether a teenager smokes, ask how many of the teen's friends smoke. One explanation for this correlation is peer influence. What's another?
ANSWER: There may also be a *selection effect*. Adolescents tend to sort themselves into like-minded groups—the jocks, the geeks, the druggies, and so forth. Those who smoke may similarly seek out other teenagers who also smoke.

2. How do individualist and collectivist cultures differ?
ANSWER: A culture that favors individualism gives priority to personal goals over group goals; people in that culture will tend to define their identity in terms of their own personal attributes. A culture that favors collectivism gives priority to group goals over individual goals; people in collectivist cultures tend to define their identity in terms of group identifications. Cultures vary in the extent to which they favor individualism or collectivism.

3. What are gender roles, and what do their variations tell us about our human capacity for learning and adaptation?
ANSWER: *Gender roles* are social rules or norms for accepted and expected behavior for females and males. The norms associated with various roles, including gender roles, vary widely in different cultural contexts, which is proof that we are very capable of learning and adapting to the social demands of different environments.

MODULE 7 Developmental Issues, Prenatal Development, and the Newborn

1. Your friend—a heavy smoker—hopes to become pregnant soon and has stopped smoking. Why is this a good idea?
ANSWER: If a woman is a heavy smoker during her pregnancy, the fetus may receive fewer nutrients and be born underweight and at risk for health problems. Your friend is wise to quit smoking before there is a chance that the pregnancy has begun.

MODULE 8 Infancy and Childhood

1. Use Piaget's first three stages of cognitive development to explain why young children are *not* just miniature adults in the way they think.
ANSWER: Infants in the *sensorimotor stage* tend to be focused only on their own perceptions of the world and may, for example, be unaware that objects continue to exist when unseen. A *preoperational* child is still egocentric and incapable of appreciating simple logic, such as the reversibility of operations. A preteen in the *concrete operational stage* is beginning to think logically about concrete events but not about abstract concepts.

MODULE 9 Adolescence

1. How has the transition from childhood to adulthood changed in Western cultures in the last 100 years?

ANSWER: In the last 100 years, the transition to adulthood has started earlier and lasted longer, so that adolescence has lengthened from a period of about 7 years in 1890 to about 12 years in the 1990s.

MODULE 10 Adulthood

1. Research has shown that living together before marriage predicts an increased likelihood of future divorce. Can you imagine two possible explanations for this correlation?

ANSWER: William Axinn and Arland Thornton (1992) report data that support two explanations. (1) The first explanation is an example of a *selection effect*—our tendency to seek out others who are similar to us. Cohabitation attracts people who are more open to terminating unsatisfying relationships. People who cohabit bring a more individualistic ethic to marriage, are more likely to see close relationships as temporary and fragile, are more accepting of divorce, and are about three times more likely after marriage to have an affair (Forste & Tanfer, 1996). (2) Axinn and Thornton's second explanation illustrates the *causal effect* of the experience of cohabitation. Over time, those who cohabit tend to become more approving of dissolving an unfulfilling union. This divorce-accepting attitude increases the odds of later divorce.

MODULE 11 Introduction to Sensation and Perception: Vision

1. What is the rough distinction between sensation and perception?

ANSWER: *Sensation* is the bottom-up process by which the physical sensory system receives and represents stimuli. *Perception* is the top-down mental process of organizing and interpreting sensory input. But in our everyday experiences, sensation and perception are different aspects of one continuous process.

2. What is the rapid sequence of events that occurs when you see and recognize someone you know?

ANSWER: Light waves reflect off the person and travel into your eye, where the rods and cones convert the light waves' energy into neural impulses sent to your brain. Your brain then processes the subdimensions of this visual input—including color, depth, movement, and form—separately but simultaneously, and integrates this information (along with previously stored information) into a conscious perception of the person you know.

MODULE 12 Other Important Senses

1. In a nutshell, how do we transform sound waves into perceived sound?

ANSWER: A simple figure offers a synopsis:

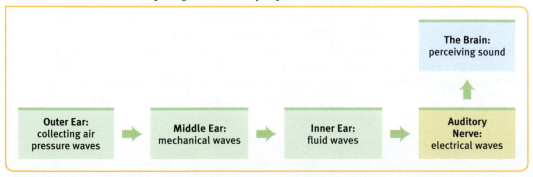

2. **What does the biopsychosocial approach to pain teach us?**
ANSWER: Considering the biological, psychological, and social-cultural influences on the perception of pain teaches us that our experience of pain is much more than neural messages sent to the brain.

3. **How does our system for sensing smell differ from our sensory systems for touch and taste?**
ANSWER: We have four basic touch senses and five taste sensations. But we have no basic smell receptors. Instead, 350 or so receptor proteins, individually and in combination, recognize some 10,000 discernible odors.

MODULE 13 Perceptual Organization

1. **What do we mean when we say that, in perception, the whole is greater than the sum of its parts?**
ANSWER: Gestalt psychologists used this saying to describe our perceptual tendency to organize clusters of sensations into meaningful forms or coherent groups.

MODULE 14 Perceptual Interpretation

1. **What type of evidence shows that, indeed, "there is more to perception than meets the senses"?**
ANSWER: We construct our perceptions based on both sensory input and—experiments show—on our assumptions, expectations, schemas, and perceptual sets, often influenced by the surrounding context.

MODULE 15 Waking and Sleeping Rhythms

1. **During psychology's history, what were the ups and downs of "consciousness"?**
ANSWER: Psychology began as the study of consciousness, but during the behaviorist era (for much of the first half of the twentieth century) psychologists focused on observations of behavior. After 1960, driven by discoveries in cognitive psychology and neuroscience, the study of consciousness (our awareness of ourselves and our environment) reemerged as a major topic in psychology.

2. **Are you getting enough sleep? What might you ask yourself to answer this question?**
ANSWER: You could start with the true/false questions in James Mass' sleep-deprivation quiz in Table 15.1 in Module 15. Also, William Dement (1999, p. 73) invites you to consider these questions: "How often do you think about taking a quick snooze? How often do you rub your eyes and yawn during the day? How often do you feel like you really need some coffee?" Dement concludes that "each of these is a warning of a sleep debt that you ignore at your peril."

MODULE 16 Hypnosis

1. **When is the use of hypnosis potentially harmful, and when can hypnosis be used to help?**
ANSWER: Hypnosis is potentially harmful when some therapists, seeking to "hypnotically refresh" memories, plant false memories. But posthypnotic suggestions have helped alleviate some ailments, and hypnosis can also help control pain.

MODULE 17 Drugs and Consciousness

1. **A U.S. government survey of 27,616 current or former alcohol drinkers found that 40 percent of those who began drinking before age 15 grew dependent on alcohol. The same was true of only 10 percent of those who first imbibed at ages 21 or 22 (Grant & Dawson, 1998). What possible explanations might there be for this correlation between early use and later abuse?**

ANSWER: Possible explanations include (1) a biological predisposition to both early use and later abuse, (2) brain changes and taste preferences induced by early use, and (3) enduring habits, attitudes, activities, and/or peer relationships that are conducive to alcohol use.

2. **In what ways are near-death experiences similar to drug-induced hallucinations?**
ANSWER: Reports of near-death experiences and drug-induced hallucinations feature similar experiences: replay of old memories, out-of-body sensations, and visions of tunnels or funnels of bright light or beings of light.

MODULE 18 Classical Conditioning

1. **As we develop, we learn cues that lead us to expect and prepare for good and bad events. We learn to repeat behaviors that bring rewards. And we watch others and learn. What do psychologists call these three types of learning?**
ANSWER: Through *classical conditioning,* we learn cues that lead us to expect and prepare for good and bad events. Through *operant conditioning,* we learn to repeat behaviors that bring rewards. Through *observational learning,* we watch others and learn.

2. **In slasher movies, sexually arousing images of women are sometimes paired with violence against women. Based on classical conditioning principles, what might be an effect of this pairing?**
ANSWER: If viewing an attractive nude or semi-nude woman (a US) elicits sexual arousal (a UR), then pairing the US with a new stimulus (violence) could turn the violence into a conditioned stimulus (CS) that also becomes sexually arousing, a conditioned response (CR).

MODULE 19 Operant Conditioning

1. *Positive reinforcement, negative reinforcement,* and *punishment* are tricky concepts for many students. Can you fit the right term in the four boxes in this table? I've done the first one (positive reinforcement) for you.

Type of Stimulus	Give It	Take It Away
Desired (for example, a compliment):	**Positive reinforcement**	*Punishment (e.g., time-out)*
Undesired/aversive (for example, an insult):	*Punishment*	*Negative reinforcement*

MODULE 20 Learning by Observation

1. **Jason's parents and older friends all smoke, but they advise him not to. Juan's parents and friends don't smoke, but they say nothing to deter him from doing so. Will Jason or Juan be more likely to start smoking?**
ANSWER: Although both saying and doing can influence people, experiments suggest that children more often do as others do and say as they say. Generalizing this finding to smoking, we can expect that Jason will be more likely to start smoking.

MODULE 21 Information Processing

1. **Memory includes (in alphabetical order) long-term memory, sensory memory, and working/short-term memory. What's the correct order of these three memory stores?**
ANSWER: Sensory memory, working/short-term memory, long-term memory.

2. **What would be the most effective strategy to learn and retain a list of names of key historical figures for a week? For a year?**
ANSWER: For a week: Make the names personally meaningful. For a year: Overlearn the list and space out rehearsals over the course of several weeks.

3. **Your friend tells you that her father experienced brain damage in an accident. She wonders if psychology can explain why he can still play checkers very well but has a hard time holding a sensible conversation. What can you tell her?**
ANSWER: Our *explicit* (declarable) memories differ from our *implicit* memories of skills and procedures, such as checkers. Our implicit memories are processed by more ancient brain areas, which apparently escaped damage during the accident.

4. **What is priming?**
ANSWER: *Priming* is the activation (often without our awareness) of associations. Seeing a gun, for example, might temporarily predispose someone to interpret an ambiguous face as threatening or to recall a boss as nasty. Although the person might not consciously remember the gun, it may prime how that individual interprets or recalls events.

MODULE 22 Forgetting, Memory Construction, and Improving Memory

1. **Can you offer an example of proactive interference?**
ANSWER: *Proactive* (forward-acting) interference occurs when earlier learning disrupts your recall of a later experience. Proactive interference has occurred if learning the names of new classmates in your first class makes it more difficult to learn the new names in your second class.

2. **What—given the commonality of source amnesia—might life be like if we remembered all our waking experiences and all our dreams?**
ANSWER: Real experiences would be confused with those we dreamed. When meeting someone, we might therefore be unsure whether we were reacting to something they previously had done or to something we dreamed they had done. William Dement (1999, p. 298) thinks this "would put a great burden on your sanity. . . . I truly believe that the wall of memory is a blessed protection."

3. **What are the recommended memory strategies you just read about? (One advised rehearsing to-be-remembered material. What were the others?)**
ANSWER: Study repeatedly to boost long-term recall. Spend more time rehearsing or actively thinking about the material. Make the material personally meaningful. To remember a list of unfamiliar items, use mnemonic devices. Refresh your memory by activating retrieval cues. Recall events while they are fresh, before you encounter possible misinformation. Minimize interference. Test your own knowledge, both to rehearse it and to help determine what you do not yet know.

MODULE 23 Thinking

1. **The availability heuristic is a quick-and-easy but sometimes misleading guide to judging reality. What is the availability heuristic?**
ANSWER: The *availability heuristic* is our tendency to judge the likelihood of an event by how easily we can recall instances of it. Like all heuristics, this guide is efficient. But it can mislead, as it does when we attempt to judge various risks (for example, of plane travel).

MODULE 24) Language and Thought

1. If children are not yet speaking, is there any reason to think they would benefit from parents and other caregivers reading to them?

ANSWER: Indeed there is, because well before age 1 children are learning to detect words among the stream of spoken sounds, and to discern grammatical rules. Before age 1, they also are babbling with the phonemes of their own language. More than many parents realize, their infants are soaking up language. As researcher Peter Jusczyk reminds us, "Little ears are listening."

2. To say that "words are the mother of ideas" assumes the truth of what concept?

ANSWER: This phrase supports the linguistic determinism hypothesis, which asserts that language determines thought. Research indicates that this position is too extreme, but language does *influence* what we perceive and think.

3. If your dog barks at a stranger at the front door, does this qualify as language? What if the dog yips in a telltale way to let you know she needs to go out?

ANSWER: These are definitely communications. But if language consists of words and the grammatical rules we use to combine them to communicate meaning, few scientists would label a dog's barking and yipping as language.

MODULE 25) Intelligence

1. Joseph is a straight-A student at Harvard Law School, writes a small column for the *Harvard Law Review*, and will be working for a Supreme Court justice next year. Judith is very proud of her grandson and says he is way more intelligent than she ever was. But Joseph is also very proud of his grandmother, who had been imprisoned by the Nazis. When the war ended, she walked out of Germany, contacted a relief agency, traveled to the United States, and began a new life. According to the definition of *intelligence* in this module, is Joseph the only intelligent person in this story? Why or why not?

ANSWER: Joseph is not the only intelligent person in this story. *Intelligence* is the ability to learn from experience, solve problems, and use knowledge to adapt to new situations. Judith certainly fits this description, given all that she accomplished after her release.

2. What was the purpose of Binet's pioneering intelligence test?

ANSWER: Binet's original test was designed to predict school achievement.

3. The Smiths have enrolled their 2-year-old son in a special program that promises to assess his IQ and, if he places in the top 5 percent of test-takers, to create a plan that will guarantee his admission to a top university at age 18. Is this a good plan?

ANSWER: The Smiths would be wasting their time and money. Two years is too young an age for reliably predicting future intelligence.

4. As society succeeds in creating equality of opportunity, it will also increase the heritability of ability. The heritability of intelligence scores will be greater in a society marked by equal opportunity than in a society of peasants and aristocrats. Why?

ANSWER: Perfect environmental equality would create 100 percent heritability— because genes alone would account for any remaining human differences.

MODULE 26) Introduction to Motivation: Hunger

1. While on a long road trip, you consider pulling over to call a loved one. But it's getting late and you are hungry, so you drive on ahead to the next town. What motivational perspective would most easily explain this behavior and why?

ANSWER: *Drive-reduction theory*—the idea that physical needs create an aroused state that drives us to reduce the need—helps explain your behavior.

2. **You are traveling and have not eaten anything in eight hours. As your long-awaited favorite dish is placed in front of you, your mouth waters. Even imagining this may set your mouth to watering. What triggers this anticipatory drooling?**

   ANSWER: You, like Pavlov's dogs, have learned through *classical conditioning* to respond to the cues—the sight and aroma—that signal the food about to enter your mouth. Both *physiological cues* (eight hours of deprivation have left you with low blood sugar) and *psychological cues* (the anticipation of the tasty meal) have heightened your experienced hunger.

MODULE 27 Sexual Motivation

1. **How might the evolutionary psychology perspective explain sexual motivation and our need to affiliate?**

   ANSWER: Evolutionary psychologists attempt to explain behaviors in terms of their survival value. From this perspective, sexual motivation and the need to affiliate can be interpreted as behaviors that help ensure the transmission (and therefore survival) of our DNA to future generations.

MODULE 28 Motivation at Work

1. **Given a choice of tasks, high achievers usually select one that is moderately challenging, but low achievers tend to choose very easy or very difficult tasks. What would explain this difference?**

   ANSWER: High achievers tend to choose tasks where success is possible, but it will be attributed to their talents and efforts. Low achievers are likely to choose tasks where they cannot fail, or where their failure will not be embarrassing because the task was very difficult.

MODULE 29 Theories and Physiology of Emotion

1. **Christine is holding her 8-month-old baby when a fierce dog appears out of nowhere and, with teeth bared, leaps for the baby's face. Christine immediately ducks for cover to protect the baby, screams at the dog, then notices that her heart is banging in her chest and she's broken out in a cold sweat. How would the James-Lange, Cannon-Bard, and two-factor theories explain Christine's emotional reaction?**

   ANSWER: The James-Lange theory would say that Christine's emotional reaction consists of her awareness of her physiological responses to the dog attack. The Cannon-Bard theory would say that her fear experience happened simultaneously with her physiological arousal. Schacter's two-factor theory would presume that her emotional reaction stemmed from her interpreting and labeling the arousal.

2. **How do the two divisions of the autonomic nervous system help us respond to and recover from a crisis, and why is this relevant to the study of emotions?**

   ANSWER: The sympathetic division of the ANS arouses us in a crisis, and the parasympathetic division of the ANS calms us when the crisis has passed. Researchers study these physiological responses, in combination with brain pattern indicators, to reach a more complete understanding of the feeling component of emotions.

MODULE 30 Expressing and Experiencing Emotion

1. **Who tends to express more emotion—men or women? How do we know the answer to that question?**

   ANSWER: Women tend to surpass men not only as emotion detectors but also at expressing certain emotions. Researchers discovered this by using such methods as showing people brief, silent clips of faces expressing various emotions and by observing who is most skilled at reading and sending emotions.

2. **What things do (and do not) predict self-reported happiness?**
ANSWER: People's age, gender, education level, parenthood, and physical attractiveness are not closely related to their happiness. Predictors of happiness include high self-esteem; optimism and an agreeable, outgoing personality; close friendships or a satisfying marriage; satisfying work and leisure activities; a meaningful religious faith; and adequate sleep and exercise.

MODULE 31 Stress and Illness

1. **What are the basic links in our stress response system?**
ANSWER: When alerted to a threat (to negative, uncontrollable events), our sympathetic nervous system arouses us. Heart rate and respiration increase. Blood is diverted from digestion to the skeletal muscles. The body releases sugar and fat to prepare for fight or flight. Simultaneously, the brain orders a sudden outpouring of hormones. The system is wonderfully adaptive, but if stress is continuous, health consequences and exhaustion may result.

MODULE 32 Promoting Health

1. **Those who frequently attend religious services live longer than those who attend infrequently or not at all. What type of research finding is this, and what explanations might it have?**
ANSWER: This is a correlational finding—frequent attendance at religious services is associated with (and predicts) health and longevity. But this is not a cause-effect statement. Longevity may be associated with religiosity because women (who tend to live longer than men) attend services more regularly, or because people in poor health are not able to attend services. But even controlling for these factors, the relationship remains, which indicates that the connection could reflect the healthy behaviors, stress-reducing social support, relaxed meditative state, optimistic outlook, and enhanced well-being often experienced by religiously active people.

MODULE 33 The Psychoanalytic Perspective

1. **What, according to Freud, were some of the important defense mechanisms, and what do they defend against? How many of these find support in modern research?**
ANSWER: Freud believed repression to be the basic defense mechanism. Others include regression, reaction formation, projection, rationalization, and displacement. All supposedly serve to reduce anxiety. Modern research supports the phenomenon Freud called *projection* and current researchers call the *false consensus effect*. Some evidence also supports self-esteem defenses, such as reaction formation. But there is little support for the others.

MODULE 34 The Humanistic Perspective

1. **What does it mean to be "empathic"? To be "self-actualized"?**
ANSWER: To be *empathic* is to share and mirror another person's feelings. Carl Rogers believed that people nurture growth in others by being empathic. Abraham Maslow viewed *self-actualization* as the ultimate psychological need—the motivation to fulfill one's potential.

MODULE 35 Contemporary Research on Personality

1. **How many trait dimensions are currently used to describe personality, and what are those dimensions?**

   ANSWER: "The Big Five" trait dimensions—*emotional stability, extraversion, openness, agreeableness,* and *conscientiousness*—provide a reasonably complete personality description.

2. **How do learned helplessness and optimism influence behavior?**

   ANSWER: Learned helplessness produces passive resignation after organisms find themselves unable to avoid aversive events. Nursing homes, prisons, colleges, and autocratic companies and countries have all been observed to produce symptoms of learned helplessness. Optimism has the opposite effect, leading to better moods, more persistence, and better health. Excessive optimism, however, can expose us to risks.

3. **In a 1997 Gallup poll, white Americans estimated 44 percent of their fellow white Americans to be high in prejudice (scoring them 5 or higher on a 10-point scale). How many rated themselves similarly high in prejudice? Just 14 percent. What phenomenon does this illustrate? Explain.**

   ANSWER: This illustrates the general tendency to see oneself as superior to the average other, which is one example of the *self-serving bias.*

MODULE 36 Introduction to Psychological Disorders

1. **What is the biopsychosocial approach, and why is it important in our understanding of psychological disorders?**

   ANSWER: This contemporary approach assumes that biological, psychological, and social-cultural influences combine to produce psychological disorders. Genes matter. The brain matters. Inner thoughts and feelings matter. Social and cultural influences matter. To get the whole integrated picture, a biopsychosocial perspective helps.

2. **Does poverty cause psychological disorders? Explain.**

   ANSWER: Poverty-related stresses can indeed help trigger disorders. But disabling disorders can also contribute to poverty. Thus, poverty and disorders are often a chicken-and-egg situation, and it's hard to know which came first.

MODULE 37 Anxiety, Dissociative, and Personality Disorders

1. **How do generalized anxiety disorder, phobias, and obsessive-compulsive disorder differ?**

   ANSWER: *Generalized anxiety disorder* is unfocused tension, apprehension, and arousal. *Phobias* focus anxiety on specific feared objects or situations. *Obsessive-compulsive disorder* expresses anxiety through unwanted repetitive thoughts (obsessions) or actions (compulsions).

2. **Is antisocial personality disorder an inherited condition?**

   ANSWER: *Antisocial personality disorder*—in which a person exhibits a lack of conscience for wrongdoing—seems to have both biological and psychological components. Twin and adoption studies show that biological relatives of people with this disorder are at increased risk for antisocial behavior. But the tendency to be fearless, when combined with a sense of social responsibility, can lead to heroism, adventurism, or athletic success.

MODULE 38) Mood Disorders

1. What does it mean to say that "depression is the common cold of psychological disorders"?

ANSWER: Saying that "depression is the common cold of psychological disorders" is a quick way to state that this serious disorder is the most common condition in those seeking mental health treatment—with almost 6 percent of men and nearly 10 percent of women reporting a depressive episode each year. Worldwide, depression is the leading cause of disability.

MODULE 39) Schizophrenia

1. What do we know about the causes of schizophrenia?

ANSWER: Brain abnormalities, such as an excess of dopamine receptors, are common among people with schizophrenia. Brain scans also reveal abnormal brain structures, such as enlarged, fluid-filled areas and smaller-than-normal cortexes. The disorders clustered under the label "schizophrenia" have a genetic component: lifetime risk of developing schizophrenia increases for those related to a person with the disease. But other factors, such as prenatal viral infections, nutritional deprivation, and oxygen deprivation during birth, may act as triggers to "turn on" genes that predispose some people to schizophrenia. Research continues on causes of this disorder, which is found worldwide.

MODULE 40) The Psychological Therapies

1. What is the major distinction between the underlying assumption in psychoanalytic and humanistic therapies and the underlying assumption in behavior therapies?

ANSWER: Psychoanalytic and humanistic therapies seek to relieve problems by providing insight into their origins. Behavior therapies assume the problem behavior *is* the problem and treat it directly, paying less attention to its origins.

MODULE 41) Evaluating Psychotherapies

1. How does the placebo effect bias clients' appraisals of the effectiveness of psychotherapies?

ANSWER: The *placebo effect* is the healing power of *belief* in a treatment. Patients who expect a treatment to be effective may believe it was.

MODULE 42) The Biomedical Therapies

1. How do researchers evaluate the effectiveness of particular drug therapies?

ANSWER: Ideally, researchers assign people to treatment and no-treatment conditions to see if those who receive therapy improve more than those who don't. In many studies, the no-treatment comparison includes a placebo condition, which allows a double-blind controlled study. If neither the therapist nor the client knows for sure whether the client has received the experimental treatment (for example, a drug), then any difference between the treated and untreated groups will reflect the treatment's actual effect.

2. What are the influences to keep in mind for successful therapeutic intervention?

ANSWER: Successful therapeutic intervention—or prevention—can intervene at many different levels because biological, psychological, and social-cultural influences can combine and interact to produce psychological disorders. Bodily (for example, neurochemical) imbalances can affect mental states, and both biochemical and mental states may be affected by environmental conditions.

MODULE 43 Social Thinking

1. **Driving to school one wintry day, Marco narrowly misses a car that slides through a red light. "Slow down! What a terrible driver," he thinks to himself. Moments later, Marco himself slips through an intersection and yelps, "Wow! These roads are awful. The city snow plows need to get out here." What social psychology principle has Marco just demonstrated? Explain.**

   ANSWER: By attributing the other person's behavior to the person ("he's a terrible driver") and his own to the situation ("these roads are awful"), Marco has exhibited the *fundamental attribution error*.

MODULE 44 Social Influence

1. **You are organizing a Town Hall–style meeting of fiercely competitive political candidates. To add to the fun, friends have suggested handing out masks of the candidates' faces for supporters to wear. What phenomenon might these masks engage?**

   ANSWER: The anonymity provided by the masks, combined with the arousal of the contentious setting, might create *deindividuation* (lessened self-awareness and self-restraint in a group setting).

MODULE 45 Social Relations

1. **Why didn't anybody help Kitty Genovese? What social relations principle did this incident illustrate?**

   ANSWER: The incident illustrated the *bystander effect*. In the presence of others, an individual is less likely to notice a situation, correctly interpret it as an emergency, and then take responsibility for offering help. Many of Kitty Genovese's neighbors noticed the situation and recognized it as an emergency but they apparently assumed others would help, and they did not feel responsible for offering help.

GLOSSARY

absolute threshold the minimum stimulation needed to detect a particular stimulus 50 percent of the time. (p. 144)

accommodation adapting one's current understandings (schemas) to incorporate new information. (p. 107)

accommodation the process by which the eye's lens changes shape to focus near or far objects on the retina. (p. 148)

achievement motivation a desire for significant accomplishment: for mastery of things, people, or ideas; for attaining a high standard. (p. 398)

achievement test a test designed to assess what a person has learned. (p. 338)

acquisition the initial stage in classical conditioning; the phase associating a neutral stimulus with an unconditioned stimulus so that the neutral stimulus comes to elicit a conditioned response. (p. 237)

action potential a neural impulse; a brief electrical charge that travels down an axon. (p. 38)

active listening empathic listening in which the listener echoes, restates, and clarifies. A feature of Rogers' client-centered therapy. (p. 544)

adaptation-level phenomenon our tendency to form judgments (of sounds, of lights, of income) relative to a neutral level defined by our prior experience. (p. 429)

addiction compulsive drug craving and use. (p. 217)

adolescence the transition period from childhood to adulthood, extending from puberty to independence. (p. 120)

adrenal [ah-DREEN-el] glands a pair of endocrine glands just above the kidneys. The adrenals secrete the hormones epinephrine (adrenaline) and norepinephrine (noradrenaline), which help to arouse the body in times of stress. (p. 45)

aerobic exercise sustained exercise that increases heart and lung fitness; may also alleviate depression and anxiety. (p. 449)

aggression any physical or verbal behavior intended to hurt or destroy. (pp. 88, 599)

algorithm a methodical, logical rule or procedure that guarantees solving a particular problem. Contrasts with the usually speedier—but also more error-prone—use of *heuristics*. (p. 308)

alpha waves the relatively slow brain waves of a relaxed, awake state. (p. 198)

altruism unselfish regard for the welfare of others. (p. 613)

amnesia the loss of memory. (p. 281)

amphetamines drugs that stimulate neural activity, causing speeded-up body functions and associated energy and mood changes. (p. 220)

amygdala [uh-MIG-duh-la] two lima bean-sized neural clusters that are components of the limbic system and are linked to emotion. (p. 52)

anorexia nervosa an eating disorder in which a normal-weight person (usually an adolescent female) diets and becomes significantly (15 percent or more) underweight, yet, still feeling fat, continues to starve. (p. 364)

antisocial personality disorder a personality disorder in which the person (usually a man) exhibits a lack of conscience for wrongdoing, even toward friends and family members. May be aggressive and ruthless or a clever con artist. (p. 517)

anxiety disorders psychological disorders characterized by distressing, persistent anxiety or maladaptive behaviors that reduce anxiety. (p. 509)

aphasia impairment of language, usually caused by left hemisphere damage either to Broca's area (impairing speaking) or to Wernicke's area (impairing understanding). (p. 58)

applied research scientific study that aims to solve practical problems. (p. 8)

aptitude test a test designed to predict a person's future performance; *aptitude* is the capacity to learn. (p. 338)

assimilation interpreting one's new experience in terms of one's existing schemas. (p. 107)

association areas areas of the cerebral cortex that are not involved in primary motor or sensory functions; rather, they are involved in higher mental functions such as learning, remembering, thinking, and speaking. (p. 57)

associative learning learning that certain events occur together. The events may be two stimuli (as in classical conditioning) or a response and its consequences (as in operant conditioning). (pp. 235, 246)

attachment an emotional tie with another person; shown in young children by their seeking closeness to the caregiver and showing distress on separation. (p. 113)

attention-deficit hyperactivity disorder (ADHD) a psychological disorder marked by the appearance by age 7 of one or more of three key symptoms: extreme inattention, hyperactivity, and impulsivity. (p. 501)

attitude feelings, often based on our beliefs, that predispose us to respond in a particular way to objects, people, and events. (p. 577)

attribution theory suggests how we explain someone's behavior—by crediting either the situation or the person's disposition. (p. 575)

audition the sense or act of hearing. (p. 157)

autism a disorder that appears in childhood and is marked by deficient communication, social interaction, and understanding of others' states of mind. (p. 111)

automatic processing unconscious encoding of incidental information, such as space, time, and frequency, and of well-learned information, such as word meanings. (p. 271)

autonomic [aw-tuh-NAHM-ik] **nervous system** the part of the peripheral nervous system that controls the glands and the muscles of the internal organs (such as the heart). Its sympathetic division arouses; its parasympathetic division calms. (p. 42)

availability heuristic estimating the likelihood of events based on their availability in memory; if instances come readily to mind (perhaps because of their vividness), we presume such events are common. (p. 311)

aversive conditioning a type of counterconditioning that associates an unpleasant state (such as nausea) with an unwanted behavior (such as drinking alcohol). (p. 547)

axon the extension of a neuron, ending in branching terminal fibers, through which messages pass to other neurons or to muscles or glands. (p. 37)

babbling stage beginning at about 4 months, the stage of speech development in which the infant spontaneously utters various sounds at first unrelated to the household language. (p. 320)

barbiturates drugs that depress the activity of the central nervous system, reducing anxiety but impairing memory and judgment. (p. 219)

basal metabolic rate the body's resting rate of energy expenditure. (p. 362)

basic research pure science that aims to increase the scientific knowledge base. (p. 8)

basic trust according to Erik Erikson, a sense that the world is predictable and trustworthy; said to be formed during infancy by appropriate experiences with responsive caregivers. (p. 116)

behavior genetics the study of the relative power and limits of genetic and environmental influences on behavior. (p. 66)

behavior therapy therapy that applies learning principles to the elimination of unwanted behaviors. (p. 545)

behaviorism the view that psychology (1) should be an objective science that (2) studies behavior without reference to mental processes. Most research psychologists today agree with (1) but not with (2). (pp. 5, 235)

belief perseverance clinging to one's initial conceptions after the basis on which they were formed has been discredited. (p. 313)

binocular cues depth cues, such as retinal disparity, that depend on the use of two eyes. (p. 174)

biofeedback a system for electronically recording, amplifying, and feeding back information regarding a subtle physiological state, such as blood pressure or muscle tension. (p. 451)

biological psychology a branch of psychology concerned with the links between biology and behavior. (Some biological psychologists call themselves *behavioral neuroscientists, neuropsychologists, behavior geneticists, physiological psychologists,* or *biopsychologists.*) (p. 37)

biomedical therapy prescribed medications or medical procedures that act directly on the patient's nervous system. (p. 565)

biopsychosocial approach an integrated approach that incorporates biological, psychological, and social-cultural levels of analysis. (p. 6)

bipolar disorder a mood disorder in which the person alternates between the hopelessness and lethargy of depression and the overexcited state of mania. (Formerly called manic-depressive disorder.) (p. 522)

blind spot the point at which the optic nerve leaves the eye, creating a "blind" spot because no receptor cells are located there. (p. 149)

bottom-up processing analysis that begins with the sensory receptors and works up to the brain's integration of sen sory information. (p. 143)

brainstem the oldest part and central core of the brain, beginning where the spinal cord swells as it enters the skull; the brainstem is responsible for automatic survival functions. (p. 48)

Broca's area controls language expression—an area of the frontal lobe, usually in the left hemisphere, that directs the muscle movements involved in speech. (p. 58)

bulimia nervosa an eating disorder characterized by episodes of overeating, usually of high-calorie foods, followed by vomiting, laxative use, fasting, or excessive exercise. (p. 364)

bystander effect the tendency for any given bystander to be less likely to give aid if other bystanders are present. (p. 614)

Cannon-Bard theory the theory that an emotion-arousing stimulus simultaneously triggers (1) physiological responses and (2) the subjective experience of emotion. (p. 407)

case study an observation technique in which one person is studied in depth in the hope of revealing universal principles. (p. 19)

catharsis emotional release. In psychology, the catharsis hypothesis maintains that "releasing" aggressive energy (through action or fantasy) relieves aggressive urges. (p. 424)

central nervous system (CNS) the brain and spinal cord. (p. 41)

cerebellum [sehr-uh-BELL-um] the "little brain" attached to the rear of the brainstem; its functions include processing sensory input and coordinating movement output and balance. (p. 49)

cerebral [seh-REE-bruhl] **cortex** the intricate fabric of interconnected neural cells that covers the cerebral hemispheres; the body's ultimate control and information-processing center. (p. 53)

chromosomes threadlike structures made of DNA molecules that contain the genes. (p. 67)

chunking organizing items into familiar, manageable units; often occurs automatically. (p. 276)

circadian [ser-KAY-dee-an] **rhythm** the biological clock; regular bodily rhythms (for example, of temperature and wakefulness) that occur on a 24-hour cycle. (p. 196)

classical conditioning a type of learning in which an organism comes to associate stimuli. A neutral stimulus that signals an unconditioned stimulus (US) begins to produce a response that anticipates and prepares for the unconditioned stimulus. Also called *Pavlovian* or *respondent conditioning.* (p. 235)

client-centered therapy a humanistic therapy, developed by Carl Rogers, in which the therapist uses techniques such as active listening within a genuine, accepting, empathic environment to facilitate clients' growth. (Also called *person-centered therapy.*) (p. 543)

clinical psychology a branch of psychology that studies, assesses, and treats people with psychological disorders. (p. 9)

cochlea [KOHK-lee-uh] a coiled, bony, fluid-filled tube in the inner ear through which sound waves trigger nerve impulses. (p. 159)

cognition all the mental activities associated with thinking, knowing, remembering, and communicating. (pp. 107, 307)

cognitive dissonance theory the theory that we act to reduce the discomfort (dissonance) we feel when two of our thoughts (cognitions) are inconsistent. For example, when our awareness of our attitudes and of our actions clash, we can reduce the resulting dissonance by changing our attitudes. (p. 579)

cognitive map a mental representation of the layout of one's environment. For example, after exploring a maze, rats act as if they have learned a cognitive map of it. (p. 253)

cognitive therapy therapy that teaches people new, more adaptive ways of thinking and acting; based on the assumption that thoughts intervene between events and our emotional reactions. (p. 549)

cognitive-behavior therapy a popular integrated therapy that combines cognitive therapy (changing self-defeating thinking) with behavior therapy (changing behavior). (p. 551)

collective unconscious Carl Jung's concept of a shared, inherited reservoir of memory traces from our species' history. (p. 462)

collectivism giving priority to goals of one's group (often one's extended family or work group) and defining one's identity accordingly. (p. 84)

color constancy perceiving familiar objects as having consistent color, even if changing illumination alters the wavelengths reflected by the object. (p. 176)

companionate love the deep affectionate attachment we feel for those with whom our lives are intertwined. (p. 611)

complementary and alternative medicine (CAM) as yet unproven health care treatments intended to supplement (complement) or serve as alternatives to conventional medicine, and which typically are not widely taught in medical schools, used in hospitals, or reimbursed by insurance companies. When research shows a therapy to be safe and effective, it usually then becomes part of accepted medical practice. (p. 452)

concept a mental grouping of similar objects, events, ideas, or people. (p. 307)

concrete operational stage in Piaget's theory, the stage of cognitive development (from about 6 or 7 to 11 years of age) during which children gain the mental operations that enable them to think logically about concrete events. (p. 111)

conditioned reinforcer a stimulus that gains its reinforcing power through its association with a primary reinforcer; also known as *secondary reinforcer*. (p. 249)

conditioned response (CR) in classical conditioning, the learned response to a previously neutral (but now conditioned) stimulus (CS). (p. 236)

conditioned stimulus (CS) in classical conditioning, an originally irrelevant stimulus that, after association with an unconditioned stimulus (US), comes to trigger a conditioned response. (p. 236)

cones retinal receptor cells that are concentrated near the center of the retina and that function in daylight or in well-lit conditions. The cones detect fine detail and give rise to color sensations. (p. 149)

confirmation bias a tendency to search for information that confirms one's preconceptions. (p. 309)

conflict a perceived incompatibility of actions, goals, or ideas. (p. 615)

conformity adjusting one's behavior or thinking to coincide with a group standard. (p. 583)

consciousness our awareness of ourselves and our environment. (p. 193)

conservation the principle (which Piaget believed to be a part of concrete operational reasoning) that properties such as mass, volume, and number remain the same despite changes in the forms of objects. (p. 109)

content validity the extent to which a test samples the behavior that is of interest (such as a driving test that samples driving tasks). (p. 339)

continuous reinforcement reinforcing the desired response every time it occurs. (p. 250)

control group the group in an experiment that contrasts with the experimental group and serves as a comparison for evaluating the effect of the treatment. (p. 25)

coronary heart disease the clogging of the vessels that nourish the heart muscle; the leading cause of death in many developed countries. (p. 438)

corpus callosum [KOR-pus kah-LOW-sum] the large band of neural fibers connecting the two brain hemispheres and carrying messages between them. (p. 60)

correlation a measure of the extent to which two factors vary together, and thus of how well either factor predicts the other. The *correlation coefficient* is the mathematical expression of the relationship, ranging from –1 to +1. (p. 21)

correlation coefficient a statistical measure of the extent to which two factors vary together, and thus of how well either factor predicts the other. Scores with a *positive correlation coefficient* go up and down together (as with high school and college GPAs). A *negative correlation coefficient* indicates that one score falls as the other rises (as in the relationship between self-esteem and depression). (p. A-4)

counseling psychology a branch of psychology that assists people with problems in living (often related to school, work, or marriage) and in achieving greater well-being. (p. 9)

counterconditioning a behavior therapy procedure that conditions new responses to stimuli that trigger unwanted behaviors; based on classical conditioning. Includes *exposure therapies* and *aversive conditioning*. (p. 545)

creativity the ability to produce novel and valuable ideas. (p. 334)

critical period an optimal period shortly after birth when an organism's exposure to certain stimuli or experiences produces proper development. (p. 114)

critical thinking thinking that does not blindly accept arguments and conclusions. Rather, it examines assumptions, discerns hidden values, evaluates evidence, and assesses conclusions. (p. 16)

cross-sectional study a study in which people of different ages are compared with one another. (p. A-7)

crystallized intelligence one's accumulated knowledge and verbal skills; tends to increase with age. (p. 133)

culture the enduring behaviors, ideas, attitudes, values, and traditions shared by a group of people and transmitted from one generation to the next. (pp. 28, 82)

defense mechanisms in psychoanalytic theory, the ego's protective methods of reducing anxiety by unconsciously distorting reality. (p. 462)

deindividuation the loss of self-awareness and self-restraint occurring in group situations that foster arousal and anonymity. (p. 589)

déjà vu that eerie sense that "I've experienced this before." Cues from the current situation may subconsciously trigger retrieval of an earlier experience. (p. 286)

delta waves the large, slow brain waves associated with deep sleep. (p. 198)

delusions false beliefs, often of persecution or grandeur, that may accompany schizophrenia and other disorders. (p. 531)

dendrite the bushy, branching extensions of a neuron that receive messages and conduct impulses toward the cell body. (p. 37)

dependent variable the outcome factor; the variable that may change in response to manipulations of the independent variable. (p. 26)

depressants drugs (such as alcohol, barbiturates, and opiates) that reduce neural activity and slow body functions. (p. 218)

depth perception the ability to see objects in three dimensions although the images that strike the retina are two-dimensional; allows us to judge distance. (p. 173)

developmental psychology a branch of psychology that studies physical, cognitive, and social change throughout the life span. (p. 99)

difference threshold the minimum difference between two stimuli required for detection 50 percent of the time. We experience the difference threshold as a *just noticeable difference* (or *jnd*). (p. 145)

discrimination in classical conditioning, the learned ability to distinguish between a conditioned stimulus and stimuli that do not signal an unconditioned stimulus. (p. 239)

discrimination unjustifiable negative behavior toward a group or its members. (p. 594)

displacement psychoanalytic defense mechanism that shifts sexual or aggressive impulses toward a more acceptable or less threatening object or person, as when redirecting anger toward a safer outlet. (p. 462)

dissociation a split in consciousness, which allows some thoughts and behaviors to occur simultaneously with others. (p. 213)

dissociative disorders disorders in which conscious awareness becomes separated (dissociated) from previous memories, thoughts, and feelings. (p. 515)

dissociative identity disorder (DID) a rare dissociative disorder in which a person exhibits two or more distinct and alternating personalities. Also called *multiple personality disorder*. (p. 515)

DNA (deoxyribonucleic acid) a complex molecule containing the genetic information that makes up the chromosomes. (p. 67)

double-blind procedure an experimental procedure in which both the research participants and the research staff are ignorant (blind) about whether the research participants have received the treatment or a placebo. Commonly used in drug-evaluation studies. (p. 25)

Down syndrome a condition of retardation and associated physical disorders caused by an extra chromosome in one's genetic makeup. (p. 340)

dream a sequence of images, emotions, and thoughts passing through a sleeping person's mind. Dreams are notable for their hallucinatory imagery, discontinuities, and incongruities, and for the dreamer's delusional acceptance of the content and later difficulties remembering it. (p. 206)

drive-reduction theory the idea that a physiological need creates an aroused tension state (a drive) that motivates an organism to satisfy the need. (p. 358)

DSM-IV the American Psychiatric Association's *Diagnostic and Statistical Manual of Mental Disorders* (Fourth Edition), a widely used system for classifying psychological disorders. Presently distributed in an updated "text revision" (DSM-IV-TR). (p. 503)

echoic memory a momentary sensory memory of auditory stimuli; if attention is elsewhere, sounds and words can still be recalled within 3 or 4 seconds. (p. 277)

eclectic approach an approach to psychotherapy that, depending on the client's problems, uses techniques from various forms of therapy. (p. 541)

Ecstasy (MDMA) a synthetic stimulant and mild hallucinogen. Produces euphoria and social intimacy, but with short-term health risks and longer-term harm to serotonin-producing neurons and to mood and cognition. (p. 223)

effortful processing encoding that requires attention and conscious effort. (p. 271)

ego the largely conscious, "executive" part of personality that, according to Freud, mediates among the demands of the id, superego, and reality. The ego operates on the *reality principle,* satisfying the id's desires in ways that will realistically bring pleasure rather than pain. (p. 460)

egocentrism in Piaget's theory, the preoperational child's difficulty taking another's point of view. (p. 110)

electroconvulsive therapy (ECT) a biomedical therapy for severely depressed patients in which a brief electric current is sent through the brain of an anesthetized patient. (p. 568)

electroencephalogram (EEG) an amplified recording of the waves of electrical activity that sweep across the brain's surface. These waves are measured by electrodes placed on the scalp. (p. 50)

embryo the developing human organism from about 2 weeks after fertilization through the second month. (p. 101)

emotion a response of the whole organism, involving (1) physiological arousal, (2) expressive behaviors, and (3) conscious experience. (p. 407)

emotional intelligence the ability to perceive, understand, manage, and use emotions. (p. 335)

empirically derived test a test (such as the MMPI) developed by testing a pool of items and then selecting those that discriminate between groups. (p. 477)

encoding the processing of information into the memory system—for example, by extracting meaning. (p. 270)

endocrine [EN-duh-krin] system the body's "slow" chemical communication system; a set of glands that secrete hormones into the bloodstream. (p. 44)

endorphins [en-DOR-fins] "morphine within"—natural, opiatelike neurotransmitters linked to pain control and to pleasure. (p. 40)

environment every nongenetic influence, from prenatal nutrition to the people and things around us. (p. 66)

equity a condition in which people receive from a relationship in proportion to what they give to it. (p. 612)

estrogen a sex hormone, secreted in greater amounts by females than by males. In nonhuman female mammals, estrogen levels peak during ovulation, promoting sexual receptivity. (p. 376)

evolutionary psychology the study of the evolution of behavior and the mind, using principles of natural selection. (p. 73)

experiment a research method in which an investigator manipulates one or more factors (independent variables) to observe the effect on some behavior or mental process (the dependent variable). By random assignment of participants, the experimenter aims to control other relevant factors. (p. 25)

experimental group the group in an experiment that is exposed to the treatment, that is, to one version of the independent variable. (p. 25)

explicit memory memory of facts and experiences that one can consciously know and "declare." (Also called *declarative memory*.) (p. 282)

exposure therapies behavioral techniques, such as systematic desensitization, that treat anxieties by exposing people (in imagination or actuality) to the things they fear and avoid. (p. 546)

external locus of control the perception that chance or outside forces beyond one's personal control determine one's fate. (p. 485)

extinction the diminishing of a conditioned response; occurs in classical conditioning when an unconditioned stimulus (US) does not follow a conditioned stimulus (CS). (p. 238)

extrasensory perception (ESP) the controversial claim that perception can occur apart from sensory input. Said to include *telepathy, clairvoyance,* and *precognition.* (p. 186)

extrinsic motivation a desire to perform a behavior due to promised rewards or threats of punishment. (p. 253)

family therapy therapy that treats the family as a system. Views an individual's unwanted behaviors as influenced by or directed at other family members. (p. 551)

feature detectors nerve cells in the brain that respond to specific features of the stimulus, such as shape, angle, or movement. (p. 151)

feel-good, do-good phenomenon people's tendency to be helpful when already in a good mood. (p. 425)

fetal alcohol syndrome (FAS) physical and cognitive abnormalities in children caused by a pregnant woman's heavy drinking. In severe cases, symptoms include noticeable facial misproportions. (p. 102)

fetus the developing human organism from 9 weeks after conception to birth. (p. 102)

figure-ground the organization of the visual field into objects (the *figures*) that stand out from their surroundings (the *ground*). (p. 171)

fixation according to Freud, a lingering focus of pleasure-seeking energies at an earlier psychosexual stage, in which conflicts were unresolved. (p. 462)

fixation the inability to see a problem from a new perspective; an impediment to problem solving. (p. 310)

fixed-interval schedule in operant conditioning, a reinforcement schedule that reinforces a response only after a specified time has elapsed. (p. 251)

fixed-ratio schedule in operant conditioning, a reinforcement schedule that reinforces a response only after a specified number of responses. (p. 250)

flashbulb memory a clear memory of an emotionally significant moment or event. (p. 281)

flow a completely involved, focused state of consciousness, with diminished awareness of self and time, resulting from optimal engagement of one's skills. (p. 392)

fluid intelligence one's ability to reason speedily and abstractly; tends to decrease during late adulthood. (p. 133)

fMRI (functional magnetic resonance imaging) a technique for revealing blood flow and, therefore, brain activity by comparing successive MRI scans. MRI scans show brain anatomy; fMRI scans show brain function. (p. 51)

foot-in-the-door phenomenon the tendency for people who have first agreed to a small request to comply later with a larger request. (p. 577)

formal operational stage in Piaget's theory, the stage of cognitive development (normally beginning about age 12) during which people begin to think logically about abstract concepts. (p. 112)

fovea the central focal point in the retina, around which the eye's cones cluster. (p. 149)

framing the way an issue is posed; how an issue is framed can significantly affect decisions and judgments. (p. 313)

fraternal twins twins who develop from separate fertilized eggs. They are genetically no closer than brothers and sisters, but they share a fetal environment. (p. 68)

free association in psychoanalysis, a method of exploring the unconscious in which the person relaxes and says whatever comes to mind, no matter how trivial or embarrassing. (p. 459)

frequency the number of complete wavelengths that pass a point in a given time (for example, per second). (p. 158)

frontal lobes the portion of the cerebral cortex lying just behind the forehead; involved in speaking and muscle movements and in making plans and judgments. (p. 54)

frustration-aggression principle the principle that frustration—the blocking of an attempt to achieve some goal—creates anger, which can generate aggression. (p. 601)

functional fixedness the tendency to think of things only in terms of their usual functions; an impediment to problem solving. (p. 310)

fundamental attribution error the tendency for observers, when analyzing another's behavior, to underestimate the impact of the situation and to overestimate the impact of personal disposition. (p. 575)

gate-control theory the theory that the spinal cord contains a neurological "gate" that blocks pain signals or allows them to pass on to the brain. The "gate" is opened by the activity of pain signals traveling up small nerve fibers and is closed by activity in larger fibers or by information coming from the brain. (p. 163)

gender in psychology, the biologically and socially influenced characteristics by which people define *male* and *female.* (p. 75)

gender-typing the acquisition of a traditional masculine or feminine role. (p. 92)

gender identity one's sense of being male or female. (p. 92)

gender role a set of expected behaviors for males or for females. (p. 90)

gender schema theory the theory that children learn from their cultures a concept of what it means to be male and female and that they adjust their behavior accordingly. (p. 92)

general adaptation syndrome (GAS) Selye's concept of the body's adaptive response to stress in three states—alarm, resistance, exhaustion. (p. 436)

general intelligence (g) a general intelligence factor that, according to Spearman and others, underlies specific mental abilities and is therefore measured by every task on an intelligence test. (p. 331)

generalization in classical conditioning, the tendency, once a response has been conditioned, for stimuli similar to the conditioned stimulus to elicit similar responses. (p. 239)

generalized anxiety disorder an anxiety disorder in which a person is continually tense, apprehensive, and in a state of autonomic nervous system arousal. (p. 510)

genes the biochemical units of heredity that make up the chromosomes; a segment of DNA capable of synthesizing a protein. (p. 67)

genome the complete instructions for making an organism, consisting of all the genetic material in that organism's chromosomes. (p. 67)

gestalt an organized whole. Gestalt psychologists emphasized our tendency to integrate pieces of information into meaningful wholes. (p. 171)

glucose the form of sugar that circulates in the blood and provides the major source of energy for body tissues. When its level is low, we feel hunger. (p. 361)

GRIT Graduated and Reciprocated Initiatives in Tension-Reduction—a strategy designed to decrease international tensions. (p. 618)

group polarization the enhancement of a group's prevailing inclinations through discussion within the group. (p. 590)

grouping the perceptual tendency to organize stimuli into coherent groups. (p. 172)

groupthink the mode of thinking that occurs when the desire for harmony in a decision-making group overrides a realistic appraisal of alternatives. (p. 591)

hallucinations false sensory experiences, such as seeing something in the absence of an external visual stimulus. (p. 198)

hallucinogens psychedelic ("mind-manifesting") drugs, such as LSD, that distort perceptions and evoke sensory images in the absence of sensory input. (p. 223)

heritability the proportion of variation among individuals that we can attribute to genes. The heritability of a trait may vary, depending on the range of populations and environments studied. (p. 343)

heuristic a simple thinking strategy that often allows us to make judgments and solve problems efficiently; usually speedier but also more error-prone than *algorithms.* (p. 308)

hierarchy of needs Maslow's pyramid of human needs, beginning at the base with physiological needs that must first be satisfied before higher-level safety needs and then psychological needs become active. (p. 359)

hindsight bias the tendency to believe, after learning an outcome, that one would have foreseen it. (Also known as the I-knew-it-all-along phenomenon.) (p. 13)

hippocampus a neural center that is located in the limbic system and helps process explicit memories for storage. (p. 282)

homeostasis a tendency to maintain a balanced or constant internal state; the regulation of any aspect of body chemistry, such as blood glucose, around a particular level. (p. 358)

hormones chemical messengers, mostly those manufactured by the endocrine glands, that are produced in one tissue and affect another. (p. 44)

hue the dimension of color that is determined by the wavelength of light; what we know as the color names *blue, green,* and so forth. (p. 148)

humanistic psychology historically significant perspective that emphasized the growth potential of healthy people; used personalized methods to study personality in hopes of fostering personal growth. (p. 4)

hypnosis a social interaction in which one person (the hypnotist) suggests to another (the subject) that certain perceptions, feelings, thoughts, or behaviors will spontaneously occur. (p. 211)

hypothalamus [hi-po-THAL-uh-muss] a neural structure lying below (*hypo*) the thalamus; it directs several maintenance activities (eating, drinking, body temperature), helps govern the endocrine system via the pituitary gland, and is linked to emotion. (p. 52)

hypothesis a testable prediction, often implied by a theory. (p. 17)

iconic memory a momentary sensory memory of visual stimuli; a photographic or picture-image memory lasting no more than a few tenths of a second. (p. 277)

id contains a reservoir of unconscious psychic energy that, according to Freud, strives to satisfy basic sexual and aggressive drives. The id operates on the *pleasure principle,* demanding immediate gratification. (p. 460)

identical twins twins who develop from a single fertilized egg that splits in two, creating two genetically identical organisms. (p. 67)

identification the process by which, according to Freud, children incorporate their parents' values into their developing superegos. (p. 462)

identity one's sense of self; according to Erikson, the adolescent's task is to solidify a sense of self by testing and integrating various roles. (p. 124)

illusory correlation the perception of a relationship where none exists. (p. 23)

imagery mental pictures; a powerful aid to effortful processing, especially when combined with semantic encoding. (p. 275)

implicit memory retention independent of conscious recollection. (Also called *nondeclarative memory.*) (p. 282)

imprinting the process by which certain animals form attachments during a critical period very early in life. (p. 114)

inattentional blindness failing to see visible objects when our attention is directed elsewhere. (p. 194)

incentive a positive or negative environmental stimulus that motivates behavior. (p. 358)

independent variable the experimental factor that is manipulated; the variable whose effect is being studied. (p. 26)

individualism giving priority to one's own goals over group goals and defining one's identity in terms of personal attributes rather than group identifications. (p. 84)

industrial-organizational (I/O) psychology the application of psychological concepts and methods to optimizing human behavior in workplaces. (p. 393)

informational social influence influence resulting from one's willingness to accept others' opinions about reality. (p. 584)

ingroup "Us"—people with whom one shares a common identity. (p. 597)

ingroup bias the tendency to favor one's own group. (p. 597)

inner ear the innermost part of the ear, containing the cochlea, semicircular canals, and vestibular sacs. (p. 159)

insight a sudden and often novel realization of the solution to a problem; it contrasts with strategy-based solutions. (p. 308)

insomnia recurring problems in falling or staying asleep. (p. 204)

instinct a complex behavior that is rigidly patterned throughout a species and is unlearned. (p. 357)

intelligence mental quality consisting of the ability to learn from experience, solve problems, and use knowledge to adapt to new situations. (p. 331)

intelligence quotient (IQ) defined originally as the ratio of mental age (*ma*) to chronological age (*ca*) multiplied by 100 (thus, IQ = *ma/ca* x 100). On contemporary intelligence tests, the average performance for a given age is assigned a score of 100. (p. 337)

intelligence test a method for assessing an individual's mental aptitudes and comparing them with those of others, using numerical scores. (p. 336)

intensity the amount of energy in a light or sound wave, which we perceive as brightness or loudness, as determined by the wave's amplitude. (p. 148)

interaction in psychology, occurs when the effect of one factor (such as environment) depends on another factor (such as heredity). (p. 71)

internal locus of control the perception that one controls one's own fate. (p. 485)

interneurons central nervous system neurons that internally communicate and intervene between the sensory inputs and motor outputs. (p. 42)

interpretation in psychoanalysis, the analyst's noting supposed dream meanings, resistances, and other significant behaviors and events in order to promote insight. (p. 542)

intimacy in Erikson's theory, the ability to form close, loving relationships; a primary developmental task in late adolescence and early adulthood. (p. 125)

intrinsic motivation a desire to perform a behavior for its own sake. (p. 253)

James-Lange theory the theory that our experience of emotion is our awareness of our physiological responses to emotion-arousing stimuli. (p. 407)

just-world phenomenon the tendency of people to believe the world is just and that people therefore get what they deserve and deserve what they get. (p. 599)

kinesthesis [kin-ehs-THEE-sehs] the system for sensing the position and movement of individual body parts. (p. 167)

language our spoken, written, or signed words and the ways we combine them to communicate meaning. (p. 319)

latent content according to Freud, the underlying meaning of a dream (as distinct from its manifest content). (p. 207)

latent learning learning that occurs but is not apparent until there is an incentive to demonstrate it. (p. 253)

learned helplessness the hopelessness and passive resignation an animal or human learns when unable to avoid repeated aversive events. (p. 485)

learning a relatively permanent change in an organism's behavior due to experience. (pp. 235, 247, 261)

lesion [LEE-zhuhn] tissue destruction. A brain lesion is a naturally or experimentally caused destruction of brain tissue. (p. 50)

levels of analysis the differing complementary views, from biological to psychological to social-cultural, for analyzing any given phenomenon. (p. 6)

limbic system a doughnut -shaped system of neural structures below the cerebral hemispheres; associated with emotions such as fear and aggression and drives such as those for food and sex. Includes the *hippocampus, amygdala,* and *hypothalamus.* (p. 50)

linguistic determinism Whorf's hypothesis that language determines the way we think. (p. 323)

lobotomy a now-rare psychosurgical procedure once used to calm uncontrollably emotional or violent patients. The procedure cut the nerves connecting the frontal lobes to the emotion-controlling centers of the inner brain. (p. 570)

long-term memory the relatively permanent and limitless storehouse of the memory system. Includes knowledge, skills, and experiences. (p. 270)

long-term potentiation (LTP) an increase in a synapse's firing potential after brief, rapid stimulation. Believed to be a neural basis for learning and memory. (p. 280)

longitudinal study research in which the same people are restudied and retested over a long period of time. (p. A-7)

LSD a powerful hallucinogenic drug; also known as *acid* (*lysergic acid diethyl-amide*). (p. 223)

lymphocytes the two types of white blood cells that are part of the body's immune system: *B lymphocytes* form in the bone marrow and release antibodies that fight bacterial infections; *T lymphocytes* form in the thymus and other lymphatic tissue and attack cancer cells, viruses, and foreign substances. (p. 440)

major depressive disorder a mood disorder in which a person experiences, in the absence of drugs or a medical condition, two or more weeks of significantly depressed moods, feelings of worthlessness, and diminished interest or pleasure in most activities. (p. 521)

mania a mood disorder marked by a hyperactive, wildly optimistic state. (p. 522)

manifest content according to Freud, the remembered story line of a dream (as distinct from its latent, or hidden, content). (p. 207)

maturation biological growth processes that enable orderly changes in behavior, relatively uninfluenced by experience. (p. 105)

mean the arithmetic average of a distribution, obtained by adding the scores and then dividing by the number of scores. (p. A-1)

median the middle score in a distribution; half the scores are above it and half are below it. (p. A-1)

medical model the concept that diseases, in this case psychological disorders, have physical causes that can be *diagnosed, treated,* and, in most cases, *cured,* often through treatment in a hospital. (p. 500)

medulla [muh-DUL-uh] the base of the brainstem; controls heartbeat and breathing. (p. 48)

memory the persistence of learning over time through the storage and retrieval of information. (p. 269)

menarche [meh-NAR-key] the first menstrual period. (p. 121)

menopause the time of natural cessation of menstruation; also refers to the biological changes a woman experiences as her ability to reproduce declines. (p. 129)

mental age measure of intelligence test performance devised by Binet; the chronological age that most typically corresponds to a given level of performance. Thus, a child who does as well as the average 8-year-old is said to have a mental age of 8. (p. 337)

mental retardation a condition of limited mental ability, indicated by an intelligence score of 70 or below and difficulty in adapting to the demands of life; varies from mild to profound. (p. 340)

mere exposure effect the phenomenon that repeated exposure to novel stimuli increases liking of them. (p. 607)

methamphetamine a powerfully addictive drug that stimulates the central nervous system, with speeded-up body functions and associated energy and mood changes; over time, appears to reduce baseline dopamine levels. (p. 220)

middle ear the chamber between the eardrum and cochlea containing three tiny bones (hammer, anvil, and stirrup) that concentrate the vibrations of the eardrum on the cochlea's oval window. (p. 159)

Minnesota Multiphasic Personality Inventory (MMPI) the most widely researched and clinically used of all personality tests. Originally developed to identify emotional disorders (still considered its most appropriate use), this test is now used for many other screening purposes. (p. 477)

mirror neurons frontal lobe neurons that fire when performing certain actions or when observing another doing so. The brain's mirroring of another's action may enable imitation and empathy. (p. 261)

misinformation effect incorporating misleading information into one's memory of an event. (p. 296)

mnemonics [nih-MON-iks] memory aids, especially those techniques that use vivid imagery and organizational devices. (p. 275)

mode the most frequently occurring score(s) in a distribution. (p. A-1)

modeling the process of observing and imitating a specific behavior. (p. 261)

monocular cues depth cues, such as interposition and linear perspective, available to either eye alone. (p. 174)

mood-congruent memory the tendency to recall experiences that are consistent with one's current good or bad mood. (p. 287)

mood disorders psychological disorders characterized by emotional extremes. See *major depressive disorder*, *mania*, and *bipolar disorder*. (p. 521)

motivation a need or desire that energizes and directs behavior. (p. 357)

motor cortex an area at the rear of the frontal lobes that controls voluntary movements. (p. 55)

motor neurons neurons that carry outgoing information from the central nervous system to the muscles and glands. (p. 42)

MRI (magnetic resonance imaging) a technique that uses magnetic fields and radio waves to produce computer-generated images that distinguish among different types of soft tissue; allows us to see structures within the brain. (p. 51)

mutation a random error in gene replication that leads to a change. (p. 73)

narcolepsy a sleep disorder characterized by uncontrollable sleep attacks. The sufferer may lapse directly into REM sleep, often at inopportune times. (p. 205)

natural selection the principle that, among the range of inherited trait variations, those that lead to increased reproduction and survival will most likely be passed on to succeeding generations. (p. 73)

naturalistic observation observing and recording behavior in naturally occurring situations without trying to manipulate and control the situation. (p. 20)

nature-nurture issue the longstanding controversy over the relative contributions that genes and experience make to the development of psychological traits and behaviors. Today's science sees traits and behaviors arising from the interaction of nature and nurture. (p. 6)

near-death experience an altered state of consciousness reported after a close brush with death (such as through cardiac arrest); often similar to drug-induced hallucinations. (p. 223)

negative reinforcement increasing behaviors by stopping or reducing negative stimuli, such as shock. A negative reinforcer is any stimulus that, when *removed* after a response, strengthens the response. (Note: negative reinforcement is *not* punishment.) (p. 249)

nerves neural "cables" containing many axons. These bundled axons, which are part of the peripheral nervous system, connect the central nervous system with muscles, glands, and sense organs. (p. 42)

nervous system the body's speedy, electrochemical communication network, consisting of all the nerve cells of the peripheral and central nervous systems. (p. 41)

neuron a nerve cell; the basic building block of the nervous system. (p. 37)

neurotransmitters chemical messengers that traverse the synaptic gaps between neurons. When released by the sending neuron, neurotransmitters travel across the synapse and bind to receptor sites on the receiving neuron, thereby influencing whether that neuron will generate a neural impulse. (p. 38)

night terrors a sleep disorder characterized by high arousal and an appearance of being terrified; unlike nightmares, night terrors occur during Stage 4 sleep, within two or three hours of falling asleep, and are seldom remembered. (p. 205)

norm an understood rule for accepted and expected behavior. Norms prescribe "proper" behavior. (p. 83)

normal curve the symmetrical bell-shaped curve that describes the distribution of many physical and psychological attributes. Most scores fall near the average, and fewer and fewer scores lie near the extremes. (pp. 339, A-4)

normative social influence influence resulting from a person's desire to gain approval or avoid disapproval. (p. 584)

object permanence the awareness that things continue to exist even when not perceived. (p. 108)

observational learning learning by observing others. (p. 261)

obsessive-compulsive disorder (OCD) an anxiety disorder characterized by unwanted repetitive thoughts (obsessions) and/or actions (compulsions). (p. 511)

occipital [ahk-SIP-uh-tuhl] lobes the portion of the cerebral cortex lying at the back of the head; includes the visual areas, each receiving information from the opposite visual field. (p. 54)

Oedipus [ED-uh-puss] complex according to Freud, a boy's sexual desires toward his mother and feelings of jealousy and hatred for the rival father. (p. 461)

one-word stage the stage in speech development, from about age 1 to 2, during which a child speaks mostly in single words. (p. 320)

operant behavior behavior that operates on the environment, producing consequences. (p. 246)

operant chamber a chamber also known as a *Skinner box*, containing a bar or key that an animal can manipulate to obtain a food or water reinforcer, with attached devices to record the animal's rate of bar pressing or key pecking. Used in operant conditioning research. (p. 247)

operant conditioning a type of learning in which behavior is strengthened if followed by a reinforcer or diminished if followed by a punisher. (p. 246)

operational definition a statement of the procedures (operations) used to define research variables. For example, *human intelligence* may be operationally defined as what an intelligence test measures. (p. 18)

opiates opium and its derivatives, such as morphine and heroin; they depress neural activity, temporarily lessening pain and anxiety. (p. 219)

opponent-process theory the theory that opposing retinal processes (red-green, yellow-blue, white-black) enable color vision. For example, some cells are stimulated by green and inhibited by red; others are stimulated by red and inhibited by green. (p. 154)

optic nerve the nerve that carries neural impulses from the eye to the brain. (p. 149)

organizational psychology a subfield of I/O psychology that examines organizational influences on worker satisfaction and productivity and facilitates organizational change. (p. 393)

outgroup "Them"—those perceived as different or apart from one's ingroup. (p. 597)

overconfidence the tendency to be more confident than correct—to overestimate the accuracy of one's beliefs and judgments. (p. 312)

panic disorder an anxiety disorder marked by unpredictable minutes-long episodes of intense dread in which a person experiences terror and accompanying chest pain, choking, or other frightening sensations. (p. 510)

parallel processing the processing of many aspects of a problem simultaneously; the brain's natural mode of information processing for many functions, including vision. Contrasts with the step-by-step (serial) processing of most computers and of conscious problem solving. (p. 152)

parapsychology the study of paranormal phenomena, including ESP and psychokinesis. (p. 187)

parasympathetic nervous system the division of the autonomic nervous system that calms the body, conserving its energy. (p. 42)

parietal [puh-RYE-uh-tuhl] lobes the portion of the cerebral cortex lying at the top of the head and toward the rear; receives sensory input for touch and body position. (p. 54)

partial (intermittent) reinforcement reinforcing a response only part of the time; results in slower acquisition of a response but much greater resistance to extinction than does continuous reinforcement. (p. 250)

passionate love an aroused state of intense positive absorption in another, usually present at the beginning of a love relationship. (p. 611)

perception the process of organizing and interpreting sensory information, enabling us to recognize meaningful objects and events. (p. 143)

perceptual adaptation in vision, the ability to adjust to an artificially displaced or even inverted visual field. (p. 182)

perceptual constancy perceiving objects as unchanging (having consistent color, shape, size, or lightness) even as illumination and retinal images change. (p. 176)

perceptual set a mental predisposition to perceive one thing and not another. (p. 183)

peripheral nervous system (PNS) the sensory and motor neurons that connect the central nervous system (CNS) to the rest of the body. (p. 42)

personal control our sense of controlling our environment rather than feeling helpless. (p. 484)

personal space the buffer zone we like to maintain around our bodies. (p. 83)

personality an individual's characteristic pattern of thinking, feeling, and acting. (p. 458)

personality disorders psychological disorders characterized by inflexible and enduring behavior patterns that impair social functioning. (p. 517)

personality inventory a questionnaire (often with true-false or agree-disagree items) on which people respond to items designed to gauge a wide range of feelings and behaviors; used to assess selected personality traits. (p. 477)

personnel psychology a subfield of I/O psychology that focuses on employee recruitment, selection, placement, training, appraisal, and development. (p.393)

PET (positron emission tomography) scan a visual display of brain activity that detects where a radioactive form of glucose goes while the brain performs a given task. (p. 50)

phobia an anxiety disorder marked by a persistent, irrational fear and avoidance of a specific object or situation. (p. 510)

physical dependence a physiological need for a drug, marked by unpleasant withdrawal symptoms when the drug is discontinued. (p. 216)

pitch a tone's experienced highness or lowness; depends on frequency. (p. 158)

pituitary gland the endocrine system's most influential gland. Under the influence of the hypothalamus, the pituitary regulates growth and controls other endocrine glands. (p. 45)

placebo [pluh-SEE-bo; Latin for "I shall please"] effect experimental results caused by expectations alone; any effect on behavior caused by the administration of an inert substance or condition, which is assumed to be an active agent. (p. 25)

plasticity the brain's capacity for modification, as evident in brain reorganization following damage (especially in children) and in experiments on the effects of experience on brain development. (p. 59)

polygraph a machine, commonly used in attempts to detect lies, that measures several of the physiological responses accompanying emotion (such as perspiration and cardiovascular and breathing changes). (p. 412)

population all the cases in a group, from which samples may be drawn for a study. (*Note:* Except for national studies, this does *not* refer to a country's whole population.) (p. 20)

positive psychology the scientific study of optimal human functioning; aims to discover and promote strengths and virtues that enable individuals and communities to thrive. (p. 487)

positive reinforcement increasing behaviors by presenting positive stimuli, such as food. A positive reinforcer is any stimulus that, when *presented* after a response, strengthens the response. (p. 249)

post-traumatic stress disorder (PTSD) an anxiety disorder characterized by haunting memories, nightmares, social withdrawal, jumpy anxiety, and/or insomnia that lingers for four weeks or more after a traumatic experience. (p. 512)

posthypnotic suggestion a suggestion, made during a hypnosis session, to be carried out after the subject is no longer hypnotized; used by some clinicians to help control undesired symptoms and behaviors. (p. 212)

predictive validity the success with which a test predicts the behavior it is designed to predict; it is assessed by computing the correlation between test scores and the criterion behavior. (Also called *criterion-related validity*.) (p. 339)

prejudice an unjustifiable (and usually negative) attitude toward a group and its members. Prejudice generally involves stereotyped beliefs, negative feelings, and a predisposition to discriminatory action. (p. 594)

preoperational stage in Piaget's theory, the stage (from about 2 to 6 or 7 years of age) during which a child learns to use language but does not yet comprehend the mental operations of concrete logic. (p. 109)

primary reinforcer an innately reinforcing stimulus, such as one that satisfies a biological need. (p. 249)

primary sex characteristics the body structures (ovaries, testes, and external genitalia) that make sexual reproduction possible. (p. 120)

priming the activation, often unconsciously, of certain associations, thus predisposing one's perception, memory, or response. (pp. 144, 285)

proactive interference the disruptive effect of prior learning on the recall of new information. (p. 293)

projection psychoanalytic defense mechanism by which people disguise their own threatening impulses by attributing them to others. (p. 462)

projective test a personality test, such as the Rorschach or TAT, that provides ambiguous stimuli designed to trigger projection of one's inner dynamics. (p. 463)

prosocial behavior positive, constructive, helpful behavior. The opposite of antisocial behavior. (p. 263)

prototype a mental image or best example of a category. Matching new items to the prototype provides a quick and easy method for including items in a category (as when comparing feathered creatures to a prototypical bird, such as a robin). (p. 307)

psychiatry a branch of medicine dealing with psychological disorders; practiced by physicians who sometimes provide medical (for example, drug) treatments as well as psychological therapy. (p. 9)

psychoactive drug a chemical substance that alters perceptions and mood. (p. 216)

psychoanalysis Freud's theory of personality and therapeutic technique that attributes thoughts and actions to unconscious motives and conflicts. Freud believed the patient's free associations, resistances, dreams, and transferences—and the therapist's interpretations of them—released previously repressed feelings, allowing the patient to gain self-insight. (pp. 459, 541)

psychological dependence a psychological need to use a drug, such as to relieve negative emotions. (p. 216)

psychological disorder deviant, distressful, and dysfunctional behavior patterns. (p. 499)

psychology the scientific study of behavior and mental processes. (p.5)

psychoneuroimmunology (PNI) the study of how psychological, neural, and endocrine processes together affect the immune system and resulting health. (p. 440)

psychopharmacology the study of the effects of drugs on mind and behavior. (p. 565)

psychophysics the study of relationships between the physical characteristics of stimuli, such as their intensity, and our psychological experience of them. (p. 144)

psychophysiological illness literally, "mind-body" illness; any stress-related physical illness, such as hypertension and some headaches. (p. 440)

psychosexual stages the childhood stages of development (oral, anal, phallic, latency, genital) during which, according to Freud, the id's pleasure-seeking energies focus on distinct erogenous zones. (p. 461)

psychosurgery surgery that removes or destroys brain tissue in an effort to change behavior. (p. 570)

psychotherapy treatment involving psychological techniques; consists of interactions between a trained therapist and someone seeking to overcome psychological difficulties or achieve personal growth. (pp. 541, 554)

puberty the period of sexual maturation, during which a person becomes capable of reproducing. (p. 120)

punishment an event that *decreases* the behavior that it follows. (p. 251)

random assignment assigning research participants to experimental and control conditions by chance, thus minimizing preexisting differences between those assigned to the different groups. (p. 25)

random sample a sample that fairly represents a population because each member has an equal chance of inclusion. (p. 20)

range the difference between the highest and lowest scores in a distribution. (p. A-3)

rationalization defense mechanism that offers self-justifying explanations in place of the real, more threatening, unconscious reasons for one's actions. (p. 462)

reaction formation psychoanalytic defense mechanism by which the ego unconsciously switches unacceptable impulses into their opposites. Thus, people may express feelings that are the opposite of their anxiety-arousing unconscious feelings. (p. 462)

recall a measure of memory in which the person must retrieve information learned earlier, as on a fill-in-the-blank test. (p. 283)

reciprocal determinism the interacting influences between personality and environmental factors. (p. 483)

recognition a measure of memory in which the person need only identify items previously learned, as on a multiple-choice test. (p. 283)

reflex a simple, automatic response to a sensory stimulus, such as the knee-jerk response. (p. 43)

refractory period a resting period after orgasm, during which a man cannot achieve another orgasm. (p. 376)

regression psychoanalytic defense mechanism in which an individual faced with anxiety retreats to a more infantile psychosexual stage, where some psychic energy remains fixated. (p. 462)

regression toward the mean the tendency for extremes of unusual scores or events to fall back (regress) toward the average. (p. A-6)

rehearsal the conscious repetition of information, either to maintain it in consciousness or to encode it for storage. (p. 272)

reinforcer in operant conditioning, any event that *strengthens* the behavior it follows. (p. 248)

relative deprivation the perception that one is worse off relative to those with whom one compares oneself. (p. 430)

relearning a memory measure that assesses the amount of time saved when learning material for a second time. (p. 283)

reliability the extent to which a test yields consistent results, as assessed by the consistency of scores on two halves of the test, on alternate forms of the test, or on retesting. (p. 339)

REM rebound the tendency for REM sleep to increase following REM sleep deprivation (created by repeated awakenings during REM sleep). (p. 208)

REM sleep rapid eye movement sleep, a recurring sleep stage during which vivid dreams commonly occur. Also known as *paradoxical sleep,* because the muscles are relaxed (except for minor twitches) but other body systems are active. (p. 197)

repetitive transcranial magnetic stimulation (rTMS) the application of repeated pulses of magnetic energy to the brain; used to stimulate or suppress brain activity. (p. 569)

replication repeating the essence of a research study, usually with different participants in different situations, to see whether the basic finding extends to other participants and circumstances. (p. 18)

representativeness heuristic judging the likelihood of things in terms of how well they seem to represent, or match, particular prototypes; may lead one to ignore other relevant information. (p. 311)

repression in psychoanalytic theory, the basic defense mechanism that banishes anxiety-arousing thoughts, feelings, and memories from consciousness. (pp. 295, 462)

resistance in psychoanalysis, the blocking from consciousness of anxiety-laden material. (p. 542)

respondent behavior behavior that occurs as an automatic response to some stimulus. (p. 246)

reticular formation a nerve network in the brainstem that plays an important role in controlling arousal. (p. 49)

retina the light-sensitive inner surface of the eye, containing the receptor rods and cones plus layers of neurons that begin the processing of visual information. (p. 148)

retinal disparity a binocular cue for perceiving depth: By comparing images from the two eyeballs, the brain computes distance—the greater the disparity (difference) between the two images, the closer the object. (p. 174)

retrieval the process of getting information out of memory storage. (p. 270)

retroactive interference the disruptive effect of new learning on the recall of old information. (p. 293)

rods retinal receptors that detect black, white, and gray; necessary for peripheral and twilight vision, when cones don't respond. (p. 149)

role a set of expectations (norms) about a social position, defining how those in the position ought to behave. (pp. 90, 578)

Rorschach inkblot test the most widely used projective test, a set of 10 inkblots, designed by Hermann Rorschach; seeks to identify people's inner feelings by analyzing their interpretations of the blots. (p. 465)

savant syndrome a condition in which a person otherwise limited in mental ability has an exceptional specific skill, such as in computation or drawing. (p. 332)

scapegoat theory the theory that prejudice offers an outlet for anger by providing someone to blame. (p. 598)

scatterplot a graphed cluster of dots, each of which represents the values of two variables. The slope of the points suggests the direction of the relationship between the two variables. The amount of scatter suggests the strength of the correlation (little scatter indicates high correlation). (p. A-5)

schema a concept or framework that organizes and interprets information. (p. 107)

schizophrenia a group of severe disorders characterized by disorganized and delusional thinking, disturbed perceptions, and inappropriate emotions and actions. (p. 531)

secondary sex characteristics nonreproductive sexual characteristics, such as female breasts and hips, male voice quality, and body hair. (p. 121)

selective attention the focusing of conscious awareness on a particular stimulus. (p. 193)

self-actualization according to Maslow, the ultimate psychological need that arises after basic physical and psychological needs are met and self-esteem is achieved; the motivation to fulfill one's potential. (p. 471)

self-concept all our thoughts and feelings about ourselves, in answer to the question, "Who am I?" (p. 472)

self-disclosure revealing intimate aspects of oneself to others. (p. 612)

self-esteem one's feelings of high or low self-worth. (p. 491)

self-serving bias a readiness to perceive oneself favorably. (p. 492)

sensation the process by which our sensory receptors and nervous system receive and represent stimulus energies from our environment. (p. 143)

sensorimotor stage in Piaget's theory, the stage (from birth to about 2 years of age) during which infants know the world mostly in terms of their sensory impressions and motor activities. (p. 108)

sensory adaptation diminished sensitivity as a consequence of constant stimulation. (p. 146)

sensory cortex the area at the front of the parietal lobes that registers and processes body touch and movement sensations. (p. 56)

sensory interaction the principle that one sense may influence another, as when the smell of food influences its taste. (p. 165)

sensory memory the immediate, very brief recording of sensory information in the memory system. (p. 270)

sensory neurons neurons that carry incoming information from the sense receptors to the central nervous system. (p. 42)

serial position effect our tendency to recall best the last and first items in a list. (p. 273)

set point the point at which an individual's "weight thermostat" is supposedly set. When the body weight falls below this level, an increase in hunger and a lowered metabolic rate may act to restore the lost weight. (p. 362)

sexual disorder a problem that consistently impairs sexual arousal or functioning. (p. 376)

sexual orientation an enduring sexual attraction toward members of either one's own sex (homosexual orientation) or the other sex (heterosexual orientation). (p. 380)

sexual response cycle the four stages of sexual responding described by Masters and Johnson—excitement, plateau, orgasm, and resolution. (p. 375)

shaping an operant conditioning procedure in which reinforcers guide behavior toward closer and closer approximations of the desired behavior. (p. 247)

short-term memory activated memory that holds a few items briefly, such as the seven digits of a phone number while dialing, before the information is stored or forgotten. (p. 270)

sleep periodic, natural, reversible loss of consciousness—as distinct from unconsciousness resulting from a coma, general anesthesia, or hibernation. (Adapted from Dement, 1999.) (p. 198)

sleep apnea a sleep disorder characterized by temporary cessations of breathing during sleep and repeated momentary awakenings. (p. 205)

social-cognitive perspective views behavior as influenced by the interaction between persons (and their thinking) and their social context. (p. 483)

social clock the culturally preferred timing of social events such as marriage, parenthood, and retirement. (p. 135)

social facilitation stronger responses on simple or well-learned tasks in the presence of others. (p. 588)

social leadership group-oriented leadership that builds teamwork, mediates conflict, and offers support. (p. 401)

social learning theory the theory that we learn social behavior by observing and imitating and by being rewarded or punished. (p. 92)

social loafing the tendency for people in a group to exert less effort when pooling their efforts toward attaining a common goal than when individually accountable. (p. 589)

social psychology the scientific study of how we think about, influence, and relate to one another. (pp. 575, 582, 594)

somatic nervous system the division of the peripheral nervous system that controls the body's skeletal muscles. Also called the *skeletal nervous system.* (p. 42)

source amnesia attributing to the wrong source an event we have experienced, heard about, read about, or imagined. (Also called *source misattribution.*) Source amnesia, along with the misinformation effect, is at the heart of many false memories. (p. 298)

spacing effect the tendency for distributed study or practice to yield better long-term retention than is achieved through massed study or practice. (p. 272)

split brain a condition in which the brain's two hemispheres are isolated by cutting the fibers (mainly those of the corpus callosum) connecting them. (p. 61)

spontaneous recovery in classical conditioning, the reappearance, after a pause, of an extinguished conditioned response. (p. 238)

spotlight effect overestimating others' noticing and evaluating our appearance, performance, and blunders (as if we presume a spotlight shines on us). (p.490)

SQ3R a study method incorporating five steps: Survey, Question, Read, Rehearse, Review. (p. 10)

standard deviation a computed measure of how much scores vary around the mean score. (p. A-3)

standardization defining meaningful scores by comparison with the performance of a pretested standardization group. (p. 338)

Stanford-Binet the widely used American revision (by Terman at Stanford University) of Binet's original intelligence test. (p. 337)

statistical significance a statistical statement of how likely it is that an obtained result occurred by chance. (p. A-8)

stereotype a generalized (sometimes accurate but often overgeneralized) belief about a group of people. (p. 594)

stereotype threat a self-confirming concern that one will be evaluated based on a negative stereotype. (p. 350)

stimulants drugs (such as caffeine, nicotine, and the more powerful amphetamines, methamphetamine, cocaine, and Ecstasy) that excite neural activity and speed up body functions. (p. 220)

storage the retention of encoded information over time. (p. 270)

stranger anxiety the fear of strangers that infants commonly display, beginning by about 8 months of age. (p. 113)

stress the process by which we perceive and respond to certain events, called stressors, that we appraise as threatening or challenging. (p. 435)

structured interviews interview process that asks the same job-relevant questions of all applicants, each of whom is rated on established scales. (p. 396)

subjective well-being self-perceived happiness or satisfaction with life. Used along with measures of objective well-being (for example, physical and economic indicators) to evaluate people's quality of life. (p. 426)

subliminal below one's absolute threshold for conscious awareness. (p. 144)

superego the part of personality that, according to Freud, represents internalized ideals and provides standards for judgment (the conscience) and for future aspirations. (p. 461)

superordinate goals shared goals that override differences among people and require their cooperation. (p. 616)

survey a technique for ascertaining the self-reported attitudes or behaviors of people, usually by questioning a representative, random sample of them. (p. 19)

sympathetic nervous system the division of the autonomic nervous system that arouses the body, mobilizing its energy in stressful situations. (p. 42)

synapse [SIN-aps] the junction between the a xon tip of the sending neuron and the dendrite or cell body of the receiving neuron. The tiny gap at this junction is called the *synaptic gap* or *cleft.* (p. 38)

systematic desensitization a type of exposure therapy that associates a pleasant relaxed state with gradually increasing anxiety-triggering stimuli. Commonly used to treat phobias. (p. 546)

task leadership goal-oriented leadership that sets standards, organizes work, and focuses attention on goals. (p. 401)

telegraphic speech early speech stage in which a child speaks like a telegram—"go car"—using mostly nouns and verbs and omitting auxiliary words. (p. 320)

temporal lobes the portion of the cerebral cortex lying roughly above the ears; includes the auditory areas, each receiving information primarily from the opposite ear. (p. 54)

teratogens agents, such as chemicals and viruses, that can reach the embryo or fetus during prenatal development and cause harm. (p. 102)

testosterone the most important of the male sex hormones. Both males and females have it, but the additional testosterone in males stimulates the growth of the male sex organs in the fetus and the development of the male sex characteristics during puberty. (pp. 90, 376)

thalamus [THAL-uh-muss] the brain's sensory switchboard, located on top of the brainstem; it directs messages to the sensory receiving areas in the cortex and transmits replies to the cerebellum and medulla. (p. 49)

THC the major active ingredient in marijuana; triggers a variety of effects, including mild hallucinations. (p. 224)

Thematic Apperception Test (TAT) a projective test in which people express their inner feelings and interests through the stories they make up about ambiguous scenes. (p. 465)

theory an explanation using an integrated set of principles that organizes observations and predicts behaviors or events. (p. 17)

theory of mind people's ideas about their own and others' mental states—about their feelings, perceptions, and thoughts, and the behavior these might predict. (p. 110)

threshold the level of stimulation required to trigger a neural impulse. (p. 38)

token economy an operant conditioning procedure in which people earn a token of some sort for exhibiting a desired behavior and can later exchange the tokens for various privileges or treats. (p. 548)

tolerance the diminishing effect with regular use of the same dose of a drug, requiring the user to take larger and larger doses before experiencing the drug's effect. (p. 216)

top-down processing information processing guided by higher-level mental processes, as when we construct perceptions drawing on our experience and expectations. (p. 143)

trait a characteristic pattern of behavior or a disposition to feel and act, as assessed by self-report inventories and peer reports. (p. 475)

transference in psychoanalysis, the patient's transfer to the analyst of emotions linked with other relationships (such as love or hatred for a parent). (p. 542)

two-factor theory Schachter-Singer's theory that to experience emotion one must (1) be physically aroused and (2) cognitively label the arousal. (p. 408)

two-word stage beginning about age 2, the stage in speech development during which a child speaks mostly two-word statements. (p. 320)

Type A Friedman and Rosenman's term for competitive, hard-driving, impatient, verbally aggressive, and anger-prone people. (p. 438)

Type B Friedman and Rosenman's term for easygoing, relaxed people. (p. 438)

unconditional positive regard according to Rogers, an attitude of total acceptance toward another person. (p. 472)

unconditioned response (UR) in classical conditioning, the unlearned, naturally occurring response to the unconditioned stimulus (US), such as salivation when food is in the mouth. (p. 236)

unconditioned stimulus (US) in classical conditioning, a stimulus that unconditionally (naturally and automatically) triggers a response. (p. 236)

unconscious according to Freud, a reservoir of mostly unacceptable thoughts, wishes, feelings, and memories. According to contemporary psychologists, information processing of which we are unaware. (p. 459)

validity the extent to which a test measures or predicts what it is supposed to. (See also *content validity* and *predictive validity*.) (p. 339)

variable-interval schedule in operant conditioning, a reinforcement schedule that reinforces a response at unpredictable time intervals. (p. 251)

variable-ratio schedule in operant conditioning, a reinforcement schedule that reinforces a response after an unpredictable number of responses. (p. 251)

vestibular sense the sense of body movement and position, including the sense of balance. (p. 168)

virtual reality exposure therapy An anxiety treatment that progressively exposes people to simulations of their greatest fears, such as airplane flying, spiders, or public speaking. (p. 546)

visual cliff a laboratory device for testing depth perception in infants and young animals. (p. 173)

wavelength the distance from the peak of one light or sound wave to the peak of the next. Electromagnetic wavelengths vary from the short blips of cosmic rays to the long pulses of radio transmission. (p. 148)

Weber's law the principle that, to be perceived as different, two stimuli must differ by a constant minimum percentage (rather than a constant amount). (p. 145)

Wechsler Adult Intelligence Scale (WAIS) the WAIS is the most widely used intelligence test; contains verbal and performance (nonverbal) subtests. (p. 337)

Wernicke's area controls language reception—a brain area involved in language comprehension and expression; usually in the left temporal lobe. (p. 58)

withdrawal the discomfort and distress that follow discontinuing the use of an addictive drug. (p. 216)

working memory a newer understanding of short-term memory that involves conscious, active processing of incoming auditory and visual-spatial information, and of information retrieved from long-term memory. (p. 271)

X chromosome the sex chromosome found in both men and women. Females have two X chromosomes; males have one. An X chromosome from each parent produces a female child. (p. 90)

Y chromosome the sex chromosome found only in males. When paired with an X chromosome from the mother, it produces a male child. (p. 90)

Young-Helmholtz trichromatic (three-color) theory the theory that the retina contains three different color receptors—one most sensitive to red, one to green, one to blue—which when stimulated in combination can produce the perception of any color. (p. 154)

zygote the fertilized egg; it enters a 2-week period of rapid cell division and develops into an embryo. (p. 101)

REFERENCES

Aas, H., & Klepp, K-I. (1992). Adolescents' alcohol use related to perceived norms. *Scandinavian Journal of Psychology, 33,* 315–325. (p. 227)

Abbey, A. (1991). Acquaintance rape and alcohol consumption on college campuses: How are they linked? *Journal of American College Health, 39,* 165–169. (p. 218)

Abrams, D. B. (1991). AIDS: What young people believe and what they do. Paper presented at the British Association for the Advancement of Science conference. (p. 488)

Abrams, D. B., & Wilson, G. T. (1983). Alcohol, sexual arousal, and self-control. *Journal of Personality and Social Psychology, 45,* 188–198. (p. 219)

Abrams, M. (2002, June). Sight unseen—Restoring a blind man's vision is now a real possibility through stem-cell surgery. But even perfect eyes cannot see unless the brain has been taught to use them. *Discover, 23,* 54–60. (p. 182)

Abramson, L. Y., Metalsky, G. I., & Alloy, L. B. (1989). Hopelessness depression: A theory-based subtype. *Psychological Review, 96,* 358–372. (p. 528)

Ackerman, D. (2004). *An alchemy of mind: The marvel and mystery of the brain.* New York: Scribner. (pp. 37, 48)

Actkinson, T. R. (2000). Master's and myth. *Eye on Psi Chi, 4,* 19–25. (p. B-9)

Adelmann, P. K., Antonucci, T. C., Crohan, S. F., & Coleman, L. M. (1989). Empty nest, cohort, and employment in the well-being of midlife women. *Sex Roles, 20,* 173–189. (p. 136)

Ader, R., & Cohen, N. (1985). CNS-immune system interactions: Conditioning phenomena. *Behavioral and Brain Sciences, 8,* 379–394. (p. 247)

Affleck, G., Tennen, H., Urrows, S., & Higgins, P. (1994). Person and contextual features of daily stress reactivity: Individual differences in relations of undesirable daily events with mood disturbance and chronic pain intensity. *Journal of Personality and Social Psychology, 66,* 329–340. (p. 426)

Agid, O., Shapira, B., Zislin, J., Ritsner, M., Hanin, B., Murad, H., Troudart, T., Bloch, M., Heresco-Levy, U., & Lerer, B. (1999). Environment and vulnerability to major psychiatric illness: A case control study of early parental loss in major depression, bipolar disorder and schizophrenia. *Molecular Psychiatry, 4,* 163–172. (p. 523)

Aiello, J. R., Thompson, D. D., & Brodzinsky, D. M. (1983). How funny is crowding anyway? Effects of room size, group size, and the introduction of humor. *Basic and Applied Social Psychology, 4,* 193–207. (p. 589)

Ainsworth, M. D. S. (1973). The development of infant-mother attachment. In B. Caldwell & H. Ricciuti (Eds.), *Review of child development research* (Vol. 3). Chicago: University of Chicago Press. (p. 115)

Ainsworth, M. D. S. (1979). Infant-mother attachment. *American Psychologist, 34,* 932–937. (p. 115)

Ainsworth, M. D. S. (1989). Attachments beyond infancy. *American Psychologist, 44,* 709–716. (p. 115)

Albee, G. W. (1986). Toward a just society: Lessons from observations on the primary prevention of psychopathology. *American Psychologist, 41,* 891–898. (p. 562)

Albert, B., Brown, S., & Flanigan, C. M. (Eds.) (2003). *14 and younger: The sexual behavior of young adolescents.* Washington, DC: National Campaign to Prevent Teen Pregnancy. (p. 379)

Alcock, J. E. (1981). *Parapsychology: Science or magic?* Oxford: Pergamon. (p. 286)

Aldrich, M. S. (1989). Automobile accidents in patients with sleep disorders. *Sleep, 12,* 487–494. (p. 205)

Aldridge-Morris, R. (1989). *Multiple personality: An exercise in deception.* Hillsdale, NJ: Erlbaum. (p. 516)

Aleman, A., Kahn, R. S., & Selten, J-P. (2003). Sex differences in the risk of schizophrenia: Evidence from meta-analysis. *Archives of General Psychiatry, 60,* 565–571. (p. 532)

Alexander, C. N., Langer, E. J., Newman, R. I., Chandler, H. M., & Davies, J. L. (1989). Transcendental meditation, mindfulness, and longevity: An experimental study with the elderly. *Journal of Personality and Social Psychology, 57,* 950–964. (p. 454)

Allard, F., & Burnett, N. (1985). Skill in sport. *Canadian Journal of Psychology, 39,* 294–312. (p. 276)

Allen, J. B., Repinski, D. J., Ballard, J. C., & Griffin, B. W. (1996). Beliefs about the etiology of homosexuality may influence attitudes toward homosexuals. Paper presented to the American Psychological Society convention. (p. 386)

Allen, K. (2003). Are pets a healthy pleasure? The influence of pets on blood pressure. *Current Directions in Psychological Science, 12,* 236–239. (p. 448)

Allen, L. S., & Gorski, R. A. (1992). Sexual orientation and the size of the anterior commisure in the human brain. *Proceedings of the National Academy of Sciences, 89,* 7199–7202. (p. 383)

Allen, N. B., & Badcock, P. B. T. (2003). The social risk hypothesis of depressed mood: Evolutionary, psychosocial, and neurobiological perspectives. *Psychological Bulletin, 129,* 887–913. (p. 521)

Alloy, L. B., Abramson, L. Y., Whitehouse, W. G., Hogan, M. E., Tashman, N. A., Steinberg, D. L., Rose, D. T., & Donovan, P. (1999). Depressogenic cognitive styles: Predictive validity, information processing and personality characteristics, and developmental origins. *Behaviour Research and Therapy, 37,* 503–531. (p. 528)

Allport, G. W. (1954). *The nature of prejudice.* New York: Addison-Wesley. (pp. 19, 596)

Allport, G. W., & Odbert, H. S. (1936). Trait-names: A psycho-lexical study. *Psychological Monographs, 47(1).* (p. 476)

Altman, L. K. (2004, November 24). Female cases of HIV found rising worldwide. *New York Times* (www.nytimes.com). (p. 441)

Alwin, D. F. (1990). Historical changes in parental orientations to children. In N. Mandell (Ed.), *Sociological studies of child development* (Vol. 3). Greenwich, CT: JAI Press. (p. 86)

Amabile, T. M. (1983). *The social psychology of creativity.* New York: Springer-Verlag. (p. 491)

Amabile, T. M., & Hennessey, B. A. (1992). The motivation for creativity in children. In A. K. Boggiano & T. S. Pittman (Eds.), *Achievement and motivation: A social-developmental perspective.* New York: Cambridge University Press. (p. 335)

Ambady, N., & Rosenthal, R. (1992). Thin slices of expressive behavior as predictors of interpersonal consequences: A meta-analysis. *Psychological Bulletin, 111,* 256–274. (p. 482)

Ambady, N., & Rosenthal, R. (1993). Half a minute: Predicting teacher evaluations from thin slices of nonverbal behavior and physical attractiveness. *Journal of Personality and Social Psychology, 64,* 431–441. (p. 482)

Ambady, N., Hallahan, M., & Rosenthal, R. (1995). On judging and being judged accurately in zero-acquaintance situations. *Journal of Personality and Social Psychology, 69,* 518–529. (p. 417)

Amedi, A., Floel, A., Knect, S., Zohary, E., & Cohen, L. (2004). Transcranial magnetic stimulation of the occipital pole interferes with verbal processing in blind subjects. *Nature Neuroscience, 7,* 1266–1270. (p. 59)

Amen, D. G., Stubblefield, M., Carmichael, B., & Thisted, R. (1996). Brain SPECT findings and aggressiveness. *Annals of Clinical Psychiatry, 8,* 129–137. (p. 600)

American Enterprise. (1992, January/February). Women, men, marriages & ministers. p. 106. (p. 86)

American Psychiatric Association. (1994). *Diagnostic and statistical manual of mental disorders (Fourth Edition).* Washington, DC: American Psychiatric Press. (p. 340)

American Psychological Association. (1991). *Medical cost offset.* Washington, DC: American Psychological Association Practice Directorate. (p. 556)

American Psychological Association. (1992). Ethical principles of psychologists and code of conduct. *American Psychologist, 47,* 1597–1611. (p. 30)

American Psychological Association. (2002). *Ethical principles of psychologists and code of conduct.* Washington, DC: American Psychological Association. (p. 30)

American Psychological Association. (2003). *Careers for the twenty-first century.* Washington, DC. (p. B-9)

American Psychological Association. (2005). *Graduate study in psychology.* Washington, DC. (p. B-9)

Andersen, R. E., Crespo, C. J., Bartlett, S. J., Cheskin, L. J., & Pratt, M. (1998). Relationship of physical activity and television watching with body weight and level of fatness among children. *Journal of the American Medical Association, 279,* 938–942. (p. 372)

Andersen, S. M. (1998). *Service Learning: A National Strategy for Youth Development.* A position paper issued by the Task Force on Education Policy. Washington, DC: Institute for Communitarian Policy Studies, George Washington University. (p. 124)

Anderson, A. K., & Phelps, E. A. (2000). Expression without recognition: Contributions of the human amygdala to emotional communication. *Psychological Science, 11,* 106–111. (p. 52)

Anderson, B. L. (2002). Biobehavioral outcomes following psychological interventions for cancer patients. *Journal of Consulting and Clinical Psychology, 70,* 590–610. (p. 442)

Anderson, C. A. (2004a). An update on the effects of playing violent video games. Journal of *Adolescence, 27,* 113–122. (p. 605)

Anderson, C. A., & Anderson, D. C. (1984). Ambient temperature and violent crime: Tests of the linear and curvilinear hypotheses. *Journal of Personality and Social Psychology, 46,* 91–97. (p. 602)

Anderson, C. A., & Dill, K. E. (2000). Video games and aggressive thoughts, feelings, and behavior in the laboratory and in life. *Journal of Personality and Social Psychology, 78,* 772–790. (p. 605)

Anderson, C. A., Anderson, K. B., Dorr, N., DeNeve, K. M., & Flanagan, M. (2000). Temperature and aggression. In M. P. Zanna (Ed.), *Advances in Experimental Social Psychology.* San Diego: Academic Press. (p. 602)

Anderson, C. A., Berkowitz, L., Donnerstein, E., Huesmann, L. R., Johnson, J. D., Linz, D., Malamuth, N. M., & Wartella, E. (2003). The influence of media violence on youth. *Psychological Science in the Public Interest, 4(3),* 81–110. (p. 264)

Anderson, C. A., Carnagey, N. L., Flanagan, M., Benjamin, A. J. ,Jr., Eubanks, J., & Valentine, J. C. (2004). Violent video games: Specific effects of violent content on aggressive thoughts and behavior. *Advances in Experimental Social Psychology, 36,* 199–249. (p. 605)

Anderson, C. A., Lindsay, J. J., & Bushman, B. J. (1999). Research in the psychological laboratory: Truth or triviality? *Current Directions in Psychological Science, 8,* 3–9. (p. 28)

Anderson, I. M. (2000). Selective serotonin reuptake inhibitors versus tricyclic antidepressants: A meta-analysis of efficacy and tolerability. *Journal of Affective Disorders, 58,* 19–36. (p. 567)

Anderson, J. R., Myowa-Yamakoshi, M., & Matsuzawa, T. (2004). Contagious yawning in chimpanzees. *Biology Letters, 271,* S468–S470. (p. 582)

Anderson, R. C., Pichert, J. W., Goetz, E. T., Schallert, D. L., Stevens, K. V., & Trollip, S. R. (1976). Instantiation of general terms. *Journal of Verbal Learning and Verbal Behavior, 15,* 667–679. (p. 284)

Anderson, S. R. (2004). *Doctor Dolittle's delusion: Animals and the uniqueness of human language.* New Haven: Yale University Press. (p. 328)

Andreasen, N. C. (1997). Linking mind and brain in the study of mental illnesses: A project for a scientific psychopathology. *Science, 275,* 1586–1593. (p. 534)

Andreasen, N. C. (2001). *Brave new brain: Conquering mental illness in the era of the genome.* New York: Oxford University Press. (p. 534)

Andreasen, N. C., Arndt, S., Swayze, V., II, Cizadlo, T., & Flaum, M. (1994). Thalamic abnormalities in schizophrenia visualized through magnetic resonance image averaging. *Science, 266,* 294–298. (p. 534)

Andrews, G., Hall, W., Teesson, M., & Henderson, S. (1999, April). *The mental health of Australians.* Canberra: Mental Health Branch, Commonwealth Department of Health and Aged Care. (p. 506)

Angell, M., & Kassirer, J. P. (1998). Alternative medicine: The risks of untested and unregulated remedies. *New England Journal of Medicine, 17,* 839–841. (p. 453)

Angelsen, N. K., Vik, T., Jacobsen, G., & Bakketeig, L. S. (2001). Breast feeding and cognitive development at age 1 and 5 years. *Archives of Disease in Childhood, 85,* 183–188. (p. 24)

Angoff, W. H. (1987). The nature-nurture debate, aptitudes, and group differences. Presidential address to American Psychological Association Division 5. (p. 346)

Antony, M. M., Brown, T. A., & Barlow, D. H. (1992). Current perspectives on panic and panic disorder. *Current Directions in Psychological Science, 1,* 79–82. (p. 513)

Antrobus, J. (1991). Dreaming: Cognitive processes during cortical activation and high afferent thresholds. *Psychological Review, 98,* 96–121. (p. 208)

APA. (2003, November). *Psychology careers for the twenty-first century.* Washington, DC: American Psychological Association. (p. 9)

Appleby, D. C. (2002). *The savvy psychology major.* Dubuque, IA: Kendall/Hunt.

Archer, J. (2004). Sex differences in aggression in real-world settings: A meta-analytic review. Review of *General Psychology, 8,* 291–322. (p. 88)

Arenson, K. W. (1997, May 4). Romanian woman breaks male grip on top math prize. *New York Times News Service* (in *Grand Rapids Press,* p. A7). (p. 348)

Arent, S. M., Landers, D. M., & Etnier, J. L. (2000). The effects of exercise on mood in older adults: A meta-analytic review. *Journal of Aging and Physical Activity, 8,* 407–430. (p. 450)

Aries, E. (1987). Gender and communication. In P. Shaver & C. Henrick (Eds.), *Review of Personality and Social Psychology, 7,* 149–176. (p. 88)

Armel, K. C., & Ramachandran, V. S. (2003). Projecting sensations to external objects: Evidence from skin conductance response. *Proceedings of the Royal Society of London. Series B. Biological Sciences, 270,* 1499–1506. (p. 162)

Armony, J. L., Quirk, G. J., & LeDoux, J. E. (1998). Differential effects of amygdala lesions on early and late plastic components of auditory cortex spike trains during fear conditioning. *Journal of Neuroscience, 18,* 2592–2601. (p. 514)

Arnett, J. J. (1999). Adolescent storm and stress, reconsidered. *American Psychologist, 54,* 317–326. (p. 120)

Arnett, J. J. (2000). Emerging adulthood: A theory of development from the late teens through the twenties. *American Psychologist, 55,* 469–480. (p. 127)

Arnold, K., & Horrigan, K. (2002). Gaining admission into the graduate program of your choice. *Eye on Psi Chi,* 30–33. (pp. B-8, B-9)

Aron, A., Melinat, E., Aron, E. N., Vallone, R. D., & Bator, R. J. (1997). The experimental generation of interpersonal closeness: A procedure and some preliminary findings. *Personality and Social Psychology Bulletin, 23,* 363–377. (p. 612)

Aronson, E. (2001, April 13). Newsworthy violence. E-mail to SPSP discussion list, drawing from *Nobody Left to Hate.* New York: Freeman, 2000. (p. 126)

Arseneault, L., Cannon, M., Poulton, R., Murray, R., Caspi, A., & Moffitt, T. E. (2002). Cannabis use in adolescence and risk for adult psychosis: Longitudinal prospective study. *British Medical Journal, 325,* 1212–1213. (p. 224)

Asch, S. E. (1955). Opinions and social pressure. *Scientific American, 193,* 31–35. (p. 583)

Aserinsky, E. (1988, January 17). Personal communication. (p. 197)

ASHA. (2003). STD statistics. American Social Health Association (www.ashastd.org/stdfaqs/statistics.html). (p. 379)

Ashtari, M., Kumra, S., Clarke, T., Ardekani, B., Bhaskar, S., & Rhinewine, J. (2004, November 29). Diffusion tensor imaging of children with attention deficit/hyperactivity disorder. Paper presented to the Radiological Society of North America convention. (p. 501)

Assanand, S., Pinel, J. P. J., & Lehman, D. R. (1998). Personal theories of hunger and eating. *Journal of Applied Social Psychology, 28,* 998–1015. (p. 362)

Associated Press. (2006, October 4). Man recites pi to 100,000 places. (p. 279)

Atkinson, R. C., & Shiffrin, R. M. (1968). Human memory: A control system and its control processes. In K. Spence (Ed.), *The psychology of learning and motivation (Vol. 2).* New York: Academic Press. (p. 270)

Atwell, R. H. (1986, July 28). *Drugs on campus: A perspective.* Higher Education & National Affairs, p. 5. (p. 218)

Aubrecht, L. (2001). What can you do with a BA in psychology? *Eye on Psi Chi, 5,* 29–31.

Austin, E. J., Deary, I. J., Whiteman, M. C., Fowkes, F. G. R., Pedersen, N. L., Rabbitt, P., Bent, N., & McInnes, L. (2002). Relationships between ability and personality: Does intelligence contribute positively to personal and social adjustment? *Personality and Individual Differences, 32,* 1391–1411. (p. 340)

Australian Bureau of Statistics. (1999). Australia now—A statistical profile: Health—overweight and obesity (www.abs.gov.au). (p. 366)

Averill, J. R. (1983). Studies on anger and aggression: Implications for theories of emotion. *American Psychologist, 38,* 1145–1160. (p. 423)

Averill, J. R. (1993). William James's other theory of emotion. In M. E. Donnelly (Ed.), *Reinterpreting the legacy of William James.* Washington, DC: American Psychological Association. (p. 408)

Avery, R. D., & others. (1994, December 13). Mainstream science on intelligence. *Wall Street Journal,* p. A–18. (p. 345)

Ax, A. F. (1953). The physiological differentiation of fear and anger in humans. *Psychosomatic Medicine, 15,* 433–442. (p. 410)

Axinn, W. & Thornton, A. (1992). The relationship between cohabitation and divorce: Selectivity or causal influence? *Demography, 29,* 357–374. (p. C-4)

Azar, B. (1998, June). Why can't this man feel whether or not he's standing up? *APA Monitor* (www.apa.org/monitor/jun98/touch.html). (p. 168)

Babad, E., Bernieri, F., & Rosenthal, R. (1991). Students as judges of teachers' verbal and nonverbal behavior. *American Educational Research Journal, 28,* 211–234. (p. 418)

Babyak, M., Blumenthal, J. A., Herman, S., Khatri, P., Doraiswamy, M., Moore, K., Craighead, W. W., Baldewics, T. T., & Krishnan, K. R. (2000). Exercise treatment for major depression: Maintenance of therapeutic benefit at ten months. *Psychosomatic Medicine, 62,* 633–638. (p. 450)

Bachman, J., Wadsworth, K., O'Malley, P., Johnston, L., & Schulenberg, J. (1997). *Smoking, drinking, and drug use in young adulthood: The impact of new freedoms and new responsibilities.* Mahwah, NJ: Erlbaum. (p. 226)

Baddeley, A. D. (1982). *Your memory: A user's guide.* New York: Macmillan. (pp. 272, 273)

Bagemihl, B. (1999). *Biological exuberance: Animal homosexuality and natural diversity.* New York: St. Martins. (p. 382)

Bahrick, H. P. (1984). Semantic memory content in permastore: 50 years of memory for Spanish learned in school. *Journal of Experimental Psychology: General, 111,* 1–29. (p. 292)

Bahrick, H. P., Bahrick, L. E., Bahrick, A. S., & Bahrick, P. E. (1993). Maintenance of foreign language vocabulary and the spacing effect. *Psychological Science, 4,* 316–321. (p. 272)

Bahrick, H. P., Bahrick, P. O., & Wittlinger, R. P. (1975). Fifty years of memory for names and faces: A cross-sectional approach. *Journal of Experimental Psychology: General, 104,* 54–75. (p. 284)

Bailey, J. M., & Zucker, K. J. (1995). Childhood sex-typed behavior and sexual orientation: A conceptual analysis and quantitative review. *Developmental Psychology, 31,* 43–55. (p. 380)

Bailey, J. M., Gaulin, S., Agyei, Y., & Gladue, B. A. (1994). Effects of gender and sexual orientation on evolutionary relevant aspects of human mating psychology. *Journal of Personality and Social Psychology, 66,* 1081–1093. (p. 76)

Bailey, J. M., Kirk, K. M., Zhu, G., Dunne, M. P., & Martin, N. G. (2000). Do individual differences in sociosexuality represent genetic or environmentally contingent strategies? Evidence from the Australian twin registry. *Journal of Personality and Social Psychology, 78,* 537–545. (p. 76)

Baillargeon, R. (1995). A model of physical reasoning in infancy. In C. Rovee-Collier & L. P. Lipsitt (Eds.), *Advances in infancy research (Vol. 9).* Stamford, CT: Ablex. (p. 109)

Baillargeon, R. (1998). Infants' understanding of the physical world. In M. Sabourin, F. I. M. Craik, & M. Roberts (Eds.), *Advances in psychological science, Vol. 2: Biological and cognitive aspects.* Hove, England: Psychology Press. (p. 109)

Baillargeon, R. (2004). Infants' physical world. *Current Directions in Psychological Science, 13,* 89–94. (p. 109)

Baker, E. L. (1987). The state of the art of clinical hypnosis. *International Journal of Clinical and Experimental Hypnosis, 35,* 203–214. (p. 212)

Baker, T. B., Piper, M. E., McCarthy, D. E., Majeskie, M. R., & Fiore, M. C. (2004). Addiction motivation reformulated: An affective processing model of negative reinforcement. *Psychological Review, 111,* 33–51. (p. 249)

Bakermans-Kranenburg, M. J., van Ijzendoorn, M. H., & Juffer, F. (2003). Less is more: Meta-analyses of sensitivity and attachment interventions in early childhood. *Psychological Bulletin, 129,* 195–215. (p. 115)

Ballard, M. E., & Wiest, J. R. (1998). Mortal Kombat: The effects of violent videogame play on males' hostility and cardiovascular responding. *Journal of Applied Social Psychology, 26,* 717–730. (p. 605)

Bancroft, J., Loftus, J., & Long, J. S. (2003). Distress about sex: A national survey of women in heterosexual relationships. *Archives of Sexual Behavior, 32,* 193–208. (p. 376)

Bandura, A. (1982). The psychology of chance encounters and life paths. *American Psychologist, 37,* 747–755. (p. 135)

Bandura, A. (1986). *Social foundations of thought and action: A social-cognitive theory.* Englewood Cliffs, NJ: Prentice-Hall. (p. 483)

Bandura, A. (2001). Social cognitive theory: An agentic perspective. *Annual Review of Psychology, 52,* 1–26. (p. 483)

Bandura, A. (2005) The evolution of social cognitive theory. In K. G. Smith & M. A. Hitt (Eds.), *Great minds in management: The process of theory development.* Oxford: Oxford University Press. (pp. 135, 263, 483)

Bandura, A., Ross, D., & Ross, S. A. (1961). Transmission of aggression through imitation of aggressive models. *Journal of Abnormal and Social Psychology, 63,* 575–582. (p. 262)

Barber, T. X. (2000). A deeper understanding of hypnosis: Its secrets, its nature, its essence. American *Journal of Clinical Hypnosis, 42,* 208–272. (p. 214)

Barinaga, M. B. (1992a). The brain remaps its own contours. *Science, 258,* 216–218. (p. 59)

Barinaga, M. B. (1997). How exercise works its magic. *Science, 276,* 1325. (p. 450)

Barker, S. L., Funk, S. C., & Houston, B. K. (1988). Psychological treatment versus nonspecific factors: A meta-analysis of conditions that engender comparable expectations for improvement. *Clinical Psychology Review, 8,* 579–594. (p. 559)

Barkley, R. A., & 74 others. (2002). International consensus statement (January 2002). *Clinical Child and Family Psychology Review, 5,* 2. (p. 501)

Barlow, D. H. (1988). *Anxiety and its disorders: The nature and treatment of anxiety and panic.* New York: Guilford. (p. 514)

Barnes, M. L., & Sternberg, R. J. (1989). Social intelligence and decoding of nonverbal cues. *Intelligence, 13,* 263–287. (p. 419)

Barnett, P. A., & Gotlib, I. H. (1988). Psychosocial functioning and depression: Distinguishing among antecedents, concomitants, and consequences. *Psychological Bulletin, 104,* 97–126. (p. 528)

Barnier, A. J., & McConkey, K. M. (2004). Defining and identifying the highly hypnotizable person. In M. Heap, R. J. Brown, & D. A. Oakley (Eds.), *High hypnotisability: Theoretical, experimental and clinical issues.* London: Brunner-Routledge. (p. 211)

Baron, R. A. (1988). Negative effects of destructive criticism: Impact on conflict, self-efficacy, and task performance. *Journal of Applied Psychology, 73,* 199–207. (p. 257)

Baron, R. S., Cutrona, C. E., Hicklin, D., Russell, D. W., & Lubaroff, D. M. (1990). Social support and immune function among spouses of cancer patients. *Journal of Personality and Social Psychology, 59,* 344–352. (p. 448)

Baron-Cohen, S. (2004). *The essential difference: Men, women, and the extreme male brain.* London: Penguin Books. (p. 111)

Baron-Cohen, S. (2005, April 6 and May 19). The assortative mating theory: A talk with Simon Baron-Cohen. *The Edge* (www.edge.org). (p. 111)

Barrett, L. F., Lane, R. D., Sechrest, L., & Schwartz, G. E. (2000). Sex differences in emotional awareness. *Personality and Social Psychology Bulletin, 26,* 1027–1035. (p. 419)

Barry, D. (1995, September 17). *Teen smokers, too, get cool, toxic, waste-blackened lungs.* Asbury Park Press, p. D3. (p. 221)

Bashore, T. R., Ridderinkhof, K. R., & van der Molen, M. W. (1997). The decline of cognitive processing speed in old age. *Current Directions in Psychological Science, 6,* 163–169. (p. 131)

Baskind, D. E. (1997, December 14). Personal communication, from Delta College. (p. 547)

Bass, L. E., & Kane-Williams, E. (1993). Stereotype or reality: Another look at alcohol and drug use among African American children. *U.S. Department of Health and Human Services, Public Health Reports, 108* (Supplement 1), 78–84. (p. 227)

Bassett, D. R., Schneider, P. L., & Huntington, G. E. (2004). Physical activity in an Old Order Amish community. *Medicine and Science in Sports and Exercise, 36,* 79–85. (p. 370)

Baum, A., & Posluszny, D. M. (1999). Health psychology: Mapping biobehavioral contributions to health and illness. *Annual Review of Psychology, 50,* 137–163. (p. 441)

Baumeister, R. F. (1989). The optimal margin of illusion. *Journal of Social and Clinical Psychology, 8,* 176–189. (pp. 312, 494)

Baumeister, R. F. (1996). Should schools try to boost self-esteem? Beware the dark side. *American Educator, 20,* 14019, 43. (p. 493)

Baumeister, R. F. (2001, April). Violent pride: Do people turn violent because of self-hate, or self-love? *Scientific American,* pp. 96–101. (p. 493)

Baumeister, R. F. (2005). *The cultural animal: Human nature, meaning, and social life.* New York: Oxford University Press. (p. 82))

Baumeister, R. F., & Bratslavsky, E. (1999). Passion, intimacy, and time: Passionate love as a function of change in intimacy. *Personality and Social Psychology Review, 3,* 49–67. (p. 612)

Baumeister, R. F., & Exline, J. J. (2000). Self-control, morality, and human strength. *Journal of Social and Clinical Psychology, 19,* 29–42. (p. 485)

Baumeister, R. F., & Leary, M. R. (1995). The need to belong: Desire for interpersonal attachments as a fundamental human motivation. *Psychological Bulletin, 117,* 497–529. (pp. 387, 389)

Baumeister, R. F., & Tice, D. M. (1986). How adolescence became the struggle for self: A historical transformation of psychological development. In J. Suls & A. G. Greenwald (Eds.), *Psychological perspectives on the self (Vol. 3).* Hillsdale, NJ: Erlbaum. (p. 126)

Baumeister, R. F., Campbell, J. D., Krueger, J. I., & Vohs, K. D. (2005, January). Exploding the self-esteem myth. *Scientific American,* pp. 84–91. (p. 491)

Baumeister, R. F., Campbell, J., Krueger, J. I., & Vohs, K. D. (2003). Does high self-esteem cause better performance, interpersonal success, happiness, or healthier lifestyles? *Psychological Science in the Public Interest, 4(1),* 1–44. (p. 491)

Baumeister, R. F., Catanese, K. R., & Vohs, K. D. (2001). Is there a gender difference in strength of sex drive? Theoretical views, conceptual distinctions, and a review of relevant evidence. *Personality and Social Psychology Review, 5,* 242–273. (p. 76)

Baumeister, R. F., Dale, K., & Sommer, K. L. (1998). Freudian defense mechanisms and empirical findings in modern personality and social psychology: Reaction formation, projection, displacement, undoing, isolation, sublimation, and denial. *Journal of Personality, 66,* 1081–1125. (p. 467)

Baumeister, R. F., Stillwell, A., & Wotman, S. R. (1990). Victim and perpetrator accounts of interpersonal conflict: Autobiographical narratives about anger. *Journal of Personality and Social Psychology, 59,* 994–1005. (p. 425)

Baumeister, R. F., Twenge, J. M., & Nuss, C. K. (2002). Effects of social exclusion on cognitive processes: Anticipated aloneness reduces intelligent thought. *Journal of Personality and Social Psychology, 83,* 817–827. (p. 389)

Baumgardner, A. H., Kaufman, C. M., & Levy, P. E. (1989). Regulating affect interpersonally: When low esteem leads to greater enhancement. *Journal of Personality and Social Psychology, 56,* 907–921. (p. 491)

Baumrind, D. (1982). Adolescent sexuality: Comment on Williams' and Silka's comments on Baumrind. *American Psychologist, 37,* 1402–1403. (p. 387)

Baumrind, D. (1996). The discipline controversy revisited. *Family Relations, 45,* 405–414. (p. 117)

Baumrind, D., Larzelere, R. E., & Cowan, P. A. (2002). Ordinary physical punishment: Is it harmful? Comment on Gershoff (2002). *Psychological Bulletin, 128,* 602–611. (p. 253)

Bavelier, D., Newport, E. L., & Supalla, T. (2003). Children need natural languages, signed or spoken. *Cerebrum, 5(1),* 19–32. (p. 321)

Beaman, A. L., & Klentz, B. (1983). The supposed physical attractiveness bias against supporters of the women's movement: A meta-analysis. *Personality and Social Psychology Bulletin, 9,* 544–550. (p. 610)

Beardsley, L. M. (1994). Medical diagnosis and treatment across cultures. In W. J. Lonner & R. Malpass (Eds.), *Psychology and culture.* Boston: Allyn & Bacon. (p. 502)

Beardsley, T. (1996, July). Waking up. *Scientific American,* pp. 14, 18. (p. 201)

Beauchamp, G. K. (1987). The human preference for excess salt. *American Scientist, 75,* 27–33. (p. 363)

Beck, A. J., Kline, S. A., & Greenfeld, L. A. (1988). *Survey of youth in custody, 1987.* U.S. Department of Justice, Bureau of Justice Statistics Special Report. (p. 603)

Beck, A. T., & Steer, R. A. (1989). Clinical predictors of eventual suicide: A 5- to 10-year prospective study of suicide attempters. *Journal of Affective Disorders, 17,* 203–209. (p. 525)

Beck, A. T., Rush, A. J., Shaw, B. F., & Emery, G. (1979). *Cognitive therapy of depression.* New York: Guilford Press. (pp. 549, 550)

Becklen, R., & Cervone, D. (1983). Selective looking and the noticing of unexpected events. *Memory and Cognition, 11,* 601–608. (p. 194)

Beckman, M. (2004). Crime, culpability, and the adolescent brain. *Science, 305,* 596–599. (p. 122)

Beeman, M. J., & Chiarello, C. (1998). Complementary right- and left-hemisphere language comprehension. *Current Directions in Psychological Science, 7,* 2–8. (p. 63)

Beilin, H. (1992) Piaget's enduring contribution to developmental psychology. *Developmental Psychology, 28,* 191–204. (p. 112)

Beitman, B. D., Goldfried, M. R., & Norcross, J. C. (1989). The movement toward integrating the psychotherapies: An overview. *American Journal of Psychiatry, 146,* 138–147. (p. 541)

Bell, A. P., Weinberg, M. S., & Hammersmith, S. K. (1981). *Sexual preference: Its development in men and women.* Bloomington: Indiana University Press. (p. 382)

Belsher, G., & Costello, C. G. (1988). Relapse after recovery from unipolar depression: A critical review. *Psychological Bulletin, 104,* 84–96. (p. 523)

Bem, D. J. (1984). Quoted in *The Skeptical Inquirer, 8,* 194. (p. 187)

Bem, D. J. (1996). Exotic becomes erotic: A developmental theory of sexual orientation. *Psychological Review, 103,* 320–335. (p. 385)

Bem, D. J. (1998). Is EBE theory supported by the evidence? Is it androcentric? A reply to Peplau et al. (1998). *Psychological Review, 105,* 395–398. (p. 385)

Bem, D. J. (2000). Exotic becomes erotic: Interpreting the biological correlates of sexual orientation. *Archives of Sexual Behavior, 29,* 531–548. (p. 385)

Bem, D. J., & Honorton, C. (1994). Does psi exist? Replicable evidence for an anomalous process of information transfer. *Psychological Bulletin, 115,* 4–18. (p. 187)

Bem, D. J., Palmer, J., & Broughton, R. S. (2001). Updating the Ganzfeld database: A victim of its own success? *Journal of Parapsychology, 65,* 207–218. (p. 187)

Bem, S. L. (1987). Masculinity and femininity exist only in the mind of the perceiver. In J. M. Reinisch, L. A. Rosenblum, & S. A. Sanders (Eds.), *Masculinity/femininity: Basic perspectives.* New York: Oxford University Press. (p. 92)

Bem, S. L. (1993). *The lenses of gender.* New Haven: Yale University Press. (p. 92)

Benbow, C. P., Lubinski, D., Shea, D. L., & Eftekhari-Sanjani, H. (2000). Sex differences in mathematical reasoning ability at age 13: Their status 20 years later. *Psychological Science, 11,* 474–2000. (p. 349)

Bennett, W. I. (1995). Beyond overeating. *New England Journal of Medicine, 332,* 673–674. (p. 372)

Ben-Shakhar, G., & Elaad, E. (2003). The validity of psychophysiological detection of information with the guilt knowledge test: A meta-analytic review. *Journal of Applied Psychology, 88,* 131–151. (p. 412)

Benson, H. (1996). *Timeless healing: The power and biology of belief.* New York: Scribner. (p. 452)

Benson, K., & Feinberg, I. (1977). The beneficial effect of sleep in an extended Jenkins and Dallenbach paradigm. *Psychophysiology, 14,* 375–384. (p. 294)

Benson, P. L., Sharma, A. R., & Roehlkepartain, E. C. (1994). *Growing up adopted: A portrait of adolescents and their families.* Minneapolis: Search Institute. (p. 72)

Berenbaum, S. A., Korman, K., & Leveroni, C. (1995). Early hormones and sex differences in cognitive abilities. *Learning and Individual Differences, 7,* 303–321. (p. 349)

Berger, B. G., & Motl, R. W. (2000). Exercise and mood: A selective review and synthesis of research employing the profile of mood states. *Journal of Applied Sports Psychology, 12,* 69–92. (p. 450)

Bergin, A. E. (1980). Psychotherapy and religious values. *Journal of Consulting and Clinical Psychology, 48,* 95–105. (p. 563)

Bergsholm, P., Larsen, J. L., Rosendahl, K., & Holsten, F. (1989). Electroconvulsive therapy and cerebral computed tomography. *Acta Psychiatrica Scandinavia, 80,* 566–572. (p. 569)

Berk, L. S., Felten, D. L., Tan, S. A., Bittman, B. B., & Westengard, J. (2001). Modulation of neuroimmune parameters during the eustress of humor-associated mirthful laughter. *Alternative Therapies, 7,* 62–76. (p. 446)

Berkel, J., & de Waard, F. (1983). Mortality pattern and life expectancy of Seventh Day Adventists in the Netherlands. *International Journal of epidemiology, 12,* 455–459. (p. 455)

Berkowitz, L. (1983). Aversively stimulated aggression: Some parallels and differences in research with animals and humans. *American Psychologist, 38,* 1135–1144. (p. 601)

Berkowitz, L. (1989). Frustration-aggression hypothesis: Examination and reformulation. *Psychological Bulletin, 106,* 59–73. (p. 601)

Berkowitz, L. (1990). On the formation and regulation of anger and aggression: A cognitive-neoassociationistic analysis. *American Psychologist, 45,* 494–503. (p. 423)

Berman, M., Gladue, B., & Taylor, S. (1993). The effects of hormones, Type A behavior pattern, and provocation on aggression in men. *Motivation and Emotion, 17,* 125–138. (p. 601)

Berndt, T. J. (1992). Friendship and friends' influence in adolescence. *Current Directions in Psychological Science, 1,* 156–159. (p. 89)

Bernhardt, P. C., Dabbs, J. M., Jr., Fielden, J. A., & Lutter, C. D. (1998). Testosterone changes during vicarious experiences of winning and losing among fans at sporting events. *Physiology and Behavior, 65,* 59–62. (p. 601)

Bernstein, D. M., Atance, C., Loftus, G. R., & Meltzoff, A. (2004). We saw it all along: Visual hindsight bias in children and adults. *Psychological Science, 15,* 264–267. (p. 14)

Berridge, K. C., & Winkielman, P. (2003). What is an unconscious emotion? (The case of unconscious "liking"). *Cognition and Emotion, 17,* 181–211. (p. 413)

Berry, D. S., & McArthur, L. Z. (1986). Perceiving character in faces: The impact of age-related craniofacial changes on social perception. *Psychological Bulletin, 100,* 3–18. (p. 241)

Berscheid, E. (1981). An overview of the psychological effects of physical attractiveness and some comments upon the psychological effects of knowledge of the effects of physical attractiveness. In G. W. Lucker, K. Ribbens, & J. A. McNamara (Eds.), *Psychological aspects of facial form (Craniofacial growth series).* Ann Arbor: Center for Human Growth and Development, University of Michigan. (p. 609)

Berscheid, E. (1985). Interpersonal attraction. In G. Lindzey & E. Aronson (Eds.), *The handbook of social psychology.* New York: Random House. (p. 388)

Berscheid, E., Gangestad, S. W., & Kulakowski, D. (1984). Emotion in close relationships: Implications for relationship counseling. In S. D. Brown & R. W. Lent (Eds.), *Handbook of counseling psychology.* New York: Wiley. (p. 611)

Bértolo, H., Paiva, T., Pessoa, L., Mestre, T., Marques, R., & Santos, R. (2003). Visual dream content, graphical representation and EEG alpha activity in congenitally blind subjects. *Cognitive Brain Research, 15,* 277–284. (p. 206)

Bettencourt, B. A., & Dorr, N. (1997). Collective self-esteem as a mediator of the relationship between allocentrism and subjective well-being. *Personality and Social Psychology Bulletin, 23,* 955–964. (p. 86)

Bettencourt, B. A., & Kernahan, C. (1997). A meta-analysis of aggression in the presence of violent cues: Effects of gender differences and aversive provocation. *Aggressive Behavior, 23,* pp. 447–457. (p. 88)

Beyerstein, B., & Beyerstein, D. (Eds.) (1992). *The write stuff: Evaluations of graphology.* Buffalo, NY: Prometheus Books. (p. 480)

Bhatt, R. S., Wasserman, E. A., Reynolds, W. F., Jr., & Knauss, K. S. (1988). Conceptual behavior in pigeons: Categorization of both familiar and novel examples from four classes of natural and artificial stimuli. *Journal of Experimental Psychology: Animal Behavior Processes, 14,* 219–234. (p. 247)

Bialystok, E. (2001). *Bilingualism in development, language, literacy, and cognition.* New York: Cambridge University Press. (p. 324)

Bickman, L. (1999). Practice makes perfect and other myths about mental health services. *American Psychologist, 54,* 965–978. (p. 557)

Biederman, J., Wilens, T., Mick, E., Spencer, T., & Faraone, S. V. (1999). Pharmacotherapy of Attention-Deficit/Hyperactivity Disorder reduces risk for substance use disorder. *Pediatrics, 104,* 1–5. (p. 501)

Biello, S. M., & Dafters, R. I. (2001). MDMA and fenfluramine alter the response of the circadian clock to a serotonin agonist in vitro. *Brain Research, 920,* 202–209. (p. 223)

Biggs, V. (2001, April 13). Murder suspect captured in Grand Marais. *Cook County News-Herald.* (p. 419)

Binet, A., & Simon, T. (1905; reprinted 1916). New methods for the diagnosis of the intellectual level of subnormals. In A. Binet & T. Simon, *The development of intelligence in children.* Baltimore: Williams & Wilkins. (p. 336)

Birnbaum, S. G., Yuan, P. X., Wang, M., Vijayraghavan, S., Bloom, A. K., Davis, D. J., Gobeski, K. T., Sweatt, J. D., Manhi, H. K., & Arnsten, A. F. T.

(2004). Protein kinase C overactivity impairs prefrontal cortical regulation of working memory. *Science, 306,* 882–884. (p. 280)

Bishop, B. (2004, November 22). Personal correspondence, and earlier articles on "The great divide" in the *Austin Statesman.* (p. 590)

Bishop, G. D. (1991). Understanding the understanding of illness: Lay disease representations. In J. A. Skelton & R. T. Croyle (Eds.), *Mental representation in health and illness.* New York: Springer-Verlag. (p. 308)

Biswas-Diener, R., & Diener, E. (2001). Making the best of a bad situation: Satisfaction in the slums of Calcutta. *Social Indicators Research, 55,* 329–352. (p. 427)

Bjork, R. A. (1999). Assessing our own competence: Heuristics and illusions. In D. Gopher & A. Koriat (Eds.), *Attention and performance XVII. Cognitive regulation of performance: Interaction of theory and application.* Cambridge, MA: MIT Press. (p. 272)

Bjork, R. A. (2000, July/August). Toward one world of psychological science. *APS Observer,* p. 3. (p. 5)

Bjorklund, D. F., & Green, B. L. (1992). The adaptive nature of cognitive immaturity. *American Psychologist, 47,* 46–54. (p. 112)

Blakemore, S-J., Wolpert, D. M., & Frith, C. D. (1998). Central cancellation of self-produced tickle sensation. *Nature Neuroscience, 1,* 635–640. (p. 161)

Blakeslee, S. (2005, February 8). Focus narrows in search for autism's cause. *New York Times* (www.nytimes.com). (p. 111)

Blanchard, R. (1997). Birth order and sibling sex ratio in homosexual versus heterosexual males and females. *Annual Review of Sex Research, 8,* 27–67. (p. 382)

Blanchard, R. (2001). Fraternal birth order and the maternal immunie hypothesis of male homosexuality. *Hormones and Behavior, 40,* 105–114. (p. 382)

Blankenburg, F., Taskin, B., Ruben, J., Moosmann, M., Ritter, P., Curio, G., & Villringer, A. (2003). Imperceptive stimuli and sensory processing impediment. *Science, 299,* 1864. (p. 145)

Blascovich, J., Seery, M. D., Mugridge, C. A., Norris, R. K., & Weisbuch, M. (2004). Predicting athletic performance from cardiovascular indexes of challenge and threat. *Journal of Experimental Social Psychology, 40,* 683–688. (p. 436)

Blass, T. (1996). Stanley Milgram: A life of inventiveness and controversy. In G. A. Kimble, C. A. Boneau, & M. Wertheimer (Eds.), *Portraits of pioneers in psychology (Vol. II).* Washington, DC and Mahwah, NJ: American Psychological Association and Lawrence Erlbaum Publishers. (p. 585)

Blass, T. (1999). The Milgram paradigm after 35 years: Some things we now know about obedience to authority. *Journal of Applied Social Psychology, 29,* 955–978. (p. 585)

Blatt, S. J., Sanislow, C. A., III, Zuroff, D. C., & Pilkonis, P. (1996). Characteristics of effective therapists: Further analyses of data from the National Institute of Mental Health Treatment of Depression Collaborative Research Program. *Journal of Consulting and Clinical Psychology, 64,* 1276–1284. (p. 561)

Bleustein, J. (2002, June 15). Quoted in "Harley retooled," by S. S. Smith, *American Way Magazine.* (p. 402)

Bloom, F. E. (1993, January/February). What's new in neurotransmitters. *BrainWork,* pp. 7–9. (p. 38)

Bloom, P. (2000). *How children learn the meanings of words.* Cambridge, MA: MIT Press. (p. 319)

Blum, K., Cull, J. G., Braverman, E. R., & Comings, D. E. (1996). Reward deficiency syndrome. *American Scientist, 84,* 132–145. (p. 53)

Bodenhausen, G. V., Sheppard, L. A., & Kramer, G. P. (1994). Negative affect and social judgment: The differential impact of anger and sadness. *European Journal of Social Psychology, 24,* 45–62. (p. 618)

Bodkin, J. A., & Amsterdam, J. D. (2002). Transdermal selegiline in major depression: A double-blind, placebo-controlled, parallel-group study in outpatients. *American Journal of Psychiatry, 159,* 1869–1875. (p. 567)

Boehm, K. E., Schondel, C. K., Marlowe, A. L., & Manke-Mitchell, L. (1999). Teens' concerns: A national evaluation. *Adolescence, 34,* 523–528. (p. 126)

Boesch-Achermann, H., & Boesch, C. (1993). Tool use in wild chimpanzees: New light from dark forests. *Current Directions in Psychological Science, 2,* 18–21. (p. 326)

Bogaert, A. F. (2003). Number of older brothers and sexual orientation: New texts and the attraction/behavior distinction in two national probability samples. *Journal of Personality and Social Psychology, 84,* 644–652. (p. 382)

Bogaert, A. F. (2004). Asexuality: Prevalence and associated factors in a national probability sample. *Journal of Sex Research, 41,* 279–287. (p. 380)

Bogaert, A. F., Friesen, C., & Klentrou, P. (2002). Age of puberty and sexual orientation in a national probability sample. *Archives of Sexual Behavior, 31,* 73–81. (p. 382)

Boggiano, A. K., Barrett, M., Weiher, A. W., McClelland, G. H., & Lusk, C. M. (1987). Use of the maximal-operant principle to motivate children's intrinsic interest. *Journal of Personality and Social Psychology, 53,* 866–879. (p. 254)

Boggiano, A. K., Harackiewicz, J. M., Bessette, M. M., & Main, D. S. (1985). Increasing children's interest through performance-contingent reward. *Social Cognition, 3,* 400–411. (p. 255)

Bogin, B. (1998, February). The tall and the short of it (range of height in humans demonstrates plasticity of human species). *Discover.* (p. 345)

Bohman, M., & Sigvardsson, S. (1990). Outcome in adoption: Lessons from longitudinal studies. In D. Brodzinsky & M. Schechter (Eds.), *The psychology of adoption.* New York: Oxford University Press. (p. 72)

Bolger, N., DeLongis, A., Kessler, R. C., & Schilling, E. A. (1989). Effects of daily stress on negative mood. *Journal of Personality and Social Psychology, 57,* 808–818. (p. 426)

Bonanno, G. A. (2001). Grief and emotion: Experience, expression, and dissociation. In M. Stroebe, W. Stroebe, R. O. Hansson, & H. Schut (Eds.), *New handbook of bereavement: Consciousness, coping, and care.* Cambridge: Cambridge University Press. (p. 139)

Bonanno, G. A. (2004). Loss, trauma, and human resilience: Have we underestimated the human capacity to thrive after extremely aversive events? *American Psychologist, 59,* 20–28. (pp. 139, 512)

Bonanno, G. A. (2005). Adult resilience to potential trauma. *Current Directions in Psychological Science, 14,* 135–137. (p. 512)

Bonanno, G. A., & Kaltman, S. (1999). Toward an integrative perspective on bereavement. *Psychological Bulletin, 125,* 760–777. (p. 139)

Bond, M. H. (1988). Finding universal dimensions of individual variation in multi-cultural studies of values: The Rokeach and Chinese values surveys. *Journal of Personality and Social Psychology, 55,* 1009–1015. (p. 85)

Bond, R., & Smith, P. B. (1996). Culture and conformity: A meta-analysis of studies using Asch's (1952b, 1956) line judgment task. *Psychological Bulletin, 119,* 111–137. (p. 584)

Bono, J. E., & Judge, T. A. (2004). Personality and transformational and transactional leadership: A meta-analysis. *Journal of Applied Psychology, 89,* 901–910. (p. 402)

Booth, F. W., & Neufer, P. D. (2005). Exercise controls gene expression. *American Scientist, 93,* 28–35. (p. 366)

Boring, E. G. (1930). A new ambiguous figure. *American Journal of Psychology, 42,* 444–445. (p. 183)

Bornstein, M. H., Cote, L. R., Maital, S., Painter, K., Park, S-Y., Pascual, L., Pecheux, M-G., Ruel, J., Venute, P., & Vyt, A. (2004). Cross-linguistic analysis of vocabulary in young children: Spanish, Dutch, French, Hebrew, Italian, Korean, and American English. *Child Development, 75,* 1115–1139. (p. 321)

Bornstein, M. H., Tal, J., Rahn, C., Galperin, C. Z., Pecheux, M-G., Lamour, M., Toda, S., Azuma, H., Ogino, M., & Tamis-LeMonda, C. S. (1992a). Functional analysis of the contents of maternal speech to infants of 5 and 13 months in four cultures: Argentina, France, Japan, and the United States. *Developmental Psychology, 28,* 593–603. (p. 87)

Bornstein, M. H., Tamis-LeMonda, C. S., Tal, J., Ludemann, P., Toda, S., Rahn, C. W., Pecheux, M-G., Azuma, H., Vardi, D. (1992b). Maternal responsiveness to infants in three societies: The United States, France, and Japan. *Child Development, 63,* 808–821. (p. 87)

Bornstein, R. F. (1989). Exposure and affect: Overview and meta-analysis of research, 1968–1987. *Psychological Bulletin, 106*, 265–289. (p. 607)

Bornstein, R. F. (1999). Source amnesia, misattribution, and the power of unconscious perceptions and memories. *Psychoanalytic Psychology, 16*, 155–178. (p. 607)

Bornstein, R. F. (2001). The impending death of psychoanalysis. *Psychoanalytic Psychology, 18*, 3–20. (p. 468)

Bornstein, R. F., Galley, D. J., Leone, D. R., & Kale, A. R. (1991). The temporal stability of ratings of parents: Test-retest reliability and influence of parental contact. *Journal of Social Behavior and Personality, 6*, 641–649. (p. 287)

Boroditsky, R., Fisher, W., & Sand, M. (1995, July). Teenagers and contraception. Section of The Canadian contraception study. *Journal of the Society of Obstetricians and Gynaecologists of Canada, Special Supplement*, pp. 22–25. (p. 379)

Boscarino, J. A. (1997). Diseases among men 20 years after exposure to severe stress: Implications for clinical research and medical care. *Psychosomatic Medicine, 59*, 605–614. (p. 436)

Bosma, H., Marmot, M. G., Hemingway, H., Nicolson, A. C., Brunner, E., & Stansfeld, S. A. (1997). Low job control and risk of coronary heart disease in Whitehall II (prospective cohort) study. *British Medical Journal, 314*, 558–565. (p. 446)

Bosma, H., Peter, R., Siegrist, J., & Marmot, M. (1998). Two alternative job stress models and the risk of coronary heart disease. *American Journal of Public Health, 88*, 68–74. (p. 446)

Bostwick, J. M., & Pankratz, V. S. (2000). Affective disorders and suicide risk: A re-examination. *American Journal of Psychiatry, 157*, 1925–1932. (p. 524)

Bosworth, R. G., & Dobkins, K. R. (1999). Left-hemisphere dominance for motion processing in deaf signers. *Psychological Science, 10*, 256–262. (p. 59)

Bothwell, R. K., Brigham, J. C., & Malpass, R. S. (1989). Cross-racial identification. *Personality and Social Psychology Bulletin, 15*, 19–25. (p. 598)

Bouchard, T. J., Jr. (1981, December 6). Interview on Nova: Twins [program broadcast by the Public Broadcasting Service]. (p. 70)

Bouchard, T. J., Jr. (1995). Longitudinal studies of personality and intelligence: A behavior genetic and evolutionary psychology perspective. In D. H. Saklofske & M. Zeidner (Eds.), *International handbook of personality and intelligence*. New York: Plenum. (p. 343)

Bouchard, T. J., Jr. (1996a). IQ similarity in twins reared apart: Finding and responses to critics. In R. Sternberg & C. Grigorenko (Eds.), *Intelligence: Heredity and environment*. New York: Cambridge University Press. (p. 342)

Bouchard, T. J., Jr. (1996b). Behavior genetic studies of intelligence, yesterday and today: The long journey from plausibility to proof. *Journal of Biosocial Science, 28*, 527–555. (p. 343)

Bouchard, T. J., Jr. (2004). Genetic influence on human psychological traits. *Current Directions in Psychological Science, 13*, 148–151. (p. 69)

Bouchard, T. J., Jr., & McGue, M. (1990). Genetic and rearing environmental influences on adult personality: An analysis of adopted twins reared apart. *Journal of Personality, 58*, 263. (p. 70)

Bouton, M. E., Mineka, S., & Barlow, D. H. (2001). A modern learning theory perspective on the etiology of panic disorder. *Psychological Review, 108*, 4–32. (p. 513)

Bowden, E. M., & Beeman, M. J. (1998). Getting the right idea: Semantic activation in the right hemisphere may help solve insight problems. *Psychological Science, 9*, 435–440. (p. 63)

Bower, B. (2003, November 22). Vision seekers. *Science News, 164*, pp. 331, 332. (p. 181)

Bower, G. H. (1983). *Affect and cognition*. Philosophical Transaction: Royal Society of London, Series B, 302, 387–402. (p. 287)

Bower, G. H. (1986). Prime time in cognitive psychology. In P. Eelen (Ed.), *Cognitive research and behavior therapy: Beyond the conditioning paradigm*. Amsterdam: North Holland Publishers. (p. 285)

Bower, G. H., & Morrow, D. G. (1990). Mental models in narrative comprehension. *Science, 247*, 44–48. (p. 274)

Bower, G. H., Clark, M. C., Lesgold, A. M., & Winzenz, D. (1969). Hierarchical retrieval schemes in recall of categorized word lists. *Journal of Verbal Learning and Verbal Behavior, 8*, 323–343. (p. 276)

Bower, J. E., Kemeny, M. E., Taylor, S. E., & Fahey, J. L. (1998). Cognitive processing, discovery of meaning, CD4 decline, and AIDS-related mortality among bereaved HIV-seropositive men. *Journal of Consulting and Clinical Psychology, 66*, 979–986. (p. 441)

Bower, J. M., & Parsons, L. M. (2003, August). Rethinking the "lesser brain." *Scientific American*, pp. 50–57. (p. 49)

Bowers, K. S. (1984). Hypnosis. In N. Endler & J. M. Hunt (Eds.), *Personality and behavioral disorders (2nd ed.)*. New York: Wiley. (pp. 211, 212)

Bowers, K. S. (1987, July). Personal communication. (p. 212)

Bowers, T. G., & Clum, G. A. (1988). Relative contribution of specific and nonspecific treatment effects: Meta-analysis of placebo-controlled behavior therapy research. *Psychological Bulletin, 103*, 315–323. (p. 557)

Bowles, S., & Kasindorf, M. (2001, March 6). Friends tell of picked-on but 'normal' kid. *USA Today*, p. 4A. (p. 389)

Bowman, H. (2003, Fall). Interactions between chimpanzees and their human caregivers in captive settings: The effects of gestural communication on reciprocity. *Friends of Washoe, 25(1)*, 7–16. (p. 327)

Boyatzis, C. J., Matillo, G. M., & Nesbitt, K. M. (1995). Effects of the 'Mighty Morphin Power Rangers' on children's aggression with peers. *Child Study Journal, 25*, 45–55. (p. 265)

Boynton, R. M. (1979). *Human color vision*. New York: Holt, Rinehart & Winston. (p. 154)

Braden, J. P. (1994). *Deafness, deprivation, and IQ*. New York: Plenum. (p. 345)

Brainerd, C. J. (1996). Piaget: A centennial celebration. *Psychological Science, 7*, 191–195. (p. 107)

Brandon, S., Boakes, J., Glaser, & Green, R. (1998). Recovered memories of childhood sexual abuse: Implications for clinical practice. *British Journal of Psychiatry, 172*, 294–307. (p. 300)

Brannon, L. A., & Brock, T. C. (1994). Perilous underestimation of sex partners' sexual histories in calculating personal AIDS risk. Paper presented to the American Psychological Society convention. (p. 379)

Bransford, J. D., & Johnson, M. K. (1972). Contextual prerequisites for understanding: Some investigations of comprehension and recall. *Journal of Verbal Learning and Verbal Behavior, 11*, 717–726. (p. 274)

Braun, S. (1996). New experiments underscore warnings on maternal drinking. *Science, 273*, 738–739. (p. 102)

Braun, S. (2001, Spring). Seeking insight by prescription. *Cerebrum*, pp. 10–21. (p. 223)

Bray, D. W., & Byham, W. (1997). Insights into the history and future of assessment centers: An interview with Dr. Douglas W. Bray and Dr. William Byham. *Journal of Social Behavior and Personality, 12*, 3–12. (p. 489)

Bray, D. W., & Byham, W. C. (1991, Winter). Assessment centers and their derivatives. *Journal of Continuing Higher Education*, pp. 8–11. (p. 489)

Bray, G. A. (1969). Effect of caloric restriction on energy expenditure in obese patients. *Lancet, 2*, 397–398. (p. 369)

Brayne, C., Spiegelhalter, D. J., Dufouil, C., Chi, L-Y., Dening, T. R., Paykel, E. S., O'Connor, D.W., Ahmed, A., McGee, M. A., & Huppert, F.A. (1999). Estimating the true extent of cognitive decline in the old old. *Journal of the American Geriatrics Society, 47*, 1283–1288. (p. A-7)

Breedlove, S. M. (1997). Sex on the brain. *Nature, 389*, 801. (p. 383)

Brehm, S., & Brehm, J. W. (1981). *Psychological reactance: A theory of freedom and control*. New York: Academic Press. (p. 591)

Breland, K., & Breland, M. (1961). The misbehavior of organisms. *American Psychologist, 16*, 661–664. (p. 255)

Breslau, N., & Klein, D. F. (1999). Smoking and panic attacks: An epidemiologic investigation. *Archives of General Psychiatry, 56*, 1141–1147. (p. 510)

Bressan, P., & Dal Martello, M. F. (2002). Talis pater, talis filius: Perceived resemblance and the belief in genetic relatedness. *Psychological Science, 13*, 213–218. (p. 183)

Brewer, C. L. (1990). Personal correspondence. (p. 73)

Brewer, C. L. (1996). Personal communication. (p. 6)

Brewer, W. F. (1977). Memory for the pragmatic implications of sentences. *Memory & Cognition, 5*, 673–678. (p. 274)

Brewin, C. R., Andrews, B., & Valentine, J. D. (2000). Meta-analysis of risk factors for posttraumatic stress disorder in trauma-exposed adults. *Journal of Consulting and Clinical Psychology, 68*, 748–766. (p. 512)

Brewin, C. R., Andrews, B., Rose, S., & Kirk, M. (1999). Acute stress disorder and posttraumatic stress disorder in victims of violent crime. *American Journal of Psychiatry, 156*, 360–366. (p. 512)

Brickman, P., Coates, D., & Janoff-Bulman, R. J. (1978). Lottery winners and accident victims: Is happiness relative? *Journal of Personality and Social Psychology, 36*, 917–927. (p. 427)

Brief, A. P., & Weiss, H. M. (2002). Organizational behavior: Affect in the workplace. *Annual Review of Psychology, 53*, 279–307. (p. 399)

Brinson, S. L. (1992). The use and opposition of rape myths in prime-time television dramas. *Sex Roles, 27*, 359–375. (p. 603)

Briscoe, D. (1997, February 16). Women lawmakers still not in charge. *Associated Press* (in *Grand Rapids Press*, p. A23). (p. 91)

Brislin, R. (1993). *Understanding culture's influence on behavior.* Fort Worth, TX: Harcourt Brace. (p. 502)

Brislin, R. W. (1988). Increasing awareness of class, ethnicity, culture, and race by expanding on students' own experiences. In I. Cohen (Ed.), *The G. Stanley Hall Lecture Series.* Washington, DC: American Psychological Association. (p. 82)

Brissette, I., & Cohen, S. (2002). The contribution of individual differences in hostility to the associations between daily interpersonal conflict, affect, and sleep. *Personality and Social Psychology Bulletin, 28*, 1265–1274. (p. 204)

Brissette, I., Scheier, M. F., & Carver, C. S. (2002). The role of optimism in social network development, coping, and psychological adjustment during a life transition. *Journal of Personality and Social Psychology, 82*, 102–111. (p. 528)

British Psychological Society. (1993). Ethical principles for conducting research with human participants. *The Psychologist: Bulletin of the British Psychological Society, 6*, 33–36. (pp. 30, 480)

Brody, J. E. (1999, November 30). Yesterday's precocious puberty is norm today. *New York Times* (www.nytimes.com). (p. 121)

Brody, J. E. (2000, March 21). When post-traumatic stress grips youth. *New York Times* (www.nytimes.com). (p. 512)

Brody, J. E. (2002, November 26). When the eyelids snap shut at 65 miles an hour. *New York Times* (www.nytimes.com). (p. 202)

Brody, J. E. (2003, August 19). Skipping a college course: Weight gain 101. *New York Times* (www.nytimes.com). (p. 370)

Brody, J. E. (2003, December 23). Stampede of diabetes as U.S. races to obesity. *New York Times* (www.nytimes.com). (p. 370)

Brody, J. E. (2003, September). Addiction: A brain ailment, not a moral lapse. *New York Times* (www.nytimes.com). (p. 217)

Brodzinsky, D. M., & Schechter, M. D. (Eds.) (1990). *The psychology of adoption.* New York: Oxford University Press. (p. 71)

Bronner, E. (1998, February 25). U.S. high school seniors among worst in math and science. *New York Times* (www.nytimes.com). (p. 348)

Brooks, D. J. (2002, October 8). Running down the road to happiness. *Gallup Tuesday Briefing* (www.gallup.com). (p. 449)

Brown, A. S. (2003). A review of the déjà vu experience. *Psychological Bulletin, 129*, 394–413. (p. 286)

Brown, A. S. (2004). *The déjà vu experience.* East Sussex, England: Psychology Press. (p. 286)

Brown, A. S., Begg, M. D., Gravenstein, S., Schaefer, C. A., Wyatt, R. J., Bresnahan, M., Babulas, V. P., & Susser, E. S. (2004). Serologic evidence of prenatal influenza in the etiology of schizophrenia. *Archives of General Psychiatry, 61*, 774–780. (p. 535)

Brown, A. S., Bracken, E., Zoccoli, S., & Douglas, K. (2004). Generating and remembering passwords. *Applied Cognitive Psychology, 18*, 641–651. (p. 293)

Brown, A. S., Schaefer, C. A., Wyatt, R. J., Goetz, R., Begg, M. D., Gorman, J. M., & Susser, E. S. (2000). Maternal exposure to respiratory infections and adult schizophrenia spectrum disorders: A prospective birth cohort study. *Schizophrenia Bulletin, 26*, 287–295. (p. 534)

Brown, E. L., & Deffenbacher, K. (1979). *Perception and the senses.* New York: Oxford University Press. (p. 160)

Brown, G. K., Ten Have, T., Henriques, G. R., Xie, S. X., Hollander, J. E., & Beck, A. T. (2005). Cognitive therapy for the prevention of suicide attempts. *JAMA: Journal of the American Medical Association, 294*, 563–570. (p. 557)

Brown, J. D. (1991). Accuracy and bias in self-knowledge. In C. R. Snyder & D. F. Forsyth (Eds.), *Handbook of social and clinical psychology: The health perspective.* New York: Pergamon Press. (p. 494)

Brown, J. D., Steele, J. R., & Walsh-Childers, K. (2002). *Sexual teens, sexual media: Investigating media's influence on adolescent sexuality.* Mahwah, NJ: Erlbaum. (p. 379)

Brown, J. L., & Pollitt, E. (1996, February). Malnutrition, poverty and intellectual development. *Scientific American*, pp. 38–43. (p. 344)

Brown, R. (1986). Linguistic relativity. In S. H. Hulse & B. F. Green, Jr. (Eds.), *One hundred years of psychological research in America.* Baltimore: Johns Hopkins University Press. (p. 323)

Brown, S. W., Garry, M., Loftus, E., Silver, B., DuBois, K., & DuBreuil, S. (1996). People's beliefs about memory: Why don't we have better memories? Paper presented at the American Psychological Society convention. (p. 295)

Brownell, K. D., & Wadden, T. A. (1992). Etiology and treatment of obesity: Understanding a serious, prevalent, and refractory disorder. *Journal of Consulting and Clinical Psychology, 60*, 505–517. (p. 370)

Browning, C. (1992). *Ordinary men: Reserve police battalion 101 and the final solution in Poland.* New York: HarperCollins. (p. 586)

Brownmiller, S. (1975). *Against our will: Men, women, and rape.* New York: Simon and Schuster. (p. 378)

Bruce, D., Dolan, A., & Phillips-Grant, K. (2000). On the transition from childhood amnesia to the recall of personal memories. *Psychological Science, 11*, 360–364. (p. 106)

Bruck, M., & Ceci, S. (2004). Forensic developmental psychology: Unveiling four common misconceptions. *Current Directions in Psychological Science, 15*, 229–232. (p. 298)

Bruck, M., & Ceci, S. J. (1999). The suggestibility of children's memory. *Annual Review of Psychology, 50*, 419–439. (p. 298)

Bruer, J. T. (1999). *The myth of the first three years: A new understanding of early brain development and lifelong learning.* New York: Free Press. (p. 344)

Brumberg, J. J. (2000). *Fasting girls: The history of anorexia nervosa.* New York: Vintage. (p. 364)

Brune, K., & Handwerker, H. (2004). Hyperalgesia: Molecular mechanisms and clinical implications. *Special issue of Progress in Pain Research and Management, 30.* Seattle, WA: International Association for the Study of Pain, IASP Press. (p. 162)

Bryant, R. A. (2001). Posttraumatic stress disorder and traumatic brain injury: Can they co-exist? *Clinical Psychology Review, 21*, 931–948. (p. 300)

Buck, L., & Axel, R. (1991). A novel multigene family may encode odorant receptors: A molecular basis for odor recognition. *Cell, 65*, 175–187. (p. 167)

Buckingham, M. (2001, August). Quoted by P. LaBarre, "Marcus Buckingham thinks your boss has an attitude problem." *The Magazine* (fastcompany.com/online/49/buckingham.html). (pp. 399, 400)

Buckingham, M., & Clifton, D. O. (2001). *Now, discover your strengths.* New York: Free Press. (pp. 394, 395)

Buckley, K. E., & Leary, M. R. (2001). Perceived acceptance as a predictor of social, emotional, and academic outcomes. Paper presented at the Society of Personality and Social Psychology annual convention. (p. 389)

Buehler, R., Griffin, D., & Ross, M. (1994). Exploring the "planning fallacy": Why people underestimate their task completion times. *Journal of Personality and Social Psychology, 67*, 366–381. (p. 312)

Bugelski, B. R., Kidd, E., & Segmen, J. (1968). Image as a mediator in one-trial paired-associate learning. *Journal of Experimental Psychology, 76,* 69–73. (p. 275)

Bugental, D. B. (1986). Unmasking the "polite smile": Situational and personal determinants of managed affect in adult-child interaction. *Personality and Social Psychology Bulletin, 12,* 7–16. (p. 418)

Buka, S. L., Goldstein, J. M., Seidman, L. J., Zornberg, G., Donatelli, J-A. A., Denny, L. R., & Tsuang, M. T. (1999). Prenatal complications, genetic vulnerability, and schizophrenia: The New England longitudinal studies of schizophrenia. *Psychiatric Annals, 29,* 151–156. (p. 534)

Buka, S. L., Tsuang, M. T., Torrey, E. F., Klebanoff, M. A., Wagner, R. L., & Yolken, R. H. (2001). Maternal infections and subsequent psychosis among offspring. *Archives of General Psychiatry, 58,* 1032–1037. (pp. 489, 535)

Bullough, V. (1990). The Kinsey scale in historical perspective. In D. P. McWhirter, S. A. Sanders, & J. M. Reinisch (Eds.), *Homosexuality/heterosexuality: Concepts of sexual orientation.* New York: Oxford University Press. (p. 380)

Buquet, R. (1988). Le reve et les deficients visuels (Dreams and the visually-impaired). *Psychanalyse-a-l'Universite, 13,* 319–327. (p. 206)

Bureau of Labor Statistics. (2004, September 14). *American time-user survey summary.* Washington, DC: United States Department of Labor (www.bls.gov). (p. 91)

Bureau of Labor Statistics, U.S. Department of Labor. (2004–2005). *Occupational Outlook Handbook, 2004–05 Edition.* (p. B-2)

Bureau of the Census. (2004). *Statistical abstract of the United States 2004.* Washington, DC: U.S. Government Printing Office. (pp. 136, 505, 565)

Burger, J. M. (1987). Increased performance with increased personal control: A self-presentation interpretation. *Journal of Experimental Social Psychology, 23,* 350–360. (p. 401)

Burgess, M., Enzle, M. E., & Schmaltz, R. (2004). Defeating the potentially deleterious effects of externally imposed deadlines: Practitioners' rules-of-thumb. *Personality and Social Psychology Bulletin, 30,* 868–877. (p. 401)

Buri, J. R., Louiselle, P. A., Misukanis, T. M., & Mueller, R. A. (1988). Effects of parental authoritarianism and authoritativeness on self-esteem. *Personality and Social Psychology Bulletin, 14,* 271–282. (p. 117)

Burish, T. G., & Carey, M. P. (1986). Conditioned aversive responses in cancer chemotherapy patients: Theoretical and developmental analysis. *Journal of Counseling and Clinical Psychology, 54,* 593–600. (p. 246)

Burke, D. M., & Shafto, M. A. (2004). Aging and language production. *Current Directions in Psychological Science, 13,* 21–24. (p. 133)

Burkholder, R. (2005a, January 11). Chinese far wealthier than a decade ago—but are they happier? *Gallup Poll News Service* (www.gallup.com). (p. 430)

Burkholder, R. (2005b, January 18). China's citizens optimistic, yet not entirely satisfied. *Gallup Poll News Service* (www.gallup.com). (p. 430)

Burns, B. C. (2004). The effects of speed on skilled chess performance. *Psychological Science, 15,* 442–447. (p. 316)

Bush, G. W. (2001, May 1). Speech to the National Defense University, Washington, DC. (p. 615)

Bushman, B. J. (1993). Human aggression while under the influence of alcohol and other drugs: An integrative research review. *Current Directions in Psychological Science, 2,* 148–152. (p. 601)

Bushman, B. J. (2002). Does venting anger feed or extinguish the flame? Catharsis, rumination, distraction, anger, and aggressive responding. *Personality and Social Psychology Bulletin, 28,* 724–731. (p. 424)

Bushman, B. J., & Anderson, C. A. (2001). Media violence and the American public: Scientific facts versus media misinformation. *American Psychologist, 56,* 477–489. (p. 606)

Bushman, B. J., & Bonaci, A. M. (2002). Violence and sex impair memory for television ads. *Journal of Applied Psychology, 87,* 557–564. (pp. 294, 378)

Bushman, B. J., Baumeister, R. F., & Stack, A. D. (1999). Catharsis, aggression, and persuasive influence: Self-fulfilling or self-defeating prophecies? *Journal of Personality and Social Psychology, 76,* 367–376. (p. 424)

Buss, A. H. (1989). Personality as traits. *American Psychologist, 44,* 1378–1388. (p. 482)

Buss, D. M. (1991). Evolutionary personality psychology. *Annual Review of Psychology, 42,* 459–491. (p. 72)

Buss, D. M. (1994). The strategies of human mating: People worldwide are attracted to the same qualities in the opposite sex. p 238–249. (pp. 76, 77)

Buss, D. M. (1995). Evolutionary psychology: A new paradigm for psychological science. *Psychological Inquiry, 6,* 1–30. (p. 76)

Buss, D. M. (1996). Sexual conflict: Evolutionary insights into feminism and the "battle of the sexes." In D. M. Buss & N. M. Malamuth (Eds.), *Sex, power, conflict: Evolutionary and feminist perspectives.* New York: Oxford University Press. (p. 77)

Buss, D. M. (2000). *The dangerous passion: Why jealousy is as necessary as love and sex.* New York: Free Press. (p. 77)

Butler, A. C., Hokanson, J. E., & Flynn, H. A. (1994). A comparison of self-esteem lability and low trait self-esteem as vulnerability factors for depression. *Journal of Personality and Social Psychology, 66,* 166–177. (p. 527)

Butler, R. A. (1954, February). Curiosity in monkeys. *Scientific American,* pp. 70–75. (p. 358)

Butterfield, F. (1999, July 12). Experts say study confirms prison's new role as mental hospital. *New York Times* (www.nytimes.com). (p. 505)

Byne, W., & Parsons, B. (1993). Human sexual orientation: The biologic theories reappraised. *Archives of General Psychiatry, 50,* 228–239. (p. 385)

Bynum, R. (2004, November 1). Associated Press article. (p. 162)

Byrne, D. (1971). *The attraction paradigm.* New York: Academic Press. (p. 610)

Byrne, D. (1982). Predicting human sexual behavior. In A. G. Kraut (Ed.), *The G. Stanley Hall Lecture Series (Vol. 2).* Washington, DC: American Psychological Association. (pp. 238, 377)

Byrne, J. (2003, September 21). From correspondence reported by Michael Shermer, E-Skeptic for September 21, 2003, from The Skeptics Society. (p. 187)

Byrne, R. W. (1991, May/June). Brute intellect. *The Sciences,* pp. 42–47. (p. 327)

Cable, D. M., & Gilovich, T. (1998). Looked over or overlooked? Prescreening decisions and postinterview evaluations. *Journal of Personality and Social Psychology, 83,* 501–508. (p. 395)

Cacioppo, J. T., Berntson, G. G., Klein, D. J., & Poehlmann, K. M. (1997). The psychophysiology of emotion across the lifespan. *Annual Review of Gerontology and Geriatrics, 17,* 27. (p. 410)

Cahill, L. (1994). (Beta)-adrenergic activation and memory for emotional events. *Nature, 371,* 702–704. (p. 280)

Cahill, L. (2005, May). His brain, her brain. *Scientific American,* pp. 40–47. (p. 90)

Cale, E. M., Lilienfeld, S. O. (2002). Sex differences in psychopathy and antisocial personality disorder: A review and integration. *Clinical Psychology Review, 22,* 1179–1207. (p. 517)

Call, K. T., Riedel, A. A., Hein, K., McLoyd, V., Petersen, A., & Kipke, M. (2002). Adolescent health and well-being in the twenty-first century: A global perspective. *Journal of Research on Adolescence, 12,* 69–98. (p. 379)

Callaghan, T., Rochat, P., Lillard, A., Claux, M. L., Odden, H., Itakura, S., Tapanya, S., & Singh, S. (2005). Synchrony in the onset of mental-state reasoning. *Psychological Science, 16,* 378–384. (p. 110)

Calle, E. E., Thun, M. J., Petrelli, J. M., Rodriguez, C., & Health, C. W., Jr. (1999). Body-mass index and mortality in a prospective cohort of U.S. adults. *New England Journal of Medicine, 341,* 1097–1105. (p. 367)

Callicott, J. H., & 11 others. (2005). Variation in DISC1 affects hippocampal structure and function and increased risk for schizophrenia. *Proceedings of the National Academy of Sciences, 102,* 8627–8632. (p. 536)

Calvo-Merino, B., Glaser, D. E., Grèzes, J., Passingham, R. E., & Haggard, P. (2004). Action observation and acquired motor skills: An fMRI study with expert dancers. *Cerebral Cortex, 15,* 1243–1249. (p. 325)

Camerer, C. F., Loewenstein, G., & Weber, M. (1989). The curse of knowledge in economic settings: An experimental analysis. *Journal of Political Economy, 97,* 1232–1254. (p. 188)

Campbell, D. T. (1975). On the conflicts between biological and social evolution and between psychology and moral tradition. *American Psychologist, 30,* 1103–1126. (p. 429)

Campbell, D. T., & Specht, J. C. (1985). Altruism: Biology, culture, and religion. *Journal of Social and Clinical Psychology, 3(1),* 33–42. (p. 473)

Campbell, S. (1986). *The Loch Ness Monster: The evidence.* Willingborough, Northamptonshire, U.K.: Acquarian Press. (p. 183)

Camper, J. (1990, February 7). Drop pompom squad, U. of I. rape study says. *Chicago Tribune,* p. 1. (p. 218)

Camperio-Ciani, A., Corna, F., & Capiluppi, C. (2004). Evidence for maternally inherited factors favouring male homosexuality and promoting female fecundity. *Proceedings of the Royal Society of London B, 271,* 2217–2221. (p. 384)

Campos, J. J., Bertenthal, B. I., & Kermoian, R. (1992). Early experience and emotional development: The emergence of wariness and heights. *Psychological Science, 3,* 61–64. (p. 513)

Canli, T., Desmond, J. E., Zhao, Z., & Gabrieli, J. D. E. (2002). Sex differences in the neural basis of emotional memories. *Proceedings of the National Academy of Sciences, 99,* 10789–10794. (p. 420)

Cannon, J. (2005). Career planning and opportunities: The bachelor's degree in psychology. *Eye on Psi Chi,* 26–28. (p. B-1)

Cannon, W. B. (1929). *Bodily changes in pain, hunger, fear, and rage.* New York: Branford. (pp. 361, 436)

Cannon, W. B., & Washburn, A. (1912). An explanation of hunger. *American Journal of Physiology, 29,* 441–454. (p. 361)

Cantor, N., & Kihlstrom, J. F. (1987). *Personality and social intelligence.* Englewood Cliffs, NJ: Prentice-Hall. (p. 335)

Cantril, H., & Bumstead, C. H. (1960). *Reflections on the human venture.* New York: New York University Press. (p. 592)

Caplan, N., Choy, M. H., & Whitmore, J. K. (1992, February). Indochinese refugee families and academic achievement. *Scientific American,* pp. 36–42. (pp. 81, 347)

Caputo, D., & Dunning, D. (2005). What you don't know: The role played by errors of omission in imperfect self-assessments. *Journal of Experimental Social Psychology,* 488–505. (p. 488)

Carducci, B. J., Cosby, P. C., & Ward, D. D. (1978). Sexual arousal and interpersonal evaluations. *Journal of Experimental Social Psychology, 14,* 449–457. (p. 611)

Carey, G. (1990). Genes, fears, phobias, and phobic disorders. *Journal of Counseling and Development, 68,* 628–632. (p. 514)

Carlezon, W. A., Jr., Mague, S. D., & Andersen, S. L. (2003). Enduring behavioral effects of early exposure to methylphenidate in rats. *Biological Psychiatry, 54,* 1330–1337. (p. 501)

Carli, L. L., & Leonard, J. B. (1989). The effect of hindsight on victim derogation. *Journal of Social and Clinical Psychology, 8,* 331–343. (p. 599)

Carlson, C. L. (2000). ADHD is overdiagnosed. In R. L. Atkinson, R. C. Atkinson, E. E. Smith, D. J. Bem, & S. Nolen-Hoeksema (Eds.), *Hilgard's introduction to psychology, Thirteenth edition.* Fort Worth: Harcourt. (p. 501)

Carlson, M. (1995, August 29). Quoted by S. Blakeslee, In brain's early growth, timetable may be crucial. *New York Times,* pp. C1, C3. (p. 116)

Carlson, M., Charlin, V., & Miller, N. (1988). Positive mood and helping behavior: A test of six hypotheses. *Journal of Personality and Social Psychology, 55,* 211–229. (p. 615)

Carlson, R. (1984). What's social about social psychology? Where's the person in personality research? *Journal of Personality and Social Psychology, 47,* 1304–1309. (p. 489)

Carlson, S. (1985). A double-blind test of astrology. *Nature, 318,* 419–425. (p. 480)

Carnegie Council on Adolescent Development. (1989, June). *Turning points: Preparing American youth for the 21st century.* (The report of the Task Force on Education of Young Adolescents.) New York: Carnegie Corporation. (p. 617)

Carrière, G. (2003). Parent and child factors associated with youth obesity. *Statistics Canada, Catalogue 82-003,* Supplement to Health Reports, 2003. (p. 369)

Carroll, D., Davey Smith, G., & Bennett, P. (1994, March). Health and socio-economic status. *The Psychologist,* pp. 122–125. (p. 446)

Carroll, J. (2005, January 14). Terrorism concerns fade. *The Gallup Organization* (www.gallup.com). (p. 315)

Carroll, J. M., & Russell, J. A. (1996). Do facial expressions signal specific emotions? Judging emotion from the face in context. *Journal of Personality and Social Psychology, 70,* 205–218. (p. 421)

Carskadon, M. (2002). *Adolescent sleep patterns: Biological, social, and psychological influences.* New York: Cambridge University Press. (p. 201)

Carter, R. (1998). *Mapping the mind.* Berkeley, CA: University of California Press. (p. 38)

Carter, S., & Snow, C. (2004, May). Helping singles enter better marriages using predictive models of marital success. Presented to the American Psychological Society convention. (p. 610)

Cartwright, R. D. (1978). *A primer on sleep and dreaming.* Reading, MA: Addison-Wesley. (p. 199)

CASA. (2003). *The formative years: Pathways to substance abuse among girls and young women ages 8–22.* New York, NY: National Center on Addiction and Substance Use, Columbia University. (pp. 218, 226)

Cash, T. F., & Henry, P. E. (1995). Women's body images: The results of a national survey in the U.S.A. *Sex Roles, 33,* 19–28. (p. 365)

Cash, T., & Janda, L. H. (1984, December). The eye of the beholder. *Psychology Today,* pp. 46–52. (p. 608)

Caspi, A. (2000). The child is father of the man: Personality continuities from childhood to adulthood. *Journal of Personality and Social Psychology, 78,* 158–172. (p. 72)

Caspi, A., Harrington, H., Milne, B., Amell, J. W., Theodore, R. F., & Moffitt, T. E. (2003). Children's behavioral styles at age 3 are linked to their adult personality traits at age 26. *Journal of Personality, 71,* 496–513. (pp. 100, 526)

Caspi, A., Moffitt, T. E., Newman, D. L., & Silva, P. A. (1996). Behavioral observations at age 3 years predict adult psychiatric disorders: Longitudinal evidence from a birth cohort. *Archives of General Psychiatry, 53,* 1033–1039. (p. 518)

Cassandro, V. J., & Simonton, D. K. (2003). Creativity and genius. In C. L. M. Keyes & J. Haidt (Eds.), *Flourishing: Positive psychology and the life well-lived.* Washington, DC: American Psychological Association. (p. 340)

Cassidy, J., & Shaver, P. R. (1999). *Handbook of attachment.* New York: Guilford. (p. 114)

Castillo, R. J. (1997). *Culture and mental illness: A client-centered approach.* Pacific Grove, CA: Brooks/Cole. (pp. 502, 506)

Castonguay, L. G., & Goldfried, M. R. (1994). Psychotherapy integration: An idea whose time has come. *Applied & Preventive Psychology, 3,* 159–172. (p. 541)

Catanese, K. R., & Tice, D. M. (2005). The effect of rejection on anti-social behaviors: Social exclusion produces aggressive behaviors. In K. D. Williams, J. P. Forgas, & W. Von Hippel (Eds.), *The social outcast: Ostracism, social exclusion, rejection, and bullying.* New York: Psychology Press. (p. 602)

Cattell, R. B. (1963). Theory of fluid and crystallized intelligence: A critical experiment. *Journal of Educational Psychology, 54,* 1–22. (p. 134)

Cavalli-Sforza, L., Menozzi, P., & Piazza, A. (1994). *The history and geography of human genes.* Princeton, NJ: Princeton University Press. (p. 346)

Cavigelli, S. A., & McClintock, M. K. (2003). Fear of novelty in infant rats predicts adult corticosterone dynamics and an early death. *Proceedings of the National Academy of Sciences, 100,* 16131–16136. (p. 437)

CDC. (2004). Teenagers in the United States: Sexual activity, contraceptive use, and childbearing, 2002. A fact sheet for series 23, number 24. DHHS Publication (PHS) 2005–1976. (pp. 379, 380)

CDC. (2004, December 16). Prevalence of overweight and obesity among adults: United States, 1999–2002. Centers for Disease Control and Prevention, National Center for Health Statistics (www.cdc.gov). (p. 366)

Ceci, S. J. (1993). Cognitive and social factors in children's testimony. Master Lecture, American Psychological Association convention. (pp. 298, 299)

Ceci, S. J., & Bruck, M. (1993). Child witnesses: Translating research into policy. *Social Policy Report (Society for Research in Child Development), 7(3),* 1–30. (p. 298)

Ceci, S. J., & Bruck, M. (1995). *Jeopardy in the courtroom: A scientific analysis of children's testimony.* Washington, DC: American Psychological Association. (p. 298)

Ceci, S. J., & Williams, W. M. (1997). Schooling, intelligence, and income. *American Psychologist, 52,* 1051–1058. (pp. 344, 345)

Ceci, S. J., Huffman, M. L. C., Smith, E., & Loftus, E. F. (1994). Repeatedly thinking about a non-event: Source misattributions among preschoolers. *Consciousness and Cognition, 3,* 388–407. (p. 298)

Centers for Disease Control Vietnam Experience Study. (1988). Health status of Vietnam veterans. *Journal of the American Medical Association, 259,* 2701–2709. (p. 512)

Centers for Disease Control. (1992, September 16). Serious mental illness and disability in the adult household population: United States, 1989. Advance Data No. 218 from *Vital and Health Statistics,* National Center for Health Statistics. (p. 506)

Centers for Disease Control. (2003). Who should get a flu shot (influenza vaccine). National Center for Infectious Diseases (http://www.cdc.gov/ncidod/diseases/flu/who.htm). (p. 535)

Centerwall, B. S. (1989). Exposure to television as a risk factor for violence. *American Journal of Epidemiology, 129,* 643–652. (p. 264)

Cerella, J. (1985). Information processing rates in the elderly. *Psychological Bulletin, 98,* 67–83. (p. 131)

CFI. (2003, July). International developments. Report. Amherst, NY: Center for Inquiry International. (p. 187)

Chambless, D. L., Baker, M. J., Baucom, D. H., Beutler, L. E., Calhoun, K. S., Crits-Christoph, P., Daiuto, A., DeRubeis, R., Detweiler, J., Haaga, D. A. F., Johnson, S. B., McCurry, S., Mueser, K. T., Pope, K. S., Sanderson, W. C., Shoham, V., Stickle, T., Williams, D. A., & Woody, S. R. (1997). Update on empirically validated therapies, II. *The Clinical Psychologist, 51(1),* 3–16. (p. 558)

Chamove, A. S. (1980). Nongenetic induction of acquired levels of aggression. *Journal of Abnormal Psychology, 89,* 469–488. (p. 263)

Chang, E. C. (2001). Cultural influences on optimism and pessimism: Differences in Western and Eastern construals of the self. In E. C. Chang (Ed.), *Optimism and pessimism.* Washington, DC: APA Books. (p. 488)

Chang, P. P., Ford, D. E., Meoni, L. A., Wang, N-Y., & Klag, M. J. (2002). Anger in young men and subsequent premature cardiovascular disease: The precursors study. *Archives of Internal Medicine, 162,* 901–906. (p. 439)

Chaplin, W. F., Phillips, J. B., Brown, J. D., Clanton, N. R., & Stein, J. L. (2000). Handshaking, gender, personality, and first impressions. *Journal of Personality and Social Psychology, 79,* 110–117. (p. 417)

Charles, S. T., Reynolds, C. A., & Gatz, M. (2001). Age-related differences and change in positive and negative affect over 23 years. *Journal of Personality and Social Psychology, 80,* 136–151. (p. 138)

Charpak, G., & Broch, H. (2004). *Debunked! ESP, telekinesis, and other pseudoscience.* Baltimore, MD: Johns Hopkins University Press. (p. 187)

Chartrand, T. L., & Bargh, J. A. (1999). The chameleon effect: The perception-behavior link and social interaction. *Journal of Personality and Social Psychology, 76,* 893–910. (p. 582)

Chase, W. G., & Simon, H. A. (1973). Perception in chess. *Cognitive Psychology, 4,* 55–81. (p. 276)

Chaudhari, N., Landin, A. M., & Roper, S. D. (2000). A metabotropic glutamate receptor variant functions as a taste receptor. *Nature Neuroscience, 3,* 113–119. (p. 165)

Cheek, J. M., & Melchior, L. A. (1990). Shyness, self-esteem, and self-consciousness. In H. Leitenberg (Ed.), *Handbook of social and evaluation anxiety.* New York: Plenum. (p. 85)

Cheit, R. E. (1998). Consider this, skeptics of recovered memory. *Ethics & Behavior, 8,* 141–160. (p. 466)

Chen, E. (2004). Why socioeconomic status affects the health of children: A psychosocial perspective. *Current Directions in Psychological Science, 13,* 112–115. (p. 446)

Chess, S., & Thomas, A. (1987). *Know your child: An authoritative guide for today's parents.* New York: Basic Books. (pp. 72, 115)

Child Trends. (2001, August). Facts at a glance. (www.childtrends.org). (p. 379)

Chiles, J. A., Lambert, M. J., & Hatch, A. L. (1999). The impact of psychological interventions on medical cost offset: A meta-analytic review. *Clinical Psychology: Science and Practice, 6,* 204–220. (p. 556)

Chisholm, K. (1998). A three year follow-up of attachment and indiscriminate friendliness in children adopted from Romanian orphanages. *Child Development, 69,* 1092–1106. (p. 116)

Choi, I., & Choi, Y. (2002). Culture and self-concept flexibility. *Personality and Social Psychology Bulletin, 28,* 1508–1517. (p. 84)

Chomsky, N. (1959). Review of B. F. Skinner's Verbal behavior. *Language, 35,* 26–58. (p. 321)

Chomsky, N. (1972). *Language and mind.* New York: Harcourt Brace (p. 319)

Chomsky, N. (1987). Language in a psychological setting. Sophia Linguistic Working Papers in Linguistics, No. 22, Sophia University, Tokyo. (p. 321)

Chorpita, B. F., & Barlow, D. H. (1998). The development of anxiety: The role of control in the early environment. *Psychological Bulletin, 124,* 3–21. (p. 513)

Christakis, D. S., Zimmerman, F. J., DiGiuseppe, D. L., & McCarty, C. A. (2004). Early television exposure and subsequent attentional problems in children. *Pediatrics, 113,* 708–713. (p. 501)

Christensen, A., & Jacobson, N. S. (1994). Who (or what) can do psychotherapy: The status and challenge of nonprofessional therapies. *Psychological Science, 5,* 8–14. (p. 561)

Christophersen, E. R., & Edwards, K. J. (1992). Treatment of elimination disorders: State of the art 1991. *Applied & Preventive Psychology, 1,* 15–22. (p. 545)

Chugani, H. T., & Phelps, M. E. (1986). Maturational changes in cerebral function in infants determined by 18FDG Positron Emission Tomography. *Science, 231,* 840–843. (p. 105)

Cialdini, R. B. (1993). *Influence: Science and practice (3rd ed.).* New York: HarperCollins. (p. 578)

Cialdini, R. B., & Richardson, K. D. (1980). Two indirect tactics of image management: Basking and blasting. *Journal of Personality and Social Psychology, 39,* 406–415. (p. 598)

Cialdini, R. B., Eisenberg, N., Green, B. L., Rhoads, K., & Bator, R. (1998). Undermining the undermining effect of reward on sustained interest. *Journal of Applied Social Psychology, 28,* 249–263. (p. 398)

Clack, B., Dixon, J., & Tredoux, C. (2005). Eating together apart: Patterns of segregation in a multi-ethnic cafeteria. *Journal of Community and Applied Social Psychology, 15,* 1–16. (p. 616)

Clancy, S. A., McNally, R. J., Schachter, D. L., Lenzenweger, M. F., & Pitman, R. K. (2002). Memory distortion in people reporting abduction by aliens. *Journal of Abnormal Psychology, 111,* 455–461. (p. 297)

Clancy, S. A., Schacter, D. L., McNally, R. J., & Pitman, R. K. (2000). False recognition in women reporting recovered memories of sexual abuse. *Psychological Science, 11,* 26–31. (p. 297)

Clark, A., Seidler, A., & Miller, M. (2001). Inverse association between sense of humor and coronary heart disease. *International Journal of Cardiology, 80,* 87–88. (p. 446)

Clark, R., Anderson, N. B., Clark, V. R., & Williams, D. R. (1999). Racism as a stressor for African Americans: A biopsychosocial model. *American Psychologist, 54,* 805–816. (p. 438)

Coffey, C. E. (Ed.) (1993). *Clinical science of electroconvulsive therapy.* Washington, DC: American Psychiatric Press. (p. 569)

Coffey, C. E., Lucke, J. F., Saxton, J. A., Ratcliff, G., Unitas, L. J., Billig, B., & Bryan, R. N. (1998). Sex differences in brain aging: A quantitative magnetic resonance imagine study. *Archives of Neurology, 55,* 169–179. (p. 131)

Coffey, C. E., Wilkinson, W. E., Weiner, R. D., Parashos, I. A., Djang, W. T., Webb, M. C., Figiel, G. S., & Spritzer, C. E. (1993). Quantitative cerebral anatomy in depression: A controlled magnetic resonance imaging study. *Archives of General Psychiatry, 50,* 7-16. (p. 481, 526)

Cogan, J. C., Bhalla, S. K., Sefa-Dedeh, A., & Rothblum, E. D. (1996). A comparison study of United States and African students on perceptions of obesity and thinness. *Journal of Cross-Cultural Psychology, 27,* 98-113. (p. 365)

Cohen, D. (1995, June 17). Now we are one, or two, or three. *New Scientist,* pp. 14-15. (p. 516)

Cohen, G., Conway, M. A., & Maylor, E. A. (1994, September). Flashbulb memories in older adults. *Psychology & Aging, 9*(3), 454-463. (p. 133)

Cohen, H., Kaplan, Z., Kotler, M., Kouperman, I., Moisa, R., & Grisaru, N. (2005). Repetitive transcranial magnetic stimulation of the right dorsolaterial prefrontal cortex in posttraumatic stress disorder: A double-blind, placebo-controlled study. *American Journal of Psychiatry, 16,* 515-524. (p. 570)

Cohen, K. M. (2002). Relationships among childhood sex-atypical behavior, spatial ability, handedness, and sexual orientation in men. *Archives of Sexual Behavior, 31,* 129-143. (p. 385)

Cohen, S. (1988). Psychosocial models of the role of social support in the etiology of physical disease. *Health Psychology, 7,* 269-297. (p. 447)

Cohen, S. (2004). Social relationships and health. *American Psychologist, 59,* 676-684. (p. 448)

Cohen, S., Doyle, W. J., Skoner, D. P., Rabin, B. S., & Gwaltney, J. M., Jr. (1997). Social ties and susceptibility to the common cold. *Journal of the American Medical Association, 277,* 1940-1944. (p. 448)

Cohen, S., Doyle, W. J., Turner, R., Alper, C. M., & Skoner, D. P. (2003). Sociability and susceptibility to the common cold. *Psychological Science, 14,* 389-395. (p. 441)

Cohen, S., Kaplan, J. R., Cunnick, J. E., Manuck, S. B., & Rabin, B. S. (1992). Chronic social stress, affiliation, and cellular immune response in nonhuman primates. *Psychological Science, 3,* 301-304. (p. 440)

Cohen, S., Line, S., Manuck, S. B., Rabin, B. S., Heise, E. R., & Kaplan, J. R. (1997). Chronic social stress, social status, and susceptibility to upper respiratory infections in nonhuman primates. *Psychosomatic Medicine, 59,* 213-221. (p. 446)

Cohen, S., Tyrrell, D. A. J., & Smith, A. P. (1991). Psychological stress and susceptibility to the common cold. *New England Journal of Medicine, 325,* 606-612. (p. 441)

Colapinto, J. (2000). *As nature made him: The boy who was raised as a girl.* New York: HarperCollins. (p. 90)

Colarelli, S. M., & Dettman, J. R. (2003). Intuitive evolutionary perspectives in marketing. *Psychology and Marketing, 20,* 837-865. (p. 75)

Colarelli, S. M., Spranger, J. L., & Hechanova, M. R. (2006). Women, power, and sex composition in small groups: An evolutionary perspective. *Journal of Organizational Behavior, 27,* 163-184. (p. 88)

Colcombe, S. J., Kramer, A. F., Erickson, K. I., Scalf, P., McAuley, E., Cohen, N. J., Webb, A., Jerome, G. J., Marquex, D. X., & Elavsky, S. (2004). Cardiovascular fitness, cortical plasticity, and aging. *Proceedings of the National Academy of Sciences, 101,* 3316-3321. (p. 132)

Colcombe, S., & Kramer, A. F. (2003). Fitness effects on the cognitive function of older adults: A meta-analytic study. *Psychological Science, 14,* 125-130. (p. 132)

Coleman, P. D., & Flood, D. G. (1986). Dendritic proliferation in the aging brain as a compensatory repair mechanism. In D. F. Swaab, E. Fliers, M. Mirmiram, W. A. Van Gool, & F. Van Haaren (Eds.), *Progress in brain research* (Vol. 20). New York: Elsevier. (p. 132)

Collins, D. W., & Kimura, D. (1997). A large sex difference on a two-dimensional mental rotation task. *Behavioral Neuroscience, 111,* 845-849. (p. 349)

Collins, N. L., & Miller, L. C. (1994). Self-disclosure and liking: A meta-analytic review. *Psychological Bulletin, 116,* 457-475. (p. 612)

Collins, R. L., Elliott, M. N., Berry, S. H., Danouse, D. E., Kunkel, D., Hunter, S. B., & Miu, A. (2004). Watching sex on television predicts adolescent initiation of sexual behavior. *Pediatrics, 114,* 280-289. (p. 21)

Collinson, S. L., MacKay, C. E., James, A. C., Quested, D. J., Phillips, T., Roberts, N., & Crow, T. J. (2003). Brain volume, asymmetry and intellectual impairment in relation to sex in early-onset schizophrenia. *British Journal of Psychiatry, 183,* 114-120. (p. 534)

Colombo, J. (1982). The critical period concept: Research, methodology, and theoretical issues. *Psychological Bulletin, 91,* 260-275. (p. 114)

Comer, R. J. (2004). *Abnormal psychology.* New York: Worth Publishers. (p. 499)

Commissioner of Official Languages. (1999). Annual Report 1998. Minister of Public Works and Government Services Canada, Cat. No. SF1-1998. (p. 324)

Conner, M., & McMillan, B. (1999). Interaction effects in the theory of planned behaviour: Studying cannabis use. *British Journal of Social Psychology, 38,* 195-222. (p. 225)

Consensus Conference. (1985). Electroconvulsive therapy. *Journal of the American Medical Association, 254,* 2103-2108. (p. 569)

Consumer Reports. (1995, November). Does therapy help? Pp. 734-739. (p. 554)

Conway, M. A., Wang, Q., Hanyu, K., & Haque, S. (2005). A cross-cultural investigation of autobiographical memory. On the universality and cultural variation of the reminiscence bump. *Journal of Cross-Cultural Psychology, 36,* 739-749. (p. 132)

Conway, M., & Ross, M. (1984). Getting what you want by revising what you had. *Journal of Personality and Social Psychology, 47,* 738-748. (p. 294)

Cooke, L. J., Wardle, J., & Gibson, E. L. (2003). Relationship between parental report of food neophobia and everyday food consumption in 2-6-year-old children. *Appetite, 41,* 205-206. (p. 165)

Cooper, K. J. (1999, May 1). This time, copycat wave is broader. *Washington Post* (www.washingtonpost.com). (pp. 265, 583)

Cooper, W. H. (1983). An achievement motivation nomological network. *Journal of Personality and Social Psychology, 44,* 841-861. (p. 398)

Coopersmith, S. (1967). *The antecedents of self-esteem.* San Francisco: Freeman. (p. 117)

Coren, S. (1996). *Sleep thieves: An eye-opening exploration into the science and mysteries of sleep.* New York: Free Press. (pp. 203, 204)

Corey, D. P., & 15 others. (2004). TRPA1 is a candidate for the mechanosensitive transduction channel of vertebrate hair cells. *Nature* (advance online publication, October 13, at www.nature.com). (p. 159)

Corina, D. P. (1998). The processing of sign language: Evidence from aphasia. In B. Stemmer & H. A. Whittaker (Eds.), *Handbook of neurolinguistics.* San Diego: Academic Press. (p. 62)

Corina, D. P., Vaid, J., & Bellugi, U. (1992). The linguistic basis of left hemisphere specialization. *Science, 255,* 1258-1260. (p. 62)

Correll, J., Park, B., Judd, C. M., & Wittenbrink, B. (2002). The police officer's dilemma: Using ethnicity to disambiguate potentially threatening individuals. *Journal of Personality and Social Psychology, 83,* 1314-1329. (p. 595)

Costa, P. T., Jr., Terracciano, A., & McCrae, R. R. (2001). Gender differences in personality traits across cultures: Robust and surprising findings. *Journal of Personality and Social Psychology, 81,* 322-331. (p. 419)

Costello, E. J., Compton, S. N., Keeler, G., & Angold, A. (2003). Relationships between poverty and psychopathology: A natural experiment. *Journal of the American Medical Association, 290,* 2023-2029. (pp. 21, 507)

Coughlin, J. F., Mohyde, M., D'Ambrosio, L. A., & Gilbert, J. (2004). *Who drives older driver decisions?* Cambridge, MA: MIT Age Lab. (p. 131)

Couli, J. T., Vidal, F., Nazarian, B., & Macar, F. (2004). Functional anatomy of the attentional modulation of time estimation. *Science, 303,* 1506-1508. (p. 392)

Courneya, K. S., & Carron, A. V. (1992). The home advantage in sports competitions: A literature review. *Journal of Sport and Exercise Psychology, 14,* 13-27. (p. 589)

Courtney, J. G., Longnecker, M. P., Theorell, T., & de Verdier, M. G. (1993). Stressful life events and the risk of colorectal cancer. *Epidemiology, 4,* 407-414. (p. 442)

Covington, M. V., & Omelich, C. L. (1988). I can resist anything but temptation: Adolescent expectations for smoking cigarettes. *Journal of Applied Social Psychology, 18,* 203–227. (p. 221)

Cowan, G., Lee, C., Levy, D., & Snyder, D. (1988). Dominance and inequality in X-rated videocassettes. *Psychology of Women Quarterly, 12,* 299–311. (p. 603)

Cowan, N. (1988). Evolving conceptions of memory storage, selective attention, and their mutual constraints within the human information-processing system. *Psychological Bulletin, 104,* 163–191. (p. 277)

Cowan, N. (1994). Mechanisms of verbal short-term memory. *Current Directions in Psychological Science, 3,* 185–189. (p. 278)

Cowan, N. (2001). The magical number 4 in short-term memory: A reconsideration of mental storage capacity. *Behavioral and Brain Sciences, 24,* 87–185. (p. 278)

Cowart, B. J. (1981). Development of taste perception in humans: Sensitivity and preference throughout the life span. *Psychological Bulletin, 90,* 43–73. (p. 165)

Crabbe, J. C. (2002). Genetic contributions to addiction. *Annual Review of Psychology, 53,* 435–462. (p. 225)

Crabtree, S. (2005, January 13). Engagement keeps the doctor away. *Gallup Management Journal* (gmj.gallup.com). (p. 400)

Craik, F. I. M., & Tulving, E. (1975). Depth of processing and the retention of words in episodic memory. *Journal of Experimental Psychology: General, 104,* 268–294. (p. 274)

Craik, F. I. M., & Watkins, M. J. (1973). The role of rehearsal in short-term memory. *Journal of Verbal Learning and Verbal Behavior, 12,* 599–607. (p. 273)

Crandall, C. S. (1988). Social contagion of binge eating. *Journal of Personality and Social Psychology, 55,* 588–598. (p. 364)

Crandall, C. S. (1994). Prejudice against fat people: Ideology and self-interest. *Journal of Personality and Social Psychology, 66,* 882–894. (p. 368)

Crandall, C. S. (1995). Do parents discriminate against their heavyweight daughters? *Personality and Social Psychology Bulletin, 21,* 724–735. (p. 368)

Crandall, J. E. (1984). Social interest as a moderator of life stress. *Journal of Personality and Social Psychology, 47,* 164–174. (p. 473)

Crawford, M., Chaffin, R., & Fitton, L. (1995). Cognition in social context. *Learning and Individual Differences, Special Issue: Psychological and psychobiological perspectives on sex differences in cognition: 1. Theory and Research, 7,* 341–362. (p. 350)

Crews, F. (Ed.) (1998). *Unauthorized Freud: Doubters confront a legend.* New York: Viking. (p. 468)

Crocker, J., & Major, B. (1989). Social stigma and self-esteem: The self-protective properties of stigma," *Psychological Review, 89,* 608–630. (p. 492)

Crocker, J., & Park, L. E. (2004). The costly pursuit of self-esteem. *Psychological Bulletin, 130,* 392–414. (p. 494)

Crocker, J., & Wolfe, C. (1999). Rescuing self-esteem: A contingencies of worth perspective. Unpublished manuscript, University of Michigan. (p. 451, 491)

Crocker, J., Thompson, L. L., McGraw, K. M., & Ingerman, C. (1987). Downward comparison, prejudice, and evaluation of others: Effects of self-esteem and threat. *Journal of Personality and Social Psychology, 52,* 907–916. (p. 598)

Croft, R. J., Klugman, A., Baldeweg, T., & Gruzelier, J. H. (2001). Electrophysiological evidence of serotonergic impairment in long-term MDMA ("Ecstasy") users. *American Journal of Psychiatry, 158,* 1687–1692. (p. 223)

Crook, T. H., & West, R. L. (1990). Name recall performance across the adult life-span. *British Journal of Psychology, 81,* 335–340. (pp. 132)

Cross, S., & Markus, H. (1991). Possible selves across the life span. *Human Development, 34,* 230–255. (p. 490)

Crossen, C. (1994). *Tainted truth: The manipulation of fact in America.* New York: Simon & Schuster. (p. A-1)

Cross-National Collaborative Group. (1992). The changing rate of major depression. *Journal of the American Medical Association, 268,* 3098–3105. (p. 523)

Crowell, J. A., & Waters, E. (1994). Bowlby's theory grown up: The role of attachment in adult love relationships. *Psychological Inquiry, 5,* 1–22. (p. 114)

Csikszentmihalyi, M. (1990). *Flow: The psychology of optimal experience.* New York: Harper & Row. (p. 392)

Csikszentmihalyi, M. (1999). If we are so rich, why aren't we happy? *American Psychologist, 54,* 821–827. (pp. 392, 427)

Csikszentmihalyi, M., & Hunter, J. (2003). Happiness in everyday life: The uses of experience sampling. *Journal of Happiness Studies, 4,* 185–199. (p. 125)

Cunningham, M. R., & others. (2005). "Their ideas of beauty are, on the whole, the same as ours": Consistency and variability in the cross-cultural perception of female physical attractiveness. *Journal of Personality and Social Psychology, 68,* 261–279. (p. 609)

Cunningham, W. A., Johnson, M. K., Raye, C. L., Gatenby, J. C., Gore, J. C., & Banaji, M. R. (2004). Separable neural components in the processing of Black and White faces. *Psychological Science, 15,* 806–813. (p. 595)

Curtis, G. C., Magee, W. J., Eaton, W. W., Wittchen, H-U., & Kessler, R. C. (1998). Specific fears and phobias: Epidemiology and classification. *British Journal of Psychiatry, 173,* 212–217. (p. 510)

Curtis, R. C., & Miller, K. (1986). Believing another likes or dislikes you: Behaviors making the beliefs come true. *Journal of Personality and Social Psychology, 51,* 284–290. (p. 610)

Czeisler, C. A., Allan, J. S., Strogatz, S. H., Ronda, J. M., Sanchez, R., Rios, C. D., Freitag, W. O., Richardson, G. S., & Kronauer, R. E. (1986). Bright light resets the human circadian pacemaker independent of the timing of the sleep-wake cycle. *Science, 233,* 667–671. (p. 197)

Czeisler, C. A., Duffy, J. F., Shanahan, T. L., Brown, E. N., Mitchell, J. F., Rimmer, D. W., Ronda, J. M., Silva, E. J., Allan, J. S., Emens, J. S., Dijk, D-J., & Kronauer, R. E. (1999). Stability, precision, and near-24-hour period of the human circadian pacemaker. *Science, 284,* 2177–2181. (p. 197)

Czeisler, C. A., Kronauer, R. E., Allan, J. S., & Duffy, J. F. (1989). Bright light induction of strong (type O) resetting of the human circadian pacemaker. *Science, 244,* 1328–1333. (p. 197)

Dabbs, J. M., Jr. (2000). *Heroes, rogues, and lovers: Testosterone and behavior.* New York: McGraw-Hill. (p. 377)

Dabbs, J. M., Jr., & Morris, R. (1990). Testosterone, social class, and antisocial behavior in a sample of 4,462 men. *Psychological Science, 1,* 209–211. (p. 601)

Dabbs, J. M., Jr., Bernieri, F. J., Strong, R. K., Campo, R., & Milun, R. (2001b). Going on stage: Testosterone in greetings and meetings. *Journal of Research in Personality, 35,* 27–40. (p. 601)

Dabbs, J. M., Jr., Riad, J. K., & Chance, S. E. (2001a). Testosterone and ruthless homicide. *Personality and Individual Differences, 31,* 599–603. (p. 600)

Dabbs, J. M., Jr., Ruback, R. B., & Besch, N. F. (1987). Male saliva testosterone following conversations with male and female partners. Paper presented at the American Psychological Association convention. (p. 377)

Daley, T. C., Whaley, S. E., Sigman, M. D., Espinosa, M. P., & Neumann, C. (2003). IQ on the rise: The Flynn effect in rural Kenyan children. *Psychological Science, 14,* 215–219. (p. 340)

Damasio, A. (2003). *Looking for Spinoza: Joy, sorrow, and the feeling brain.* New York: Harcourt. (p. 408)

Damasio, A. R. (1994). *Descartes error: Emotion, reason, and the human brain.* New York: Grossett/Putnam & Sons. (p. 336)

Damasio, H., Grabowski, T., Frank, R., Galaburda, A. M., & Damasio, A. R. (1994). The return of Phineas Gage: Clues about the brain from the skull of a famous patient. *Science, 264,* 1102–1105. (p. 57)

Damon, W. (1995). *Greater expectations: Overcoming the culture of indulgence in America's homes and schools.* New York: Free Press. (p. 491)

Danner, D. D., Snowdon, D. A., & Friesen, W. V. (2001). Positive emotions in early life and longevity: Findings from the Nun Study. *Journal of Personality and Social Psychology, 80,* 804–813. (p. 447)

Danso, H., & Esses, V. (2001). Black experimenters and the intellectual test performance of white participants: The tables are turned. *Journal of Experimental Social Psychology, 37,* 158–165. (p. 350)

Darley, J. M., & Latané, B. (1968a). Bystander intervention in emergencies: Diffusion of responsibility. *Journal of Personality and Social Psychology, 8,* 377–383. (p. 613, 614)

Darley, J. M., & Latané, B. (1968b, December). When will people help in a crisis? *Psychology Today,* pp. 54–57, 70–71. (p. 613)

Darrach, B., & Norris, J. (1984, August). An American tragedy. *Life,* pp. 58–74. (p. 517)

Darwin, C. (1859). *On the origin of species by means of natural selection.* London: John Murray. (p. 75)

Daum, I., & Schugens, M. M. (1996). On the cerebellum and classical conditioning. *Psychological Science, 5,* 58–61. (p. 283)

Davey, G. C. L. (1992). Classical conditioning and the acquisition of human fears and phobias: A review and synthesis of the literature. *Advances in Behavior Research and Therapy, 14,* 29–66. (p. 246)

Davey, G. C. L. (1995). Preparedness and phobias: Specific evolved associations or a generalized expectancy bias? *Behavioral and Brain Sciences, 18,* 289–297. (p. 514)

Davidoff, J. (2004). Coloured thinking. *The Psychologist, 17,* 570–572. (p. 323)

Davidson, R. J. (2000). Affective style, psychopathology, and resilience: Brain mechanisms and plasticity. *American Psychologist, 55,* 1196–1209. (p. 411)

Davidson, R. J. (2003). Affective neuroscience and psychophysiology: Toward a synthesis. *Psychophysiology, 40,* 655–665. (p. 411)

Davidson, R. J., Kabat-Zinn, J., Schumacher, J., Rosenkranz, M., Muller, D., Santorelli, S. F., Urbanowski, F., Harrington, A., Bonus, K., & Sheridan, J. F. (2003). Alterations in brain and immune function produced by mindfulness meditation. *Psychosomatic Medicine, 65,* 564–570. (p. 453)

Davidson, R. J., Pizzagalli, D., Nitschke, J. B., & Putnam, K. (2002). Depression: Perspectives from affective neuroscience. *Annual Review of Psychology, 53,* 545–574. (p. 526)

Davidson, R. J., Putnam, K. M., & Larson, C. L. (2000). Dysfunction in the neural circuitry of emotion regulation—a possible prelude to violence. *Science, 289,* 591–594. (p. 600)

Davies, D. R., Matthews, G., & Wong, C. S. K. (1991). Aging and work. *International Review of Industrial and Organizational Psychology, 6,* 149–211. (p. 135)

Davies, M. F. (1997). Positive test strategies and confirmatory retrieval processes in the evaluation of personality feedback. *Journal of Personality and Social Psychology, 73,* 574–583. (pp. 480, 481)

Davies, P. (1992). *The mind of God: The scientific basis for a rational world.* New York: Simon & Schuster. (p. 95)

Davies, P. (1999). *The fifth miracle: The search for the origin and meaning of life.* New York: Simon & Schuster. (p. 95)

Davies, P. (2004, April 14). Into the 21st century. *Metaviews* (www.metanexus.net). (p. 95)

Davis, B. E., Moon, R. Y., Sachs, H. C., & Ottolini, M. C. (1998). Effects of sleep position on infant motor development. *Pediatrics, 102,* 1135–1140. (p. 105)

Davis, J. O., & Phelps, J. A. (1995a). Twins with schizophrenia: Genes or germs? *Schizophrenia Bulletin, 21,* 13–18. (p. 535)

Davis, J. O., Phelps, J. A., & Bracha, H. S. (1995b). Prenatal development of monozygotic twins and concordance for schizophrenia. *Schizophrenia Bulletin, 21,* 357–366. (p. 535)

Davis, S., Rees, M., Ribot, J., Moufarege, A., Rodenberg, C., & Purdie, D. (2003). Efficacy and safety of testosterone patches for the treatment of low sexual desire in surgically menopausal women. Presented to the American Society for Reproductive Medicine, San Antonio, October 11–15. (p. 376)

Dawes, R. M. (1994). *House of cards: Psychology and psychotherapy built on myth.* New York: Free Press. (p. 465, 491)

Dawkins, R. (1998). *Unweaving the rainbow.* Boston: Houghton Mifflin. (p. 94)

Dawkins, R. (1999, April 8). Is science killing the soul (a discussion with Richard Dawkins and Steven Pinker). www.edge.org. (p. 192)

de Boysson-Bardies, B., Halle, P., Sagart, L., & Durand, C. (1989). A cross linguistic investigation of vowel formats in babbling. *Journal of Child Language, 16,* 1–17. (p. 320)

de Courten-Myers, G. M. (2005, February 4). Personal correspondence (estimating total brain neurons, extrapolating from her carefully estimated 20 to 23 billion cortical neurons). (pp. 42, 54)

de Hoogh, A. H. B., den Hartog, D. N., Koopman, P. L., Thierry, H., van den Berg, P. T., van der Weide, J. G., & Wilderom, C. P. M. (2004). Charismatic leadership, environmental dynamism, and performance. *European Journal of Work and Organisational Psychology, 13,* 447–471. (p. 402)

De Koninck, J. (2000). Waking experiences and dreaming. In M. Kryger, T. Roth, & W. Dement (Eds.), *Principles and practice of sleep medicine, 3rd ed.* Philadelphia: Saunders. (p. 206)

de Waal, F. B. M. (1999, December). The end of nature versus nurture. *Scientific American,* pp. 94–99. (p. 93)

Deacon, B. J., & Abramowitz, J. S. (2004). Cognitive and behavioral treatments for anxiety disorders: A review of meta-analytic findings. *Journal of Clinical Psychology, 60,* 429–441. (p. 546)

Dean, G. A., Kelly, I. W., Saklofske, D. H., & Furnham, A. (1992). Graphology and human judgment. In B. Beyerstein & D. Beyerstein (Eds.), *The write stuff: Evaluations of graphology.* Buffalo, NY: Prometheus Books. (p. 480)

Deary, I. J., & Matthews, G. (1993). Personality traits are alive and well. *The Psychologist: Bulletin of the British Psychological Society, 6,* 299–311. (p. 482)

Deary, I. J., Thorpe, G., Wilson, V., Starr, J. M., & Whalley, L. J. (2003). Population sex differences in IQ at age 11: The Scottish mental survey 1932. *Intelligence, 31,* 533–541. (p. 348)

DeBruine, L. M. (2002). Facial resemblance enhances trust. *Proceedings of the Royal Society of London, 269,* 1307–1312. (p. 608)

DeBruine, L. M. (2004). Facial resemblance increases the attractiveness of same-sex faces more than other-sex faces. *Proceedings of the Royal Society of London B, 271,* 2085–2090. (p. 608)

Deci, E. L., & Ryan, R. M. (1985). *Intrinsic motivation and self-determination in human behavior.* New York: Plenum Press. (p. 255)

Deci, E. L., & Ryan, R. M. (1992). The initiation and regulation of intrinsically motivated learning and achievement. In A. K. Boggiano & T. S. Pittman (Eds.), *Achievement and motivation: A social-developmental perspective.* New York: Cambridge University. (p. 255)

Deci, E. L., & Ryan, R. M. (2000). The "what" and "why" of goal pursuits: Human needs and the self-determination of behavior. *Psychological Inquiry, 11,* 227–268. (p. 255)

Deci, E. L., Koestner, R., & Ryan, R. M. (1999, November). A meta-analytic review of experiments examining the effects of extrinsic rewards on intrinsic motivation. *Psychological Bulletin, 125(6),* 627–668. (p. 254)

Delaney, P. F., Ericsson, K. A., Weaver, G. E., & Mahadevan, S. (1999). Accounts of the memorist Rajan's exceptional performance: Comparing three theoretical proposals. Paper presented to the American Psychological Society convention. (p. 278)

Delgado, J. M. R. (1969). *Physical control of the mind: Toward a psychocivilized society.* New York: Harper & Row. (p. 55)

DeLoache, J. S. (1995). Early understanding and use of symbols: The model model. *Current Directions in Psychological Science, 4,* 109–113. (p. 109)

DeLoache, J. S., & Brown, A. L. (1987, October–December). Differences in the memory-based searching of delayed and normally developing young children. *Intelligence, 11(4),* 277–289. (p. 109)

DeLoache, J. S., Uttal, D. H., & Rosengren, K. S. (2004). Scale errors offer evidence for a perception-action dissociation early in life. *Science, 304,* 1027–1029. (p. 107)

Dement, W. C. (1978). *Some must watch while some must sleep.* New York: Norton. (pp. 197, 198, 205)

Dement, W. C. (1997, September). What all undergraduates should know about how their sleeping lives affect their waking lives. Stanford University: www.leland.stanford.edu/~dement/sleepless.html. (p. 201)

Dement, W. C. (1999). *The promise of sleep.* New York: Delacorte Press. (pp. 197, 198, 200, 201, 202, 205, C-5, C-7)

Dement, W. C., & Wolpert, E. A. (1958). The relation of eye movements, body mobility, and external stimuli to dream content. *Journal of Experimental Psychology, 55,* 543–553. (p. 206)

Demir, E., & Dickson, B. J. (2005). Fruitless splicing specifies male courtship behavior in Drosophila. *Cell, 121,* 785–794. (p. 383)

Dempster, F. N. (1988). The spacing effect: A case study in the failure to apply the results of psychological research. *American Psychologist, 43,* 627–634. (p. 272)

Denes-Raj, V., Epstein, S., & Cole, J. (1995). The generality of the ratio-bias phenomenon. *Personality and Social Psychology Bulletin, 21,* 1083–1092. (p. 313)

DeNeve, K. M., & Cooper, H. (1998). The happy personality: A meta-analysis of 137 personality traits and subjective well-being. *Psychological Bulletin, 124,* 197–229. (p. 432)

Dennett, D. C. (1991). *Consciousness explained.* Boston: Little, Brown. (p. 240)

Denton, K., & Krebs, D. (1990). From the scene to the crime: The effect of alcohol and social context on moral judgment. *Journal of Personality and Social Psychology, 59,* 242–248. (p. 218)

DePaulo, B. M. (1994). Spotting lies: Can humans learn to do better? *Current Directions in Psychological Science 3,* 83–86. (p. 419)

Dermer, M., & Pyszczynski, T. A. (1978). Effects of erotica upon men's loving and liking responses for women they love. *Journal of Personality and Social Psychology, 36,* 1302–1309. (p. 611)

Dermer, M., Cohen, S. J., Jacobsen, E., & Anderson, E. A. (1979). Evaluative judgments of aspects of life as a function of vicarious exposure to hedonic extremes. *Journal of Personality and Social Psychology, 37,* 247–260. (p. 430)

Deroche-Garmonet, V., Belin, D., & Piazza, P. V. (2004). Evidence for addiction-like behavior in the rat. *Science, 305,* 1014–1017. (p. 217)

DeRubeis, R. J., & 10 others, (2005). Cognitive therapy vs. medications in the treatment of moderate to severe depression. *Archives of General Psychiatry, 62,* 409–416. (p. 557)

DeSteno, D., Dasgupta, N., Bartlett, M. Y., & Cajdric, A. (2004). Prejudice from thin air: The effect of emotion on automatic intergroup attitudes. *Psychological Science, 15,* 319–324. (p. 424)

DeSteno, D., Petty, R. E., Wegener, D. T., & Rucker, D. D. (2000). Beyond valence in the perception of likelihood: The role of emotion specificity. *Journal of Personality and Social Psychology, 78,* 397–416. (p. 287)

Deutsch, J. A. (1972, July). Brain reward: ESP and ecstasy. *Psychology Today,* 46–48. (p. 53)

Deutsch, M. (1991). Egalitarianism in the laboratory and at work. In R. Vermunt & H. Steensma (Eds.), *Social justice in human relations.* New York: Plenum. (p. 257)

DeValois, R. L., & DeValois, K. K. (1975). Neural coding of color. In E. C. Carterette & M. P. Friedman (Eds.), *Handbook of perception: Vol. V. Seeing.* New York: Academic Press. (p. 154)

Devilly, G. J. (2003). Eye movement desensitization and reprocessing: A chronology of its development and scientific standing. *Scientific Review of Mental Health Practice, 1,* 113–118. (p. 558)

Devine, P. G. (1995). Prejudice and outgroup perception. In A. Tesser (Ed.), *Advanced social psychology.* New York: McGraw-Hill. (p. 608)

Devlin, B., Daniels, M., & Roeder, K. (1997). The heritability of IQ. *Nature, 388,* 468–471. (p. 342)

Dew, M. A., Hoch, C. C., Buysse, D. J., Monk, T. H., Begley, A. E., Houck, P. R., Hall, M., Kupfer, D. J., Reynolds, C. F., III (2003). Healthy older adults' sleep predicts all-cause mortality at 4 to 19 years of follow-up. *Psychosomatic Medicine, 65,* 63–73. (p. 201)

Dey, E. L., Astin, A. W., & Korn, W. S. (1991). *The American freshman: Twenty-five year trends.* Los Angeles: Higher Education Research Institute, UCLA. (p. 91)

Diaconis, P. (2002, August 11). Quoted by L. Belkin, The odds of that. *New York Times* (www.nytimes.com). (p. 24)

Diaconis, P., & Mosteller, F. (1989). Methods for studying coincidences. *Journal of the American Statistical Association, 84,* 853–861. (p. 24)

Diamond, J. (1989, May). The great leap forward. *Discover,* pp. 50–60. (p. 319)

Diamond, J. (2001, February). A tale of two reputations: Why we revere Darwin and give Freud a hard time. *Natural History,* pp. 20–24. (p. 75)

Diamond, R. (1993). Genetics and male sexual orientation (letter). *Science, 261,* 1258. (p. 386)

Dickerson, S. S., & Kemeny, M. E. (2004). Acute stressors and cortisol responses: A theoretical integration and synthesis of laboratory research. *Psychological Bulletin, 130,* 355–391. (p. 445)

Dickson, B. J. (2005, June 3). Quoted in E. Rosenthal, For fruit flies, gene shift tilts sex orientation. *New York Times* (www.nytimes.com). (p. 383)

Diener, E., & Biswas-Diener, R. (2002). Will money increase subjective well-being? A literature review and guide to needed research. *Social Indicators Research, 57,* 119–169. (p. 428)

Diener, E., & Oishi, S. (2000). Money and happiness: Income and subjective well-being across nations. In E. Diener & E. M. Suh (Eds.), *Subjective well-being across cultures.* Cambridge, MA: MIT Press. (p. 429)

Diener, E., & Seligman, M. E. P. (2002). Very happy people. *Psychological Science, 13,* 81–84. (p. 388)

Diener, E., Diener, M., & Diener, C. (1995). Factors predicting the subjective well-being of nations. *Journal of Personality and Social Psychology, 69,* 851–864. (pp. 85, 85, 609)

Diener, E., Oishi, S., & Lucas, R. E. (2003). Personality, culture, and subjective well-being: Emotional and cognitive evaluations of life. *Annual Review of Psychology, 54,* 403–425. (p. 432)

Diener, E., Wirtz, D., & Oishi, S. (2001). End effects of rated life quality: The James Dean effect. *Psychological Science, 12,* 124–128. (p. 164)

Diener, M. L., & Lucas, R. E. (2004). Adults' desires for children's emotions across 48 countries: Associations with individual and national characteristics. *Journal of Cross-Cultural Psychology, 35,* 525–547. (p. 425)

Dietz, W. H., Jr., & Gortmaker, S. L. (1985). Do we fatten our children at the television set? Obesity and television viewing in children and adolescents. *Pediatrics, 75,* 807–812. (p. 372)

Dijksterhuis, A., & Aarts, H. (2003). On wildebeests and humans: The preferential detection of negative stimuli. *Psychological Science, 14,* 14–18. (p. 417)

DiLalla, D. L., Carey, G., Gottesman, I. I., & Bouchard, T. J., Jr. (1996). Heritability of MMPI personality indicators of psychopathology in twins reared apart. *Journal of Abnormal Psychology, 105,* 491–499. (pp. 70, 525)

Dimberg, U., Thunberg, M., & Elmehed, K. (2000). Unconscious facial reactions to emotional facial expressions. *Psychological Science, 11,* 86–89. (pp. 261, 414, 422)

Dimberg, U., Thunberg, M., & Grunedal, S. (2002). Facial reactions to emotional stimuli: Automatically controlled emotional responses. *Cognition and Emotion, 16,* 449–472. (p. 261)

Dindia, K., & Allen, M. (1992). Sex differences in self-disclosure: A meta-analysis. *Psychological Bulletin, 112,* 106–124. (p. 89)

Dinges, N. G., & Hull, P. (1992). Personality, culture, and international studies. In D. Lieberman (Ed.), *Revealing the world: An interdisciplinary reader for international studies.* Dubuque, IA: Kendall-Hunt. (p. 323)

Dion, K. K., & Dion, K. L. (1993). Individualistic and collectivistic perspectives on gender and the cultural context of love and intimacy. *Journal of Social Issues, 49,* 53–69. (p. 86)

Dion, K. K., & Dion, K. L. (2001). Gender and cultural adaptation in immigrant families. *Journal of Social Issues, 57,* 511–521. (p. 92)

Discover (1996, May). A fistful of risks. Pp. 82–83. (p. 220)

Doherty, E. W., & Doherty, W. J. (1998). Smoke gets in your eyes: Cigarette smoking and divorce in a national sample of American adults. *Families, Systems, and Health, 16,* 393–400. (p. 222)

Dohrenwend, B. P., Levav, I., Shrout, P. E., Schwartz, S., Naveh, G., Link, B. G., Skodol, A. E., & Stueve, A. (1992). Socioeconomic status and psychiatric disorders: The causation-selection issue. *Science, 255,* 946–952. (p. 506)

Dohrenwend, B. P., Turner, J. B., Turse, N. A., Adams, B. G., Koenen, K. C., & Marshall, R. (2006). The psychological risks of Vietnam for U.S. veterans: A revisit with new data and methods. *Science, 313,* 979–982. (p. 512)

Dohrenwend, B., Pearlin, L., Clayton, P., Hamburg, B., Dohrenwend, B. P., Riley, M., & Rose, R. (1982). Report on stress and life events. In G. R. Elliott & C. Eisdorfer (Eds.), *Stress and human health: Analysis and implications of research* (A study by the Institute of Medicine/National Academy of Sciences). New York: Springer. (p. 437)

Dolcos, F., LaBar, K. S., & Cabeza, R. (2004). Interaction between the amygdala and the medial temporal lobe memory system predicts better memory for emotional events. *Neuron, 42,* 855–863. (p. 280)

Dole, R. (1996, April 20). Quoted by M. Duffy, Look who's talking. *Time,* p. 48. (p. 576)

Dolezal, H. (1982). *Living in a world transformed.* New York: Academic Press. (p. 183)

Domhoff, G. W. (1996). *Finding meaning in dreams: A quantitative approach.* New York: Plenum. (p. 206)

Domhoff, G. W. (1999). New directions in the study of dream content using the Hall and Van de Castle coding system. *Dreaming, 9,* 115–137. (p. 206)

Domhoff, G. W. (2000). Moving Dream Theory Beyond Freud and Jung. Paper presented to the symposium "Beyond Freud and Jung?" Graduate Theological Union, Berkeley, CA, 9/23/2000. (p. 207)

Domhoff, G. W. (2003). *The scientific study of dreams: Neural networks, cognitive development, and content analysis.* Washington, DC: APA Books. (p. 208)

Domjan, M. (1992). Adult learning and mate choice: Possibilities and experimental evidence. *American Zoologist, 32,* 48–61. (p. 238)

Domjan, M. (1994). Formulation of a behavior system for sexual conditioning. *Psychonomic Bulletin & Review, 1,* 421–428. (p. 238)

Domjan, M. (2005). Pavlovian conditioning: A functional perspective. *Annual Review of Psychology, 56.* (p. 238)

Domjan, M., Blesbois, E., & Williams, J. (1998). The adaptive significance of sexual conditioning: Pavlovian control of sperm release. *Psychological Science, 9,* 411–415. (p. 238)

Donahoe, J. W., & Vegas, R. (2004). Pavlovian conditioning: The CS-UR relation. *Journal of Experimental Psychology: Animal Behavior, 30,* 17–33. (p. 258)

Donnellan, M. B., Trzesniewski, K. H., Robins, R. W., Moffitt, T. E., & Caspi, A. (2005). Low self-esteem is related to aggression, antisocial behavior, and delinquency. *Psychological Science, 16,* 328–335. (pp. 484, 494)

Donnerstein, E. (1998). Why do we have those new ratings on television. Invited address to the National Institute on the Teaching of Psychology. (pp. 264, 265)

Donnerstein, E., Linz, D., & Penrod, S. (1987). *The question of pornography.* New York: Free Press. (p. 265)

Dorner, G. (1976). *Hormones and brain differentiation.* Amsterdam: Elsevier Scientific. (p. 384)

Dorner, G. (1988). Neuroendocrine response to estrogen and brain differentiation in heterosexuals, homosexuals, and transsexuals. *Archives of Sexual Behavior, 17,* 57–75. (p. 384)

Doty, R. L., Shaman, P., Applebaum, S. L., Giberson, R., Siksorski, L., & Rosenberg, L. (1984). Smell identification ability: Changes with age. *Science, 226,* 1441–1443. (p. 131)

Dovidio, J. F., & Gaertner, S. L. (1999). Reducing prejudice: Combating intergroup biases. *Current Directions in Psychological Science, 8,* 101–105. (p. 617)

Dovidio, J. F., ten Vergert, M., Stewart, T. L., Gaertner, S. L., Johnson, J. D., Esses, V. M., Riek, B. M., & Pearson, A. R. (2004). Perspective and prejudice: Antecedents and mediating mechanisms. *Personality and Social Psychology Bulletin, 30,* 1537–154 (p. 617)

Downing, P. E., Jiang, Y., & Shuman, M. (2001). A cortical area selective for visual processing of the human body. Science, 293, 2470–2473. (p. 151)

Doyle, R. (2005, March). Gay and lesbian census. *Scientific American,* p. 28. (p. 76)

Draguns, J. G. (1990a). Normal and abnormal behavior in cross-cultural perspective: Specifying the nature of their relationship. *Nebraska Symposium on Motivation 1989, 37,* 235–277. (pp. 506, 528)

Draguns, J. G. (1990b). Applications of cross-cultural psychology in the field of mental health. In R. W. Brislin (Ed.), *Applied cross-cultural psychology.* Newbury Park, CA: Sage. (pp. 502, 506)

Draguns, J. G. (1997). Abnormal behavior patterns across cultures: Implications for counseling and psychotherapy. *International Journal of Intercultural Relations, 21,* 213–248. (p. 506)

Druckman, D., & Bjork, R. A. (1991). *In the mind's eye: Enhancing human performance.* National Academy Press: Washington, DC. (p. 475)

Druckman, D., & Bjork, R. A. (Eds.) (1994). *Learning, remembering, believing: Enhancing human performance.* Washington, DC: National Academy Press. (p. 212)

Duclos, S. E., Laird, J. D., Sexter, M., Stern, L., & Van Lighten, O. (1989). Emotion-specific effects of facial expressions and postures on emotional experience. *Journal of Personality and Social Psychology, 57,* 100–108. (p. 422)

Duenwald, M. (2004, October 26). The dorms may be great, but how's the counseling? *New York Times* (www.nytimes.com). (p. 567)

Duffy, M. (2003, June 9). Weapons of mass disappearance. *Time,* pp. 28–33. (p. 579)

Duggan, J. P., & Booth, D. A. (1986). Obesity, overeating, and rapid gastric emptying in rats with ventromedial hypothalamic lesions. *Science, 231,* 609–611. (p. 361)

Dugger, C. W. (2005, January 18). U.N. proposes doubling of aid to cut poverty. *New York Times* (www.nytimes.com). (p. 315)

Duncan, B. L. (1976). Differential social perception and attribution of intergroup violence: Testing the lower limits of stereotyping of blacks. *Journal of Personality and Social Psychology, 34,* 590–598. (p. 594)

Duncker, K. (1945). On problem solving. *Psychological Monographs, 58* (Whole no. 270). (pp. 310, 312)

Dunn, A. L., Trivedi, M. H., Kampert, J. B., Clark, C. G., & Chambliss, H. O. (2005). Exercise treatment for depression: Efficacy and dose response. *American Journal of Preventive Medicine, 28,* 1–8. (p. 450)

Dunson, D. B., Colombo, B., & Baird, D. D. (2002). Changes with age in the level and duration of fertility in the menstrual cycle. *Human Reproduction, 17,* 1399–1403. (p. 129)

Dush, C. M. K., Cohan, C. L., & Amato, P. R. (2003). The relationship between cohabitation and marital quality and stability: Change across cohorts? *Journal of Marriage and Family, 65,* 539–549. (p. 136)

Dutton, D. G., & Aron, A. (1989). Romantic attraction and generalized liking for others who are sources of conflict-based arousal. *Canadian Journal of Behavioural Sciences, 21,* 246–257. (p. 611)

Dutton, D. G., & Aron, A. P. (1974). Some evidence for heightened sexual attraction under conditions of high anxiety. *Journal of Personality and Social Psychology, 30,* 510–517. (p. 611)

Eagly, A. H. (1994). Are people prejudiced against women? Donald Campbell Award invited address, American Psychological Association convention. (p. 596)

Eagly, A. H., & Crowley, M. (1986). Gender and helping behavior: A meta-analytic review of the social psychological literature. *Psychological Bulletin, 100,* 283–308. (p. 614)

Eagly, A. H., & Johnson, B. T. (1990). Gender and leadership style: A meta-analysis. *Psychological Bulletin, 108,* 233–256. (p. 88)

Eagly, A. H., & Wood, W. (1999). The origins of sex differences in human behavior: Evolved dispositions versus social roles. *American Psychologist, 54,* 408–423. (p. 78)

Eagly, A. H., Ashmore, R. D., Makhijani, M. G., & Kennedy, L. C. (1991). What is beautiful is good, but . . .: A meta-analytic review of research on the physical attractiveness stereotype. *Psychological Bulletin, 110,* 109–128. (p. 608)

Eastman, C. L., Boulos, Z., Terman, M., Campbell, S. S., Dijk, D-J., & Lewy, A. J. (1995). Light treatment for sleep disorders: Consensus report. VI. Shift work. *Journal of Biological Rhythms, 10,* 157–164. (p. 197)

Eastman, C. L., Young, M. A., Fogg, L. F., Liu, L., & Meaden, P. M. (1998). Bright light treatment of winter depression: A placebo-controlled trial. *Archives of General Psychiatry, 55,* 883–889. (p. 559)

Ebbesen, E. B., Duncan, B., & Konecni, V. J. (1975). Effects of content of verbal aggression on future verbal aggression: A field experiment. *Journal of Experimental Social Psychology, 11,* 192–204. (p. 424)

Ebbinghaus, H. (1885). Über das Gedachtnis. Leipzig: Duncker & Humblot. Cited in R. Klatzky (1980), *Human memory: Structures and processes.* San Francisco: Freeman. (pp. 272, 291)

Eberhardt, J. L. (2005). Imaging race. *American Psychologist, 60,* 181–190. (p. 595)

Eberhardt, J. L., Goff, P. A., Purdie, V. J., & Davies, P. G. (2004). Seeing Black: Race, crime, and visual processing. *Journal of Personality and Social Psychology, 87,* 876–893. (p. 595)

Eccles, J. S., Jacobs, J. E., & Harold, R. D. (1990). Gender role stereotypes, expectancy effects, and parents' socialization of gender differences. *Journal of Social Issues, 46,* 183–201. (p. 350)

Eckensberger, L. H. (1994). Moral development and its measurement across cultures. In W. J. Lonner & R. Malpass (Eds.), *Psychology and culture.* Boston: Allyn and Bacon. (p. 123)

Eckersley, R. (2000). The mixed blessings of material progress: Diminishing returns in the pursuit of happiness. *Journal of Happiness Studies, 1,* 267–292. (p. 428)

Eckersley, R., & Dear, K. (2002). Correlates of youth suicide. *Social Science and Medicine, 55,* 1891–1935. (p. 524)

Eckert, E. D., Heston, L. L., & Bouchard, T. J., Jr. (1981). MZ twins reared apart: Preliminary findings of psychiatric disturbances and traits. In L. Gedda, P. Paris, & W. D. Nance (Eds.), *Twin research: Vol. 3. Pt. B. Intelligence, personality, and development.* New York: Alan Liss. (p. 514)

Economist. (2001, December 20). An anthropology of happiness. *The Economist* (www.economist.com/world/asia). (p. 388)

Edelman, S., & Kidman, A. D. (1997). Mind and cancer: Is there a relationship? A review of the evidence. *Australian Psychologist, 32,* 1–7. (p. 442)

Edison, T. A. (1948). *The diary and sundry observations of Thomas Alva Edison,* edited by D. D. Runes. New York: Philosophical Library. Cited by S. Coren (1996). *Sleep Thieves.* New York: Free Press. (p. 200)

Edwards, C. P. (1981). The comparative study of the development of moral judgment and reasoning. In R. H. Munroe, R. L. Munroe, & B. B. Whiting (Eds.), *Handbook of cross-cultural human development.* New York: Garland Press. (p. 123)

Edwards, C. P. (1982). Moral development in comparative cultural perspective. In D. A. Wagner & H. W. Stevenson (Eds.), *Cultural perspectives on child development.* San Francisco: Freeman. (p. 123)

Egan, M. F., & 16 others. (2004). Variation in GRM3 affects cognition, prefrontal glutamate, and risk for schizophrenia. *Proceedings of the National Academy of Sciences, 101,* 12604–12609. (p. 536)

Ehrlichman, H., & Halpern, J. N. (1988). Affect and memory: Effects of pleasant and unpleasant odors on retrieval of happy and unhappy memories. *Journal of Personality and Social Psychology, 55,* 769–779. (p. 167)

Eibl-Eibesfeldt, I. (1971). *Love and hate: The natural history of behavior patterns.* New York: Holt, Rinehart & Winston. (p. 421)

Eich, E. (1990). Learning during sleep. In R. B. Bootzin, J. F. Kihlstrom, & D. L. Schacter (Eds.), *Sleep and cognition.* Washington, DC: American Psychological Association. (p. 206)

Eisenberg, N., & Lennon, R. (1983). Sex differences in empathy and related capacities. *Psychological Bulletin, 94,* 100–131. (p. 419)

Eisenberger, R., & Rhoades, L. (2001). Incremental effects of reward on creativity. *Journal of Personality and Social Psychology, 81,* 728–741. (p. 255)

Eiser, J. R. (1985). Smoking: The social learning of an addiction. *Journal of Social and Clinical Psychology, 3,* 446–457. (p. 221)

Ekman, P. (1994). Strong evidence for universals in facial expressions: A reply to Russell's mistaken critique. *Psychological Bulletin, 115,* 268–287. (p. 420)

Ekman, P., Friesen, W. V. (1975). *Unmasking the face.* Englewood Cliffs, NJ: Prentice-Hall. (p. 420)

Ekman, P., Friesen, W. V., O'Sullivan, M., Chan, A., Diacoyanni-Tarlatzis, I., Heider, K., Krause, R., LeCompte, W. A., Pitcairn, T., Ricci-Bitti, P. E., Scherer, K., Tomita, M., & Tzavaras, A. (1987). Universals and cultural differences in the judgments of facial expressions of emotion. *Journal of Personality and Social Psychology, 53,* 712–717. (p. 420)

Elbert, T., Pantev, C., Wienbruch, C., Rockstroh, B., & Taub, E. (1995). Increased cortical representation of the fingers of the left hand in string players. *Science, 270,* 305–307. (p. 80)

Elfenbein, H. A., & Ambady, N. (1999). Does it take one to know one? A meta-analysis of the universality and cultural specificity of emotion recognition. Unpublished manuscript, Harvard University. (p. 420)

Elfenbein, H. A., & Ambady, N. (2002). On the universality and cultural specificity of emotion recognition: A meta-analysis. *Psychological Bulletin, 128,* 203–235. (p. 421)

Elfenbein, H. A., & Ambady, N. (2003a). When familiarity breeds accuracy: Cultural exposure and facial emotion recognition. *Journal of Personality and Social Psychology, 85,* 276–290. (p. 421)

Elfenbein, H. A., & Ambady, N. (2003b). Universals and cultural differences in recognizing emotions. *Current Directions in Psychological Science, 12,* 159–164. (p. 421)

Elkin, I., Shea, T., Watkins, J. T., Imber, S. D., Sotsky, S. M., Collins, J. F., Glass, D. R., Pilkonis, P. A., Leber, W. R., Docherty, J. P., Fiester, S. J., & Parloff, M. B. (1989). National Institute of Mental Health treatment of depression collaborative research program. *Archives of General Psychiatry, 46,* 971–983. (p. 556)

Elkind, D. (1970). The origins of religion in the child. *Review of Religious Research, 12,* 35–42. (p. 122)

Elkind, D. (1978). *The child's reality: Three developmental themes.* Hillsdale, NJ: Erlbaum. (p. 122)

Ellis, A. (1980). Psychotherapy and atheistic values: A response to A. E. Bergin's "Psychotherapy and religious values." *Journal of Consulting and Clinical Psychology, 48,* 635–639. (p. 562)

Ellis, B. J. (2004). Timing of pubertal maturation in girls: An integrated life history approach. *Psychological Bulletin, 130,* 920–958. (p. 126)

Ellis, B. J., Bates, J. E., Dodge, K. A., Fergusson, D. M., John, H. L., Pettit, G. S., & Woodward, L. (2003). Does father absence place daughters at special risk for early sexual activity and teenage pregnancy? *Child Development, 74,* 801–821. (p. 380)

Ellis, L., & Ames, M. A. (1987). Neurohormonal functioning and sexual orientation: A theory of homosexuality-heterosexuality. *Psychological Bulletin, 101,* 233–258. (p. 384)

Emde, R. N., Plomin, R., Robinson, J., Corley, R., DeFries, J., Fulker, D. W., Reznick, J. S., Campos, J., Kagan, J., & Zahn-Waxler, C. (1992). Temperament, emotion, and cognition at fourteen months: The MacArthur Longitudinal Twin Study. *Child Development, 63,* 1437–1455. (p. 72)

EMDR. (2002, September 19). Description for professionals. (www.emdr.org). (p. 558)

Emerging Trends. (1997, September). *Teens turn more to parents than friends on whether to attend church.* Princeton, NJ: Princeton Religion Research Center, p. 5. (p. 126)

Emery, G. (2004). Psychic predictions 2004. Committee for the Scientific Investigation of Claims of the Paranormal (www.csicop.org). (p. 186)

Emmons, S., Geisler, C., Kaplan, K. J., & Harrow, M. (1997). *Living with schizophrenia.* Muncie, IN: Taylor and Francis (Accelerated Development). (pp. 498, 532)

Empson, J. A. C., & Clarke, P. R. F. (1970). Rapid eye movements and remembering. *Nature, 227,* 287–288. (p. 207)

Emslie, C., Hunt, K., & Macintyre, S. (2001). Perceptions of body image among working men and women. *Journal of Epidemiology and Community Health, 55,* 406–407. (p. 365)

Endler, N. S. (1982). Holiday of darkness: *A psychologist's personal journey out of his depression.* New York: Wiley. (pp. 482, 526, 569)

Endler, N. S., & Speer, R. L. (1998). Personality psychology: Research trends for 1993–1995. *Journal of Personality, 66,* 621–669. (p. 478)

Engemann, K. M., & Owyang, M. T. (2005, April). So much for that merit raise: The link between wages and appearance. *Regional Economist* (www.stlouisfed.org). (p. 608)

Engen, T. (1987). Remembering odors and their names. *American Scientist, 75,* 497–503. (p. 167)

Engle, R. W. (2002). Working memory capacity as executive attention. *Current Directions in Psychological Science, 11,* 19–23. (p. 271)

Epley, N., & Dunning, D. (2000). Feeling "holier than thou": Are self-serving assessments produced by errors in self- or social prediction? *Journal of Personality and Social Psychology, 79,* 861–875. (p. 493)

Epley, N., Keysar, B., Van Boven, L., & Gilovich, T. (2004). Perspective taking as egocentric anchoring and adjustment. *Journal of Personality and Social Psychology, 87,* 327–339. (p. 110)

EPOCH. (2000). Legal reforms: Corporal punishment of children in the family (www.stophitting.com/laws/legalReform.php). (p. 253)

Epstein, J., Stern, E., & Silbersweig, D. (1998). Mesolimbic activity associated with psychosis in schizophrenia: Symptom-specific PET studies. In J. F. McGinty (Ed.), *Advancing from the ventral striatum to the extended amygdala: Implications for neuropsychiatry and drug use: In honor of Lennart Heimer.* Annals of the New York Academy of Sciences, 877, 562–574. (p. 534)

Epstein, S. (1983a). Aggregation and beyond: Some basic issues on the prediction of behavior. *Journal of Personality, 51,* 360–392. (p. 482)

Epstein, S. (1983b). The stability of behavior across time and situations. In R. Zucker, J. Aronoff, & A. I. Rabin (Eds.), *Personality and the prediction of behavior.* San Diego: Academic Press. (p. 482)

Erdberg, P. (1990). Rorschach assessment. In G. Goldstein & M. Hersen (Eds.), *Handbook of psychological assessment, 2nd ed.* New York: Pergamon. (p. 465)

Erdelyi, M. H. (1985). *Psychoanalysis: Freud's cognitive psychology.* New York: Freeman. (p. 467)

Erdelyi, M. H. (1988). Repression, reconstruction, and defense: History and integration of the psychoanalytic and experimental frameworks. In J. Singer (Ed.), *Repression: Defense mechanism and cognitive style.* Chicago: University of Chicago Press. (p. 467)

Erel, O., & Burman, B. (1995). Interrelatedness of marital relations and parent-child relations: A meta-analytic review. *Psychological Bulletin, 118,* 108–132. (p. 136)

Erickson, M. F., & Aird, E. G. (2005). *The motherhood study: Fresh insights on mothers' attitudes and concerns.* New York: The Motherhood Project, Institute for American Values. (p. 136)

Ericsson, K. A. (2002). Attaining excellence through deliberate practice: Insights from the study of expert performance. In C. Desforges & R. Fox (Eds.), *Teaching and learning: The essential readings.* Malden, MA: Blackwell Publishers. (p. 333)

Ericsson, K. A., & Lehmann, A. C. (1996). Expert and exceptional performance: Evidence of maximal adaptations to task constraints. *Annual Review of Psychology, 47,* 273–305. (p. 333)

Erikson, E. H. (1963). *Childhood and society.* New York: Norton. (p. 124)

Erikson, E. H. (1983, June). A conversation with Erikson (by E. Hall). *Psychology Today,* pp. 22–30. (p. 116)

Ernsberger, P., & Koletsky, R. J. (1999). Biomedical rationale for a wellness approach to obesity: An alternative to a focus on weight loss. *Journal of Social Issues, 55,* 221–260. (p. 371)

ESPAD. (2003). Summary of the 2003 findings. European School Survey Project on Alcohol and Other Drugs (www.espad.org). (p. 225)

Esser, J. K., & Lindoerfer, J. S. (1989). Groupthink and the space shuttle Challenger accident: Toward a quantitative case analysis. *Journal of Behavioral Decision Making, 2,* 167–177. (p. 591)

Esterson, A. (2001). The mythologizing of psychoanalytic history: Deception and self-deception in Freud's accounts of the seduction theory episode. *History of Psychiatry, 12,* 329–352. (p. 466)

Eszterhas, J. (2002, August 9). Hollywood's responsibility for smoking deaths. *New York Times* (www.nytimes.com). (p. 221)

Etnier, J. L., Salazar, W., Landers, D. M., Petruzzello, S. J., Han, M., & Nowell, P. (1997). The influence of physical fitness and exercise upon cognitive functioning: A meta-analysis. *Journal of Sport & Exercise Psychology, 19,* 249–277. (p. 450)

Evans, C. R., & Dion, K. L. (1991). Group cohesion and performance: A meta-analysis. *Small Group Research, 22,* 175–186. (p. 401)

Evans, G. W., Palsane, M. N., & Carrere, S. (1987). Type A behavior and occupational stress: A cross-cultural study of blue-collar workers. *Journal of Personality and Social Psychology, 52,* 1002–1007. (p. 438)

Evans, G. W., Palsane, M. N., Lepore, S. J., & Martin, J. (1989). Residential density and psychological health: The mediating effects of social support. *Journal of Personality and Social Psychology, 57,* 994–999. (p. 447)

Evans, R. I., Dratt, L. M., Raines, B. E., & Rosenberg, S. S. (1988). Social influences on smoking initiation: Importance of distinguishing descriptive versus mediating process variables. *Journal of Applied Social Psychology, 18,* 925–943. (p. 221)

Ewing, R., Schmid, T., Killingsworth, R., Zlot, A., & Raudenbush, S. (2003). Relationship between urban sprawl and physical activity, obesity, and morbidity. *American Journal of Health Promotion, 18,* 47–57. (p. 370)

Exner, J. E. (2003). *The Rorschach: A comprehensive system, 4th edition.* Hoboken, NJ: Wiley. (p. 465)

Eysenck, H. J. (1952). The effects of psychotherapy: An evaluation. *Journal of Consulting Psychology, 16,* 319–324. (p. 555)

Eysenck, H. J. (1990, April 30). An improvement on personality inventory. *Current Contents: Social and Behavioral Sciences, 22*(18), 20. (p. 476)

Eysenck, H. J. (1992). Four ways five factors are not basic. *Personality and Individual Differences, 13,* 667–673. (p. 476)

Eysenck, H. J., & Grossarth-Maticek, R. (1991). Creative novation behaviour therapy as a prophylactic treatment for cancer and coronary heart disease: Part II—Effects of treatment. *Behaviour Research and Therapy, 29,* 17–31. (p. 413), 452)

Eysenck, H. J., Wakefield, J. A., Jr., & Friedman, A. F. (1983). Diagnosis and clinical assessment: The DSM-III. *Annual Review of Psychology, 34,* 167–193. (p, 503)

Eysenck, M. W., MacLeod, C., & Mathews, A. (1987). Cognitive functioning and anxiety. *Psychological Research, 49,* 189–195. (p. 484)

Eysenck, S. B. G., & Eysenck, H. J. (1963). The validity of questionnaire and rating assessments of extraversion and neuroticism, and their factorial stability. *British Journal of Psychology, 54,* 51–62. (p. 476)

Faber, N. (1987, July). Personal glimpse. *Reader's Digest,* p. 34. (p. 334)

Fagan, J. F., III. (1992). Intelligence: A theoretical viewpoint. *Current Directions in Psychological Science, 1,* 82–86. (p. 347)

Fairburn, C. G., Cowen, P. J., & Harrison, P. J. (1999). Twin studies and the etiology of eating disorders. *International Journal of Eating Disorders, 26,* 349–358. (p. 364)

Fantz, R. L. (1961, May). *The origin of form perception.* Scientific American, pp. 66–72. (p. 103)

Farah, M. J., Rabinowitz, C., Quinn, G. E., & Liu, G. T. (2000). Early commitment of neural substrates for face recognition. *Cognitive Neuropsychology, 17,* 117–124. (p. 59)

Farina, A. (1982). The stigma of mental disorders. In A. G. Miller (Ed.), *In the eye of the beholder.* New York: Praeger. (pp. 500, 503)

Farina, A., & Fisher, J. D. (1982). Beliefs about mental disorders: Findings and implications. In G. Weary & H. L. Mirels (Eds.), *Integrations of clinical and social psychology.* New York: Oxford University Press. (p. 554)

Farley, M., Baral, I., Kiremire, M., & Sezgin, U. (1998). Prostitution in five countries: Violence and post-traumatic stress disorder. *Feminism and Psychology, 8,* 405–426. (p. 512)

Farley, T., & Cohen, D. (2001, December). Fixing a fat nation. *Washington Monthly* (www.washingtonmonthly.com/features/2001/0112.farley.cohen.html). (p. 370)

Farrington, D. P. (1991). Antisocial personality from childhood to adulthood. *The Psychologist: Bulletin of the British Psychological Society, 4,* 389–394. (p. 517)

FBI. (2004). *Crime in the United States 2003, Five-Year Arrest Trends by Sex, 1999–2003.* Table 35. (p. 88)

Feder, H. H. (1984). Hormones and sexual behavior. *Annual Review of Psychology, 35,* 165–200. (p. 376)

Feeney, D. M. (1987) Human rights and animal welfare. *American Psychologist, 42,* 593–599. (p. 29)

Feeney, J. A., & Noller, P. (1990). Attachment style as a predictor of adult romantic relationships. *Journal of Personality and Social Psychology, 58,* 281–291. (p. 116)

Feigenson, L., Carey, S., & Spelke, E. (2002). Infants' discrimination of number vs. continuous extent. *Cognitive Psychology, 44,* 33–66. (p. 109)

Feingold, A. (1990). Gender differences in effects of physical attractiveness on romantic attraction: A comparison across five research paradigms. *Journal of Personality and Social Psychology, 59,* 981–993. (p. 608)

Feingold, A. (1992). Good-looking people are not what we think. *Psychological Bulletin, 111,* 304–341. (p. 608)

Feingold, A., & Mazzella, R. (1998). Gender differences in body image are increasing. *Psychological Science, 9,* 190–195. (pp. 364, 609)

Fellowes, D., Barnes, K., & Wilkinson, S. (2004). Aromatherapy and massage for symptom relief in patients with cancer. *The Cochrane Library, 3,* Oxford, UK: Update Software. (p. 452)

Fenn, K. M., Nusbaum, H. C., & Margoliash, D. (2003). Consolidation during sleep of perceptual learning of spoken language. *Nature, 425,* 614–616. (p. 203)

Fenton, W. S., & McGlashan, T. H. (1991). Natural history of schizophrenia subtypes: II. Positive and negative symptoms and long-term course. *Archives of General Psychiatry, 48,* 978–986. (p. 533)

Fenton, W. S., & McGlashan, T. H. (1994). Antecedents, symptom progression, and long-term outcome of the deficit syndrome in schizophrenia. *American Journal of Psychiatry, 151,* 351–356. (p. 533)

Ferguson, E. D. (1989). Adler's motivational theory: An historical perspective on belonging and the fundamental human striving. *Individual Psychology, 45,* 354–361. (p. 387)

Fergusson, D. M., & Woodward, L. G. (2002). Mental health, educational, and social role outcomes of adolescents with depression. *Archives of General Psychiatry, 59,* 225–231. (p. 523)

Fernandex-Dols, J-M., & Ruiz-Belda, M-A. (1995). Are smiles a sign of happiness? Gold medal winners at the Olympic Games. *Journal of Personality and Social Psychology, 69,* 1113–1119. (p. 421)

Fernandez, E., & Turk, D. C. (1989). The utility of cognitive coping strategies for altering pain perception: A meta-analysis. *Pain, 38,* 123–135. (p. 164)

Ferris, C. F. (1996, March). The rage of innocents. *The Sciences,* pp. 22–26. (p. 117)

Fiedler, F. E. (1981). Leadership effectiveness. *American Behavioral Scientist, 24,* 619–632. (p. 401)

Fiedler, F. E. (1987, September). When to lead, when to stand back. *Psychology Today,* pp. 26–27. (p. 401)

Fiedler, K., Nickel, S., Muehlfriedel, T., & Unkelbach, C. (2001). Is mood congruency an effect of genuine memory or response bias? *Journal of Experimental Social Psychology, 37,* 201–214. (p. 287)

Field, T. (2001). Massage therapy facilitates weight gain in preterm infants. *Current Directions in Psychological Science, 10,* 51–54. (p. 80)

Field, T., Hernandez-Reif, M., Diego, M., Feijo, L., Vera, Y., & Gil, K. (2004). Massage therapy by parents improves early growth and development. *Infant Behaviour and Development, 27,* 435–442. (p. 80)

Fincham, F. D., & Bradbury, T. N. (1993). Marital satisfaction, depression, and attributions: A longitudinal analysis. *Journal of Personality and Social Psychology, 64,* 442–452. (p. 576)

Fink, G. R., Markowitsch, H. J., Reinkemeier, M., Bruckbauer, T., Kessler, J., & Heiss, W-D. (1996). Cerebral representation of one's own past: Neural networks involved in autobiographical memory. *Journal of Neuroscience, 16,* 4275–4282. (p. 283)

Fink, M. (1998). ECT and managed care. *Journal Watch Psychiatry, 4,* 73, 76. (p. 569)

Fischhoff, B. (1982). Debiasing. In D. Kahneman, P. Slovic, & A. Tversky (Eds.), *Judgment under uncertainty: Heuristics and biases.* New York: Cambridge University Press. (p. 313)

Fischhoff, B., Slovic, P., & Lichtenstein, S. (1977). Knowing with certainty: The appropriateness of extreme confidence. *Journal of Experimental Psychology: Human Perception and Performance, 3,* 552–564. (p. 312)

Fisher, H. E. (1993, March/April). After all, maybe it's biology. *Psychology Today,* pp. 40–45. (p. 136)

Fisher, H. E., Aron, A., Mashek, D., Li, H., & Brown, L. L. (2002). Defining the brain systems of lust, romantic attraction, and attachment. *Archives of Sexual Behavior, 31,* 413–419. (p. 375)

Fisher, H. T. (1984). Little Albert and Little Peter. *Bulletin of the British Psychological Society, 37,* 269. (p. 546)

Fiske, S. T., Harris, L. T., & Cuddy, A. J. C. (2004). Why ordinary people torture enemy prisoners. *Science, 306,* 1482–1483. (p. 579)

Fleming, I., Baum, A., & Weiss, L. (1987). Social density and perceived control as mediator of crowding stress in high-density residential neighborhoods. *Journal of Personality and Social Psychology, 52,* 899–906. (p. 446)

Fleming, J. H. (2001, Winter/Spring). Introduction to the special issue on linkage analysis. *The Gallup Research Journal,* pp. i–vi. (p. 400)

Fletcher, G. J. O., Fitness, J., & Blampied, N. M. (1990). The link between attributions and happiness in close relationships: The roles of depression and explanatory style. *Journal of Social and Clinical Psychology, 9,* 243–255. (p. 576)

Fletcher, P. C., Zafiris, O., Frith, C. D., Honey, R. A. E., Corlett, P. R., Zilles, K., & Fink, G. R. (2005). On the benefits of not trying: Brain activity and connectivity reflecting the interactions of explicit and implicit sequence learning. *Cerebral Cortex, 7,* 1002–1015. (p. 467)

Flora, S. R. (2004). *The power of reinforcement.* Albany, NJ: SUNY Press. (p. 256)

Flouri, E., & Buchanan, A. (2004). Early father's and mother's involvement and child's later educational outcomes. *British Journal of Educational Psychology, 74,* 141–153. (p. 115)

Flynn, J. R. (1987). Massive IQ gains in 14 nations: What IQ tests really measure. *Psychological Bulletin, 101,* 171–191. (p. 340)

Flynn, J. R. (1999). Searching for justice: The discovery of IQ gains over time. *American Psychologist, 54,* 5–20. (p. 340)

Flynn, J. R. (2003). Movies about intelligence: The limitations of g. *Current Directions in Psychological Science, 12,* 95–99. (p. 343)

Foa, E. B., & Kozak, M. J. (1986). Emotional processing of fear: Exposure to corrective information. *Psychological Bulletin, 99,* 20–35. (p. 546)

Fogg, N. P., Harrington P. E., & Harrington T. F. (2004). *The college majors' handbook.* Indianapolis, IN: JIST Works, Inc. (pp. B-1, B-2, B-3)

Ford, E. S. (2002). Does exercise reduce inflammation? Physical activity and B-reactive protein among U.S. adults. *Epidemiology, 13,* 561–569. (p. 450)

Foree, D. D., & LoLordo, V. M. (1973). Attention in the pigeon: Differential effects of food-getting versus shock-avoidance procedures. *Journal of Comparative and Physiological Psychology, 85,* 551–558. (p. 255)

Forer, B. R. (1949). The fallacy of personal validation: A classroom demonstration of gullibility. *Journal of Abnormal and Social Psychology, 44,* 118–123. (p. 480)

Forgas, J. P., Bower, G. H., & Krantz, S. E. (1984). The influence of mood on perceptions of social interactions. *Journal of Experimental Social Psychology, 20,* 497–513. (p. 287)

Forman, D. R., Aksan, N., & Kochanska, G. (2004). Toddlers' responsive imitation predicts preschool-age conscience. *Psychological Science, 15,* 699–704. (p. 263)

Forste, R. & Tanfer, K. (1996). Sexual exclusivity among dating, cohabiting, and married women. *Journal of Marriage and the Family 58*, 33–47. (p. C-4)

Foss, D. J., & Hakes, D. T. (1978). *Psycholinguistics: An introduction to the psychology of language.* Englewood Cliffs, NJ: Prentice-Hall. (p. 466)

Foster, J. D., Campbell, W. K., & Twenge, J. M. (2003). Individual differences in narcissism: Inflated self-views across the lifespan and around the world. *Journal of Research in Personality, 37*, 469–486. (p. 86)

Foster, R. G. (2004). Are we trying to banish biological time? *Cerebrum, 6(2)*, 7–26. (p. 196)

Foulkes, D. (1999). *Children's dreaming and the development of consciousness.* Cambridge, MA; Harvard University Press. (p. 208)

Fouts, R. S. (1992). Transmission of a human gestural language in a chimpanzee mother-infant relationship. *Friends of Washoe, 12/13*, pp. 2–8. (p. 328)

Fouts, R. S. (1997). *Next of kin: What chimpanzees have taught me about who we are.* New York: Morrow. (p. 328)

Fouts, R. S., & Bodamer, M. (1987). Preliminary report to the National Geographic Society on "Chimpanzee intrapersonal signing." *Friends of Washoe, 7(1)*, 4–12. (p. 328)

Fowler, M. J., Sullivan, M. J., & Ekstrand, B. R. (1973). Sleep and memory. *Science, 179*, 302–304. (p. 294)

Fowler, R. C., Rich, C. L., & Young, D. (1986). San Diego suicide study: II. Substance abuse in young cases. *Archives of General Psychiatry, 43*, 962–965. (p. 525)

Fowles, D. C. (1992). Schizophrenia: Diathesis-stress revisited. *Annual Review of Psychology, 43*, 303–336. (p. 533)

Fox, B. H. (1998). Psychosocial factors in cancer incidence and prognosis. In P. M. Cinciripini & others (Eds.), *Psychological and behavioral factors in cancer risk.* New York: Oxford University Press. (p. 442)

Fox, J. L. (1984). The brain's dynamic way of keeping in touch. *Science, 225*, 820–821. (p. 59)

Fozard, J. L., & Popkin, S. J. (1978). Optimizing adult development: Ends and means of an applied psychology of aging. *American Psychologist, 33*, 975–989. (p. 130)

Fracassini, C. (2000, August 27). Holidaymakers led by the nose in sales quest. *Scotland on Sunday.* (p. 167)

Fraley, R. C. (2002). Attachment stability from infancy to adulthood: Meta-analysis and dynamic modeling of developmental mechanisms. *Personality and Social Psychology Review, 6*, 123–151. (p. 116)

Franek, R., Meltzer, T., & Maier, C. (2005). The Best 361 Colleges. For *Princeton Review.* (p. B-1)

Frank, J. D. (1982). Therapeutic components shared by all psychotherapies. In J. H. Harvey & M. M. Parks (Eds.), *The Master Lecture Series: Vol. 1. Psychotherapy research and behavior change.* Washington, DC: American Psychological Association. (pp. 559, 561)

Frank, R. (1999). *Luxury fever: Why money fails to satisfy in an era of excess.* New York: Free Press. (p. 84)

Frank, S. J. (1988). Young adults' perceptions of their relationships with their parents: Individual differences in connectedness, competence, and emotional autonomy. *Developmental Psychology, 24*, 729–737. (p. 126)

Frankel, A., Strange, D. R., & Schoonover, R. (1983). CRAP: Consumer rated assessment procedure. In G. H. Scherr & R. Liebmann-Smith (Eds.), *The best of The Journal of Irreproducible Results.* New York: Workman Publishing. (p. 477)

Frankenburg, W., Dodds, J., Archer, P., Shapiro, H., & Bresnick, B. (1992). The Denver II: A major revision and restandardization of the Denver Developmental Screening Test. *Pediatrics, 89*, 91–97. (p. 105)

Franz, E. A., Waldie, K. E., & Smith, M. J. (2000). The effect of callosotomy on novel versus familiar bimanual actions: A neural dissociation between controlled and automatic processes? *Psychological Science, 11*, 82–85. (p. 62)

Frasure-Smith, N., & Lespérance, F. (2005). Depression and coronary heart disease: Complex synergism of mind, body, and environment. *Current Directions in Psychological Science, 14*, 39–43. (p. 439)

Fredrickson, B. L., & Kahneman, D. (1993). Duration neglect in retrospective evaluations of affective episodes. *Journal of Personality and Social Psychology, 65*, 45–55. (p. 275)

Fredrickson, B. L., Roberts, T-A., Noll, S. M., Quinn, D. M., & Twenge, J. M. (1998). That swimsuit becomes you: Sex differences in self-objectification, restrained eating, and math performance. *Journal of Personality and Social Psychology, 75*, 269–284. (p. 365)

Freedman, D. J., Riesenhuber, M., Poggio, T., & Miller, E. K. (2001). Categorical representation of visual stimuli in the primate prefrontal cortex. *Science, 291*, 312–316. (p. 326)

Freedman, J. L. (1988). Television violence and aggression: What the evidence shows. In S. Oskamp (Ed.), *Television as a social issue.* Newbury Park, CA: Sage. (p. 264)

Freedman, J. L., & Fraser, S. C. (1966). Compliance without pressure: The foot-in-the-door technique. *Journal of Personality and Social Psychology, 4*, 195–202. (p. 578)

Freedman, J. L., & Perlick, D. (1979). Crowding, contagion, and laughter. *Journal of Experimental Social Psychology, 15*, 295–303. (p. 589)

Freeman, W. J. (1991, February). The physiology of perception. *Scientific American*, pp. 78–85. (p. 157)

Frensch, P. A., & Rünger, D. (2003). Implicit learning. Current *Directions in Psychological Science, 12*, 13–18. (p. 467)

Freud, S. (1935; reprinted 1960). *A general introduction to psychoanalysis.* New York: Washington Square Press. (p. 135)

Freyd, J. J., Putnam, F. W., Lyon, T. D., Becker-Blease, K. A., Cheit, R. E., Siegel, N. B., & Pezdek, K. (2005). The science of child sexual abuse. *Science, 308*, 501. (p. 117)

Friedman, M., & Ulmer, D. (1984). *Treating Type A behavior—and your heart.* New York: Knopf. (pp. 438, 451)

Friedrich, O. (1987, December 7). New age harmonies. *Time*, pp. 62–72. (p. 499)

Friend, T. (2004). *Animal talk: Breaking the codes of animal language.* New York: Free Press. (p. 329)

Frith, U., & Frith, C. (2001). The biological basis of social interaction. *Current Directions in Psychological Science, 10*, 151–155. (p. 111)

Fromkin, V., & Rodman, R. (1983). *An introduction to language (3rd ed.).* New York: Holt, Rinehart & Winston. (p. 320)

Fry, A. F., & Hale, S. (1996). Processing speed, working memory, and fluid intelligence: Evidence for a developmental cascade. *Psychological Science, 7*, 237–241. (p. 131)

Fuhriman, A., & Burlingame, G. M. (1994). Group psychotherapy: Research and practice. In A. Fuhriman & G. M. Burlingame (Eds.), *Handbook of group psychotherapy.* New York: Wiley. (p. 551)

Fuller, M. J., & Downs, A. C. (1990). *Spermarche is a salient biological marker in men's development.* Poster presented at the American Psychological Society convention. (p. 121)

Fulmer, I. S., Gerhart, B., & Scott, K. S. (2003). Are the 100 best better? An empirical investigation fo the relationship between being a "great place to work" and firm performance. *Personnel Psychology, 56*, 965–993. (p. 399)

Funder, D. C. (2001). Personality. *Annual Review of Psychology, 52*, 197–221. (p. 478)

Funder, D. C., & Block, J. (1989). The role of ego-control, ego-resiliency, and IQ in delay of gratification in adolescence. *Journal of Personality and Social Psychology, 57*, 1041–1050. (p. 123)

Furlow, F. B., & Thornhill, R. (1996, January/February). The orgasm wars. *Psychology Today*, pp. 42–46. (p. 375)

Furnham, A. (1982). Explanations for unemployment in Britain. *European Journal of Social Psychology, 12*, 335–352. (p. 576)

Furnham, A. (2001). Self-estimates of intelligence: Culture and gender difference in self and other estimates of both general (g) and multiple intelligences. *Personality and Individual Differences, 31*, 1381–1405. (p. 347)

Furnham, A., & Baguma, P. (1994). Cross-cultural differences in the evaluation of male and female body shapes. *International Journal of Eating Disorders, 15*, 81–89. (p. 366)

Furnham, A., & Mottabu, R. (2004). Sex and culture differences in the estimates of general and multiple intelligence: A study comparing British and Egyptian students. *Individual Differences Research, 3,* 82–96. (p. 347)

Furnham, A., & Rawles, R. (1995). Sex differences in the estimation of intelligence. *Journal of Social Behavior and Personality, 10,* 741–748. (p. 596)

Furnham, A., & Taylor, L. (1990). Lay theories of homosexuality: Aetiology, behaviours, and 'cures.' *British Journal of Social Psychology, 29,* 135–147. (p. 386)

Furnham, A., & Thomas, C. (2004). Parents' gender and personality and estimates of their own and their children's intelligence. *Personality and Individual Differences, 37,* 887–903. (p. 347)

Furnham, A., Callahan, I., & Akande, D. (2004). Self-estimates of intelligence: A study in two African countries. *Journal of Psychology, 138,* 265–285. (p. 347)

Furnham, A., Hosoe, T., & Tang, T. L-P. (2002a). Male hubris and female humility? A cross-cultural study of ratings of self, parental, and sibling multiple intelligence in American, Britain, and Japan. *Intelligence, 30,* 101–115. (p. 347)

Furnham, A., Reeves, E., & Bughani, S. (2002b). Parents think their sons are brighter than their daughters: Sex differences in parental self-estimations and estimations of their children's multiple intelligences. *Journal of Genetic Psychology, 163,* 24–39. (p. 347)

Furr, R. M., & Funder, D. C. (1998). A multimodal analysis of personal negativity. *Journal of Personality and Social Psychology, 74,* 1580–1591. (p. 528)

Gabbay, F. H. (1992). Behavior-genetic strategies in the study of emotion. *Psychological Science, 3,* 50–55. (p. 72)

Gabrieli, J. D. E., Desmond, J. E., Demb, J. E., Wagner, A. D., Stone, M. V., Vaidya, C. J., & Glover, G. H. (1996). Functional magnetic resonance imaging of semantic memory processes in the frontal lobes. *Psychological Science, 7,* 278–283. (p. 283)

Gaertner, L., & Iuzzini, J. (2005). Rejection and entitativity: A synergistic model of mass violence. In K. D. Williams, J. P. Forgas, & W. von Hippel (Eds.). *The social outcast: Ostracism, social exclusion, rejection, and bullying.* New York: Psychology Press. (p. 602)

Gage, F. H. (2003, September). Repair yourself. *Scientific American,* pp. 46–53. (p. 60)

Galambos, N. L. (1992). Parent-adolescent relations. *Current Directions in Psychological Science, 1,* 146–149. (p. 125)

Galanter, E. (1962). Contemporary psychophysics. In R. Brown, E. Galanter, E. H. Hess, & G. Mandler (Eds.), *New directions in psychology.* New York: Holt Rinehart, & Winston. (p. 144)

Galati, D., Scherer, K. R., & Ricci-Bitti, P. E. (1997). Voluntary facial expression of emotion: Comparing congenitally blind with normally sighted encoders. *Journal of Personality and Social Psychology, 73,* 1363–1379. (p. 421)

Galea, S., Boscarino, J., Resnick, H., & Vlahov, D. (2002). Mental health in New York City after the September 11 terrorist attacks: Results from two population surveys. Chapter 7. In *Mental-Health, United States, 2001, R. W. Manderscheid, & M. J. Henderson (Eds.).* Washington, DC: Superintendent of Documents, U.S. Government Printing Office. (p. 512)

Gallup. (2002, February 21). Homosexual relations. The Gallup Organization (www.gallup.com/poll/topics/homosexual.asp). (p. 385)

Gallup. (2002, June 11). Poll insights: The gender gap—post Sept. 11th fear. The Gallup Organization (www.gallup.com/poll/pollInsights). (p. 510)

Gallup Organization. (2003, July 8). American public opinion about Iraq. *Gallup Poll News Service* (www.gallup.com) (p. 579, 580)

Gallup Organization. (2004, August 16). 65% of Americans receive NO praise or recognition in the workplace. E-mail from Tom Rath: bucketbook@gallup.com. (p. 400)

Gallup, G. H. (1972). *The Gallup poll: Public opinion 1935–1971 (Vol. 3).* New York: Random House. (p. 616)

Gallup, G., Jr. (2002, April 30). Education and youth. *Gallup Tuesday Briefing* (www.gallup.com/poll/tb/educaYouth/20020430.asp). (p. 264)

Gallup. (2005, May 5). The gender gap: President Bush's handling of Iraq. *The Gallup Poll* (www.gallup.com). (p. 88)

Gangestad, S. W., & Simpson, J. A. (2000). The evolution of human mating: Trade-offs and strategic pluralism. *Behavioral and Brain Sciences, 23,* 573–587. (p. 77)

Garcia, J., & Gustavson, A. R. (1997, January). Carl R. Gustavson (1946–1996): Pioneering wildlife psychologist. *APS Observer,* pp. 34–35. (p. 245)

Garcia, J., & Koelling, R. A. (1966). Relation of cue to consequence in avoidance learning. *Psychonomic Science, 4,* 123–124. (p. 243)

Gardner, H. (1983). *Frames of mind: The theory of multiple intelligences.* New York: Basic Books. (p. 332)

Gardner, H. (1998, March 19). An intelligent way to progress. *The Independent (London),* p. E4. (pp. 81, 332, 333)

Gardner, H. (1998, November 5). Do parents count? *New York Review of Books* (www.nybooks.com). (p. 332)

Gardner, H. (1999). *Multiple views of multiple intelligence.* New York: Basic Books. (pp. 332, 336)

Gardner, R. A., & Gardner, B. I. (1969). Teaching sign language to a chimpanzee. *Science, 165,* 664–672. (p. 327)

Gardner, R. M., & Tockerman, Y. R. (1994). A computer-TV video methodology for investigating the influence of somatotype on perceived personality traits. *Journal of Social Behavior and Personality, 9,* 555–563. (p. 368)

Garfield, C. (1986). *Peak performers: The new heroes of American business.* New York: Morrow. (p. 325)

Garner, D. M., & Wooley, S. C. (1991). Confronting the failure of behavioral and dietary treatments for obesity. *Clinical Psychology Review, 11,* 729–780. (p. 371)

Garnets, L., & Kimmel, D. (1990). Lesbian and gay dimensions in the psychological study of human diversity. Master lecture, American Psychological Association convention. (p. 380)

Garry, M., & Loftus, E. F., & Brown, S. W. (1994). Memory: A river runs through it. *Consciousness and Cognition, 3,* 438–451. (p. 466)

Garry, M., Manning, C. G., Loftus, E. F., & Sherman, S. J. (1996). Imagination inflation: Imagining a childhood event inflates confidence that it occurred. *Psychonomic Bulletin & Review, 3,* 208–214. (p. 297)

Gates, W. (1998, July 20). Charity begins when I'm ready (interview). *Fortune* (www.pathfinder.com/fortune/1998/980720/bil7.html). (p. 332)

Gawin, F. H. (1991). Cocaine addiction: Psychology and neurophysiology. *Science, 251,* 1580–1586. (p. 222)

Gazzaniga, M. S. (1967, August). The split brain in man. *Scientific American,* pp. 24–29. (p. 61)

Gazzaniga, M. S. (1983). Right hemisphere language following brain bisection: A 20-year perspective. *American Psychologist, 38,* 525–537. (p. 61)

Gazzaniga, M. S. (1988). Organization of the human brain. *Science, 245,* 947–952. (pp. 62, 217)

Gazzaniga, M. S. (1997). Brain, drugs, and society. *Science, 275,* 459. (p. 217)

Geary, D. C. (1995). Sexual selection and sex differences in spatial cognition. *Learning and Individual Differences, 7,* 289–301. (p. 349)

Geary, D. C. (1996). Sexual selection and sex differences in mathematical abilities. *Behavioral and Brain Sciences, 19,* 229–247. (p. 349)

Geary, D. C. (1998). *Male, female: The evolution of human sex differences.* Washington, DC: American Psychological Association. (p. 77)

Geary, D. C., Salthouse, T. A., Chen, G-P., & Fan, L. (1996). Are East Asian versus American differences in arithmetical ability a recent phenomenon? *Developmental Psychology, 32,* 254–262. (p. 347)

Geen, R. G. (1984). Human motivation: New Perspectives on old problems. In A. M. Rogers & C. J. Scheirer (Eds.), *The G. Stanley Hall Lecture Series (Vol. 4).* Washington DC: American Psychological Association. (p. 398)

Geen, R. G., & Quanty, M. B. (1977). The catharsis of aggression: An evaluation of a hypothesis. In L. Berkowitz (Ed.), *Advances in experimental social psychology (Vol. 10).* New York: Academic Press. (p. 424)

Geen, R. G., & Thomas, S. L. (1986). The immediate effects of media violence on behavior. *Journal of Social Issues, 42(3),* 7–28. (p. 265)

Gehring, W. J., Wimke, J., & Nisenson, L. G. (2000). Action monitoring dysfunction in obsessive-compulsive disorder. *Psychological Science, 11(1),* 1–6. (p. 514)

Geldard, F. A. (1972). *The human senses (2nd ed.).* New York: Wiley. (p. 154)

Gelman, D. (1989, May 15). Voyages to the unknown. *Newsweek,* pp. 66–69. (p. 421)

Genesee, F., & Gándara, P. (1999). Bilingual education programs: A cross-national perspective. *Journal of Social Issues, 55,* 665–685. (p. 324)

Genevro, J. L. (2003). *Report on bereavement and grief research.* Washington, DC: Center for the Advancement of Health. (p. 139)

Gentile, D. A., Lynch, P. J., Linder, J. R., & Walsh, D. A. (2004). The effects of violent video game habits on adolescent hostility, aggressive behaviors, and school performance. *Journal of Adolescence, 27,* 5–22. (pp. 265, 605)

George, L. K., Ellison, C. G., & Larson, D. B. (2002). Explaining the relationships between religious involvement and health. *Psychological Inquiry, 13,* 190–200. (p. 455)

George, L. K., Larson, D. B., Koenig, H. G., & McCullough, M. E. (2000). Spirituality and health: What we know, what we need to know. *Journal of Social and Clinical Psychology, 19,* 102–116. (p. 455)

George, M. S. (2003, September). Stimulating the brain. *Scientific American,* pp. 67–73. (p. 570)

Gerbner, G. (1990). Stories that hurt: Tobacco, alcohol, and other drugs in the mass media. In H. Resnik (Ed.), *Youth and drugs: Society's mixed messages.* Rockville, MD: Office for Substance Abuse Prevention, U.S. Department of Health and Human Services. (p. 227)

Gerbner, G., Morgan, M., & Signorielli, N. (1993). Television violence profile No. 16: The turning point from research to action. Annenberg School for Communication, University of Pennsylvania. (p. 604)

Gerhart, K. A., Koziol-McLain, J., Lowenstein, S. R., & Whiteneck, G. G. (1994). Quality of life following spinal cord injury: Knowledge and attitudes of emergency care providers. *Annals of Emergency Medicine, 23,* 807–812. (p. 426)

Gerrard, M., & Luus, C. A. E. (1995). Judgments of vulnerability to pregnancy: The role of risk factors and individual differences. *Personality and Social Psychology Bulletin, 21,* 160–171. (p. 379)

Gershoff, E. T. (2002). Parental corporal punishment and associated child behaviors and experiences: A meta-analytic and theoretical review. *Psychological Bulletin, 128,* 539–579. (p. 253)

Gershon, J., Anderson, P., Graap, K., Zimand, E., Hodges, L., & Rothbaum, B. O. (2002). Virtual reality exposure therapy in the treatment of anxiety disorders. *Scientific Review of Mental Health Practice, 1,* 76–81. (p. 547)

Gfeller, J. D., Lynn, S. J., & Pribble, W. E. (1987). Enhancing hypnotic susceptibility: Interpersonal and rapport factors. *Journal of Personality and Social Psychology, 52,* 586–595. (p. 214)

Gibbons, F. X. (1986). Social comparison and depression: Company's effect on misery. *Journal of Personality and Social Psychology, 51,* 140–148. (p. 430)

Gibbs, W. W. (1996, June). Mind readings. *Scientific American,* pp. 34–36. (p. 55)

Gibbs, W. W. (2002, August). Saving dying languages. *Scientific American,* pp. 79–85. (p. 321)

Gibbs, W. W. (2005, June). Obesity: An overblown epidemic? *Scientific American,* pp. 70–77. (p. 366)

Gibson, E. J., & Walk, R. D. (1960, April). The "visual cliff." *Scientific American,* pp. 64–71. (p. 173)

Gibson, H. B. (1995, April). Recovered memories. *The Psychologist,* pp. 153–154. (p. 212)

Gigerenzer, G. (2004). Fast and frugal heuristics: The tools of bounded rationality. In D. Koehler & N. Harvey (Eds.), *Handbook of judgment and decision making.* Oxford, UK: Blackwell. (pp. 314, 316)

Gilbert, D. T., Pelham, B. W., & Krull, D. S. (2003). The psychology of good ideas. *Psychological Inquiry, 14,* 258–260. (p. 14)

Gilbert, D. T., Pinel, E. C., Wilson, T. D., Blumberg, S. J., & Wheatley, T. P. (1998). Immune neglect: A source of durability bias in affective forecasting. *Journal of Personality and Social Psychology, 75,* 617–638. (p. 427)

Giles, D. E., Dahl, R. E., & Coble, P. A. (1994). Childbearing, developmental, and familial aspects of sleep. In J. M. Oldham & M. B. Riba (Eds.), *Review of Psychiatry, (Vol. 13).* Washington, DC: American Psychiatric Press. (p. 198)

Gilligan, C. (1982). *In a different voice: Psychological theory and women's development.* Cambridge, MA: Harvard University Press. (p. 89)

Gilligan, C., Lyons, N. P., & Hanmer, T. J. (Eds.). (1990). *Making connections: The relational worlds of adolescent girls at Emma Willard School.* Cambridge, MA: Harvard University Press. (p. 89)

Gilovich, T. (1991). *How we know what isn't so: The fallibility of human reason in everyday life.* New York: Free Press. (p. 23)

Gilovich, T., & Medvec, V. H. (1995). The experience of regret: What, when, and why. *Psychological Review, 102,* 379–395. (p. 137)

Gilovich, T., & Savitsky, K. (1999). The spotlight effect and the illusion of transparency: Egocentric assessments of how we are seen by others. *Current Directions in Psychological Science, 8,* 165–168. (p. 490)

Gilovich, T., Kruger, J., & Medvec, V. H. (2002). The spotlight effect revisited: Overestimating the manifest variability of our actions and appearance. *Journal of Experimental Social Psychology, 38,* 93–99. (p. 490)

Gilovich, T., Vallone, R., & Tversky, A. (1985). The hot hand in basketball: On the misperception of random sequences. *Cognitive Psychology, 17,* 295–314. (p. 24)

Gilovich, T. D. (1996). The spotlight effect: Exaggerated impressions of the self as a social stimulus. Unpublished manuscript, Cornell University. (p. 490)

Gingerich, O. (1999, February 6). Is there a role for natural theology today? *The Real Issue* (www.origins.org/real/n9501/natural.html). (p. 94)

Gladue, B. A. (1990). Hormones and neuroendocrine factors in atypical human sexual behavior. In J. R. Feierman (Ed.), *Pedophilia: Biosocial dimensions.* New York: Springer-Verlag. (p. 384)

Gladue, B. A. (1994). The biopsychology of sexual orientation. *Current Directions in Psychological Science, 3,* 150–154. (pp. 383, 385)

Gladwell, M. (2000, May 9). The new-boy network: What do job interviews really tell us? *New Yorker,* pp. 68–86. (p. 396)

Gladwell, M. (2004, September 20). Personality plus. *New Yorker,* pp. 42–48. (p. 475)

Glass, R. I. (2004). Perceived threats and real killers. *Science, 304,* 927. (p. 315)

Glass, R. M. (2001). Electroconvulsive therapy: Time to bring it out of the shadows. *Journal of the American Medical Association, 285,* 1346–1348. (p. 569)

Glater, J. D. (2001, March 26). Women are close to being majority of law students. *New York Times* (www.nytimes.com). (p. 91)

Gleaves, D. H. (1996). The sociocognitive model of dissociative identity disorder: A reexamination of the evidence. *Psychological Bulletin, 120,* 42–59. (p. 517)

Glenn, N. D. (1975). Psychological well-being in the postparental stage: Some evidence from national surveys. *Journal of Marriage and the Family, 37,* 105–110. (p. 136)

Glick, P., & 15 others. (2004). Bad but bold: Ambivalent attitudes toward men predict gender inequality in 16 nations. *Journal of Personality and Social Psychology, 86,* 713–728. (p. 596)

Glick, P., Gottesman, D., & Jolton, J. (1989). The fault is not in the stars: Susceptibility of skeptics and believers in astrology to the Barnum effect. *Personality and Social Psychology Bulletin, 15,* 572–583. (p. 481)

Godden, D. R., & Baddeley, A. D. (1975). Context-dependent memory in two natural environments: On land and underwater. *British Journal of Psychology, 66,* 325–331. (pp. 285, 286)

Goel, V., & Dolan, R. J. (2001). The functional anatomy of humor: Segregating cognitive and affective components. *Nature Neuroscience, 4,* 237–238. (p. 58)

Goff, D. C. (1993). Reply to Dr. Armstrong. *Journal of Nervous and Mental Disease, 181,* 604–605. (p. 516)

Goff, D. C., & Simms, C. A. (1993). Has multiple personality disorder remained consistent over time? *Journal of Nervous and Mental Disease, 181,* 595–600. (p. 516)

Goff, L. M., & Roediger, H. L., III. (1998). Imagination inflation for action events: Repeated imaginings lead to illusory recollections. *Memory and Cognition, 26,* 20–33. (p. 297)

Gold, M., & Yanof, D. S. (1985). Mothers, daughters, and girlfriends. *Journal of Personality and Social Psychology, 49,* 654–659. (p. 125)

Goldapple, K., Segal, Z., Garson, C., Lau, M., Bieling, P., Kennedy, S., & Mayberg, H. (2004). Modulation of cortical-limbic pathways in major depression. *Archives of General Psychiatry, 61,* 34–41. (p. 567)

Golden, R. N., Gaynes, B. N., Ekstrom, R. D., Hamer, R. M., Jacobsen, F. M., Suppes, T., Wisner, K. L., & Nemeroff, C. B. (2005). The efficacy of light therapy in the treatment of mood disorders: A review and meta-analysis of the evidence. *American Journal of Psychiatry, 162,* 656–662. (p. 559)

Goldfried, M. R. (2001). Integrating gay, lesbian, and bisexual issues into mainstream psychology. *American Psychologist, 56,* 977–988. (p. 524)

Goldfried, M. R., & Padawer, W. (1982). Current status and future directions in psychotherapy. In M. R. Goldfried (Ed.), *Converging themes in psychotherapy: Trends in psychodynamic, humanistic, and behavioral practice.* New York: Springer. (p. 559)

Goldfried, M. R., Raue, P. J., & Castonguay, L. G. (1998). The therapeutic focus in significant sessions of master therapists: A comparison of cognitive-behavioral and psychodynamic-interpersonal interventions. *Journal of Consulting and Clinical Psychology, 66,* 803–810. (p. 560)

Golding, J. M. (1996). Sexual assault history and women's reproductive and sexual health. *Psychology of Women Quarterly, 20,* 101–121. (p. 603)

Golding, J. M. (1999). Sexual-assault history and the long-term physical health problems: Evidence from clinical and population epidemiology. *Current Directions in Psychological Science, 8,* 191–194. (p. 512)

Goldstein, I. (2000, August). Male sexual circuitry. *Scientific American,* pp. 70–75. (p. 43)

Goldstein, I., Lue, T. F., Padma-Nathan, H., Rosen, R. C., Steers, W. D., & Wicker, P. A. (1998). Oral sildenafil in the treatment of erectile dysfunction. *New England Journal of Medicine, 338,* 1397–1404. (pp. 26, 603)

Goleman, D. (1995). *Emotional intelligence.* New York: Bantam. (p. 411)

Gonsalves, B., Reber, P. J., Gitelman, D. R., Parrish, T. B., Mesulam, M-M., & Paller, K. A. (2004). Neural evidence that vivid imagining can lead to false remembering. *Psychological Science, 15,* 655–659. (p. 297)

Goodall, J. (1968). The behaviour of free-living chimpanzees in the Gombe Stream Reserve. *Animal Behaviour Monographs, 1,* 161–311. (p. 80)

Goodall, J. (1986). *The chimpanzees of Gombe: Patterns of behavior.* Cambridge, MA: Harvard University Press. (p. 597)

Goodall, J. (1998). Learning from the chimpanzees: A message humans can understand. *Science, 282,* 2184–2185. (p. 20)

Goodchilds, J. (1987). Quoted by Carol Tavris, Old age is not what it used to be. *The New York Times Magazine: Good Health Magazine,* September 27, pp. 24–25, 91–92. (p. 130)

Goode, E. (1999, April 13). If things taste bad, 'phantoms' may be at work. *New York Times* (www.nytimes.com). (p. 163)

Goode, E. (2003, January 28). Even in the age of Prozac, some still prefer the couch. *New York Times* (www.nytimes.com). (p. 542)

Goodhart, D. E. (1986). The effects of positive and negative thinking on performance in an achievement situation. *Journal of Personality and Social Psychology, 51,* 117–124. (p. 488)

Goodman, G. S., Ghetti, S., Quas, J. A., Edelstein, R. S., Alexander, K. W., Redlich, A. D., Cordon, I. M., & Jones, D. P. H. (2003). A prospective study of memory for child sexual abuse: New findings relevant to the repressed-memory controversy. *Psychological Science, 14,* 113–118. (p. 300)

Goodman, G. S., Rudy, L., Bottoms, B. L., & Aman, B. (1990). Children's concerns and memory: Issues of ecological validity in the study of children's eyewitness testimony. In R. Fivush & J. A. Hudson (Eds.), *Knowing and remembering in young children.* New York: Cambridge University Press. (p. 299)

Goodstein, L., & Glaberson, W. (2000, April 9). The well-marked roads to homicidal rage. *New York Times* (www.nytimes.com). (p. 489)

Goodwin, F. K., & Morrison, A. R. (1999). Scientists in bunkers: How appeasement of animal rights activism has failed. *Cerebrum, 1(2),* 50–62. (p. 29)

Goodwin, R., & Hamilton, S. P. (2002). Cigarette smoking and panic: The role of neuroticism. *American Journal of Psychiatry, 159,* 1208–1213. (p. 510)

Gopnik, A., & Meltzoff, A. N. (1986). Relations between semantic and cognitive development in the one-word stage: The specificity hypothesis. *Child Development, 57,* 1040–1053. (p. 324)

Goranson, R. E. (1978). The hindsight effect in problem solving. Unpublished manuscript, cited by G. Wood (1984), Research methodology: A decision-making perspective. In A. M. Rogers & C. J. Scheirer (Eds.), *The G. Stanley Hall Lecture Series (Vol. 4).* Washington, DC: American Psychological Association. (p. 15)

Gordon, P. (2004). Numerical cognition without words: Evidence from Amazonia. *Science, 306,* 496–499. (p. 323)

Gore-Felton, C., Koopman, C., Thoresen, C., Arnow, B., Bridges, E., & Spiegel, D. (2000). Psychologists' beliefs and clinical characteristics: Judging the veracity of childhood sexual abuse memories. *Professional Psychology: Research and Practice, 31,* 372–377. (p. 300)

Gortmaker, S. L., Must, A., Perrin, J. M., Sobol, A. M., & Dietz, W. H. (1993). Social and economic consequences of overweight in adolescence and young adulthood. *New England Journal of Medicine, 329,* 1008–1012. (p. 368)

Gosling, S. D., Ko, S. J., Mannarelli, T., & Morris, M. E. (2002). A room with a cue: Personality judgments based on offices and bedrooms. *Journal of Personality and Social Psychology, 82,* 379–398. (p. 482)

Gosling, S. D., Kwan, V. S. Y., & John, O. P. (2003). A dog's got personality: A cross-species comparative approach to personality judgments in dogs and humans. *Journal of Personality and Social Psychology, 85,* 1161–1169. (p. 476)

Gotlib, I. H., & Hammen, C. L. (1992). *Psychological aspects of depression: Toward a cognitive-interpersonal integration.* New York: Wiley. (p. 528)

Gottesman, I. I. (1991). *Schizophrenia genesis: The origins of madness.* New York: Freeman. (p. 536)

Gottesman, I. I. (2001). Psychopathology through a life span—genetic prism. *American Psychologist, 56,* 867–881. (p. 489), 535)

Gottfredson, L. S. (2002a). Where and why g matters: Not a mystery. *Human Performance, 15,* 25–46. (p. 332)

Gottfredson, L. S. (2002b). g: Highly general and highly practical. In R. J. Sternberg & E. L. Grigorenko (Eds.), *The general factor of intelligence: How general is it?* Mahwah, NJ: Erlbaum. (p. 332)

Gottfredson, L. S. (2003a). Dissecting practical intelligence theory: Its claims and evidence. *Intelligence, 31,* 343–397. (p. 332)

Gottfredson, L. S. (2003b). On Sternberg's "Reply to Gottfredson." *Intelligence, 31,* 415–424. (p. 332)

Gottfried, J. A., O'Doherty, J., & Dolan, R. J. (2003). Encoding predictive reward value in human amygdala and orbitofrontal cortex. *Science, 301,* 1104–1108. (p. 237)

Gould, E., Reeves, A. J., Graziano, M. S. A., & Gross, C. G. (1999). Neurogenesis in the neocortex of adult primates. *Science, 286,* 548–552. (p. 60)

Gould, S. J. (1981). *The mismeasure of man.* New York: Norton. (p. 337)

Gould, S. J. (1997, June 12). Darwinian fundamentalism. *The New York Review of Books, XLIV(10),* 34–37. (p. 77)

Grady, C. L., & McIntosh, A. R., Horwitz, B., Maisog, J. M., Ungeleider, L. G., Mentis, M. J., Pietrini, P., Schapiro, M. B., & Haxby, J. V. (1995). Age-related reductions in human recognition memory due to impaired encoding. *Science, 269,* 218–221. (p. 291)

Graf, P. (1990). Life-span changes in implicit and explicit memory. *Bulletin of the Psychonomic Society, 28,* 353–358. (p. 133)

Graham, J. W., Marks, G., & Hansen, W. B. (1991). Social influence processes affecting adolescent substance use. *Journal of Applied Psychology, 76,* 291–298. (p. 227)

Grant, B. F., & Dawson, D. A. (1998). Age of onset of drug use and its association with DSM-IV drug abuse and dependence: Results from the national Longitudinal Alcohol Epidemiologic Survey. *Journal of Substance Abuse, 10,* 163–173. (pp. 229, C-5)

Grant, B. F., Stinson, F. S., Hasin, D. S., Dawson, D. A., Chou, S. P., & Anderson, K. (2004). Immigration and lifetime prevalence of DSM-IV psychiatric disorders among Mexican Americans and non-Hispanic Whites in the United States. *Archives of General Psychiatry, 61,* 1226–1233. (p. 506)

Gray-Little, B., & Burks, N. (1983). Power and satisfaction in marriage: A review and critique. *Psychological Bulletin, 93,* 513–538. (p. 612)

Gray-Little, B., & Hafdahl, A. R. (2000). Factors influencing racial comparisons of self-esteem: A quantitative review. *Psychological Bulletin, 126,* 26–54. (p. 492)

Green, B. (2002). Listening to leaders: Feedback on 360-degree feedback one year later. *Organizational Development Journal, 20,* 8–16. (p. 397)

Green, J. T., & Woodruff-Pak, D. S. (2000). Eyeblink classical conditioning: Hippocampal formation is for neutral stimulus associations as cerebellum is for association-response. *Psychological Bulletin, 126,* 138–158. (p. 283)

Greene, R. L. (1987). Effects of maintenance rehearsal on human memory. *Psychological Bulletin, 102,* 403–413. (p. 273)

Greenfeld, L. A. (1998). *Alcohol and crime: An analysis of national data on the prevalence of alcohol involvement in crime.* Washington, DC: Document NCJ–168632, Bureau of Justice Statistics (www.ojp.usdoj.gov/bjs). (p. 601),

Greenwald, A. G. (1992). Subliminal semantic activation and subliminal snake oil. Paper presented to the American Psychological Association Convention, Washington, DC. (pp. 141, 145, 467)

Greenwald, A. G., McGhee, D. E., & Schwartz, J. L. K. (1998). Measuring individual differences in implicit cognition: The implicit association test. *Journal of Personality and Social Psychology, 74,* 1464–1480. (p. 595)

Greenwald, A. G., Oakes, M. A., & Hoffman, H. (2003). Targets of discrimination: Effects of race on responses to weapons holders. *Journal of Experimental Social Psychology, 39,* 399. (p. 595)

Greenwald, A. G., Spangenberg, E. R., Pratkanis, A. R., & Eskenazi, J. (1991). Double-blind tests of subliminal self-help audiotapes. *Psychological Science, 2,* 119–122. (p. 145)

Greenwood, M. R. C. (1989). Sexual dimorphism and obesity. In A. J. Stunkard & A. Baum (Eds.). *Perspectives in behavioral medicine: Eating, sleeping, and sex.* Hillsdale, NJ: Erlbaum. (p. 366)

Greers, A. E. (2004). Speech, language, and reading skills after early cochlear implantation. *Archives of Otolaryngology—Head & Neck Surgery, 130,* 634–638. (p. 321)

Gregory, R. L. (1978). *Eye and brain: The psychology of seeing (3rd ed.).* New York: McGraw-Hill. (p. 181)

Gregory, R. L., & Gombrich, E. H. (Eds.). (1973). *Illusion in nature and art.* New York: Charles Scribner's Sons. (p. 185)

Greif, E. B., & Ulman, K. J. (1982). The psychological impact of menarche on early adolescent females: A review of the literature. *Child Development, 53,* 1413–1430. (p. 121)

Greist, J. H., Jefferson, J. W., & Marks, I. M. (1986). *Anxiety and its treatment: Help is available.* Washington, DC: American Psychiatric Press. (p. 510)

Grewal, D., & Salovey, P. (2005). Feeling smart: The science of emotional intelligence. *American Scientist, 93,* 330–339. (p. 335)

Grèzes, J., & Decety, J. (2001). Function anatomy of execution, mental simulation, observation, and verb generation of actions: A meta-analysis. *Human Brain Mapping, 12,* 1–19. (p. 325)

Griffiths, M. (2001). Sex on the Internet: Observations and implications for Internet sex addiction. *Journal of Sex Research, 38,* 333–342. (p. 217)

Grill-Spector, K., & Kanwisher, N. (2005). Visual recognition: As soon as you know it is there, you know what it is. *Psychological Science, 16,* 152–160. (p. 307)

Grilo, C. M., & Pogue-Geile, M. F. (1991). The nature of environmental influences on weight and obesity: A behavior genetic analysis. *Psychological Bulletin, 110,* 520–537. (p. 369)

Grobstein, C. (1979, June). External human fertilization. *Scientific American,* pp. 57–67. (p. 101)

Groothuis, T. G. G., & Carere, C. (2005). Avian personalities: Characterization and epigenesis. *Neuroscience and Biobehavioral Reviews, 29,* 137–150. (p. 477)

Gross, A. E., & Crofton, C. (1977). What is good is beautiful. *Sociometry, 40,* 85–90. (p. 610)

Grossberg, S. (1995). The attentive brain. *American Scientist, 83,* 438–449. (p. 184)

Grossman, M., & Wood, W. (1993). Sex differences in intensity of emotional experience: A social role interpretation. *Journal of Personality and Social Psychology, 65,* 1010–1022. (p. 419)

Gruder, C. L. (1977). Choice of comparison persons in evaluating oneself. In J. M. Suls & R. L. Miller (Eds.), *Social comparison processes.* New York: Hemisphere. (p. 430)

Grunebaum, M. F., Ellis, S. P., Li, S., O(quendo, M. A., Mann, J. J. (2004). Antidepressants and suicide risk in the United States, 1985–1999. *Journal of Clinical Psychiatry, 65,* 1456–1462. (p. 568)

Guerin, B. (1986). Mere presence effects in humans: A review. *Journal of Personality and Social Psychology, 22,* 38–77. (p. 588)

Guerin, B. (2003). Language use as social strategy: A review and an analytic framework for the social sciences. *Review of General Psychology, 7,* 251–298. (p. 319)

Guilbault, R. L., Bryant, F. B., Brockway, J. H., & Posavac, E. J. (2004). A meta-analysis of research on hindsight bias. *Basic and Applied Social Psychology, 26,* 103–117. (p. 14)

Guisinger, S. (2004). Adapted to flee famine: Adding an evolutionary perspective on anorexia nervosa. *Psychological Review, 110,* 745–761. (p. 364)

Gundersen, E. (2001, August 1). MTV is a many splintered thing. *USA Today,* pp. D1, D2. (p. 264)

Gustafson, D., Lissner, L., Bengtsson, C., Björkelund, C., & Skoog, I. (2004). A 24-year follow-up of body mass index and cerebral atrophy. *Neurology, 63,* 1876–1881. (p. 366)

Gustafson, D., Rothenberg, E., Blennow, K., Steen, B., & Skoog, I. (2003). An 18-year follow-up of overweight and risk of Alzheimer disease. *Archives of Internal Medicine, 163,* 1524–1528. (p. 366)

Gustavson, C. R., Garcia, J., Hankins, W. G., & Rusiniak, K. W. (1974). Coyote predation control by aversive conditioning. *Science, 184,* 581–583. (p. 245)

Gustavson, C. R., Kelly, D. J., & Sweeney, M. (1976). Prey-lithium aversions I: Coyotes and wolves. *Behavioral Biology, 17,* 61–72. (p. 245)

Guttmacher Institute. (1994). *Sex and America's teenagers.* New York: Alan Guttmacher Institute. (pp. 127, 379)

Guttmacher Institute. (2000). *Fulfilling the promise: Public policy and U.S. family planning clinics.* New York: Alan Guttmacher Institute. (p. 127)

H., Sally. (1979, August). Videotape recording number T–3, Fortunoff Video Archive of Holocaust Testimonies. New Haven, CT: Yale University Library. (p. 466)

Haber, R. N. (1970, May). How we remember what we see. *Scientific American,* pp. 104–112. (p. 269)

Haddock, G., & Zanna, M. P. (1994). Preferring "housewives" to "feminists." *Psychology of Women Quarterly, 18,* 25–52. (p. 596)

Hakuta, K., Bialystok, E., & Wiley, E. (2003). Critical evidence: A test of the critical-period hypothesis for second-language acquisition. *Psychological Science, 14,* 31–38. (p. 322)

Halberstadt, J. B., Niedenthal, P. M., & Kushner, J. (1995). Resolution of lexical ambiguity by emotional state. *Psychological Science, 6,* 278–281. (p. 184)

Haldeman, D. C. (1994). The practice and ethics of sexual orientation conversion therapy. *Journal of Consulting and Clinical Psychology, 62,* 221–227. (p. 381)

Haldeman, D. C. (2002). Gay rights, patient rights: The implications of sexual orientation conversion therapy. *Professional Psychology: Research and Practice, 33,* 260–264. (p. 381)

Hall, C. S., & Lindzey, G. (1978). *Theories of personality (2nd ed.).* New York: Wiley. (p. 467)

Hall, C. S., Dornhoff, W., Blick, K. A., & Weesner, K. E. (1982). The dreams of college men and women in 1950 and 1980: A comparison of dream contents and sex differences. *Sleep, 5,* 188–194. (p. 206)

Hall, G. (1997). Context aversion, Pavlovian conditioning, and the psychological side effects of chemotherapy. *European Psychologist, 2,* 118–124. (p. 246)

Hall, G. S. (1904). *Adolescence: Its psychology and its relations to physiology, anthropology, sex, crime, religion and education (Vol. I).* New York: Appleton-Century-Crofts. (p. 120)

Hall, J. A. (1984). *Nonverbal sex differences: Communication accuracy and expressive style.* Baltimore: Johns Hopkins University Press. (p. 419)

Hall, J. A. (1987). On explaining gender differences: The case of nonverbal communication. In P. Shaver & C. Hendrick (Eds.), *Review of Personality and Social Psychology, 7,* 177–200. (pp. 88, 419)

Hall, J. A. Y., & Kimura, D. (1994). Dermatoglyphic assymetry and sexual orientation in men. *Behavioral Neuroscience, 108,* 1203–1206. (p. 385)

Hall, S. S. (2004, May). The good egg. *Discover,* pp. 30–39. (p. 101)

Halpern, C. T., Joyner, K., Udry, J. R., & Suchindran, C. (2000). Smart teens don't have sex (or kiss much either). *Journal of Adolescent Health, 26,* 213–225. (p. 380)

Halpern, D. F. (1991). Cognitive sex differences: Why diversity is a critical research issue. Paper presented to the American Psychological Association convention. (p. 348)

Halpern, D. F. (2000). *Sex-related ability differences: Changing perspectives, changing minds.* Mahwah, NJ: Erlbaum. (pp. 347, 349)

Halpern, D. F. (2005, May 20). Response to Drs. Pinker and Spelke. www.edge.org. (p. 350)

Halsey, A. H., & Webb, J. (2000). *Twentieth-century British social trends.* Basingstoke: Macmillan. (p. 366)

Hamann, S., Herman, R. A., Nolan, C. L., & Wallen, K. (2004). Men and women differ in amygdala response to visual sexual stimuli. *Nature Neuroscience, 7,* 411–416. (p. 378)

Hamann, S., Monarch, E. S., & Goldstein, F. C. (2002). Impaired fear conditioning in Alzheimer's disease. *Neuropsychologica, 40,* 1187–1195. (p. 280)

Hammer, E. (2003). How lucky you are to be a psychology major. *Eye on Psi Chi, 4–5.* (p. B-8)

Hammersmith, S. K. (1982, August). Sexual preference: An empirical study from the Alfred C. Kinsey Institute for Sex Research. Paper presented at the meeting of the American Psychological Association, Washington, DC. (p. 382)

Hampson, R. (2000, April 10). In the end, people just need more room. *USA Today,* p. 19A. (p. 370)

Hankin, B. L., & Abramson, L. Y. (2001). Development of gender differences in depression: An elaborated cognitive vulnerability-transactional stress theory. *Psychological Bulletin, 127,* 773–796. (p. 527)

Hansen, C. H., & Hansen, R. D. (1988). Finding the face-in-the-crowd: An anger superiority effect. *Journal of Personality and Social Psychology, 54,* 917–924. (p. 417)

Harber, K. D. (1998), Feedback to minorities: Evidence of a positive bias. *Journal of Personality and Social Psychology, 74,* 622–628. (p. 595)

Hardin, C., & Banaji, M. R. (1993). The influence of language on thought. *Social Cognition, 11,* 277–308. (p. 323)

Hare, R. D. (1975). Psychophysiological studies of psychopathy. In D. C. Fowles (Ed.), *Clinical applications of psychophysiology.* New York: Columbia University Press. (p. 518)

Harkins, S. G., & Szymanski, K. (1989). Social loafing and group evaluation. *Journal of Personality and Social Psychology, 56,* 934–941. (p. 589)

Harlow, H. F., Harlow, M. K., & Suomi, S. J. (1971). From thought to therapy: Lessons from a primate laboratory. *American Scientist, 59,* 538–549. (p. 113)

Harmon-Jones, E., Abramson, L. Y., Sigelman, J., Bohlig, A., Hogan, M. E., & Harmon-Jones, C. (2002). Proneness to hypomania/mania symptoms or depression symptoms and asymmetrical frontal cortical responses to an anger-evoking event. *Journal of Personality and Social Psychology, 82,* 610–618. (p. 411)

Harris, B. (1979). Whatever happened to Little Albert? *American Psychologist, 34,* 151–160. (p. 247)

Harris, J. A. (1999). Review and methodological considerations in research on testosterone and aggression. *Aggression and Violent Behavior, 4,* 273–291. (p. 601)

Harris, J. R. (1998). *The nurture assumption.* New York: Free Press. (pp. 81)

Harris, J. R. (2006). *No two are alike: Human nature and human individuality.* New York: Norton. (p. 70)

Harris, R. J. (1994). The impact of sexually explicit media. In J. Brant & D. Zillmann (Eds.), *Media effects: Advances in theory and research.* Hillsdale, NJ: Erlbaum. (p. 603)

Harrison, Y., & Horne, J. A. (2000). The impact of sleep deprivation on decision making: A review. *Journal of Experimental Psychology: Applied, 6,* 236–249. (p. 202)

Harter, J. K. (2000, Winter/Spring). The linkage of employee perceptions to outcomes in a retail environment—cause and effect? *Gallup Research Journal,* pp. 25–38. (p. 400)

Harter, J. K., Schmidt, F. L., & Hayes, T. L. (2002). Business-unit-level relationship between employee satisfaction, employee engagement, and business outcomes: A meta-analysis. *Journal of Applied Psychology, 87,* 268–279. (p. 399)

Hartmann, E. (1981, April). The strangest sleep disorder. *Psychology Today,* pp. 14, 16, 18. (p. 205)

Hassan, R., & Carr, J. (1989). Changing patterns of suicide in Australia. *Australian and New Zealand Journal of Psychiatry, 23,* 226–234. (p. 524)

Hatfield, E. (1988). Passionate and companionate love. In R. J. Sternberg & M. L. Barnes (Eds.), *The psychology of love.* New Haven: Yale University Press. (p. 611)

Hatfield, E., & Sprecher, S. (1986). *Mirror, mirror . . . The importance of looks in everyday life.* Albany: State University of New York Press. (p. 608)

Hathaway, S. R. (1960). *An MMPI Handbook* (Vol. 1, Foreword). Minneapolis: University of Minnesota Press. (Revised edition, 1972). (p. 477)

Haxby, J. V. (2001, July 7). Quoted by B. Bower, Faces of perception. *Science News,* pp. 10–12. See also J. V. Haxby, M. I. Gobbini, M. L. Furey, A. Ishai, J. L. Schouten & P. Pietrini, Distributed and overlapping representations of faces and objects in ventral temporal cortex. *Science, 293,* 2425–2430. (p. 151)

Head Start. (2005). Head Start program fact sheet. www.acf.hhs.gov/. (p. 344)

Healey, J. (2004). *Overweight and obesity.* Thirroul, NSW, Australia: Spinney Press. (p. 366)

Heaps, C. M., & Nash, M. (2001). Comparing recollective experience in true and false autobiographical memories. *Journal of Experimental Psychology: Learning, Memory, and Cognition, 27,* 920–930. (p. 300)

Hebb, D. O. (1980). *Essay on mind.* Hillsdale, NJ: Erlbaum. 9–16. (pp. 246, 406)

Hebl, M. R., & Mannix, L. M. (2003). The weight of obesity in evaluating others: A mere proximity effect. *Personality and Social Psychology Bulletin, 29,* 28–38. (p. 368)

Hedges, L. V., & Nowell, A. (1995). Sex differences in mental test scores, variability, and numbers of high-scoring individuals. *Science, 269,* 41–45. (pp. 347, 348)

Heider, F. (1958). *The psychology of interpersonal relations.* New York: Wiley. (p. 575)

Heiman, J. R. (1975, April). The physiology of erotica: Women's sexual arousal. *Psychology Today,* 90–94. (p. 378)

Heins, M. (2004, December 14). Quoted by B. Kloza, Violent Christmas games. *ScienCentralNews* (www.sciencecentral.com). (p. 605)

Hejmadi, A., Davidson, R. J., & Rozin, P. (2000). Exploring Hindu Indian emotion expressions: Evidence for accurate recognition by Americans and Indians. *Psychological Science, 11,* 183–187. (p. 418)

Heller, W. (1990, May/June). Of one mind: Second thoughts about the brain's dual nature. *The Sciences,* pp. 38–44. (p. 63)

Helmreich, W. B. (1992). *Against all odds: Holocaust survivors and the successful lives they made in America.* New York: Simon & Schuster. (pp. 116, 466)

Helmreich, W. B. (1994). Personal correspondence. Department of Sociology, City University of New York. (p. 466)

Helms, J. E., Jernigan, M., & Mascher, J. (2005). The meaning of race in psychology and how to change it: A methodological perspective. *American Psychologist, 60,* 27–36. (p. 346)

Helmuth, L. (2001). Boosting brain activity from the outside in. *Science, 292,* 1284–1286. (p. 570)

Hembree, R. (1988). Correlates, causes, effects, and treatment of test anxiety. *Review of Educational Research, 58,* 47–77. (p. 410)

Hemenover, S. H. (2003). The good, the bad, and the healthy: Impacts of emotional disclosure of trauma on resilient self-concept and psychological distress. *Personality and Social Psychology Bulletin, 29,* 1236–1244. (p. 449)

Henderlong, J., & Lepper, M. R. (2002). The effects of praise on children's intrinsic motivation: A review and synthesis. *Psychological Bulletin, 128,* 774–795. (p. 255)

Henkel, L. A., Franklin, N., & Johnson, M. K. (2000, March). Cross-modal source monitoring confusions between perceived and imagined events. *Journal of Experimental Psychology: Learning, Memory, & Cognition, 26,* 321–335. (p. 298)

Henley, N. M. (1989). Molehill or mountain? What we know and don't know about sex bias in language. In M. Crawford & M. Gentry (Eds.), *Gender and thought: Psychological perspectives.* New York: Springer-Verlag. (p. 324)

Henninger, P. (1992). Conditional handedness: Handedness changes in multiple personality disordered subject reflect shift in hemispheric dominance. *Consciousness and Cognition, 1,* 265–287. (p. 516)

Herbert, B. (2001, July 23). Economics 202 at Big Tobacco U. *New York Times* (www.nytimes.com). (p. 220)

Herbert, J. D., Lilienfeld, S. O., Lohr, J. M., Montgomery, R. W., O'Donohue, W. T., Rosen, G. M., & Tolin, D. F. (2000). Science and pseudoscience in the development of eye movement desensitization and reprocessing: Implications for clinical psychology. *Clinical Psychology Review, 20,* 945–971. (p. 558)

Herman, C. P., & Polivy, J. (1980). Restrained eating. In A. J. Stunkard (Ed.), *Obesity.* Philadelphia: Saunders. (p. 372)

Herman-Giddens, M. E., Wang, L., & Koch, G. (2001). Secondary sexual characteristics in boys: Estimates from the National Health and Nutrition Examination Survey III, 1988–1994. *Archives of Pediatrics and Adolescent Medicine, 155,* 1022–1028. (p. 120)

Herrmann, D. (1982). Know thy memory: The use of questionnaires to assess and study memory. *Psychological Bulletin, 92,* 434–452. (p. 301)

Herrnstein, R. J., & Loveland, D. H. (1964). Complex visual concept in the pigeon. *Science, 146,* 549–551. (p. 247)

Herrnstein, R. J., & Murray, C. A. (1994). *The bell curve: Intelligence and class structure in American life.* NY: Free Press. (p. 346)

Hershenson, M. (1989). *The moon illusion.* Hillsdale, NJ: Erlbaum. (p. 178)

Hertenstein, M. J. (2002). Touch: Its communicative functions in infancy. *Human Development, 45,* 70–94. (p. 114)

Herz, R. S. (2001). Ah sweet skunk! Why we like or dislike what we smell. *Cerebrum, 3(4),* 31–47. (p. 167)

Herz, R. S., Schankler, C., & Beland, S. (2004). Olfaction, emotion and associative learning: Effects on motivated behavior. *Motivation and Emotion, 28(4),* 363–383. (p. 167)

Hess, E. H. (1956, July). Space perception in the chick. *Scientific American,* pp. 71–80. (p. 182)

Hettema, J. M., Neale, M. C., & Kendler, K. S. (2001). A review and meta-analysis of the genetic epidemiology of anxiety disorders. *American Journal of Psychiatry, 158,* 1568–1578. (p. 514)

Hewlett, B. S. (1991). *Intimate fathers: The nature and context of Aka Pygmy.* Ann Arbor: University of Michigan Press. (p. 115)

Hickok, G., Bellugi, U., & Klima, E. S. (2001, June). Sign language in the brain. *Scientific American,* pp. 58–65. (p. 62)

Hilgard, E. R. (1986). *Divided consciousness: Multiple controls in human thought and action.* New York: Wiley. (p. 215)

Hilgard, E. R. (1992). Dissociation and theories of hypnosis. In E. Fromm & M. R. Nash (Eds.), *Contemporary hypnosis research.* New York: Guilford. (p. 215)

Hill, C. E., & Nakayama, E. Y. (2000). Client-centered therapy: Where has it been and where is it going? A comment on Hathaway. *Journal of Clinical Psychology, 56,* 961–875. (p. 544)

Hill, H., & Johnston, A. (2001). Categorizing sex and identity from the biological motion of faces. *Current Biology, 11,* 880–885. (p. 420)

Hines, M. (2004). *Brain gender.* New York: Oxford University Press. (p. 90)

Hingson, R. W., Heeren, T., Zakocs, R. C., Kopstein, A., & Wechsler, H. (2002). Magnitude of alcohol-related mortality and morbidity among U.S. college students ages 18–24. *Journal of Studies on Alcohol, 63,* 136–144. (p. 219)

Hintzman, D. L. (1978). *The psychology of learning and memory.* San Francisco: Freeman. (p. 276)

Hinz, L. D., & Williamson, D. A. (1987). Bulimia and depression: A review of the affective variant hypothesis. *Psychological Bulletin, 102,* 150–158. (p. 364)

Hirsch, J. (2003). Obesity: Matter over mind? *Cerebrum, 5(1),* 7–18. (p. 368)

HMHL. (2002, August). Smoking and depression. *Harvard Mental Health Letter,* pp. 6–7. (p. 526)

HMHL. (2002, January). Disaster and trauma. *Harvard Mental Health Letter,* pp. 1–5. (p. 437)

Hobson, J. A. (1995, September). Quoted by C. H. Colt, The power of dreams. *Life,* pp. 36–49. (p. 207)

Hobson, J. A. (2003). *Dreaming: An introduction to the science of sleep.* New York: Oxford. (p. 208)

Hobson, J. A. (2004). *13 dreams Freud never had: The new mind science.* New York: Pi Press. (p. 208)

Hoebel, B. G., & Teitelbaum, P. (1966). Effects of forcefeeding and starvation on food intake and body weight in a rat with ventromedial hypothalamic lesions. *Journal of Comparative and Physiological Psychology, 61,* 189–193. (p. 361)

Hoffman, C., & Hurst, N. (1990). Gender stereotypes: Perception or rationalization? *Journal of Personality and Social Psychology, 58,* 197–208. (p. 596)

Hoffman, D. D. (1998). *Visual intelligence: How we create what we see.* New York: Norton. (p. 152)

Hoffman, H. G. (2004, August). Virtual-reality therapy. *Scientific American,* pp. 58–65. (pp. 158, 164)

Hoffman, H. G. (2004, August). Virtual-reality therapy. *Scientific American,* pp. 58–65. (pp. 158, 547)

Hogan, J. (1995, November). Get smart, take a test. *Scientific American,* pp. 12, 14. (p. 341)

Hogan, R. (1998). Reinventing personality. *Journal of Social and Clinical Psychology, 17,* 1–10. (p. 482)

Hoge, C. W., Castro, C. A., Messer, S. C., McGurk, D., Cotting, D. I., & Koffman, R. L. (2004). Combat duty in Iraq and Afghanistan, mental health problems, and barriers to care. *New England Journal of Medicine, 35,* 13–22. (p. 512)

Hogg, M. A. (1996). Intragroup processes, group structure and social identity. In W. P. Robinson (Ed.), *Social groups and identities: Developing the legacy of Henri Tajfel.* Oxford: Butterworth Heinemann. (p. 597)

Hohmann, G. W. (1966). Some effects of spinal cord lesions on experienced emotional feelings. *Psychophysiology, 3,* 143–156. (p. 408)

Hokanson, J. E., & Edelman, R. (1966). Effects of three social responses on vascular processes. *Journal of Personality and Social Psychology, 3,* 442–447. (p. 424)

Holahan, C. K., & Sears, R. R. (1995). *The gifted group in later maturity.* Stanford, CA: Stanford University Press. (p. 340)

Holden, C. (1980a). Identical twins reared apart. *Science, 207,* 1323–1325. (p. 70)

Holden, C. (1980b, November). Twins reunited. *Science, 80,* 55–59. (p. 70)

Holden, C. (1986). Researchers grapple with problems of updating classic psychological test. *Science, 233,* 1249–1251. (p. 473)

Holden, C. (1993). Wake-up call for sleep research. *Science, 259,* 305. (p. 201)

Holliday, R. E., & Albon, A. J. (2004). Minimizing misinformation effects in young children with cognitive interview mnemonics. *Applied Cognitive Psychology, 18,* 263–281. (p. 299)

Hollis, K. L. (1997). Contemporary research on Pavlovian conditioning: A "new" functional analysis. *American Psychologist, 52,* 956–965. (p. 238)

Hollon, S. D., & 10 others. (2005). Prevention of relapse following cognitive therapy vs. medications in moderate to severe depression. *Archives of General Psychiatry, 62,* 417–422. (p. 557)

Hollon, S. D., Thase, M. E., & Markowitz, J. C. (2002). Treatment and prevention of depression. *Psychological Science in the Public Interest, 3,* 39–77. (p. 567)

Holstege, G., Georgiadis, J. R., Paans, A. M. J., Meiners, L. C., van der Graaf, F. H. C. E., & Reinders, A. A. T. S. (2003a). Brain activation during male ejaculation. *Journal of Neuroscience, 23,* 9185–9193. (p. 375)

Holstege, G., Reinders, A. A. T., Paans, A. M. J., Meiners, L. C., Pruim, J., & Georgiadis, J. R. (2003b). *Brain activation during female sexual orgasm. Program No. 727.7.* Washington, DC: Society for Neuroscience. (p. 375)

Holzman, P. S., & Matthysse, S. (1990). The genetics of schizophrenia: A review. *Psychological Science, 1,* 279–286. (p. 146)

Home Office. (2003). *Prevalence of drug use: Key findings from the 2002/2003 British Crime Survey.* London: Research, Development and Statistics Directorate, Home Office. (p. 222)

Hooper, J., & Teresi, D. (1986). *The three-pound universe.* New York: Macmillan. (p. 53)

Hooykaas, R. (1972). *Religion and the rise of modern science.* Grand Rapids, MI: Eerdmans. (p. 16)

Horn, J. L. (1982). The aging of human abilities. In J. Wolman (Ed.), *Handbook of developmental psychology.* Englewood Cliffs, NJ: Prentice-Hall. (p. 134)

Horowitz, T. S., Cade, B. E., Wolfe, J. M., & Czeisler, C. A. (2003). Searching night and day: A dissociation of effects of circadian phase and time awake on visual selective attention and vigilance. *Psychological Science, 14,* 549–557. (p. 202)

Horwood, L. J., & Fergusson, D. M. (1998). Breastfeeding and later cognitive and academic outcomes. *Pediatrics, 101(1).* (p. 21)

House, J. S., Landis, K. R., & Umberson, D. (1988). *Social relationships and health. Science, 241,* 540–545. (p. 447)

House, R. J., & Singh, J. V. (1987). Organizational behavior: Some new directions for I/O psychology. *Annual Review of Psychology, 38,* 669–718. (p. 402)

Houts, A. C., Berman, J. S., & Abramson, H. (1994). Effectiveness of psychological and pharmacological treatments for nocturnal enuresis. *Journal of Consulting and Clinical Psychology, 62,* 737–745. (p. 545)

Howe, M. L. (1997). Children's memory for traumatic experiences. *Learning and Individual Differences, 9,* 153–174. (p. 299)

Hoyer, G., & Lund, E. (1993). Suicide among women related to number of children in marriage. *Archives of General Psychiatry, 50,* 134–137. (p. 524)

Hu, F. B., Li, T. Y., Colditz, G. A., Willett, W. C., & Manson, J. E. (2003). Television watching and other sedentary behaviors in relation to risk of obesity and type 2 diabetes mellitus in women. *Journal of the American Medical Association, 289,* 1785–1791. (p. 370)

Hubel, D. H. (1979, September). The brain. *Scientific American,* pp. 45–53. (p. 146)

Hubel, D. H., & Wiesel, T. N. (1979, September). Brian mechanisms of vision. *Scientific American,* pp. 150–162. (p. 151)

Hublin, C., Kaprio, J., Partinen, M., & Koskenvuo, M. (1998). Sleeptalking in twins: Epidemiology and psychiatric comorbidity. *Behavior Genetics, 28,* 289–298. (p. 205)

Hublin, C., Kaprio, J., Partinen, M., Heikkila, K., & Koskenvuo, M. (1997). Prevalence and genetics of sleepwalking—A population-based twin study. *Neurology, 48,* 177–181. (p. 205)

Hucker, S. J., & Bain, J. (1990). Androgenic hormones and sexual assault. In W. Marshall, R. Law, & H. Barbaree (Eds.), *The handbook on sexual assault.* New York: Plenum. (p. 377)

Huffcutt, A. I., Conway, J. M., Roth, P. L., & Stone, N. J. (2001). Identification and meta-analytic assessment of psychological constructs measured in employment interviews. *Journal of Applied Psychology, 86,* 897–913. (p. 396)

Hugenberg, K., & Bodenhausen, G. V. (2003). Facing prejudice: Implicit prejudice and the perception of facial threat. *Psychological Science, 14,* 640–643. (p. 595)

Hughes, H. C. (1999). *Sensory exotica: A world beyond human experience.* Cambridge, MA: MIT Press. (p. 144)

Hugick, L. (1989, July). Women play the leading role in keeping modern families close. *Gallup Report, No. 286,* pp. 27–34. (p. 89)

Hull, J. G., & Bond, C. F., Jr. (1986). Social and behavioral consequences of alcohol consumption and expectancy: A meta-analysis. *Psychological Bulletin, 99,* 347–360. (p. 218)

Hull, J. M. (1990). *Touching the rock: An experience of blindness.* New York: Vintage Books. (pp. 285, 609)

Hulme, C., & Tordoff, V. (1989). Working memory development: The effects of speech rate, word length, and acoustic similarity on serial recall. *Journal of Experimental Child Psychology, 47,* 72–87. (p. 278)

Hummer, R. A., Rogers, R. G., Nam, C. B., & Ellison, C. G. (1999). Religious involvement and U.S. adult mortality. *Demography, 36,* 273–285. (pp. 415, 455)

Hunsley, J., & Di Giulio, G. (2002). Dodo bird, phoenix, or urban legend? The question of psychotherapy equivalence. *Scientific Review of Mental Health Practice, 1,* 11–22. (p. 557)

Hunt, C., Slade, T., & Andrews, G. (2004). Generalized anxiety disorder and major depressive disorder comorbidity in the *National Survey of Mental Health and Well-Being. Depression and Anxiety, 20,* 23–31. (p. 510)

Hunt, J. M. (1982). Toward equalizing the developmental opportunities of infants and preschool children. *Journal of Social Issues, 38(4),* 163–191. (p. 344)

Hunt, M. (1974). *Sexual behavior in the 1970s.* Chicago: Playboy Press. (p. 378)

Hunt, M. (1990). *The compassionate beast: What science is discovering about the humane side of humankind.* New York: William Morrow. (p. 9)

Hunt, M. (1993). *The story of psychology.* New York: Doubleday. (pp. 3, 247)

Hunter, J. E. (1997). Needed: A ban on the significance test. *Psychological Science, 8,* 3–7. (p. A-8)

Hunter, S., & Sundel, M. (Eds.). (1989). *Midlife myths: Issues, findings, and practice implications.* Newbury Park, CA: Sage. (p. 135)

Huss, M. (1996). Secrets to standing out from the pile: Getting into graduate school. *Psi Chi Newsletter,* 6–7.

Hussein, S. (2002, July 17 and August 28). Speeches to the Iraqi people as reported by various media. (p. 615)

Huston, A. C., Donnerstein, E., Fairchild, H., Feshbach, N. D., Katz, P. A., & Murray, J. P. (1992). *Big world, small screen: The role of television in American society.* Lincoln, NE: University of Nebraska Press. (p. 264)

Hyde, J. S. (1983, November). Bem's gender schema theory. Paper presented at GLCA Women's Studies Conference, Rochester, IN. (p. 296)

Hyde, J. S., Fennema, E., & Lamon, S. J. (1990). Gender differences in mathematics performance: A meta-analysis. *Psychological Bulletin, 107,* 139–155. (p. 348)

Hyler, S., Gabbard, G. O., & Schneider, I. (1991). Homicidal maniacs and narcissistic parasites: Stigmatization of mentally ill persons in the movies. *Hospital and Community Psychiatry, 42,* 1044–1048. (p. 505)

Hyman, R. (1981). Cold reading: How to convince strangers that you know all about them. In K. Frazier (Ed.), *Paranormal borderlands of science.* Buffalo, NY: Prometheus. (p. 480)

Ickes, W., Snyder, M., & Garcia, S. (1997). Personality influences on the choice of situations. In R. Hogan, J. Johnson, & S. Briggs (Eds.). *Handbook of Personality Psychology.* San Diego, CA: Academic Press. (p. 484)

Idson, L. C., & Mischel, W. (2001). The personality of familiar and significant people: The lay perceiver as a social-cognitive theorist. *Journal of Personality and Social Psychology, 80,* 585–596. (p. 576)

Ikonomidou, C., Bittigau, P., Ishimaru, M. J., Wozniak, D. F., Koch, C., Genz, K., Price, M. T., Stefovska, V., Hoerster, F., Tenkova, T., Dikranian, K., & Olney, J. W. (2000). Ethanol-induced apoptotic neurodegeneration and fetal alcohol syndrome. *Science, 287,* 1056–1060. (p. 102)

Immen, W. (1995, July 16). Canadians ignore 'safe sex' warning. *Toronto Globe and Mail* (in *Grand Rapids Press,* p. A22). (p. 379)

Ingham, A. G., Levinger, G., Graves, J., & Peckham, V. (1974). The Ringelmann effect: Studies of group size and group performance. *Journal of Experimental Social Psychology, 10,* 371–384. (p. 589)

Inglehart, R. (1990). *Culture shift in advanced industrial society.* Princeton, NJ: Princeton University Press. (pp. 137, 138, 389, 392, 393, 486)

Inglehart, R., Basañez, M., Diez-Medrano, J., Halman, L., & Luijkx, R. (Eds.). (2004). *Human beliefs and values: A sourcebook based on the 1999-2001 values surveys.* Mexico City: Siglo XXI. (p. 428)

Inman, M. L., & Baron, R. S. (1996). Influence of prototypes on perceptions of prejudice. *Journal of Personality and Social Psychology, 70,* 727–739. (p. 308)

Insana, R. (2005, February 21). Coach says honey gets better results than vinegar (interview with Larry Brown). *USA Today,* p. 4B. (p. 401)

Inzlicht, M., & Ben-Zeev, T. (2000). A threatening intellectual environment: Why females are susceptible to experiencing problem-solving deficits in the presence of males. *Psychological Science, 11,* 365–371. (p. 350)

IPU. (2005). Women in national parliaments: Situation as of 28 February 2005. *Inter-Parliamentary Union* (www.ipu.org). (p. 88)

Ironson, G., Solomon, G. F., Balbin, E. G., O'Cleirigh, C., George, A., Kumar, M., Larson, D., & Woods, T. E. (2002). The Ironson-Woods spiritual/ religiousness index is associated with long survival, health behaviors, less distress, and low cortisol in people with HIV/AIDS. *Annals of Behavioral Medicine, 24,* 34–48. (p. 455)

Irwin, M., Mascovich, A., Gillin, J. C., Willoughby, R., Pike, J., & Smith, T. L. (1994). Partial sleep deprivation reduces natural killer cell activity in humans. *Psychosomatic Medicine, 56,* 493–498. (p. 201)

Isensee, B., Wittchen, H-U., Stein, M. B., Hofler, M., & Lieb, R. (2003). Smoking increases the risk of panic: Findings from a prospective community study. *Archives of General Psychiatry, 60,* 692–700. (p. 510)

ISR. (2003, Spring). *Drug use: Religion plays role for White as well as Black teens (data from 70,000 seniors surveyed 1997-2001, ISR Monitoring the Future Study).* Ann Arbor, MI: Institute for Social Research Newsletter, University of Michigan. (p. 227)

Ito, T. A., Miller, N., & Pollock, V. E. (1996). Alcohol and aggression: A meta-analysis on the moderating effects of inhibitory cues, triggering events, and self-focused attention. *Psychological Bulletin, 120,* 60–82. (p. 601)

Iversen, L. L. (2000). *The science of marijuana.* New York: Oxford. (p. 224)

Iyengar, S. S., & Lepper, M. R. (2000). When choice is demotivating: Can one desire too much of a good thing? *Journal of Personality and Social Psychology, 79,* 995–1006. (p. 486)

Iyer, P. (1993, April). The soul of an intercontinental wanderer. *Harper's, 286,* 13–17. (p. 83)

Izard, C. E. (1977). *Human emotions.* New York: Plenum Press. (pp. 420, 423)

Izard, C. E. (1994). Innate and universal facial expressions: Evidence from developmental and cross-cultural research. *Psychological Bulletin, 114,* 288–299. (p. 420)

Jablensky, A. (1999). Schizophrenia: Epidemiology. *Current Opinion in Psychiatry, 12,* 19–28. (p. 534)

Jackson, J. M., & Williams, K. D. (1988). Social loafing: A review and theoretical analysis. Unpublished manuscript, Fordham University. (p. 589)

Jackson, J. S., Brown, K. T., Brown, T. N., & Marks, B. (2001). Contemporary immigration policy orientations among dominant-group members in western Europe. *Journal of Social Issues, 57,* 431–456. (p. 595)

Jackson, S. W. (1992). The listening healer in the history of psychological healing. *American Journal Psychiatry, 149,* 1623–1632. (p. 559)

Jacobi, C., Hayward, C., deZwaan, M., Kraemer, H. C., & Agras, W. S. (2004). Coming to terms with risk factors for eating disorders: Application of risk terminology and suggestions for a general taxonomy. *Psychological Bulletin, 130,* 19–65. (p. 364)

Jacobs, B. L. (1987). How hallucinogenic drugs work. *American Scientist, 75,* 386–392. (p. 223)

Jacobs, B. L. (1994). Serotonin, motor activity, and depression-related disorders. *American Scientist, 82,* 456–463. (pp. 411, 450)

Jacobs, B. L. (2004). Depression: The brain finally gets into the act. *Current Directions in Psychological Science, 13,* 103–106. (p. 567)

Jacobs, B., van Praag, H., & Gage, F. H. (2000). Adult brain neurogenesis and psychiatry: A novel theory of depression. *Molecular Psychiatry, 5,* 262–269. (p. 526)

Jacobs, W. J., & Nadel, L. (1985). Stress-induced recovery of fears and phobias. *Psychological Bulletin, 92,* 512–531. (p. 513)

Jacoby, L. L., Bishara, A. J., Hessels, S., & Toth, J. P. (2005). Aging, subjective experience, and cognitive control: Dramatic false remembering by older adults. *Journal of Experimental Psychology: General, 154,* 131–148. (p. 297)

Jaffe, E. (2004, October). Peace in the Middle East may be impossible: Lee D. Ross on naive realism and conflict resolution. *APS Observer,* pp. 9–11. (p. 184)

Jakicic, J. M., Winters, C., Lang, W., & Wing R. R. (1999). Effects of intermittent exercise and use of home exercise equipment on adherence, weight loss, and fitness in overweight women. *Journal of the American Medical Association, 282,* 1554–1560. (p. 372)

James, K. (1986). Priming and social categorizational factors: Impact on awareness of emergency situations. *Personality and Social Psychology Bulletin, 12,* 462–467. (p. 285)

James, W. (1890). *The principles of psychology (Vol. 2).* New York: Holt. (pp. 161, 215, 290, 407, 580)

James, W. (1902; reprinted 1958). *Varieties of religious experience.* New York: Mentor Books. (p. 425)

Jameson, D. (1985). Opponent-colors theory in light of physiological findings. In D. Ottoson & S. Zeki (Eds.), *Central and peripheral mechanisms of color vision.* New York: Macmillan. (p. 176)

Jamison, K. R. (1993). *Touched with fire: Manic-depressive illness and the artistic temperament.* New York: Free Press. (p. 522)

Jamison, K. R. (1995, February). Manic-depressive illness and creativity. *Scientific American,* pp. 62–67. (p. 522)

Janicak, P. G. (2005). Treating psychiatric disorders using transcranial magnetic stimulation. *Psychiatric Annals, 35,* 102–108. (p. 570)

Janis, I. L. (1982). *Groupthink: Psychological studies of policy decisions and fiascoes.* Boston: Houghton Mifflin. (p. 591)

Janis, I. L. (1986). Problems of international crisis management in the nuclear age. *Journal of Social Issues, 42(2),* 201–220. (p. 310)

Janoff-Bulman, R., Timko, C., & Carli, L. L. (1985). Cognitive biases in blaming the victim. *Journal of Experimental Social Psychology, 21,* 161–177. (p. 599)

Javitt, D. C., & Coyle, J. T. (2004, January). Decoding schizophrenia. *Scientific American,* pp. 48–55. (p. 533)

Jeffery, R. W., Drewnowski, A., Epstein, L. H., Stunkard, A. J., Wilson, G. T., Wing, R. R., & Hill, D. R. (2000). Long-term maintenance of weight loss: Current status. *Health Psychology, 19,* No. 1 (Supplement), 5–16. (pp. 371, 372)

Jenkins, J. G., & Dallenbach, K. M. (1924). Oblivescence during sleep and waking. *American Journal of Psychology, 35,* 605–612. (pp. 293, 294)

Jenkins, J. M., & Astington, J. W. (1996). Cognitive factors and family structure associated with theory of mind development in young children. *Developmental Psychology, 32,* 70–78. (p. 110)

Jensen, J. P., & Bergin, A. E. (1988). Mental health values of professional therapists: A national interdisciplinary survey. *Professional Psychology: Research and Practice, 19,* 290–297. (p. 561)

Jervis, R. (1985, April 2). Quoted in D. Goleman, Political forces come under new scrutiny of psychology. *The New York Times,* pp. C1, C4. (p. 313)

Jing, H. (1999, Summer). China faces myriad psychological challenges of modernization. *Psychology International* (APA newsletter), p. 7. (p. 5)

Johansson, P., Hall, L., Sikström, S., & Olsson, A. (2005). Failure to detect mismatches between intention and outcome in a simple decision task. *Science, 310,* 116–119. (p. 194)

John, O. P., & Srivastava, S. (1999). The Big Five trait taxonomy: History, measurement, and theoretical perspectives. In L. A. Pervin & O. P. John (Eds.), *Handbook of personality: Theory and research.* New York: Guilford. (p. 477)

Johnson, D. L., Wiebe, J. S., Gold, S. M., Andreasen, N. C., Hichwa, R. D., Watkins, G. L., & Ponto, L. L. B. (1999). Cerebral blood flow and personality: A Positron Emission Tomography study. *American Journal of Psychiatry, 156,* 252–257. (p. 476)

Johnson, D. W., & Johnson, R. T. (1989). *Cooperation and competition: Theory and research.* Edina, MN: Interaction Book. (p. 617)

Johnson, D. W., & Johnson, R. T. (1994). Constructive conflict in the schools. *Journal of Social Issues, 50(1),* 117–137. (p. 617)

Johnson, J. G., Cohen, P., Kotler, L., Kasen, S., & Brook, J. S. (2002). Psychiatric disorders associated with risk for the development of eating disorders during adolescence and early adulthood. *Journal of Consulting and Clinical Psychology, 70,* 1119–1128. (p. 364)

Johnson, J. S., & Newport, E. L. (1991). Critical period effects on universal properties of language: The status of subjacency in the acquisition of a second language. *Cognition, 39,* 215–258. (p. 322)

Johnson, L. C. (2001, July 10). The declining terrorist threat. *New York Times* (www.nytimes.com). (p. 314)

Johnson, M. E., & Hauck, C. (1999). Beliefs and opinions about hypnosis held by the general public: A systematic evaluation. *American Journal of Clinical Hypnosis, 42,* 10–20. (p. 212)

Johnson, M. H. (1992). Imprinting and the development of face recognition: From chick to man. *Current Directions in Psychological Science, 1,* 52–55. (p. 114)

Johnson, M. H., & Morton, J. (1991). *Biology and cognitive development: The case of face recognition.* Oxford: Blackwell Publishing. (p. 103)

Johnson, W., McGue, M., & Krueger, R. F. (2005). Personality stability in late adulthood: A behavioral genetic analysis. *Journal of Personality, 73,* 523–552. (p. 100)

Johnston, L. D., O'Malley, P. M., Bachman, J. G., & Schulenberg, J. E. (2005). *Monitoring the future: National results on adolescent drug use: Overview of key findings, 2004.* Bethesda, MD: National Institute on Drug Abuse. (pp. 222, 226)

Johnston, L. D., O'Malley, P. M., Bachman, J. G., & Schulenberg, J. E. (2005). *Teen drug use down but progress halts among youngest teens.* University of Michigan News and Information Services: Ann Arbor, MI. (pp. 225)

Joiner, T. E., Pettit, J. W., Walker, R. L., Voelz, Z. R., Cruz, J., Rudd, M. D., & Lester, D. (2002). Perceived burdensomeness and suicidality: Two studies on the suicide notes of those attempting and those completing suicide. *Journal of Social and Clinical Psychology, 21,* 531–545. (p. 525)

Jones, E. E., Cumming, J. D., & Horowitz, M. J. (1988). Another look at the nonspecific hypothesis of therapeutic effectiveness. *Journal of Consulting and Clinical Psychology, 56,* 48–55. (p. 559)

Jones, J. M. (2003, February 12). Fear of terrorism increases amidst latest warning. *Gallup News Service* (www.gallup.com/releases/pr030212.asp). (p. 510)

Jones, J. M., & Moore, D. W. (2003, June 17). Generational differences in support for a woman president. The Gallup Organization (www.gallup.com). (p. 594)

Jones, J. T., Pelham, B. W., Carvallo, M., & Mirenberg, M. C. (2004). How do I love thee? Let me count the Js: Implicit egotism and interpersonal attraction. *Journal of Personality and Social Psychology, 87,* 665–683. (p. 607)

Jones, L. (2000, December). Skeptics New Year quiz. *Skeptical Briefs,* p. 11. (p. 481)

Jones, M. C. (1924). A laboratory study of fear: The case of Peter. *Journal of Genetic Psychology, 31,* 308–315. (p. 546)

Jones, M. V., Paull, G. C., & Erskine, J. (2002). The impact of a team's aggressive reputation on the decisions of association football referees. *Journal of Sports Sciences, 20,* 991–1000. (p. 184)

Jones, S. S., Collins, K., & Hong, H-W. (1991). An audience effect on smile production in 10-month-old infants. *Psychological Science, 2,* 45–49. (p. 421)

Jones, W. H., Carpenter, B. N., & Quintana, D. (1985). Personality and interpersonal predictors of loneliness in two cultures. *Journal of Personality and Social Psychology, 48,* 1503–1511. (p. 28)

Jordan, C. H., Spencer, S. J., Zanna, M. P., Hoshino-Browne, E., & Correll, J. (2003). Secure and defensive high self-esteem. *Journal of Personality and Social Psychology, 85,* 969–978. (p. 494)

Joseph, J. (2001). Separated twins and the genetics of personality differences: A critique. *American Journal of Psychology, 114,* 1–30. (p. 70)

Judge, T. A., Thoresen, C. J., Bono, J. E., & Patton, G. K. (2001). The job satisfaction/job performance relationship: A qualitative and quantitative review. *Psychological Bulletin, 127,* 376–407. (p. 399)

Jung-Beeman, M., Bowden, E. M., Haberman, J., Frymiare, J. L., Arambel-Liu, S., Greenblatt, R., Reber, P. J., & Kounios, J. (2004). Neural activity when people solve verbal problems with insight. *PloS Biology 2(4): e111.* (p. 308)

Kagan, J. (1976). Emergent themes in human development. *American Scientist, 64,* 186–196. (p. 116)

Kagan, J. (1984). *The nature of the child.* New York: Basic Books. (p. 113)

Kagan, J. (1995). On attachment. *Harvard Review of Psychiatry, 3,* 104–106. (p. 115)

Kagan, J. (1998). *Three seductive ideas.* Cambridge, MA: Harvard University Press. (p. 100)

Kagan, J., & Snidman, N. (2004). *The long shadow of temperament.* Cambridge, MA: Belknap Press. (p. 72)

Kagan, J., Arcus, D., Snidman, N., Feng, W. Y., Hendler, J., & Greene, S. (1994). Reactivity in infants: A cross-national comparison. *Developmental Psychology, 30,* 342–345. (p. 72)

Kagan, J., Lapidus, D. R., & Moore, M. (December, 1978). Infant antecedents of cognitive functioning: A longitudinal study. *Child Development, 49(4),* 1005–1023. (p. 100)

Kagan, J., Snidman, N., & Arcus, D. M. (1992). Initial reactions to unfamiliarity. *Current Directions in Psychological Science, 1,* 171–174. (p. 72)

Kahneman, D. (1999). Assessments of objective happiness: A bottom-up approach. In D. Kahneman, E. Diener, & N. Schwartz (Eds.), *Understanding well-being: Scientific perspectives on enjoyment and suffering.* New York: Russell Sage Foundation. (p. 163)

Kahneman, D. (2005, February 10). Are you happy now? *Gallup Management Journal* interview (www.gmj.gallup.com). (p. 426)

Kahneman, D. (2005, January 13). What were they thinking? Q&A with Daniel Kahneman. *Gallup Management Journal* (gmj.gallup.com). (p. 310)

Kahneman, D., & Tversky, A. (1972). Subjective probability: A judgment of representativeness. *Cognitive Psychology, 3,* 430–454. (p. 23)

Kahneman, D., Fredrickson, B. L., Schreiber, C. A., & Redelmeier, D. A. (1993). When more pain is preferred to less: Adding a better end. *Psychological Science, 4,* 401–405. (p. 163)

Kahneman, D., Krueger, A. B., Schkade, D. A., Schwarz, N., & Stone, A. A. (2004). A survey method for characterizing daily life experience: The day reconstruction method. *Science, 306,* 1776–1780. (p. 426)

Kail, R. (1991). Developmental change in speed of processing during childhood and adolescence. *Psychological Bulletin, 109,* 490–501. (p. 131)

Kaiser. (2001). Inside-out: A report on the experiences of lesbians, gays and bisexuals in America and the public's views on issues and policies related to sexual orientation. The Henry J. Kaiser Foundation (www.kff.org). (p. 386)

Kaiser Family Foundation. (2003, October 28). New study finds children age zero to six spend as much time with TV, computers and video games as playing outside. www.kff.org/entmedia/entmedia102803nr.cfm. (p. 21)

Kalin, N. H. (1993, May). The neurobiology of fear. *Scientific American,* pp. 94–101. (p. 411)

Kamarck, T., & Jennings, J. R. (1991). Biobehavioral factors in sudden cardiac death. *Psychological Bulletin, 109,* 42–75. (p. 439)

Kamena, M. (1998). Repressed/false childhood sexual abuse memories: A survey of therapists. Paper presented to the Sexual Abuse memories Symposium at the American Psychological Association convention. (p. 299)

Kaminski, J., Cali, J., & Fischer, J. (2004). Word learning in a domestic dog: Evidence for "fast mapping." *Science, 304,* 1682–1683. (p. 327)

Kanaya, T., Scullin, M. H., & Ceci, S. J. (2003). The Flynn effect and U.S. policies: The impact of rising IQ scores on American society via mental retardation diagnoses. *American Psychologist, 58,* 778–790. (p. 341)

Kandel, D. B., & Raveis, V. H. (1989). Cessation of illicit drug use in young adulthood. *Archives of General Psychiatry, 46,* 109–116. (p. 227)

Kandel, E. R., & Schwartz, J. H. (1982). Molecular biology of learning: Modulation of transmitter release. *Science, 218,* 433–443. (p. 280)

Kann, L., Warren, W., Collins, J. L., Ross, J., Collins, B., Kolbe, L. J. (1993). Results from the national school-based 1991 Youth Risk Behavior Survey and progress toward achieving related health objectives for the nation. U.S. Department of Health and Human Services, *Public Health Reports, 108* (Supplement 1), 47–55. (p. 227)

Kaplan, A. (2004). Exploring the gene-environment nexus in anorexia, bulimia. *Psychiatric Times, 21* (www.psychiatrictimes.com/p040801b.html). (p. 364)

Kaplan, H. I., & Saddock, B. J. (Eds.). (1989). *Comprehensive textbook of psychiatry.* V. Baltimore, MD: Williams and Wilkins. (p. 566)

Kaprio, J., Koskenvuo, M., & Rita, H. (1987). Mortality after bereavement: A prospective study of 95,647 widowed persons. *American Journal of Public Health, 77,* 283–287. (p. 437)

Karacan, I., Aslan, C., & Hirshkowitz, M. (1983). Erectile mechanisms in man. *Science, 220,* 1080–1082. (p. 199)

Karacan, I., Goodenough, D. R., Shapiro, A., & Starker, S. (1966). Erection cycle during sleep in relation to dream anxiety. *Archives of General Psychiatry, 15,* 183–189. (p. 199)

Karau, S. J., & Williams, K. D. (1993). Social loafing: A meta-analytic review and theoretical integration. *Journal of Personality and Social Psychology, 65,* 681–706. (p. 589)

Kark, J. D., Shemi, G., Friedlander, Y., Martin, O., Manor, O., & Blondheim, S. H. (1996). Does religious observance promote health? Mortality in secular vs. religious kibbutzim in Israel. *American Journal of Public Health, 86,* 341–346. (p. 454)

Karni, A., & Sagi, D. (1994). Dependence on REM sleep for overnight improvement of perceptual skills. *Science, 265,* 679–682. (p. 207)

Karni, A., Meyer, G., Rey-Hipolito, C., Jezzard, P., Adams, M. M., Turner, R., & Ungerleider, L. G. (1998). The acquisition of skilled motor performance: Fast and slow experience-driven changes in primary motor cortex. *Proceedings of the National Academy of Sciences, 95,* 861–868. (p. 80)

Karno, M., Golding, J. M., Sorenson, S. B., & Burnam, A. (1988). The epidemiology of obsessive-compulsive disorder in five US communities. *Archives of General Psychiatry, 45,* 1094–1099. (p. 511)

Kashima, Y., Siegal, M., Tanaka, K., & Kashima, E. S. (1992). Do people believe behaviours are consistent with attitudes? Towards a cultural psychology of attribution processes. *British Journal of Social Psychology, 31,* 111–124. (p. 85)

Kasser, T. (2000). Two version of the American dream: Which goals and values make for a high quality of life? In E. Diener (Ed.), *Advances in quality of life theory and research.* Dordrecht, Netherlands: Kluwer. (p. 429)

Kasser, T. (2002). *The high price of materialism.* Cambridge, MA: MIT Press. (p. 429)

Kaufman, J. C., & Baer, J. (2002). I bask in dreams of suicide: Mental illness, poetry, and women. *Review of General Psychology, 6,* 271–286. (p. 522)

Kaufman, J., & Zigler, E. (1987). Do abused children become abusive parents? *American Journal of Orthopsychiatry, 57,* 186–192. (p. 116)

Kaufman, L., & Kaufman, J. H. (2000). Explaining the moon illusion. *Proceedings of the National Academy of Sciences, 97,* 500–505. (p. 178)

Kazdin, A. E., & Benjet, C. (2003). Spanking children: Evidence and issues. *Current Directions in Psychological Science, 12,* 99–103. (p. 253)

Keesey, R. E., & Corbett, S. W. (1983). Metabolic defense of the body weight set-point. In A. J. Stunkard & E. Stellar (Eds.), *Eating and its disorders.* New York: Raven Press. (p. 362)

Keller, M. B., McCullough, J. P., Klein, D. N., Arnow, B., Dunner, D. L., Gelenberg, A. J., Markowitz, J. C., Nemeroff, C. B., Russell, J. M., Thase, M. E., Trivedi, M. H., & Zajecka J. (2000), A comparison of nefazodone, the cognitive behavioral-analysis system of psychotherapy, and their combination for the treatment of chronic depression. *New England Journal of Medicine, 342,* 1462–1470. (p. 567)

Kellerman, J., Lewis, J., & Laird, J. D. (1989). Looking and loving: The effects of mutual gaze on feelings of romantic love. *Journal of Research in Personality, 23,* 145–161. (p. 417)

Kellermann, A. L. (1997). Comment: Gunsmoke—changing public attitudes toward smoking and firearms. *American Journal of Public Health, 87,* 910–913. (p. 599)

Kellermann, A. L., Rivara, F. P., Rushforth, N. B., Banton, H. G., Feay, D. T., Francisco, J. T., Locci, A. B., Prodzinski, J., Hackman, B. B., & Somes, G. (1993). Gun ownership as a risk factor for homicide in the home. *New England Journal of Medicine, 329,* 1084–1091. (p. 599)

Kellermann, A. L., Somes, G. Rivara, F. P., Lee, R. K., & Banton, J. G. (1998). Injuries and deaths due to firearms in the home. *Journal of Trauma, 45,* 263–267. (p. 599)

Kelley, J., & De Graaf, N. D. (1997). National context, parental socialization, and religious belief: Results from 15 nations. *American Sociological Review, 62,* 639–659. (p. 71)

Kelling, S. T., & Halpern, B. P. (1983). Taste flashes: Reaction times, intensity, and quality. *Science, 219,* 412–414. (p. 165)

Kellner, C. H., & 15 others. (2005). Relief of expressed suicidal intent by ECT: A consortium for research in ECT study. *American Journal of Psychiatry, 162,* 977–982. (p. 569)

Kelly, A. E. (2000). Helping construct desirable identities: A self-presentational view of psychotherapy. *Psychological Bulletin, 126,* 475–494. (p. 549)

Kelly, I. W. (1997). Modern astrology: A critique. *Psychological Reports, 81,* 1035–1066. (p. 480)

Kelly, I. W. (1998). Why astrology doesn't work. *Psychological Reports, 82,* 527–546. (p. 480)

Kelly, T. A. (1990). The role of values in psychotherapy: A critical review of process and outcome effects. *Clinical Psychology Review, 10,* 171–186. (p. 561)

Kempe, R. S., & Kempe, C. C. (1978). *Child abuse.* Cambridge, MA: Harvard University Press. (p. 116)

Kempermann, G., & Gage, F. H. (1999, May). New nerve cells for the adult brain. *Scientific American,* pp. 48–53. (pp. 60, 450)

Kempermann, G., Kuhn, H. G., & Gage, F. H. (May, 1998). Experience-induced neurogenesis in the senescent dentate gyrus. *Journal of Neuroscience, 18(9),* 3206–3212. (p. 132)

Kendall-Tackett, K. A., Williams, L. M., & Finkelhor, D. (1993). Impact of sexual abuse on children: A review and synthesis of recent empirical studies. *Psychological Bulletin, 113,* 164–180. (pp. 114, 117)

Kendall-Tackett, K. A., Williams, L. M., & Finkelhor, D. (1993). Impact of sexual abuse on children: A review and synthesis of recent empirical studies. *Psychological Bulletin, 113,* 164–180. (pp. 114, 300)

Kendler, K. S. (1997). Social support: A genetic-epidemiologic analysis. *American Journal of Psychiatry, 154,* 1398–1404. (p. 484)

Kendler, K. S. (1998, January). Major depression and the environment: A psychiatric genetic perspective. *Pharmacopsychiatry, 31(1),* 5–9. (p. 523)

Kendler, K. S., Jacobson, K. C., Myers, J., & Prescott, C. A. (2002a). Sex differences in genetic and environmental risk factors for irrational fears and phobias. *Psychological Medicine, 32,* 209–217. (p. 514)

Kendler, K. S., Karkowski, L. M., & Prescott, C. A. (1999). Fears and phobias: Reliability and heritability. *Psychological Medicine, 29,* 539–553. (p. 514)

Kendler, K. S., Myers, J., & Prescott, C. A. (2002b). The etiology of phobias: An evaluation of the stress-diathesis model. *Archives of General Psychiatry, 59,* 242–248. (p. 514)

Kendler, K. S., Neale, M. C., Kessler, R. C., Heath, A. C., & Eaves, L. J. (1992). Generalized anxiety disorder in women: A population-based twin study. *Archives of General Psychiatry, 49,* 267–272. (p. 514)

Kendler, K. S., Neale, M. C., Thornton, L. M., Aggen, S. H., Gilman, S. E., & Kessler, R. C. (2002). Cannabis use in the last year in a U.S. national sample of twin and sibling pairs. *Psychological Medicine, 32,* 551–554. (p. 225)

Kendler, K. S., Thornton, L. M., & Gardner, C. O. (2001). Genetic risk, number of previous depressive episodes, and stressful life events in predicting onset of major depression. *American Journal of Psychiatry, 158,* 582–586. (p. 523)

Kennedy, S., & Over, R. (1990). Psychophysiological assessment of male sexual arousal following spinal cord injury. *Archives of Sexual Behavior, 19,* 15–27. (p. 43)

Kenrick, D. T., & Funder, D. C. (1988). Profiting from controversy: Lessons from the person-situation debate. *American Psychologist, 43,* 23–34. (p. 482)

Kenrick, D. T., & Gutierres, S. E. (1980). Contrast effects and judgments of physical attractiveness: When beauty becomes a social problem. *Journal of Personality and Social Psychology, 38,* 131–140. (p. 378)

Kenrick, D. T., Gutierres, S. E., & Goldberg, L. L. (1989). Influence of popular erotica on judgments of strangers and mates. *Journal of Experimental Social Psychology, 25,* 159–167. (p. 378)

Keough, K. A., Zimbardo, P. G., & Boyd, J. N. (1999). Who's smoking, drinking, and using drugs? Time perspective as a predictor of substance use. *Basic and Applied Social Psychology, 2,* 149–164. (p. 460)

Kernis, M. H. (2003). Toward a conceptualization of optimal self-esteem. *Psychological Inquiry, 14,* 1–26. (p. 494)

Kerr, N. L., & Bruun, S. E. (1983). Dispensability of member effort and group motivation losses: Free-rider effects. *Journal of Personality and Social Psychology, 44,* 78–94. (p. 589)

Kessler, M., & Albee, G. (1975). Primary prevention. *Annual Review of Psychology, 26,* 557–591. (p. 562)

Kessler, R. C. (2000). Posttraumatic stress disorder: The burden to the individual and to society. *Journal of Clinical Psychiatry, 61*(suppl. 5), 4–12. (p. 512)

Kessler, R. C. (2001). Epidemiology of women and depression. *Journal of Affective Disorders, 74,* 5–13. (p. 527)

Kessler, R. C., Foster, C., Joseph, J., Ostrow, D., Wortman, C., Phair, J., & Chmiel, J. (1991). Stressful life events and symptom onset in HIV infection. *American Journal of Psychiatry, 148,* 733–738. (p. 442)

Kessler, R. C., Soukup, J., Davis, R. B., Foster, D. F., Wilkey, S. A., Van Rompay, M. I., & Eisenberg, D. M. (2001). The use of complementary and alternative therapies to treat anxiety and depression in the United States. *American Journal of Psychiatry, 158,* 289–294. (p. 558)

Kestenbaum, R. (1992). Feeling happy versus feeling good: The processing of discrete and global categories of emotional expressions by children and adults. *Developmental Psychology, 28,* 1132–1142. (p. 417)

Keynes, M. (1980, December 20/27). Handel's illnesses. *The Lancet,* pp. 1354–1355. (p. 522)

Keys, A., Brozek, J., Henschel, A., Mickelsen, O., & Taylor, H. L. (1950). *The biology of human starvation.* Minneapolis: University of Minnesota Press. (p. 360)

Khan, A., Warner, H. A., & Brown, W. A. (2000). Symptom reduction and suicide risk inpatients treated with placebo in antidepressant clinical trials. *Archives of General Psychiatry, 57,* 311–317. (p. 568)

Kho, K. H., van Vreeswijk, M. F., Simpson, S., & Zwinderman, A. H. (2003). A meta-analysis of electroconvulsive therapy efficacy in depression. *Journal of ECT, 19,* 139–147. (p. 569)

Kiecolt-Glaser, J. K., & Glaser, R. (1995). Psychoneuroimmunology and health consequences: Data and shared mechanisms. *Psychosomatic Medicine, 57,* 269–274. (p. 441)

Kiecolt-Glaser, J. K., & Newton, T. L. (2001). Marriage and health: His and hers. *Psychological Bulletin, 127,* 472–503. (p. 447)

Kiecolt-Glaser, J. K., Page, G. G., Marucha, P. T., MacCallum, R. C., & Glaser, R. (1998). Psychological influences on surgical recovery: Perspectives from psychoneuroimmunology. *American Psychologist, 53,* 1209–1218. (p. 440)

Kihlstrom, J. F. (1990). Awareness, the psychological unconscious, and the self. Address to the American Psychological Association convention. (p. 295)

Kihlstrom, J. F. (1990). The psychological unconscious. In L. A. Pervin (Ed.), *Handbook of personality: Theory and research.* New York: Guilford Press. (p. 467)

Kihlstrom, J. F. (1994). The social construction of memory. Paper presented at the American Psychological Society convention. (p. 297)

Kihlstrom, J. F. (1997, November 11). Freud as giant pioneer on whose shoulders we should stand. Social Psychology listserv posting (spsp@stolaf.edu). (p. 468)

Kihlstrom, J.F. (2005) Dissociative disorders. *Annual review of Clinical Psychology, 1,* 227–253. (p. 517)

Kihlstrom, J.F., & McConkey, K. M. (1990). William James and hypnosis: A centennial reflection. *Psychological Science, 1,* 174–177. (p. 215)

Killeen, P. R., & Nash, M. R. (2003). The four causes of hypnosis. *Internal Journal of Clinical and Experimental Hypnosis, 51,* 195–231. (p. 215)

Kim, B. S. K., Ng, G. F., & Ahn, A. J. (2005). Effects of client expectation for counseling success, client-counselor worldview match, and client adherence to Asian and European American cultural values on counseling process with Asian Americans. *Journal of Counseling Psychology, 52,* 67–76. (p. 561)

Kim, H., & Markus, H. R. (1999). Deviance or uniqueness, harmony or conformity? A cultural analysis. *Journal of Personality and Social Psychology, 77,* 785–800. (p. 85)

Kimata, H. (2001). Effect of humor on allergen-induced wheal reactions. *Journal of the American Medical Association, 285,* 737. (p. 446)

Kimble, G. A. (1956). *Principles of general psychology.* New York: Ronald. (p. 243)

Kimble, G. A. (1981). *Biological and cognitive constraints on learning.* Washington, DC: American Psychological Association. (p. 243)

King, R. N., & Koehler, D. J. (2000). Illusory correlations in graphological interference. *Journal of Experimental Psychology: Applied, 6,* 336–348. (p. 480)

Kinnier, R. T., & Metha, A. T. (1989). Regrets and priorities at three stages of life. *Counseling and Values, 33,* 182–193. (p. 137)

Kirby, D. (2002). Effective approaches to reducing adolescent unprotected sex, pregnancy, and childbearing. *Journal of Sex Research, 39,* 51–57. (p. 380)

Kirkpatrick, L. (1999). Attachment and religious representations and behavior. In J. Cassidy & P. R. Shaver (Eds.), *Handbook of attachment.* New York: Guilford. (p. 114)

Kirsch, I. (1996). Hypnotic enhancement of cognitive-behavioral weight loss treatments: Another meta-reanalysis. *Journal of Consulting and Clinical Psychology, 64,* 517–519. (p. 212)

Kirsch, I., & Braffman, W. (2001). Imaginative suggestibility and hypnotizability. *Current Directions in Psychological Science, 10,* 57–61. (p. 211)

Kirsch, I., & Lynn, S. J. (1995). The altered state of hypnosis. *American Psychologist, 50,* 846–858. (p. 215)

Kirsch, I., & Lynn, S. J. (1998a). Dissociation theories of hypnosis. *Psychological Bulletin, 123,* 100–115. (p. 215)

Kirsch, I., & Lynn, S. J. (1998b). Social-cognitive alternatives to dissociation theories of hypnotic induction. *Review of General Psychology, 2,* 66–80. (p. 215)

Kirsch, I., & Sapirstein, G. (1998). Listening to Prozac but hearing placebo: A meta-analysis of antidepressant medication. *Prevention and Treatment, 1,* posted June 26 at (journals.apa.org/prevention/volume1). (pp. 25, 568)

Kirsch, I., Montgomery, G., & Sapirstein, G. (1995). Hypnosis as an adjunct to cognitive-behavioral psychotherapy: A meta-analysis. *Journal of Consulting and Clinical Psychology, 63,* 214–220. (p. 212)

Kirsch, I., Moore, T. J., Scoboria, A., & Nicholls, S. S. (2002, July 15). New study finds little difference between effects of antidepressants and placebo. *Prevention and Treatment* (journals.apa.org/prevention). (p. 568)

Kivimaki, M., Leino-Arjas, P., Luukkonen, R., Rihimaki, H., & Kirjonen, J. (2002). Work stress and risk of cardiovascular mortality: Prospective cohort study of industrial employees. *British Medical Journal, 325,* 857. (p. 446)

Klayman, J., & Ha, Y-W. (1987). Confirmation, disconfirmation, and information in hypothesis testing. *Psychological Review, 94,* 211–228. (p. 309)

Klein, D. N., & 16 others. (2003). Therapeutic alliance in depression treatment: Controlling for prior change and patient characteristics. *Journal of Consulting and Clinical Psychology, 71,* 997–1006. (p. 561)

Klein, S. B., & Kihlstrom, J. F. (1998). On bridging the gap between social-personality psychology and neuropsychology. *Personality and Social Psychology Review, 2,* 228–242. (p. 111)

Kleinfeld, J. (1998). *The myth that schools shortchange girls: Social science in the service of deception.* Washington, DC: Women's Freedom Network. Available from ERIC, Document ED423210, and via www.uaf.edu/northern/schools/myth.html. (p. 348)

Kleinke, C. L. (1986). Gaze and eye contact: A research review. *Psychological Bulletin, 1000,* 78–100. (p. 417)

Kleinmuntz, B., & Szucko, J. J. (1984). A field study of the fallibility of polygraph lie detection. *Nature, 308,* 449–450. (p. 412)

Kleitman, N. (1960, November). Patterns of dreaming. *Scientific American,* pp. 82–88. (p. 197)

Klemm, W. R. (1990). Historical and introductory perspectives on brainstem-mediated behaviors. In W. R. Klemm & R. P. Vertes (Eds.), *Brainstem mechanisms of behavior.* New York: Wiley. (p. 48)

Kline, D., & Schieber, F. (1985). Vision and aging. In J. E. Birren & K. W. Schaie (Eds.), *Handbook of the psychology of aging.* New York: Van Nostrand Reinhold. (p. 130)

Kline, G. H., Stanley, S. M., Markman, J. H., Olmos-Gallo, P. A., St. Peters, M., Whitton, S. W., & Prado, L. M. (2004). Timing is everything: Pre-engagement cohabitation and increased risk for poor marital outcomes. *Journal of Family Psychology, 18,* 311–318. (p. 136)

Kline, N. S. (1974). *From sad to glad.* New York: Ballantine Books. (p. 529)

Klineberg, O. (1938). Emotional expression in Chinese literature. *Journal of Abnormal and Social Psychology, 33,* 517–520. (p. 420)

Klineberg, O. (1984). Public opinion and nuclear war. *American Psychologist, 39,* 1245–1253. (p. 617)

Klinke, R., Kral, A., Heid, S., Tillein, J., & Hartmann, R. (1999). Recruitment of the auditory cortex in congenitally deaf cats by long-term cochlear electrostimulation. *Science, 285,* 1729–1733. (p. 182)

Kluft, R. P. (1991). Multiple personality disorder. In A. Tasman & S. M. Goldfinger (Eds.), *Review of Psychiatry, (Vol. 10).* Washington, DC: American Psychiatric Press. (p. 516)

Knapp, S., & VandeCreek, L. (2000, August). Recovered memories of childhood abuse: Is there an underlying professional consensus? *Professional Psychology: Research and Practice, 31,* 365–371. (p. 300)

Knecht, S., Floeel, A., Draeger, B., Breitenstein, C., Sommer, J., Henningsen, H., Ringelstein, E. F., & Pascual-Leone, A. (2002). Degree of language lateralization determines susceptibility to unilateral brain lesions. *Nature Neuroscience, 5,* 695–699. (p. 62)

Knickmeyer, E. (2001, August 7). In Africa, big is definitely better. *Associated Press* (Seattle Times, p. A7). (p. 364)

Knight, W. (2004, August 2). Animated face helps deaf with phone chat. NewScientist.com. (p. 165)

Koenig, H. G. (2002, October 9). Personal communication, from Director of Center for the Study of Religion/Spirituality and Health, Duke University. (p. 454)

Koenig, H. G., & Larson, D. B. (1998). Use of hospital services, religious attendance, and religious affiliation. *Southern Medical Journal, 91,* 925–932. (p. 455)

Koenig, L. B., McGue, M., Krueger, R. F., & Bouchard, T. J., Jr. (2005). Genetic and environmental influences on religiousness: Findings for retrospective and current religiousness ratings. *Journal of Personality, 73,* 471–488. (p. 71)

Koestner, R., Lekes, N., Powers, T. A., & Chicoine, E. (2002). Attaining personal goals: Self-concordance plus implementation intentions equals success. *Journal of Personality and Social Psychology, 83,* 231–244. (p. 401)

Kohlberg, L. (1981). *The philosophy of moral development: Essays on moral development (Vol. I).* San Francisco: Harper & Row. (p. 123)

Kohler, I. (1962, May). Experiments with goggles. *Scientific American,* pp. 62–72. (p. 183)

Köhler, W. (1925; reprinted 1957). *The mentality of apes.* London: Pelican. (p. 326)

Kohn, P. M., & Macdonald, J. E. (1992). The survey of recent life experiences: A decontaminated hassles scale for adults. *Journal of Behavioral Medicine, 15,* 221–236. (p. 438)

Kohout, J., & Wicherski, M. (2004). 2001 *Doctorate employment survey,* Washington, DC: American Psychological Association. (p. B-4)

Kolata, G. (1986). Youth suicide: New research focuses on a growing social problem. *Science, 233,* 839–841. (p. 525)

Kolata, G. (1987). Metabolic catch-22 of exercise regimens. *Science, 236,* 146–147. (p. 372)

Kolata, G. (2004, September 30). Health and money issues arise over who pays for weight loss. *New York Times* (www.nytimes.com). (p. 371)

Kolb, B. (1989). Brain development, plasticity, and behavior. *American Psychologist, 44,* 1203–1212. (p. 59)

Kolb, B., & Whishaw, I. Q. (2006). *An introduction to brain and behavior, 2nd edition.* New York: Worth Publishers. (p. 334)

Kolodziej, M. E., & Johnson, B. T. (1996). Interpersonal contact and acceptance of persons with psychiatric disorders: A research synthesis. *Journal of Consulting and Clinical Psychology, 64,* 1387–1396. (p. 504)

Koole, S., & Spijker, M. (2000). Overcoming the planning fallacy through willpower: Effects of implementation intentions on actual and predicted task-completion times. *European Journal of Social Psychology, 30,* 873–888. (p. 401)

Kopta, S. M., Lueger, R. J., Saunders, S. M., & Howard, K. I. (1999). Individual psychotherapy outcome and process research: Challenges leading to greater turmoil or a positive transition? *Annual Review of Psychology, 30,* 441–469. (p. 556)

Kosslyn, S. M., & Koenig, O. (1992). *Wet mind: The new cognitive neuroscience.* New York: Free Press. (p. 42, 43)

Kosslyn, S. M., Thompson, W. L., Costantini-Ferrando, M. F., Alpert, N. M., & Spiegel, D. (2000). Hypnotic visual illusion alters color processing in the brain. *American Journal of Psychiatry, 157,* 1279–1284. (p. 215)

Kotchick, B. A., Shaffer, A., & Forehand, R. (2001). Adolescent sexual risk behavior: A multi-system perspective. *Clinical Psychology Review, 21,* 493–519. (p. 379)

Kotkin, M., Daviet, C., & Gurin, J. (1996). The Consumer Reports mental health survey. *American Psychologist, 51,* 1080–1082. (p. 554)

Kotva, H. J., & Schneider, H. G. (1990). Those "talks"—general and sexual communication between mothers and daughters. *Journal of Social Behavior and Personality, 5,* 603–613. (p. 379)

Kraft, C. (1978). A psychophysical approach to air safety: Simulator studies of visual illusions in night approaches. In H. L. Pick, H. W. Leibowitz, J. E. Singer, A. Steinschneider, & H. W. Stevenson (Eds.), *Psychology: From research to practice.* New York: Plenum Press. (pp. 188, 189)

Kraft, R. (1996, December 2, and 1994, July 20). Personal correspondence (from Otterbein College) regarding Holocaust memories. (p. 466)

Kraus, N., Malmfors, T., & Slovic, P. (1992). Intuitive toxicology: Expert and lay judgments of chemical risks. *Risk Analysis, 12,* 215–232. (p. 313)

Kraut, R. E., & Johnston, R. E. (1979). Social and emotional messages of smiling: An ethological approach. *Journal of Personality and Social Psychology, 37,* 1539–1553. (p. 421)

KRC Research & Consulting. (2001, August 7). Memory isn't quite what it used to be (survey for General Nutrition Centers). *USA Today,* p. D1. (p. 133)

Krebs, D. L., & Van Hesteren, F. (1994). The development of altruism: Toward an integrative model. *Developmental Review, 14,* 103–158. (p. 123)

Krijn, M., Emmelkamp, P. M. G., Olafsson, R. P., & Biemond, R. (2004). Virtual reality exposure therapy of anxiety disorders: A review. *Clinical Psychology Review, 24,* 259–281. (p. 547)

Kring, A. M., & Gordon, A. H. (1998). Sex differences in emotion: Expression, experience, and physiology. *Journal of Personality and Social Psychology, 74,* 686–703. (p. 419)

Kristof, N. D. (2004, July 21). Saying no to killers. *New York Times* (www.nytimes.com). (p. 613)

Kroll, R., Danis, S., Moreau, M., Waldbaum, A., Shifren, J., & Wekselman, K. (2004). Testosterone transdermal patch (TPP) significantly improved sexual function in naturally menopausal women in a large Phase III study. Presented to the American Society of Reproductive Medicine annual meeting, Philadelphia, October. (p. 376)

Krosnick, J. A., Betz, A. L., Jussim, L. J., & Lynn, A. R. (1992). Subliminal conditioning of attitudes. *Personality and Social Psychology Bulletin, 18,* 152–162. (p. 144)

Kruger J., Epley, N., Parker, J., & Ng, Z-W. (2005). Egocentrism over e-mail: Can we communicate as well as we think? *Journal of Personality and Social Psychology, 89,* 925–936. (p. 110)

Kruger, J., & Dunning, D. (1999). Unskilled and unaware of it: How difficulties in recognizing one's own incompetence lead to inflated self-assessments. *Journal of Personality and Social Psychology, 77,* 1121–1134. (p. 488)

Kruger, J., Epley, N., & Gilovich, T. (1999). Egocentrism over email. Paper presented at the American Psychological Society meeting. (p. 418)

Krugman, P. (2003, September 14). The tax-cut con. *New York Times* (www.nytimes.com). (p. A-2)

Krugman, P. (2005, July 4). Girth of a nation. *New York Times* (www.nytimes.com). (p. 367)

Krupa, D. J., Thompson, J. K., & Thompson, R. F. (1993). Localization of a memory trace in the mammalian brain. *Science, 260,* 989–991. (p. 283)

Krützen, M., Mann, J., Heithaus, M. R., Connor, R. C., Bejder, L., & Sherwin, W. B. (2005). Cultural transmission of tool use in bottlenose dolphins. *Proceedings of the National Academy of Sciences, 102,* 8939–8943. (p. 327)

Kubey, R., & Csikszentmihalyi, M. (2002, February). Television addiction is no mere metaphor. *Scientific American,* pp. 74–80. (p. 264)

Kübler, A., Winter, S., Ludolph, A. C., Hautzinger, M., & Birbaumer, N. (2005). Severity of depressive symptoms and quality of life in patients with amyotrophic lateral sclerosis. *Neurorehabilitation and Neural Repair, 19(3),* 182–193. (p. 426)

Kubzansky, L. D., Sparrow, D., Vokanas, P., Kawachi, I. (2001). Is the glass half empty or half full? A prospective study of optimism and coronary heart disease in the normative aging study. *Psychosomatic Medicine, 63,* 910–916. (pp. 401, 439)

Kuhl, P. K., & Meltzoff, A. N. (1982). The bimodal perception of speech in infancy. *Science, 218,* 1138–1141. (p. 320)

Kujala, U. M., Kaprio, J., Sarna, S., & Koskenvuo, M. (1998). Relationship of leisure-time physical activity and mortality: The Finnish twin cohort. *Journal of the American Medical Association, 279,* 440–444. (p. 450)

Kulkin, H. S., Chauvin, E. A., & Percle, G. A. (2000). Suicide among gay and lesbian adolescents and young adults: A review of the literature. *Journal of Homosexuality, 40,* 1–29. (p. 381)

Kuncel, N. R., Nezlett, S. A., & Ones, D. S. (2004). Academic performance, career potential, creativity, and job performance: Can one construct predict them all? *Journal of Personality and Social Psychology, 86,* 148–161. (p. 332)

Kunkel, D. (2001, February 4). *Sex on TV.* Menlo Park, CA: Henry J. Kaiser Family Foundation (www.kff.org). (p. 379)

Kunkel, D., Cope-Farrar, K., Biely, E., Farinola, W. J. M., & Donnerstein, E. (2001). *Sex on TV (2): A biennial report to the Kaiser Family Foundation.* Menlo Park, CA: Kaiser Family Foundation. (p. 604)

Kurtz, P. (1983, Spring). Stars, planets, and people. *The Skeptical Inquirer,* pp. 65–68. (p. 481)

L'Engle, M. (1972). *A wind in the door.* Bantam Doubleday Dell Books for Young Readers. (p. 13)

Labouvie-Vief, G., & Schell, D. A. (1982). Learning and memory in later life. In B. B. Wolman (Ed.), *Handbook of developmental psychology.* Englewood Cliffs, NJ: Prentice-Hall. (p. 133)

Lacayo, R. (1995, June 12). Violent reaction. *Time Magazine,* pp. 25–39. (p. 19)

Lachman, M. E. (2004). Development in midlife. *Annual Review of Psychology, 55,* 305–331. (p. 135)

Lachman, M. E., & Weaver, S. L. (1998). The sense of control as a moderator of social class differences in health and well-being. *Journal of Personality and Social Psychology, 74,* 763–773. (p. 485)

Ladd, E. C. (1998, August/September). The tobacco bill and American public opinion. *The Public Perspective,* pp. 5–19. (p. 227)

Ladd, G. T. (1887). *Elements of physiological psychology.* New York: Scribner's. (p. 193)

Laird, J. D. (1974). Self-attribution of emotion: The effects of expressive behavior on the quality of emotional experience. *Journal of Personality and Social Psychology, 29,* 475–486. (p. 422)

Laird, J. D. (1984). The real role of facial response in the experience of emotion: A reply to Tourangeau and Ellsworth, and others. *Journal of Personality and Social Psychology, 47,* 909–917. (p. 422)

Laird, J. D., Cuniff, M., Sheehan, K., Shulman, D., & Strum, G. (1989). Emotion specific effects of facial expressions on memory for life events. *Journal of Social Behavior and Personality, 4,* 87–98. (p. 422)

Lakin, J. L., & Chartrand, T. L. (2003). Using nonconscious behavioral mimicry to create affiliation and rapport. *Psychological Science, 14,* 334–339. (p. 582)

Lalumière, M. L., Blanchard, R., & Zucker, K. J. (2000). Sexual orientation and handedness in men and women: A meta-analysis. *Psychological Bulletin, 126,* 575–592. (p. 385)

Lambert, W. E. (1992). Challenging established views on social issues: The power and limitations of research. *American Psychologist, 47,* 533–542. (p. 324)

Lambert, W. E., Genesee, F., Holobow, N., & Chartrand, L. (1993). Bilingual education for majority English-speaking children. *European Journal of Psychology of Education, 8,* 3–22. (p. 324)

Lamberth, J. (1998, August 6). Driving while black: A statistician proves that prejudice still rules the road. *Washington Post,* p. C1. (p. 596)

Lampinen, J. M. (2002). What exactly is déjà vu? *Scientific American* (scieam.com/askexpert/biology/biology63). (p. 286)

Lammers, B. (2000). Quick tips for applying to graduate school in psychology. *Eye onPsi Chi, 4,* 40–42.

Landau, M. J., Solomon, S., Greenberg, J., Cohen, F., Pyszczynski, T., Arndt, J., Miller, C. H., Ogilvie, D. M., & Cook, A. (2004). Deliver us from evil: The effects of mortality salience and reminders of 9/11 on support for President George W. Bush. *Personality and Social Psychology Bulletin, 30,* 1136–1150. (p. 598)

Landauer, T. (2001, September). Quoted by R. Herbert, You must remember this. *APS Observer,* p. 11. (p. 302)

Landauer, T. K., & Whiting, J. W. M. (1979). Correlates and consequences of stress in infancy. In R. Munroe, B. Munroe & B. Whiting (Eds.), *Handbook of Cross-Cultural Human Development.* New York: Garland. (p. 436)

Landers, A. (1969, April 8). Syndicated newspaper column. Cited by L. Berkowitz, The case for bottling up rage. *Psychology Today,* September, 1973, pp. 24–31. (p. 424)

Landrum, E. (2001). I'm getting my bachelor's degree in psychology. What can I do with it? *Eye on Psi Chi,* 22–24. (pp. B-1, B-9)

Landry, M. J. (2002). MDMA: A review of epidemiologic data. *Journal of Psychoactive Drugs, 34,* 163–169. (p. 223)

Lang, E. V., Benotsch, E. G., Fick, L. J., Lutgendorf, S., Berbaum, M. L., Logan, H., & Spiegel, D. (2000). Adjunctive non-pharmacological analgesia for invasive medical procedures: A randomised trial. *Lancet, 355,* 1486–1490. (p. 214)

Langer, E. J. (1983). *The psychology of control.* Beverly Hills, CA: Sage. (p. 486)

Langer, E. J., & Abelson, R. P. (1974). A patient by any other name . . .: Clinician group differences in labeling bias. *Journal of Consulting and Clinical Psychology, 42,* 4–9. (p. 504)

Langer, E. J., & Imber, L. (1980). The role of mindlessness in the perception of deviance. *Journal of Personality and Social Psychology, 39,* 360–367. (p. 504)

Langlois, J. H., Kalakanis, L., Rubenstein, A. J., Larson, A., Hallam, M., & Smoot, M. (2000). Maxims or myths of beauty? A meta-analytic and theoretical review. *Psychological Bulletin, 126,* 390–423. (pp. 608, 609)

Langlois, J. H., Roggman, L. A., Casey, R. J., Ritter, J. M., Rieser-Danner, L. A., & Jenkins, V. Y. (1987). Infant preferences for attractive faces: Rudiments of a stereotype? *Developmental Psychology, 23,* 363–369. (p. 609)

Larkin, K., Resko, J. A., Stormshak, F., Stellflug, J. N., & Roselli, C. E. (2002). Neuroanatomical correlates of sex and sexual partner preference in sheep. Society for Neuroscience convention. (p. 383)

Larrance, D. T., & Twentyman, C. T. (1983). Maternal attributions and child abuse. *Journal of Abnormal Psychology, 92,* 449–457. (p. 110)

Larsen, R. J., & Diener, E. (1987). Affect intensity as an individual difference characteristic: A review. *Journal of Research in Personality, 21,* 1–39. (p. 72)

Larsen, R. J., Kasimatis, M., & Frey, K. (1992). Facilitating the furrowed brow: An unobtrusive test of the facial feedback hypothesis applied to unpleasant affect. *Cognition and Emotion, 6,* 321–338. (p. 422)

Larson, R. W. (2001). How U.S. children and adolescents spend time: What it does (and doesn't) tell us about their development. *Current Directions in Psychological Science, 10,* 160–164. (p. 125)

Larson, R. W., & Verma, S. (1999). How children and adolescents spend time across the world: Work, play, and developmental opportunities. *Psychological Bulletin, 125,* 701–736. (p. 347)

Larzelere, R. E. (1996). A review of the outcomes of parental use of nonabusive or customary physical punishment. *Pediatrics, 78,* 824–828. (p. 253)

Larzelere, R. E. (2000). Child outcomes of non-abusive and customary physical punishment by parents: An updated literature review. *Clinical Child and Family Psychology Review, 3,* 199–221. (p. 253)

Larzelere, R. E., Kuhn, B. R., & Johnson, B. (2004). The intervention selection bias: An underrecognized confound in intervention research. *Psychological Bulletin, 130,* 289–303. (p. 253)

Lashley, K. S. (1950). In search of the engram. In *Symposium of the Society for Experimental Biology (Vol. 4).* New York: Cambridge University Press. (p. 279)

Lassiter, G. D., & Irvine, A. A. (1986). Video-taped confessions: The impact of camera point of view on judgments of coercion. *Journal of Personality and Social Psychology, 16,* 268–276. (p. 576)

Latané, B. (1981). The psychology of social impact. *American Psychologist, 36,* 343–356. (p. 589)

Latané, B., & Dabbs, J. M., Jr. (1975). Sex, group size and helping in three cities. *Sociometry, 38,* 180–194. (p. 614)

Laudenslager, M. L., & Reite, M. L. (1984). Losses and separations: Immunological consequences and health implications. *Review of Personality and Social Psychology, 5,* 285–312. (p. 445)

Laumann, E. O., Gagnon, J. H., Michael, R. T., & Michaels, S. (1994). *The social organization of sexuality: Sexual practices in the United States.* Chicago: University of Chicago Press. (pp. 76, 381)

Lazarus, R. S. (1990). Theory-based stress measurement. *Psychological Inquiry, 1,* 3–13. (p. 438)

Lazarus, R. S. (1991). Progress on a cognitive-motivational-relational theory of emotion. *American Psychologist, 46,* 352–367. (p. 414)

Lazarus. R. S. (1998). *Fifty years of the research and theory of R. S. Lazarus: An analysis of historical and perennial issues.* Mahwah, NJ: Erlbaum. (pp. 414, 435)

Le Grand, R., Mondloch, C. J., Maurer, D., & Brent, H. P. (2004). Impairment in holistic face processing following early visual deprivation. *Psychological Science, 15,* 762–768. (p. 181)

Lea, S. E. G. (2000). Towards an ethical use of animals. *The Psychologist, 13,* 556–557. (p. 30)

Leach, P. (1993). Should parents hit their children? *The Psychologist: Bulletin of the British Psychological Society, 6,* 216–220. (p. 253)

Leach, P. (1994). *Children first.* New York: Knopf. (p. 253)

Leary, M. R. (1999). The social and psychological importance of self-esteem. In R. M. Kowalski & M. R. Leary (Eds.), *The social psychology of emotional and behavioral problems.* Washington, DC: APA Books. (p. 491)

Leary, M. R., Haupt, A. L., Strausser, K. S., & Chokel, J. T. (1998). Calibrating the sociometer: The relationship between interpersonal appraisals and state self-esteem. *Journal of Personality and Social Psychology, 74,* 1290–1299. (p. 388)

Leary, W. E. (1998, September 28). Older people enjoy sex, survey says. *New York Times* (www.nytimes.com). (p. 130)

LeDoux, J. (1996). *The emotional brain: The mysterious underpinnings of emotional life.* New York: Simon & Schuster. (p. 283)

LeDoux, J. E., & Armony, J. (1999). Can neurobiology tell us anything about human feelings? In D. Kahneman, E. Diener, & N. Schwartz (Eds.), *Well-being: The foundations of hedonic psychology.* New York: Sage. (p. 414)

Lefcourt, H. M. (1982). *Locus of control: Current trends in theory and research.* Hillsdale, NJ: Erlbaum. (p. 485)

Legrand, L. N., Iacono, W. G., & McGue, M. (2005). Predicting addiction. *American Scientist, 93,* 140–147. (p. 227)

Lehman, A. F., Steinwachs, D. M., Dixon, L. B., Goldman, H. H., Osher, F., Postrado, L., Scott, J. E., Thompson, J. W., Fahey, M., Fischer, P., Kasper, J. A., Lyles, A., Skinner, E. A., Buchanan, R., Carpenter, W. T., Jr., Levine, J., McGlynn, E. A., Rosenheck, R., & Zito, J. (1998). Translating research into practice: The schizophrenia patient outcomes research team (PORT) treatment recommendations. *Schizophrenia Bulletin, 24,* 1–10. (p. 566)

Lehman, D. R., Wortman, C. B., & Williams, A. F. (1987). Long-term effects of losing a spouse or child in a motor vehicle crash. *Journal of Personality and Social Psychology, 52,* 218–231. (p. 139)

Leigh, B. C. (1989). In search of the seven dwarves: Issues of measurement and meaning in alcohol expectancy research. *Psychological Bulletin, 105,* 361–373. (p. 219)

Leitenberg, H., & Henning, K. (1995). Sexual fantasy. *Psychological Bulletin, 117,* 469–496. (pp. 377, 378)

Lemonick, M. D. (2002, June 3). Lean and hungrier. *Time,* p. 54. (p. 362)

Lennox, B. R., Bert, S., Park, G., Jones, P. B., & Morris, P. G. (1999). Spatial and temporal mapping of neural activity associated with auditory hallucinations. *Lancet, 353,* 644. (p. 56)

Lenzenweger, M. F., Dworkin, R. H., & Wethington, E. (1989). Models of positive and negative symptoms in schizophrenia: An empirical evaluation of latent structures. *Journal of Abnormal Psychology, 98,* 62–70. (p. 566)

Lerner, M. J. (1980). *The belief in a just world: A fundamental delusion.* New York: Plenum Press. (p. 599)

Leserman, J., Jackson, E. D., Petitto, J. M., Golden, R. N., Silva, S. G., Perkins, D. O., Cai, J., Folds, J. D., & Evans, D. L. (1999). Progression to AIDS: The effects of stress, depressive symptoms, and social support. *Psychosomatic Medicine, 61,* 397–406. (p. 441)

Lester, W. (2004, May 26). AP polls: Nations value immigrant workers. *Associated Press* release. (p. 595)

Leucht, S., Barnes, T. R. E., Kissling, W., Engel, R. R., Correll, C., & Kane, J. M. (2003). Relapse prevention in schizophrenia with new-generation antipsychotics: A systematic review and exploratory meta-analysis of randomized, controlled trials. *American Journal of Psychiatry, 160,* 1209–1222. (p. 566)

LeVay, S. (1991). A difference in hypothalamic structure between heterosexual and homosexual men. *Science, 253,* 1034–1037. (p. 383)

LeVay, S. (1994, March). Quoted in D. Nimmons, Sex and the brain. *Discover,* pp. 64–71. (p. 383)

Levenson, R. W. (1992). Autonomic nervous system differences among emotions. *Psychological Science, 3,* 23–27. (p. 410)

Lever, J. (2003, November 11). Personal correspondence reporting data responses volunteered to Elle/MSNBC.com survey of weight perceptions. (p. 365)

Levin, I. P., & Gaeth, G. J. (1988). How consumers are affected by the framing of attribute information before and after consuming the product. *Journal of Consumer Research, 15,* 374–378. (p. 313)

Levine, J. A., Eberhardt, N. L., & Jensen, M. D. (1999). Role of nonexercise activity thermogenesis in resistance to fat gain in humans. *Science, 283,* 212–214. (p. 369)

Levine, J. A., Lanningham-Foster, L. M., McCrady, S. K., Krizan, A. C., Olson, L. R., Kane, P. H., Jensen, M. D., & Clark, M. M. (2005). Interindividual variation in posture allocation: Possible role in human obesity. *Science, 307,* 584–586. (p. 369)

Levine, R. V., & Norenzayan, A. (1999). The pace of life in 31 countries. *Journal of Cross-Cultural Psychology, 30,* 178–205. (pp. 21, 83)

Levine, R., Sato, S., Hashimoto, T., & Verma, J. (1995). Love and marriage in eleven cultures. *Journal of Cross-Cultural Psychology, 26,* 554–571. (p. 612)

Levy, P. E. (2003). *Industrial/organizational psychology: Understanding the workplace.* Boston: Houghton Mifflin. (p. 397)

Lewinsohn, P. M., & Rosenbaum, M. (1987). Recall of parental behavior by acute depressives, remitted depressives, and nondepressives. *Journal of Personality and Social Psychology, 52,* 611–619. (p. 287)

Lewinsohn, P. M., Hoberman, H., Teri, L., & Hautziner, M. (1985). An integrative theory of depression. In S. Reiss & R. Bootzin (Eds.), *Theoretical issues in behavior therapy.* Orlando, FL: Academic Press. (p. 522)

Lewinsohn, P. M., Rohde, P., & Seeley, J. R. (1998). Major depressive disorder in older adolescents: Prevalence, risk factors, and clinical implications. *Clinical Psychology Review, 18,* 765–794. (p. 522)

Lewis, C. S. (1967). *Christian reflections.* Grand Rapids, MI: Eerdmans. (p. 290)

Lewis, D. O., Pincus, J. H., Bard, B., Richardson, E., Prichep, L. S., Feldman, M., & Yeager, C. (1988). Neuropsychiatric, psychoeducational, and family characteristics of 14 juveniles condemned to death in the United States. *American Journal of Psychiatry, 145,* 584–589. (p. 116)

Lewis, D. O., Pincus, J. H., Feldman, M., Jackson, L., & Bard, B. (1986). Psychiatric, neurological, and psychoeducational characteristics of 15 death row inmates in the United States. *American Journal of Psychiatry, 143,* 838–845. (p. 600)

Lewis, D. O., Yeager, C. A., Swica, Y., Pincus, J. H., & Lewis, M. (1997). Objective documentation of child abuse and dissociation in 12 murderers with dissociative identity disorder. *American Journal of Psychiatry, 154,* 1703–1710. (p. 517)

Lewis, M. (1992). Commentary. *Human Development, 35,* 44–51. (p. 287)

Lewontin, R. (1976). Race and intelligence. In N. J. Block & G. Dworkin (Eds.), *The IQ controversy: Critical readings.* New York: Pantheon. (p. 346)

Lewontin, R. (1982). *Human diversity.* New York: Scientific American Library. (pp. 75, 346)

Li, J. C., Dunning, D., & Malpass, R. L. (1996). Cross-racial identification among European-Americans Basketball fandom and the contact hypothesis. Unpublished manuscript, Cornell University. (p. 598)

Li, J., Laursen, T. M., Precht, D. H., Olsen, J., & Mortensen, P. B. (2005). Hospitalization for mental illness among parents after the death of a child. *New England Journal of Medicine, 352,* 1190–1196. (p. 139)

Licata, A., Taylor, S., Berman, M., & Cranston, J. (1993). Effects of cocaine on human aggression. *Pharmacology Biochemistry and Behavior, 45,* 549–552. (p. 222)

Lichtman, S. W., Pisarska, K., Berman, E. R., Pestone, M., Dowling, H., Offenbacher, E., Weisel, H., Heshka, S., Matthews, D. E., & Heymsfield, S. B. (1992). Discrepancy between self-reported and actual caloric intake and exercise in obese subjects. *New England Journal of Medicine, 327,* 1893–1898. (p. 370)

Lieberman, J. A., & 11 others. (2005). Effectiveness of antipsychotic drugs in patients with chronic schizophrenia. *New England Journal of Medicine, 353,* 1209–1223. (p. 566)

Lilienfeld, S. O., Lynn, S. J., Kirsch, I., Chaves, J. F., Sarbin, T. R., Ganaway, G. K., & Powell, R. A. (1999). Dissociative identity disorder and the sociocognitive model: Recalling the lessons of the past. *Psychological Bulletin, 125,* 507–523. (p. 517)

Lilienfeld, S. O., Wood, J. M., & Garb, H. N. (2000). The scientific status of projective techniques. *Psychological Science in the Public Interest, 1,* 27–66. (p. 465)

Lilienfeld, S. O., Wood, J. M., & Garb, H. N. (2001, May). What's wrong with this picture? *Scientific American,* pp. 81–87. (p. 465)

Linde, K., & 10 others. (2005). Acupuncture for patients with migraine: A randomized controlled trial. *Journal of the American Medical Association, 293,* 2118–2125. (p. 452)

Lindskold, S. (1978). Trust development, the GRIT proposal, and the effects of conciliatory acts on conflict and cooperation. *Psychological Bulletin, 85,* 772–793. (p. 618)

Lindskold, S., & Han, G. (1988). GRIT as a foundation for integrative bargaining. *Personality and Social Psychology Bulletin, 14,* 335–345. (p. 618)

Linville, P. W., Fischer, G. W., & Fischhoff, B. (1992). AIDS risk perceptions and decision biases. In J. B. Pryor & G. D. Reeder (Eds.), *The social psychology of HIV infection.* Hillsdale, NJ: Erlbaum. (p. 313)

Lippa, R. A. (2002). Gender-related traits of heterosexual and homosexual men and women. *Archives of Sexual Behavior, 31,* 83–98. (p. 385)

Lippman, J. (1992, October 25). Global village is characterized by a television in every home. *Los Angeles Times Syndicate* (in *Grand Rapids Press,* p. F9). (p. 264)

Lipps, H. M. (1999). *A new psychology of women: Gender, culture, and ethnicity.* Mountain View, CA: Mayfield Publishing. (p. 596)

Lipsitt, L. P. (2003). Crib death: A biobehavioral phenomenon? *Current Directions in Psychological Science, 12,* 164–170. (p. 105)

Lipton, J. S., & Spelke, E. S. (2003). Origins of number sense: Large-number discrimination in human infants. *Psychological Science, 14,* 296–401. (p. 109)

Livingstone, M., & Hubel, D. (1988). Segregation of form, color, movement, and depth: Anatomy, physiology, and perception. *Science, 240,* 740–749. (p. 152)

Locke, E. A., & Latham, G. P. (2002). Building a practically useful theory of goal setting and task motivation. *American Psychologist, 57,* 705–717. (p. 401)

Loehlin, J. C., & Nichols, R. C. (1976). *Heredity, environment, and personality.* Austin: University of Texas Press. (p. 69)

Loehlin, J. C., McCrae, R. R., & Costa, P. T., Jr. (1998). Heritabilities of common and measure-specific components of the Big Five personality factors. *Journal of Research in Personality, 32,* 431–453. (p. 478)

Loewenstein, G., & Furstenberg, F. (1991). Is teenage sexual behavior rational? *Journal of Applied Social Psychology, 21,* 957–986. (p. 250)

Loftus, E. F. (1979). The malleability of human memory. *American Scientist, 67,* 313–320. (p. 296)

Loftus, E. F. (1980). *Memory: Surprising new insights into how we remember and why we forget.* Reading, MA: Addison-Wesley. (p. 212)

Loftus, E. F. (1993). The reality of repressed memories. *American Psychologist, 48,* 518–537. (p. 301)

Loftus, E. F. (1995, March/April). Remembering dangerously. *Skeptical Inquirer,* pp. 20–29. (p. 466)

Loftus, E. F. (2001, November). Imagining the past. *The Psychologist, 14,* 584–587. (p. 297)

Loftus, E. F., & Ketcham, K. (1994). *The myth of repressed memory.* New York: St. Martin's Press. (p. 279, 301)

Loftus, E. F., & Loftus, G. R. (1980). On the permanence of stored information in the human brain. *American Psychologist, 35,* 409–420. (p. 279)

Loftus, E. F., & Palmer, J. C. (October, 1974). Reconstruction of automobile destruction: An example of the interaction between language and memory. *Journal of Verbal Learning & Verbal Behavior, 13(5),* 585–589. (p. 296)

Loftus, E. F., Coan, J., & Pickrell, J. E. (1996). Manufacturing false memories using bits of reality. In L. Reder (Ed.), *Implicit memory and metacognition.* Mahway, NJ: Erlbaum. (p. 300)

Loftus, E. F., Levidow, B., & Duensing, S. (1992). Who remembers best? Individual differences in memory for events that occurred in a science museum. *Applied Cognitive Psychology, 6,* 93–107. (p. 296)

Loftus, E. F., Milo, E. M., & Paddock, J. R. (1995). The accidental executioner: Why psychotherapy must be informed by science. *The Counseling Psychologist, 23,* 300–309. (p. 299)

Loftus, G. R. (1992). When a lie becomes memory's truth: Memory distortion after exposure to misinformation. *Current Directions in Psychological Science, 1,* 121–123. (p. 296)

Logan, T. K., Walker, R., Cole, J., & Leukefeld, C. (2002). Victimization and substance abuse among women: Contributing factors, interventions, and implications. *Review of General Psychology, 6,* 325–397. (p. 226)

Logue, A. W. (1998a). Laboratory research on self-control: Applications to administration. *Review of General Psychology, 2,* 221–238. (p. 250)

Logue, A. W. (1998b). Self-control. In W. T. O'Donohue, (Ed.), *Learning and behavior therapy.* Boston, MA: Allyn & Bacon. (p. 250)

London, P. (1970). The rescuers: Motivational hypotheses about Christians who saved Jews from the Nazis. In J. Macaulay & L. Berkowitz (Eds.), *Altruism and helping behavior.* New York: Academic Press. (p. 263)

Looy, H. (2001). Sex differences: Evolved, constructed, and designed. *Journal of Psychology and Theology, 29,* 301–313. (p. 77)

Lopes, P. N., Brackett, M. A., Nezlek, J. B., Schutz, A., Sellin, II, & Salovey, P. (2004). Emotional intelligence and social interaction. *Personality and Social Psychology Bulletin, 30,* 1018–1034. (p. 335)

Lopez, A. D. (1999). Measuring the health hazards of tobacco: Commentary. *Bulletin of the World Health Organization, 77(1),* 82–83. (p. 220)

Lord, C. G., Lepper, M. R., & Preston, E. (1984). Considering the opposite: A corrective strategy for social judgment. *Journal of Personality and Social Psychology, 47,* 1231–1247. (p. 313)

Lord, C. G., Ross, L., & Lepper, M. (1979). Biased assimilation and attitude polarization: The effects of prior theories on subsequently considered evidence. *Journal of Personality and Social Psychology, 37,* 2098–2109. (p. 313)

Lorenz, K. (1937). The companion in the bird's world. *Auk, 54,* 245–273. (p. 114)

Los Angeles Times. *(1998, 14 March). Daughters give birth on same day, p. A15. (p. 24)*

Louie, K., & Wilson, M. A. (2001). Temporally structured replay of awake hippocampal ensemble activity during rapid eye movement sleep. *Neuron, 29,* 145–156. (p. 207)

Lourenco, O., & Machado, A. (1996). In defense of Piaget's theory: A reply to 10 common criticisms. *Psychological Review, 103,* 143–164. (p. 112)

Lovaas, O. I. (1987). Behavioral treatment and normal educational and intellectual functioning in young autistic children. *Journal of Consulting and Clinical Psychology, 55,* 3–9. (p. 548)

Lowry, P. E. (1997). The assessment center process: New directions. *Journal of Social Behavior and Personality, 12,* 53–62. (489)

Lu, Z.-L., Williamson, S. J., & Kaufman, L. (1992). Behavioral lifetime of human auditory sensory memory predicted by physiological measures. *Science, 258,* 1668–1670. (p. 261), 277)

Lubinski, D., & Benbow, C. P. (1992). Gender differences in abilities and preferences among the gifted: Implications for the math-science pipeline. *Current Directions in Psychological Science, 1,* 61–66. (p. 347)

Lubinski, D., & Benbow, C. P. (2000). States of excellence. *American Psychologist,* 137–150. (p. 340)

Luborsky, L., Rosenthal, R., Diguer, L., Andrusyna, T. P., Berman, J. S., Levitt, J. T., Seligman, D. A., & Krause, E. D. (2002). The dodo bird verdict is alive and well—mostly. *Clinical Psychology: Science and Practice, 9,* 2–34. (p. 557)

Lucas, A., Morley, R., Cole, T. J., Lister, G., & Leeson-Payne, C. (1992). Breast milk and subsequent intelligence quotient in children born preterm. *Lancet, 339,* 261–264. (p. 25)

Lucas, R. E. (2005). Long-term disability has lasting effects on subjective well-being: Evidence from two nationally representative longitudinal studies. Unpublished manuscript, Michigan State University. (p. 426)

Lucas, R. E., Clark, A. E., Georgellis, Y., & Diener, E. (2003). Re-examining adaptation and the setpoint model of happiness: Reactions to changes in marital status. *Journal of Personality and Social Psychology, 84,* 527–539. (Figure courtesy of R. E. Lucas.) (p. 139)

Lucas, R. E., Clark, A. E., Georgellis, Y., & Diener, E. (2004). Unemployment alters the set point for life satisfaction. *Psychological Science, 15,* 8–13. (p. 432)

Ludwig, A. M. (1995). *The price of greatness: Resolving the creativity and madness controversy.* New York: Guilford Press. (pp. 382, 522)

Ludwig, J. (2004, June 1). Acceptance of interracial marriage at record high. *Gallup Poll Tuesday Briefing* (www.gallup.com). (p. 594)

Luntz, F. (2003, June 10). Quoted by T. Raum, "Bush insists banned weapons will be found." *Associated Press* (story.news.yahoo.com). (p. 580)

Luria, A. M. (1968). In L. Solotaroff (Trans.), *The mind of a mnemonist.* New York: Basic Books. (p. 269)

Lustig, C., & Buckner, R. L. (2004). Preserved neural correlates of priming in old age and dementia. *Neuron, 42,* 865–875. (p. 282)

Lutgendorf, S. K., Russell, D., Ullrich, P., Harris, T. B., & Wallace, R. (2004). Religious participation, Interleukin-6, and mortality in older adults. *Health Psychology, 23,* 465–475. (p. 455)

Luthar, S. S., & Latendresse, S. J. (2005). Children of the affluent: Challenges to well-being. *Current Directions in Psychological Science, 14,* 49–53. (p. 427)

Lykken, D. T. (1991). Science, lies, and controversy: An epitaph for the polygraph. Invited address upon receipt of the Senior Career Award for Distinguished Contribution to Psychology in the Public Interest, American Psychological Association convention. (p. 412)

Lykken, D. T. (1995). *The antisocial personalities.* Hillsdale, NJ: Erlbaum. (p. 518, 601)

Lykken, D. T. (1999). *Happiness.* New York: Golden Books. (p. 342)

Lykken, D. T. (2001). Happiness—stuck with what you've got? *The Psychologist, 14,* 470–473. (p. 71)

Lykken, D. T., & Tellegen, A. (1993) Is human mating adventitious or the result of lawful choice? A twin study of mate selection. *Journal of Personality and Social Psychology, 65,* 56–68. (p. 135)

Lykken, D. T., & Tellegen, A. (1996). Happiness is a stochastic phenomenon. *Psychological Science, 7,* 186–189. (p. 432)

Lyman, D. R. (1996). Early identification of chronic offenders: Who is the fledgling psychopath? *Psychological Bulletin, 120,* 209–234. (p. 518)

Lynch, G. (2002). Memory enhancement: The search for mechanism-based drugs. *Nature Neuroscience, 5* (suppl.), 1035–1038. (p. 280)

Lynch, G., & Staubli, U. (1991). Possible contributions of long-term potentiation to the encoding and organization of memory. *Brain Research Reviews, 16,* 204–206. (p. 280)

Lynn, M. (1988). The effects of alcohol consumption on restaurant tipping. *Personality and Social Psychology Bulletin, 14,* 87–91. (p. 218)

Lynn, R. (1987). Japan: Land of the rising IQ. A reply to Flynn. *Bulletin of the British Psychological Society, 40,* 464–468. (p. 346)

Lynn, R. (1991, Fall/Winter). The evolution of racial differences in intelligence. *The Mankind Quarterly, 32,* 99–145. (p. 346)

Lynn, R. (2001). *Eugenics: A reassessment.* Westport, CT: Praeger/Greenwood. (p. 346)

Lynn, S. J., Rhue, J. W., & Weekes, J. R. (1990). Hypnotic involuntariness: A social cognitive analysis. *Psychological Review, 97,* 169–184. (p. 214)

Lyons, L. (2002, June 25). Are spiritual teens healthier? *Gallup Tuesday Briefing,* Gallup Organization (www.gallup.com/poll/tb/religValue/20020625b.asp). (p. 455)

Lyons, L. (2003, September 23). Oh, boy: Americans still prefer sons. *Gallup Poll Tuesday Briefing* (www.gallup.com). (p. 596)

Lyons, L. (2005, January 4). Teens stay true to parents' political perspectives. *Gallup Poll News Service* (www.gallup.com). (p. 126)

Lytton, H., & Romney, D. M. (1991). Parents' differential socialization of boys and girls: A meta-analysis. *Psychological Bulletin, 109,* 267–296. (p. 92)

Lyubomirsky, S. (2001). Why are some people happier than others? The role of cognitive and motivational processes in well-being. *American Psychologist, 56,* 239–249. (p. 430)

Lyubomirsky, S., King, L., & Diener, E. (2005). The benefits of frequent positive affect: Does happiness lead to success? *Psychological Bulletin, 131,* 803–855. (p. 425)

Lyubomirsky, S., Sousa, L., & Dickerhoof, R. (2006). The costs and benefits of writing, talking, and thinking about life's triumphs and defeats. *Journal of Personality and Social Psychology, 90,* 692–708. (p. 449)

Ma, L. (1997, September). On the origin of Darwin's ills. *Discover,* p. 27. (p. 511)

Maas, J. B. (1999). *Power sleep. The revolutionary program that prepares your mind for peak performance.* New York: HarperCollins. (pp. 201, 202, 204)

Maass, A., & Russo, A. (2003). Directional bias in the mental representation of spatial events: Nature or culture? *Psychological Science, 14,* 296–301. (p. 324)

Macaluso, E., Frith, C. D., & Driver, J. (2000). Modulation of human visual cortex by crossmodal spatial attention. *Science, 289,* 1206–1208. (p. 165)

Macan, T. H., & Dipboye, R. L. (1994). The effects of the application on processing of information from the employment interview. *Journal of Applied Social Psychology, 24,* 1291. (p. 395)

Maccoby, E. E. (1990). Gender and relationships: A developmental account. *American Psychologist, 45,* 513–520. (p. 89)

Maccoby, E. E. (1995). Divorce and custody: The rights, needs, and obligations of mothers, fathers, and children. *Nebraska Symposium on Motivation, 42,* 135–172. (p. 91)

Maccoby, E. E. (1998). *The paradox of gender.* Cambridge, MA: Harvard University Press. (p. 88)

Maccoby, E. E. (2002). Gender and group process: A developmental perspective. *Current Directions in Psychological Science, 11,* 54–58. (p. 590)

MacDonald, N. (1960). Living with schizophrenia. *Canadian Medical Association Journal, 82,* 218–221. (p. 531)

MacDonald, T. K., Fong, G. T., Zanna, M. P., & Martineau, A. M. (2000). Alcohol myopia and condom use: Can alcohol intoxication be associated with more prudent behavior? *Journal of Personality and Social Psychology, 78,* 605–619. (p. 218)

MacDonald, T. K., Zanna, M. P., & Fong, G. T. (1995). Decision making in altered states: Effects of alcohol on attitudes toward drinking and driving. *Journal of Personality and Social Psychology, 68,* 973–985. (p. 218)

MacDonald, T. K., Zanna, M. P., & Fong, G. T. (1996). Why common sense goes out the window: The effects of alcohol on intentions to use condoms. *Personality and Social Psychology Bulletin, 22,* 763–775. (p. 218)

MacFarlane, A. (1978, February). What a baby knows. *Human Nature,* pp. 74–81. (p. 103)

Macfarlane, J. W. (1964). Perspectives on personality consistency and change from the guidance study. *Vita Humana, 7,* 115–126. (p. 120)

MacKinnon, D. W., & Hall, W. B. (1972). Intelligence and creativity. In *Proceedings, XVIIth International Congress of Applied Psychology (Vol. 2).* Brussels: Editest. (p. 334)

MacLeod, C., & Campbell, L. (1992). Memory accessibility and probability judgments: An experimental evaluation of the availability heuristic. *Journal of Personality and Social Psychology, 63,* 890–902. (p. 311)

MacNeilage, P. F., & Davis, B. L. (2000). On the origin of internal structure of word forms. *Science, 288,* 527–531. (p. 320)

Maddox, K. B. (2004). Perspectives on racial phenotypicality bias. *Personality and Social Psychology Review, 8,* 383–401. (p. 595)

Maes, H. H. M., Neale, M. C., & Eaves, L. J. (1997). Genetic and environmental factors in relative body weight and human adiposity. *Behavior Genetics, 27,* 325–351. (p. 369)

Maestripieri, D. (2003). Similarities in affiliation and aggression between cross-fostered rhesus macaque females and their biological mothers. *Developmental Psychobiology, 43,* 321–327. (p. 71)

Magnusson, D. (1990). Personality research—challenges for the future. *European Journal of Personality, 4,* 1–17. (p. 518)

Maguire, E. A., Spiers, H. J., Good, C. D., Hartley, T., Frackowiak, R. S. J., & Burgess, N. (2003a). Navigation expertise and the human hippocampus: A structural brain imaging analysis. *Hippocampus, 13,* 250–259. (p. 283)

Maguire, E. A., Valentine, E. R., Wilding, J. M., & Kapur, N. (2003b). Routes to remembering: The brains behind superior memory. *Nature Neuroscience, 6,* 90–95. (pp. 275, 283)

Mahowald, M. W., & Ettinger, M. G. (1990). Things that go bump in the night: The parsomias revisited. *Journal of Clinical Neurophysiology, 7,* 119–143. (p. 198)

Maier, S. F., Watkins, L. R., & Fleshner, M. (1994). Psychoneuroimmunology: The interface between behavior, brain, and immunity. *American Psychologist, 49,* 1004–1017. (pp. 440, 441)

Major, B., Carrington, P. I., & Carnevale, P. J. D. (1984). Physical attractiveness and self-esteem: Attribution for praise from an other-sex evaluator. *Personality and Social Psychology Bulletin, 10,* 43–50. (p. 609)

Major, B., Schmidlin, A. M., & Williams, L. (1990). Gender patterns in social touch: The impact of setting and age. *Journal of Personality and Social Psychology, 58,* 634–643. (p. 88)

Malamuth, N. M. (1996). Sexually explicit media, gender differences, and evolutionary theory. *Journal of Communication, 46,* 8–31. (p. 603)

Malamuth, N. M., & Check, J. V. P. (1981). The effects of media exposure on acceptance of violence against women: A field experiment. *Journal of Research in Personality, 15,* 436–446. (p. 378)

Malamuth, N. M., Linz, D., Heavey, C. L., Barnes, G., & Acker, M. (1995). Using the confluence model of sexual aggression to predict men's conflict with women: A 10-year follow-up study. *Journal of Personality and Social Psychology, 69,* 353–369. (p. 604)

Malamuth, N. M., Sockloskie, R. J., Koss, M. P., & Tanaka, J. S. (1991). Characteristics of aggressors against women: Testing a model using a national sample of college students. *Journal of Consulting and Clinical Psychology, 59,* 670–681. (p. 604)

Malan, D. H. (1978). "The case of the secretary with the violent father." In H. Davanloo (Ed.), *Basic principles and techniques in short-term dynamic psychotherapy.* New York: Spectrum. (p. 543)

Malinosky-Rummell, R., & Hansen, D. J. (1993). Long-term consequences of childhood physical abuse. *Psychological Bulletin, 114,* 68–79. (p. 116)

Malkiel, B. (2004). *A random walk down Wall Street (8th ed.).* New York: Norton. (p. 312)

Malkiel, B. G. (1989). Is the stock market efficient? *Science, 243,* 1313–1318. (p. 24)

Malkiel, B. G. (1995, June). Returns from investing in equity mutual funds 1971 to 1991. *Journal of Finance,* pp. 549–572. (p. 24)

Malloy, E. A. (1994, June 7). Report of the Commission on Substance Abuse at Colleges and Universities, reported by *Associated Press.* (p. 218)

Malmquist, C. P. (1986). Children who witness parental murder: Posttraumatic aspects. *Journal of the American Academy of Child Psychiatry, 25,* 320–325. (p. 466)

Malnic, B., Hirono, J., Sato, T., & Buck, L. B. (1999). Combinatorial receptor codes for odors. *Cell, 96,* 713–723. (p. 167)

Manber, R., Bootzin, R. R., Acebo, C., & Carskadon, M. A. (1996). The effects of regularizing sleep-wake schedules on daytime sleepiness. *Sleep, 19,* 432–441. (p. 204)

Mandel, D. (1983, March 13). One man's holocaust: Part II. The story of David Mandel's journey through hell as told to David Kagan. *Wonderland Magazine (Grand Rapids Press),* pp. 2–7. (p. 360)

Mann, J. J. (2003). Neurobiology of suicidal behaviour. *Nature Reviews Neuroscience, 4,* 819–828. (p. 524)

Manson, J. E. (2002). Walking compared with vigorous exercise for the prevention of cardiovascular events in women. *New England Journal of Medicine, 347,* 716–725. (p. 450)

Maquet, P. (2001). The role of sleep in learning and memory. *Science, 294,* 1048–1052. (p. 207)

Maquet, P., Peters, J-M., Aerts, J., Delfiore, G., Degueldre, C., Luxen, A., & Franck, G. (1996). Functional neuroanatomy of human rapid-eye-movement sleep and dreaming. *Nature, 383,* 163–166. (p. 208)

Marangell, L. B., Rush, A. J., George, M. S., Sackeim, H. A., Johnson, C. R., Husain, M. M., Nahas, Z., & Lisanby, S. H. (2002). Vagus nerve stimulation (VNS) for major depressive episodes: One year outcomes. *Biological Psychiatry, 51,* 280–287. (p. 569)

Marcus, G. (2004). *The birth of the mind: How a tiny number of genes creates the complexity of human thought.* New York: Basic Books. (p. 72)

Margolis, M. L. (2000). Brahms' lullaby revisited: Did the composer have obstructive sleep apnea? *Chest, 118,* 210–213. (p. 205)

Markowitsch, H. J. (1995). Which brain regions are critically involved in the retrieval of old episodic memory? *Brain Research Reviews, 21,* 117–127. (p. 283)

Markus, G. B. (1986). Stability and change in political attitudes: Observe, recall, and "explain." *Political Behavior, 8,* 21–44. (p. 298)

Markus, H., & Kitayama, S. (1991). Culture and the self: Implications for cognition, emotion, and motivation. *Psychological Review, 98,* 224–253. (pp. 85, 323, 424)

Markus, H., & Nurius, P. (1986). Possible selves. *American Psychologist, 41,* 954–969. (p. 490)

Marlatt, G. A. (1991). Substance abuse: Etiology, prevention, and treatment issues. Master lecture, American Psychological Association convention. (p. 218)

Marley, J., & Bulia, S. (2001). Crimes against people with mental illness: Types, perpetrators and influencing factors. *Social Work, 46,* 115–124. (p. 505)

Marmot, M. G., Bosma, H., Hemingway, H., Brunner, E., & Stansfeld, S. (1997). Contribution to job control and other risk factors to social variations in coronary heart disease incidents. *Lancet, 350,* 235–239. (p. 446)

Marschark, M., Richman, C. L., Yuille, J. C., & Hunt, R. R. (1987). The role of imagery in memory: On shared and distinctive information. *Psychological Bulletin, 102,* 28–41. (p. 275)

Marsh, A. A., Elfenbein, H. A., & Ambady, N. (2003). Nonverbal "accents": Cultural differences in facial expressions of emotion. *Psychological Science, 14,* 373–376. (p. 421)

Marsh, H. W., & Parker, J. W. (1984). Determinants of student self-concept: Is it better to be a relatively large fish in a small pond even if you don't learn to swim as well? *Journal of Personality and Social Psychology, 47,* 213–231. (p. 431)

Marshall, M. J. (2002). *Why spanking doesn't work.* Springville, UT: Bonneville Books. (p. 253)

Marteau, T. M. (1989). Framing of information: Its influences upon decisions of doctors and patients. *British Journal of Social Psychology, 28,* 89–94. (p. 313)

Marti, M. W., Robier, D. M., & Baron, R. S. (2000). Right before our eyes: The failure to recognize non-prototypical forms of prejudice. *Group Processes and Intergroup Relations, 3,* 403–418. (p. 308)

Martin, C. L., & Ruble, D. (2004). Children's search for gender cues. *Current Directions in Psychological Science, 13,* 67–70. (p. 92)

Martin, C. L., Ruble, D. N., & Szkrybalo, J. (2002). Cognitive theories of early gender development. *Psychological Bulletin, 128,* 903–933. (p. 92)

Martin, J. L. R., Barbanojh, M. J., Schlaepfer, T. E., Thompson, E., Perez, V., & Kulisevsky, J. (2005). Repetitive transcranial magnetic stimulation for the treatment of depression: Systematic review and meta-analysis. *British Journal of Psychiatry, 182,* 480–491. (p. 570)

Martin, R. J., White, B. D., & Hulsey, M. G. (1991). The regulation of body weight. *American Scientist, 79,* 528–541. (p. 370)

Martin, S. J., Kelly, I. W., & Saklofske, D. H. (1992). Suicide and lunar cycles: A critical review over 28 years. *Psychological Reports, 71,* 787–795. (p. 506)

Martins, Y., Preti, G., Crabtree, C. R., & Wysocki, C. J. (2005). Preference for human body odors is influenced by gender and sexual orientation. *Psychological Science, 16,* 694–701. (p. 383)

Maruta, T., Colligan, R. C., Malinchoc, M., & Offord, K. P. (2002). Optimists vs. pessimists: Survival rate among medical patients over a 30-year period. *Mayo Clinic Proceedings, 75,* 140–143. (p. 446)

Maslow, A. H. (1970). *Motivation and personality (2nd ed.).* New York: Harper & Row. (pp. 359, 471)

Maslow, A. H. (1971). *The farther reaches of human nature.* New York: Viking Press. (p. 359)

Mason, C., & Kandel, E. R. (1991). Central visual pathways. In E. R. Kandel, J. H. Schwartz, & T. M. Jessell (Eds.), *Principles of neural science (3rd ed.).* New York: Elsevier. (pp. 41, 42)

Mason, H. (2003, March 25). Wake up, sleepy teen. *Gallup Poll Tuesday Briefing* (www.gallup.com). (p. 201)

Mason, H. (2003, September 2). Americans, Britons at odds on animal testing. *Gallup Poll News Service* (www.gallup.com). (p. 29)

Mason, H. (2005, February 22). How many teens are on mood medication? The Gallup Organization (www.gallup.com). (p. 501)

Mason, H. (2005, January 25). Who dreams, perchance to sleep? *Gallup Poll News Service* (www.gallup.com). (p. 201)

Mason, R. A., & Just, M. A. (2004). How the brain processes causal inferences in text. *Psychological Science, 15,* 1–7. (p. 63)

Masse, L. C., & Tremblay, R. E. (1997). Behavior of boys in kindergarten and the onset of substance use during adolescence. *Archives of General Psychiatry, 54,* 62–68. (p. 225)

Massimini, M., Ferrarelli, F., Huber, R., Esser, S. K., Singh, H., & Tononi, G. (2005). Breakdown of cortical effective connectivity during sleep. *Science, 309,* 2228–2232. (p. 197)

Masten, A. S. (2001). Ordinary magic: Resilience processes in development. *American Psychologist, 56,* 227–238. (p. 116)

Masters, W. H., & Johnson, V. E. (1966). *Human sexual response.* Boston: Little, Brown. (p. 375)

Mastroianni, G. R. (2002). Milgram and the Holocaust: A reexamination. *Journal of Theoretical and Philosophical Psychology, 22,* 158–173. (p. 586)

Masuda, T., & Kitayama, S. (2004). Perceiver-induced constraint and attitude attribution in Japan and the US: A case for the cultural dependence of the correspondence bias. *Journal of Experimental Social Psychology, 40,* 409–416. (p. 575)

Mataix-Cols, D., Rosario-Campos, M. C., & Leckman, J. F. (2005). A multidimensional model of obsessive-compulsive disorder. *American Journal of Psychiatry, 162,* 228–238. (p. 514)

Mataix-Cols, D., Wooderson, S., Lawrence, N., Brammer, M. J., Speckens, A., & Phillips, M. L. (2004). Distinct neural correlates of washing, checking, and hoarding symptom dimensions in obsessive-compulsive disorder. *Archives of General Psychiatry, 61,* 564–576. (p. 514)

Mather, M., & Carstensen, L. L. (2003). Aging and attentional biases for emotional faces. *Psychological Science, 14,* 409–415. (p. 138)

Mather, M., Canli, T., English, T., Whitfield, S., Wais, P., Ochsner, K., Gabrieli, J. D. E., & Carstensen, L. L. (2004). Amygdala responses to emotionally valenced stimuli in older and younger adults. *Psychological Science, 15,* 259–263. (p. 138)

Matsumoto, D. (1994). *People: Psychology from a cultural perspective.* Pacific Grove, CA: Brooks/Cole. (p. 323)

Matsumoto, D., & Ekman, P. (1989). American-Japanese cultural differences in intensity ratings of facial expressions of emotion. *Motivation and Emotion, 13,* 143–157. (p. 420)

Maurer, D., & Maurer, C. (1988). *The world of the newborn.* New York: Basic Books. (p. 103)

Maurer, D., Lewis, T. L., Brent, H. P., & Levin, A. V. (1999). Rapid improvement in the acuity of infants after visual input. *Science, 286,* 108–110. (p. 182)

May, C. P., Hasher, L., & Stoltzfus, E. R. (1993). Optimal time of day and the magnitude of age differences in memory. *Psychological Science, 4,* 326–330. (p. 133)

May, C., & Hasher, L. (1998). Synchrony effects in inhibitory control over thought and action. *Journal of Experimental Psychology: Human Perception and Performance, 24*, 363–380. (p. 196)

Mayberry, R. I., Lock, E., & Kazmi, H. (2002). Linguistic ability and early language exposure. *Nature, 417*, 38. (p. 322)

Mayer, J. D. Salovey, P., & Caruso, D. (2002). *The Mayer-Salovey-Caruso emotional intelligence test (MSCEIT).* Toronto: Multi-Health Systems, Inc. (p. 335)

Mazur, A., & Booth, A. (1998). Testosterone and dominance in men. *Behavioral and Brain Sciences, 21*, 353–363. (p. 601)

Mazure, C., Keita, G., & Blehar, M. (2002). *Summit on women and depression: Proceedings and recommendations.* Washington, DC: American Psychological Association (www.apa.org/pi/wpo/women&depression.pdf). (p. 527)

Mazzoni, G., & Memon, A. (2003). Imagination can create false autobiographical memories. *Psychological Science, 14*, 186–188. (p. 297)

Mazzuca, J. (2002, July 2). Same-sex parenting: Does public back Rosie? The Gallup Organization (www.gallup.com/poll/tb/religValue/20020702.asp). (pp. 248, 264, 386)

McAneny, L. (1996, September). Large majority think government conceals information about UFO's. *Gallup Poll Monthly*, pp. 23–26. (p. 286)

McBurney, D. H. (1996). *How to think like a psychologist: Critical thinking in psychology.* Upper Saddle River, NJ: Prentice-Hall. (p. 57)

McBurney, D. H., & Collings, V. B. (1984). *Introduction to sensation and perception (2nd ed.).* Englewood Cliffs, NJ: Prentice-Hall. (pp. 178, 179)

McBurney, D. H., & Gent, J. F. (1979). On the nature of taste qualities. *Psychological Bulletin, 86*, 151–167. (p. 164)

McCall, R. B. (1994). Academic underachievers. *Current Directions in Psychological Science, 3*, 15–19. (p. 398)

McCann, I. L., & Holmes, D. S. (1984). Influence of aerobic exercise on depression. *Journal of Personality and Social Psychology, 46*, 1142–1147. (p. 449, 450)

McCann, U. D., Eligulashvili, V., & Ricaurte, G. A. (2001). (+-)3,4-Methylenedioxymethamphetamine ('Ecstasy')-induced serotonin neurotoxicity: Clinical studies. *Neuropsychobiology, 42*, 11–16. (p. 211), 223)

McCarthy, P. (1986, July). Scent: The tie that binds? *Psychology Today*, pp. 6, 10. (p. 166)

McCaul, K. D., & Malott, J. M. (1984). Distraction and coping with pain. *Psychological Bulletin, 95*, 516–533. (p. 164)

McCauley, C. R. (2002). Psychological issues in understanding terrorism and the response to terrorism. In C. E. Stout (Ed.), *The psychology of terrorism, Vol. 3.* Westport, CT: Praeger/Greenwood. (p. 590)

McCauley, C. R., & Segal, M. E. (1987). Social psychology of terrorist groups. In C. Hendrick (Ed.), *Group processes and intergroup relations.* Beverly Hills, CA: Sage. (p. 590)

McClearn, G. E., Johansson, B., Berg, S., Pedersen, N. L., Ahern, F., Petrill, S. A., & Plomin, R. (1997). Substantial genetic influence on cognitive abilities in twins 80 or more years old. *Science, 276*, 1560–1563. (p. 343)

McClintock, M. K., & Herdt, G. (December, 1996). Rethinking puberty; The development of sexual attraction. *Current Directions in Psychological Science, 5(6)*, 178–183. (p. 121)

McClure, E. B. (2000). A meta-analytic review of sex differences in facial expression processing and their development in infants, children, and adolescents. *Psychological Bulletin, 126*, 424–453. (p. 347)

McConkey, K. M. (1995). Hypnosis, memory, and the ethics of uncertainty. *Australian Psychologist, 30*, 1–10. (p. 212)

McConnell, R. A. (1991). National Academy of Sciences opinion on parapsychology. *Journal of the American Society for Psychical Research, 85*, 333–365. (p. 186)

McCool, G. (1999, October 26). Mirror-gazing Venezuelans top of vanity stakes. *Toronto Star* (via web.lexis-nexis.com). (p. 608)

McCormick, C. M., & Witelson, S. F. (1991). A cognitive profile of homosexual men compared to heterosexual men and women. *Psychoneuroendocrinology, 16*, 459–473. (p. 385)

McCrae, R. R. (2001). Trait psychology and culture. *Journal of Personality, 69*, 819–846. (p. 478)

McCrae, R. R., & Costa, P. T., Jr. (1986). Clinical assessment can benefit from recent advances in personality psychology. *American Psychologist, 41*, 1001–1003. (p. 478)

McCrae, R. R., & Costa, P. T., Jr. (1990). *Personality in adulthood.* New York: Guilford. (p. 135)

McCrae, R. R., & Costa, P. T., Jr. (1994). The stability of personality: Observations and evaluations. *Current Directions in Psychological Science, 3*, 173–175. (pp. 100, 479)

McCrae, R. R., & Costa, P. T., Jr. (1999). A five-factor theory of personality. In L. A. Pervin & O. P. John (Eds.), *Handbook of personality: Theory and research.* New York: Guilford. (p. 477)

McCrae, R. R., Costa, P. T., Jr., de Lirna, M. P., Simoes, A., Ostendorf, F., Angleitner, A., Marusic, I., Bratko, D., Caprara, G. V., Barbaranelli, C., Chae, J-H., & Piedmont, R. L. (1999). Age differences in personality across the adult life span: Parallels in five cultures. *Developmental Psychology, 35*, 466–477. (p. 478)

McCrae, R. R., Costa, P. T., Jr., Ostendorf, F., Angleitner, A., Hrebickova, M., Avia, M. D., Sanz, J., Sanchez-Bernardos, M. L., Kusdil, M. E., Woodfield, R., Saunders, P. R., & Smith, P. B. (2000). Nature over nurture: Temperament, personality, and life span development. *Journal of Personality and Social Psychology, 78*, 173–186. (p. 72)

McCrae, R. R., Terracciano, A., & 78 others. (2005). Universal features of personality traits from the observer's perspective: Data from 50 cultures. *Journal of Personality and Social Psychology, 88*, 547–561. (p. 478)

McCrink, K., & Wynn, K. (2004). Large-number addition and subtraction by 9-month-old infants. *Psychological Science, 15*, 776–781. (p. 109)

McCullough, M. E., & Laurenceau, J-P. (2005). Religiousness and the trajectory of self-rated health across adulthood. *Personality and Social Psychology Bulletin, 31*, 560–573. (p. 454)

McCullough, M. E., Hoyt, W. T., Larson, D. B., Koenig, H. G., & Thoresen, C. (2000). Religious involvement and mortality: A meta-analytic review. *Health Psychology, 19*, 211–222. (p. 454)

McCullough, M. E., Tsang, J-A., & Emmons, R. A. (2004). Gratitude in intermediate affective terrain: Links of grateful moods to individual differences and daily emotional experience. *Journal of Personality and Social Psychology, 86*, 295–309. (p. 429)

McFadden, D. (2002). Masculinization effects in the auditory system. *Archives of Sexual Behavior, 31*, 99–111. (p. 385)

McFarland, C., & Ross, M. (1987). The relation between current impressions and memories of self and dating partners. *Psychological Bulletin, 13*, 228–238. (p. 298)

McGaugh, J. I. (2003). *Memory and emotion: The making of lasting memories.* New York: Columbia University Press. (pp. 268)

McGaugh, J. L. (1994). Quoted by B. Bower, Stress hormones hike emotional memories. *Science News, 146*, 262. (p. 280)

McGhee, P. E. (June, 1976). Children's appreciation of humor: A test of the cognitive congruency principle. *Child Development, 47(2)*, 420–426. (p. 111)

McGrath, J. J., & Welham, J. L. (1999). Season of birth and schizophrenia: A systematic review and meta-analysis of data from the Southern hemisphere. *Schizophrenia Research, 35*, 237–242. (p. 534)

McGrath, J., Welham, J., & Pemberton, M. (1995). Month of birth, hemisphere of birth and schizophrenia. *British Journal of Psychiatry, 167*, 783–785. (p. 534)

McGrath, M. J., & Cohen, D. B. (1978). REM sleep facilitation of adaptive waking behavior: A review of the literature. *Psychological Bulletin, 85*, 24–57. (p. 207)

McGue, M., & Bouchard, T. J., Jr. (1998). Genetic and environmental influences on human behavioral differences. *Annual Review of Neuroscience, 21*, 1–24. (p. 71)

McGue, M., Bouchard, T. J., Jr., Iacono, W. G., & Lykken, D. T. (1993). Behavioral genetics of cognitive ability: A life-span perspective. In R. Plomin & G. E. McClearn (Eds.), *Nature, nurture and psychology.* Washington, DC: American Psychological Association. (pp. 342, 343)

McGuire, M. T., Wing, R. R., Klem, M. L., Lang, W., & Hill, J. O. (1999). What predicts weight regain in a group of successful weight losers? *Journal of Consulting and Clinical Psychology, 67,* 177–185. (p. 372)

McGuire, W. J. (1986). The myth of massive media impact: Savings and salvagings. In G. Comstock (Ed.), *Public communication and behavior.* Orlando, FL: Academic Press. (p. 264)

McGurk, H., & MacDonald, J. (1976). Hearing lips and seeing voices. *Nature, 264,* 746–748. (p. 165)

McHugh, P. R. (1995a). Witches, multiple personalities, and other psychiatric artifacts. *Nature Medicine, 1(2),* 110–114. (p. 516)

McHugh, P. R. (1995b). Resolved: Multiple personality disorder is an individually and socially created artifact. *Journal of the American Academy of Child and Adolescent Psychiatry, 34,* 957–959. (p. 517)

McKenna, K. Y. A., & Bargh, J. A. (1998). Coming out in the age of the Internet: Identity "demarginalization" through virtual group participation. *Journal of Personality and Social Psychology, 75,* 681–694. (p. 590)

McLaughlin, C. S., Chen, C., Greenberger, E., & Biermeier, C. (1997). Family, peer, and individual correlates of sexual experience among Caucasian and Asian American late adolescents. *Journal of Personality and Social Psychology: Journal of Research on Adolescence, 7,* 33–53. (p. 379)

McMurray, C. (2004, January 13). U.S., Canada, Britain: Who's getting in shape? *Gallup Poll Tuesday Briefing* (www.gallup.com). (p. 449)

McNally, R. J. (1999). EMDR and Mesmerism: A comparative historical analysis. *Journal of Anxiety Disorders, 13,* 225–236. (p. 558)

McNally, R. J. (2003). *Remembering trauma.* Cambridge, MA: Harvard University Press. (pp. 297, 300, 513)

McNally, R. J., Bryant, R. A., & Ehlers, A. (2003). Does early psychological intervention promote recovery from posttraumatic stress? *Psychological Science in the Public Interest, 4,* 45–79. (p. 513)

McNeil, B. J., Pauker, S. G., & Tversky, A. (1988). On the framing of medical decisions. In D. E. Bell, H. Raiffa, & A. Tversky (Eds.), *Decision making: Descriptive, normative, and prescriptive interactions.* New York: Cambridge, 1988. (p. 313)

Meador, B. D., & Rogers, C. R. (1984). Person-centered therapy. In R. J. Corsini (Ed.), *Current psychotherapies (3rd ed.).* Itasca, IL: Peacock. (p. 544)

Medical Institute for Sexual Health. (1994, April). Condoms ineffective against human papilloma virus. *Sexual Health Update, 2.* (p. 379)

Medland, S. E., Perelle, I., De Monte, V., & Ehrman, L. (2004). Effects of culture, sex, and age on the distribution of handedness: An evaluation of the sensitivity of three measures of handedness. *Laterality: Asymmetries of Body, Brain, and Cognition, 9,* 287–297. (p. 62)

Mednick, S. A., Huttunen, M. O., & Machon, R. A. (1994). Prenatal influenza infections and adult schizophrenia. *Schizophrenia Bulletin, 20,* 263–267. (p. 534)

Meece, J. L., Anderman, E. M., & Anderman, L. H. (2006). Classroom goal structure, student motivation, and academic achievement. *Annual Review of Psychology, 57,* 487–503. (p. 398)

Mehl, M. R., & Pennebaker, J. W. (2003). The sounds of social life: A psychometric analysis of students' daily social environments and natural conversations. *Journal of Personality and Social Psychology, 84,* 857–870. (p. 21)

Meichenbaum, D. (1977). *Cognitive-behavior modification: An integrative approach.* New York: Plenum Press. (p. 550)

Meichenbaum, D. (1985). *Stress inoculation training.* New York: Pergamon. (p. 550)

Meltzoff, A. N. (1988). Infant imitation after a 1-week delay: Long-term memory for novel acts and multiple stimuli. *Developmental Psychology, 24,* 470–476. (p. 262)

Meltzoff, A. N., & Moore, M. K. (1989). Imitation in newborn infants: Exploring the range of gestures imitated and the underlying mechanisms. *Developmental Psychology, 25,* 954–962. (p. 262)

Meltzoff, A. N., & Moore, M. K. (1997). Explaining facial imitation: A theoretical model. *Early Development and Parenting, 6,* 179–192. (p. 262)

Melzack, R. (1990, February). The tragedy of needless pain. *Scientific American,* pp. 27–33. (p. 217)

Melzack, R. (1992, April). Phantom limbs. *Scientific American,* pp. 120–126. (p. 163)

Melzack, R. (1993). Distinguished contribution series. *Canadian Journal of Experimental Psychology, 47,* 615–629. (p. 163)

Melzack, R. (1998, February). Quoted in Phantom limbs. *Discover,* p. 20. (p. 163)

Melzack, R. (1999). Pain and Stress: A new perspective. In R. J. Gatchel, & D. C. Turk (Eds.), *Psychosocial factors in pain: Critical perspectives.* New York: Guilford Press. (p. 163)

Melzack, R., & Wall, P. D. (1965). Pain mechanisms: A new theory. *Science, 150,* 971–979. (p. 163)

Melzack, R., & Wall, P. D. (1983). *The challenge of pain.* New York: Basic Books. (p. 163)

Mendolia, M., & Kleck, R. E. (1993). Effects of talking about a stressful event on arousal: Does what we talk about make a difference? *Journal of Personality and Social Psychology, 64,* 283–292. (p. 449)

Merari, A. (2002). Explaining suicidal terrorism: Theories versus empirical evidence. Invited address to the American Psychological Association. (p. 590)

Merskey, H. (1992). The manufacture of personalities: The production of multiple personality disorder. *British Journal of Psychiatry, 160,* 327–340. (p. 516)

Merton, R. K. (1938; reprinted 1970). *Science, technology and society in seventeenth-century England.* New York: Fertig. (p. 16)

Merton, R. K., & Kitt, A. S. (1950). Contributions to the theory of reference group behavior. In R. K. Merton & P. F. Lazarsfeld (Eds.), *Continuities in social research: Studies in the scope and method of the American soldier.* Glencoe, IL: Free Press. (p. 430)

Mestel, R. (1997, April 26). Get real, Siggi. *New Scientist* (www.newscientist.com/ns/970426/siggi.html). (p. 206)

Meston, C. M., & Frohlich, P. F. (2000). The neurobiology of sexual function. *Archives of General Psychiatry, 57,* 1012–1030. (p. 376)

Meston, C. M., Trapnell, P. D., & Gorzalka, B. B. (1996). Ethnic and gender differences in sexuality: Variations in sexual behavior between Asian and non-Asian university students. *Archives of Sexual Behavior, 25,* 33–72. (p. 379)

Metcalfe, J. (1998). Cognitive optimism: Self-deception or memory-based processing heuristics. *Personality and Social Psychology Review, 2,* 100–110. (p. 312)

Meyer, I. H. (2003). Prejudice, social stress, and mental health in lesbian, gay, and bisexual populations: Conceptual issues and research evidence. *Psychological Bulletin, 129,* 674–697. (p. 500)

Meyer-Bahlburg, H. F. L. (1995). Psychoneuroendocrinology and sexual pleasure: The aspect of sexual orientation. In P. R. Abramson & S. D. Pinkerton (Eds.), *Sexual nature/sexual culture.* Chicago: University of Chicago Press. (p. 384)

Mezulis, A. M., Abramson, L. Y., Hyde, J. S., & Hankin, B. L. (2004). Is there a universal positivity bias in attributions? A meta-analytic review of individual, developmental, and cultural differences in the self-serving attributional bias. *Psychological Bulletin, 130,* 711–747. (p. 492)

Michaels, J. W., Bloomel, J. M., Brocato, R. M., Linkous, R. A., & Rowe, J. S. (1982). Social facilitation and inhibition in a natural setting. *Replications in Social Psychology, 2,* 21–24. (p. 588)

Middlebrooks, J. C., & Green, D. M. (1991). Sound localization by human listeners. *Annual Review of Psychology, 42,* 135–159. (p. 160)

Mikulincer, M., & Shaver, P. R. (2001). Attachment theory and intergroup bias: Evidence that priming the secure base schema attenuates negative reactions to our-groups. *Journal of Personality and Social Psychology, 81,* 97–115. (p. 598)

Mikulincer, M., & Shaver, P. R. (2005). Attachment theory and emotions in close relationships: Exploring the attachment-related dynamics of emotional reactions to relational events. *Personal Relationships, 12,* 149–168. (p. 116)

Mikulincer, M., Babkoff, H., Caspy, T., & Sing, H. (1989). The effects of 72 hours of sleep loss on psychological variables. *British Journal of Psychology, 80,* 145–162. (p. 201)

Milan, R. J., Jr., & Kilmann, P. R. (1987). Interpersonal factors in premarital contraception. *Journal of Sex Research, 23,* 289–321. (p. 379)

Miles, D. R., & Carey, G. (1997). Genetic and environmental architecture of human aggression. *Journal of Personality and Social Psychology, 72,* 207–217. (p. 600)

Milgram, S. (1963). Behavioral study of obedience. *Journal of Abnormal & Social Psychology, 67(4),* 371–378. (p. 584)

Milgram, S. (1974). *Obedience to authority.* New York: Harper & Row. (pp. 586)

Miller, E. J., Smith, J. E., & Trembath, D. L. (2000). The "skinny" on body size requests in personal ads. *Sex Roles, 43,* 129–141. (p. 368)

Miller, G. (2004). Axel, Buck share award for deciphering how the nose knows. *Science, 306,* 207. (p. 167)

Miller, G. A. (1956). The magical number seven, plus or minus two: Some limits on our capacity for processing information. *Psychological Review, 63,* 81–97. (p. 278)

Miller, G. A. (1962). *Psychology: The science of mental life.* New York: Harper & Row. (p. 468)

Miller, J. G., & Bersoff, D. M. (1995). Development in the context of everyday family relationships: Culture, interpersonal morality and adaptation. In M. Killen and D. Hart (Eds.), *Morality in everyday life: A developmental perspective.* New York: Cambridge University Press. (p. 123)

Miller, K. I., & Monge, P. R. (1986). Participation, satisfaction, and productivity: A meta-analytic review. *Academy of Management Journal, 29,* 727–753. (p. 486)

Miller, L. (2005, January 4). U.S. airlines have 34 deaths in 3 years. *Associated Press.* (p. 314)

Miller, L. K. (1999). The Savant Syndrome: Intellectual impairment and exceptional skill. *Psychological Bulletin, 125,* 31–46. (p. 332)

Miller, N. E. (1985, February). Rx: biofeedback. *Psychology Today,* pp. 54–59. (p. 451)

Miller, N. E. (1995). Clinical-experimental interactions in the development of neuroscience: A primer for nonspecialists and lessons for young scientists. *American Psychologist, 50,* 901–911. (p. 362)

Miller, N. E., & Brucker, B. S. (1979). A learned visceral response apparently independent of skeletal ones in patients paralyzed by spinal lesions. In N. Birbaumer & H. D. Kimmel (Eds.), *Biofeedback and self-regulation.* Hillsdale, NJ: Erlbaum. (p. 451)

Miller, P. A., Eisenberg, N., Fabes, R. A., & Shell, R. (1996). Relations of moral reasoning and vicarious emotion to young children's prosocial behavior toward peers and adults. *Developmental Psychology, 32,* 210–219. (p. 123)

Miller, P. C., Lefcourt, H. M., Holmes, J. G., Ware, E. E., & Saleh, W. E. (1986). Marital locus of control and marital problem solving. *Journal of Personality and Social Psychology, 51,* 161–169. (p. 485)

Miller, S. D., Blackburn, T., Scholes, G., White, G. L., & Mamalis, N. (1991). Optical differences in multiple personality disorder: A second look. *Journal of Nervous and Mental Disease, 179,* 132–135. (p. 516)

Mills, M., & Melhuish, E. (1974). Recognition of mother's voice in early infancy. *Nature, 252,* 123–124. (p. 103)

Milner, D. A. (2003). Visual awareness and the primate brain. In M. A. Jeeves (Ed.), *Human nature.* London: Routledge. (p. 153)

Milton, J., & Wiseman, R. (2002). A response to Storm and Ertel (2002). *Journal of Parapsychology, 66,* 183–185. (p. 187)

Mineka, S. (1985). The frightful complexity of the origins of fears. In F. R. Brush & J. B. Overmier (Eds.), *Affect, conditioning and cognition: Essays on the determinants of behavior.* Hillsdale, NJ: Erlbaum. (p. 514)

Mineka, S., & Zinbarg, R. (1996). Conditioning and ethological models of anxiety disorders: Stress-in-dynamic-context anxiety models. In D. Hope (Ed.), *Perspectives on anxiety, panic, and fear.* Nebraska symposium on motivation. Lincoln, NE: University of Nebraska Press. (pp. 512, 513, 514)

Miner-Rubino, K., & Winter, D. G., & Stewart, A. J. (2004). Gender, social class, and the subjective experience of aging: Self-perceived personality change from early adulthood to late midlife. *Personality and Social Psychology Bulletin, 30,* 1599–1610. (p. 137)

Mirescu, C., Peters, J. D., & Gould, E. (2004). Early life experience alters response of adult neurogenesis to stress. *Nature Neuroscience, 7,* 841–846. (p. 117)

Mischel, W. (1968). *Personality and assessment.* New York: Wiley. (p. 479)

Mischel, W. (1981). Current issues and challenges in personality. In L. T. Benjamin, Jr. (Ed.), *The G. Stanley Hall Lecture Series (Vol. 1).* Washington, DC: American Psychological Association. (p. 489)

Mischel, W. (1984). Convergences and challenges in the search for consistency. *American Psychologist, 39,* 351–364. (p. 479)

Mischel, W. (2004). Toward an integrative science of the person. *Annual Review of Psychology, 55,* 1–22. (p. 479)

Mischel, W., Shoda, Y., & Peake, P. K. (1988). The nature of adolescent competencies predicted by preschool delay of gratification. *Journal of Personality and Social Psychology, 54,* 687–696. (p. 124)

Mischel, W., Shoda, Y., & Rodriguez, M. L. (1989). Delay of gratification in children. *Science, 244,* 933–938. (pp. 124, 250)

Miserandino, M. (1991). Memory and the seven dwarfs. *Teaching of Psychology, 18,* 169–171. (p. 284)

Mita, T. H., Dermer, M., & Knight, J. (1977). Reversed facial images and the mere-exposure hypothesis. *Journal of Personality and Social Psychology, 35,* 597–601. (p. 607)

Mitchell, T. R., Thompson, L., Peterson, E., & Cronk, R. (1997). Temporal adjustments in the evaluation of events: The "rosy view." *Journal of Experimental Social Psychology, 33,* 421–448. (p. 275)

Moffitt, T. E., Caspi, A., Harrington, H., & Milne, B. J. (2002). Males on the life-course-persistent and adolescence-limited antisocial pathways: Follow-up at age 26 years. *Development and Psychopathology, 14,* 179–207. (p. 100)

Moghaddam, F. M. (2005). The staircase to terrorism: A psychological exploration. *American Psychologist, 60,* 161–169. (p. 590)

Mohn, J. K., Tingle, L. R., & Finger, R. (2003). An analysis of the causes of the decline in non-marital birth and pregnancy rates for teens from 1991 to 1995. *Adolescent and Family Health, 3,* 39–47. (p. 380)

Moises, H. W., Zoega, T., & Gottesman, I. I. (2002, 3 July). The glial growth factors deficiency and synaptic destabilization hypothesis of schizophrenia. *BMC Psychiatry, 2(8)* (www.biomedcentral.com/1471-244X/2/8). (p. 535)

Monaghan, P. (1992, September 23). Professor of psychology stokes a controversy on the reliability and repression of memory. *Chronicle of Higher Education,* pp. A9–A10. (p. 301)

Mondloch, C. J., Lewis, T. L., Budreau, D. R., Maurer, D., Dannemiller, J. L., Stephens, B. R., & Kleiner-Gathercoal, K. A. (1999). Face perception during early infancy. *Psychological Science, 10,* 419–422. (p. 103)

Money, J. (1987). Sin, sickness, or status? Homosexual gender identity and psychoneuroendocrinology. *American Psychologist, 42,* 384–399. (pp. 382, 384)

Money, J., Berlin, F. S., Falck, A., & Stein, M. (1983). *Antiandrogenic and counseling treatment of sex offenders.* Baltimore: Department of Psychiatry and Behavioral Sciences, The Johns Hopkins University School of Medicine. (p. 377)

Moody, R. (1976). *Life after life.* Harrisburg, PA: Stackpole Books. (p. 224)

Mook, D. G. (1983). In defense of external invalidity. *American Psychologist, 38,* 379–387. (p. 27)

Moorcroft, W. (1993). *Sleep, dreaming, and sleep disorders: An introduction (2nd ed.).* Landam, MD: University Press of America. (p. 202)

Moorcroft, W. H. (2003). *Understanding sleep and dreaming.* New York: Kluwer/Plenum. (pp. 197, 203, 208)

Moore, D. W. (2003, November 23). Many Americans deluding themselves about weight. *Gallup Poll* (poll.gallup.com). (p. 371)

Moore, D. W. (2004, December 17). Sweet dreams go with a good night's sleep. *Gallup News Service* (www.gallup.com). (p. 200)

Mor, N., & Winquist, J. (2002). Self-focused attention and negative affect: A meta-analysis. *Psychological Bulletin, 128,* 638–662. (p. 527)

Moreland, R. L., & Beach, S. R. (1992). Exposure effects in the classroom: The development of affinity among students. *Journal of Experimental Social Psychology, 28,* 255–276. (p. 607)

Moreland, R. L., & Zajonc, R. B. (1982). Exposure effects in person perception; Familiarity, similarity, and attraction. *Journal of Experimental Social Psychology, 18,* 395–415. (p. 607)

Morell, V. (1995). Attacking the causes of "silent" infertility. *Science, 269,* 775–776. (p. 379)

Morell, V. (1995). Zeroing in on how hormones affect the immune system. *Science, 269,* 773–775. (p. 440)

Morelli, G. A., Rogoff, B., Oppenheim, D., & Goldsmith, D. (1992). Cultural variation in infants' sleeping arrangements: Questions of independence. *Developmental Psychology, 26,* 604–613. (p. 86)

Morey, R. A., Inan, S., Mitchell, T. V., Perkins, D. O., Lieberman, J. A., & Belger, A. (2005). Imaging frontostriatal function in ultra-high-risk, early, and chronic schizophrenia during executive processing. *Archives of General Psychiatry, 62,* 254–262. (p. 533)

Morgan, A. B., & Lilienfeld, S. O. (2000). A meta-analytic review of the relation between antisocial behavior and neuropsychological measures of executive function. *Clinical Psychology Review, 20,* 113–136. (p. 518)

Morgan, B., & Korschgen, A. (2001). Psychology career exploration made easy. *Eye on Psi Chi, 35–36.* (pp B-1, B-9)

Morin, R., & Brossard, M. A. (1997, March 4). Communication breakdown on drugs. *Washington Post,* pp. A1, A6. (p. 125)

Morrison, A. R. (2003). The brain on night shift. *Cerebrum, 5(3),* 23–36. (p. 199)

Mortensen, E. L., Michaelsen, K. F., Sanders, S. A., & Reinisch, J. M. (2002). The association between duration of breastfeeding and adult intelligence. *Journal of the American Medical Association, 287,* 2365–2371. (p. 24)

Mortensen, P. B. (1999). Effects of family history and place and season of birth on the risk of schizophrenia. *New England Journal of Medicine, 340,* 603–608. (p. 534)

Moscovici, S. (1985). Social influence and conformity. In G. Lindzey & E. Aronson (Eds.), *The handbook of social psychology (3rd ed).* Hillsdale, N.J.: Erlbaum. (p. 592)

Moser, P. W. (1987, May). Are cats smart? Yes, at being cats. *Discover,* pp. 77–88. (p. 150)

Mosher, D. L., & Anderson, R. D. (1986). Macho personality, sexual aggression, and reactions to guided imagery of realistic rape. *Journal of Research in Personality, 20,* 77–94. (p. 218)

Moss, A. J., Allen, K. F., Giovino, G. A., & Mills, S. L. (1992, December 2). Recent trends in adolescent smoking, smoking-update correlates, and expectations about the future. *Advance Data No. 221* (from Vital and Health Statistics of the Centers for Disease Control and Prevention). (p. 221)

Moss, H. A., & Susman, E. J. (1980). Longitudinal study of personality development. In O. G. Brim, Jr., & J. Kagan (Eds.), *Constancy and change in human development.* Cambridge, MA: Harvard University Press. (p. 100)

Moyer, K. E. (1983). The physiology of motivation: Aggression as a model. In C. J. Scheier & A. M. Rogers (Eds.), *G. Stanley Hall Lecture Series (Vol. 3).* Washington, DC: American Psychological Association. (p. 600)

Mroczek, D. K. (2001). Age and emotion in adulthood. *Current Directions in Psychological Science, 10,* 87–90. (p. 138)

Mroczek, D. K., & Kolarz, D. M. (1998). The effect of age on positive and negative affect: A developmental perspective on happiness. *Journal of Personality and Social Psychology, 75,* 1333–1349. (p. 135)

Mroczek, D. K., & Spiro, A., III. (2005). Change in life satisfaction during adulthood: Findings from the Veterans Affairs normative aging study. *Journal of Personality and Social Psychology, 88,* 189–202. (p. 432)

Muhlnickel, W. (1998). Reorganization of auditory cortex in tinnitus. *Proceedings of the National Academy of Sciences, 95,* 10340–10343. (p. 56)

Muller, J. E., & Verrier, R. L. (1996). Triggering of sudden death—Lessons from an earthquake. *New England Journal of Medicine, 334,* 461. (p. 437)

Muller, J. E., Mittleman, M. A., Maclure, M., Sherwood, J. B., & Tofler, G. H. (1996). Triggering myocardial infarction by sexual activity. *Journal of the American Medical Association, 275,* 1405–1409. (p. 375)

Mullin, C. R., & Linz, D. (1995). Desensitization and resensitization to violence against women: Effects of exposure to sexually violent films on judgments of domestic violence victims. *Journal of Personality and Social Psychology, 69,* 449–459. (p. 265)

Mulrow, C. D. (1999, March). Treatment of depression—newer pharmacotherapies, summary. *Evidence Report/Technology Assessment, 7.* Agency for Health Care Policy and Research, Rockville, MD. (http://www.ahrq.gov/clinic/depsumm.htm). (p. 567)

Murphy, G. E., & Wetzel, R. D. (1990). The lifetime risk of suicide in alcoholism. *Archives of General Psychiatry, 47,* 383–392. (p. 524)

Murphy, S. T., Monahan, J. L., & Miller, L. C. (1998). Inference under the influence: The impact of alcohol and inhibition conflict on women's sexual decision making. *Personality and Social Psychology Bulletin, 24,* 517–528. (p. 218)

Murphy, S. T., Monahan, J. L., & Zajonc, R. B. (1995). Additivity of nonconscious affect: Combined effects of priming and exposure. *Journal of Personality and Social Psychology, 69,* 589–602. (p. 413)

Murphy, T. N. (1982). Pain: Its assessment and management. In R. J. Gatchel, A. Baum, & J. E. Singer (Eds.), *Handbook of psychology and health: Vol. I. Clinical psychology and behavioral medicine: Overlapping disciplines.* Hillsdale, NJ: Erlbaum. (p. 163)

Murray, B. (1998, May). Psychology is key to airline safety at Boeing. *The APA Monitor,* p. 36. (p. 188)

Murray, C. A., & Herrnstein, R. J. (1994, October 31). Race, genes and I.Q.—An apologia. New Republic, pp. 27–37. (p. 345)

Murray, C. J., & Lopez, A. D. (Eds.) (1996). *The global burden of disease: A comprehensive assessment of mortality and disability from diseases, injuries, and risk factors in 1990 and projected to 2020.* Cambridge, MA: Harvard University Press. (p. 506)

Murray, H. (1938). *Explorations in personality.* New York: Oxford University Press. (p. 398)

Murray, H. A., & Wheeler, D. R. (1937). A note on the possible clairvoyance of dreams. *Journal of Psychology, 3,* 309–313. (pp. 19, 186)

Murray, J. E. (2000). Marital protection and marital selection: Evidence from a historical-prospective sample of American men. *Demography, 37,* 511–521. (p. 447)

Murray, R., Jones, P., O'Callaghan, E., Takei, N., & Sham, P. (1992). Genes, viruses, and neurodevelopmental schizophrenia. *Journal of Psychiatric Research, 26,* 225–235. (p. 534)

Murray, S. L., Bellavia, G. M., Rose, P., & Griffin, D. W. (2003). Once hurt, twice hurtful: How perceived regard regulates daily marital interactions. *Journal of Personality and Social Psychology, 84,* 126–147. (p. 184)

Murray, S. L., Rose, P., Bellavia, G. M., Holmes, J. G., & Kusche, A. G. (2002). When rejection stings: How self-esteem constrains relationship-enhancement processes. *Journal of Personality and Social Psychology, 83,* 556–573. (p. 491)

Musick, M. A., Herzog, A. R., & House, J. S. (1999). Volunteering and mortality among older adults: Findings from a national sample. *Journals of Gerontology, 54B,* 173–180. (p. 455)

Mustanski, B. S., & Bailey, J. M. (2003). A therapist's guide to the genetics of human sexual orientation," *Sexual and Relationship Therapy, 18,* 1468–1479. (p. 383)

Mustanski, B. S., Bailey, J. M., & Kaspar, S. (2002). Dermatoglyphics, handedness, sex, and sexual orientation. *Archives of Sexual Behavior, 31,* 113–122. (p. 385)

Mydans, S. (2002, May 17). In Pakistan, rape victims are the 'criminals.' *New York Times* (www.nytimes.com). (p. 599)

Myers, D. G. (1993). *The pursuit of happiness.* New York: Avon Books. (pp. 425, 426, 432)

Myers, D. G. (2000). *The American paradox: Spiritual hunger in an age of plenty.* New Haven: Yale University Press. (pp. 432, 603)

Myers, D. G. (2001, December). Do we fear the right things? *American Psychological Society Observer*, p. 3. (p. 314)

Myers, D. G. (2002). *Intuition: Its powers and perils*. New Haven: Yale University Press. (p. 24)

Myers, D. G. (2005). *Social psychology, 8th edition*. New York: McGraw-Hill. (p. 492, 493)

Myers, D. G., & Bishop, G. D. (1970). Discussion effects on racial attitudes. *Science, 169*, 78–779. (p. 590)

Myers, D. G., & Diener, E. (1995). Who is happy? *Psychological Science, 6*, 10–19. (p. 432)

Myers, D. G., & Diener, E. (1996, May). The pursuit of happiness. *Scientific American*. (p. 432)

Myers, D. G., & Scanzoni, L. D. (2005). *What God has joined together?* San Francisco: HarperSanFrancisco. (pp. 136, 381)

Myers, I. B. (1987). *Introduction to type: A description of the theory and applications of the Myers-Briggs Type Indicator*. Palo Alto, CA: Consulting Psychologists Press. (p. 475)

Nagourney, A. (2002, September 25). For remarks on Iraq, Gore gets praise and scorn. *New York Times* (www.nytimes.com). (p. 577)

Napolitan, D. A., & Goethals, G. R. (1979). The attribution of friendliness. *Journal of Experimental Social Psychology, 15*, 105–113. (p. 575)

Narrow, W. E., Rae, D. S., Robins, L. N., & Regier, D. A. (2002). Revised prevalence estimates of mental disorders in the United States. *Archives of General Psychiatry, 59*, 115–123. (p. 506)

Nash, M. R. (2001, July). The truth and the hype of hypnosis. *Scientific American*, pp. 47–55. (p. 212)

National Academy of Sciences, Institute of Medicine. (1982). *Marijuana and health*. Washington, DC: National Academic Press. (p. 224)

National Academy of Sciences. (1999). *Marijuana and medicine: Assessing the science base* (by J. A. Benson, Jr. & S. J. Watson, Jr.). Washington, DC: National Academy Press. (p. 224)

National Academy of Sciences. (2001). *Exploring the biological contributions to human health: Does sex matter?* Washington, DC: Institute of Medicine, National Academy Press. (p. 90)

National Center for Complementary and Alternative Medicine. (2006). What is complementary and alternative medicine. nccam.nih.gov/health/whatiscam. (p. 453)

National Center for Health Statistics. (1990). *Health, United States, 1989*. Washington, DC: U.S. Department of Health and Human Services. (p. 131)

National Center for Health Statistics. (1991). Family structure and children's health: United States, 1988, *Vital and Health Statistics, Series 10*, No. 178, CHHS Publication No. PHS 91-1506 by Deborah A. Dawson. (p. 381)

National Center for Health Statistics. (2004, December 15). Marital status and health: United States, 1999–2002 (by Charlotte A. Schoenborn). *Advance Data from Vital and Human Statistics, number 351*. Centers for Disease Control and Prevention. (p. 447)

National Institute of Mental Health. (1982). *Television and behavior: Ten years of scientific progress and implications for the eighties*. Washington, DC: U. S. Government Printing Office. (p. 264)

National Institute of Mental Health. (1999). *ADHD: Attention deficit hyperactivity disorder*. Bethesda, MD: National Institute of Health Publication No. 96-3572, 1994, update July 1, 1999. (p. 501)

National Institute of Mental Health. (2003). *Attention deficit hyperactivity disorder*. Bethesda, MD: National Institute of Mental Health. (p. 501)

National Institute on Drug Abuse. (2004). NIDA InfoFacts: Marijuana. www.nida.nih.gov/Infofax/marijuana.html. (p. 224)

National Institutes of Health. (1998). Clinical guidelines on the identification evaluation and treatment of overweight and obesity in adults. Executive summary, Obesity Education Initiative, National Heart, Lung, and Blood Institute. (p. 371)

National Research Council. (1987). *Risking the future: Adolescent sexuality, pregnancy, and childbearing*. Washington, DC: National Academy Press. (p. 379)

National Research Council. (1990). *Human factors research needs for an aging population*. Washington, DC: National Academy Press. (p. 130)

National Safety Council. (2005, October 3). Passenger deaths and death rates, from Injury Facts (via correspondence with Kevin T. Fearn, Research & Statistical Services Department). (p. 314)

Naylor, T. H. (1990). Redefining corporate motivation, Swedish style. *Christian Century, 107*, 566–570. (p. 402)

NCTV News. (1987, July-August). More research links harmful effects to non-violent porn, p. 12. (p. 555), 603)

Neese, R. M. (1991, November/December). What good is feeling bad? The evolutionary benefits of psychic pain. *The Sciences*, pp. 30–37. (pp. 162, 245)

Neisser, U. (1979). The control of information pickup in selective looking. In A. D. Pick (Ed.), *Perception and its development: A tribute to Eleanor J. Gibson*. Hillsdale, NJ: Erlbaum. (p. 194)

Neisser, U. (1997). The ecological study of memory. *Philosophical Transactions of the Royal Society of London, 352*, 1697–1701. (p. 340)

Neisser, U. (1998). *The rising curve: Long-term gains in IQ and related measures*. Washington, DC: American Psychological Association. (p. 340)

Neisser, U., Boodoo, G., Bouchard, T. J., Jr., Boykin, A. W., Brody, N., Ceci, S. J., Halpern, D. F., Loehlin, J. C., Perloff, R., Sternberg, R. J., & Urbina, S. (1996). Intelligence: Knowns and unknowns. *American Psychologist, 51*, 77–101. (pp. 342, 345, 350)

Neisser, U., Winograd, E., & Weldon, M. S. (1991). Remembering the earthquake: "What I experienced" vs. "How I heard the news." Paper presented to the Psychonomic Society convention. (p. 281)

Neitz, J., Geist, T., & Jacobs, G. H. (1989). Color vision in the dog. *Visual Neuroscience, 3*, 119–125. (p. 154)

Nelson, G., Hoon, M. A., Chandrashekar, J., Zhang, Y., Ryba, N. J., Nicholas, J. P., & Zuker, C. S. (2001). Mammalian sweet taste receptors. *Cell, 106*, 381–390. (p. 165)

Nelson, M. D., Saykin, A. J., Flashman, L. A., & Riordan, H. J. (1998). Hippocampal volume reduction in schizophrenia as assessed by magnetic resonance imaging. *Archives of General Psychiatry, 55*, 433–440. (p. 534)

Nelson, N. (1988). *A meta-analysis of the life-event/health paradigm: The influence of social support*. Philadelphia: Temple University Ph.D. dissertation. (p. 447)

Nesca, M., & Koulack, D. (1994). Recognition memory, sleep and circadian rhythms. *Canadian Journal of Experimental Psychology, 48*, 359–379. (p. 294)

Neumann, R., & Strack, F. (2000). "Mood contagion": The automatic transfer of mood between persons. *Journal of Personality and Social Psychology, 79*, 211–223. (pp. 422, 582)

Nevin, J. A. (1988). Behavioral momentum and the partial reinforcement effect. *Psychological Bulletin, 103*, 44–56. (p. 250)

Newberg, A., & D'Aquili, E. (2001). *Why God won't go away: Brain science and the biology of belief*. New York: Simon and Schuster. (p. 453)

Newcomb, M. D., & Harlow, L. L. (1986). Life events and substance use among adolescents: Mediating effects of perceived loss of control and meaninglessness in life. *Journal of Personality and Social Psychology, 51*, 564–577. (p. 225)

Newcombe, N. S., Drummey, A. B., Fox, N. A., Lie, E., & Ottinger-Alberts, W. (2000). Remembering early childhood: How much, how, and why (or why not). *Current Directions in Psychological Science, 9*, 55–58. (p. 106)

Newman, A. J., Bavelier, D., Corina, D., Jezzard, P., & Neville, H. J. (2002). A critical period for right hemisphere recruitment in American Sign Language processing. *Nature Neuroscience, 5*, 76–80. (p. 323)

Newman, L. S., & Baumeister, R. F. (1996). Toward an explanation of the UFO abduction phenomenon: Hypnotic, elaboration, extraterrestrial sadomasochism, and spurious memories. *Psychological Inquiry, 7*, 99–126. (p. 212)

Newport, E. L. (1990). Maturational constraints on language learning. *Cognitive Science, 14*, 11–28. (p. 323)

Newport, F. (2001, February). Americans see women as emotional and affectionate, men as more aggressive. *The Gallup Poll Monthly*, pp. 34–38. (p. 419)

Newport, F. (2002, July 29). Bush job approval update. *Gallup News Service* (www.gallup.com/poll/releases/pr020729.asp). (p. 617)

Newport, F., Moore, D. W., Jones, J. M., & Saad, L. (2003, March 21). Special release: American opinion on the war. *Gallup Poll Tuesday Briefing* (www.gallup.com). (p. 579)

Newton, I. (1704). *Opticks, or a treatise of the reflections, refractions, inflections & colours of light.* Oxford, England Whittlesey House, McGraw-Hill, 1931. (p. 154)

Neylan, T. C., Metzler, T. J., Best, S. R., Weiss, D. S., Fagan, J. A., Liberman, A., Rogers, C., Vedantham, K., Brunet, A., Lipsey, T. L., & Marmar, C. R. (2002). Critical incident exposure and sleep quality in police officers. *Psychosomatic Medicine, 64,* 345–352. (p. 204)

Nezlek, J. B. (2001). Daily psychological adjustment and the planfulness of day-to-day behavior. *Journal of Social and Clinical Psychology, 20,* 452–475. (p. 485)

Ng, S. H. (1990). Androcentric coding of man and his in memory by language users. *Journal of Experimental Social Psychology, 26,* 455–464. (p. 324)

NHTSA. (2000). *Traffic safety facts 1999: Older population.* Washington, DC: National Highway Traffic Safety Administration (National Transportation Library: www.ntl.bts.gov). (p. 131)

Nickell, J. (1996, May/June). A study of fantasy proneness in the thirteen cases of alleged encounters in John Mack's Abduction. *Skeptical Inquirer,* pp. 18–20, 54. (p. 212)

Nickerson, R. S. (1998). Applied experimental psychology. *Applied Psychology: An International Review, 47,* 155–173. (p. 188)

Nickerson, R. S. (1999). How we know—and sometimes misjudge—what others know: Imputing one's own knowledge to others. *Psychological Bulletin, 125,* 737–759. (p. 188)

Nicol, S. E., & Gottesman, I. I. (1983). Clues to the genetics and neurobiology of schizophrenia. *American Scientist, 71,* 398–404. (p. 536)

NIDA. (2002). Methamphetamine abuse and addiction. *Research Report Series.* National Institute on Drug Abuse, NIH Publication Number 02-4210. (p. 220)

NIDA. (2005, May). Methamphetamine. *NIDA Info Facts.* National Institute on Drug Abuse. (p. 220)

Nier, J. A. (2004). Why does the "above average effect" exist? Demonstrating idiosyncratic trait definition. *Teaching of Psychology, 31,* 53–54. (p. 493)

Nightingale, F. (1860/1969). *Notes on nursing.* Mineola, NY: Dover. (p. 448)

NIH. (2001, July 20). Workshop summary: Scientific evidence on condom effectiveness for sexually transmitted disease (STD) prevention. Bethesda: National Institute of Allergy and Infectious Diseases, National Institutes of Health. (p. 379)

NIMH. (2002, April 26). U.S. suicide rates by age, gender, and racial group. National Institute of Mental Health (www.nimh.nih.gov/research/suichart.cfm). (p. 524)

Nisbett, R. E. (1987). Lay personality theory: Its nature, origin, and utility. In N. E. Grunberg, R. E. Nisbett, & others, *A distinctive approach to psychological research: The influence of Stanley Schachter.* Hillsdale, NJ: 1987. (p. 395)

Nisbett, R. E., & Cohen, D. (1996). *Culture of honor: The psychology of violence in the South.* Boulder, CO: Westview Press. (p. 602)

Nisbett, R. E., & Ross, L. (1980). *Human inference: Strategies and shortcomings of social judgment.* Englewood Cliffs, NJ: Prentice-Hall. (p. 311)

Noel, J. G., Forsyth, D. R., & Kelley, K. N. (1987). Improving the performance of failing students by overcoming their self-serving attributional biases. *Basic and Applied Social Psychology, 8,* 151–162. (p. 487)

Nolen-Hoeksema, S. (2001). Gender differences in depression. *Current Directions in Psychological Science, 10,* 173–176. (p. 527)

Nolen-Hoeksema, S. (2003). *Women who think too much: How to break free of overthinking and reclaim your life.* New York: Holt. (p. 527)

Nolen-Hoeksema, S., & Larson, J. (1999). *Coping with loss.* Mahwah, NJ: Erlbaum. (p. 139)

NORC (National Opinion Research Center). (1985, October/November). Images of the world. *Public Opinion,* p. 38. (p. 473)

NORC (National Opinion Research Center). (2002). Percent saying sex with person other than spouse is always or almost always wrong. National Opinion Research Center General Social Survey of 2000 (www.csa.berkeley.edu:7502). (p. 386)

Norem, J. K. (2001). *The positive power of negative thinking: Using defensive pessimism to harness anxiety and perform at your peak.* Basic Books. (p. 488)

Norman, D. A. (1988). *The psychology of everyday things.* New York: Basic Books. (p. 188)

Norman, D. A. (2001). The perils of home theater (www.jnd.org/dn.mss/ProblemsOfHomeTheater.html). (p. 188)

Norton, K. L., Olds, T. S., Olive, S., & Dank, S. (1996). Ken and Barbie at life size. *Sex Roles, 34,* 287–294. (p. 365)

Norton, M. B. (2002, October 31). They called it witchcraft. *New York Times* (www.nytimes.com). (p. 598)

Nowak, R. (1994). Nicotine scrutinized as FDA seeks to regulate cigarettes. *Science, 263,* 1555–1556. (p. 221)

Nowell, A., & Hedges, L. V. (1998). Trends in gender differences in academic achievement from 1960 to 1994: An analysis of differences in mean, variance, and extreme scores. *Sex Roles, 39,* 21–43. (p. 350)

NSF. (2001, October 24). Public bounces back after Sept. 11 attacks, national study shows. *NSF News,* National Science Foundation (www.nsf.gov/od/lpa/news/press/ol/pr0185.htm). (p. 437)

Nuttin, J. M., Jr. (1987). Affective consequences of mere ownership: The name letter effect in twelve European languages. *European Journal of Social Psychology, 17,* 381–402. (p. 607)

O'Connor, A. (2004, February 6). Study details 30-year increase in calorie consumption. *New York Times* (www.nytimes.com). (p. 370)

O'Connor, A. (2004, May 14). Pressure to go along with abuse is strong, but some soldiers find strength to refuse. *New York Times* (www.nytimes.com). (p. 591)

O'Connor, P., & Brown, G. W. (1984). Supportive relationships: Fact or fancy? *Journal of Social and Personal Relationships, 1,* 159–175. (p. 561)

O'Donnell, L., Stueve, A., O'Donnell, C., Duran, R., San Doval, A., Wilson, R. F., Haber, D., Perry, E., & Pleck, J. H. (2002). Long-term reduction in sexual initiation and sexual activity among urban middle schoolers in the reach for health service learning program. *Journal of Adolescent Health, 31,* 93–100. (p. 380)

O'Keeffe, C., & Wiseman, R. (2005). Testing alleged mediumship: Methods and results. *British Journal of Psychology, 96,* 165–179. (p. 481)

O'Neil, J. (2002, September 3). Vital Signs: Behavior: Parent smoking and teenage sex. *New York Times.* (p. 22)

O'Neill, M. J. (1993). The relationship between privacy, control, and stress responses in office workers. Paper presented to the Human Factors and Ergonomics Society convention. (p. 446)

Oetting, E. R., & Beauvais, F. (1987). Peer cluster theory, socialization characteristics, and adolescent drug use: A path analysis. *Journal of Counseling Psychology, 34,* 205–213. (p. 227)

Oetting, E. R., & Beauvais, F. (1990). Adolescent drug use: Findings of national and local surveys. *Journal of Social and Personal Relationships, 1,* 159–175. (p. 227)

Oettingen, G., & Mayer, D. (2002). The motivating function of thinking about the future: Expectations versus fantasies. *Journal of Personality and Social Psychology, 83,* 1198–1212. (p. 487)

Oettingen, G., & Seligman, M. E. P. (1990). Pessimism and behavioural signs of depression in East versus West Berlin. *European Journal of Social Psychology, 20,* 207–220. (p. 486)

Offer, D., Ostrov, E., Howard, K. I., & Atkinson, R. (1988). *The teenage world: Adolescents' self-image in ten countries.* New York: Plenum. (p. 125)

Office of National Statistics. (2002). *The social and economic circumstances of adults with mental disorders* (report based on the analysis of the ONS Survey of Psychiatric Morbidity Among Adults in Great Britain carried out in 2000). Norwich: HMSO. (p. 506)

Ogden, C. L., Fryar, C. D., Carroll, M. D., & Flegal, K. M. (2004, October 27). Mean body weight, heights, and body mass index, Unites States 1960–2002. *Advance Data from Vital and Health Statistics, No. 347.* (p. 370)

Öhman, A. (1986). Face the beast and fear the face: Animal and social fears as prototypes for evolutionary analyses of emotion. *Psychophysiology, 23,* 123–145. (p. 514)

Öhman, A., Lundqvist, D., & Esteves, F. (2001). The face in the crowd revisited: A threat advantage with schematic stimuli. *Journal of Personality and Social Psychology, 80,* 381–396. (p. 417)

Oishi, S., Diener, E. F., Lucas, R. E., & Suh, E. M. (1999). Cross-cultural variations in predictors of life satisfaction: Perspectives from needs and values. *Personality and Social Psychology Bulletin, 25,* 980–990. (p. 360)

Olds, J. (1958). Self-stimulation of the brain. *Science, 127,* 315–324. (p. 52)

Olds, J. (1975). Mapping the mind onto the brain. In F. G. Worden, J. P. Swazey, & G. Adelman (Eds.), *The neurosciences: Paths of discovery.* Cambridge, MA: MIT Press. (p. 52)

Olds, J., & Milner, P. (1954). Positive reinforcement produced by electrical stimulation of the septal area and other regions of rat brain. *Journal of Comparative and Physiological Psychology, 47,* 419–427. (p. 52)

Olfson, M., Gameroff, M. J., Marcus, S. C., & Jensen, P. S. (2003). National trends in the treatment of attention deficit hyperactivity disorder. *American Journal of Psychiatry, 160,* 1071–1077. (p. 567)

Olfson, M., Marcus, S. C., Wan, G. J., & Geissler, E. C. (2004). National trends in the outpatient treatment of anxiety disorders. *Journal of Clinical Psychiatry, 65,* 1166–1173. (p. 566)

Olfson, M., Shaffer, D., Marcus, S. C., & Greenberg, T. (2003). Relationship between antidepressant medication treatment and suicide in adolescents. *Archives of General Psychiatry, 60,* 978–982. (p. 501)

Oliner, S. P., & Oliner, P. M. (1988). *The altruistic personality: Rescuers of Jews in Nazi Europe.* New York: Free Press. (p. 263)

Olshansky, S. J., Passaro, D. J., Hershow, R. C., Layden, J., Carnes, B. A., Brody, J., Hayflick, L., Butler, R. N., Allison, D. B., & Ludwig, D. S. (2005). A potential decline in life expectancy in the United States in the 21st century. *New England Journal of Medicine, 352,* 1138–1145. (p. 366)

Olson, S. (2005). Brain scans raise privacy concerns. *Science, 307,* 1548–1550. (p. 476)

Olsson, A., & Phelps, E. A. (2004). Learned fear of "unseen" faces after Pavlovian, observational, and instructed fear. *Psychological Science, 15,* 822–828. (p. 514)

Olweus, D., Mattsson, A., Schalling, D., & Low, H. (1988). Circulating testosterone levels and aggression in adolescent males: A causal analysis. *Psychosomatic Medicine, 50,* 261–272. (p. 601)

Oman, D., Kurata, J. H., Strawbridge, W. J., & Cohen, R. D. (2002). Religious attendance and cause of death over 31 years. *International Journal of Psychiatry in Medicine, 32,* 69–89. (p. 454)

Oren, D. A., & Terman, M. (1998). Tweaking the human circadian clock with light. *Science, 279,* 333–334. (p. 196)

Orne, M. T., & Evans, F. J. (1965). Social control in the psychological experiment: Antisocial behavior and hypnosis. *Journal of Personality and Social Psychology, 1,* 189–200. (p. 212)

Osborne, J. W. (1997). Race and academic disidentification. *Journal of Educational Psychology, 89,* 728–735. (p. 351)

Osborne, L. (1999, October 27). A linguistic big bang. *New York Times Magazine* (www.nytimes.com). (p. 321)

Osgood, C. E. (1962). *An alternative to war or surrender.* Urbana: University of Illinois Press. (p. 618)

Osgood, C. E. (1980). GRIT: A strategy for survival in mankind's nuclear age? Paper presented at the Pugwash Conference on New Directions in Disarmament. (p. 618)

OSS Assessment Staff. (1948). *The assessment of men.* New York: Rinehart. (p. 489)

Ost, L. G., & Hugdahl, K. (1981). Acquisition of phobias and anxiety response patterns in clinical patients. *Behaviour Research and Therapy, 16,* 439–447. (p. 513)

Ostfeld, A. M., Kasl, S. V., D'Atri, D. A., & Fitzgerald, E. F. (1987). *Stress, crowding, and blood pressure in prison.* Hillsdale, NJ: Erlbaum. (p. 446)

Ouellette, J. A., & Wood, W. (1998). Habit and intention in everyday life: The multiple processes by which past behavior predicts future behavior. *Psychological Bulletin, 124,* 54–74. (pp. 395, 489)

Overmier, J. B., & Murison, R. (1997). Animal models reveal the "psych" in the psychosomatics of peptic ulcers. *Current Directions in Psychological Science, 6,* 180–184. (p. 445)

Oxfam (2005, March 26). Three months on: New figures show tsunami may have killed up to four times as many women as men. *Oxfam Press Release* (www.oxfam.org.uk). (p. 91)

Ozer, E. J., & Weiss, D. S. (2004). Who develops posttraumatic stress disorder. *Current Directions in Psychological Science, 13,* 169–172. (p. 512)

Ozer, E. J., Best, S. R., Lipsey, T. L., & Weiss, D. S. (2003). Predictors of posttraumatic stress disorder and symptoms in adults: A meta-analysis. *Psychological Bulletin, 129,* 52–73. (p. 512)

Özgen, E. (2004). Language, learning, and color perception. *Current Directions in Psychological Science, 13,* 95–98. (pp. 323, 324)

Pacifici, R., Zuccaro, P., Farre, M., Pichini, S., Di Carlo, S., Roset, P. N., Ortuno, J., Pujadas, M., Bacosi, A., Menoyo, E., Segura, J., & de la Torre, R. (2001). Effects of repeated doses of MDMA ("Ecstasy") on cell-mediated immune response in humans. *Life Sciences, 69,* 2931–2941. (p. 223)

Padgett, V. R. (1989). Predicting organizational violence: An application of 11 powerful principles of obedience. Paper presented to the American Psychological Association convention. (p. 586)

Page, S. (1977). Effects of the mental illness label in attempts to obtain accommodation. *Canadian Journal of Behavioral Science, 9,* 84–90. (p. 504)

Paikoff, R. L., & Brooks-Gunn, J. (1991). Do parent-child relationships change during puberty? *Psychological Bulletin, 110,* 47–66. (p. 125)

Paivio, A. (1986). *Mental representations: A dual coding approach.* New York: Oxford University Press. (p. 275)

Palace, E. M. (1995). Modification of dysfunctional patterns of sexual response through autonomic arousal and false physiological feedback. *Journal of Consulting and Clinical Psychology, 63,* 604–615. (p. 413)

Palladino, J. J., & Carducci, B. J. (1983). "Things that go bump in the night": Students' knowledge of sleep and dreams. Paper presented at the meeting of the Southeastern Psychological Association. (p. 196)

Pallier, C., Colomé, A., & Sebastián-Gallés, N. (2001). The influence of native-language phonology on lexical access: Exemplar-based versus abstract lexical entries. *Psychological Science, 12,* 445–448. (p. 320)

Palmer, S., Schreiber, C., & Box, C. (1991). Remembering the earthquake: "Flashbulb" memory for experienced vs. reported events. Paper presented to the Psychonomic Society convention. (p. 281)

Pandey, J., Sinha, Y., Prakash, A., & Tripathi, R. C. (1982). Right-left political ideologies and attribution of the causes of poverty. *European Journal of Social Psychology, 12,* 327–331. (p. 576)

Panksepp, J. (1982). Toward a general psychobiological theory of emotions. *Behavioral and Brain Sciences, 5,* 407–467. (p. 411)

Pantelis, C., Velakoulis, D., McGorry, P. D., Wood, S. J., Suckling, J., Phillips, L. J., Yung, A. R., Bullmore, E. T., Brewer, W., Soulsby, B., Desmond, P., & McGuire, P. K. (2002). Neuroanatomical abnormalities before and after onset of psychosis: A cross-sectional and longitudinal MRI comparison. *The Lancet,* published online at image.thelancet.com/extras/01art9092web.pdf. (p. 534)

Park, D. C., Lautenschlager, G., Hedden, T., Davidson, N. S., Smith, A. D., & Smith, P. K. (2002). Models of visuospatial and verbal memory across the adult life span. *Psychology and Aging, 17,* 299–320. (p. 134)

Park, R. L. (1999). Liars never break a sweat. *New York Times,* July 12, 1999 (www.nytimes.com). (p. 412)

Parker, C. P., Baltes, B. B., Young, S. A., Huff, J. W., Altmann, R. A., LaCost, H. A., & Roberts, J. E. (2003). Relationships between psychological climate perceptions and work outcomes: A meta-analytic review. *Journal of Organizational Behavior, 24,* 389–416. (p. 399)

Parker, S., Nichter, M., Nichter, M., & Vuckovic, N. (1995). Body image and weight concerns among African American and white adolescent females: Differences that make a difference. *Human Organization, 54,* 103–114. (p. 365)

Passell, P. (1993, March 9). Like a new drug, social programs are put to the test. *New York Times,* pp. C1, C10. (p. 26)

Pate, J. E., Pumariega, A. J., Hester, C., & Garner, D. M. (1992). Cross-cultural patterns in eating disorders: A review. *Journal of the American Academy of Child and Adolescent Psychiatry, 31,* 802–809. (p. 364)

Patoine, B. (2005, January-February). Imagine that! Neural prosthetics harness thoughts to control computers and robotics. *Brain Work,* pp. 1–3. (p. 55)

Patterson, D. R. (2004). Treating pain with hypnosis. *Current Directions in Psychological Science, 13,* 252–255. (p. 212)

Patterson, D. R., & Jensen, M. (2003). Hypnosis for clinical pain control. *Psychological Bulletin, 129,* 495–521. (p. 214)

Patterson, F. (1978, October). Conversations with a gorilla. *National Geographic,* pp. 438–465. (p. 328)

Patterson, G. R., Chamberlain, P., & Reid, J. B. (1982). A comparative evaluation of parent training procedures. *Behavior Therapy, 13,* 638–650. (pp. 253, 603)

Patterson, G. R., Reid, J. B., & Dishion, T. J. (1992). *Antisocial boys.* Eugene, OR: Castalia. (p. 603)

Patterson, M., Warr, P., & West, M. (2004). Organizational climate and company productivity: The role of employee affect and employee level. *Journal of Occupational and Organizational Psychology, 77,* 193–216. (p. 399)

Patterson, R. (1951). *The riddle of Emily Dickinson.* Boston: Houghton Mifflin. (p. 529)

Patton, G. C., Coffey, C., Carlin, J. B., Degenhardt, L., Lynskey, M., & Hall, W. (2002). Cannabis use and mental health of young people: Cohort study. *British Medical Journal, 325,* 1195–1198. (p. 224)

Paulesu, E., Demonet, J-F., Fazio, F., McCrory, E., Chanoine, V., Brunswick, N., Cappa, S. F., Cossu, G., Habib, M., Frith, C. D., & Frith, U. (2001). Dyslexia: Cultural diversity and biological unity. *Science, 291,* 2165–2167. (p. 28)

Paulos, J. A. (1995). *A mathematician reads the newspaper.* New York: Basic Books. (p. 568)

Paunonen, S. V., Zeidner, M., Engvik, H. A., Oosterveld, P., & Maliphant, R. (2000). The nonverbal assessment of personality in five cultures. *Journal of Cross-Cultural Psychology, 31,* 220–239. (p. 478)

Paus, T., Zijdenbos, A., Worsley, K., Collins, D. L., Blumenthal, J., Giedd, J. N., Rapoport, J. L., & Evans, A. C. (1999) Structural maturation of neural pathways in children and adolescents: In vivo study. *Science, 283,* 1908–1911. (p. 105)

Pavlidis, G. T. (2005, January 17). Eye movements can diagnose preschoolers at high risk for attention deficit/hyperactivity disorder (ADHD). Press release, Brunel University (www.brunel.ac.uk). (p. 501)

Pavlov, I. (1927). *Conditioned reflexes: An investigation of the physiological activity of the cerebral cortex.* Oxford: Oxford University Press. (p. 236)

Pedersen, N. L., Plomin, R., McClearn, G. E., & Friberg, L. (1988). Neuroticism, extraversion, and related traits in adult twins reared apart and reared together. *Journal of Personality and Social Psychology, 55,* 950–957. (p. 70)

Peeters, A., Barendregt, J. J., Willekens, F., Mackenbach, J. P., & Mamum, A. A. (2003). Obesity in adulthood and its consequences for life expectancy: A life-table analysis. *Annals of Internal Medicine, 138,* 24–32. (p. 367)

Peigneux, P., Laureys, S., Fuchs, S., Collette, F., Perrin, F., Reggers, J., Phillips, C., Degueldre, C., Del Fiore, G., Aerts, J., Luxen, A., & Maquet, P. (2004). Are spatial memories strengthened in the human hippocampus during slow wave sleep? *Neuron, 44,* 535–545. (pp. 203, 283)

Pekkanen, J. (1982, June). Why do we sleep? *Science, 82,* p. 86. (p. 203)

Pelham, B. W. (1993). On the highly positive thoughts of the highly depressed. In R. F. Baumeister (Ed.), *Self-esteem: The puzzle of low self-regard.* New York: Plenum. (p. 491)

Pendick, D. (1994, January/February). The mind of violence. *Brain Work: The Neuroscience Newsletter,* pp. 1–3, 5. (p. 600)

Pennebaker, J. (1990). *Opening up: The healing power of confiding in others.* New York: William Morrow. (pp. 449, 466)

Pennebaker, J. W. (2002, January 28). Personal communication. (p. 617)

Pennebaker, J. W., & O'Heeron, R. C. (1984). Confiding in others and illness rate among spouses of suicide and accidental death victims. *Journal of Abnormal Psychology, 93,* 473–476. (p. 448)

Pennebaker, J. W., & Stone, L. D. (2003). Words of wisdom: Language use over the life span. *Journal of Personality and Social Psychology, 85,* 291–301. (p. 138)

Pennebaker, J. W., Barger, S. D., & Tiebout, J. (1989). Disclosure of traumas and health among Holocaust survivors. *Psychosomatic Medicine, 51,* 577–589. (p. 449)

Peplau, L. A. (1982). Research on homosexual couples: An overview. *Journal of Homosexuality, 8*(2), 3–8. (p. 381)

Perkins, A., & Fitzgerald, J. A. (1997). Sexual orientation in domestic rams: Some biological and social correlates. In L. Ellis and L. Ebertz (Eds.), *Sexual orientation: Toward biological understanding.* Westport, CT: Praeger Publishers. (p. 382)

Perlmutter, M. (1983). Learning and memory through adulthood. In M. W. Riley, B. B. Hess, & K. Bond (Eds.), *Aging in society: Selected reviews of recent research.* Hillsdale, NJ: Erlbaum. (p. 133)

Perls, T., & Silver, M. H., with Lauerman, J. F. (1999). *Living to 100: Lessons in living to your maximum potential.* Thorndike, ME: Thorndike Press. (p. 441)

Perrett, D. I., Harries, M., Misflin, A. J., & Chitty, A. J. (1988). Three stages in the classification of body movements by visual neurons. In H. B. Barlow, C. Blakemore, & M. Weston Smith (Eds.), *Images and understanding.* Cambridge: Cambridge University Press. (p. 152)

Perrett, D. I., Hietanen, J. K., Oram, M. W., & Benson, P. J. (1992). *Organization and functions of cells responsive to faces in the temporal cortex.* Philosophical Transactions of the Royal Society of London: Series B, 335, 23–30. (p. 152)

Perrett, D. I., Lee, K. J., Penton-Voak, I., Rowland, D., Yoshikawa, S., Burt, D. M., Henzi, S. P., Castles, D. L., Akamatsu, S. (1998, August). Effects of sexual dimorphism on facial attractiveness. *Nature, 394,* 884–887. (p. 596)

Perrett, D. I., May, K. A., & Yoshikawa, S. (1994). Facial shape and judgments of female attractiveness. *Nature, 368,* 239–242. (p. 152)

Persky, S., & Blascovich, J. (2005). Consequences of playing violent video games in immersive virtual environments, In A. Axelsson & Ralph Schroeder (Eds.). *Work and Play in Shared Virtual Environments.* New York: Springer. (p. 605)

Pert, C. B., & Snyder, S. H. (1973). Opiate receptor: Demonstration in nervous tissue. *Science, 179,* 1011–1014. (p. 39)

Perugini, E. M., Kirsch, I., Allen, S. T., Coldwell, E., Meredith, J., Montgomery, G. H., & Sheehan, J. (1998). Surreptitious observation of responses to hypnotically suggested hallucinations: A test of the compliance hypothesis. *International Journal of Clinical and Experimental Hypnosis, 46,* 191–203. (p. 215)

Peschel, E. R., & Peschel, R. E. (1987). Medical insights into the castrati in opera. *American Scientist, 75,* 578–583. (p. 377)

Peters, T. J., & Waterman, R. H., Jr. (1982). *In search of excellence: Lessons from America's best-run companies.* New York: Harper & Row. (p. 257)

Peterson, C., & Barrett, L. C. (1987). Explanatory style and academic performance among university freshmen. *Journal of Personality and Social Psychology, 53,* 603–607. (p. 487)

Peterson, C., & Seligman, M. E. P. (2004). *Character strengths and virtues: A handbook and classification.* New York: Oxford. (p. 504)

Peterson, C., Peterson, J., & Skevington, S. (1986). Heated argument and adolescent development. *Journal of Social and Personal Relationships, 3,* 229–240. (p. 122)

Peterson, L. R., & Peterson, M. J. (1959). Short-term retention of individual verbal items. *Journal of Experimental Psychology, 58,* 193–198. (pp. 277, 278)

Petitto, L. A., & Marentette, P. F. (1991). Babbling in the manual mode: Evidence for the ontogeny of language. *Science, 251,* 1493–1496. (p. 320)

Pettegrew, J. W., Keshavan, M. S., & Minshew, N. J. (1993). 31P nuclear magnetic resonance spectroscopy: Neurodevelopment and schizophrenia. *Schizophrenia Bulletin, 19,* 35–53. (p. 533)

Petticrew, C., Bell, R., & Hunter, D. (2002). Influence of psychological coping on survival and recurrence in people with cancer: Systematic review. *British Medical Journal, 325,* 1066. (p. 442)

Petticrew, M., Fraser, J. M., & Regan, M. F. (1999). Adverse life events and risk of breast cancer: A meta-analysis. *British Journal of Health Psychology, 4,* 1–17. (p. 442)

Pettigrew, T. F. (1969). Racially separate or together? *Journal of Social Issues, 25,* 43–69. (p. 616)

Pettigrew, T. F. (1998). Reactions toward the new minorities of western Europe. *Annual Review of Sociology, 24,* 77–103. (p. 595)

Pettigrew, T. F. (2004). Justice deferred a half century after Brown v. Board of Education. *American Psychologist, 59,* 521–529. (p. 616)

Pew. (2003). *Views of a changing world 2003. The Pew Global Attitudes Project.* Washington, DC: Pew Research Center for the People and the Press (http://people-press.org/reports/pdf/185.pdf). (p. 91)

Phelps, J. A., Davis J. O., & Schartz, K. M. (1997). Nature, nurture, and twin research strategies. *Current Directions in Psychological Science, 6,* 117–120. (p. 535)

Philip Morris. (2003). Philip Morris USA youth smoking prevention. Teenage attitudes and behavior study, 2002. In "Raising kids who don't smoke," vol. 1(2). (p. 221)

Phillips, D. P. (1985). Natural experiments on the effects of mass media violence on fatal aggression: Strengths and weaknesses of a new approach. In L. Berkowitz (Ed.), *Advances in experimental social psychology* (Vol. 19). Orlando, FL: Academic Press. (p. 583)

Phillips, D. P., Carstensen, L. L., & Paight, D. J. (1989). Effects of mass media news stories on suicide, with new evidence on the role of story content. In D. R. Pfeffer (Ed.), *Suicide among youth: Perspectives on risk and prevention.* Washington, DC: American Psychiatric Press. (p. 583)

Phillips, J. L. (1969). *Origins of intellect: Piaget's theory.* San Francisco: Freeman. (p. 110)

Piaget, J. (1932). *The moral judgment of the child.* New York: Harcourt, Brace & World. (p. 123)

Pickar, D., Labarca, R., Linnoila, M., Roy, A., Hommer, D., Everett, D., & Payl, S. M. (1984). Neuroleptic-induced decrease in plasma homovanillic acid and antipsychotic activity in schizophrenic patients. *Science, 225,* 954–957. (p. 566)

Pike, K. M., & Rodin, J. (1991). Mothers, daughters, and disordered eating. *Journal of Abnormal Psychology, 100,* 198–204. (p. 364)

Piliavin, J. A. (2003). Doing well by doing good: Benefits for the benefactor. In C. L. M. Keyes & J. Haidt (Eds.), *Flourishing: Positive psychology and the life well-lived.* Washington, DC: American Psychological Association. (p. 124)

Pillemer, D. G. (1998). *Momentous events, vivid memories.* Cambridge: Harvard University Press, 1998. (p. 132)

Pillemer, D. G. (1995). *What is remembered about early childhood events?* Invited paper presentation to the American Psychological Society convention. (p. 106)

Pillsworth, M. G., Haselton, M. G., & Buss, D. M. (2004). Ovulatory shifts in female desire. *Journal of Sex Research, 41,* 55–65. (p. 376)

Pincus, H. A. (1997) Commentary: Spirituality, religion, and health: Expanding, and using the knowledge base. *Mind/Body Medicine, 2,* 49. (p. 456)

Pinel, J. P. J. (1993). *Biopsychology (2nd ed).* Boston: Allyn & Bacon. (p. 362)

Pingitore, R., Dugoni, B. L., Tindale, R. S., & Spring, B. (1994). Bias against overweight job applicants in a simulated employment interview. *Journal of Applied Psychology, 79,* 909–917. (p. 368)

Pinker, S. (1990, September-October). Quoted by J. de Cuevas, "No, she holded them loosely." *Harvard Magazine,* pp. 60–67. (p. 319)

Pinker, S. (1995). The language instinct. *The General Psychologist, 31,* 63–65. (p. 328, 329)

Pinker, S. (1998). Words and rules. *Lingua, 106,* 219–242. (p. 319)

Pinker, S. (2002). *The blank slate.* New York: Viking. (p. 75)

Pinker, S. (2002, September 9). A biological understanding of human nature: A talk with Steven Pinker. *The Edge Third Culture Mail List* (www.edge.org). (pp. 71, 321)

Pinker, S. (2005, April 22). The science of gender and science: A conversation with Elizabeth Spelke. *Harvard University* (www.edge.org). (p. 349)

Pinkerton, S. D., & Abramson, P. R. (1997). Condoms and the prevention of AIDS. *American Scientist, 85,* 364–373. (p. 380)

Pipe, M-E. (1996). Children's eyewitness memory. *New Zealand Journal of Psychology, 25,* 36–43. (p. 299)

Pipe, M-E., Lamb, M. E., Orbach, Y., & Esplin, P. W. (2004). Recent research on children's testimony about experienced and witnessed events. *Developmental Review, 24,* 440–468. (p. 299)

Piper, A., Jr. (1998, Winter). Multiple personality disorder: Witchcraft survives in the twentieth century. *Skeptical Inquirer,* pp. 44–50. (p. 516)

Pipher, M. (2002). *The middle of everywhere: The world's refugees come to our town.* New York: Harcourt Brace. (pp. 389, 437)

Pittenger, D. J. (1993). The utility of the Myers-Briggs Type Indicator. *Review of Eduational Research, 63,* 467–488. (p. 475)

Pliner, P. (1982). The effects of mere exposure on liking for edible substances. *Appetite: Journal for Intake Research, 3,* 283–290. (p. 363)

Pliner, P., Pelchat, M., & Grabski, M. (1993). Reduction of neophobia in humans by exposure to novel foods. *Appetite, 20,* 111–123. (p. 363)

Plomin, R. (1999). Genetics and general cognitive ability. *Nature, 402* (Suppl), C25–C29. (pp. 331, 342)

Plomin, R. (2001). Genetics and behaviour. *The Psychologist, 14,* 134–139. (p. 342)

Plomin, R. (2003). General cognitive ability. In R. Plomin, J. C. DeFries, I. W. Craig, & P. McGuffin (Eds.), *Behavioral genetics in a postgenomic world.* Washington, DC: APA Books. (p. 342)

Plomin, R., & Bergeman, C. S. (1991). The nature of nurture: Genetic influence on "environmental" measures. *Behavioral and Brain Sciences, 14,* 373–427. (p. 73)

Plomin, R., & Crabbe, J. (2000). DNA. *Psychological Bulletin, 126,* 806–828. (p. 67)

Plomin, R., & Daniels, D. (1987). Why are children in the same family so different from one another? *Behavioral and Brain Sciences, 10,* 1–60. (p. 81)

Plomin, R., & DeFries, J. C. (1998, May). The genetics of cognitive abilities and disabilities. *Scientific American,* pp. 62–69. (p. 343)

Plomin, R., & McGuffin, P. (2003). Psychopathology in the postgenomic era. *Annual Review of Psychology, 54,* 205–228. (pp. 525, 526)

Plomin, R., Corley, R., Caspi, A., Fulker, D. W., & DeFries, J. (1998). Adoption results for self-reported personality: Evidence for nonadditive genetic effects? *Journal of Personality and Social Psychology, 75,* 211–219. (p. 71)

Plomin, R., DeFries, J. C., McClearn, G. E., & Rutter, M. (1997). *Behavioral genetics.* New York: Freeman. (pp. 69, 343, 369, 383, 384, 535)

Plomin, R., Fulker, D. W., Corley, R., & DeFries, J. C. (1997). Nature, nurture and cognitive development from 1 to 16 years: A parent-offspring adoption study. *Psychological Science, 8,* 442–447. (p. 74)

Plomin, R., McClearn, G. E., Pedersen, N. L., Nesselroade, J. R., & Bergeman, C. S. (1988). Genetic influence on childhood family environment perceived retrospectively from the last half of the life span. *Developmental Psychology, 24,* 37–45. (p. 73)

Plomin, R., Reiss, D., Hetherington, E. M., & Howe, G. W. (January, 1994). Nature and nurture: Genetic contributions to measures of the family environment. *Developmental Psychology, 30(1),* 32–43. (p. 73)

Plous, S., & Herzog, H. A. (2000). Poll shows researchers favor lab animal protection. *Science, 290,* 711. (p. 30)

Polivy, J., & Herman, C. P. (1985). Dieting and binging: A causal analysis. *American Psychologist, 40,* 193–201. (p. 372)

Polivy, J., & Herman, C. P. (1987). Diagnosis and treatment of normal eating. *Journal of Personality and Social Psychology, 55,* 635–644. (p. 372)

Polivy, J., & Herman, C. P. (2002). Causes of eating disorders. *Annual Review of Psychology, 53,* 187–213. (p. 364)

Pollack, A. (2004, April 13). With tiny brain implants, just thinking may make it so. *New York Times* (www.nytimes.com). (p. 55)

Pollak, S. D., & Kistler, D. J. (2002). Early experience is associated with the development of categorical representations for facial expressions of emotion. *Proceedings of the National Academy of Sciences, 99,* 9072–9076. (p. 418)

Pollak, S. D., & Tolley-Schell, S. A. (2003). Selective attention to facial emotion in physically abused children. *Journal of Abnormal Psychology, 112,* 323–328. (p. 418)

Pollak, S. D., Cicchetti, D., & Klorman, R. (1998). Stress, memory, and emotion: Developmental considerations from the study of child maltreatment. *Developmental Psychopathology, 10,* 811–828. (p. 241)

Pollard, R. (1992). 100 years in psychology and deafness: A centennial retrospective. Invited address to the American Psychological Association convention, Washington, DC. (p. 324)

Polusny, M. A., & Follette, V. M. (1995). Long-term correlates of child sexual abuse: Theory and review of the empirical literature. *Applied & Preventive Psychology, 4,* 143–166. (p. 117)

Poole, D. A., & Lindsay, D. S. (1995). Interviewing preschoolers: Effects of nonsuggestive techniques, parental coaching and leading questions on reports of nonexperienced events. *Journal of Experimental Child Psychology, 60,* 129–154. (p. 298)

Poole, D. A., & Lindsay, D. S. (2001). Children's eyewitness reports after exposure to misinformation from parents. *Journal of Experimental Psychology: Applied, 7,* 27–50. (p. 298)

Poole, D. A., & Lindsay, D. S. (2002). Reducing child witnesses' false reports of misinformation from parents. *Journal of Experimental Child Psychology, 81,* 117–140. (p. 298)

Poole, D. A., Lindsay, D. S., Memon, A., & Bull, R. (1995). Psychotherapy and the recovery of memories of childhood sexual abuse: U.S. and British practitioners' opinions, practices, and experiences. *Journal of Consulting and Clinical Psychology, 63,* 426–437. (p. 299)

Poon, L. W. (1987). *Myths and truisms: Beyond extant analyses of speed of behavior and age.* Address to the Eastern Psychological Association convention. (p. 131)

Pope, H. G., & Yurgelun-Todd, D. (1996). The residual cognitive effects of heavy marijuana use in college students. *Journal of the American Medical Association, 275,* 521–527. (p. 224)

Popenoe, D. (1993). *The evolution of marriage and the problem of stepfamilies: A biosocial perspective.* Paper presented at the National Symposium on Stepfamilies, Pennsylvania State University. (p. 86)

Popenoe, D., & Whitehead, B. D. (2002). *Should We Live Together?, 2nd Ed.* New Brunswick, NJ: The National Marriage Project, Rutgers University. (p. 136)

Poremba, A., & Gabriel, M. (2001). Amygdalar efferents initiate auditory thalamic discriminative training-induced neuronal activity. *Journal of Neuroscience, 21,* 270–278. (p. 52)

Porter, D., & Neuringer, A. (1984). Music discriminations by pigeons. *Journal of Experimental Psychology: Animal Behavior Processes, 10,* 138–148. (p. 247)

Porter, S., Birt, A. R., Yuille, J. C., & Lehman, D. R. (2000, Nov.). Negotiating false memories: Interviewer and rememberer characteristics relate to memory distortion. *Psychological Science, 11,* 507–510. (p. 297)

Porter, S., Yuille, J. C., & Lehman, D. R. (1999). The nature of real, implanted, and fabricated memories for childhood events: Implications for the recovered memory debate. *Law and Human Behavior, 23,* 517–537. (p. 300)

Posavac, H. D., Posavac, S. S., & Posavac, E. J. (1998). Exposure to media images of female attractiveness and concern with body weight among young women. *Sex Roles, 38,* 187–201. (p. 365)

Posner, M. I., & Carr, T. H. (1992). Lexical access and the brain: Anatomical constraints on cognitive models of word recognition. *American Journal of Psychology, 105,* 1–26. (p. 58)

Poulton, R., & Milne, B. J. (2002). Low fear in childhood is associated with sporting prowess in adolescence and young adulthood. *Behaviour Research and Therapy, 40,* 1191–1197. (p. 518)

Powell, J. (1989). *Happiness is an inside job.* Valencia, CA: Tabor. (p. 493)

Powell, K. E., Thompson, P. D., Caspersen, C. J., & Kendrick, J. S. (1987). Physical activity and the incidence of coronary heart disease. *Annual Review of Public Health, 8,* 253–287. (p. 450)

Powell, L. H., Schahabi, L., & Thoresen, C. E. (2003). Religion and spirituality: Linkages to physical health. *American Psychologist, 58,* 36–52. (p. 455)

Powell, R. A., & Boer, D. P. (1994). Did Freud mislead patients to confabulate memories of abuse? *Psychological Reports, 74,* 1283–1298. (p. 466)

Pratkanis, A. R., & Greenwald, A. G. (1988). Recent perspectives on unconscious processing: Still no marketing applications. *Psychology and Marketing, 5,* 337–353. (p. 145)

PRB. (2002). *2002 Women of our world.* Population Reference Bureau (www.prb.org). (p. 596)

Prentice, D. A., & Miller, D. T. (1993). Pluralistic ignorance and alcohol use on campus: Some consequences of misperceiving the social norm. *Journal of Personality and Social Psychology, 64,* 243–256. (p. 227)

Presley, C. A., Meilman, P. W., & Lyerla, R. (1997). *Alcohol and drugs on American college campuses: Issues of violence and harrassment.* Carbondale, IL: Core Institute, Southern Illinois University. (p. 218)

Presson, P. K., & Benassi, V. A. (1996). Locus of control orientation and depressive symptomatology: A meta-analysis. *Journal of Social Behavior and Personality, 11,* 201–212. (p. 485)

Pringle, P. J., Geary, M. P., Rodeck, C. H., Kingdom, J. C., Kayamba-Kay's, S., & Hindmarsh, P. C. (2005). The influence of cigarette smoking on antenatal growth, birth size, and the insulin-like growth factor axis. *Journal of Clinical Endocrinology and Metabolism, 90,* 2556–2562. (p. 102)

Prioleau, L., Murdock, M., & Brody, N. (1983). An analysis of psychotherapy versus placebo studies. *The Behavioral and Brain Sciences, 6,* 275–310. (p. 559)

Pronin, E., Lin, D. Y., & Ross, L. (2002). The bias blind spot: Perceptions of bias in self versus others. *Personality and Social Psychology Bulletin, 28,* 369–381. (p. 493)

Provine, R. R. (2001). *Laughter: A scientific investigation.* New York: Penguin. (p. 21)

Pryor, J. H., Hurtado, S., Saenz, V. B., Lindholm, J. A., Korn, W. S., & Mahoney, K. M. (2005). *The American freshman: National norms for fall 2005.* Los Angeles: Higher Education Research Institute, UCLA. (pp. 76, 91)

Psychologist. (2003, April). Who's the greatest? *The Psychologist, 16,* 17. (p. 112)

Puchalski, C. (2005, March 12). Personal correspondence from Director, George Washington Institute for Spirituality and Health. (p. 454)

Putnam, F. W. (1991). Recent research on multiple personality disorder. *Psychiatric Clinics of North America, 14,* 489–502. (p. 516)

Putnam, F. W. (1995). Rebuttal of Paul McHugh. *Journal of the American Academy of Child and Adolescent Psychiatry, 34,* 963. (p. 517)

Putnam, R. (2000). *Bowling alone.* New York: Simon and Schuster. (p. 84)

Pyszczynski, T. A., Solomon, S., & Greenberg, J. (2002). *In the wake of 9/11: The psychology of terror.* Washington, DC: American Psychological Association. (p. 598)

Pyszczynski, T., Hamilton, J. C., Greenberg, J., & Becker, S. E. (1991). Self-awareness and psychological dysfunction. In C. R. Snyder & D. O. Forsyth (Eds.), *Handbook of social and clinical psychology: The health perspective.* New York: Pergamon. (p. 527)

Qirko, H. N. (2004). "Fictive kin" and suicide terrorism. *Science, 304,* 49–50. (p. 590)

Quinn, P. C., Bhatt, R. S., Brush, D., Grimes, A., & Sharpnack, H. (2002). Development of form similarity as a Gestalt grouping principle in infancy. *Psychological Science, 13,* 320–328. (p. 172)

Quinn, P. J., Williams, G. M., Najman, J. M., Andersen, M. J., & Bor, W. (2001). The effect of breastfeeding on child development at 5 years: A cohort study. *Journal of Pediatrics & Child Health, 3,* 465–469. (p. 24)

Rahman, Q., & Wilson, G. D. (2003). Born gay? The psychobiology of human sexual orientation. *Personality and Individual Differences, 34,* 1337–1382. (pp. 383, 385)

Rahman, Q., Wilson, G. D., & Abrahams, S. (2003). Biosocial factors, sexual orientation and neurocognitive functioning. *Psychoneuroendocrinology, 29,* 867–881. (p. 385)

Raine, A. (1999). Murderous minds: Can we see the mark of Cain? *Cerebrum: The Dana Forum on Brain Science 1(1),* 15–29. (pp. 518, 600)

Raine, A., Lencz, T., Bihrle, S., LaCasse, L., & Colletti, P. (2000). Reduced prefrontal gray matter volume and reduced autonomic activity in antisocial personality disorder. *Archives of General Psychiatry, 57,* 119–127. (p. 518)

Rainville, P., Duncan, G. H., Price, D. D., Carrier, B., & Bushnell, M. C. (1997). Pain affect encoded in human anterior cingulate but not somatosensory cortex. *Science, 277,* 968–971. (p. 214)

Raison, C. L., Klein, H. M., & Steckler, M. (1999). The mood and madness reconsidered. *Journal of Affective Disorders, 53,* 99–106. (p. 506)

Ralston, A. (2004). Enough rope. Interview for ABC TV, Australia, by Andrew Denton (www.abc.net.au/enoughrope/stories/s1227885.htm). (p. 356)

Ramachandran, V. S., & Blakeslee, S. (1998). *Phantoms in the brain: Probing the mysteries of the human mind.* New York: Morrow. (pp. 42, 59, 163)

Rand, C. S. W., & Macgregor, A. M. C. (1990). Morbidly obese patients' perceptions of social discrimination before and after surgery for obesity. *Southern Medical Journal, 83,* 1390–1395. (p. 368)

Rand, C. S. W., & Macgregor, A. M. C. (1991). Successful weight loss following obesity surgery and perceived liability or morbid obesity. *Internal Journal of Obesity, 15,* 577–579. (p. 368)

Randi, J. (1999, February 4). 2000 Club mailing list e-mail letter. (p. 187)

Rapoport, J. L. (1989, March). The biology of obsessions and compulsions. *Scientific American,* pp. 83–89. (pp. 511, 514)

Räsänen, S., Pakaslahti, A., Syvalahti, E., Jones, P. B., & Isohanni, M. (2000). Sex differences in schizophrenia: A review. *Nordic Journal of Psychiatry, 54,* 37–45. (p. 533)

Ray, J. (2005, April 12). U.S. teens walk away from anger: Boys and girls manage anger differently. The Gallup Organization (www.gallup.com). (p. 424)

Raynor, H. A., & Epstein, L. H. (2001). Dietary variety, energy regulation, and obesity. *Psychological Bulletin, 127,* 325–341. (p. 362)

Reason, J. (1987). The Chernobyl errors. *Bulletin of the British Psychological Society, 40,* 201–206. (p. 591)

Reason, J., & Mycielska, K. (1982). *Absent-minded? The psychology of mental lapses and everyday errors.* Englewood Cliffs, NJ: Prentice-Hall. (p. 184)

Reed, P. (2000). Serial position effects in recognition memory for odors. *Journal of Experimental Psychology: Learning, Memory, and Cognition, 26,* 411–422. (p. 273)

Reeve, C. L., & Hakel, M. D. (2002). Asking the right questions about g. *Human Performance, 15,* 47–74. (p. 332)

Regier, D. A., Kaelber, C. T., Rae, D. S., Farmer, M. E., Knauper, B., Kessler, R. C., & Norquist, G. S. (1998). Limitations of diagnostic criteria and assessment instruments for mental disorders: Implications for research and policy. *Archives of General Psychiatry, 55,* 109–115. (p. 503)

Reichman, J. (1998). *I'm not in the mood: What every woman should know about improving her libido.* New York: Morrow. (p. 376)

Reiner, W. G., & Gearhart, J. P. (2004). Discordant sexual identity in some genetic males with cloacal exstrophy assigned to female sex at birth. *New England Journal of Medicine, 350,* 333–341. (p. 90)

Reisenzein, R. (1983). The Schachter theory of emotion: Two decades later. *Psychological Bulletin, 94,* 239–264. (p. 413)

Reiser, M. (1982). *Police psychology.* Los Angeles: LEHI. (p. 186)

Remafedi, G. (1999). Suicide and sexual orientation: Nearing the end of controversy? *Archives of General Psychiatry, 56,* 885–886. (p. 381)

Remley, A. (1988, October). From obedience to independence. *Psychology Today,* pp. 56–59. (p. 86)

Reneman, L., Lavalaye, J., Schmand, B., De Wolff, F. A., Van Den Brink, W., Den Heeten, G., & Booij, J. (2001). Cortical serotonin transporter density and verbal memory in individuals who stopped using 3, 4-methylenedioxy-methampetamine. *Archives of General Psychiatry, 58,* 901–908. (p. 223)

Renner, M. J. (1992). Curiosity and exploration. In L. R. Squire (Ed.), *Encyclopedia of Learning and Memory.* New York: Macmillan. (p. 358)

Renner, M. J., & Renner, C. H. (1993). Expert and novice intuitive judgments about animal behavior. *Bulletin of the Psychonomic Society, 31,* 551–552. (p. 79)

Renner, M. J., & Rosenzweig, M. R. (1987). *Enriched and impoverished environments: Effects on brain and behavior.* New York: Springer-Verlag. (p. 79)

Rentfrow, P. J., & Gosling, S. D. (2003). The Do Re Mi's of everyday life: The structure and personality correlates of music preferences. *Journal of Personality and Social Psychology, 84,* 1236–1256. (p. 482)

Repetti, R. L., Taylor, S. E., & Seeman, T. E. (2002). Risky families: Family social environments and the mental and physical health of offspring. *Psychological Bulletin, 128,* 330–366. (p. 436)

Rescorla, R. A., & Wagner, A. R. (1972). A theory of Pavlovian conditioning: Variations in the effectiveness of reinforcement and nonreinforcement. In A. H. Black & W. F. Perokasy (Eds.), *Classical conditioning II: Current theory.* New York: Appleton-Century-Crofts. (p. 241)

Resnick, M. D., Bearman, P. S., Blum, R. W., Bauman, K. E., Harris, K. M., Jones, J., Tabor, J., Beuhring, T., Sieving, R., Shew, M., Bearinger, L. H., & Udry, J. R. (1997). Protecting adolescents from harm: Findings from the National Longitudinal Study on Adolescent Health. *Journal of the American Medical Association, 278,* 823–832. (pp. 22, 125)

Resnick, R. A., O'Regan, J. K., & Clark, J. J. (1997). To see or not to see: The need for attention to perceive changes in scenes. *Psychological Science, 8,* 368–373. (p. 194)

Resnick, S. M. (1992). Positron emission tomography in psychiatric illness. *Current Directions in Psychological Science, 1,* 92–98. (p. 533)

Responsive Community. (1996, Fall). Age vs. weight. Page 83 (reported from a *Wall Street Journal* survey). (p. 371)

Reuters. (2000, July 5). Many teens regret decision to have sex (National Campaign to Prevent Teen Pregnancy survey). www.washingtonpost.com. (p. 379)

Reynolds, A. J., Temple, J. A., Robertson, D. L., & Manri, E. A. (2001). Long-term effects of an early childhood intervention on educational achievement and juvenile arrest. *Journal of the American Medical Association, 285,* 2339–2346. (p. 344)

Rhee, S. H., & Waldman, I. D. (2002). Genetic and environmental influences on antisocial behavior: A meta-analysis of twin and adoption studies. *Psychological Bulletin, 128,* 490–529. (p. 518)

Rhodes, S. R. (1983). Age-related differences in work attitudes and behavior: A review and conceptual analysis. *Psychological Bulletin, 93,* 328–367. (p. 131)

Rholes, W. S., & Simpson, J. A. (Eds.) (2004). *Adult attachment: Theory, research, and clinical implications.* New York: Guilford. (p. 116)

Ribeiro, R., Gervasoni, D., Soares, E. S., Zhou, Y., & Lin S-C., Pantoja, J., Lavine, M., & Nicolelis, M. A. L. (2004). Long-lasting novelty-induced neuronal reverberation during slow-wave sleep in multiple forebrain areas. *PloS Biology, 2(1),* e37 (www.plosbiology.org). (p. 203)

Ricciardelli, L. A., & McCabe, M. P. (2004). A biopsychosocial model of disordered eating and the pursuit of muscularity in adolescent boys. *Psychological Bulletin, 130,* 179–205. (p. 364)

Rice, B. (1985, September). Performance review: The job nobody likes. *Psychology Today,* pp. 30–36. (p. 577)

Rice, M. E., & Grusec, J. E. (1975). Saying and doing: Effects on observer performance. *Journal of Personality and Social Psychology, 32,* 584–593. (p. 263)

Rieff, P. (1979). *Freud: The mind of a moralist (3rd ed.).* Chicago: University of Chicago Press. (p. 468)

Rieger, G., Chivers, M. L., & Bailey, J. M. (2005). Sexual arousal patterns of bisexual men. *Psychological Science, 16,* 579–584. (p. 381)

Riis, J., Loewenstein, G., Baron, J., Jepson, C., Fagerlin, A., & Ubel, P. A. (2005). Ignorance of hedonic adaptation to hemodialysis: A study using ecological momentary assessment. *Journal of Experimental Psychology: General, 134,* 3–9. (p. 426)

Ring, K. (1980). *Life at death: A scientific investigation of the near-death experience.* New York: Coward, McCann & Geoghegan. (p. 224)

Ripple, C. H., & Zigler, E. F. (2003). Research, policy, and the federal role in prevention initiatives for children. *American Psychologist, 58,* 482–490. (p. 344)

Riskind, J. H., Beck, A. T., Berchick, R. J., Brown, G., & Steer, R. A. (1987). Reliability of DSM-III diagnoses for major depression and generalized anxiety disorder using the structured clinical interview for DSM-III. *Archives of General Psychiatry, 44,* (p. 503)

Rizzolatti, G., Fadiga, L., Fogassi, L., & Gallese, V. (2002). From mirror neurons to imitation: Facts and speculations. In A. N. Meltzoff & W. Prinz (Eds.), *The imitative mind: Development, evolution, and brain bases.* Cambridge: Cambridge University Press, 2002. (p. 261)

Roberson, D., Davidoff, J., Davies, I. R. L., & Shapiro, L. R. (2004). The development of color categories in two languages: A longitudinal study. *Journal of Experimental Psychology: General, 133,* 554–571. (p. 323)

Roberts, A. H., Kewman, D. G., Mercier, L., & Hovell, M. (1993). The power of nonspecific effects in healing: Implications for psychosocial and biological treatments. *Clinical Psychology Review, 13,* 375–391. (p. 559)

Roberts, B. W., & DelVecchio, W. F. (2000). The rank-order consistency of personality traits from childhood to old age: A quantitative review of longitudinal studies. *Psychological Bulletin, 126,* 3–25. (p. 479)

Roberts, B. W., Caspi, A., & Moffitt, T. E. (2001). The kids are alright: Growth and stability in personality development from adolescence to adulthood. *Journal of Personality and Social Psychology, 81,* 670–683. (p. 100)

Roberts, B. W., Caspi, A., & Moffitt, T. E. (2003). Work experiences and personality development in young adulthood. *Journal of Personality and Social Psychology, 84,* 582–593. (pp. 100, 137)

Roberts, B. W., Walton, K. E., & Viechtbauer, W. (2006). Patterns of mean-level change in personality traits across the life course: A meta-analysis of longitudinal studies. *Psychological Bulletin, 132,* 1–25. (p. 100)

Roberts, L. (1988). Beyond Noah's ark: What do we need to know? *Science, 242,* 1247. (p. 446)

Roberts, T-A. (1991). Determinants of gender differences in responsiveness to others' evaluations. *Dissertation Abstracts International, 51*(8–B). (p. 89)

Robins, L. N., Davis, D. H., & Goodwin, D. W. (1974). Drug use by U.S. Army enlisted men in Vietnam: A follow-up on their return home. *American Journal of Epidemiology, 99,* 235–249. (p. 227)

Robins, L., & Regier, D. (Eds.). (1991). *Psychiatric disorders in America.* New York: Free Press. (p. 507)

Robins, R. W., & Trzesniewski, K. H. (2005). Self-esteem development across the lifespan. *Current Directions in Psychological Science, 14*(3), 158–162. (p. 137)

Robins, R. W., Gosling, S. D., & Craik, K. H. (1999). An empirical analysis of trends in psychology. *American Psychologist, 54,* 117–128. (p. 459)

Robins, R. W., Trzesniewski, K. H., Tracy, J. L., Gosling, S. D., & Potter, J. (2002). Global self-esteem across the lifespan. *Psychology and Aging, 17,* 423–434. (p. 125)

Robinson, F. P. (1970). *Effective study.* New York: Harper & Row. (p. 10)

Robinson, J. (2002, October 8). What percentage of the population is gay? *Gallup Tuesday Briefing* (www.gallup.com/poll/tb/religValue/20021008b.asp). (p. 380)

Robinson, J. L., Kagan, J., Reznick, J. S., & Corley, R. (1992). The heritability of inhibited and uninhibited behavior: A twin study. *Developmental Psychology, 28,* 1030–1037. (p. 72)

Robinson, T. E., & Berridge, K. C. (2003). Addiction. *Annual Review of Psychology, 54,* 25–53. (p. 217)

Robinson, T. N. (1999). Reducing children's television viewing to prevent obesity. *Journal of the American Medical Association, 282,* 1561–1567. (p. 372)

Robinson, V. M. (1983). Humor and health. In P. E. McGhee & J. H. Goldstein (Eds.), *Handbook of humor research: Vol. II. Applied studies.* New York: Springer-Verlag. (p. 446)

Rochat, F. (1993). How did they resist authority? Protecting refugees in Le Chambon during World War II. Paper presented at the American Psychological Association convention. (p. 587)

Rock, I., & Palmer, S. (1990, December). The legacy of Gestalt psychology. *Scientific American,* pp. 84–90. (p. 172)

Rodin, J. (1986). Aging and health: Effects of the sense of control. *Science, 233,* 1271–1276. (pp. 446, 486)

Roediger, H. (2001, September). Quoted by R. Herbert, Doing a number on memory. *APS Observer,* pp. 1, 7–11. (p. 293)

Roediger, H. L., III, Wheeler, M. A., & Rajaram, S. (1993). Remembering, knowing, and reconstructing the past. In D. L. Medin (Ed.), *The psychology of learning and motivation: Advances in research and theory (Vol. 30).* Orlando, FL: Academic Press. (p. 297)

Roehling, M. V. (1999). Weight-based discrimination in employment: Psychological and legal aspects. *Personnel Psychology, 52,* 969–1016. (p. 368)

Roehling, P. V., Roehling, M. V., & Moen, P. (2001). The relationship between work-life policies and practices and employee loyalty: A life course perspective. *Journal of Family and Economic Issues, 22,* 141–170. (p. 402)

Roenneberg, T., Kuehnle, T., Pramstaller, P. P., Ricken, J., Havel, M., Guth, A., Merrow, M. (2004). A marker for the end of adolescence. *Current Biology, 14,* R1038–9. (p. 196)

Roese, N. J., & Summerville, A. (2005). What we regret most . . . and why. *Personality and Social Psychology Bulletin, 31,* 1273–1285. (p. 137)

Roesser, R. (1998). What you should know about hearing conservation. *Better Hearing Institute* (www.betterhearing.org). (p. 160)

Rogers, C. R. (1958). Reinhold Niebuhr's The self and the dramas of history: A criticism. *Pastoral Psychology, 9,* 15–17. (p. 492)

Rogers, C. R. (1961). *On becoming a person: A therapist's view of psychotherapy.* Boston: Houghton Mifflin. (p. 543)

Rogers, C. R. (1980). *A way of being.* Boston: Houghton Mifflin. (pp. 471, 472, 543, 544)

Rohan, M. J., & Zanna, M. P. (1996). Value transmission in families," in C. Seligman, J. M. Olson, & M. P. Zanna (Eds.), *The psychology of values: The Ontario Symposium (Vol. 8).* Malwah, NJ: Erlbaum. (p. 71)

Rohner, R. P. (1986). *The warmth dimension: Foundations of parental acceptance-rejection theory.* Newbury Park, CA:Sage. (p. 87)

Rohner, R. P., & Veneziano, R. A. (2001). The importance of father love: History and contemporary evidence. *Review of General Psychology, 5,* 382–405. (pp. 115, 117)

Roiser, J. P., Cook, L. J., Cooper, J. D., Rubinsztein, D. C., & Sahakian, B. J. (2005). Association of a functional polymorphism in the serotonin transporter gene with abnormal emotional processing in ecstasy users. *American Journal of Psychiatry, 162,* 609–612. (p. 223)

Rokach, A., Orzeck, T., Moya, M., & Exposito, F. (2002). Causes of loneliness in North America and Spain. *European Psychologist, 7,* 70–79. (p. 28)

Rosch, E. (1978). Principles of categorization. In E. Rosch & B. L. Lloyd (Eds.), *Cognition and categorization.* Hillsdale, NJ: Erlbaum. (p. 307)

Rose, J. S., Chassin, L., Presson, C. C., & Sherman, S. J. (1999). Peer influences on adolescent cigarette smoking: A prospective sibling analysis. *Merrill-Palmer Quarterly, 45,* 62–84. (pp. 81, 221)

Rose, R. J., Kaprio, J., Winter, T., Dick, D. M., Viken, R. J., Pulkkinen, L., & Koskenvuo, M. (2002). Femininity and fertility in sisters with twin brothers: Prenatal androgenization? Cross-sex socialization? *Psychological Science, 13,* 263–266. (p. 382)

Rose, S. (1999). Precis of Lifelines: Biology, freedom, determinism. *Behavioral and Brain Sciences, 22,* 871–921. (p. 77)

Rose, S., Bisson, J., & Wessely, S. (2003). A systematic review of single-session psychological interventions ('debriefing') following trauma. *Psychotherapy and Psychosomatics, 72*, 176–184. (pp. 81, 513)

Roselli, C. E., Resko, J. A., & Stormshak, F. (2002). Hormonal influences on sexual partner preference in rams. *Archives of Sexual Behavior, 31*, 43–49. (p. 383)

Rosenbaum, M. (1986). The repulsion hypothesis: On the nondevelopment of relationships. *Journal of Personality and Social Psychology, 51*, 1156–1166. (p. 610)

Rosenberg, N. A., Pritchard, J. K., Weber, J. L., Cann, H. M., Kidd, K. K., Zhivotosky, L. A., & Feldman, M. W. (2002). Genetic structure of human populations. *Science, 298*, 2381–2385. (p. 75)

Rosenhan, D. L. (1973). On being sane in insane places. *Science, 179*, 250–258. (p. 503)

Rosenthal, R., Hall, J. A., Archer, D., DiMatteo, M. R., & Rogers, P. L. (1979). The PONS test: Measuring sensitivity to nonverbal cues. In S. Weitz (Ed.), *Nonverbal communication* (2nd ed.). New York: Oxford University Press. (pp. 347, 417)

Rosenzweig, M. R. (1984). Experience, memory, and the brain. *American Psychologist, 39*, 365–376. (p. 79)

Ross, M., McFarland, C., & Fletcher, G. J. O. (1981). The effect of attitude on the recall of personal histories. *Journal of Personality and Social Psychology, 40*, 627–634. (p. 294)

Ross, M., Xun, W. Q. E., & Wilson, A. E. (2002). Language and the bicultural self. *Personality and Social Psychology Bulletin, 28*, 1040–1050. (p. 323)

Rossi, P. J. (1968). Adaptation and negative after effect to lateral optical displacement in newly hatched chicks. *Science, 160*, 430–432. (p. 182)

Rostosky, S. S., Wilcox, B. L., Wright, M. L. C., & Randall, B. A. (2004). The impact of religiosity on adolescent sexual behavior: A review of the evidence. *Journal of Adolescent Research, 19*, 677–697. (p. 380)

Roth, T., Roehrs, T., Zwyghuizen-Doorenbos, A., Stpeanski, E., & Witting, R. (1988). Sleep and memory. In I. Hindmarch & H. Ott (Eds.), *Benzodiazepine receptor ligans, memory and information processing.* New York: Springer-Verlag. (p. 206)

Rothbart, M. K., Ahadi, S. A., & Evans, D. E. (2000). Temperament and personality: Origins and outcomes. *Journal of Personality and Social Psychology, 78*, 122–135. (p. 72)

Rothbart, M., Fulero, S., Jensen, C., Howard, J., & Birrell, P. (1978). From individual to group impressions: Availability heuristics in stereotype formation. *Journal of Experimental Social Psychology, 14*, 237–255. (p. 598)

Rothbaum, B. O., Hodges, L., Anderson, P. L., Price, L., & Smith, S. (2002). Twelve-month followup of virtual reality and standard exposure therapies for the fear of flying. *Journal of Consulting and Clinical Psychology, 70*, 428–432. (p. 503), 547)

Rothbaum, F., & Tsang, B. Y-P. (1998). Lovesongs in the United States and China: On the nature of romantic love. *Journal of Cross-Cultural Psychology, 29*, 306–319. (p. 86), 86)

Rothman, A. J., & Salovey, P. (1997). Shaping perceptions to motivate healthy behavior: The role of message framing. *Psychological Bulletin, 121*, 3–19. (p. 313)

Rothstein, W. G. (1980). The significance of occupations in work careers: An empirical and theoretical review. *Journal of Vocational Behavior, 17*, 328–343. (p. 137)

Rotton, J., & Kelly, I. W. (1985). Much ado about the full moon: A meta-analysis of lunar-lunacy research. *Psychological Bulletin, 97*, 286–306. (p. 506)

Rovee-Collier, C. (1989). The joy of kicking: Memories, motives, and mobiles. In P. R. Solomon, G. R. Goethals, C. M. Kelley, & B. R. Stephens (Eds.), *Memory: Interdisciplinary approaches.* New York: Springer-Verlag. (p. 106)

Rovee-Collier, C. (1993). The capacity for long-term memory in infancy. *Current Directions in Psychological Science, 2*, 130–135. (p. 286)

Rovee-Collier, C. (1997). Dissociations in infant memory: Rethinking the development of implicit and explicit memory. *Psychological Review, 104*, 467–498. (p. 106)

Rowe, D. C. (1990). As the twig is bent? The myth of child-rearing influences on personality development. *Journal of Counseling and Development, 68*, 606–611. (p. 71)

Rowe, D. C. (2005). Under the skin: On the impartial treatment of genetic and environmental hypotheses of racial differences. *American Psychologist, 60*, 60–70. (p. 346)

Rowe, D. C., Almeida, D. M., & Jacobson, K. C. (1999). School context and genetic influences on aggression in adolescence. *Psychological Science, 10*, 277–280. (p. 600)

Rowe, D. C., Jacobson, K. C., & Van den Oord, E. J. C. G. (1999). Genetic and environmental influences on vocabulary IQ: Parental education level as moderator. *Child Development, 70(5)*, 1151–1162. (p. 343)

Rowe, D. C., Vazsonyi, A. T., & Flannery, D. J. (1994). No more than skin deep: Ethnic and racial similarity in developmental process. *Psychological Review, 101(3)*, 396. (p. 87)

Rowe, D. C., Vazsonyi, A. T., & Flannery, D. J. (1995). Ethnic and racial similarity in developmental process: A study of academic achievement. *Psychological Science, 6*, 33–38. (p. 87)

Rozin, P., Dow, S., Mosovitch, M., & Rajaram, S. (1998). What causes humans to begin and end a meal? A role for memory for what has been eaten, as evidenced by a study of multiple meal eating in amnesic patients. *Psychological Science, 9*, 392–396. (p. 363)

Rozin, P., Millman, L., & Nemeroff, C. (1986). Operation of the laws of sympathetic magic in disgust and other domains. *Journal of Personality and Social Psychology, 50*, 703–712. (p. 241)

Ruback, R. B., Carr, T. S., & Hopper, C. H. (1986). Perceived control in prison: Its relation to reported crowding, stress, and symptoms. *Journal of Applied Social Psychology, 16*, 375–386. (p. 486)

Rubenstein, J. S., Meyer, D. E., & Evans, J. E. (2001). Executive control of cognitive processes in task switching. *Journal of Experimental Psychology: Human Perception and Performance, 27*, 763–797. (p. 194)

Rubin, J. Z., Pruitt, D. G., & Kim, S. H. (1994). *Social conflict: Escalation, stalemate, and settlement.* New York: McGraw-Hill. (p. 617)

Rubin, L. B. (1985). *Just friends: The role of friendship in our lives.* New York: Harper & Row. (p. 89)

Rubin, Z. (1970). Measurement of romantic love. *Journal of Personality and Social Psychology, 16*, 265–273. (p. 417)

Rubonis, A. V., & Bickman, L. (1991). Psychological impairment in the wake of disaster: The disaster-psychopathology relationship. *Psychological Bulletin, 109*, 384–399. (p. 437)

Ruchlis, H. (1990). *Clear thinking: A practical introduction.* Buffalo, NY: Prometheus Books. (p. 308)

Rudman, L. A., & Goodwin, S. A. (2004). Gender differences in automatic in-group bias: Why do women like women more than men like men? *Journal of Personality and Social Psychology, 87*, 494–509. (p. 596)

Ruffin, C. L. (1993). Stress and health—little hassles vs. major life events. *Australian Psychologist, 28*, 201–208. (p. 438)

Rule, B. G., & Ferguson, T. J. (1986). The effects of media violence on attitudes, emotions, and cognitions. *Journal of Social Issues, 42(3)*, 29–50. (p. 265)

Rumbaugh, D. M. (1977). *Language learning by a chimpanzee: The Lana project.* New York: Academic Press. (p. 328)

Rumbaugh, D. M., & Savage-Rumbaugh, S. (1978). Chimpanzee language research: Status and potential. *Behavior Research Methods & Instrumentation, 10*, 119–131. (p. 328)

Rumbaugh, D. M., & Savage-Rumbaugh, S. (1994, January/February). Language and apes. *Psychology Teacher Network*, pp. 2–5, 9. (p. 329)

Rumbaugh, D. M., & Washburn, D. A. (2003). *Intelligence of apes and other rational beings.* New Haven, CT: Yale University Press. (p. 329)

Rupp, R. (1998). *How we remember and why we forget.* New York: Three Rivers Press. (p. 268)

Rush, A. J., & 15 others. (2005). Vagus nerve stimulation for treatment-resistant depression: A randomized, controlled acute phase trial. *Biological Psychiatry, 58*, 347–354. (p. 569)

Rushton, J. P. (1975). Generosity in children: Immediate and long-term effects of modeling, preaching, and moral judgment. *Journal of Personality and Social Psychology, 31,* 459–466. (p. 263)

Rushton, J. P. (1998). The "Jensen effect" and the "Spearman-Jensen hypothesis" of black-white IQ differences. *Intelligence, 26,* 217–225. (p. 346)

Rushton, J. P. (2003). Race, brain size, and IQ: The case for consilience. *Behavioral and Brain Sciences, 26,* 648–649. (p. 346)

Russell, B. (1930/1985). *The conquest of happiness.* London: Unwin Paperbacks. (p. 430)

Rusting, C. L., & Nolen-Hoeksema, S. (1998). Regulating responses to anger: Effects of rumination and distraction on angry mood. *Journal of Personality and Social Psychology, 74,* 790–803. (p. 425)

Rutter, M., and the English and Romanian Adoptees (ERA) study team. (1998). Developmental catch-up, and deficit, following adoption after severe global early privation. *Journal of Child Psychology and Psychiatry, 39,* 465–476. (p. 116)

Ryan, L., Hatfield, C., & Hofstetter, M. (2002). Caffeine reduces time-of-day effects on memory performance in older adults. *Psychological Science, 13,* 68–71. (p. 133)

Ryan, R. (1999, February 2). Quoted by Alfie Kohn, In pursuit of affluence, at a high price. *New York Times* (www.nytimes.com). (pp. 429, 430)

Ryan, R. M., & Deci, E. L. (2004). Avoiding death or engaging life as accounts of meaning and culture: Comment on Pyszczynski et al. (2004). *Psychological Bulletin, 130,* 473–477. (p. 494)

Ryckman, R. M., Robbins, M. A., Kaczor, L. M., & Gold J. A. (1989). Male and female raters' stereotyping of male and female physiques. *Personality and Social Psychology Bulletin, 15,* 244–251. (p. 368)

Saad, L. (2001, December 17). Americans' mood: Has Sept. 11 made a difference? *Gallup Poll News* Service (www.gallup.com/poll/releases/pr011217.asp). (pp. 435, 437)

Saad, L. (2002, November 21). Most smokers wish they could quit. *Gallup News Service* (www.gallup.com). (p. 221)

Sabini, J. (1986). Stanley Milgram (1933–1984). *American Psychologist, 41,* 1378–1379. (p. 585)

Sachdev, P., & Sachdev, J. (1997). Sixty years of psychosurgery: Its present status and its future. *Australian and New Zealand Journal of Psychiatry, 31,* 457–464. (p. 571)

Sacks, O. (1985). *The man who mistook his wife for a hat.* New York: Summit Books. (pp. 168, 281)

Sadato, N., Pascual-Leone, A., Grafman, J., Ibanez, V., Deiber, M-P., Dold, G., & Hallett, M. (1996). Activation of the primary visual cortex by Braille reading in blind subjects. *Nature, 380,* 526–528. (p. 59)

Salmon, P. (2001). Effects of physical exercise on anxiety, depression, and sensitivity to stress: A unifying theory. *Clinical Psychology Review, 21,* 33–61. (p. 450)

Salovey, P. (1990, January/February). Interview. *American Scientist,* pp. 25–29. (p. 425)

Salovey, P., & Grewal, D. (2005). The science of emotional intelligence. *Current Directions in Psychological Science, 14,* 281-285. (p. 335)

Salovey, P., & Mayer, J. D. (1990). Emotional intelligence. *Imagination, Cognition, and Personality, 9,* 185–211. (p. 335)

Sampson, E. E. (2000). Reinterpreting individualism and collectivism: Their religious roots and monologic versus dialogic person–other relationship. *American Psychologist, 55,* 1425–1432. (p. 84)

Samuels, J., & Nestadt, G. (1997). Epidemiology and genetics of obsessive-compulsive disorder. *International Review of Psychiatry, 9,* 61–71. (p. 511)

Samuels, S., & McCabe, G. (1989). Quoted by P. Diaconis & F. Mosteller, Methods for studying coincidences. *Journal of the American Statistical Association, 84,* 853–861. (p. 24)

Sanders, G., & Wright, M. (1997). Sexual orientation differences in cerebral asymmetry and in the performance of sexually dimorphic cognitive and motor tasks. *Archives of Sexual Behavior, 26,* 463–479. (p. 385)

Sanders, G., Sjodin, M., & de Chastelaine, M. (2002). On the elusive nature of sex differences in cognition hormonal influences contributing to within-sex variation. *Archives of Sexual Behavior, 31,* 145–152. (p. 385)

Sandfort, T. G. M., de Graaf, R., Bijl, R., & Schnabel, P. (2001). Same-sex sexual behavior and psychiatric disorders. *Archives of General Psychiatry, 58,* 85–91. (pp. 356, 381)

Sandler, W., Meir, I., Padden, C., & Aronoff, M. (2005). The emergence of grammar: Systematic structure in a new language. *Proceedings of the National Academy of Sciences, 102,* 2261–2265. (p. 321)

Sanford, A. J., Fray, N., Stewart, A., & Moxey, L. (2002). Perspective in statements of quantity, with implications for consumer psychology. *Psychological Science, 13,* 130–134. (p. 313)

Santarelli, L., & 11 others. (2003). Requirement of hippocampal neurogenesis for the behavioral effects of antidepressants. *Science, 301,* 805–809. (p. 567)

Sanz, C., Blicher, A., Dalke, K., Gratton-Fabri, L., McClure-Richards, T., & Fouts, R. (1998, Winter-Spring). Enrichment object use: Five chimpanzees' use of temporary and semi-permanent enrichment objects. *Friends of Washoe, 19(1,2),* 9–14. (p. 327)

Sanz, C., Morgan, D., Gulick, S. (2004). New insights into chimpanzees, tools, and termites from the Congo Basin. *American Naturalist, 164,* 567–581. (p. 326)

Sapadin, L. A. (1988). Friendship and gender: Perspectives of professional men and women. *Journal of Social and Personal Relationships, 5,* 387–403. (p. 89)

Sapolsky, B. S., & Tabarlet, J. O. (1991). Sex in primetime television: 1979 versus 1989. *Journal of Broadcasting and Electronic Media, 35,* 505–516. (pp. 379, 604)

Sapolsky, R. (2003, September). Taming stress. *Scientific American,* pp. 87–95. (p. 523)

Sapolsky, R. (2005). The influence of social hierarchy on primate health. *Science, 308,* 648–652. (pp. 446)

Saudino, K. J., Wertz, A. E., Gagne, J. R., & Chawla, S. (2004). Night and day: Are siblings as different in temperament as parents say they are? *Journal of Personality and Social Psychology, 87,* 698–706. (p. 72)

Savage-Rumbaugh, E. S., Murphy, J., Sevcik, R. A., Brakke, K. E., Williams, S. L., & Rumbaugh, D. M., with commentary by Bates, E. (1993). Language comprehension in ape and child. *Monographs of the Society for Research in Child Development, 58* (no. 233), 1–254. (p. 328)

Savic, I., Berglund, H., & Lindstrom, P. (2005). Brain response to putative pheromones in homosexual men. *Proceedings of the National Academy of Sciences, 102,* 7356–7361. (p. 383)

Savitsky, K., & Gilovich, T. (2003). The illusion of transparency and the alleviation of speech anxiety. Journal *of Experimental Social Psychology, 39,* 618–625. (p. 491)

Savitsky, K., Epley, N., & Gilovich, T. (2001). Do others judge us as harshly as we think? Overestimating the impact of our failures, shortcomings, and mishaps. *Journal of Personality and Social Psychology, 81,* 44–56. (p. 490)

Savoy, C., & Beitel, P. (1996). Mental imagery for basketball. *International Journal of Sport Psychology, 27,* 454–462. (p. 325)

Sawyer, M. G., Arney, F. M., Baghurst, P. A., Clark, J. J., Graetz, B. W., Kosky, R. J., Nurcombe, B., Patton, G. C., Prior, M. R., Raphael, B., Rey, J., Whaites, L. C., & Zubrick, S. R. (2000). *The mental health of young people in Australia.* Canberra: Mental Health and Special Programs Branch, Commonwealth Department of Health and Aged Care. (pp. 506, 523)

Sax, L. J., Hurtado, S., Lindholm, J A., Astin, A. W., Korn, W. S., & Mahoney, K. M. (2004). *The American freshman: National norms for Fall, 2004.* Los Angeles: Cooperative Institutional Research Program, UCLA. (p. 527)

Scarr, S. (1984, May). What's a parent to do? A conversation with E. Hall. *Psychology Today,* pp. 58–63. (p. 344)

Scarr, S. (1989). Protecting general intelligence: Constructs and consequences for interventions. In R. J. Linn (Ed.), *Intelligence: Measurement, theory, and public policy.* Champaign: University of Illinois Press. (p. 332)

Scarr, S. (1990). Back cover comments on J. Dunn & R. Plomin (1990). *Separate lives: Why siblings are so different.* New York: Basic Books. (p. 73)

Scarr, S. (1993, May/June). Quoted by *Psychology Today,* Nature's thumbprint: So long, superparents, p. 16. (p. 81)

Schab, F. R. (1991). Odor memory: Taking stock. *Psychological Bulletin, 109,* 242–251. (p. 167)

Schachter, S., & Singer, J. E. (1962). Cognitive, social and physiological determinants of emotional state. *Psychological Review, 69,* 379–399. (pp. 408, 411)

Schacter, D. L. (1992). Understanding implicit memory: A cognitive neuroscience approach. *American Psychologist, 47,* 559–569. (p. 282)

Schacter, D. L. (1996). *Searching for memory: The brain, the mind, and the past.* New York: Basic Books. (pp. 131, 282, 298, 466)

Schacter, D. L. (1999). The seven sins of memory: Insights from psychology and cognitive neuroscience. *American Psychologist, 54,* 182–201. (p. 290)

Schafer, G. (2005). Infants can learn decontextualized words before their first birthday. *Child Development, 76,* 87–96. (p. 320)

Schaie, K.W., & Geiwitz, J. (1982). *Adult development and aging.* Boston: Little, Brown. (A-7)

Schall, T., & Smith, G. (2002, Fall). Career trajectories in baseball. *Chance,* pp. 35–38. (pp. 130, A-6)

Scheier, M. F., & Carver, C. S. (1992). Effects of optimism on psychological and physical well-being: Theoretical overview and empirical update. *Cognitive Therapy and Research, 16,* 201–228. (p. 446)

Schein, E. H. (1956). The Chinese indoctrination program for prisoners of war: A study of attempted brainwashing. *Psychiatry, 19,* 149–172. (p. 577)

Scherer, K. R., Banse, R., & Wallbott, H. G. (2001). Emotion inferences from vocal expression correlate across languages and cultures. *Journal of Cross-Cultural Psychology, 32,* 76–92. (p. 417)

Schiavi, R. C., & Schreiner-Engel, P. (1988). Nocturnal penile tumescence in healthy aging men. *Journal of Gerontology: Medical Sciences, 43,* M146–150. (p. 199)

Schiffenbauer, A., & Schiavo, R. S. (1976). Physical distance and attraction: An intensification effect. *Journal of Experimental Social Psychology, 12,* 274–282. (p. 589)

Schimel, J., Arndt, J., Pyszczynski, T., & Greenberg, J. (2001). Being accepted for who we are: Evidence that social validation of the intrinsic self reduces general defensiveness. *Journal of Personality and Social Psychology, 80,* 35–52. (p. 473)

Schlaug, G., Jancke, L., Huang, Y., & Steinmetz, H. (1995). In vivo evidence of structural brain asymmetry in musicians. *Science, 267,* 699–701. (p. 51)

Schmidt, F. L. (2002). The role of general cognitive ability and job performance: Why there cannot be a debate. *Human Performance, 15,* 187–210. (p. 395)

Schmidt, F. L., & Hunter, J. E. (1998). The validity and utility of selection methods in personnel psychology: Practical and theoretical implications of 85 years of research findings. *Psychological Bulletin, 124,* 262–274. (pp. 395, 396, 489)

Schmidt, F. L., & Zimmerman, R. D. (2004). A counterintuitive hypothesis about employment interview validity and some supporting evidence. *Journal of Applied Psychology, 89,* 553–561. (p. 396)

Schmitt, D. P., & Pilcher, J. J. (2004). Evaluating evidence of psychological adaptation: How do we know one when we see one? *Psychological Science, 15,* 643–649. (p. 75)

Schnaper, N. (1980). Comments germane to the paper entitled "The reality of death experiences" by Ernst Rodin. *Journal of Nervous and Mental Disease, 168,* 268–270. (p. 224)

Schneider, R. H., Alexander, C. N., Staggers, F., Rainforth, M., Salerno, J. W., Hartz, A., Arndt, S., Barnes, V. A., & Nidich, S. (2005). Long-term effects of stress reduction on mortality in persons > or = 55 years of age with systemic hypertension. *American Journal of Cardiology, 95,* 1060–1064. (p. 454)

Schneider, S. L. (2001). In search of realistic optimism: Meaning, knowledge, and warm fuzziness. *American Psychologist, 56,* 250–263. (p. 488)

Schneiderman, N. (1999). Behavioral medicine and the management of HIV/AIDS. *International Journal of Behavioral Medicine, 6,* 3–12. (p. 441)

Schoeneman, T. J. (1994). Individualism. In V. S. Ramachandran (Ed.), *Encyclopedia of human behavior.* San Diego: Academic Press. (pp. 473)

Schofield, J. W. (1986). Black-White contact in desegregated schools. In M. Hewstone & R. Brown (Eds.), *Contact and conflict in intergroup encounters.* Oxford: Basil Blackwell. (p. 616)

Schonfield, D., & Robertson, B. A. (1966). Memory storage and aging. *Canadian Journal of Psychology, 20,* 228–236. (p. 133)

Schooler, J. W., Gerhard, D., & Loftus, E. F. (1986). Qualities of the unreal. *Journal of Experimental Psychology: Learning, Memory, and Cognition, 12,* 171–181. (p. 296)

Schuman, H., & Scott, J. (June, 1989). Generations and collective memories. *American Sociological Review, 54(3),* 359–381. (p. 132)

Schwartz, B. (1984). *Psychology of learning and behavior (2nd ed.).* New York: Norton. (pp. 246, 513)

Schwartz, B. (2000). Self-determination: The tyranny of freedom. *American Psychologist, 55,* 79–88. (p. 486)

Schwartz, B. (2004). *The paradox of choice: Why more is less.* New York: Ecco/HarperCollins. (p. 486)

Schwartz, J. M., Stoessel, P. W., Baxter, L. R., Jr., Martin, K. M., & Phelps, M. E. (1996). Systematic changes in cerebral glucose metabolic rate after successful behavior modification treatment of obsessive-compulsive disorder. *Archives of General Psychiatry, 53,* 109–113. (pp. 551, 571)

Schwartz, J., & Estrin, J. (2004, November 7). *Living for today, locked in a paralyzed body.* New York Times (www.nytimes.com). (p. 426)

Schwarz, N., Strack, F., Kommer, D., & Wagner, D. (1987). Soccer, rooms, and the quality of your life: Mood effects on judgments of satisfaction with life in general and with specific domains. *European Journal of Social Psychology, 17,* 69–79. (p. 287)

Sclafani, A. (1995). How food preferences are learned: Laboratory animal models. *Proceedings of the Nutrition Society, 54,* 419–427. (p. 363)

Scott, D. J., & others. (2004, November 9). U-M team reports evidence that smoking affects human brain's natural "feel good" chemical system (press release by Kara Gavin). University of Michigan Medical School (www.med.umich.edu). (p. 221)

Scott, W. A., Scott, R., & McCabe, M. (1991). Family relationships and children's personality: A cross-cultural, cross-source comparison. *British Journal of Social Psychology, 30,* 1–20. (p. 87)

Sechrest, L., Stickle, T. R., & Stewart, M. (1998). The role of assessment in clinical psychology. In A. Bellack, M. Hersen (Series eds.) & C. R. Reynolds (Vol. ed.), *Comprehensive clinical psychology: Vol 4: Assessment.* New York: Pergamon. (p. 465)

Seeman, P., Guan, H-C., & Van Tol, H. H. M. (1993). Dopamine D4 receptors elevated in schizophrenia. *Nature, 365,* 441–445. (p. 533)

Segal, N. L. (1999). *Entwined lives: Twins and what they tell us about human behavior.* New York: Dutton. (p. 70)

Segal, N. L. (2000). Virtual twins: New findings on within-family environmental influences on intelligence. *Journal of Educational Psychology, 92,* 442–448. (p. 70)

Segall, M. H., Dasen, P. R., Berry, J. W., & Poortinga, Y. H. (1990). *Human behavior in global perspective: An introduction to cross-cultural psychology.* New York: Pergamon. (pp. 76, 91, 112)

Segerstrom, S. C., Taylor, S. E., Kemeny, M. E., & Fahey, J. L. (1998). Optimism is associated with mood, coping, and immune change in response to stress. *Journal of Personality and Social Psychology, 74,* 1646–1655. (p. 446)

Segerstrom, S., & Miller, G. E. (2004). Psychological stress and the human immune system: A meta-analytic study of 30 years of inquiry. *Psychological Bulletin, 130,* 601–630. (p. 436)

Seidlitz, L., & Diener, E. (1998). Sex differences in the recall of affective experiences. *Journal of Personality and Social Psychology, 74,* 262–271. (p. 527)

Self, C. E. (1994). *Moral culture and victimization in residence halls.* Dissertation: Thesis (M.A.). Bowling Green University. (p. 227)

Seligman, M. E. P. (1974, May). Submissive death: Giving up on life. Psychology Today, pp. 80–85. (p. 410)

Seligman, M. E. P. (1975). Helplessness: On depression, development and death. San Francisco: Freeman. (p. 485, 527)

Seligman, M. E. P. (1991). *Learned optimism.* New York: Knopf. (pp. 193, 485, 527, 528)

Seligman, M. E. P. (1994). *What you can change and what you can't.* New York: Knopf. (pp. 450, 468, 491)

Seligman, M. E. P. (1995). The effectiveness of psychotherapy: The Consumer Reports study. *American Psychologist, 50,* 965–974. (pp. 528, 554, 557)

Seligman, M. E. P. (2002). *Authentic happiness: Using the new positive psychology to realize your potential for lasting fulfillment.* New York: Free Press. (pp. 487, 491, 551)

Seligman, M. E. P. (2004). Eudaemonia, the good life. A talk with Martin Seligman. www.edge.org. (p. 487)

Seligman, M. E. P., & Yellen, A. (1987). What is a dream? Behavior Research and Therapy, 25, 1–24. (p. 197)

Seligman, M. E. P., Steen, T. A., Park, N., & Peterson, C. (2005). Positive psychology progress: Empirical validation of interventions. *American Psychologist, 60,* 410–421. (p. 487)

Selye, H. (1936). A syndrome produced by diverse nocuous agents. *Nature, 138,* 32. (p. 436)

Selye, H. (1976). *The stress of life.* New York: McGraw-Hill. (p. 436)

Sen, A. (2003). Missing women—revisited. *British Medical Journal, 327,* 1297–1298. (p. 596)

Senghas, A., & Coppola, M. (2001). Children creating language: How Nicaraguan Sign Language acquired a spatial grammar. *Psychological Science, 12,* 323–328. (p. 321)

Sengupta, S. (2001, October 10). Sept. 11 attack narrows the racial divide. *New York Times* (www.nytimes.com). (p. 617)

Serdula, M. K., Mokdad, A., Williamson, D. F., Galuska, D. A., Mendlein, J. M., & Heath, G. W. (1999). Prevalence of attempting weight loss and strategies for controlling weight. *Journal of the American Medical Association, 282,* 1353–1358. (p. 371)

Service, R. F. (1994). Will a new type of drug make memory-making easier? *Science, 266,* 218–219. (p. 280)

Seto, M. C., & Barbaree, H. E. (1995). The role of alcohol in sexual aggression. *Clinical Psychology Review, 15,* 545–566. (p. 218)

Shadish, W. R., 556, 557

Shadish, W. R., Baldwin, S. A. (2005). Effects of behavioral marital therapy: A meta-analysis of randomized controlled trials. *Journal of Consulting and Clinical Psychology, 73,* 6–14. (p. 557)

Shadish, W. R., Matt, G. E., Navarro, A. M., & Phillips, G. (2000). The effects of psychological therapies under clinically representative conditions: A meta-analysis. *Psychological Bulletin, 126,* 512–529. (p. 556)

Shafir, E., & LeBoeuf, R. A. (2002). Rationality. *Annual Review of Psychology, 53,* 491–517. (p. 315)

Shamir, B., House, R. J., & Arthur, M. B. (1993). The motivational effects of charismatic leadership: A self-concept based theory. *Organizational Science, 4(4),* 577–594. (p. 402)

Shapiro, F. (1989). Efficacy of the eye movement desensitization procedure in the treatment of traumatic memories. *Journal of Traumatic Stress, 2,* 199–223. (p. 558)

Shapiro, F. (1995). *Eye movement desensitization and reprocessing: Basic principles, protocols, and procedures.* New York: Guilford. (p. 558)

Shapiro, F. (1999). Eye movement desensitization and reprocessing (EMDR) and the anxiety disorders: Clinical and research implications of an integrated psychotherapy treatment. *Journal of Anxiety Disorders, 13,* 35–67. (p. 558)

Shapiro, F. (Ed.) (2002). *EMDR as an integrative psychotherapy approach: Experts of diverse orientations explore the paradigm prism.* Washington, DC: APA Books. (p. 558)

Sharma, A. R., McGue, M. K., & Benson, P. L. (1998). The psychological adjustment of United States adopted adolescents and their nonadopted siblings. *Child Development, 69,* 791–802. (p. 72)

Shaver, P. R., Morgan, H. J., & Wu, S. (1996). Is love a basic emotion? *Personal Relationships, 3,* 81–96. (p. 423)

Shaw, H. L. (1989–90). Comprehension of the spoken word and ASL translation by chimpanzees (Pan troglodytes). *Friends of Washoe, 9(1/2),* 8–19. (p. 328)

Sheehan, S. (1982). *Is there no place on earth for me?* Boston: Houghton Mifflin. (p. 531)

Sheldon, K. M., Elliot, A. J., Kim, Y., & Kasser, T. (2001). What is satisfying about satisfying events? Testing 10 candidate psychological needs. *Journal of Personality and Social Psychology, 80,* 325–339. (p. 388)

Shelton, J. N., & Richeson, J. A. (2005). Intergroup contact and pluralistic ignorance. *Journal of Personality and Social Psychology, 88,* 91–107. (p. 616)

Shenton, M. E. (1992). Abnormalities of the left temporal lobe and thought disorder in schizophrenia: A quantitative magnetic resonance imaging study. *New England Journal of Medicine, 327,* 604–612. (p. 534)

Shepard, R. N. (1990). *Mind sights.* New York: Freeman. (p. 31)

Shepherd, C. (1997, April). News of the weird. *Funny Times,* p. 15. (p. 69)

Shepherd, C. (1999, June). News of the weird. *Funny Times,* p. 21. (p. 370)

Sherif, M. (1966). *In common predicament: Social psychology of intergroup conflict and cooperation.* Boston: Houghton Mifflin. (p. 616)

Sherman, P. W., & Flaxman, S. M. (2001). Protecting ourselves from food. *American Scientist, 89,* 142–151. (p. 366)

Sherry, D., & Vaccarino, A. L. (1989). Hippocampus and memory for food caches in black-capped chickadees. *Behavioral Neuroscience, 103,* 308–318. (p. 282)

Shettleworth, S. J. (1973). Food reinforcement and the organization of behavior in golden hamsters. In R. A. Hinde & J. Stevenson-Hinde (Eds.), *Constraints on learning.* London: Academic Press. (p. 255)

Shettleworth, S. J. (1993). Where is the comparison in comparative cognition? Alternative research programs. *Psychological Science, 4,* 179–184. (p. 278)

Shneidman, E. (1987, March). At the point of no return. *Psychology Today,* pp. 54–58. (p. 525)

Showers, C. (1992). The motivational and emotional consequences of considering positive or negative possibilities for an upcoming event. *Journal of Personality and Social Psychology, 63,* 474–484. (p. 488)

Shulman, P. (2000, June). The girl who loved math. *Discover,* pp. 67–70. (p. 348)

Sieff, E. M., Dawes, R. M., & Loewenstein, G. (1999). Anticipated versus actual reaction to HIV test results. *The American Journal of Psychology, 112,* 297–313. (p. 426)

Siegel, J. M. (1990). Stressful life events and use of physician services among the elderly: The moderating role of pet ownership. *Journal of Personality and Social Psychology, 58,* 1081–1086. (pp. 447)

Siegel, J. M. (2003, November). Why we sleep. *Scientific American,* pp. 92–97. (p. 203)

Siegel, R. K. (1977, October). Hallucinations. *Scientific American,* pp. 132–140. (p. 224)

Siegel, R. K. (1980). The psychology of life after death. *American Psychologist, 35,* 911–931. (p. 224)

Siegel, R. K. (1982, October). Quoted by J. Hooper, Mind tripping. *Omni,* pp. 72–82, 159–160. (p. 223)

Siegel, R. K. (1984, March 15). Personal communication. (p. 211), 223)

Siegel, R. K. (1990). Intoxication. New York: Pocket Books. (pp. 205, 210), 217, 222, 224)

Siegler, R. S., & Ellis, S. (1996). Piaget XE "Piaget, J." on childhood. *Psychological Science, 7,* 211–215. (p. 107)

Silbersweig, D. A., Stern, E., Frith, C., Cahill, C., Holmes, A., Grootoonk, S., Seaward, J., McKenna, P., Chua, S. E., Schnorr, L., Jones, T., & Frackowiak, R. S. J. (1995). A functional neuroanatomy of hallucinations in schizophrenia. *Nature, 378,* 176–179. (p. 534)

Silva, A. J., Stevens, C. F., Tonegawa, S., & Wang, Y. (1992). Deficient hippocampal long-term potentiation in alpha-calcium-calmodulin kinase II mutant mice. *Science, 257,* 201–206. (p. 280)

Silva, C. E., & Kirsch, I. (1992). Interpretive sets, expectancy, fantasy proneness, and dissociation as predictors of hypnotic response. *Journal of Personality and Social Psychology, 63,* 847–856. (p. 211)

Silver, M., & Geller, D. (1978). On the irrelevance of evil: The organization and individual action. *Journal of Social Issues, 34,* 125–136. (p. 587)

Silverman, I., & Eals, M. (1992). Sex differences in spatial abilities: Evolutionary theory and data. In J. H. Barkow, L. Cosmides, & J. Tooby (Eds.), *The adapted mind: Evolutionary psychology and the generation of culture.* New York: Oxford University Press. (p. 349)

Silverman, I., & Phillips, K. (1998). The evolutionary psychology of spatial sex differences. In C. Crawford & D. L. Krebs (Eds.), *Handbook of Evolutionary Psychology: Ideas, Issues, and Applications.* Mahwah, NJ: Erlbaum. (p. 349)

Silverman, K., Evans, S. M., Strain, E. C., & Griffiths, R. R. (1992). Withdrawal syndrome after the double-blind cessation of caffeine consumption. *New England Journal of Medicine, 327,* 1109–1114. (p. 220)

Simon, H. (2001, February). Quoted by A. M. Hayashi, "When to trust your gut." *Harvard Business Review,* pp. 59–65. (p. 316)

Simons, D. J. (1996). In sight, out of mind: When object representations fail. *Psychological Science, 7,* 301–305. (p. 194)

Simons, D. J., & Ambinder, M. S. (2005). Change blindness: Theory and consequences. *Current Directions in Psychological Science, 14,* 44–48. (p. 194)

Simons, D. J., & Chabris, C. F. (1999). Gorillas in our midst: Sustained inattentional blindness for dynamic events. *Perception, 28,* 1059–1074. (p. 194)

Simonton, D. K. (1988). Age and outstanding achievement: What do we know after a century of research? *Psychological Bulletin, 104,* 251–267. (p. 134)

Simonton, D. K. (1990). Creativity in the later years: Optimistic prospects for achievement. *The Gerontologist, 30,* 626–631. (p. 134)

Simonton, D. K. (1992). The social context of career success and course for 2,026 scientists and inventors. *Personality and Social Psychology Bulletin, 18,* 452–463. (p. 335)

Simonton, D. K. (2000). Creativity: Cognitive, personal, developmental, and social aspects. *American Psychologist, 55,* 151–158. (pp. 249, 265, 334)

Sinclair, R. C., Hoffman, C., Mark, M. M., Martin, L. L., & Pickering, T. L. (1994). Construct accessibility and the misattribution of arousal: Schachter and Singer revisited. *Psychological Science, 5,* 15–18. (p. 413)

Singelis, T. M., & Sharkey, W. F. (1995). Culture, self-construal, and embarrassability. *Cross-Cultural Psychology, 26,* 622–644. (p. 85)

Singelis, T. M., Bond, M. H., Sharkey, W. F., & Lai, C. S. Y. (1999). Unpackaging culture's influence on self-esteem and embarrassability: The role of self-construals. *Journal of Cross-Cultural Psychology, 30,* 315–341. (p. 85)

Singer, J. L. (1981). Clinical intervention: New developments in methods and evaluation. In L. T. Benjamin, Jr. (Ed.), *The G. Stanley Hall Lecture Series (Vol. 1).* Washington, DC: American Psychological Association. (p. 557)

Singer, T., Seymour, B., O'Doherty, J., Kaube, H., Dolan, R. J., & Frith, C. (2004). Empathy for pain involves the affective but not sensory components of pain. *Science, 303,* 1157–1162. (p. 261)

Singh, D. (1993). Adaptive significance of female physical attractiveness: Role of waist-to-hip ratio. *Journal of Personality and Social Psychology, 65,* 293–307. (p. 77)

Singh, D. (1995). Female health, attractiveness, and desirability for relationships: Role of breast asymmetry and waist-to-hip ratio. *Ethology and Sociobiology, 16,* 465–481. (p. 77)

Singh, S. (1997). *Fermat's enigma: The epic quest to solve the world's greatest mathematical problem.* New York: Bantam Books. (p. 334)

Singh, S., & Riber, K. A. (1997, November). Fermat's last stand. *Scientific American,* pp. 68–73. (p. 335)

Singleton, D., Tate, A., & Kohout, J. (2003). *2002 Master's, specialist's, and related degrees employment survey.* Washington, DC: American Psychological Association. (p. B-4)

Sipski, M. L., & Alexander, C. J. (1999). Sexual response in women with spinal cord injuries: Implications for our understanding of the able bodied. *Journal of Sex and Marital Therapy, 25,* 11–22. (p. 43)

Sirenteanu, R. (1999). Switching on the infant brain. *Science, 286,* 59, 61. (p. 182)

Sjöstrum, L. (1980). Fat cells and body weight. In A. J. Stunkard (Ed.), *Obesity.* Philadelphia: Saunders. (p. 368)

Skinner, B. F. (1953). *Science and human behavior.* New York: Macmillan. (p. 250)

Skinner, B. F. (1956). A case history in scientific method. *American Psychologist, 11,* 221–233. (p. 252)

Skinner, B. F. (1957). *Verbal behavior.* Englewood Cliffs, NJ: Prentice-Hall. (p. 321)

Skinner, B. F. (1961, November). Teaching machines. *Scientific American,* pp. 91–102. (p. 250)

Skinner, B. F. (1983, September). Origins of a behaviorist. *Psychology Today,* pp. 22–33. (pp. 256, 527)

Skinner, B. F. (1985). *Cognitive science and behaviorism.* Unpublished manuscript, Harvard University. (p. 321)

Skinner, B. F. (1986). What is wrong with daily life in the western world? *American Psychologist, 41,* 568–574. (p. 257)

Skinner, B. F. (1988). The school of the future. Address to the American Psychological Association convention. (p. 257)

Skinner, B. F. (1989). Teaching machines. *Science, 243,* 1535. (p. 257)

Skinner, B. F. (1990). Address to the American Psychological Association convention. (p. 254)

Skitka, L. J., Bauman, C. W., & Mullen, E. (2004). Political tolerance and coming to psychological closure following the September 11, 2001, terrorist attacks: An integrative approach. *Personality and Social Psychology Bulletin, 30,* 743–756. (p. 424)

Sklar, L. S., & Anisman, H. (1981). Stress and cancer. *Psychological Bulletin, 89,* 369–406. (p. 442)

Skoog, G., & Skoog, I. (1999). A 40-year follow-up of patients with obsessive-compulsive disorder. *Archives of General Psychiatry, 56,* 121–127. (p. 511)

Skov, R. B., & Sherman, S. J. (1986). Information-gathering processes: Diagnosticity, hypothesis-confirmatory strategies, and perceived hypothesis confirmation. *Journal of Experimental Social Psychology, 22,* 93–121. (p. 309)

Slater, E., & Meyer, A. (1959). *Confinia Psychiatra.* Basel: S. Karger AG. (p. 522)

Slater, L. (2000, November 19). How do you cure a sex addict? *New York Times Magazine* (www.nytimes.com). (p. 567)

Slavin, R. E., Hurley, E. A., & Chamberlain, A. (2003). Cooperative learning and achievement: Theory and research. In W. M. Reynolds & G. E. Miller (Eds.), *Handbook of psychology: Educational psychology, Vol. 7.* New York: Wiley. (p. 617)

Sloan, R. P. (2005). Field analysis of the literature on religion, spirituality, and health. Columbia University (available at www.metanexus.net/tarp). (p. 454)

Sloan, R. P., & Bagiella, E. (2002). Claims about religious involvement and health outcomes. *Annals of Behavioral Medicine, 24,* 14–21. (p. 454)

Sloan, R. P., Bagiella, E., & Powell, T. (1999). Religion, spirituality, and medicine. *Lancet, 353,* 664–667. (p. 454)

Sloan, R. P., Bagiella, E., VandeCreek, L., & Poulos, P. (2000). Should physicians prescribe religious activities? *New England Journal of Medicine, 342,* 1913–1917. (p. 454)

Slovic, P., & Fischhoff, B. (1977). On the psychology of experimental surprises. *Journal of Experimental Psychology: Human Perception and Performance, 3,* 544–551. (p. 13)

Slovic, P., Finucane, M., Peters, E., & MacGregor, D. G. (2002). The affect heuristic. In T. Gilovich, D. Griffin, & D. Kahneman (Eds.), *Intuitive judgment: Heuristics and biases.* New York: Cambridge University Press. (p. 221)

Slutske, W. S. (2005). Alcohol use disorders among U.S. college students and their non-college-attending peers. *Archives of General Psychiatry, 62,* 321–327. (p. 218)

Small, M. F. (1997). Making connections. *American Scientist, 85,* 502–504. (p. 87)

Small, M. F. (2002, July). What you can learn from drunk monkeys. *Discover*, pp. 40–45. (p. 226)

Smart, R. G., Adlaf, E. M., & Walsh, G. W. (1991). *The Ontario student drug use survey: Trends between 1977 and 1991.* Toronto: Addiction Research Foundation. (p. 225)

Smedley, A., & Smedley, B. D. (2005). Race as biology is fiction, racism as a social problem is real: Anthropological and historical perspectives on the social construction of race. *American Psychologist, 60,* 16–26. (p. 346)

Smelser, N. J., & Mitchell, F. (Eds.) (2002). *Terrorism: Perspectives from the behavioral and social sciences.* Washington, DC: National Research Council, National Academies Press. (p. 599)

Smith, A. (1983). Personal correspondence. (p. 533)

Smith, D. V., & Margolskee, R. F. (2001, March). Making sense of taste. *Scientific American,* pp. 32–39. (p. 165)

Smith, E., & Delargy, M. (2005). Locked-in syndrome. *British Medical Journal, 330,* 406–409. (p. 426)

Smith, J. E., Waldorf, V. A., & Trembath, D. L. (1990). "Single white male looking for thin, very attractive . . ." *Sex Roles, 23,* 675–685. (p. 368)

Smith, M. B. (1978). Psychology and values. *Journal of Social Issues, 34,* 181–199. (p. 473)

Smith, M. L., & Glass, G. V. (1977). Meta-analysis of psychotherapy outcome studies. *American Psychologist, 32,* 752–760. (p. 557)

Smith, M. L., Glass, G. V., & Miller, R. L. (1980). *The benefits of psychotherapy.* Baltimore: Johns Hopkins Press. (pp. 556, 557)

Smith, P. B., & Tayeb, M. (1989). Organizational structure and processes. In M. Bond (Ed.), *The cross-cultural challenge to social psychology.* Newbury Park, CA: Sage. (p. 402)

Smith, P. F. (1995). Cannabis and the brain. *New Zealand Journal of Psychology, 24,* 5–12. (p. 224)

Smith, S. M., McIntosh, W. D., & Bazzini, D. G. (1999). Are the beautiful good in Hollywood? An investigation of the beauty-and-goodness stereotype on film. *Basic and Applied Social Psychology, 21,* 69–80. (p. 608)

Smith, T. W. (1998, December). American sexual behavior: Trends, sociodemographic differences, and risk behavior. National Opinion Research Center GSS Topical Report No. 25. (pp. 379, 380, 381)

Smith, T. W., & Ruiz, J. M. (2002). Psychosocial influences on the development and course of coronary heart disease: Current status and implications for research and practice. *Journal of Consulting and Clinical Psychology, 70,* 548–568. (pp. 424, 439)

Smolak, L., & Murnen, S. K. (2002). A meta-analytic examination of the relationship between child sexual abuse and eating disorders. *International Journal of Eating Disorders, 31,* 136–150. (p. 364)

Smoreda, Z., & Licoppe, C. (2000). Gender-specific use of the domestic telephone. *Social Psychology Quarterly, 63,* 238–252. (p. 89)

Snarey, J. R. (1985). Cross-cultural universality of social-moral development: A critical review of Kohlbergian research. *Psychological Bulletin, 97,* 202–233. (p. 123)

Snarey, J. R. (1987, June). A question of morality. *Psychology Today,* pp. 6–7. (p. 123)

Snodgrass, S. E., Higgins, J. G., & Todisco, L. (1986). The effects of walking behavior on mood. Paper presented at the American Psychological Association convention. (p. 422)

Snyder, M. (1984). When belief creates reality. In L. Berkowitz (Ed.), *Advances in experimental social psychology (Vol. 18).* New York: Academic Press. (pp. 37, 505)

Snyder, S. H. (1986). *Drugs and the brain.* New York: Scientific American Library. (p. 521), 568)

Solomon, D. A., Keitner, G. I., Miller, I. W., Shea, M. T., & Keller, M. B. (1995). Course of illness and maintenance treatments for patients with bipolar disorder. *Journal of Clinical Psychiatry, 56,* 5–13. (p. 568)

Solomon, J. (1996, May 20). Breaking the silence. *Newsweek,* pp. 20–22. (p. 504)

Solomon, M. (1987, December). Standard issue. *Psychology Today,* pp. 30–31. (p. 608)

Sommer, R. (1969). *Personal space.* Englewood Cliffs, NJ: Prentice-Hall. (p. 83)

Sonenstein, F. L. (1992). Condom use. *Science, 257,* 861. (p. 379)

Sontag, S. (1978). *Illness as metaphor.* New York: Farrar, Straus, & Giroux. (p. 442)

Soussignan, R. (2001). Duchenne smile, emotional experience, and autonomic reactivity: A test of the facial feedback hypothesis. *Emotion, 2,* 52–74. (p. 422)

Sowell, T. (1991, May/June). Cultural diversity: A world view. *American Enterprise,* pp. 44–55. (p. 618)

Spanos, N. P. (1982). A social psychological approach to hypnotic behavior. In G. Weary & H. L. Mirels (Eds.), *Integrations of clinical and social psychology.* New York: Oxford. (p. 212)

Spanos, N. P. (1986). Hypnosis, nonvolitional responding, and multiple personality: A social psychological perspective. *Progress in Experimental Personality Research, 14,* 1–62. (p. 516)

Spanos, N. P. (1991). Hypnosis, hypnotizability, and hypnotherapy. In C. R. Snyder & D. R. Forsyth (Eds.), *Handbook of social and clinical psychology: The health perspective.* New York: Pergamon Press. (p. 212)

Spanos, N. P. (1994). Multiple identity enactments and multiple personality disorder: A sociocognitive perspective. *Psychological Bulletin, 116,* 143–165. (pp. 214, 516)

Spanos, N. P. (1996). *Multiple identities and false memories: A sociocognitive perspective.* Washington, DC: American Psychological Association Books. (pp. 212, 214)

Spanos, N. P., & Coe, W. C. (1992). A Social-psychological approach to hypnosis. In E. Fromm & M. R. Nash (Eds.), *Contemporary hypnosis research.* New York: Guilford. (p. 214)

Spector, P. E. (1986). Perceived control by employees: A meta-analysis of studies concerning autonomy and participation at work. *Human Relations, 39,* 1005–1016. (p. 401)

Spelke, E. (2005, April 22). *The science of gender and science.* Harvard University (www.edge.org). (pp. 111, 349)

Spelke, E. S. (2000). Core knowledge. *American Psychologist, 55,* 1233–1243. (p. 109)

Spencer, K. M., Nestor, P. G., Perlmutter, R., Niznikiewicz, M. A., Klump, M. C., Frumin, M., Shenton, M. E., & McCarley, R. W. (2004). Neural synchrony indexes disordered perception and cognition in schizophrenia. *Proceedings of the National Academy of Sciences, 101,* 17288–17293. (p. 533)

Spencer, S. J., Steele, C. M., & Quinn, D. M. (1997). Stereotype threat and women's math performance. Unpublished manuscript, Hope College. (p. 350)

Sperling, G. (1960). The information available in brief visual presentations. *Psychological Monographs, 74* (Whole No. 498). (p. 277)

Sperry, R. W. (1964). Problems outstanding in the evolution of brain function. James Arthur Lecture, American Museum of Natural History, New York. Cited by R. Ornstein (1977), *The psychology of consciousness (2nd ed.).* New York: Harcourt Brace Jovanovich. (p. 62)

Sperry, R. W. (1985). Changed concepts of brain and consciousness: Some value implications. *Zygon, 20,* 41–57. (p. 153)

Spiegel, K., Leproult, R., & Van Cauter, E. (1999). Impact of sleep debt on metabolic and endrocrine function. *Lancet, 354,* 1435–1439. (p. 202)

Spielberger, C., & London, P. (1982). Rage boomerangs. *American Health, 1,* 52–56. (p. 439)

Spradley, J. P., & Phillips, M. (1972). Culture and stress: A quantitative analysis. *American Anthropologist, 74,* 518–529. (p. 83)

Sprecher, S. (1989). The importance to males and females of physical attractiveness, earning potential, and expressiveness in initial attraction. *Sex Roles, 21,* 591–607. (p. 608)

Sprecher, S., & Sedikides, C. (1993). Gender differences in perceptions of emotionality: The case of close heterosexual relationships. *Sex Roles, 28,* 511–530. (p. 419)

Spring, B., Pingitore, R., Bourgeois, M., Kessler, K. H., & Bruckner, E. (1992). The effects and non-effects of skipping breakfast: Results of three studies. Paper presented at the American Psychological Association convention. (p. 372)

Springer, S. P., & Deutsch, G. (1985). *Left brain, right brain.* San Francisco: Freeman. (p. 62)

Spychalski, A., Quinones, M. A., & Gaugler, B. B. (1997). A survey of assessment center practices in the United States. *Personnel Psychology, 50,* 71–90. (p. 489)

Squire, L. R. (1992). Memory and the hippocampus: A synthesis from findings with rats, monkeys, and humans. *Psychological Review, 99,* 195–231. (p. 282)

Srivastava, A., Locke, E. A., & Bartol, K. M. (2001). Money and subject well-being: It's not the money, it's the motives. *Journal of Personality and Social Psychology, 80,* 959–971. (p. 429)

Srivastava, S., John, O. P., Gosling, S. D., & Potter, J. (2003). Development of personality in early and middle adulthood: Set like plaster or persistent change? *Journal of Personality & Social Psychology, 84,* 1041–1053. (pp. 100, 478)

St. Clair, D., Xu, M., Wang, P., Yu, Y., Fang, Y., Zhang, F., Zheng, X., Gu, N., Feng, G., Sham, P., & He, L. (2005). Rates of adult schizophrenia following prenatal exposure to the Chinese famine of 1959–1961. *Journal of the American Medical Association, 294,* 557–562. (p. 534)

Stack, S. (1992). Marriage, family, religion, and suicide. In R. Maris, A. Berman, J. Maltsberger, & R. Yufit (Eds.), *Assessment and prediction of suicide.* New York: Guilford Press. (p. 524)

Stafford, R. S., MacDonald, E. A., & Finkelstein, S. N. (2001). National patterns of medication treatment for depression, 1987 to 2001. *Primary Care Companion Journal of Clinical Psychiatry, 3,* 232–235. (p. 567)

Stanford University Center for Narcolepsy. (2002). Narcolepsy is a serious medical disorder and a key to understanding other sleep disorders (www.med.stanford.edu/school/Psychiatry/narcolepsy). (p. 205)

Stanley, J. C. (1997). Varieties of intellectual talent. *Journal of Creative Behavior, 31,* 93–119. (p. 340)

Stanovich, K. (1996). *How to think straight about psychology.* New York: HarperCollins. (p. 459)

Staples, B. (1999a, May 2). When the 'paranoids' turn out to be right. *New York Times* (www.nytimes.com). (p. 596)

Staples, B. (1999b, May 24). Why 'racial profiling' will be tough to fight. *New York Times* (www.nytimes.com). (p. 596)

Stark, R. (2003a). *For the glory of God: How monotheism led to reformations, science, witch-hunts, and the end of slavery.* Princeton, NJ: Princeton University Press. (p. 16)

Stark, R. (2003b, October-November). False conflict: Christianity is not only compatible with science—it created it. *American Enterprise,* pp. 27–33. (p. 16)

Statistics Canada. (1999). *Statistical report on the health of Canadians.* Prepared by the Federal, Provincial and Territorial Advisory Committee on Population Health for the Meeting of Ministers of Health, Charlottetown, PEI, September 16–17, 1999. (pp. 126, 366)

Statistics Canada. (2002). (www.statcan.ca). (p. 83)

Statistics Canada. (2003). *Victims and persons accused of homicide, by age and sex.* Table 253–0003. www.statcan.ca (p. 88)

Staub, E. (1989). *The roots of evil: The psychological and cultural sources of genocide.* New York: Cambridge University Press. (p. 578)

Steele, C. (1990, May). A conversation with Claude Steele. *APS Observer,* pp. 11–17. (p. 345)

Steele, C. M. (1995, August 31). Black students live down to expectations. *New York Times.* (p. 350)

Steele, C. M. (1997). A threat in the air: How stereotypes shape intellectual identity and performance. *American Psychologist, 52,* 613–629. (p. 350)

Steele, C. M., & Josephs, R. A. (1990). Alcohol myopia: Its prized and dangerous effects. *American Psychologist, 45,* 921–933. (p. 218)

Steele, C. M., Spencer, S. J., & Aronson, J. (2002). Contending with group image: The psychology of stereotype and social identity threat. *Advances in Experimental Social Psychology, 34,* 379–440. (p. 350)

Steinberg, L. (1987, September). Bound to bicker. *Psychology Today,* pp. 36–39. (p. 125)

Steinberg, L., & Morris, A. S. (2001). Adolescent development. *Annual Review of Psychology, 52,* 83–110. (pp. 117, 121, 125)

Steinberg, L., & Scott, E. S. (2003). Less guilty by reason of adolescence: Developmental immaturity, diminished responsibility, and the juvenile death penalty. *American Psychologist, 58,* 1009–1018. (p. 22)

Steinberg, N. (1993, February). Astonishing love stories (from an earlier United Press International report). *Games,* p. 47. (p. 607)

Steinmetz, J. E. (1999). The localization of a simple type of learning and memory: The cerebellum and classical eyeblink conditioning. *Contemporary Psychology, 7,* 72–77. (p. 283)

Stengel, E. (1981). Suicide. In *The new Encyclopaedia Britannica, macropaedia* (Vol. 17, pp. 777–782). Chicago: Encyclopaedia Britannica. (p. 524)

Stern, M., & Karraker, K. H. (1989). Sex stereotyping of infants: A review of gender labeling studies. *Sex Roles, 20,* 501–522. (p. 185)

Stern, S. L., Dhanda, R., & Hazuda, H. P. (2001). Hopelessness predicts mortality in older Mexican and European Americans. *Psychosomatic Medicine, 63,* 344–351. (p. 446)

Sternberg, E. M. (2001). *The balance within: The science connecting health and emotions.* New York: Freeman. (p. 440)

Sternberg, R. (Ed.) (2002). *Career paths in psychology: Where your degree can take you.* Washington, DC: APA.

Sternberg, R. J. (1985). *Beyond IQ: A triarchic theory of human intelligence.* New York: Cambridge University Press. (p. 333)

Sternberg, R. J. (1988). Applying cognitive theory to the testing and teaching of intelligence. *Applied Cognitive Psychology, 2,* 231–255. (p. 334)

Sternberg, R. J. (1998). Principles of teaching for successful intelligence. *Educational Psychologist, 33,* 65–72. (p. 333)

Sternberg, R. J. (1999). The theory of successful intelligence. *Review of General Psychology, 3,* 292–316. (pp. 333)

Sternberg, R. J. (2000). Presidential aptitude in Science. (p. 333)

Sternberg, R. J. (2003). Our research program validating the triarchic theory of successful intelligence: Reply to Gottfredson. *Intelligence, 31,* 399–413. (pp. 333)

Sternberg, R. J., & Grajek, S. (1984). The nature of love. *Journal of Personality and Social Psychology, 47,* 312–329. (p. 612)

Sternberg, R. J., & Kaufman, J. C. (1998). Human abilities. *Annual Review of Psychology, 49,* 479–502. (p. 331)

Sternberg, R. J., & Lubart, T. I. (1991). An investment theory of creativity and its development. *Human Development,* 1–31. (p. 334)

Sternberg, R. J., & Lubart, T. I. (1992). Buy low and sell high: An investment approach to creativity. *Psychological Science, 1,* 1–5. (p. 334)

Sternberg, R. J., & Wagner, R. K. (1993). The g-ocentric view of intelligence and job performance is wrong. *Current Directions in Psychological Science, 2,* 1–5. (p. 333)

Sternberg, R. J., Grigorenko, E. L., & Kidd, K. K. (2005). Intelligence, race, and genetics. *American Psychologist, 60,* 46–59. (p. 346)

Sternberg, R. J., Wagner, R. K., Williams, W. M., & Horvath, J. A. (1995). Testing common sense. *American Psychologist, 50,* 912–927. (p. 333)

Stetter, F., & Kupper, S. (2002). Autogenic training: A meta-analysis of clinical outcome studies. *Applied Psychophysiology and Biofeedback, 27,* 45–98. (p. 451)

Stevenson, H. W. (1992, December). Learning from Asian schools. *Scientific American,* pp. 70–76. (p. 347)

Stewart, B. (2002, April 6). Recall of the wild. *New York Times* (www.nytimes.com). (p. 30)

Stice, E. (2002). Risk and maintenance factors for eating pathology: A meta-analytic review. *Psychological Bulletin, 128,* 825–848. (pp. 364, 365)

Stice, E., & Shaw, H. E. (1994). Adverse effects of the media portrayed thin-ideal on women and linkages to bulimic symptomatology. *Journal of Social and Clinical Psychology, 13,* 288–308. (p. 365)

Stice, E., Spangler, D., & Agras, W. S. (2001). Exposure to media-portrayed thin-ideal images adversely affects vulnerable girls: A longitudinal experiment. *Journal of Social and Clinical Psychology, 20,* 270–288. (p. 365)

Stickgold, R. (2000, March 7). Quoted by S. Blakeslee, For better learning, researchers endorse "sleep on it" adage. *New York Times,* p. F2. (p. 206, 207)

Stickgold, R., Hobson, J. A., Fosse, R., & Fosse, M. (2001). Sleep, learning, and dreams: Off-line memory processing. *Science, 294,* 1052–1057. (p. 207)

Stickgold, R., Malia, A., Maquire, D., Roddenberry, D., & O'Connor, M. (2000, October 13). Replaying the game: Hypnagogic images in normals and amnesics. *Science, 290,* 350–353. (p. 207)

Stith, S. M., Rosen, K. H., Middleton, K. A., Busch, A. L., Lunderberg, K., & Carlton, R. P. (2000). The intergenerational transmission of spouse abuse: A meta-analysis. *Journal of Marriage and the Family, 62,* 640–654. (p. 263)

Stockton, M. C., & Murnen, S. K. (1992). Gender and sexual arousal in response to sexual stimuli: A meta-analytic review. Presented at the American Psychological Society convention. (p. 378)

Stone, A. A., & Neale, J. M. (1984). Effects of severe daily events on mood. *Journal of Personality and Social Psychology, 46,* 137–144. (p. 426)

Stoolmiller, M. (1999). Implications of the restricted range of family environments for estimates of heritability and nonshared environment in behavior-genetic adoption studies. *Psychological Bulletin, 125,* 392–409. (p. 71)

Stoppard, J. M., & Gruchy, C. D. G. (1993). Gender, context, and expression of positive emotion. *Personality and Social Psychology Bulletin, 19,* 143–150. (p. 419)

Storm, L. (2000). Research note: Replicable evidence of psi: A revision of Milton's (1999) meta-analysis of the ganzfeld data bases. *Journal of Parapsychology, 64,* 411–416. (p. 187)

Storm, L. (2003). Remote viewing by committee: RV using a multiple agent/multiple percipient design. *Journal of Parapsychology, 67,* 325–342. (p. 187)

Storms, M. D. (1973). Videotape and the attribution process: Reversing actors' and observers' points of view. *Journal of Personality and Social Psychology, 27,* 165–175. (p. 576)

Storms, M. D. (1981). A theory of erotic orientation development. *Psychological Review, 88,* 340–353. (p. 382)

Storms, M. D. (1983). *Development of sexual orientation.* Washington, DC: Office of Social and Ethical Responsibility, American Psychological Association. (p. 382)

Storms, M. D., & Thomas, G. C. (1977). Reactions to physical closeness. *Journal of Personality and Social Psychology, 35,* 412–418. (p. 589)

Strack, F., Martin, L., & Stepper, S. (1988). Inhibiting and facilitating conditions of the human smile: A nonobtrusive test of the facial feedback hypothesis. *Journal of Personality and Social Psychology, 54,* 768–777. (p. 422)

Strack, S., & Coyne, J. C. (1983). Social confirmation of dysphoria: Shared and private reactions to depression. *Journal of Personality and Social Behavior, 44,* 798–806. (p. 528)

Strahan, E. J., Spencer, S. J., & Zanna, M. P. (2002). Subliminal priming and persuasion: Striking while the iron is hot. *Journal of Experimental Social Psychology, 38,* 556–568. (p. 145)

Strange, B. A., & Dolan, R. J. (2004). b-Adrenergic modulation of emotional memory-evoked human amygdala and hippocampal responses. *Proceedings of the National Academy of Sciences, 101,* 11454–11458. (p. 280)

Stratton, G. M. (1896). Some preliminary experiments on vision without inversion of the retinal image. *Psychological Review, 3,* 611–617. (p. 183)

Straub, R. O., Seidenberg, M. S., Bever, T. G., & Terrace, H. S. (1979). Serial learning in the pigeon. *Journal of the Experimental Analysis of Behavior, 32,* 137–148. (p. 328)

Straus, M. A., & Gelles, R. J. (1980). *Behind closed doors: Violence in the American family.* New York: Anchor/Doubleday. (p. 253)

Straus, M. A., Sugarman, D. B., & Giles-Sims, J. (1997). Spanking by parents and subsequent antisocial behavior of children. *Archives of Pediatric Adolescent Medicine, 151,* 761–767. (p. 253)

Strawbridge, W. J. (1999). Mortality and religious involvement: A review and critique of the results, the methods, and the measures. Paper presented at a Harvard University conference on religion and health, sponsored by the National Institute for Health Research and the John Templeton Foundation. (p. 454)

Strawbridge, W. J., Cohen, R. D., & Shema, S. J. (1997). Frequent attendance at religious services and mortality over 28 years. *American Journal of Public Health, 87,* 957–961. (p. 454)

Strawbridge, W. J., Shema, S. J., Cohen, R. D., & Kaplan, G. A. (2001). Religious attendance increases survival by improving and maintaining good health behaviors, mental health, and social relationships. *Annals of Behavioral Medicine, 23,* 68–74. (p. 455)

Strayer, D. L., & Johnston, W. A. (2001). Driven to distraction: Dual-task studies of simulated driving and conversing on a cellular telephone. *Psychological Science, 12,* 462–466. (p. 194)

Strayer, D. L., Drews, F. A., & Johnston, W. A. (2003). Cell phone-induced failures of visual attention during simulated driving. *Journal of Experimental Psychology: Applied, 9,* 23–32. (p. 194)

Striegel-Moore, R. H., Silberstein, L. R., & Rodin, J. (1993). The social self in bulimia nervosa: Public self-consciousness, social anxiety, and perceived fraudulence. *Journal of Abnormal Psychology, 102,* 297–303. (p. 364)

Stroebe, M., Stroebe, W., & Schut, H. (2001). Gender differences in adjustment to bereavement: An empirical and theoretical review. *Review of General Psychology, 5,* 62–83. (p. 139)

Stroebe, M., Stroebe, W., Schut, H., Zech, E., & van den Bout, J. (2002). Does disclosure of emotions facilitate recovery from bereavement? Evidence from two prospective studies. *Journal of Consulting and Clinical Psychology, 70,* 169–178. (p. 139)

Stroebe, W., Schut, H., & Stroebe, M. S. (2005). Grief work, disclosure and counseling: Do they help the bereaved? *Clinical Psychology Review, 25,* 395–414. (p. 139)

Strupp, H. H. (1986). Psychotherapy: Research, practice, and public policy (How to avoid dead ends). *American Psychologist, 41,* 120–130. (p. 559)

Stumpf, H., & Jackson, D. N. (1994). Gender-related differences in cognitive abilities: Evidence from a medical school admissions testing program. *Personality and Individual Differences, 17,* 335–344. (p. 347)

Stumpf, H., & Stanley, J. C. (1998). Stability and change in gender-related differences on the college board advanced placement and achievement tests. *Current Directions in Psychology, 7,* 192–196. (p. 349)

Stunkard, A. J., Harris, J. R., Pedersen, N. L., & McClearn, G. E. (1990). A separated twin study of the body mass index. *New England Journal of Medicine, 322,* 1483–1487. (p. 369)

Sturm, R. (2003). Increases in clinically severe obesity in the United States, 1986–2000. *Archives of Internal Medicine, 163,* 2146–2148. (p. 366)

Subiaul, F., Cantlon, J. F., Holloway, R. L., & Terrace, H. S. (2004). Cognitive imitation in rhesus macaques. *Science, 305,* 407–410. (p. 261)

Suddath, R. L., Christison, G. W., Torrey, E. F., Casanova, M. F., & Weinberger, D. R. (1990). Anatomical abnormalities in the brains of monozygotic twins discordant for schizophrenia. *New England Journal of Medicine, 322,* 789–794. (p. 536)

Sue, S. (2006). Research to address racial and ethnic disparities in mental health: Some lessons learned. In S. Il. Donaldson, D. E. Berger, & K. Pezdek (Eds.), *Applied psychology: New frontiers and rewarding careers.* Mahwah, NJ: Erlbaum. (p. 561)

Suedfeld, P. (1998). Homo invictus: The indomitable species. *Canadian Psychology, 38,* 164–173. (p. 512)

Suedfeld, P. (2000). Reverberations of the Holocaust fifty years later: Psychology's contributions to understanding persecution and genocide. *Canadian Psychology, 41,* 1–9. (p. 512)

Suedfeld, P., & Mocellin, J. S. P. (1987). The "sensed presence" in unusual environments. *Environment and Behavior, 19,* 33-52. (p. 224)

Sugita, Y. (2004). Experience in early infancy is indispensable for color perception. *Current Biology. 14,* 1267-1271. (p. 176)

Suhail, K., & Chaudry, H. R. (2004). Predictors of subjective well-being in an Eastern Muslim culture. *Journal of Social and Clinical Psychology, 23,* 359. (p. 427)

Suinn, R. M. (1997). Mental practice in sports psychology: Where have we been, Where do we go? *Clinical Psychology: Science and Practice, 4,* 189-207. (p. 325)

Sullivan, P. F., Neale, M. C., & Kendler, K. S. (2000). Genetic epidemiology of major depression: Review and meta-analysis. *American Journal of Psychiatry, 157,* 1552-1562. (p. 524)

Suls, J. M., & Tesch, F. (1978). Students' preferences for information about their test performance: A social comparison study. *Journal of Experimental Social Psychology, 8,* 189-197. (p. 430)

Summers, M. (1996, December 9). Mister clean. *People Weekly,* pp. 139-142. (p. 498)

Sundstrom, E., De Meuse, K. P., & Futrell, D. (1990). Work teams: Applications and effectiveness. *American Psychologist, 45,* 120-133. (p. 402)

Suomi, S. J. (1986). Anxiety-like disorders in young nonhuman primates. In R. Gettleman (Ed.), *Anxiety disorders of childhood.* New York: Guilford Press. (p. 514)

Suomi, S. J. (1987). Genetic and maternal contributions to individual differences in rhesus monkey biobehavioral development. In N. A. Krasnegor & others (Eds.), *Perinatal development: A psychobiological perspective.* Orlando, FL: Academic Press. (p. 462)

Super, C., & Super, D. (2001). *Education and Training. Opportunities in psychology careers,* pp. 68-80. Chicago, IL:VGM Career Books. (p. B-3)

Suppes, P. Quoted by R. H. Ennis. (1982). Children's ability to handle Piaget XE "Piaget, J." 's propositional logic: A conceptual critique. In S. Modgil & C. Modgil (Eds.), *Jean Piaget: Consensus and controversy.* New York: Praeger. (p. 112)

Surgeon General. (1986). *The Surgeon General's workshop on pornography and public health, June 22-24.* Report prepared by E. P. Mulvey & J. L. Haugaard and released by Office of the Surgeon General on August 4, 1986. (p. 604)

Surgeon General. (1999). *Mental health: A report of the Surgeon General.* Rockville, MD: U.S. Department of Health and Human Services. (p. 505, 525)

Susser, E. S., Herman, D. B., & Aaron, B. (2002, August). Combating the terror of terrorism. *Scientific American,* pp. 70-77. (p. 512)

Susser, E., Neugenbauer, R., Hoek, H. W., Brown, A. S., Lin, S., Labovitz, D., & Gorman, J. M. (1996). Schizophrenia after prenatal famine. *Archives of General Psychiatry, 53(1),* 25-31. (p. 534)

Sweat, J. A., & Durm, M. W. (1993). Psychics: Do police departments really use them? *Skeptical Inquirer, 17,* 148-158. (p. 186)

Swerdlow, N. R., & Koob, G. F. (1987). Dopamine, schizophrenia, mania, and depression: Toward a unified hypothesis of cortico-stiato-pallido-thalamic function (with commentary). *Behavioral and Brain Sciences, 10,* 197-246. (p. 533)

Swim, J. K. (1994). Perceived versus meta-analytic effect sizes: An assessment of the accuracy of gender stereotypes. *Journal of Personality and Social Psychology, 66,* 21-36. (p. 596)

Swindle, R., Jr., Heller, K., Bescosolido, B., & Kikuzawa, S. (2000). Responses to nervous breakdowns in America over a 40-year period: Mental health policy implications. *American Psychologist, 55,* 740-749. (p. 523)

Symond, M. B., Harris, A. W. F., Gordon, E., & Williams, L. M. (2005). "Gamma synchrony" in first-episode schizophrenia: A disorder of temporal connectivity? *American Journal of Psychiatry, 162,* 459-465. (p. 533)

TADS (Treatment for Adolescents with Depression Study Team). (2004). Fluoxetine, cognitive-behavioral therapy, and their combination for adolescents with depression: Treatment for adolescents with depression study (TADS) randomized controlled trial. *Journal of the American Medical Association, 292,* 807-820. (p. 567)

Taha, F. A. (1972). A comparative study of how sighted and blind perceive the manifest content of dreams. *National Review of Social Sciences, 9(3),* 28. (p. 206)

Taheri, S. (2004). The genetics of sleep disorders. *Minerva Medica, 95,* 203-212. (p. 202)

Tajfel, H. (Ed.). (1982). *Social identity and intergroup relations.* New York: Cambridge University Press. (p. 597)

Talal, N. (1995). Quoted by V. Morell, Zeroing in on how hormones affect the immune system. *Science, 269,* 773-775. (p. 440)

Talarico, J. M., & Rubin, D. C. (2003). Confidence, not consistency, characterizes flashbulb memories. *Psychological Science, 14,* 455-461. (p. 281)

Talbot, M. (2002, June 2). Hysteria hysteria. *New York Times* (www.nytimes.com). (p. 582)

Tamres, L. K., Janicki, D., & Helgeson, V. S. (2002). Sex differences in coping behavior: A meta-analytic review and an examination of relative coping. *Personality and Social Psychology Review, 6,* 2-30. (p. 89)

Tang, S-H., & Hall, V. C. (1995). The overjustification effect: A meta-analysis. *Applied Cognitive Psychology, 9,* 365-404. (p. 254)

Tangney, J. P., Baumeister, R. F., & Boone, A. L. (2004). High self-control predicts good adjustment, less pathology, better grades, and interpersonal success. *Journal of Personality, 72,* 271-324. (p. 485)

Tannen, D. (1990). *You just don't understand: Women and men in conversation.* New York: Morrow. (pp. 28, 89)

Tannenbaum, P. (2002, February). Quoted by R. Kubey & M. Csikszentmihalyi, Television addiction is no mere metaphor. *Scientific American,* pp. 74-80. (p. 147)

Tanner, J. M. (1978). *Fetus into man: Physical growth from conception to maturity.* Cambridge, MA: Harvard University Press. (p. 120)

Tarbert, J. (2004, May 14). Bad apples, bad command, or both? *Dart Center for Journalism and Trauma* (www.dartcenter.org). (p. 579)

Tarmann, A. (2002, May/June). Out of the closet and onto the Census long form. *Population Today, 30,* pp. 1, 6. (p. 381)

Taubes, G. (1994). Will new dopamine receptors offer a key to schizophrenia? *Science, 265,* 1034-1035. (p. 566)

Taubes, G. (2001). The soft science of dietary fat. *Science, 291,* 2536-2545. (p. 372)

Taubes, G. (2002, July 7). What if it's all been a big fat lie? *New York Times* (www.nytimes.com). (p. 372)

Tavris, C. (1982, November). Anger defused. *Psychology Today,* pp. 25-35. (p. 425)

Taylor, S. E. (1989). Positive illusions. New York: Basic Books. (pp. 312, 447, 493, 494)

Taylor, S. E. (2002). *The tending instinct: How nurturing is essential to who we are and how we live.* New York: Times Books. (p. 89)

Taylor, S. E., Cousino, L. K., Lewis, B. P., Gruenewald, T. L., Gurung, R. A. R., & Updegraff, J. A. (2000). Biobehavioral responses to stress in females: Tend-and-befriend, not fight-or-flight. *Psychological Review, 107,* 411-430. (p. 436)

Taylor, S. E., Lerner, J. S., Sherman, D. K., Sage, R. M., & McDowell, N. K. (2003). Portrait of the self-enhancer: Well adjusted and well liked or maladjusted and friendless? *Journal of Personality and Social Psychology, 84,* 165-176. (p. 494)

Taylor, S. E., Pham, L. B., Rivkin, I. D., & Armor, D. A. (1998). Harnessing the imagination: Mental simulation, self-regulation, and coping. *American Psychologist, 53,* 429-439. (p. 325)

Taylor, S. P., & Chermack, S. T. (1993). Alcohol, drugs and human physical aggression. *Journal of Studies on Alcohol, Supplement No. 11,* 78-88. (p. 601)

Taylor, S., Kuch, K., Koch, W. J., Crockett, D. J., & Passey, G. (1998). The structure of posttraumatic stress symptoms. *Journal of Abnormal Psychology, 107,* 154-160. (p. 512)

Tedeschi, R. G., & Calhoun, L. G. (2004). Posttraumatic growth: Conceptual foundations and empirical evidence. *Psychological Inquiry, 15,* 1–18. (p. 512)

Teerlink, R., & Ozley, L. (2000). *More than a motorcycle: The leadership journey at Harley-Davidson.* Cambridge, MA: Harvard Business School Press. (p. 402)

Teevan, R. C., & McGhee, P. E. (1972) Childhood development of fear of failure motivation. *Journal of Personality and Social Psychology, 21,* 345–348. (p. 398)

Teghtsoonian, R. (1971). On the exponents in Stevens' law and the constant in Ekinan's law. *Psychological Review, 78,* 71–80. (p. 146)

Teicher, M. (2002). McLean motion and attention test (M-MAT): A new test to diagnose a troubling disorder. *McLean Hospital Annual Report* (www.mclean.harvard.edu). (p. 501)

Teicher, M. H. (2002, March). The neurobiology of child abuse. *Scientific American,* pp. 68–75. (p. 117)

Tenopyr, M. L. (1997). Improving the workplace: Industrial/organizational psychology as a career. In R. J. Sternberg (Ed.), *Career paths in psychology: Where your degree can take you.* Washington, DC: American Psychological Association. (p. 393)

Teran-Santos, J., Jimenez-Gomez, A., & Cordero-Guevara, J. (1999). The association between sleep apnea and the risk of traffic accidents. *New England Journal of Medicine, 340,* 847–851. (p. 205)

Terman, J. S., Terman, M., Lo, E-S., & Cooper, T. B. (2001). Circadian time of morning light administration and therapeutic response in winter depression. *Archives of General Psychiatry, 58,* 69–73. (p. 559)

Terman, M., Terman, J. S., & Ross, D. C. (1998). A controlled trial of timed bright light and negative air ionization for treatment of winter depression. *Archives of General Psychiatry, 55,* 875–882. (p. 559)

Terrace, H. S. (1979, November). How Nim Chimpsky changed my mind. *Psychology Today,* pp. 65–76. (p. 328)

Terre, L., & Stoddart, R. (2000). Cutting edge specialties for graduate study in psychology. *Eye on Psi Chi, 23–26.* (p. B-4)

Tesser, A., Forehand, R., Brody, G., & Long, N. (1989). Conflict: The role of calm and angry parent-child discussion in adolescent development. *Journal of Social and Clinical Psychology, 8,* 317–330. (p. 125)

Tetlock, P. E. (1988). Monitoring the integrative complexity of American and Soviet policy rhetoric: What can be learned? *Journal of Social Issues, 44,* 101–131. (p. 618)

Thatcher, R. W., Walker, R. A., & Giudice, S. (1987). Human cerebral hemispheres develop at different rates and ages. *Science, 236,* 1110–1113. (pp. 99, 105)

Thayer, R. E. (1987). Energy, tiredness, and tension effects of a sugar snack versus moderate exercise. *Journal of Personality and Social Psychology, 52,* 119–125. (p. 449)

Thayer, R. E. (1993). Mood and behavior (smoking and sugar snacking) following moderate exercise: A partial test of self-regulation theory. *Personality and Individual Differences, 14,* 97–104. (p. 449)

Thiele, T. E., Marsh, D.J., Ste. Marie, L., Bernstein, I. L., & Palmiter, R. D. (1998). Ethanol consumption and resistance are inversely related to neuropeptide Y levels. *Nature, 396,* 366–369. (p. 225)

Thomas, A., & Chess, S. (1986). The New York Longitudinal Study: From infancy to early adult life. In R. Plomin & J. Dunn (Eds.), *The study of temperament: Changes, continuities, and challenges.* Hillsdale, NJ: Erlbaum. (p. 100)

Thomas, L. (1992). The fragile species. New York: Scribner's. (pp. 95, 322, 555)

Thompson, C. P., Frieman, J., & Cowan, T. (1993). Rajan's memory. Paper presented to the American Psychological Society convention. (p. 278)

Thompson, G. (1998, December 14). As obesity in children increases, so do cases of adult-onset diabetes. *New York Times* (www.nytimes.com). (p. 370)

Thompson, J. K., & Stice, E. (2001). Thin-ideal internalization: Mounting evidence for a new risk factor for body-image disturbance and eating pathology. *Current Directions in Psychological Science, 10,* 181–183. (p. 365)

Thompson, J. K., Jarvie, G. J., Lahey, B. B., & Cureton, K. J. (1982). Exercise and obesity: Etiology, physiology, and intervention. *Psychological Bulletin, 91,* 55–79. (p. 372)

Thompson, P. M., Cannon, T. D., Narr, K. L., van Erp, T., Poutanen, V-P., Huttunen, M., Lönnqvist, J., Standerskjöld-Nordenstam, C-G., Kaprio, J., Khaledy, M., Dail, R., Zoumalan, C. I., & Toga, A. W. (2001). Genetic influences on brain structure. *Nature Neuroscience, 4,* 1253–1258. (p. 342)

Thompson, P. M., Giedd, J. N., Woods, R. P., MacDonald, D., Evans, A. C., & Toga, A. W. (2000). Growth patterns in the developing brain detected by using continuum mechanical tensor maps. *Nature, 404,* 190–193. (p. 105)

Thompson, R., Emmorey, K., & Gollan, T. H. (2005). "Tip of the fingers" experiences by Deaf signers. *Psychological Science, 16,* 856–860. (p. 292)

Thorndike, A. L., & Hagen, E. P. (1977). *Measurement and evaluation in psychology and education.* New York: Macmillan. (p. 338)

Thorne, J., with Larry Rothstein. (1993). *You are not alone: Words of experience and hope for the journey through depression.* New York: HarperPerennial. (p. 498)

Thornton, B., & Moore, S. (1993). Physical attractiveness contrast effect: Implications for self-esteem and evaluations of the social self. *Personality and Social Psychology Bulletin, 19,* 474–480. (p. 609)

Thorpe, W. H. (1974). *Animal nature and human nature.* London: Metheun. (p. 329)

Tiedens, L. Z. (2001). Anger and advancement versus sadness and subjugation: The effect of negative emotion expressions on social status conferral. *Journal of Personality and Social Psychology, 80,* 86–94. (p. 425)

Tikkanen, T. (2001). Psychology in Europe: A growing profession with high standards and a bright future. *European Psychologist, 6,* 144–146. (p. 5)

Time. (1997, December 22). Greeting card association data, p. 19. (p. 89)

Tinbergen, N. (1951). *The study of instinct.* Oxford: Clarendon. (p. 357)

Tirrell, M. E. (1990). Personal communication. (p. 238)

Tollefson, G. D., Fawcett, J., Winokur, G., Beasley, C. M., et al. (1993). Evaluation of suicidality during pharmacologic treatment of mood and non-mood disorders. *Annals of Clinical Psychiatry, 5(4),* 209–224. (p. 568)

Tollefson, G. D., Rampey, A. H., Beasley, C. M., & Enas, G. G. (1994). Absence of a relationship between adverse events and suicidality during pharmacotherapy for depression. *Journal of Clinical Psychopharmacology, 14,* 163–169. (p. 568)

Tolman, E. C., & Honzik, C. H. (1930). Introduction and removal of reward, and maze performance in rats. *University of California Publications in Psychology, 4,* 257–275. (p. 254)

Tolstoy, L. (1904). *My confessions.* Boston: Dana Estes. (p. 8)

Tondo, L., Jamison, K. R., & Baldessarini, R. J. (1997). Effect of lithium maintenance on suicidal behavior in major mood disorders. In D. M. Stoff & J. J. Mann (Eds.), *The neurobiology of suicide: From the bench to the clinic.* New York: New York Academy of Sciences. (p. 568)

Toni, N., Buchs, P.-A., Nikonenko, I., Bron, C. R., & Muller, D. (1999). LTP promotes formation of multiple spine synapses between a single axon terminal and a dendrite. *Nature, 402,* 421–42. (p. 280)

Torrey, E. F. (1986). *Witchdoctors and psychiatrists.* New York: Harper & Row. (p. 561)

Torrey, E. F., & Miller, J. (2002). *The invisible plague: The rise of mental illness from 1750 to the present.* New Brunswick, NJ: London: Rutgers University Press. (p. 534)

Torrey, E. F., Miller, J., Rawlings, R., & Yolken, R. H. (1997). Seasonality of births in schizophrenia and bipolar disorder: A review of the literature. *Schizophrenia Research, 28,* 1–38. (p. 534)

Totterdell, P., Kellett, S., Briner, R. B., & Teuchmann, K. (1998). Evidence of mood linkage in work groups. *Journal of Personality and Social Psychology, 74,* 1504–1515. (p. 582)

Tovee, M. J., Mason, S. M., Emery, J. L., McCluskey, S. E., & Cohen-Tovee, E. M. (1997). Supermodels: Stick insects or hourglasses? *The Lancet, 350,* 1474–1475. (p. 365)

Towler, G. (1986). From zero to one hundred: Coaction in a natural setting. *Perceptual and Motor Skills, 62,* 377–378. (p. 588)

Tracey, J. L., & Robins, R. W. (2004). Show your pride: Evidence for a discrete emotion expression. *Psychological Science, 15*, 194–197. (p. 423)

Tranel, D., Bechara, A., & Denburg, N. L. (2002). Asymmetric functional roles of right and left ventromedial prefrontal cortices in social conduct, decision-making and emotional processing. *Cortex, 38*, pp. 589–613. (p. 63)

Treffert, D. A., & Wallace, G. L. **(2002).** Island of genius—The artistic brilliance and dazzling memory that sometimes accompany autism and other disorders hint at how all brains work. *Scientific American, 286*, 76–86. (p. 332)

Treisman, A. (1987). Properties, parts, and objects. In K. R. Boff, L. Kaufman, & J. P. Thomas (Eds.), *Handbook of perception and human performance.* New York: Wiley. (p. 172)

Tremblay, R. E., Pihl, R. O., Vitaro, F., & Dobkin, P. L. (1994). Predicting early onset of male antisocial behavior from preschool behavior. *Archives of General Psychiatry, 51*, 732–739. (p. 518)

Trewin, D. (2001). *Australian social trends 2001.* Canberra: Australian Bureau of Statistics. (p. 83, 91)

Triandis, H. C. (1981). *Some dimensions of intercultural variation and their implications for interpersonal behavior.* Paper presented at the American Psychological Association convention. (p. 83)

Triandis, H. C. (1994). *Culture and social behavior.* New York: McGraw-Hill. (pp. 85, 421, 486, 602, 603)

Triandis, H. C., Bontempo, R., Villareal, M. J., Asai, M., & Lucca, N. (1988). Individualism and collectivism: Cross-cultural perspectives on self-ingroup relationships. *Journal of Personality and Social Psychology, 54*, 323–338. (p. 86)

Trickett, P. K., & McBride-Chang, C. (1995). The developmental impact of different forms of child abuse and neglect. *Developmental Review, 15*, 311–337. (p. 117)

Trimble, J. E. (1994). Cultural variations in the use of alcohol and drugs. In W. J. Lonner & R. Malpass (Eds.), *Psychology and culture.* Boston: Allyn & Bacon. (p. 227)

Triplett, N. (1898). The dynamogenic factors in pacemaking and competition. *American Journal of Psychology, 9*, 507–533. (p. 588)

Trolier, T. K., & Hamilton, D. L. (1986). Variables influencing judgments of correlational relations. *Journal of Personality and Social Psychology, 50*, 879–888. (p. 23)

Trut, L. N. (1999). Early canid domestication: The farm-fox experiment. *American Scientist, 87*, 160–169. (p. 74)

Tsai, J. L., & Chentsova-Dutton, Y. (2003). Variation among European Americans in emotional facial expression. *Journal of Cross-Cultural Psychology, 34*, 650–657. (p. 421)

Tsang, Y. C. (1938). Hunger motivation in gastrectomized rats. *Journal of Comparative Psychology, 26*, 1–17. (p. 361)

Tsien, J. Z. (April, 2000). Building a brainier mouse. *Scientific American*, 62–68. (p. 342)

Tsuang, M. T., & Faraone, S. V. (1990). *The genetics of mood disorders.* Baltimore, MD: Johns Hopkins University Press. (p. 525)

Tuber, D. S., Miller, D. D., Caris, K. A., Halter, R., Linden, F., & Hennessy, M. B. (1999). Dogs in animal shelters: Problems, suggestions, and needed expertise. *Psychological Science, 10*, 379–386. (p. 30)

Tucker, K. A. (2002). I believe you can fly. *Gallup Management Journal* (www.gallupjournal.com/CA/st/20020520.asp). (p. 400)

Tuerk, P. W. (2005). Research in the high-stakes era: Achievement, resources, and no child left behind. *Psychological Science, 16*, 419–425. (p. 344)

Turkheimer, E., Haley, A., Waldron, M., D'Onofrio, B., & Gottesman, I. I. (2003). Socioeconomic status modifies heritability of IQ in young mothers. *Psychological Science, 14*, 623–628. (p. 344)

Turner, J. C. (1987). *Rediscovering the social group: A self-categorization theory.* New York: Basil Blackwell. (p. 597)

Turner, N., Barling, J., & Zacharatos, A. (2002). Positive psychology at work. In C. R. Snyder & S. J. Lopez (Eds.), *The handbook of positive psychology.* New York: Oxford University Press. (p. 402)

Tutu, D. (1999). *No future without forgiveness.* New York: Doubleday. (p. 388)

Tversky, A. (1985, June). Quoted in K. McKean, Decisions, decisions. *Discover*, pp. 22–31. (p. 310)

Tversky, A., & Kahneman, D. (1974). Judgment under uncertainty: Heuristics and biases. *Science, 185*, 1124–1131. (pp. 292, 310, A-6)

Twenge, J. M. (1997). Changes in masculine and feminine traits over time: A meta-analysis. *Sex Roles 36(5–6)*, 305–325. (p. 93)

Twenge, J. M. (2000). The age of anxiety? Birth cohort change in anxiety and neuroticism, 1952–1993. *Journal of Personality and Social Psychology, 79*, 1007–1021. (p. 515)

Twenge, J. M., & Campbell, W. K. (2001). Age and birth cohort differences in self-esteem: A cross-temporal meta-analysis. *Personality and Social Psychology Review, 5*, 321–344. (p. 125)

Twenge, J. M., & Crocker, J. (2002). Race and self-esteem: Meta-analyses comparing Whites, Blacks, Hispanics, Asians, and American Indians and comment on Gray-Little and Hafdahl (2000). *Psychological Bulletin, 128*, 371–408. (p. 492)

Twenge, J. M., & Nolen-Hoeksema, S. (2002). Age, gender, race, socioeconomic status, and birth cohort differences on the children's depression inventory: A meta-analysis. *Journal of Abnormal Psychology, 111*, 578–588. (p. 125)

Twenge, J. M., Baumeister, R. F., Tice, D. M., & Stucke, T. S. (2001). If you can't join them, beat them: Effects of social exclusion on aggressive behavior. *Journal of Personality and Social Psychology, 81*, 1058–1069. (pp. 365, 389, 602)

Twenge, J. M., Catanese, K. R., & Baumeister, R. F. (2002). Social exclusion causes self-defeating behavior. *Journal of Personality and Social Psychology, 83*, 606–615. (pp. 389, 602)

Twenge, J. M., Catanese, K. R., & Baumeister, R. F. (2003). Social exclusion and the deconstructed state: Time perception, meaninglessness, lethargy, lack of emotion, and self-awareness. *Journal of Personality and Social Psychology, 85*, 409–423. (p. 602)

Twiss, C., Tabb, S., & Crosby, F. (1989). Affirmative action and aggregate data: The importance of patterns in the perception of discrimination. In F. Blanchard & F. Crosby (Eds.), *Affirmative action: Social psychological perspectives.* New York: Springer-Verlag. (p. A-6)

Tyler, K. A. (2002). Social and emotional outcomes of childhood sexual abuse: A review of recent research. *Aggression and Violent Behavior, 7*, 567–589. (p. 117)

U.S. Senate Select Committee on Intelligence. (2004, July 9). *Report of the U.S. Intelligence Community's prewar intelligence assessments on Iraq.* www.gpoaccess.gov/serialset/creports/iraq.html (pp. 18, 310, 591)

Uchino, B. N., Cacioppo, J. T., & Kiecolt-Glaser, J. K. (1996). The relationship between social support and physiological processes: A review with emphasis on underlying mechanisms and implications for health. *Psychological Bulletin, 119*, 488–531. (p. 448)

Uchino, B. N., Uno, D., & Holt-Lunstad, J. (1999). Social support, physiological processes, and health. *Current Directions in Psychological Science, 8*, 145–148. (p. 448)

Udry, J. R. (2000). Biological limits of gender construction. *American Sociological Review, 65*, 443–457. (p. 90)

UK ECT Review Group. (2003). Efficacy and safety of electroconvulsive therapy in depressive disorders: A systematic review and meta-analysis. *Lancet, 361*, 799–808. (p. 569)

Ullman, E. (2005, October 19). The boss in the machine. *New York Times* (www.nytimes.com). (p. 392)

Ulrich, R. E. (1991). Animal rights, animal wrongs and the question of balance. *Psychological Science, 2*, 197–201. (p. 29)

UNAIDS. (2005). *AIDS epidemic update, December 2005.* United Nations (www.unaids.org). (p. 441)

UNAIDS. (2005). *AIDS in Africa: Three scenarios to 2025.* United Nations (www.unaids.org). (p. 441)

UNAIDS. (2005). *Epidemiology.* Joint United Nations Programme on HIV/AIDS (www.unaids.org). (p. 441)

United Nations. (1992). *1991 demographic yearbook.* New York: United Nations. (p. 135)

Urbany, J. E., Bearden, W. O., & Weilbaker, D. C. (1988). The effect of plausible and exaggerated reference prices on consumer perceptions and price search. *Journal of Consumer Research, 15,* 95–110. (p. 313)

Urry, H. L., Nitschke, J. B., Dolski, I., Jackson, D. C., Dalton, K. M., Mueller, C. J., Rosenkranz, M. A., Ryff, C. D., Singer, B. H., & Davidson, R. J. (2004). Making a life worth living: Neural correlates of well-being. *Psychological Science, 15,* 367–372. (p. 411)

Ursu, S., Stenger, V. A., Shear, M. K., Jones, M. R., & Carter, C. S. (2003). Overactive action monitoring in obsessive-compulsive disorder: Evidence from functional magnetic resonance imaging. *Psychological Science, 14,* 347–353. (p. 514, 515)

USAID. (2004, January). *The ABCs of HIV prevention.* www.usaid.gov. (p. 441)

Vaidya, J. G., Gray, E. K., Haig, J., & Watson, D. (2002). On the temporal stability of personality: Evidence for differential stability and the role of life experiences. *Journal of Personality and Social Psychology, 83,* 1469–1484. (pp. 100, 478)

Vaillant, G. E. (1977). *Adaptation to life.* New York: Little, Brown. (p. 298)

Vaillant, G. E. (2002). *Aging well: Surprising guideposts to a happier life from the landmark Harvard study of adult development.* Boston: Little, Brown. (p. 447)

Valenstein, E. S. (1986). *Great and desperate cures: The rise and decline of psychosurgery.* New York: Basic Books. (p. 571)

Vallerand, R. J., Fortier, M. S., & Guay, F. (1997). Self-determination and persistence in a real-life setting: Toward a motivational model of high school dropout. *Journal of Personality and Social Psychology, 72,* 1161–1176. (p. 398)

Vallone, R. P., Griffin, D. W., Lin, S., & Ross, L. (1990). Overconfident prediction of future actions and outcomes by self and others. *Journal of Personality and Social Psychology, 58,* 582–592. (p. 15)

van Boxtel, H. W., Orobio de Castro, B., & Goossens, F. A. (2004). High self-perceived social competence in rejected children is related to frequent fighting. *European Journal of Developmental Psychology, 1,* 205–214. (p. 493)

van den Boom, D. (1990). Preventive intervention and the quality of mother-infant interaction and infant exploration in irritable infants. In W. Koops, H. J. G. Soppe, J. L. van der Linden, P. C. M. Molenaar, & J. J. F. Schroots (Eds.), *Developmental psychology research in The Netherlands.* The Netherlands: Uitgeverij Eburon. Cited by C. Hazan & P. R. Shaver (1994). Deeper into attachment theory. *Psychological Inquiry, 5,* 68–79. (p. 115)

van den Bos, K., & Spruijt, N. (2002). Appropriateness of decisions as a moderator of the psychology of voice. *European Journal of Social Psychology, 32,* 57–72. (p. 402)

Van Dyke, C., & Byck, R. (1982, March). Cocaine. *Scientific American,* pp. 128–141. (p. 222)

van Engen, M. L., & Willemsen, T. M. (2004). Sex and leadership styles: A meta-analysis of research published in the 1990s. *Psychological Reports, 94,* 3–18. (p. 88)

Van IJzendoorn, M. H., & Juffer, F. (2005). Adoption is a successful natural intervention enhancing adopted children's IQ and school performance. *Current Directions in Psychological Science, 14,* 326–330. (p. 342)

van IJzendoorn, M. H., & Kroonenberg, P. M. (1988). Cross-cultural patterns of attachment: A meta-analysis of the strange situation. *Child Development, 59,* 147–156. (p. 115)

Van Leeuwen, M. S. (1978). A cross-cultural examination of psychological differentiation in males and females. *International Journal of Psychology, 13,* 87–122. (p. 91)

Van Rooy, D. L., & Viswesvaran, C. (2004). Emotional intelligence: A meta-analytic investigation of predictive validity and nomological net. *Journal of Vocational Behavior, 65,* 71–95. (p. 335)

van Schaik, C. P., Ancrenaz, M., Borgen, G., Galdikas, B., Knott, C. D., Singleton, I., Suzuki, A., Utami, S. S., & Merrill, M. (2003). Orangutan cultures and the evolution of material culture. *Science, 299,* 102–105. (p. 327)

Van Yperen, N. W., & Buunk, B. P. (1990). A longitudinal study of equity and satisfaction in intimate relationships. *European Journal of Social Psychology, 20,* 287–309. (p. 612)

Van Praag, H., Schinder, A. F., Christie, B. R., Toni, N., Palmer, T. D., & Gage, F. H. (2002). Neurogenesis: Functional neurons in adult hippocampus. *Nature, 415,* 1030–1034. (p. 60)

Vance, E. B., & Wagner, N. N. (1976). Written descriptions of orgasm: A study of sex differences. *Archives of Sexual Behavior, 5,* 87–98. (p. 375)

Vandenberg, S. G., & Kuse, A. R. (1978). Mental rotations: A group test of three-dimensional spatial visualization. *Perceptual and Motor Skills, 47,* 599–604. (p. 349, 354)

Vanman, E. J., Saltz, J. L., Nathan, L. R., & Warren, J. A. (2004). Racial discrimination by low-prejudiced Whites. *Psychological Science, 15,* 711–714. (p. 595)

Vaughn, K. B., & Lanzetta, J. T. (1981). The effect of modification of expressive displays on vicarious emotional arousal. *Journal of Experimental Social Psychology, 17,* 16–30. (p. 422)

Vazire, S., & Gosling, S. D. (2004). e-Perceptions: Personality impressions based on personal websites. *Journal of Personality and Social Psychology, 87,* 123–132. (p. 482)

Vecera, S. P., Vogel, E. K., & Woodman, G. F. (2002). Lower region: A new cue for figure-ground assignment. *Journal of Experimental Psychology: General, 13,* 194–205. (p. 175)

Vega, W. A., Kolody, B., Aguilar-Gaxiola, S., Alderete, E., Catalano, R., & Caraveo-Anduaga, J. (1998). Lifetime prevalence of DSM-III-R psychiatric disorders among urban and rural Mexican Americans in California. *Archives of General Psychiatry, 55,* 771–778. (p. 506)

Vekassy, L. (1977). Dreams of the blind. *Magyar Pszichologiai Szemle, 34,* 478–491. (p. 206)

Verbeek, M. E. M., Drent, P. J., & Wiepkema, P. R. (1994). Consistent individual differences in early exploratory behaviour of male great tits. *Animal Behaviour, 48,* 1113–1121. (p. 477)

Verhaeghen, P., & Salthouse, T. A. (1997). Meta-analyses of age-cognition relations in adulthood: Estimates of linear and nonlinear age effects and structural models. *Psychological Bulletin, 122,* 231–249. (p. 131)

Viding, E., Blair, R., James, R., Moffitt, T. E., & Plomin, R. (2005). Evidence for substantial genetic risk for psychopathy in 7-year-olds. *Journal of Child Psychology & Psychiatry, 46,* 592–597. (p. 518)

Vigliocco, G., & Hartsuiker, R. J. (2002). The interplay of meaning, sound, and syntax in sentence production. *Psychological Bulletin, 128,* 442–472. (p. 319)

Vining, E. P. G., Freeman, J. M., Pillas, D. J., Uematsu, S., Carson, B. S., Brandt, J., Boatman, D., Pulsifer, M. B., & Zukerberg, A. (1997). Why would you remove half a brain? The outcome of 58 children after hemispherectomy—The Johns Hopkins Experience: 1968 to 1996. *Pediatrics, 100,* 163–171. (p. 59)

Vita, A. J., Terry, R. B., Hubert, H. B., & Fries, J. F. (1998). Aging, health risks, and cumulative disability. *New England Journal of Medicine, 338,* 1035–1041. (p. 222)

Vohs, K., Voelz, Z., Pettit, J., Bardone, A., Katz, J., Abramson, L., Heatherton, T., & Joiner, T. (2001). Perfectionism, body dissatisfaction, and self-esteem: An interactive model of bulimic symptom development. *Journal of Social and Clinical Psychology, 20,* 476–497. (p. 365)

von Senden, M. (1932). *The perception of space and shape in the congenitally blind before and after operation.* Glencoe, IL: Free Press. (p. 181)

Vreeland, C. N., Gallagher, B. J., III, & McFalls, J. A., Jr. (1995). The beliefs of members of the American Psychiatric Association on the etiology of male homosexuality: A national survey. *Journal of Psychology, 129,* 507–517. (p. 385)

Wadden, T. A., Vogt, R. A., Foster, G. D., & Anderson, D. A. (1998). Exercise and the maintenance of weight loss: 1-year follow-up of a controlled clinical trial. *Journal of Consulting and Clinical Psychology, 66,* 429–433. (p. 372)

Wager, T. D., Rilling, J. K., Smith, E. E., Sokolik, A., Casey, K. L., Davidson, R. J., Kosslyn, S. M., Rose, R. M., & Cohen, J. D. (2004).

Placebo-induced changes in fMRI in the anticipation and experience of pain. *Science, 303,* 1162–1167. (p. 164)

Wagner, U., Gais, S., Haider, H., Verleger, R., & Born, J. (2004). Sleep inspires insight. *Nature, 427,* 352–355. (p. 203)

Wagstaff, G. (1982). Attitudes to rape: The "just world" strikes again? *Bulletin of the British Psychological Society, 13,* 275–283. (p. 576)

Wahl, O. F. (1992). Mass media images of mental illness: A review of the literature. *Journal of Community Psychology, 20,* 343–352. (p. 505)

Wahlberg, D. (2001, October 11). *We're more depressed, patriotic, poll finds.* Grand Rapids Press, p. A15. (p. 437)

Wakefield, J. C., & Spitzer, R. L. (2002). Lowered estimates—but of what? *Archives of General Psychiatry, 59,* 129–130. (p. 513)

Walker, W. R., Skowronski, J. J., Gibbons, J. A., Vogl, R. J., & Thompson, C. P. (2003). On the emotions that accompany autobiographical memories: Dysphoria disrupts the fading affect bias. *Cognition and Emotion, 17,* 703–723. (pp. 138, 275)

Wall Street Journal. (1999, December 17). Money and misery. Editorial, p. A14. (p. 554)

Wall, B. (2002, August 24–25). Profit matures along with baby boomers. *International Herald Tribune,* p. 13. (p. 609)

Wall, P. D. (2000). *Pain: The science of suffering.* New York: Columbia University Press. (p. 163)

Wallace, D. S., Paulson, R. M., Lord, C. G., & Bond, C. F., Jr. (2005). Which behaviors do attitudes predict? Meta-analyzing the effects of social pressure and perceived difficulty. *Review of General Psychology, 9(3),* 214–227. (p. 577)

Wallach, M. A., & Wallach, L. (1983). *Psychology's sanction for selfishness: The error of egoism in theory and therapy.* New York: Freeman. (p. 473)

Wallach, M. A., & Wallach, L. (1985, February). How psychology sanctions the cult of the self. *Washington Monthly,* pp. 46–56. (p. 473)

Wallis, C. (1983, June 6). Stress: Can we cope? *Time,* pp. 48–54. (p. 438)

Walster (Hatfield), E., Aronson, V., Abrahams, D., & Rottman, L. (1966). Importance of physical attractiveness in dating behavior. *Journal of Personality and Social Psychology, 4,* 508–516. (p. 608)

Wampold, B. E. (2001). *The great psychotherapy debate: Models, methods, and findings.* Mahwah, NJ: Erlbaum. (pp. 559, 561)

Wampold, B. E., Mondin, G. W., Moody, M., & Ahn, H. (1997). The flat earth as a metaphor for the evidence for uniform efficacy of bona fide psychotherapies: Reply to Crits-Christoph (1997) and Howard et al. (1997). *Psychological Bulletin, 122,* 226–230. (p. 557)

Ward, A., & Mann, T. (2000). Don't mind if I do: Disinhibited eating under cognitive load. *Journal of Personality and Social Psychology, 78,* 753–763. (p. 372)

Ward, C. (1994). Culture and altered states of consciousness. In W. J. Lonner & R. Malpass (Eds.), *Psychology and culture.* Boston: Allyn & Bacon. (p. 219)

Ward, K. D., Klesges, R. C., & Halpern, M. T. (1997). Predictors of smoking cessation and state-of-the-art smoking interventions. *Journal of Socies Issues, 53,* 129–145. (p. 222)

Wardle, J., Cooke, L. J., Gibson, L., Sapochnik, M., Sheiham, A., Lawson, M. (2003). Increasing children's acceptance of vegetables; a randomized trial of parent-led exposure. *Appetite, 40,* 155–162. (p. 165)

Warner, J., McKeown, E., Johnson, K., Ramsay, A., Cort, C., & King, M. (2004). Rates and predictors of mental illness in gay men, lesbians and bisexual men and women. *British Journal of Psychiatry, 185,* 479–485. (p. 381)

Warr, P., & Payne, R. (1982). Experiences of strain and pleasure among British adults. *Social Science and Medicine, 16,* 1691–1697. (p. 447)

Warren, N. C. (2005, March 4). Personal correspondence from founder of eHarmony.com. (p. 610)

Wason, P. C. (1960). On the failure to eliminate hypotheses in a conceptual task. *Quarterly Journal of Experimental Psychology, 12,* 129–140. (p. 309)

Wason, P. C. (1981). The importance of cognitive illusions. *The Behavioral and Brain Sciences, 4,* 356. (p. 309)

Wasserman, E. A. (1993). Comparative cognition: Toward a general understanding of cognition in behavior. *Psychological Science, 4,* 156–161. (p. 247)

Wasserman, E. A. (1995). The conceptual abilities of pigeons. *American Scientist, 83,* 246–255. (p. 326)

Wastell, C. A. (2002). Exposure to trauma: The long-term effects of suppressing emotional reactions. *Journal of Nervous and Mental Disorders, 190,* 839–845. (p. 448)

Waterhouse, R. (1993, July 19). Income for 62 percent is below average pay. *The Independent,* p. 4. (p. A-2)

Waterman, A. S. (1988). Identity status theory and Erikson's theory: Commonalities and differences. *Developmental Review, 8,* 185–208. (p. 125)

Watkins, C. E., Campbell, V. L., Nieberding, R., & Hallmark, R. (1995). Contemporary practice of psychological assessment by clinical psychologists. *Professional Psychology: Research and Practice, 26,* 54–60. (p. 465)

Watkins, J. G. (1984). The Bianchi (L. A. Hillside Strangler) case: Sociopath or multiple personality? *International Journal of Clinical and Experimental Hypnosis, 32,* 67–101. (p. 515)

Watkins, P. C. (2004). Gratitude and subjective well-being. In R. A. Emmons and M. E. McCullough (Eds.), *The psychology of gratitude.* New York: Oxford University Press. (p. 429)

Watson, D. (2000). *Mood and temperament.* New York: Guilford Press. (pp. 426, 449)

Watson, D., Suls, J., & Haig, J. (2002). Global self-esteem in relation to structural models of personality and affectivity. *Journal of Personality and Social Psychology, 83,* 185–197. (p. 491)

Watson, J. B. (1913). Psychology as the behaviorist views it. *Psychological Review, 20,* 158–177. (pp. 193, 247)

Watson, J. B. (1924). The unverbalized in human behavior. *Psychological Review, 31,* 339–347. (p. 247)

Watson, J. B., & Rayner, R. (1920). Conditioned emotional reactions. *Journal of Experimental Psychology, 3,* 1–14. (p. 247)

Watson, R. I., Jr. (1973). Investigation into deindividuation using a cross-cultural survey technique. *Journal of Personality and Social Psychology, 25,* 342–345. (p. 589)

Wayment, H. A., & Peplau, L. A. (1995). Social support and well-being among lesbian and heterosexual women: A structural modeling approach. *Personality and Social Psychology Bulletin, 21,* 1189–1199. (p. 136)

Weaver, J. B., Masland, J. L., & Zillmann, D. (1984). Effect of erotica on young men's aesthetic perception of their female sexual partners. *Perceptual and Motor Skills, 58,* 929–930. (p. 378)

Webb, W. B. (1992). *Sleep: The gentle tyrant.* Bolton, MA: Anker Publishing. (pp. 199, 204)

Webb, W. B., & Campbell, S. S. (1983). Relationships in sleep characteristics of identical and fraternal twins. *Archives of General Psychiatry, 40,* 1093–1095. (p. 200)

Wechsler, H., Davenport, A., Dowdall, G., Moeykens, B., & Castillo, S. (1994). Health and behavioral consequences of binge drinking in college. *Journal of the American Medical Association, 272,* 1672–1677. (p. 219)

Wechsler, H., Lee, J. E., Kuo, M., Seibring, M., Nelson, T. F., & Lee, H. (2002). Trends in college binge drinking during a period of increased prevention efforts. *Journal of American College Health, 50,* 203–217. (p. 219)

Wee, C. C., Phillips, R. S., Legedza, A. T. R., Davis, R. B., Soukup, J. R., Colditz, G. A., & Hamel, M. B. (2005). Health care expenditures associated with overweight and obesity among US adults: Importance of age and race. *American Journal of Public Health, 95,* 159–165. (p. 367)

Weinberg, M. S., & Williams, C. (1974). *Male homosexuals: Their problems and adaptations.* New York: Oxford University Press. (p. 381)

Weingarten, G. (2002, March 10). Below the beltway. *Washington Post,* p. WO3. (p. 392)

Weinstein, N. D. (1980). Unrealistic optimism about future life events. *Journal of Personality and Social Psychology, 39,* 806–820. (p. 488)

Weinstein, N. D. (1982). Unrealistic optimism about susceptibility to health problems. *Journal of Behavioral Medicine, 5,* 441–460. (p. 488)

Weinstein, N. D. (1996, October 4). 1996 optimistic bias bibliography. Distributed via internet (weinstein_c A case study and implications. *Oxford, UK: Oxford University Press. (p. 152)*

Weiss, A., King, J. E., & Enns, R. M. (2002). Subjective well-being is heritable and genetically correlated with dominance in chimpanzees (Pan troglodytes). *Journal of Personality and Social Psychology, 83,* 1141-1149. (p. 432)

Weiss, A., King, J. E., & Figueredo, A. J. (2000). The heritability of personality factors in chimpanzees (Pan troglodytes). *Behavior Genetics, 30,* 213-221. (p. 432)

Weissman, M. M. (1999). Interpersonal psychotherapy and the health care scene. In D. S. Janowsky (Ed.), *Psychotherapy indications and outcomes.* Washington, DC: American Psychiatric Press. (p. 543)

Weissman, M. M., Bland, R. C., Canino, G. J., Faravelli, C., Greenwald, S., Hwu, H-G., Joyce, P. R., Karam, E. G., Lee, C-K., Lellouch, J., Lepine, J-P., Newman, S. C., Rubio-Stepic, M., Wells, J. E., Wickramaratne, P. J., Wittchen, H-U., & Yeh, E-K. (1996). Cross-national epidemiology of major depression and bipolar disorder. *Journal of the American Medical Association, 276,* 293-299. (p. 523)

Weisz, J. R., Rothbaum, F. M., & Blackburn, T. C. (1984). Standing out and standing in: The psychology of control in America and Japan. *American Psychologist, 39,* 955-969. (p. 82)

Wellman, H. M., & Gelman, S. A. (1992). Cognitive development: Foundational theories of core domains. *Annual Review of Psychology, 43,* 337-375. (p. 109)

Wellman, H. M., Cross, D., & Watson, J. (2001). Meta-analysis of theory-of-mind development: The truth about false belief. *Child Development, 72,* 655-684. (p. 110)

Wells, G. L. (1981). Lay analyses of causal forces on behavior. In J. Harvey (Ed.), *Cognition, social behavior and the environment.* Hillsdale, NJ: Erlbaum. (p. 233)

Wender, P. H., Kety, S. S., Rosenthal, D., Schulsinger, F., Ortmann, J., & Lunde, I. (1986). Psychiatric disorders in the biological and adoptive families of adopted individuals with affective disorders. *Archives of General Psychiatry, 43,* 923-929. (p. 525)

Wener, R., Frazier, W., & Farbstein, J. (1987, June). Building better jails. *Psychology Today,* pp. 40-49. (p. 486)

Westen, D. (1996). Is Freud really dead? Teaching psychodynamic theory to introductory psychology. Presentation to the Annual Institute on the Teaching of Psychology, St. Petersburg Beach, Florida. (p. 464)

Westen, D. (1998). The scientific legacy of Sigmund Freud: Toward a psychodynamically informed psychological science. *Psychological Bulletin, 124,* 333-371. (pp. 459, 465)

Westen, D., & Morrison, K. (2001). A multidimensional meta-analysis of treatments for depression, panic, and generalized anxiety disorder: An empirical examination of the status of empirically supported therapies. *Journal of Consulting and Clinical Psychology, 69,* 875-899. (p. 557)

Weuve, J., Kang, J. H., Manson, J. E., Breteler, M. M. B., Ware, J. H., & Grodstein, F. (2004). Physical activity, including walking, and cognitive function in older women. *Journal of the American Medical Association, 292,* 1454-1460. (p. 132)

Whalen, P. J., Kagan, J., Cook, R. G., Davis, F. C., Kim, H., Polis, S., McLaren, D. G., Somerville, L. H., McLean, A. A., Maxwell, J. S., & Johnstone, T. (2004). Human amygdala responsibility to masked fearful eye whites. *Science, 302,* 2061. (p. 414)

Whalen, P. J., Shin, L. M., McInerney, S. C., Fisher, H., Wright, C. I., & Rauch, S. L. (2001). A functional MRI study of human amygdala responses to facial expressions of fear versus anger. *Emotion, 1,* 70-83. (p. 411)

Wheelwright, J. (2004, August). Study the clones first. *Discover,* pp. 44-50. (p. 69)

White, G. L., & Kight, T. D. (1984). Misattribution of arousal and attraction: Effects of salience of explanations for arousal. *Journal of Experimental Social Psychology, 20,* 55-64. (p. 611)

White, H. R., Brick, J., & Hansell, S. (1993). A longitudinal investigation of alcohol use and aggression in adolescence. *Journal of Studies on Alcohol, Supplement No. 11,* 62-77. (p. 601)

White, K. M. (1983). Young adults and their parents: Individuation to mutuality. *New Directions for Child Development, 22,* 61-76. (p. 126)

White, L., & Edwards, J. (1990). Emptying the nest and parental well-being: An analysis of national panel data. *American Sociological Review, 55,* 235-242. (p. 136)

White, P. H., Kjelgaard, M. M., & Harkins, S. G. (1995). Testing the contribution of self-evaluation to goal-setting effects. *Journal of Personality and Social Psychology, 69,* 69-79. (p. 401)

Whitehead, B. D., & Popenoe, D. (2001). *The state of our unions 2001: The social health of marriage in America.* Rutgers University: The National Marriage Project. (p. 136)

Whiten, A., & Boesch, C. (2001, January). Cultures of chimpanzees. *Scientific American,* pp. 60-67. (p. 327)

Whiten, A., & Byrne, R. W. (1988). Tactical deception in primates. *Behavioral and Brain Sciences, 11,* 233-244, 267-273. (p. 20)

Whiting, B. B., & Edwards, C. P. (1988). *Children of different worlds: The formation of social behavior.* Cambridge, MA: Harvard University Press. (p. 86)

Whitley, B. E., Jr. (1990). The relationships of heterosexuals' attributions for the causes of homosexuality to attitudes toward lesbians and gay men. *Personality and Social Psychology Bulletin, 16,* 369-377. (p. 386)

Whitley, B. E., Jr. (1999). Right-wing authoritarianism, social dominance orientation, and prejudice. *Journal of Personality and Social Psychology, 77,* 126-134. (p. 597)

WHO. (2002). The global burden of disease. Geneva: World Health Organization (www.who.int/msa/mnh/ems/dalys/intro.htm). (p. 521)

WHO. (2002a, September 4). Suicide rates. World Health Organization (www5.who.int/mental_health). (pp. 524, 525)

WHO. (2002c, December 9). China: WHO lauds launch of nation's first suicide prevent center: Xinhua news. World Health Organization (www5.who.int/mental_health). (p. 524)

WHO. (2002d). Schizophrenia. World Health Organization (www5.who.int/mental_health). (p. 532)

WHO. (2004). Prevalence, severity, and unmet need for treatment of mental disorders in the World Health Organization World Mental Health Surveys. *Journal of the American Medical Association, 291,* 2581-2590. (pp. 506, 524)

WHO. (2005, February 24). Global tobacco treaty enters into force with 57 countries already committed. World Health Organization media centre (www.who.int). (p. 220)

Whooley, M. A., & Browner, W. S. (1998). Association between depressive symptoms and mortality in older women. *Archives of Internal Medicine, 158,* 2129-2135. (p. 439)

Whorf, B. L. (1956). Science and linguistics. In J. B. Carroll (Ed.), *Language, thought, and reality: Selected writings of Benjamin Lee Whorf.* Cambridge, MA: MIT Press. (p. 323)

Wickelgren, I. (2005). Autistic brains out of sync? *Science, 308,* 1856-1858. (p. 111)

Wickelgren, W. A. (1977). *Learning and memory.* Englewood Cliffs, NJ: Prentice-Hall. (p. 274)

Widom, C. S. (1989a). Does violence beget violence? A critical examination of the literature. *Psychological Bulletin, 106,* 3-28. (p. 116)

Widom, C. S. (1989b). The cycle of violence. *Science, 244,* 160-166. (p. 116)

Wiens, A. N., & Menustik, C. E. (1983). Treatment outcome and patient characteristics in an aversion therapy program for alcoholism. *American Psychologist, 38,* 1089-1096. (p. 547)

Wierson, M., & Forehand, R. (1994). Parent behavioral training for child noncompliance: Rationale, concepts, and effectiveness. *Current Directions in Psychological Science, 3,* 146-149. (p. 257)

Wiertelak, E. P., Smith K. P., Furness, L., Mooney-Heiberger, K., Mayr, T., Maier, S. F., & Watkins, L. R. (1994). Acute and conditioned hyperalgesic responses to illness. *Pain, 56,* 227-234. (p. 162)

Wierzbicki, M. (1993). Psychological adjustment of adoptees: A meta-analysis. *Journal of Clinical Child Psychology, 22,* 447-454. (p. 72)

Wiesel, T. N. (1982). Postnatal development of the visual cortex and the influence of environment. *Nature, 299,* 583-591. (p. 182)

Wiesner, W. H., & Cronshow, S. P. (1988). A meta-analytic investigation of the impact of interview format and degree of structure on the validity of the employment interview. *Journal of Occupational Psychology, 61,* 275–290. (p. 396)

Wigdor, A. K., & Garner, W. R. (1982). *Ability testing: Uses, consequences, and controversies.* Washington, DC: National Academy Press. (p. 350)

Wilcox, A. J., Baird, D. D., Dunson, D. B., McConnaughey, D. R., Kesner, J. S., & Weinberg, C. R. (2004). On the frequency of intercourse around ovulation: Evidence for biological influences. *Human Reproduction, 19,* 1539–1543. (p. 376)

Wilder, D. A. (1981). Perceiving persons as a group: Categorization and intergroup relations. In D. L. Hamilton (Ed.), *Cognitive processes in stereotyping and intergroup behavior.* Hillsdale, NJ: Erlbaum. (p. 597)

Wilford, J. N. (1999, February 9). New findings help balance the cosmological books. *New York Times* (www.nytimes.com). (p. 94)

Williams, C. L., & Berry, J. W. (1991). Primary prevention of acculturative stress among refugees. *American Psychologist, 46,* 632–641. (p. 437)

Williams, J. E., & Best, D. L. (1990). *Measuring sex stereotypes: A multination study.* Newbury Park, CA: Sage. (p. 88)

Williams, J. E., Paton, C. C., Siegler, I. C., Eigenbrodt, M. L., Nieto, F. J., & Tyroler, H. A. (2000). Anger proneness predicts coronary heart disease risk: Prospective analysis from the artherosclerosis risk in communities (ARIC) study. *Circulation, 101,* 17, 2034–2040. (p. 439)

Williams, K. D. (2002). *Ostracism: The power of silence.* New York: Guilford. (p. 389)

Williams, K. D., & Zadro, L. (2001). Ostracism: On being ignored, excluded and rejected. In M. Leary (Ed.), *Rejection.* New York: Oxford University Press. (p. 389)

Williams, R. (1993). Anger kills. New York: Times Books. (p. 400), 424, 439)

Williams, S. L. (1987). Self-efficacy and mastery-oriented treatment for severe phobias. Paper presented to the American Psychological Association convention. (p. 546)

Willmuth, M. E. (1987). Sexuality after spinal cord injury: A critical review. *Clinical Psychology Review, 7,* 389–412. (p. 378)

Wilson, A. E., & Ross, M. (2001). From chump to champ: People's appraisals of their earlier and present selves. *Journal of Personality and Social Psychology, 80,* 572–584. (p. 494)

Wilson, C. M., & Oswald, A. J. (2002). How does marriage affect physical and psychological health? A survey of the longitudinal evidence. Working paper, University of York and Warwick University. (p. 447)

Wilson, R. C., Gaft, J. G., Dienst, E. R., Wood, L., & Bavry, J. L. (1975). *College professors and their impact on students.* New York: Wiley. (p. 590)

Wilson, R. S. (1979). Analysis of longitudinal twin data: Basic model and applications to physical growth measures. *Acta Geneticae medicae et Gemellologiae, 28,* 93–105. (p. 105)

Wilson, R. S., & Matheny, A. P., Jr. (1986). Behavior-genetics research in infant temperament: The Louisville twin study. In R. Plomin & J. Dunn (Eds.), *The study of temperament: Changes, continuities, and challenges.* Hillsdale, NJ: Erlbaum. (p. 72)

Wilson, T. D. (2002). *Strangers to ourselves: Discovering the adaptive unconscious.* Cambridge: Harvard University Press. (p. 193)

Windholz, G. (1989, April-June). The discovery of the principles of reinforcement, extinction, generalization, and differentiation of conditional reflexes in Pavlov's laboratories. *Pavlovian Journal of Biological Science, 26,* 64–74. (p. 241)

Windholz, G. (1997). Ivan P. Pavlov: An overview of his life and psychological work. *American Psychologist, 52,* 941–946. (p. 238)

Winner, E. (2000). The origins and ends of giftedness. *American Psychologist, 55,* 159–169. (p. 340)

Wiseman, R. (2002). *Laugh Lab—final results.* University of Hertfordshire (www.laughlab.co.uk). (p. 309)

Wiseman, R., Jeffreys, C., Smith, M., & Nyman, A. (1999). The psychology of the seance. *The Skeptical Inquirer, 23*(2), 30–33. (p. 297)

Wisman, A., & Goldenberg, J. L. (2005). From the grave to the cradle: Evidence that mortality salience engenders a desire for offspring. *Journal of Personality and Social Psychology, 89,* 46–61. (p. 118)

Witelson, S. F., Kigar, D. L., & Harvey, T. (1999). The exceptional brain of Albert Einstein. *The Lancet, 353,* 2149–2153. (p. 57)

Witvliet, C. V. O., & Vrana, S. R. (1995). Psychophysiological responses as indices of affective dimensions. *Psychophysiology, 32,* 436–443. (p. 410)

Witvliet, C. V. O., Ludwig, T., & Vander Laan, K. (2001). Granting forgiveness or harboring grudges: Implications for emotions, physiology, and health. *Psychological Science, 12,* 117–123. (p. 425)

Wixted, J. T., & Ebbesen, E. B. (1991). On the form of forgetting. *Psychological Science, 2,* 409–415. (p. 292)

Wolfson, A. R., & Carskadon, M. A. (1998). Sleep schedules and daytime functioning in adolescents. *Child Development, 69,* 875–887. (p. 207)

Woll, S. (1986). So many to choose from: Decision strategies in videodating. *Journal of Social and Personal Relationships, 3,* 43–52. (p. 608)

Wolpe, J. (1958). *Psychotherapy by reciprocal inhibition.* Stanford, CA: Stanford University Press. (p. 546)

Wolpe, J., & Plaud, J. J. (1997). Pavlov's contributions to behavior therapy: The obvious and the not so obvious. *American Psychologist, 52,* 966–972. (p. 546)

Wong, D. F., Wagner, H. N., Tune, L. E., Dannals, R. F., & others. (1986). Positron emission tomography reveals elevated D2 dopamine receptors in drug-naive schizophrenics. *Science, 234,* 1588–1593. (p. 533)

Wong, M. M., & Csikszentmihalyi, M. (1991). Affiliation motivation and daily experience: Some issues on gender differences. *Journal of Personality and Social Psychology, 60,* 154–164. (p. 89)

Wood, J. (2003, May 19). Quoted by R. Mestel, Rorschach tested: Blot out the famous method? Some experts say it has no place in psychiatry. *Los Angeles Times* (www.latimes.com). (p. 465)

Wood, J. M., Bootzin, R. R., Kihlstrom, J. F., & Schacter, D. L. (1992). Implicit and explicit memory for verbal information presented during sleep. *Psychological Science, 3,* 236–239. (p. 294)

Wood, J. M., Nezworski, M. T., Garb, H. N., & Lilienfeld, S. O. (2006). The controversy over the Exner Comprehensive System and the Society for Personality Assessment's white paper on the Rorschach. *Independent Practitioner,* in press. (p. 465)

Wood, J. V., Saltzberg, J. A., & Goldsamt, L. A. (1990a). Does affect induce self-focused attention? *Journal of Personality and Social Psychology, 58,* 899–908. (p. 527)

Wood, J. V., Saltzberg, J. A., Neale, J. M., Stone, A. A., & Rachmiel, T. B. (1990b). Self-focused attention, coping responses, and distressed mood in everyday life. *Journal of Personality and Social Psychology, 58,* 1027–1036. (p. 527)

Wood, W. (1987). Meta-analytic review of sex differences in group performance. *Psychological Bulletin, 102,* 53–71. (p. 88)

Wood, W., & Eagly, A. (2002). A cross-cultural analysis of the behavior of women and men: Implications for the origins of sex differences. *Psychological Bulletin, 128,* 699–727. (pp. 78, 88, 89, 93)

Wood, W., Lundgren, S., Ouellette, J. A., Busceme, S., & Blackstone, T. (1994). Minority influence: A meta-analytic review of social influence processes. *Psychological Bulletin, 115,* 323–345. (p. 592)

Woods, N. F., Dery, G. K., & Most, A. (1983). Recollections of menarche, current menstrual attitudes, and premenstrual symptoms. In S. Golub (Ed.), *Menarche: The transition from girl to woman.* Lexington, MA: Lexington Books. (p. 121)

Woody, E. Z., & McConkey, K. M. (2003). What we don't know about the brain and hypnosis, but need to: A view from the Buckhorn Inn. *International Journal of Clinical and Experimental Hypnosis, 51,* 309–338. (p. 215)

World Federation for Mental Health. (2005). ADHD: The hope behind the hype. www.wfmh.org. (p. 501)

World Health Organization. (1979). *Schizophrenia: An international follow-up study.* Chicester, England: Wiley. (p. 533)

World Health Organization. (2004). *Prevention of mental disorders: Effective interventions and policy options. Summary report.* Geneva: World Health Organization, Department of Mental Health and Substance Abuse. (p. 507)

Worobey, J., & Blajda, V. M. (1989). Temperament ratings at 2 weeks, 2 months, and 1 year: Differential stability of activity and emotionality. *Developmental Psychology, 25,* 257–263. (p. 72)

Worthington, E. L., Jr. (1989). Religious faith across the life span: Implications for counseling and research. *The Counseling Psychologist, 17,* 555–612. (p. 122)

Worthington, E. L., Jr., Kurusu, T. A., McCullogh, M. E., & Sandage, S. J. (1996). Empirical research on religion and psychotherapeutic processes and outcomes: A 10-year review and research prospectus. *Psychological Bulletin, 119,* 448–487. (p. 562, 563)

Wortman, C. B., & Silver, R. C. (1989). The myths of coping with loss. *Journal of Consulting and Clinical Psychology, 57,* 349–357. (p. 139)

Wren, C. S. (1999, April 8). Drug survey of children finds middle school a pivotal time. *New York Times* (www.nytimes.com). (p. 227)

Wright, I. C., Rabe-Hesketh, S., Woodruff, P. W. R., David, A. S., Murray, R. M., & Bullmore, E. T. (2000). Meta-analysis of regional brain volumes in schizophrenia. *American Journal of Psychiatry, 157,* 16–25. (p. 534)

Wright, P. H. (1989). Gender differences in adults' same- and cross-gender friendships. In R. G. Adams & R. Blieszner (Eds.), *Older adult friendships: Structure and process.* Newbury Park, CA: Sage. (p. 89)

Wright, P., Takei, N., Rifkin, L., & Murray, R. M. (1995). Maternal influenza, obstetric complications, and schizophrenia. *American Journal of Psychiatry, 152,* 1714–1720. (p. 534)

Wright, W. (1998). *Born that way: Genes, behavior, personality.* New York: Knopf. (p. 70)

Wrzesniewski, A., & Dutton, J. E. (2001). Crafting a job: Revisioning employees as active crafters of their work. *Academy of Management Review, 26,* 179–201. (p. 392)

Wrzesniewski, A., McCauley, C. R., Rozin, P., & Schwartz, B. (1997). Jobs, careers, and callings: People's relations to their work. *Journal of Research in Personality, 31,* 21–33. (p. 392)

Wuethrich, B. (2001, March). Features—GETTING STUPID—Surprising new neurological behavioral research reveals that teenagers who drink too much may permanently damage their brains and seriously compromise their ability to learn. *Discover, 56,* 56–64. (p. 218)

Wulsin, L. R., Vaillant, G. E., & Wells, V. E. (1999). A systematic review of the mortality of depression. *Psychosomatic Medicine, 61,* 6–17. (p. 439)

Wyatt, J. K., & Bootzin, R. R. (1994). Cognitive processing and sleep: Implications for enhancing job performance. *Human Performance, 7,* 119–139. (pp. 206, 294)

Wyatt, R. J., Henter, I., & Sherman-Elvy, E. (2001). Tantalizing clues to preventing schizophrenia. *Cerebrum: The Dana Forum on Brain Science, 3,* pp. 15–30. (p. 535)

Wynn, K. (1992). Addition and subtraction by human infants. *Nature, 358,* 749–759. (p. 109)

Wynn, K. (2000). Findings of addition and subtraction in infants are robust and consistent: reply to Wakeley, Rivera, and Langer. *Child Development, 71,* 1535–1536. (p. 109)

Wynn, K., Bloom, P., & Chiang, W-C. (2002). Enumeration of collective entities by 5-month-old infants. *Cognition, 83,* B55–B62. (p. 109)

Wynne, C. D. L. (2004). *Do animals think?* Princeton, NJ: Princeton University Press. (p. 328)

Xu, Y., & Corkin, S. (2001). H.M. revisits the Tower of Hanoi puzzle. *Neuropsychology, 15,* 69–79. (p. 282)

Yang, N., & Linz, D. (1990). Movie ratings and the content of adult videos: The sex-violence ratio. *Journal of Communication, 40(2),* 28–42. (p. 603)

Yankelovich Partners. (1995, May/June). Growing old. *American Enterprise,* p. 108. (p. 129)

Yardley, J. (2005, January 31). Fearing future, China starts to give girls their due. *New York Times* (www.nytimes.com). (p. 596)

Yarnell, P. R., & Lynch, S. (1970, April 25). Retrograde memory immediately after concussion. *Lancet,* pp. 863–865. (p. 280)

Yates, A. (1989). Current perspectives on the eating disorders: I. History, psychological and biological aspects. *Journal of the American Academy of Child and Adolescent Psychiatry, 28,* 813–828. (p. 364)

Yates, A. (1990). Current perspectives on the eating disorders: II. Treatment, outcome, and research directions. *Journal of the American Academy of Child and Adolescent Psychiatry, 29,* 1–9. (p. 364)

Yates, W. R. (2000). Testosterone in psychiatry. *Archives of General Psychiatry, 57,* 155–156. (p. 377)

Ybarra, O. (1999). Misanthropic person memory when the need to self-enhance is absent. *Personality and Social Psychology Bulletin, 25,* 261–269. (p. 491)

Yip, P. S. F. (1998). Age, sex, marital status and suicide: An empirical study of east and west. *Psychological Reports, 82,* 311–322. (p. 525)

Yirmiya, N., Erel, O., Shaken, M., & Solomonica-Levi, D. (1998). Meta-analyses comparing theory of mind abilities of individuals with autism, individuals with mental retardation, and normally developing individuals. *Psychological Bulletin, 124,* 283–307. (p. 111)

Zajonc, R. B. (1965). Social facilitation. *Science, 149,* 269–274. (p. 588)

Zajonc, R. B. (1980). Feeling and thinking: Preferences need no inferences. *American Psychologist, 35,* 151–175. (p. 413)

Zajonc, R. B. (1984a). On the primacy of affect. *American Psychologist, 39,* 117–123. (p. 413)

Zajonc, R. B. (1984b, July 22). Quoted by D. Goleman, Rethinking IQ tests and their value. *The New York Times,* p. D22. (p. 337)

Zajonc, R. B. (1998). Emotions. In D. Gilbert, S. T. Fiske, & G. Lindzey (Eds.), *Handbook of social psychology, 4th ed.* New York: McGraw-Hill. (p. 608)

Zajonc, R. B. (2001). Mere exposure: A gateway to the subliminal. *Current Directions in Psychological Science, 10,* 224–228. (p. 607)

Zajonc, R. B., & Markus, G. B. (1975). Birth order and intellectual development. *Psychological Review, 82,* 74–88. (p. A-8)

Zammit, S., Allebeck, P., Andreasson, S., Lundberg, I., & Lewis, G. (2002). Self reported cannabis use as a risk factor for schizophrenia in Swedish conscripts of 1969: Historical cohort study. *British Medical Journal, 325,* 1199. (p. 224)

Zauberman, G., & Lynch, J. G., Jr. (2005). Resource slack and propensity to discount delayed investments of time versus money. *Journal of Experimental Psychology: General, 134,* 23–37. (p. 312)

Zeidner, M. (1990). Perceptions of ethnic group modal intelligence: Reflections of cultural stereotypes or intelligence test scores? *Journal of Cross-Cultural Psychology, 21,* 214–231. (p. 345)

Zeineh, M. M., Engel, S. A., Thompson, P. M., & Bookheimer, S. Y. (2003). Dynamics of the hippocampus during encoding and retrieval of face-name pairs. *Science, 299,* 577–580. (p. 283)

Zigler, E. F. (1987). Formal schooling for four-year-olds? No. *American Psychologist, 42,* 254–260. (p. 344)

Zigler, E. F., & Styfco, S. J. (2001). Extended childhood intervention prepared children for school and beyond. *Journal of the American Medical Association, 285,* 2378–2380. (p. 344)

Zilbergeld, B. (1983). *The shrinking of America: Myths of psychological change.* Boston: Little, Brown. (pp. 555, 557)

Zillmann, D. (1986). Effects of prolonged consumption of pornography. Background paper for *The Surgeon General's workshop on pornography and public health,* June 22–24. Report prepared by E. P. Mulvey & J. L. Haugaard and released by Office of the Surgeon General on August 4, 1986. (pp. 410, 413)

Zillmann, D. (1989). Effects of prolonged consumption of pornography. In D. Zillmann & J. Bryant (Eds.), *Pornography: Research advances and policy considerations.* Hillsdale, NJ: Erlbaum. (pp. 378, 604)

Zillmann, D., & Bryant, J. (1984). Effects of massive exposure to pornography. In N. Malamuth & E. Donnerstein (Eds.), *Pornography and sexual aggression.* Orlando, FL: Academic Press. (p. 604)

Zimbardo, P. G. (1970). The human choice: Individuation, reason, and order versus deindividuation, impulse, and chaos. In W. J. Arnold & D. Levine (Eds.), *Nebraska Symposium on Motivation, 1969.* Lincoln, NE: University of Nebraska Press. (p. 589)

Zimbardo, P. G. (1972, April). Pathology of imprisonment. *Transaction/Society,* pp. 4–8. (p. 578)

Zimbardo, P. G. (2001, September 16). Fighting terrorism by understanding man's capacity for evil. Op Ed Essay distributed by spsp-discuss Abu Ghraib prison abuses: Eleven answers to eleven questions. Unpublished manuscript, Stanford University. (p. 579)

Zimbardo, P. G. (2005, January 18). You can't be a sweet cucumber in a vinegar barrel. *The Edge* (www.edge.org). (p. 579)

Zimmer, C. (2003). How the mind reads other minds. *Science, 300,* 1079–1080. (p. 110)

Zornberg, G. L., Buka, S. L., & Tsuang, M. T. (2000). At issue: The problem of obstetrical complications and schizophrenia. *Schizophrenia Bulletin, 26,* 249–256. (p. 534)

Zubieta, J-K., Heitzeg, M. M., Smith, Y. R., Bueller, J. A., Xu, K., Xu, Y., Koeppe, R. A., Stohler, C. S., & Goldman, D. (2003). COMT val158met genotype affects μ-opioid neurotransmitter responses to a pain stressor. *Science, 299,* 1240–1243. (p. 163)

Zucker, G. S., & Weiner, B. (1993). Conservatism and perceptions of poverty: An attributional analysis. *Journal of Applied Social Psychology, 23,* 925–943. (p. 576)

Zuckerman, M. (1979). *Sensation seeking: Beyond the optimal level of arousal.* Hillsdale, NJ: Erlbaum. (p. 358)

Name Index

SUBJECT INDEX